Chinese Maritime Cases Series

Series Editors

Martin Davies, Tulane University Law School, New Orleans, LA, USA

Jiang Lin, Law School, Shanghai Maritime University, Shanghai, China

The primary aim of this series is to, for the first time, provide the academics, practitioners and businessmen worldwide with a crucial source to perceive how the specially designed Chinese maritime courts apply, interpretate and develop the shipping law in practice to strike a balance of interest among the domestic and international market players. Each year, China trades with other states in trillions of USD, and more than 90% of the cargoes are carried by ocean-going ships. In view of the enormous trade volume and maritime activities, foreign trading houses, shipping companies and marine underwriters, as well as their legal advisors, are keen to track down the developments of Chinese maritime law and court practice so as to predicate and avoid the potential problems or resolve the emerging disputes properly. Cases and judgments are regarded as a crucial source of learning. However, so far, no serial Chinese casebooks, which contain full English translation of selected judgments, have been published. The authors try to make an audacious break-through in this field. This series has a secondary aim: to establish a core part of the database, which can be further developed to be an innovative tool for the foreign students, professors and lawyers to have a systematic study of Chinese maritime law.

More information about this series at https://link.springer.com/bookseries/16710

Martin Davies · Jiang Lin
Editors

Chinese Maritime Cases

Selection for Year of 2015

Volume 2

 Springer

Editors
Martin Davies
Law School
Tulane University
New Orleans, LA, USA

Jiang Lin
Law School
Shanghai Maritime University
Shanghai, China

ISSN 2730-9851   ISSN 2730-986X (electronic)
Chinese Maritime Cases Series
ISBN 978-3-662-63715-9   ISBN 978-3-662-63716-6 (eBook)
https://doi.org/10.1007/978-3-662-63716-6

© The Editor(s) (if applicable) and The Author(s), under exclusive license to Springer-Verlag GmbH, DE, part of Springer Nature 2021
This work is subject to copyright. All rights are solely and exclusively licensed by the Publisher, whether the whole or part of the material is concerned, specifically the rights of translation, reprinting, reuse of illustrations, recitation, broadcasting, reproduction on microfilms or in any other physical way, and transmission or information storage and retrieval, electronic adaptation, computer software, or by similar or dissimilar methodology now known or hereafter developed.
The use of general descriptive names, registered names, trademarks, service marks, etc. in this publication does not imply, even in the absence of a specific statement, that such names are exempt from the relevant protective laws and regulations and therefore free for general use.
The publisher, the authors and the editors are safe to assume that the advice and information in this book are believed to be true and accurate at the date of publication. Neither the publisher nor the authors or the editors give a warranty, expressed or implied, with respect to the material contained herein or for any errors or omissions that may have been made. The publisher remains neutral with regard to jurisdictional claims in published maps and institutional affiliations.

This Springer imprint is published by the registered company Springer-Verlag GmbH, DE part of Springer Nature.
The registered company address is: Heidelberger Platz 3, 14197 Berlin, Germany

Preface

To provide the legal professions worldwide with a good reference of Chinese maritime adjudication, this book, being the second in the series, delicately selects dozens of influential maritime cases heard by Chinese Maritime Courts and their appeal courts – Provincial High People's Courts and the Supreme People's Court of China. The selection covers a wide scope of disputes including carriage of goods by sea contract, charterparty, shipbuilding, ship sale and purchase, marine insurance, mortgage and collision.

Reading the judgments in this book, which are literally translated from the original Chinese version, readers will gain a better comprehension of the Chinese maritime law and a real sense how Chinese maritime judges apply the law to decide the issues in practice. This book offers excellent case study materials and will benefit the personnel engaged in the shipping, legal, judicial, arbitral and educational sectors. It is expected to promote mutual understanding and exchange of views, on which basis the international maritime justice will be further credited and enhanced.

It is worth noting that with the prosperous developments of international trade and shipping in the past decades, China has experienced steady growth of cross-board disputes arising from maritime transactions and admiral affairs. Those emerging disputes and the underlying causes seem to be distinctive in comparison with their counterparts in foreign countries. That is largely due to the fact that the scale of the shipping and circumferential markets in China is impressive and their operation is unique, which are clearly demonstrated in this book.

The selected cases involve multiple parties, and between them, there exist complicated business and legal relationships. Thus, while trialing the cases, Chinese judges interpret and apply the law in a creative way to resolve the novel questions, the answers to which cannot be found in international conventions or customs or foreign statutes or caselaw. In one sense, Chinese maritime courts are in an unrivaled situation to analyze and assess, in depth and breadth, the evolving disputes in the trade and shipping world and promote Chinese maritime judgments, as well as domestic legislative instruments, to be precedents for reference purpose worldwide.

This book does not only show the fruitful outcomes of Chinese maritime adjudication, but also casts a light on the trend of evolution of Chinese maritime legislation. For every maritime nation, the previous judgments make valuable contributions to present interpretation and application of the law and future legislation.

April, 2021

Dong Nian Yin
Professor in Law
Shanghai Maritime University
Shanghai, China

Acknowledgments

The editors would like to acknowledge the following for their assistance with the Chinese end of this project: from Shanghai Maritime University Law School, Prof. Dong Nian Yin, Prof. Shi Cheng Yu and Prof. Cun Qiang Cai; from Shanghai Maritime Court, Judge Tong Wang, Judge Zhen Kun Jia and Judge Hai Long Lin; Assistants to Editors in particular Hui Zeng, Yu Ming Wang, Yun Fei Han, Rui Ying Chen, Yu Tong Wang and Mu Fan Jia Yang.

The editors would also like to acknowledge the following present and former students of Tulane University Law School, who have served as Assistant Editors for the American part of this project: Richard Beaumont (2014–2015); Scott Ferrier (2015–2016); Guyer Bogen (2017–2018); Lindsey Magee Gordley and Katherine Kaplan (2018–2019); Erica Endlein (2019–2020); Robert Bradley and Mary Katherine Koch (2020–2021).

The editors also acknowledge the efforts of Jocelyn Mahan and Andrea Felice of IQNection for their work in building the companion Web site for this project, www.chinesemaritimecases.com.

About the Editors

Professor Martin Davies is Admiralty Law Institute Professor of Maritime Law at Tulane University Law School in New Orleans and Director of the Tulane Maritime Law Center.

He holds the degrees of M.A. and B.C.L. from Oxford University, England, and an LL.M. from Harvard Law School. Before joining Tulane, he was Harrison Moore Professor of Law at The University of Melbourne in Australia and before that he taught at Monash University, The University of Western Australia and Nottingham University. He has also been a visiting professor at universities in China, Italy, Azerbaijan and Singapore. In 2019, he was elected to be Titulary Member of the Comité Maritime International (CMI).

He is the author (or co-author) of books on maritime law, international trade law, conflict of laws and the law of torts. He has also published many journal articles on these topics. He has extensive practical experience as a consultant for over 30 years on maritime matters and general international litigation and arbitration, in Australia, Hong Kong, Singapore and the USA.

Associate Professor Jiang Lin (John Lin) is Associate Professor of Maritime Law at Shanghai Maritime University and Deputy Director of Shipping Policy and Law Research Center of Shanghai International Shipping Institute. He is also Adjunct Professor at Tulane University Law School.

After graduation with a B.Sc. degree from Shanghai Maritime University in 1996 and an LL.M. degree from Southampton University in 1999, he commenced his legal career at Sinclair Roche & Temperley (SRT) and later jointed Ince & Co. He was dually qualified as English solicitor and Chinese lawyer. In 2008, he came back to his mother college to be a lecturer and researcher. Meanwhile, he keeps practicing English and Chinese laws at Sinopar Law Firm. He is also an arbitrator with China Maritime Arbitration Association, Shanghai Arbitration Commission and Shanghai International Arbitration Center and a supporting member of London Maritime Arbitrators' Association.

He is the author and chief editor of two serial books: *Shanghai Shipping Policy and Law Development White Book* and *Shipping Finance Law Review*. He also writes books and articles on cruise commerce, off-shore trade and insurance.

John Lin is a member of Jiusan Society, one of the eight democratic parties in China.

Table of Contents

Table of Cases by Name of Plaintiff in Judgment of First Instance...... xiii
Table of Cases by Jurisdiction (Which Chinese Court Makes the Effective Judgment).. xxiii
Table of Cases by Cause of Action for Maritime Cases in the People's Republic of China... xxxiii
List of Maritime Courts and Their Appeal and Petition Courts in the People's Republic of China................................. xliii
List of Causes of Action for Maritime Cases in the People's Republic of China (Extracted from the Regulations on Causes of Action for Civil Disputes made by The Supreme People's Court of the People's Republic of China 2020)... xlv
Table of References li

Table of Cases by Name of Plaintiff in Judgment of First Instance

AIG Europe Ltd. v. Shanghai Heming Shipping Service Co., Ltd. Tianjin Branch et al. (2014) Hu Hai Fa Shang Chu Zi No. 116, *judgment of first instance of Shanghai Maritime Court* 1

Allianz China General Insurance Co., Ltd. v. Youda (Shanghai) International Freight Co., Ltd. et al. (2014) Hu Hai Fa Shang Chu Zi No. 361, *judgment of first instance of Shanghai Maritime Court* 11

A.P. Moller-Maersk A/S v. Shanghai Chanlian Xieyun Logistics Co., Ltd. et al. (2012) Guang Hai Fa Chu Zi No. 329, *judgment of first instance of Guangzhou Maritime Court* 45

A.P. Moller-Maersk A/S v. Shanghai Chanlian Xieyun Logistics Co., Ltd. et al. (2013) Yue Gao Fa Min Si Zhong Zi No. 162, *judgment of second instance of Guangdong High People's Court* 58

A.P. Moller-Maersk A/S v. Shanghai Chanlian Xieyun Logistics Co., Ltd. et al. (2015) Min Ti Zi No. 119, *judgment of retrial of The Supreme People's Court* 76

China Transport Groupage International (Shenzhen) Limited v. Shenzhen Zhongyi Freight Forwarding Co., Ltd. (2014) Guang Hai Fa Chu Zi No. 102, *judgment of first instance of Guangzhou Maritime Court* 83

China Transport Groupage International (Shenzhen) Limited v. Shenzhen Zhongyi Freight Forwarding Co., Ltd. (2015) Yue Gao Fa Min Si Zhong Zi No. 138, *judgment of second instance of Guangdong High People's Court* 93

China Transport Groupage International (Shenzhen) Limited v. Shenzhen Zhongyi Freight Forwarding Co., Ltd. (2017) Zui Gao Fa Min Shen Zi No. 104, *judgment of retrial of The Supreme People's Court* 107

Changhang Phoenix Co., Ltd. v. Wuhan Tairun Marine Service Co., Ltd. et al. (2014) Wu Hai Fa Shang Zi No. 01755, *judgment of first instance of Wuhan Maritime Court* 121

China Geology and Mining Corporation v. Tianjin Kangjie Import and Export Trade Co., Ltd. et al. (2014) Jin Hai Fa Shang Chu Zi No. 153, *judgment of first instance of Tianjin Maritime Court* 131

China Geology and Mining Corporation v. Tianjin Kangjie Import and Export Trade Co., Ltd. et al. (2015) Jin Gao Min Si Zhong Zi No. 77, *judgment of second instance of Tianjin High People's Court* ... 152

China Guangfa Bank Stock Co., Ltd. Nanjing Chengxi Branch v. Nanjing Hengshunda Shipping Co., Ltd. et al. (2015) Wu Hai Fa Shang Zi No. 00205, *judgment of first instance of Wuhan Maritime Court* 171

China Minsheng Bank Co., Ltd. (Xiamen Branch) v. Fujian Guanhai Shipping Co., Ltd. et al. (2015) Xia Hai Fa Shang Chu Zi No. 216, *judgment of first instance of Xiamen Maritime Court* 179

China Ping An Property Insurance Co., Ltd. Guangdong Branch v. Guangzhou Hang Jie Logistics Co., Ltd. (2013) Guang Hai Fa Chu Zi No. 1014, *judgment of first instance of Guangzhou Maritime Court* 199

China Ping An Property Insurance Co., Ltd. Guangdong Branch v. Guangzhou Hang Jie Logistics Co., Ltd. (2014) Yue Gao Fa Min Si Zhong Zi No. 204, *judgment of second instance of Guangdong High People's Court* 207

China Shipping Logistics Co., Ltd. v. Jiangsu Zhongtai Bridge Steel Structure Co., Ltd. (2014) Hu Hai Fa Shang Chu Zi No. 1068, *judgment of first instance of Shanghai Maritime Court* 215

China Shipping Logistics Co., Ltd. v. Jiangsu Zhongtai Bridge Steel Structure Co., Ltd. (2015) Hu Gao Min Si (Hai) Zhong Zi No. 25, *judgment of second instance of Shanghai High People's Court* 240

Chongqing Red Dragonfly Oil Limited Liability Company v. PICC Property and Casualty Company Limited Chongqing Branch (2015) Wu Hai Fa Shang Zi No. 00151, *judgment of first instance of Wuhan Maritime Court* 267

Connexions (Asia) Limited v. J&S Worldwide Logistics Co., Ltd. et al. (2012) Guang Hai Fa Shang Chu Zi No. 704, *judgment of first instance of Guangzhou Maritime Court* 283

Connexions (Asia) Limited v. J&S Worldwide Logistics Co., Ltd. et al. (2015) Yue Gao Fa Min Si Zhong Zi No. 10, *judgment of second instance of Guangdong High People's Court* 293

Table of Cases by Name of Plaintiff in Judgment of First Instance   xv

Connexions (Asia) Limited v. Shenzhen J&S Worldwide Logistics
Ltd. et al. (2015) Min Shen Zi No. 3206, *ruling of retrial of The
Supreme People's Court* 309

COSCO Container Lines Co., Ltd. v. Shenzhen Finigate Integrated
Logistics Co., Ltd. Qingdao Branch et al. (2014) Qing Hai Fa Hai
Shang Chu Zi No. 751, *judgment of first instance of Qingdao Maritime
Court* 313

COSCO Container Lines Co., Ltd. v. Shenzhen Finigate Integrated
Logistics Co., Ltd. Qingdao Branch et al. (2015) Lu Min Si Zhong Zi
No. 152, *judgment of second instance of Shandong High
People's Court*... 324

COSCO Container Lines Co., Ltd. v. Shenzhen Finigate Integrated
Logistics Co., Ltd. Qingdao Branch et al. (2016) Zui Gao Fa Min
Shen No. 2157, *ruling of retrial of The Supreme People's Court* 334

Daewoo Shipbuilding & Maritime Engineering Co., Ltd. v. Glory
Advance Corporation (2014) Xia Hai Fa Que Zi No. 1, *judgment
of first instance of Xiamen Maritime Court*..................... 339

Export-Import Bank of China et al. v. Nanjing Wujiazui Ship
Building Co., Ltd. et al. (2014) Wu Hai Fa Shang Chu Zi No. 00470,
judgment of first instance of Wuhan Maritime Court 349

Fan Sen (V.S) Shanghai International Freight Forwarding Co., Ltd.
v. Zhongman Petroleum & Natural Gas Group Co., Ltd. (2014) Hu
Hai Fa Shang Chu Zi No. 1112, *judgment of first instance of Shanghai
Maritime Court* 363

Fujian Guanhai Shipping Co., Ltd. v. Shanghai Huaya Ship Fuel
Company (2015) Hu Hai Fa Shang Chu Zi No. 47, *judgment of first
instance of Shanghai Maritime Court* 381

GUO Jiangbao v. Xiamen Chengyi Shipping Co., Ltd. (2014) Xia Hai
Fa Shang Chu Zi No. 452, *judgment of first instance of Xiamen
Maritime Court* 393

Hainan Weilong Shipping Engineering Co., Ltd. v. Hainan Yuehai
Shipping Logistics Co., Ltd. (2014) Qiong Hai Fa Shang Chu Zi No.
87, *judgment of first instance of Haikou Maritime Court* 407

Hainan Weilong Shipping Engineering Co., Ltd. v. Hainan Yuehai
Shipping Logistics Co., Ltd. (2015) Qiong Min San Zhong Zi No. 2,
judgment of second instance of Hainan High People's Court 418

Hong Kong Everglory Shipping Co., Ltd. et al. v. TAN Dingzhao
et al. (2014) Guang Hai Fa Shang Chu Zi No. 340, *judgment of first
instance of Guangzhou Maritime Court* 433

Hongxin (HK) Container Development Limited v. Shanghai
Hongsheng Gangtai Shipping Co., Ltd. et al. (2015) Xia Hai Fa
Shang Chu Zi No. 378, *judgment of first instance of Xiamen Maritime
Court* 453

Huayu Electrical Appliance Group Co., Ltd. v. JC Logistics Service
Co., Ltd. Ningbo Branch (2013) Yong Hai Fa Shang Chu Zi No. 579,
judgment of first instance of Ningbo Maritime Court 469

Huayu Electrical Appliance Group Co., Ltd. v. JC Logistics Service
Co., Ltd. Ningbo Branch (2014) Zhe Hai Zhong Zi No. 72, *judgment
of second instance of Zhejiang High People's Court* 476

Huayu Electrical Appliance Group Co., Ltd. v. JC Logistics Service
Co., Ltd. Ningbo Branch (2015) Min Ti Zi No. 19, *judgment of retrial
of The Supreme People's Court* 485

Hunan Zoomlion International Trade Co., Ltd. et al. v. Shanghai
GCL International Co., Ltd. et al. (2012) Hu Hai Fa Shang Chu Zi
No. 1208, *judgment of first instance of Shanghai Maritime Court* 491

Hunan Zoomlion International Trade Co., Ltd. et al. v. Shanghai
GCL International Co., Ltd. et al. (2014) Hu Gao Min Si (Hai) Zhong
Zi No. 119, *judgment of second instance of Shanghai High
People's Court*... 552

Hunan Zoomlion International Trade Co., Ltd. et al. v. Shanghai
GCL International Co., Ltd. et al. (2016) Zui Gao Fa Min Shen No.
1602, *ruling of retrial of The Supreme People's Court* 600

JIANG Haiping v. Shanghai New Qiao Insurance Brokers Ltd.
(2014) Hu Hai Fa Shang Chu Zi No. 1410, *judgment of first instance
of Shanghai Maritime Court* 607

JIANG Haiping v. Shanghai New Qiao Insurance Brokers Ltd.
(2015) Hu Gao Min Si (Hai) Zhong Zi No. 57, *judgment of second
instance of Shanghai High People's Court*...................... 615

Jiangsu Eastern Heavy Industry Co., Ltd. v. Nanjing Twin Rivers
Shipping Co., Ltd. (2012) Jin Hai Fa Shang Chu Zi No. 784, *judgment
of first instance of Tianjin Maritime Court* 625

Jianxin Finance Leasing Co., Ltd. v. Wenzhou Changjiang Energy
Shipping Co., Ltd. (2015) Jin Hai Fa Shang Chu Zi No. 663, *judgment
of first instance of Tianjin Maritime Court*....................... 647

LI Chunjiang et al. v. Tanggu Water Conservancy Project Company
et al. (2013) Jin Hai Fa Shang Chu Zi No. 521, *judgment of first
instance of Tianjin Maritime Court* 661

Table of Cases by Name of Plaintiff in Judgment of First Instance   xvii

LI Xuelan et al. v. Ningbo Jialili Shipping Co., Ltd. (2015) Guang Hai Fa Chu Zi No. 397, *judgment of first instance of Guangzhou Maritime Court* 675

LIN Guihe v. PICC Property and Casualty Company Limited Shunde Branch (2008) Guang Hai Fa Chu Zi No. 259, *judgment of first instance of Guangzhou Maritime Court* 689

LIN Guihe v. PICC Property and Casualty Company Limited Shunde Branch (2014) Yue Gao Min Si Zhong Zi No. 112, *judgment of second instance of Guangdong High People's Court* 701

LIN Guihe v. PICC Property and Casualty Company Limited Shunde Branch (2016) Zui Gao Fa Min Shen No. 1452, *ruling of retrial of The Supreme People's Court*........................... 727

LIU Fengxi v. Ningbo Junsheng Yuanda Shipping Co., Ltd. et al. (2015) Wu Hai Fa Shang Zi No. 00599, *judgment of first instance of Wuhan Maritime Court* 731

MAO Chuanwu v. Fengdu County Fengping Shipping Investment Co., Ltd. (2015) Wu Hai Fa Shang Zi No. 00134, *judgment of first instance of Wuhan Maritime Court* 737

Mitsui O.S.K. Lines, Ltd. v. Guangdong Shunde Local Product Import and Export Co., Ltd. et al. (2014) Guang Hai Fa Chu Zi No. 339, *judgment of first instance of Guangzhou Maritime Court* 747

Mund & Fester GmbH & Co. KG v. Pangang Group World Trade Panzhihua Co., Ltd. et al. (2011) Wu Hai Fa Shang Zi No. 00300, *judgment of first instance of Wuhan Maritime Court* 761

Nanjing Jinan Welding Technology Co., Ltd. v. Nanjing Lansheng Shipbuilding Co., Ltd. (2014) Wu Hai Fa Shang Zi No. 00369, *judgment of first instance of Wuhan Maritime Court* 781

Nanjing Jinan Welding Technology Co., Ltd. v. Nanjing Lansheng Shipbuilding Co., Ltd. (2015) E Min Si Zhong Zi No. 00064, *judgment of second instance of Hubei High People's Court* 788

Operating Department of China Continent Property & Casualty Insurance Co., Ltd. v. China Shipping Logistics Co., Ltd. (2014) Hu Hai Fa Shang Chu Zi No. 1509, *judgment of first instance of Shanghai Maritime Court* 799

People's Insurance Company of China Hangzhou Branch v. Tribute Ship Holding S.A. (2014) Da Hai Shang Chu Zi No. 21, *judgment of first instance of Dalian Maritime Court* 811

Qingdao Huashun Shipping Co., Ltd. v. Marc Loud Schiffahrts
Gesellschaft mbH & Co. KG. et al. (2014) Qing Hai Fa Que Zi
No. 7-1, *judgment of first instance of Qingdao Maritime Court* 823

Qinhuangdao Heshun Shipping Co., Ltd. v. China People's Property
Insurance Co., Ltd. Qinhuangdao City Branch (2015) Jin Hai Fa
Shang Chu Zi No. 287, *judgment of first instance of Tianjin
Maritime Court* 831

Qinhuangdao Heshun Shipping Co., Ltd. v. China People's Property
Insurance Co., Ltd. Qinhuangdao City Branch (2015) Jin Gao Min Si
Zhong Zi No. 93, *judgment of second instance of Tianjin High
People's Court*.. 842

Qinhuangdao Heshun Shipping Co., Ltd. v. China People's Property
Insurance Co., Ltd. Qinhuangdao City Branch (2016) Zui Gao
Fa Min Shen No. 1395, *ruling of retrial of The Supreme
People's Court*.. 854

Shandong Xianglong Industrial Group Co., Ltd. v. NCS Co., Ltd.
et al. (2011) Jin Hai Fa Shang Chu Zi No. 465, *judgment of first
instance of Tianjin Maritime Court* 859

Shanghai Eastern Shipping Material Co., Ltd. v. Beihai Honghai
Shipping Co., Ltd. et al. (2009) Guang Hai Fa Chu Zi No. 97,
judgment of first instance of Guangzhou Maritime Court 877

Shanghai Eastern Shipping Material Co., Ltd. v. Beihai Honghai
Shipping Co., Ltd. et al. (2012) Yue Gao Fa Min Si Zhong Zi No. 148,
judgment of second instance of Guangdong High People's Court 891

Shanghai Wan Feng International Freight Forwarding Co., Ltd.
v. Fujian Hongxing Electronic Technology Co., Ltd. (2014) Hu Hai
Fa Shang Chu Zi No. 1496, *judgment of first instance of Shanghai
Maritime Court* 925

Shanghai Yizhou Waterway Engineering Co., Ltd. v. QIU Guohua
(2013) Hu Hai Fa Hai Chu Zi No. 60, *judgment of first instance
of Shanghai Maritime Court* 943

Shanghai Yizhou Waterway Engineering Co., Ltd. v. QIU Guohua
(2015) Hu Gao Min Si (Hai) Zhong Zi No. 32, *judgment of second
instance of Shanghai High People's Court*................................. 967

Shanghai Jielong Industrial Group Co., Ltd. Yutian Packaging and
Printing Branch v. Norasia Container Lines Limited et al. (2012) Hu
Hai Fa Shang Chu Zi No. 1011, *judgment of first instance of Shanghai
Maritime Court* 987

Shanghai Jielong Industrial Group Co., Ltd. Yutian Packaging and
Printing Branch v. Norasia Container Lines Limited et al. (2013) Hu
Gao Min Si (Hai) Zhong Zi No. 132, *judgment of second instance
of Shanghai High People's Court* 999

Shanghai Jielong Industrial Group Co., Ltd. Yutian Packaging and
Printing Branch v. Norasia Container Lines Limited et al. (2015) Min
Shen Zi No. 573, *ruling of retrial of The Supreme People's Court* 1010

SHAN Yongzhen et al. v. LIANG Mingren (2014) Da Hai Shi Chu Zi
No. 121, *judgment of first instance of Dalian Maritime Court* 1015

SHAN Yongzhen et al. v. LIANG Mingren (2015) Liao Min San
Zhong Zi No. 201, *judgment of second instance of Liaoning High
People's Court* 1022

Shenzhen COSCO Logistics Co., Ltd. v. Guangdong Yanlin Energy
Limited by Share Ltd. (2012) Guang Hai Fa Chu Zi No. 910,
judgment of first instance of Guangzhou Maritime Court 1031

Shenzhen COSCO Logistics Co., Ltd. v. Guangdong Yanlin Energy
Limited by Share Ltd. (2014) Yue Gao Fa Min Si Zhong Zi No. 197,
judgment of second instance of Guangdong High People's Court 1042

Silvery Dragon Prestressed Materials Co., Ltd. (Tianjin) v. Dalian
Pei Hua International Logistics Co., Ltd. (2014) Jin Hai Fa
Shang Chu Zi No. 698, *judgment of first instance of Tianjin
Maritime Court* 1053

Station Ocean Administration Beihai Branch v. Wang Jianlong et al.
(2013) Qing Hai Fa Hai Shang Chu Zi No. 986, *judgment of first
instance of Qingdao Maritime Court* 1067

Suqian Rongxiang Shipping Co., Ltd. v. China United Property
Insurance Co., Ltd. Jiangsu Branch (2014) Wu Hai Fa Shang Zi
No. 01351, *judgment of first instance of Wuhan Maritime Court* 1079

Tai-I Jiangtong (Guangzhou) Co., Ltd. v. American President Lines,
Ltd. (2013) Guang Hai Fa Chu Zi No. 552, *judgment of first instance
of Guangzhou Maritime Court* 1089

Tai-I Jiangtong (Guangzhou) Co., Ltd. v. American President Lines,
Ltd. (2015) Yue Gao Fa Min Si Zhong Zi No. 24, *judgment
of second instance of Guangdong High People's Court* 1107

Tianjin Tianguan Ocean International Freight Forwarding Co., Ltd.
v. Yantai Fuhai International Ship Management Co., Ltd. et al.
(2014) Jin Hai Fa Shang Chu Zi No. 772, *judgment of first instance
of Tianjin Maritime Court* 1117

WANG Hong v. Jiangsu Yuanhai Logistics Co., Ltd. et al. (2014)
Wu Hai Fa Shi Zi No. 00040, *judgment of first instance of Wuhan
Maritime Court* 1127

WANG Jun v. Dalian Tiger Beach Tourism Development Co., Ltd.
(2013) Da Hai Shi Chu Zi No. 78, *judgment of first instance of Dalian
Maritime Court* 1143

WU Guangbao et al. v. Anqing City Yingjiang District Xinzhou
Country Ferry Station (2015) Wu Hai Fa Shang Chu Zi No. 00827,
judgment of first instance of Wuhan Maritime Court 1153

Wuhan Ling Da Compressor Co., Ltd. v. Falcon Insurance Company
(Hong Kong) Limited (2014) Wu Hai Fa Shang Zi No. 01268,
judgment of first instance of Wuhan Maritime Court 1163

WU Jinya v. Nanjing Haijing Shipping Co., Ltd. (2015) Wu Hai Fa
Shang Chu Zi No. 00123, *judgment of first instance of Wuhan
Maritime Court* 1177

Xiamen Yida Sihai Import & Export Co., Ltd. v. A.P. Moller—
Maersk A/S Co., Ltd. (2014) Xia Hai Fa Shang Chu Zi No. 583,
judgment of first instance of Xiamen Maritime Court 1193

XIE Hongjian v. WENG Kaiheng (2015) Qiong Hai Fa Shang Chu Zi
No. 80, *judgment of first instance of Haikou Maritime Court* 1205

XIE Hongjian v. WENG Kaiheng (2015) Qiong Min San Zhong Zi
No. 84, *judgment of second instance of Hainan High People's Court* ... 1214

XUE Haibing et al. v. Sun Shell Shipping Co., Ltd. (2015) Hai Shi
Chu Zi No. 3, *judgment of first instance of Beihai Maritime Court* 1221

Yantai Maritime Safety Administration of the People's Republic
of China v. China People's Property Insurance Co., Ltd. Qingdao
Branch (2011) Qing Hai Fa Shang Chu Zi No. 187, *judgment of first
instance of Qingdao Maritime Court* 1241

Yantai Maritime Safety Administration of the People's Republic
of China v. China People's Property Insurance Co., Ltd. Qingdao
Branch (2014) Lu Min Si Zhong Zi No. 107, *judgment of second
instance of Shandong High People's Court* 1250

Yue Hai (Fan Yu) Petrochemicals Storage Transportation
Development Co., Ltd. v. Shanghai Port Fuxing Shipping Co., Ltd.
(2014) Guang Hai Fa Zhong Zi No. 55, *judgment of first instance of
Guangzhou Maritime Court* 1263

Zhuhai Jiaxun Saite Electronic Co., Ltd. v. Shenzhen Shi Chang
Freight Co., Ltd. et al. (2015) Guang Hai Fa Chu Zi No. 182,
judgment of first instance of Guangzhou Maritime Court 1309

Table of Cases by Name of Plaintiff in Judgment of First Instance

Zhuhai Xiangzhou Haiyun Co., Ltd. v. Sanya Hongrui Engineer Co., Ltd. et al. (2014) Qiong Hai Fa Shang Chu Zi No. 80, *judgment of first instance of Haikou Maritime Court* 1321

Zhuhai Xiangzhou Haiyun Co., Ltd. v. Sanya Hongrui Engineer Co., Ltd. et al. (2015) Qiong Min San Zhong Zi No. 25, *judgment of second instance of Hainan High People's Court* 1337

Zhumadian South China Sea Shipping Co., Ltd. v. People's Insurance Company of China Property and Casualty Co., Ltd. Zhumadian Branch (2014) Wu Hai Fa Shang Chu Zi No. 00795, *judgment of first instance of Wuhan Maritime Court* 1355

Zhumadian South China Sea Shipping Co., Ltd. v. People's Insurance Company of China Property and Casualty Co., Ltd. Zhumadian Branch (2015) E Min Si Zhong Zi No. 00058, *judgment of second instance of Hubei High People's Court* 1377

ZHONG Kangqiu v. Fujian Chengxing Fuel Oil Co., Ltd. (2014) Hai Shang Chu Zi No. 203, *judgment of first instance of Beihai Maritime Court* 1395

Table of Cases by Jurisdiction (Which Chinese Court Makes the Effective Judgment)

Effective Judgments Made by Maritime Courts

Shanghai Maritime Court

AIG Europe Ltd. v. Shanghai Heming Shipping Service Co., Ltd. Tianjin Branch et al. (2014) Hu Hai Fa Shang Chu Zi No. 116, *judgment of first instance of Shanghai Maritime Court* 1

Allianz China General Insurance Co., Ltd. v. Youda (Shanghai) International Freight Co., Ltd. et al. (2014) Hu Hai Fa Shang Chu Zi No. 361, *judgment of first instance of Shanghai Maritime Court* 11

Fan Sen (V.S) Shanghai International Freight Forwarding Co., Ltd. v. Zhongman Petroleum & Natural Gas Group Co., Ltd. (2014) Hu Hai Fa Shang Chu Zi No. 1112, *judgment of first instance of Shanghai Maritime Court* 363

Fujian Guanhai Shipping Co., Ltd. v. Shanghai Huaya Ship Fuel Company (2015) Hu Hai Fa Shang Chu Zi No. 47, *judgment of first instance of Shanghai Maritime Court* 381

Operating Department of China Continent Property & Casualty Insurance Co., Ltd. v. China Shipping Logistics Co., Ltd. (2014) Hu Hai Fa Shang Chu Zi No. 1509, *judgment of first instance of Shanghai Maritime Court* 799

Shanghai Wan Feng International Freight Forwarding Co., Ltd. v. Fujian Hongxing Electronic Technology Co., Ltd. (2014) Hu Hai Fa Shang Chu Zi No. 1496, *judgment of first instance of Shanghai Maritime Court* 925

Tianjin Maritime Court

Jiangsu Eastern Heavy Industry Co., Ltd. v. Nanjing Twin Rivers Shipping Co., Ltd. (2012) Jin Hai Fa Shang Chu Zi No. 784, *judgment of first instance of Tianjin Maritime Court* 625

Jianxin Finance Leasing Co., Ltd. v. Wenzhou Changjiang Energy Shipping Co., Ltd. (2015) Jin Hai Fa Shang Chu Zi No. 663, *judgment of first instance of Tianjin Maritime Court* 647

LI Chunjiang et al. v. Tanggu Water Conservancy Project Company et al. (2013) Jin Hai Fa Shang Chu Zi No. 521, *judgment of first instance of Tianjin Maritime Court* 661

Shandong Xianglong Industrial Group Co., Ltd. v. NCS Co., Ltd. et al. (2011) Jin Hai Fa Shang Chu Zi No. 465, *judgment of first instance of Tianjin Maritime Court* 859

Silvery Dragon Prestressed Materials Co., Ltd. (Tianjin) v. Dalian Pei Hua International Logistics Co., Ltd. (2014) Jin Hai Fa Shang Chu Zi No. 698, *judgment of first instance of Tianjin Maritime Court* 1053

Tianjin Tianguan Ocean International Freight Forwarding Co., Ltd. v. Yantai Fuhai International Ship Management Co., Ltd. et al. (2014) Jin Hai Fa Shang Chu Zi No. 772, *judgment of first instance of Tianjin Maritime Court* 1117

Qingdao Maritime Court

Qingdao Huashun Shipping Co., Ltd. v. Marc Loud Schiffahrts Gesellschaft mbH & Co. KG et al. (2014) Qing Hai Fa Que Zi No. 7-1, *judgment of first instance of Qingdao Maritime Court* 823

Station Ocean Administration Beihai Branch v. WANG Jianlong et al. (2013) Qing Hai Fa Hai Shang Chu Zi No. 986, *judgment of first instance of Qingdao Maritime Court* 1067

Dalian Maritime Court

People's Insurance Company of China Hangzhou Branch v. Tribute Ship Holding S.A. (2014) Da Hai Shang Chu Zi No. 21, *judgment of first instance of Dalian Maritime Court* 811

WANG Jun v. Dalian Tiger Beach Tourism Development Co., Ltd. (2013) Da Hai Shi Chu Zi No. 78, *judgment of first instance of Dalian Maritime Court* 1143

Guangzhou Maritime Court

Hong Kong Everglory Shipping Co., Ltd. et al. v. TAN Dingzhao et al. (2014) Guang Hai Fa Shang Chu Zi No. 340, *judgment of first instance of Guangzhou Maritime Court* 433

LI Xuelan et al. v. Ningbo Jialili Shipping Co., Ltd. (2015) Guang Hai Fa Chu Zi No. 397, *judgment of first instance of Guangzhou Maritime Court* 675

Mitsui O.S.K. Lines, Ltd. v. Guangdong Shunde Local Product Import and Export Co., Ltd. et al. (2014) Guang Hai Fa Chu Zi No. 339, *judgment of first instance of Guangzhou Maritime Court* 747

Yue Hai (Fan Yu) Petrochemicals Storage Transportation Development Co., Ltd. v. Shanghai Port Fuxing Shipping Co., Ltd. (2014) Guang Hai Fa Zhong Zi No. 55, *judgment of first instance of Guangzhou Maritime Court*.. 1263
Zhuhai Jiaxun Saite Electronic Co., Ltd. v. Shenzhen Shi Chang Freight Co., Ltd. et al. (2015) Guang Hai Fa Chu Zi No. 182, *judgment of first instance of Guangzhou Maritime Court* 1309

Wuhan Maritime Court

Changhang Phoenix Co., Ltd. v. Wuhan Tairun Marine Service Co., Ltd. et al. (2014) Wu Hai Fa Shang Zi No. 01755, *judgment of first instance of Wuhan Maritime Court*....................................... 121
China Guangfa Bank Stock Co., Ltd. Nanjing Chengxi Branch v. Nanjing Hengshunda Shipping Co., Ltd. et al. (2015) Wu Hai Fa Shang Zi No. 00205, *judgment of first instance of Wuhan Maritime Court*............ 171
Chongqing Red Dragonfly Oil Limited Liability Company v. PICC Property and Casualty Company Limited Chongqing Branch (2015) Wu Hai Fa Shang Zi No. 00151, *judgment of first instance of Wuhan Maritime Court*......... 267
Export-Import Bank of China et al. v. Nanjing Wujiazui Ship Building Co., Ltd. et al. (2014) Wu Hai Fa Shang Chu Zi No. 00470, *judgment of first instance of Wuhan Maritime Court*............................. 349
LIU Fengxi v. Ningbo Junsheng Yuanda Shipping Co., Ltd. et al. (2015) Wu Hai Fa Shang Zi No. 00599, *judgment of first instance of Wuhan Maritime Court*.. 731
MAO Chuanwu v. Fengdu County Fengping Shipping Investment Co., Ltd. (2015) Wu Hai Fa Shang Zi No. 00134, *judgment of first instance of Wuhan Maritime Court*....................................... 737
Mund & Fester GmbH & Co. KG v. Pangang Group World Trade Panzhihua Co., Ltd. et al. (2011) Wu Hai Fa Shang Zi No. 00300, *judgment of first instance of Wuhan Maritime Court*................... 761
Suqian Rongxiang Shipping Co., Ltd. v. China United Property Insurance Co., Ltd. Jiangsu Branch (2014) Wu Hai Fa Shang Zi No. 01351, *judgment of first instance of Wuhan Maritime Court* 1079
WANG Hong v. Jiangsu Yuanhai Logistics Co., Ltd. et al. (2014) Wu Hai Fa Shi Zi No. 00040, *judgment of first instance of Wuhan Maritime Court*... 1127
WU Guangbao et al. v. Anqing City Yingjiang District Xinzhou Country Ferry Station (2015) Wu Hai Fa Shang Chu Zi No. 00827, *judgment of first instance of Wuhan Maritime Court*............................ 1153
Wuhan Ling Da Compressor Co., Ltd. v. Falcon Insurance Company (Hong Kong) Limited (2014) Wu Hai Fa Shang Zi No. 01268, *judgment of first instance of Wuhan Maritime Court* 1163
WU Jinya v. Nanjing Haijing Shipping Co., Ltd. (2015) Wu Hai Fa Shang Chu Zi No. 00123, *judgment of first instance of Wuhan Maritime Court* 1177

Xiamen Maritime Court

China Minsheng Bank Co., Ltd. (Xiamen Branch) v. Fujian Guanhai
Shipping Co., Ltd. et al. (2015) Xia Hai Fa Shang Chu Zi No. 216,
judgment of first instance of Xiamen Maritime Court 179
Daewoo Shipbuilding & Maritime Engineering Co., Ltd. v. Glory Advance
Corporation (2014) Xia Hai Fa Que Zi No. 1, *judgment of first instance
of Xiamen Maritime Court* 339
GUO Jiangbao v. Xiamen Chengyi Shipping Co., Ltd. (2014) Xia Hai Fa
Shang Chu Zi No. 452, *judgment of first instance of Xiamen Maritime
Court*... 393
Hongxin (HK) Container Development Limited v. Shanghai Hongsheng
Gangtai Shipping Co., Ltd. et al. (2015) Xia Hai Fa Shang Chu Zi No. 378,
judgment of first instance of Xiamen Maritime Court 453
Xiamen Yida Sihai Import & Export Co., Ltd. v. A.P. Moller—Maersk
A/S Co., Ltd. (2014) Xia Hai Fa Shang Chu Zi No. 583, *judgment of first
instance of Xiamen Maritime Court* 1193

Beihai Maritime Court

XUE Haibing et al. v. Sun Shell Shipping Co., Ltd. (2015) Hai Shi Chu Zi
No. 3, *judgment of first instance of Beihai Maritime Court*............. 1221
ZHONG Kangqiu v. Fujian Chengxing Fuel Oil Co., Ltd. (2014) Hai Shang
Chu Zi No. 203, *judgment of first instance of Beihai Maritime Court*....... 1395

Effective Judgments Made by Appeal Courts

Shanghai High People's Court

China Shipping Logistics Co., Ltd. v. Jiangsu Zhongtai Bridge Steel
Structure Co., Ltd. (2014) Hu Hai Fa Shang Chu Zi No. 1068, *judgment
of first instance of Shanghai Maritime Court* 215
China Shipping Logistics Co., Ltd. v. Jiangsu Zhongtai Bridge Steel
Structure Co., Ltd. (2015) Hu Gao Min Si (Hai) Zhong Zi No. 25,
judgment of second instance of Shanghai High People's Court 240
JIANG Haiping v. Shanghai New Qiao Insurance Brokers Ltd. (2014)
Hu Hai Fa Shang Chu Zi No. 1410, *judgment of first instance of Shanghai
Maritime Court* 607
JIANG Haiping v. Shanghai New Qiao Insurance Brokers Ltd. (2015)
Hu Gao Min Si (Hai) Zhong Zi No. 57, *judgment of second instance
of Shanghai High People's Court*................................... 615
Shanghai Yizhou Waterway Engineering Co., Ltd. v. QIU Guohua (2013)
Hu Hai Fa Hai Chu Zi No. 60, *judgment of first instance of Shanghai
Maritime Court*... 943
Shanghai Yizhou Waterway Engineering Co., Ltd. v. QIU Guohua (2015)
Hu Gao Min Si (Hai) Zhong Zi No. 32, *judgment of second instance
of Shanghai High People's Court* 967

Tianjin High People's Court

China Geology and Mining Corporation v. Tianjin Kangjie Import and Export Trade Co., Ltd. et al. (2014) Jin Hai Fa Shang Chu Zi No. 153, *judgment of first instance of Tianjin Maritime Court* 131

China Geology and Mining Corporation v. Tianjin Kangjie Import and Export Trade Co., Ltd. et al. (2015) Jin Gao Min Si Zhong Zi No. 77, *judgment of second instance of Tianjin High People's Court* 152

Shandong High People's Court

Yantai Maritime Safety Administration of the People's Republic of China v. China People's Property Insurance Co., Ltd. Qingdao Branch (2011) Qing Hai Fa Shang Chu Zi No. 187, *judgment of first instance of Qingdao Maritime Court*.. 1241

Yantai Maritime Safety Administration of the People's Republic of China v. China People's Property Insurance Co., Ltd. Qingdao Branch (2014) Lu Min Si Zhong Zi No. 107, *judgment of second instance of Shandong High People's Court*.. 1250

Liaoning High People's Court

SHAN Yongzhen et al. v. LIANG Mingren (2014) Da Hai Shi Chu Zi No. 121, *judgment of first instance of Dalian Maritime Court* 1015

SHAN Yongzhen et al. v. LIANG Mingren (2015) Liao Min San Zhong Zi No. 201, *judgment of second instance of Liaoning High People's Court* 1022

Guangdong High People's Court

China Ping An Property Insurance Co., Ltd. Guangdong Branch v. Guangzhou Hang Jie Logistics Co., Ltd. (2013) Guang Hai Fa Chu Zi No. 1014, *judgment of first instance of Guangzhou Maritime Court* 199

China Ping An Property Insurance Co., Ltd. Guangdong Branch v. Guangzhou Hang Jie Logistics Co., Ltd. (2014) Yue Gao Fa Min Si Zhong Zi No. 204, *judgment of second instance of Guangdong High People's Court* 207

Shanghai Eastern Shipping Material Co., Ltd. v. Beihai Honghai Shipping Co., Ltd. et al. (2009) Guang Hai Fa Chu Zi No. 97, *judgment of first instance of Guangzhou Maritime Court* 877

Shanghai Eastern Shipping Material Co., Ltd. v. Beihai Honghai Shipping Co., Ltd. et al. (2012) Yue Gao Fa Min Si Zhong Zi No. 148, *judgment of second instance of Guangdong High People's Court* 891

Shenzhen COSCO Logistics Co., Ltd. v. Guangdong Yanlin Energy Limited by Share Ltd. (2012) Guang Hai Fa Chu Zi No. 910, *judgment of first instance of Guangzhou Maritime Court*....................... 1031

Shenzhen COSCO Logistics Co., Ltd. v. Guangdong Yanlin Energy
Limited by Share Ltd. (2014) Yue Gao Fa Min Si Zhong Zi No. 197,
judgment of second instance of Guangdong High People's Court 1042
Tai-I Jiangtong (Guangzhou) Co., Ltd. v. American President Lines, Ltd.
(2013) Guang Hai Fa Chu Zi No. 552, *judgment of first instance
of Guangzhou Maritime Court* 1089
Tai-I Jiangtong (Guangzhou) Co., Ltd. v. American President Lines, Ltd.
(2015) Yue Gao Fa Min Si Zhong Zi No. 24, *judgment of second instance
of Guangdong High People's Court* 1107

Hubei High People's Court

Nanjing Jinan Welding Technology Co., Ltd. v. Nanjing Lansheng
Shipbuilding Co., Ltd. (2014) Wu Hai Fa Shang Zi No. 00369, *judgment
of first instance of Wuhan Maritime Court* 781
Nanjing Jinan Welding Technology Co., Ltd. v. Nanjing Lansheng
Shipbuilding Co., Ltd. (2015) E Min Si Zhong Zi No. 00064, *judgment
of second instance of Hubei High People's Court*. 788
Zhumadian South China Sea Shipping Co., Ltd. v. People's Insurance
Company of China Property and Casualty Co., Ltd. Zhumadian Branch
(2014) Wu Hai Fa Shang Chu Zi No. 00795, *judgment of first instance
of Wuhan Maritime Court*. 1355
Zhumadian South China Sea Shipping Co., Ltd. v. People's Insurance
Company of China Property and Casualty Co., Ltd. Zhumadian Branch
(2015) E Min Si Zhong Zi No. 00058, *judgment of second instance
of Hubei High People's Court*. 1377

Hainan High People's Court

Hainan Weilong Shipping Engineering Co., Ltd. v. Hainan Yuehai
Shipping Logistics Co., Ltd. (2014) Qiong Hai Fa Shang Chu Zi No. 87,
judgment of first instance of Haikou Maritime Court 407
Hainan Weilong Shipping Engineering Co., Ltd. v. Hainan Yuehai
Shipping Logistics Co., Ltd. (2015) Qiong Min San Zhong Zi No. 2,
judgment of second instance of Hainan High People's Court. 418
XIE Hongjian v. WENG Kaiheng (2015) Qiong Hai Fa Shang Chu Zi No.
80, *judgment of first instance of Haikou Maritime Court* 1205
XIE Hongjian v. WENG Kaiheng (2015) Qiong Min San Zhong Zi No. 84,
judgment of second instance of Hainan High People's Court. 1214
Zhuhai Xiangzhou Haiyun Co., Ltd. v. Sanya Hongrui Engineer Co., Ltd.
et al. (2014) Qiong Hai Fa Shang Chu Zi No. 80, *judgment of first instance
of Haikou Maritime Court*. 1321
Zhuhai Xiangzhou Haiyun Co., Ltd. v. Sanya Hongrui Engineer Co., Ltd.
et al. (2015) Qiong Min San Zhong Zi No. 25, *judgment of second instance
of Hainan High People's Court* 1337

Effective Judgments Made by Petition Court

The Supreme People's Court

A.P. Moller-Maersk A/S v. Shanghai Chanlian Xieyun Logistics Co., Ltd. et al. (2012) Guang Hai Fa Chu Zi No. 329, *judgment of first instance of Guangzhou Maritime Court* 45

A.P. Moller-Maersk A/S v. Shanghai Chanlian Xieyun Logistics Co., Ltd. et al. (2013) Yue Gao Fa Min Si Zhong Zi No. 162, *judgment of second instance of Guangdong High People's Court* 58

A.P. Moller-Maersk A/S v. Shanghai Chanlian Xieyun Logistics Co., Ltd. et al. (2015) Min Ti Zi No. 119, *judgment of retrial of The Supreme People's Court* 76

China Transport Groupage International (Shenzhen) Limited v. Shenzhen Zhongyi Freight Forwarding Co., Ltd. (2014) Guang Hai Fa Chu Zi No. 102, *judgment of first instance of Guangzhou Maritime Court* 83

China Transport Groupage International (Shenzhen) Limited v. Shenzhen Zhongyi Freight Forwarding Co., Ltd. (2015) Yue Gao Fa Min Si Zhong Zi No. 138, *judgment of second instance of Guangdong High People's Court* 93

China Transport Groupage International (Shenzhen) Limited v. Shenzhen Zhongyi Freight Forwarding Co., Ltd. (2017) Zui Gao Fa Min Shen Zi No. 104, *judgment of retrial of The Supreme People's Court* 107

Connexions (Asia) Limited v. J&S Worldwide Logistics Co., Ltd. et al. (2012) Guang Hai Fa Shang Chu Zi No. 704, *judgment of first instance of Guangzhou Maritime Court* 283

Connexions (Asia) Limited v. J&S Worldwide Logistics Co., Ltd. et al. (2015) Yue Gao Fa Min Si Zhong Zi No. 10, *judgment of second instance of Guangdong High People's Court* 293

Connexions (Asia) Limited v. Shenzhen J&S Worldwide Logistics Ltd. et al. (2015) Min Shen Zi No. 3206, *ruling of retrial of The Supreme People's Court* 309

COSCO Container Lines Co., Ltd. v. Shenzhen Finigate Integrated Logistics Co., Ltd. Qingdao Branch et al. (2014) Qing Hai Fa Hai Shang Chu Zi No. 751, *judgment of first instance of Qingdao Maritime Court* 313

COSCO Container Lines Co., Ltd. v. Shenzhen Finigate Integrated Logistics Co., Ltd. Qingdao Branch et al. (2015) Lu Min Si Zhong Zi No. 152, *judgment of second instance of Shandong High People's Court* 324

COSCO Container Lines Co., Ltd. v. Shenzhen Finigate Integrated Logistics Co., Ltd. Qingdao Branch et al. (2016) Zui Gao Fa Min Shen No. 2157, *ruling of retrial of The Supreme People's Court* 334

Huayu Electrical Appliance Group Co., Ltd. v. JC Logistics Service Co., Ltd. Ningbo Branch (2013) Yong Hai Fa Shang Chu Zi No. 579, *judgment of first instance of Ningbo Maritime Court* 469

Huayu Electrical Appliance Group Co., Ltd. v. JC Logistics Service Co.,
Ltd. Ningbo Branch (2014) Zhe Hai Zhong Zi No. 72, *judgment of second
instance of Zhejiang High People's Court* 476
Huayu Electrical Appliance Group Co., Ltd. v. JC Logistics Service Co.,
Ltd. Ningbo Branch (2015) Min Ti Zi No. 19, *judgment of retrial
of The Supreme People's Court* 485
Hunan Zoomlion International Trade Co., Ltd. et al. v. Shanghai GCL
International Co., Ltd. et al. (2012) Hu Hai Fa Shang Chu Zi No. 1208,
judgment of first instance of Shanghai Maritime Court................. 491
Hunan Zoomlion International Trade Co., Ltd. et al. v. Shanghai GCL
International Co., Ltd. et al. (2014) Hu Gao Min Si (Hai) Zhong Zi No.
119, *judgment of second instance of Shanghai High People's Court* 552
Hunan Zoomlion International Trade Co., Ltd. et al. v. Shanghai GCL
International Co., Ltd. et al. (2016) Zui Gao Fa Min Shen No. 1602,
ruling of retrial of The Supreme People's Court..................... 600
LIN Guihe v. PICC Property and Casualty Company Limited Shunde
Branch (2008) Guang Hai Fa Chu Zi No. 259, *judgment of first instance
of Guangzhou Maritime Court* 689
LIN Guihe v. PICC Property and Casualty Company Limited Shunde
Branch (2014) Yue Gao Min Si Zhong Zi No. 112, *judgment of second
instance of Guangdong High People's Court* 701
LIN Guihe v. PICC Property and Casualty Company Limited Shunde
Branch (2016) Zui Gao Fa Min Shen No. 1452, *ruling of retrial
of The Supreme People's Court* 727
Qinhuangdao Heshun Shipping Co., Ltd. v. China People's Property
Insurance Co., Ltd. Qinhuangdao City Branch (2015) Jin Hai Fa Shang
Chu Zi No. 287, *judgment of first instance of Tianjin Maritime Court*..... 831
Qinhuangdao Heshun Shipping Co., Ltd. v. China People's Property
Insurance Co., Ltd. Qinhuangdao City Branch (2015) Jin Gao Min Si
Zhong Zi No. 93, *judgment of second instance of Tianjin High
People's Court* 842
Qinhuangdao Heshun Shipping Co., Ltd. v. China People's Property
Insurance Co., Ltd. Qinhuangdao City Branch (2016) Zui Gao Fa Min
Shen No. 1395, *ruling of retrial of The Supreme People's Court*......... 854
Shanghai Jielong Industrial Group Co., Ltd. Yutian Packaging and Printing
Branch v. Norasia Container Lines Limited et al. (2012) Hu Hai Fa
Shang Chu Zi No. 1011, *judgment of first instance of Shanghai
Maritime Court*... 987
Shanghai Jielong Industrial Group Co., Ltd. Yutian Packaging and Printing
Branch v. Norasia Container Lines Limited et al. (2013) Hu Gao Min Si
(Hai) Zhong Zi No. 132, *judgment of second instance of Shanghai High
People's Court* 999

Shanghai Jielong Industrial Group Co., Ltd. Yutian Packaging and Printing
Branch v. Norasia Container Lines Limited et al. (2015) Min Shen Zi
No. 573, *ruling of retrial of The Supreme People's Court* 1010

Table of Cases by Cause of Action for Maritime Cases in the People's Republic of China

193. Dispute over liability for ship collision damage

Hong Kong Everglory Shipping Co., Ltd. et al. v. TAN Dingzhao et al. (2014) Guang Hai Fa Shang Chu Zi No. 340, *judgment of first instance of Guangzhou Maritime Court* 433
LI Xuelan et al. v. Ningbo Jialili Shipping Co., Ltd. (2015) Guang Hai Fa Chu Zi No. 397, *judgment of first instance of Guangzhou Maritime Court* 675
Shanghai Eastern Shipping Material Co., Ltd. v. Beihai Honghai Shipping Co., Ltd. et al. (2009) Guang Hai Fa Chu Zi No. 97, *judgment of first instance of Guangzhou Maritime Court*. 877
Shanghai Eastern Shipping Material Co., Ltd. v. Beihai Honghai Shipping Co., Ltd. et al. (2012) Yue Gao Fa Min Si Zhong Zi No. 148, *judgment of second instance of Guangdong High People's Court*. 891
XUE Haibing et al. v. Sun Shell Shipping Co., Ltd. (2015) Hai Shi Chu Zi No. 3, *judgment of first instance of Beihai Maritime Court*. 1221

194. Dispute over liability for contact of vessel

Yue Hai (Fan Yu) Petrochemicals Storage Transportation Development Co., Ltd. v. Shanghai Port Fuxing Shipping Co., Ltd. (2014) Guang Hai Fa Zhong Zi No. 55, *judgment of first instance of Guangzhou Maritime Court* 1263

196. Dispute over liability for damage of ship pollution

WANG Jun v. Dalian Tiger Beach Tourism Development Co., Ltd. (2013) Da Hai Shi Chu Zi No. 78, *judgment of first instance of Dalian Maritime Court* 1143

200. Dispute over liability for personal injury at sea

SHAN Yongzhen et al. v. LIANG Mingren (2014) Da Hai Shi Chu Zi No. 121, *judgment of first instance of Dalian Maritime Court* 1015

SHAN Yongzhen et al. v. LIANG Mingren (2015) Liao Min San Zhong Zi
No. 201, *judgment of second instance of Liaoning High People's Court* ... 1022

201. Dispute over illegal lien on ship, cargoes carried by ship, bunkers and stores of ship

Shandong Xianglong Industrial Group Co., Ltd. v. NCS Co., Ltd. et al.
(2011) Jin Hai Fa Shang Chu Zi No. 465, *judgment of first instance
of Tianjin Maritime Court*.. 859
WANG Hong v. Jiangsu Yuanhai Logistics Co., Ltd. et al. (2014)
Wu Hai Fa Shi Zi No. 00040, *judgment of first instance of Wuhan
Maritime Court*.. 1127
ZHONG Kangqiu v. Fujian Chengxing Fuel Oil Co., Ltd. (2014)
Hai Shang Chu Zi No. 203, *judgment of first instance of Beihai
Maritime Court*.. 1395

202. Dispute over contract of carriage of goods by sea or sea-connected waters

AIG Europe Ltd. v. Shanghai Heming Shipping Service Co., Ltd. Tianjin
Branch et al. (2014) Hu Hai Fa Shang Chu Zi No. 116, *judgment of first
instance of Shanghai Maritime Court*............................. 1
Allianz China General Insurance Co., Ltd. v. Youda (Shanghai)
International Freight Co. Ltd. et al. (2014) Hu Hai Fa Shang Chu Zi No.
361, *judgment of first instance of Shanghai Maritime Court*..... 11
A.P. Moller-Maersk A/S v. Shanghai Chanlian Xieyun Logistics Co., Ltd.
et al. (2012) Guang Hai Fa Chu Zi No. 329, *judgment of first instance
of Guangzhou Maritime Court*..................................... 45
A.P. Moller-Maersk A/S v. Shanghai Chanlian Xieyun Logistics Co., Ltd.
et al. (2013) Yue Gao Fa Min Si Zhong Zi No. 162, *judgment of second
instance of Guangdong High People's Court*....................... 58
A.P. Moller-Maersk A/S v. Shanghai Chanlian Xieyun Logistics Co., Ltd.
et al. (2015) Min Ti Zi No. 119, *judgment of retrial of The Supreme
People's Court*.. 76
China Shipping Logistics Co., Ltd. v. Jiangsu Zhongtai Bridge Steel
Structure Co., Ltd. (2014) Hu Hai Fa Shang Chu Zi No. 1068, *judgment
of first instance of Shanghai Maritime Court*.................... 215
China Shipping Logistics Co., Ltd. v. Jiangsu Zhongtai Bridge Steel
Structure Co., Ltd. (2015) Hu Gao Min Si (Hai) Zhong Zi No. 25,
judgment of second instance of Shanghai High People's Court.... 240
Connexions (Asia) Limited v. J&S Worldwide Logistics Co., Ltd. et al.
(2012) Guang Hai Fa Shang Chu Zi No. 704, *judgment of first instance
of Guangzhou Maritime Court*..................................... 283

Connexions (Asia) Limited v. J&S Worldwide Logistics Co., Ltd. et al.
(2015) Yue Gao Fa Min Si Zhong Zi No. 10, *judgment of second instance
of Guangdong High People's Court*.............................. 293
Connexions (Asia) Limited v. J&S Worldwide Logistics Co., Ltd. et al.
(2015) Min Shen Zi No. 3206, *ruling of retrial of The Supreme
People's Court* 309
COSCO Container Lines Co., Ltd. v. Shenzhen Finigate Integrated
Logistics Co., Ltd. Qingdao Branch et al. (2014) Qing Hai Fa Hai Shang
Chu Zi No. 751, *judgment of first instance of Qingdao Maritime Court*.... 313
COSCO Container Lines Co., Ltd. v. Shenzhen Finigate Integrated
Logistics Co., Ltd. Qingdao Branch et al. (2015) Lu Min Si Zhong Zi
No. 152, *judgment of second instance of Shandong High People's Court*.... 324
COSCO Container Lines Co., Ltd. v. Shenzhen Finigate Integrated
Logistics Co., Ltd. Qingdao Branch et al. (2016) Zui Gao Fa Min Shen
No. 2157, *ruling of retrial of The Supreme People's Court* 334
Fan Sen (V.S) Shanghai International Freight Forwarding Co., Ltd. v.
Zhongman Petroleum & Natural Gas Group Co., Ltd. (2014) Hu Hai Fa
Shang Chu Zi No. 1112, *judgment of first instance of Shanghai
Maritime Court*.. 363
Hunan Zoomlion International Trade Co., Ltd. et al. v. Shanghai GCL
International Co., Ltd. et al. (2012) Hu Hai Fa Shang Chu Zi No. 1208,
judgment of first instance of Shanghai Maritime Court................ 491
Hunan Zoomlion International Trade Co., Ltd. et al. v. Shanghai GCL
International Co., Ltd. et al. (2014) Hu Gao Min Si (Hai) Zhong Zi No.
119, *judgment of second instance of Shanghai High People's Court* 552
Hunan Zoomlion International Trade Co., Ltd. et al. v. Shanghai GCL
International Co., Ltd. et al. (2016) Zui Gao Fa Min Shen No. 1602,
ruling of retrial of The Supreme People's Court..................... 600
Mitsui O.S.K. Lines, Ltd. v. Guangdong Shunde Local Product Import
and Export Co., Ltd. et al. (2014) Guang Hai Fa Chu Zi No. 339, *judgment
of first instance of Guangzhou Maritime Court*....................... 747
Mund & Fester GmbH & Co. KG v. Pangang Group World Trade
Panzhihua Co., Ltd. et al. (2011) Wu Hai Fa Shang Zi No. 00300,
judgment of first instance of Wuhan Maritime Court.................. 761
Operating Department of China Continent Property & Casualty Insurance
Co., Ltd. v. China Shipping Logistics Co., Ltd. (2014) Hu Hai Fa Shang Chu
Zi No. 1509, *judgment of first instance of Shanghai Maritime Court* 799
People's Insurance Company of China Hangzhou Branch v. Tribute Ship
Holding S.A. (2014) Da Hai Shang Chu Zi No. 21, *judgment of first
instance of Dalian Maritime Court*................................ 811
Shanghai Jielong Industrial Group Co., Ltd. Yutian Packaging and Printing
Branch v. Norasia Container Lines Limited et al. (2012) Hu Hai Fa
Shang Chu Zi No. 1011, *judgment of first instance of Shanghai
Maritime Court*.. 987

Shanghai Jielong Industrial Group Co., Ltd. Yutian Packaging and Printing
Branch v. Norasia Container Lines Limited et al. (2013) Hu Gao Min Si
(Hai) Zhong Zi No. 132, *judgment of second instance of Shanghai High
People's Court* 999
Shanghai Jielong Industrial Group Co., Ltd. Yutian Packaging and Printing
Branch v. Norasia Container Lines Limited et al. (2015) Min Shen Zi
No. 573, *ruling of retrial of The Supreme People's Court* 1010
Silvery Dragon Prestressed Materials Co., Ltd. (Tianjin) v. Dalian Pei Hua
International Logistics Co., Ltd. (2014) Jin Hai Fa Shang Chu Zi No. 698,
judgment of first instance of Tianjin Maritime Court 1053
Tai-I Jiangtong (Guangzhou) Co., Ltd. v. American President Lines, Ltd.
(2013) Guang Hai Fa Chu Zi No. 552, *judgment of first instance
of Guangzhou Maritime Court* 1089
Tai-I Jiangtong (Guangzhou) Co., Ltd. v. American President Lines, Ltd.
(2015) Yue Gao Fa Min Si Zhong Zi No. 24, *judgment of second instance
of Guangdong High People's Court* 1107
Tianjin Tianguan Ocean International Freight Forwarding Co., Ltd.
v. Yantai Fuhai International Ship Management Co., Ltd. et al. (2014)
Jin Hai Fa Shang Chu Zi No. 772, *judgment of first instance of Tianjin
Maritime Court*... 1117
Xiamen Yida Sihai Import & Export Co., Ltd. v. A.P. Moller—Maersk
A/S Co., Ltd. (2014) Xia Hai Fa Shang Chu Zi No. 583, *judgment of first
instance of Xiamen Maritime Court* 1193
Zhuhai Jiaxun Saite Electronic Co., Ltd. v. Shenzhen Shi Chang Freight
Co., Ltd. et al. (2015) Guang Hai Fa Chu Zi No. 182, *judgment of first
instance of Guangzhou Maritime Court* 1309

205. Dispute over ship operation contract

WU Guangbao et al. v. Anqing City Yingjiang District Xinzhou Country
Ferry Station (2015) Wu Hai Fa Shang Chu Zi No. 00827, *judgment of first
instance of Wuhan Maritime Court*................................. 1153

206. Dispute over ship sales and purchases contract

Shanghai Yizhou Waterway Engineering Co., Ltd. v. QIU Guohua (2013)
Hu Hai Fa Hai Chu Zi No. 60, *judgment of first instance of Shanghai
Maritime Court*... 943
Shanghai Yizhou Waterway Engineering Co., Ltd. v. QIU Guohua (2015)
Hu Gao Min Si (Hai) Zhong Zi No. 32, *judgment of second instance
of Shanghai High People's Court*................................... 967

207. Dispute over shipbuilding contract

Export-Import Bank of China et al. v. Nanjing Wujiazui Ship Building Co.,
Ltd. et al. (2014) Wu Hai Fa Shang Chu Zi No. 00470, *judgment of first
instance of Wuhan Maritime Court* 349
Hainan Weilong Shipping Engineering Co., Ltd. v. Hainan Yuehai
Shipping Logistics Co., Ltd. (2014) Qiong Hai Fa Shang Chu Zi No. 87,
judgment of first instance of Haikou Maritime Court. 407
Hainan Weilong Shipping Engineering Co., Ltd. v. Hainan Yuehai
Shipping Logistics Co., Ltd. (2015) Qiong Min San Zhong Zi No. 2,
judgment of second instance of Hainan High People's Court. 418
Jiangsu Eastern Heavy Industry Co., Ltd. v. Nanjing Twin Rivers Shipping
Co., Ltd. (2012) Jin Hai Fa Shang Chu Zi No. 784, *judgment of first
instance of Tianjin Maritime Court.* 625
MAO Chuanwu v. Fengdu County Fengping Shipping Investment Co.,
Ltd. (2015) Wu Hai Fa Shang Zi No. 00134, *judgment of first instance
of Wuhan Maritime Court*. 737
Nanjing Jinan Welding Technology Co., Ltd. v. Nanjing Lansheng
Shipbuilding Co., Ltd. (2014) Wu Hai Fa Shang Zi No. 00369, *judgment
of first instance of Wuhan Maritime Court* 781
Nanjing Jinan Welding Technology Co., Ltd. v. Nanjing Lansheng
Shipbuilding Co., Ltd. (2015) E Min Si Zhong Zi No. 00064, *judgment
of second instance of Hubei High People's Court*. 788

210. Dispute over ship dismantling contract

XIE Hongjian v. WENG Kaiheng (2015) Qiong Hai Fa Shang Chu Zi No.
80, *judgment of first instance of Haikou Maritime Court* 1205
XIE Hongjian v. WENG Kaiheng (2015) Qiong Min San Zhong Zi No. 84,
judgment of second instance of Hainan High People's Court. 1214

211. Dispute over ship mortgage contract

China Guangfa Bank Stock Co., Ltd. Nanjing Chengxi Branch v. Nanjing
Hengshunda Shipping Co., Ltd. et al. (2015) Wu Hai Fa Shang Zi No.
00205, *judgment of first instance of Wuhan Maritime Court*. 171
China Minsheng Bank Co., Ltd. (Xiamen Branch) v. Fujian Guanhai
Shipping Co., Ltd. et al. (2015) Xia Hai Fa Shang Chu Zi No. 216,
judgment of first instance of Xiamen Maritime Court 179
Daewoo Shipbuilding & Maritime Engineering Co., Ltd. v. Glory Advance
Corporation (2014) Xia Hai Fa Que Zi No. 1, *judgment of first instance
of Xiamen Maritime Court* 339

212. Dispute over voyage charter party

Shenzhen COSCO Logistics Co., Ltd. v. Guangdong Yanlin Energy
Limited by Share Ltd. (2012) Guang Hai Fa Chu Zi No. 910, *judgment
of first instance of Guangzhou Maritime Court*...... 1031
Shenzhen COSCO Logistics Co., Ltd. v. Guangdong Yanlin Energy
Limited by Share Ltd. (2014) Yue Gao Fa Min Si Zhong Zi No. 197,
judgment of second instance of Guangdong High People's Court 1042

213(1) Dispute over time charter party

Zhuhai Xiangzhou Haiyun Co., Ltd. v. Sanya Hongrui Engineer Co., Ltd.
et al. (2014) Qiong Hai Fa Shang Chu Zi No. 80, *judgment of first instance
of Haikou Maritime Court*....... 1321
Zhuhai Xiangzhou Haiyun Co., Ltd. v. Sanya Hongrui Engineer Co., Ltd.
et al. (2015) Qiong Min San Zhong Zi No. 25, *judgment of second instance
of Hainan High People's Court*....... 1337

213(2) Dispute over bareboat charter party

Changhang Phoenix Co., Ltd. v. Wuhan Tairun Marine Service Co., Ltd.
et al. (2014) Wu Hai Fa Shang Zi No. 01755, *judgment of first instance
of Wuhan Maritime Court*........ 121

214. Dispute over ship financial leasing contract

Jianxin Finance Leasing Co., Ltd. v. Wenzhou Changjiang Energy
Shipping Co., Ltd. et al. (2015) Jin Hai Fa Shang Chu Zi No. 663,
judgment of first instance of Tianjin Maritime Court 647

219. Dispute over contract on lease of shipping container

Hongxin (HK) Container Development Limited v. Shanghai Hongsheng
Gangtai Shipping Co., Ltd. et al. (2015) Xia Hai Fa Shang Chu Zi No. 378,
judgment of first instance of Xiamen Maritime Court 453

221. Dispute over contract on custody of cargo in port

China Geology and Mining Corporation v. Tianjin Kangjie Import and
Export Trade Co., Ltd. et al. (2014) Jin Hai Fa Shang Chu Zi No. 153,
judgment of first instance of Tianjin Maritime Court 131
China Geology and Mining Corporation v. Tianjin Kangjie Import and
Export Trade Co., Ltd. et al. (2015) Jin Gao Min Si Zhong Zi No. 77,
judgment of second instance of Tianjin High People's Court 152

223. Dispute over freight forwarding contract on the sea or sea-connected waters

China Transport Groupage international (Shenzhen) Limited v. Shenzhen Zhongyi Freight Forwarding Co., Ltd. (2014) Guang Hai Fa Chu Zi No. 102, *judgment of first instance of Guangzhou Maritime Court*........ 83
China Transport Groupage international (Shenzhen) Limited v. Shenzhen Zhongyi Freight Forwarding Co., Ltd. (2015) Yue Gao Fa Min Si Zhong Zi No. 138, *judgment of second instance of Guangdong High People's Court*... 93
China Transport Groupage international (Shenzhen) Limited v. Shenzhen Zhongyi Freight Forwarding Co., Ltd. (2017) Zui Gao Fa Min Shen Zi No. 104, *judgment of retrial of The Supreme People's Court*............ 107
China Ping An Property Insurance Co., Ltd. Guangdong Branch v. Guangzhou Hang Jie Logistics Co., Ltd. (2013) Guang Hai Fa Chu Zi No. 1014, *judgment of first instance of Guangzhou Maritime Court*....... 199
China Ping An Property Insurance Co., Ltd. Guangdong Branch v. Guangzhou Hang Jie Logistics Co., Ltd. (2014) Yue Gao Fa Min Si Zhong Zi No. 204, *judgment of second instance of Guangdong High People's Court*........... 207
Huayu Electrical Appliance Group Co., Ltd. v. JC Logistics Service Co., Ltd. Ningbo Branch (2013) Yong Hai Fa Shang Chu Zi No. 579, *judgment of first instance of Ningbo Maritime Court*........................... 469
Huayu Electrical Appliance Group Co., Ltd. v. JC Logistics Service Co., Ltd. Ningbo Branch (2014) Zhe Hai Zhong Zi No. 72, *judgment of second instance of Zhejiang High People's Court*............................ 476
Huayu Electrical Appliance Group Co., Ltd. v. JC Logistics Service Co., Ltd. Ningbo Branch (2015) Min Ti Zi No. 19, *judgment of retrial of The Supreme People's Court*.. 485
Shanghai Wan Feng International Freight Forwarding Co., Ltd. v. Fujian Hongxing Electronic Technology Co., Ltd. (2014) Hu Hai Fa Shang Chu Zi No. 1496, *judgment of first instance of Shanghai Maritime Court*....... 925

225. Dispute over contract for marine stores and spare parts supply

Fujian Guanhai Shipping Co., Ltd. v. Shanghai Huaya Ship Fuel Company (2015) Hu Hai Fa Shang Chu Zi No. 47, *judgment of first instance of Shanghai Maritime Court*.................................... 381

226. Dispute over contract for employment of seaman

GUO Jiangbao v. Xiamen Chengyi Shipping Co., Ltd. (2014) Xia Hai Fa Shang Chu Zi No. 452, *judgment of first instance of Xiamen Maritime Court*... 393
LIU Fengxi v. Ningbo Junsheng Yuanda Shipping Co., Ltd. et al. (2015) Wu Hai Fa Shang Zi No. 00599, *judgment of first instance of Wuhan Maritime Court*... 731

230. Dispute over marine insurance contract on the sea or sea-connected waters

JIANG Haiping v. Shanghai New Qiao Insurance Brokers Ltd. (2014) Hu Hai Fa Shang Chu Zi No. 1410, *judgment of first instance of Shanghai Maritime Court*.. 607

JIANG Haiping v. Shanghai New Qiao Insurance Brokers Ltd. (2015) Hu Gao Min Si (Hai) Zhong Zi No. 57, *judgment of second instance of Shanghai High People's Court*.................................... 615

LIN Guihe v. PICC Property and Casualty Company Limited Shunde Branch (2008) Guang Hai Fa Chu Zi No. 259, *judgment of first instance of Guangzhou Maritime Court* 689

LIN Guihe v. PICC Property and Casualty Company Limited Shunde Branch (2014) Yue Gao Min Si Zhong Zi No. 112, *judgment of second instance of Guangdong High People's Court*........................ 701

LIN Guihe v. PICC Property and Casualty Company Limited Shunde Branch (2016) Zui Gao Fa Min Shen No. 1452, *ruling of retrial of The Supreme People's Court* 727

Qinhuangdao Heshun Shipping Co., Ltd. v. China People's Property Insurance Co., Ltd. Qinhuangdao City Branch (2015) Jin Hai Fa Shang Chu Zi No. 287, *judgment of first instance of Tianjin Maritime Court* 831

Qinhuangdao Heshun Shipping Co., Ltd. v. China People's Property Insurance Co., Ltd. Qinhuangdao City Branch (2015) Jin Gao Min Si Zhong Zi No. 93, *judgment of second instance of Tianjin High People's Court*.. 842

Qinhuangdao Heshun Shipping Co., Ltd. v. China People's Property Insurance Co., Ltd. Qinhuangdao City Branch (2016) Zui Gao Fa Min Shen No. 1395, *ruling of retrial of The Supreme People's Court*......... 854

Suqian Rongxiang Shipping Co., Ltd. v. China United Property Insurance Co., Ltd. Jiangsu Branch (2014) Wu Hai Fa Shang Zi No. 01351, *judgment of first instance of Wuhan Maritime Court* 1079

Wuhan Ling Da Compressor Co., Ltd. v. Falcon Insurance Company (Hong Kong) Limited (2014) Wu Hai Fa Shang Zi No. 01268, *judgment of first instance of Wuhan Maritime Court* 1163

Zhumadian South China Sea Shipping Co., Ltd. v. People's Insurance Company of China Property and Casualty Co., Ltd. Zhumadian Branch (2014) Wu Hai Fa Shang Chu Zi No. 00795, *judgment of first instance of Wuhan Maritime Court*.. 1355

Zhumadian South China Sea Shipping Co., Ltd. v. People's Insurance Company of China Property and Casualty Co., Ltd. Zhumadian Branch (2015) E Min Si Zhong Zi No. 00058, *judgment of second instance of Hubei High People's Court*.................................... 1377

231. Dispute over contract for protection and indemnity insurance on the sea or sea-connected waters

Chongqing Red Dragonfly Oil Limited Liability Company v. PICC Property and Casualty Company Limited Chongqing Branch (2015) Wu Hai Fa Shang Zi No. 00151, *judgment of first instance of Wuhan Maritime Court* 267

Yantai Maritime Safety Administration of the People's Republic of China v. China People's Property Insurance Co., Ltd. Qingdao Branch (2011) Qing Hai Fa Shang Chu Zi No. 187, *judgment of first instance of Qingdao Maritime Court* 1241

Yantai Maritime Safety Administration of the People's Republic of China v. China People's Property Insurance Co., Ltd. Qingdao Branch (2014) Lu Min Si Zhong Zi No. 107, *judgment of second instance of Shandong High People's Court* 1250

236. Dispute over contract for construction of dock or harbor

Station Ocean Administration Beihai Branch v. WANG Jianlong et al. (2013) Qing Hai Fa Hai Shang Chu Zi No. 986, *judgment of first instance of Qingdao Maritime Court* 1067

243. Dispute over marine development and utilization of sea

LI Chunjiang v. Tanggu Water Conservancy Project Company et al. (2013) Jin Hai Fa Shang Chu Zi No. 521, *judgment of first instance of Tianjin Maritime Court* 661

245. Dispute over ownership of ship

WU Jinya v. Nanjing Haijing Shipping Co., Ltd. (2015) Wu Hai Fa Shang Chu Zi No. 00123, *judgment of first instance of Wuhan Maritime Court* ... 1177

247. Dispute over confirmation of maritime claim

Qingdao Huashun Shipping Co., Ltd. v. Marc Loud Schiffahrts-Gesellschaft mbH & Co. KG. (2014) Qing Hai Fa Que Zi No. 7-1, *judgment of first instance of Qingdao Maritime Court* 823

List of Maritime Courts and Their Appeal and Petition Courts in the People's Republic of China

Maritime Courts	Appeal Courts	Petition Court
Shanghai Maritime Court http://shhsfy.gov.cn/hsfyytwx/hsfyytwx/	Shanghai High People's Court http://www.hshfy.sh.cn/	The Supreme People's Court of the People's Republic of China http://www.court.gov.cn/
Tianjin Maritime Court http://tjhsfy.chinacourt.gov.cn/index.html	Tianjin High People's Court http://tjfy.chinacourt.gov.cn/index.shtml	
Qingdao Maritime Court http://qdhsfy.sdcourt.gov.cn/qdhsfy/sjb/index.html	Shandong High People's Court http://sdcourt.gov.cn/	
Dalian Maritime Court http://www.dlhsfy.gov.cn/court/	Liaoning High People's Court http://lnfy.chinacourt.gov.cn/index.shtml	
Guangzhou Maritime Court http://www.gzhsfy.gov.cn/	Guangdong High People's Court http://www.gdcourts.gov.cn/	
Wuhan Maritime Court http://whhsfy.hbfy.gov.cn/	Hubei High People's Court http://www.hbfy.gov.cn/	
Haikou Maritime Court http://www.hkhsfy.gov.cn/	Hainan High People's Court http://www.hicourt.gov.cn/	
Xiamen Maritime Court http://www.xmhsfy.gov.cn/	Fujian High People's Court http://www.fjcourt.gov.cn/	
Ningbo Maritime Court https://www.nbhsfy.cn/court/index.html	Zhejiang High People's Court http://www.zjsfgkw.cn/	
Beihai Maritime Court http://www.bhhsfy.gov.cn/platformData/infoplat/pub/bhhs_32/shouye_1003/index.html	Guangxi Zhuang Autonomous Region High People's Court http://www.gxcourt.gov.cn/	
Nanjing Maritime Court www.njhsfy.gov.cn/	Jiangsu High People's Court http://www.jsfy.gov.cn/	

List of Causes of Action for Maritime Cases in the People's Republic of China (Extracted from the Regulations on Causes of Action for Civil Disputes made by The Supreme People's Court of the People's Republic of China 2020)

Part 6 Ownership Dispute	
49. Dispute over return of property buried underground	
Part 7 Usufruct Dispute	
55. Dispute over exploration right	
Part 8 Mortgage Dispute	
67. Dispute over mortgage	
(8) Dispute over mortgage of movables	
(9) Dispute over mortgage of vessels and aircrafts under manufacture	
(10) Dispute over floating charge of movables	
(11) Dispute over right of mortgage of ceiling amount	
68. Dispute over right of pledge	
(1) Dispute over right of pledge of movables	
(2) Dispute over right of re-pledge	
(3) Dispute over right of pledge of ceiling amount	
(7) Dispute over right of pledge of warehouse receipts	
(8) Dispute over right of pledge of bills of lading	
(9) Dispute over right of pledge of equity interest	
(12) Dispute over right of pledge of receivables	
69. Dispute over right of lien	
Part 10 Contract Dispute	
74. Dispute over liability for fault in contracting	
76. Dispute over confirming the validity of contract	
(1) Dispute over confirming the validity of contract	
(2) Dispute over confirming the invalidity of contract	
77. Dispute over contract for assignment of creditor's rights	
103. Dispute over contract of loan	
(1) Dispute over contract of financial loan	
104. Dispute over contract of suretyship	
106. Dispute over pledge contract	
114. Dispute over contract for contracting work	
(1) Dispute over contract for processing	

(continued)

(continued)

(2) Dispute over contract for manufacturing	
(5) Dispute over contract for testing	
(6) Dispute over contract for inspecting	
116. Dispute over contract for carriage	
(3) Dispute over contract for carriage of passengers by waterway	
(4) Dispute over contract for carriage of goods by waterway	
(10) Dispute over contract for combined transport	
(11) Dispute over contract for combined transport by multiple way	
118. Dispute over contract of warehouse	
119. Dispute over agency contract	
(1) Dispute over contract for agency contract for import/ export	
121. Dispute over commission contract	
123. Dispute over intermediary contract	
143. Dispute over right of recourse	
Part 19 Maritime Dispute	
193. Dispute over liability for ship collision damage	
194. Dispute over liability for contact of vessel	
195. Dispute over liability for damage to facility in the air or under water	
196. Dispute over liability for damage of ship pollution	
197. Dispute over liability for marine pollution damage on the sea or sea-connected waters	
198. Dispute over liability for damage to breeding on the sea or sea-connected waters	
199. Dispute over liability for damage to property on the sea or sea-connected waters	
200. Dispute over liability for personal injury at sea	
201. Dispute over illegal lien on ship, cargoes carried by ship, bunkers and stores of ship	
202. Dispute over contract of carriage of goods by sea or sea-connected waters	
203. Dispute over contract of carriage of passenger by sea or sea-connected waters	
204. Dispute over contract of carriage of luggage by sea or sea-connected waters	
205. Dispute over ship operation contract	
206. Dispute over ship sales and purchases contract	
207. Dispute over shipbuilding contract	
208. Dispute over ship repairing contract	
209. Dispute over ship rebuilding contract	
210. Dispute over ship dismantling contract	
211. Dispute over ship mortgage contract	
212. Dispute over voyage charter party	
213. Dispute over charter party	
(1) Dispute over time charter party	
(2) Dispute over bareboat charter party	
214. Dispute over ship financial leasing contract	
215. Dispute over undertaking contract of transporting ship on the sea or sea-connected waters	
216. Dispute over undertaking contract of fishing ships	
217. Dispute over contract for lease of utensils affixed to ship	
218. Dispute over contract for custody of utensils affixed to ship	
219. Dispute over contract on lease of shipping container	
220. Dispute over contract on custody of shipping container	

(continued)

List of Causes of Action for Maritime Cases in the People's Republic of China … xlvii

(continued)

221. Dispute over contract on custody of cargo in port
222. Dispute over shipping agency contract
223. Dispute over freight forwarding contract on the sea or sea-connected waters
224. Dispute over tally contract
225. Dispute over contract for marine stores and spare parts supply
226. Dispute over contract for employment of seaman
227. Dispute over salvage contract
228. Dispute over contract on refloatation on the sea or sea-connected waters
229. Dispute over towage contract on the sea or sea-connected waters
230. Dispute over marine insurance contract on the sea or sea-connected waters
231. Dispute over contract for protection and indemnity insurance on the sea or sea-connected waters
232. Dispute over contract for joint transport on the sea or sea-connected waters
233. Dispute over ship operation loan contract
234. Dispute over maritime security contract
235. Dispute over channel and port dredging contract
236. Dispute over contract for construction of dock or harbor
237. Dispute over contract for inspection of ship
238. Dispute over maritime security
239. Dispute over liability for major transport accident on the sea or sea-connected waters
240. Dispute over liability for major accident of port operation
241. Dispute over port operation
242. Dispute over general average
243. Dispute over marine development and utilization of sea
244. Dispute over joint ownership of ship
245. Dispute over ownership of ship
246. Dispute over maritime fraud
247. Dispute over confirmation of maritime claim
Part 20 Business-related Dispute
256. Dispute over contract for affiliated operation
258. Dispute over contract for joint operation
Part 27 Insurance Dispute
333. Dispute over contract for property insurance
(4) Dispute over contract for guarantee insurance
(5) Dispute over insurer's right of subrogation
335. Dispute over contract for reinsurance
336. Dispute over contract for insurance brokerage
337. Dispute over contract for insurance agency
Part 31 Tort Liability Dispute
390. Dispute over liability for damage caused by water transport
(1) Dispute over liability for personal injury caused by water transport
(2) Dispute over liability for property damage caused by water transport
392. Dispute over damage caused by application for pre-litigation property preservation
393. Dispute over damage caused by application for pre-litigation evidence preservation
395. Dispute over damage caused by application for advance execution
Part 32 Cases of Declaration of Missing and Declaration of Death

(continued)

(continued)

400. Application for adjudication of death of citizen	
401. Application for revocation of adjudication of death of citizen	
Part 36 Cases of Holding Properties Unclaimed	
407. Application for determining certain property as ownerless	
408. Application for revocation of determination of certain property as ownerless	
Part 40 Cases of Procedure for Hastening	
418. Application for payment orders	
Part 41 Cases of Procedure of Public Summons for Exhortation	
419. Application for public summons for exhortation	
Part 45 Cases of Application for Preservation	
431. Application for pre-litigation property preservation	
432. Application for pre-litigation behaviors preservation	
433. Application for pre-litigation evidence preservation	
434. Application for pre-arbitration property preservation	
435. Application for pre-arbitration behaviors preservation	
436. Application for pre-arbitration evidence preservation	
437. Property preservation in arbitration proceedings	
438. Evidence preservation in arbitration proceedings	
439. Application for suspending payment of the amount under a letter of credit	
441. Application for suspending payment of the amount under a letter of guarantee	
Part 48 Arbitration Cases	
444. Application for confirmation of effectiveness of arbitration agreements	
445. Application for revocation in arbitral award	
Part 49 Special Maritime Procedure Cases	
446. Application for reservation of maritime claims	
(1) Application for detention of vessels	
(2) Application for auction of detained vessels	
(3) Application for seizure of vessel cargoes	
(4) Application for auction of seizure vessel cargoes	
(5) Application for seizure of bunker oil and ship's stores	
(6) Application for auction of seizure bunker oil and ship's stores	
447. Application for maritime payment orders	
448. Application for maritime injunctions	
449. Application for maritime evidence preservation	
450. Application for establishment of a fund for limitation liability for maritime claims	
451. Application for publicizing notices for assertion of maritime priority rights	
452. Application for registration and repayment of maritime claims	
Part 50 Application for Recognition and Enforcement of Judgments and Awards Cases	
453. Application for enforcement of maritime arbitral award	
454. Application for enforcement of intellectual property arbitral award	
455. Application for enforcement of foreign affairs arbitral award	
456. Application for recognition and enforcement of civil judgment rendered by court of the Hong Kong Special Administrative Region	
457. Application for recognition and enforcement of arbitration award rendered by court of the Hong Kong Special Administrative Region	

(continued)

(continued)

458. Application for recognition and enforcement of civil judgment rendered by court of the Macao Special Administrative Region
459. Application for recognition and enforcement of arbitration award rendered by court of the Macao Special Administrative Region
460. Application for recognition and enforcement of civil judgment rendered by court of Taiwan Special Administrative Region
461. Application for recognition and enforcement of arbitration award rendered by court of Taiwan Special Administrative Region
462. Application for recognition and enforcement of civil judgment rendered by foreign court
463. Application for recognition and enforcement of foreign arbitration award
Part 54 Action of Opposition to Enforcement Cases
471. Offense against enforcement
(1) Offense against enforcement by an outsider
(1) Application for enforcement of objection
472. Objection over the implementation of the distribution plan

Table of References

Chinese Legislation

(2015) Min Si Ta Zi Reply of the Supreme People's Court
Item 2...... People's Insurance (p. 818, p. 819)

Administrative Measures of the Customs of the People's Republic of China for Manifests of Inward and Outward Means of Transport
Art. 9 Para. 3......Tai-I Jiangtong (p. 1110)
Art. 13......Tai-I Jiangtong (p. 1105)

Administrative Measures of the Customs of the People's Republic of China for the Inspection of Imported and Exported Goods
Art. 2......Tai-I Jiangtong (p. 1105)
Art. 17 Para. 2......Tai-I Jiangtong (p. 1105)

Civil Procedure Law of the People's Republic of China
Art. 13 Para. 1......LIN Guihe (p. 721)
Art. 21 Para. 1.......WU Jinya (p. 1178)
Art. 23......China Transport Groupage (p. 90, p. 98, p. 111) China Guangfa (p. 173) Export-Import (p. 350) Nanjing Jinan (p. 782)
Art. 24......Chongqing Red (p. 268) Suqian Rongxiang (p. 1080)
Art. 27......A.P. Moller-Maersk (p. 53, p. 66) Connexions (Asia) (p. 290, p. 300, p. 306) Tai-I Jiangtong (p. 1103) Xiamen Yida (p. 1200)
Art. 28......Mund & Fester (p. 762)
Art. 30......Hong Kong (p. 447) Qingdao Huashun (p. 828)
Art. 56 Para. 2......Jiangsu Eastern (p. 645)
Art. 64......Connexions (Asia) (p. 292, p. 302) MAO Chuanwu (p. 745)
Art. 64 Para. 1......AIG Europe (p. 8) Allianz China (p. 39) China Transport Groupage (p. 91, p. 99, p. 100, p. 103, p. 104, p. 112, p. 113, p. 115, p.116) China Geology p. 151, p. 160) China Shipping (p. 237, p. 262) Daewoo Shipbuilding (p. 346) Fan Sen (p. 377) Fujian Guanhai (p. 390) GUO Jiangbao (p. 402) Hong Kong (p. 450) Hongxin (HK) (p. 465) Hunan Zoomlion (p. 548, p. 586) JIANG Haiping (p. 614, p. 619) Jianxin Finance (p. 658) LI Chunjiang (p. 672) LI Xuelan (p. 686) LIN Guihe (p. 699, p. 720, p. 722) Mund & Fester (p. 779) Operating Department (p. 808) Qinhuangdao Heshun (p. 841, p. 848) Shandong Xianglong (p. 875) Shanghai Wan (p. 940) Shanghai Yizhou (p. 965, p. 979) Shanghai Jielong (p. 997, p. 1005) Shenzhen COSCO (p. 1047) Silvery Dragon

(continued)

(continued)

(p. 1064) Tai-I Jiangtong (p. 1106) Tianjin Tianguan (p. 1124) WANG Hong (p. 1141) WU Guangbao (p. 1161) Xiamen Yida (p. 1203) XUE Haibing (p. 1238) Yue Hai (p. 1306) Zhumadian South (p. 1373, p. 1385)
Art. 65 Para. 2 Zhumadian South (p. 1362)
Art. 67 Para. 1......LIN Guihe (p. 708)
Art. 70 Sub-Para. 1......Hongxin (HK) (p. 458)
Art. 78......LIN Guihe (p. 712)
Art. 124......WANG Hong (p. 1141)
Art. 137......China Ping (p. 213)
Art. 142......Changhang Phoenix (p. 129) China Guangfa (p. 177) Chongqing Red (p. 281) Export-Import (p. 361) MAO Chuanwu (p. 745) Mund & Fester (p. 779) Nanjing Jinan (p. 787, p. 792) Suqian Rongxiang (p. 1086) WU Guangbao (p. 1161) Wuhan Ling (p. 1175) WU Jinya (p. 1191) Zhumadian South (p. 1375, p. 1387)
Art. 144......China Minsheng (p. 195) COSCO Container (p. 333) Daewoo Shipbuilding (p. 346) Export-Import (p. 361) Hongxin (HK) (p. 465) Jianxin Finance (p. 658) LIU Fengxi (p. 735) Mitsui O.S.K. (p. 758) Tianjin Tianguan (p. 1124)
Art. 152......Export-Import (p. 361)
Art. 153......Qingdao Huashun (p. 829)
Art. 170 Para. 1......JIANG Haiping (p. 623) Yantai Maritime (p. 1261)
Art. 170 Para. 1 Sub-Para. 1......AP. Moller-Maersk (p. 75) China Geology (p. 170) China Shipping Logistics (p. 264) COSCO Container (p. 333) Hainan Weilong (p. 430) Huayu Electrical (p. 484) Hunan Zoomlion (p. 598) Nanjing Jinan (p. 797) Qinhuangdao Heshun (p. 853) Shanghai Eastern (p. 918) Shanghai Yizhou (p. 985) Shanghai Jielong (p. 1009) SHAN Yongzhen (p. 1030) Shenzhen COSCO (p. 1048) Tai-I Jiangtong (p. 1115) Zhuhai Xiangzhou (p. 1352) Zhumadian South (p. 1393)
Art. 170 Para. 1 Sub-Para. 2......China Transport Groupage (p. 104, p. 116, p. 120) Huayu Electrical (p. 490) LIN Guihe (p. 722) Shanghai Eastern (p. 918) Shenzhen COSCO (p. 1048) XIE Hongjian (p. 1219)
Art. 171 Para. 1......Connexions (Asia) (p. 308)
Art. 175......China Shipping (p. 264) Hunan Zoomlion (p. 598) JIANG Haiping (p. 623) Shanghai Yizhou (p. 985) Shanghai Jielong (p. 1009)
Art. 200......COSCO Lines (p. 336) Hunan Zoomlion (p. 605) LIN Guihe (p. 730) Qinhuangdao Heshun (p. 858)
Art. 200 Para. 1......Connexions (Asia) (p. 311) Shanghai Jielong (p. 1012, p. 1013, p. 1014)
Art. 200 Para. 2......Connexions (Asia) (p. 311) Shanghai Jielong (p. 1012, p. 1014)
Art. 200 Para. 6......Connexions (Asia) (p. 311) Shanghai Jielong (p. 1012, p. 1014)
Art. 204 Para. 1......Connexions (Asia) (p. 312) COSCO Lines (p. 336) Hunan Zoomlion (p. 605) LIN Guihe (p. 730) Qinhuangdao Heshun (p. 858) Shanghai Jielong (p. 1014)
Art. 207 Para. 1......A.P. Moller-Maersk (p. 81) China Transport Groupage (p. 120)
Art. 227......ZHONG Kangqiu (p. 1402, p. 1403)
Art. 229......China Transport Groupage (p. 92, p. 100, p. 113) Shanghai Eastern (p. 890) Tianjin Tianguan (p. 1125)
Art. 241......Shanghai Eastern (p. 885, p.899)
Art. 253......AIG Europe (p. 9) Allianz China (p. 40) A.P. Moller-Maersk (p. 57) Changhang Phoenix (p. 130) China Guangfa (p. 178) China Minsheng (p. 196) China Ping (p. 206) China Shipping (p. 238) Chongqing Red (p. 282) Fujian Guanhai (p. 390) GUO Jiangbao (p. 402) Hainan Weilong(p. 416) Hong Kong (p. 451) Huayu Electrical (p. 474, p. 480) Hunan Zoomlion (p. 549) Jianxin Finance (p. 659) LI Chunjiang (p. 672) LIN Guihe (p. 700) LIU Fengxi (p. 735) Mitsui O.S.K. (p. 759) Nanjing Jinan (p. 787, p. 793) Operating Department (p. 808) Shandong Xianglong (p. 876) Shanghai Eastern (p. 919) Shanghai Wan (p. 940) Shanghai Jielong (p. 997) Shenzhen COSCO (p. 1041, p. 1049) Silvery Dragon (p. 1065) Station Ocean (p. 1077) Suqian Rongxiang (p. 1086) WANG Jun (p. 1151) XIE Hongjian (p. 1213, p. 1216, p. 1219) Yantai Maritime (p. 1249) Zhuhai Jiaxun (p. 1319) Zhuhai Xiangzhou (p. 1336) Zhumadian South (p. 1376)

Contract Law of the People's Republic of China
General......Operating Department (p. 808) Shanghai Yizhou (p. 982)
Art. 6 ......Jiangsu Eastern (p. 645) Shanghai Yizhou (p. 965, p. 979)
Art. 8......China Shipping (p. 237, p. 262)

(continued)

Table of References

(continued)

Art. 8 Para. 1	......Shanghai Yizhou (p. 965, p. 979)
Art. 41	......LIN Guihe (p. 703) Zhuhai Xiangzhou (p. 1346)
Art. 44	......Zhuhai Xiangzhou (p. 1336)
Art. 49	......China Transport Groupage (p. 90, p. 98, p. 102, p. 112, p. 114)
Art. 52	......China Ping (p. 204)
Art. 56	......LIN Guihe (p. 721, p. 722)
Art. 60	......MAO Chuanwu (p. 745) Nanjing Jinan (p. 795) Zhuhai Xiangzhou (p. 1344)
Art. 60 Para. 1	......China Shipping (p. 237, p. 262) Zhuhai Xiangzhou (p. 1335, p. 1336)
Art. 61	......Fujian Guanhai (p. 387, p. 388, p. 390)
Art. 62 Para. 1	......Fujian Guanhai (p. 387)
Art. 65	......A.P. Moller-Maersk (p. 57, p. 70)
Art. 73	......Yantai Maritime (p. 1261)
Art. 77	......Zhuhai Xiangzhou (p. 1342, p. 1344)
Art. 79	......Export-Import (p. 360, p. 361)
Art. 80	......Export-Import (p. 360, p. 361)
Art. 93	......Hongxin (HK) (p. 465) Jianxin Finance (p. 658)
Art. 93 Para. 2	......Hongxin (HK) (p. 463) Jiangsu Eastern (p. 645) Zhuhai Xiangzhou (p. 1349)
Art. 94	......Zhuhai Xiangzhou (p. 1349, p. 1350)
Art. 94 Para. 4	......Changhang Phoenix (p. 127, p. 129) XIE Hongjian (p. 1212, p. 1216, p.1218)
Art. 96	......Changhang Phoenix (p. 127) Zhuhai Xiangzhou (p. 1349)
Art. 96 Para. 1	......XIE Hongjian (p. 1212, p. 1216)
Art. 97	......Changhang Phoenix (p. 127, p. 129) China Geology (p. 148, p. 157) Hongxin (HK) (p. 463, p. 465) Jianxin Finance (p. 658) XIE Hongjian (p. 1212, p. 1216)
Art. 97 Para. 2	......Hongxin (HK) (p. 465)
Art. 107	......A.P. Moller-Maersk (p. 57, p. 70) China Guangfa (p. 177) China Minsheng (p. 194) China Shipping (p. 237, p. 262) Export-Import (p. 361) Hainan Weilong (p. 430) Jianxin Finance (p. 658) LI Chunjiang (p. 672) Nanjing Jinan (p. 787, p. 792, p. 795) Shanghai Wan (p. 940) Zhuhai Xiangzhou (p. 1351)
Art. 108	......Zhuhai Xiangzhou (p. 1351)
Art. 109	......Hainan Weilong (p. 416, p. 423)
Art. 111	......Fujian Guanhai (p. 388, p. 389, p. 390)
Art. 113	......A.P. Moller-Maersk (p. 56, p. 57 p. 69, p. 70) China Shipping (p. 232, p. 235, p. 257, p.260) Fan Sen (p. 377) Hunan Zoomlion (p. 541, p. 579) Nanjing Jinan (p. 796) Silvery Dragon (p. 1063)
Art. 113 Para. 1	......Allianz China (p. 39) China Shipping (p. 237, p. 262) Fan Sen (p. 377) Shenzhen COSCO (p. 1039) Silvery Dragon (p. 1064)
Art. 114 Para. 1	......Hainan Weilong (p. 416,p.423) Hongxin (HK) (p. 464, p. 465)
Art. 119	......Nanjing Jinan (p. 787, p. 792) Shanghai Eastern (p. 906)
Art. 119 Para. 1	......A.P. Moller-Maersk (p. 57, p. 70)
Art. 120	......Zhuhai Xiangzhou (p. 1335)
Art. 121	......A.P. Moller-Maersk (p. 55, p. 68)
Art. 125 Para. 1	......Silvery Dragon (p. 1062, p. 1064) Zhuhai Xiangzhou (p. 1342)
Art. 126 Para. 1	......China Transport Groupage (p. 90, p. 98, p. 111)
Art. 132	......ZHONG Kangqiu (p. 1401, p. 1403)
Art. 133	......ZHONG Kangqiu (p. 1401, p. 1403)
Art. 174	......Fan Sen (p. 377)
Art. 205	......China Guangfa (p. 177) China Minsheng (p. 194)
Art. 206	......China Guangfa (p. 177) China Minsheng (p. 194)
Art. 207	......China Guangfa (p. 177) China Minsheng (p. 194)
Art. 215	......SHAN Yongzhen (p. 1028)
Art. 226	......Hongxin (HK) (p. 465)
Art. 227	......Hongxin (HK) (p. 463, p. 465)
Art. 248	......Jianxin Finance (p. 658)

(continued)

(continued)

Art. 251......Jiangsu Eastern (p. 645) SHAN Yongzhen (p. 1018, p. 1025)
Art. 253......Jiangsu Eastern (p. 645) SHAN Yongzhen (p. 1018, p. 1025)
Art. 260......Jiangsu Eastern (p. 645)
Art. 263......Hainan Weilong (p. 416, p. 423)
Art. 264......Jiangsu Eastern (p. 642, p. 645)
Art. 292......China Shipping (p. 234, p. 237, p. 259, p. 262)
Art. 304......Shanghai Jielong (p. 997, p. 1005)
Art. 311......China Ping (p. 204, p. 205) Hunan Zoomlion (p. 538, p. 576) Operating Department (p. 805, p. 808)
Art. 398......China Transport Groupage (p. 91, p. 99, p. 100, p. 104, p. 112, p. 113, p. 115, p. 116, p. 120) Shanghai Wan (p. 940)
Art. 402......JIANG Haiping (p. 614, p. 619)
Art. 403 Para. 1......Zhuhai Jiaxun (p. 1317)
Art. 403 Para. 2......China Transport Groupage (p. 119)
Art. 405......Shanghai Wan (p. 940)
Art. 406 Para. 1......Huayu Electrical (p. 474, p. 480)

Customs Law of the People's Republic of China
General...... Shandong Xianglong (p. 870)
Art. 14......Tai-I Jiangtong (p. 1105)
Art. 24 Para. 1......Tai-I Jiangtong (p. 1104)
Art. 24 Para. 2......Tai-I Jiangtong (p. 1105)
Art. 24 Para. 3......Tai-I Jiangtong (p. 1105)
Art. 86 Para. 3......Tai-I Jiangtong (p. 1104)

Domestic Waterway Cargo Carriage Insurance Clauses (2009 Edition)
Art. 6......Chongqing Red (p. 280)
Art. 20......Chongqing Red (p. 281)

Fishery Law of the People's Republic of China
Art. 11 Para. 1......WANG Jun (p. 1149, p. 1151)

General Principles of the Civil Law of the People's Republic of China
Art. 63......Mund & Fester (p. 776, p. 779)
Art. 63 Para. 2......LI Chunjiang (p. 672)
Art. 87......Hongxin (HK) (p. 461, p. 465)
Art. 106......Station Ocean (p. 1077)
Art. 106 Para. 1......Nanjing Jinan (p. 787, p. 792)
Art. 134 Para. 1 Sub-Para. 4......Nanjing Jinan (p. 787, p. 792)
Art. 135......China Ping (p. 212)
Art. 137......China Ping (p. 212)
Art. 140......China Ping (p. 205) Hainan Weilong (p.424) Operating Department (p. 808)
Art. 170 Para. 1 Sub-Para. 2......China Ping (p. 213)
Art. 170 Para. 1 Sub-Para. 3......China Ping (p. 213)

General Rules of Judicial Appraisal Procedure of the Ministry of Justice
General......LIN Guihe (p. 718)
Art. 22......LIN Guihe (p. 718, p. 729)

Guaranty Law of the People's Republic of China
General......Changhang Phoenix (p. 126)
Art. 18......China Guangfa (p. 177) China Minsheng (p. 193, p. 194) Jianxin Finance (p. 658)

(continued)

(continued)

Art. 21 Para. 1......China Guangfa (p. 177)
Art. 31......China Minsheng (p. 193, p. 194) Jianxin Finance (p. 658)
Art. 41......LIN Guihe (p. 697)
Art. 42......LIN Guihe (p. 697)

Hong Kong Arbitration Ordinance
General......Shenzhen COSCO (p. 1036)

Hong Kong Companies Ordinance
Part XI......Shanghai Eastern (p. 909)

Implementation Measures of the Regulations on Management of Ocean Dumping of the People's Republic of China
General......Station Ocean (p. 1076)

Insurance Law of the People's Republic of China *[Nb. This statute was enacted in 1995, and revised in 2002, 2009, 2014 and 2015.]*
General......Qinhuangdao Heshun (p. 840, p. 848) LIN Guihe (p. 698) Yantai Maritime (p. 1246, p. 1247, p. 1254, p. 1256, p. 1257, p. 1258)
Art. 10......Shanghai Eastern (p. 915) Wuhan Ling (p. 1175)
Art. 12......LIN Guihe (p. 719, p. 729)
Art. 12 Para. 1......LIN Guihe (p. 720, p. 722)
Art. 12 Para. 2......Chongqing Red (p. 279) Lin Guihe (p. 722)
Art. 12 Para. 6......Chongqing Red (p. 281)
Art. 13......Chongqing Red (p. 278) Suqian Rongxiang (p. 1086)
Art. 13 Para. 1......Chongqing Red (p. 281)
Art. 13 Para. 3......Chongqing Red (p. 281)
Art. 17......Zhumadian South (p. 1370, p. 1375, p. 1383, p. 1387)
Art. 17 Para. 2......Zhumadian South (p. 1375, p. 1387, p. 1391)
Art. 23......Chongqing Red (p. 281) Suqian Rongxiang (p. 1086)
Art. 23 Para. 1......Chongqing Red (p. 281) Zhumadian South (p. 1373, p. 1375, p. 1385, p. 1387)
Art. 23 Para. 2......Zhumadian South (p. 1375, p. 1387)
Art. 23 Para. 3......Chongqing Red (p. 281)
Art. 24 Para. 1......LIN Guihe (p. 699)
Art. 25......Shanghai Eastern (p. 906) Zhumadian South (p. 1373, p. 1375, p. 1385, p. 1387, p. 1389, p. 1392)
Art. 26......Shanghai Eastern (p. 916)
Art. 30......Suqian Rongxiang (p. 1086)
Art. 31......LIN Guihe (p. 703, p. 704)
Art. 40......LIN Guihe (p. 699)
Art. 44......Yantai Maritime (p. 1261)
Art. 50......Yantai Maritime (p. 1248, p. 1255, p. 1256)
Art. 52......Zhumadian South (p. 1388)
Art. 52 Para. 1......Zhumadian South (p. 1390)
Art. 52 Para. 3......Zhumadian South (p. 1390)
Art. 57......Zhumadian South (p. 1392)
Art. 60......Shanghai Eastern (p. 909) Yantai Maritime (p. 1261)
Art. 60 Para. 1......Allianz China (p. 39) Yue Hai (p. 1293)
Art. 60 Para. 3......Yue Hai (p. 1293)

(continued)

(continued)

Art. 65......Yantai Maritime (p. 1246, p. 1247, p. 1248, p. 1249, p. 1254, p. 1255, p. 1256, p. 1259)
Art. 65 Para. 2......Yantai Maritime (p. 1247, p. 1260, p. 1261)
Art. 128......JIANG Haiping (p. 614, p. 618, p. 619)
Art. 184......Yantai Maritime (p. 1260)

Interpretation of the Supreme People's Court on Certain Issues concerning the Application of Law in the Trial of Cases Involving Compensation for Personal Injury
General......LI Xuelan (p. 677) SHAN Yongzhen (p. 1020, p. 1027)
Art. 10......SHAN Yongzhen (p. 1018, p. 1021, p. 1025, p. 1028, p. 1029)
Art. 11......SHAN Yongzhen (p. 1018, p. 1025)
Art. 11 Para. 3......GUO Jiangbao (p. 400)
Art. 17 Para. 1......LI Xuelan (p. 685)
Art. 17 Para. 3......LI Xuelan (p. 685)
Art. 18......LI Xuelan (p. 683) SHAN Yongzhen (p. 1021, p. 1028)
Art. 22......SHAN Yongzhen (p. 1021, p. 1028)
Art. 27......LI Xuelan (p. 681)
Art. 28......LI Xuelan (p. 682) SHAN Yongzhen (p. 1021, p. 1028)
Art. 29......LI Xuelan (p. 681) SHAN Yongzhen (p. 1020, p. 1021, p. 1027 p. 1028)

Interpretation of the Supreme People's Court on Certain Issues concerning the Application of the Guaranty Law of the People's Republic of China
Art. 42......China Minsheng (p. 194)
Art. 80......Shandong Xianglong (p. 875)
Art. 85......Changhang Phoenix (p. 127, p. 129)
Art. 88......China Geology (p. 150, p. 159, p. 168)
Art. 114......Shandong Xianglong (p. 875)

Interpretation of the Supreme People's Court on Issues concerning the Application of Law for the Trial of Cases of Disputes over Sales Contracts
Art 2......Shanghai Fan Sen (p. 377)

Interpretation of the Supreme People's Court on Several Issues concerning the Application of the Contract Law of the People's Republic of China (II)
Art. 19......China Geology (p. 169)
Art. 29 Para. 1......Hongxin (HK) (p. 464)
Art. 29......A.P. Moller-Maersk (p. 74) Hainan Weilong (p. 425)

Interpretation of the Supreme People's Court on Several Issues concerning the Application of the Insurance Law of the People's Republic of China (I)
Art. 1......Yantai Maritime (p. 1246, p. 1254, p. 1260)
Art. 3......Yantai Maritime (p. 1247, p. 1254)

Interpretation of the Supreme People's Court on Several Issues concerning the Application of the Insurance Law of the People's Republic of China (II)
Art. 9......Zhumadian South (p. 1391)
Art. 16......Operating Department (p. 808)
Art. 16 Para. 2......China Ping (p. 205)

(continued)

(continued)

Interpretation of the Supreme People's Court on Several Issues concerning the Application of the Law of the Application of Law for Foreign-related Civil Relations of the People's Republic of China (I)
Art. 8 Para. 2......Xiamen Yida (p. 1201)
Art. 19......Hongxin (HK) (p. 460) Wuhan Ling (p. 1171)

Interpretation of the Supreme People's Court on the Application of the Civil Procedure Law of the People's Republic of China
Article 25 Zhumadian South China (p. 1356)
Art. 90......China Transport Groupage (p. 103, p. 104, P. 115, P. 116) China Minsheng (p. 195) LIN Guihe (p. 720, p. 722) Shenzhen COSCO (p. 1047, p. 1048)
Art. 90 Para 2......Huayu Electrical (p. 490)
Art. 91 Para 1......Hongxin (HK) (p. 458)
Art. 92......China Minsheng (p. 193)
Art. 92 Para 2......WU Guangbao (p. 1161)
Art. 93......China Geology (p. 166)
Art. 93 Para 1......Hongxin (HK) (p. 462)
Art. 93 Para 1 Sub Para 5......Shanghai Eastern (p. 914)
Art. 99 Para 3......XIE Hongjian (p. 1228)
Art. 102......XIE Hongjian (p. 1217)
Art. 105......Hongxin (HK) (p. 462)
Art. 115......Zhuhai Xiangzhou (p. 1347)
Art 121 Para 1......LIN Guihe (p. 716, p. 717)
Art. 196......Shanghai Eastern (p.919)
Art. 202 Para 1......Shanghai Eastern (p.919)
Art. 304......ZHONG Kangqiu (p. 1403)
Art. 307......ZHONG Kangqiu (p. 1403)
Art. 312......ZHONG Kangqiu (p. 1403)
Art. 395 Para 2......COSCO Container (p. 336) Hunan Zoomlion (p. 605)
Art. 407 Para 2......A.P. Moller-Maersk (p. 81)

Interpretation of the Supreme People's Court on the Application of the Special Maritime Procedure Law of the People's Republic of China
Art. 1......Connexions (Asia) (p. 290, p. 300) WANG Hong (p. 1128)

Interpretation on Certain Issues concerning the Determination of Compensation Liability for Mental Damage in Civil Torts of the Supreme People's Court
General......LI Xuelan (p. 677)
Art. 8 Para. 2......LI Xuelan (p. 684)
Art. 10......LI Xuelan (p. 684)
Art. 11......SHAN Yongzhen (p. 1020, p. 1027)

Labor Contract Law of the People's Republic of China
Art. 30 Para. 1......LIU Fengxi (p. 735)
Art. 36......Guo Jiangbao (p. 399, p. 402)
Art. 66......LIU Fengxi (p. 734)
Art. 92......LIU Fengxi (p. 735)

Law of the Application of Law for Foreign-related Civil Relations of the People's Republic of China
Art. 3......Tianjin Tianguan (p. 1121)
Art. 4......Daewoo Shipbuilding (p. 346)

(continued)

(continued)

Art. 41......Daewoo Shipbuilding (p. 346) Hongxin (HK) (p. 460) Shandong Xianglong (p. 871, p. 875) Wuhan Ling (p. 1171) Xiamen Yida (p. 1201)
Art. 44......Mund & Fester (p. 773) Shandong Xianglong (p. 872, p. 875) XUE Haibing (p. 1232)

Law of the People's Republic of China on the Administration of the Use of Sea Areas
Art. 2 Para. 1......WANG Jun (p. 1149, p. 1151)
Art. 3 Para. 2......WANG Jun (p. 1149, p. 1151)

Maritime Code of the People's Republic of China
General...... China Geology (p. 149, p. 158) Shandong Xianglong (p. 873) Shanghai Eastern (p. 912) XUE Haibing (p. 1232)
Art. 3......LIN Guihe (p. 697)
Art. 7......WU Jinya (p. 1190, p. 1191)
Art. 9......WU Jinya (p. 1190, p. 1191) ZHONG Kangqiu(p. 1401, p. 1403)
Art. 11......China Minsheng (p. 194)
Art. 13......Operating Department (p. 807, p. 808)
Art. 21......LIU Fengxi (p. 735)
Art. 22 Para. 1......LIU Fengxi (p. 735)
Chapter 4......Operating Department (p. 808)
Art. 41......AIG Europe (p. 8) Hunan Zoomlion (p. 548, p. 586) Shanghai Jielong (p. 997, p. 1005)
Art. 42......Hunan Zoomlion (p. 544, p. 582)
Art. 42 Sub-Para. 1......Hunan Zoomlion (p. 548, p. 586)
Art. 42 Para. 4......COSCO Container (p. 333)
Art. 46......Allianz China (p. 39) Xiamen Yida (p. 1202)
Art. 46 Para. 1......AIG Europe (p. 8) Hunan Zoomlion (p. 548, p. 586) Zhuhai Jiaxun (p. 1318, p. 1319)
Art. 47......Hunan Zoomlion (p. 539, p. 577) Qinhuangdao Heshun (p. 839, p. 847, p. 857)
Art. 48......Hunan Zoomlion (p. 544, p. 582) Shanghai Jielong (p. 997, p. 1005) Xiamen Yida (p. 1202)
Art. 49 Para. 1......Silvery Dragon (p. 1062, p. 1064)
Art. 51......Hunan Zoomlion (p. 538, p. 576) Xiamen Yida (p. 1202) Zhuhai Jiaxun (p. 1318)
Art. 51 Para. 1 Sub-Para. 1......Hunan Zoomlion (p. 538, p. 539, p. 548, p. 576, p. 577, p. 586, p. 604)
Art. 51 Para. 1 Sub-Para. 3......Hunan Zoomlion (p. 538, p. 548, p. 576, p. 586)
Art. 51 Para. 1 Sub-Para. 8......People's Insurance (p. 821)
Art. 51 Para. 1 Sub-Para. 9......People's Insurance (p. 819, p. 821)
Art. 51 Para. 1 Sub-Para. 12......People's Insurance (p. 821)
Art. 51 Para. 2......People's Insurance (p. 820)
Art. 51 Para. 5......Xiamen Yida (p. 1202)
Art. 54......Hunan Zoomlion (p. 548, p. 586)
Art. 55......Allianz China (p. 39) Zhuhai Jiaxun (p. 1318)
Art. 55 Para. 1......Connexions (Asia) (p. 291, p. 301, p. 307) Hunan Zoomlion (p. 548, p. 586) Zhuhai Jiaxun (p. 1318, p. 1319)
Art. 55 Para. 2......Connexions (Asia) (p. 291, p. 301, p. 307) Hunan Zoomlion (p. 548, p. 586) Zhuhai Jiaxun (p. 1318, p. 1319)
Art. 56......AIG Europe (p. 8) Allianz China (p. 34, p. 36, p. 39)
Art. 57......Allianz China (p. 34)
Art. 58......Mund & Fester (p. 778, p. 779)
Art. 59......Allianz China (p. 34) Hunan Zoomlion (p. 547, p. 585)
Art. 59 Para. 1......AIG Europe (p. 8)
Art. 60 Para. 1......Allianz China (p. 39)
Art. 61......Hunan Zoomlion (p. 603, p. 604)
Art. 64......Allianz China (p. 39)
Art. 69 Para. 1......China Shipping (p. 234, p. 237, p. 259, p. 262)

(continued)

Table of References   lix

(continued)

Art. 71......Allianz China (p. 39) Connexions (Asia) (p. 291, p. 301) People's Insurance (p. 817, p. 820)
Art. 72......Connexions (Asia) (p. 306) Mund & Fester (p. 775)
Art. 72 Para. 2......Shandong Xianglong (p. 872)
Art. 75......Mund & Fester (p. 774, p. 775, p. 779)
Art. 76......Mund & Fester (p. 774, p. 775, p. 779)
Art. 78......COSCO Container (p. 333) People's Insurance (p. 817) Shandong Xianglong (p. 872, p. 875)
Art. 83......Allianz China (p. 39)
Art. 86......COSCO Container (p. 322, p. 328, p. 330, p. 336) Mitsui O.S.K. (p. 757, p. 758)
Art. 87......A.P. Moller-Maersk (p. 56, p. 69) COSCO Container (p. 322, p. 328) Shandong Xianglong (p. 874)
Art. 88......A.P. Moller-Maersk (p. 56, p. 69)
Art. 92......Tianjin Tianguan (p. 1124)
Art. 98......Shandong Xianglong (p. 875)
Art. 100 Para. 2......Shenzhen COSCO (p. 1038, p. 1041, p. 1048)
Art. 102......Allianz China (p. 28,p.39)
Art. 103......Allianz China (p. 39)
Art. 104......Allianz China (p. 39)
Art. 105......Allianz China (p. 36,p.39)
Art. 106......Allianz China (p. 39)
Art. 166......LI Xuelan (p. 686)
Art. 169......LI Xuelan (p. 678, p. 686) Qingdao Hua (p. 828, p. 829)
Art. 169 Para. 1......Hong Kong (p. 448, p. 450) Shanghai Eastern (p.886, p.889, p. 899, p. 903, p. 918) XUE Haibing (p. 1237, p. 1238)
Art. 169 Para. 2......Shanghai Eastern (p. 886, p,889, p. 899, p. 903, p. 918) XUE Haibing (p. 1237, p. 1238)
Art. 204......Shanghai Eastern (p. 886, p.889, p. 899, p. 900, p. 903, p. 918)
Art. 207......Shanghai Eastern (p. 886, p. 887, p. 900)
Art. 207 Para. 1 Sub-Para. 1...... Shanghai Eastern (p. 889, p. 903, p. 918)
Art. 209......Hunan Zoomlion (p. 547, p. 585) Shanghai Eastern (p. 887, p. 900, p. 904, p. 905, p. 914)
Art. 210......Hunan Zoomlion (p. 547, p. 586)
Art. 216......Shanghai Eastern (p. 915)
Art. 224......Operating Department (p. 806)
Art. 229......Wuhan Ling (p. 1175)
Art. 231......Operating Department (p. 806)
Art. 232......Hunan Zoomlion (p. 542, p. 580)
Art. 237......Yantai Maritime (p. 1249, p. 1256)
Art. 238......Yantai Maritime (p. 1249, p. 1256)
Art. 244 Para. 1 Sub-Para. 1......Qinhuangdao Heshun (p. 841, p. 848)
Art. 246......LIN Guihe (p. 703)
Art. 249......LIN Guihe (p. 703)
Art. 252......AIG Europe (p. 8) China Ping (p. 205) Shanghai Eastern (p. 887, p. 901, p. 906, p. 908) Yantai Maritime (p. 1260, p. 1261)
Art. 252 Para. 1......China Ping (p. 203, p.205, p. 208) Hong Kong (p. 449, p. 450) Hunan Zoomlion (p. 548, p. 586) People's Insurance (p. 817) Shanghai Eastern (p. 916)
Art. 255......LIN Guihe (p. 704)
Art. 257......China Ping (p. 205) Mund & Fester (p. 777, p. 778)
Art. 257 Para. 1......A.P. Moller-Maersk (p. 54, p. 67, p. 74) China Ping (p. 205) Mund & Fester (p. 779) Tai-I Jiangtong (p. 1104)
Art. 264......Yantai Maritime (p. 1248, p. 1255, p. 1261)
Art. 267......A.P. Moller-Maersk (p. 80) China Ping (p. 209, p. 213)
Art. 269......Allianz China (p. 39) A.P. Moller-Maersk (p. 53, p. 66) Connexions (Asia) (p. 290, p. 300, p. 306) Hong Kong (p. 447) Mitsui O.S.K. (p. 757) People's Insurance (p. 817, p. 821) Shenzhen COSCO (p. 1038) Tai-I Jiangtong (p. 1103, p.1113) Zhuhai Jia (p. 1316)

(continued)

(continued)

Art. 271 Para. 1......China Minsheng (p. 194)
Art. 273......Qingdao Hua (p. 828) Shanghai Eastern (p. 886, p. 899)
Art. 277......Allianz China (p. 39))

Maritime Traffic Safety Management Regulations of Fuzhou City
Art. 15......XUE Haibing (p. 1232)

Measures for the Implementation of the Regulations on Work-Related Injury Insurance in Fujian Province
Art. 26......GUO Jiangbao (p. 401)
Art. 27......GUO Jiangbao (p. 401)

Measures on the Payment of Litigation Costs
Art. 6......LIN Guihe (p. 721) WANG Hong (p. 1141)
Art. 10......Shenzhen COSCO (p. 1048)
Art. 10 Sub-Para. 2......Shenzhen COSCO (p. 1048)
Art. 12......LIN Guihe (p. 721)
Art. 13 Para. 1......Changhang Phoenix (p. 130) China Guangfa (p. 178) Chongqing Red (p. 282) Export-Import (p. 361) LIU Fengxi (p. 736) MAO Chuanwu (p. 745) Mund & Fester (p. 780) Nanjing Jinan (p. 787) Suqian Rongxiang (p. 1086) WANG Hong (p. 1141) WU Guangbao (p. 1161) Wuhan Ling (p. 1175) WU Jinya (p. 1191) Zhumadian South (p. 1376)
Art. 14......WANG Hong (p. 1141)
Art. 29 Para. 1......LIN Guihe (p. 721)
Art. 29 Para. 2......Shanghai Eastern (p. 919) Shenzhen COSCO (p. 1048)
Art. 38 Para. 3......Shenzhen COSCO (p. 1040, p. 1048)

No.256 Response to Claim Limitation and Related Questions made by China Insurance Regulatory Commission (CIRC) (1999)
General......Yantai Maritime (p. 1248, p. 1256)

Notice of Liaoning High People's Court on Issuing the Minutes of Meeting for Civil Trial of the Courts in the Province [Liao Gao Fa (2009) No. 120]
General......SHAN Yongzhen (p. 1020, p. 1027)

Notice of the Supreme People's Court on Adjustment of the Jurisdiction and the Scope of Cases Entertained by Dalian, Wuhan and Beihai Maritime Courts
General...... WANG Hong (p. 1128)
Art. 2......Chongqing Red (p. 268) Zhumadian South (p. 1356)

Official Reply of the Supreme People's Court on the Limitation of Action of the Carrier's Claim for Compensation against the Consignor, Consignee, or Holder of the Bill of Lading under Carriage of Goods by Sea
General......A.P. Moller-Maersk (p. 54, p. 67, p. 71, p. 79)

Opinions of Xiamen Labor and Social Security Bureau on Several Issues concerning Coverage of Work-Related Injury Insurance
Art. 3......GUO Jiangbao (p. 401)

Property Law of the People's Republic of China
General......LIN Guihe (p. 697)
Art. 5......China Geology (p. 149, p. 159)

(continued)

Table of References

(continued)

Art. 23......Shandong Xianglong (p. 874)
Art. 24......WU Jinya (p. 1190, p. 1191)
Art. 26......China Geology (p. 150, p. 159, p. 162, p. 168) Shandong Xianglong (p. 874)
Art. 28......China Geology (p. 166)
Art. 35......China Geology (p. 151, p. 160, p. 170)
Art. 39......WU Jinya (p. 1191)
Art. 106......China Geology (p. 167)
Art. 106 Para. 1......China Geology (p. 148, p. 158)
Art. 173......China Guangfa (p. 177)
Art. 176......China Guangfa (p. 177)
Art. 179......China Guangfa (p. 177)
Art. 179 Para. 2......China Minsheng (p. 194)
Art. 187......Changhang Phoenix (p. 128, p. 129)
Art. 195......China Guangfa (p. 177)
Provisions of the National Bureau of Statistics on the Composition of Wages
Art. 4......GUO Jiangbao (p. 400)
Provisions of the Supreme People's Court on Several Issues about the Trial of Cases concerning Marine Insurance Disputes
Art. 1......Yantai Maritime (p. 1260)
Art. 14......AIG Europe (p. 8) China Ping (p. 204) Hunan Zoomlion (p. 542, p.581)
Art. 15......Hunan Zoomlion (p. 542, p. 581)
Provisions of the Supreme People's Court on Several Issues concerning the Application of Law in the Trial of Cases of Disputes arising from Delivery of Goods without Original Bill of Lading
Art. 2......Connexions (Asia) (p. 291, p. 301, p. 307)
Art. 14......Mund & Fester (p. 778)
Provisions of the Supreme People's Court on Several Issues Concerning the Trial of Cases of Disputes over Marine Freight Forwarding
Art. 9......Shanghai Wan (p. 940)
Art. 8......Huayu Electrical (p. 474, p. 480, p. 486)
Art. 10......Huayu Electrical (p. 474, p. 480)
Art. 13......China Transport Groupage (p. 89, p. 98, p. 111)
Provisions of the Supreme People's Court on Several Issues concerning the Trial of Injury Insurance Administrative Cases
Art. 3 Para. 1 Sub-Para. 4......MAO Chuanwu (p. 744)
Art. 3 Para. 2......MAO Chuanwu (p. 744)
Provisions of the Supreme People's Court on Some Issues Concerning the Trial of Cases of Disputes over Letter of Credit
Art. 8......Mund & Fester (p. 774)
Provisions of the Supreme People's Court on the Sealing, Seizure and Freezing of Property in the Civil Enforcement of the People's Court
General......China Geology (p. 162)
Art. 8......China Geology (p. 166)
Art. 26......China Geology (p. 162)
Art. 26 Para. 3......China Geology (p. 167)

(continued)

(continued)

Provisions of the Supreme People's Court on the Trial of Certain Issues in Cases of Disputes over Collision of Ships
Art. 4......Hong Kong (p. 448, p. 449, p. 450) Qingdao Huashun (p. 828) XUE Haibing (p. 1238)
Art. 6......Shanghai Eastern (p. 912)
Art. 11......Shanghai Eastern (p. 910)

Provisions of the Supreme People's Court on the Trial of Compensation for Property Damage in Cases of Collision and Contact of Ships
Art. 3 Para. 2......XUE Haibing (p. 1234, p. 1235, p. 1236)
Art. 7......XUE Haibing (p. 1237)
Art. 9 Para. 1......Shanghai Eastern (p. 917)
Art. 12......Yue Hai (p. 1304)
Art. 13......XUE Haibing (p. 1237)
Art. 16 Para. 6......XUE Haibing (p. 1236)
Art. 16 Para. 7......XUE Haibing (p. 1237)

Regulations for Safe Navigation in the Waters of the Pearl River Estuary
Art. 8......Hong Kong (p. 441, p. 448)

Regulations Made by the Supreme People's Court for the Application of Laws relating to Hearing the Taiwan-related Civil and Commercial Cases
Art. 1......XUE Haibing (p. 1231)

Regulations of the People's Republic of China Governing the Registration of Ships
General......LIN Guihe (p. 697, p. 720)

Regulations on the Handling of Medical Accidents
Art. 50 Sub-Para. 11......SHAN Yongzhen (p. 1020, p. 1027)

Regulations on the Management of Shipboard Electronic Chart System and Automatic Identification System Equipment for Domestic Sailing Ship
General......Qinhuangdao Heshun (p. 856)
Art. 19......Qinhuangdao Heshun (p. 839, p. 847, p. 851, p. 857)
Art. 21......Qinhuangdao Heshun (p. 849, p. 852, p. 855, p. 857)

Regulations on Work-Related Injury Insurance
General......GUO Jiangbao (p. 399, p. 400)
Art. 33 Para. 1......GUO Jiangbao (p. 400, p.402)
Art. 37 Para. 1 Sub-Para. 2......GUO Jiangbao (p. 402)
Art. 37 Para. 2......GUO Jiangbao (p. 400)

Reply of the China Insurance Regulatory Commission on the Definition of Illegal Acts as Excluded Liabilities in Insurance Clauses
Art. 3......LIN Guihe (p. 698)

Reply of the Supreme People's Court on How to Determine the Statute of Limitation of Right of Demanding Compensation for Coastal and Inland Waterway Goods Transport
General......Operating Department (p. 807, p. 808)

(continued)

(continued)

Safety Production Act of the People's Republic of China
[Nb. This statute is enacted in 2002, and revised in 2009, 2014 and 2015.]
Art. 23......SHAN Yongzhen (p. 1019, p. 1025)

Several Provisions of the Supreme People's Court concerning the Trial of Dispute Cases in relation to Maritime Compensation Liability Limitation
Art. 7......Shanghai Eastern (p. 903)
Art. 11......Qingdao Huashun (p. 829)
Art. 19......Shanghai Eastern (p. 914)

Some Provisions of the Supreme People's Court on Evidence in Civil Procedures
Art. 2......Allianz China (p. 39) Fan Sen (p. 377) Hunan Zoomlion (p. 548, p. 586) Tai-I Jiangtong (p. 1106) Xiamen Yida (p. 1203)
Art. 27 Para. 1......LIN Guihe (p. 715, p. 716, p. 717, p. 730)
Art. 29......LIN Guihe (p.712)
Art. 71......LIN Guihe (p. 718, p. 729)
Art. 41......Hainan Weilong (p. 427)
Art. 74......Allianz China (p. 39)
Art. 76......Hunan Zoomlion (p. 548, p. 586)
Art. 77......Zhuhai Xiangzhou (p. 1341)

Some Provisions of the Supreme People's Court on the Scope of Cases to be Entertained by Maritime Courts
Art. 1......Hong Kong (p. 447) Shanghai Eastern (p. 885, p. 898)
Art. 2 Para. 11......Tai-I Jiangtong (p. 1103)
Art. 11......A.P. Moller-Maersk (p. 53, p. 66) Connexions (Asia) (p. 290, p. 300)
Art. 16......Shenzhen COSCO (p. 1038)

Special Maritime Procedure Law of the People's Republic of China
Art. 2 Para. 3......Shenzhen COSCO (p. 1038)
Art. 6 Para. 1......Tai-I Jiangtong (p. 1103)
Art. 6 Para. 2 Sub-Para. 2......Xiamen Yida (p. 1200)
Art. 6 Para. 2 Sub-Para. 5 ......LIU Fengxi (p. 732)
Art. 19......Daewoo Shipbuilding (p. 346)
Art. 93......China Ping (p. 204, p. 205) Hong Kong (p. 449, p. 450) People's Insurance (p. 817) Shanghai Eastern (p. 916)
Art. 95......Hunan Zoomlion (p. 541, p. 580)
Art. 116......Daewoo Shipbuilding (p. 346, p. 347) Yue Hai (p. 1306)

Special Operation Directory of the Provisions on the Examination and Management of Safety Technical Training for Special Operation Personnel (No.30 Decree of the State Production Safety Supervision and Administration)
Art. 2.1......SHAN Yongzhen (p. 1019, p. 1026)

The People's Republic of China GB/T11253-2007
General...... Mund & Fester (p. 766, p. 767, p. 776)

The People's Republic of China GB/T5526
General......People's Insurance (p. 814)

(continued)

(continued)

The People's Republic of China GB/T17411:2012
General......Fujian Guanhai (p. 386, p. 387)

Tort Liability Law of the People's Republic of China
General......LI Xuelan (p. 677) Operating Department (p. 808)
Art. 2......WANG Hong (p. 1140)
Art. 6......COSCO Container (p. 330)
Art. 6 Para. 1......Yue Hai (p. 1294, p. 1306)
Art. 16......LI Xuelan (p. 685)
Art. 18 Para. 2......LI Xuelan (p. 685)
Art. 26......WANG Jun (p. 1151)
Art. 34......Hong Kong Everglory (p. 437)
Art. 65......WANG Jun (p. 1148, p. 1151)
Art. 66......WANG Jun (p. 1148, p. 1151)

Vessel's Minimum Safety Manning Regulation
General......LIN Guihe (p. 695)
Art. 5......Qingdao Huashun (p. 827)
Art. 7......Qingdao Huashun (p. 827)
Art. 15......Qingdao Huashun (p. 827)

International Conventions and Customs

International Convention for the Unification of Certain Rules of Law Relating to Bills of Lading 1924 (Hague Rules)
Art. 4 Sub-Para. 5......Allianz China (p. 37)

International Convention on Standards of Training, Certification, and Watchkeeping for Seafarers (the STWC Convention)
Chapter 8......Qingdao Huashun (p. 827)

International Hydrographic Organization S-57
General......Qinhuangdao Heshun (p. 839, p. 847, p. 851, p. 857)

International Regulations for Preventing Collisions at Sea, 1972 (COLREG)
General......Qingdao Huashun (p. 828) Shanghai Eastern (p. 903, p. 904) XUE Haibing (p. 1232, p. 1234)
Art. 2 Para. 1......Hong Kong (p. 441, p. 448)
Art. 5......Hong Kong (p. 441, p. 442, p. 448) Qingdao Huashun (p. 827)
Art. 6......Hong Kong (p. 441, p. 442, p. 448) Qingdao Huashun (p. 827) Shanghai Eastern (p. 904, p. 913)
Art. 7......Qingdao Huashun (p. 827)
Art. 8......Shanghai Eastern (p. 904)
Art. 8 Para. 1......Hong Kong (p. 441, p. 448) Shanghai Eastern (p. 907, p. 913)
Art. 9......Qingdao Huashun (p. 828)
Art. 10......Shanghai Eastern (p. 903)

(continued)

(continued)

Art. 10 Para. 1......Shanghai Eastern (p. 907, p. 913)
Art. 13......Qingdao Huashun (p. 827)
Art. 15......Qingdao Huashun (p.827) Shanghai Eastern (p. 907, p. 913)
Art. 16......Shanghai Eastern (p. 904, p. 913)
Art. 17......Shanghai Eastern (p. 913)
Art. 17 Para. 1 Sub Para 2......Shanghai Eastern (p. 907)
Art. 19......Qingdao Huashun (p.827, p. 828)
Art. 34......Shanghai Eastern (p. 904, p. 913)
Art. 35......Qingdao Huashun (p.827)
Art. 35 Para. 1......Hong Kong (p. 441, p. 442, p. 448)

ISO8217:2012
General......Fujian Guanhai (p. 383, p. 386)

Protocol to Amend the International Convention for the Unification of Certain Rules of Law Relating to Bills of Lading 1968 (Hague-Visby Rules)
General......Mund & Fester (p. 778, p. 779)
Art. 2......Allianz China (p. 37)
Chapter IV......Mund & Fester (p. 778)

United Nations Convention on the Carriage of Goods by Sea 1978 (Hamburg Rules)
Art. 6 Sub-Para. 1(a)......Allianz China (p. 37)

Chinese Judgments

(2007) Guang Hai Fa Chu Zi No. 332-3 Civil Ruling......LIN Guihe (p.696)
(2008) Guang Hai Fa Chu Zi No. 234-3 Civil Judgment......LIN Guihe (p. 710, p. 712, p. 713)
(2008) Qing Hai Fa Hai Yan Shang Chu Zi No. 46 Civil Judgment......Yantai Maritime (p. 1246, p. 1253, p. 1260)
(2009) Guang Hai Fa Chu Zi No. 4......Shanghai Eastern (p. 884, p. 897, p. 909, p. 910)
(2009) Guang Hai Fa Chu Zi No. 116......Shanghai Eastern (p. 884, p. 897)
(2009) Guang Hai Fa Chu Zi No. 292......Shanghai Eastern (p. 884, p. 897, p. 909, p. 910)
(2009) Yue Gao Fa Min Si Zhong Zi No. 267 Civil Ruling......Shanghai Eastern (p. 884. P. 897)
(2010) Hai Xing Chu Zi No. 661......LIN Guihe (p. 696)
(2010) Yue Gao Fa Min Si Zhong Zi No. 86 Civil Judgement......Shanghai Eastern (p. 884, p. 886, p. 889, p. 897, p.899, p. 902, p. 906, p. 909, p. 910, p. 911)
(2010) Yue Gao Fa Min Si Zhong Zi No. 87 Civil Judgement......Shanghai Eastern (p. 884, p. 886, p. 889, p. 897,p. 899, p. 902, p. 906, p. 909, p. 910, p. 911)
(2012) Hui Zhong Fa Xing Yi Zhong Zi No. 111 Criminal Ruling......LIN Guihe (p. 692, p. 696)
(2012) Jin Hai Fa Shang Chu Zi No. 836......Shandong Xianglong (p. 871)
(2012) Min Ti Zi No. 142 Civil Judgment......Shanghai Eastern (p. 907, p. 909, p. 910, p. 911, p. 914)
(2013) Jin Hai Fa Shang Chu Zi No. 310 Civil Judgment......Shanghai Yizhou (p. 984)

(continued)

(continued)

(2013) Wu Hai Fa Shang Zi No. 00264 Civil Judgment......MAO Chuanwu (p. 741, p. 743)
(2013) Xia Hai Fa Shang Chu Zi No. 333 Civil Judgment......ZHONG Kangqiu (p. 1396, p. 1398, p. 1402)
(2013) Zhe Hai Zhong Zi No. 72 Civil Judgment......Huayu Electrical (p. 486)
(2014) Guang Hai Fa Chu Zi No. 704 Civil Judgment......Connexions (Asia) (p. 294)
(2014) Hai Fa Zhi Zi No. 1 of Civil Ruling...... ZHONG Kangqiu (p. 1398, p. 1402)
(2014) Hai Fa Zhi Zi No. 1-2 of Civil Ruling......ZHONG Kangqiu (p. 1398)
(2014) Hai Fa Zhi Zi No. 3 Executive Ruling......ZHONG Kangqiu (p. 1402)
(2014) Hong Min Wu (Shang) Chu Zi No. 554 Civil Judgmen......Operating Department (p. 800)
(2014) Min Shen Zi No. 2229 Civil Ruling...... Connexions (Asia) (p. 310) Huayu Electrical (p. 485)
(2014) Qing Hai Fa Deng Zi No. 168 Civil Ruling......Qingdao Huashun (p. 824, p. 825)
(2014) Wu Hai Fa Shi Zi No. 00040 Civil Ruling......WANG Hong (p. 1128)
(2014) Xia Hai Fa Ren Zi No. 13 Civil Ruling......Daewoo Shipbuilding (p. 340, p. 345)
(2014) Xia Hai Fa Ren Zi No. 14 Civil Ruling......Daewoo Shipbuilding (p. 340, p. 345)
(2014) Yue Gao Fa Min Si Zhong Zi No. 122 Civil Judgment......LIN Guihe (p. 728)
(2015) Min Min Zhong Zi No. 319 Civil Ruling......Xiamen Yida (p. 1194)
(2015) Min Shen Zi No. 559 Civil Ruling......A.P. Moller-Maersk (p. 77)
(2015) Wu Hai Fa Bao Zi No. 00149 Civil Ruling......Changhang Phoenix (p. 123)
(2016) Zui Gao Fa Min Shen No. 1885 Civil Ruling......China Transport Groupage (p. 108)

Foreign Legislation and Judgments

Arbitration Act 1996 of the United Kingdom
General......Daewoo Shipbuilding (p. 343, p.344, p. 345)

Britain Law of Property Act 1925
Art. 136......Shandong Xianglong (p. 871, p. 875)

Maritime Law of the Republic of Panama (the 5th Version of 2008)
Art. 244......Daewoo Shipbuilding (p. 346)
Art. 260......Daewoo Shipbuilding (p. 346)

United States Carriage of Goods by Sea Act 1936 (COGSA)
General......Connexions (Asia) (p. 286, p. 288, p. 291, p. 296, p. 298, p. 301, p. 311)

Wuhan Maritime Court
Civil Judgment

Mund & Fester GmbH & Co. KG
v.
Pangang Group World Trade Panzhihua Co., Ltd. et al.

(2011) Wu Hai Fa Shang Zi No.00300

Related Case(s) None.

Cause(s) of Action 202. Dispute over contract of carriage of goods by sea or sea-connected waters.

Headnote Carrier's agent and shipper's agent held not liable in fraud for issuing clean bill of lading for rust-damaged cargo of steel, because bill of lading had been issued on basis of external packaging.

Summary The Plaintiff cargo insurer claimed that a cargo of steel coil was damaged with rust before being loaded but a clean bill of lading was issued. The Plaintiff alleged that the Defendants, the agent of the carrier and the shipper, conspired to fraudulently sign a clean bill while knowing that the goods were damaged. It was held that the Plaintiff should not have sued the two Defendants, as their action did not directly cause the Plaintiff's loss. The court noted the importance of efficiency in carriers signing clean bills of lading, and held that the Defendants did not commit fraud by signing the clean bill of lading based on the outward appearance of the goods' packages.

Judgment

The Plaintiff: Mund & Fester GmbH & Co. KG
Domicile: Trostbrucke 1, 20457, Hamburg, Germany.
Legal representative: HERBERT PAWLIK and SVEN GATHMANN, directors.
Agent *ad litem*: WANG Huaijiang, lawyer of Shanghai Sloma & Co.
Agent *ad litem*: SHU Liang, lawyer of Shanghai Sloma & Co.

The Defendant: Pangang Group World Trade Panzhihua Co., Ltd.
Domicile: Eastern Dadukou Panzhihua City, Sichuan, China Building 7-12 levels
Organization Code: 74692999-1.

Legal representative: ZHANG Hu, chairman.
Agent *ad litem*: GOU Xiaoming, lawyer of Sichuan Daohe Law Firm.

The Defendant: Changshu Tongshenxing International Shipping Agency Co., Ltd.
Domicile: Changshu Economic Development Zone, Jiangsu, Fuhua Road, Hi-tech Innovation Service Center Organization Code: 79085295-2.
Legal representative: ZHI Zhenhua, general manager.
Agent *ad litem*: LIU Weijun, lawyer of Jiangsu Putai Law Firm.

With respect to the tort dispute over carriage of goods by sea under bill of lading filed by the Plaintiff Mund & Fester GmbH & Co. KG (hereinafter referred to as MFG Company) against the Defendant Pangang Group World Trade Panzhihua Co., Ltd. (hereinafter referred to as Pangang Company) and Changshu Tongshenxing International Shipping Agency Co., Ltd. (hereinafter referred to as Tongshenxing Company) to the court on March 23, 2011. This case is the dispute over bill of lading of carriage of goods by sea, and it should be ruled by the maritime court. The issuing place of bill of lading and Defendant Tongshenxing Company are both located in Changshu, Jiangsu, and it was within the jurisdiction of the court's region. According to the provision of Article 28 of the Civil Procedure Law of People's Republic of China, the court has jurisdiction on this case. The court, after accepting this case, constituted the collegiate panel, including Judges HOU Wei, ZHANG Yu and YI Lu, and HOU Wei served as Presiding Judge. The court had a hearing publicly on December 28, 2012. Because of the adjustment of personnel, the collegiate panel was changed, which included Judges HOU Wei, YANG Qing and Acting Judge DENG Yi, HOU Wei still served as the presiding judge. And, the court had a hearing publicly on May 29, 2014. Agents *ad litem* of Plaintiff, WANG Huaijiang and SHU Liang, agent *ad litem* of the Defendant Pangang Company, GOU Xiaoming, and agent *ad litem* of Defendant Tongshenxing Company, LIU Weijun, attended the court hearing. After several court mediation failed, now the case has been concluded.

The Plaintiff alleged that, on May 2008, the German buyer Coutinho & Ferrostaal GmbH (hereinafter referred to as CFG Company) ordered 1,500 tons coil steel from Defendant Pangang Company. And agreement was made that Defendant Pangang Company was responsible for the loading and transportation at Changshu, China. At the end of July in 2008, after loading the goods on board in Changshu China, Defendant Tongshenxing Company signed No.HDMUCGOAW8050103 shipped B/L. The B/L stated as follows: the loading port was Changshu China, other discharging port was Antwerpen Belgium, the voyage number was DORIC SPIRIT V.805C. The goods, after arriving at the port of destination, were accepted by CFG Company, and wet damage and rust to the goods were found. So CFG Company entrusted related personnel to examine the damaged goods on October 2, 2008, and the examiner issued Report on Examination. According to the final examination conclusion, the wet damage, rust to the goods and so on took place before loading at Changshu port. Moreover, according to the related loaded

B/L that were obtained through MFG Company applied Wuhan Maritime Court for preserving maritime evidence, it was true that the damage to the goods took place before loading. Obviously, the two Defendants collaborated to sign the loaded B/L on purpose while they had already known that the damage to the goods had took place before loading. Then the risk, which Pangang Company should have assumed, were transferred illegally to the consignee of the B/L through settlement procedure of foreign exchange account of the bank. As for the tort, the two Defendants shall bear joint and several liability for the consignee. CFG Company, as the buyer (consignee of the B/L), had bought marine cargo transportation insurance on the above goods for Plaintiff. After noticing the damage, CFG Company asked Plaintiff for claim on the goods insurance. With the insurance verification, the Plaintiff completed the claim to the assured, with a compensation €660,901.96(6,106,734.11 yuan) CFG Company, as the consignee, confirmed the acceptation of insurance claim and had an agreement on creditor's right subrogation. For this, the Plaintiff sued to the court and requested judgment as followed: 1. To order the two Defendants to pay for losses of cargo RMB6,106,734.11 (totally €660,901.96 calculated at the exchange rate from RMB to EUR on May 19, 2009) and interests. 2. The two Defendants should be responsible for the legal cost in this lawsuit.

The Defendant Pangang Company argued that: 1. the Plaintiff claimed that the damage to the goods took place before loading, the claim of Plaintiff had been beyond the insured liability, so it was not the right of Plaintiff to execute the right of subrogation. 2. The Plaintiff should sue the carrier or the agent of the carrier, and Pangang Company, as the shipper, was not the proper Defendant in this case. 3. The B/L in this case included remarks in the mate's receipt, which had endorsed the B/L, so it was not true that the two Defendants collaborated and colluded to sign the clean loaded B/L on purpose. 4. The Plaintiff had no evidence to prove that the damage to the goods took place before arriving at the port. 5. The *Report on Examination* offered by the Plaintiff could not prove that there were damages before loading, and the examining company had no examination qualification. 6. The sue from the Plaintiff was beyond the limitation.

The Defendant Tongshenxing Company argued that: 1. the sue from the Plaintiff was beyond the one-year limitation which has been provided in Article 257 of the Maritime Code. 2. As for the damage in this case, the Plaintiff should not ask for claim according to the insurance contract, and the Plaintiff did not have right to execute the right of subrogation. 3. The Defendant Pangang Company's *Letter of Guarantee* was issued for carrier, instead of the agent, so the carrier shall bear the responsibility. 4. In the *Report on Examination* offered by the Plaintiff, it was unfair that the goods owner dealt the goods by himself, and it could not show the real situation in which the damage had taken place. 5. The B/L that Defendant signed for carrier was a loaded B/L, instead of a clean B/L, and the B/L in this case has included remarks in the mate's receipt, so it was not true that the two Defendants collaborated and colluded to sign the clean loaded B/L on purpose. Above all, the Defendant Tongshenxing Company requested the court to reject the claims of Plaintiff.

To support its lawsuit, the Plaintiff submitted such evidence as follows:

Evidence No.1: Receipt and Letter of Subrogation and the attachment B/L (No. HDMUCGOAW8050103) issued by CFG Company, Report on Shipment Status, Policy (No.7888STEEL) and Bill of Credit Evidence of Payment, to prove that: 1. CFG Company, as the insured, was the holder and consignee of the B/L in this case. 2. Some of the goods as referred in this case were in bad situation such as damage and broken package when shipped. 3. There was an insurance contract relationship between the Plaintiff (also the insurer in this case) and the assured, and the Plaintiff was the insurer of the goods as referred 4. The Plaintiff has paid CFG Company the insurance indemnity about €660,901.96, so it had the right of subrogation legally.

The Defendant Pangang Company raised no objection to the authenticity of Receipt and Letter of Subrogation and the B/L: as for other evidence, the company held the opinion that it had no procedures on notarial certification and its form was illegal. So the company raised objection to the authenticity of other evidence.

The Defendant Tongshenxing Company raised no objection to the authenticity of Receipt and Letter of Subrogation and the B/L. However, Tongshenxing Company thought that there should have been official seal on Receipt and Letter of Subrogation and the Plaintiff could not prove the identity of the lawful holder of B/L; As for other evidence, the company held the opinion that it had no procedures on notarial certification and its form was illegal. So the company raised objection to the authenticity of other evidence.

The court holds that: the first group evidence provided by the Plaintiff is formally legal through procedures on notarial certification and its form is legal, so it shall serve as the basis of establishment of facts.

Evidence No.2: Authentic Act of the alteration of the name of the assured CFG Company, to prove that assured CFG Company's status about business registration and change in company's name.

The Defendants Pangang Company and Tongshenxing Company raised no objection to the authenticity of the evidence, but they argued that there should be official document and seal issued by specialized agency.

The court holds that, as for the evidence No.2 provided by Plaintiff, the two Defendants raised no objection to the authenticity of it, so it shall serve as the basis of establishment of facts.

Evidence No.3: Business Registration File of assured CFG Company, to prove that assured CFG Company's status about business registration.

The Defendants Pangang Company and Tongshenxing Company to the authenticity of the evidence, but they argued that there should be official document and seal issued by specialized agency.

The court holds that, as for the Evidence No.3 provided by Plaintiff,, the two Defendants raised no objection to the authenticity of it, so it shall serve as the basis of establishment of facts.

Evidence No.4: *Confirmation Letter* of insurance broker, to prove that insurer had paid for the insurance indemnity to the external, and had the right to sue the court for insurance subrogation as the chief insurer.

The Defendant Pangang Company raised objection to the authenticity of the evidence facticity, and the Plaintiff could not prove that it had paid to the external actually.

The Defendant Tongshenxing Company raised objection to the authenticity of evidence. The evidence just notarized the signatures of the two, which could not prove that they had the right to issue the document in the name of other insurers.

The court holds that the evidence provided by the Plaintiff is formally legal through procedures on notarial certification and its form is legal, so it shall serve as the basis of establishment of facts.

Evidence No.5, Sales Contract and Business Receipt signed between assured CFG Company and Defendant Pangang Company, to prove that there was a sales contract relationship between assured CFG Company and the Defendant Pangang Company, and it was clearly prescribed in the contract that the Defendant should offer clean loaded B/L.

The Defendant Pangang Company and Tongshenxing Company raised no objection to the authenticity of, however, Tongshenxing Company argued that FERROSTAAL METALS GmbH Company (hereinafter referred to as FMG Company), the buyer in this sales contract, was not the assured CFG Company.

The court holds that, as for evidence No.5 provided by the Plaintiff, the two Defendants raised no objection to its authenticity, so it shall serve as the basis of establishment of facts. the evidence above can be basis for the court to make judgment. About the relationship between FMG Company and CFG Company, evidence No.2 provided by the Plaintiff could prove the process of change of registration between the two patties.

Evidence No.6: *Letter of Credit*, to prove that according to Sales Contract and Letter of Credit, if marine B/L noted the damaged condition as goods really were accurately when loading the goods, it would lead to failure in exchange settlement procedure.

Both the Defendants Pangang Company and Tongshenxing Company raised objection to the authenticity of the evidence. However, both the Defendants argued that L/C should include "approval in mate's receipt" in the B/L's note, and the sign and issue of B/L met the needs of L/C, so Plaintiff's object of proof could not set up during the hearing, the Plaintiff argued that the *Letter of Credit* offered by Defendant Pangang Company was more consistent with the loading time in this case.

The court holds that, as for the evidence above provided by the Plaintiff, both the two Defendants raised objection to its authenticity, and the Plaintiff argued that the L/C offered by Defendant Pangang Company was more consistent with the loading time in this case, so the evidence shall not serve as the basis of establishment of facts.

Evidence No.7: Mate's Receipt and Report on Goods Status obtained in evidence preservation by Wuhan Maritime Court, to prove that the goods damage had taken place before loading.

The Defendants Pangang Company and Tongshenxing Company raised no objection to the authenticity of the evidence.

The court holds that, the evidence is obtained legally in evidence preservation by the court, so the evidence shall serve as the basis of establishment of facts.

Evidence No.8: Report on Examination issued by JORAS European Examination Company (hereinafter referred to as JORAS Company), to prove that both the heavy wet damage and rust took place before loading and the value of the damage of goods was €660,901.96.

The Defendants Pangang Company and Tongshenxing Company argued that: 1. the two Defendants raised objection to the effect of the report because the examiner was not qualified, and the report was a unilateral authorization. 2. The time when examination was executed was too long since discharging, which led to a huger loss.

The court holds that report on examination offered by JORAS Company can prove the examination has been executed. Whether the examination conclusion can be the reasons for loss identification and the basis of loss amount recognition, the court will discuss in the reasoning Section.

Evidence No.9: Lawyer's Letter and EMS records, to prove that the Plaintiff asked Defendant Pangang Company for claim again in written on September 1, 2001.

The Defendant Pangang Company argued that it did not receive related e-mails, and raised objection to the authenticity.

The Defendant Tongshenxing Company argued that the evidence was delivered to Defendant Pangang Company, and was not related to itself.

The court holds that the Plaintiff could not prove that it really sent Lawyer's Letter to the Defendant Pangang Company, so the evidence shall not serve as the basis of establishment of facts.

To object against the Plaintiff's lawsuit, Defendant Pangang Company submitted such evidence as follows to the court:

Evidence No.1: Sales Contract, to prove that there was a sales contract relationship between Defendant Pangang Company and FMG Company. In the contract, it was agreed that dispute over the contract should be referred to arbitration in China International Economic and Trade Arbitration Commission.

Both the Plaintiff MFG Company and the Defendant Tongshenxing Company raised no objection to the authenticity of the evidence.

The court holds that the evidence shall serve as the basis of establishment of facts.

Evidence No.2: Information on company standard of the steel (Q/72322100-X.007-2006), German standard (DIN 1623) and national standard of the People's Republic of China GB/T11253-2007, to prove that Pangang Company produced goods according to the contract standard; German standard required that there would be no oxidation for 3 months in condition of usual package, transport, loading, discharging and storage; moreover, it was common sense that refrigerated rolled steel would rust if stored for 3 to 6 months in condition of usual package, transport, loading, discharging and storage.

The Plaintiff MFG Company raised objection to the authenticity of company standard Q/72322100-X.007-2006 and German standard (DIN 1623) but no objection to national standard of the People's Republic of China GB/T11253-2007.

The Defendant Tongshenxing Company raised no objection to the authenticity of the evidence.

The court holds that Plaintiff CFG raised objection to the authenticity of the company standard and German standard offered by Defendant Pangang Company, and Defendant did not offer other evidence to support, so Evidence No.2 shall not serve as the basis of establishment of facts. As for the national standard of the People's Republic of China GB/T11253-2007 offered by Defendant Pangang Company, both Plaintiff MFG Company and Defendant Tongshenxing Company raised no objection, so the evidence shall serve as the basis of establishment of facts.

Evidence No.3: Proof of packaging sound of goods, Product Package Instruction, Company Standard QG/LZ2008-2007 of cold rolling factory product package and Implementation Rules for Management on Mark Quality, to prove that products of Defendant Pangang Company were in intact package when they were manufactured; The manufacturer had packed the rolled steel strictly according to the technical requirement.

Both the Plaintiff MFG Company and the Defendant Tongshenxing Company raised no objection to the authenticity of the evidence.

The court holds that the evidence shall serve as the basis of establishment of facts.

Evidence No.4: Agreement and its appendix between the Defendant Pangang Company and Chongqing Luhang Shipping Co., Ltd. (hereinafter referred to as Chongqing Luhang Company), to prove that the Defendant Pangang Company entrusted Chongqing Luhang Company to load, discharge and stow according to technical requirement strictly.

The Plaintiff MFG Company could not confirm the authenticity of the evidence meanwhile, Plaintiff argued that this evidence had no relation with this case.

The Defendant Tongshenxing Company raised no objection to the authenticity of the evidence.

The court holds that: the evidence offered by the Defendant Pangang Company was just a copy, and the Plaintiff CFG raised objection to the authenticity of the evidence. What's more, the Defendant did not offer other evidence to support, so the evidence shall not serve as the basis of establishment of facts.

Evidence No.5: Agreement and related technical requirement between the Defendant Pangang Company and Changshu Foreign Transport Co., Ltd. (hereinafter referred to as Changshu Transport Company), to prove that the Defendant Pangang Company entrusted Changshu Transport Company as the goods agent, and to handle according to technical requirement strictly.

The Plaintiff MFG Company could not confirm the authenticity of evidence, meanwhile, the Plaintiff argued that this evidence had no relation with this case.

The Defendant Tongshenxing Company raised no objection to the authenticity of the evidence.

The court holds that the Plaintiff CFG raised objection to the authenticity of evidence for the Defendant Pangang Company offered just a copy, and the Defendant did not offer other evidence to support, so the evidence shall not serve as the basis of establishment of facts.

Evidence No.6: Receipt, Packing List, Certificate of Origin, Inspection Certificate of Quality, Goods Declaration, Customs Tariff of People Republic of China and Regulatory Document Code Description, to prove that the goods Pangang Company exported met the quality requirement and exported goods, whose code was 7209, were not legal examine goods.

The Plaintiff MFG Company raised objection to Receipt, Packing List, Certificate of Origin and Inspection Certificate of Quality and could not confirm the authenticity of Goods Declaration, Customs Tariff of People Republic of China and Regulatory Document Code Description, which Plaintiff argued, had no relationship with this case.

The Defendant Tongshenxing Company raised no objection to the authenticity of evidence.

The court holds that Receipt, Packing List, Certificate of Origin and Inspection Certificate of Quality, offered by Defendant Pangang Company, were origin, and Defendant did not offer related counter evidence, though it raised objection to the authenticity of evidence, so the evidence above shall serve as the basis of establishment of facts. Goods Declaration, Customs Tariff of People Republic of China and Regulatory Document Code Description offered by Defendant Pangang Company were not original, and Pangang Company did not offer other evidence to support, so the evidence shall not serve as the basis of establishment of facts.

Evidence No.7: Report on Goods Status of China Marine Services Co., Ltd. in Beijing, to prove that there was only slight package problem before loading on board so it was not true that the two Defendants cheated the Plaintiff together.

The Plaintiff MFG Company raised objection to the object of proof instead of the authenticity of the evidence.

The Defendant Tongshenxing Company raised no objection to the authenticity of evidence, however, it argued that this evidence was not complete.

The court holds that, this evidence was same as evidence No.7 offered by the Plaintiff, and since both the Plaintiff MFG Company and the Defendant Tongshenxing Company raised no objection. Therefore the evidence shall serve as the basis of establishment of facts.

Evidence No.8: Bill of lading, mate's receipt of Defendant Tongshenxing Company, Letter of Guarantee and Letter of Credit, to prove that the Defendant Pangang Company had a long-term relationship with the buyer, and issuing *Letter of Guarantee* was to meet the need of *Letter of Credit*. So it was not true that the two Defendants cheated the Plaintiff together.

Both the Plaintiff MFG Company and the Defendant Tongshenxing Company raised no objection to the authenticity of the evidence.

The court holds that the evidence shall serve as the basis of establishment of facts.

Evidence No.9: Business materials (contracts, L/C, B/L and MR) between the Defendant Pangang Company and FMG Company from 2006 to 2008 to prove that the Defendant Pangang Company had a long-term relationship with FMG Company, and the L/C was issued and negotiated according to years' cooperation practice of both parties. So there was no fraud in this case.

The Plaintiff MFG Company raised objection to the authenticity and relevancy of evidence.

The Defendant Tongshenxing Company raised no objection to the authenticity of the evidence.

The court holds that this group evidence can prove that there was long-term trade relationship between Defendant Pangang Company and FMG Company, but what the Defendant Pangang Company wanted to prove could not realize.

Evidence No.10: CRU News Monthly, to prove that the price of coil steel has decreased sharply after the financial crisis. Also, without handling the goods in time, FMG contributed to larger loss.

The Plaintiff MFG Company raised objection to the authenticity and relevancy of the evidence.

The Defendant Tongshenxing Company raised no objection the authenticity of the evidence.

The court holds that evidence No.10 was obtained from Internet and had no direct relation with this case, so the evidence shall not serve as the basis of establishment of facts.

Evidence No.11: Evidence from the two following witnesses, YE Kaimin (male, the Han nationality, was born on September 25, 1975, lived in Panzhihua City, and works for Pangang Company), and QU Guoxing (male, Han, born on September 8, 1977, lived in Changshu City Jiangsu, and works for Changshu Transport Company). During the hearing, witness YE Kaimin stated the process of packing of coil steel, namely firstly, put coil steel on anti-tarnish paper and there was a sheeting outside the coil steel, and added outside package after inside package was done, meanwhile, installed both inside and outside plastic corners. During the hearing, witness QU Guoxing stated that it was common to appear package rust and fracture in tying band in refrigerated rolled steel, and fracture in tying band was one kind of slight damage.

The Plaintiff argued that evidence No.11 was not related with this case. The Defendant Tongshenxing Company raised no objection to evidence No.11.

The court holds that what witness YE Kaimin stated proved the process of packing of coil steel, so the evidence shall serve as the basis of establishment of facts. And what witness QU Guoxing stated was his own opinion, it shall serve as the basis of establishment of facts, for judging a heavy damage needed the particular situation.

Evidence No.12: e-mails, to prove that the buyer would inform Defendant Pangang Company if there was any damage took place.

The Plaintiff MFG Company raised objection to the authenticity of the evidence.

The Defendant Tongshenxing Company raised no objection to the authenticity of the evidence.

The court holds that Plaintiff CFG raised objection to the authenticity of the evidence, and the Defendant did not offer any other evidence to support, so evidence No.12 shall not serve as the basis of establishment of facts.

To reject against the Plaintiff's lawsuit, the Defendant Tongshenxing Company submitted such evidence as follows:

Evidence No.1: Agency Agreement, Confirmation of Letter of Guarantee, E-mails of issuing B/L, B/L and Letter of Guarantee regarding vessel in this case between Sino Far East Shipping Co., Ltd. and the Defendant Tongshenxing Company, to prove that issuing B/L of the Defendant Tongshenxing Company had got conformation from the shipowner.

The Plaintiff MFG Company raised no objection to the authenticity of B/L and L/G, but raised objection to the authenticity of E-mails.

The Defendant Pangang Company raised objection to the authenticity of L/G, for there was no the Defendant's seal on it. And the Defendant raised no objection to the authenticity of e-mails and B/L.

The court holds that apart from B/L, the authenticity of the evidence above referred by Defendant Tongshenxing Company could not be sure, so the evidence shall not serve as the basis of establishment of facts.

According to the Plaintiff's evidence and Defendant's cross-examination, also authentication opinions from the court, the court went into investigation, and ascertains as follows:

1. Facts related to sales of goods.

On May 20, 2008, the Defendant Pangang Company signed steel sales contract with CFG Company. The main contract clauses were as follows: Goods were refrigerated rolled steel; The amount was 1,500 tons; the unit price of 250 tons of goods with 0.8 mm × 1,000 mm was FOB ST USD1,060/metric ton, unit price of other goods was FOB ST USD1,050/metric ton, totally USD1,577,500; package was according to factory standard; deadline for loading was 25 August 2008; The Loading Port was Changshu port, China; discharging Port was Antwerpen Port, Belgium; the buyer was responsible for the insurance; the mode of payment was at sight letter of credit; the seller should submit materials to the negotiating bank, including clean loaded B/L, Receipt, Certificate of Quality, amount, weight expertise report, the certificate of origin issued by China Council for the Promotion of International Trade (CCPIT); after arriving at the destination port, in case the quality, quantity or weight of the goods was found not in conformity with those stipulated in this Contract, the buyer could raise objection according to the examination certification issued by examination organization which both the buyer and the seller agreed. And the buyer should raise objection within 60 days after the goods arrived at the destination port to quality, quantity and weight, within 30 days. The seller should respond within 30 days.

On May 27, 2008, according to application from FMG Company, the bank issued documentary credit as follows: the validity deadline was September 15, 2008; applicant was CFG Company; beneficiary was the Defendant Pangang Company; loading deadline was August 25, 2008; unit price of 250 tons of goods with 0.8 mm × 1,000 mm was FOB ST USD1,060/ metric ton, unit price of other goods was FOB ST USD1,050/metric ton, totally USD1,577,500; loading port was Changshu Port, China; discharging port was Antwerpen Port, Belgium; the negotiating L/C asked for 3 copies of marine B/L; B/L would be made according to FMG Company's order, freight payable as per charter party, and remarks as per mate's receipt,

On September 30, 2008, the Defendant Pangang Company issued business receipt for CFG Company, as provided in the receipt that net weight of the goods was 1,505.77 metric ton, totally 191 rolls; Loading Port was Changshu Port, China; destination port: was Antwerpen Port, Belgium; total value was USD1,583,587.4.

2. Facts related to goods transport.

Before loading the goods, China Marine Services Company Ltd, representing the shipowner, did the pre-shipment inspection on MV DORIC SPIRIT. Among the facts, as prescribed in the B/L (No.HDMUCGOAW8050103) in this case: 1. rust on the coil steel appearance. 2. Break on 5 rolls of the coil steel edge. 3. Lost of 1 to 2 pieces of 9 rolls. 4. Scratch on 25 pieces of coil steel. 5. Quantity was offered by tallying. 6. Weight, measure and quality were offered by shipper. The content was unknown. The shipowner issued Mate's Receipt and included all the examination above before loading on board.

On August 19, 2008, the Defendant Tongshenxing Company, representing shipowner of MV DORIC SPIRIT, issued No.HDMUCGOAW8050103 bill of lading after loading on board. As provided in the bill of lading, shipper was Defendant Pangang Company; Consignee took action according to the order of FMG Company; Notifying Party: was FMG Company; Vessel for carriage was MV DORIC SPIRIT; Loading port was Changshu port, China; Discharging port was Antwerpen Port, Belgium; Goods: were refrigerated rolled steel; gross weight was 1,513.41 metric ton; net weight was 1,505.77 metric ton; total was 191 rolls; freight payable as per charter party. And remarks as per mate's receipt.

On September 24, 2008, the vessel for carriage arrived at the destination port. On September 29, 2008, CFG Company entrusted JORAS Company, as the examiner, to examine the goods on MV DORIC SPIRIT that arrived at the port. JORAS Company was informed that examiner of the consignee found package rust on some of the goods during and after discharging. On October 2, 2008, examiner of consignee, JORAS Company, representative of shipowner and representative of charted party examined the goods jointly. During the joint examination, 2 of 3 heavily damaged goods showed wet damage and rust in different degree on the inside and bottom of package, but the goods were not polluted from the sea water. After that, besides 78 rolls were stored in Antwerpen Port, the other goods were sold to ended users by CFG Company. JORAS Company examined the goods at Duisburg, Bönen, Deggendorf and Bochum because of the claims from the ended users. Report on Examination described as follows for the damage reason: the damage to the goods was obviously found by the examiner entrusted by CFG Company after the goods arrived at the port. During the joint examination, there was obvious rust on the goods package. During the examination, there was no any blisters on the package due to seepage into goods in the cabin, which could exclude the possibility of rust during the shipping. According to this, the goods got wet before loading or during the storage process instead of during shipping period.

About the management on the goods. About the goods in Duisburg, since the consignee needed the goods in a hurry, he agreed to deduct 5 rolls steel with rust which would be handled in shortage, and the shortage of goods would be handled by residual value. About the goods in Bönen, since the examination result and appearance of opened goods, the consignee refused to accept the goods as prime quality. Therefore, related parties agreed to sell out the goods on-site at residual value to decrease loss. As for the goods delivered to Kermi Company, all parties agreed to sell by inviting bids in the best solution. As for the goods delivered to Schutz Company, all parties agreed to sell at residual value in the best solution. The goods stored in Antwerpen Port would be sold out by inviting bids in the best solution. Finally, according to benefit after deducting costs associated with handling of the goods, JORAS Company ascertained that the total loss value of the goods was USD660,901.96.

3. Facts related to goods insurance.

In January 2002, GOSSLER, GOBERT & WOLTERS Insurance Broker Co., Ltd. (hereinafter referred to as GGW Company) issued No.7888 Steel Transport Policy. As provided in this Policy: the assured were CCC Steel GmbH Company and its subsidiary; the assured goods were different kinds of specialized steel products, coal, mineral and chemical materials; types of shipping were water, land and air; And the contract shall automatically continue. According to clauses provided in the policy, distribution of assured proportion was like this: the Plaintiff MFG Company, as the first insurer, accounted for 55%, GOSSLER GEBR GMBH 35% and Burmester, Dunchey & Joly 10%. On July 1, 2008, related parties modified the contents in the policy, and CFG Company (the old CCC Steel GmbH) became the insurer. At the same time, there was an adjustment about the assured proportion: Plaintiff MFG Company accounted for 50%, GOSSLER GEBR GMBH 32%, Paul Sleveking 10% and Burmester, Dunchey & Joly 8%.

Based on the damage to the goods, CFG Company asked Plaintiff MFG Company for settlement of claims. On August 18, 2010, CFG Company issued Receipt and Letter of Subrogation, and confirmed receiving the insurance claim of €660,901.96 on May 19. Moreover, CFG Company agreed to transfer all its rights, relief and right of claim that were related the goods and B/Ls to the first insurer namely the Plaintiff MFG Company (whether it was based on contract or tort, but the arbitration agreement was excepted).

At the same time, on September 14, 2010, GGW Company issued Confirmation Letter, and confirmed that the B/L involved in this case was recorded and managed in the name of Plaintiff MFG Company. Also, the insurer has already paid for assured CFG Company all the insurance claims.

Moreover, on January 29, 2008, CCC Steel GmbH & Co. KG was changed into Coutinho & Ferrostaal GmbH & Co. KG, and registered at Commercial Registrar of Local Court at Hamburg Germany. After this, steel trade of Coutinho & Ferrostaal GmbH & Co. KG was imparted to CFG Company, and completed the registration of business separation on September 12, 2008. CFG Company once developed business in the name of FMG Company.

The court holds that the Plaintiff, as the first insurer, after completing the insurance claim and obtaining the right of subrogation, still collaborated and colluded to sign the clean B/L on purpose while the shipper (the Defendant Pangang Company) and agent of carrier(the Defendant Tongshenxing Company) already knew that damage had taken place before loading, then transferred illegally the risk that should have been taken by the Defendant Pangang Company to consignee of B/L. So the court holds that the two Defendants should take joint and several liability for the tort. As provided in Article 44 of the Law of the Application of Law for Foreign-related Civil Relations of the People's Republic of China, the laws at the place of tort shall apply to liabilities for tort, but if the parties have a mutual habitual residence, the laws at the mutual habitual residence shall apply. If the parties choose the applicable laws by agreement after any tort takes place, the agreement shall prevail. This is a tort case, during the hearing, all the Plaintiff and the two Defendants proposed to apply to China's law, the court would regard that all parties agreed to choose law that this case applied to, so dealing with issues in this case should apply to China's law.

1. Plaintiff's right to appeal

The Plaintiff, as the first insurer in the insurance contract, could have the right of recourse on the third party on behalf of other insurers after the insurer had affected payment of indemnity to the assured. During the hearing, the Plaintiff proposed that after obtaining the right of subrogation, the Plaintiff required that the Defendants should take joint and several liability with the reason that what Defendant has done was fraud. The court holds that the right of subrogation provided in Maritime Code or Insurance Law is a kind of legal debenture transfer, which means that, if the insurance accident was caused by third party due to damage of insured object, then from the day when the insurer paid the insurance claim to the assured, the insurer had the right of subrogation to ask third party for claim within the aggregate amount of claim. In this case, the insurance accident was arising from damage to goods, and it was obvious that it was not arising from Defendant Tongshenxing Company's issuing B/L and Defendant Pangang Company's issuing L/G. The two Defendants were not the third party that caused the insurance accident, so the Plaintiff had no right to propose rights from the Defendants by executing the right of subrogation. However, according to the nature of rights of recovery, it was necessary to distinguish the legal right of subrogation from the right of subrogation obtained by debenture transfer. The Defendant was not the third party that caused the insurance accident. The Plaintiff had no right to execute the legal right of subrogation, but according to debenture transfer contract, it had the right to sue the Defendant for its action in tort for the loss caused by Defendant. Therefore, the court shall accept what Plaintiff's lawsuit according to the law.

2. Whether what defendants have done was maritime fraud.

During the hearing, the Plaintiff argued that the two Defendants collaborated and colluded to sign the clean B/L on purpose which was maritime fraud, then required the two Defendants to take joint and several liability for the goods loss. Maritime fraud, refers to cheating actions for the purpose to obtain illegal interests during international maritime transport and trade activities. Maritime fraud includes different types, maritime fraud designed by merchants themselves, maritime fraud co-designed by merchant, as the seller and shipowner, maritime fraud designed by shipowner and maritime fraud designed by charted party. In this case, according to what Plaintiff stated, what the two Defendants did was a maritime fraud co-designed by merchant and shipowner.

Among the civil wrongs, fraud is the most serious. In the international legal trade, fraud can lead to cease on paying for L/C. For this, we can refer to the Provision of the Supreme People's Court on Some Issues concerning the Trial of Cases of Disputes over Letter of Credit, and as provided in Article 8, there are different ways to identify L/C fraud, 1. The documents forged by the beneficiary or false documents submitted by beneficiary; 2. The beneficiary refused to deliver the goods on purpose or the delivered goods are blank; 3. There was no real transaction basis but just false document submitted by beneficiary and applicant of document or other third party; and 4. Other situations. Article 8 sets strict conditions for composing L/C fraud, such as without real basic business relation, blank delivered goods, refusing of delivery of goods, forgery of document or document with false contents. Although this case was not L/C fraud, the judicial interpretation which defined fraud still could still be reference for the court. In this case, the Defendant Pangang Company sold goods to the buyer, which was a real transaction. Although damage to the goods had existed before loading, this could only be deemed that the Defendant Pangang Company did not offer goods as provided. So it was not fraud for what the Defendant Pangang Company had done.

Whether what the Defendant Tongshenxing Company had done was maritime fraud. According to Article 75 and Article 76 provided in Maritime Code, the carrier or its agent should issue bill of lading as the appearance of goods really are. In this case, according to the tally report from the loading port, the appearance of goods were not in good condition before loading, and the main problems were as follows: rust in coil steel appearance; broke on 5 rolls of coil steel's edge; loss of 1-2 pieces of 9 rolls; scrape on 25 pieces of coil steel. However, according to the Report on Examination of JORAS Company, the main reason for the damage was rust on the coil steel in this case. Technically, in the loading port, the examination of goods appearance was just from eye-measurement. But JORAS Company opened the outside package and then examined directly, to examine that whether the goods met the standard. This was why the examination report in loading port was seriously different from the report in destination port. As for refrigerated rolled steel, the specialized goods, the carrier or its agent could not judge the real situation inside the package according to the outside package, for it was common to have flaw on the outside package due to the store and transport before loading on board. Therefore, in the condition that refrigerated rolled steel had flaw on outside package, the Defendant Tongshenxing Company issued the clean B/L was to meet the need of Letter of Credit, and it is according to the shipping practice. So it was not fraud for what the Defendant Tongshenxing Company had done.

3. Identity of legal relation in this case.

This case was arising from issuing the bill of lading. About the issue of B/L, the carrier is responsible for two obligations. Firstly, according to Article 72 as provided in Maritime Code, when the goods have been taken over by the carrier or have been loaded on board, the carrier shall, on demand of the shipper, issue to the shipper a bill of lading. According to Article 75 and Article 76 as provided in Maritime Code, the carrier should issue bill of lading as the appearance of goods really are. The carrier or its agent would adjust according to Chapter IV as provided in Maritime Law once violating the obligation of issuing B/L. Although the Plaintiff sued the shipper and carrier's agent, being the Defendants together, instead of suing the carrier, this still was a case arising from dispute over bill of lading of carriage of goods by sea. Although what the Defendants Pangang Company and Tongshenxing Company had done was not fraud, it was sure that they would not be free from their responsibility for the tort over bill of lading of carriage of goods by sea.

4. Whether the Defendants Pangang Company and Tongshenxing company should be responsible for the tort.

1) Identity for the tort of the Defendant. The Defendant Tongshenxing Company did not include the description of goods appearance, which was in the mate's receipt, into the B/L in the condition that it already knew there was flow on the package before loading on board. Due to the mate's receipt was not a part of the B/L, so the Remarks as per Mate's Receipt was not effective remarks in B/L. The Defendant Tongshenxing Company did not include remarks into the B/L, which regarded that the appearance of goods were in good condition; The carrier should deliver the goods according to records in the B/L strictly, otherwise the carrier should take corresponding responsibility for claim. The Defendant Pangang Company, as the shipper, should assumed liabilities as provided in the contract, even there was damage in the goods delivered, but the Defendant did not carry out in tort.

According to the facts that the court has identified, the shipowner had entrusted professional examination company to examine the goods before loading on board, and signed and confirmed the mate's receipt. It could be judged that the shipowner knew exactly about the goods appearance before they were loaded on board. Due to the goods had been delivered at destination port, and the representative of the shipowner had co-examined the goods at destination port, so the carrier should know clearly that the Defendant Tongshenxing Company had issued the clean B/L, however, the carrier had no objection ever. So this action should be deemed that the carrier had accepted issuing clean B/L of the Defendant Tongshenxing Company. According to Article 63 as provided in the General Principles of the Civil Law, the Defendant Tongshenxing Company, as the agent, issued B/L in the name of carrier within the power of agent, the principal, that was the carrier, should be responsible for the legal consequence of this action. The Plaintiff had no power to claim the Defendant Tongshenxing Company for the right.

2) Loss for the Plaintiff. The Plaintiff proposed the Defendant for tort liability of B/L of carriage of goods by sea, which should base on the value of damage to goods when discharging. To prove the reason for damage and the value of the goods, the Plaintiff offered Report on Examination from JORAS Company to the court. However, the court raised objection to examination qualification of JORAS Company, examination process, examination method and the way how to judge the damage. Firstly, about the examination qualification. The Plaintiff did not offer any evidence about the examination qualification of JORAS Company, so as for the report on examination, the court would not believe according to the law. Secondly, about the examination process. According to provision in national standard of the People's Republic of China GB/T11253-2007, the refrigerated rolled steel in this case would rust during 3 to 6 months in the condition of general package, transport, loading, discharging and storage. In this case, Although JORAS Company knew clearly that there was flow on the goods, it did not examine the goods immediately after discharging instead of 2 to 3 months later. So *Report on Examination* from JORAS Company could not prove exactly the real condition of damage when discharging, and could not exclude the possibilities such as natural rust due to goods features and expanded loss happened the period from destination port to warehouse of ended users or period of storage in the warehouse of destination port. Thirdly, about the examination method. Totally 191 rolls coil steel were involved in this case, however, in the Report on Examination, JORAS Company only opened and examined part of them, so the report could not reflect the damage of the whole goods. Fourthly. About the way how to judge the damage. JORAS Company did not evaluate the goods price according to the conditions when discharging, and part of the goods were sold without public bid, it was just confirmed by deducting corresponding cost from the profit earned by CFG Company, the entrusted party, sold out goods unilaterally. This way to handle the goods unilaterally was unfair, and it could not reflect the real market value of the damaged goods when discharging. Although there was a public bid of part goods as provided in *Report on Examination*, there were not details about the process of inviting bids, so it could not prove that publicly inviting bids to reduce loss had been adopted. Therefore, the loss value of the goods identified in Report on Examination could not be the basis for the court to calculate the loss of Plaintiff.

3) The cause and effect. Although the court does not recognize the loss of Plaintiff, it is necessary to analyze whether there is legal cause and effect between what Defendant has done and the loss that Plaintiff has claimed. According to the Plaintiff's logic, if the Defendant Tongshenxing Company had made notes in the B/

L accurately, then the bank would have right to refuse to pay because of documents not conferring to the provisions of L/C, and the Defendant Pangang Company would take responsibility for corresponding damage risk. Therefore, what the Defendant had done impaired the buyer's right of refusing to pay for the *Letter of Credit*.

The court holds that, in the international trade, Letter of Credit is relatively independent from the basic contract, and bank has the obligation to censor the document strictly. If the document offered by the seller is not correspond with the *Letter of Credit*, even the buyer agrees to accept the goods, the bank still can refuse to pay externally. To avoid impediment during the transaction of Letter of Credit, when there is slight flow on the goods appearance, the carrier accepts the shipper's Letter of Guarantee and issues clean B/L to meet the requirement of L/C. The action that carrier accepts L/G and issues clean B/L kindly is according to the practice of international shipping. If the carrier is required to take strictly legal liability for above conducts, even there is only slight flow on the appearance of goods, the carrier will refuse to issue clean B/L no matter what condition it is to avoid self risks. And this will severely affect the function of L/C, give impediment to regular international trade, and violate the purpose that shipping serves the trade. If the consignee required the carrier to take responsibility for claim with the reason that the consignee has lost its right to refuse to pay for the goods under L/C, it is not true to follow corresponding principles simply under L/C, but consider fully whether it has composed fraud for the carrier to issue B/L incorrectly, and whether there is direct cause and effect between carrier's dutifully including remarks and buyer's right to refuse accepting the goods according to the sales contract or dissolution of sales contract. In this case, Defendant the scope of the remarks in the B/L made by the Defendant Tongshenxing Company was only about the outside appearance package of the goods, instead of the quality of inside goods, thus the action of the incorrect issue of clean B/L did not compose fraud, and the Plaintiff did not offer evidence to prove that the action that the Defendant Tongshenxing Company did not make notes into the B/L resulted in losing right to refuse to accept the goods or dissolution of contract in the international sales contract. So there was no direct cause and effect between what the Defendant had done and the Plaintiff's losing the right to refuse to pay for the goods under L/C.

5. The limitation period of this case.

The Defendant Tongshenxing Company demurred that, according to Article 257 as provided in Maritime Code, the limitation period for claims against the carrier with regard to the carriage of goods by sea is one year, counting from the day on which the goods were delivered or should have been delivered by the carrier. So the sue from Plaintiff has been beyond the limitation. The Plaintiff argued that, its sue reasoning for maritime fraud from the Defendant should apply a two-year limitation, instead of one-year as Article 257 provided in Maritime Code.

Due to the court has identified that what the Defendant has done did not compose maritime fraud and this case is still arising from dispute over bill of lading of carriage of goods by sea, so entertaining this case should prevail to apply to related regulations as provided in Maritime Law. According to Article 257 as provided in Maritime Code, the limitation period for claims against the carrier with regard to the carriage of goods by sea is one year, counting from the day on which the goods were delivered or should have been delivered by the carrier. Although this provision does not distinguish lawsuit for contract from lawsuit for tort, according to the spirit of Article 14 as provided in Provisions of the Supreme People's Court on Several Issues concerning the Application of Law in the Trial of Cases arising from Delivery of Goods without Orginal Bill of Lading, if carrier releases goods without original Bills of Lading, it shall apply to one-year limitation due to lawsuit against the carrier. Therefore, as for the right of claim against the carrier for the maritime transport, the limitation will be one-year whether it is based on lawsuit for contract or for tort.

This case is arising from dispute over bill of lading of carriage of goods by sea tort, and issuing B/L is one of the basic act of agent for the carrier's agent. So the legal relation of tort arising from dispute over bill of lading of carriage of goods by sea among the Plaintiff and shipper or carrier's agent was within the adjusting scope as provided in Chapter V of Maritime Code of the People's Republic of China. Also, it is provided clearly in Article 58 of Maritime Code, the defence and limitation of liability provided for in this Chapter shall apply to any legal action brought against the carrier with regard to the loss of or damage to or delay in delivery of the goods covered by the contract of carriage of goods by sea, whether the applicant is a party to the contract or whether the action is founded for contract or for tort.

But, as for whether the carrier's servant and its agent can cite the carrier's demurrer against the lawsuit, there is no clear provision in Maritime Law. The court holds that the carrier's servant and its agent can cite the carrier's demurrer against the lawsuit. The main reasons are as follows: when Maritime Code was drafted, Article 58 fully borrowed the contents of Chapter IV bis in Protocol to Amend the International Convention for the Unification of Certain Rules of Law Relating to Bills of Lading (Also Hague-Visby Rules). As provided of Chapter IV bis in Hague-Visby Rules, "if such an action is brought against a servant or the agent of the carrier (such servant or agent is not an independent contractor), such servant or agent shall be entitled to avail himself of the defence and limits of liability which the carrier is entitled to invoke under this Convention". In contrast, the lawsuit against the carrier's servant or its agent, if applied to Hague-Visby Rules, the carrier's servant or its agent can cite the carrier's demurrer reasons and limitation of liability in the convention; if applied to Maritime law, the carrier's servant or its agent can only cite the carrier's demurrer reasons and limitation of liability provided in Chapter IV. The limitation period of lawsuit against the carrier in maritime transport is one-year both provided in Hague-Visby Rules and Maritime Law, which is one important demurrer reason of the carrier, and this limitation period is different from that of common lawsuit. Under Hague-Visby Rules, the carrier's servant and its agent can cite the carrier's demurrer against the lawsuit. If applied to Article 58 in Maritime Law, for the limitation period is provided in Chapter XIII, so the carrier's demurrer reason provided in Chapter IV seems not to include the matter about demurrer reason. According to interpretation, the carrier's servant and its agent cannot cite the carrier's demurrer against the lawsuit. China reasonably referred to related international convention when Maritime Law was drafted. However, during the process of bringing related international convention into domestic law, changes in legislation model has resulted in different interpretations on some provisions. So, when interpreting related provisions, full consideration should been taken on why Maritime Law referred to the international convention. In fact, the added IV bis provisions in Hague-Visby Rules were to protect the carrier, its servant and agent, and to prevent obligee from directly suing the carrier's servant and agent, which may result in the loss of the right of demurrer reason and limitation of liability of the carrier. Furthermore, if the carrier's servant and agent could not cite one-year limitation, it would result in disunity between limitation against the carrier and that against the carrier's servant and agent. Supposed that the carrier's servant and agent are sued after the goods were delivered for one year, they would have right to recover against the carrier after they have taken responsible for the external claim, and the carrier would also lose protection of one-year limitation. Article 58 in Maritime Law is referred to Hague-Visby Rules, and it is aimed at the same purpose and has no intention to make specific provisions. Including the limitation period into the chapter accords with the characteristic of China's legislation during the process of drafting Maritime Law. However, there is no limitation period for the carrier's demurrer reason as provided in Article 58 of Maritime Code, which is not the original intention of legislation. Therefore, when interpreting Article 58 in Maritime Code, it should take the above elements fully into consideration, and it should allow the carrier's servant and agent to cite the demurrer reason about limitation period.

So, in this case, about the dispute over bill of lading of carriage of goods by sea, the Plaintiff asked for the right of claim against the Defendants Tongshenxing Company and Pangang Company, this also shall apply to provision in Article 257 Paragraph 1 of the Maritime Code, the limitation period for claims against the carrier with regard to the carriage of goods by sea is one year, counting from the day on which the goods were delivered or should have been delivered by the carrier. The goods involved in this case was delivered around the date of September 24, 2008, but the Plaintiff sued to the court on March 23, 2011, which was already beyond the limitation period.

Above all, it lacks legal and fact basis for the Plaintiff to ask the two Defendants to take liabilities for tort, moreover, the sue from Plaintiff has been beyond the limitation period. Therefore the court shall not support the Plaintiff's claim according to the law.

According to Article 63 as provided in the General Principles of the Civil Law of the People's Republic of China, Articles 58, 75, 76 and 257 Paragraph 1 as provided in the Maritime Code of the People's Republic of China, and Article 64 Paragraph 1, Article 142 as provided in the Civil Procedure Law of the People's Republic of China, the judgment is as follows:

Reject the claims of the Plaintiff Mund & Fester GmbH & Co. KG against the Defendants Pangang Company and Tongshenxing Company.

Court acceptance fee in amount of RMB54,547, shall be born by Plaintiff Mund & Fester GmbH & Co. KG.

In event of dissatisfaction with this judgment, the Plaintiff shall within 30 days as of the service of this judgment, while the Defendant shall within 15 days, submit a Statement of Appeal to the court, together with copies in the number of the counter parties to make an appeal before the Hubei High People's Court. The appellant shall submit the appeal according to the volume of dissatisfaction with this judgment and Article 13 Paragraph 1 in Measures on the Payment of Litigation Costs, and pay the court acceptance fee in advance to Non-tax Revenue Settlement Account of Hubei Province Finance Department, Bank of Deposit: Agricultural Bank of China Wuhan City Donghu Branch. Account Name: special bank account of Non-tax Revenue Settlement Account of Hubei Province Finance Department. Number of account: 052101040000369. The payer shall pay through bank transfer, remittance and other ways. And it shall remark Hubei High People's Court or its code 103001 in the purpose of bank voucher blank. In the case of the appellant's failure to submit the fee of appeal in advance, the appeal shall be deemed to be withdrawn automatically.

Presiding Judge: HOU Wei
Judge: YANG Qing
Acting Judge: DENG Yi

March 27, 2015

Clerk: YANG Cheng

Wuhan Maritime Court
Civil Judgment

Nanjing Jinan Welding Technology Co., Ltd.
v.
Nanjing Lansheng Shipbuilding Co., Ltd.

(2014) Wu Hai Fa Shang Zi No.00369

Related Case(s) This is the judgment of first instance and the judgment of second instance is on page 788.

Cause(s) of Action 207. Dispute over shipbuilding contract.

Headnote The Plaintiff subcontractor successful in claim for damages against the Defendant shipbuilder for losses resulting from delays caused by the Defendant's delayed delivery of shipbuilding materials.

Summary The Plaintiff subcontractor completed approximately 90% of a project before ceasing work, alleging that the Defendant shipbuilder delayed delivery of shipbuilding materials. Plaintiff filed suit, seeking damages for the losses it sustained in the delay of construction, including compensation it paid to its staff while construction was paused. Defendant argued that it had paid the Plaintiff properly according to the contract and was not responsible for the losses incurred by the Plaintiff. The court found that the Defendant's failure to provide materials in a timely manner caused the delay and constituted a breach of contract. It was therefore responsible for the losses incurred by the Plaintiff and ordered to pay damages.

Judgment

The Plaintiff: Nanjing Jinan Welding Technology Co., Ltd.
Domicile: 201-A, Bldg. 5, Hengsheng Road, Gaochun County Economic Development Zone, Nanjing City, Jiangsu.
Organization Code: 69462842-4.
Legal representative: ZHANG Mengya, general manager .
Agent *ad litem*: SHAN Aiping, lawyer of Jiangsu Yuanshenghan Law Firm.
Agent *ad litem*: YANG Peixiu, lawyer of Jiangsu Yuanshenghan Law Firm.

The Defendant: Nanjing Lansheng Shipbuilding Co., Ltd.
Domicile: Dongjiang Village, Baguazhou Street, Xixia District, Nanjing City, Jiangsu.
Organization Code: 75945548-1.
Legal representative: YAN Wei, general manager.
Agent *ad litem*: KE Xiaosong, lawyer of Jiangsu Deshan Law Firm.

With respect to the case arising from dispute over a shipbuilding contract, the Plaintiff, Nanjing Jinan Welding Technology Co., Ltd. (hereinafter referred to as "Jinan Company") filed an action against the Defendant, Nanjing Lansheng Shipbuilding Co., Ltd. (hereinafter referred to as "Lansheng Company") before the Nanjing Xixia People's Court on November 14, 2013, and the court transferred this case to the court. This case is concerning maritime dispute, it is under specialized jurisdiction of maritime court, and the address, being Nanjing, of the Defendant, is under the jurisdiction of the court, according to Article 23 of the Civil Procedure Law of the People's Republic of China, the court has jurisdiction to this case. The court, after entertaining this case on January 20, 2014, constituted the collegiate panel consisted of Presiding Judge ZHOU Yanhua, Judge YANG Qing, and Acting Judge DENG Yi, and heard the case in public on June 10, 2014. SHAN Aiping and YANG Peixiu as agents *ad litem* of the Plaintiff, and KE Xiaosong as agent *ad litem* of the Defendant appeared in court and participated in the lawsuit. This case now has been concluded.

The Plaintiff claimed that it signed *Contract for Work for the Construction of Hull -2# of a 4,300 DWT Bunker* (hereinafter referred to as *Contract for Work*) with the Defendant on August 18, 2011, and came to an agreement that the Plaintiff should complete the labor service, such as the construction of the steel structure of the vessel's hull, and the Defendant was responsible to provide the drawings, technical documents, materials, etc. for the construction; the Plaintiff should provide the added-value tax invoices with tax rate being 3.5% of equal amount when the Defendant made payment, and if it failed, the Defendant should withhold and remit the tax. At the same time, the contract determined the construction period as 180 days; the Defendant should pay the labor costs in time, and if the construction by the Plaintiff was affected due to the cause of the Defendant and the construction period was delayed, the delayed days calculated according to the record on spot should be on the account of the Defendant. After signing the contract, the Plaintiff carried out the construction actively and completed 90% of the whole construction, but Lansheng Company delayed in the materials for construction and failed to provide the engine equipment and the outfitting materials, as a result, the construction period delayed and the construction had not been completed, which caused a great loss to the Plaintiff. the Defendant also withheld the added-value taxes (5.5%) of the Plaintiff. Therefore, Jinan Company requested the court to rule that the Defendant should pay the Plaintiff the outstanding construction payment in amount of RMB351,532 yuan, and compensate the Plaintiff RMB1,018,512.5 yuan for the losses, and return RMB27,083 yuan as 2% of the added-value taxes additionally deducted; and the Defendant should undertake the court fees of this case.

The Defendant argued that it had already fully paid the Plaintiff for the completed construction according to the contract, and there was no construction payment in arrears. There was no evidence that could prove the losses claimed by the Plaintiff, and such losses were unconcerned with the Defendant. Because the Plaintiff did not provide the invoices of the added-value taxes, the Defendant withheld the corresponding taxes, and would be willing to return them totally after the Plaintiff provide the invoices to the Defendant.

The Plaintiff, in order to prove its claim, presented the following evidence to the court:

1. *Contract for Work* and Safety Production Responsibility Agreement, to prove that the content of *Contract for Work* signed by the Plaintiff and the Defendant on August 18, 2011.

   The Defendant had no objection to the authenticity of this evidence.

2. Wage table of the year 2012 and 2013 (65 pages in total) and *Contract for Work* (37 pages in total), to prove the workers' wages starting from March 2012 extra paid by the Plaintiff due to the cause of the Defendant.

   The Defendant denied the authenticity of this evidence, and held that this evidence was the contract signed between the Plaintiff and its workers, and it was an internal file of the Plaintiff which was irrelevant to the case.

3. Accident Injury Insurance Policy of PICC (2012 and 2013), to prove that the Plaintiff purchased accident insurance for the workers according the contract.

   The Defendant held that the evidence was concerning the contents of the contract signed by the two parties, but it had no relevancy to the dispute over the construction payment involved.

4. Advice of settlement of partial construction payment and the application for payment to prove that after March 2012, the Plaintiff had to continue to perform the obligations according to the contract because of the Defendant, and had to pay for the labor services; and the Defendant paid partial construction payment as agreed.

   The Defendant had no dissension to the authenticity of this evidence, but it held that this evidence could not prove the construction period claimed by the Plaintiff, and the time of payment was inconsistent with the construction period, and the final statement of the construction was provided according to the procedures of performing the contract for the two parties.

5. Inspection list, to prove that the Plaintiff had performed its obligations according to the contract, and it was qualified upon inspection by the Defendant.

   The Defendant denied this evidence because it held that the list was just a copy.

6. QI Xianglin (male, Han, born on June 25, 1987, living in Jiangsu) appeared in court as a witness, to prove that the workers still worked on the ship involved after March 2012.

   The Defendant held that there was no evidence to prove that the witness, QI Xianglin, was the worker of the Plaintiff; and if he was the worker of the Plaintiff, his testimony could not be confirmed because of the stakes.

The court, after certification, holds that the Defendant, did not have any objection to the authenticity of evidence 1 and 4 presented by the Plaintiff, and therefore the court admits the authenticity thereof according to law. Even though evidence 2, the wage table and the labor contract, was formed by the Plaintiff internally, there are originals and workers' signatures, of which the source is legal and they are related to this case, and the Defendant could not present any rebuttal evidence to deny their authenticity, therefore the court confirms this evidence. Evidence 3 was the original copy, which was formed during the process of the Plaintiff's performing the obligation according the contract involved, and it is relevant with this case and possessed the features of validity and authenticity, and therefore the court affirms the probative force thereof. Even though evidence 5 is a copy, its content was about the inspection record of the completed construction, and the original copy was archived at the Defendant; combined with the inspection requirements provided in evidence 1 and the fact that the Defendant had already paid the construction payment according to the application of the Plaintiff (after being tested as qualified), the court confirmed that evidence 5 could be regarded as the evidence to prove the facts in this case. Evidence 6 is the witness' testimony, and the witness, QI Xianglin, appeared in the court as a witness, and his identity and the content of his testimony and evidence 2 could corroborate mutually, so the court admits this evidence.

The Defendant did not present any evidence.

According to the Plaintiff's evidence, the Defendant's cross-examination and the court's certification opinion, and additionally combining the investigation of the court hearing, the court finds out the following facts about the case:

On August 18, 2011, the Plaintiff signed *Contract for Work* with the Defendant in Baguazhou, Nanjing. It was provided that the Plaintiff should complete the labor service, including the hull steel structure of 4300-ton tanker 2# etc., according to the engineering drawing and the construction list provided by the Defendant; the total price in the contract was RMB1,740,000 yuan, and for each payment the Plaintiff, should provide the invoices of local added-value tax (rate being 3.5%) in equal amount, and otherwise the Defendant should withhold and remit the tax. The Plaintiff should pay the workers exactly and fully at the time of settling the construction payment, and one copy of the wage table, after the workers signed and put their fingerprints on it, should be handed over to the finance department of the Defendant (the Defendant should appoint person to supervise the payment of the workers' wages). Advice of settlement could be made at the production department of the Defendant by surrendering the inspection sheet of the quality supervision department of the Defendant, and application for inspection having been signed and admitted by the surveyor and the shipowner, and after being approved by the person in charge of the Defendant, the Plaintiff could get the payments of this contract from the finance department of the Defendant. The construction period was 180 days, from the day of signing the contract and receiving the notice to commence the construction issued by the Defendant to the day of passing the inspection, and in order to ensure the period of shipbuilding, the Plaintiff must provide sufficient constructors and construct in strict accordance with the milestones made by the

Defendant. The Plaintiff should organize workers to enter into the construction site within 3 days after signing the contract, and the number of workers for the construction should be 50-70 in principle, and additionally, the Plaintiff should add the workers at any time subject to the arrangement of the Defendant. If the construction could not be finished on schedule due to the Plaintiff, it should compensate the Defendant for the loss in amount RMB2,000 yuan each day for the delay. If the construction period delayed due to the Defendant, it should undertake the responsibility according to the time recorded on the spot, and the delivery day should be extended correspondingly. The two parties also made clear provisions about the contents of the construction, inspection requirements, responsibilities, modification of the contract and so on. On the same day, the Plaintiff and the Defendant reached an agreement on the safety responsibility in production.

After the signing of *Contract for Work*, the Plaintiff organized workers to enter into the construction according to the agreement on August 20, 2011, and arranged the personal insurance, including accident injury insurance, accident hospitalization benefit insurance, accident medical insurance and so on, for the workers. Due to the fact that the Defendant delayed to provide the construction materials and equipment, the construction period was extended again and again, and the construction was stopped on September 30, 2013. In order to perform the obligation to ensure the number of workers according to the contract, the Plaintiff paid wages by raising money, and the Defendant also paid directly the partial workers' wages, totally RMB172,000 yuan, from September 2012 to January 2013. During the process of construction, both of the Plaintiff and the Defendant inspected the completed blocks according to the provision of the contract, and after the Plaintiff submitted the application for the payment of the construction, the Defendant appropriated the exact amount of money (RMB1,216,468 yuan). The Plaintiff paid the extra workers' wages in amount of RMB1,018,512.5 yuan (having deducted the wages in amount of RMB172,000 yuan directly paid by the Defendant) from the day the 180-day construction period expired to the day the construction stopped. Due to the fact that Plaintiff did not provide the invoices for the added-value taxes of equal amount when receiving the construction payment, the Defendant withheld the taxes by the tax rate of 5.5%, which was RMB25,745 yuan higher than that calculated on the basis of the agreed rate of 3.5%. Besides, the Plaintiff itself estimated that 95% of the whole shipbuilding construction had already been completed when the construction stopped, however the Defendant only admitted that about 80% of the whole construction had been completed.

So far, the left construction of shipbuilding involved is mainly the installation of the main engine and auxiliary engines and outfitting. Due to the fact that the Defendant could not provide the corresponding equipment and materials, the Plaintiff lodged an action after demanding the construction payment and losses in vain. The court had carried out mediation for many times during the hearing of this case, the two parties could not reach an agreement about the amount of compensation for the losses.

The court holds that this case is concerning dispute over a shipbuilding contract. *Contract for Work* signed by the Plaintiff and the Defendant, showed the true intention of the two parties, formed legally and shall be valid and effective. The two parties shall exercise the civil rights according to the provisions of the contract and the law, and should fully perform the civil obligations with integrity. According the fact found out during the court hearing, the Defendant's failure to provide the materials and the equipment in time caused the repeated extension and the stopping of the construction in the final, the act has already constituted a breach of contract, therefore the Defendant, should take the liability to compensate for the loss of the Plaintiff according to the law. As for the amount of the losses claimed by the Plaintiff, it was calculated on the basis of the amount of wages of the workers from the construction period from the day the 180-day construction period expired to the day the construction stopped, namely the extension period of the construction. In order to perform the obligation to ensure the number of workers according to the contract, the Plaintiff calculated and paid the wages on the basis of the attendance days, and it not only conforms to the contract purpose for ensuring the construction progress and the practice of shipbuilding, but also has evidence for the actual wage payment of RMB1,018,512.5 yuan during the extension, therefore it is authentic and believable that the losses of the extra paid wages were caused by the construction extension. According to the provision of the contract, where the construction by the Plaintiff was affected due to the cause of the Defendant and the construction period was delayed, the delayed days calculated according to the record on spot should be on the Defendant's account. Considering that the wages of the workers belong to internal management of the Plaintiff, the Plaintiff shall perform the obligation to mitigate losses after the Defendant breached the contract according to the law, and shall take appropriate measures to avoid further loss; at the same time, in view of the whole quantity of the construction for shipbuilding and the principle of equality, the court comprehensively determines that the Defendant should compensate the Plaintiff for the losses in amount of RMB611,107.5 yuan (1,018,512.5 × 60%).

As for the claim of the Plaintiff that the Defendant should pay the defaulted sum of RMB351,532 yuan, the Defendant had appropriated the full amount of money according to provision on the payment procedure after the Plaintiff submitted the application for payment, and the Plaintiff did not submit any evidence to prove that the Defendant did not pay the construction payment according to the application for payment, and also it could not present any evidence to prove it had already completed 95% of the construction, therefore there was no factual basis for this claim of the Plaintiff and the court will dismiss this claim according to law.

As for the claim of the Plaintiff that the Defendant should return additionally deducted added-value taxes, it was provided in the contract that the Plaintiff should provide the invoices for the local added-value taxes (the tax rate being 3.5%) of equal amount at the time of payment, and if not, the Defendant should with hold and remit the taxes, therefore it was against the provision that the Defendant should withhold the taxes by the tax rate of 5.5% in the case where the Plaintiff failed to provide added-value taxes' invoices, and the Defendant should return the added-value taxes additionally deducted (2%) in amount of RMB25,745 yuan.

From the above, the claim of the Plaintiff, was legal and can be proved by evidence, therefore the court supports part of them according to the law. According to according to Article 107 and Article 119 of the Contract Law of the People's Republic of China, Article 106 Paragraph 1 and Article 134 Paragraph 1 Sub-paragraph 4 of the General Principles of the Civil Law of the People's Republic of China and Article 142 of the Civil Procedure Law of the People's Republic of China, the judgment is as follows:

1. The Defendant Nanjing Lansheng Shipbuilding Co., Ltd. shall compensate the Plaintiff Nanjing Jinan Welding Technology Co., Ltd. for the loss in amount of RMB611,107.5 yuan;
2. The Defendant Nanjing Lansheng Shipbuilding Co., Ltd. shall return the Plaintiff Nanjing Jinan Welding Technology Co., Ltd. the value-added taxes in amount of RMB25,745 yuan;
3. Reject other claims of the Plaintiff Nanjing Jin An Welding Technology Co., Ltd.

The Defendant, Nanjing Lansheng Shipbuilding Co., Ltd., shall fulfill the pecuniary obligation within ten days after this judgment comes into effect.

If the Defendant, Nanjing Lansheng Shipbuilding Co., Ltd., fails to fulfill obligations with respect to pecuniary payment within the period specified by the judgment, it shall double pay the interest on debt for the delayed period according to Article 253 of the Civil Procedure Law of the People's Republic of China.

Court acceptance fee in amount of 16,076 yuan, the Plaintiff Nanjing Jinan Welding Technology Co., Ltd. shall pay RMB8,748, and the Defendant Nanjing Lansheng Shipbuilding Co., Ltd. shall pay RMB7,328.

In the event of dissatisfaction with this judgment, any party may within 15 days upon the service of this judgment submit a statement of appeal to the court, together with copies according to the number of the opposite parties and lodge an appeal to the Hubei High People's Court. When submitting the statement of appeal, in terms of the claim amount in the appeal that dissatisfies this judgment, the appellant shall prepay the appeal costs according to Article 13 Paragraph 1 of the Measures on the Payment of Litigation Costs. [Payee of the remittance: Non-tax Revenue Special Account of Hubei High People's Court; bank of deposit: Wuhan East Lake Branch of Agricultural Bank of China; account number: 052101040000369. When paying the cost in bank transfer, bank remittance and so on, the payer shall note "Hubei High People's Court" or Hubei High People's Court's unit number "103001" on the blank of purpose of the voucher]. If the appellant fails to prepay the litigation costs within 7 days after the expiration of appeal, the appeal would be deemed to be withdrawn automatically.

Presiding Judge: ZHOU Yanhua
Judge: YANG Qing
Acting Judge: DENG Yi

December 29, 2014

Clerk: ZHENG Wenhui

Hubei High People's Court
Civil Judgment

Nanjing Jinan Welding Technology Co., Ltd.
v.
Nanjing Lansheng Shipbuilding Co., Ltd.

(2015) E Min Si Zhong Zi No.00064

Related Case(s) This is the judgment of second instance, and the judgment of first instance is on page 781.

Cause(s) of Action 207. Dispute over shipbuilding contract.

Headnote Affirming lower court ruling in favor of Plaintiff subcontractor, which successfully claimed damages against Defendant shipbuilder for losses resulting from delays caused by Defendant's delayed delivery of shipbuilding materials.

Summary The Respondent subcontractor completed approximately 90% of the project before ceasing work, alleging that the Appellant shipbuilder delayed delivery of shipbuilding materials. Respondent filed suit seeking damages for the losses it sustained in the delay of construction, including compensation it paid to its staff while construction was paused. Appellant argued that it had paid the Respondent properly according to the contract and was not responsible for the losses incurred by the Respondent. The court of first instance found that the Appellant's failure to provide materials in a timely manner caused the delay and constituted a breach of contract and was therefore responsible for the losses incurred by the Respondent. Appellant appealed, putting forth its original argument and asserting that there was no evidence to prove the losses claimed by the Respondent. The court of appeal rejected this argument, citing Appellant's inability to prove that Respondent was in noncompliance with the contract, and upheld the original judgment.

Judgment

The Appellant (the Defendant of first instance): Nanjing Lansheng Shipbuilding Co., Ltd.
Domicile: Dongjiang Village, Baguazhou Street, Xixia District, Nanjing, Jiangsu.
Organization Code: 75945548-1.

Legal representative: YAN Wei, general manager.
Agent *ad litem*: KE Xiaosong, lawyer of Jiangsu Deshan Law Firm.

The Respondent (the Plaintiff of first instance): Nanjing Jinan Welding Technology Co., Ltd.
Domicile: 201-A, Building 5, Hengsheng Road, Gaochun County Economic Development Zone, Nanjing, Jiangsu.
Organization Code: 69462842-4.
Legal representative: ZHANG Mengya, general manager.
Agent *ad litem*: SHAN Aiping, lawyer of Jiangsu Yuanshenghan Law Firm.
Agent *ad litem*: YANG Peixiu, lawyer of Jiangsu Yuanshenghan Law Firm.

Dissatisfied with the Civil Judgment (2014) Wu Hai Fa Shang Zi No.00369 rendered by Wuhan Maritime Court with respect to the case of dispute over a shipbuilding contract the Appellant, Nanjing Lansheng Shipbuilding Co., Ltd. (hereinafter referred to as "Lansheng Company"), filed an appeal against the Respondent, Nanjing Jinan Welding Technology Co., Ltd. (hereinafter referred to as "Jinan Company") before the court. After docketing this case on April 9, 2015, the court constituted the collegiate panel consisted of Presiding Judge GUO Zaiyu, Judge CHEN Zhuo and Acting Judge YU Jun to try this case on May 8, 2015. KE Xiaosong, agent *ad litem* of the Appellant Lansheng Company, SHAN Aiping and YANG Peixiu, agents *ad litem* of the Respondent Jinan Company, appeared in court and participated in the action. After the mediation conducted by the court, the parties failed to reach an agreement. This case has now been concluded.

Jinan Company claimed in first instance that it signed *Contract for Work for the Construction of Hull -2# of a 4,300 DWT Bunker* (hereinafter referred to as *Contract for Work*) with Lansheng Company on August 18, 2011, and came to an agreement that Jinan Company should complete the labor services such as the construction of the steel structure of the vessel's hull, and Lansheng Company was responsible to provide the drawings, technical documents, materials, etc. for the construction; Jinan Company should provide the added-value tax invoices of equal amount with tax rate being 3.5% when Lansheng Company made payment, and if it failed, Lansheng Company should withhold and remit the tax. At the same time, the contract determined the construction period as 180 days; Lansheng Company should pay the labor costs in time, and if the construction by Jinan Company was affected due to Lansheng Company and the construction period was delayed, the delayed days calculated according to the record on spot should be on the account of Lansheng Company. After signing the contract, Jinan Company carried out the construction actively and completed 90% of the whole construction, but Lansheng Company delayed in delivering the materials for construction and failed to provide the engine equipment and the outfitting materials, as a result, the construction period delayed and the construction had not been completed, which caused a great losses to Jinan Company. Lansheng Company also withheld the added-value taxes (5.5%) of Jinan Company. Therefore, Jinan Company requested the court to rule that Lansheng Company should pay Jinan Company the outstanding construction payment in amount of RMB351,532 yuan, compensate Jinan Company RMB1,018,512.5 yuan for the losses and return 2% of the added-value taxes extra deducted in amount of RMB27,083 yuan; and Lansheng Company should undertake the court fees of this case.

Lansheng Company argued in first instance that it had already fully paid Jinan Company for the completed construction according to the contract, and there was no construction payment in arrears. No evidence could prove the losses claimed by Jinan Company, and such losses were unconcerned with Lansheng Company. Because Jinan Company did not provide the invoices of the added-value taxes, Lansheng Company withheld the corresponding taxes, and would be willing to return them totally after Jinan Company provide the invoices to Lansheng Company.

The court of first instance found out the following facts about the case:

On August 18, 2011, Jinan Company signed *Contract for Work* with Lansheng Company in Baguazhou, Nanjing. It was provided that Jinan Company should complete the labor services, including the hull steel structure of 4300-ton tanker 2# etc. according to the engineering drawing and the construction list provided by Lansheng Company; the total contract price was RMB1,740,000 yuan, and for each payment Jinan Company, should provide the invoice of local added-value tax (rate being 3.5%) in equal amount, otherwise Lansheng Company should withhold and remit the tax. Jinan Company should pay the workers exactly and fully at the time of settling the construction payment, and one copy of the wage table, after the workers signed and put their fingerprints on it, Jinan Company should be handed over to the finance department of Lansheng Company (Lansheng Company should appoint person to supervise the payment of the workers' wages). Advice of settlement could be made at the production department of Lansheng Company by surrendering the inspection sheet of the quality supervision department of Lansheng Company, and application for inspection having been signed and admitted by the surveyor and the shipowner, and after being approved by the person in charge of Lansheng Company, Jinan Company could get the payments of this contract from the finance department of Lansheng Company. The construction period was 180 days, from the day of signing the contract and receiving the notice to commence the construction issued by Lansheng Company to the day of passing the inspection, and in order to ensure the period of shipbuilding, Jinan Company should provide sufficient constructors and construct in strict accordance with the milestones made by Lansheng Company. Jinan Company should organize workers to enter into the construction site within 3 days after signing the contract, and the number of workers for the construction should be 50-70 in principle, and additionally, Jinan Company should add the workers at any time subject to the arrangement of Lansheng Company. If the construction could not be finished on schedule due to Jinan Company, it should compensate Lansheng Company for the losses in amount RMB2,000 yuan each day for the delay. If the construction period delayed due to Lansheng Company, it should undertake the responsibility according to the time recorded on the spot, and the delivery day should be extended correspondingly. The two parties also made clear provisions about the contents of the construction, inspection requirements, responsibilities, modification of the contract and so on. On the same day, Jinan Company and Lansheng Company reached an agreement on the safety responsibility in production.

After the signing of *Contract for Work*, Jinan Company organized workers to enter into the construction according to the agreement on 20 August 2011, and arranged the personal insurance, including accident injury insurance, accident hospitalization benefit insurance, accident medical insurance and so on, for the workers. Due to the fact that Lansheng Company delayed to provide the construction materials and equipment, the construction period was extended again and again, and the construction was stopped on September 30, 2013. In order to perform the obligation to ensure the number of workers according to the contract, Jinan Company paid wages by raising money, and Lansheng Company also paid directly the partial workers' wages, totally RMB172,000 yuan, from September 2012 to January 2013. During the process of construction, both of Jinan Company and Lansheng Company inspected the completed blocks according to the provision of the contract, and after Jinan Company submitted the application for the payment of the construction, Lansheng Company appropriated the exact amount of money (RMB1,216,468 yuan). Jinan Company paid the extra workers' wages in amount of RMB1,018,512.5 yuan (having deducted the wages in amount of RMB172,000 yuan directly paid by Lansheng Company) from the day the 180-day construction period expired to the day the construction stopped. Due to the fact that Plaintiff did not provide the invoices for the added-value taxes of equal amount when receiving the construction payment, Lansheng Company withheld the taxes by the tax rate of 5.5%, which was RMB25,745 yuan higher than that calculated on the basis of the agreed rate of 3.5%. Besides, Jinan Company itself estimated that 95% of the whole shipbuilding construction had already been completed when the construction stopped, however Lansheng Company only admitted that about 80% of the whole construction had been completed.

So far, the left construction of shipbuilding involved was mainly the installation of the main engine and auxiliary engines and outfitting. Due to the fact that Lansheng Company could not provide the corresponding equipment and materials, Jinan Company lodged an action after demanding the construction payment and losses in vain. the court of first instance had carried out mediation for many times during the hearing of this case, the two parties could not reach an agreement about the amount of compensation for the losses.

The court of first instance held that this case was concerning dispute over a shipbuilding contract. *Contract for Work* signed by Jinan Company and Lansheng Company, showed the true intention of the two parties, formed legally and should be valid and effective. The two parties should exercise the civil rights according to the provisions of the contract and the law, and should fully perform the civil obligations with integrity. According the fact found out during the court hearing, Lansheng Company's failure to provide the materials and the equipment in time caused the repeated extension and the stopping of the construction in the final, the act had already constituted a breach of contract, therefore Lansheng Company, should take the liability to compensate for the losses of Jinan Company according to the law. As for the amount of the losses claimed by Jinan Company, it was calculated on the basis of the amount of wages of the workers from the construction period from the day the 180-day construction period expired to the day the construction stopped, namely the extension period of the construction. In order to perform the obligation to ensure the number of workers according to the contract, Jinan Company calculated and paid the wages on the basis of the attendance days, and it not only conformed to the contract purpose for ensuring the construction progress and the practice of shipbuilding, but also had evidence for the actual wage payment of RMB1,018,512.5 yuan during the extension, therefore it was authentic and believable that the losses of the extra paid wages were caused by the construction extension. According to the provision of the contract, where the construction by Jinan Company was affected due to Lansheng Company and the construction period was delayed, the delayed days calculated according to the record on spot should be on Lansheng Company's account. Considering that the wages of the workers belong to internal management of Jinan Company, Jinan Company should perform the obligation to mitigate losses after Lansheng Company breached the contract according to the law, and should take appropriate measures to avoid further losses; at the same time, in view of the whole quantity of the construction for shipbuilding and the principle of equality, the court of first instance comprehensively determined that Lansheng Company should compensate Jinan Company for the losses in amount of RMB611,107.5 yuan (1,018,512.5 × 60%).

As for the claim of Jinan Company that Lansheng Company should pay the defaulted sum of RMB351,532 yuan, Lansheng Company had appropriated the full amount of money according to provision on the payment procedure after Jinan Company submitted the application for payment, and Jinan Company did not submit any evidence to prove that Lansheng Company did not pay the construction payment according to the application for payment, and also it could not present any evidence to prove it had already completed 95% of the construction, therefore there was no factual basis for this claim of Jinan Company and the court of first instance dismissed this claim according to law.

As for the claim of Jinan Company that Lansheng Company should return additionally deducted added-value taxes, it was provided in the contract that Jinan Company should provide the invoices for the local added-value taxes (the tax rate being 3.5%) of equal amount at the time of payment, and if not, Lansheng Company should withhold and remit the taxes, therefore it was against the provision that Lansheng Company should withhold the taxes by the tax rate of 5.5% in the case where the Jinan Company failed to provide added-value taxes' invoices, and Lansheng Company should return the added-value taxes additionally deducted (2%) in amount of RMB25,745 yuan.

From the above, the claim of Jinan Company, was legal and could be proved by evidence, therefore the court of first instance supported part of them according to the law. According to Article 107 and Article 119 of the Contract Law of the People's Republic of China, Article 106 Paragraph 1 and Article 134 Paragraph 1 Sub-paragraph 4 of the General Principles of the Civil Law of the People's Republic of China and Article 142 of the Civil Procedure Law of the People's Republic of China, the court of first instance judged that: 1. Lansheng Company should compensate Jinan Company for the losses in amount of RMB611,107.5 yuan; 2. Lansheng Company should return Jinan Company the value-added taxes in amount of RMB25,745 yuan; 3. reject other claims of Jinan Company should be rejected. Lansheng Company should make one-off performance of the above obligation for pecuniary payment within 10 days after the judgment came into effect. If Lansheng Company failed to perform the obligation with respect to pecuniary payment within the period specified by the judgment, it shall double pay the interest on debt for the delayed period according to Article 253 of the Civil Procedure Law of the People's Republic of China. As for court acceptance fee of this case, Jinan Company should pay RMB8,748, and Lansheng Company should pay RMB7,328.

Lansheng Company was dissatisfied with the judgment of first instance, and filed appeal requesting to revoke Item 1 and Item 2 of the judgment of first instance, and amend the judgment to reject Jinan Company's claim and rule that Jinan Company should undertake the court acceptance fees of the first and second instance. The reasons were as follows:

1. The original judgment found facts incorrectly. Firstly, the construction period 180 days as prescribed in the Contract for Work was just a general description, and actually it was unfixed period, and the construction period should be counted from "the day when the contract is signed and Party B receives the Notice of Commencement from Party A"; it was wrong that the court of first instance counted the time from the signing time of contract, and the actual time of commencement was later than that time; secondly, Jinan Company had no evidence to prove that the extension of construction was caused by Lansheng Company; thirdly, it was wrong that the court of first instance calculated the amount of workers' wages brought by the extension of construction as RMB1,018,512.5 according to the workers' wage table of the year 2012 and 2013 submitted by Jinan Company. The wage table, which contained numerous corrections, was Jinan Company's internal file, and Lansheng Company merely accepted RMB68,968.5 thereof.
2. The application of law was incorrect. Even if the construction is caused by Lansheng Company, the wages of the workers extra paid by Jinan Company should not be undertaken by Lansheng Company. Firstly, this case was concerning contract for work, Jinan Company, as the contractor, in order to achieve specific result of work, signed the labor contract with the workers and paid them wages, those were specific internal management activities for specific work carried out by the contractor for the purpose of achieving specific work result, which had no direct relationship with the ordering party. Secondly, according to Article 7.9 of *Contract for Work*, "if Party A affects Party B and the extension of construction to Party B, the extended days or time of the construction recorded on spot should be on Party B's account, and the construction period for Party B should be extended backward accordingly. The legal consequence of such extension caused by Lansheng Company was to extend the construction period accordingly, while, there was no agreement on that Jinan Company could request Lansheng Company to compensate its losses. Thirdly, in the event of no

agreement thereon, the loss of construction period did not fall into the scope of loss, it was common commercial risk; Jinan Company should have foreseen reasonably the consequence of the extension of construction period caused by the change of Lansheng Company's construction planning at the time of signing the Contract for Work, and it should arrange workers and equipment reasonably, and prevent risks thereby.

Without submitting written defense, Jinan Company argued in the court trial as follows: firstly, according to the Contract for Work signed by both parties, Jinan Company should arrange workers to the construction site within 3 days after signing the contract, therefore Jinan Company arranged workers to the construction site on 20 August 2011, and the calculation of the starting time in the first instance is consistent with the facts.; secondly, it was explicitly stipulated in the Contract for Work that if the construction could not be completed on schedule due to Jinan Company, it should compensate Lansheng Company RMB2,000 per day; if the extension of the construction period was caused by Lansheng Company, Lansheng Company should take the corresponding responsibility for the extended time; thirdly, Jinan Company counted the cost according to the construction period of 180 days, however Lansheng Company delayed the construction again and again, as a result, Jinan Company extra paid more wages for the workers and the losses were far more than the original wages. The facts were clearly recognized in the first instance, and the substantial issues are objective and impartial. Therefore, Jinan Company required to reject the appeal and affirm the original judgment.

Neither Lansheng Company nor Jinan Company did not submit any evidence to the court during the period of adducing evidence in the second instance.

It is found in the second instance that the facts found in the first instance are clear and therefore the court hereby affirms.

Considering both the opinions of the Appellant and the defender, the court concludes that the outstanding issues in the second instance as follows: 1. whether the construction period involved is extended; if so, should the wages for the workers extra paid by Jinan Company be undertaken by Lansheng Company or not? 2. The amount of the more wages extra paid by Jinan Company for the workers.

1. Whether the construction period involved is extended; if so, should the wages of the workers extra paid by Jinan Company be undertaken by Lansheng Company or not?

    The court is of the opinion that *Contract for Work* signed by Jinan Company and Lansheng Company shows the true intention of the two parties, and it was lawfully established and shall be valid and effective. Both parties shall fully perform *Contract for Work* according to the principle of good faith; Lansheng Company delayed to provide the materials, it caused the construction period involved extended, and the wages of the workers extra paid by Jinan Company should be undertaken by Lansheng Company. Firstly, in *Contract for Work*, Article 5. Construction Period provides that "the whole construction is undertaken by Party B (Jinan Company), the construction period is 180 days, from the day when the contract is signed and the Notice of Commencement issued by Party A (Lansheng Company) is received to the day when the construction finishes and passes inspection, of which 75 days is for block construction and 45 days is for the block assembly... Article 7. Change, Rewards and Punishments provides "Party B (Jinan Company) shall organize workers to the construction site within 3 days after signing the shipbuilding contact..." The above provisions show that both parties have made clear agreement about the construction period in the contract, it is no unfixed construction period alleged by Lansheng Company. *Contract for Work* was signed on August 18, 2011, and according to the agreement between the two parties that the workers should be arranged to the construction site within 3 day after signing the contract, the court of first instance recognized the date of commencement was August 20, 2011, and adopted this date as the starting point, it is not improper to calculate the 180-day construction period as prescribed in the contract; up to September 30, 2013, the construction involved had not been completely finished, and hereby the court affirms the fact of the extension of construction. Lansheng Company claimed in the appeal that the commencement time recognized by the first instance was improper, and the construction period should be calculated from the date of receiving *Notice of Commencement*; however it did not present any evidence to prove the date of Notice of Commencement, so the court does not support Lansheng Company's reason for appeal. Secondly, according to the Article 60 of the Contract Law, a party should fully perform its obligations as agreed. According to the Contract for Work signed by the two parties, Article 6.1.1 Responsibilities provides that "Party A (Lansheng Company) shall take the responsibility to provide the drawings, technical documents and materials for the construction", and Article 6.1.5 provides that "Party A (Lansheng Company) should pay Party B (Jinan Company) the labor costs in time; Lansheng Company shall provide materials needed for the construction and pay Jinan Company the labor costs in time". Lansheng Company did not provide relevant materials in time, the construction could not be commenced on schedule. Up to the day that the action was filed, Lansheng Company still failed to provide marine engine and outfitting materials, it led to the construction's not being fully completed. Both parties recognized this fact. even though Lansheng Company denied the causality between its delay to provide materials and the extension of construction, it neither presented other reasons for the extension of construction nor Jinan Company's noncompliance with the contract. Therefore, the court holds that Lansheng Company shall undertake the losses of Jinan Company caused by the extension of construction. Thirdly, according to Article 107 of the Contract Law, "if a party fails to perform its obligations under a contract, or its performance fails to satisfy the terms of the contract, it shall bear the liabilities for breach of contract such as to continue to perform its obligations, to take remedial measures, or to compensate for losses", Lansheng Company could not provide the corresponding materials in time as agreed, the construction period therefore was extended again and again, and due to its failure to provide the engine and outfitting materials, the construction could not be completed; the extra paid workers' wages by Jinan Company are expenses arising from performance of the contract, and according to Article 113 of the Contract Law, "where a party fails to perform its obligations under the contract or its performance fails to conform to the agreement and cause losses to the other party, the amount of compensation for losses shall be equal to the losses caused by the breach of contract, including the interests receivable after the performance of the contract, provided not exceeding the probable losses caused by the breach of contract which has been foreseen or ought to be foreseen when the party in breach concludes the contract", the court holds that it has a legal basis that Jinan Company demanded Lansheng Company to compensate for the extra paid workers' wages due to the extension of the construction period, and the court hereby supports.

2. The amount of the wages extra paid by Jinan Company for the workers.

Jinan Company submitted the workers' wage table of the year 2012 and 2013, according to which it advocated that the wages extra paid for the workers was RMB1,018,512.5. Lansheng Company argued that the wage table was an internal file of Jinan Company and there were many corrections therein, and therefore denied the authenticity and relevancy thereof. The court finds that Paragraph 2 of Article 4.1.1 Contract Price and Payment Methods of the Contract for Work provides that "Party B (Jinan Company) shall pay workers exactly and fully for every time to settle the construction payments and after the workers sign and leave fingerprints on the wage table, one copy shall be handed over to the finance department of Party A (Lansheng Company), and Party A shall send person to supervise when Party B pays for the workers". Article 6.2.3 Responsibilities provides that "workers only by virtue of fingerprint identification at the gate keepers of Party A (Lansheng Company) can enter into and leave the factory of Party A". Seeing from the above agreements, Lansheng Company should take hold of the attendance of the workers at the construction site as well as the records of payroll. Though Lansheng Company denied the authenticity of the wage table submitted by Jinan Company, it neither provided opposing evidence to prove the wage table, was not authentic, nor did it present the corresponding evidence to prove that the workers recorded on the wage table did not work at the construction site. Besides, in the court trial, Lansheng Company pointed out that 11 workers, including ZHANG Faqin, YI Jinhong and so on, were not in the list of the workers' life insurance contract submitted by Jinan Company, and ZHANG Faqin etc. did not work at the construction site; however, after verification in the court, ZHANG Faqin, YI Jinhong etc. mentioned by Lansheng Company, were all in the list of the insurance contract. Hence, the court holds that Jinan Company provided the original wage table and the workers' signatures for receiving wages, and the wage table can be admitted as the evidence to affirm the amount of the workers' wages extra paid by Jinan Company under the condition that Lansheng Company did not provide any valid opposing evidence. As for the allegation of Lansheng Company that the losses of construction period in *Contract for Work* was commercial risk and the reason of appeal that Jinan Company should have foreseen the risk and arranged reasonably workers and equipment to prevent risks at the time of signing the contract, the court holds that it is agreed in Article 7.1 Change, Rewards and Punishment, "the number of workers for the construction from Party B (Jinan Company) shall be 50-70 in principle and workers shall be added at any time subject to the arrangement of Party B (Jinan Company); otherwise Party B (Jinan Company) constitute breach of contract and Party A (Lansheng Company) is entitled to terminate the contract and refuse to settle the construction having been completed and pay Party B (Jinan Company) any costs having happened (including the workers' wages), and all economic losses shall be undertaken by Party B. Jinan Company kept the number of workers at the construction site as agreed is promise-keeping behavior of fully performing the obligations of the contract, and in the case where Lansheng Company had been aware of the possibility of delay in providing materials, Lansheng Company have the obligation to notify Jinan Company to reduce the number of workers to lower the losses of both parties, and therefore, the court does not support the reason of Lansheng Company's appeal. The workers' wages extra paid due to the extension of the construction period are increased costs for the purpose of performing the contract and they are actual cost. What's more, Lansheng Company has no evidence to prove that the expanded costs are caused by Jinan Company's improper behavior, and it's unreasonably that the first instance determined by discretion that Lansheng Company should compensate for Jinan Company RMB611,107.5 (1,018,512.5×60%). Considering that Jinan Company did not lodge appeal in terms of the amount of compensation, and it has disposed its interest in this part, so the court affirms this amount.

To sum up, the grounds of Lansheng Company's appeal cannot stand. In the first instance, the fact affirmation is clear and the judicial procedure is legitimate; though there is inappropriateness in the entity dealing, Jinan Company did not appeal thereto. According to Article 170 Paragraph 1 Sub-paragraph 1 of the Civil Procedure Law of the People's Republic of China, the judgment is as follows:

Reject the appeal, and affirm the original judgment.

Court acceptance fee of second instance in amount of RMB16,076, shall be undertaken by the Appellant Nanjing Lansheng Shipbuilding Co., Ltd.

The judgment is final.

Presiding Judge: GUO Zaiyu
Judge: CHEN Zhuo
Acting Judge: YU Jun

August 24, 2015

Clerk: CHEN Yinhua

Shanghai Maritime Court
Civil Judgment

Operating Department of China Continent Property & Casualty Insurance Co., Ltd.
v.
China Shipping Logistics Co., Ltd.

(2014) Hu Hai Fa Shang Chu Zi No.1509

Related Case(s) None.

Cause(s) of Action 202. Dispute over contract of carriage of goods by sea or sea-connected waters.

Headnote Carrier held liable for water damage to cargo caused by defective container seals, rejecting carrier's argument that cargo owner bore a responsibility to inspect the container before loading.

Summary The Plaintiff, a cargo insurer, sued the Defendant for damages arising from water damage to a cargo of sequoia paper belonging to the Plaintiff's insured, the shipper of the goods. The cargo was carried "door to door" by the Defendant, and was damaged by water while on the wharf at the port of loading because of a defective seal on the container. The Court found for the Plaintiff, holding that the damage happened within the Defendant's period of responsibility. The Court rejected the Defendant's argument that the Plaintiff should have inspected the container more carefully, as it was the Defendant's obligation, as carrier, to provide containers in satisfactory condition. The Plaintiff was entitled to be subrogated to the shipper's rights, having paid the claim in full. The claim had been brought within the limitation period.

Judgment

The Plaintiff: Operating Department of China Continent Property & Casualty Insurance Co., Ltd.
Domicile: Pudong New Area, Shanghai.
Legal representative: HUANG Le, general manager of the Operating Department.
Agent *ad litem*: SHAO Changhui, lawyer of Shanghai Zhontianyang Law Firm.

The Defendant: China Shipping Logistics Co., Ltd.
Domicile: Hongkou District, Shanghai.
Legal representative: ZHAO Bangtao, chairman.
Agent *ad litem*: SHAO Jingshu, lawyer of Shanghai Rolmax & Co.
Agent *ad litem*: LUO Congrui, lawyer of Shanghai Rolmax & Co.

With respect to the case of dispute over contract of carriage of goods by sea the Plaintiff, Operating Department of China Continent Property & Casualty Insurance Co., Ltd. instituted an action against the Defendant China Shipping Logistics Co., Ltd. before the Shanghai Hongkou District People's Court (herein after referred to as the Hongkou Court) on August 27, 2014. The Defendant challenged the jurisdiction of Hongkou Court, the court made (2014) Hong Min Wu (Shang) Chu Zi No.554 Civil Judgment on November 3, 2014 and transferred this case to the court. After being transferred, this case was entertained and docketed by the court on December 1, 2014, and was tried under summary procedure according to law. On December 25, 2014, the court summoned all parties concerned to exchange evidence and held a court hearing on January 13. SHAO Changhui, agent *ad litem* of the Plaintiff and SHAO Jingshu, agent *ad litem* of the Defendant appeared in court and participated in the action. The case has been concluded now.

The Plaintiff alleged that: the sixteen volumes of sequoia A level 140-140 grams paper were underwritten by the Plaintiff. The insured Jian Group Co., Ltd. (hereinafter referred to as Jian Company) entrusted the Defendant to carry the goods from door to door. On October 21, 2012, the goods were loaded on board and transported from Shanghai port to Jinzhou Port. On October 26, 2012, the goods arrived at the place of consignee. After unpacking the goods, the consignee found the bottom of the goods were wet on a large scale and refused to accept the goods. The goods were sold at lower price by the Defendant and thus caused economic loss of RMB45,330.30. The Plaintiff compensated the insured Jian Company RMB45,330.30 according to insurance contract. The Plaintiff claimed that the loss of goods happened during the period of responsibility of the Defendant and the Defendant should bear the liability. After payment of the insurance compensation to Jian Company, the Plaintiff lawfully gained the right of subrogation to Jian Company. Thus The Plaintiff requested the court to rule the Defendant to pay the Plaintiff RMB45,330.30 in terms of the loss of goods and burden the court fee.

The Defendant alleged that: 1. the Plaintiff's compensation exceeded the scope of insurance liability; 2. the ascertainment of amounts of damage goods is lack of evidence; 3. the shipper Jian Company should burden part of liability of the goods loss; and 4. the Plaintiff's filing the action exceeded the statute of limitations and thus the Defendant requested the court to reject the Plaintiff's claims.

In terms of this case, the Plaintiff's evidence, the Defendant's cross-examination and the court's ascertainment are as follows:

1. Original copy of the carriage contract, to prove Jian Company established a relationship of contract of carriage of goods by sea with the Defendant, and Jian Company was the shipper and the Defendant was carrier of through carriage.

The Defendant ascertained the authenticity, legality of this evidence, but did not ascertain it can prove that the Defendant shall bear the liability for the recourse of the Plaintiff.

2. Original purchase and sales contract between Jian Company and Senxin Paper (Beijing) Co., Ltd. Shenyang Branch (hereinafter referred to as Senxin Company), to prove the value of the goods involved. The Defendant claimed that the purchase and sales contract was the original, but the seal of the buyer, Senxin Company, a party not involved in this case, was not the original seal and thus it did not ascertain the authenticity of this evidence. What's more, it was agreed in the purchase and sales contract there would be rebate when the amount of goods reaches certain quantities, thus the unit price of the goods involved claimed by the Plaintiff was little higher.
3. Original shipper's order of domestic coastal container goods, to prove that Jian Company entrusted the Defendant to transport the goods involved from the warehouse of the shipper Jian Company to the warehouse of the consignee Senxin Company. The Defendant ascertained the authenticity and legality of this evidence, but held it could not that the Defendant should bear the liability for the recourse by the Plaintiff.
4. Original delivery order, to prove the condition when the goods involved were sent out. The Defendant ascertained the authenticity and legality of this evidence, but held it could not prove that the Defendant should burden the liability for the recourse by the Plaintiff.
5. Original container freight bill, to prove the condition when the goods involved departed from port. The Defendant ascertained the authenticity and legality of this evidence, but held it could not prove that the Defendant should bear the liability for the recourse by the Plaintiff.
6. Original purchase and sales contract between the Defendant and Hangzhou Tianxin Paper Co., Ltd. (hereinafter referred to as Tianxin Company), to prove the price of the goods involved sold at a discount after being damaged. The Defendant ascertained the authenticity and legality and content of proof of this evidence.
7. Original statement of goods damaged by sea water issued by the Defendant, to prove that the Defendant ascertained the damage fact, cause and loss amount of the goods involved. The Defendant ascertained the authenticity and legality of this evidence, but considered that this statement just estimated the cause of damage of the goods involved which is subjective assume but could not prove the real cause of the damaged goods.
8. Weather forecast, to prove the damage cause of the goods involved. The Defendant considered this evidence was just a printed material without notarization from website, thus did not ascertain the authenticity of this evidence. What's more, the Defendant considered that this evidence just forecasted local light rain, but did not prove that the damage was caused by rain infiltrated into container.

9. Original survey report, to prove the fact and cause of the damage and the loss amount of the goods involved. The Defendant ascertained the authenticity and legality of this evidence, but considered that in the survey report, the identification could not identify the cause of the damage to the goods involved, which lacked evidence and was subjective assume, and in terms of the identification of the amount of the damaged goods, since the original value of the goods had not been verified, the calculation of loss was not reasonable.
10. (1) Statement of wet damage processing situations issued the Defendant. (2) Original purchase and sales contract between Jian Company and the Defendant, to prove that the Defendant agreed to take the obligations for compensation on 15 April 2013. The Defendant considered that 10 (1) was not the original copy thus did not ascertain the authenticity of this evidence and the 10 (2) was the original copy thus ascertained the authenticity and legality of that evidence, but the two pieces of evidence could not prove that the Defendant had committed to undertake the obligation for compensation.
11. Original bank payment voucher, to prove that the Plaintiff had actually paid insurance indemnity. The Defendant ascertained the probative force and content of proof of this evidence.
12. Original of subrogation form, to prove the Defendant had obtain the subrogation right. The Defendant ascertained the probative force and content of proof of this evidence.
13. Copy of goods transportation open cover of 2012, to prove that the Plaintiff and Shanghai Gangsong International Logistics Co., Ltd. (hereinafter referred to as Gangsong Company) established a relationship of insurance contract, under which the insured is stated as Jian Company. The Defendant considered this evidence was just the copy but not the original, thus did not ascertain the authenticity of this evidence. In addition, the Defendant held, according to the insurance contract, the involved accident exceeded the coverage.
14. Copy of the supplementary agreement, to prove that the Defendant and Gangsong Company had modified part of the clauses of the open cover. The Defendant considered this evidence was just a copy but not the original, thus did not ascertain the authenticity of this evidence.
15. Original copy of domestic waterway and land goods transportation insurance slip, to prove that Gangsong Company had insured the goods involved on the Plaintiff. The Defendant considered that the title "9060978" had the defacement at the "Danger Box/Title" of this evidence and the number of insurance slip "PYDL201231090004000385" was filled in the original copy, but there was no number on the copy, it could prove that the number was added by hand. Thus the Defendant did not ascertain the authenticity of this evidence.
16. Original copy of the policy, to prove the legal insurance contract relationship in terms of the goods involved. The Defendant considered that the insurance policy was solely made but the Plaintiff and thus did not ascertain its authenticity. In addition, the Defendant considered that the issuing date of the policy

was on October 29, 2012, which was after October 26, 2012 when the accident happened. Thus this evidence proved that the goods were not insured before the damages to the goods happened.
17. Original copy of goods transportation open cover of 2013, to prove that the Plaintiff and Gangsong Company have long-term insurance contract relationship under which the insured was Jian Company. The Defendant considered that this evidence was just a color printed copy and thus did not ascertain its authenticity or legality; this evidence was an open cover of 2013, it had nothing to do with this case and thus did not ascertain its relevancy.

The ascertainment of the court are as follows: evidence 1, 3-7, 9, 10.2, 11-12 is original and the Defendant ascertained the authenticity and legality of the evidence and the evidence materials all have relevancy to the facts to be proved. Thus the court ascertains probative force of the evidence. The seal of the buyer Senxin Company in evidence 2 is not the original, but the unit price of goods recorded in this evidence corroborates the calculation of the original value of the goods in the survey report of evidence 9 and the original value of the goods calculated by this criteria is also ascertained in evidence 7 by the Defendant. Evidence 2 can corroborate evidence 7 and 9, the court ascertains the probative force of evidence 2.

Evidence 10 (1) is the copy but it could corroborate evidence 1, 2 and 10 (2) and the court ascertained the probative force of evidence 10 (1).

Evidence 15 and 16 is original copies. The number of policy in evidence 15 is added by hand and the seal has defacement, but the transportation information of the goods involved recorded in the insurance slip can corroborate with evidence 3 and 5. The number of the insurance policy, number of shipping document and the information of goods recorded in evidence 16 can corroborate evidence 3, 5 and 12, thus the court ascertains the probative force of evidence 15 and 16.

Evidence 13 and 14 are copies but they can corroborate evidence 12, 15 and 16, thus the court ascertains the probative force of these two pieces of evidence.

Evidence 8 is printed copy from website and its authenticity cannot be verified. It is just the weather forecast but not the objective reflection of weather condition, thus the court does not ascertain the probative force thereof.

The court holds the evidence with probative force include evidence 1-7, 9-16. In terms of the probative force of the evidence, the court ascertains as follows: evidence 1 and 3 proves Jian Company set up contract of carriage of goods by sea relationship with the Defendant, Jian Company is the shipper and the Defendant is the carrier. Evidence 2 proves the unit price of the goods involved. Evidence 4 proves the quantity and condition when the goods involved were sent out. Evidence 5 proves the surface of container was in good condition when the goods involved departed from port. Evidence 6 proves the amount of the goods involved sold at a discount after being damaged. Evidence 7 proves the Defendant estimated the damage fact, cause and loss amount of the goods involved. Evidence 9 proves the damage fact and damage to the goods involved took place during the Defendant's performance of the carriage of contract, the amount of damaged goods and the identification of the damage cause. Evidence 11-12 proves the Plaintiff had actually paid insurance indemnity and obtained the subrogation right. Evidence 13-16 proves the Plaintiff had insurance contract relationship with Gangsong Company under which the insured was Jian Company. Evidence 10 (1) and 10 (2) have no receiver and the obligation for compensation and amount thereof were unclear, thus it cannot prove that the Defendant agreed to perform the duty of compensation and it just proves that the Defendant would negotiate with Jian Company to confirm the compensation amount after Jian Company obtained insurance claims. Thus, the court ascertains the probative force of evidence 1-7, 9 and 11-16.

The Defendant did not submit any evidence.

Based on the aforementioned evidence and investigation and cross-examination in the court trial, the court ascertains the following facts:

Jian Company, a party not involved in this case, signed a goods transportation contract with the Defendant in which Jian Company was the shipper and the Defendant was the carrier and the transportation mean was "door to door" ocean shipping container transportation and the validity period was from August 1, 2012 to May 31, 2013. According to the contract, Jian Company entrusted the Defendant to transport a batch of A-level sequoia 140-140 grams papers and the place of receipt was Jian Company's warehouse and the place of delivery was Senxin Company's warehouse. On October 17, 2012, the Defendant arranged a container truck to tow a 40 feet empty container to pick up at Jian Company's warehouse. There are sixteen volumes of goods with a total weight of 26,620 kgs, among which the 140 grams paper are 13,933 kgs and 170 grams paper are 12,687 kgs. The goods were loaded in the container with container number of HCIU8009644. There was no delivery receipt during the process of container transition. The Defendant transported the goods to Zhang Huabin Wharf, Shanghai Port. The goods was loaded on the board to transport to Jinzhou Port on October 25, 2012. The container goods bill issued by Shanghai ZGXL Industrial Company Co., Ltd. (hereinafter referred to as ZGXL Company), stated: the shipper as the Defendant, the carrier as ZGXL Company, the place of consignee was the address of Senxin Company's warehouse, the vessel name M.V. "Xin He Chang 1", the voyage "1256N", Loading port was Shanghai Port, discharging port was Jinzhou Port, goods carton number was HCIU8009644 and transportation clause was CY-DO. The transportation bill did not have a special notation on goods status. The goods arrived Jinzhou Port and discharged on October 25, 2012. The goods delivered to the consignee Senxin Company on October 26, 2012. After unpacked the goods, the consignee found the bottom of the goods and container were largely wet and refused to accept goods. The goods was sold at lower price by the Defendant to Tianxin Company with resale price of RMB50,564.

In terms of the damage cause of the goods involved, the Plaintiff entrusted Shenzhen McLarens Young Insurance Survey Co., Ltd. Shanghai Branch (hereinafter referred to as McLarens Company) to survey the reason. McLarens Company considered that there was a sealing gap at the container's door. During the storage of the container at Shanghai Port, the rain in Shanghai immersed the container through that gap and caused goods wet. The Defendant also analyzed the cause of this case and issued the statement of the goods wet, in which the conclusion is consistent with that of the survey report.

The court also finds that Gangsong Company had insured the domestic waterway and land goods transportation of comprehensive risk for the goods involved with the Plaintiff in which the insured was Jian Company, the period of insured liability was from warehouse to warehouse, the insured amount was RMB100,000 and deductible amount was RMB1,000. The Plaintiff paid insurance compensation of RMB44,330.30 to Jian Company of August 12, 2012. Jian Company had issued subrogation form to Plaintiff and confirmed the receipt of the forwarding compensation and agreed to transfer claim right of the goods involved to the Plaintiff.

The court also finds that the Plaintiff submitted a complaint to the Hongkou Court in terms of the goods involved on March 31, 2014 and applied to withdraw the suit on August 25, 2014. The Hongkou Court ruled to withdraw the suit on the same day. The Plaintiff initialed an action before the Hongkou Court again in terms of the goods involved on August 27, 2014.

The court holds that this case is arising from dispute over a contract of carriage of goods by sea. Jian Company is the shipper and the Defendant is the carrier. According to the survey report submitted by the Plaintiff and the statement of accident issued by the Defendant can identify the damages happened during the period of the Defendant's performance of the contract of carriage. According to Article 311 of the Contract Law of People's Republic of China (hereinafter referred to as the Contract Law), The carrier is liable for damages in case of damage to or loss of the goods in the course of carriage, provided that it is not liable for damages if it proves that such damage to or loss of the goods is caused by force majeure, the intrinsic characteristics of the goods, reasonable depletion, or the fault of the consignor or consignee. The Defendant failed to prove statutory exemptions, thus it shall undertake the compensation liability of goods losses.

The main issues in this case are as follows: 1. whether the shipper shall bear part of liability for the goods damage; 2. the amount of goods loss; 3. whether the Plaintiff obtained the right of subrogation; 4. whether the action filed by the Plaintiff exceeded the statute of limitations.

In terms of whether the shipper shall bear part of liability of the goods damage, the Defendant holds, according to Article 79 of the Rules on Carriage of Goods by Domestic Waterway, the shipper shall have the obligation for inspection of the container. If the Plaintiff's claim in respect of the damage reason is tenable, that is, because the container door has a seal gap through which the rain immersed the container and caused goods wet. The shipper Jian Company did not check out the seal gap when delivering the empty container and shall bear part of responsibility for goods loss. The Plaintiff held that Jian Company had checked the basic status of the container and did not find obvious abnormality and the shipper has no obligation to make strict inspection on container sealing strip, on the contrary, the carrier shall have the duty to provide container in good condition. The court ascertained that the shipper has the obligation to check the container provided by the carrier but this kind of examination obligation is just a general duty of care which only limited to the surface inspection. The sealing strip gap in the door belongs to undetectable and less-visible flaw. If without special duty of care, it is difficult to find this defect. In this case, the container is provided by the carrier and carrier shall have the obligation to ensure the container in good condition. With the examination obligation, the shipper did not find faulty parts of container or crack on the box through visual inspection which deemed the shipper had performed the examination obligation of container. The court did not support the Defendant's claim that the shipper shall bear part of responsibility of goods loss due to its inaction of examination obligation of container.

In terms of the amount of the loss of goods, the Plaintiff and the Defendant both confirmed the re-sale price of the damaged goods was RMB50,564, but they had controversy over the original price of the goods. The Plaintiff held that the original price should be calculated on the basis of the agreed unit price between Jian Company and Senxin Company, namely the total price was RMB95,894.30. The Defendant argued that the original price was lack of evidence and the purchase and sales contract between Jian Company and Senxin Company prescribed that when goods sent out reached a certain amount then there would be a rebate, so the original price should be lower than the price as agreed in the contract. The court holds that the Plaintiff submitted a sales contract and the invoice, which respectively proves the unit price and quantity of the goods involved. There are two types of the goods involved among which 140 grams of paper are 13,933 kilograms, 170 grams of paper are 12,687 kilograms. In terms of the original prices of the two types of paper in the contract, Jian Company and Senxin Company agreed as follows: 140 grams of paper is RMB3,650 per ton and 170 grams of paper is RMB3,550 per ton. These two kinds of paper multiplied by the unit price and quantities is amounting to RMB95,894.30. The Defendant also confirmed the amount in the statement of the accident issued by itself. The Plaintiff claimed that the calculation of the original price had basis and the Defendant also confirmed that. Thus, the court does not adopt the Defendant's allegation that the calculation of the loss of the goods was lack of evidence. The original price of the goods involved shall be RMB95,894.30, the re-sale price of the damaged goods shall be RMB50,564 and the loss of the goods shall be RMB45,330.30.

In terms of whether the Plaintiff has obtained the right of subrogation, the Defendant argued that: 1. the Plaintiff did not issue open cover in terms of open insurance contract which contradicted Article 231 of the Maritime Code of the People's Republic of China (hereinafter referred to as the Maritime Code) and thus the open insurance contract had not concluded. 2. The Plaintiff solely issued the policy in terms of the involved transportation on October 29, 2012, it was late after the damage accident happened, namely October 26, 2012. According to Article 224 of the Maritime Code, the Plaintiff should not compensate. 3. The compensation claimed by the Plaintiff was beyond the scope of compensation agreed in the open insurance contract and thus the Plaintiff did not obtain subrogation right according to law. The Plaintiff claimed that it signed open insurance contract with Gangsong Company on May 22, 2012 of which the period of validity was from June 1, 2012 to May 31, 2013 and the insured is Jian Company and subject matter insured was paper products. In terms of the transportation of the goods involved, the Plaintiff issued policy according to procedures as provided in the open insurance contract. After the accident, the Plaintiff had compensated Jian Company and should obtain the subrogation right. The court ascertains that this case is concerning the dispute over the subrogation right of the insurer and the court shall only try the lawful relationship between the insured and the third party who caused insurance accident. In terms of insurance contract validity and the defense that whether the Plaintiff shall pay the insurance compensation extend the scope of the trial, the court will not review that. During the trial, the Plaintiff submitted the copy of open insurance contract, insurance slip, original insurance policy and original bank payment voucher paid by the insured Jian Company, through which the court holds the Plaintiff has obtained the subrogation right and the Plaintiff is entitled to recourse against the Defendant according to the law from the date of making the insurance compensation.

In terms of whether the action filed by the Plaintiff exceeded the statute of limitations. The Defendant considered this case was concerning dispute that the insured exercise the subrogation right under marine insurance contract and the insured and the carrier had the coastal goods transportation contract relationship, thus this case shall apply the statute of limitation prescribed in the Maritime Code, namely, the statute of limitation is one year from the date that carrier deliver the goods or the date that the goods shall be delivered. The goods involved were delivered to the consignee on October 26, 2012 and the Plaintiff sued to the court on March 31, 2013 it had exceeded the statute of limitation. The Plaintiff held that the statute of limitation should apply the relevant judicial interpretations of the General Principles of the Civil Law and the Insurance Law of the People's Republic of China, namely, the statute of limitation is two years from the date that the insured obtains the subrogation right. The Plaintiff compensated Jian Company on August 12, 2013, thus the Plaintiff's filing this case did not exceed the statute of limitation. The court holds that, according to the Reply of the Supreme People's Court on How to Determine the Statute of Limitation of Right of Demanding Compensation for Coastal and Inland Waterway goods Transport, the time limitation of compensation for coastal goods transport is one year.

The main dispute of this case is the starting point of statute of limitation. The Defendant claimed the Official Reply of the Supreme People's Court on the Starting Date of the Statute of Limitations in Which the Insurer of a Marine Insurance Contract Exercises the Right of Subrogation to Claim for Compensation should apply, in which the statute of limitation is from the date that carrier deliver the goods or the date that the goods shall be delivered. The court holds, according to this reply, if the legal relationship of the insured and the third party involved in the subrogation under marine insurance shall subject to of the Maritime Code, then the Maritime Code shall apply. The statute of limitation that the insured exercise subrogation right shall apply the provision of Article 13 of the Maritime Code, that is from the date that carrier delivers the goods or the date that the goods shall be delivered. If the legal relationship between the insured and the third party exceeds the adjustment scope of the Maritime Code, then it did not apply Maritime Code but apply the descriptions of the Contract Law or the Tort Liability Law of the People's Republic of China. The starting point of statute of limitation that the insured performs subrogation right shall apply to Article 16 of the Interpretation of the Supreme People's Court on Several Issues concerning the Application of the Insurance Law of the People's Republic of China (II) (hereinafter referred to as the Interpretation II), that is from the date that the insured obtained the subrogation right. The involved transportation is carried by sea between the ports of the People's Republic of China, the contractual rights and obligations of goods transport relationship between the insured Jian Company and the Defendant is not under the adjustment of chapter 4 of the Maritime Code and shall apply the Contract Law. Thus the start point of statute of limitation that the insured exercises the subrogation right shall not apply to chapter 13 of the Maritime Code but apply to the Interpretation II of the Insurance Law, that is from the date that the insured obtains the subrogation right. The Plaintiff claimed to the court on March 31, 2014 which is under the one-year statute of limitation when obtained the subrogation right on August 12, 2013. According to Article 140 of the General Principles of the Civil Law of the People's Republic (hereinafter referred to the Civil Law), the statute of limitation in this case was interrupted by the Plaintiff's lawsuit. The Plaintiff refiled on August 27, 2014 after withdrawal which did not exceed the statute of limitation. The court did not support the Defendant's claim that the Plaintiff's prosecution exceeded the limitation.

To sum up, according to Article 140 of the General Principles of the Civil Law of the People's Republic, Article 311 of the Contract Law of People's Republic of China, the Reply of the Supreme People's Court on How to Determine the Statute of Limitation of Right of Demanding Compensation for Coastal and Inland Waterway goods Transport and Article 64 Paragraph 1 of the Civil Procedure Law of the People's Republic of China, the judgment is as follows:

The Defendant China Shipping Logistics Co., Ltd. shall pay the Plaintiff Operating Department of China Continent Property & Casualty Insurance Co., Ltd. the loss of RMB44,330.30 within 10 days after this judgment comes into effect.

For failure to fulfill the obligation of payment within the period designated by this judgment, interest on the debt for the delayed period shall be doubled, pursuant to Article 253 of the Civil Procedure Law of the People's Republic of China.

Court acceptance fee in amount of RMB908.26, the Defendant China Shipping Logistics Co., Ltd. shall bear it.

In case of dissatisfaction with this judgment, the Plaintiff Operating Department of China Continent Property & Casualty Insurance Co., Ltd and the Defendant China Shipping Logistics Co., Ltd may within 15 days upon the service of this judgment, submit a statement of appeal to the court, with duplicates in the number of the opposing parties, to lodge an appeal to the Shanghai High People's Court.

Acting Judge: XU Wei
January 27, 2015
Clerk: GU Chanyan

Appendix: Relevant Law

1. General Principles of the Civil Law of the People's Republic of China
Article 140 A statute of limitation shall be discontinued if suit is brought or if one party makes a claim for or agrees to fulfillment of obligations. A new limitation shall be countered from the time of the discontinuance.

2. Contract Law of People's Republic of China
Article 311 The carrier is liable for damages in case of damage to or loss of the goods in the course of carriage, provided that it is not liable for damages if it proves that such damage to or loss of the goods is caused by force majeure, the intrinsic characteristics of the goods, reasonable depletion, or the fault of the consignor or consignee.

3. Reply of the Supreme People's Court on How to Determine the Statute of Limitation of Right of Demanding Compensation for Coastal and Inland Waterway goods Transport
……

According to the spirit prescribed in Article 257 Paragraph 1 of the Maritime Code of the People's Republic of China and combined the trial practice, the statute of limitation that the shipper or consignee claimed the compensation against the carrier in terms of coastal and inland waterway goods transport contract or the carrier claimed the compensation against the shipper and consignee in terms of coastal and inland waterway goods transport is one year which started from the date that carrier deliver the goods or the date that the goods shall be delivered.

4. Interpretation II of the Supreme People's Court on Several Issues concerning the Application of the Insurance Law of the People's Republic of China
……

Article 16 According to Article 60 Paragraph 1 of Insurance Law, the statute of limitation of the insured's subrogation right shall be counted from the date that the insured obtained the subrogation right.

5. Civil Procedure Law of People's Republic of China
Article 64 A party shall have the burden to provide evidence for its claims.

……

Dalian Maritime Court
Civil Judgment

People's Insurance Company of China Hangzhou Branch
v.
Tribute Ship Holding S.A.

(2014) Da Hai Shang Chu Zi No.21

Related Case(s) None.

Cause(s) of Action 202. Dispute over contract of carriage of goods by sea or sea-connected waters.

Headnote Subrogated cargo insurer failed in an action for losses incurred due to a shortage of refined palm oil discovered after discharge; insurer relied on density calculations done at the discharge port, whereas carrier relied on a density table, but court preferred carrier's calculations because there was no evidence that they were not done in good faith.

Summary The Plaintiff-Cargo Insurer compensated its Assured for losses incurred due to a shortage of goods discovered after discharging operations. Assured transferred all its rights against Carrier to Plaintiff. In this case, the Plaintiff-Insurer sued the Defendant-Carrier.

Here, whether there was a shortage of goods depended on which method of density calculation was valid. Plaintiff relied on the density calculation at the port of discharge; whereas, Defendant relied on a density table.

The court held that the Plaintiff could not rely on its evidence because the evidence was derived from an impermissible density test. The court also held that, so long as a Carrier acted in good faith, the court presumes the density table Carrier relies upon is accurate. Rejecting Plaintiff's claims, the court held no actual shortage of the goods happened.

Judgment

The Plaintiff: People's Insurance Company of China Hangzhou Branch
Domicile: No.27 Tiyuchang Road, Xiacheng District, Hangzhou City, Zhejiang Province, China.
Legal representative: XU Bin, general manager.
Agent *ad litem*: CHEN Lei, lawyer of Shanghai RICC & Co.
Agent *ad litem*: YAO Yanan, lawyer of Shanghai RICC & Co.

The Defendant: Tribute Ship Holding S.A.
Domicile: 53rd E Street Urbanization Marbella MMG Tower, 16th Floor Panama, Republic of Panama.
Legal representative: MasafumiAbo, manager.
Agent *ad litem*: LI Yingchun, lawyer of Beijing Dentons Law Offices (Shanghai).
Agent *ad litem*: PAN Rui, lawyer of Beijing Dentons Law Offices (Shanghai).

With respect to the case arising from dispute over contract of carriage of goods by sea, the Plaintiff People's Insurance Company of China Hangzhou Branch (hereinafter referred to as PICC Hangzhou), filed a litigation against the Defendant Tribute Ship Holding S.A. (hereinafter referred to as Tribute). The court entertained the case, and constituted the collegiate panel according to the law, and held a hearing to try this case. CHEN Lei and YAO Yanan, agents *ad litem* of the Plaintiff PICC Hangzhou, LI Yingchun and PAN Rui, agents *ad litem* of the Defendant Tribute, appeared in court and participated in the hearing. Now the case has been concluded.

PICC Hangzhou claimed that the refined palm oil it insured was loaded on M.V. "Botany Tribute" (now renamed as M.V. "ASL Tribute") from Indonesia to Yingkou (Bayuquan) in China on October 6, 2012. Tribute's agent issued No. LBGY1N001 clean bill of lading. On October 21, 2012, after the goods arrived at the port of discharge, it was found the goods was in serious shortage. Pursuant to the insurance contract, PICC Hangzhou compensated the insured USD10,324.72, and obtained right of subrogation according to the law. Tribute was the carrier under the contract of carriage of goods by sea involved, ASP Tander Management Co., Ltd. (hereinafter referred to as ASP) was the operator of the carrying ship (PICC Hangzhou sued ASP in this case, and withdrew the suit against ASP on June 23, 2014), they should be responsible for the short occurring during the period of liability of the carrier. PICC Hangzhou requested the court to order them to compensate for the loss of shortage of goods in sum of USD10,324.72 (equivalent to RMB649,371.69) and the interest from January 7, 2013 to the date the court ordered Tribute to assume the obligation for compensation which should be calculated at the term deposit interest rate of the People's Bank of China over the same period; and bear the court fees of this case.

Tribute argued that PICC Hangzhou could not prove that the shortage of goods happened during the period of the carrier's liability, and the goods did not actually fall into short. It requested the court to reject PICC Hangzhou's claims.

PICC Hangzhou provided the following evidence to support its claims:

1. No.LBGY1N001 B/L clean bill of lading, to prove that Tribute is the carrier;
2. Commercial invoices and import declarations, to prove that the unit price of the goods involved is (CFR Yingkou) USD1,080/ton;
3–4. Weight Inspection Certificate numbered with 211000112004097 and Dead Space Certificate issued by China Bayuquan Entry-Exit Inspection and Quarantine Bureau (hereinafter referred to as CIQ) on November 21, 2012, to prove that the goods involved is unloaded on October 22, 2012, the quantity of unloading was 11,355.255 metric tons;
5. A cargo transport insurance policy issued by PICC Hangzhou and the insured Lighthouse Northern Chemical Co., Ltd. (hereinafter referred to as the Northern Chemical), to prove that PICC Hangzhou was the insurer of the goods involved;
6. Payment voucher and receipt of insurance compensation, and Letter of Subrogation, to prove that PICC Hangzhou compensated Northern Chemical USD10,324.72on January 7, 2013 and obtained right of subrogation;
7. Ship registration website information, to prove that tribute was the shipowner of M.V. "Botany Tribute";
8. Letter of guarantee, to prove that QBE Insurance (Europe) Co., Ltd. issued a letter of guarantee in terms of the claim for the shortage of the goods involved, the amount was USD13,1986.80, to the holder the bill of lading/the insurer;
9. CIQ shore tank survey report, to prove that the quantity of port of discharge was identified as 11,379.418 metric tons, PICC Hangzhou made insurance compensation to Northern Chemical. PICC Hangzhou applied to the court for investigation and collection of evidence, the court collected the record of checking weight by volume, the Ullage Measurement Record Sheet, the Dry Certificate, and the Density Test Report (20 °C laboratory) of the goods involved from CIQ.

Tribute had no objection to the authenticity of the evidence provided by PICC Hangzhou. But it held that the shortage of goods could not be proved due to the agreement in the sales contract, the difference of the density adopted at the port of loading and the port of discharging, lack of rationality to identify the shortage on basis of shore tank quantity, and incorrect data of density calculation CIQ and other factors, on the contrary, the evidence of Tribute could prove that the actual shortage of goods did not occur.

Tribute submitted the following evidence to support its defences:

1. Dead Space Certificate of the port of loading (notarized by the Indonesian Embassy), to prove that Intertek, the surveyor at the port of loading confirmed the cargo tank was clean and dry, and signed the Dead Space Certificate together with the mate;

2. Density Table the goods provided by the consignor (notarized by the Indonesian Embassy), which recorded the density of the goods involved at different temperatures, and the quantity having been loaded estimated according to the Density Table by Intertek;
3. Weight Inspection Certificate issued by Intertek, the surveyor at the port of loading, which records the weight of the goods was 11,500.858 tonnes, and set out the actually measured temperatures and the density adopted, and bore the seal of Northern Chemical;
4. Ullage Report and Ullage Measurement Record Sheet jointly signed by the ship side and CIQ, to prove that the ship side and CIQ jointly carried out ullage measurement, test results, calculated according to the Density Table of the port of loading, respectively came out from the two sides were exactly the same, the quantity of goods at the port of discharge was 11,502.104 metric tons, 1.264 metric tons more than that in the bill of lading;
5. Ullage Report and Dead Space Certificate at the port of discharge, to prove that after the unloading of the goods, CIQ confirmed that all of the cargo holds were empty after unloading, Tribute had fulfilled the obligation for delivery under the bill of lading;
6. *Sales Contract of Goods* signed by Northern Chemical and the seller, Article 4 thereof stipulated that the quantity of goods should be determined by the designated independent international surveyor at the port of loading according to the standard at the port of loading, such determination should bind the parties to the contract, Intertek, the surveyor designated by shipper was in compliance with the sales contract. Therefore, the method to determine the quantity having been unloaded at the port of discharge shall be measured on the basis of the same Density Table as that of the port of loading;
7. *Survey Report* issued by Burton Shanghai Poseidon Insurance Co., Ltd. (hereinafter referred to as "Poseidon Company") which was entrusted by Tribute, to prove that the shortage of goods according to the measurement of PICC Hangzhou carried out according to the CIQ Weight Inspection Certificate may be resulted from two reasons: (1) the density adopted by CIQ was different from that of the Density Table;(2) CIQ's result was shore tank rather than hold;
8. Emails and attachments (including insurance policy, insurance claim payment voucher, Contract of the Sales and Purchase of Goods concluded by Northern Chemical and the Seller, and the Weight and Quality Certificate of the port of loading etc.) the agent of PICC Hangzhou sent to the agent of Tribute, to prove that evidence 3 of Tribute was from PICC Hangzhou;
9. Provisions on Authentication of Weight of Import and Export Goods Part I: General Rules for Static Weighing of Ships (SN/T3023.1–2011), according to the Provisions, density determination method of liquid animal and vegetable oil should meet such inspection rules;
10. Methods for Determination of Specific Gravity (The People's Republic of China GB/T5526), according to the Methods 0.00064 was the expansion coefficient of in 10–30 °C, which should not be applied in the case where the measured temperature had exceeded 30 °C;

11. Query result from the national standard network service platform, to prove that the density test standard ZBX04012-86 adopted in the Test Report issued by CIQ was null and void as of May 1, 2000;
12. Ullage Report of the port of loading jointly signed by the mate and the surveyor Intertek, and Calculation Report of Containers Loaded in Holds (notarized by the Indonesian Embassy), to prove that the weight of the goods at the port of loading was calculated on the basis of the Density Table provided by the seller, rather than the actual measured density.

In terms of Tribute's evidence, PICC Hangzhou held that: Tribute only underwent notarization for evidence 1, 2, and 12 at the Indonesian Embassy, but there was no authentication of Chinese Embassy in Indonesia, it did not meet the requirements of form of evidence, the authenticity was involved; Tribute explained as for objection that Chinese embassy required authentication could only be undergone in the presence of the handler of the formation of evidence, but it could not find the mate and the surveyor of Intertek, the requirement of authentication could not be satisfied, but in the case where the original of the evidence had been presented, the authenticity of evidence 1, 2, 12 should be admitted in conjunction with the signature of the mate and evidence 3. PICC Hangzhou has no objection to the authenticity of evidence 3, 5–6, and 8–10. Ullage Report in evidence 4 had no and the authenticity thereof should not be confirmed. There was no objection to the formal authenticity of the evidence 7, but the conclusion could not be admitted. The authenticity of the evidence 11 should be did not recognized.

According to the cross-examination opinions of the Plaintiff PICC Hangzhou and Tribute, the court admits the authenticity of the evidence of PICC Hangzhou, and evidence 3, and 5–10 of Tribute. Since the originals of evidence 1–2 and evidence 12 have been notarized by the Indonesian Embassy, and the contents thereof corroborate evidence 3 of Tribute,, the court admits the authenticity of the evidence, Ullage Report in evidence 4 shall not be admitted for lack of original, but Ullage Measurement Record Sheet is consistent with the evidence collected by the court, the authenticity shall be admitted. The authenticity of evidence 11 shall be admitted.

After trial, the court finds the following facts: on September 19, 2012, the buyer Northern Chemical signed a contract of the sale of goods with the seller Huaxing Group (Singapore) Pte. Ltd., to purchase bulk RBD palm oil from Indonesia by Northern Chemical, which agreed the weight, quantity, specifications, unit price of goods and so on. Article 4 Quality and Quantity thereof provides: "according to the bill of lading, the quantity is 11,500 tons, 2% of overweight or shortage is permitted, subject to the seller; the quantity of goods shall be determined by the designated independent internationally recognized surveyor at the port of loading according to the standard at the port of loading, such determination shall be final and binding up on the parties to the contract, the loading quantity and quality shall be final". From October 4 to 6, 2012, Intertek, the surveyor designated by the shipper, examined the RBD palm oil carried by M.V. "Botany Tribute" at the port of Lubukgaung, Indonesia. The density values corresponding to temperatures of the goods in each cabin (44 °C, 43 °C, 42 °C) recorded in Ullage Report and Container Ullage Calculation Report signed by Intertek and the mate of M.V. "Botany Tribute" and those listed on the Density Table are exactly the same. On October 6, 2012, the agent of Tribute issued the clean bill of lading No.LBGYIN. The bill of lading records: the port of loading port is Lubukgaung, the port of unloading is Yingkou port, the cargo is 11,500.858 tons of RBD palm oil (bulk cargo), the notify party is Northern Chemical.

Intertek issued the Weight Inspection Certificate on October 8, 2012, which records the temperatures of shore tank actually measured are 49 °C, 48 °C, 46 °C, 43 °C and 44 °C, and corresponding density values and volume, and the quantity estimated to be delivered is 11,500.858 metric tons, as well as the quality test data of the sample of the goods, while the density actually measured is not specified. Northern Chemical confirmed the Weight Inspection Certificate with signature. The density at each temperature recorded in *Weight Inspection Certificate*, *Ullage Report* and the Calculation Report of Containers Loaded in Holds at the port of loading are consistent with corresponding density values listed in the Density Table.

On October 21, 2012, the goods arrived at Yingkou (Bayuquan) port, and were all discharged on the next day. Northern Chemical as a holder of the bill of lading took delivery of the goods with the import customs declaration price was USD1,080/ton. Before discharge, CIQ and the mate jointly signed the Ullage Measurement Record Sheet, the temperatures of the goods in th hold actually measured were 44 °C and 45 °C, the mate's receipt only confirmed the ullage and temperatures. CIQ conducted a laboratory density test on the sample of goods on the basis of ZBX04012-86 standard, it was measured that the density at 20 °C was 0.9178 g/ml. CIQ issued a Dead Space Certificate on October 24, 2012, confirming the holds of M.V. "Botany Tribute" were empty and there was no remaining goods, and the goods had been delivered in good condition. CIQ calculated the quantity of the goods on board on the basis of the density at 20 °C tested in laboratory and correction factor 0.00064/°C before unloading, the basis of calculation includes the measured ullage, temperatures of the goods in hold, volume, laboratory density at 20 °C 0.9178 g/ml, density correction coefficient of 0.00064/20 °C, weight (density) correction factor (WCF) and other data, upon calculation, the quantity of goods arriving at the port was 11,355.255 tons. CIQ issued a Weight Inspection Certificate, a Dry Certificate and Survey Report of Shore Tank on November 21, 2012, which recorded the goods loaded on board was 11,355.255 metric tons, and the quantity of shore tank was 11,379.418 metric tons.

The insured Northern Chemical signed a cargo transport insurance policy with PICC Hangzhou on September 27, 2012, PICC Hangzhou underwrote insurance for the goods involved against all risks, the quantity of the goods underwritten was 11,500.858 metric tons, the amount of insurance was USD13,663,020, and the deductible of shortage was 0.3%. On January 7, 2013, PICC Hangzhou paid compensation in sum of USD10,324.72 to Northern Chemical. Northern Chemical agreed to transfer all the interests on the subject matter insured within the scope of the compensation to PICC Hangzhou. The compensation of PICC Hangzhou was calculated on the basis of quantity came out of the quantity stated in the bill of lading, namely 11,500.858 metric tons by deducting the shore tank quantity of 11,759.81 metric tons at the unloaded and the deductible amount of 34.50 metric tons (0.3% of the quantity of bill of lading) at a unit price of USD 1,080 per metric ton plus 10%.

Poseidon Company was entrusted by Beijing Dentons (Shanghai) Law Firm under the commission of Tribute to evaluate the shortage of goods. Poseidon Company issued a Survey Report, based on Sales Contract of Goods, Density Table, Ullage Reports of loading and unloading ports, Calculation Report of Containers Loaded in Holds, Holds Measurement Report, CIQ Weight Inspection Certificate and Ullage Certificate and other documents, its opinions on the shortage alleged by the Appellant mainly attributed to two causes: (1) the difference caused by different calculation of density at the loading and unloading ports that is to say, CIQ usually used its own laboratory to test the density of goods, the values were often lower than those provided by the shipper; (2) the difference between measurement on board and shore, namely the difference between the results of the measurement in ship's hold and shore tank (volume). If being calculated according to the ship's hold measurement report at the port of unloading and the Density Table of the port of loading, there was no shortage of goods when comparing the quantity arriving at the port with the that stated in the bill of lading, there was even 1.264 tons more than that of the bill of lading. The assessment concluded that the ship side was not obliged to compensate the so-called shortage of goods.

It is otherwise found that the query information from the national standard network service platform suggests ZBX04012-86 is no longer in force from May 1, 2000.

The court holds that this case is an action filed by the insurer for exercise of right of subrogation, PICC Hangzhou is not a party to the contract of carriage of goods by sea with the carrier Tribute, regardless of whether there is any provisions on applicable law in the bill of lading, the contract cannot bind PICC Hangzhou. Because the object of litigation is shortage of the goods delivered by the carrier in China, according to Article 269 of the Maritime Code of the People's Republic of China(hereinafter referred to as "Maritime Code"), the law of the People's Republic of China which has the closest connection with the dispute of this case shall apply.

According to Articles 71 and 78 of the Maritime Code, Northern Chemical as the holder of the bill of lading established a relationship of contract of carriage of goods by sea with Tribute, it shall be legal and effective. PICC Hangzhou, after paying insurance compensation pursuant to the marine insurance contract it concluded with the Northern Chemical, has obtained the right of subrogation within the scope of the insurance compensation according to Article 252 Paragraph 1 of the Maritime Code and Article 93 of the Special Maritime Procedure Law of the People's Republic of China, Tribute is entitled to defence against Northern Chemical. Whether the insurance claim between PICC Hangzhou and Northern Chemical complies with the insurance contract and the provisions of the law does not fall into the scope of trial in this case.

According to the claims and defences of the parties, the court holds the issues in this case are: whether a shortage happened during the carrier's liability and whether Tribute shall bear the liability for compensation.

1. Whether a shortfall happened in the period during which Tribute is responsible for the goods.

PICC Hangzhou claimed although the shore tank quantity determined by CIQ was adopted in the insurance compensation by Northern Chemical, its claim was based on the quantity arriving at the port. namely of 11,355.255 tons, which was identified by the Ullage Report, Dead Space Certificate and the density upon correction, there was a shortfall of 145.603 tons compared with the quantity as stated in the bill of lading, the amount of loss was USD157,251.24. The amount Hangzhou claimed was within the scope of insurance compensation and lower than the liability Tribute should assume. The evidence such as the Dead Space Certificate, the Density Table, the Ullage Report and the calculation report of containers loaded in ship's holds at the port of loading was not been authenticated by the Chinese embassy. The sales contract of goods only confirmed the weight at the port of loading, and it did not affect the buyer's determination of the weight at the port of unloading and the bill of lading did not state the weight of delivery should be determined subject to the calculation at the port of loading. Inconsistency in the calculation of cargo weight between the loading and unloading ports does not affect the final determination of the weight of the goods.

Tribute argued although the evidence at the port of loading it provided did not undergo authentication for failure to meet the requirements of the Chinese embassy, the authenticity of the evidence cannot be denied, and it could be corroborated by the Weight and Quality Inspection Certificate issued by Intertek which had been confirmed by Northern Chemical. It could be confirmed that Intertek, the surveyor did not measure the density of the goods at the port of loading, and it calculated the weight of the goods based on the Density Table provided by the consignor. CIQ calculated out the weight of the goods at the port of unloading based on the corrected 20 °C laboratory density. As a result of different methods used by the loading and unloading ports, the claim of PICC Hangzhou on the shortage of goods should not be admitted. CIQ on the density and correction calculation error, 20 °C laboratory density test method was a null and void standard, so the accuracy of the two sets of data should be admitted. By virtue of calculation in light of the ullage report at the port of unloading and the density table at the port of loading, the weight of the goods actually arrived at the port was 1.264 tons more than that, stated in the bill of lading, the goods did not occur actual shortage.

The court considers that the case is concerning carriage of bulk liquid cargo, according to item 2 of (2015) Min Si Ta Zi Reply of the Supreme People's Court (hereinafter referred to as the Reply"), as for determination of effectiveness of the evidence for delivery quantity of bulk liquid cargo, where the consignee fails to provide effective evidence to prove the shortage of goods occurs during the period of the carrier's responsibility, the Dry Certificate and the Ullage Certificate submitted by the carrier shall have the effectiveness to prove the quantity of bulk liquid cargo delivered. The shore tank quantity certificate provided by the consignee, unless the carrier approves, shall not have the effectiveness to prove the quantity of bulk liquid cargo delivered, when examining and confirming the quantity of bulk liquid cargo delivered, two evidence identification rules shall be adopted when the applicable condition as stipulated in the Reply achieves. The applicable condition is that the consignee fails to provide effective evidence to prove the shortage of goods occurs during the period of the carrier's liability. As for the two evidence identification rules, one is direct determination in the event the carrier accepts or agrees the shore tank quantity certificate, and the other is the presumption bases on the evidence like dry certificate and ullage report in the event the carrier does not agree with the shore tank quantity.

2. Whether the applicable condition are achieved.

Although the Weight Inspection Certificate at the port of unloading provided by PICC Hangzhou is not the certificate of the quantity of shore tank, except for the difference between the inspection time and the period of the carrier's responsibility, the density of the weight inspection certificate before unloading and that of the weight inspection certificate of the quantity of shore tank are calculated based on the laboratory density at 20 °C after correction. According to the Weight and Quality Inspection Certificate issued by Intertek which has been confirmed by the insured Northern Chemical, and the density table confirmed by the court, it can be found the weight of the goods recorded in the bill of lading came from the density table and Ullage Report provided by the consignor, the consignor and Intertek only measured the temperature of the goods on board but not the density of the goods. Due to the different density values adopted by the loading and unloading ports, as well as the sampling method, test method, test standard and measurement error used by the surveyor at the port of unloading, which may lead to the difference between the quantity of the bill of lading and the weight inspected at the port of unloading. Therefore the Weight Inspection Certificate at the port of unloading cannot be used as a valid basis to decide whether a shortage of goods happened during the period of the carrier's liability. The conditions to apply to the Reply have achieved.

3. Whether there is an actual shortage of the goods.

Although the record of quantity stated in the bill of lading is the carrier's confirmation of the goods it has received, the carrier has no statutory obligations for inspection and guarantee of the nature (including density and quality) of the goods when taking over bulk liquid cargo. Therefore, the carrier is not obliged to mark the temperature and density of the goods loaded on board. However, the carrier may, according to the provisions of Article 51 Paragraph 1 Sub-paragraph 9 of the Maritime Code, defend against the allegation for shortage proposed by the holder of bill of lading or the consignee of goods based on the report issued by a survey at the port of loading on the temperature and density which can represent the nature of the goods. according to item 2 of the Reply, the Ullage Report and Density Table of the unloading port shows that the goods have been fully unloaded, and in the absence of evidence to prove changes in the quality of the goods (quality standards) arising from causes other than the nature or inherent vice, it shall be presumed that the quality of the goods has not changed, shortage shall be calculated on basis of the Density Table which can represent the nature of the goods at the unloading port, even if the Density Table may not accurately reflect the nature of goods, it shall be presumed to be true for a carrier in good faith. According to CIQ Ullage Report and Density Table, combined with the Dead Space Certificate, the quantity actually unloaded is 11,502.104 metric tons, 1.246 metric tons more than the amount recorded on the bill of lading, the goods did not actually fall in short.

4. Whether Tribute is liable for compensation.

According to Article 71 of the Maritime Code, the carrier has the obligation to deliver the goods in the quantities stated on the bill of lading. Although the goods involved after the arriving at the port did not occur actual shortage of weight, however, there is a superficial difference between the quantity stated on the bill of lading and quantity recorded in the CIQ Weight Inspection Certificate, the form of goods on the shortage. PICC Hangzhou held that even if there was a difference between the results calculated on the basis of different density at the port of loading and the port of unloading, according to the law of mass conservation, the results should be within a reasonable range of measurement error, and the shortage of the goods involved obviously exceeded a reasonable calculation error, so such shortage of goods which was inconsistent with the law of mass conservation, should be identified as actual shortage, Tribute should be liable therefor.

The court holds that according to Article 51 Paragraph 2 of the Maritime Code, Tribute shall bear the burden of proof for the reason of shortage of goods in form or in fact. After the delivery of the goods, no one claimed that the quality of the goods changed during the period of the carrier's liability, it shall be presumed that the quality of the goods has not changed. In this case, the evidence provided by Tribute can prove that the reason of shortage of goods in form may be attributable to the following three reasons: (1) the reason for the consignor, that is to say, the density table provided by the consignor is untrue; (2) the nature of goods (density, liquid evaporation, etc.) has changed; and (3) the survey at the unloading port is incorrect. According to Article 51 Paragraph 1 Sub-paragraph 8, Paragraph 1 Sub-paragraph 9, Paragraph 1 Sub-paragraph 12, the above three reasons pertain to the circumstances that the carrier may be entitled to exemption of liability, namely act of the shipper, the nature of goods or inherent vice, and other causes arising without the fault of the carrier. Tribute shall not be liable for compensation for the formal shortage which does not match the law of mass conservation, but fall into exemption of liability.

In conclusion, the evidence of PICC Hangzhou is not sufficient to prove that the actual shortage of goods happened during the period of responsibility of Tribute, and the evidence of Tribute can prove that it should not bear the liability for the difference between the quantity in the bill of lading quantity and that in the CIQ

Weight Inspection Certificate. According to Article 51 Paragraph 1 Sub-paragraph 8, Paragraph 1 Sub-paragraph 9, Paragraph 1 Sub-paragraph 12, Article 269 of the Maritime Code of the People's Republic of China, the judgment is as follows:

Reject the claims of People's Insurance Company of China Hangzhou Branch against Tribute Ship Holding S.A.

Court acceptance fee in amount of RMB10,294 (PICC Hangzhou prepaid), shall be born by PICC Hangzhou.

In the event of dissatisfaction with this judgment, People's Insurance Company of China Hangzhou Branch may within 15 days upon the service of this judgment, Tribute Ship Holding S.A. may within 30 days upon the service of this judgment, submit a Statement of Appeal and duplicates in the amount of the opposing parties to the court, so as to file an appeal to Liaoning High People's Court of the People's Republic of China.

Presiding Judge: SUN Guang
Judge: XIN Xin
Acting Judge: DONG Shihua

December 11, 2015

Clerk: WANG Cuicui

Qingdao Maritime Court
Civil Judgment

Qingdao HuaShun Shipping Co., Ltd.
v.
Marc Loud Schiffahrts Gesellschaft mbH & Co. KG. et al.

(2014) Qing Hai Fa Que Zi No.7-1

Related Case(s) None.

Cause(s) of Action 247. Dispute over confirmation of maritime claim.

Headnote Collision case in which court apportioned 60% of responsibility to overtaking vessel and 40% to overtaken vessel.

Summary The Plaintiff Huashun Company sued two Defendants, Marc Loud Company (the Shipowner) and Chenoas Company (the Demise Charterer), for full maritime liability arising from a collision accident. The Plaintiff alleged that Defendant should compensate it for the losses that resulted from the sinking of its vessel. Plaintiff argued that M.V. "Hua Shun 88" (the Plaintiff's ship) was being overtaken by the Defendants' M.V. "Marc Loud" and that M.V. "Hua Shun 88" had taken reasonable measures to prevent the collision, but M.V. "Marc Loud" had failed to fulfill its obligation as the overtaking ship under Article 13 of the 1972 Preventing Collisions Regulations to avoid collision and acted inappropriately after the accident happened. The Defendant counter-argued that Article 13 should not apply in heavy fog, and the Plaintiff should bear at least 50% of the collision liability for its misconduct before and after the accident. The court held that both ships were to blame, and apportioned responsibility 60% to M.V. "Marc Loud" and 40% to M.V. "Hua Shun 88".

Judgment

The Plaintiff: Qingdao Huashun Shipping Co., Ltd.
Domicile: 1105 Room, No.537 Building, Taihang Mountain Road, Qingdao Economic and Technological Development Zone, the People's Republic of China.
Legal representative: SUN Jingfang, General Manager.
Agents *ad litem*: CHU Beiping and SHA Lezhang, lawyers of Boning & Co.

The Defendant: Marc Loud Schiffahrts Gesellschaft mbH & Co. KG.
Domicile: GASSTRA BETA E4BHALLEK522761HAMBURG, Germany.
Legal representative: Matthias Dabelstein, director.

The Defendant: Chenoas Shipping Co., Ltd.
Domicile: 60 Nevis Street, St. John's, Antigua & Barbuda, West Indies.
Legal representative: JORG-HEINERWULFF, authorized representative.
Agents *ad litem* of the Defendants: XU Xianglong and LIU Huali, lawyers of Shandong Minyang Law Firm.

At about 1430 h on 12 April 2014, M.V. "Marc Loud", owned by the Defendant Marc Loud, and bareboat charter by the Defendant Chenoas Shipping Co., Ltd. (hereinafter referred to as Chenoas Company), collided with M.V. "Hua Shun 88", a ship of Chinese nationality owned by Qingdao Huashun Shipping Co., Ltd. (hereinafter referred to as Huashun Company) in the sea area near Qingdao Port (the position was approximate about 35°57.8′N, 120°40.9′E). The accident resulted in M.V. "Hua Shun 88" sunk. On April 18, 2014, the Defendant Marc Loud and Chenoas Company applied to the court for setting up a limitation fund for maritime claims. After entertaining the case, the court severed a notice to the parties concerned, and published an announcement on the Chinese Daily for three times respectively on May 8, 9 and 10 of the same year. On June 20 of the same year, the court made (2014) Qing Hai Fa Xian Zi No.2-1 Civil Ruling, allowing the establishment of a limitation fund for maritime claims as applied by the Defendants Marc Loud and Chenoas Company. On July 9, 2014, the Plaintiff Huashun Company applied for registration of creditor's rights to the court, requesting the court to allow registration for the legal creditor's rights in sum of RMB31,636,717 and the interest thereon. The court made (2014) Qing Hai Fa Deng Zi No.168 Civil Ruling, allowing the Plaintiff's claim for the registration of the creditor's rights. Afterwards the Plaintiff Huashun Company filed an affirmative petitory action before the court. After entertaining this case, the court formed a collegiate panel and heard the case in public. SHA Lezhang, agent *ad litem* of the Plaintiff, and XU Xianglong and LIU Huali, agents *ad litem* jointly of the two Defendants appeared in court and participated in the hearing. The court has heard the case in terms of the responsibility in the collision of two ships and made a judgment.

The Plaintiff alleged that: on April 12, 2014, M.V. "Marc Loud", owned by the Defendant Marc Loud and bareboat chartered by the Defendant Chenoas Company collided with M.V. "Hua Shun 88" owned by Plaintiff in Qingdao Port, which resulted in the sinking of M.V. "Hua Shun 88". Due to the accident, the Plaintiff suffered huge losses, including the losses of the ship, wreck salvage charge charges, wreck pollution clean-up costs, wreck rescue charge, etc., summing to RMB31,636,717 yuan. On April 18, 2014, the two Defendants applied to the court for constituting a limitation fund for maritime claims, on June 20, Qingdao Maritime Court made (2014) Qing Hai Fa Xian Zi No.2-1 Civil Ruling, allowing the establishment of a limitation fund for maritime claims as applied by the two Defendants and published the notice of registration of the creditor's rights. On July

9, the Plaintiff applied to the court according to the law for a registration of creditor's rights with regard to the losses caused by the collision accident in sum of RMB31,636,717 yuan and the interest thereon, which was allowed by the court in (2014) Qing Hai Fa Deng Zi No.168 Civil Ruling. Therefore, the Plaintiff filed an affirmative petitory action, and requested the court to order: 1. the two Defendants should compensate the Plaintiff for the losses of ship, wreck salvage charge, wreck pollution clean-up costs, wreck rescue charge, etc., in total sum of RMB31,636,717 yuan and the corresponding interest, which should be recovered from the limitation fund of maritime claims established by the two Defendants according to law; 2. the application fee of the case for registration of creditor's rights, court fees and other legal costs should be borne by the two Defendants. In addition, the wreck salvage due to the collision accident had not yet been completed, the following pollution clean-up costs could not be confirmed, so the Plaintiff retained the right to add claims after confirmation of the following pollution clean-up costs.

The Defendants argued that: firstly, M.V. "Marc Loud" was under bareboat charter, which had been registered according to law, so the Defendant Chenoas Company should bear the liability of collision, and the Defendant Marc Loud as the registered owner should be out of the liability; secondly, as for the liability ratio of the collision accident, the Defendant insisted that M.V. "Hua Shun 88" should bear at least fifty percent proportion. The Defendants had established a fund and should have the right to limit the liability for maritime claims according to the law; thirdly, the evidence submitted by the Plaintiff was not sufficient to prove that the losses claimed by the Plaintiff had actually occurrence and been paid.

The court ascertains the following facts about the collision of two ships:

M.V. "Hua Shun 88" is a steel tanker, whose port of registry is Qingdao Port in Shandong Province of the People's Republic of China, length is 60.90 m, width is 10 m, depth is 5.10 m, the gross tonnage is 669 tons, net tonnage is 375 tons, gross power is 850 KW. The ship was built on June 18, 1989 in Japan, and re-built in Jiangx Jiujiang Shipyard on October 1, 1996. The owner is the Plaintiff in this case. The ship's legal certificates are complete and effective.

M.V. "Marc Loud" is a container ship, whose port of registry is Antigua and Barbuda / STJOHN, length is 142.70 m, width is 22.60 m, depth is 11.20 m, the gross tonnage is 9610 tons, net tonnage is 4745 tons, deadweight is 12,779 tons, main power is 7,860.00 KW. The ship was built in September 2007 in Busan Korea. The owner of the ship is Marc Loud and the bareboat charterer is Chenoas Company. The ship's statutory certificates are complete and effective.

At about 1428 h on April 12, 2014, on the way heading from the waters of Chaolian island for the Qingdao Port, M.V. "Marc Loud" and M.V. "Hua Shun 88" collided at the place about 6 nautical miles (35°57′N, 120°41′E) to the east of the line between Xiaogong Island and Dagong Island. The accident caused the sinking of M.V. "Hua Shun 88" due to hull rupture and water seepage, and the left upper part of the bulbous bow of M.V. "Marc Loud" depressed. When the collision accident happened, the visibility of the sea was about 50–100 m.

The second mate and one sailor of M.V. "Marc Loud" were on duty in the bridge, while the chief officer and one of their sailor of M.V. "Hua Shun 88" were on duty in the bridge.

Before the collision, M.V. "Marc Loud" and M.V. "Hua Shun 88" did not make any sound signals, nor contacted with each other by wireless telephone.

According to the records of voyage data recorder, before a period of time of the collision, the second mate and the sailor of M.V. "Marc Loud" on duty were talking about irrelevant topics to the safety of navigation. The captain of the ship was not in command of the ship during a period of time before the collision and when the collision happened.

M.V. "Marc Loud" was manned with a total of 16 crew members for the voyage involved all of them were competent, and the certificates were complete and effective, the manning of crew satisfied the requirements of the Minimum Manning of Safety Certificate issued by Antigua and Barbuda authorities. M.V. "Hua Shun 88" was manned with a total of 6 crew members, but no captain, it does not meet the requirements of the Minimum Manning of Safety Certificate issued by the authorities. The certificate of competency held by the chief officer applied to ships of which gross tonnage are less than 500 tons, but does not meet the requirements of the ship (the gross tonnage was 669 tons), the tonnage grade does not meet the requirements of the Minimum Manning of Safety Certificate issued by the authorities.

At 2330 h on April 9, 2014, M.V. "Marc Loud" loaded 2,362.4 tons of goods was away from Osaka Port in Japan to Qingdao Port of Shandong. At 0442 h on April 12, the ship dropped anchor in the east area of Chaolian island, and raised anchor and sailed into the port at 1300 h on April 12.

At 1400 h on April 7, 2014, M.V. "Hua Shun 88" was away from the Kaohsiung pier of Qingdao Port to the Chaolian island waters. The crew involved claimed that the ship sailed to Chaolian island waters, during the whole sailing out of the port, the ship's AIS (automatic identification system of the ship) was closed, as also did not report to the Qingdao traffic control center. At 2300 h on April 12, the ship returned to the Kaohsiung pier of Qingdao Port from the south-east waters of Chaolian island.

During 1352 h and 1428 h on April 12, 2014, the relevant data about the two ships are as follows:

In respect of M, HM, VS, HS,, V, the two ships' distance is 1352280 degrees, 16.7 knots 6.30 nautical miles (nm) 1401281 degrees, 16.7 knots 304.6 degrees 7.2 knots 4.34 nm 1410281 degrees 16.8 knots 7.8 knots 244.5 degrees 2.89 nm 1417281 degrees 16.8 knots 286.8 degrees 7.2 knots 1.88 nm 1425283 degree 16.8 knots 286.1 degrees 7.2 knots 0.44 nm 1427283 degrees 16.8 knots 290.8 degrees 7.1 knots 0.27 nm 1428286.1 degrees 16.1 knots 0 nm. Note: M is M.V. "Marc Loud", S is M.V. "Hua Shun 88", H is course, V is speed.

After the collision, M.V. "Marc Loud" turned hard starboard, the turn made its bulbous bow divorce from M.V. "Hua Shun 88", which resulted in water seepage into the hull of M.V. "Hua Shun 88" and quick tilt. Subsequently, M.V. "Marc Loud" halted.

Qingdao Maritime Safety Administration of the People's Republic of China determined the responsibility for the collision accident as follows:

M.V. "Marc Loud", a motor ship sailing in the visibility under adverse conditions, did not keep a proper and continuous watch out or sailed at a safe speed, nor did it not make a full judgment on the collision risk; in addition, it failed to carefully navigate and take any action to avoid, as well as to make sound signals according to the requirements. The action violated the provisions of Articles 5, 6, 7, 19 and 35 of the International Regulations For Preventing Collisions At Sea, 1972. In the waters connected with the port in poor visibility under the condition of biggish traffic density, the captain of M.V. "Marc Loud" did not perform his duties in the bridge, it was in violation of the relevant provisions of Chapter 8 (Duty) of the STCW Convention.

M.V. "Hua Shun 88", a motor ship sailing in poor visibility under adverse conditions, did not keep a proper lookout, nor made a full judgment on the collision risk, or took any action to avoid. The action has violated Articles 15 and 19 of the International Regulations For Preventing Collisions At Sea, 1972. The voyage of M.V. "Hua Shun 88" was not manned with captain, which violated the relevant provisions of Chapter 8 (Duty) of the STCW Convention, as well as the provisions of Articles 5, 7 and 15 of the Vessel's Minimum Safety Manning Regulation (hereinafter referred to as the MSM Regulations). The tonnage grade the chief mate of M.V. "Hua Shun 88" is allowed to serve for has exceeded the that allowed by the certificate he held, it violated the provisions of Articles 5 and 15 of the MSM Regulations.

In summary, the fault of M.V. "Marc Loud" was larger than that of M.V. "Hua Shun 88", so M.V. "Marc Loud" should bear the main responsibility in the accident and M.V. "Hua Shun 88" should bear secondary responsibility.

The Plaintiff in the trial claimed as follows: firstly, M.V. "Hua Shun 88" was the overtaken ship, it had been keeping safe speed before the collision, although the course had some change, but it was the crew's reasonable error of course in the process of sailing. The ship remained cautious driving, repeatedly took measures to avoid collision such as making sound signal, turning fog lights, and strengthening lookout, etc. The crews of the Plaintiff had done their best to fulfill their obligations. The main cause of the accident lied in the Defendant's ship. According to the Article 13 of Chapter 2 of the Internation Regulations for Preventing Collisions at Sea, 1972 (hereinafter referred to as the Preventing Collisions Regulations), the Plaintiff insisted that M.V. "Hua Shun 88" was the overtaken ship, and M.V. "Marc Loud" was the overtaking ship, M.V. "Marc Loud" should give way to M.V. "Hua Shun 88". Secondly, after the accident, M.V. "Marc Loud" did not identify the specific circumstances of the accident, and wrongly reversed and turned hard starboard in the condition its bulbous bow inserted into M.V. "Hua Shun 88", as a result, the ship being hit instantly lost support. A large number of water was flooded into the ship from the broken hull, causing the ship sunk quickly, M.V. "Marc Loud" should bear full responsibility.

In this regard, the Defendant argued that: the Plaintiff should bear at least 50% of the collision liability. The reasons are as follows: the collision happened in heavy fog, Article 9 but not Article 13 of the International Regulations for Preventing Collisions at Sea, 1972 should apply. M.V. "Hua Shun 88" turned blindly in the fog, it led to an urgent situation, M.V. "Hua Shun 88" turned off the AIS without reporting to the VTS of traffic control center M.V. "Hua Shun 88" was not manned with captain when the accident happened. The competency certificate held by the chief officer was not suitable for the ship, so the ship was unseaworthy. After the accident, M.V. "Hua Shun 88" did not stop, the crew blindly abandoned the ship, resulting in the sinking of M.V. "Hua Shun 88", the Plaintiff should bear responsibility for the expanded losses.

The court holds that this case is concerning dispute over liability caused by ship collision, since the Defendant is foreign company, this case is involved with foreign-related tort dispute. The place where the tort and result happened is in the waters of Qingdao, according to Article 30 of the Civil Procedure Law of the PRC, the court has jurisdiction over this case. according to Article 273 of the Maritime Code of the People's Republic of China, the court applies to the People's Republic of China law and the International Regulation for Preventing Collisions at Sea, 1972 and its amendments to settle substantial dispute of this case.

The court holds that in the case, when determining the ratio of fault, in addition to the factors that whether the two ships kept proper lookout, safe speed, whether the two ships have taken any action to avoid collision and whether the captain has performed duties, the particularity of sail in fog should be taken into consideration, that's to say there is no argument for overtaking ship or overtaken ship, the two ships should bear equal obligations to ensure the safe navigation on the sea. In this case, the two ships were on the route of entering port, if M.V. "Hua Shun 88" opened automatic identification system (AIS) and reported to maritime traffic control center (VTS) before setting sail, then the safety coefficient of the ship will be greatly improved. M.V. "Hua Shun 88" shall bear the corresponding legal liability for the above acts. In addition, after the collision accident, M.V. "Marc Loud" failed to use good seamanship to jack M.V. "Hua Shun 88" and to avoid large quantity of water entering in at dead slow speed, it should bear the corresponding responsibility. So the court, in combination of the determination on the responsibility for the collision accident of Qingdao Maritime Safety Administration, decides the ratio of collision liability of M.V. "Marc Loud" and M.V. "Hua Shun 88" shall be 6: 4, namely, M.V. "Marc Loud" should bear 60% liability and M.V. "Hua Shun 88" remain 40% liability in this collision accident. According to provision that if the colliding ships are all in fault, each ship shall be liable in proportion to the extent of its fault of Article 169 of the Maritime Code of the People's Republic of China, M.V. "Marc Loud" contributed to 60% liability.

Pursuant to the provision that where a colliding ship is under bareboat charter which has been registered according to law, its bareboat charterer shall undertake the compensation liability as prescribed in Article 4 of the Provisions of the Supreme People's Court on the Trial of Certain Issues in Cases of Disputes over Collision of Ships (hereinafter referred to as the Ship Collision Provisions), the liability of M.V. "Marc Loud" in this collision shall be born by the bareboat charterer Chenoas Company.

The allegation of the Defendants that M.V. "Hua Shun 88" should bear at least 50% liability has no factual basis, and the court shall not support.

In summary, according to Article 169 of the Maritime Code of the People's Republic of China, Article 4 of the Ship Collision Provisions, Article 11 of the Several Provisions of the Supreme People's Court concerning the Trial of Dispute Cases in relation to Maritime Compensation Liability Limitation, Article 153 of the Civil Procedure Law of the People's Republic of China, the judgment is as follows:

1. M.V. "Marc Loud" shall bear 60% liability for the ship collision accident;
2. Reject the claims of the Plaintiff Qingdao Huashun Shipping Co., Ltd. in terms of the liability of Marc Loud Schiffahrts Gesellschaft mbH & Co. KG. for the ship collision accident.

In event of dissatisfaction with this judgment, the Plaintiff may, within 15 days upon service of this judgment, and the Defendant within 30 days upon the service of this judgment submit a Statement of Appeal and duplicates according to the number of the opposing parties to the court, to lodge an appeal to the Shandong High People's Court.

Presiding Judge: CHI Huande
Judge: LI Hua
Judge: WANG Keke

August 3, 2015

Clerk: XU Wenwen

Tianjin Maritime Court
Civil Judgment

Qinhuangdao Heshun Shipping Co., Ltd.
v.
China People's Property Insurance Co., Ltd. Qinhuangdao City Branch

(2015) Jin Hai Fa Shang Chu Zi No.287

Related Case(s) This is the judgment of first instance, and the judgment of second instance and the ruling of retrial are on page 842 and page 854 respectively.

Cause(s) of Action 230. Dispute over marine insurance contract on the sea or sea-connected waters.

Headnote Assured's claim for indemnity under a hull insurance policy denied because of its knowledge of the unseaworthy condition of the vessel, which was the cause of the vessel's grounding.

Summary The Plaintiff-Insured's insurance policy with the Defendant-Insurer provided for protection for all risks of coastal and inland waterways. The Plaintiff-Insured's vessel was equipped with two electronic charts and was certified as seaworthy by government bodies. During the voyage, the Plaintiff-Insured's vessel made contact with a reef, which caused significant damage.

The Defendant-Insurer denied coverage since the Plaintiff-Insured was not the first beneficiary of the insurance policy because of an outstanding mortgage over the vessel. Therefore, the Plaintiff-Insured had no right to file suit. Also, the vessel was not equipped with the proper charts to put its crew on notice of the reef's location. Lacking the proper charts rendered the vessel unseaworthy, which was an exclusion under the policy.

Even though the Plaintiff-Insured was not the first beneficiary under the policy due to a mortgage over the vessel, the court held the Plaintiff-Insured still had an insurable interest in the vessel. Accordingly, the Plaintiff-Insured had a right to bring suit because it still had an insured interest in the vessel. However, rejecting the Plaintiff-Insured's claim, the court also held the vessel was unseaworthy since the Plaintiff-Insured failed to exercise due diligence to make the vessel seaworthy because it was not timely equipped with proper charts, which was the direct cause of the allision. Had the vessel been equipped with the most recent charts, its crew would have known about the reef with which it allided. The court stated the vessel's certification of seaworthiness was not determinative.

Judgment

The Plaintiff: Qinhuangdao Heshun Shipping Co., Ltd.
Domicile: Qinhuangdao City, Hebei, China.
Legal representative: LIU Wanzhong, general managerm.
Agent *ad litem*: ZHAO Yong, lawyer of Hebei Gaojun Law Firm.
Agent *ad litem*: LI Xia, lawyer of Hebei Gaojun Law Firm.

The Defendant: China People's Property Insurance Co., Ltd. Qinhuangdao City Branch
Domicile: Qinhuangdao City, Hebei, China.
Legal representative: ZHANG Youlin, general manager.
Agent *ad litem*: WANG Peng, lawyer of Beijing Gaopeng (Tianjin) Law Firm.
Agent *ad litem*: SHANG Weiwei, lawyer of Beijing Gaopeng (Tianjin) Law Firm.

With respect to the case arising from dispute over ship insurance contract between the Plaintiff Qinhuangdao Heshun Shipping Co., Ltd. (hereinafter referred to as "Heshun") and the Defendant China People's Property Insurance Co., Ltd. Qinhuangdao City Branch (hereinafter referred to as "PICC Qinghuangdao"), the court accepted the case on April 7, 2015. According to the law to apply summary procedure, Acting Judge OUYANG Hongwei tried the case independently. The case was heard on June 8, 2015. Legal representative of the Plaintiff, LIU Wanzhong, agents *ad litem* of the Plaintiff, ZHAO Yong and LI Xia, and agents *ad litem* of the Defendant, WANG Peng and SHANG Weiwei, attended the hearing. Now the case has been concluded.

The Plaintiff claimed that: on May 10, 2014, the Plaintiff insured M.V. "Jin Run 988" with the Defendant against all risks of coastal and inland waterway and the Defendant issued an insurance policy of all risks of coastal and inland waterway ship numbered Ji 13001300233905. The insurance policy recorded that: the insured was the Plaintiff; the insurance was all risks of coastal and inland waterway ship; the additional risks were a quarter of the collision, touch liability and individual loss of insurance liability such as propeller; insurance conditions and special agreement that the deductible for each accident was RMB100,000 yuan or 10% of the amount of the loss, whichever was higher. The insurance period was from 0:00, May 11, 2014 to 24:00, May 10, 2015. The insured amount was RMB24 million yuan. The insurance premium totaled RMB153,840 yuan. The resolution of dispute was litigation. After the policy was signed, the Plaintiff paid the insurance premium.

On November 3, 2014, after granted a visa by Marine Department of Honghai Bay of Shanwei Port, M.V. "Jin Run 988", on voyage 1430, headed to Jingjiang Port from Shanwei Port, Shenzhen, with 4,775 tons of argil on board. At 00:30 on November 5, 2014, when the vessel sailed through the southeast of Nan'ao Island, a collision ("Xinjiao Reef") happened at the waters located at 23°17′5″ N, 117°11′0″ E. At 00:35, the hull was tilted and made a sound of the friction of steel plate. The captain applied for maritime rescue immediately. At 07:00, the vessel docked at Guang'ao Port in Shantou by the designation of maritime department for which the

Plaintiff paid the berthing fee of RMB40,000 yuan. On November 6, 2014, in order to found out the damage of the ship, the Plaintiff entrusted Xiamen Xia Min Diving Engineering Co., Ltd. to do the underwater video detection inspection to the outside of the hull. It cost RMB27,500 yuan. On November 9, 2014, the Plaintiff asked Hebei Ship Inspection Bureau for an additional inspection to the damage of the hull in the collision. The Inspection Report issued by the Bureau indicated that though there was a deformation of the shell plate and a concave bending of frame, the hull plate was not damaged and did not have water penetration. The ship could meet the voyage of sailing to the port of discharge to unload the goods and to the dockyard for a repair. But the vessel should sail under the sea conditions of Beaufort scale below level 7 and of wave height less than 3 m. After unloaded, the vessel sailed to Zhoushan Jinping Shipbuilding Co., Ltd. to be repaired and applied for survey. On November 10, 2014, the thickness measurement of hull issued by Xiamen Ke Wei Detection Co., Ltd. showed the thickness of bow bottom plate and corrosion of starboard and portside were in reasonable range. The survey cost RMB15,000 yuan. According to the Inspection Report of Hebei Shipping Inspection Bureau and the Supervision and Inspection Report of Shantou MSA, the Plaintiff got a visa granted by Shantou Guang'ao Marine Department to enter the port onNovember 13, 2014 and got a visa to depart from the port on November 20, 2014. After unloaded at Jingjiang Port, the vessel sailed to Zhoushan Jinping Shipbuilding Co., Ltd. to be repaired and paid RMB953,444.95 yuan for the repair. The accident caused a total loss of RMB1,035,944.95 yuan to the Plaintiff. The Plaintiff asked the Defendant for an insurance compensation to the property losses caused by the collision happened to M.V. "Jin Run 988". The Defendant refused to pay compensation on grounds of unseaworthiness. The Plaintiff sued to the court to protect its legitimate rights and interests and requested the court to order that: 1. the Defendant should pay the ship insurance compensation of RMB932,350 yuan and the interest according to the People's Bank of China at the same time the interest rate of RMB from December 17, 2014 until the date of actual payment to the Plaintiff; 2. the costs of litigation in this case should be born by the Defendant.

The Defendant argued that: 1. the Plaintiff was an unqualified subject; 2. the direct cause of the accident was that the vessel was not equipped with paper chart. This situation belonged to the unseaworthiness of the vessel which was an exclusion of the insurer. The insurer should have the right to refuse to pay; 3. the amount claimed by the Plaintiff was too high and there was no basis for the claims. The Defendant requested the court to reject the Plaintiff's claims.

According to the Plaintiff's claims and the Defendant's defense, the issue of the dispute in this case could be summarized as: 1. whether the Plaintiff had the right to claim insurance compensation to the Defendant; 2. whether the vessel involved in the collision belonged to the unseaworthiness and whether the Defendant should bear insurance liability to the Plaintiff; 3. if the Defendant bore liability, what the exact amount of the insurance proceed shall be.

The Plaintiff submitted the following evidence to the court to support its claims:

Evidence 1. certificate of ship's nationality, to prove the ship's basic information.

Evidence 2. Insurance policies, payment agreements, insurance invoices of all risks of coastal and inland waterway ship, to prove that the Plaintiff assured to the Defendant for M.V. "Jin Run 988" and the Plaintiff had the right to claim for compensation against the Defendant.

Evidence 3. Notice of refusal of payment made by the Defendant, to prove that the reason for refusing to compensate insurance of the Defendant was the unseaworthiness.

Evidence 4. Certificate of maritime ship inspection and relevant certificates, to prove that M.V. "Jin Run 988" passed the inspection and was seaworthy.

Evidence 5. Certificate of seafarer, to prove that the equipment of crew met the requirements.

Evidence 6. Endorsement book of vessels, to prove that the voyage involved of M.V. "Jin Run 988" got visas granted by marine departments which ensured the seaworthiness of the vessel and the voyage.

Evidence 7. Maritime traffic accident report, to prove that the occurrence of the collision was caused by the boisterous wind and waves and the complex condition of navigation.

Evidence 8. Electronic chart certificate, to prove that M.V. "Jin Run 988" was equipped with a standard electronic chart system.

Evidence 9. Electronic chart picture, to prove that the navigation trajectory and the formulation of shipping line of the voyage of M.V. "Jin Run 988" involved should refer to the navigational aids. It showed that another electronic chart system of M.V. "Jin Run 988" had marked the "Xinjiao Reef".

Evidence 10. Berthing agreement and its fee invoice, to prove that the collision of M.V. "Jin Run 988" resulted in berthing fee of RMB40,000 yuan.

Evidence 11. Reports of underwater hull video inspection and its fee invoices issued by Xiamen Xia Min Diving Engineering Co., Ltd., to prove that the Plaintiff entrusted Xiamen Xia Min Diving Engineering Co., Ltd. to do the underwater hull video inspection and it cost RMB27,500 yuan.

Evidence 12. Reports of hull thickness inspection and fee invoices issued by Xiamen Ke Wei Detection Co., Ltd., to prove that the hull thickness inspection of M.V. "Jin Run 988" was done by Xiamen Ke Wei Detection Co., Ltd. and it cost RMB15,000 yuan.

Evidence 13. Repair statements, completion acceptance list and its cost invoices of M.V. "Jin Run 988", to prove that the Plaintiff had paid RMB953,444.95 yuan for repair of M.V. "Jin Run 988".

The Defendant's opinions on the evidence provided by the Plaintiff: Recognize the authenticity, relevancy and legality of evidence 1. Recognize the authenticity of evidence 2 but not recognize the propose of proof thereof, holding that the first beneficiary of the policy was not the Plaintiff. Recognize the authenticity, relevancy and legality of evidence 3. Recognize the authenticity of evidence 4 but holding that the certificate of inspection issued in November 2010 had been invalidated.

Recognize the authenticity, relevancy and legality of evidence 5. Recognize the authenticity of evidence 6 but not recognize the propose of proof thereof, holding that the acquisition of visas could not prove the actual seaworthiness of the vessel. Recognize the authenticity of evidence 7 but not recognize the propose of proof thereof, holding that the reason for the collision was "Xinjiao Reef" on the shipping line which was not marked in the electronic chart and the vessel was not equipped with a paper chart. Not recognize the authenticity and the propose of proof of evidence 8. Not recognize the authenticity and the purpose of proof of evidence 9. Recognize the authenticity, relevancy and legality of evidence 10, 11, 12. Recognize the authenticity of evidence 13 but not recognize the cost of repair.

The Defendant submitted the following evidence to the Court to support its pleas:

Evidence 1. Insurance policy, insurance slip and endorsement of the policy, to prove that the Plaintiff was not a qualified subject with the right of claim and the Defendant had the right to refuse to pay according to the insurance contract agreement.

Evidence 2. Assessment report, to prove that the proximate cause of the accident was unseaworthiness of the vessel which was an excluded liability of insured. The claim amount requested by the Plaintiff was too high and should not be supported.

Evidence 3. Screenshot of the image of waters involved from the Shipping News Network and Chart No.14370 of Navigation Guarantee Department, to prove that "Xinjiao Reef" which caused the collision was not marked in the paper chart and the chart on an open website. The situation that Plaintiff was not equipped with a paper chart belonged to unseaworthiness of the vessel.

The Plaintiff's opinions on the evidence provided by the Defendant: Recognize the authenticity and legality of evidence 1 but not recognize the propose of proof thereof; not recognize the authenticity and the propose of proof of evidence 2; recognize the authenticity and legality of evidence 3 but not recognize the propose of proof thereof.

The court's opinions on the Plaintiff's evidence: confirming the authenticity of evidence 1 which can prove the basic information of the vessel; confirm the authenticity of evidence 2 which can prove that the Plaintiff insured M.V. "Jin Run 988" with the Defendant and the relationship of insurance contract between the Plaintiff and the Defendant was established; confirm the authenticity of evidence 3 which can prove that the Defendant refused to compensate insurance on the grounds of unseaworthiness; confirm the authenticity of evidence 4 which can prove that M.V. "Jin Run 988" had been inspected and got the certificate of seaworthiness; confirm the authenticity of evidence 5 which can prove that the crew of M.V. "Jin Run 988" was equipped to meet the requirements; confirm the authenticity of evidence 6 which can prove that M.V. "Jin Run 988" had got visas granted by maritime departments; confirm the authenticity of evidence 7 which can prove that the wind and waves was boisterous and the navigation condition was complex during the voyage involved; confirm the authenticity of evidence 8 which can prove that M.V. "Jin Run 988" was equipped with a standard electronic chart system; confirm the authenticity of evidence 9 but hold that Xin Ma electronic chart was obtained on June 7, 2015 which cannot prove that "Xinjiao Reef" was marked on the electronic chart system when the accident happened and M.V. "Jin Run 988" was using that electronic chart system and other images of charts can prove the navigation trajectory of M.V. "Jin Run 988"; confirm the authenticity of evidence 10 which can prove that the berthing charge of RMB40,000 yuan was incurred after the collision of M.V. "Jin Run 988"; confirm the authenticity of evidence 11 which can prove that the Plaintiff entrusted Xiamen Xia Min Diving Engineering Co., Ltd. to do the underwater video detection inspection and it cost RMB27,500 yuan; confirm the authenticity of evidence 12 which can prove that Xiamen Ke Wei Detection Co., Ltd. measured the thickness of hull and it cost RMB15,000 yuan; confirm the authenticity of evidence 13 which can prove that the Plaintiff paid RMB953,444.95 yuan for the repair of M.V. "Jin Run 988".

The court's opinions on the Defendant's evidence: confirm the authenticity of evidence 1 which can prove that the relationship of insurance contract between the Plaintiff and the Defendant was established; about evidence 2, GAO Yongge, the appraiser of the assessment report, appeared in the court for inquiry and submitted the corresponding proof of qualification to the court, combined with the evidence provided by the Plaintiff, the authenticity of the evidence 2 can be confirmed. But the validity thereof needs to be identified. The Plaintiff held that the application of the law and the handling suggestion of Item 1560 of the flag state supervision and inspection report in the assessment report was erroneous, which could not be used as a standard for determining the seaworthiness of the vessel. The court holds that the legality review of administrative acts is not the scope of the case. The flag state supervision and inspection report made by the maritime department with the objective authenticity can be used as evidence to be accepted. The Plaintiff also held that the shipping line in the assessment report was not planned based on important navigation aids and inflection point of Nanpeng archipelago therefore the planned shipping line was untrue and had no authenticity. The court holds that, first of all, not all the planned shipping lines of the vessels navigating in this sea area should be planned based on navigation aids and inflection point of Nanpeng archipelago. Secondly, according to Item 1599 of the flag state supervision and inspection report that "the shipping line was not planned according to the requirements of the system to make full use of the required information of nautical books, the crew on duty was not confirmed by signature, the captain did not assess and verify the planned the shipping line" and Item 2525 that "the third mate did not operate according to the operation notice of system chart (chart operations from Shanwei to Jingjiang)", the planned shipping line had been developed but the third mate did not operate according to the operation notice of system chart and the captain did not assess and verify the planned shipping line. However, it did not mean that the planned shipping line was untrue. Accordingly, the reason the Plaintiff held that the planned shipping line was untrue could not be established. Confirm the authenticity of evidence 3 which can prove that "Xinjiao Reef" was clearly marked in Chart No.14370 of Chinese People's Liberation Army Navy Navigation Guarantee Department and in the screenshot of the track.

The court finds out that:

On May 10, 2014, the Plaintiff insured M.V. "Jin Run 988" with the Defendant against all risks of coastal and inland waterway ship and the Defendant issued an insurance policy of all risks of coastal and inland waterway ship numbered Ji 13001300233905. The insurance policy recorded that: the insured was the Plaintiff; the insurance was all risks of coastal and inland waterway ship; the additional risks were a quarter of the collision, touch liability and individual loss of insurance liability such as propeller; insurance conditions and special agreement that the deductible for each accident was RMB100,000 yuan or 10% of the amount of the loss, whichever was higher. The insurance period was from 0:00, May 11, 2014 to 24:00, May 10, 2015. The insured amount was RMB24 million yuan. The insurance premium totaled RMB153,840 yuan. The resolution of dispute was litigation. According to hull insurance clauses for ships engaging in coastal and inland river transportation (2009 Edition), "the insurer has provided and in detail introduced the applicable terms of the insurance, and has made specific notification to the insured about exemption liabilities (include but not limited to exemptions, obligations, compensations, etc.). The insurer also informed the insured of the payment agreement and special agreements in the insurance contract. The insured fully understood and accepted the content above, and placed the insurance voluntarily based on the conclusion of contract." The contract was sealed by the Plaintiff. The hull insurance clauses (2009 Edition) of PICC demonstrated the exemption liabilities in bold, "the insurance shall not be liable for any losses, liabilities or expenses due to the following circumstances: firstly, the unseaworthiness and untowworthiness of the ship (non-liable losses include losses caused by technology, manning, loading, as well as expenses resulted from tug and tugboat towing." The Plaintiff affixed the official seal on this page. After the contract was concluded, the Plaintiff paid the total insurance premium.

On November 3, 2014, after granted a visa by Marine Department of Honghai Bay of Shanwei Port, M.V. "Jin Run 988", on voyage 1430, headed to Jingjiang Port from Shanwei Port, Shenzhen, with 4,775 tons of argil on board. At 00:30 on November 5, 2014, when the vessel sailed through the southeast of Nan'ao Island, a collision ("Xinjiao Reef") happened at the waters located at 23°17'5" N, 117°11'0" E. At 00:35, the hull was tilted and made a sound of the friction of steel plate. The captain applied for maritime rescue immediately. At 07:00, the vessel docked at Guang'ao Port in Shantou by the designation of maritime department for which the Plaintiff paid the berthing fee of RMB40,000 yuan. On November 6, 2014, in order to found out the damage of the ship, the Plaintiff entrusted Xiamen Xia Min Diving Engineering Co., Ltd. to do the underwater video detection inspection to the outside of the hull. It cost RMB27,500 yuan. On the same day, Shantou Maritime Safety Administration carried out an inspection on the vessels involved and issued the inspection report under the supervision of the flag state. From the report, the 1560 defect was described as lacking a majority of the paper navigation maps (15110, 14370, 14310, etc.) from Shanwei to Jingjiang, the processing code of which was 30 (departure prohibited). The 1599 defect described that the route planning did not make full use of the information from the required navigation book and was not followed the system requirements, the crew on duty did not signed the confirmation, and the captain did not estimate and verify the route, the processing code of which was 17 (to be redressed before sailing). The 2525 defect described that the third mate did not follow the work instructions (Shanwei to Jingjiang chart), the processing code of which was 60 (crew score). On November 9, 2014, the Plaintiff asked Hebei Ship Inspection Bureau for an additional inspection to the damage of the hull in the collision. The inspection report issued by the Bureau indicated that though there were a deformation of the shell plate and a concave bending of frame, the hull plate was not damaged and did not take in water. The ship could meet the voyage of sailing to the port of discharge to unload the goods and to the dockyard for a repair. But the vessel should sail under the sea conditions of Beaufort scale below level 7 and of wave height less than 3 m. After unloaded, the vessel sailed to Zhoushan Jinping Shipbuilding Co., Ltd. to be repaired and applied for survey. On November 10, 2014, the thickness measurement of hull issued by Xiamen Ke Wei detection Co., Ltd. showed the thickness of bow bottom plate and corrosion of starboard were in reasonable range. The survey cost RMB15,000 yuan. According to the inspection report of Hebei Shipping Inspection Bureau and the supervision and inspection report of Shantou Maritime Bureau, the Plaintiff got a visa granted by Shantou Guang'ao Marine Department to enter the port on November 13, 2014 and got a visa to depart from the port on November 20, 2014. After unloaded at Jingjiang Port, the vessel sailed to Zhoushan Jinping Shipbuilding Co., Ltd. to be repaired and RMB953,444.95 yuan was paid for the repair. After the accident, the Plaintiff updated the ECS157 electronic chart system. The updated version 9.3.1 showed that the accident water area had been marked as "1-meter reef". According to the paper chart (3rd edition, from Guleitou to Biaojiao) in July 2013, the People's Liberation Army Navy Command Navigation Department of China marked "New Reef" near the accident water area.

On November 5, 2014, Tianjin Jiulian Insurance Appraisal Co., Ltd., entrusted by PICC Qinhuangdao, appointed GAO Yongge as surveyor of the accident insurance assessor, to assess the scene of M.V. "Jin Run 988" from November 6, 2014 to November 13, 2014. The final report was issued on November 15, 2014, which deemed that M.V. "Jin Run 988" failed to meet the requirements of paper chart before and at the beginning of the voyage. The vessel was unseaworthy, which directly caused the accident. The losses caused by the accident were within the scope of the exclusion liability clauses.

The court also finds out that:

Hebei Ship Inspection Bureau issued a seaworthy certificate for M.V. "Jin Run 988" on December 31, 2013. The certification was valid until January 2, 2015. Tianjin Jiulian Insurance Assessment Co., Ltd. obtained the business license for insurance assessment on April 11, 2014, and the certificate was valid until April 10, 2017. GAO Yongge and DU Peng obtained the insurance assessor qualification certificates on July 2, 2014.

The court holds that:

This case is the dispute arising from vessel insurance contract, and the contract between the Plaintiff and the Defendant is ship insurance contract.

As for whether the Plaintiff has the right to claim the compensation, in this case, the Plaintiff effected insurance with Defendant against all risks of coastal and inland river ship on May 10, 2014. The Plaintiff was the insured and the Defendant was the insurer. The Plaintiff had delivered insurance premiums to the Defendant as contracted and the Defendant had the obligation to take the responsibility at the appointed time. Although Qinhuangdao Branch of China Construction Bank Co., Ltd become the first beneficiary since the mortgage issued on M.V. "Jin Run 988". However, the Plaintiff, as the shipowner of M.V. "Jin Run 988", did not lose the insurable interest on it. When the accident happened, the Plaintiff, as the insured, had the insurable interest on M.V. "Jin Run 988". As a result, the Plaintiff has the right to claim insurance compensation against the Defendant.

As for whether the accident ship is seaworthy, as well as whether the Defendant should bear the insurance liability to the Plaintiff, the Plaintiff held that M.V. "Jin Run 988" had the certificate of seaworthiness and other relevant certifications about the crew, vessels, properly manning, and cargo. Meanwhile, the vessel was certified by Shanwei Port Red Bay Marine Department before the voyage of the accident, so M.V. "Jin Run 988" was seaworthy. In addition, M.V. "Jin Run 988" was equipped with two sets of electronic chart system, it had a clear mark on "New Reef" in Xinhaima electronic chart system which was equipped at the time of shipping out of factory. The Plaintiff used both sets of electronic chart system at the same time. The court holds that, first of all, the Plaintiff failed to provide evidence to prove that Xinhaima electronic chart system had a clear mark on "New Reef", and M.V. "Jin Run 988" was using the electronic chart system when the accident happened. Secondly, according to Article 19 of the Regulations on the Management of Shipboard Electric chart System and Automatic Identification System Equipment for Domestic Sailing Ship, an official issued coastal ship electronic chart system should be used and updated timely according to the International Hydrographic Organization S-57 format requirements of electronic chart to ensure the accuracy and integrity of the chart data. M.V. "Jin Run 988" should use the required ECS157 electronic chart system instead of two sets of systems at the same time. Therefore, the justifications held by the Plaintiff stating that two sets of electronic chart system were used at the same time and a clear mark was on "New Reef" on the electronic chart of M.V. "Jin Run 988" were not established. Despite the fact that M.V. "Jin Run 988" had the certification of seaworthiness and was certified by Marine Department before the voyage, the certification and the Marine Department visa were not the final evidence of the ship's seaworthiness. according to Article 47 of the Maritime Code of People's Republic of China, the carrier shall, before and at the beginning of the voyage, exercise due diligence to make the ship seaworthy, properly man, equip and supply the ship and to make the holds, refrigerating and cool chambers and all other parts of the ship in which goods are carried, fit and safe for their reception, carriage and preservation. The carrier had due diligence to make the ship seaworthy, properly equip the ship, and to make radar, compass and other navigational instruments, mooring accessories, such as anchor, mooring rope, as well as charts, route guide and other navigational materials, all items listed above should exist and be in good condition. According to flag state supervision and inspection report No.1560 (processing code: 30, departure prohibits), it was necessary for the vessel to have paper chart. The Plaintiff did not update and install the electronic chart system on a timely basis, which led to the incompleteness and the unreliability of the navigation data. As a result, before the beginning of the involved voyage, the Plaintiff failed to exercise due diligence to update the electronic chart system in time and to equip the ship with paper chart, the ship should be deemed to be unseaworthy. The Plaintiff claimed that the accident was caused by poor navigation condition and low operating skills of the crew rather than the unseaworthiness of the vessel. The court holds that even though the accident vessel sailed under 6/7 winds and 2–2.5 m waves, the conditions was not the direct cause of the accident. Since the ship involved did not update the electronic chart system in time and install the paper chart, the crew could not see "New Reef" label when planning routes, and formulated a route plan near the "New Reef" label area, which directly caused the unseaworthiness of the vessel involved.

The Plaintiff claimed that the Defendant failed to fulfill the obligation of full disclosure about the exemption clause, which should be considered to be legally ineffective. The court holds that the insured stated in the insurance policy on coastal inland waterway insurance (2009 Edition): The insurer had introduced the applicable terms and informed the insured of insurer's liabilities (including but not limited to the liability exemption, the insured's obligation, compensation processing and other matters, etc.), as well as the insurance contract payment agreement and special agreement. The insured had fully understood and accepted the content above, and had placed the insurance voluntarily based on the conclusion of contract. The contract was sealed by the Plaintiff. The hull insurance clauses (2009 Edition) of PICC demonstrated the exemption liabilities in bold, "based on the section 3, the insurance shall not be liable for any losses, liabilities or expenses due to the following circumstances: firstly, the unseaworthiness and untowworthiness of the ship (non-liable losses include losses caused by technology, manning, loading, as well as expenses resulted from tug and tugboat towing." The Plaintiff affixed the official seal on this page. As an insurer, the Defendant had drew the Plaintiff's attention to the terms of insurance and exemption clauses in a reasonable manner. Therefore, the insurer had fulfilled the responsibility of full disclosure requirement provided by the Insurance Law of the People's Republic of China. The signature of the Plaintiff, should be assumed as fully understood and accepted the terms in the process of insurance contract negotiation. As a result, the Plaintiff's argument about the ineffectiveness of exclusion clause cannot be established.

The Plaintiff claimed that the daily operation of the ship was carried out by the captain and the crew. The Plaintiff was not responsible for the daily management of the ship. Even if the ship was unseaworthy at the beginning of the voyage, under the condition of insured's unawareness of the insurance term, the insurer should still be liable for compensation. The court holds that though the daily operation of the ship was carried out by the master and the crew, as the carrier, the Plaintiff had the obligation to manage the ship. The carrier should perform due diligence to make the ship seaworthy. It was a basic requirement for maritime navigation that the electronic chart system should be update timely and the vessel should be equipped with paper charts, the involved ship was not seaworthy because the Plaintiff did not perform due diligence before the beginning of the voyage, therefore the argument that the Plaintiff did not know the ship's unseaworthiness should not be established. M.V. "Jin Run 988" was not seaworthy at the beginning of the voyage, which caused the occurrence of the insurance accidents. The loss of accident belonged to exclusion clauses. So the court shall not support the Plaintiff's claim that the Plaintiff requested the Defendant to pay the ship insurance indemnity in amount of RMB932,350 yuan and the interest calculated from December 17, 2014 up to the actual payment day based on the loan interest rate set by People's Bank of China for the same period.

Pulling the threads together, there is a ship insurance contract between the Plaintiff and the Defendant, the Plaintiff has insurable interest on M.V. "Jin Run 988" and should be entitled to claim compensation against the Defendant. M.V. "Jin Run 988" was not seaworthy at the beginning of the involved voyage, and this is the direct cause of the accidents, the loss of which is within the scope of exclusion clauses. According to the Maritime Code of People's Republic of China Article 244 Paragraph 1 Sub-paragraph 1 and the Civil Procedure Law of People's Republic of China Article 64 Paragraph 1, the judgment is as follows:

Reject the claims of the Plaintiff, Qinhuangdao Heshun Shipping Co., Ltd.

Court acceptance fee in amount of RMB6,562 yuan, shall be born by the Plaintiff, Qinhuangdao Heshun Shipping Co., Ltd.

In the event of dissatisfaction with this judgment, a statement of appeal and six copies should be filed to Tianjin High People's Court for instituting legal procedures, within 15 days after the service of the judgment, and within seven days from the date of filing the appeal. Appellant should pay the cost of appeal. (Deposit Bank: Agricultural Bank of Tiancheng Branch 02200501040006269, Account name: Tianjin High People's Court Financial Services). The appeal will be considered withdrawn automatically if the cost is not paid on time.

Acting Judge: OUYANG Hongwei
June 29, 2015
Clerk: SONG Wenjie

Tianjin High People's Court
Civil Judgment

Qinhuangdao Heshun Shipping Co., Ltd.
v.
China People's Property Insurance Co., Ltd. Qinhuangdao City Branch

(2015) Jin Gao Min Si Zhong Zi No.93

Related Case(s) This is the judgment of second instance, and the judgment of first instance and the ruling of retrial are on page 831 and page 854 respectively.

Cause(s) of Action 230. Dispute over marine insurance contract on the sea or sea-connected waters.

Headnote Affirming lower court's decision denying assured's claim for indemnity under a hull insurance policy because of its knowledge of the unseaworthy condition of the vessel, which was the cause of the vessel's grounding.

Summary Qinhuangdao Heshun Shipping Co., Ltd. (Plaintiff) filed suit against China People's Property Insurance Co., Ltd. Qinhuangdao Branch (Defendant) to compel the Defendant to honor the terms of their insurance policy agreement after the Plaintiff's vessel allided with a reef ("New Reef") along its planned route. This allision happened due to the Plaintiff's failure to equip its vessel with updated charts that depicted the "New Reef." For this reason, the Defendant refused to compensate the Plaintiff due to this unseaworthy condition, excluding the Defendant from liability under the exclusion clause of the parties' insurance contract. The Court of first instance ruled that the Defendant was not liable due to this unseaworthy condition, and the Plaintiff was liable for all relevant litigation costs of the suit.

On appeal, the appeal court recognized the judgment of the court of first instance, the Plaintiff, again, bearing all liability for the relevant costs of the appeal.

Judgment

The Appellant (the Plaintiff of first instance): Qinhuangdao Heshun Shipping Co., Ltd.
Domicile: Qinhuangdao City, Hebei, China.
Legal representative: LIU Wanzhong, general manager of the company.

Agent *ad litem*: ZHAO Yong, lawyer of Hebei Gao Junxia Law Firm.
Agent *ad litem*: LI Xia, lawyer of Hebei Gao Junxia Law Firm.

The Respondent (the Defendant of first instance): China People's Property Insurance Co., Ltd. Qinhuangdao City Branch
Domicile: Qinhuangdao City, Hebei, China.
Legal representative: ZHANG Youlin, general manager of the branch.
Agent *ad litem*: WANG Peng, lawyer of Beijing Gaopeng Law Firm.
Agent *ad litem*: SHANG Weiwei, lawyer of Beijing Gaopeng Law Firm.

With respect to the case arising from dispute over ship insurance contract between the Appellant, Qinhuangdao Heshun Shipping Co., Ltd. (hereinafter referred to as Heshun), and the Respondent, China People's Property Insurance Co., Ltd. Qinhuangdao City Branch (hereinafter referred to as PICC Qinghuangdao), the Appellant disagreed with the Tianjin Maritime Court (hereinafter referred to as the court of first instance) (2015) Jin Hai Fa Shang Chu Zi No.287 Civil Judgment (hereinafter referred to as judgment of first instance), and appealed to the court. After accepting it, the court the court formed a collegiate panel, and held a hearing in public on September 1, 2015. Legal representative of the Appellant Heshun, LIU Wanzhong, agents *ad litem*, ZHAO Yong and LI Xia, agents *ad litem* of the Respondent PICC Qinghuangdao, WANG Peng and SHANG Weiwei, appeared in court to attend the hearing. Now the case has been concluded.

Heshun claimed that: on May 10, 2014, Heshun claimed that it insured M.V. "Jin Run 988" with PICC Qinghuangdao against all risks of coastal and inland waterway, and PICC Qinghuangdao issued an insurance policy for all risks of coastal and inland waterway. The insurance policy recorded as follows. Heshun was the insured, and the insurance was for all risks of coastal and inland waterways. The additional risks were a quarter of the collision, grounding and individual losses such as propeller damage. The insurance conditions and special agreement provide that the deductible for each accident was RMB100,000 yuan or 10% of the amount of the loss, whichever was higher. The insurance period was from 0:00, May 11, 2014 to 24:00, May 10, 2015. The insured amount was RMB24 million yuan. The insurance premium totaled RMB153,840 yuan. Dispute resolution required litigation. After the policy was signed, Heshun paid the insurance premium. On November 3, 2014, after the Marine Department of Honghai Bay of Shanwei Port granted a visa, M.V. "Jin Run 988" (on voyage 1430), headed to Jingjiang Port from Shanwei Port, Shenzhen with 4,775 tons of argil clay onboard. At 00:30 on November 5, 2014, when the vessel sailed through the southeast of Nan'ao Island, an collision (at "Xinjiao Reef") happened at the waters located at 23°17'5" N, 1177°11'0" E. At 00:35, the hull was tilted and the friction of the steel plate could be heard. The captain applied for maritime rescue immediately. At 07:00, the vessel docked at Guang'ao Port in Shantou, which was designated by the maritime department. Heshun paid the berthing fee, which was RMB40,000 yuan. On November 6, 2014, in order to assess the ship's damage, Heshun entrusted Xiamen Xia Min Diving Engineering Co., Ltd. to do the underwater video detection inspection on the outside of the hull. It cost RMB27,500 yuan. On November 9, 2014, Heshun asked Hebei Ship Inspection Bureau for additional inspection of the damage to the hull. The Inspection Report issued by the Bureau indicated that, although the shell plate was deformed and the frame had a concave bend, the hull plate was not damaged and did not suffer water penetration. The ship could sail to the port of discharge to unload the goods and proceed to the dockyard for repair. But the vessel should sail under Beaufort scale 7 sea conditions and when wave heights were less than 3 m. After unloading, the vessel sailed to Zhoushan Jinping Shipbuilding Co., Ltd. to be repaired, and a survey was applied for. On November 10, 2014, the thickness measurement of the hull issued by Xiamen Ke Wei Detection Co., Ltd. showed the thickness of the bow bottom plate and corrosion of the starboard and portside to be within a reasonable range. The survey cost RMB15,000 yuan. According to the Hebei Shipping Inspection Bureau's Inspection Report and Shantou MSA's Supervision and Inspection Report, Shantou Guang'ao Marine Department granted Heshun a visa enter the port on November 13, 2014 a visa to depart from the port on November 20, 2014. After discharging at Jingjiang Port, the vessel sailed to Zhoushan Jinping Shipbuilding Co., Ltd. for repairs. It cost RMB953,444.95 yuan for the repairs. The accident caused Heshun a total loss of RMB1,035,944.95 yuan. Heshun asked PICC Qinghuangdao for insurance compensation for the property losses caused by the collision. PICC Qinghuangdao refused to pay on grounds of the unseaworthiness. Heshun requested that the court to order that: 1. PICC Qinghuangdao should pay for ship insurance compensation totaling RMB932,350 yuan and the interest from December 17, 2014 until the date of actual payment to Heshun; 2. PICC Qinghuangdao should bear litigation costs.

PICC Qinghuangdao argued that: Heshun was an unqualified subject. 2. The direct cause of the accident was that the vessel was not equipped with paper chart. This situation belonged to the unseaworthiness of the vessel which was an exclusion of the insurer. The insurer should have the right to refuse to pay. 3. The amount claimed by Heshun was too high and there was no basis for the claims. PICC Qinghuangdao requested the court to reject Heshun's claims.

The court of first instance found out that: on May 10, 2014, Heshun insured M.V. "Jin Run 988" with PICC Qinghuangdao against all risks of coastal and inland waterways. PICC Qinghuangdao issued an insurance policy for all risks of coastal and inland waterway No.13xxx233905. The insurance policy provided that Heshun was the insured, and the insurance was for all risks of coastal and inland waterways. Additional risks were a quarter of the collision, touch liability and individual loss such as propeller. The deductible for each accident was RMB100,000 yuan or 10% of the amount of the loss, whichever was higher. The insurance period was from 0:00, May 11, 2014 to 24:00, May 10, 2015. The insured amount was RMB24 million yuan. The insurance premium totaled RMB153,840 yuan. Resolving disputes required litigation. According to hull insurance clauses for ships engaging in coastal and inland river transportation (2009 Edition), "the insurer has provided and in detail introduced the applicable terms of the insurance and has made specific notification to the insured about exemption liabilities (including, but not limited to, exemptions, obligations, compensations, etc.). The insurer also informed the insured of the payment agreement and special agreements in the insurance contract. The insured has fully understood and accepted the content above, and has placed the insurance voluntarily based on the conclusion of contract." Heshun sealed the contract. The hull insurance clauses (2009 Edition) of the People's Insurance Company of China (PICC) demonstrated the exemption liabilities in bold that "the insurance shall not be liable for any losses, liabilities or expenses due to the following circumstances: firstly, the unseaworthiness and untowworthiness of the ship (non-liable losses include losses caused by technology, manning, loading, as well as expenses resulted from tug and tugboat towing." Heshun affixed the official seal on this page. After the contract was concluded, Heshun paid the total insurance premium.

On November 3, 2014, after marine department's granted a visa, M.V. "Jin Run 988" headed to Jingjiang Port from Shanwei Port, Shenzhen with 4,775 tons of argil on board. At 00:30 on November 5, 2014, when the vessel sailed through the southeast of Nan'ao Island, an collision (at "Xinjiao Reef") happened at the waters located at 23°17′5″ N, 117°11′0″ E. At 00:35, the hull was tilted and the friction of the steel plate could be heard. The captain applied for maritime rescue immediately. At 07:00, the vessel docked at Guang'ao Port in Shantou, which was designated by maritime departments. Heshun paid berthing fees totaling RMB40,000 yuan. On November 6, 2014, in order to found out the damage of the ship, Heshun entrusted Xiamen Xia Min Diving Engineering Co., Ltd. to make the underwater video detection inspection to the outside of the hull. It cost RMB27,500 yuan. On the same day, the Shantou Maritime Safety Administration carried out an inspection on the vessels involved and issued the Inspection Report under the Supervision of the Flag State. From the report, the 1560 defect was described as lacking a majority of paper navigation maps (15110, 14370, 14310, etc.) from Shanwei to Jingjiang, the processing code of which was 30. The 1599 defect described that the route planning did not make full use of the information from the required navigation book and was not followed the system requirements, the crew on duty did not signed the confirmation, and the captain did not estimate and verify the route, the processing code of which was 17 (to be redressed before sailing). The 2525 defect stated that the third mate did not follow work instructions (Shanwei to Jingjiang chart), the processing code of which was 60 (crew score). On November 9, 2014, Heshun asked Hebei Ship Inspection Bureau for an additional inspection regarding the hull's damage. The Inspection Report issued by the Bureau indicated that, though the shell plate was deformed and the frame had a concave bend, the hull plate was not damaged and did not take in water. The ship could sail to the port of discharge to unload the goods and then to the dockyard for repairs. However, the vessel should sail under the sea conditions of Beaufort scale below level 7 and with wave heights less than 3 m. After unloading, the vessel sailed to Zhoushan Jinping Shipbuilding Co., Ltd. to be repaired and applied for a survey. On 10th November 2014, the hull thickness measurement issued by Xiamen Ke Wei detection Co., Ltd. showed the thickness of bow bottom plate and starboard's corrosion were in reasonable ranges. The survey cost RMB15,000 yuan. According MSA, Heshun got a visa granted by Shantou Guang'ao Marine Department to enter the port on November 13, 2014 and a visa to depart from the port on November 20, 2014. After unloading at Jingjiang

Port, the vessel sailed to Zhoushan Jinping Shipbuilding Co., Ltd. to be repaired and paid RMB953,444.95 yuan for the repair. After the accident, Heshun updated the ECS157 electronic chart system. The updated version 9.3.1 showed that the accident area had been marked as a "1-meter reef". According to the paper chart (3rd edition, from Guleitou to Biaojiao) in July 2013, the People's Liberation Army Navy Command Navigation Department of China marked the "new reef" near the accident water area.

On November 5, 2014, Tianjin Jiulian Insurance Appraisal Co., Ltd., entrusted by PICC Qinhuangdao, appointed GAO Yongge, a surveyor for the insurance assessor, to assess the scene of M.V. "Jin Run 988" from November 6, 2014 to November 13, 2014. The final report was issued on November 15, 2014. It stated that M.V. "Jin Run 988" failed to meet the requirements of the paper chart before and at the beginning of the voyage. Furthermore, the vessel was unseaworthy, which directly caused the accident. The losses caused by the accident were within the scope of the exclusion liability clauses.

The court of first instance also found out that:

Hebei Ship Inspection Bureau issued a seaworthy certificate for M.V. "Jin Run 988" on December 31, 2013. The certification was valid until January 2, 2015. Tianjin Jiulian Insurance Assessment Co., Ltd. obtained the business license for insurance assessment on April 11, 2014, and the certificate was valid until April 10, 2017. GAO Yongge and DU Peng obtained the insurance assessor qualification certificates on July 2, 2014.

The court of first instance held that:

This case was the dispute arising from vessel insurance contract, and the contract between Heshun and PICC Qinghuangdao was ship insurance contract.

As for whether Heshun had the right to claim the compensation, in this case, Heshun effected insurance with Defendant against all risks of coastal and inland river ship on May 10, 2014. Heshun was the insured and PICC Qinghuangdao was the insurer. Heshun had delivered insurance premiums to PICC Qinghuangdao as contracted and PICC Qinghuangdao had the obligation to take the responsibility at the appointed time. Although Qinhuangdao Branch of China Construction Bank Co., Ltd become the first beneficiary since the mortgage issued on M.V. "Jin Run 988". However, Heshun, as the shipowner of M.V. "Jin Run 988", did not lose the insurable interest on it. When the accident happened, Heshun, as the insured, had the insurable interest on M.V. "Jin Run 988". As a result, Heshun had the right to claim insurance compensation against PICC Qinghuangdao.

As for whether the accident ship was seaworthy, as well as whether PICC Qinghuangdao should bear the insurance liability to Heshun, Heshun held that M. V. "Jin Run 988" had the certificate of seaworthiness and other relevant certifications about the crew, vessels, properly manning, and cargo. Meanwhile, the vessel was certified by Shanwei Port Red Bay Marine Department before the voyage of the accident, so M.V. "Jin Run 988" was seaworthy. In addition, M.V. "Jin Run 988" was equipped with two sets of electronic chart system, it had a clear mark on "New Reef" in Xinhaima electronic chart system which was equipped at the time of shipping out of factory. Heshun used both sets of electronic chart system at the same time. The court of first instance held that, first of all, Heshun failed to provide evidence to prove that Xinhaima electronic chart system had a clear mark on "New Reef", and M.V. "Jin Run 988" was using the electronic chart system when the accident happened. Secondly, according to Article 19 of the Regulations on the Management of Shipboard Electronic Chart System and Automatic Identification System Equipment for Domestic Sailing Ship, an official issued coastal ship electronic chart system should be used and updated timely according to the International Hydrographic Organization S-57 format requirements of electronic chart to ensure the accuracy and integrity of the chart data. M.V. "Jin Run 988" should use the required ECS157 electronic chart system instead of two sets of systems at the same time. Therefore, the justifications held by Heshun stating that two sets of electronic chart system were used at the same time and a clear mark was on "New Reef" on the electronic chart of M.V. "Jin Run 988" were not established. Despite the fact that M.V. "Jin Run 988" had the certification of seaworthiness and was certified by Marine Department before the voyage, the certification and the Marine Department visa were not the final evidence of the ship's seaworthiness. according to Article 47 of the Maritime Code of People's Republic of China, the carrier should, before and at the beginning of the voyage, exercise due diligence to make the ship seaworthy, properly man, equip and supply the ship and to make the holds, refrigerating and cool chambers and all other parts of the ship in which goods are carried, fit and safe for their reception, carriage and preservation. The carrier had due diligence to make the ship seaworthy, properly equip the ship, and to make radar, compass and other navigational instruments, mooring accessories, such as anchor, mooring rope, as well as charts, route guide and other navigational materials, all items listed above should exist and be in good condition. According to flag state supervision and inspection report No.1560 (processing code: 30, departure prohibits), it was necessary for the vessel to have paper chart. Heshun did not update and install the electronic chart system on a timely basis, which led to the incompleteness and the unreliability of the navigation data. As a result, before the beginning of the involved voyage, Heshun failed to exercise due diligence to update the electronic chart system in time and to equip the ship with paper chart, the ship should be deemed to be unseaworthy. Heshun claimed that the accident was caused by poor navigation condition and low operating skills of the crew rather than the unseaworthiness of the vessel. The court of first instance held that even though the accident vessel sailed under 6/7 winds and 2–2.5 m waves, the conditions was not the direct cause of the accident. Since the ship involved did not update the electronic chart system in time and install the paper chart, the crew could not see "New Reef" label when planning routes, and formulated a route plan near the "New Reef" label area, which directly caused the unseaworthiness of the vessel involved.

Heshun claimed that PICC Qinghuangdao failed to fulfill the obligation of full disclosure about the exemption clause, which should be considered to be legally ineffective. The court of first instance held that the insured stated in the insurance policy on coastal inland waterway insurance (2009 Edition): the insurer had introduced the applicable terms and informed the insured of insurer's liabilities (including but not limited to the liability exemption, the insured's obligation, compensation processing and other matters, etc.), as well as the insurance contract payment agreement and special agreement. The insured had fully understood and accepted the content above, and had placed the insurance voluntarily based on the conclusion of contract. The contract was sealed by Heshun. The hull insurance clauses (2009 Edition) of PICC demonstrated the exemption liabilities in bold, "based on the section 3, the insurance shall not be liable for any losses, liabilities or expenses due to the following circumstances: firstly, the unseaworthiness and untowworthiness of the ship (non-liable losses include losses caused by technology, manning, loading, as well as expenses resulted from tug and tugboat towing." Heshun affixed the official seal on this page. As an insurer, PICC Qinghuangdao had drew Heshun's attention to the terms of insurance and exemption clauses in a reasonable manner. Therefore, the insurer had fulfilled the responsibility of full disclosure requirement provided by the Insurance Law of the People's Republic of China. The signature of Heshun, should be assumed as fully understood and accepted the terms in the process of insurance contract negotiation. As a result, Heshun's claim about the ineffectiveness of exclusion clause cannot be established.

Heshun claimed that the daily operation of the ship was carried out by the captain and the crew. Heshun was not responsible for the daily management of the ship. Even if the ship was unseaworthy at the beginning of the voyage, under the condition of insured's unawareness of the insurance term, the insurer should still be liable for compensation. The court of first instance held that though the daily operation of the ship was carried out by the master and the crew, as the carrier, Heshun had the obligation to manage the ship. The carrier should perform due diligence to make the ship seaworthy. It was a basic requirement for maritime navigation that the electronic chart system should be update timely and the vessel should be equipped with paper charts, the involved ship was not seaworthy because Heshun did not perform due diligence before the beginning of the voyage, therefore the argument that Heshun did not know the ship's unseaworthiness should not be established. M.V. "Jin Run 988" was not seaworthy at the beginning of the voyage, which caused the occurrence of the insurance accidents. The loss of accident belonged to exclusion clauses. So the court of first instance should not support Heshun's claim that Heshun requested PICC Qinghuangdao to pay the ship insurance indemnity in amount of RMB932,350 yuan and the interest calculated from December 17, 2014 up to the actual payment day based on the loan interest rate set by People's Bank of China for the same period.

Pulling the threads together, there was a ship insurance contract between Heshun and PICC Qinghuangdao, Heshun had insurable interest on M.V. "Jin Run 988" and should be entitled to claim compensation against PICC Qinghuangdao. M.V. "Jin Run 988" was not seaworthy at the beginning of the involved voyage, and this was the direct cause of the accidents, the loss of which was within the scope of exclusion clauses. According to the Maritime Code of People's Republic of China Article 244 Paragraph 1 Sub-paragraph 1 and the Civil Procedure Law of People's Republic of China Article 64 Paragraph 1, the judgment was as follows: reject the claims of Heshun. Court acceptance fee in amount of 6,562 yuan should be born by Heshun.

Heshun disagreed with judgment of first instance, and appealed to the court. It required the court to revoke judgment of first instance and change to judge that PICC Qinghuangdao should pay ship insurance indemnity 932,350 yuan and the interest calculated from the RMB loan interest rate of the People's Bank of China for the same period from December 17, 2014 to the date of actual payment, court acceptance fees of two cases should be born by PICC Qinghuangdao. Facts and reasons: firstly, the court of first instance confirmed that the ship was not equipped with paper charts, which caused the ship to be unseaworthy and had a causal relationship with the reef accident, which was wrong. According to the Regulations on the Management of Ship Electronic Chart System and Automatic Identification System Equipment for Domestic Sailing Ship Article 21, for ships involved with electronic charts, paper charts were only used for backup and supplementary purposes. They were not necessary and the only chart data. The lack of paper charts did not cause the ship to become unseaworthy. Moreover, The Xinhaima electronic charts and navigation data on the ship had marked "New Reef", and there was no causal relationship between the lack of paper charts and accident. Secondly, the court of first instance confirmed that there was a causal relationship between the failure to update the electronic chart and the occurrence of the reef accident, which was wrong. The electronic chart ECS157 used by the ship involved had been updated to the latest version 9.3.1 when the adjuster boarded the ship for insurance assessment. This version also had no "New Reef" label, only "1-meter Dark Reef" manually added by the captain. Since then, Heshun updated the electronic chart system several times, and there was no "New Reef" and "1-meter Dark Reef" label. There was no causal relationship with the occurrence of the reef accident. Thirdly, The "ship planned route" determined by the court of first instance was a false route for the captain to evade responsibility instructions. In the waters where the incident happened, the Nanpeng Island was an important turning point and the basis for the planned route. According to the route formulation guidelines and waterway navigation laws, the captain could not make a route through "New Reef". Fourthly, the court of first instance confirmed that the ship was unseaworthy, which was wrong. Heshun provided the Sea Cargo Ship Seaworthiness Certificate, Ship Minimum Safety Manning Certificate, ship's exit visa and other documents, which could prove that the ship was in a seaworthy state. Fifthly, the Inspection Report under the Supervision of the Flag State and Ship Insurance Assessment Report accepted by the court of first instance had no authenticity or objectivity, they could not be used as evidence to confirm the facts of the case. Sixthly, the losses claimed by Heshun were real and reasonable, and PICC Qinhuangdao should compensate in full.

PICC Qinghuangdao argued that: firstly, the electronic charts used by the ship involved in the incident were not updated and were not equipped with the necessary paper charts. As a result, the crew could not see "New Reef" mark when planning the route and planned the route through the new reef, therefore, the ship involved was not equipped with the necessary navigation charts, which caused the ship to be unseaworthy and had a direct causal relationship with the occurrence of this accident. Secondly, the inability of the ship to be unseaworthy was the exclusive responsibility of the insurer, and the insurer had the right not to compensate. The ship seaworthiness documents provided by Heshun could not prove that the ship was in seaworthiness when the ship was in operation, The Inspection Report under the Supervision of the Flag State issued by the Shantou Maritime Department identified the lack of paper charts as a serious violation of the seaworthiness of the ship, and made a decision to detain and prohibit departure, which could prove that the ship involved was not seaworthy. Thirdly, the unit and the valuer of the insurance assessment report in this case had qualifications for assessment, and the assessment report was objective, fair and true. Fourthly, Heshun repaired the ship without authorization, incurred repair costs not related to the accident, and there was no reasonable basis for determining the repair price, and the amount of the claim was too high. So the facts confirmed by the court of first instance were clear, and application of law was correct, it required the court to dismiss the appeal of Heshun.

During second instance, Heshun submitted three pieces of new evidence, evidence 1, two electronic chart photos taken on November 30, 2014 and August 31, 2015, to prove that the red route and the "1-meter Reef" label on the electronic chart were added manually by the captain, not the contents of the electronic chart. Evidence 2, Chinese Navigation Guide: South China Sea (2011 Edition), to prove that as the necessary navigation information for ships, it had recorded the situation about the new reef and the waterway navigation law. The actual route of the ship was in violation of the navigation law. Evidence 3, China Coastal Mileage (2006 Edition), to prove that there was a turning point near the southern Penglie Island in the waters involved, and the planned route indicated by the captain did not refer to the turning point against common sense, so the planned route was false.

PICC Qinghuangdao cross-examined that, it recognized the photo taken on November 30, 2014 in evidence 1, but did not recognize the purpose of proof, it could not prove that the label of "1-meter Reef" was added manually, it did not recognize the authenticity, legality or relevancy of the photo taken on August 31, 2015, it could not be recognized that the photo was an electronic chart being used by the ship involved. It did not recognized the authenticity and relevancy of evidence 2 and 3, it could not prove that the above-mentioned information was provided by the ship involved at the time of the incident, and the information was not nautical chart data, which could not be used to deny the authenticity of the planned navigation determined by the court of first instance.

Combined with the proving of evidence and cross-examination of the parties, the court holds that, PICC Qinghuangdao had no objection to the authenticity of the photo taken on November 30, 2014 in evidence 1, so the court confirms it. The photo taken on August 31, 2015 cannot prove that it was the electronic chart system currently used by the ship involved, so the court does not confirm the authenticity. The comparison of the two photos cannot prove that the "1-meter Reef" was added manually, and the purpose of proof is not confirmed by the court. The court confirms the authenticity of evidence 2 and 3, but the evidence cannot prove that when the ship was equipped with the navigation information, the planned route indicated by the captain was false, and the purpose of proof is not confirmed by the court.

In addition, Heshun applied to the court for investigation and evidence collection of Nanjing Junlu Technology Co., Ltd. (hereinafter referred to as Junlu), a manufacturer of electronic chart ESC157, to prove that the updated chart of the ship involved had not been marked with "New Reef" in the waters where the incident happened. After investigation, the court holds that, Heshun stated in its Information Statement for investigation and evidence collection submitted to the court that the chart data produced by Junlu were all from the Shanghai Sea Chart Center of the East China Sea Navigation Support Center of the Ministry of Transport, which confirmed that the electronic chart data source was consistent with the paper chart, "New Reef" was now marked on the electronic charts that were now issued. Accordingly, the court holds that it is no longer necessary to investigate and obtain evidence from Junlu.

PICC Qinghuangdao did not submit new evidence.

The facts confirmed by the court of first instance can be proved by evidence, so the court confirms the facts found out by the court of first instance.

The court holds that:

The case is the dispute over ship insurance contract, the coastal inland ship insurance contract concluded by Heshun and PICC Qinhuangdao is legal and valid, and the two parties have established a ship insurance contract relationship. The issue of the case is whether the accident involved is the excluded liability agreed in the insurance contract.

Whether the ship involved is seaworthy.

Firstly, the seaworthiness of the ship is a factual state. In addition to complying with the relevant requirements during the ship survey, the carrier is also required to take care to ensure that the ship is in an actual seaworthy state before and when the ship sails. The holding of seaworthiness certificate and exit visa by Heshun is only the preliminary evidence of the seaworthiness of the ship, not the final proof. Having a valid ship inspection certificate is the minimum obligation that the carrier should fulfill. The ship's actual seaworthiness should be reviewed in terms of crewing, ship equipment, supplies, cargo loading, etc.

Secondly, the carrier's seaworthiness obligations include the necessary equipment to complete the scheduled voyage of the ship. According to the Regulations on the Management of Shipboard Electronic Chart System and Automatic Identification System Equipment for Domestic Sailing Ship Article 19, in order to ensure the accuracy and completeness of the electronic chart data, the electronic chart system equipment onboard ships on coastal navigation should use the officially issued electronic charts that meet the requirements of the International Hydrographic Organization S-57 format and should be updated in time, the electronic charts equipped on ships should be updated in time. At the time of the accident, the ECS157 electronic chart system used by the ship was version 9.0.1 instead of the latest version 9.3.1. The carrier did not fulfill its responsibility of updating in time, and did not guarantee that the ship was equipped to achieve seaworthiness. Although Heshun advocated that the ship involved also used the Xinhaima electronic chart system with "New Reef" label, the ship met the seaworthiness conditions, but the ship inspection department and the insurance adjuster's boarding inspection results did not confirm it, and Heshun failed to provide evidence to prove this, so the court does not support the claim.

Thirdly, according to the Regulations on the Management of Shipboard Electronic Chart System and Automatic Identification System Equipment for Domestic Sailing Ship Article 21, ships equipped with shipborne electronic chart system equipment should keep appropriate paper charts as backup and update them in time. In order to ensure that the shipboard electronic chart system equipment can safely return to the port in the event of a failure. The above regulations make it mandatory for ships to be equipped with paper charts to ensure safe navigation. In the case where the electronic chart used at the time of the ship's incident does not match the actual water area, it is particularly necessary to equip the corresponding paper chart to set the correct route and ensure safe navigation. The Shantou Maritime Safety Administration, as the competent ship supervision and inspection department that understands the specific navigation conditions in the waters where the incident happened, made the decision on "Prohibition of Departure (Detention)" based on the Inspection Report under the Supervision of the Flag State on the ship involved because of the "lack of most paper navigation charts from Shanwei to Jingjiang". Based on this, it can be determined that the ship is not seaworthy due to the lack of appropriate paper charts during this voyage.

In conclusion, M.V. "Jin Run 988" is not equipped with the necessary equipment to complete the voyage involved, and the ship is in a state of being unseaworthy.

Whether there is a causal relationship between the unseaworthy ship and the accident involved.

People's Liberation Army Naval Command Navigation Guarantee Department 2013 version of the paper charts are marked "New Reef" in the water area, but the ship involved was not equipped with the paper chart required for the route, and the electronic chart used by it was not marked with "New Reef". After the accident, the results of the surveyor's boarding inspection showed that the planned route of the voyage indicated by the captain passed the location of "New Reef", and the updated electronic chart showed the label of "1-meter Reef" at that location. The fact that Heshun failed to provide sufficient evidence to prove that its claimed that the captain had indicated a false route, and the ECS157 electronic chart was still updated without "New Reef" label. Therefore, due to the absence of paper charts and the failure to update the electronic charts, the ship involved did not avoid the location of "New Reef" when planning the route, resulting in a collision accident with ships traveling along the planned route. So there is a causal relationship between the unseaworthy ship and the accident involved.

As to the problem that whether can the ship involved refer to the Chinese Navigation Guide: South China Sea Area and China Coastal Mileage to plan the route, so as to avoid the accident of reef collision. Since none of the above-mentioned materials have marked the specific location of "New Reef", it cannot replace the role of paper charts. With reference to this data, the location of "New Reef" cannot be accurately determined, so that a safe route can be planned to avoid accidents of reef contact. So the provision of the aforesaid navigational information cannot prevent the causal relationship between the unseaworthy ship and the accident involved.

Pulling the threads together, the facts confirmed by the court of first instance are clear, the appeal reasons of Heshun lack factual or legal basis, so the court does not support them. According to the Civil Procedure Law of the People's Republic of China Article 170 Paragraph 1 Sub-paragraph 1, the judgment is as follows:

Dismiss the appeal, and affirm the original judgment.

Court acceptance fee of first instance in amount of RMB6,562 yuan, shall be born according to judgment of first instance, court acceptance fee of second instance in amount of RMB13,124 yuan, shall be born by the Appellant, Qinhuangdao Heshun Shipping Co., Ltd.

The judgment is final.

Presiding Judge: ZHAI Hong
Acting Judge: YANG Zeyu
Acting Judge: YU Yinan

November 9, 2015

Clerk: YIN Qi

The Supreme People's Court of the People's Republic of China Civil Ruling

Qinhuangdao Heshun Shipping Co., Ltd.
v.
China People's Property Insurance Co., Ltd. Qinhuangdao City Branch

(2016) Zui Gao Fa Min Shen No.1395

Related Case(s) This is the ruling of retrial, and the judgment of first instance and the judgment of second instance are on page 831 and page 842 respectively.

Cause(s) of Action 230. Dispute over marine insurance contract on the sea or sea-connected waters.

Headnote The Supreme People's Court dismissed assured's application for retrial, affirming lower court decisions denying assured's claim for indemnity under a hull insurance policy because of its knowledge of the unseaworthy condition of the vessel, which was the cause of the vessel's grounding.

Summary Qinhuangdao Heshun Shipping Co., Ltd. (Plaintiff) filed suit against China People's Property Insurance Co., Ltd. Qinhuangdao Branch (Defendant) to compel the Defendant to honor the terms of their insurance policy agreement after the Plaintiff's vessel allided with a reef ("New Reef") along its planned route. This allision happened due to the Plaintiff's failure to equip its vessel with updated charts that depicted the "New Reef." For this reason, the Defendant refused to compensate the Plaintiff due to this unseaworthy condition, denying liability under the exclusion clause of the parties' insurance contract. The Court of first instance ruled that the Defendant was not liable due to this unseaworthy condition, and the Plaintiff was liable for all relevant litigation costs of the suit. On appeal, the appeal Court recognized the judgment of the court of first instance, the Plaintiff, again, bearing all liability for the relevant costs of the appeal.

The Plaintiff filed an application for retrial. The Plaintiff failed in its challenge to the trial court's finding that the Plaintiff lacked sufficient equipment for a safe voyage and the Supreme People's Court dismissed petition for a retrial.

Ruling

The Claimant of Retrial (the Plaintiff of first instance, the Appellant of second instance): Qinhuangdao Heshun Shipping Co., Ltd.
Domicile: Qinhuangdao City, Hebei, China.
Legal representative: LIU Wanzhong, general manager.
Agent *ad litem*: ZHAO Yong, lawyer of Hebei Runqian Law Firm.
Agent *ad litem*: TIAN Junmei, lawyer of Hebei Runqian Law Firm.

The Respondent of Retrial (the Defendant of first instance, the Respondent of second instance): China People's Property Insurance Co., Ltd. Qinhuangdao City Branch
Domicile: Qinhuangdao City, Hebei, China.
Legal representative: ZHANG Youlin, general manager.
Agent *ad litem*: WANG Peng, lawyer of Beijing Gaopeng Law Firm.
Agent *ad litem*: SHANG Weiwei, lawyer of Beijing Gaopeng Law Firm.

With respect to the case arising from dispute over ship insurance contract between the Claimant of Retrial, Qinhuangdao Heshun Shipping Co., Ltd. (hereinafter referred to as Heshun), and the Respondent of Retrial, China People's Property Insurance Co., Ltd. Qinhuangdao City Branch (hereinafter referred to as PICC Qinghuangdao), the Claimant of Retrial disagreed with the Tianjin High People's Court (2015) Jin Gao Min Si Zhong Zi No.93 Civil Judgment and applied for retrial. The court formed a collegiate panel to investigate the case, now the case has been concluded.

Heshun claimed that: firstly, the court of second instance held that M.V. "Jin Run 988" was unseaworthy, which was wrong. 1. The Sea Cargo Ship Seaworthiness Certificate, Ship Nationality Certificate, Marine Ship Inspection Certificate, Ship Minimum Safety Manning Certificate submitted by Heshun and visa issued by the administrative department indicated that the ship involved was seaworthy. 2. According to the Guidelines for Handling Defects in Ship Safety Inspection, ECS157 electronic charts on the ship involved were not updated but not cause the ship to become unseaworthy, and after the electronic charts of Heshun were updated to the latest, "New Reef" logo was still not displayed, and the label of "1-meter Reef" on the updated electronic charts was added manually by the captain. The updating of electronic charts had nothing to do with seaworthiness. 3. The ship involved was equipped with two sets of electronic chart systems, of which "New Reef" was clearly marked in the electronic chart system equipped at the factory, meanwhile, the navigation information such as the China Navigation Guide: South China Sea Area and China Coastal Mileage provided on board also clearly marked the location of "New Reef", so the absence of paper charts for the voyage did not result in the absence of "New Reef" information on board. According to the Regulations on the Management of Shipboard Electronic Chart System and Automatic Identification System Equipment for Domestic Sailing Ship Article 21, paper charts were just backups, and the lack of paper charts did not necessarily cause the ship to become unseaworthy. Secondly, the facts confirmed by the court of second instance had no evidence to prove, and part of evidence was forged, which could not be used to prove the facts. 1. The Inspection Report under the Supervision of the Flag State issued by Shantou MSA and the Assessment Report made by Tainjin Jiulian Insurance Surveyors & Adjusters Co., Ltd. could not be used as basis to confirm the case. 2. The "ship planned route" confirmed by the judgment of second instance was forged by the captain after the accident of collision. 3. There was no causal relationship between the unupdated electronic charts, the absence of paper charts and the occurrence of reef accident. The collision accident was caused by the captain and crew using the autopilot and negligent driving behavior. Thirdly, the ship involved was seaworthy, and Heshun fulfilled the obligations of the shipowner. According to the Maritime Code of the People's Republic of China, it should be liable. In conclusion, it required the court to retry the case.

PICC Qinghuangdao argued that: the facts confirmed by the court of second instance are clear, and application of law was correct.

Firstly, the facts that Heshun claimed for retrial had no evidence to prove. 1. The fact that the label of "1-meter Reef" on ECS157 was manually updated did not exist, and whether the electronic charts were updated manually did not affect the result of the ship being unseaworthy at the time of the accident. 2. The fact that the ship used two electronic chart systems simultaneously did not exist. 3. The fact that the planned route made by the crew was false did not exist, and whether or not to make a planned route does not affect the final result of the ship's unseaworthinessness leading to an accident.

Secondly, M.V. "Jin Run 988" involved in the case was unseaworthy at the time of the accident, and there was a causal relationship between the unseaworthiness ship and the accident. 1. Shipowners were obliged to properly equip ships to make them seaworthy, according to the Regulations on the Management of Shipboard Electronic Chart System and Automatic Identification System Equipment for Domestic Sailing Ship, the provision of paper charts was a mandatory requirement. For the lack of nautical data, Heshun had an unshirkable responsibility as a carrier. 2. Shantou Maritime Safety Administration was the department in charge of ship supervision and inspection, and its decision on the handling of Heshun in the Inspection Report under the Supervision of the Flag State was an administrative penalty. Heshun's dissatisfaction with the administrative punishment resulted should be appealed through legal channels. The company's unilateral defense did not affect the validity of the report. 3. The seaworthiness of a ship referred to the factual status. Obtaining a seaworthiness certificate or entry and exit visa did not mean that the ship was actually seaworthy. 4. The ship involved was not equipped with a paper chart, and there was no "New Reef" sign on the electronic chart, even the discreet crew, because they could not accurately determine the existence of "New Reef", it was possible to formulate a route through "New Reef, which could not prevent the occurrence of the reef accident. Therefore, the unseaworthy ship was the direct cause of the accident. It required the court to dismiss the application for retrial.

After investigation, the court holds that, the case is the dispute over ship insurance contract, according to the application for retrial of Heshun, the main issues is that: the court of second instance confirmed that the ship involved was unseaworthy and there was a causal relationship between the ship's unseaworthiness and the accident, whether there is lack of evidence to prove the facts and wrong application of law.

According to the Maritime Code of the People's Republic of China Article 47, the carrier shall, before and at the beginning of the voyage, exercise due diligence to make the ship seaworthy, properly man, equip and supply the ship and to make the holds, refrigerating and cool chambers and all other parts of the ship in which goods are carried, fit and safe for their reception, carriage and preservation. Accordingly, it is the legal obligation of the carrier to make the ship seaworthy before and at the time of sailing. In this case, ECS157 electronic chart system used by M.V. "Jin Run 988" owned by Heshun was version 9.0.1 instead of the latest version 9.3.1 when the accident involving the reef collision happened. Heshun Company failed to fulfill its responsibility for timely updating, and the ship was not equipped with the paper charts required for the voyage. Heshun failed to fulfill its responsibility for timely updating, and the ship was not equipped with the paper charts required for the voyage. According to the Regulations on the Management of Shipboard Electronic Chart System and Automatic Identification System Equipment for Domestic Saling Ship Article 19 and Article 21, in order to ensure the accuracy and completeness of the electronic chart data, the electronic chart system equipment onboard ships on coastal navigation should use the officially issued electronic charts that meet the requirements of the International Hydrographic Organization S-57 format and should be updated in time; ships equipped with Shipboard electronic chart system equipment should keep appropriate paper charts as backup and update them in time. In order to ensure that the shipboard electronic chart system equipment can be safely returned to the port. As the carrier, Heshun did not have the necessary equipment to complete the scheduled voyage of the ship, the map set the correct route and ensure the safety of navigation to ensure that the ship was equipped to reach the seaworthiness state, which eventually led to the accident of reef collision. The court of second instance confirmed that the ship involved was unseaworthy and there was a causal relationship between the ship's unseaworthiness and the accident, whether there is no lack of evidence to prove the facts or wrong application of law.

The Sea Cargo Ship Seaworthiness Certificate, Ship Nationality Certificate, Marine Ship Inspection Certificate, Ship Minimum Safety Manning Certificate submitted by Heshun and visa issued by the administrative department only indicated that the ship involved was seaworthy. A valid inspection certificate is not the only requirement for a ship to be seaworthy, and it cannot fully prove that the ship involved is in a seaworthy state; Heshun advocated that the ship involved also use Xinhaima electronic chart system with "New Reef" label, but the fact was not confirmed in the ship inspection department and the insurance adjuster's boarding inspection results. Heshun also failed to provide evidence to prove this; Heshun advocated that the captain falsify the "ship planned route", and the label of "1-meter

Reef" on the updated electronic chart was added by the captain, but it did not provide evidence; Heshun advocated that the Inspection Report under the Supervision of the Flag State of Shantou Maritime Safety Administration and the evaluation report issued by Tianjin Jiulian Insurance Surveyors & Adjusters Co., Ltd. cannot be used as the basis for the determination, but the reasons provided are not sufficient to deny the authenticity of the two reports; the Chinese Navigation Guide: South China Sea Area and China Coastal Mileage do not mark the specific location of "New Reef" and cannot replace the role of paper charts. Reference to this information cannot accurately determine the location of "New Reef" in order to plan a safe route and avoid accidents that hit the rocks. The reasons of Heshun that the ship involved was seaworthy cannot be established.

Pulling the threads together, the application for retrial of Heshun is not consistent with the Civil Procedure Law of the People's Republic of China Article 200. According to the Civil Procedure Law of the People's Republic of China Article 204 Paragraph 1, the ruling is as follows:

Dismiss the application for retrial of Qinhuangdao Heshun Shipping Co., Ltd.

Presiding Judge: HU Fang
Judge: LI Guishun
Acting Judge: HOU Wei

September 1, 2016

Clerk: LI Na

Tianjin Maritime Court
Civil Judgment

Shandong Xianglong Industrial Group Co., Ltd.
v.
NCS Co., Ltd. et al.

(2011) Jin Hai Fa Shang Chu Zi No.465

Related Case(s) None.

Cause(s) of Action 201. Dispute over illegal lien on ship, cargoes carried by ship, bunkers and stores of ship.

Headnote Ocean carrier held to be entitled to exercise a lien over cargo for freight that had not been paid by the cargo shipper; receiver held liable to pay carrier's costs of delay at the port of destination but not the unpaid freight itself, which was still owed by the shipper.

Summary The Plaintiffs-Receivers and Sellers entered into a sales contract. Sellers entered into an agreement with the Defendants-Carrier to transport the goods from Indonesia to the People's Republic of China. The bill of lading specified that Sellers would pay freight. Defendants-Carrier transferred all its rights regarding the applicable bills of lading to the Defendants-Assignees. Upon discharging in the People's Republic of China, the Defendants-Assignees claimed they had a lien over the cargo because Seller never fully paid freight. The claim that there may be a lien over the cargo precluded Plaintiffs-Receivers from immediately taking possession of the cargo. As a result, the court sold the cargo at auction, and Plaintiffs-Receivers were given the proceeds.

The Plaintiffs-Receivers sued the Defendants-Carrier and the Defendants-Assignees to recover losses resulting from an illegal lien. The Defendants-Assignees counterclaimed for freight and expenses incurred by the cargo's delayed transfer at the port of destination.

The court determined that an agreement between Sellers and the Defendants-Carrier specified the procedure for freight payment. That agreement was incorporated in the relevant bills of lading. As such, that agreement specified Sellers would pay freight, and the obligation to pay freight never shifted to Plaintiffs-Receivers. Consequently, the court rejected the Defendants-Assignees' counterclaim for unpaid freight. However, the court ordered Plaintiffs-Receivers to compensate the Defendants-Assignees for the expenses it incurred because of the cargo's delay after discharging. The Defendants-Assignees were to be compensated from the cargo auction's proceeds.

Rejecting Plaintiff-Receivers' claim, the court held the Defendants-Assignees had a valid lien over the cargo. Whether the Defendants-Assignees had a valid lien depended on if Sellers, who were obliged to pay freight, were the rightful titleholders when the lien arose. According to the People's Republic of China law, the court determined the creation or transfer of a property right occurs upon delivery of a movable. The court reasoned that when the Plaintiffs-Receivers obtained the full set of bills of lading, they also obtained ownership of the cargo. Because Plaintiffs-Receivers could not prove the exact moment they received the full set of bills of lading, the court determined cargo ownership transferred to the Plaintiffs-Receivers when they reminded the Defendants-Carrier to take delivery of the goods. The Plaintiffs-Receivers reminded the Defendants-Carrier to take delivery of the goods after a lien arose over the goods due to Sellers not timely paying the Defendants-Carrier freight. For that reason, the Defendants-Assignees had a valid lien.

Judgment

The Plaintiff (the counterclaim Defendant): Shandong Xianglong Industrial Group Co., Ltd.
Domicile: No.174, Jinqueshan Road, Linyi City, Shandong, the People's Republic of China.
Legal representative: XIE Yongjun, chairman of the company.
Agent *ad litem*: LI Xuebing, lawyer of Shandong Yahetai Law Firm.
Agent *ad litem*: ZHANG Yunke, lawyer of Tianjing Sifang Junhui Law Firm.

The Defendant (the counterclaim Plaintiff): NCS CO., Ltd.
Domicile: 35/F, West Tower, Shun Tak Centre, 168-200 Connaught Road C, Hong Kong of the People's Republic of China.
Legal representative: LUO Jing, chairman of the company.
Agent *ad litem*: YI Yuefeng, male, Han, born on July 22, 1965, the vice president of the North Shipping Shareholding Co., Ltd., living in Shahekou District, Dalian City Liaoning, the People's Republic of China.
Agent *ad litem*: QIU Ximing, male, Han, born on July 22, 1976, manager of the North Shipping Shareholding Co., Ltd., living in Haigang District, Qinghuangdao City, Hebei, the People's Republic of China.

The Defendant: JINYUAN Marine INC.
Domicile: Floor 15, Banco General Tower, Aquilino de la Guardia Street, Marbella, Panama City, Republic of Panama.
Legal representative: CEN Erkang, director of the company.
Agent *ad litem*: YANG Wengui, lawyer of Beijing Haitong Law Firm.
Agent *ad litem*: PENG Xianwei, lawyer of Beijing Haitong Law Firm.

With respect to the case arising from dispute over the damage compensation for the incorrect lien of the marine transported cargoes between the Plaintiff, Shandong Xianglong Industrial Group Co., Ltd. (hereinafter referred to as "Shandong Xianglong") and the Defendant, NCS Co., Ltd. (hereinafter referred to as NCS), after accepting it on October 11, 2011, the court legitimately constituted the collegiate panel to try the case. During hearing, NCS lodged a counterclaim; the court accepted it and tried the counterclaim together with the original claim according to the related regulations of Civil Procedure Law of the People's Republic of China. On September 20, 2012, Shandong Xianglong made an application of suspending the hearing to the court taking it as a reason that the cargoes involved in the case was in the procedure of customs auction and the amount of loss for cargoes should be determined by the result of the auction. Later after the application of NCS, the case was resumed to hear on December 8, 2014. On September 10, 2014, Shandong Xianglong made an application of taking JINYUAN Marine INC. as an additional Defendant, and the court permitted legally. The evidence of this case were exchanged on September 17, 2012, and the court heard the case in public on September 18, 2012, December 12, 2014 and June 8, 2015. Agents *ad litem*, LI Xuebing (failing to attend the third trial) and ZHANG Yunke, entrusted by Shandong Xianglong, agents *ad litem*, YI Yuefeng (failing to attend the third trial) and QIU Ximing, entrusted by NCS and agents *ad litem*, YANG Wengui (failing to attend the first and third trial) and PENG Xianwei (failing to attend the first trial) appeared in the court to attend the hearings. Now the case has been concluded.

The Plaintiff, Shandong Xianglong claimed as follows. It signed a sales contract of nickel minerals with PT.KRESNA INTI CIPTA Company (hereinafter referred to as PT company), the seller in Indonesia on Mar 22, 2011; PT Company sold 5,000 tons (±10%) of nickel minerals to Shandong Xianglong. It was agreed that nickel content was 1.6%-1.7%, lower than 1.6%, and the buyer had the right to reject and the price was 56 dollars/ton and the payment method was letter of credit. Two parties signed the supplemental agreement on April 20, 2011, that the price was changed into 58.5 dollars/ton and the payment method was changed into 30% T/T, 70% letter of credit. The buyer and seller signed a supplemental agreement again on July 29, 2011 that INTERTEK was regarded as the surveyor to inspect the quality of nickel minerals at the destination port. After Shandong Xianglong paid 877,500 dollars, PT Company loaded 53,952 tons of nickel minerals on M.V. JIN YUAN on July 12, 2012, and JINYUAN MARINE INC. as the carrier, authorized the captain to issue a bill of lading. After M.V. JIN YUAN arrived at Tianjin Port, nickel content involved in this case was 1.34% after inspected by INTERTEK. According to the market price at that time, the price of the whole wheel of nickel minerals involved in this case was less than 11,329,920 RMB. Therefore, the two parties consulted orally that Shandong Xianglong did not need to pay for goods. After that, PT Company posted the lading bill involved in this case to Shandong Xianglong. NCS CO., LIMITED sent the lien notice to Shandong Xianglong on September 1, 2011 to claim that they would reject deliver goods if Shandong Xianglong did not pay the freight and demurrage charge. Shandong Xianglong thought that JINYUAN MARINE INC., as the carrier on the lading bill, and NCS CO., LIMITED, as the actual lien operator, should assume the compensation liability for loss caused by the wrong lien on the goods of Shandong Xianglong. Therefore, it is requested to judge as follows. 1. NCS CO., LIMITED and JINYUAN MARINE INC. should make a joint compensation for Shandong Xianglong the surcharge 243,169 RMB, valuation fee 98,376.26 RMB and storage charge 6,490,652.8 RMB, totally 6,832,198.06 RMB; 2. NCS CO., LIMITED and JINYUAN MARINE INC. should make a joint compensation for Shandong Xianglong the loss of interest, of which the cargo value is 16,688,131 RMB, according to the loan interest rate stipulated by the People's Bank of China for the corresponding period and 1164 days, and of which storage fee is 6,832,198.06 RMB according to the loan interest rate stipulated by the People's Bank of China for the corresponding period and calculated from December 5, 2014 to the date of compensation; 3. The court cost should be bare by NCS CO., LIMITED and JINYUAN MARINE INC.

The Defendant, NCS Co., LTD argued as follows: 1. The freight term in the lease of May 18, 201, which was incorporated into the bill does not have the feature of freight prepaid, therefore Shandong Xianglong should pay the unpaid freight by the lading bill; 2. Shandong Xianglong has the responsibility to pay the demurrage charge in the port of discharge; 3. NCS Co., LTD has the lien right of the cargoes involved in this case; 4. NCS Co., LTD pushed Shandong Xianglong to make the customs clearance and sale the cargoes as soon as possible many times, but Shandong Xianglong did not take any measures to reduce the loss till now. NCS Co., LTD should not take the responsibility as for the additional losses due to not taking the measure of reducing loss; and 5. The real reason why the cargo could not be sold lies in the quality problem and has nothing to do with NCS Co., LTD's cargo lien. Therefore, the claim to reject the appeal of Shandong Xianglong is promoted.

The Defendant, JINYUAN MARINE INC. lodged a claim as follows: 1. JINYUAN MARINE INC. does not have any entity relevancy with this case and did not implement any infringement, so it should not undertake any tortious liability. The lien of the goods is implemented by NCS Co., LTD and under its actual control, and JINYUAN MARINE INC. has just signed the rights transfer agreement and transferred the right under the lading bill involved in the case to NCS Co., LTD, and it does not have any faults; 2. Shandong Xianglong did not fulfill the mitigate damage obligation and it should undertake the responsibility of the extended loss caused by its fault; 3. Shandong Xianglong has just paid 30% for goods and the compensation scope should not go beyond the actual loss; and 4. Shandong Xianglong's appeal has already been beyond the prescribed period for litigation.

The counterclaim Plaintiff, NCS Co., LTD, lodged the following claim. The lading bill in this case is the master bill of lading, issued by the loading port agent under a series of charter parties on behalf of the captain. JINYUAN MARINE INC. has already transferred all the rights under the bill of the lading items, including the right to charge the freight and demurrage fees, to NCS Co., LTD, therefore, NCS Co., LTD gained all of the rights of carrier under the bill of lading items. It is stated clearly in the lading bill that the freight is paid according to the charter party and the lease incorporated on May 18, 2011 is exclusive and clear and additionally Shandong Xianglong should know, foresee and agree clearly to accept the incorporation of freight item in the charter party into lading bill and therefore think that the incorporation is valid. According to the agreement of the charter party, Shandong Xianglong, as the lading bill holder, is responsible to pay the remainder freight, and NCS Co., LTD has the lien on the goods involved in this case. Therefore, the following judgment is requested. 1. Shandong Xianglong should pay NCS Co., LTD the 1,233,545 dollars as the freight and interest (from July 24, 2011 to the date of actual payment and calculated according to the loan interest rate stipulated by the People's Bank of China for the corresponding period); 2. The court costs should be undertaken by Shandong Xianglong.

The counterclaim Defendant, Shandong Xianglong, lodged the following claim: 1. Shandong Xianglong has ownership of nickel minerals. The nickel content is only 1.34%, so it's reasonable for the seller, PT Company to agree not to pay the NCS CO., LIMITED has an actual control of operation of ship, and the lien was implemented in the name of their own, but it did not acquire the right of lading bill, transferred from JINYUAN MARINE INC. at the time of implementing lien, so its lien is illegal. At the same time, NCS CO., LIMITED has no right to implement the lien on the nickel minerals involved in this case according to the lease; 3. Shandong Xianglong's prosecution of JINYUAN MARINE INC. is not beyond the prescribed period for litigation. JINYUAN MARINE INC. did not stop NCS CO., LIMITED's illegal lien under the condition of knowing about that, and it transferred its right of lading bill to NCS CO., LIMITED, which constitutes indulge and cooperation behavior, and it is joint infringement of right and it is continued, which is not beyond the prescribed period for litigation; and 4. The lading bill involved in this case is the freight prepaid bill of lading, and the lease of May 18, 2011 could not be incorporated into the lading bill, therefore NCS CO., LIMITED has no right to ask for freight under the lease from Shandong Xianglong, the non-lease party.

According to the claim of Shandong Xianglong, the defence of NCS CO., LIMITED and JINYUAN MARINE INC. and the claim of NCS CO., LIMITED, the defence of Shandong Xianglong and the dispute focus of this case are as follows: 1. whether have NCS CO., LIMITED and JINYUAN MARINE INC. lien to the cargoes resolved in this case and whether will this kind of the action constitute tort to Shandong Xianglong; 2. if it is constituted the tort and whether will Shandong Xianglong endure any loss from this and what are the amount and its evidence; 3. whether does Shandong Xianglong have the duty to pay freight to NCS CO., LIMITED; 4. if it does, what are the amount and the basis of calculation.

In order to prove its claim, Shandong Xianglong provided the following evidential material: evidence one: Sales Contract; evidence two: Supplementary Agreement One of Sales Contract; evidence three: Supplementary Agreement Two of Sales Contract; evidence four: The commercial invoice of 30% payment for goods; evidence five: Remittance Single; evidence six: Original bill of lading; evidence seven: letter of Shandong Xianglong's request for taking delivery of goods in August 2011. The above evidence proved that Shandong Xianglong, as the lading bill holder, have paid for the goods, and gained the full set of original lading bill involved in this case, and has the right to request NCS CO., LIMITED and JINYUAN MARINE INC. to release cargoes. Evidence Eight: lien notice, which proves NCS CO., LIMITED still had an illegal lien on goods involved in the case under the condition of knowing the above and JINYUAN MARINE INC. let the lien, caused a great loss to Shandong Xianglong. evidence nine: the quality certificate and translation of cargo, whose aim is the same with the first seven evidence; evidence ten: customs instruction and the standard of delayed declaration fee selected by the court, which prove the charge standard and amount of delayed declaration fee. Evidence four is original copy and Evidence eight is fax.

NCS CO., LIMITED put forward the following cross-examining opinions to Shandong Xianglong. It has no objection to the legality and authenticity of the first three evidence, but only the sale contract is not enough to prove that Shandong Xianglong gained the ownership of the cargo. It has no objection to the authenticity and relevancy of Evidence Four and it has no objection to evidence five, six, seven and eight. It has no objection to the authenticity and legality of evidence nine but its purpose of proof is not accepted; the quality of cargo caused that the cargo could not be sold out, and this case caused by the dispute of sale contract. Evidence ten cannot prove the claim of Shandong Xianglong, therefore it should take charge of all of the delayed declaration fee; goods under lien does not affect Shandong Xianglong's customs clearance; even though it does, Shandong Xianglong refused NCS CO., LIMITED's request for customs clearance on December 15, 2011, from when the delayed declaration fee should be taken charge of by Shandong Xianglong.

JINYUAN MARINE INC. put forward the following cross-examining opinions to Shandong Xianglong. It has no objection to the legality and authenticity of the first seven evidence, but it has objection to the relevancy. It has no objection to the authenticity and legality of evidence eight and nine, and there no relevancy with JINYUAN MARINE INC., and the lien has already been carried out on September 1, and it was on December 18 that JINYUAN MARINE INC. issued rights transfer agreement; the cost of evidence ten should be born by NCS CO., LIMITED.

The court's authentication opinions on Shandong Xianglong's evidence are as follows. NCS CO., LIMITED and JINYUAN MARINE INC. have no objection to the authenticity of Shandong Xianglong's ten evidence, and the court confirmed that. Evidence one to five can prove that Shandong Xianglong signed the business contract and the supplementary agreement of nickel minerals involved in this case with PT Company, and it was agreed in the contract that Shandong Xianglong could accept the congenbill, and it was noted clearly on the bill that the freight should be paid according to charter party. The 30% of the funds should be paid through telegraphic transfer and the other 70% should be paid through letter of Credit. Shandong Xianglong paid PT Company 708,5000 dollars and NCS CO., LIMITED 169,000 dollars according to the agreement; evidence six could prove the nickel minerals was loaded on M.V. JIN YUAN and the loading port agent signed the bill involved in this case on behalf of the captain; evidence seven could prove that Shandong Xianglong requested the carrier to pick up the goods after receiving the full set of original bill of lading; evidence eight could prove that NCS CO.,

LIMITED informed Shandong Xianglong of having implemented the lien on the goods involved in this case on Sept 1, 2011; evidence nine could prove the nickel content, 1.34%, did not meet the quality requirement stipulated in the sales contract; evidence ten could prove that the nickel minerals involved in this case has already been auctioned by Tianjin Customs, and the proceeds, deducting the related fees, like tariff and storage charges, etc., RMB8,795,964.24 has already been returned to Shandong Xianglong.

In order to prove its claim, NCS CO., LIMITED provided the following evidential materials. Evidence one: the certified transcripts of M.V. JIN YUAN to prove that the registered ship owner and the carrier under the lading bill is JINYUAN MARINE INC.; evidence two: the voyage charter party of the seller, PT Company and Lanyang International Shipping Co., LTD (hereinafter referred to as Lanyang Company); evidence three: the voyage charter party of Lanyang Company and NCS CO., LIMITED; evidence four: the time charter party of NCS CO., LIMITED and Timeplus Limited (hereinafter referred to as Timeplus Company). Evidence two to four prove that the lease of May 18, 2011, incorporated into the lading bill, can only be the voyage charter party of Lanyang Company and NCS CO., LIMITED; evidence five: the e-mail of the port changing and freight adding to prove that the port changing needs additional payment for the freight; evidence six: transfer notice and agreement to prove that JINYUAN MARINE INC. has transferred the right under the lading bill to NCS CO., LIMITED; evidence seven: the proof of the demurrage at the loading port to prove the demurrage fee at the loading port; evidence eight: the proof of the demurrage at the unloading port to prove the time of ship's arriving at the port and the time of unloading finishing; evidence nine: the correspondence of confirming the first customs declaration to prove that the loss was further expanded due to it that Shandong Xianglong rejected the suggestion of NCS CO., LIMITED unreasonably; evidence ten: certificate of quality to prove that the goods' quality is the root cause of the failure to sell; evidence twelve: the Xinhua news to prove that there appeared changes in the nickel mineral market and the price of nickel mineral was very low when it arrived at the unloading port, but the auction price became very high after Indonesia prohibited the export of nickel later; evidence thirteen: the lawyer comment letter through the notarial certification to prove that the right transfer of JINYUAN MARINE INC. is valid and effective; evidence fourteen: the Supreme Court case to prove that the signing and issuing of the lading bill is necessary for the recognition of the carrier; evidence fifteen: the excerpt and translation of authoritative book about English law to prove that the behavior of NCS CO., LIMITED did not cause any loss to the Plaintiff; evidence sixteen: the lien notice from NCS CO., LIMITED to Lanyang Company to prove that NCS CO., LIMITED had a lien on the goods involved in this case. There are original copies for evidence one, two, three, eleven and thirteen; evidence four, five, six and nine are e-mails; evidence sixteen is fax, and other evidence are all copies.

Shandong Xianglong put forward the following cross-examining opinion to NCS CO., LIMITED. The authenticity of evidence one cannot be confirmed. It accepted the authenticity of evidence two and three. It confused the authenticity of evidence four and the aim of evidence two to four. Evidence five is the e-mail of the port changing; its authenticity cannot be checked and this evidence is inconsistent with the claim of NCS CO., LIMITED; the freight' adding for the port changing is the basis of counting the rent and there is no relevancy for this evidence that NCS CO., LIMITED stated that its claim came from the claim right for lading bill. It accepts the authenticity of evidence six, and if it is transferred to the foreign, the notarial certification is needed. It does not confirm the purpose of proof of loading port demurrage in evidence seven and the loading port demurrage have no relevancy with Shandong Xianglong. It has no objection to the authenticity of evidence eight. It confirmed the authenticity of the correspondence in evidence nine but refused its aim. It accepted the authenticity of evidence ten but refused its aim. It accepted the authenticity of evidence eleven but refused the legality and purpose of proof. It accepted the authenticity of evidence twelve but thought that its aim is unrelated with this case. It accepted the notarial certification form of evidence thirteen but as for this case, Law of the People's Republic of China should be applied and the expert opinion could not be regarded as the legal basis. It had no objection to the authenticity of evidence fourteen but refused the purpose of proof and relevancy. Evidence fifteen belongs to the foreign law and has no referential value. Evidence sixteen is formed overseas without the notarial certification, therefore its authenticity cannot be decided; it was formed on July 25, 2011, with no relevancy with this case, and NCS CO., LIMITED's claim of the lien on goods to Lanyang Company is before the right transfer, and its lien behavior has no right basis.

JINYUAN MARINE INC. put forward the following cross-examining opinions to the evidence of NCS CO., LIMITED. It has no objection to evidence one, but refuses its purpose. It cannot make sure the authenticity of evidence two to five. It has no objection to evidence six. It does not confirm the authenticity of evidence seven and eight. It has no objection to evidence nine. It has no objection to the authenticity and validity of evidence ten and eleven but refuses their purpose of proof. It has no objection to the authenticity and validity of evidence twelve but it is unrelated with this case. It has no objection to the authenticity and validity of evidence thirteen. Evidence fourteen has no relevancy with this case. It has no objection to evidence fifteen, but refused its purpose of proof. It accepted the authenticity and validity of evidence sixteen but refused its relevancy, and this lien notice has no any relevancy with JINYUAN MARINE INC.

The court holds the following authentication opinions on the evidence from NCS CO., LIMITED. JINYUAN MARINE INC. had no objection to the authenticity of evidence one and the court confirmed that it could prove that JINYUAN MARINE INC. was the owner of M.V. JIN YUAN involved in this case; Shandong Xianglong had no objection to the authenticity of evidence two and three and NCS CO., LIMITED also provided the original copy of the evidence, and the court confirmed the authenticity of the two evidence and thought that they could prove that PT Company signed the voyage charter party with Lanyang Company and Lanyang Company signed the voyage charter party with NCS CO., LIMITED about the transportation of the goods involved in this case; NCS CO., LIMITED could not prove the identity to the two parties of the e-mail in evidence four and it also did not notarize the content of the e-mail, therefore the court did not confirm the authenticity of this evidence; Shandong Xianglong had no objection to the authenticity of the transfer notice, and JINYUAN MARINE INC., as one party of the right transfer agreement, had no objection to the authenticity of the transfer agreement, therefore the court confirmed the authenticity of evidence six; evidence seven and the evidence seven from JINYUAN MARINE INC., logbook, could mutually verify, and the court confirm the authenticity of this evidence and thought that it could prove that there had appeared demurrage fees, 559,187.5 dollars, at the loading port; evidence eight is a copy, so the court did not confirm its authenticity; Shandong Xianglong and JINYUAN MARINE INC. had no objection to the authenticity of evidence nine to twelve, and the court confirmed that. Evidence eleven us the testimony of witness, and the witness had no warrant and had not appeared at the court, therefore the court did not confirm the its effect of evidence; evidence twelve had no relevancy with the court, therefore the court did not confirm its probative force; evidence fourteen and fifteen had no relevancy with this case, so the court did not confirm the effect of evidence of the two evidence; evidence sixteen combined with evidence eight from Shandong Xianglong, so the court confirms the probative force. The specific reasons are as follows. Firstly, according the stipulation of lading bill and lease, freight should be paid within three bank days (before July 15, 2011) after the cargo shipment finished. When the ship arrived at Tianjin Port, NCS CO., LIMITED still had not received most of the freight, and on the second day after arriving at the port, the payment notice and the lien notice, send to the lessee of the lease, Lanyang Company, are up to the common sense and the habit of shipping industry; secondly, the ship arrived at Tianjin Port on July 24, 2011, but Shandong Xianglong did not remind the delivery till August 22, 2011. Before Shandong Xianglong showed its original lading bill to NCS CO., LIMITED, NCS CO., LIMITED could not confirm the receiver, and it also could not send the lien notice to Shandong Xianglong before August 22, 2011; lastly, it was written clearly on the lien notice to Shandong Xianglong, that NCS CO., LIMITED had already had a lien on all of the goods, which could mutually verify with the lien notice to Lanyang Company on July 25, 2011.

In order to prove its claim, JINYUAN MARINE INC. provided the following evidential materials. Evidence one: the certificate of registration to prove the identity of the subject; evidence two: the Supreme Court reply to prove that Shandong Xianglong has no right to claim the loss of loan interest; evidence three: the e-mails on November 18, 2011; evidence four: the e-mails on November 21, 2011; evidence five: the facsimile record on November 23, 2011 to prove that JINYUAN MARINE INC. sent the right transfer agreement to the lawyer of Shandong Xianglong through E-mail; evidence six: the facsimile record on November 25, 2011 to prove that the typewriting of the right transfer agreement is incorrect and JINYUAN MARINE INC. sent a letter to the lawyer of Shandong Xianglong to explain; and evidence seven: logbook to prove the condition and the time of loading and unloading, and demurrage fees of the ships involved in the case at the loading port.

Shandong Xianglong's cross-examining evidence to JINYUAN MARINE INC. are as follows. It accepts the authenticity of evidence one; it does not accept the purpose of proof of evidence two; it accepts the authenticity of evidence three to six but denies the purpose of proof, and JINYUAN MARINE INC. still colluded with NCS CO., LIMITED under the condition that it had known the realization of its right, which is the evidence for its bearing the joint liability; it does not accept the authenticity and the relevancy of evidence seven.

JINYUAN MARINE INC.'s cross-examining evidence to Shandong Xianglong are as follows. It has no objection to evidence three to seven; it has no objection to evidence two, and Shandong Xianglong has no right to claim the loss of loan interest.

The court's authentication opinions on JINYUAN MARINE INC.'s evidence are as follows. Shandong Xianglong and NCS CO., LIMITED have no objection to the authenticity of the six evidence from JINYUAN MARINE INC. and the court confirmed that. Evidence three to six can prove that JINYUAN MARINE INC. transferred the right under the bill of lading items to NCS CO., LIMITED and informed the Shandong Xianglong of the fact; JINYUAN MARINE INC. provided the original copy of evidence seven and the court confirmed its authenticity.

The court finds out the following facts.

On March 22, 2011, Shandong Xianglong, as the buyer, signed a nickel purchase contract, with the number, KRESNA-XL-201101, with the seller, PT Company and it agreed as follows. The specification and quality is the nickel content being 1.6%-1.7%, iron content being 17% and water content being 33%; according to the CNF FO Term, the basic price of wet ton being 56 dollars/ton (nickel content being 1.6% and water content being 33%), if the nickel content is lower than 1.6%, the two parties could not reach an agreement on the price through friendly negotiation and the buyer could reject to receive the goods; the buyer should entrust Indonesia CCIC to inspect the quality of the nickel quality at the loading port, and provide the inspection certificate, including the details of the goods and the percent of the water content, the buyer at the unloading port paid the fees themselves and appointed the CCIC of the People's Republic of China to sample and analyze; the CCIC of the People's Republic of China tested the sample and issued the analysis report within 40 days after the date on the lading bill, and this certificate was regarded as the final payment basis; within five working days after signing the contract, the buyer issued the irrevocable sight letter of credit of 100% contract amount through the international bank with level 1, and the format of signing L/C needed the mutual confirmation of the two parties. Interim payment is 100% of the whole CNF FO value, and the buyer need provide the provisional invoice at the time of paying; the value on the provisional invoice was based on the inspection certificate of the loading port. It must be noted on the lease that the lading bill can be accepted; the full set of clean on board bills of lading, blank heading and the blank endorsement need providing at the time of paying and it should be noted that the freight was paid on the base of the charter party; this contract can only be modified or supplemented through the written explanation, signed by the two parties, except the written form, any partial or whole abandoning of any items in this contract would be ineffective. On May 20, 2011, the buyer and the seller reached a supplementary agreement on the above contract to make some modification on partial items as follows. The total CNF FO value of the 50,000 wet tons of cargoes is 2,925,000 dollars, and the payment instruction is 30% telegraphic transfer and the latest payment date is May 20, 2011; 169,000 dollars belongs to the owner of M.V. JIN YUAN, and the reminder 708,500 dollars belongs to the bank of the seller; 70% of the amount is paid through letter of credit (the credit no is ic384141100147). On the same day, PT Company issued the commercial invoice with the number: 057/KIC/XL/V/2011 to Shandong Xianglong, and it was noted clearly on the invoice that the price of nickel mineral is 36 dollars/ton, and the total amount is 1,800,000 dollars. The freight is 22.5 dollars/ton, totally 1,125,000 dollars. The 30% of the amount, 877,500 dollars, was paid as the deposit, 708,500 dollars to the seller and 169,000 dollars to the ship owner. Shandong Xianglong paid the bank of the seller RMB4,608,792.5 and the bank of the ship owner RMB1,099,345 according to the invoice. On July 29, 2011, the buyer and the seller signed a complementary agreement as for the contract and reached the agreement that the buyer appointed the INTERTEK to inspect the amount and quality of nickel mineral on behalf of CCIC on the unloading port. Due to it that the seller did not prepare the certificate with standard quality at the loading port, the payment was according to the certificate issued by INTERTEK at the unloading port. After M.V. JIN YUAN arrived at Tianjin Port, INTERTEK had an inspection on the revolved nickel mineral and issued the quality certificate on August 11, 2011 and proved that it contained 1.34% nickel, 15.51% iron and 31.47% water. Shandong Xianglong claimed in the indictment that the value of the whole ship of goods was less than 11,329,920 RMB according to the market price of that time, and so PT Company agreed by word of mouth that they would not ask the reminder 70% amount from Shandong Xianglong.

In order to ship the goods involved in this case from Indonesia to Tianjin Port, Lanyang Company and the lessee, PT Company, signed the voyage charter party on April 11, 2011, and agreed about the freight, 23.25 dollars/ton. Lanyang Company and NCS CO., LIMITED signed the voyage charter party on May 18, 2011, and reached the following agreement. The freight is 21.95 dollars/ton (shipping to Rizhao/Luanshan/Lianyungang); 300,000 dollars should be paid to received by the account, designated by the ship owner, before 18:00, May 20, 2011, otherwise the ship owner would have the right to cancel the lease and to claim for compensation for any loss cause by this. All of the freight and loading port demurrage, after deducting the address commission and 270,000 dollars (partially margin) and after finishing loading, should been paid to the designated account within three banking days, but the freight should not be later than the date of unloading. The lading bill should give the note that the freight is paid according to the charter party. Within five banking days after unloading, the reminder 30,000 dollars should be returned to the charterer if there is still reminder after deducting the unloading port demurrage. Whether the charterer pays the freight or not, the ship owner should sign and issue the lading bill that the freight is paid according to the charter party within two days after loading. The charterer does not full pay the freight to the account of the ship owner before the ship arrives, the ship owner have the right to refuse to unload and all of the loss caused by the time delay should be undertaken by the charterer; and the lease should be strictly confidential. NCS CO., LIMITED and Timeplus Company signed the time charter party, and NCS CO., LIMITED and Timeplus Company confirmed the condition of voyage transportation on May 19, 2011. NCS CO., LIMITED confirmed the following during the court hearing. The account to receive the freight from Shandong Xianglong is theirs. It has received the 300,000 dollars as the deposit from Lanyang Company, which was offset in the demurrage cause at the loading port; it has paid Jin Yuan Marine INC. all of the time charter rent, including this voyage.

The 53,952 tons of nickel minerals involved in this case was loaded on M.V. JIN YUAN on July 12, 2011, and the ship agent signed the lading bill with the No, 001/PML-CHN/7/11 on behalf of the captain; it was recorded at the upper right of this bill of lading that it was used together with the lease, at the upper right that the consignor was PT Company and at the bottom left that the freight was paid according to the lease if May 18, 2011. M.V. JIN YUAN arrived at Tianjin Port on July 24, 2011. NCS CO., LIMITED sent a notice to Lanyang Company on July 25, 2011 to claim that it should not be regarded as the rejection to the lien on goods due to Lanyang Company back pay for the demurrage fees and freight at the loading port and it unloaded when the ship was moored at the berth. The goods involved in this case were unloaded at the Hengwei Storage and Service Center in Tianjin Port Free Trade Zone on July 30, 2011. On July 12, 2011, Shandong Xianglong sent the correspondence to all parties of M.V. JIN YUAN to claim that it would manage the cargo delivery procedure after receiving the full set of original bill of lading, send by PT Company. On September 1, 2011, NCS CO., LIMITED sent a lien notice to Shandong Xianglong to claim that the lease had already been incorporated into the lading bill on May 18, 2011, and it has already had a lien on all of the cargoes under the bill of lading items due to not receive the freight and demurrage fees, totally 1,551,822.08 dollars. On December 10, 2011, Tianjing Xingang Customs issued (2011) Jin Xin Guan Chao Zi No.534 Tianjin Xingang Customs Extract Expired Goods Imported Certificate to claim that the goods involved in this case has already been beyond the time limited for the customs clearance, stipulated by the Customs Law of the People's Republic of China and these goods should be taken over and sold off the customs. On November 18, 2011, Shandong Xianglong sent a application about the maintaining the goods of M.V. JIN YUAN that Tianjin Customs should not be disposed and auctioned. On January 9, 2012, NCS CO., LIMITED sent correspondences to Shandong Xianglong to request to arrange the clearance as soon as possible and NCS CO., LIMITED will provide the necessary assistance but Shandong Xianglong rejected the clearance and resold. On December 14, 2014, Tianjin Customs replied the court by e-mail that the nickel minerals involved in this case had already been auctioned legally the price was RMB16,688,131; the balance payment, RMB8,795,964.24, has already been given back to Shandong Xianglong after deducting the customs tax, RMB1,303,137.7 (value-added tax on imports: RMB16,688,131, Delayed Declaration Fee: RMB243,169) and paying the related fees, RMB6,589,029.06 (price valuation fee: RMB98,376.26, the storage charge of

Tianjin Port Free Trade Zone Hengwei Storage and Service Center: RMB642,256, the storage charge of Pengfa Freight Agency Co., Ltd. at Tianjing Development Zone: RMB5,848,396.8).

Shandong Xianglong thought that the wrong lien on goods involved of NCS CO., LIMITED and JINYUAN MARINE INC. caused its loss, and NCS CO., LIMITED thought its lien was established and Shandong Xianglong should pay the remainder freight, therefore the lawsuit came into being.

Additionally, it was found out that NCS CO., LIMITED and JINYUAN MARINE INC. signed the right transfer agreement on November 18, 2011, and JINYUAN MARINE transferred the right and interests under the bill of lading items to NCS CO., LIMITED absolutely and irrepealably; the taking effect of the transferred traced back to the date of lading bill signing; the agreement is applicable to English law. On the same day, JINYUAN MARINE INC. informed Shandong Xianglong of the transferring. G D winter, as the lawyer of Winter Scott Law Firm, provided the following legal advice to the above transfer agreement in Dec, 2014. According to Article 136 of the Britain Law of Property Act 1925, any through the assignor issued by the written, involving the transfer of any debt or other intangible personal property rights and interests of absolute transfer (not just for guarantee), and the debtor Trust, the trustee or other assignor shall have the right to recover the debt or intangible personal property rights and interests of persons issued a written notice of assignment, the method has been effective from the date on which the notice of assignment (subject to equity law takes precedence over the rights of the assignee): a) according to the above debt or intangible personal property rights and legal rights; B) on the debt or intangible personal property rights and interests of all the legal or other remedy; C) without a transferor to help relieve the debt or the power of intangible personal property rights, the transfer agreement.

JINYUAN MARINE INC. was the ship owner of M.V. JIN YUAN, registered in the Republic of Panama.

On May 2, 2013, the court made the judgment that Shandong Xianglong should pay Tianjing Tanghe Logistics Co., Ltd. (hereinafter referred to as Tanghe Company) the forced dispatch and port local charge of the goods involved, RMB2,778,528, in terms of (2012) Jin Hai Fa Shang Chu Zi No.836, and this judgment has already taken effect.

The court holds that this case is the compensation dispute about the wrong lien on goods carried by sea.

1. Law application of this case.

    The court holds that JINYUAN MARINE INC. was the legal person, registered in the Republic of Panama, and this case is case concerning foreign interests. As for the force of the right transferring agreement between JINYUAN MARINE INC. and NCS CO., LIMITED, two parties agreed to apply English law; according to Article 41 of the Law of the Application of Law for Foreign-related Civil Relations of the People's Republic of China, "parties can agree to choose the law to apply to the contracts", therefore the force of this case should be identified by English law; with regard to the other substantial issues, like the legal status and the establishment of lien, etc., of the three parties involved in this case, the three parties chose to apply the Law of the People's Republic of China during the case hearing, and to quote the Law of the People's Republic of China to state proposal and opinion; according to Article 44 of the Law of the Application of Law for Foreign-related Civil Relations of the People's Republic of China, "tortious liability is applicable to the law of the place where an infringing act is committed, but as for the condition that parties share the same habitual residence, the laws at the mutual habitual residence shall apply". After the infringement act, parties agreed to choose applied law according to their agreement, and the above disputes should be dealt with the laws of the People's Republic of China shall apply.

2. The legal status of Shandong Xianglong, NCS CO., LIMITED and JINYUAN MARINE INC.

   Shandong Xianglong, as the buyer of goods involved in this case, holding a full set of original bill of lading, is the receiver. Even though it was recorded in the upper right part of the involved lading bill to make a joint use with the lease, the specific lease was unclear, therefore the carrier involved in this case could not be identified according to the content of the lease. According to Article 78 of the Maritime Code of the People's Republic of China, the right-duty relationship between the carrier and the receiver, lading bill holder is identified according the regulation of bill of lading; Shandong Xianglong, as the holder of the full set of original bill of lading involved in this case, lodged a complaint based on the bill of lading, therefore the bill of lading involved in this case constituted the final evidence for its recording content. The recording of the involved lading bill was signed by the ship agent on behalf of the captain, who was in the employ of JINYUAN MARINE INC., and according to Article 72 Paragraph 2 of the Maritime Code of the People's Republic of China, the bill of lading may be signed by a person authorized by the carrier. A bill of lading signed by the Master of the ship carrying the goods is deemed to have been signed on behalf of the carrier.

   JINYUAN MARINE INC., and NCS CO., LIMITED signed the right transferring agreement to transfer the rights to charge the related funds, under bill of lading items involved in this case and the other rights related to the lading bill to NCS CO., LIMITED. The agreement of the transfer agreement is applied to English law; according to the identified English law, this transfer law is valid, therefore NCS CO., LIMITED gained the right to charge the freight, demurrage fee and to have the lien on goods under this lading bill, and this right took effect from the date of bill's signing. Shandong Xianglong claimed that NCS CO., LIMITED had paid JINYUAN MARINE INC. all the rent, including the involved voyage, therefore JINYUAN MARINE INC. had no right to charge the freight and lost the basis of transferring right. The court holds that JINYUAN MARINE INC., as the carrier under the lading bill involved in this case, have the right to charge the freight from the consignor or the receiver under the bill of lading items; as for this case, the obligor of the freight payment is PT Company, and NCS CO., LIMITED's payment of rent for JINYUAN MARINE INC., did not mean to replace PT Company to pay the freight for JINYUAN MARINE INC., therefore, JINYUAN MARINE INC. still has the right to charge freight from PT Company, and the court does not support Shandong Xianglong's claims.

To sum up, according to the record of the lading bill involved, the consignor is PT Company, and the carrier is JINYUAN MARINE INC., and NCS CO., LIMITED gained the right to charge the freight and have lien on goods from JINYUAN MARINE INC. through rights transferring, and Shandong Xianglong is the receiver.

3. Whether should Shandong Xianglong undertake the responsibility of freight payment.

It was agreed in the contract between Shandong Xianglong and the seller, PT, that the price term is CNF and the amount will be 100% paid by L/C, and the bill of the transporting cargoes is charter party one and it will be noted that the freight will be paid according to the charter-party. Later both of the buyer and the seller modified the payment in the supplementary agreement to the following: 30% of the amount will be paid through telegraphic transfer, and PT instructed Shandong Xianglong to pay the partial freight, USD169,000 directly for NCS CO., LIMITED and pay the left 70% through L/C. It can be seen from the above agreement that Shandong Xianglong has already known the freight under the bill involved in case being paid according the lease. Bill of this case was issued after checked and recognized correct by the ship owner and the agent of PT, that is to say that PT has confirmed the terms on the till and Shandong Xianglong accepted the charter party bill of the contract and the term, the freight being paid according to the lease was noted on the bill, which indicated that Shandong Xianglong accepted that the freight payment term of lease of May 18, 2011 was incorporated into the bill involved in the case. The court support NCS CO., LIMITED's claim to incorporate the freight payment term of the lease of May 18, 2011 into the bill involved in the case.

According to the Maritime Code of the People's Republic of China, as the certification of the transporting contract, bill has a binding effect on both of the carrier and the bill owner. The freight payment term in the lease of May 18, 2011 has already been incorporated into the bill, so the agreement of this term that the ship owner have the right to refuse unloading, bringing the binding effect on both sides of the lading bill, if the charterer does not fully pay the freight before the ship's arriving; that is to say that, the carrier can refuse to deliver the goods to the lading bill holder according the above. Even though the carrier have the right of defense, there is not any agreement in the term of shifting the freight payment obligation to the lading bill holder; what's more, there is also an agreement in the price term in the purchase and sale agreement of the cargoes involved that PT shoulder the responsibility to pay the freight; therefore, the court holds that Shandong Xianglong does not have the obligation to pay the freight involved in this case.

4. Whether does NCS CO., LIMITED have the lien on the cargoes involved.
   According to Article 87 of the Maritime Code of the People's Republic of China, "the carrier can have the retention of the cargoes within reasonable limits under the circumstance that the freight, which should be paid to the carrier, general average contribution, demurrage charge, the necessary fees paid for the goods by the carrier and the other fees, which should be paid for the carrier, were not paid off and were not given appropriate assurance". On the basis of this stipulation, the elements of the lien include the following: 1. Creditors legitimately possesses the debtor's movables; 2. It has been the amortization period for the creditor's rights but the debtor fails to fulfill its debt. In terms of this case, according to the stipulation about the freight payment in the lading bill involved in this case, PT should pay all the freight within three bank working days, July 15, 2011, after the cargoes shipment; NCS CO., LIMITED had legal possession of the cargoes involved when it detained those cargoes on July 25, 2011; PT did not fully pay the freight and it was the amortization period for creditor's rights, therefore the key of the lien establishment is whether PT is the titleholder of the cargoes involved in this case. The court believes that, according to stipulation, in Article 23 of the Property Law of the People's Republic of China, that the creation or transfer of the property right of the movables shall become valid as of the time of their delivery, unless otherwise provided for by law, the cargoes involved in this case, which need to be transported to Tianjin Port of the People's Republic of China from Indonesia by sea, belongs to the movable property, and the carrier issued a full set of original bill of lading at the lading port after receiving the cargoes and the seller, PT, took the physical delivery by means of transferring the lading bill.
   According to Article 26 of the Property Law of the People's Republic of China, the ownership of cargoes involved should be operated in terms of draft delivery, and the time, when the ownership is transferred from the seller, PT, to Shandong Xianglong, is that, when Shandong Xianglong receives the full set of original bill of lading; due to the fact that Shandong Xianglong could not present the evidence to prove the exact time, when they received the lading bill, therefore the court determined it as the time, when Shandong Xianglong reminded the carrier to take delivery of goods, that is August 22, 2011, and the ownership of the cargoes involved in this case was transferred from the seller, PT, to Shandong Xianglong till August 22,2011, and PT was still the owner of the cargoes involved in this case till July 25, 2011. To sum up, NCS CO., LIMITED's lien on goods involved in this case confirms to the establishment essentials of lien, so the lien was valid, and therefore the court does not support Shandong Xianglong's claim that NCS CO., LIMITED and JINYUAN MARINE INC. caused its loss due to the wrong lien. As for whether Shandong Xianglong's prosecution to JINYUAN MARINE INC. is beyond the prescribed period for litigation, the court won't confirm any more since it does not affect the results of this case.

5. The amount of preferred payment under the condition that NCS performs the lien.

The lien is the legal security interest. According to Article 114 of the Interpretation of the Supreme People's Court on Certain Issues concerning the Application of the Guaranty Law of the People's Republic of China, "Article 64, 80, 87, 91 and 93 under this law apply to lien". According to Article 80, "when the pledge is lost, destroyed or expropriated, the mortgagee will have the priority to be paid for the insurance, indemnity or compensation". Since the cargoes involved in the case has been in the forced auction of Tianjin Customs, NCS CO., LIMITED has a priority right to be repaid for the auction within its power.

According the recordation for the lading bill, there is 53,952 tons of cargoes involved in the case and the it was agreed that the freight was USD21.95/ton in the freight payment term of the lease on May 18, 2011, therefore the total freight of the cargoes involved in the case is USD1,184,246.4, and after the deduction of paid amount of USD169,000, the balance is USD1,015,246.4. Even though NCS CO., LIMITED claimed to increase USD1.5/ton for the freight due to the change of port, it could not provide the valid evidence to prove that, therefore the court did not support this claim. Lanyang has paid USD300,000 for the deposit, but the demurrage charge at loading port has already been higher than the deposit, so the deposit cannot be used to offset the freight. Above all, the freight amount, which NCS CO., LIMITED was paid preferentially after performing the lien, should be USD1,015,246.4. Now, the nickel minerals has already been auctioned by the customs, and the auction balance, after deducting the relevant costs, was RMB8,795,964.24; as for the port charges of RMB2,778,528 including the forced dispatch money at Tianjin Port of cargoes involved in the case paid for Tanghe by Shandong Xianglong and the necessary expenses paid for the retained property, they should be paid from the auction firstly; therefore, the surplus auction of the cargoes involved in the case was RMB6,017,436.24. According to the exchange rate, being 1:6.1251, between the U.S. dollar and the Chinese Renminbi of the date, when Tianjin Customs reply the court, NCS CO., LIMITED's freight of 1,015,246.4 dollars, equivalence renminbi 6,218,485.7 yuan, is higher than the surplus auction of the cargoes, so NCS CO., LIMITED can has a priority to be paid for only in amount of RMB6,017,436.24. Since Tianjin Customs has already paid the surplus auction for Shandong Xianglong, Shandong Xianglong should paid RMB6,017,436.24 for NCS CO., LIMITED.

Hereby, according to Article 41 and 44 of the Law of the Application of Law for Foreign-related Civil Relations of the People's Republic of China, Article 136 of the Britain Law of Property Act 1925, Article 78 and 98 of the Maritime Code of the People's Republic of China, Article 80 and 114 of the Interpretation of the Supreme People's Court on Certain Issues concerning the Application of the Guaranty Law of the People's Republic of China, Article 64 Paragraph 1 of the Civil Procedure Law of the People's Republic of China, the judgment is as follows:

1. The Plaintiff (the counterclaim Defendant) Shandong Xianglong should pay RMB6,017,436.24 as the auction for the Defendant (the counterclaim Plaintiff) within 10 days after the judgment comes into effect;
2. Reject the claims of the Plaintiff (the counterclaim Defendant) Shandong Xianglong.
3. Reject other counterclaims of the Defendant (the counterclaim Plaintiff) NCS.

If the paying duties during the specified period according to this judgment are not performed, the interest on debt during the period of delaying in performance should be doubled according to Article 253 of the Civil Procedure Law of the People's Republic of China.

Court acceptance fee of this claim in amount of 59,625 yuan, shall be born by the Plaintiff (the counterclaim Defendant) Shandong Xianglong. Court acceptance fee of the counterclaim in amount of 34,722 yuan, shall be compensated preferentially from the realized lien by the Defendant (the counterclaim Plaintiff) NCS.

If not satisfy with the judgment, Shandong Xianglong can submit petition for appeal and its copies in octuplicate to the court and lodge an appeal to the Tianjin High People's Court within 15 day before the day when the judgments is delivered; and NCS and Jinyuan Marine Inc. can also do the same action within 30 days. And they should pay the appeal cost to the Tianjin High People's Court according to the partial amount of arresting the judgment of first instance within 7 days after the submitting the petition for appeal (bank of deposit: Tiancheng Branch of Agriculture Bank of China 02-200501012001686; account name: the finance section of Tianjin High People's Court). If overdue, the appeal will be withdrawn automatically.

Presiding Judge: CHEN Shunping
Acting Judge: ZHANG Lina
Acting Judge: HU Yingjie

June 18, 2015

Clerk: MA Jihai

Guangzhou Maritime Court
Civil Judgment

Shanghai Eastern Shipping Material Co., Ltd.
v.
Beihai Honghai Shipping Co., Ltd. et al.

(2009) Guang Hai Fa Chu Zi No.97

Related Case(s) this is the judgment of first instance and the judgment of second instance is on page 891.

Cause(s) of Action 193. Dispute over liability for ship collision damage.

Headnote one of two ships involved in both-to-blame collision held entitled to limit its liability for cargo damage.

Summary The Plaintiff's goods were totally lost after the ship on which they were being carried, M.V. "Xinghai 668" collided with M.V. "OOCL EUROPE". The Court held that M.V. "Xinghai 668" was 40% responsible and M.V. "OOCL EUROPE" 60%. The owner of M.V. "Xinghai 668" was entitled to limit its liability. The bareboat charterer of M.V. "OOCL EUROPE" was ordered to pay its 60% share, 9,575,098.34 RMB, in full. The 40% share of the owner of M.V. "Xinghai 668" was reduced from 6,383,398.90 RMB to 2,642,925.24 RMB by virtue of the owner's right to limit its liability.

Judgment

The Plaintiff: Shanghai Eastern Shipping Material Co., Ltd.
Domicile: #3, 4160 Shangnan Road, Pudong District, Shanghai.
Legal representative: XU Hongyi, director.
Agent *ad litem*: WU Jinjun, clerk.
Agent *ad litem*: LUAN Jianping, lawyer of Shanghai Gong & Mao Law Firm.

The Defendant: Beihai Honghai Shipping Co., Ltd.
Domicile: C Building, Fl.9, Panorama Tower, Beihai Avenue, Haicheng District, Beihai, Zhuang Autonomous Region, Guangxi.
Legal representative: CHEN Feijing, general manager.
Agent *ad litem*: CHEN Yusheng, lawyer of Guangdong Yonghang Law Firm.
Agent *ad litem*: WANG Silv, lawyer of Guangdong Yonghang Law Firm.

The Defendant: Orient Overseas Container Line (U.K.) Limited
Domicile: Fl.33, Harbor Center, No.25 Harbor Road, Wanchai, Hong Kong S.A.R.
Legal representative: DAI Shengjian, Chairman.
Agent *ad litem*: CHEN Xiangyong, lawyer of Guangdong Wang Jing & Co.
Agent *ad litem*: CAO Yanghui, lawyer of Guangdong Wang Jing & Co.

With respect to the case arising from dispute over liability for ship collision damage filed by the Plaintiff, Shanghai Eastern Shipping Material Co., Ltd. against the Defendants, Shanghai Hailian Transportation Co., Ltd. (hereinafter referred to as Hailian Company), Beihai Honghai Shipping Co., Ltd. (hereinafter referred to as Honghai Company), Tiane National Leasing Co., Ltd., and Orient Overseas Container Line (U.K.) Limited (hereinafter referred to as Orient U.K.), the court, after accepting the case, organized the collegiate panel according to law. Since the hearing of the case must base on the trial result of another case concerning the dispute over damage compensation arising from ship collision, the court made a Civil Ruling (2009) Guang Hai Fa Chu Zi No.97-3 on May 26, 2009 and discontinued the action. The stay of the action was eliminated on March 12, 2012 and this case resumed. On May 23, 2012, the Plaintiff applied for the withdrawal of claims against Hailian Company, and Tiane National Leasing Co., Ltd. The court ruled its permission. On April 16 and June 11, 2012, the court summoned all parties concerned to exchange evidence before hearing and held an open trial. WU Jinjun and LUAN Jianping as agents *ad litem* of the Plaintiff, CHEN Yusheng as agent *ad litem* of the Defendant Honghai Company, CHEN Xiangyong and CAO Yanghui as agents *ad litem* of the Defendant Orient U.K., attended the first hearing; WU Jinjun and LUAN Jianping as agents *ad litem* of the Plaintiff, CHEN Yusheng as agent *ad litem* of the Defendant Honghai Company, CAO Yanghui as agent *ad litem* of the Defendant Orient U.K., attended the second hearing. The case has been concluded.

The Plaintiff alleged that: on August 6, 2008, the Plaintiff signed a transport protocol with Hailian Company. The Plaintiff entrusted Hailian Company to transport 6,421.981 tons of steel plates by partial shipment from Zhangjiagang Harbor to the wharf of China State Shipbuilding Corporation of Guangzhou Longxue (hereinafter referred as Longxue Corporation). On October 16, 2008, the Defendant Honghai Company signed and issued the Water Freight Bill and recognized the acceptance of carriage by the subordinate M.V. "Xinhai 668" with 209 pieces of steel plates weighing 1,780.704 tons altogether. On October 21, 2008, while sailing for Guangzhou Harbor, M.V. "Xinhai 668" was crashed by the Defendant Orient U.K.'s M.V. "OOCL EUROPE" which was in bareboat charter period. The ship collision caused M.V. "Xinhai 668" and its consignments to be sunk and brought about huge financial loss. According to the final judgment by Guangdong High People's Court, the cognizance of involved ship collision was that the Defendant Honghai Company took responsibility of 40% and the Defendant Orient U.K. took responsibility of 60%. The Plaintiff requested the court to adjudge the two Defendants to compensate the Plaintiff RMB16,458,186.83 and its interests based on the proportion of each responsibility (interests shall take effect from October 21, 2008 to the payment day prescribed herein at the loan interest rate of working capital of enterprises for the same period as published by the People's Bank of China). The court hearing fee, property preservation application fee, registration of claims application fee and etc. shall be born by the two Defendants.

In the court hearing, the Plaintiff requested that the financial losses shall be changed to RMB16,260,865.40 including RMB15,958,497.24 as payment of goods in this case, RMB293,816.16 as transportation expenses and RMB8,552 as insurance expenses. Other claims remained unchanged.

The Plaintiff submitted the following evidential documents within the time limit for burden of proof: 1. Transportation Protocol; 2. Water Freight Bill; 3. Receipt; 4. B/L of Products; 5. Detail Packing List of Manufacture; 6. Notice of Loss and Damage; 7. Sales Contract; 8. Procurement Contract; 9. Income Invoice; 10. Written Warranty; 11. Statement of Cargo Ownership Transfer; 12. Official Letter from Hong Kong Marine Department; 13. Correspondences between the Plaintiff and the Defendant Honghai Company; 14. Correspondences between the Plaintiff and Hong Kong Marine Department; 15. Longxue Company's Statement; 16. Ship Registration from North Sea Marine Bureau; 17. Prepayment Insurance Indemnity Protocol; 18. The Second Prepayment Insurance Indemnity Protocol; 19. Insurance Certificate.

The Defendant Honghai Company defended that: 1. since the Plaintiff did not submit any evidence to affirm the ownership of the subject cargo damage, it shall be requested to overrule the Plaintiff's claim; 2. the Plaintiff did not provide sufficient evidence to prove the alleged damage and loss hereby it shall be requested to overrule the application of the subject prosecution; 3. in respect to the cargo value, the Plaintiff submitted value add tax invoice. If the subject damage and loss can be verified, 17% of the sum in value added tax invoice shall be deducted; 4. with the aforesaid views no changed, Honghai Company shall be entitled to the limitation of liability for maritime compensation which shall not exceed the amount of RMB2,642,925.24. The reasonable expenses for underwater detection, salvaging the wreck and the subject cargo shall be deducted from the limitation of liability pro rata.

The Defendant Honghai Company submitted the following evidential documents within the time limit for burden of proof: 1. Underwater Detection Protocol signed by the Defendant Honghai Company and Shenzhen Xinlong Diving Engineering Co., Ltd. (hereinafter referred as Xinlong Company), Underwater Detection Report, and the Payment Voucher; 2. Protocol and Payment Voucher for Salvaging the Wreck and the Subject Cargo; 3. Correspondences among the Defendant Honghai Company, Hong Kong Marine Department and etc.; 4. Underwater Detection Protocol signed by the Defendant Honghai Company and Guangzhou Salvage Bureau, Underwater Detection Report, Payment Voucher and the Quotation; 5. correspondences between the Defendant and the Plaintiff.

The Defendant Orient U.K. defended that: 1. the Plaintiff did not submit cargo payment voucher and thereby it was not entitled to claim for compensation; 2. the primary and immediate cause was gross negligence of M.V. "Xinghai 668" concerning the equipment of the crew. It further caused the collision accident. Although the Guangdong High People's Court has made a final judgment on the dispute arising from the two vessels' liability proportion, with no true evidence submitted by the Defendant Honghai Company, the court did not find out the truth and mistakenly recognized the liability in respect to M.V. "Xinghai 668". With regard to the cargo loss and damage caused by the ship collision, the whole liability shall be born by the Defendant Honghai Company; 3. the amount of the subject loss applied by the Plaintiff shall not be approved. On the one hand, the Plaintiff did not submit the Payment Voucher of the subject cargo to the seller. On the other hand, the Plaintiff's claim for compensation was about RMB16.3 million. However, pursuant to the Defendant Honghai Company's evidence, salvaging cargo only needed RMB5 million. The Plaintiff did not fulfill the obligation to reduce the losses. Therefore, the Plaintiff shall not be entitled to claim for total loss and shall claim for compensation of RMB5 million at most.

The Defendant Orient U.K. submitted the following evidential documents within the time limit for burden of proof: 1. Registration Certificate of M.V. "OOCL EUROPE", Logbook, Engine Logbook, Maritime Investigation Report from Hong Kong Marine Department and etc.; 2. correspondences of Hong Kong Marine Department; 3. Correspondences from the Plaintiff requiring the Defendant Honghai Company to salvage the subject cargo; 4. Quotation Letter from Guangzhou Salvage Bureau; 5. Salvaging Cargo and Wrecks Protocol signed by the Defendant Honghai Company and Xinglong Company.

Upon the adducing evidence and cross-examinations by the Plaintiff and Defendants, the court ascertains the following facts through investigation:

1. Transactions of Ships involved in the Accident

The Plaintiff stated that the subject goods, 209 pieces of steel plates, were purchased by the Plaintiff and China's Shipbuilding Industry Materials Co., Ltd. (East China) which was entrusted by the Plaintiff. The subject goods were purchased from Jiangsu Shagang Group Co., Ltd. (hereinafter referred to as Shagang Company). The Plaintiff paid RMB15,958,497.24 for 209 pieces of steel plates, 1,780.704 tons in total. The Plaintiff therewith sold the subject goods, in total RMB16,458,186.83, to Longxue Company. The Plaintiff therefor submitted Procurement Contract, Receipts Voucher, Written Warranty and etc.

The foregoing evidence recorded: on June 6 and July 7, 2008, the Plaintiff as the demander signed *Products Purchase & Sales Contract* No.D080608 and No. K0808I2 with the supplier Shagang Company. They made an agreement that the demander purchased respectively 1,296.291 tons and 1,656.225 tons from the supplier; the sums were respectively RMB11,295,653.15 and RMB14,653,695.90; the demander needed pick up goods in Shagang Company. Each Products Purchase & Sales Contract attached *Products Purchase & Sales Lists* including Products Specializations and models, Products Pieces, Weight, Unit Price, Sums and etc. On October 19, 2008, Shagang Company issued the VAT invoice for RMB7,146,815.38 including the subject 7 pieces of steel plates, in total 37.694 tons and in the amount of RMB342,891.25. On August 28 and October 8, 2008, the Plaintiff as the demander signed the Industrial and Mineral Products Purchase & Sales Contract with the supplier China's Shipbuilding Industry Materials Co., Ltd.

(East China). They made an agreement that the demander purchased respectively 2,021.013 tons and 1,448.452 tons from the supplier; the sums were respectively RMB18,097,982.30 and RMB13,385,130.40; the demander needed pick up goods in Shagang Company. Each *Products Purchase & Sales Contract* attached the Products Purchase & Sales Lists including Products Specializations and models, Products Pieces, Weight, Unit Price, Sums and etc. each contract recorded the subject steel plates 195 pieces and 7 pieces. On November 18, 2008 and on March 17, 2009, China's Shipbuilding Industry Materials Co., Ltd. (East China) issued the VAT invoices to the Plaintiff. The 13 VAT invoices, with the No.01615967—01615979, were issued for the subject 195 pieces of steel plates, totally weighing 1,673.779 tons and in the amount of RMB14,973,626.93. The VAT invoice No.00199267 recorded the subject 7 pieces of steel plates, totally weighing 69.231 tons and in the amount of RMB641,979.06. The foresaid 209 pieces of steel plates totaled 1780.704 tons and amounted to RMB15,958,497.24.

On June 6, July 3, August 7, and September 18, 2008, the Plaintiff as the supplier signed 4 pieces of *Products Purchase & Sales Contract* with the demander Longxue Company; the contract number was 07GLS230—01C155, 07GLS230—01C158, 07GLS230—01C163 and 07GLS230—01C172 respectively corresponding to the weight of 1,296.291 tons, 1,656.225 tons, 2,106.578 tons and 1,443.452 tons; it respectively corresponded to the amount of RMB11,691,021.91, RMB14,993,222.05, RMB19,446,850.57 and RMB13,803,142.22. Each *Products Purchase & Sales Contract* attached *Products Purchase & Sales Lists* including Products Specializations and models, Weight, Products Pieces, Unit Price, Sums and etc. In the contracts, the subject 209 pieces of steel plates were sold to Longxue Company with the total sum of RMB16,458,186.83.

On April 20, 2012, Longxue Company's statements were verified by the court: the Company signed the contract No.07GLS230—01C155, No.07GLS230—01C158, No.07GLS230—01C163, No.07GLS230—01C172 with the Plaintiff. Pursuant to the third article in the 4 pieces of Purchases & Sales Contract, the demander's specified wharf for delivery points and delivery means referred to the Wharf of Longxue Company; both sides fulfilled the 4 pieces of *Purchases & Sales Contract*. With regard to the 209 pieces of steel plates, totaling 1,780.704 tons, loaded in the wreck "Xinghai 668", Longxue Company had no liability. In the court hearing, the agents *ad litem* from the Plaintiff claimed that the Plaintiff rearranged the supply of goods to the Longxue Company after the subject accident.

The two Defendants did not file the objection to the foregoing evidence and the content of the evidence can be mutually verified. The foregoing evidence and facts were recognized by the collegiate panel.

2. Cargo Transport involved in the Accident

On August 6, 2008, the Plaintiff signed the transport protocol with Hailian Company. They made an agreement that the Plaintiff entrusted Hailian Company to ship the 6,421.981 tons of steel plates, including the subject goods, by partial shipment from Zhangjiagang to the Longxue Company's wharf. The whole waterage were RMB165 per ton (including pilotage dues, insurance expenses and freights). When goods arrived at the Longxue Company's wharf, the Plaintiff would pay all the waterage to Hailian Company within one month.

On October 15, 2008, the subject goods started to be loaded into M.V. "Xinghai 668" on Shagang Company's wharf. Pursuant to the product bills of lading issued by Shagang Company, it recorded various specialization and weight of the goods. Among all the bills of lading, 4 pieces of steel plates with 19.349 tons in No.6880 B/L, 3 pieces of steel plates with 18.3 tons in No.6882 B/L, 195 pieces of steel plates with 1,637.779 tons in No.6860 B/L, 7 pieces of steel plates with 69.231 tons in No.6887 B/L. The 4 pieces of bills of lading totally recorded the 209 pieces of steel plates with the amount of 1,780.704 tons. One bill of lading was handwritten with the content "209 pieces of steel plates were actually received, without scratching and buckling, by GAO Huaqiang". The Defendant Honghai Company recognized that GAO Huaqiang was one of Honghai Company's staff. Shagang Company issued 30 pieces of detailed packing lists. The contents including cargo names, specialization, weight and etc. were according to the product bills of lading.

On October 16, 2008, the Defendant as carrier signed and issued the Water Freight Bill. It recorded that the Plaintiff as the shipper, Longxue Company as the consignee, goods, 209 pieces of steel plates totaling 1,780.704 tons, were shipped to Longxue Company's wharf. In the Water Freight Bill, there was the handwritten content "the specialization of the wide and thick plates can be seen on B/L"; the Defendant Honghai Company stamped the seal of M.V. "Xinghai 668" at the point of the carrier's signature.

On November 21, 2008, the Defendant Honghai Company issued the Notice of Loss to Shanghai Branch of China Pacific Property Insurance Co., Ltd. (hereinafter referred as Pacific Shanghai Branch). It was stated that, on October 17, 2008, M.V. "Xinghai 668" shipped about 1780 tons of steel plates from Zhangjiagang to Guangzhou Longxue Shipyard; around 0600 on October 21, the vessel was collided to sink by the foreign vessel near the Hong Kong waters; the Defendant requested the Insurance Company should send members to make an examination.

Pursuant to the foregoing evidence, the Plaintiff held that the subject goods were actually accepted for carriage by M.V. "Xinghai 668" subordinate to the Defendant Honghai Company and on October 21, 2008 sank with the vessel in the subject collision accident. However, the two Defendants held that the foresaid evidence cannot fully prove M.V. "Xinghai 668" actually accepted for carriage of the subject goods. The collegiate panel held that the evidence including Products Purchase & Sales Protocol, Products Purchase & Sales Lists, Product Bills of Lading, Factory Detailed Packing Lists, Water Freight Bill and etc. can form the complete evidence chain; and the evidence can affirm that the Plaintiff purchased the subject 209 pieces of steel plates in number of 1,780.704 tons and the goods were loaded into M.V. "Xinghai 668"; also, the Notice of Loss issued by the Defendant Honghai Company verified the subject goods were loaded by M.V. "Xinghai 668". Hence, the defense that the Plaintiff did not fully prove M.V. "Xinghai 668" actual acceptance for the subject goods' carriage cannot stand.

3. Cargo Insurance involved in the Accident

Pursuant to the insurance certificate of domestic waterway and landway cargo transportation submitted by the Plaintiff: on October 17, 2008, the Plaintiff as the insurer, Hailian Company as the Policy holder, requested Pacific Shanghai Branch to insure the comprehensive risk for the subject goods pursuant to the domestic waterway and landway cargo transportation insurance clause (February 2, 1995). The insurance amount totaled RMB10,690,000 and its premiums were RMB8,552. After the insurance accident, on May 4 and October 26, 2009, Pacific Shanghai Branch respectively prepaid the insurance indemnities RMB2 million and RMB2.5 million; the two parties respectively signed the Prepaid Insurance Indemnity Protocol and the Second Prepaid Insurance Indemnity Protocol; since the specific loss amount of the subject goods cannot be confirmed and the Plaintiff purchased the substitute cargo which caused the extra expenses, the Plaintiff requested the Pacific Shanghai Branch to prepay the insurance indemnity. For this, the two parties reached the following agreement: 1. Pacific Shanghai Branch shall respectively prepay the Plaintiff the insurance indemnities RMB2 million and RMB2.5 million within 10 days after the agreement took effect; 2. the two parties jointly confirmed that the Plaintiff shall firstly bring a lawsuit against the responsible party in order to claim for compensation. Pacific Shanghai Branch's prepayment for the insurance indemnity shall not affect the Plaintiff to exercise the lawsuit claim of the subject goods against the responsible party. The loss amount of the Plaintiff in the accident shall be confirmed according to the court's binding judgment or the two parties' negotiation and rules from the insurance policy No.ASHH101043080001015N; due to the Plaintiff's underinsurance, if the Plaintiff's loss in this accident finally cannot be fully compensated, as for the unreceived compensation, Pacific Shanghai Branch shall undertake the insurance liability pursuant to the insurance policy agreement and the proportion of the insured amount and the cargo value; if the Plaintiff's fault enlarged the loss or could not receive compensation by recourse, Pacific Shanghai Branch shall have right to deduct the relevant indemnity. 3. Within 30 days from the Plaintiff's receiving all the indemnity from the responsible party, the two parties shall complete the settlement of the insurance indemnity and shall settle the indemnity with the difference based on the settlement result; 4. the Plaintiff shall confirm and promise to further contact with Hong Kong Marine Department and strive to gain the permission of salvaging goods alone; after gaining the permission from Hong Kong Marine Department, the Plaintiff shall actively implement salvage assessment and the salvage of cargo in order to reduce cargo loss. The Plaintiff confirmed that, after signing the two pieces of Prepaid Insurance Indemnity Protocol with Pacific Shanghai Branch, had received the prepayment of insurance indemnities from Pacific Shanghai Branch with the total number of RMB4.5 million.

4. Hearing the Liability on Ship Collision

With respect to the dispute over damage compensation arising from ship collision between M.V. "Xinghai 668" and M.V. "OOCL EUROPE", the Defendant

Honghai Company filed an action to request OOCL UK as the bareboat charterer of M.V. "OOCL EUROPE" to assume the compensation liability; Orient U.K. and other company instituted a counter claim against the Defendant Honghai Company with the (2009) Guang Hai Fa Chu Zi No.4 and (2009) Guang Hai Fa Chu Zi No.292. According to the first instance by the court, the Defendant Honghai Company shouldered responsibility of 40% on the collision accident and the Defendant Orient U.K. shouldered responsibility of 60%. The Defendant Orient U. K. refused the first instance and then lodged an appeal. During the second instance, the Defendant Orient U.K. filed an application to request the Guangdong High People's Court to obtain evidence material from Guangdong Marine Safety Administration. The application requested the court to draw up the verification that it was part of the unreal evidence, concerning the collision accident, submitted by the Defendant Honghai Company that misdirected the court's affirmation on the accident liability. According to the fact that the Defendant Orient U.K. had submitted the confirmation of evidence completion in the first trial, Guangdong High People's Court refused the Defendant Orient U.K.'s application on obtaining evidence. On December 20, 2011, Guangdong High People's Court made a Civil Ruling (2010) Yue Gao Fa Min Si Zhong Zi No.86 and No.87 and the appeal shall be dismissed and the original judgment shall be affirmed.

5. Limitation Fund for Maritime Claims Liability Applied by the Defendant Honghai Company and Property Preservation Applied by the Plaintiff

On February 11, 2009, the Defendant Honghai Company applied to the court for constituting the limitation fund for maritime claims liability; after accepting and hearing the application, on May 19, 2009, the court made a civil ruling (2009) Guang Hai Fa Chu Zi No.116 which permitted that the Defendant Honghai Company should constitute limitation fund for liability pursuant to the SDRs limitation of the Article 249 and 832; based on the date of the accident on October 21, 2008, the exchange rate of SDRs to US Dollar shall be calculated and finally equivalent to RMB2,642,925.24. The Defendant Orient U.K. refused the judgment and then lodged an appeal. Guangdong High People's Court made a civil ruling (2009) Yue Gao Fa Min Si Zhong Zi No.267; the appeal shall be dismissed and the original judgment shall be affirmed. However, the Defendant Honghai Company did not constitute the limitation fund for maritime claims liability pursuant to the effective judgment in the court.

In the period of the announcement published by the court on the Defendant's constituting limitation fund for maritime claims liability, the Plaintiff handled the registration formalities of creditor's right and rendered its registration fee in sum of RMB1,000. Besides, after the Defendant Honghai Company did not constitute the limitation fund for maritime claims liability pursuant to the effective judgment in the court, the Plaintiff successively submitted 4 times the application to the court for property preservation; the court decided that the Plaintiff's application for property preservation shall be permitted and the Defendant Honghai Company's handling ownership disposal formalities shall be forbidden. The Plaintiff therefor rendered the property preservation application fee in sum of RMB20,000.

6. M.V. "Xinghai 668" and goods Salvage Involved in This Case

After M.V. "Xinghai 668" sank, the Defendant Honghai Company signed *Shipwreck Detection Protocol* with Xinlong Company on December 1, 2008. Pursuant to the Protocol, Xinlong Company was entrusted to conduct detection of M.V. "Xinghai 668" sinking near the Hong Kong East Lamma Channel, confirm the situation of the shipwreck and goods and submit detection report. The detection fee was RMB85,000 by appointment.

On December 11, 2008, Hong Kong Youli Engineering Co., Ltd. submitted *Detection Report* on M.V. "Xinghai 668".

On February 8, 2009, the Defendant Honghai Company signed the shipwreck and goods salvage protocol with Xinlong Company. Pursuant to the protocol, Xinlong Company was entrusted to conduct the salvage of M.V. "Xinghai 668" and goods. The lump sum of shipwreck salvage was RMB2,900,000. The lump sum of goods salvage, freshwater flushing and shipping to Longxue Wharf was RMB5,000,000.

Pursuant to the correspondences between the Defendant Honghai Company and Hong Kong Marine Department, the Defendant Honghai Company filed extension for several times towards Hong Kong Marine Department in the process of entrusting Xinlong Company to salvage the shipwreck and the subject goods.

Agents *ad litem* of the Defendant Honghai Company claimed that since Xinlong Company was unfamiliar with the procedure of the relevant license application for salvaging in Hong Kong Waters and underestimated the difficulties of salvage, finally the salvage of shipwrecks and sunken objects was not implemented. Afterwards, the Defendant Honghai Company inquired Guangzhou Salvage Bureau of the salvage expenses for the shipwrecks and the subject goods. Guangzhou Salvage Bureau quoted that the salvage expenses were in sum of RMB9,180,000 if it entered the areas before the date of January 25, 2009; the salvage expenses were in sum of RMB8,380,000 if it entered the areas after the March of 2009. Since incapable to pay the mentioned expenses, the Defendant Honghai Company did not sign the salvage agreement with Guangzhou Salvage Bureau.

However, the Plaintiff claimed that the Defendant Honghai Company owned several ships and its incapability to pay the salvage expenses was not true. The delay of the salvage caused the entire loss of the subject goods. Therefore, the Defendant Honghai Company should shoulder the full liability and not be entitled to enjoy the limitation liability for maritime claims.

The Defendant Honghai Company recognized that M.V. "Xinghai 668" and the subject goods were not salvaged until the hearing the case.

The members of collegiate panel reached an agreement that: this case is a dispute over damage compensation arising from ship collision related with Hong Kong. Pursuant to Article 1 of the Some provisions of the Supreme People's Court on the Scope of Cases to be Entertained by Maritime Courts, this case is regarded to the scope of maritime court's specific jurisdiction. The subject collision accident took place at the junction of Guangzhou Waters and Hong Kong Waters. Pursuant to Article 241 of the Civil Procedure Law of the People's Republic of China, the court has the jurisdiction to this case. Pursuant to Article 273 of the Maritime Code of the People's Republic of China, this case shall apply the law of the People's Republic of China to treat the substantive dispute.

The issues of the subject dispute mainly include that: the suit qualification of the Plaintiff; whether the Defendant Honghai Company shall be entitled to enjoy the limitation liability for maritime claims; whether the insurance company's prepayment to the Plaintiff for the insurance indemnity shall be deducted from the Plaintiff's claims.

In respect to the suit qualification of the Plaintiff, the facts in this case show that the Plaintiff is the seller and shipper of the subject goods and entitled to claim for goods loss by law because the goods have been damaged on passage. Longxue Company, as the Consignee, makes it clear that it is not the Obligee of the subject goods. Hence, the two Defendants' claims that the Plaintiffis not the obligee of the subject goods do not base on facts and law and shall not be assisted.

The evidence involved shows that the subject goods have sunken with M.V. "Xinghai 668" due to the collision between M.V. "Xinghai 668" and M.V. "OOCL EUROPE" and the accident has caused the damage of the subject goods. Pursuant to Guangdong High People's Court's civil order in (2010) Yue Gao Fa Min Si Zhong Zi No.86 and No.87, the court recognized that M.V. "Xinghai 668" and M.V. "OOCL EUROPE" are both to blame for collision and shall respectively shoulder 40% and 60% of the negligence liability. Pursuant to Article 169 Paragraph 1 of the Maritime Code of the People's Republic of China, if the colliding ships are all in fault, each ship shall be liable in proportion to the extent of its fault; according to Article 169 Paragraph 2 of the Maritime Code of the People's Republic of China, if the respective faults are equal in proportion or it is impossible to determine the extent of the proportion of the respective faults, the liability of the colliding ships shall be apportioned equally. The Defendant Honghai Company, as the owner of M.V. "Xinghai 668", and the Defendant Orient U.K., as the bareboat charterer of M.V. "OOCL EUROPE", shall respectively shoulder the indemnity liability to the subject goods of the Plaintiff in this collision by the proportion of 40% and 60%.

In respect to whether the Defendant Honghai Company shall be entitled to enjoy the limitation liability for maritime claims, according to the provisions of Chap. 11 of the Maritime Code of the People's Republic of China on limitation liability for maritime claims, if the subject wants to enjoy the limitation liability for maritime claims, he shall confirm with Article 204 of the Maritime Code of the People's Republic of China; maritime claims shall belong to the limited claims in Article 207 of the Law and there shall not exist the situation in Article 209 of the Law. When the collision accident about M.V. "Xinghai 668" took place, the vessel loading the subject goods was bounding from Zhangjiagang to Guangzhou. It subordinates to the freightage between domestic ports. The Defendant Honghai Company, as the owner of M.V. "Xinghai 668", the subject confirms with the provisions of Article 204 of Maritime Code of the People's Republic of China. According to Article 207 of the Maritime Code of the People's Republic of China, limitation liability for maritime claims herein include as follows: claims in respect of loss of life or personal injury or loss of or damage to property including damage to harbour works, basins and waterways and aids to navigation occurring on board or in direct connection with the operation of the ship or with salvage operations, as well as consequential damages resulting there from. It is during the operation of ship that the subject goods were caused to sink by ship collision. Hence, it confirms with the foregoing provisions and subordinates to limitation liability. According to Article 209 of Maritime Code of the People's Republic of China, the Defendant Honghai Company shall be entitled to limit his liability, if it is not proved that the loss resulted from his act or omission done with the intent to cause such loss or recklessly and with knowledge that such loss would probably result. According to the available evidence in this case, the subject goods loss or damage by ship collision is caused by the fault of two vessels; there is no evidence to show that the loss results from the Defendant Honghai Company's act or omission done with the intent to cause such loss or recklessly and with knowledge that such loss would probably result. Hence, the Defendant Honghai Company shall be entitled to limit his liability for maritime claims according to Article 207 of the Maritime Code of the People's Republic of China. The Plaintiff blames the Defendant Honghai Company on not fulfilling the obligations of goods salvage and then claims that the Defendant Honghai Company shall not be entitled to enjoy the limitation liability for maritime claims. Since whether the subject goods are salvaged is affiliated to whether the Defendant Honghai Company fulfills the obligation of loss reduction and also affiliated with the affirmation range of the loss and its nature category; it has nothing to do with whether the Defendant Honghai Company shall be entitled to limit his liability for maritime claims; it does not affect the Defendant Honghai Company to enjoy limitation liability for maritime claims due to the goods loss arising from ship collision. If there is sufficient evidence that the Defendant Honghai Company's fault expands the range of goods loss, then, the expanding loss is neither affiliated to goods loss arising from ship collision nor limitation liability for claims. What's more, pursuant to the evidence in this case, although the amount of salvage charges in the salvage protocol signed by the Defendant Honghai Company and the salvage part is less than money for goods purchase, since the subject goods are not yet salvaged, it cannot be recognized whether the salvage has been completed and the final expenses for salvaging and cleaning goods; there is also no evidence to prove the devaluation degree of goods loss and its residual value and thus it cannot be recognized that the loss or the scope of loss will be expanded without salvaging the goods. Therefore, based on the Plaintiff's insufficient evidence, there is no factual basis for the Plaintiff's claim that the Defendant Honghai Company expands the loss and the goods loss in this case shall be all confirmed to the loss caused by ship collision. Hence, the Plaintiff's claim that the Defendant Honghai Company should not enjoy the limitation liability for claims due to the Company's not salvaging goods lacks basis and shall not be supported by the Court.

In respect to whether the insurance company's prepayment to the Plaintiff for the insurance indemnity shall be deducted from the Plaintiff's claims, during the Plaintiff's sue for this case, the Pacific Shanghai Branch has totally prepaid RMB4,500,000 as insurance indemnity. According to Article 252 of the Maritime Code of the People's Republic of China, the right of the insured to demand compensation from the third person shall be subrogated to the insurer from the time the indemnity is paid. Hence, under the circumstance that Pacific Shanghai Branch has prepaid RMB4,500,000 as the insurance indemnity, Pacific Shanghai Branch has obtained the right of subrogation in the herein claims scope; thus, the Plaintiff shall not be entitled to lodge the claim to the Defendant for the acquired settlement of claims once again. However, according to the Prepaid Insurance Indemnity Protocol signed with Pacific Shanghai Branch, the Plaintiff holds that the prepayment of insurance indemnity does not affect the Plaintiff to exercise the claim for the subject goods towards responsible party. Within 30 days from the Plaintiff's receiving all the indemnity from the responsible party, the two parties shall complete the settlement of the insurance indemnity and shall settle the indemnity with the difference based on the settlement result. Since the amount of RMB4,500,000 paid the insurer belongs to prepayment, the insurance contract between the Plaintiff and Pacific Shanghai Branch does not actually settle the claim and the Plaintiff is entitled to claim for the total loss of the subject goods to the two Defendants. The collegiate panel holds that the Plaintiff takes the two Defendants as the persons responsible for the ship collision accident and shall claim for the responsibility to the loss of the subject goods consigned by the Plaintiff due to the ship collision; this case arises from infringement dispute. The Plaintiff, as the obligee of the cargo carried by a ship, is entitled to claim for the loss of the subject goods towards the two Defendants who are regarded as responsible parties. According to the agreement between the Plaintiff and Pacific Shanghai Branch, the prepayment of insurance indemnity made by Pacific Shanghai Branch does not affect the Plaintiff to exercise the claim for the subject goods towards responsible parties; after receiving all the owing indemnity of the responsible parties, the Plaintiff shall complete the settlement of the insurance indemnity and shall settle the indemnity with the difference based on the settlement result with Pacific Shanghai Branch. Hence, the amount of RMB4,500,000, which Pacific Shanghai Branch pays to the Plaintiff, belongs to prepaid insurance indemnity rather than the final indemnity for the defined insurance accident. What's more, the two Defendants, as the responsible parties of infringement, shall not enhance obligation because of the protocol between the Plaintiff and the insurer. After the Plaintiff receives the insurance indemnity prepaid by Pacific Shanghai Branch, he shall still claim for the total loss of the subject goods towards the responsible parties in the name of his own. It does not violate the provisions of law and shall be permitted. Thus, the two Defendants' claim that the insurer's prepayment to the Plaintiff for the insurance indemnity shall be deducted from the Plaintiff's claims shall be established pursuant to law and shall not be supported.

It shall be reasonable that the Plaintiff requests the purchase price of the subject goods as the goods loss according to the submitted evidence like *Product Purchase & Sales Contract*, VAT Invoice and etc.; the collegiate panel affirms that the sum of the subject goods totals RMB15,958,497.24. The Defendant Honghai Company's claim that the goods loss of the Plaintiff should deduct 17% of VAT lacks legal basis and shall not be supported. In respect to the freight claimed by the Plaintiff, the freight shall be paid within one month after the goods arrive at the destination port pursuant to the transport protocol between the Plaintiff and Hailian Company.

The goods in this case have been damaged on the way and the Plaintiff has not paid the herein expenses. Hence, there is no basis for the Plaintiff's claim for the freight. According to the transport protocol between the Plaintiff and Hailian Company, the freight shall cover the insurance expenses; moreover, according to the evidence in this case, the applicant of the insurance in this case shall be Hailian Company; the Plaintiff does not submit any evidence to show that he has paid the insurance expenses; hence, there is no basis for the Plaintiff's claim for the insurance expenses loss. Pursuant to the civil order (2010) Yue Gao Fa Min Si Zhong Zi No.86 and No.87 made by the Guangdong High People's Court, the Defendant Honghai Company shall shoulder 40% of responsibility and the Defendant Orient U.K. shall shoulder 60% of responsibility; it is hereby calculated that the Defendant Honghai Company shall pay the Plaintiff RMB6,383,398.90 as compensation and the Defendant Orient U.K. shall pay the Plaintiff RMB9,575,098.34 as compensation. Since the Defendant Honghai Company is entitled to limit the liability for damage, also, pursuant to the first and second instance judged by the court and the Guangdong High People's Court, the Defendant Honghai Company's limitation fund for maritime claims shall be RMB2,642,925.24 as for the loss caused by ship collision; hence, the Defendant Honghai Company shall only compensate for RMB2,642,925.24 within the limitation fund for maritime claims and shall not pay for the excess part. In respect to the Defendant Honghai Company's claim that the reasonable expenses including detecting and salvaging the shipwrecks and the subject goods shall be deducted in proportion from the liability limitation, there is no legal basis and shall not be supported. The Plaintiff claims that, from the date October 21, 2008 to the date of payment set by this judgment, the two Defendants shall shoulder the interest based on the interest rate for enterprise working capital loans over the corresponding period as promulgated by the People's Bank of China; the foregoing claim is reasonable and shall be supported. The Plaintiff's claim for property preservation is aimed at the property of the Defendant Honghai Company; the court has recognized that the Defendant Honghai Company shall shoulder responsibility to the Plaintiff's goods loss; hence, the application fee for preservation is caused by the Defendant Honghai Company and shall be shouldered by the Defendant Honghai Company. According to Article 7 of the Regulations of the Supreme People's Court on Issues concerning the Trial of Liability Limitation for Maritime Claims, the registration fee of the claims paid by the Plaintiff shall be born by the Defendant Honghai Company.

According to Article 169 Paragraph 1 and Paragraph 2, Article 204 and Article 207 Paragraph 1 Sub-paragraph 1 of the Maritime Code of the People's Republic of China, the judgment is as follows:

1. The Defendant Beihai Honghai Shipping Co., Ltd. shall indemnify the Plaintiff Shanghai Eastern Shipping Material Co., Ltd. in amount of RMB2,642,925.24 and the interest thereof (calculated from the date October 21, 2008 to the date of payment set by this judgment and based on the interest rate for enterprise working capital loans over the corresponding period as promulgated by the People's Bank of China);

2. The Defendant Orient Overseas Container Line (U.K.) Limited shall indemnify the Plaintiff Shanghai Eastern Shipping Material Co., Ltd. in amount of RMB9,575,098.40 and the interest thereof (calculated from the date October 21, 2008 to the date of payment set by this judgment and based on the interest rate for enterprise working capital loans over the corresponding period as promulgated by the People's Bank of China);
3. The application fee of property preservation in amount of RMB20,000 paid by the Plaintiff shall be born by the Defendant Beihai Honghai Shipping Co., Ltd.;
4. The registration fee of the claims in amount of RMB1,000 paid by the Plaintiff shall be shouldered by the Defendant Beihai Honghai Shipping Co., Ltd.;
5. Reject other claims filed by the Plaintiff Shanghai Eastern Shipping Material Co., Ltd.

The Plaintiff prepaid court acceptance fee in amount of RMB120,549 and requested to reduce the amount of claims before the finality of the court investigation; calculated by the reduced amount of claims, court acceptance fee in amount of RMB1,183.81 shall be returned to the Plaintiff. Actual court acceptance fee in amount of RMB119,365.19, RMB29,841.30 shall be born by the Plaintiff, RMB19,098.43 by the Defendant Honghai Company and RMB70,425.46 by the Defendant Orient U.K.

The above obligation of payment shall be fulfilled within 10 days after this judgment comes into effect.

Where any party fails to perform the obligation of paying above-mentioned amounts within the period prescribed herein, such party shall, according to Article 229 of the Civil Procedure Law of the People's Republic of China, double pay the interest for the period of delayed performance.

In event of dissatisfaction with this judgment, the Plaintiff and the Defendant Honghai Company may, within 15 days upon service of this judgment, and the Defendant Orient U.K. may, within 30 days upon service of this judgment, file an application to the court, with duplicates being submitted in terms of the number of the other parties, to lodge an appeal to the Guangdong High People's Court.

Presiding Judge: XU Yuanping
Judge: ZHANG Kexiong
Acting Judge: WU Guining

August 20, 2012

Clerk: YANG Qian

Guangdong High People's Court
Civil Judgment

Shanghai Eastern Shipping Material Co., Ltd.
v.
Beihai Honghai Shipping Co., Ltd. et al.

(2012) Yue Gao Fa Min Si Zhong Zi No.148

Related Case(s) this is the judgment of second instance, and the judgment of first instance is on page 877.

Cause(s) of Action 193. Dispute over liability for ship collision damage.

Headnote Plaintiff cargo-owner recovered damages from shipowner involved in a "both to blame" collision in proportion to the shipowner's responsibility for the collision causing loss of the Plaintiff's cargo.

Summary the Plaintiff, Shanghai Eastern Shipping Materials Co., Ltd. (hereinafter referred to as Shanghai Eastern Company) filed suit against Orient Overseas Container Line (U.K.) Limited (hereinafter referred to as OOCL UK) and Beihai Honghai Shipping Co., Ltd. (hereinafter referred to as Honghai Company) for reimbursement for the loss of 209 panels of steel plate which were lost after a collision between two vessels operated by the Defendants. This "both-to-blame" collision happened when the stand-on vessel, M.V. "OOCL EUROPE" collided with the give-way vessel, M.V. "Xinghai 668", which was the vessel carrying the Plaintiff's steel plates. Not only did M.V. "Xinghai 668" fail to give way, but M.V. "OOCL EUROPE" upon notice of M.V. "Xinghai 668"'s failure to give way, did not take action to avoid collision as required for the stand-by vessel under the Collision Regulations. Therefore, the court determined that M.V. "Xinghai 668" should bear 60% of the liability, with M.V. "OOCL EUROPE" bearing 40% of the liability for the goods lost by the Plaintiff as a result of the collision.

Because the goods were never salvaged, they were deemed as lost, therefore the value of their loss was calculated based on the actual value of the goods. Therefore, the court ruled that both Defendants should reimburse Shanghai for their proportion of fault in the collision (minus the RMB4.5 million Shanghai had already received as insurance).

Judgment

The Appellant (the Plaintiff of first instance): Shanghai Eastern Shipping Materials Co., Ltd.
Domicile: #3, 4160 Shanghan Road, Pudong District, Shanghai City, P.R. China.
Legal representative: XU Hongyi, chairman.
Agent *ad litem*: WU Jinjun, employee.
Agent *ad litem*: LUAN Jianping, lawyer of Shanghai Gongmao Law Firm.

The Appellant (the Defendant of first instance): Orient Overseas Container Line (U.K.) Limited
Registration place: Scotia Centre, 4th Floor, P.O.Box 2804, George Town, Grand Cayman, Cayman Islands.
Domicile: 33 floor, No.25 Harbour centre, Harbour Road, Wan Chai, Hong Kong Special Administrative Region of the People's Republic of China.
Legal representative: DAI Shengjian, Chairman.
Agent *ad litem*: CHEN Xiangyong, lawyer of Guangdong Wang Jing & Co.
Agent *ad litem*: CAO Yanghui, lawyer of Guangdong Wang Jing & Co. (Nansha).

The Respondent (the Defendant of first instance): Beihai Honghai Shipping Co., Ltd.
Domicile: C Building, Fig, Panoroma Toner, Beihai Avenue, Beihai, Guangxi Zhuang Autonomous Region, the People's Republic of China.
Legal representative: CHEN Fu, general manager.
Agent *ad litem*: CHEN Yusheng, lawyer of Guangdong Yonghang Law Firm.
Agent *ad litem*: WANG Silv, lawyer of Guangdong Yonghang Law Firm.

With respect to the case arising from dispute over liability for ship collision damage between the Appellants Shanghai Eastern Shipping Materials Co., Ltd. (hereinafter referred to as Shanghai Eastern Company), Orient Overseas Container Line (U.K.) Limited (hereinafter referred to as OOCL UK), and the Respondent, Beihai Honghai Shipping Co., Ltd. (hereinafter referred to as Honghai Company), the Appellants disagreed with the Guangzhou Maritime Court (2009) Guang Hai Fa Chu Zi No.97 Civil Judgment and appealed to the court. The court formed a collegiate bench to try the case according to law. In this case, the collegiate panel consisted of WANG Jianping, ZHANG Yiyin, MO Fei, WANG Jianping served as Presiding Judge. Then due to job demand members changed into DU Yixing, ZHANG Yiyin, MO Fei, DU Yixing served as Presiding Judge. Agents *ad litem* of the Appellant Shanghai Eastern Company, LUAN Jianping and WU Jinjun, agents *ad litem* of the Appellant OOCL UK, CHEN Xiangyong and CAO Yanghui, and agent ad litem of the Respondent Honghai Company, CHEN Yusheng, attended the court investigation on March 26, 2013. Thereafter, LUAN Jianping, CAO Yanghui, CHEN Yusheng attended the supplementary cross-examination on June 27, 2013. Now the case has been concluded.

Shanghai Eastern Company alleged in first instance that: on August 6, 2008, Shanghai Eastern Company signed a transport protocol with Hailian Company. Shanghai Eastern Company entrusted Hailian Company to transport 6,421.981 tons of steel plates by partial shipment from Zhangjiagang Harbor to the wharf of China State Shipbuilding Corporation of Guangzhou Longxue (hereinafter referred as Longxue Corporation). On October 16, 2008, Honghai Company signed and issued the Water Freight Bill and recognized the acceptance of carriage by the subordinate M.V. "Xinhai 668" with 209 pieces of steel plates weighing 1,780.704 tons altogether. On October 21, 2008, while sailing for Guangzhou Harbor, M.V. "Xinhai 668" was crashed by OOCL UK's M.V. "OOCL EUROPE" which was in bareboat charter period. The ship collision caused M.V. "Xinhai 668" and its consignments to be sunk and brought about huge financial loss. According to the final judgment by Guangdong High People's Court, the cognizance of involved ship collision was that Honghai Company took responsibility of 40% and OOCL UK took responsibility of 60%.Shanghai Eastern Company requested the court of first instance to adjudge the two Defendants to compensate Shanghai Eastern Company RMB16,458,186.83 and its interests based on the proportion of each responsibility (interests shall take effect from October 21, 2008 to the payment day prescribed herein at the loan interest rate of working capital of enterprises for the same period as published by the People's Bank of China). Court acceptance fee, property preservation application fee, registration of claims application fee and etc. shall be born by OOCL UK and Honghai Company.

The court found out that:

1. Transactions of Ships involved in the Accident

Shanghai Eastern Company stated that the subject goods, 209 pieces of steel plates, were purchased by Shanghai Eastern Company and China's Shipbuilding Industry Materials Co., Ltd. (East China) which was entrusted by Shanghai Eastern Company. The subject goods were purchased from Jiangsu Shagang Group Co., Ltd. (hereinafter referred to as Shagang Company). Shanghai Eastern Company paid RMB15,958,497.24 for 209 pieces of steel plates, 1,780.704 tons in total. Shanghai Eastern Company therewith sold the subject goods, in total RMB16,458,186.83, to Longxue Corporation. Shanghai Eastern Company therefor submitted Procurement Contract, Receipts Voucher, Written Warranty and etc.

The foregoing evidence recorded: on June 6 and July 7, 2008, Shanghai Eastern Company as the demander signed *Products Purchase & Sales Contract* No. D080608 and No.K0808I2 with the supplier Shagang Company. They made an agreement that the demander purchased respectively 1,296.291 tons and 1,656.225 tons from the supplier; the sums were respectively RMB11,295,653.15 and RMB14,653,695.90; the demander needed pick up goods in Shagang Company. Each Products Purchase & Sales Contract attached *Products Purchase & Sales Lists* including Products Specializations and models, Products Pieces, Weight, Unit Price, Sums and etc. On October 19, 2008, Shagang Company issued the VAT invoice for RMB7,146,815.38 including the subject 7 pieces of steel plates, in total 37.694 tons and in the amount of RMB342,891.25. On August 28 and October 8, 2008, Shanghai Eastern Company as the demander signed the Industrial and

Mineral Products Purchase & Sales Contract with the supplier China's Shipbuilding Industry Materials Co., Ltd. (East China). They made an agreement that the demander purchased respectively 2,021.013 tons and 1,448.452 tons from the supplier; the sums were respectively RMB18,097,982.30 and RMB13,385,130.40; the demander needed pick up goods in Shagang Company. Each *Products Purchase & Sales Contract* attached the Products Purchase & Sales Lists including Products Specializations and models, Products Pieces, Weight, Unit Price, Sums and etc. each contract recorded the subject steel plates 195 pieces and 7 pieces. On November 18, 2008 and on March 17, 2009, China's Shipbuilding Industry Materials Co., Ltd. (East China) issued the VAT invoices to Shanghai Eastern Company. The 13 VAT invoices, with the No.01615967—01615979, were issued for the subject 195 pieces of steel plates, totally weighing 1,673.779 tons and in the amount of RMB14,973,626.93. The VAT invoice No.00199267 recorded the subject 7 pieces of steel plates, totally weighing 69.231 tons and in the amount of RMB641,979.06. The foresaid 209 pieces of steel plates totaled 1780.704 tons and amounted to RMB15,958,497.24.

On June 6, July 3, August 7, and September 18, 2008, Shanghai Eastern Company as the supplier signed 4 pieces of *Products Purchase & Sales Contract* with the demander Longxue Corporation; the contract number was 07GLS230—01C155, 07GLS230—01C158, 07GLS230—01C163 and 07GLS230—01C172 respectively corresponding to the weight of 1,296.291 tons, 1,656.225 tons, 2,106.578 tons and 1,443.452 tons; it respectively corresponded to the amount of RMB11,691,021.91, RMB14,993,222.05, RMB19,446,850.57 and RMB13,803,142.22. Each *Products Purchase & Sales Contract* attached *Products Purchase & Sales Lists* including Products Specializations and models, Weight, Products Pieces, Unit Price, Sums and etc. In the contracts, the subject 209 pieces of steel plates were sold to Longxue Corporation with the total sum of RMB16,458,186.83.

On April 20, 2012, Longxue Corporation's statements were verified by the court of first instance: the company signed the contract No.07GLS230—01C155, No.07GLS230—01C158, No.07GLS230—01C163, No.07GLS230—01C172 with Shanghai Eastern Company. Pursuant to the third article in the 4 pieces of Purchases & Sales Contract, the demander's specified wharf for delivery points and delivery means referred to the Wharf of Longxue Corporation; both sides fulfilled the 4 pieces of *Purchases & Sales Contract*. With regard to the 209 pieces of steel plates, totaling 1,780.704 tons, loaded in the wreck M.V. "Xinghai 668", Longxue Corporation had no responsibility. In the court hearing, the agents *ad litem* from Shanghai Eastern Company claimed that Shanghai Eastern Company rearranged the supply of goods to the Longxue Corporation after the subject accident.

The two Defendants did not file the objection to the foregoing evidence and the content of the evidence can be mutually verified. The foregoing evidence and facts were recognized by the trial bench.

2. Cargo Transport involved in the Accident

On August 6, 2008, Shanghai Eastern Company signed the transport protocol with Hailian Company. They made an agreement that Shanghai Eastern Company entrusted Hailian Company to ship the 6,421.981 tons of steel plates, including the subject goods, by partial shipment from Zhangjiagang to the Longxue Corporation's wharf. The whole waterage were RMB165 per ton (including pilotage dues, insurance expenses and freights). When goods arrived at the Longxue Corporation's wharf, Shanghai Eastern Company would pay all the waterage to Hailian Company within one month.

On October 15, 2008, the subject goods started to be loaded into M.V. "Xinghai 668" on Shagang Company's wharf. Pursuant to the product bills of lading issued by Shagang Company, it recorded various specialization and weight of the goods. Among all the bills of lading, 4 pieces of steel plates with 19.349 tons in No.6880 B/L, 3 pieces of steel plates with 18.3 tons in No.6882 B/L, 195 pieces of steel plates with 1,637.779 tons in No.6860 B/L, 7 pieces of steel plates with 69.231 tons in No.6887 B/L. The 4 pieces of bills of lading totally recorded the 209 pieces of steel plates with the amount of 1,780.704 tons. One bill of lading was handwritten with the content "209 pieces of steel plates were actually received, without scratching and buckling, by GAO Huaqiang". Honghai Company recognized that GAO Huaqiang was one of Honghai Company's staff. Shagang Company issued 30 pieces of detailed packing lists. The contents including cargo names, specialization, weight and etc. were according to the product bills of lading.

On October 16, 2008, Honghai Company as carrier signed and issued the Water Freight Bill. It recorded that Shanghai Eastern Company as the shipper, Longxue Corporation as the consignee, goods, 209 pieces of steel plates totaling 1,780.704 tons, were shipped to Longxue Corporation's wharf. In the Water Freight Bill, there was the handwritten content "the specialization of the wide and thick plates can be seen on B/L"; the Defendant Honghai Company stamped the seal of M.V. "Xinghai 668" at the point of the carrier's signature.

On November 21, 2008, Honghai Company issued the Notice of Loss to Shanghai Branch of China Pacific Property Insurance Co., Ltd. (hereinafter referred as Pacific Shanghai Branch). It was stated that, on October 17, 2008, M.V. "Xinghai 668" shipped about 1780 tons of steel plates from Zhangjiagang to Guangzhou Longxue Shipyard; around 0600 on October 21, the vessel was collided to sink by the foreign vessel near the Hong Kong waters; Honghai Company requested the Insurance Company should send members to make an examination.

Pursuant to the foregoing evidence, Shanghai Eastern Company held that the subject goods were actually accepted for carriage by M.V. "Xinghai 668" subordinate to Honghai Company and on October 21, 2008 sank with the vessel in the subject collision accident. However, OOCL UK and Honghai Company held that the foresaid evidence could not fully prove M.V. "Xinghai 668" actually accepted for carriage of the subject goods. The trial bench held that the evidence including Products Purchase & Sales Protocol, Products Purchase & Sales Lists, Product Bills of Lading, Factory Detailed Packing Lists, Water Freight Bill and etc. can form the complete evidence chain; and the evidence can affirm that Shanghai Eastern Company purchased the subject 209 pieces of steel plates in number of 1,780.704 tons and the goods were loaded into M.V. "Xinghai 668"; also, the *Notice of Loss* issued by Honghai Company verified the subject goods were loaded by M.V.

"Xinghai 668". Hence, the defense that Shanghai Eastern Company did not fully prove M.V. "Xinghai 668" actual acceptance for the subject goods' carriage could not stand.

3. Cargo Insurance involved in the Accident

Pursuant to the insurance certificate of domestic waterway and landway cargo transportation submitted by Shanghai Eastern Company: on October 17, 2008, Shanghai Eastern Company as the insurer, Hailian Company as the Policy holder, requested Pacific Shanghai Branch to insure the comprehensive risk for the subject goods pursuant to the domestic waterway and landway cargo transportation insurance clause (February 2, 1995). The insurance amount totaled RMB10,690,000 and its premiums were RMB8,552. After the insurance accident, on May 4 and October 26, 2009, Pacific Shanghai Branch respectively prepaid the insurance indemnities RMB2 million and RMB2.5 million; the two parties respectively signed the Prepaid Insurance Indemnity Protocol and the Second Prepaid Insurance Indemnity Protocol; since the specific loss amount of the subject goods cannot be confirmed and Shanghai Eastern Company purchased the substitute cargo which caused the extra expenses, Shanghai Eastern Company requested the Pacific Shanghai Branch to prepay the insurance indemnity. For this, the two parties reached the following agreement: 1. Pacific Shanghai Branch shall respectively prepay Shanghai Eastern Company the insurance indemnities RMB2 million and RMB2.5 million within 10 days after the agreement took effect; 2. the two parties jointly confirmed that Shanghai Eastern Company shall firstly bring a lawsuit against the responsible party in order to claim for compensation. Pacific Shanghai Branch's prepayment for the insurance indemnity shall not affect Shanghai Eastern Company to exercise the lawsuit claim of the subject goods against the responsible party. The loss amount of Shanghai Eastern Company in the accident shall be confirmed according to the court's binding judgment or the two parties' negotiation and rules from the insurance policy No. ASHH101043080001015N; due to Shanghai Eastern Company's underinsurance, if Shanghai Eastern Company's loss in this accident finally cannot be fully compensated, as for the unreceived compensation, Pacific Shanghai Branch shall undertake the insurance responsibility pursuant to the insurance policy agreement and the proportion of the insured amount and the cargo value; if Shanghai Eastern Company's fault enlarged the loss or could not receive compensation by recourse, Pacific Shanghai Branch shall have right to deduct the relevant indemnity. 3. Within 30 days from Shanghai Eastern Company's receiving all the indemnity from the responsible party, the two parties shall complete the settlement of the insurance indemnity and shall settle the indemnity with the difference based on the settlement result; 4. Shanghai Eastern Company shall confirm and promise to further contact with Hong Kong Marine Department and strive to gain the permission of salvaging goods alone; after gaining the permission from Hong Kong Marine Department, Shanghai Eastern Company shall actively implement salvage assessment and the salvage of cargo in order to reduce cargo loss. Shanghai Eastern Company confirmed that, after signing the two pieces of Prepaid Insurance Indemnity Protocol with Pacific Shanghai Branch, had received the prepayment of insurance indemnities from Pacific Shanghai Branch with the total number of RMB4.5 million.

4. Hearing the responsibility on Ship Collision

With respect to the dispute over damage compensation arising from ship collision between M.V. "Xinghai 668" and M.V. "OOCL EUROPE", Honghai Company filed an action to request OOCL UK as the bareboat charterer of M.V. "OOCL EUROPE" to assume the compensation responsibility; OOCL UK and other company instituted a counter claim against the Defendant Honghai Company with the (2009) Guang Hai Fa Chu Zi No.4 and (2009) Guang Hai Fa Chu Zi No.292. According to the first instance by the court, Honghai Company shouldered responsibility of 40% on the collision accident and OOCL UK shouldered responsibility of 60%. OOCL UK refused the first instance and then lodged an appeal. During the second instance, OOCL UK filed an application to request the Guangdong High People's Court to obtain evidence material from Guangdong Marine Safety Administration. The application requested the court to draw up the verification that it was part of the unreal evidence, concerning the collision accident, submitted by Honghai Company that misdirected the court's affirmation on the accident responsibility. According to the fact that OOCL UK had submitted the confirmation of evidence completion in the first trial, Guangdong High People's Court refused OOCL UK's application on obtaining evidence. On December 20, 2011, Guangdong High People's Court made a civil ruling (2010) Yue Gao Fa Min Si Zhong Zi No.86 and No.87 and the appeal shall be dismissed and the original judgment shall be affirmed.

5. Limitation Fund for Maritime Claims responsibility Applied by the Defendant Honghai Company and Property Preservation Applied by Shanghai Eastern Company

On February 11, 2009, Honghai Company applied to the court for constituting the limitation fund for maritime claims responsibility; after accepting and hearing the application, on May 19, 2009, the court made a civil ruling (2009) Guang Hai Fa Chu Zi No.116 which permitted that Honghai Company should constitute limitation fund for responsibility pursuant to the SDRs limitation of the Article 249 and 832; based on the date of the accident on October 21, 2008, the exchange rate of SDRs to US Dollar shall be calculated and finally equivalent to RMB2,642,925.24. OOCL UK refused the judgment and then lodged an appeal. Guangdong High People's Court made a Civil Ruling (2009) Yue Gao Fa Min Si Zhong Zi No.267; the appeal shall be dismissed and the original judgment shall be affirmed. However, Honghai Company did not constitute the limitation fund for maritime claims responsibility pursuant to the effective judgment in the court.

In the period of the announcement published by the court on Honghai Company's constituting limitation fund for maritime claims responsibility, Shanghai Eastern Company handled the registration formalities of creditor's right and rendered its registration fee in sum of RMB1,000. Besides, after Honghai Company did not constitute the limitation fund for maritime claims responsibility pursuant to the effective judgment in the court, Shanghai Eastern Company successively submitted 4 times the application to the court for property preservation;

the court of first instance decided that Shanghai Eastern Company's application for property preservation shall be permitted and the Defendant Honghai Company's handling ownership disposal formalities shall be forbidden. Shanghai Eastern Company therefor rendered the property preservation application fee in sum of RMB20,000.

6. M.V. "Xinghai 668" and goods Salvage Involved in this Case

After M.V. "Xinghai 668" sank, Honghai Company signed *Shipwreck Detection Protocol* with Xinlong Company on December 1, 2008. Pursuant to the Protocol, Xinlong Company was entrusted to conduct detection of M.V. "Xinghai 668" sinking near the Hong Kong East Lamma Channel, confirm the situation of the shipwreck and goods and submit detection report. The detection fee was RMB85,000 by appointment.

On December 11, 2008, Hong Kong Youli Engineering Co., Ltd. submitted *Detection Report* on M.V. "Xinghai 668".

On February 8, 2009, Honghai Company signed the shipwreck and goods salvage protocol with Xinlong Company. Pursuant to the protocol, Xinlong Company was entrusted to conduct the salvage of M.V. "Xinghai 668" and goods. The lump sum of shipwreck salvage was RMB2,900,000. The lump sum of goods salvage, freshwater flushing and shipping to Longxue Wharf was RMB5,000,000.

Pursuant to the correspondences between Honghai Company and Hong Kong Marine Department, Honghai Company filed extension for several times towards Hong Kong Marine Department in the process of entrusting Xinlong Company to salvage the shipwreck and the subject goods.

Agents *ad litem* of Honghai Company claimed that since Xinlong Company was unfamiliar with the procedure of the relevant license application for salvaging in Hong Kong Waters and underestimated the difficulties of salvage, finally the salvage of shipwrecks and sunken objects was not implemented. Afterwards, Honghai Company inquired Guangzhou Salvage Bureau of the salvage expenses for the shipwrecks and the subject goods. Guangzhou Salvage Bureau quoted that the salvage expenses were in sum of RMB9,180,000 if it entered the areas before the date of January 25, 2009; the salvage expenses were in sum of RMB8,380,000 if it entered the areas after the March of 2009. Since incapable to pay the mentioned expenses, the Defendant Honghai Company did not sign the salvage agreement with Guangzhou Salvage Bureau.

However, Shanghai Eastern Company claimed that Honghai Company owned several ships and its incapability to pay the salvage expenses was not true. The delay of the salvage caused the entire loss of the subject goods. Therefore, Honghai Company should bear the full responsibility and not be entitled to enjoy the limitation responsibility for maritime claims.

The Defendant Honghai Company recognized that M.V. "Xinghai 668" and the subject goods were not salvaged until the hearing the case.

The court of first instance held that:

This case was a dispute over damage compensation arising from ship collision related with Hong Kong. Pursuant to Article 1 of the Some Provisions of the Supreme People's Court on the Scope of Cases to be Entertained by Maritime

Courts, this case was regarded to the scope of maritime court's specific jurisdiction. The subject collision accident took place at the junction of Guangzhou Waters and Hong Kong Waters. Pursuant to Article 241 of the Civil Procedure Law of the People's Republic of China, the court of first instance had the jurisdiction to this case. Pursuant to Article 273 of the Maritime Code of the People's Republic of China, this case should apply the law of the People's Republic of China to treat the substantive dispute.

The issues of the subject dispute mainly included that: the suit qualification of Shanghai Eastern Company; whether Honghai Company should be entitled to enjoy the limitation responsibility for maritime claims; whether the insurance company's prepayment to Shanghai Eastern Company for the insurance indemnity shall be deducted from Shanghai Eastern Company's claims.

In respect to the suit qualification of Shanghai Eastern Company, the facts in this case showed that Shanghai Eastern Company as the seller and shipper of the subject goods and entitled to claim for goods loss by law because the goods have been damaged on passage. Longxue Corporation, as the consignee, makes it clear that it was not the obligee of the subject goods. Hence, the two Defendants' claims that the Plaintiff was not the obligee of the subject goods do not base on facts and law and should not be assisted.

The evidence involved showed that the subject goods have sunken with M.V. "Xinghai 668" due to the collision between M.V. "Xinghai 668" and M.V. "OOCL EUROPE" and the accident has caused the damage of the subject goods. Pursuant to Guangdong High People's Court's civil order in (2010) Yue Gao Fa Min Si Zhong Zi No.86 and No.87, the court of first instance recognized that M.V. "Xinghai 668" and M.V. "OOCL EUROPE" are both to blame for collision and shall respectively shoulder 40% and 60% of the negligence responsibility. Pursuant to Article 169 Paragraph 1 of the Maritime Code of the People's Republic of China, if the colliding ships are all in fault, each ship shall be liable in proportion to the extent of its fault; according to Article 169 Paragraph 2 of the Maritime Code of the People's Republic of China, if the respective faults are equal in proportion or it is impossible to determine the extent of the proportion of the respective faults, the responsibility of the colliding ships shall be apportioned equally. Honghai Company, as the owner of M.V. "Xinghai 668", and OOCL UK, as the bareboat charterer of M.V. "OOCL EUROPE", shall respectively shoulder the indemnity responsibility to the subject goods of Shanghai Eastern Company in this collision by the proportion of 40% and 60%.

In respect to whether Honghai Company shall be entitled to enjoy the limitation responsibility for maritime claims, according to the provisions of Chap. 11 of the Maritime Code of the People's Republic of China on limitation responsibility for maritime claims, if the subject wants to enjoy the limitation responsibility for maritime claims, he shall confirm with Article 204 of the Maritime Code of the People's Republic of China; maritime claims shall belong to the limited claims in Article 207 of the Law and there shall not exist the situation in Article 209 of the Law. When the collision accident about M.V. "Xinghai 668" took place, the vessel loading the subject goods was bounding from Zhangjiagang to Guangzhou. It subordinates to the freightage between domestic ports. Honghai Company, as the owner of M.V. "Xinghai 668", the subject confirms with the provisions of Article 204 of the Maritime Code of the People's Republic of China. According to Article 207 of the Maritime Code of the People's Republic of China, limitation responsibility for maritime claims herein include as follows: claims in respect of loss of life or personal injury or loss of or damage to property including damage to harbour works, basins and waterways and aids to navigation occurring on board or in direct connection with the operation of the ship or with salvage operations, as well as consequential damages resulting there from. It is during the operation of ship that the subject goods were caused to sink by ship collision. Hence, it confirms with the foregoing provisions and subordinates to limitation responsibility. According to Article 209 of Maritime Code of the People's Republic of China, Honghai Company shall be entitled to limit his responsibility, if it is not proved that the loss resulted from his act or omission done with the intent to cause such loss or recklessly and with knowledge that such loss would probably result. According to the available evidence in this case, the subject goods loss or damage by ship collision is caused by the fault of two vessels; there is no evidence to show that the loss results from Honghai Company's act or omission done with the intent to cause such loss or recklessly and with knowledge that such loss would probably result. Hence, Honghai Company shall be entitled to limit his responsibility for maritime claims according to Article 207 of the Maritime Code of the People's Republic of China. Shanghai Eastern Company blames Honghai Company on not fulfilling the obligations of goods salvage and then claims that Honghai Company shall not be entitled to enjoy the limitation responsibility for maritime claims. Since whether the subject goods are salvaged is affiliated to whether Honghai Company fulfills the obligation of loss reduction and also affiliated with the affirmation range of the loss and its nature category; it has nothing to do with whether Honghai Company shall be entitled to limit his responsibility for maritime claims; it does not affect Honghai Company to enjoy limitation responsibility for maritime claims due to the goods loss arising from ship collision. If there is sufficient evidence that Honghai Company's fault expands the range of goods loss, then, the expanding loss is neither affiliated to goods loss arising from ship collision nor limitation responsibility for claims. What's more, pursuant to the evidence in this case, although the amount of salvage charges in the salvage protocol signed by Honghai Company and the salvage part is less than money for goods purchase, since the subject goods are not yet salvaged, it cannot be recognized whether the salvage has been completed and the final expenses for salvaging and cleaning goods; there is also no evidence to prove the devaluation degree of goods loss and its residual value and thus it cannot be recognized that the loss or the scope of loss will be expanded without salvaging the goods. Therefore, based on Shanghai Eastern Company's insufficient evidence, there is no factual basis for Shanghai Eastern Company's claim that Honghai Company expands the loss and the goods loss in this case shall be all confirmed to the loss caused by ship collision. Hence, Shanghai Eastern Company's claim that Honghai Company should not enjoy the limitation responsibility for claims due to the Company's not salvaging goods lacks basis and shall not be supported by the court.

In respect to whether the insurance company's prepayment to Shanghai Eastern Company for the insurance indemnity shall be deducted from Shanghai Eastern Company's claims, during Shanghai Eastern Company's sue for this case, the Pacific Shanghai Branch has totally prepaid RMB4,500,000 as insurance indemnity. According to Article 252 of the Maritime Code of the People's Republic of China, the right of the insured to demand compensation from the third person shall be subrogated to the insurer from the time the indemnity is paid. Hence, under the circumstance that Pacific Shanghai Branch has prepaid RMB4,500,000 as the insurance indemnity, Pacific Shanghai Branch has obtained the right of subrogation in the herein claims scope; thus, Shanghai Eastern Company shall not be entitled to lodge the claim to the Defendant for the acquired settlement of claims once again. However, according to the Prepaid Insurance Indemnity Protocol signed with Pacific Shanghai Branch, Shanghai Eastern Company holds that the prepayment of insurance indemnity does not affect Shanghai Eastern Company to exercise the claim for the subject goods towards responsible party. Within 30 days from Shanghai Eastern Company's receiving all the indemnity from the responsible party, the two parties shall complete the settlement of the insurance indemnity and shall settle the indemnity with the difference based on the settlement result. Since the amount of RMB4,500,000 paid the insurer belongs to prepayment, the insurance contract between Shanghai Eastern Company and Pacific Shanghai Branch does not actually settle the claim and Shanghai Eastern Company is entitled to claim for the total loss of the subject goods to OOCL UK and Honghai Company. The court of first instance held that Shanghai Eastern Company took OOCL UK and Honghai Company as the persons responsible for the ship collision accident and shall claim for the responsibility to the loss of the subject goods consigned by Shanghai Eastern Company due to the ship collision; this case arises from infringement dispute. Shanghai Eastern Company, as the obligee of the cargo carried by a ship, was entitled to claim for the loss of the subject goods towards OOCL UK and Honghai Company who are regarded as responsible parties. According to the agreement between Shanghai Eastern Company and Pacific Shanghai Branch, the prepayment of insurance indemnity made by Pacific Shanghai Branch did not affect Shanghai Eastern Company to exercise the claim for the subject goods towards responsible parties; after receiving all the owing indemnity of the responsible parties, Shanghai Eastern Company shall complete the settlement of the insurance indemnity and shall settle the indemnity with the difference based on the settlement result with Pacific Shanghai Branch. Hence, the amount of RMB4,500,000, which Pacific Shanghai Branch paid to Shanghai Eastern Company, belonged to prepaid insurance indemnity rather than the final indemnity for the defined insurance accident. What's more, OOCL UK and Honghai Company, as the responsible parties of infringement, shall not enhance obligation because of the protocol between Shanghai Eastern Company and the insurer. After Shanghai Eastern Company receives the insurance indemnity prepaid by Pacific Shanghai Branch, he shall still claim for the total loss of the subject goods towards the responsible parties in the name of his own. It does not violate the provisions of law and shall be permitted. Thus, OOCL UK and Honghai Company's claim that the insurer's prepayment to Shanghai Eastern Company for the insurance indemnity shall be deducted from Shanghai Eastern Company's claims shall be established pursuant to law and shall not be supported.

It shall be reasonable that Shanghai Eastern Company requested the purchase price of the subject goods as the goods loss according to the submitted evidence like *Product Purchase & Sales Contract*, VAT Invoice and etc.; the trial bench affirms that the sum of the subject goods totaled RMB15,958,497.24. Honghai Company's claim that the goods loss of Shanghai Eastern Company should deduct 17% of VAT lacked legal basis and shall not be supported. In respect to the freight claimed by Shanghai Eastern Company, the freight shall be paid within one month after the goods arrive at the destination port pursuant to the transport protocol between Shanghai Eastern Company and Hailian Company. The goods in this case had been damaged on the way and Shanghai Eastern Company had not paid the herein expenses. Hence, there was no basis for Shanghai Eastern Company's claim for the freight. According to the transport protocol between Shanghai Eastern Company and Hailian Company, the freight shall cover the insurance expenses; moreover, according to the evidence in this case, the applicant of the insurance in this case shall be Hailian Company; Shanghai Eastern Company does not submit any evidence to show that he has paid the insurance expenses; hence, there is no basis for Shanghai Eastern Company's claim for the insurance expenses loss. Pursuant to the civil ruling (2010) Yue Gao Fa Min Si Zhong Zi No.86 and No.87 made by the Guangdong High People's Court, Honghai Company shall shoulder 40% of responsibility and OOCL UK shall shoulder 60% of responsibility; it is hereby calculated that Honghai Company shall pay Shanghai Eastern Company RMB6,383,398.90 as compensation and OOCL UK shall pay Shanghai Eastern Company RMB9,575,098.34 as compensation. Since Honghai Company is entitled to limit the responsibility for damage, also, pursuant to the first and second instance judged by the court and the Guangdong High People's Court, Honghai Company's limitation fund for maritime claims shall be RMB2,642,925.24 as for the loss caused by ship collision; hence, Honghai Company shall only compensate for RMB2,642,925.24 within the limitation fund for maritime claims and shall not pay for the excess part. In respect to Honghai Company's claim that the reasonable expenses including detecting and salvaging the shipwrecks and the subject goods shall be deducted in proportion from the responsibility limitation, there is no legal basis and shall not be supported. Shanghai Eastern Company claims that, from the date October 21, 2008 to the date of payment set by this judgment, OOCL UK and Honghai Company shall shoulder the interest based on the interest rate for enterprise working capital loans over the corresponding period as promulgated by the People's Bank of China; the foregoing claim was reasonable and shall be supported. Shanghai Eastern Company's claim for property preservation was aimed at the property of Honghai Company; the court of first instance had recognized that Honghai Company shall shoulder responsibility to Shanghai Eastern Company's goods loss; hence, the application fee for preservation was caused by Honghai Company and shall be shouldered by Honghai Company.

According to Article 7 of the Several Provisions of the Supreme People's Court concerning the Trial of Dispute Cases in relation to Maritime Compensation Liability Limitation, the registration fee of the claims paid by Shanghai Eastern Company shall be born by Honghai Company.

According to Article 169 Paragraph 1 and Paragraph 2, Article 204 and Article 207 Paragraph 1 Sub-paragraph 1 of the Maritime Code of the People's Republic of China, the judgment was as follows:

1. Honghai Company should indemnify Shanghai Eastern Company in amount of RMB2,642,925.24 and the interest thereof (calculated from the date October 21, 2008 to the date of payment set by this judgment and based on the interest rate for enterprise working capital loans over the corresponding period as promulgated by the People's Bank of China);
2. OOCL UK shall indemnify Shanghai Eastern Company in amount of RMB9,575,098.40 and the interest thereof (calculated from the date October 21, 2008 to the date of payment set by this judgment and based on the interest rate for enterprise working capital loans over the corresponding period as promulgated by the People's Bank of China);
3. The application fee of property preservation in amount of RMB20,000 paid by Shanghai Eastern Company shall be born by Honghai Company;
4. The registration fee of the claims in amount of RMB1,000 paid by Shanghai Eastern Company shall be born by Honghai Company;
5. Reject other claims filed by Shanghai Eastern Company.

Shanghai Eastern Company prepaid court acceptance fee in amount of RMB120,549 and requested to reduce the amount of claims before the finality of the court investigation; calculated by the reduced amount of claims, court acceptance fee in amount of RMB1,183.81 shall be returned to Shanghai Eastern Company. Actual court acceptance fee in amount ofRMB119,365.19, RMB29,841.30 shall be born by Shanghai Eastern Company, RMB19,098.43 by Honghai Company and RMB70,425.46 by OOCL UK.

The above obligation of payment shall be fulfilled within 10 days after this judgment came into effect.

Shanghai Eastern Company refused to accept judgment of first instance and filed an appeal to the court, claiming to revoke the first item of judgment of first instance, and the judgment should be changed to that Honghai Company to compensate the loss of goods by RMB6,383,389.90. The reasons are as follows: 1. the ship involved violated the relevant provisions of the International Regulations for Preventing Collisions at Sea, 1972 (hereinafter referred to as the COLREG) and was obviously at fault for the occurrence of the collision. According to Article 10 of the COLREG, ships should be particularly cautious when driving near the end of the traffic separation system. In the case, M.V. "OOCL EUROPE" and M. V."Xinghai 668" were in a state of high-speed navigation during encounters when crossing the warning zone, namely the end of the East Boliao Waterway. After the first sighting, they did not maintain a safe speed and use good boatmanship actively and early to avoid collisions according to Article 6 and Article 8 of the COLREG, and its fault was obvious. When the two ships crossed each other, M.V. "OOCL EUROPE" was on the starboard side of M.V."Xinghai 668", so M.V. "OOCL EUROPE" was a direct sailing ship and M.V."Xinghai 668" was a giving way ship. M.V."Xinghai 668" did not take any action within 6 minutes of the first sighting of the two ships, and violated Article 16 of the COLREG, which stipulated that the giving way ship should take large action as early as possible and give way to the direct sailing ship with ample allowance. When turning, the horns were not sounded or the lights were used according to Article 34 of the COLREG, so that M. V. "OOCL EUROPE" was unable to know its steering intention-M.V."Xinghai 668" failed to perform its responsibility as a giving way ship, which was the main reason for the urgent situation of the two ships and the collision. The captain of M. V."Xinghai 668" failed to take correct and standardized driving measures according to the requirements of the COLREG. He knew that it might cause an accident within ample time, but first did not act and then acted recklessly (turning to the left) and caused the serious consequences of that the ship sank and goods was lost. In addition, M.V."Xinghai 668" still had serious unseaworthy conditions such as the crew was insufficient and most of the crew did not hold a certificate of competency, Honghai Company still hired the crew knowing that the crew did not have the corresponding qualifications, and it should bear the corresponding legal consequences. The illegal navigation of M.V."Xinghai 668" had a direct cause and effect relationship with the collision accident involved. As the owner of the ship, Honghai Company was obviously at fault for the ship sinking and goods loss caused by the accident. 2. Honghai Company refused to perform its obligations as the main salvage responsibility entity only on the grounds of "lack of funds", and did not actually salvage the goods, resulting in increased loss. According to the above, according to Article 209 of the Maritime Code of the People's Republic of China, the loss that caused the claim for compensation was resulted from its act or omission done with the intent to cause such loss or recklessly and with knowledge that such loss would probably result, and the liable person had no right to limit the responsibility of compensation. Honghai Company had no right to enjoy the limitation of responsibility for maritime compensation.

In response to the appeal of Shanghai Eastern Company, OOCL UK did not issue a reply on the grounds that Shanghai Eastern Company did not file an appeal against it in second instance.

In response to the appeal of Shanghai Eastern Company, Honghai Company replied in second instance: 1. the fundamental cause of the accident involved was that M.V. "OOCL EUROPE", as a ship crossing the channel, failed to evade the ship at the direction of the general flow of the channel when crossing the Dangan Waterway, and sailed in the opposite direction outside the approach channel of the Dangan Waterway. The reason claimed by Shanghai Eastern Company in the appeal was not the main reason for the accident, and the "cross-encounter pattern" was not applicable in the traffic separation system. Regarding the issue of the proportion of responsibility for accidents between the two ships, the effective judgment in another case confirmed, so it was not appropriate to re-examine or make other different determinations in the case. Although Shanghai Eastern Company claimed that M.V."Xinghai 668" did have sufficient crew and Honghai Company was aware of the lack of crew, it did not provide evidence to prove it, so it could not be established. According to Article 209 of the Maritime Code of the People's Republic of China, the circumstances that cause the person liable to not have the right to enjoy the limitation of maritime compensation responsibility were limited to its reckless act or omission deliberately or knowingly that may cause loss, even if Shanghai Eastern Company's reason had a causal relationship with the collision accident involved, but this kind of minor navigational negligence did not belong to the circumstances stipulated by the above-mentioned law and was not sufficient to affect Honghai Company's right to limit maritime compensation responsibility. 2. After the accident, who had the obligation to reduce loss was the owner of the goods. If the owner of the goods involved was determined to be Shanghai Eastern Company, the goods should be salvaged by Shanghai Eastern Company. Honghai Company contacted and explored the salvage in time. As Xinlong Company did not have the qualifications for salvage operations in the accident water areas and the amount required by the Guangzhou Salvage Bureau was beyond the scope of Honghai Company's capabilities, the salvage work could not actually be carried out. However, Honghai Company informed Shanghai Eastern Company of the relevant situation, and had fulfilled its reasonable notification obligation. It was the failure of Shanghai Eastern Company to perform the derogation obligations that caused the loss to expand. The appeal of Shanghai Eastern Company lacked factual and legal basis and should be dismissed.

OOCL UK refused to accept judgment of first instance and filed an appeal before the court, claiming to revoke judgment of first instance, and the judgment should be changed to dismiss all claims of Shanghai Eastern Company against OOCL UK. Honghai Company should bear all the responsibility of compensation for the accident involved. The litigation fee of first instance and second instance should be born by Shanghai Eastern Company and Honghai Company. The reasons were as follows: 1. Shanghai Eastern Company was not an eligible claimant in the case. The case was a dispute over compensation for goods loss caused by a ship collision, which was an infringement action. Only the owner of the goods or the person who had the right from the owner of the goods may suffer loss had the right to claim. Shanghai Eastern Company resold the steel ordered from Shagang Company to Longxue Corporation. As an intermediary, it only paid part of the deposit to Shagang Company and collected part of the deposit from Longxue Corporation. There was no evidence that the entire payment was paid. It did not obtain the ownership of the goods involved. Correspondingly, Longxue Corporation, which was the buyer, did not obtain the ownership of the goods, and the statement issued by Longxue Corporation that it was not the owner of the goods was meaningless. Judgment of first instance failed to find out whether Shanghai Eastern Company paid for the goods and obtained the ownership of the goods. It was clearly improper that Shanghai Eastern Company had the right to lodge claims based on the statement of the consignee Longxue Corporation. 2. Judgment of first instance wrongly confirmed Shanghai Eastern Company's loss. Shanghai Eastern Company only provided invoices without providing proof of payment, which was not enough to prove that it actually paid the goods. According to the agreement of the product purchase and sale contract concluded with Longxue Corporation, it received 50% of the payment from Longxue Corporation in advance, and according to the agreement of the product purchase and sale contract concluded with Shagang Company, it only paid 30% of the payment to Shagang Company. This showed that Shanghai Eastern Company did not actually suffer loss. According to the agreements concluded by Honghai Company with Xinlong Company and Guangzhou Salvage Bureau, the salvage cost was lower than the value of the goods. Shanghai Eastern Company and Honghai Company shirk each other's responsibility for the ship and goods salvage. Although the goods involved sank with the ship, if the two companies could cooperate with each other, they could still significantly reduce loss through timely salvage. According to Article 119 of the Contract Law of the People's Republic of China, Shanghai Eastern Company had no right to claim compensation for the enlarged loss caused by failure to take reasonable measures. The amount of goods loss involved should be limited in a reasonable goods salvage cost of RMB5 million. The excess part was an enlarged loss and should not be born by the ship. 3. After receiving part of the insurance indemnity, Shanghai Eastern Company had no right to claim for all loss. Article 25 of the Insurance Law of the People's Republic of China (2009) stipulated that if the insurer was unable to determine the amount of the compensation after receiving the claim and related materials, it should pay the amount that could be determined according to the existing certificates and materials, and then pay the corresponding difference after the final compensation amount was determined. Even if the insurer was temporarily unable to determine the exact amount of compensation, it should pay a certain amount of compensation firstly. This kind of "advance payment" was part of the insurance indemnity. According to Article 252 of the Maritime Code of the People's Republic of China, since the date of receipt of the insurance indemnity of RMB4.5 million, the right to claim for this part of the loss should be transferred to the insurer involved CPIC Shanghai Branch. CPIC Shanghai Branch should file a claim in its own name. The transfer of the aforesaid right of compensation should not be changed by the agreement of the parties concerned. Article 14 of China Pacific Insurance Co., Ltd. the Domestic Waterway and Land Goods Transportation Insurance Clauses also stated that "if the insured requests, the insurer can pay compensation firstly, but the insured shall issue a transfer of rights and interests to the insurer and assist the insurer to recover from the liable party". Judgment of first instance did not deduct RMB4.5 million from the compensation received by Shanghai Eastern Company, which was equivalent to allowing Shanghai Eastern Company and CPIC Shanghai Branch to file a claim for this part of the loss at the same time. This violated the provisions of the law and the insurance clauses, and aggravated the ship's responsibility, which was obviously inappropriate. 4. Inappropriate division of the responsibility proportion for the collision of the ship involved. Regarding the collision between M.V. "OOCL EUROPE" and M.V. "Xinghai 668", (2010) Yue Gao Fa Min Si Zhong Zi No.86 and No.87 Civil Judgments confirmed that the two ships were at fault in the accident and should bear 60% and 40% respectively. According to the analysis of the ship's seaworthiness and the layout of the two ships, the confirmation was obviously inappropriate. On the one hand, according to the investigations by the Guangdong Maritime Safety Administration and the Hong Kong Maritime Department, the minimum safe crew requirement for M.V. "Xinghai 668" was 12. However, in fact, the ship was equipped with only 11 crew, of which only 4 had certificates; the second officer on duty at the time of the accident did not hold a pilot's competency certificate and the sailor on duty did not hold a duty certificate and were not qualified for navigation duty; the second officer on duty did not master the basic navigation skills and was unable to operate the radar, which directly led to the accident. Honghai Company knew that most of the crew did not hold certificates and still hired them, and even used other crew to replace the crew who were actually on board under investigation by the Guangdong Maritime Safety Administration. There were serious frauds. On the other hand, regarding the layout of the two ships at the time of the accident, Article 10 Paragraph 1 of the COLREG stipulated that ships navigating in the water areas of the traffic separation system must comply with the requirements of the traffic separation system and other provisions. It was stipulated that a ship could not enjoy privileges or become a direct sailing ship because it sailed along a traffic lane. The warning zone involved was relatively independent, and neither belonged to the Boliao Waterway nor the Dangan Waterway. The two ships should fulfill their obligation of giving way according to the pattern of encounters. M.V. "OOCL EUROPE" was located in front of the starboard side of M.V. "Xinghai 668", and the two ships formed a cross encounter situation. According to Article 15 of the COLREG, M.V. "OOCL EUROPE" was a direct sailing ship, and M.V. "Xinghai 668" was a giving way ship, and the latter should fulfill the obligation of giving way. In terms of the current course and speed of M.V. "Xinghai 668" and the respective lengths of the two ships, M.V. "Xinghai 668" took evasive measures too late, which violated Article 8 Paragraph 1 of the COLREG "early and wide" requirements. When M.V. "Xinghai 668" began to turn to the right, M.V. "OOCL EUROPE" was about to enter the warning zone. After observing that the other party had obviously not gave way in time, M.V. "OOCL EUROPE" had to turn to the left. It complied with Article 17 Paragraph 1 Sub-paragraph 2 of the COLREG, "can take manipulative actions alone to avoid collisions". The urgent situation between the two ships was caused by the failure of M.V. "Xinghai 668" as a giving way ship to give way in time. When the collision was unavoidable, M.V. "OOCL EUROPE" turned to the left, which was as the last effort to reduce loss. It should not be held liable. Therefore, Honghai Company should bear full responsibility for the collision accident of the ship involved. OOCL UK applied for a retrial regarding the confirmation of the proportion of responsibility for collision between two ships in the above effective judgment. After the Supreme People's Court accepted it, it issued a trial with (2012) Min Ti Zi No.142 Civil Ruling and suspended the enforcement of the original judgment.

In response to the appeal of OOCL UK, Shanghai Eastern Company replied in second instance: 1. Shanghai Eastern Company provided evidence such as contracts, invoices, ownership transfer instructions, which was sufficient to prove that it fulfilled its payment obligations and had ownership of the goods involved. 2. After the accident involved, Shanghai Eastern Company reorganized the supply of goods to Longxue Corporation and actively performed its obligation to reduce loss. Upon contact, the main body responsible for the salvage the accident involved in the Hong Kong Maritime Department's response was the shipowner. The official letter from the Hong Kong Maritime Department provided by Shanghai Eastern Company in first instance and the correspondence between it and the Hong Kong Maritime Department and other evidence could prove it; and the relevant Chinese laws also stipulated that: the main body responsible for the salvage of such accidents was the shipowner. As the goods owner, Shanghai Eastern Company was unable to salvage the sunk goods involved, and OOCL UK's claim that Shanghai Eastern Company failed to salvage and perform its derogation obligations could not be established. 3. Since the goods involved was not salvaged and their residual value could not be ascertained, it was objectively difficult to determine the specific amount of loss, and repurchase of similar goods to deliver to Longxue Corporation also required funds. For this reason, CPIC Shanghai Branch paid part of the payment in advance for Shanghai Eastern Company, and the two parties also agreed through an agreement that the payment of the payment would not affect the exercise of the right of Shanghai Eastern Company to claim compensation from the liable party. After the specific loss was determined, the settlement would be based on the principle of more refund and less compensation. Therefore, judgment of first instance that the RMB4.5 million was prepayment and not deducted was correct. OOIL UK's appeal was unreasonable and should be dismissed.

In response to the appeal of OOCL UK, Honghai Company replied in second instance: 1. Honghai Company agreed with the first, second and third appeal reasons raised by OOCL UK, namely, Shanghai Eastern Company was not eligible claimant for this case and the judgment of first instance made an error in the loss of Shanghai Eastern Company and Shanghai Eastern Company had no right to claim all loss after receiving part of the insurance indemnity. Regarding the confirmation of the loss of Shanghai Eastern Company, Shanghai Eastern Company's view that the sunk goods with the ship should be salvaged by the shipowner was wrong. Even if the shipowner had certain obligations for the salvage of the sunk goods with the ship, Honghai Company clearly informed Shanghai Eastern Company that it lacked the required funds, was unable to arrange salvage, and the Guangzhou Salvage Bureau's price quotation and said that it could assist in handling the application for salvage to the Hong Kong Maritime Department. Shanghai Eastern Company knew that Honghai Company was unable to salvage, but did not actively organize the salvage itself, nor did it request Honghai Company to assist in handling the application for salvage to the Hong Kong Maritime Department. This was clearly required by law that the party bore loss did not take effective measures to reduce the loss, so Shanghai Eastern Company should bear the enlarged part of the loss by itself. Regarding the RMB4.5 million paid by CPIC Shanghai Branch, even if judgment of first instance determined that it was prepaid, it could not change its nature as an insurance indemnity. According to Article 252 of the Maritime Code of the People's Republic of China, and Article 60 of the Insurance Law of the People's Republic of China (2009), the right of the insured to claim compensation from the liable person should be transferred to the insurer from the date the insurer paid the insurance indemnity. The signing of the agreement of CPIC Shanghai Branch and Shanghai Eastern Company did not make an agreement contrary to the above-mentioned legal provisions, so from the date of payment of this part of the insurance indemnity, CPIC Shanghai Branch would obtain the corresponding right of subrogation, and Shanghai Eastern Company had no right to continue claiming the compensation for this part of the loss which was compensated. Judgment of first instance failed to deduct this part when calculating the amount of compensation available to Shanghai Eastern Company, which was that the loss was improperly determined. 2. The proportion of responsibility for collision between the two ships should be determined based on the trial result of (2012) Min Ti Zi No.142. OOIL UK's appeal was partly reasonable, and judgment of first instance should be adjusted for its reasonable part.

After the trial, the court finds that the facts found in judgment of first instance were corroborated by relevant evidence, and the court confirms the facts found in first instance.

The court also finds out that: OOCL UK was a limited responsibility company incorporated in the Cayman Islands. It was registered in Hong Kong region under Part XI of the Hong Kong Companies Ordinance on March 13, 2003, and held an overseas company registration certificate. The declaration form showed that the company was a non-Hong Kong company.

During the trial of second instance, OOCL UK submitted the following evidence to prove the proportion of liabilities of M.V. "OOCL EUROPE" and M.V. "Xinghai 668" in the collision accident of the ships involved: Supreme People's Court (2012) Min Ti Zi No.142 No. Civil Judgment. Shanghai Eastern Company and Honghai Company had no objection to the evidence, and the court confirms its probative force. According to the trial situation of first instance, second instance, and retrial of the case involving ship collision accident and (2012) Min Ti Zi No.142 Civil Judgment, the court finds out the following facts that:

Honghai Company filed an action against OOCL UK, OOCL Container Shipping Company, Swan Country Commercial Leasing Co., Ltd., on the claim for loss caused by the ship collision accident involved between M.V. "OOCL EUROPE" and M.V. "Xinghai 668" and OOCL UK and others jointly filed counterclaims against Honghai Company's action. The court of first instance accepted the case with (2009) Guang Hai Fa Chu Zi No.4 and (2009) Guang Hai Fa Chu Zi No.292 respectively. After trial, it was confirmed that M.V. "OOCL EUROPE" was liable for 60% of the collision accident and M.V. "Xinghai 668" was liable for 40%, and a judgment was made accordingly. OOCL UK refused to accept the judgment and filed an appeal. The court accepted and affirmed the judgment with (2010) Yue Gao Fa Min Si Zhong Zi No.86 and (2010) Yue Gao Fa Min Si Zhong Zi No.87. OOCL UK refused to accept the (2010) Yue Gao Fa Min Si Zhong Zi No.86 and No.87 Civil Judgments, and filed an application for retrial to the Supreme People's Court, which approved it. During the retrial, OOCL UK submitted a notarized the *Maritime Investigation Report* made by the Hong Kong Maritime Department on July 20, 2011 in order to prove that M.V. "Xinghai 668" was seriously unseaworthy. In addition, OOCL UK also applied to the Supreme People's Court to obtain relevant accident investigation data from Guangdong Maritime Safety Administration. The court of first instance was entrusted by the Supreme People's Court to obtain ship certificates, crew certificates, interview transcripts and other relevant materials. After trial, the Supreme People's Court ruled to revoke the court's (2010) Yue Gao Fa Min Si Zhong Zi No.86 and No.87 Civil Judgments, and partially changed the court of first instance (2009) Guang Hai Fa Chu Zi No.4 and No.292 Civil Judgments.

The registered shipping area of M.V. "Xinghai 668" was the coastal area, and the operating area was A1 + A2. Honghai Company held the seaworthiness certificate of the ship. M.V. "OOCL EUROPE" was a steel container ship with a gross tonnage of 89,097 tons and a net tonnage of 55,204 tons. The port of registration was Hong Kong. When the accident happened, the ship classification certificate, international load line certificate, international oil pollution prevention certificate, safety management certificates were within the validity period. The facts confirmed in (2010) Yue Gao Fa Min Si Zhong Zi No. 86 and No. 87 Civil Judgments contained no content regarding the unseaworthiness of M.V. "Xinghai 668" and the unfitness of the crew.

The Supreme People's Court (2012) Min Ti Zi No.142 Civil Judgment held that: although the authenticity of the *Maritime Investigation Report* issued by the Hong Kong Maritime Department could be confirmed, the information on the crew stated on it was based on the investigation of the crew by the China Maritime Safety Administration. Because the report did not contain the corresponding crew investigation data, it could not prove that the crew of M.V. "Xinghai 668" was unsuitable; the multiple interview transcripts in the relevant accident investigation data obtained from the Guangdong Maritime Safety Administration were witness testimonies. They were not recognized by Honghai Company, and the crew and related personnel under investigation did not appear in court as witnesses to accept the inquiries from the parties, and the competent authority did not make an investigation report on the accident, and did not confirm the unfitness of the crew. The investigation data did not belong to Article 11 of the Provisions of the Supreme People's Court on the Trial of Certain Issues in Cases of Disputes over Collision of Ships on evidence for determining the facts of the case. Therefore, the judgment did not confirm the fact that OOCL UK claimed that M.V. "Xinghai 668" was unseaworthy. The facts confirmed in No.86 and No.87 Civil Judgments of (2010) Yue Gao Fa Min Si Zhong Zi were basically clear and the judgement confirmed. Based on this, the relevant circumstances of the collision involved are as follows: on October 21, 2008, M.V. "OOCL EUROPE" sailed along the exit channel of the East Boliao Waterway and sailed to Singapore via the Dangan Waterway; M.V. "Xinghai 668" sailed along the entrance of Dangan Waterway from east to west. Both ships used radar and manual observation methods. At about 0537, M.V. "Xinghai 668" and M.V. "OOCL EUROPE" first met. The distance between the two ships was about 3 nautical miles. At this time, M.V. "Xinghai 668" was heading about 272°and the speed was about 7.5 knots. M.V. "OOCL EUROPE" was heading about 148°and the speed was about 16 knots. M.V. "OOCL EUROPE" started to turn to the left and slowed down at 0544, with a heading of 146° and a speed of 16 knots; at 0545, a heading of 100° and a speed of 12.5 knots. M.V. "Xinghai 668" started to turn right at 0543 with a heading of 272° and a speed of 8 knots; at 0545, a heading of 329° and a speed of 7 knots. At about 0545, the starboard side of M.V. "OOCL EUROPE" collided with the bow of M.V. "Xinghai 668" at the junction of Hong Kong water areas and Guangzhou water areas, approximately 114° 12.67′ east longitude and 22° 08.9′ north latitude. M.V. "Xinghai 668" sank in the bow, and sank near Light Buoy No.1 at about 0615, about 1.1 nautical miles from the collision location, belonging to Hong Kong water areas. When the accident happened, the water areas had good visibility. According to the relevant circumstances of the collision accident, the Supreme People's Court (2012) Min Ti Zi No.142 Civil Judgment held that: (2010) Yue Gao Fa Min Si Zhong Zi No.86 and No.87 Civil Judgments concerning the leftward steering of M. V. "OOCL EUROPE" was the main reason for the urgent situation of two ships, the fact that the failure of M.V. "Xinghai 668" to give way was the secondary cause of the accident, and its facts confirmed and legal basis are insufficient. Accordingly, the confirmation that M.V. "OOCL EUROPE" bore 60% of the responsibility of the collision accident and M.V. "Xinghai 668" bore 40% of the responsibility was also inappropriate and should be corrected. M.V. "Xinghai 668" should bear 60% of the responsibility of the collision accident and M.V. "OOCL EUROPE" should bear 40% of the responsibility. Accordingly, the judgment on the amount of compensation involved was changed.

In order to prove the nature of the payment of RMB4.5 million by CPIC Shanghai Branch, Shanghai Eastern Company submitted 1 piece of evidence: a statement issued by CPIC Shanghai Branch. OOIL UK and Honghai Company had no objection to the authenticity of the evidence, but they did not recognize the content contained therein. The court holds that the evidence is the original and the content contained in it is related to the facts involved, so the court confirms its probative power. Based on this piece of evidence, the following facts are additionally found out:

On April 16, 2013, CPIC Shanghai Branch issued a statement stating that: CPIC Shanghai Branch, as the insurer of the sunk goods, clearly held that the insured, Shanghai Eastern Company, had economic loss, but before the sunk goods were successfully salvaged, the specific loss amount of the goods could not be determined. The amount of RMB4.5 million paid by CPIC Shanghai Branch to Shanghai Eastern Company was an advance payment made by the insurer to help the insured reduce loss, and was not an insurance indemnity. After receiving the payment, Shanghai Eastern Company did not issue a receipt and sign the transfer of rights and interests, and it did not request Shanghai Eastern Company to issue a receipt and sign the transfer of rights and interests. According to the two prepaid insurance indemnity agreements concluded between the two parties, the right to claim compensation from the liable party for goods loss caused by the accident still belonged to Shanghai Eastern Company.

In addition, the parties concerned unanimously recognized in second instance court investigation that the goods involved have not been salvaged since they sank.

The court holds that:

Although the Appellant OOCL UK was registered as an overseas company in Hong Kong region, this did not change its nature as a company incorporated in the Cayman Islands. Therefore, the case is a dispute over responsibility for foreign ship collision damage. The parties did not raise any objection to the court of first instance in handling the substantive disputes with the laws of the People's Republic of China. After review by the court, the handling was not obviously improper, so it is affirmed. Based on the appeals, defenses and court investigations, the court confirmed that the disputes in second instance in this case mainly lie in whether Shanghai Eastern Company is the eligible subject of the claim for loss to the goods involved, the proportion of responsibility for the collision accident of the ship involved, and whether Honghai Company has the right to enjoy the limitation of maritime compensation responsibility, whether Shanghai Eastern Company has the right to claim compensation for the corresponding loss of the amount paid by CPIC Shanghai Branch, and the amount of compensation for the goods loss involved.

1. Whether Shanghai Eastern Company is the eligible subject of the claim for loss to the goods involved

The case is a dispute over compensation for goods loss caused by a ship collision. The transportation involved was goods transportation along domestic coastal ports between Zhangjiagang and Guangzhou. M.V. "OOCL EUROPE" and M.V. "Xinghai 668" involved in the collision were all sea ships. Therefore, the rights, obligations, and liabilities of all parties involved in the accident should be determined according to the *Maritime Code of the People's Republic of China* and the *Provisions of the Supreme People's Court on the Trial of Certain Issues in Cases of Disputes over Collision of Ships*. Shanghai Eastern Company delivered the steel goods legally purchased by it for transportation. Honghai Company actually carried and issued the corresponding transportation documents with its own M.V. "Xinghai 668". The shipper stated on the transportation document was Shanghai Eastern Company. It was sufficient to show that Shanghai Eastern Company had rights to the goods involved transported by M.V. "Xinghai 668". The negligent collision of M.V. "OOCL EUROPE" and M.V. "Xinghai 668" caused the goods involved loaded on M.V. "Xinghai 668" to fall into the sea, according to Article 6 of the Provisions of the Supreme People's Court on the Trial of Certain Issues in Cases of Disputes over Collision of Ships "Where the damage caused to the goods on board due to collided ships with the fault of each other, and the right holder of the goods on board files an action of compensation for breach of contract against the ship carrying the goods, or files an action of compensation for infringement against one or both of the parties to the collision, the people's court shall accept the action according to the law.", Shanghai Eastern Company had the right to lodge a claim against OOCL UK and Honghai Company for the loss of goods caused by the collision. The provisions of Chapter VIII of the *Maritime Code of the People's Republic of China* on ship collision and the *Provisions of the Supreme People's Court on the Trial of Certain Issues in Cases of Disputes over Collision of Ships* have not limited the scope of the "owner of goods on board" to the owner of the goods. Therefore, whether Shanghai Eastern Company paid the price of the goods and whether it actually obtained the ownership of the goods involved did not affect the exercise of its right of claim for compensation. The goods involved, as the subject matter of the transportation contract, fell into the sea due to a ship collision accident and have not been salvaged so far. As a result, the purpose of the transportation contract of the shipper Shanghai Eastern Company to deliver the goods to the consignee could not be realized, and Shanghai Eastern Company was lost control of the goods; moreover, it can be seen from the evidence and facts of first instance that, in order to perform its contract with the outsider, Shanghai Eastern Company separately organized similar goods to complete the original delivery. The above situation is sufficient to show that the falling of the goods involved objectively caused loss to Shanghai Eastern Company, and Shanghai Eastern Company had a direct interest in the collision accident and is entitled to corresponding compensation. OOCL UK and Honghai Company claim that Shanghai Eastern Company did not pay for the goods and was not the owner of the goods, and therefore was not the eligible subject of claim for loss of the goods involved, which has no legal basis and cannot be established.

2. The proportion of responsibility for the collision accident of the ship involved

According to Article 6 of the COLREG, ships should be particularly cautious when sailing near the end of the traffic separation system. In the collision involved, M.V. "OOCL EUROPE" and M.V. "Xinghai 668" were in a high-speed state when sailing in the alert zone at the end of the East Boliao waterway, namely the intersection of the two channels, and did not maintain a safe speed after the first sighting and actively and early use good craftsmanship to avoid collisions, failing to sound the horn or use lights when taking steering measures, so that the other ship could not know the intention of the ship's steering, which violated Article 6, Articles 8 Paragraph 1 and Article 34 of the COLREG, both ships were at fault for the occurrence of the collision. According to Article 8, Article 15, Article 16, and Article 17 of the COLREG, in the situation of intersection, giving way ships have a greater obligation to avoid collisions than direct sailing ships. If an urgent situation is formed due to that giving way ships fail to early fulfill the obligation to give way, the main responsibility for the collision should be born; according to Article 10 Paragraph 1 of the COLREG, the provisions of the traffic separation system cannot remove the obligation to give way of giving way ship in the cross encounter situation. After the first encounter, the two ships formed a cross encounter situation. M. V. "OOCL EUROPE" was located on the starboard side of M.V. "Xinghai 668", so M.V. "OOCL EUROPE" was a direct sailing ship and M.V. "Xinghai 668" was a giving way ship. M.V. "Xinghai 668" should take action as soon as possible to give way to M.V. "OOCL EUROPE". However, M.V. "Xinghai 668" did not take any action within 6 minutes after the two ships first met, and only started to turn to the right until 2 minutes before the collision, which led to the formation of an urgent situation, and it should bear the main responsibility for the accident. According to Article 17 of the COLREG, a direct sailing ship should maintain course and speed. When the giving way ship fails to take appropriate actions to fulfill its obligation to give way, it can independently take maneuvering action to avoid collisions; if the circumstances permit at the time, it should not take a left turn operation for the ship on the port side of the ship. After M.V. "Xinghai 668" failed to give way in time and caused an urgent situation, M.V. "OOCL EUROPE" violated the above regulations when taking collision avoidance actions and suddenly turned to the left, which was an important cause of the accident. OOCL UK's claim that M.V. "Xinghai 668" should bear full responsibility for the collision lacks factual and legal basis, and the court does not support it. In the absence of sufficient evidence to prove that M.V. "Xinghai 668" was unseaworthy and the crew was unfit, comprehensively considering the degree of negligence of the two ships, M.V. "Xinghai 668" should bear 60% of the responsibility for the collision. M.V. "OOCL EUROPE" should bear 40% of the responsibility. Judgment of first instance that M.V. "OOCL EUROPE" bore 60% of the responsibility for the collision accident and M.V. "Xinghai 668" bore 40% of the responsibility is improper, and the court corrects it.

3. Whether Honghai Company has the right to enjoy the limitation of maritime compensation responsibility

During the trial of the dispute over compensation for loss caused by the ship collision between M.V. "OOCL EUROPE" and M.V. "Xinghai 668", the parties concerned failed to provide effective evidence to prove that M.V. "Xinghai 668" was unseaworthy and the crew was not suitable. The effective Civil Judgment (2012) Min Ti Zi No.142 confirmed the facts confirmed in the judgment of first instance of the case, and at the same time confirmed that the *Maritime Investigation Report* made by the Hong Kong Marine Department provided by OOCL UK on the collision involved could not prove the crew of M.V. "Xinghai 668" was not suitable, and the accident investigation materials of the Guangdong Maritime Safety Administration requested by the court it applied were not sufficient to prove that the ship was unseaworthy. According to Article 93 Paragraph 1 Sub-paragraph 5 of the Interpretation of the Supreme People's Court on the Application of the Civil Procedure Law of the People's Republic of China regarding facts confirmed by the people's court in a legally effective judgment, the parties do not need to provide evidence to prove. In the case that neither party provided relevant other evidence in this case, it can be confirmed that there was no unseaworthy ship or unfit crew of M.V. "Xinghai 668". Article 209 of the Maritime Code of the People's Republic of China stipulates that only the loss that caused the claim for compensation was caused by the liable person's act or omission done with the intent to cause such loss or recklessly and with knowledge that such loss would probably result, and the liable person has no right to comply with the provisions of Chap. 11 of the law to limit the responsibility for compensation; Article 19 of the Several Provisions of the Supreme People's Court concerning the Trial of Dispute Cases in relation to Maritime Compensation Liability Limitation stipulates that the people's court shall not support the maritime claimant's claim that the person liable has no right to limit the responsibility for compensation on the ground that the ship in a maritime accident is unseaworthy, but it cannot prove that the loss resulted from his act or omission done with the intent to cause such loss or recklessly and with knowledge that such loss would probably result. Although the goods loss involved was caused by the negligent collision between M.V. "OOCL EUROPE" and M.V. "Xinghai 668", and M.V. "Xinghai 668" was primarily liable for the collision, there was no case that the ship was unseaworthy or its crew was unfit. There is no evidence or facts that show that the improper operation of the crew of M.V. "Xinghai 668" was caused by Honhai Company's intentional or knowingly possible loss and still reckless act or omission. Shanghai Eastern Company claimed that it was not entitled to the limitation of maritime compensation responsibility only on the grounds that Honhai Company was obviously at fault for the occurrence of the collision, which lacked factual and legal basis and could not be established. Judgment of first instance that Honhai Company had the right to enjoy the limitation of maritime compensation responsibility within the limit of RMB2,642,925.24 was not improper, and the court supports it.

4. Whether Shanghai Eastern Company has the right to claim compensation for the corresponding loss of the amount paid by CPIC Shanghai Branch

According to Article 10 of the Insurance Law of the People's Republic of China (2002) "An insurance contract is an agreement whereby the insurance rights and obligations are specified and agreed by the applicant and the insurer." "An insurer refers to the insurance company which enters into an insurance contract with an applicant and is obligated to make indemnity or payments of the insurance benefits.", Article 216 of the Maritime Code of the People's Republic of China "A contract of marine insurance is a contract whereby the insurer undertakes, as agreed, to indemnify the loss to the subject matter insured and the responsibility of the insured caused by perils covered by the insurance against the payment of an insurance premium by the insured.", "The covered perils referred to in the preceding paragraph mean any maritime perils agreed upon between the insurer and the insured, including perils occurring in inland rivers or on land which is related to a maritime adventure.", in the marine insurance contract, the payment obligation that the insurer should bear to the insured is limited to the loss or responsibility caused by the insured accident. After the collision involved, CPIC Shanghai Branch paid a total of RMB4.5 million to Shanghai Eastern Company twice in 2009, according to the contents of the *Prepayment insurance indemnity Agreement* and the *Second Prepayment insurance indemnity Agreement* concluded by both parties at that time, Shanghai Eastern Company's claim to CPIC Shanghai Branch was "prepayment of insurance indemnity", and CPIC Shanghai Branch agreed to "prepay insurance indemnity" to Shanghai Eastern Company, indicating that both parties agreed that the payment was insurance indemnity, even if it was "prepaid", it was not enough to change the nature of the payment; the two parties agreed to settle the claim after Shanghai Eastern Company received the compensation due from the liable party, and implement more refunds and less compensation, indicating that the payment was actually paid and there was no possibility of that CPIC Shanghai Branch withdrew in the future. The two parties had no objection to the occurrence of the insured accident involved and the establishment of insurance responsibility. The two agreements and the statement submitted by CPIC Shanghai Branch in second instance also made it clear that the reason for the prepayment of compensation was that the specific loss of the goods could not be determined, not otherwise. Article 26 of the Insurance Law of the People's Republic of China (2002) stipulates that if the insurer cannot determine the amount after receiving a claim for compensation or insurance payment and relevant certificates and materials, payment should be made in advance on the basis of the minimum amount that can be determined on the basis of evidence and information, and the corresponding difference will be paid after the final amount is determined. The payment of RMB4.5 million paid by CPIC Shanghai Branch to Shanghai Eastern Company complied with the provisions of the above-mentioned law on advance compensation. Although Shanghai Eastern Company and CPIC Shanghai Branch denied that the payment was an insurance indemnity and claimed that it was an advance payment, the court holds that, in the absence of evidence to prove that the two parties involved in the insurance contract, in addition to fulfilling the insurance payment responsibility, in the case of other reasonable and legal commercial arrangements, the amount paid by CPIC Shanghai Branch as the insurer to Shanghai Eastern Company as the insured should be insurance indemnity. According to Article 252 Paragraph 1 of the Maritime Code of the People's Republic of China, "Where the loss of or damage to the subject matter insured within the insurance converage is caused by a third person, the right of the insured to demand compensation from the third person shall be subrogated to the insurer from the time the compensation is paid.", Article 93 of the Special Maritime Procedure Law of the People's Republic of China "In the event of an insured event caused by a third party, the insurer shall, within the scope of the insurance indemnity, exercise the subrogation right of the insured to claim compensation against the third party after paying the insurance indemnity to the insured.", starting from when CPIC Shanghai Branch paid RMB2,000,000 on May 4, 2009 and RMB2.5 million on October 26, 2009, the right to claim for the loss of the corresponding amount was transferred to CPIC Shanghai Branch. CPIC Shanghai Branch could substitute Shanghai Eastern Company to exercise the right of claim and claim compensation from the Third Party that caused the loss. The transfer of the right to claim is a statutory transfer, and the agreement of CPIC Shanghai Branch and Shanghai Eastern Company regarding the exercise of the right of compensation by CPIC Shanghai Branch after prepayment of insurance indemnity does not comply with the law. Shanghai Eastern Company does not have the right to claim compensation for the loss corresponding to the RMB4.5 million insurance indemnity it obtained. Its claim for this part of the loss lacks a legal basis and the court does not support it. The scope of the loss that Shanghai Eastern Company has the right to claim is directly related to the specific compensation liabilities of OOCL UK and Honghai Company in the case. Judgment of first instance about RMB4.5 million is not the final compensation of the insured accident involved. OOCL UK and Honghai Company did not aggravate its responsibility due to the contract between Shanghai Eastern Company and CPIC Shanghai Branch for the exercise of the right of compensation. The confirmation that Shanghai Eastern Company still had the right to claim for this is improper and the court corrects it.

5. The amount of compensation for the goods loss involved

The 209 pieces of steel plates carried by M.V. "Xinghai 668" were the subject matter under the involved transportation contract. All of them fell into the sea and sank due to the collision of the ship and have not been salvaged so far. As analyzed before, Shanghai Eastern Company, as the buyer and shipper under the transportation contract lost its actual control and organized a separate source of goods to complete the original delivery, and objectively suffered loss. OOCL UK and Honghai claimed that Shanghai Eastern Company had no actual loss on the grounds that Shanghai Eastern Company did not pay the full payment. This is inconsistent with the objective situation and is not supported. The judgment of first instance determined the specific price, quantity, weight, of the goods involved based on evidence such as the purchase contract, VAT invoice, waterway goods waybill, bill of lading, and ex-factory code sheet, and determined that the value of the goods fell into sea involved was RMB15,958,497.24. There is nothing wrong, the court confirms it. The goods involved was sunk with the ship in Hong Kong water areas due to a collision accident. There is no evidence in this case that Shanghai Eastern Company and Honghai had agreed in advance on the handling of the goods falling into the sea and damaged, or that the ship and goods parties had negotiated and reached an agreement after the accident on goods salvage matters, and the parties failed to provide sufficient evidence to prove the subject of the obligation to salvage sunken goods in Hong Kong water areas and related procedure requirements, and the goods involved fell into the sea due to a negligent collision between the two ships, Honghai Company and OOCL UK are the parties liable for the accident, and the goods that has fallen into the sea has not been salvaged so far. The actual salvage cost, the extent of loss to the goods, and the residual value cannot be determined. Therefore, the claim of Honghai Company that after the accident, it contacted the salvage company and notified the relevant situation to Shanghai Eastern Company, it had fulfilled its reasonable notification obligations and as the owner of the goods, Shanghai Eastern Company did not perform its de obligations by organizing salvage and OOCL UK's claim on Shanghai Eastern Company and Honghai Company failed to cooperate with each other to complete the procedures, payment of fee and other matters and actually organize the salvage, which led to the expansion of the loss, and the amount of goods loss involved should be limited to a reasonable salvage cost of RMB5 million both lack factual and legal basis and reasonableness, the court does not support it.

The goods involved fell into the sea and sank in October 2008 due to a collision accident. All parties recognized that the goods had not been salvaged so far. There is no evidence and facts in the case that the other parties actually salvaged the goods, so it can be confirmed as the goods involved have been lost. Article 9 of the Provisions of the Supreme People's Court on the Trial of Compensation for Property Damage in Cases of Collision and Contact of Ships "Calculation of loss of property on board" Paragraph (1) stipulates that "if the goods are lost, the actual value of the goods, namely, shall be calculated on the basis of the value of the goods at the time of shipment plus freight and the insurance premium paid by the claimer for the goods, and any savings shall be saved", Shanghai Eastern Company did not provide evidence to prove that it actually paid the freight, insurance premium and the specific amount of the goods involved. There is no evidence in the case to prove that there was a cost that could be saved, so the loss of the goods involved should be determined based on its value of RMB15,958,497.24. As mentioned above, Shanghai Eastern Company received the insurance indemnity RMB4.5 million from the outsider CPIC Shanghai Branch. The right to claim the corresponding amount of loss was transferred. Shanghai Eastern Company had no right to claim compensation for the loss was already compensated. Therefore, the loss amount it had the right to claim from OOCL UK and Honghai Company, the parties liable for the accident was RMB11,458,497.24 (RMB15,958,497.24 − RMB4,500,000 = RMB11,458,497.24). According to Article 169 Paragraph 1 of the Maritime Code of the People's Republic of China, "if the colliding ships are all in fault, each ship shall be liable in proportion to the extent of its fault; if the respective faults are equal in proportion or it is impossible to determine the extent of the proportion of the respective faults, the responsibility of the colliding ships shall be apportioned equally.", Paragraph 2 "The ships in fault shall be liable for the damage to the ship, the goods and other property on board pursuant to the proportions prescribed in the preceding paragraph. Where damage is caused to the property of a third party, the responsibility for compensation of any of the colliding ships shall not exceed the proportion it shall bear.", M.V. "Xinghai 668" should bear 60% of the responsibility for the collision accident, and Honghai should pay Shanghai Eastern Company the compensation for the loss of goods RMB6,875,098.34 (RMB11,458,497.24 × 60% = RMB6,875,098.34) and the corresponding interest; M.V. "OOCL EUROPE" should bear 40% of the responsibility for the collision accident, and the loss of goods that OOIL UK should compensate Shanghai Eastern Company is RMB4,583,389.90 (RMB11,458,497.24 × 40% = RMB4,583,389.90) and the corresponding interest. Since Honghai Company has the right to enjoy the limitation of maritime compensation responsibility within the range of RMB2,642,925.24 for the accident involved, the amount of goods loss that it should eventually compensate Shanghai Eastern Company should be RMB2,642,925.24 and the corresponding interest. The confirmation of judgment of first instance regarding the amount of compensation for loss of goods of OOIL UK is improper, and is corrected by the court.

Pulling the threads together, the facts confirmed in the judgment of first instance is basically clear, but the application of the law is wrong and the handling results are partially improper. The court will correct the improper parts. The appeals of Shanghai Eastern Company was not well-founded, and the court does not support it. The appeals of OOCL UK was partly justified, and the court supports the reasonable part of it, and does not support the unreasonable part. According to Article 169 Paragraph 1 and Paragraph 2, Article 204 and Article 207 Paragraph 1 Sub-paragraph 1 of the Maritime Code of the People's Republic of China, Article 170 Paragraph 1 Sub-paragraph 1 and Sub-paragraph 2 of the Civil Procedure Law of the People's Republic of China, Article 196 and Article 202 Paragraph 1 of the Interpretation of the Supreme People's Court on the Application of the Civil Procedure Law of the People's Republic of China, Article 29 Paragraph 2 of the Measures on the Payment of Litigation Costs, the judgement is as follows:

1. Affirm the 1st, 3rd and 4th items of Civil Judgment of Guangzhou Maritime Court (2009) Guang Hai Fa Chu Zi No.97;
2. Revoke the 5th item of Civil Judgment of Guangzhou Maritime Court (2009) Guang Hai Fa Chu Zi No.97;
3. Change the 2nd item of Civil Judgment of Guangzhou Maritime Court (2009) Guang Hai Fa Chu Zi No.97 to that: Orient Overseas Container Line (U.K.) Limited. shall compensate Shanghai Eastern Shipping Materials Co., Ltd. for goods loss RMB4,583,389.90 and its interest (from October 21, 2008 to the date when the payment is confirmed in the judgment, calculated at the current fund loan interest rate of the same period of the People's Bank of China);
4. Reject other claims of Shanghai Eastern Shipping Materials Co., Ltd.;
5. Dismiss appeal of Shanghai Eastern Shipping Materials Co., Ltd.

The above obligation to pay money shall be fulfilled within 10 days after the judgment comes into effect.

If the Defendant fails to perform the obligation to pay money according to the period specified in this judgment, it shall double the payment of interest on the debt during the period of delay according to Article 253 of the Civil Procedure Law of the People's Republic of China.

Court acceptance fee of first instance RMB119,365.19, and Shanghai Eastern Shipping Materials Co., Ltd. shall beliable for RMB66,844.51, Beihai Honghai Shipping Co., Ltd. shall beliable for RMB19,432.65, and Orient Overseas Container Line (U.K.) Limited. shall beliable for RMB33,088.03. Shanghai Eastern Shipping Materials Co., Ltd. actually paid court acceptance fee of first instance RMB120,549 in advance, and the court of first instance returned RMB53,704.49 to it; Beihai Honghai Shipping Co., Ltd. shall pay RMB19,432.65 it should bear and Orient Overseas Container Line (U.K.) Limited. shall pay RMB33,088.03 it should bear to the court of first instance.

Court acceptance fee of second instance of Shanghai Eastern Shipping Materials Co., Ltd. RMB36,723.79 shall be born by Shanghai Eastern Shipping Materials Co., Ltd.; Shanghai Eastern Shipping Materials Co., Ltd. actually paid RMB56,483.79 in advance, and the court returned RMB19,670 to it. Court acceptance fee of second instance of Orient Overseas Container Line (U.K.) Limited. shall be RMB78,825.69. Orient Overseas Container Line (U.K.) Limited. shall beliable for RMB37,836.33, and Shanghai Eastern Shipping Materials Co., Ltd. shall beliable for RMB40,989.36. Orient Overseas Container Line (U.K.) Limited. actually paid court acceptance fee of second instance RMB70,425.46 in advance, and the court returned RMB32,589.13 to it; Shanghai Eastern Shipping Materials Co., Ltd. shall pay court acceptance fee of second instance RMB40,989.36 it should bear to the court. After the above two offsets, Shanghai

Eastern Shipping Materials Co., Ltd. still shall pay court acceptance fee of second instance RMB21,229.36 to the court.

The judgement is final

Presiding Judge: DU Yixing
Acting Judge: ZHANG Yiyin
Acting Judge: MO Fei

July 10, 2015

Clerks: WANG Qian
Clerks: LI Junsong

Appendix: Relevant Laws

1. Maritime Code of the People's Republic of China

Article 169 If the colliding ships are all in fault, each ship shall be liable in proportion to the extent of its fault; if the respective faults are equal in proportion or it is impossible to determine the extent of the proportion of the respective faults, the responsibility of the colliding ships shall be apportioned equally.

The ships in fault shall be liable for the damage to the ship, the goods and other property on board pursuant to the proportions prescribed in the preceding paragraph. Where damage is caused to the property of a third party, the responsibility for compensation of any of the colliding ships shall not exceed the proportion it shall bear.

If the ships in fault have caused loss of life or personal injury to a third party, they shall be jointly and severally liable therefor. If a ship has paid an amount of compensation in excess of the proportion prescribed in paragraph 1 of this Article, it shall have the right of recourse against the other ship(s) in fault.

Article 209 A person liable shall not be entitled to limit his responsibility according to the provisions of this Chapter, if it is proved that the loss resulted from his act or omission done with the intent to cause such loss or recklessly and with knowledge that such loss would probably result.

Article 216 A contract of marine insurance is a contract whereby the insurer undertakes, as agreed, to indemnify the loss to the subject matter insured and the responsibility of the insured caused by perils covered by the insurance against the payment of an insurance premium by the insured.

The covered perils referred to in the preceding paragraph mean any maritime perils agreed upon between the insurer and the insured, including perils occurring in inland rivers or on land which is related to a maritime adventure.

Article 252 Where the loss of or damage to the subject matter insured within the insurance converage is caused by a third person, the right of the insured to demand compensation from the third person shall be subrogated to the insurer from the time the compensation is paid.

The insured shall furnish the insurer with necessary documents and information that should come to his knowledge and shall endeavour to assist the insurer in pursuing recovery from the third person.

2. Insurance Law of the People's Republic of China (2002)

Article 10 An insurance contract is an agreement whereby the insurance rights and obligations are specified and agreed by the applicant and the insurer.

An applicant refers to the party who enters into an insurance contract with an insurer and is obligated to pay the premiums under the insurance contract.

An insurer refers to the insurance company which enters into an insurance contract with an applicant and is obligated to make indemnity or payments of the insurance benefits.

Article 26 If the amount of indemnity or payment of the insurance benefits cannot be determined within sixty (60) days of receipt of the claim for indemnity or payment of the insurance benefits, and relevant evidence and information thereof, then the insurer shall effect payment of the minimum amount which can be determined by the evidence and information obtained. The insurer shall pay the balance after the final amount of indemnity or payment of the insurance benefits is determined.

Provisions of the Supreme People's Court on the Trial of Certain Issues in Cases of Disputes over Collision of Ships.

Article 6 Where the damage caused to the goods on board due to collided ships with the fault of each other, and the right holder of the goods on board files an action of compensation for breach of contract against the ship carrying the goods, or files an action of compensation for infringement against one or both of the parties to the collision, the people's court shall accept the action according to the law.

Article 11 After the occurrence of a ship collision, the materials of the collision fact investigation obtained by the competent authority through investigation according to the law and recognized by the parties to the accident and relevant personnel may be used as evidence for confirming the facts of the case by the people's court, unless there is evidence to the contrary which is sufficient to refute the facts.

3. Regulations of the Supreme People's Court on Issues Concerning the Trial of Responsibility Limitation for Maritime Claims

Article 19 The people's court shall not support the maritime claimant's claim that the person liable has no right to limit the responsibility for compensation on the ground that the ship in a maritime accident is unseaworthy, but it cannot prove that the loss resulted from his act or omission done with the intent to cause such loss or recklessly and with knowledge that such loss would probably result.

4. Provisions of the Supreme People's Court on the Trial of Compensation for Property Damage in Cases of Collision and Touching of Ships

Article 9 Calculation of loss of property on board:

(1) if the goods are lost, the actual value of the goods, namely, shall be calculated on the basis of the value of the goods at the time of shipment plus freight and

the insurance premium paid by the claimer for the goods, and any savings shall be saved;

(2) if the goods are damaged, it shall be calculated on the basis of the cost for repair or by that the actual value of the goods deducting the salvage value and the cost which can be saved;

(3) loss caused by delayed delivery within the agreed time as a result of the collision, shall be calculated on the basis of the difference between the actual value of the delayed goods plus the expected profit and the market price at the time of arrival, and the expected profit shall not exceed 10% of the actual value of the goods;

(4) value of the fish goods caught on board shall be calculated on the basis of the actual value of the fish goods. The value of the fish shall refer to the local market price at the time of the occurrence of maritime accident, deducting the cost which can be saved.

(5) types and quantity of fishing gear and net gear on board shall be calculated by deducting the current stock from the quantity required for the current fishing operation, but if the required amount exceeds the types and quantity prescribed or permitted by the fishery administration department, it shall not be recognized; the value of fishing gear and net gear shall be calculated on the basis of the original purchase price or the original construction cost deducting depreciation expense and salvage value;

(6) loss of passengers' luggage and articles (including cabin luggage) belongs to the loss of passengers of the ship and shall be handled according to the maritime code; the loss of passengers belonging to another ship shall be dealt with by reference to the provisions in the passenger transport contract concerning compensation for the loss of or damage to passengers' luggage;

(7) loss of personal necessities of the crew, appropriate compensation shall be made according to the actual loss;

(8) loss of money, gold, silver and jewelery, negotiable securities or other valuable articles in the custody of the carrier as agreed in writing between the carrier and the passenger shall be dealt with according to the maritime code; loss of money, gold and silver, jewelery, negotiable securities or other valuable articles carried by crew, passengers and other individuals shall not be recognized;

(9) loss of other property on the ship shall be calculated on the basis of its actual value.

5. Civil Procedure Law of the People's Republic of China

Article 170 After trying a case on appeal, the people's court of second instance shall deal with it according to the following circumstances respectively:

(1) if the facts are clearly confirmed and the law is correctly applied in the original judgment and ruling, the appeal shall be dismissed by way of judgment or ruling and the original judgment and ruling shall be affirmed;

(2) if the original judgment and ruling was wrong in confirming the facts or in applying the law, it shall be changed, revoked or corrected according to the law by the judgment or ruling;
(3) if the basic facts are not clearly confirmed in the original judgment, a ruling shall be made to revoke the original judgment and send it back to the people's court of first instance for retrial, or the judgment shall be changed after finding out the facts;
(4) if the original judgment omitted a party or seriously violated legal procedures, such as the illegal judgment by default, the original judgment shall be revoked by the ruling and sent to the people's court of first instance for retrial.

After the people's court of first instance has made a judgment on the case sent for retrial, if a party files an appeal, the people's court of second instance shall not send the case for retrial again.

6. Special Maritime Procedure Law of the People's Republic of China

Article 93 In the event of an insured event caused by a third party, the insurer shall, within the scope of the insurance indemnity, exercise the subrogation right of the insured to claim compensation against the third party after paying the insurance indemnity to the insured.

7. Interpretation of the Supreme People's Court on the Application of the Civil Procedure Law of the People's Republic of China

Article 93 Parties do not have to prove the following facts:

(1) laws of nature and theorems and laws;
(2) well-known facts;
(3) facts presumed according to the law;
(4) another fact presumed on the basis of known facts and the rules of experience in daily life;
(5) the facts confirmed by the legally effective judgments of the people's court;
(6) the facts confirmed by the effective award of the arbitration institution;
(7) facts that have been proved by valid notarial documents.

The facts set forth in Sub-paragraphs 2 to 4 of the preceding Paragraph shall be excepted where the parties have evidence to the contrary to refute them; the facts set forth in Sub-paragraphs 5 to 7 shall be excepted where the parties have evidence to the contrary sufficient to disprove them.

Article 196 If a people's court changes the result of original judgment, ruling or mediation, it shall deal with the burden of the litigation fee of first instance in the judgment document.

Article 202 If the Plaintiff, the Defendant and the Third Party appeal respectively, the court acceptance fee of second instance shall be paid in advance according to the appeal claims.

If more than one person from the same party appeals together, only one court acceptance fee of second instance shall be paid in advance; if the appeal is made respectively, the court acceptance fee of second instance shall be paid in advance respectively according to the appeal claims.

8. Measures for the Payment of Litigation Fee of the State Council

Article 29 The litigation fee shall be born by the losing party, except those voluntarily born by the winning party.

If the action is partially won or partially lost, the people's court shall, according to the specific circumstances of the case, determine the amount of litigation fee born by each party.

If a party in a joint action loses the action, the people's court shall, on the basis of its interest in the object of action, determine the amount of litigation fee born by each party.

Shanghai Maritime Court
Civil Judgment

Shanghai Wan Feng International Freight Forwarding Co., Ltd.
v.
Fujian Hongxing Electronic Technology Co., Ltd.

(2014) Hu Hai Fa Shang Chu Zi No.1496

Related Case(s) None.

Cause(s) of Action 223. Dispute over freight forwarding contract on the sea or sea-connected waters.

Headnote Freight forwarder held to be entitled to recover from customer the amount that it had paid to Customs authorities to allow for export clearance, there being a forwarding agreement, despite the Defendant's argument to the contrary.

Summary The Plaintiff, Shanghai Wan Feng International Freight Forwarding Co., Ltd. brought suit against Fujian Hongxing Electronic Technology Co. Ltd. The Court determined that a contractual relationship existed between the Plaintiff and the Defendant, where the Plaintiff provided freight forwarding services for Fujian Hongxing. The court held that the Defendant should reimburse the Plaintiff freight forwarder for the deposit it advanced to procure transportation in the amount of 30,000 RMB, less 5,000 RMB that was incurred by the Plaintiff in the form of a fine for submitting a false declaration to the Customs. This was in spite of the fact that the Customs delay caused the Plaintiff to be in breach of its obligations under the freight-forwarding contract. The court also ordered the Defendant to reimburse the Plaintiff 9,000 RMB for money advanced for towing.

Judgment

The Plaintiff: Shanghai Wan Feng International Freight Forwarding Co., Ltd.
Domicile: Room 105, 6th Building, No.235, Sanlin Road, Pudong New District, Shanghai.

Legal representative: LING Jianfeng, chairman.
Agent *ad litem*: ZHANG Hao, lawyer of Shanghai Haosheng Law Firm.
Agent *ad litem*: BAO Gengsheng, lawyer of Shanghai Haosheng Law Firm.

The Defendant: Fujian Hongxing Electronic Technology Co., Ltd.
Domicile: 5th floor, 28th building, No.89 Software Avenue, A Area, Fuzhou Software Park, Fuzhou Gulou District, Funjian.
Legal representative: XU Peilei, manager.
Agent *ad litem*: HUANG Xian, lawyer of Grandall (Fuzhou) Law Firm.

With respect to the case arising from dispute over the freight forwarding contract, the Plaintiff Shanghai Wan Feng International Freight Forwarding Co., Ltd. filed an action against the Defendant Fujian Hongxing Electronic Technology Co., Ltd. before the court on November 24, 2014. The court accepted the case on the same day, and a summary procedure for trial was conducted in accordance to the law. The Plaintiff submitted an application for property preservation to the court at the same time of filing the case, and requested to freeze the Defendant's bank deposits RMB42,320.56, or sealed up and detained other equivalent property owned by Defendant. On December 2, 2014, the court allowed the Plaintiff's application for property preservation. Due to complexity of the case, on January 28, 2015, the case was turned into general procedure. On March 17, 2015 and April 10, the court held two hearings in public. BAO Gengsheng and ZHANG hao, agents *ad litem* of the Plaintiff, and HUANG Xian, agent *ad litem* of the Defendant, attended the hearings. Now the case has been concluded.

The Plaintiff alleged in the statement of claim that, in late June 2014, the Plaintiff commissioned the Defendant to ship a batch of goods from Shanghai Yangshan Port, China to Kumport, Turkey, and the Defendant sent an application for goods shipment to the Plaintiff through QQ. After received the commission, the Plaintiff dealt with freight forwarding business of this batch of goods such as the trailer, booking, clearance, insurance and so on. On July 22, 2014, the Plaintiff declared the export matters of goods involved to Shanghai Yangshan Port, because of the Customs inspection, the goods failed to be shipped in time. The Defendant was requested by customs to pay RMB30,000 as deposit for the purpose of the final result of inspection affairs. On August 11, 2014, the Defendant asked the Plaintiff to pay the deposit to the customs, as it was not Shanghai company and it was not convenient to pay the deposit. Based on the consideration of commercial interests, On August 11, 2014, the legal representative of the Plaintiff LING Jianfeng paid 30,000 yuan deposit to the Customs instead of the Defendant under his own account. After obtaining the control of the goods involved, the Defendant entrusted other freight forwarding companies to ship goods involved again. The Plaintiff deemed that the lump sum fee caused by the lumpsum business that the Plaintiff dealt with for the Defendant should be paid by the Defendant to the Plaintiff, and the Defendant should return deposit paid by the Plaintiff for it. Accordingly, the Plaintiff requested to order the Defendant to pay the towing fee of RMB9,000, declaration charges of RMB100, insurance premiums of USD524 (equivalent to

RMB3,220.56, according to the US dollar and the RMB exchange rate 1:6.146 on November 14, 2014), and the Defendant should return deposit of RMB30,000, paid by the Plaintiff to the customs, meanwhile the Defendant should undertake court acceptance fee and property preservation application fee.

The Defendant defended that there was no freight forwarding contractual relationship between the Plaintiff and the Defendant The involved business was generated between ZHAO Wenxiang and the Defendant, the Defendant only entrusted ZHAO Wenxiang, rather than the Plaintiff; even if there was freight forwarding contractual relationship between the Plaintiff and the Defendant, because the Plaintiff was unable to provide a clear agency fee agreement between two parties, the advance fees were without authorization or after the ratification of the Defendant, so the Plaintiff's behavior should not be regarded as actual performance of the agency contract, it had no right to claim the various agent fees; deposit was paid by the Defendant, the Plaintiff had no right to ask the Defendant to return. Accordingly, the Defendant requested to reject all of the Plaintiff's claims.

To support its claims, the Plaintiff submitted the following evidence:

1. Application for goods shipment, QQ chatting records among the employees of the Plaintiff and the Defendant, and the identity information of Defendant employee CHEN Yanxiang, the situation description issued by the Plaintiff, Shanghai college graduates, postgraduates employment agreement, the labor contract signed between the Plaintiff and ZHAO Wenxiang, ZHAO Wenxiang's employment and unemployment registration certificate and the SF express waybill of sending materials from the Plaintiff to the Defendant, to prove that CHEN Yanxiang was the employee of the Defendant, which represented the Defendant to send booking note of the goods involved, to ZHAO Wenxiang, the employee of the Plaintiff company, and ZHAO Wenxiang performed duties on behalf of the Plaintiff, not in his own name did business with the Defendant. The Plaintiff accepted the entrust of the Defendant, freight forwarding contractual relationship set up between the parties, and the calculation way of premium was agreed in the chatting records by the two parties.

The Defendant had no objection to the authenticity of, the application for goods shipment, but considered it was printout, which could not prove that it was sent by the Defendant; the Defendant did not confirm the authenticity of the QQ chatting records, whose content was not complete, and there was no declaration of intention of the agency contract and agreement of agency fee, and it had no relevancy with the case; as for the identity information of CHEN Yanxiang, the Defendant deemed it as the data input by itself in QQ, its authenticity could not be confirmed, but it confirmed that CHEN Yanxiang was the employee of the Defendant; the Defendant did not confirm the authenticity of condition description issued by the Plaintiff, and held that it was made by Plaintiff itself; the Defendant did not confirm the authenticity of Shanghai college and postgraduates employment agreement, and argued that there was no signature of school party; as for the labor contract signed by the Plaintiff and ZHAO Wenxiang, the Defendant argued that it was signed by ZHAO Wenxiang and the Plaintiff, and whose authenticity could not be verified; the Defendant had no objection to the authenticity of ZHAO Wenxiang's employment and unemployment registration certificate, but it argued there was no relevancy with the case; the Defendant did not confirm the authenticity of SF express waybill, and it argued that the signature was not signed by QIU Xue, but it confirmed that QIU Xue was the employee of the Defendant.

The court confirms that the Plaintiff provided the labor contract signed with ZHAO Wenxiang and the original copy of ZHAO Wenxiang's employment and unemployment registration certificate, the condition description issued by the Plaintiff, the content of Shanghai college and postgraduates employment agreement could verify with the above two files, meanwhile, ZHAO Wenxiang also attended the court to answer questions and confirmed that he worked for the Plaintiff when he received the involved business entrusted by the Defendant, and he accepted the commission of Defendant on behalf of the Plaintiff, so the court confirms the effectiveness of the above evidence, and the involved business is proved to be formed between the Plaintiff and the Defendant and ZHAO Wenxiang's action is the professional action on behalf of Plaintiff; as for the identity information of CHEN Yanxiang, the court ascertains that although the Defendant denied the authenticity of the identity, but it did not deny the fact that CHEN Yanxiang was the employee of its company, so the fact in this section can be confirmed; as for the application of goods shipment and QQ chatting records, the court holds that the identities of two parties can be confirmed, when ZHAO Wenxiangin court answered questions, he also demonstrated his remaining QQ chatting records to the court, which are consistent with the chatting records provided by the Plaintiff. Although the Defendant argued that the chatting records were not complete, but it did not deny its authenticity, so the court confirms the effectiveness of the application for goods shipment and QQ chatting records, which can prove the fact that the Defendant entrusted Plaintiff to ship goods involved; as for the SF express waybill, the court ascertains that the Defendant did not deny the fact that QIU Xue was the employee of the Defendant, combining it with other facts of the case, which could prove that QIU Xue had participated in the involved business.

2. No.223120140811157784 customs export declaration, to prove that the Plaintiff declared the goods involved to the customs, and performed the contractual obligations of the freight forwarders, and the Defendant was the owner of the goods involved. The Defendant had no objection to the authenticity of the customs declaration, but argued it could only prove that the Defendant exported the goods involved, and it could not prove that the Plaintiff performed the obligations of agent contract. As the Defendant had no objection to the authenticity of the customs declaration, the court confirms its effect of evidence.

3. *Container Load Plan*, to prove that the Plaintiff made containers for the goods involved, and performed the contractual obligations of freight forwarder. The Defendant did not confirm the authenticity of the packing list, and argued that there was no signatures of the party that stuffed the container, it also could not prove that the Plaintiff was commissioned by the Defendant to stuff the containers, but the Defendant confirmed the authenticity of the address of the party that stuffed the containers shown on *Container Load Plan*. The court ascertains that the container numbers recorded on *Container Load Plan* were consistent with the above customs

export declaration, the Defendant also confirmed the address of the party that stuffed the containers shown on it, so the court confirms the evidence effect of the *Container Load Plan*, and it can prove the address of stuffing the containers of goods involved was No.718, Yellow River West Road, Changzhou.

4. Sales confirmation, commercial invoices, cargo shipping insurance policy, premium notices, invoices printed by general machine in local taxation, the customer receipt notification of Agricultural Bank of China that the receipt was China Pacific Property Insurance Co., Ltd. shipping insurance business operating center, to prove that the Plaintiff dealt with the insurance matters on the goods involved, and performed contractual obligations of the freight forwarder. The Defendant confirmed the amount of the disputed insurance premium, and the Plaintiff had paid the premium of goods involved.

The Defendant argued that the contents of sales confirmation and commercial invoices were made by the Plaintiff according to the blank documents sealed and provided by the Defendant, and the Defendant did not confirm the contents; the Defendant did not confirm the authenticity of the insurance policy, and argued that the goods involved were not insured by Defendant, the information filled in the insurance policy still did not get confirmation from the Defendant, the contents in the insurance policy were not consistent with *Container Load Plan*; the Defendant had no objection to the authenticity of premium notice, statements, invoices and account distribution memorandum, but argued that the amount shown in the premium notice was consistent with the amount claimed by Plaintiff, and the goods involved were not shipped at that time, insurance policy shall be revoked, the Plaintiff shall undertake the premiums paid by themselves without the consent of the Defendant.

The Court held that the Defendant did not deny the authenticity of the Defendant's stamp in sales confirmation and commercial invoice, the cargo information on which are corresponded to the contents of the customs export declaration, and confirmed the evidential effects of sales confirmation and commercial invoice; As for the evidence that was to prove that the Plaintiff c covered insurance and paid insurance premiums on behalf of the Defendant, As for the false declaration of the goods involved, which was deducted and inspected by the customs, so the shipping covered by the policy provided by the Plaintiff did not actually occur, and the amount of the premiums provide by the Plaintiff that it had paid was also inconsistent with the premium amount claimed by the Plaintiff. Under the situation that the Plaintiff did not make a reasonable explanation of this, the Court finds that these evidence could not prove the Plaintiff's factum probandum.

5. Value added tax invoices, to prove that the Plaintiff issued invoices to the Defendant and requested the Defendant to pay the lump sum fee, insurance premium. The Defendant did not confirm the authenticity of the invoice and deemed that was made by the Plaintiff. The court ascertains that the Plaintiff had provided the original invoice, and confirms its authenticity, and it can prove that the Plaintiff had claimed to the Defendant for paying freight forwarding fees.

6. Special customs deposit receipts, customs payment notice, the bank withdrawal slips and the identity information of LING Jianfeng, the legal representative

of the Plaintiff, three bank card withdrawal information involved in the case, the detailed statement of Golden Harvest debit card of Agricultural Bank of China, the historical transaction detailed list of Bank of China, the records of conversation between ZHANG Hao, agents *ad litem* of the Plaintiff and ZHAO Wenxiang, the power of attorney to handle deposit refund provided by Defendant, the special payment letter to confiscate income of Shanghai Customs and the flight ticket information of CHEN Yanxiang and QIU Xue, to prove that the Customs requested the Defendant to pay the disputed deposit, the legal representative of the Plaintiff withdrew RMB30,000 from his three bank cards to pay the deposit on behalf of the Defendant, so the Plaintiff now held the original copy of special customs deposit receipt.

The Defendant had no objection to the authenticity of special customs deposit receipt and customs payment notice, but argued that the deposit was paid by the Defendant; The Defendant did not confirm the authenticity of the bank withdrawal slips and LING Jianfeng's identity information, involved three bank cards information, and argued that it could not be verified; the Defendant had no objection to the authenticity to the detailed statement of Golden Harvest debit card of Agricultural Bank of China and the historical transaction detailed list of Bank of China, but argued that they could not prove that the money withdrew from the bank was used to pay the customs deposit; the Defendant did not object to the authenticity of records of conversation of ZHAO Wenxiang, argued that although ZHAO Wenxiang attended the Court to accept the inquiry, he had interest with the Plaintiff, so his statement was not real; the defendant did not object to the authenticity of power of attorney to refund deposit, and argued that the original copy of this power of attorney to refund deposit was not provided by Plaintiff, now this copy remained in ZHAO Wenxiang's phone has lost efficacy, and the writings such as the date and so on were printed below the power of attorney to refund deposit covered up the seal of the Plaintiff, so there was possible to use the blank paper sealed by the Plaintiff to make power of attorney;

The Defendant had no objection to the authenticity of the special payment letter to confiscate income of Shanghai Customs, but argued that it could not prove that the Plaintiff had paid customs deposits; The Defendant had no objection to the authenticity of flight ticket information of QIU Xue and CHEN Yanxiang, it argued that the fact that the deposit was paid by the Defendant was denied because the two persons had no withdrawal records.

As for the Defendant had no objection to the authenticity of the special customs deposit receipt and customs payment notice, the original copy of the receipt was also provided by the Plaintiff, the court confirms the authenticity of the two evidence materials, which can prove the fact the Plaintiff had paid deposit to the customs on the goods involved; as for the bank withdrawal slips and the identity information of LING Jianfeng, the legal representative of the Plaintiff, three bank card withdrawal information involved, the detailed statement of Golden Harvest debit card of Agricultural Bank of China and the historical transaction detailed list of Bank of China, the court considers that the contents of evidence could be confirmed with each other, which can prove the fact that LING Jianfeng withdrew totaling RMB30,000 from his three individual bank cards on August 11, 2014; as for records of conversation of ZHAO Wenxiang, the court ascertains as for ZHAO Wenxiang personally attended the court to accept the inquiry, and confirms the contents of records of conversation, so the court confirms the evidence effect of records of conversation; as for power of attorney to refund deposit, the court holds that ZHAO Wenxiang when attending the court to accept inquiry explained that the power of attorney to refund deposit was drafted by himself, and sent to the employee of Defendant, OUYANG Dan through QQ, after it was confirmed by OUYANG Dan, she sent back to ZHAO Wenxiang through QQ. ZHAO Wenxiang showed the relevant information on the phone, although the link of power of attorney to refund deposit on the phone was invalid, but at least it could prove that a document named by it was sent between OUYANG Dan and ZHAO Wenxiang when they communicated. The Defendant had no objection to the fact that OUYANG Dan was the employee of its company, on the one hand, the Defendant denied the authenticity of power of attorney to refund deposit, on the other hand, they could not explain the content of the invalid link retained in the phone, so the court did not accept the views of their cross-examination and confirmed effect of evidence of power of attorney to refund deposit; as for the Defendant had no objection to the authenticity of the special payment letter to confiscate income of Shanghai Customs, the Plaintiff also provided the original copy of it, the Plaintiff and the Defendant had no objection to the fact that the customs fined RMB5,000 for false declaration of goods involved, the court confirms the effect of evidence of the payment letter, which can proved the fact that customs fined; as for the Defendant had no objection to the authenticity of ticket information of QIU Xue and CHEN Yanxiang, the court confirms its authenticity, which could prove that the two persons had ever gone to Shanghai to deal with customs detention.

7. VAT invoices and condition description issued by the outsider Peishuo Freight Forwarding Co., Ltd. (hereinafter referred to as Peishuo Company) to the Plaintiff, Plaintiff's payment voucher, registration information of Peishuo Company, the SF waybill of sending relevant documents about tailers, the customer receipt notification of Agricultural Bank of China that the receipt was Peishuo Company, to prove that the Plaintiff got in touch with the seller of the Defendant's domestic trade contract according to the Defendant's indication, and performed the obligations under the freight forwarding contract and trailer fee for this. The Defendant did not confirm the authenticity of this group of evidence materials except for the customer receipt notification, and argued that this group of evidence had no relevancy to the case. As for the content of this group of evidence material could be confirmed with each other, the Defendant had no objection to the fact that the goods were arranged by the Plaintiff to be shipped from the Defendant's supplier location, Changzhou to Shanghai Yangshan Port, the court confirms the effect of evidence of this group of evidence, which could prove that the Plaintiff paid the towing fee of RMB9,000 to Peishuo Company for the involved cargo shipping.

8. VAT special invoice and customers debit notice issued by the third party Shanghai Xinhai declaration Co., Ltd., the payment application issued by the Third Party Shanghai Xinhai International Logistics Co., Ltd., the condition description

issued by the third party Shanghai Xinhai International Logistics Co., Ltd., to prove that the Plaintiff had fulfilled the declaration obligation under the freight forwarding contract and the customs declaration fees caused by these. The Defendant did not confirm the authenticity of this group of evidence materials and argued that even if the Plaintiff had paid the customs declaration fees, which were caused by the fault of the Plaintiff, the Plaintiff shall bear responsibility. Whereas the original copies of this group of evidence materials had been provided by the Plaintiff, the court confirms the authenticity, which can prove that the Plaintiff paid customs declaration fees of RMB100 for the declaration of goods involved.

To ascertain the facts of the case, the Plaintiff requested ZHAO Wenxiang, CHEN Yanxiang, QIU Xue to testify at the court. ZHAO Wenxiang demonstrated the formation of the operation of involved business and deposit payment process, and used the phone to demonstrate the chatting records with the employee of the Defendant during the business contact and handling goods detention. The Plaintiff believed that witness testimony of ZHAO Wenxiang was legal and effective, which shall be adopted. The Defendant believed that ZHAO Wenxiang was the employee of Plaintiff company, and there was interest between them, so the authenticity of witness testimony could not be confirmed, and some witness testimony did not match with the objective facts. The court holds that the Plaintiff provided chatting records between the Plaintiff's agents *ad litem* and ZHAO Wenxiang, and the contents of the records were basically consistent with the content stated by ZHAO Wenxiang in court, and confirmed the effect of evidence of witness testimony stated by ZHAO Wenxiang in court. CHEN Yanxiang and QIU Xue failed to appear in court as witnesses, the Defendant stated that the two persons had provided written witness testimony, and there was no need to appear in court, and there are other work arrangements, so they did not need to appear in court.

In order to justify its demurrer, the Defendant submitted the following evidence:

1. QQ chatting records between ZHAO Wenxiang and the employee of Defendant, OUYANG Dan, to prove that the Defendant did not establish a contractual relationship on freight forwarding with the Plaintiff and only contacted with ZHAO Wenxiang. Due to the fault of ZHAO Wenxiang, the goods involved were detained by customs. The Plaintiff did not confirm the authenticity, legality and relevancy of the chatting records. The court holds that the chatting records are formed between ZHAO Wenxiang and the employee of Defendant. ZHAO Wenxiang confirmed the authenticity of the chatting records, when appearing in court to answer questions, so the court confirms the effect of evidence, which can prove ZHAO Wenxiang had communicated with OUYANG Dan on the goods involved.
2. Elements of customs declaration, to prove that the Defendant provided the declaration information to ZHAO Wenxiang. The Plaintiff did not confirm the authenticity, legality and relevancy of them, and held that they were made by Defendant. The court holds that although the elements of customs declaration were made by the Defendant, the goods information on them was consistent with the goods involved, and confirms the effect of evidence.

3. QQ chatting records between OUYANG Dan and ZHAO Wenxiang, were to prove that the Plaintiff had asked the Defendant to send several blank documents sealed by Defendant. The Plaintiff had no objection to the authenticity of the chatting records, in view of this, the Court confirmed the effect of evidence of the chatting records.
4. Certificate of guarantee of Yangshan customs, to prove that after the Defendant gave deposit to Yangshan Customs, Yangshan Customs gave formal certificate of guarantee to the Defendant and the certificate of guarantee was remained by the Defendant. The Plaintiff confirmed the authenticity of this group of evidence material, but deemed that the Defendant only held the certificate of guarantee, and the Plaintiff held the original copy of the special receipt of customs deposit, which could prove that although the subject of punishment was the Defendant, but the Plaintiff still advanced deposit. As for the Plaintiff had no objection to the authenticity of certificate of guarantee, the court recognizes the authenticity of it, which can prove the fact that the Customs ever charged RMB30,000 deposit on goods involved.
5. Tickets information of QIU Xue and CHEN Yanxiang, to prove that the Defendant assigned them to go to Shanghai to deal with the administrative penalty matters of the goods involved from August 5, 2014 to August 19, 2014, and additional ticket fees were RMB3,081. The Plaintiff confirmed the authenticity of evidence material, but deemed that these two persons had no withdrawal voucher to prove they had paid the deposit, and identified that Plaintiff had advanced the deposit. Since the Plaintiff had no objection to the authenticity of ticket information, the court confirms its authenticity, which can prove that these two persons went to Shanghai to handle the matters of detained goods.
6. Social security annual and personal payment schedule of CHEN Yanxiang, QIU Xue and OUYANG Dan, and the labor contracts signed between Defendant and CHEN Yanxiang, witnesses testimony provided by CHEN Yanxiang, QIU Xue and OUYANG Dan, to prove that they were employees of the Defendant, and they all stated the fact of the formation of involved freight forwarding business and paying customs deposits. The Plaintiff did not confirm the authenticity of this group of payment schedules and labor contracts, but recognized that the three people were the employees of Defendant; as for this group of witnesses testimony, the Plaintiff believed that the witnesses shall appear in court to answer questions. Since the three people did not appear in court to answer questions, their authenticity shall not be confirmed. The court holds that the Plaintiff had no objection to the fact that the three people were the employees of the Defendant, and confirms the fact; as for the witness testimony provided by them, the court holds that CHEN Yanxiang and QIU Xue did not appear in court to answer questions, the signatures of witness testimony cannot be determined that they were signed by themselves, so the court does not confirm the effect of evidences of witness testimony.

7. Pasted list of original bill issued by the Defendant, to prove that the Defendant had withdrew RMB98,000 from company's revolving fund in July 2014. The Plaintiff did not confirm the authenticity, legality and relevancy of the pasted list. The court holds that it has no relevancy to the case from the pasted list, the court does not confirm the effect of evidences of the pasted list.
8. Administrative penalty decision of Yangshan Customs and the special payment letter to confiscate incomes of Shanghai Customs, to prove that the Defendant was fined RMB5,000 due to ZHAO Wenxiang's fault. The Plaintiff had no objection to the authenticity of evidence material, but held that the subject of administrative penalty decision was the Defendant, so the Defendant should bear the corresponding legal consequences. The original copy of the special payment letter to confiscate incomes of Shanghai Customs was held by the Plaintiff, which could prove that the Plaintiff advanced the deposit. Since the Plaintiff had no objection to the authenticity of evidence material, the court confirms the authenticity, which could prove the fact that customs fined RMB5,000 on the goods involved due to false declaration.
9. SF express waybill sent by QIU Xue to ZHAO Wenxiang, to prove that all original customs bills were handed to ZHAO Wenxiang by the Defendant to handle matters of customs deposit refunds. The Plaintiff had no objection to the authenticity, legality and relevancy of express waybill, which could prove that the Defendant knew that ZHAO Wenxiang was the employee of Plaintiff. Since the Plaintiff had no objection to the authenticity, legality and relevancy of express waybill, the court confirms the effect of evidence of the express waybill.
10. Cargo transportation insurance policy of China Ping An Property Insurance Co., Ltd., to prove that the Defendant knew nothing about the fact that ZHAO Wenxiang bought involved cargo transportation insurance, after dismissing the agency contract with ZHAO Wenxiang, the Defendant separately covered involved cargo transportation insurance. The Plaintiff had no objection to the authenticity of the insurance policy, but considered there was no relation to the case. Since the Plaintiff had no objection to the authenticity of insurance policy, the court recognizes its authenticity, which can prove that the Defendant separately bought transportation insurance for the goods involved.
11. No.223120140812083930, No.223120140811157784, No.223120140812696345 customs export declarations and No.CNSE257762 bill of lading, to prove the false declaration information provided by ZHAO Wenxiang leaded to twice false declaration, and then the goods involved successfully exported on August 21, 2014. The Plaintiff confirmed the authenticity of No.223120140811157784 customs export declaration, but did not deem it was false declaration; the Plaintiff did not confirm the authenticity of other materials in this group of evidence. The court holds that since ZHAO Wenxiang when appearing in court to answer questions, showed that the goods involved failed to declare twice, the QQ chatting records with OUYANG Dan could be confirmed with No.223120140812083930, No.223120140811157784 customs export declaration, and the Plaintiff had no objection to the authenticity of No.223120140811157784 customs export

declaration, so the court confirms the effect of evidence of the two customs export declaration; No.223120140812696345 customs export declaration and the CNSE257762 bill of lading were produced by the Defendant and the outsider in establishing freight forwarding contractual relationship, which has no association with the involved dispute, so the court does not confirm the effect of evidence of the two evidence materials in the case.
12. Freight forwarding contract, VAT special invoices and online banking business receipt, to prove that because of the fault of ZHAO Wenxiang's performing the entrusted matters, which caused the Defendant to separately entrust Shanghai Deyi International shipping Co., Ltd. To ship goods involved and pay agency fees of RMB75,645. The Plaintiff did not confirm the authenticity, legality and relevancy of the freight forwarding contract and VAT special invoice, confirmed the authenticity of the online banking business receipt, but held that it had no relevancy to the case.
13. Purchase and sales contract signed between the Defendant and the outsider Goldman Industrial Group Co., Ltd., to prove that the fault of ZHAO Wenxiang caused the Defendant's breach of contract to the buyer of goods involved, Goldman Industrial Group Co., Ltd. The insured of goods involved shall be Goldman Industrial Group Co., Ltd. And ZHAO Wenxiang did not give the involved insurance policy to the Defendant, which leaded to wrong insurance information. The Plaintiff did not confirm the authenticity, legality and relevancy of the purchases and sales contract and deemed it had no relation to the case.

As for evidence 12–13 provided by the Defendant, the court holds that the two evidence was produced by the contractual relation established between the Defendant and the outsider, and there is no relevancy to the case, so the court does not confirm the effect of evidence of the two group of evidence materials.

To find out the fact of the case, the court went to Bank of Communications Shanghai Lingang New City Branch to obtain the monitoring record on August 12, 2014, on which the involved deposit was paid. The monitoring record showed the actual situation when the employees of the Plaintiff and the Defendant paid the deposit on the payment day. The Plaintiff had no objection to the authenticity, legality and relevancy of the monitoring records, and deemed that the customs deposit was paid by ZHAO Wenxiang in cash. The Defendant had no objection to the authenticity, legality and relevancy of the monitoring records, but believed that it could only see from the monitoring records that ZHAO Wenxiang held cash, which could not prove that it belonged to him. Bank bills were filled by CHEN Yanxiang, and the cash was also directly submitted by CHEN Yanxiang, so it could prove that the deposit was paid by Defendant. The court holds that the Plaintiff and the Defendant had no objection to the authenticity, legality and relevancy of monitoring records, and the monitoring records truly reflected the involved deposit payment process, the content displayed on monitoring records shall be confirmed.

According to the analysis of the above evidence materials and combining court investigation and statements of the parties, the court ascertains the following facts:

On June 27, 2014, ZHAO Wenxiang got touch to CHEN Yanxiang, the employee of Defendant through QQ, agreed that the Defendant commissioned the Plaintiff to ship a batch of goods from Shanghai, China to Istanbul, Turkey. The Plaintiff stated, ZHAO Wenxiang worked in the Plaintiff company as an intern from March 2014 to June 2014. In July 2014, the Plaintiff and ZHAO Wenxiang signed a labor contract. ZHAO Wenxiang confirmed that he had business transaction with Defendant on behalf of the Plaintiff.

After accepting the commission of the Defendant, the Plaintiff entrusted Peishuo Company to stuff the containers on the goods involved. On July 14, 2014, Peishuo Company went to No.718 Yellow River West Road, Changzhou to stuff the containers, the goods were stuffed in two 40 feet containers, No.CXDU2124697 and PCIU4540959, which were conveyed to Shanghai Yangshan port. For this, the Plaintiff paid trailer fees of RMB9,000 to Peishuo Company.

On July 14, 2014, the Plaintiff handled the export declaration of the goods involved for the Defendant, for the amount had problems at declaration, the declaration did not succeed. On July 22, 2014, the Plaintiff handled the second declaration, but the amount still had problems, resulting the goods were seizured by the Customs to inspect for false declaration. The Plaintiff stated that the relevant declaration companies charged declaration fees of RMB100, and the Plaintiff also covered transportation insurance for the Defendant of goods involved and paid the relevant insurance premium.

From July to August 2014, ZHAO Wenxiang communicated with OUYANG Dan, the employee of the Defendant online on the declaration of goods involved. In the chatting records of both sides, OUYANG Dan urged ZHAO Wenxiang to issue bills of lading all the time, but ZHAO Wenxiang said that after goods were shipped from Shanghai, they were unloaded on dock in Hong Kong due to storms, so he was unable to issue bills of lading. The two parties had also communicated on the amount of goods. ZHAO Wenxiang in court said alleged that because the Defendants was his client, therefore, after the goods were seized by the customs due to false declaration, he did not promptly disclose the relevant facts to the Defendant, but he said the goods were detained in Hong Kong. Until August 5, 2014, the Defendant was told the truth. After knowing the goods were seized, the Defendant delegated employees CHEN Yanxiang, QIU Xue to go to Shanghai, and go to Yangshan Customs with ZHAO Wenxiang to handle related matters. In the coordination process, the customs informed that they could pay RMB30,000 as deposit in order to make the goods released in advance.

On August 11, 2014, the legal representative of the Plaintiff LING Jianfeng separately withdrew cash totaling RMB30,000 from the Agricultural Bank of China and Bank of China. ZHAO Wenxiang stated that after LING Jianfeng withdrawal the cash, LING Jianfeng handed the money to him, and he carried the money to Shanghai Lingang Branch of Bank of Communications and paid the deposit on the next day.

On August 12, 2014, ZHAO Wenxiang and CHEN Yanxiang went to Shanghai Lingang Branch of Bank of Communications to pay the deposit. The monitoring records on that day showed: CHEN Yanxiang and ZHAO Wenxiang entered into the bank door one after another, CHEN Yanxiang carried a big bag, ZHAO Wenxiang held a kraft paper bag. Then they went to payment counter, CHEN Yanxiang seated, ZHAO Wenxiang stood around, at this time, the kraft paper bag was held by ZHAO Wenxiang. According to the requirements of the bank staff, CHEN Yanxiang filled out the form. Subsequently, ZHAO Wenxiang handed kraft paper bag to CHEN Yanxiang, and CHEN Yanxiang put the kraft paper bag into the bank counter. After taking out cash from the kraft paper bag, the bank staff returned the kraft paper bags to CHEN Yanxiang. CHEN Yanxiang looked up the paper bag, and handed it to ZHAO Wenxiang. ZHAO Wenxiang put it on the counter. After bank staff had counted the cash, a seal was stamped on deposit special receipt, and handed to CHEN Yanxiang. Then CHEN Yanxiang and ZHAO Wenxiang left the counter, before leaving, ZHAO Wenxiang returned the counter from distant place, and took the aforementioned kraft paper bags with cash away. The Defendant stated that the above RMB30,000 deposit were carried from Fuzhou to Shanghai by the employee of Defendant. Currently, the first receipt and second refund of deposit special receipt both were held by the Plaintiff. The Plaintiff said that if the Defendant paid the deposit, it was willing to hand the deposit receipt to the Defendant.

After receiving deposit, Yangshan Customs permitted the goods released in advance, but the Defendant did not commission the Plaintiffs to continue to handle matters relating to the shipment of goods, but entrusted other freight forwarding company to handle customs declaration matters, and the Plaintiff also confirmed this. The Defendant also separately covered the transport insurance of goods involved.

On November 4 and November 14, 2014, the Plaintiff separately issued VAT general invoices to the Defendant, and informed the Defendant to pay agency fees, including towing fees of RMB9,000, declaration fees of RMB100, insurance premium of RMB3,220.56.

On November 10, 2014, an administrative penalty decision was issued by Yangshan Customs to the Defendant, the Defendant was fined RMB5,000 because of false declaration, the money directly deducted from the deposit paid to the Customs.

On November 18, 2014, the Defendant issued power of attorney to refund deposit to customs. In the power of attorney, the Defendant claimed that he entrusted the Plaintiff to get the deposit RMB30,000 advanced by the Plaintiff on behalf of the Defendant, and required the customs to return the deposit to the account of Defendant.

During the hearing, through the court understood from the Yangshan Customs, refunding deposit required of the second refund list of special deposit receipt, if it could not be submitted, the company applying for refunding deposit could issue condition description, such as losing the refund list etc. In November 2014, Yangshan Customs had notified the Defendant to handle related refunding matters and materials, but the Defendant had yet not to handle, and did not inquiry the customs for example, what to do if lacking the refund list. The Plaintiff asked the customs to return the deposit to Plaintiff through phone and writing, for it was paid by the Plaintiff, and the customs replied that they could only return it to the payment company showed on the special deposit receipt, which was the Defendant.

The court holds that the case is the dispute over freight forwarding contract. About whether there was a freight forwarding contractual relationship between the Plaintiff and the Defendant. The Defendant argued that the there was a freight forwarding contractual relationship between ZHAO Wenxiang and the Defendant, there was no freight forwarding contractual relationship between the Plaintiff and the Defendant. The court holds that, although ZHAO Wenxiang was only an intern of the Plaintiff, Zahowenxiang confirmed that goods involved was accepted by him on behalf of Plaintiff. The Plaintiff also confirmed that, the involved freight forwarding fees also advanced by the Plaintiff to related party, and claimed to the Defendant for issuing the invoice again, so there is a freight forwarding contractual relationship between the Plaintiff and the Defendant.

Regarding whether the trailer fees, customs declaration fees, insurance premium and other fees of freight forwarding could be supported. The Court believed that the fees claimed by Plaintiff, were all produced when it worked as freight forwarders of the Defendant. Among them, the towing fee was produced by the fact that the Plaintiff commissioned Peishuo Company to ship goods from Changzhou to Shanghai Yangshan Port. Although finally the Defendant entrusted other freight forwarding companies to ship the goods, the fact could not be changed that the goods were shipped from Changzhou to Shanghai Yangshan Port by road and the Plaintiff paid related fees. The Defendant shall pay the freight forwarding fees that it had performed to the Plaintiff. The Plaintiff had provided evidence to prove that the Plaintiff has paid the towing fee of RMB9,000 to Peishuo Company, the Defendant should bear the fee, and the court supports the Plaintiff's claim. As for the clearance fees, according to the facts found, declaration of goods involved failed twice, and the declaration was caused by the Plaintiff's fault. After the goods were released, the Defendant again entrusted other freight forwarding companies to ship the goods. Therefore, as for the declaration matters, the Plaintiff had not completed it according to the contract, so the Plaintiff had no right to claim to the Defendant as a consignor. The paid declaration charges arising from the Plaintiff's own fault, the Plaintiff shall undertake it, and the court does not support the Plaintiff's claim. As for premium, the court holds that the goods involved was seized by customs to inspect because of false declaration, so the transportation related to the insurance the Plaintiff bought for the Defendant did not actually happen, and the Defendant provided evidence to prove that when goods were arranged to be shipped again, it separately purchased cargo transportation insurance. At the same time, the amount premium the Plaintiffs claimed is not consistent with the amount actually happening, therefore the court does not support this claim of the Plaintiff.

Regarding whether the involved RMB3000 deposit shall be returned by the Defendant to Plaintiff. The court holds that the Plaintiff and the Defendant claimed that the deposit was paid by them. In the refund proxy provided by the Plaintiff, the

Defendant showed that it commissioned the Plaintiff to get the advanced deposit RMB30,000, and required the customs to return the deposit to the account of the Defendant. Although the Defendant denied the authenticity of refund proxy, reasonable excuses and rebuttal evidence were not issued by Defendant, according to this, the fact that the deposit was advanced by the Plaintiff can be confirmed. In words, even if there was doubts about the authenticity of the refund proxy, it could be presumed that the deposit was advanced by the Plaintiff from other evidence and related facts. Firstly, the goods involved were seized by customs to inspect because of the fault of the Plaintiff in dealing with the freight forwarding matters. Under the condition that the Plaintiff knew it had the fault, the Plaintiff actively handled the matters and advanced the deposit so as to make the goods released which fit for common sense. Secondly, the Plaintiff provided the bank card cash withdrawal transactions of legal representative on the day before paying deposit, there was highly articulated between the withdrawal time and payment time, the amount of withdrawal can also match with the amount of payment. Thirdly, according to the monitoring records of bank on payment day, CHEN Yanxiang carried a big bag, and ZHAO Wenxiang held a kraft paper bag with cash in it while entering the bank. When the bank asked to pay cash, ZHAO Wenxiang handed the kraft bag to CHEN Yanxiang, and CHEN Yanxiang stuffed it in counter. If the cash was carried from Fuzhou to Shanghai as the Defendant said, why it is held by ZHAO Wenxiang, the Defendant could not give reasonable explanation. In addition, for a large amount of cash, obviously, it is safer in bag than in hand. Under the condition that CHEN Yanxiang carried a bag, did not put the cash in bag but held to others which was not accord to common sense, and the Defendant could not give reasonable explanation. According to the bank's monitoring records, when bank staff took out of cash from the kraft paper bag and returned the kraft paper bags to CHEN Yanxiang, CHEN Yanxiang looked up the paper bag, and handed it to ZHAO Wenxiang. ZHAO Wenxiang put it on the counter. After completing all procedures, ZHAO Wenxiang returned counter from distant place and took the kraft paper bags away. Analysis the natural response on degree of CHEN Yanxiang and ZHAO Wenxiang concerning kraft paper bags, the behavioral characteristics of them, the cash meet the situation that the cash was prepared by the Plaintiff and put in the bag by the Plaintiff. Fourthly, the first receipt list and the second refund list of deposit special receipt were held by the Plaintiff. According to the situation learned from Yangshan Customs, after customs informed the Defendant to handle the matters of refunding the deposit. The Defendant did not handle the matters promptly. Even if the Defendant could not handle matters of refunding deposit because of lack of refund list, the Defendant could inquire the customs whether it can solve it through other methods, the Defendant did not inquire the customs on this matters. Opposite to the negative attitude of the Defendant applying for refunding deposit, the Plaintiff contacted the customs several times through writing and phone, claimed that the deposit was paid by the Plaintiff and requested the customs to refund the deposit to the Plaintiff. The contrast of the different attitudes strengthened the reliability that the deposit was advanced by the Plaintiff. According to this, the Court believed under the situation that there was no direct evidence to prove the source of involved deposit, no matter according to the evidence provided by Plaintiff, or the confirmed fact, there was a higher probability that the deposit was advanced by the Plaintiff. Since the Plaintiff advanced the deposit of RMB30,000, the Defendant shall repay it to the Plaintiff, but RMB5,000 of them had been confiscated by customs due to false declaration, so the deposit the customs returned to the Defendant shall not include the confiscation of RMB5,000. Therefore, it was difficult for the Court to support that the Plaintiff requested the Defendant to refund the confiscated money, and the Defendant shall repay the Plaintiff the remaining deposit RMB25,000.

To sum up, according to Article 107, Article 398, Article 405 of the Contract Law of the People's Republic of China, Article 9 of the Provisions of the Supreme People's Court on Several Issues concerning the Trial of Cases of Disputes over Marine Freight Forwarding, Article 64 Paragraph 1 of the Civil Procedure Law of the People's Republic of China, the judgment is as follows:

1. The Defendant Fujian Hongxing Electronic Technology Co., Ltd. shall pay towing fee of RMB9,000 to the Plaintiff Shanghai Wan Feng International Freight Forwarding Co., Ltd. within ten days after the effective day of this judgment;
2. The Defendant Fujian Hongxing Electronic Technology Co., Ltd., within ten days after the effective day of this judgment, shall repay customs deposit of RMB25,000 to the Plaintiff, Shanghai Wan Feng International Freight Forwarding Co., Ltd.;
3. Reject the other claims of the Plaintiff Shanghai Wan Feng International Freight Forwarding Co., Ltd.

If the Defendant Fujian Hongxing Electronic Technology Co., Ltd. fails to fulfill its obligation to make the said payments within the time limit provided by this judgment, the interest shall be double paid for the period of deferred payment according to Article 253 of the Civil Procedure Law of the People's Republic of China.

Court acceptance fee in amount of RMB858, property preservation fee in amount of RMB443, totaling RMB1,301, RMB255.79 shall be born by the Plaintiff Shanghai Wan Feng International Freight Forwarding Co., Ltd., and RMB1,045.21 shall be born by the Defendant Fujian Hongxing Electronic Technology Co., Ltd.

If dissatisfy with this judgment, any party shall within fifteen days as of the service of this judgment, submit a Statement of Appeal to the court, with duplicates in the number of the opposing parties, so as to make an appeal to the Shanghai High People's Court.

Presiding Judge: JIN Xiaofeng
Acting Judge: WANG Lei
People's Juror: BAO Xiaoling
May 4, 2015
Clerk: BAO Haiyue

Appendix: Relevant Law

1. Contract Law of the People's Republic of China

Article 107 If a party fails to perform its obligations under a contract, or its performance fails to satisfy the terms of the contract, it shall bear the liabilities for breach of contract such as to continue to perform its obligations, to take remedial measures, or to compensate for losses.

Article 398 The principal shall prepay the expenses for handling the commissioned affair. Any expense necessary for handling the commissioned affair advanced by the agent shall be repaid with interest by the principal.

Article 405 Upon completion of the commissioned affair by the agent, the principal shall pay the remuneration thereto. Where the agency appointment contract is terminated or the commissioned affair is not capable of being completed due to any reason not attributable to the agent, the principal shall pay to the agent an appropriate amount of remuneration. If the parties agrees otherwise, such agreement shall prevail.

2. The Provisions of the Supreme People's Court on Several Issues about the Trial of Cases concerning Marine Freight Forwarding Disputes

Article 9 If the freight agency enterprise completes the marine freight agency matters according to general powers of entrustment and requests the principal to pay relevant reasonable expenses, the people's court shall support such request.

3. Civil Procedure Law of the People's Republic of China

Article 64 A party shall have the responsibility to provide evidence in support of its own propositions.

……

Article 253 If the person subjected to execution fails to fulfil his obligations with respect to pecuniary payment within the period specified by a judgment or written order or any other legal document, he shall pay double interest on the debt for the belated payment. If the person subjected to execution fails to fulfill his other obligations within the period specified in the judgment or written order or any other legal document, he shall pay a charge for the dilatory fulfilment.

Shanghai Maritime Court
Civil Judgment

Shanghai Yizhou Waterway Engineering Co., Ltd.
v.
QIU Guohua

(2013) Hu Hai Fa Hai Chu Zi No.60

Related Case(s) This is the judgment of first instance and the judgment of second instance is on page 967.

Cause(s) of Action 206. Dispute over ship sales and purchases contract.

Headnote Settlement agreement in relation to a dispute over the purchase price of a ship held to be enforceable, requiring the Defendant to repay RMB11 million to the Plaintiff.

Summary The Plaintiff in this case agreed to purchase a vessel for RMB11 million. The Defendant argued that the excess funds that the Plaintiff transferred into his account were for the increased value of the vessel. The Third Party was the financing company that the Plaintiff used to obtain some of the funding. The Defendant gave the Plaintiff the bank card and access to the account that the Plaintiff deposited the funds in. The Defendant argued that it was for ease of payment only. The court ultimately held that the Defendant was required to remit the excess funds into the account of the Plaintiff, and the two parties agreed that the price of the vessel was a fixed amount of RMB11 million.

Judgment

The Plaintiff: Shanghai Yizhou Waterway Engineering Co., Ltd.
Legal representative: CHEN Shineng.
Agent *ad litem*: CHEN Youmu, lawyer of Shanghai Wintell & Co.
Agent *ad litem*: QUE Dongli, lawyer of Shanghai Wintell & Co.

The Defendant: QIU Guohua
Agent *ad litem*: XUE Zhicai, lawyer of Zhejiang Shiguang Law Firm.

The Third Party: Zhongxin Futong Lease Finance Co., Ltd.
Legal representative: LIU Zhiqiang.
Agent *ad litem*: YANG Wengui, lawyer of Beijing Haitong Law Firm.
Agent *ad litem*: PENG Xianwei, lawyer of Beijing Haitong Law Firm.

With respect to the case arising from dispute over ship purchase and sale contract filed by the Plaintiff Shanghai Yizhou Waterway Engineering Co., Ltd. (hereinafter referred to as Yizhou Company) and the Defendant QIU Guohua, the court, after entertaining this case, formed a collegiate panel according to law. On November 27, 2013 and December 8, 2014, the Plaintiff filed an application of preservation to the court to freeze the Defendant's bank deposits, stock right and seal up his property, for the purpose of preventing the Defendant from transferring or concealing property and avoiding difficulty in enforcing effective instruments. On November 27, 2013 and December 11, 2014, the court ruled on permission and executed preservation measures to Defendant's corresponding property. On December 6, 2013, the Defendant put forward reconsideration and dissent to the preservation ruling and jurisdiction of the case. On December 17, the court rejected the reconsideration of preservation by virtue of a notice and rendered a ruling rejecting the Defendant's challenge of jurisdiction. On January 22, 2014, Shanghai High People's Court ruled against Defendant's appeal in terms of challenge of jurisdiction. On February 8, 2014, as the results of the case had legally interests with Zhongxin Futong Lease Finance Co., Ltd. (hereinafter referred to as Zhongxin Company), the Plaintiff applied to add that company to be the third party of the case. After review, the court added Zhongxin Company to be the Third Party of the case. On September 18, 2014, the court held the first hearing in public, CHEN Shineng, legal representative of the Plaintiff, CHEN Youmu and QUE Dongli, agents *ad litem*, XUE Zhicai, agent *ad litem* of the Defendant, PENG Xianwei, agent *ad litem* of the Third Party, appeared in court and participated in the action. As the value of M.V. "Huitong 3" during the period from October 19, 2013 to January 8, 2013 was a key fact of this case, the court authorized Shanghai Maritime Judicial Expertise Center (hereinafter referred to as Expertise Center) to evaluate the value of M.V. "Huitong 3" during the aforesaid period. On November 4, 2015, the Expertise Center issues No.001 ship value and evaluation. On December 4, 2014, the court held the second hearing in public. QUE Dongli, agent *ad litem* of the Plaintiff, XUE Zhicai, agent *ad litem* of the Defendant, and PENG Xianwei, agent *ad litem* of the Third Party, attended the hearing, QU Moumou, the appraiser of Expertise Center was questioned by the parties in court. This case has now been concluded.

The Plaintiff alleged that on October 19, 2012, it signed *M.V. "Huitong 3" Purchase and Sale Contract* to purchase M.V. "Huitong 3" from the Defendant. The agreed price was RMB11,000,000, a fixed price. The ship price was arranged by the Plaintiff in way of finance; the Defendant was responsible for helping the Plaintiff to complete the financing formalities and returning the difference to the Plaintiff after receiving the ship price. After that, the Plaintiff, the Defendant and the Third Party concluded several complementary agreements of finance of M.V.

"Huitong 3" included *Purchase and Sale Contract* and *Finance Leasing Contract* with Anhui Changhui Transportation and Trade Co., Ltd. (hereinafter referred to as Changhui Company), a party not involved. According to those agreements, the ship price was RMB38,000,000, among which the down payment was RMB34,200,000, the final payment RMB38,000,000 and the deposit (RMB7,600,000) was going to be deducted from the finance payment. On January 8, 2013, the Plaintiff, the Defendant and the Third Party set up a supervision account in the bank. On January 14, 2013, the Third Party paid the down payment in amount of RMB30,400,000. On January 17, 2013, the Plaintiff and the Third Party applied to pay the price of RMB26,600,000 to the Defendant's account, of which the deposit was deducted from the down payment. Although the Defendant repeatedly promised to pay the price difference to the Plaintiff, after repeatedly urging by the Plaintiff, the Defendant only paid RMB6,000,000. The Plaintiff requested the court to order the Defendant to: 1. return the remaining ship finance RMB13,400,000 and interests to the supervision account which was set up in the Bank of Communications Beijing Sanyuan Branch (the interests should be calculated according to the current deposit interest rate over the same period of the Bank of China, starting from the finance payment is actually paid and ending at the day of the judgment effects. The actual paying date of the first payment was January 17, 2013 and November 28, 2013 for the second payment); 2. the litigation costs should be born by the Defendant.

The Defendant alleged that, the Plaintiff and the Defendant concluded the contract note of ship sale and purchase on October 19, 2012, but the Plaintiff knew that they could not afford the payment so they introduced the business to the Third Party. On January 8, 2013, the Plaintiff, the Defendant and the Third Party concluded *Ship Purchase and Sale Contract* at the price of RMB38,000,000. At that time, the previous *Purchase and Sale Contract* had been concealed, so the Plaintiff's asking for returning the ship's payment had no evidence; they did not appoint any concept of returning the price difference of the ship to the Plaintiff which was asked by the Plaintiff, and the Plaintiff knew that the business reflected by the contract note of ship sale and purchase would not succeed when they concluded this contract with the Defendant; the ship's sale contract and finance lease contract concluded by the Plaintiff, the Defendant and the Third Party had no relationship with the contract note of ship sale and purchase the Plaintiff claimed and is not the complementary agreements of the contract note of ship sale and purchase the Plaintiff claimed; it was false statement that the Defendant repeatedly promised to pay the price difference of the ship to the Plaintiff. The Defendant never promised to give the property belonging to themselves to the Plaintiff. The Plaintiff asked the Defendant to pay the discount for helping the Defendant to sale the ship, and the Defendant could not help but pay RMB12,000,000. In all, the Defendant asked to reject the Plaintiff's claims.

The Third Party alleged that it was not involved in the contract note of ship sale and purchase and did not know the existence of that contract, so they has no legal relation with the case; in the contract note of ship sale and purchase, the Plaintiff and the Defendant did not define the buyer's obligations and the transfer delivery of the subject that do not conform to the features of sale contract according to the law, so it was not strictly *Purchase and Sale Contract*. From the concept of the contract, the aim is making provision for the distribution of the finance lease price between two parties. At the same time, the Third Party has paid the price and the subject has been delivered, so *Purchase and Sale Contract* was effective and true; the Third Party agreed with the action of the Plaintiff, identify with the return of the finance payment and think it would assure that the Plaintiff repay the defaulting rent in full.

To prove the claims, the Plaintiff submitted the following evidential documents within the time limit for burden of proof:

1. Contract note of ship sale and purchase concluded by the Plaintiff and the Defendant on October 19, 2012, to prove that the Plaintiff bought M.V. "Huitong 3" from the Defendant with the unchangeable price of RMB11,000,000. The price was dealt by means of finance and the Defendant was responsible for cooperating with the Plaintiff to handle the finance;
2. *Ship Purchase and Sale Contract* and finance lease contract concluded by the Plaintiff, the Defendant and the Third Party on January 8, 2013, to prove that the agreed ship's price was RMB38,000,000, down price was RMB34,200,000 and the final price was RMB3,800,000;
3. Agreement of regulating account concluded by the Plaintiff and the Third Party, to prove that three parties set up assert supervision account in the bank, using for receiving and pay the ship's price;
4. Certificate of receipts on January 14, 2013, to prove that the Third Party pay the down price of RMB30,400,000;
5. Proof of payment on January 17, 2013, to prove that the Plaintiff and the Third Party arranged for paying the down price subtract deposit of RMB26,600,000 to the Defendant;
6. Certificate of receipts on January 29, 2013, to prove that the Defendant had paid RMB6,000,000 to the Plaintiff;
7. Civil conciliation statement of Tianjin Maritime Court and proof of payment of RMB3,800,000, to prove that on November 28, 2013, the Defendant received the final price. So far, the Defendant has received all payment of the ship;
8. Email communications and texts about the preparations of signing documents, to prove that on December 25, 2012, three parties confirmed the finance plan and got ready for signing complementary agreements of finance lease. Three parties was planned to sign the agreement and set up account before December 31;
9. Entrusting payment letter of Changhui Company and the agreement of dissolving, to prove that on December 25, 2012, the Defendant all set the complementary documents needed for signing finance lease complementary agreements. The Plaintiff and the Defendant did not show the declaration of intention and behavior of concealing the contract note of ship sale and purchase;
10. Bank card, USBK and email communication of the Defendant, to prove that after December 31, 2012, the Defendant still provided their bank card and USBK to pay the balance of ships price with the Plaintiff and continued to perform the contract note of ship sale and purchase;

11. Texts communication between the Plaintiff and the Defendant on January 17, 2013, to prove that two parties arranged for the payment of difference on that day and continued to perform the contract note of ship sale and purchase;
12. Confirming letter of four parties on January 8, 2013, to prove that the ship finance lease was implemented in terms of plans confirmed by all parties before December 31, 2012. The complementary agreement of finance lease was signed for performing the contract note of ship sale and purchase;
13. Payment documents of litigation cost, to prove that the Plaintiff has paid RMB79,000 as litigation fee and RMB5,000 as application fee for property preservation;
14. Notarizations of Defendant's QQ number, text and Email, to prove XXXXXXX@qq.com and XXXXXXXXXXX was used by the Defendant QIU Guohua. Before December 31, 2012, three parties reached agreements of complementary agreements of finance lease that the contract note of ship sale and purchase remains in force;
15. Pre-estimated valuation list of the price of M.V. "Huitong 3" (the Plaintiff provided formal estimated valuation report later, namely evidence 18), to prove the ship price, RMB11,000,000 was rational;
16. Calling records between the Plaintiff's employee GU Jiansheng and the Defendant, to prove that the Defendant knew that the complementary agreements of finance lease was concluded to perform the contract note of ship sale and purchase. The Defendant undoubtedly knew the efficiency of the contract note of ship sale and purchase and obligations of returning price difference to the Plaintiff;
17. Value estimation report of M.V. "Huitong 3", to prove that the value was RMB11,000,000;
18. Contract note of ship sale and purchase of M.V. "Jinhua 158", to prove that transaction operation mode of M.V. "Huitong 3" accorded with that contract. *Ship Purchase and Sale Contract* was real declaration of intention of buyer and seller about ship price, and the price listed in *Ship Purchase and Sale Contract* was set just for finance lease.

The Defendant objected to the authenticity and relevancy of evidence 1 and held that the contract had been concealed. RMB11,000,000 was used for tax avoidance according to the Plaintiff's asking and not true, so the evidence could not accomplish the purpose of proof of the Plaintiff;

The Defendant did not object to the authenticity and concept of *Ship Purchase and Sale Contract* and finance lease contract has been confirmed by three parties. The Defendant did not have any rights and obligations with finance lease and it was only ship sale and purchase relation with the Third Party;

The Defendant did not object to the authenticity of evidence 3 but held that it had no relationship with the case. Evidence 3 was payment account set by the Third Party, the Plaintiff and Bank of Communications, which was used for regulating performing of ship sale and purchase, so it could not accomplish the Plaintiff's purpose of proof;

The Defendant did not object to the authenticity of evidence 4, whereas RMB30,400,000 was paid by the Third Party for ship price and the Plaintiff only had the obligation of receiving the Third Party's authorization to pay the price;

The Defendant did not object to the authenticity of evidence 5, while it was that the Plaintiff received the Third Party's authorization to help the Third Party to pay for the Defendant, which had no relationship with the Plaintiff's claims;

The Defendant objected to the authenticity, legality and relevancy of evidence 6.

The Defendant did not object to the authenticity and legality of evidence 7, while it was not related to the Plaintiff's claim. On the contrary, the Plaintiff was responsible for assisting the Third Party to pay the final price (RMB3,800,000) to the Defendant in the progress of hearing and mediation of Tianjin Maritime Court and recognizing that they still defaulted the deposit RMB7,600,000 to the dependant. Now the Defendant prosecuted to Tianjin Maritime Court about the return of that deposit, which was planned to set the hearing at 0900 hrs on March 11, 2014.

The Defendant objected to the authenticity, relevancy of evidence 8; there was no signature of QIU Guohua and stamp of Changhui Company on the material; page 57 and 62 of email were communication between the Plaintiff and the Third Party, the content was limited in finance lease and had no relation with ship sale and purchase of the Defendant; page 63 and 64 of texts could not prove who was sender and whether the sending time was true; even though above-mentioned were true, they did not deny the fact that the Plaintiff gave rise to the cancellation of the contract note of ship sale and purchase for not providing financing institution within the time appointed at Article 5 of Term 3 in *Ship Purchase and Sale Contract*; nor did they deny that, after the cancellation of the contract, the Plaintiff approved the Third Party of purchasing the ship with RMB38,000,000 and lending the ship; on December 25, 2012, the Plaintiff did not provide financing institution and the contract could not be concluded, but the email asked the Plaintiff to provide *Purchase and Sale Contract*, the handover book of the ship and instruction of the ship. It's obvious that the Email was forged. As the Defendant's identification card, seal and cancelling agreement of bareboat charter was directly related to the Defendant's identity and commercial interests, before the Plaintiff decided the financing institution, the Defendant was not responsible for submitting. Because the Plaintiff could not find the financing institution, in late May, the Plaintiff, the Defendant and the Third Party discussed the sale and purchase issue about M.V. "Huitong 3"; until January 8, 2013, the Plaintiff was willing to charter.

Page 65 of evidence 9 was the email communication between GU Jiansheng and GAO Wei, which could not prove that the Plaintiff requested the Defendant to provide materials for performing the contract. Only after the cancellation of the contract and the determination of another buyer could the Plaintiff request. The Defendant objected to the authenticity, legality and relevancy of page 66 and 67 of cancelling agreement of bareboat charter and the authority to pay. The Defendant objected to the authenticity and relevancy of page 68 of texts, the reason was the same as evidence 8.

The Defendant requested the Plaintiff to provide the original copy, otherwise he objected to the authenticity of evidence 10. Even though they provide the original copy, the Defendant object to the relevancy of it, for that it could not achieve the Plaintiff's purpose of proof and proved that the Plaintiff knew that they did not meet the requirement of the contract note of ship sale and purchase but wanted to asked the Third Party to buy at RMB38,000,000 and charter to operate.

Page 71 of evidence 11 was email, and Page 72 are bank card and USBK. The time showed in the email were January 6, 2013, at which the contract had been cancelled. At the same time, the Defendant and the Third Party had agreed to sale and purchase the ship. While the Plaintiff wanted to charter for operating, which was the aim of the Third Party, so it was the Plaintiff's work to transit the ship's materials, transfer the ship and pay after the Defendant sell the ship. In all, QIU Guohua's bank card, USBK and personal seal required in the email were all used for performing the ship Purchase and Sale Contract signed on January 8, 2013 by the Defendant and the Third Party and had no relation to the contract note of ship sale and purchase signed by the Plaintiff and the Defendant before.

The Defendant objected to the authenticity, legality and relevancy of evidence 12;

The Defendant did not object to the authenticity and relevancy of evidence 13, while thought it could not accomplish the Defendant's purpose of proof. On the contrary, the confirmation was summary of the case, which was signed on every party's own accord after making the contract note of ship sale and purchase. The role of confirmation was proving relations between the Plaintiff and the Third Party was merely buyer and seller, between the Plaintiff and the Third Party was finance lease. The Plaintiff agreed to buy the ship in RMB38,000,000, and the Plaintiff wanted to charter for operation, for which the Defendant should be honest and trustworthy and never pass the commercial interest;

The Defendant did not object to the authenticity of evidence 14, but object to the relevancy;

The Defendant objected to the authenticity and relevancy of evidence 15 and made sure that the phone number, QQ number and email were both belong to the Defendant QIU Guohua, but even though the Defendant had used it, others could still use it;

The Defendant objected to the authenticity, relevancy and legality of evidence 16. Evaluating price of ships that was similar to the ship in case at standard and trading hour was RMB40,000,000, so the ship's price in case should refer to those similar ship;

The Defendant objected to the authenticity, legality and relevancy of evidence 17 that there were no reason to prove the content of evidence 17;

The Defendant objected to the authenticity, legality and relevancy of evidence 18. The reporting procedure was illegal;

The Defendant objected to the authenticity of evidence 19 because it was not original copy, on which the signature could not be confirmed. The contract of M.V. "Jinhua 158" was different from the contract in case, which had cancelling term;

The Third Party objected to the authenticity, legality and relevancy of evidence 1. There was no relation with evidence 1;

The Third Party recognized the authenticity and legality of evidence 2, while there was no relation between finance lease contract and price difference disputes of the Plaintiff and the Defendant;

Cross-examination opinions about evidence 3, 4 were the same as evidence 2;

The Third Party recognized the authenticity and legality of evidence 5, while the finance lease relation and price difference disputes should mutually independent and the behavior of payment to the Defendant was deemed as paying the ship's price. As to the legal relation and disputes between charterer (the Plaintiff) and seller(the Defendant), it did not matter to the Third Party;

The Third Party objected to the effect of evidence 6;

Cross-examination opinions about evidence 7 were the same as evidence 2;

The Third Party recognized authenticity and legality of email of evidence 8 in which the address postfix was the Third Party's and recognized GAO Wei and YAN Weiwei were staffs who operating this business as the Third Party's staff, and GU Jiansheng as the Plaintiff's staff. Cross-examination opinions about evidence that were same as evidence 2. But they objected to the authenticity and legality of texts that had no relation with the Third Party;

Cross-examination opinions about evidence 9 were the same as evidence 8;

Cross-examination opinions about evidence 10 were the same as evidence 2;

The Third Party objected to the authenticity and legality of evidence 11 that had no relation with the Third Party;

The Third Party objected to the authenticity, legality and relevancy of evidence 12;

The Third Party recognized authenticity and legality of evidence 13, while finance lease relationship had no relation to commercial relation between the Plaintiff and the Defendant. The Third Party did not know their privately trade of ship, and it could not prove that the finance lease contract was complementary agreement for performing the contract note of ship sale and purchase between the Plaintiff and the Defendant;

The Third Party recognized the effect of evidence 14;

Evidence 15-19 could merely prove that the Plaintiff and the Defendant agreed on the distribution of finance lease price but had no relation with the Third Party and could not effect real trade relation between the Third Party and the Plaintiff and the Defendant; the Third Party recognized authenticity of evidence 15, while among that were agreements of finance lease price distribution between the Plaintiff and the Defendant which had no relation with the Third Party; the Third Party objected to authenticity, legality and relevancy of evidence 16 and 17; The Third Party recognized superficial authenticity of evidence 18, while its evaluation did not follow the normal procedure and could not reflect the value of ship when three parties concluded the contract. The evaluation were merely distribution arrangement of finance lease price between the Plaintiff and the Defendant; the Third Party recognized authenticity and of evidence 19 while had no relation with the case.

The court recognizes evidence of the Plaintiff as follows: evidence 1-7, 10 and 13 can verify the relevant proofs and statements of the Defendant and the Third Party, so the court recognizes the authenticity and effect as evidence; the authenticity of evidence 8, 9, 11, 12 is proved by evidence 15, and the Defendant and the Third Party confirmed that relevant phone number, QQ, and email were used by their employees, so the court recognizes the effect as evidence; the court recognizes the effect of evidence 14, for proving the payment of evidence preservation application; evidence 17 is telephone record as to the Plaintiff while the Defendant objected to its authenticity. Moreover, the Plaintiff did not provide proof to prove its derivation and gaining method and whether the gaining was permitted by the caller, it is impossible to verify its authenticity and legality, so the court objects to its effect; evidence 16, 18 is assets appraisal reports entrusted by the Plaintiff unilaterally, the effect and demonstrability can be recognized combined with conclusion of judicial appraisal; evidence 19 is verified by part of concept of relevant statement of the Defendant and the Third Party and conclusion of judicial appraisal, so the court recognizes its authenticity. As to its demonstrability, the court will affirm separately.

The Defendant submitted the following evidence:

1. Ship Purchase and Sale Contract (same as evidence 2 of the Plaintiff), to prove that the Plaintiff did not appoint financing institute before December 31, 2012. The Plaintiff did not conclude contract with financing institute, according to Article 3 Paragraph 5 of the contract note of ship sale and purchase, the contract should be cancelled;
2. Finance lease contract, (same as evidence 2 of the Plaintiff), to prove ship sale and purchase relationship and finance lease relationship between three parties. The Plaintiff wanted to lease the ship in RMB38,000,000 which belong to the Third Party;
3. Confirmation letter (same as evidence 13 of the Plaintiff), to prove that the Defendant had no legal relationship with finance lease;
4. The contract note of ship sale and purchase (same as evidence 1 of the Plaintiff), expense invoices of ship transaction, to prove that the ship of the case bought by the Third Party was taxed legally;
5. Ship's ownership registration certificate, to prove that the ship sold by the Defendant went through formalities of transferring ownership, so the ownership belong to the Third Party;
6. Civil conciliation statement of Tianjin Maritime Court (same as evidence 7 of the Plaintiff), to prove that the dispute was ended through conciliation;
7. Record of trial of Tianjin Maritime Court, to prove that RMB7,600,000 (in RMB38,000,000 which should be paid by the Third Party confirmed by the Plaintiff) was guarantee of leasing the Defendant paid for the Plaintiff;
8. Official letter of the Third Party, October 11, 2013, to prove that the Third Party confirmed that the Defendant had comprehensively performed all obligations agreed in *Ship Purchase and Sale Contract*. At the same time, the Third Party urged the Plaintiff to perform assisting paying obligation as soon as possible;
9. Lawyer's letter in May, ship material lists the Plaintiff required the Defendant to provide during the case heard by Tianjin Maritime Court, to prove that the reason why the Plaintiff and the Third Party had rejected to pay the final price

was that the Defendant did not give ship survey certificate and technical data. The Plaintiff did not propose any rights in the case heard by Tianjin Maritime Court. Combined with civil conciliation statement, to prove that the Plaintiff has confirmed that there were no other disputes over case of *Ship Purchase and Sale Contract* between three parties;

10. Agreement of regulating account (same as evidence 3 of the Plaintiff), remittance slip, requisition for settlement, to prove that RMB30,400,000 was paid by the Third Party through the common account set by the Third Party and the Plaintiff, and the Plaintiff was remittance entrusted by the Third Party;
11. Remittance slip and transfer voucher, to prove that the Defendant paid brokerage RMB12,000,000 to the Plaintiff's legal representative CHEN Shineng and his wife ZHENG Cuiti;
12. Notice of acceptance of the case of Tianjin Maritime Court, to prove that the court had accepted and heard the case of returning guarantee RMB7,600,000;
13. Bareboat charter, to prove the monthly rent of ship similar with M.V. "Huitong 3";
14. Authorization certificate of the Plaintiff at Tianjin Maritime court, to prove that opinions of agent *ad litem* of the Plaintiff should be viewed as opinions of the Plaintiff;
15. Three records of trial of Tianjin Maritime court, to prove that the Plaintiff recognized the authenticity of ship sale and purchase relationship and price between the Plaintiff and the Defendant, the Third Party, recognized that there were no relation between the Defendant and finance leasing contract, recognized that the Plaintiff should pay the balance RMB3.8 million, but did not mention the contract note of ship sale and purchase concluded by the Plaintiff and the Defendant, did not raise independent request or plead;
16. Civil judgment (2013) Jin Hai Fa Shang Chu Zi No.66-1, Civil Judgment (2014) Jin Gao Li (Min) Zhong Zi No.0075, to prove that the ship finance leasing contract and the case were not the same legal relationship, so the Plaintiff's statement the ship sale contract and finance leasing contract were complementary to the contract note of ship sale and purchase was false;
17. Notarization stated by QIU Shifen and bill of credit, to prove that the Defendant had authorized QIU Shifen to pay RMB3 million to CHEN Shineng and CHEN Shineng had returned it after that;
18. Notarization stated by SHI Moumou and LIANG Qingfa, to prove that the contract attach to the verified written opinion were not concluded by them; and
19. Proof provided by Anhui Hengtong Shipbuilding Co., Ltd. (hereinafter referred to as Hengtong Company), to prove that the company started to use the official seal from March 2013 and they never used any other official seals after that.

The Plaintiff recognized authenticity and legality of evidence 1-4, while 38 million was paid to perform the contract note of ship sale and purchase and was complementary agreement of the contract note of ship sale and purchase;

The Plaintiff recognized the effect of evidence 5, while after the ownership was transferred to the Third Party, the Third Party should go through relative ship procedures;

The Plaintiff recognized the authenticity and legality of evidence 6, while based on the coordination of Tianjin Maritime court, the Plaintiff should participate in the lawsuit of the case. The Plaintiff signed on the reconciliation agreement was because the Third Party agreed to pay the balance;

As to evidence 7, the Plaintiff asked parties to verify it but did not voice the cross-examination during the legal term;

The Plaintiff recognized the authenticity and legality of evidence 8;

The Plaintiff objected to the first and fifth lawyer's letters among evidence 9 but recognized the second, third and fourth lawyer's letters; the Plaintiff asked to verify lists of material but did not voice the cross- examination during the legal term and thought that it was Defendant's behavior of not providing ship certificates that resulted the ship could not work;

The Plaintiff recognized the authenticity and legality of evidence 10, but the Plaintiff had the obligation of supervision but not authorized to trans-pay by the Third Party;

The Plaintiff recognized that the Defendant paid RMB6 million, while another 6 million in evidence 11 was not the money involved, and there were no discounts between the Plaintiff and the Defendant. The Defendant paid the money to the Plaintiff according to the agreement of returning price difference;

The Plaintiff could not affirm the authenticity of evidence 12 and thought it had no relationship with the case;

The Plaintiff objected to the effect of evidence 13. Even though the price was true, it could not prove that the ship price of RMB38 million was reasonable;

The Plaintiff recognized the authenticity and legality of evidence 14 but had no relationship with the case;

The authenticity of evidence 15 should be verified by Tianjin Maritime Court. But disputes of final price of *Ship Purchase and Sale Contract* had no relationship with the case;

The Plaintiff recognized the authenticity, legality and relevancy of evidence 16, which could prove that the contract note of ship sale and purchase was real and valid contract and the Defendant had started to perform;

The Plaintiff recognized the authenticity of evidence 17, but whether CHEN Shineng had received 3 million needed to be verified and 3 million was irrelevant to with the case;

The Plaintiff recognized the superficial authenticity of evidence 18, but it just proved that two people had made statement before the notary, as for whether it was true, the notary could not judge and the relevant concept should be verified by the material obtained from Maritime Administrative Center;

Evidence 19 was made by Hengtong Company and could not be verified. The case should subject to materials kept by Maritime Administrative Center;

The Third Party recognized the authenticity and legality of evidence 1-4, as for purpose of proof they agreed with the Plaintiff;

The Third Party recognized the authenticity and legality of evidence 5-9 but thought they were irrelevant to the case;

As for evidence 10, the Third Party had same opinion with the Plaintiff and there were no warranty relationships between the Plaintiff and the Third Party in account supervision agreements, business receipts and settlement applications;

The Third Party recognized the authenticity of evidence 11 but thought it was irrelevant to the Third Party;

The Third Party recognized the authenticity and legality of evidence 12 but it was irrelevant to Third Party;

The Third Party recognized the effect of evidence 13;

The Third Party recognized the authenticity, legality and relevancy of evidence 14-16 and thought the price agreed by three parties was true ship price;

The Third Party recognized the authenticity of evidence 17 but was irrelevant to the Third Party;

The Third Party recognized the authenticity of evidence 18 and 19. But references did not appear in court so the court did not affirm its concept.

The court recognizes evidence of the Plaintiff as follows: evidence 1-12, 14-17 could be mutual verified by relevant evidence and statements provided by the Plaintiff and the Third Party, so the court recognized the effect but would ascertain probative force separately; the court objects to the authenticity of evidence 13 because there are no original copy to verify; evidence 18 is witness testimony, even though it is notarized, the witness did not appear in the court to accept inquiry by parties; neither did the Defendant provide evidence to prove that the witness had legal reason to miss the hearing, so the court objects to the authenticity of evidence 18; evidence 19 is sole statement of Hengtong Company and they did not provide evidence, but the material was provided by People's Republic of China Tianjin Maritime Board, so the court objects to statement of Hengtong Company.

The Third Party submitted evidence as follows:

1. Ship Purchase and Sale Contract (same as evidence 2 of the Plaintiff and evidence 1 of the Defendant), to prove that there were real ship business between the Plaintiff and the Defendant and the contract was real meaning expression that completely stated terms of ship price, ship handover and ownership transference;
2. Account supervision agreement (same as evidence 3 of the Plaintiff and evidence 10 of the Defendant), to prove that the Third Party and the Plaintiff concluded the agreement to perform *Ship Purchase and Sale Contract*;
3. Business receipt of RMB30.4 million, to prove that, on January 14, 2013, the Third Party remitted RMB30.4 million to the account according to *Ship Purchase and Sale Contract*;
4. Ship handover paper, to prove that on January 8, 2013, parties of the contract has accomplish the ship handover of M.V. "Huitong 3" and signed the handover paper;
5. Registration certificate of ship's ownership, to prove that the ownership of M.V. "Huitong 3" had been transferred to the Third Party according to agreement.

The Plaintiff recognized the authenticity, legality and relevancy of evidence 1-4; the Plaintiff recognized the authenticity and legality of evidence 5 but thought that the period of applying for ship's ownership certificate was too long. The Defendant did not provide the certificate to the Plaintiff which resulted in that the ship could not operate;

The Defendant recognized the authenticity legality and relevancy of evidence 1-5, but thought that the Defendant actually received RMB26.6 million and another RMB3.8 million had been preserved by the court. Among the money actually received by the Defendant, the Defendant has paid RMB12 million to the Plaintiff.

The court recognizes that evidence 1-5 provided by the Third Party can mutually verify with evidence and statements of the Plaintiff and the Defendant, so the court recognizes the effect and homologous probative force.

About verified written opinion from EC, the Plaintiff recognized its authenticity, legality and relevancy and thought it objectively reflected ship's value during basic period, which was made on the basic of sufficient investigation and demonstration; The Defendant objected to its authenticity, legality and relevancy; the Third Party thought EC did not have legal connection with them and there were some defects in it: the reason was not enough, so EC could not prove its result. The court recognizes EC's effect and probative force because EC was made from Judicial Evaluation Organ on the basic of investigation and demonstration.

Upon examination and confirmation of above-mentioned evidence, the court ascertains the following facts through investigation:

On October 19, 2012, the Plaintiff Yizhou Company concluded contract note of ship sale and purchase, Article 3 Paragraph 1 two parties agreed that the ship price was invariable price - RMB11 million; in Paragraph 2, the price was paid through finance leasing and QIU Guohua was obliged to help Yizhou Company handle relevant finance leasing procedures. QIU Guohua advanced 6 million for Yizhou Company without interest the day before two parties concluded ship Purchase and Sale Contract with financial institute and the money was guarantee for finance leasing; In Paragraph 5, they agreed that if two parties did not conclude *Ship Purchase and Sale Contract* with financial institute which was designated by Yizhou Company before December 31, 2012, this contract will be cancelled.

On December 5, 2012, Yizhou Company's employee GU Jiansheng forwarded the e-mail from Zhongxin Company's employee GAO Wei to QIU Guohua, and the concept was about ship finance leasing. The concept was that: "because this finance leasing business could not provide receipt of leases, to avoid tax risk, it is necessary to change the trading mode from direct leasing to leaseback. So it is necessary to add Changhui Company as joint lessee of this leasing business, but actually Yizhou Company paid all rent, guarantee, service charge and other relative fee and Changhui Company is not obliged for paying and guarantee. Please negotiate with Changhui Company and ask it to provide material lists in attachment." There were adjusted project confirmation note and material lists which should be provided by Changhui Company attached to the e-mail. On December 7, GU Jiansheng sent e-mail to QIU Guohua to tell him materials Changhui Company needed in the joint lease business and said After negotiation of Yizhou Company, Changhui Company should just sign and seal on the contract, but in fact, they do not undertake any paying or guarantee obligations. Yizhou Company would independently conclude supplementary agreement with Changhui Company and wrote that Changhui Company did not undertake any paying or guarantee obligations. On December 25, GU Jiansheng forwarded the e-mail from Zhongxin Company's employee GAO Eei to QIU Guohua, among which GAO Wei said what documents QIU Guohua should sign asked GU Jiansheng to pre-inform QIU Guohua what materials QIU Guohua should prepare. As for the dispute whether the Plaintiff or the Defendant first negotiated with the Third Party about finance leasing business, according to the Third Party's statement and e-mails, the court did not find any evidence to prove that the Defendant had connection with the Third Party directly.

On December 25, 2012, Changhui Company made payment order and said Zhongxin Company and Yizhou Company carried out finance leasing business. Zhongxin Company bought a sand dredger M.V. "Huitong 3" from Changhui Company of 38 million and the money will be supervised by common account set by Changhui Company, Zhongxin Company and Yizhou Company; for M.V. "Huitong 3" actually belong to QIU Guohua but operated by Changhui Company, Changhui Company agreed that, after the ownership was registered to Zhongxin Company, they would remit the money of RMB38 million directly to QIU Guohua through supervision account, and the receiver account was Agricultural Bank in Ningbo Chaiqiao branch(QIU Guohua' account). On the same day, Changhui Company concluded agreement of cancelling M.V. "Huitong 3" subordination.

The bank card of QIU Guohua and USDK was left by Yizhou Company. According to the e-mail sent from GU Jiansheng to QIU Guohua on January 7, 2013, GU Jiansheng asked QIU Guohua to provide QIU Guohua's bank card, USDK and personal seal. While according to text records provided by Yizhou Company, on January 7, 2013, Yizhou Company connected with XU Xianjun (staff of Ningbo Huabu Logistics Co., Ltd., according to contact name stored in phone of Yizhou Company) through text and asked XU Xianjun to take QIU Guohua's ID card, bank card, USDK, authorization letter and seal to Bank of Communication Beijing Sanyuan branch at 1400 hrs on the next day. According to text records, at 1135 hrs on January 8, 2013, XU Xianjun said he was there and GU Jiansheng was appeared at 1450 hrs. In the hearing, the Defendant recognized that he had delivered bank card and USDK to the Plaintiff but said it was for the convenience of the Plaintiff to remit the money. The Plaintiff alleged that after they had remit the money to the Defendant's account on January 17, that is next day, the aforesaid account has been closed. The Defendant alleged that he reported loss to the bank because it was more convenient to report loss directly rather than get back from the Plaintiff.

On January 8, 2013, Changhui Company concluded *Ship Purchase and Sale Contract* with three parties: QIU Guohua(Party A), Zhongxin Company(Party B) and Yizhou Company(Party C), contract number was [ZXFT (YW) XXXXXXX-2]. They agreed that Party A and Party C applied finance leasing business to Party B and concluded finance leasing contract on January 8, 2013, the contract number was [ZXTF (YW) XXXXXXX-1]. They agreed in the contract that Party A sold lease (ship) to Party B as owner, then Party A and Party C joint lease the ship by finance leasing method. In Paragraph (1) of Article 3, the price of M.V. "Huitong 3" was RMB38 million which was made according to leasing contract and account supervision contract of Zhongxin Company and Yizhou Company, and the money should be remitted to account of Yizhou Company; in Paragraph 2, the money should be paid into 2 phases, the first payment of RMB34.2 million should be remitted by Yizhou Company to the account designated by Changhui Company and QIU Guohua after the Maritime Organ registered the transference of the ship. If the ship did not register to Zhongxin Company during agreed time, Changhui Company and QIU Guohua should return the money and interest within 10 workday after receiving Zhongxin Company's inform of returning money; in Paragraph 3, from the day of getting materials that Maritime Organ register the transference of the ship, receiving original receipt of the ship provided by Changhui Company and QIU Guohua and inform of receiving the ship made by Yizhou Company, within 3 days, Zhongxin Company should pay the final payment of 3.8 million to the seller. In Paragraph 1 of Article 5, the ship should be delivered directly from Changhui Company and QIU Guohua to Yizhou Company and the delivery details should be negotiated separately by three parties; in Paragraph 2, the ownership of the ship would belong to Zhongxin Company from the day of delivering, the risks after that would be undertook by Yizhou Company. They had also agreed that Changhui Company and QIU Guohua should deliver ship's certification certificate, marine technology drawings and other technological files, and all things on board and on shore that belong to the ship to Yizhou Company without extra paying. Aforesaid certificate, drawings and goods, equipment and standby equipments belonged to Zhongxin Company.

Then aforesaid all parties concluded finance leasing contract of M.V. "Huitong 3" [Number ZXFT(YW)XXXXXXX-1]. Zhongxin Company was Party A, as leaser; Yizhou Company, Changhui Company and QIU Guohua was Party B, as character. They agreed that the Party B transferred the lease to Party A by leaseback, for the purpose of financing, and the Party A delivered the lease to Party B according to the financing purpose. The principal of leasing was 38 million, which was price Party A paid to Party B for buying lease, and the interest was 8.32%, which was fluctuated and calculated by the three-five year benchmark loan rate of People's Bank of China multiply 1.3. The service fee was 1.9 million and guarantee was 38 million(Party B must one-off pay both to the account designated by the Party A before the leasing principal put into the circulation and the money will not return in any case; the guarantee did not calculate interest, if the Party B paid the rent by contract and did not do anything break the contract, the guarantee would automatically charge against the last rent). Nominal price of goods was 50 thousands, that was the money Party B paid to buy lease after Party B paying all rent and other dues. The whole rent, terminal rent and pay day should base on Attachment 4– Rent Paying List and Attachment 5– Adjustment of Rent Notification, which was made after the leasing interest was adjusted. Attachment 4 of the contract was blank (actually all attachments were blank) and did not had concepts. The period of paying rent was every 3 months, but they did not agree on explicit leasing period; they did not agree on paying methods of leasing principal but just wrote accounts of receiving money of two parties. The account of Party B was that supervision account set by Yizhou Company and Zhongxin Company on Bank of Communication Beijing Sanyuan Branch.

On the same day, Yizhou Company (Party A), Zhongxin Company (Party B) and Bank of Communication Beijing Sanyuan branch concluded agreement of supervising account (apply to reserved basic transaction, specimen seals of both parties are reserved seals for supervision account) and agreed that Party C provides supervision service for supervision account. The name of that supervision account was Yizhou Company, the payment of supervision account should conducted through OTC and both parties must seal on the paying receipt using reserved seal. The agreement w attached to reserved seals, include official seal of Party A, special finance seal of Party A, name seal of Party A's finance chief and name seal of Party B's finance chief, and the words of name seal of Party A's finance chief was QIU Guohua.

On the same day, Zhongxin Company, Yizhou Company, Changhui Company and QIU Guohua made confirmation note for signing finance lease contract [Number ZXFT (YW) XXXXXXX-1]. Because the actual user of lease was Yizhou Company, four parties agreed that Yizhou Company undertakes all rights and obligations of Party B under contract terms, Changhui Company and QIU Guohua did not undertake any rights or obligations.

According to registration certificate of ownership of M.V. "Huitong 3", the port of registry was Tianjin, the original port of registry was Wuhu. The type of the ship was sand dredger. Dockyard was Hengtong Company in Chaohu city Wuwei country Erba town. The completion date was June 18, 2009. Length overall was 76m, beam 13.80m, height 4m, GRT 1179 ton, NRT 354 ton. Type of 2 powers was internal-combustion engine, gross capacity was 432kilowatt. Type of 2 propellers was screw propeller. Shipowner was the Third Party Zhongxin Company, the date of acquiring ownership was January 8, 2013.

On January 14, 2013, Zhongxin Company remitted RMB30.4 million to the supervision account. On the same day, Haitian Ship Service Company in Chaohu invoiced service fee receipt of business management of RMB1.14 million (fee rate 3%). The written ship was M.V. "Huitong 3", and the payer was Zhongxin Company, Changhui Company as buyer and Zhongxin Company as seller. On January 17, the supervision account remitted RMB26.6 million to QIU Guohua's account.

According to phone record of Yizhou Company. On January 18, 2013, the employee GU Jiansheng phoned QIU Guohua and QIU Guohua referred many times that "if give the money to CHEN Shineng, it will become contract defraud", "YI Jianbo said the ship was related to defraud, and he will be in jail. If I coordinate him, I will become a swindler", "that's the end of contract defraud if I give the money to him", "Take out the original contract, that contract is useless", "I can say they did, I sell 49% to CHEN Shineng and he will finance lease to me", "I have cancelled that bank card. I will go to Beijing and say that bank card was missed."

If the bank card was missed, Beijing (branch) must give me a new one"; GU Jiansheng had asked why did QIU Guohua do this and persuaded him not to do this, it's bad for both parties.

On January 29, 2013 and February 8, the Defendant QIU Guohua remitted RMB6 million respectively to Zheng Cuidi's account (wife of the Plaintiff's legal representative) and CHEN Shineng's account (the Plaintiff's legal representative), amount to 12 million. On the hearing, the Plaintiff alleged that CHEN Shineng and Zheng Cuidi were both shareholders of the Plaintiff. The Defendant alleged that the money was discount the Defendant paid to the Plaintiff's legal representative and his wife. According to the Plaintiff, among RMB12 million, only 6million was price of goods the Defendant- QIU Guohua returned to the Plaintiff-Yizhou Company and another 6 million was other capital transaction between the Plaintiff and the Defendant. The Plaintiff alleged that he lent RMB2 million to the Defendant before the ship sale and purchase; while the Defendant alleged that they lent 3 million and provided paying receipt to the court as evidence and had been recognized by the Plaintiff and the Defendant. But that RMB3 million was not related to the case.

On May 6, 2013, Tianjin Maritime court accepted the case over disputes: QIU Guohua sue Zhongxin Company about ship sale and purchase, Yizhou Company was the Third Party. On November 20, QIU Guohua, Zhongxin Company and Yizhou Company concluded settlement agreement and agreed that, before November 26, 2013, Zhongxin Company must pay the final price of RMB3.4 million of the ship to QIU Guohua through the supervision account which was set with Yizhou Company and Yizhou Company agreed to help to perform that obligation. The performance of that obligation means the performance of obligation that Zhongxin Company paid the final price to QIU Guohua. If Zhongxin Company did not perform the paying obligation or they could not perform because Yizhou Company did not give them help, QIU Guohua has rights to apply to the court to give compulsory execution to RMB3.8 million in aforesaid supervision account. If the money in account was not enough, Zhongxin Company should pay the final price to QIU Guohua by using other properties. After performing that obligation, if there were extra money in the supervision account, it should return to Zhongxin Company and Zhongxin Company agree to use this money to charge against rent over finance leasing contract between them and Yizhou Company. Besides, Yizhou Company undertook the litigation fee of RMB18,600. On the same day, Tianjin Maritime Court issued the civil mediation and confirmed the settlement agreement.

On November 28, 2013, the supervision account remitted RMB3.8 million to QIU Guohua's account. On account of Yihzou Company's application, the court adopted the preservation measures.

Yizhou Company authorized Shanghai Jilian Asset Evaluation Company to evaluate the value of M.V. "Huitong 3" in January 2013. The evaluation work started on January 10, 2013 and ended at February 10. On October 20, 2013, Jilian Company issued Evaluation Report of the Value of M.V. "Huitong 3", the evaluating method was replacement cost method, the type of value was market value. The result was that: the evaluation value of M.V. "Huitong 3" was RMB11.5 million on the base date of assets evaluation–January31, 2013.

Authorized by the court, EC investigated and collected evidence from Hengtong Company, China Wuhu Maritime Organ and Tianjin Maritime Organ and finally collected Shipbuilding Contract of M.V. "Huitong 3", Shipbuilding Contract of M. V. "Jinhua158" (Huitong) and Ship Purchase and Sale Contract of Jinhua 158 "Huitong 3" from Tianjin Maritime Organ, then made Verified Written Paper on November 15, 2013 and shown that the value of M.V. "Huitong 3" could not surpass 12 million from October 19, 2012 to January 8, 2013.

In the hearing, the Plaintiff alleged that, before the sale and purchase business, M.V. "Huitong 3" serviced for the engineering construction of Guangdong Gangao Bridge leased by the Plaintiff. After the business, it was the Defendant did not deliver materials such as ship certificate that results in the termination of the ship operation in Zhuhai. The Third Party alleged that the Plaintiff defaulted some rent when they performed the finance leasing contract.

Besides, the Plaintiff concluded contract note of ship sale and purchase with another person SHI Moumou on July 25, 2012 and agreed that the Plaintiff bought the ship "Jinhua 158" from SHI Moumou. The price was RMB15 million and changeless. The Plaintiff first paid subscription 2 million and then paid other RMB13 million by means of finance leasing. SHI Moumou was obliged to help the Plaintiff to handle relevant procedures. On August 31, the Plaintiff, SHI Moumou and Zhongxin Company concluded *Ship Purchase and Sale Contract* and agreed that Zhongxin Company paid RMB40 million to buy M.V. "Jinhua 158" from SHI Moumou and lease it to the Plaintiff; The Plaintiff and Zhongxin Company concluded Finance Leasing Contract (direct lease) and agreed that Zhongxin Company rented out M.V. "Jinhua 158" to the Plaintiff in RMB40 million, with 8% of year-annual interest rate, RMB1.04 million of service fee and RMB5 million of guarantee. The name price was RMB50,000, after paying all rent, overdue fine, liquidated damages and other due payments, the Plaintiff would get the ownership of the lease ship. The Plaintiff and Zhongxin Company commonly set a capital supervision account in Communication Bank of China Sanyuan branch for this finance leasing business and at the column of "financial administrator's seal" in the seal specimen reserved by the bank, there were a seal presenting "SHI Moumou's seal". The Plaintiff confirmed that SHI Moumou has returned the difference to the Plaintiff, which the actual-received finance leasing money exceed the agreed money.

The court recognizes that the Plaintiff required the Defendant to return the money according to *Contract Note of Ship Sale and Purchase* concluded by the Plaintiff and the Defendant. And the money was difference between the finance leasing price the Defendant actually received and the ship price agreed in the contract note, so the case was dispute over the sale and purchase of the ship. To decide whether the Defendant should return the aforesaid difference, it was necessary to analyze and judge whether there was a real declaration of intention about the ship sale and purchase and its price between the Plaintiff and the Defendant.

According to *Contract Note of Ship Sale and Purchase*, the transaction price of M.V. "Huitong 3" was 11 million and was raise by the Plaintiff by means of finance leasing. The Defendant should help the Plaintiff to handle relevant finance leasing procedures. Even though the Defendant alleged that the price was made for avoiding taxes, they did not provide any evidence to prove it. The contract was concluded by the Plaintiff and the Defendant and was real declaration of intention of both parties, so both parties should restraint by it. And effective evidence also proved that, after the contract was concluded, the Plaintiff communicated with the Third Party immediately about relevant finance leasing business; the Plaintiff then told the Defendant that the Third Party asked the Defendant and Changhui Company to help to handle relevant procedures, while the Defendant did not show rejection or disagreement explicitly. Behaviors of the Plaintiff and the Defendant were actual performance of *Contract Note of Ship Sale and Purchase* and presented that both parties was willing to be confined by the contract. The Defendant alleged that the Plaintiff, the Defendant and the Third Party concluded *Ship Purchase and Sale Contract* on January 8, 2013, so *Contract Note of Ship Sale and Purchase* was cancelled. The court supports that according to effective evidence, from December 5, 2012 to January 8, 2013, the Plaintiff negotiated and communicated with the Third Party and the Defendant uninterruptedly about finance leasing business, repairing projects and informed the Defendant providing relevant materials and handling procedures, so the Plaintiff has fulfilled his obligations under *Contract Note of Ship Sale and Purchase*. During this period, the Defendant did not express rejection of performing obligation of helping the Plaintiff to handle finance leasing procedures. In particular, after December 31 2012, that was January 7, 2013 and January 8, 2013, the Plaintiff informed the Defendant providing bank card, USTB and personal seal. While evidence show that the Defendant has actually provided those things to the Plaintiff and concluded *Ship Purchase and Sale Contract*, *Finance Leasing Contract* and *Agreement of Supervision Account* with the Plaintiff and the Third Party on January 8, 2013. The Defendant not only did not express rejection of performing obligations under *Contract Note of Ship Sale and Purchase*, but also positively helped the Plaintiff accomplish finance leasing procedures of M.V. "Huitong 3" and concluded supplementary agreements of finance leasing successfully, that were explicit performances of obligations. To speak of, after December 31, 2013, the Defendant's behaviors of giving bank card, USTB and personal seal to the Plaintiff are expressing performances of relevant obligations according to Contract Note of Ship Sale and Purchase; if the Defendant did not want to perform the contract, or think the contract was cancelled and ineffective, he would not fulfill the Plaintiff's requirements and help handling procedures. Because behaviors of the Defendant was enough to make reliance for the Plaintiff, that was the Defendant performed and wanted to continue to perform the contract as usual and had no declaration of regret intention. Based on this reliance, the Plaintiff was willing to handle relevant finance leasing business of M.V. "Huitong 3" between the Defendant and the Third Party to promote two parties to conclude supplementary agreements. After the Third Party remitting RMB26.6 million of ship's price to the supervision account, the Plaintiff agreed to remit it to the Defendant through the supervision account under the circumstance of controlling that money. The behaviors of the Plaintiff are based on the reliance to the Defendant and subjective circumstance that the Plaintiff actually controlled the bank card and

USDK. Consequently, the pleading of the Defendant about *Contract Note of Ship Sale and Purchase* which had been cancelled did not accord with the Defendant's performance and opposites to the legal protection to the reliance interest of parties, so the court does not support.

As for real declaration of intention of the Plaintiff and the Defendant, the court confirms that, as evidence shown, the Plaintiff and the Defendant has agreed in *Contract Note of Ship Sale and Purchase* that the price of M.V. "Huitong 3" was 11 million and emphasized it was changeless price; In addition, the money was raised by the Plaintiff from the financial institute but they did not agree on specific financial price, neither did they agree that the whole financial money was used for purchasing M.V. "Huitong 3" and paid to the Defendant. As a result, both parties should be honest and perform according to the price agreed in the contract. After that, the Plaintiff negotiated with the Third Party about handling finance leasing business and the Defendant helped the Plaintiff handle according to the contract, which shows that both parties did not want to change the price of ship; After December 31, 2012, both parties performed respective obligations as contract. The Defendant did not declare any intentions to void or cancel the contract, while the Plaintiff, based on reliance to the Defendant, agreed to remit RMB26.6 million of the ship's price to the Defendant through supervision account. On the whole, the aforesaid transaction is an integrated and interrupted process and also a performing process for *Contract Note of Ship Sale and Purchase*.

In the aforesaid process, two details are essential to investigate real declaration of intention of the Plaintiff and the Defendant: firstly, the Defendant never expressly suspended or terminated contract. In particular, after 2013, the Defendant still helped the Plaintiff to handle business; secondly, the Defendant gave bank card and USDK to the Plaintiff according to the requirement of the Plaintiff in the whole process. The declaration of intention of the party is presented by language or behavior, so that the opposite could clearly receive and understand and make relevant declaration of intention, which could be legal effectively and bind force of the party's behaviors. In this case, according to the circumstance of performance of Contract Note of Ship Sale and Purchase in 2012, if the Defendant want to allege that after 2012 *Contract Note of Ship Sale and Purchase* was cancelled or ineffective, he should expressly declare this will to the Plaintiff on time and reject to requirements of the Plaintiff, so that the Plaintiff could know the Defendant's meaning and make adjustment. On the contrary, the Defendant not only prepared relevant materials positively according to the Plaintiff's requirement and concluded *Ship Purchase and Sale Contract*, *Finance Leasing Contract* with the Plaintiff and the Third Party, but gave personal bank card and USDK to the Plaintiff. The Defendant alleged that the behaviors were for the convenience of the Plaintiff to remit the money. However, as common sense, when the payer remit the money to the receiver, he should just tell the username, account number and messages of bank of deposit to the receiver instead of giving bank card and USDK to the receiver. Bank card and USDK are signs of rights of ownership and method of controlling the account, which have direct and close relationship with possessor's personal bank account. The Defendant could not give his bank card and USDK to the

Plaintiff without special reason. On January 7, 2013, the Plaintiff asked the Defendant deliver bank card and USDK. The behavior of deliver of the Defendant apparently accords with the fact alleged by the Plaintiff that the Defendant agreed to return the difference, which is between the actual finance leasing price and the agreed price of RMB11 million, while the interpretation of the Defendant that was for the convenience of the Plaintiff to remit the money, so the court does not support. In addition, the Defendant went to the bank to report the loss of the bank card and USDK after giving them to the Plaintiff. Now that the bank card and USDK were given by the Defendant voluntarily, he could get back from the Plaintiff or ask the Plaintiff to send it back without saying rather than reporting loss. The interpretation of "it was more convenient to report loss than getting back from the Plaintiff" is unreasonable. Aforesaid behaviors of the Defendant apparently show that the Defendant solely regret after the Plaintiff performing obligations on the basic of reliance and reject to perform the obligation of returning final finance leasing payment under the contract note, which break agreements of two parties and do harm to the Plaintiff's reliance interest and rights under the contract.

What's more, according to evidence, after the Defendant remitting RMB26.6 million through supervision account, on January 29 and February 8, he remitted RMB6 million to the Plaintiff's legal representative and his wife separately, in whole 12 million. The Defendant alleged that it was discount. While on the one hand, under the circumstance that the Defendant just received RMB26.6 million, the Defendant paid RMB12 million of discount to the Plaintiff, which is almost half of the ship price. It is beyond understanding of normal people because the price and percentage was so high. On the other hand, the Defendant did not provide evidence to prove that in the transaction of the ship, it is necessary for the Defendant to pay discount to the Plaintiff. The Defendant did not provide evidence to prove that RMB12 million was other payment besides the business between the Plaintiff and the Defendant. On the whole, combined with promises in *Contract Note of Ship Sale and Purchase* and performances of both parties, in particular the Defendant's behavior of giving bank card and USDK to the Plaintiff in January 2013, the behavior of the Defendant–pay RMB12 million after receiving RMB26.6 million of finance leasing payment, accords with logic, facts and requirement of the Plaintiff– require the Defendant to return the difference between actual finance leasing payment and agreed ship price (RMB11 million). It is easy to know that the Plaintiff and the Defendant has reached an agreement and subjected to real declaration of intention: the Defendant paid RMB11 million to buy M.V. "Huitong 3" from the Plaintiff and the money was obtained by financing from relevant finance institute found and associated by the Plaintiff, but the price would not change because the change of actual financing funds. Whatever based on obligations under contract or principle of honesty and credibility, the Defendant should return the difference after he had received actual financing funds.

Whereas equity of transaction, the money of the ship was obtained by financing from the Third Party. The Defendant did not provide evidence to prove that he first associated with the Third Party to get the opportunity of financing; the Third Party also confirmed that no evidence showed that the Defendant first associated with the

Third Party. Under such circumstances, the Plaintiff obtained financing funds which is higher than the ship's price agreed in *Contract Note of Ship Sale and Purchase* from cooperation and negotiation, so the funds should be used and governed by the Plaintiff. What's more, by judicial evaluation, the ship's actual value from October 19, 2012 to January 8, 2013, could not exceed RMB12 million, so the price of RMB11 million agreed in *Contract Note of Ship Sale and Purchase* was more accurate and appropriate to reflect real value of the ship. Even though the Defendant and the Third Party alleged that the value of M.V. "Huitong 3" was RMB38 million agreed by three parties in Ship Purchase and Sale Contract and Finance Leasing Contract, they did not provide any evidence to prove that; On the contrary, the Third Party put forward to use the price of a similar ship M.V. "Jinhua 158" as a reference to M.V. "Huitong 3". However, the Plaintiff has provided evidence to prove that the price of ship "Jinhua 158" was financed from the Third Party, actual financing funds exceed agreed ship price, which the Plaintiff and the actual owner SHI Moumou reached an agreement, and SHI Moumou is obliged to return the difference to the Plaintiff.

Whereas efficiency, the value of M.V. "Huitong 3" could not exceed RMB12 million in the past, while the price agreed by the Third Party, the Plaintiff and the Defendant in Ship Purchase and Sale Contract and Finance Leasing Contract was 38 million, which exceeds real value of the ship, so once the charter breached the contract and did not pay the rent, the unpaid rent that financing fund exceeds real value of the lease would undertake the risk of not guaranteed by the value of the lease. Even though the Defendant alleged that *Ship Purchase and Sale Contract* and *Finance Leasing Contract* was independent of *Contract Note of Ship Sale and Purchase*, combined all facts: the agreement that the Plaintiff financed the funds in Contract Note of Ship Sale and Purchase, the Plaintiff associated and negotiated financing business with the Third Party, the Plaintiff was only party of chartering and undertaking the obligation of paying rent, the conclusion is that the Plaintiff was who negotiated the ship's price, paid the ship's price to the Third Party by financing and finally bought and operated M.V. "Huitong 3", and was the only party to make full use of M.V. "Huitong 3". Under the circumstance that the capital of financing of M.V. "Huitong 3" exceeded its real value and the financing funds faced risks, the funds which exceeds its real value was more appropriate to be governed and use by the party who undertakes the obligation of paying rent under the finance leasing contract, or to be supervised by relevant parties in finance leasing business. It is more beneficial for the safe supervision and use of funds and avoiding risks. As a result, the Third Party, as investor of finance leasing, has recognized the claim of the Plaintiff in the hearing.

In conclusion, the court supports the Plaintiff's claim that the Defendant should return the sum exceeding agreed financing funds to supervision account, because facts and evidence and accords with the requirements of equity and efficiency. While the claimed money should deduct RMB12 million that the Defendant has proved to remit to the legal representative of the Plaintiff and his wife. RMB30.4 million has been paid to the Defendant through supervision account, which deducted agreed ship price of RMB1 million and RMB12 million that the

Defendant has paid before, the Defendant should return RMB7.4 million. The Plaintiff's claim for interest accords with rules of law, according to real paying date of two funds and the date of interest – December29, 2013, of which RMB3.8 million of the price was confirmed by Tianjin Maritime Court, other interest should be calculated from the date of return of the Defendant, that is the day after the Defendant receiving RMB26.6 million– January18, 2013. According to Article 6, Article 8 Paragraph 1 of the Contract Law of the People's Republic of China, Article 64 Paragraph 1 of the Civil Procedure Law of the People's Republic of China, the judgment is as follows:

1. The Defendant QIU Guohua shall pay RMB7,400,000 and the interest thereon (thereof RMB3,600,000 of interest started from 18 January 2013 and RMB3,800,000 of interest started from December 29, 2013. Both shall be calculated according to deposit and lending rates of the People's Bank of China for the corresponding period, ended until the judgment effects) to the supervision account which has been set by the Plaintiff Shanghai Yizhou Waterway Engineering Co., Ltd. and the Third Party Zhongxin Futong Finance Leasing Co., Ltd. in Bank of Communication Beijing Sanyuan Branch (Account name: Shanghai Yizhou Waterway Engineering Co., Ltd., Account Number: XXXXXXXXXXXXXXXXX. Opening bank: Communication Bank of China Beijing Sanyuan Branch).
2. Reject other claims of the Plaintiff Shanghai Yizhou Waterway Engineering Co., Ltd.

Court acceptance fee in amount of RMB102,200, the Plaintiff Shanghai Yizhou Waterway Engineering Co., Ltd. shall bear RMB45,761, the Defendant QIU Guohua shall bear RMB56,439. Application fee of preservative measures in amount of RMB5,000, evaluation fee in amount of RMB50,000, the Defendant QIU Guohua shall bear the fees.

In case of dissatisfaction with this judgment, both parties may within 15 days upon the service of this judgment, submit a statement of appeal to the court, together with copies according to the number of the opposite parties, and appeal to the Shanghai High People's Court.

Presiding Judge: ZHOU Gang
Judge: LIN Yan
Acting Judge: DAI Yuzhen

December 19, 2014

Clerk: SUN Ye

Appendix: Relevant Law

1. **Contract Law of the People's Republic of China**
   Article 6 The parties shall abide by the principle of good faith in exercising their rights and performing their obligations.
   Article 8 A lawfully formed contract is legally binding on the parties. The parties shall perform their respective obligations according to the contract, and neither party may arbitrarily amend or terminate the contract.
2. **Civil Procedure Law of the People's Republic of China**
   Article 64 A party shall have the responsibility to provide evidence in support of its own propositions.

   For the evidence that cannot be obtained by any parties or their litigation representatives because of some realistic reasons or for the evidence that the people's court considers necessary for adjudicating the case, the people's court shall investigate and collect such evidence.

   The people's court shall, according to the procedure prescribed by law, collect and examine evidence comprehensively and objectively.

Shanghai High People's Court
Civil Judgment

Shanghai Yizhou Waterway Engineering Co., Ltd.
v.
QIU Guohua

(2015) Hu Gao Min Si (Hai) Zhong Zi No.32

Related Case(s) This is the judgment of second instance, and the judgment of first instance is on page 943.

Cause(s) of Action 206. Dispute over ship sales and purchases contract.

Headnote Affirming lower court decision enforcing settlement agreement in relation to a dispute over the purchase price of a ship, requiring Defendant to repay 11 million RMB to Plaintiff.

Summary The Appellant Shanghai Yizhou Waterway Engineering Co., Ltd. filed this appeal against the Appellant QIU Guohua and the Third Party Zhongxin Futong Financial Leasing Co., Ltd concerning a dispute over a vessel purchase contract settlement. The dispute concerns a settlement agreement among the three parties, recognized by the court of first instance, from which the court determined that Defendant had received more than he deserved and ordered Defendant to return RMB11 million. This case is Defendant's appeal. The court held that the contract between Plaintiff and Defendant was still valid and affirm the lower court's judgment, ordering Defendant to repay RMB11 million.

Judgment

The Appellant (the Plaintiff of first instance): Shanghai Yizhou Waterway Engineering Co., Ltd.
Legal representative: CHEN Moumou.
Agent *ad litem*: FENG Wen, lawyer of Shanghai Wintell & Co.
Agent *ad litem*: QUE Dongli, lawyer of Shanghai Wintell & Co. (Guangzhou)

The Appellant (the Defendant of first instance): QIU Guohua
Agent *ad litem*: XUE Zhicai, lawyer of Zhejiang Shiguang Law Firm.

The Third Party of First Instance: Zhongxin Futong Lease Finance Co., Ltd.
Legal representative: LIU Zhiqiang.
Agent *ad litem*: YANG Wengui, lawyer of Beijing Haitong Law Firm.
Agent *ad litem*: PENG Xianwei, lawyer of Beijing Haitong Law Firm.

With respect to the case arising from dispute over vessel purchase contract among the Appellant, Shanghai Yizhou Waterway Engineering Co., Ltd. (hereinafter referred to as Yizhou Company), and the Appellant QIU Guohua as well as the Third Party of first instance, Zhongxin Futong Lease Finance Co., Ltd. (hereinafter referred to as Zhongxin Company), the Appellant, Yizhou Company challenged (2013) Hu Hai Fa Hai Chu Zi No.60 Civil Judgment made by Shanghai Maritime Court and made an appeal to the court. The court organized collegiate panel according to law, after entertained the case on February 12, 2015 and held the public trial in court on March 18, 2015. Agents *ad litem* of Yizhou Company, FENG Wen and QUE Dongli, agent *ad litem* of QIU Guohua XUE Zhicai, and agent *ad litem* of Zhongxin Company, PENG Xianwei, attended the hearing. The case has now been concluded.

Yizhou Company alleged in first instance that on October 19, 2012, it signed M.V. "Huitong 3" *Purchase and Sale Contract* to purchase M.V. "Huitong 3" from QIU Guohua. The agreed price was RMB11,000,000, a fixed price. The ship price was arranged by Yizhou Company in way of finance; QIU Guohua was responsible for helping Yizhou Company to complete the financing formalities and returning the difference to Yizhou Company after receiving the ship price. After that, Yizhou Company, QIU Guohua and Zhongxin Company concluded several complementary agreements of finance of M.V. "Huitong 3" included *Purchase and Sale Contract* and *Finance Leasing Contract* with Anhui Changhui Transportation and Trade Co., Ltd. (hereinafter referred to as Changhui Company), a party not involved in this case. According to those agreements, the ship price was RMB38,000,000, among which the down payment was RMB34,200,000, the final payment RMB38,000,000 and the deposit (RMB7,600,000) was going to be deducted from the finance payment. On January 8, 2013, Yizhou Company, QIU Guohua and Zhongxin Company set up a supervision account in the bank. On January 14, 2013, Zhongxin Company paid the down payment in amount of RMB30,400,000. On January 17, 2013, Yizhou Company and Zhongxin Company applied to pay the price of RMB26,600,000 to QIU Guohua's account, the deposit was deducted from the down payment. Although QIU Guohua repeatedly promised to pay the price difference to Yizhou Company, after repeatedly urging by Yizhou Company, QIU Guohua only paid RMB6,000,000. Yizhou Company requested the court of first instance to order QIU Guohua to: 1. return the remaining ship finance RMB13,400,000 and interests to the supervision account which was set up in the Bank of Communications Beijing Sanyuan Branch (the interests should be calculated according to the current deposit interest rate over the same period of the Bank of China, starting from the finance payment was actually paid and ending at the day of the judgment effects. The actual paying date of the first payment was January 17,

2013 and November 28, 2013 for the second payment); 2. the litigation costs should be born by QIU Guohua.

QIU Guohua alleged in first instance that, Yizhou Company and QIU Guohua concluded the contract note of *Ship Sale and Purchase* on October 19, 2012, but Yizhou Company knew that they could not afford the payment so they introduced the business to Zhongxin Company. On January 8, 2013, Yizhou Company, QIU Guohua and Zhongxin Company concluded *Ship Purchase and Sale Contract* at the price of RMB38,000,000. At that time, the previous *Purchase and Sale Contract* had been concealed, so Yizhou Company's asking for returning the ship's payment had no evidence; they did not appoint any concept of returning the price difference of the ship to Yizhou Company which was asked by Yizhou Company, and Yizhou Company knew that the business reflected by *Contract Note of Ship Sale and Purchase* would not succeed when they concluded this contract with QIU Guohua; the ship's sale contract and finance lease contract concluded by Yizhou Company, QIU Guohua and Zhongxin Company had no relationship with the contract note of ship sale and Purchase Yizhou Company claimed and was not the complementary agreements of the contract note of ship sale and Purchase Yizhou Company claimed; it was false statement that QIU Guohua repeatedly promised to pay the price difference of the ship to Yizhou Company. QIU Guohua never promised to give the property belonging to themselves to Yizhou Company. Yizhou Company asked QIU Guohua to pay the discount for helping QIU Guohua to sale the ship, and QIU Guohua could not help but pay RMB12,000,000. In all, QIU Guohua ask to dismiss Yizhou Company's action.

Zhongxin Company alleged in first instance that it was not involved in the contract note of ship sale and Purchase and did not know the existence of that contract, so they had no legal relation with the case; in *Contract Note of Ship Sale and Purchase*, Yizhou Company and QIU Guohua did not define the buyer's obligations and the transfer delivery of the subject that did not conform to the features of sale contract according to the law, so it was not strictly *Purchase and Sale Contract*. From the concept of the contract, the aim was making provision for the distribution of the finance lease price between two parties. At the same time, Zhongxin Company had paid the price and the subject had been delivered, so the Purchase and Sale Contract was effective and true; Zhongxin Company agree with the action of Yizhou Company, identify with the return of the finance payment and think it will assure that Yizhou Company should repay the defaulting rent in full.

The court of first instance ascertained the following facts through investigation:

On October 19, 2012, Yizhou Company Yizhou Company concluded *Contract Note of Ship Sale and Purchase*, Paragraph 1 of Article 3 two parties agreed that the ship price was invariable price - RMB11 million; in Paragraph 2, the price was paid through finance leasing and QIU Guohua was obliged to help Yizhou Company handle relevant finance leasing procedures. QIU Guohua advanced 6 million for Yizhou Company without interest the day before two parties concluded *Ship Purchase and Sale Contract* with financial institute and the money was guarantee for finance leasing; in Paragraph 5, they agreed that if two parties did not conclude

Ship Purchase and Sale Contract with financial institute which was designated by Yizhou Company before December 31, 2012, this contract would be cancelled.

On December 5, 2012, Yizhou Company's employee GU Jiansheng forwarded the e-mail from Zhongxin Company's employee GAO Wei to QIU Guohua, and the concept was about ship finance leasing. The concept was that: "because this finance leasing business could not provide receipt of leases, to avoid tax risk, it is necessary to change the trading mode from direct leasing to leaseback. So it is necessary to add Changhui Company as joint lessee of this leasing business, but actually Yizhou Company paid all rent, guarantee, service charge and other relative fee and Changhui Company was not obliged for paying and guarantee. Please negotiate with Changhui Company and ask it to provide material lists in attachment." There were adjusted project confirmation note and material lists which should be provided by Changhui Company attached to the e-mail. On December 7, GU Jiansheng sent e-mail to QIU Guohua to tell him materials Changhui Company needed in the joint lease business and said After negotiation of Yizhou Company, Changhui Company should just sign and seal on the contract, but in fact, they did not undertake any paying or guarantee obligations. Yizhou Company would independently conclude supplementary agreement with Changhui Company and wrote that Changhui Company did not undertake any paying or guarantee obligations. On 25 December, GU Jiansheng forwarded the e-mail from Zhongxin Company's employee GAO Wei to QIU Guohua, among which GAO Wei said what documents QIU Guohua should sign asked GU Jiansheng to pre-inform QIU Guohua what materials QIU Guohua should prepare. As for the dispute whether Yizhou Company or QIU Guohua first negotiated with Zhongxin Company about finance leasing business, according to Zhongxin Company's statement and e-mails, the court of first instance did not find any evidence to prove that QIU Guohua had connection with Zhongxin Company directly.

On December 25, 2012, Changhui Company made payment order and said Zhongxin Company and Yizhou Company carried out finance leasing business. Zhongxin Company bought a sand dredger M.V. "Huitong 3" from Changhui Company of 38 million and the money would be supervised by common account set by Changhui Company, Zhongxin Company and Yizhou Company; for M.V. "Huitong 3" actually belong to QIU Guohua but operated by Changhui Company, Changhui Company agreed that, after the ownership was registered to Zhongxin Company, they will remit the money of RMB38 million directly to QIU Guohua through supervision account, and the receiver account was Agricultural Bank in Ningbo Chaiqiao branch(QIU Guohua's account). On the same day, Changhui Company concluded agreement of cancelling M.V. "Huitong 3" subordination.

The bank card of QIU Guohua and USDK was left by Yizhou Company. According to the e-mail sent from GU Jiansheng to QIU Guohua on January 7, 2013, GU Jiansheng asked QIU Guohua to provide QIU Guohua's bank card, USDK and personal seal. While according to text records provided by Yizhou Company, on January 7, 2013, Yizhou Company connected with XU Xianjun(staff of Ningbo Huabu Logistics Co., Ltd., according to contact name stored in phone of Yizhou Company) through text and asked XU Xianjun to take QIU Guohua's ID card, bank card, USDK, authorization letter and seal to Bank of Communication Beijing Sanyuan branch at 1400 hrs on the next day. According to text records, at 1135 hrs on January 8, 2013, XU Xianjun said he was there and GU Jiansheng was appeared at 1450 hrs. In the hearing, QIU Guohua recognized that he had delivered bank card and USDK to Yizhou Company but said it was for the convenience of Yizhou Company to remit the money. Yizhou Company alleged that after they had remit the money to QIU Guohua's account on January, 17 that was next day, the aforesaid account had been closed. QIU Guohua alleged that he reported loss to the bank because it was more convenient to report loss directly rather than get back from Yizhou Company.

On January 8, 2013, Changhui Company concluded ship Purchase and Sale Contract with three parties: QIU Guohua (Party A), Zhongxin Company (Party B) and Yizhou Company (Party C), contract number was [ZXFT (YW) XXXXXXX-2]. They agreed that Party A and Party C applied finance leasing business to Party B and concluded finance leasing contract on January 8, 2013, the contract number was [ZXTF (YW) XXXXXXX-1]. They agreed in the contract that Party A sold lease (ship) to Party B as owner, then Party A and Party C joint lease the ship by finance leasing method. In Paragraph 1 of Article 3, the price of M.V. "Huitong 3" was RMB38 million which was made according to leasing contract and account supervision contract of Zhongxin Company and Yizhou Company, and the money should be remitted to account of Yizhou Company; in Paragraph 2, the money should be paid by 2 installments, the first payment of RMB34.2 million should be remitted by Yizhou Company to the account designated by Changhui Company and QIU Guohua after the Maritime Organ registered the transference of the ship. If the ship do not register to Zhongxin Company during agreed time, Changhui Company and QIU Guohua should return the money and interest within 10 workday after receiving Zhongxin Company's inform of returning money; in Paragraph 3, from the day of getting materials that Maritime Organ register the transference of the ship, receiving original receipt of the ship provided by Changhui Company and QIU Guohua and inform of receiving the ship made by Yizhou Company, within 3 days, Zhongxin Company should pay the final payment of 3.8 million to the seller. In Paragraph 1 of Article 5, the ship should be delivered directly from Changhui Company and QIU Guohua to Yizhou Company and the delivery details should be negotiated separately by three parties; in Paragraph 2, the ownership of the ship will belong to Zhongxin Company from the day of delivering, the risks after that will be undertook by Yizhou Company. They had also agreed that Changhui Company and QIU Guohua should deliver ship's certification certificate, marine technology drawings and other technological files, and all things on board and on shore that belong to the ship to Yizhou Company without extra paying. Aforesaid certificate, drawings and goods, equipment and standby equipments belonged to Zhongxin Company.

Then aforesaid all parties concluded finance leasing contract of M.V. "Huitong 3" [Number ZXFT(YW)XXXXXXX-1]. Zhongxin Company was Party A, as leaser; Yizhou Company, Changhui Company and QIU Guohua was Party B, as character. They agreed that the Party B transferred the lease to Party A by leaseback, for the purpose of financing, and the Party A delivered the lease to Party B according to the financing purpose. The principal of leasing was 38 million, which was price Party A paid to Party B for buying lease, and the interest was 8.32%, which was fluctuated and calculated by the three-five year benchmark loan rate of People's Bank of China multiply 1.3. The service fee was 1.9 million and guarantee was 38 million(Party B must one-off pay both to the account designated by the Party A before the leasing principal put into the circulation and the money would not return in any case; the guarantee do not calculate interest, if the Party B pay the rent by contract and do not do anything break the contract, the guarantee would automatically charge against the last rent). Nominal price of goods was 50 thousands, that was the money Party B paid to buy lease after Party B paying all rent and other dues. The whole rent, terminal rent and pay day should base on Attachment 4– Rent Paying List and Attachment 5– Adjustment of Rent Notification, which was made after the leasing interest was adjusted. Attachment 4 of the contract was blank (actually all attachments were blank) and did not had concepts. The period of paying rent was every 3 months, but they did not agree on explicit leasing period; they did not agree on paying methods of leasing principal but just wrote accounts of receiving money of two parties. The account of Party B was that supervision account set by Yizhou Company and Zhongxin Company on Bank of Communication Beijing Sanyuan branch.

On the same day, Yizhou Company (Party A), Zhongxin Company (Party B) and Bank of Communication Beijing Sanyuan branch concluded agreement of supervising account (apply to reserved basic transaction, specimen seals of both parties were reserved seals for supervision account) and agreed that Party C provides supervision service for supervision account. The name of that supervision account was Yizhou Company, the payment of supervision account should conducted through OTC and both parties must seal on the paying receipt using reserved seal. The agreement w attached to reserved seals, include official seal of Party A, special finance seal of Party A, name seal of Party A's finance chief and name seal of Party B's finance chief, and the words of name seal of Party A's finance chief was QIU Guohua.

On the same day, Zhongxin Company, Yizhou Company, Changhui Company and QIU Guohua made confirmation note for signing finance lease contract [Number ZXFT (YW) XXXXXXX-1]. Because the actual user of lease was Yizhou Company, four parties agreed that Yizhou Company undertakes all rights and obligations of Party B under contract terms, Changhui Company and QIU Guohua did not undertake any rights or obligations.

According to registration certificate of ownership of M.V. "Huitong 3", the port of registry was Tianjin, the original port of registry was Wuhu. The type of the ship was sand dredger. Dockyard was Hengtong Company in Chaohu city Wuwei country Erba town. The completion date was June 18, 2009. Length overall was 76m, beam 13.80m, hight 4m, GRT 1179 ton, NRT 354 ton. Type of 2 powers was internal-combustion engine, gross capacity was 432kilowatt. Type of 2 propellers was screw propeller. Shipowner was Zhongxin Company Zhongxin Company, the date of acquiring ownership was January 8, 2013.

On January 14, 2013, Zhongxin Company remitted RMB30.4 million to the supervision account. On the same day, Haitian Ship Service Company in Chaohu invoiced service fee receipt of business management of RMB1.14 million (fee rate 3%). The written ship was M.V. "Huitong 3", and the payer was Zhongxin Company, Changhui Company as buyer and Zhongxin Company as seller. On January 17, the supervision account remitted RMB26.6 million to QIU Guohua's account.

According to phone record of Yizhou Company. On January 18, 2013, the employee GU Jiansheng phoned QIU Guohua and QIU Guohua referred many times that "if give the money to CHEN Shineng, it would become contract defraud", "YI Jianbo said the ship was related to defraud, and he will be in jail. If I coordinate him, I will become a swindler", "that is the end of contract defraud if I give the money to him", "take out the original contract, that contract was useless", "I can say they did, I sell 49% to CHEN Shineng and he will finance lease to me", "I had cancelled that bank card. I will go to Beijing and say that bank card was missed. If the bank card was missed, Beijing (branch) must give me a new one"; GU Jiansheng had asked why did QIU Guohua do this and persuaded him not to do this, it's bad for both parties.

On January 29, 2013 and February 8, QIU Guohua remitted RMB6 million respectively to Zheng Cuidi's account(wife of Yizhou Company's legal representative) and CHEN Shineng's account (Yizhou Company's legal representative), amount to 12 million. On the hearing, Yizhou Company alleged that CHEN Shineng and ZHENG Cuidi were both shareholders of Yizhou Company. QIU Guohua alleged that the money was discount QIU Guohua paid to Yizhou Company's legal representative and his wife. According to Yizhou Company, among RMB12 million, only 6million was price of goods QIU Guohua- QIU Guohua returned to Yizhou Company-Yizhou Company and another 6 million was other capital transaction between Yizhou Company and QIU Guohua. Yizhou Company alleged that he lent RMB2 million to QIU Guohua before the ship sale and Purchase; while QIU Guohua alleged that they lent 3 million and provided paying receipt to the court as evidence and had been recognized by Yizhou Company and QIU Guohua. But that RMB3 million was not related to the case.

On May 6, 2013, Tianjin Maritime court accepted the case over disputes: QIU Guohua sued Zhongxin Company about ship sale and Purchase, Yizhou Company was Zhongxin Company. On November 20,QIU Guohua, Zhongxin Company and Yizhou Company concluded settlement agreement and agreed that, before November 26, 2013, Zhongxin Company must pay the final price of RMB3.4 million of the ship to QIU Guohua through the supervision account which was set with Yizhou Company and Yizhou Company agreed to help to perform that obligation. The performance of that obligation means the performance of obligation that Zhongxin Company paid the final price to QIU Guohua. If Zhongxin Company did not perform the paying obligation or they could not perform because Yizhou Company do not give them help, QIU Guohua had rights to apply to the court to give compulsory execution to RMB3.8 million in aforesaid supervision account. If the money in account was not enough, Zhongxin Company should pay the final price to QIU Guohua by using other properties. After performing that obligation, if there were extra money in the supervision account, it should return to Zhongxin Company and Zhongxin Company agree to use this money to charge against rent over finance leasing contract between them and Yizhou Company. Besides, Yizhou Company undertook the litigation fee of RMB18,600. On the same day, Tianjin Maritime Court issued the civil mediation and confirmed the settlement agreement.

On November 28, 2013, the supervision account remitted RMB3.8 million to QIU Guohua's account. On account of Yihzou Company's application, the court adopted the preservation measures.

Yizhou Company had authorized Shanghai Jilian Asset Evaluation Company to evaluate the value of M.V. "Huitong 3" in January 2013. The evaluation work started on January 10, 2013 and ended at February 10. On October 20, 2013, Jilian Company issued Evaluation Report of the Value of M.V. "Huitong 3", the evaluating method was replacement cost method, the type of value was market value. The result was that: the evaluation value of M.V. "Huitong 3" was RMB11.5 million on the base date of assets evaluation– January31, 2013.

Authorized by the court, EC investigated and collected evidence from Hengtong Company, China Wuhu Maritime Organ and Tianjin Maritime Organ and finally collected Shipbuilding Contract of M.V. "Huitong 3", Shipbuilding Contract of M. V. "Jinhua158" (Huitong) and *Ship Purchase and Sale Contract* of Jinhua 158 "Huitong 3" from Tianjin Maritime Organ, then made Verified Written Paper on November 15, 2013 and shown that the value of M.V. "Huitong 3" could not surpass 12 million from October 19, 2012 to January 8, 2013.

In the first instance hearing, Yizhou Company alleged that, before the sale and purchase business, M.V. "Huitong 3" had serviced for the engineering construction of Guangdong Gangao Bridge leased by Yizhou Company. After the business, it was QIU Guohua did not deliver materials such as ship certificate that resulted in the termination of the ship operation in Zhuhai. Zhongxin Company alleged that Yizhou Company defaulted some rent when they performed the finance leasing contract.

Besides, the first instance court found that Yizhou Company concluded contract note of ship sale and Purchase with another person SHI Moumou on July 25, 2012 and agreed that Yizhou Company bought the ship "Jinhua 158" from SHI Moumou. The price was RMB15 million and changeless. Yizhou Company first paid subscription 2 million and then paid other RMB13 million by means of finance leasing. SHI Moumou was obliged to help Yizhou Company to handle relevant procedures. On August 31, Yizhou Company, SHI Moumou and Zhongxin Company concluded *Ship Purchase and Sale Contract* and agreed that Zhongxin Company paid RMB40 million to buy M.V. "Jinhua 158" from SHI Moumou and lease it to Yizhou Company; Yizhou Company and Zhongxin Company concluded *Finance Leasing Contract*(direct lease) and agreed that Zhongxin Company rented out M.V. "Jinhua 158" to Yizhou Company in RMB40 million, with 8% of year-annual interest rate, RMB1.04 million of service fee and RMB5 million of guarantee. The name price was RMB50,000, after paying all rent, overdue fine, liquidated damages and other due payments, Yizhou Company would get the ownership of the lease ship. Yizhou

Company and Zhongxin Company commonly set a capital supervision account in Communication Bank of China Sanyuan branch for this finance leasing business and at the column of "financial administrator's seal" in the seal specimen reserved by the bank, there were a seal presenting "SHI Moumou's seal". Yizhou Company confirmed that SHI Moumou had returned the difference to Yizhou Company, which the actual-received finance leasing money exceed the agreed money.

The court of first instance recognized that Yizhou Company required QIU Guohua to return the money according to *Contract Note of Ship Sale and Purchase* concluded by Yizhou Company and QIU Guohua. And the money was difference between the finance leasing price QIU Guohua actually received and the ship price agreed in the contract note, so the case was dispute over the sale and Purchase of the ship. To decide whether QIU Guohua should return the aforesaid difference, it was necessary to analyze and judge whether there was a real declaration of intention about *Ship Sale and Purchase* and its price between Yizhou Company and QIU Guohua.

According to *Contract Note of Ship Sale and Purchase*, the transaction price of M.V. "Huitong 3" was 11 million and was raise by Yizhou Company by means of finance leasing. QIU Guohua should help Yizhou Company to handle relevant finance leasing procedures. Even though QIU Guohua alleged that the price was made for avoiding taxes, they did not provide any evidence to prove it. The contract was concluded by Yizhou Company and QIU Guohua and was real declaration of intention of both parties, so both parties should restraint by it. And effective evidence also proved that, after the contract was concluded, Yizhou Company communicated with Zhongxin Company immediately about relevant finance leasing business; Yizhou Company then told QIU Guohua that Zhongxin Company asked QIU Guohua and Changhui Company help to handle relevant procedures, while QIU Guohua did not show rejection or disagreement explicitly. Behaviors of Yizhou Company and QIU Guohua were actual performance of *Contract Note of Ship Sale and Purchase* and presented that both parties was willing to be confined by the contract. QIU Guohua alleged that Yizhou Company, QIU Guohua and Zhongxin Company concluded *Ship Purchase and Sale Contract* on January 8, 2013, so *Contract Note of Ship Sale and Purchase* was cancelled. The court of first instance supported that according to effective evidence, from December 5, 2012 to January 8, 2013, Yizhou Company negotiated and communicated with Zhongxin Company and QIU Guohua uninterruptedly about finance leasing business, repairing projects and informed QIU Guohua providing relevant materials and handling procedures, so Yizhou Company had fulfilled his obligations under *Contract Note of Ship Sale and Purchase*. During this period, QIU Guohua did not express rejection of performing obligation of helping Yizhou Company to handle finance leasing procedures. In particular, after December 31, 2012, that was January 7, 2013 and January 8, 2013, Yizhou Company informed QIU Guohua providing bank card, USTB and personal seal. While evidence show that QIU Guohua had actually provided those things to Yizhou Company and concluded *Ship Purchase and Sale Contract*, *Finance Leasing Contract* and *Agreement of Supervision Account* with Yizhou Company and Zhongxin Company on January 8, 2013. QIU

Guohua not only did not express rejection of performing obligations under *Contract Note of Ship Sale and Purchase*, but also positively helped Yizhou Company accomplish finance leasing procedures of M.V. "Huitong 3" and concluded supplementary agreements of finance leasing successfully, that were explicit performances of obligations. To speak of, after December 31, 2013, QIU Guohua's behaviors of giving bank card, USTB and personal seal to Yizhou Company were expressing performances of relevant obligations according to Contract Note of Ship Sale and Purchase; if QIU Guohua did not want to perform the contract, or think the contract was cancelled and ineffective, he would not fulfill Yizhou Company's requirements and help handling procedures. Because behaviors of QIU Guohua was enough to make reliance for Yizhou Company, that was QIU Guohua performed and wanted to continue to perform the contract as usual and had no declaration of regret intention. Based on this reliance, Yizhou Company was willing to handle relevant finance leasing business of M.V. "Huitong 3" between QIU Guohua and Zhongxin Company to promote two parties to conclude supplementary agreements. After Zhongxin Company remitting RMB26.6 million of ship's price to the supervision account, Yizhou Company agreed to remit it to QIU Guohua through the supervision account under the circumstance of controlling that money. The behaviors of Yizhou Company were based on the reliance to QIU Guohua and subjective circumstance that Yizhou Company actually controlled the bank card and USDK. Consequently, the pleading of QIU Guohua about the Contract Note of Ship Sale and Purchase which had been cancelled do not accord with QIU Guohua's performance and opposites to the legal protection to the reliance interest of parties, so the court of first instance did not support.

As for declaration of real intention of Yizhou Company and QIU Guohua, the court of first instance confirmed that, as evidence show, Yizhou Company and QIU Guohua had agreed in *Contract Note of Ship Sale and Purchase* that the price of M.V. "Huitong 3" was 11 million and emphasized it was changeless price; in addition, the money was raised by Yizhou Company from the financial institute but they did not agree on specific financial price, neither did they agree that the whole financial money was used for purchasing M.V. "Huitong 3" and paid to QIU Guohua. As a result, both parties should be honest and perform according to the price agreed in the contract. After that, Yizhou Company negotiated with Zhongxin Company about handling finance leasing business and QIU Guohua helped Yizhou Company handle according to the contract, which showed that both parties did not want to change the price of ship; after December 31, 2012, both parties performed respective obligations as contract. QIU Guohua did not declare any intentions to void or cancel the contract, while Yizhou Company, based on reliance to QIU Guohua, agreed to remit RMB26.6 million of the ship's price to QIU Guohua through supervision account. On the whole, the aforesaid transaction was a integrated and interrupted process and also a performing process for *Contract Note of Ship Sale and Purchase*.

In the aforesaid process, two details were essential to investigate real declaration of intention of Yizhou Company and QIU Guohua: firstly, QIU Guohua never expressly suspended or terminated contract. In particular, after 2013, QIU Guohua still helped Yizhou Company to handle business; secondly, QIU Guohua gave bank card and USDK to Yizhou Company according to the requirement of Yizhou Company in the whole process. The declaration of intention of the party was presented by language or behavior, so that the opposite could clearly receive and understand and make relevant declaration of intention, which could be legal effectively and bind force of the party's behaviors. In this case, according to the circumstance of performance of *Contract Note of Ship Sale and Purchase* in 2012, if QIU Guohua wanted to allege that after 2012 *Contract Note of Ship Sale and Purchase* was cancelled or ineffective, he should expressly declare this will to Yizhou Company on time and reject to requirements of Yizhou Company, so that Yizhou Company could know QIU Guohua's meaning and make adjustment. On the contrary, QIU Guohua not only prepared relevant materials positively according to Yizhou Company's requirement and concluded *Ship Purchase and Sale Contract, Finance Leasing Contract* with Yizhou Company and Zhongxin Company, but gave personal bank card and USDK to Yizhou Company. QIU Guohua alleged that the behaviors were for the convenience of Yizhou Company to remit the money. However, as common sense, when the payer remit the money to the receiver, he should just tell the username, account number and messages of bank of deposit to the receiver instead of giving bank card and USDK to the receiver. Bank card and USDK were signs of rights of ownership and method of controlling the account, which had direct and close relationship with possessor's personal bank account. QIU Guohua could not give his bank card and USDK to Yizhou Company without special reason. On January 7, 2013, Yizhou Company asked QIU Guohua deliver bank card and USDK. The behavior of deliver of QIU Guohua apparently accords with the fact alleged by Yizhou Company that QIU Guohua agreed to return the difference, which was between the actual finance leasing price and the agreed price of RMB11 million, while the interpretation of QIU Guohua that was for the convenience of Yizhou Company to remit the money, so the court of first instance did not support. In addition, QIU Guohua went to the bank to report the loss of the bank card and USDK after giving them to Yizhou Company. Now that the bank card and USDK were given by QIU Guohua voluntarily, he could get back from Yizhou Company or ask Yizhou Company to send it back without saying rather than reporting loss. The interpretation of "it was more convenient to report loss than getting back from Yizhou Company" was unreasonable. Aforesaid behaviors of QIU Guohua apparently show that QIU Guohua solely regret after Yizhou Company performing obligations on the basic of reliance and reject to perform the obligation of returning final finance leasing payment under the contract note, which break agreements of two parties and do harm to Yizhou Company's reliance interest and rights under the contract.

Further more, according to evidence, after QIU Guohua remitting RMB26.6 million through supervision account, on January 29 and February 8, he remitted RMB6 million to Yizhou Company's legal representative and his wife separately, in whole 12 million. QIU Guohua alleged that it was discount. While on the one hand, under the circumstance that QIU Guohua just received RMB26.6 million, QIU Guohua paid RMB12 million of discount to Yizhou Company, which was almost half of the ship price. It was beyond understanding of normal people because the price and percentage was so high. On the other hand, QIU Guohua did not provide evidence to prove that in the transaction of the ship, it was necessary for QIU Guohua to pay discount to Yizhou Company. QIU Guohua did not provide evidence to prove that RMB12 million was other payment besides the business between Yizhou Company and QIU Guohua. On the whole, combined with promises in *Contract Note of Ship Sale and Purchase* and performances of both parties, in particular QIU Guohua's behavior of giving bank card and USDK to Yizhou Company in January 2013, the behavior of QIU Guohua–pay RMB12 million after receiving RMB26.6 million of finance leasing payment, accorded with logic, facts and requirement of Yizhou Company–require QIU Guohua to return the difference between actual finance leasing payment and agreed ship price (RMB11 million). It was easy to know that Yizhou Company and QIU Guohua had reached an agreement and subjected to real declaration of intention: QIU Guohua paid RMB11 million to buy M.V. "Huitong 3" from Yizhou Company and the money was obtained by financing from relevant finance institute found and associated by Yizhou Company, but the price would not change because the change of actual financing funds. Whatever based on obligations under contract or principle of honesty and credibility, QIU Guohua should return the difference after he had received actual financing funds.

Whereas equity of transaction, the money of the ship was obtained by financing from Zhongxin Company. QIU Guohua did not provide evidence to prove that he first associated with Zhongxin Company to get the opportunity of financing; Zhongxin Company also confirmed that no evidence showed that QIU Guohua first associated with Zhongxin Company. Under such circumstances, Yizhou Company obtained financing funds which was higher than the ship's price agreed in *Contract Note of Ship Sale and Purchase* from cooperation and negotiation, so the funds should be used and governed by Yizhou Company. What's more, by judicial evaluation, the ship's actual value from October 19, 2012 to January 8, 2013, could not exceed RMB12 million, so the price of RMB11 million agreed in *Contract Note of Ship Sale and Purchase* was more accurate and appropriate to reflect real value of the ship. Even though QIU Guohua and Zhongxin Company alleged that the value of M.V. "Huitong 3" was RMB38 million agreed by three parties in *Ship Purchase and Sale Contract* and *Finance Leasing Contract*, they did not provide any evidence to prove that; on the contrary, Zhongxin Company put forward to use the price of a similar ship M.V. "Jinhua 158" as a reference to M.V. "Huitong 3". However, Yizhou Company had provided evidence to prove that the price of ship "Jinhua 158" was financed from Zhongxin Company, actual financing funds exceed agreed ship price, which Yizhou Company and the actual owner SHI Moumou reached an agreement, and SHI Moumou was obliged to return the difference to Yizhou Company.

Whereas efficiency, the value of M.V. "Huitong 3" could not exceed RMB12 million in the past, while the price agreed by Zhongxin Company, Yizhou Company and QIU Guohua in *Ship Purchase and Sale Contract* and *Finance Leasing Contract* was 38 million, which exceeded real value of the ship, so once the charter breached the contract and did not pay the rent, the unpaid rent that financing fund exceeded real value of the lease would undertake the risk of not guaranteed by the value of the lease. Even though QIU Guohua alleged that *Ship Purchase and Sale Contract* and *Finance Leasing Contract* was independent of *Contract Note of Ship Sale and Purchase*, combined all facts: the agreement that Yizhou Company financed the funds in *Contract Note of Ship Sale and Purchase*, Yizhou Company associated and negotiated financing business with Zhongxin Company, Yizhou Company was only party of charactering and undertaking the obligation of paying rent, the conclusion was that Yizhou Company was who negotiated the ship's price, paid the ship's price to Zhongxin Company by financing and finally bought and operated M.V. "Huitong 3", and was the only party to make full use of M.V. "Huitong 3". Under the circumstance that the capital of financing of M.V. "Huitong 3" exceeded its real value and the financing funds faced risks, the funds which exceeds its real value was more appropriate to be governed and use by the party who undertakes the obligation of paying rent under the finance leasing contract, or to be supervised by relevant parties in finance leasing business. It was more beneficial for the safe supervision and use of funds and avoiding risks. As a result, Zhongxin Company, as investor of finance leasing, had recognized the claim of Yizhou Company in the hearing.

In conclusion, the court of first instance supported Yizhou Company's claim that QIU Guohua should return the sum exceeding agreed financing funds to supervision account, because facts and evidence and accords with the requirements of equity and efficiency. While the claimed money should deduct RMB12 million that QIU Guohua had proved to remit to the legal representative of Yizhou Company and his wife. RMB30.4 million had been paid to QIU Guohua through supervision account, which deducted agreed ship price of RMB1 million and RMB12 million that QIU Guohua had paid before, QIU Guohua should return RMB7.4 million. Yizhou Company's claim for interest accords with rules of law, according to real paying date of two funds and the date of interest – December29, 2013, of which RMB3.8 million of the price was confirmed by Tianjin Maritime Court, other interest should be calculated from the date of return of QIU Guohua, that was the day after QIU Guohua receiving RMB26.6 million– January18, 2013. According to Article 6, Article 8 Paragraph 1 of the Contract Law of the People's Republic of China, Article 64 Paragraph 1 of the Civil Procedure Law of the People's Republic of China, the judgment was as follows: 1. QIU Guohua should pay RMB7,400,000 and the interest thereon (the interest on RMB3,600,000 started from January 18, 2013 and the interest on RMB3,800,000 started from December 29, 2013, calculated according to loan rate of the People's Bank of China over the corresponding period until the judgment came into effect) to the supervision account which had been set by Yizhou Company and Zhongxin Company (Account name: Shanghai Yizhou Waterway Engineering Co., Ltd., Account Number: XXXXXXX XXXXXXXXXX. Deposit bank: Communication Bank of China Beijing Sanyuan Branch); 2. reject other claims of Yizhou Company. Court acceptance fee of first instance in amount of RMB102,200, Yizhou Company should bear RMB45,761 and QIU Guohua should bear RMB56,439. The application fee of preservative measures in amount of RMB5,000 and the evaluation fee in amount of RMB50,000 should be born by QIU Guohua.

Yizhou Company dissatisfied with the judgment of first instance and filed an appeal. Yizhou Company alleged that the fund, RMB12,000,000, that had been said to be repaid by QIU Guohua consisted of three parts, including two funds of RMB3,000,000 paid to one of the stock holder of Yizhou Company, Zheng Moumou, and RMB6,000,000 which was paid to the legal representative of Yizhou Company CHEN Moumou. It was the amount of fund RMB6,000,000 which paid to ZHENG Moumou that should be repaid to Yizhou Company as the financial fund for M.V. "Huitong 3", but the amount of fund RMB6,000,000 that paid to CHEN Moumou had no relevancy with this case. The court of first instance mistakenly assigned the responsibility of proof and concluded that QIU Guohua had already repaid RMB12,000,000 to Yizhou Company, on the ground that Yizhou Company failed to prove the fund of RMB6,000,000 paid to CHEN Moumou was other current funds. The mistakes mentioned above should be corrected. Therefore, the Appellant made an appeal to the court of second instance for the following requirements: 1. revoke the (2013) Hu Hai Fa Hai Chu Zi No.60 Civil Judgment made by Shanghai Maritime Court and amend the judgment that support all the litigation claims of Yizhou Company; 2. QIU Guohua should be required to pay all the litigation fees concerned with the first instance and the second instance.

As response to the appeal of Yizhou Company, QIU Guohua contended that there existed no vessel purchase relationship between QIU Guohua and Yizhou Company. The actual price for the vessel was RMB38,000,000, rather than RMB11,000,000. The amount of fund RMB12,000,000 that QIU Guohua paid to Yizhou Company was not vessel purchase fund, but the commission fee claimed by QIU Guohua. In conclusion, the Appellant hereby appealed to the court of second instance and requested the court not to support the appeal of Yizhou Company.

As response to the appeal of Yizhou Company, Zhongxin Company stated that the dispute over the amount of fund RMB6,000,000 between Yizhou Company and QIU Guohua had nothing to do with Zhongxin Company. Zhongxin Company was not involved in two parties' deal and known little about the deal. Therefore, Zhongxin Company made no comments about the case.

QIU Guohua made an appeal and held following opinions that:

1. The ascertained facts judged by the court of first instance were wrong. *Ship Purchase Contract* was cancelled after the date of December 31, 2012, so Yizhou Company was thereafter not the counterpart under *Ship Purchase Contract*. Although *Ship Purchase Contract* had been cancelled, Yizhou Company neither paid the vessel purchase fund, nor signed or performed another vessel purchase contract or relevant agreements with QIU Guohua. Therefore, there were no obligations or right relationship between QIU Guohua and Yizhou Company. Zhongxin Company signed *Ship Purchase Contract* with QIU Guohua, so Zhongxin Company was the buyer of the vessel involved. The performance of *Ship Purchase Contract* between the two parties was completed, when Zhongxin Company paid RMB3,800,000 from its regulatory account to

QIU Guohua. Yizhou Company was the counterpart under *Financial Leasing Contract*. QIU Guohua was not connected with the financial leasing, so the agreement of *Financial Leasing Contract* could not be considered as regulations for QIU Guohua' obligations and rights. QIU Guohua gave credit card, E-bank and personal seal to Yizhou Company, which was not for the purpose of making it convenient to transferring vessel purchase fund into Yizhou Company's account. QIU Guohua did not negotiate with Zhongxin Company about the program of vessel financing. Yizhou Company and Zhongxin Company negotiated with each other on the issue of chartering, rather than vessel purchase. Under the circumstance of fund shortage, Yizhou Company turned to Zhongxin Company for leasing the vessel instead of buying the vessel involved. The court of first instance breached the common commercial practices, when ascertaining the price of the vessel. If the price of the vessel was RMB11,000,000 as agreed in *Ship Purchase Contract*, Yizhou Company could buy the vessel with the fund of RMB11,000,000, rather than obtained the ownership of the vessel through financing the amount of fund RMB38,000,000.

2. The court of first instance admitted the evidence presented by Yizhou Company beyond the time limit of evidence production, which breached the law procedure. The court of first instance entrusted identifications without application from Yizhou Company which also breached the law procedure. The identification comment on the vessel involved made by identification institution was lack of objective basis.

3. The court of first instance breached law procedure, for there was one trial with two courts involved. Tianjin Maritime Court has concluded the dispute over Ship Purchase Contract and the according paper of civil mediation was being put into effect, but the court of first instance breached the procedure law to entertain the case again on the ground of ship purchase contract dispute. In conclusion, the Appellant requested that the court of second instance shall revoke the judgment in first instance and reject all the claims made by Yizhou Company.

As response to QIU Guohua's appeal, Yizhou Company contended that:

1. Yizhou Company did not recognize the dealing-procedure of the vessel involved mentioned by QIU Guohua. The primary issue was to inspect the true meaning of payment arrangement and price on *Ship Purchase Contract* between the two parties, since QIU Guohua had already confirmed that this case was dispute over ship purchase contract. According to agreements in *Ship Purchase Contract*, the true meaning of two parties showed that the vessel price was fixed with RMB11,000,000, so QIU Guohua should cooperate with Yizhou Company so that the payment fund for vessel purchase could be gotten through financing. According to the performance of *Ship Purchase Contract*, QIU Guohua had already confirmed that *Ship Purchase Contract* was valid and knew that the obligation to repay over RMB11,000,000 to Yizhou Company should be fulfilled.

2. *Ship Purchase Contract* was still binding on Yizhou Company and QIU Guohua, since it had not been terminated. As a matter of fact, before the time of contract termination, Yizhou Company had reached an agreement with Zhongxin Company on the financial leasing program including *Ship Purchase Contract* under that framework, so it was not qualified for the requirements of contract termination.
3. *Ship Purchase Contract* and *Financial Leasing Contract* were signed and performed for the purpose of collecting vessel purchase fund under *Ship Purchase Contract*. It aimed to assist Yizhou Company of obtaining fund so as to pay RMB11,000,000 for vessel purchase. No discussion or negotiation had been conducted by QIU Guohua.
4. The essence of the ownership obtained by Zhongxin Company was to guarantee the financial fund in the financial leasing program, but Yizhou Company bear the outstanding rent that exceeded the value of lease items. Therefore, the financial fund that exceeded the amount of fund RMB11,000,000 should belong to Yizhou Company. And it was in conformity with agreements of the contract and the principles of equity and efficiency.
5. The procedure violation in first instance claimed by QIU Guohua was not the fact. Three parties all presented complementary evidence, after exchanging evidence. Therefore, the court of first instance did not breach the relevant laws or regulations, when the court made such arrangement. With respect to the issues of entrusted identifications, the fact that the court of first instance entrusted jurisdiction institution to make identification so as to ascertain the value of the vessel involved under the condition that materials and data presented by each parties were different from each other's, so the court of first instance did not breach laws and regulations. This case was different from the case entertained by Tianjin Maritime Court as claimed by the Appellant in aspects of both basic law relation among parties and appeals, thereby, the court of first instance did not violate the principle of "non bis in idem".

As response to the appeal of QIU Guohua, Zhongxin Company stated that:

The term of "vessel's actual value" used by the court of first instance should be further clarified. From the view of actual circumstance in this case, the terminally actual deal was financial deal through signing *Ship Purchase Contract* and *Financial Leasing Contract* with financial institutions. The deal between Yizhou Company and QIU Guohua was not the same purchase contract as defined in the chapter of purchase contract in the Contract Law of People's Republic of China. Zhongxin Company believed that *Ship Purchase Contract* and *Financial Leasing Contract* among three parties represented their true meanings and were all valid.

QIU Guohua presented the following materials in the second instance:

1. Copy of Shipbuilding Contract;
2. Original bareboat charter party on the same type vessel with the vessel involved. QIU Guohua presented the copy of this agreement in the first instance;

3. Copy of Cooperation Agreement on the Suction Sand.

The materials mentioned above jointly proved that the actual price of the vessel involved was RMB30,000,000.

During the cross-examination, Yizhou Company considered that:

1. *Shipbuilding Contract* appeared in the judicial appraisal conclusion in first instance and had been denied.
2. Bareboat charter party was not relevant with this case.
3. *Cooperation Agreement on the Suction Sand* was in conformity with the materials that Yizhou Company had presented in another litigation case against QIU Guohua, but the materials could not prove the price of the vessel involved.

Zhongxin Company believed that the three materials had nothing to do with Zhongxin Company, but the materials could prove that the financial leasing fund of RMB13,000,000 was reasonable.

According to the evidence having been ascertained, the court considers that:

1. *Shipbuilding Contract* is component part of judicial appraisal conclusion in first instance, rather than new evidence in second instance.
2. Bareboat charter party is original document and the authenticity of the agreement can be confirmed, but it has no relevancy with this case. The court does not admit the agreement.
3. Yizhou Company has confirmed *Cooperation Agreement on the Suction Sand* and the court ascertains the authenticity of the agreement. But the agreement can only show the possible rent revenue which has not deducted the possible expenditure cost such as crew wages, fuel costs and insurance fees. Besides, the agreement cannot guarantee the profits in the long term, so the materials alone cannot prove the value of vessel involved. Thereby, the court does not confirm the relevancy of the materials.

After trial, the court ascertains the following facts:

The seventeenth evidence presented by Yizhou Company in first instance is phone communication record between GU Moumou, the employee of Yizhou Company, and QIU Guohua. QIU Guohua challenged the authenticity, legality and relevancy of the evidence. The court of first instance can neither confirm the authenticity of evidence, nor ascertain that Yizhou Company gets the evidence through legal way, since Yizhou Company does not provide the other evidence to explain the seventeenth evidence's source and the way of obtaining, and Yi Zhou Company cannot prove that the phone speakers permit the phone-call recording. The court of first instance considers that the evidence is not valid. Therefore, it is inappropriate for the court of first instance to state the content of phone-call recording in the fact investigating part of the verdict. It should be corrected.

The court confirms that the other facts ascertained by court of first instance are clear and has been proved by relevant evidence.

The court considers that: this case is the dispute over fund payment arising from vessel purchase. The main dispute of this case is that whether QIU Guohua should return the part of fund that exceeds RMB11,000,000. according to the fact ascertained in this case, the dispute lies in the confirmation toward the effectiveness of Ship Purchase Contract between Yizhou Company and QIU Guohua. In this case, Yizhou Company claims that *Ship Purchase Contract* should be valid; the fixed price of vessel involved should be RMB11,000,000 according to agreement between two parties and QIU Guohua should return the exceeding part of fund. QIU Guohua claims that *Ship Purchase Contract* has been cancelled according to agreed conditions; the buyer of vessel involved is Zhongxin Company; QIU Guohua has rights to get RMB38,000,000 by selling the vessel but has been forced to pay RMB12,000,000 as commission fee to Yizhou Company, so QIU Guohua has no obligation to return the rest of fund. The court considers that although Yizhou Company and QIU Guohua have reached an agreement on termination date of *Ship Purchase Contract*, Yizhou Company still negotiates with Zhongxin Company on the issue of finance and QIU Guohua also still provides relevant cooperation for Yizhou Company according to the actions of two parties before and after this date. The actions of two parties are in conformity with agreement of the contract and are also continuous before and after the date. The date of termination for the contract does not make two parties stop performing the contract. Besides, the two parties have no express or implied indications toward the termination of the contract effectiveness. Therefore, the existing evidence cannot lead to the conclusion that the contract between two parties is not valid. In this case, the contract between Yizhou Company and QIU Guohua is still binding on the two parties. According to the contract, QIU Guohua can get RMB11,000,000 by selling the vessel, but Qiu Mou cannot occupy the exceeding part of fund without good reasons. Yizhou Company, thereby, has right to require QIU Guohua to return the occupied exceeding part of fund to Yizhou Company's capital regulatory account. QIU Guohua claims that the court of first instance accepts the proof beyond the time limit of evidence production and entrusts identification without parties' permission which breaches the law. In this case, according to law, the court considers that the civil court can require parties to present necessary evidence and prescribe the time limit according to the circumstance of case trial as well as entrusts the qualified institutions to identify the specific issues involving in this case on the condition that the parties do not apply for it. Therefore, the court does not admit QIU Guohua's claim which is lack of law supports. QIU Guohua also claims that the court of first instance violates the principle of "non bis in idem" in this case trial. The court considers that there are differences between the case of (2013) Jin Hai Fa Shang Chu Zi No.310 and this case in aspects of main parties and basic requirement rights. Besides, the case of (2013) Jin Hai Fa Shang Chu Zi No.310 is concluded by mediation methods on the basis that parties reach an accommodation, but relevant facts has not been ultimately ascertained. Therefore, the judgment of this case does not conflict with relevant cases entertained by Tian Jin Maritime Court. The court does not admit this ground of appeal presented by QIU Guohua. In conclusion, the court does not support QIU Guohua's appeal claims which have no basis of facts and laws. As for Yizhou Company's ground of appeal that RMB6,000,000 paid by QIU Guohua is other business fund and is irrelevant with this case, the court does not admit above mentioned appeal claims either, since Yizhou Company does not present evidence to prove it.

In conclusion, the court affirms the facts and sustains decisions ascertained by the court of first instance which are respectively clear and correct. The court does not support two parties' appeal claims, as both Yizhou Company's and QIU Guohua's appeal claims are lack of factual and legal basis. According to Article 175 and Article 170 Paragraph 1 Sub-paragraph 1 of the Civil Procedure Law of the People's Republic of China, the judgment is as follows:

Dismiss the appeal, and affirm the original judgment.

Court acceptance fee of second instance in amount of RMB102,200 yuan, the Appellant Shanghai Yizhou Waterway Engineering Co., Ltd. should bear RMB45,761 and the Appellant QIU Guohua should bear RMB56,439.

The judgment is final.

Presiding Judge: DONG Min
Acting Judge: HU Hailong
Acting Judge: XU Yijin
May 11, 2015
Clerk: CHEN Xi

Appendix: Relevant Law

1. **Civil Procedure Law of the People's Republic of China**
   Article 170 After trial, the civil court of second instance concludes the appeal case respectively according to following situations:

   (1) The ascertained facts in original judgment are clear and applies with correct law, the court shall reject the appeal and sustain the original judgment and decision in the manner of judging and ruling;

   (2) The ascertained facts in original judgment are wrong or applies with wrong law, the court shall amend, cancel or alter the original judgment and decision in the manner of judging and ruling;

   (3) The basically ascertained facts in original judgment are not clear. The original judgment shall be cancelled and be sent back to original court to have retrial; or the original judgment shall be changed, after the facts are ascertained.

   (4) If the original judgment seriously breaches the law procedure. For example, the original court omits parties or makes judgment with absence of parties. The original judgment should be cancelled and be sent back to the original court to have retrial.

After the original people's court makes judgment on the case which is sent back to have retrial, if the Party makes an appeal, the court of second instance should not send the case back to the original people's court to have retrial again.

Article 175 The judgment and ruling made by second instance People's Court are final judgment and ruling.

Shanghai Maritime Court
Civil Judgment

Shanghai Jielong Industrial Group Co., Ltd. Yutian Packaging and Printing Branch
v.
Norasia Container Lines Limited et al.

(2012) Hu Hai Fa Shang Chu Zi No.1011

Related Case(s) This is the judgment of first instance, and the judgment of second instance and the ruling of retrial are on page 999 and page 1010 respectively.

Cause(s) of Action 202. Dispute over contract of carriage of goods by sea or sea-connected waters.

Headnote The Plaintiff-shipper and the Defendant-carrier held equally responsible for loss caused by consignee's failure to collect cargo at port of destination, which ultimately led to rerouting and sale of cargo by the Defendant-carrier.

Summary The Defendant carrier, Norasia Container, transported Plaintiff's shipment of cardboard to the destination port, but the consignee did not take delivery of the goods. The Plaintiff failed to provide the carrier with the correct contact information of the consignee, so the consignee did not receive the carrier's notice of delivery. The cost of storage grew over the course of a year to exceed the value of the goods, so the carrier exercised its option stated on the back of the bill of lading to re-ship the goods. Thereafter, the carrier attempted to contact the Plaintiff regarding disposal of the goods, but received no response. The Plaintiff's buyer refused to pay for the goods, which it had not received, so the Plaintiff sued the Defendant carrier for breach of the carriage contract in failing to deliver the goods as agreed. The court held that both the Plaintiff shipper and the Defendant carrier were liable for the loss: Plaintiff, in failing to provide the correct contact information and failing to timely respond to the carrier; and the Defendant, in improperly disposing of the goods, rather than discharging them at an appropriate place or applying for a lien on the goods. Thus, each party should bear half of the loss.

Judgment

The Plaintiff: Shanghai Jielong Industrial Group Co., Ltd. Yutian Packaging and Printing Branch
Domicile: No. 1, Lane 7076, Chuanzhou Road, Pudong New District, Shanghai, the People's Republic of China.
Legal representative: FEI Yili, manager.
Agent *ad litem*: CAO Fang, lawyer of Shanghai Allbright Law Office.
Agent *ad litem*: MA Yixing, lawyer of Shanghai Allbright Law Office.

The Defendant: Norasia Container Lines Limited
Domicile: 18/2, South Street, Valletta VLT1102, the Republic of Malta.
Legal representative: Héctor Arancibia Sánchez and José Francisco Muoz, directors.

The Defendant: South American Steamship (China) Shipping Co., Ltd.
Domicile: Room 1901A, 1902–1906, Hongyi International Plaza, No. 288 Jiujiang Road, Shanghai, the People's Republic of China.
Legal representative: Andres Roberto Kulka Kuperman, general manager.
Agent *ad litem* of the two Defendants: CHEN Youmu, lawyer of Shanghai Wintell & Co.
Agent *ad litem* of the two Defendants: LIU Yujia, lawyer of Shanghai Wintell & Co.

With respect to the case of dispute over contract of carriage of goods by sea filed by the Plaintiff, Shanghai Jielong Industrial Group Co., Ltd. Yutian Packaging and Printing Branch against the Defendants, Norasia Container Lines Limited (hereinafter referred to as Norasia Container) and South American Steamship (China) Shipping Co., Ltd. (hereinafter referred to as SAC) on July 26, 2012. The court, after entertaining this case on August 1, 2012, formed a collegiate panel according to law on May 16, 2013 and held a hearing to try this case in public. The Plaintiff's agent *ad litem*, CAO Fang, the Defendants' agents *ad litem*, CHEN Youmu and LIU Yujia, appeared in court and participated in the hearing. Now the case has been concluded.

The Plaintiff claimed that: in May and June 2011, the Plaintiff entrusted the two Defendants respectively to transport four containers' goods from Shanghai Port, China to St Petersburg Port, Russia, SAC issued two sets of B/L under which Norasia Container was the carrier. After the goods arrived at the destination port, the delay in shipment led to the consignee's dissatisfaction and delay in delivery. During the negotiation between the Plaintiff and the consignee, the Defendants shipped the goods back to Shanghai Port and re-shipped the goods again without the approval of the Plaintiff. As a consequence, the consignee could not take delivery of the goods and refused to pay the price of goods. The Plaintiff claimed that Norasia Container, as the carrier, breached the carriage contract, which caused the goods missed and the loss of the Plaintiff, should be responsible for the compensation, SAC as the agent of the carrier also had fault in return shipment and re-shipment of the goods involved, should bear joint and several liability. The Plaintiff requested the court to order the Defendants to: compensate the Plaintiff RMB917,617.44 yuan (USD144,778 translated to RMB91,7617.44 yuan on the basis of the exchange rate of 1:6.3381 prevailing on July 26, 2012) and the interest thereon (the interest should be calculated at the loan interest rate over the same period from July 26, 2012 to the day of effectiveness of the judgment), and bear the court acceptance fee.

The two Defendants argued that firstly, as the Plaintiff could not provide the original bill of lading, it had no right of claim; secondly when the goods arrived at port of St Petersburg, Russia, because the consignee failed to take delivery of goods on time. According to the regulations of the Russian Customs, the Customs temporary storage period was 2 months, the Defendant Norasia Container re-loaded the goods before the expiry of the storage period, besides the Defendant also informed the shipper and the consignee to take delivery of the goods for many times during the period, but the shipper did not reply at all, the consignee also expressed abandonment of goods. It was proper that the Defendant handled the goods on his own according to the terms on the back of the B/L; thirdly, SAC was not the carrier, it was the agent of the carrier, it should not bear the responsibility under the carriage contract.

The evidence of the Plaintiff, the cross-examination of the Defendants and the authentication of the court are as follows:

1. Export agency agreement (hereinafter referred to as the agreement) signed by the Plaintiff and Shanghai Baolong International Trade Co., Ltd. (hereinafter referred to as Baolong Company), No.NDADFDK00 and No.NDADL3800 B/Ls, to prove that the Plaintiff was the shipper under the carriage contract and the destination port was St. Petersburg, Russia. the two Defendants cross-examined the evidence and held that there were original B/Ls, they objected to the authenticity thereof, but confirmed that the Plaintiff was the shipper under the carriage contract. The Defendants had no objection to the authenticity but not the relevancy of the agreement, and held the evidence could not prove that the Plaintiff was the legitimate holder of the B/Ls and have the right of claim. The court holds that even though the B/Ls are copies, the EXPORT REFERENCES (export reference number) recorded therein corresponds to the contents of the Customs declaration. And the container numbers are also the same, besides the name of the company recorded therein is same as the name of the shipper and operating unit as stated in the Customs declaration, the court confirms the effect and probative force of the evidence.
2. Email sent by the Defendant SAC to the Plaintiff, to prove that the two Defendants carried the goods away from the destination port without the permission of the Plaintiff or the order of the competent authority at the destination port. the two Defendants cross-examined the evidence and held that they had no objection to the authenticity of the evidence, on the other hand, the email also showed that they consulted with the Plaintiff in terms of how to deal with the goods for many times, but they got no reply from the Plaintiff. The court

confirms the authenticity thereof, as for the probative force, the court will identify in combination with other evidence.
3. Customs declaration, to prove the value of the goods, the two Defendants cross-examined the evidence and held that they had no objection to the authenticity thereof, but the value of the goods should be determined according to the trade documents, such as the sale and purchase contract, invoice and so on. Since the Plaintiff had no objection to the validity of the evidence, the court confirms the authenticity there the evidence. While, the probative force thereof will be identified in combination with other evidence.
4. Certificate issued by Baolong Company and a copy of its business license, to prove that the Defendant Norasia Container failed to perform the obligations of carrier, caused the missing of the goods, as a consequence, Norasia Container should bear the liability for compensation. the two Defendants cross-examined the evidence and raised no objection to the authenticity, but they held the evidence could not prove the Plaintiff was the seller under the trade contract, besides the statement that the goods did not arrive at the destination port does not match with the reality. The court confirms the authenticity of the evidence. The probative force thereof will be identified in combination with other evidence.
5. Container query records, to prove that the containers were set to be empty and used for other purposes, the goods had been disposed. the two Defendants cross-examined the evidence, they did not confirm the form of the evidence, but they had no objection to that the devanning and disposal of the goods. The court holds that although the Plaintiff objected to the authenticity, but not the contents thereof, the court confirms the effectiveness and probative force of the evidence.

The evidence of the Defendants, the cross-examination of the Plaintiff and the authentication of the court are as follows:

1. Temporary Storage Expiration Notice and a Letter on Request for Relevant Situations issued by the Baltic Customs, to prove that No.TCNU9661692 and No.TCNU9015239 containers were temporarily stored in the Customs supervision area since June 30, 2011, the storage of the goods had exceeded the two-month storage period. Baltic Customs investigated the reason for the overdue storage of goods. The Plaintiff cross-examined that the evidence had not been notarized or authenticated, it objected to the authenticity thereof, and held the evidence could not prove the nature of the temporary storage and the consequence of expiration such period. The court confirms that the document is the original, according to Article 29 of the Treaty of Civil and Criminal Judicial Assistance between the People's Republic of China and the Russian Federation, the document produced or certified by the Russian courts or competent authorities, shall be effective upon signature and official seal. The letter was signed and sealed by the Russian Customs, the court confirms the effectiveness and probative force thereof based on the contents recorded therein.
2. Delivery notice of the goods under No.NDADFDK00 and No.NDADL3800 B/Ls, the Final Notice and the Final Notice on Disposal of Goods and the postal

order, to prove that after the goods arrived at the destination port, the carrier and its agent have urged the consignee to take delivery of the goods for many times, but the shipper and the consignee never replied. The Plaintiff held that the evidence had not been notarized or authenticated, it objected to the authenticity thereof, and held the contents, which were materials between the carrier and a party not involved in this case, should not be binding upon the Plaintiff. As the above notices are produced by the Plaintiff, the court confirms the authenticity thereof, besides this evidence can corroborate evidence 1, therefore the court confirms the effectiveness of the evidence and probative force thereof.

3. Notice on goods under export procedure, to prove that the goods under No. NDADL3800 B/L had already been regarded as jettison and should be carried back to Shanghai, and the cost was USD45,572.56 in total. The Plaintiff held that the evidence had not been notarized or authenticated, it objected to the authenticity thereof, and held the contents, which were materials between the carrier and a party not involved in this case, should not be binding upon it. As the above notices are produced by the Plaintiff, the court confirms the authenticity thereof, the court confirms the effectiveness of the evidence and probative force thereof.

4. Notice of demand of payment, to prove that the goods under the two B/Lsinvolved had generated USD73,144.56 by March 12, 2012. The Plaintiff held that the evidence had not been notarized or authenticated, it objected to the authenticity of the evidence, the notice was an announcement of the two Defendants, it did not admit the content thereof. The above notice is produced by the Plaintiff, the court confirms the authenticity of the evidence, the probative force thereof will be identified in combination with other evidence.

5. Notice of abandonment of cargo, the terms on the back of the B/L and invoice list, to prove that the consignee had no relationship with the goods loaded in the container as it alleged, the Defendant, Norasia Container, as the carrier, disposed the goods according to the terms on the back of the B/L, the residual value of the goods was USD4,000, the Plaintiff held that notice of abandonment of cargo and invoice list had not been notarized or authenticated, the Plaintiff objected to the authenticity thereof, the Plaintiff had no objection to the terms on the back of the B/L, but the terms are the Defendant's unilateral intention, not an agreement arrived at with the Plaintiff, they are not binding upon the Plaintiff, and the contents of the terms were invalid because of violation of the law. As the Plaintiff had no objection to the authenticity of the terms on the back of the B/Ls, the court confirms the authenticity thereof, as for the probative force, the court will verify in combination with other evidence. The notice of abandonment of cargo is not the original and the Plaintiff objected thereto, so the court does not confirm the authenticity thereof. The content of the invoice list is correspondent with evidence 5 provided by the Plaintiff, it can prove the that the two Defendants disposed the goods, the court confirms the effectiveness of the evidence and probative force thereof.

6. Statement of fees arising from the goods involved and the appendix thereto, to prove the storage fee, transshipment freight and container detention fee arising from the goods stored in the destination port. The fees have already surpassed

the goods' value in good condition, the Plaintiff held that it was the statement of one party concerned, it could not be used as the evidence, besides the calculation of the fees was not reasonable, the court confirms that the evidence is in form a statement of the party concerned, and can be admitted as evidence, and it is reasonable to pay the storage fee and container detention fee as the result of storage at the destination port for a long period, the court confirms the probative force thereof will be identified in combination with other evidence.

7. A report issued by Shanghai Ejoy Insurance Survey Co., Ltd. (hereinafter referred to as Ejoy Survey), to prove that the residual value and the measures taken on the goods by the Defendant were appropriate. The Plaintiff held that the evidence was adduced beyond the time limit, and Ejoy Survey only had the insurance survey qualification, it had no qualification to assess the goods and the survey basis was not reasonable. The court confirms that the evidence is original, it can reinforce the original evidence, Ejoy Survey is qualified for the survey, therefore the court confirms the effectiveness thereof, Ejoy Survey held that as the goods were loaded in closed containers for a long time, it was reasonable that the goods would be damaged as a result of the temperature and humidity, but Ejoy Company did not inspect the goods, it is lack of facts to support its allegation, it held that the goods could only be disposed as wastes and it was proper that the carrier dealt with the goods as wastes. The court does not confirm that.

After examination and authentication of the above evidence, the court, in combination with the investigation in the trial, finds the following facts:

In May and June 2011, the Plaintiff entrusted the Defendant Norasia Container to transport the ivory cardboard from Shanghai port to St Petersburg Port of Russia. The Customs declarations recorded that both the export company and the operating unit were Baolong Company, the carrying ship and the voyage was SACROMERAL/1121S, the destination country was Russia. The numbers of the B/Ls were CNSULT0564 and CNSULT05933, the corresponding container numbers were TCNU9015239, TCNU9661692, CAXU9899164 and TCLU5991929. The value of the goods recorded by the two Customs declarations was respectively USD72,389, and USD144,778 in total. After the Defendant Norasia Container received the goods, it respectively issued No.NDADFDK00 B/L and No. NDADL3800 B/Ls on May 3 and June 2. As the shipper and the carrier agreed to deliver the goods subject to telex, Norasia Container just submitted a copy of the B/Ls without an original. The two copies of the B/Ls record that the shipper was the Plaintiff, the consignee was ZAOTORGOVYDOMPOKROVSKYPOLIMER (Z Company), Shanghai was the port of shipment, and St Petersburg was the destination port. The export reference numbers respectively recorded by the two B/Lswere CNSULT0593 and CNSULT05645, there was a signature of the Defendant SAS at lower right corner of the B/Ls. During the trial, both the Plaintiff and the Defendants confirmed that SAS was the agent of the carrier. It was said in the Article 20 Paragraph 6 of the terms on the back of the B/Ls that "if the owner does not take delivery of part or all of the goods within 30 days after receiving the notice of arrival of goods, or if the carrier holds that the goods may be rotten, deteriorated and unworthy, or the case exists in which the costs of storage or other disposal of the goods will exceed the value of the goods, the carrier may at own decision, without prejudice to its rights to the owner and without enhancing the liability of the carrier, sell, destroy or dispose the goods without informing the owner, and the price of the goods shall be deducted from the sum which the owner owes to the carrier under the B/Ls, or the carrier may at his discretion (but not necessarily) ship the goods to the port of shipment or the port of the destination, the expenses and the costs resulting from the voyage shall on the account of cargo".

On June 30, No.TCNU901523 and No.TCNU9661692 containers arrived at the destination, on August 5 of the same year, No.CAXU989916 and No. TCLU5991929 containers also arrived at the destination, on August 11 and September 7, the Defendant sent the notice of demanding for taking delivery of goods to the consignee's address through the Russia post, saying that it would be deemed as refusal to perform the contract and abandonment of goods if the consignee did not take delivery of the goods beyond the time limit. But the two mails failed to be delivered because the consignee did not domicile at the delivery address. On August 17, Russian Baltic Customs informed the destination agent of the Defendant, as the temporary storage of the containers fell due, the Customs was examining the issue relevant to the violation of the administrative law, the agent is required to provide the information of the consignee or the owner. On November 1, the Baltic Customs of the Russian Federation requested that the destination agent of the Defendant to provide the reason for the extension of temporary storage of the containers and the relevant information.

On October 13 and November 8, SAS sent a notice to the booking party of the carriage by courier, namely, Litong Logistics (China) Co., Ltd. (hereinafter referred to as Litong Logictics), the notice recorded the receiver was the Plaintiff and Litong Logictics, the two receivers were required to clear the Customs within 7 days, otherwise the goods would be sent to the relevant department, and the storage fee, detention fee, survey fee and lawyer's fee resulted from the goods would be recovered by the Plaintiff and Litong Logistics. On November 15 and November 25, 2011, SAS sent the final notice about the disposal of the goods to Litong Logictics by courier. The goods were regarded as abandoned goods due to the non-taking delivery of the goods, the Defendant could dispose the goods at anytime and require payment of USD27,062 and USD39,120 for non-taking delivery.

On October 4 and December 9, Norasia Container loaded the containers back to its ship, No.TCNU901523 and No.TCNU9661692 containers were sent back to Shanghai port. On January 17, 2012, SAS sent an email to the Plaintiff alleging that it had never gotten the reply from it after SAS sent the final notice to the Plaintiff trough Litong Logictics, the notice of final disposal of goods was attached thereto, the Plaintiff was requested to reply as soon as possible how to deal with the goods under the two B/Lsinvolved. On February 15 of the same year, SAS sent an email to the Plaintiff and claimed that they never get the reply from it until now, the goods were on the voyage to Shanghai, the Plaintiff might receive the goods in two days, or SAS could dispose the goods on their own and claim the loss according to the law, the Plaintiff never replied the above emails.

On December 21, 2011, the destination agent of Norasia Container sent the notice to inform the consignee that the goods were under the process of re-export formalities, the consignee should pay the warehousing fee, Customs inspection fee, re-export fee, container detention fee in total of USD45,575.26. On March 12, 2012, the destination agent of Norasia Container sent the notice to the consignee again, to inform it that the consignee should pay the fees in sum of USD73,144.56 resulted from the non-taking delivery of the four containers. The two notices have not been served because the consignee did not live in the address. On March 14, the destination agent of Norasia Container sent the final notice about the disposal of the goods to the Plaintiff, alleging that since the consignee appointed by the Plaintiff did not take delivery of the goods within the time permitted by the local Customs, the goods were regarded as abandoned goods, Norasia Container disposed the goods in order to avoid the loss expanding; in the meantime, the Plaintiff should pay the fees of USD73144.56 resulted from the non-taking delivery of the four containers, or Norasia Container would sue the Plaintiff, the Plaintiff still did not reply.

The two Defendants alleged that the storage fee, transshipment freight and container detention fee resulted from the goods exceeded the value of the goods in good condition and caused huge economic loss to the two Defendants, the goods were disposed as wasted paper at the beginning of September 2012 in Malaysia at a price of USD4,000. On July 24, 2013, Ejoy Survey assessed the goods, and held that the ivory board involved, after being contained in the closed containers for more than one year, affected by the temperature and humidity, would occur oxidation, mildew and other chemical and physical phenomena, as a consequence, the ivory board could not be normally used; it only could be recycled as wasted paper for raw material; according to the domestic market inquiry and quotation, the residual value of the goods was USD4,025, the price of wasted paper abroad was basically equal to that at home, so it is reasonable that the Defendant disposed the goods in Malaysia at a price of USD4,000.

It is also found that the Plaintiff and Baolong Company signed anexport agency agreement on February 22, 2011. It is agreed that Baolong Company would export corrugated boxes/cartons, cardboard boxes, jewelry boxes and the alike as the agent of the Plaintiff. The validity period of the contract was from January 1 to December 31, 2011. On January 4, 2012, Baolong Company issued a certificate confirming that the Plaintiff was the actual shipper of the carriage contract, the four containers under No.NDADFDK00 and No.NDADL3800 B/Ls were owned by the Plaintiff, Baolong Company was just a trading agent.

The court holds that the case is concerning dispute over a carriage contract of goods by sea, the Defendant Norasia Container is a company registered in a foreign country, the destination port is St-Petersburg Port, Russia, the case involved with foreign-related factors. According to the law of the People's Republic of China, the parties concerned may explicitly choose the applicable law to foreign-related civil legal relationship. Since the parties in the trial chose to apply the law of the People's

Republic of China, the court permits and determines the applicable law of this case shall be the law of the People's Republic of China.

As whether the Plaintiff has the right of claim, according to the available evidence, the Plaintiff is the shipper recorded in the B/L, Norasia Container is the carrier, SAS is the agent of the carrier, both the Plaintiff and the Defendants confirmed the above identities, Baolong Company, a party not involved in this case, is a trading agent, it confirmed the owner of the goods of the four containers was the Plaintiff. The court holds that the carriage contract between the Plaintiff and Norasia Container is valid, as the original B/L is not actually issued, the goods were not delivered for circulation, the Plaintiff as the shipper under the carriage contract and the owner of the goods involved, it has the right of claim in terms of the compensation according to the carriage contract, the court does not adopt the defense of the two Defendants.

As whether the two Defendants should bear the liability for compensation, the Plaintiff claimed that because of the delay in delivery in the transportation, the consignee dissatisfied and delayed in taking delivery of the goods, the Defendants also transshipped the goods to a third country without the permission of the Plaintiff, as a consequence, the consignee could not take delivery of the goods and refused to pay price of goods, the two Defendants should compensate the Plaintiff. the two Defendants argued that the goods had not been taken delivery at the destination port, in order to protect the interest of the Plaintiff, Norasia Container loaded the goods back to the ship, Norasia Container also informed the Plaintiff and the consignee to take delivery of the goods for many times, the carrier insisted that it was reasonable to dispose the goods according to the terms under the B/L. The court confirms that according to the existing evidence, after the goods arrived at the destination port, the consignee did not take delivery of the goods over almost one year, Norasia Container contacted the consignee for several times, but the mails could not be served on consignee for wrong address.

Norasia Container has contacted the shipper for several times and asked for the instruction for disposal of the goods, but the shipper did not reply. According to the law, the contract of carriage of goods by sea is a contract agreeing to carry the goods from one port to another port by sea. As the original B/L had not been issued, the goods involved were telex released, the carriage contract is agreed to deliver the goods to a specific third party namely, Z Company, Norasia Container has carried the goods to the destination port safely and fulfilled the carrier's obligations completely. In the case of non-taking delivery at the destination port, Norasia Container sent the delivery notice to the consignee's address provided by the Plaintiff, besides Norasia Container also sent the notice of disposal of goods to the Plaintiff, it can be seen that Norasia Container has exercised due diligence in taking care of the goods. At the expiry of the temporary storage at the destination port, Norasia Container for the purpose of the Plaintiff's interest and avoiding the addition of the storage fee or the warehouse fee, it is reasonable that Norasia Container loaded the goods back to the ship and informed the Plaintiff of disposal of the goods.

The Plaintiff as the counterpart of the carriage contract, it is obliged to inform Norasia Container accurately about the consignee's address and the name and the other necessary transportation information. Nevertheless, neither the Plaintiff told the right contact information to the carrier, nor did it reply Norasia Container regarding to how to disposal the goods, as a result, the goods could not be delivered in a long time, the Plaintiff was indolent to exercise the right as the shipper and the owner of the goods, it is obvious the Plaintiff's fault, the risks and the losses resulted therefrom shall be born by the Plaintiff. The goods have not been taken delivery at the destination port, according to the law, the carrier shall discharge the goods at an appropriate place or act a lien on the goods carried and apply for an action to the court. It is improper that Norasia Container disposed the goods without going through legal procedures, the Defendants should bear the corresponding liability.

To sum up, both the Plaintiff and the Defendants have faults in the performance of the contract, which led the goods to be regarded as the garage in the end, the losses resulted therefrom shall be shared by the Plaintiff and the Defendants.

As for the defense of Norasia Container that Norasia Container's delay in delivery of the goods caused the delay in taking delivery of the goods by the consignee, the court holds that the Plaintiff cannot provide relevant evidence to prove whether the goods were delayed in delivery and whether there is a causal relationship between the delay in delivery of goods and the delay in taking delivery of the goods by the consignee, the court does not adopt the defense. As for the defense of Norasia Container that it disposed the goods in according to the terms under the B/L, the court holds that the original B/Lswere not issued, the Plaintiff could not know the content of the terms of the B/Ls, no evidence can prove that the terms have been negotiated and agreed by the parties, so the defense shall not be admitted. SAS is the agent of Norasia Container, it is not the party to the contract, so it shall not bear the liability for compensation.

As the commercial value and the actual value of the goods, the Plaintiff claimed that the sum USD144,778 recorded in the Customs declaration was the value of the goods (the dollar currency translated to renminbi according to the U.S. dollar against RMB exchange rate at 1:6.3381 prevailing on July 26, 2012 was RMB917,617.44), the Defendants held that because the goods were none-taken delivery at the destination port, the goods were stored in the containers for more than one year, the value thereof was devaluated, it is proper to disposed the goods as wasted paper. The court holds that the sum recorded in the Customs declaration is expected benefit which would be gained by the Plaintiff when the trade contract is accomplished, it is the commercial value of the goods, according to the existing evidence, the goods have been stored in the destination port for several months, Norasia Container tried to contact the Plaintiff and Z Company, but there is no reply from them. The goods were under the control of Norasia Container for more than one year, Norasia Container requested the Plaintiff for taking delivery or return of the goods, but the Plaintiff never replied. The Plaintiff did not submit evidence to prove that Z Company or other consignees took delivery of the goods, that the Plaintiff did not prove that it can achieve the commercial value of the goods, and obtain the corresponding commercial benefit, according to Ejoy Survey Report, as the goods were contained in the closed containers for a long period, the temperature and humidity would cause derogation of the actual value to some extent.

As for the loss of interest, the Plaintiff claimed that it should be calculated from July 26, 2012 to the date that the judgment enters into force according to the deposit interest rate published by the People's Bank of China. As the loss of interest is the fruits derived from delay in payment, the court confirms that.

To sum up, the court holds this case is concerning dispute over a carriage contract of goods by sea, the Plaintiff has fault in performing the contract, which caused the derogation in the commercial value and the actual value of the goods, besides, it is clearly inappropriate that Norasia Container disposed the goods without undergoing legal procedures, it shall be reasonable that the Plaintiff and Norasia Container should each bear half of the loss in sum of RMB917,617.44. According to Article 304 of the Contract Law of the People's Republic of China, Articles 41 and 48 of the Maritime Code of the People's Republic of China, Article 64 Paragraph 1 of the Civil Procedure Law of the People's Republic of China, the judgment is as follows:

1. Norasia Container Lines Limited shall pay RMB458,808.72 yuan and the interest thereon (the interest shall be calculated from July 26, 2012 to the date of effectiveness of the judgment at the deposit interest rate published by the Bank of China over the same period) to Shanghai Jielong Industrial Group Co., Ltd. Yutian Packaging and Printing Branch within ten days from the date of effectiveness of the judgment;
2. Reject other claims of Shanghai Jielong Industrial Group Co., Ltd. Yutian Packaging and Printing Branch.

If Norasia Container Lines Limited fails to perform the obligation for payment of above-mentioned sum within 10 days after the judgment enters into force, Norasia Container Lines Limited shall pay double interest on the delayed sum according to Article 253 of the Civil Procedure Law of the People's Republic of China.

Court acceptance fee in amount of RMB8,605, shall be half born by the Plaintiff Shanghai Jielong Industrial Group Co., Ltd. Yutian Packaging and Printing Branch and the Defendant Norasia Container Lines Limited, namely RMB4,302.5.

In event of dissatisfaction with this judgment, the Plaintiff Shanghai Jielong Industrial Group Co., Ltd. Yutian Packaging and Printing Branch and the Defendant South American Steamship (China) Shipping Co., Ltd. may, within 15 days upon service of this judgment, the Defendant Norasia Container Lines Limited may, within 30 days upon service of this judgment, submit a letter of appeal to the court with duplicates in terms of the number of the opposing parties, to lodge an appeal to the Shanghai High People's Court.

Presiding Judge: JI Gang
Judge: ZHANG Jianchen
Acting Judge: JIANG Yun

September 9, 2013

Clerk: LI Yuanjun

Appendix: Relevant Law

1. **Contract Law of the People's Republic of China**
   Article 304 In undergoing the formalities for cargoes, the consignor shall precisely indicate to carrier the name of the consignee or the consignee by order, the name, nature weight, amount and the place for taking delivery of the cargoes, and other information necessary for cargo carriage.
   Where the carrier suffers from damage due to untrue declaration or omission of important information by the consignor, the consignor shall be liable for damages.
2. **Maritime Code of the People's Republic of China**
   Article 41 A contract of carriage of goods by sea is a contract under which the carrier, against payment of freight, undertakes to carry by sea the goods contracted for shipment by the shipper from one port to another.
   Article 48 The carrier shall properly and carefully load, handle, stow, carry, keep, care for and discharge the goods carried.
3. **Civil Procedure Law of the People's Republic of China**
   Article 64 A party shall have the responsibility to provide evidence in support of its own propositions.

Shanghai High People's Court
Civil Judgment

Shanghai Jielong Industrial Group Co., Ltd. Yutian Packaging and Printing Branch
v.
Norasia Container Lines Limited et al.

(2013) Hu Gao Min Si (Hai) Zhong Zi No.132

Related Case(s) This is the judgment of second instance, and the ruling of first instance and the judgment of retrial are on page 987 and page 1010 respectively.

Cause(s) of Action 202. Dispute over contract of carriage of goods by sea or sea-connected waters.

Headnote Affirming lower court decision holding the Plaintiff-shipper and the Defendant-carrier equally responsible for loss caused by consignee's failure to collect cargo at port of destination, which ultimately led to rerouting and sale of cargo by the Defendant-carrier.

Summary Jielong Company (Plaintiff-shipper) and Norasia Container (Defendant-carrier) both appealed a lower court decision that found both parties to be at fault in the performance of the carriage contract and held the parties to be equally liable for the resulting loss. The appeal court confirmed the facts as found by the lower court: that the consignee did not take delivery of the goods for over a year, and that the goods suffered damage from the storage conditions. The court recognized that the Plaintiff-shipper was at fault in failing to provide the consignee's correct contact information to the carrier and in failing to respond to the carrier's multiple e-mails. However, the carrier was also at fault because it illegally re-sold the goods to a scrap merchant relying on the terms of the copies of the bills of lading, the terms of which were not agreed to by the shipper and the consignee. Thus, the court dismissed both appeals and recognized the judgment of first instance apportioning liability for the loss equally between the carrier and the shipper.

Judgment

The Appellant (the Plaintiff of first instance): Shanghai Jielong Industrial Group Co., Ltd. Yutian Packaging and Printing Branch
Domicile: No.1, Lane 7076, Chuanzhou Road, Pudong New District, Shanghai, the People's Republic of China
Legal representative: WU Jiangming, Manager
Agent *ad litem*: CAO Fang, Shanghai Allbright Law Firm
Agent *ad litem*: MA Yixing, Shanghai Allbright Law Firm

The Appellant (the Defendant of first instance): Norasia Container Lines Limited
Domicile: 18/2 South Street, Valletta VLT1102, Republic of Malta.
Legal representatives: Héctor Arancibia Sánchez and José Francisco Munoz, directors.
Agent *ad litem*: Chen Yumu, Shanghai Wintell Law Firm
Agent *ad litem*: LIU Yujia, Shanghai Wintell Law Firm

The Defendant of first instance: South American Steamship (China) Shipping Co., Ltd.
Domicile: Room 1901A, 1902-1906, Hongyi International Plaza, No.288 Jiujiang Road, Shanghai, the People's Republic of China.
Legal representative: Andres Roberto Kulka Kuperman, general manager
Agent ad litem: Chen Yumu, Shanghai Wintell Law Firm
Agent ad litem: LIU Yujia, Shanghai Wintell Law Firm

Dissatisfied with (2012) Hu Hai Shang Chu Zi No.1011 Civil Judgment rendered by the Shanghai Maritime Court with respect to the case airing from dispute over a contract of carriage of goods by sea, with the Defendant of the first instance involved in, South American Steamship (China) Shipping Co., Ltd. (hereinafter referred to as SAC), the Appellant, Shanghai Jielong Industrial Group Co., Ltd. Yutian Packaging and Printing Branch (hereinafter referred to as Jielong Company), and the Appellant, Norasia Container Lines Limited (hereinafter referred to as Norasia Container) respectively filed an appeal before the court. After docketing and entertaining this case on November 21, 2013, the court constituted a collegiate panel, and held a hearing in public on May 23, 2014. CAO Fang, agent *ad litem* of Jielong Company, and LIU Yujia, agent *ad litem* of Norasia Container and ASC, appeared in court and participated in the hearing. Now the case has been concluded.

In May and June 2011, Jielong Company entrusted Norasia Container to transport the ivory cardboard from Shanghai Port to St Petersburg Port of Russia. The Customs declarations recorded that both the export company and the operating unit were Baolong Company, the carrying ship and the voyage was SACROMERAL/1121S, the destination country was Russia. The numbers of the B/Ls were CNSULT0564 and CNSULT05933, the corresponding container numbers were TCNU9015239, TCNU9661692, CAXU9899164 and TCLU5991929. The value of the goods recorded by the two Customs declarations was respectively USD72,389, and USD144,778 in total. After Norasia Container received the goods, it respectively issued No.NDADFDK00 B/L and No.NDADL3800 B/Ls on May 3 and June 2. As the shipper and the carrier agreed to deliver the goods subject to telex, Norasia Container just submitted a copy of the B/Ls without an original. The two copies of the B/Ls record that the shipper was Jielong Company, the consignee was ZAOTORGOVYDOMPOKROVSKYPOLIMER (Z Company), Shanghai was the port of shipment, and St Petersburg was the port of destination. The export reference numbers respectively recorded by the two B/Ls were CNSULT0593 and CNSULT05645, there was a signature of SAS at lower right corner of the B/Ls. During the trial, both Jielong Company and Norasia Container and SAS confirmed that SAS was the agent of the carrier. It was said in the Article 20 Paragraph 6 of the terms on the back of the B/Ls that "if the owner did not take delivery of part or all of the goods within 30 days after receiving the notice of arrival of goods, or if the carrier held that the goods may be rotten, deteriorated and unworthy, or the case exists in which the costs of storage or other disposal of the goods will exceed the value of the goods, the carrier may at own decision, without prejudice to its rights to the owner and without enhancing the liability of the carrier, sell, destroy or dispose the goods without informing the owner, and the price of the goods should be deducted from the sum which the owner owes to the carrier under the B/Ls, or the carrier may at his discretion (but not necessarily) ship the goods to the port of shipment or the port of the destination, the expenses and the costs resulting from the voyage should on the account of cargo".

On June 30, No.TCNU901523 and No.TCNU9661692 containers arrived at the destination port, on August 5 of the same year, No.CAXU989916 and No. TCLU5991929 containers also arrived at the destination, on August 11 and September 7, Norasia Container sent the notice of demanding for taking delivery of goods to the consignee's address through the Russia post, saying that it would be deemed as refusal to perform the contract and abandonment of goods if the consignee did not take delivery of the goods beyond the time limit. But the two mails failed to be delivered because the consignee did not domicile at the delivery address. On August 17, Russian Baltic Customs informed the destination agent of Norasia Container, as the temporary storage of the containers fell due, the Customs was examining the issue relevant to the violation of the administrative law, the agent was required to provide the information of the consignee or the owner. On November 1, the Baltic Customs of the Russian Federation requested that the destination agent of Norasia Container to provide the reason for the extension of temporary storage of the containers and the relevant information.

On October 13 and November 8, SAS sent a notice to the booking party of the carriage by courier, namely, Litong Logistics (China) Co., Ltd. (hereinafter referred to as Litong Logictics), the notice recorded the receiver was Jielong Company and Litong Logictics, the two receivers were required to clear the Customs within 7 days, otherwise the goods would be sent to the relevant department, and the storage fee, detention fee, survey fee and lawyer's fee resulted from the goods would be recovered by Jielong Company and Litong Logistics. On November 15 and November 25, 2011, SAS sent the final notice about the disposal of the goods to Litong Logistics by courier. The goods were regarded as abandoned goods due to the non-taking delivery of the goods, Norasia Container could dispose the goods at anytime and require payment of USD27,062 and USD39,120 for non-taking delivery.

On October 4 and December 9, Norasia Container loaded the containers back to its ship, No.TCNU901523 and No.TCNU9661692 containers were sent back to Shanghai Port. On January 17, 2012, SAS sent an email to Jielong Company alleging that it had never gotten the reply from it after SAS sent the final notice to Jielong Company through Litong Logistics, the notice of final disposal of goods was attached thereto, Jielong Company was requested to reply as soon as possible how to deal with the goods under the two B/Lsinvolved. On February 15 of the same year, SAS sent an email to Jielong Company and claimed that they had never gotten the reply from it until now, the goods were on the voyage to Shanghai, Jielong Company might receive the goods in two days, or SAS could dispose the goods on their own and claim the loss according to the law, Jielong Company never replied the above emails.

On December 21, 2011, the destination agent of Norasia Container sent the notice to inform the consignee that the goods were under the process of re-export formalities, the consignee should pay the warehousing fee, Customs inspection fee, re-export fee, container detention fee in total of USD45,575.26. On March 12, 2012, the destination agent of Norasia Container sent the notice to the consignee again, to inform it that the consignee should pay the fees in sum of USD73,144.56 resulted from the non-taking delivery of the four containers. The two notices have not been served because the consignee did not live in the address. On March 14, the destination agent of Norasia Container sent the final notice about the disposal of the goods to Jielong Company, alleging that since the consignee appointed by Jielong Company did not take delivery of the goods within the time permitted by the local Customs, the goods were regarded as abandoned goods, Norasia Container disposed the goods in order to avoid the loss expanding; in the meantime, Jielong Company should pay the fees of USD73144.56 resulted from the non-taking delivery of the four containers, or Norasia Container would sue Jielong Company, Jielong Company still did not reply.

Norasia Container and SAS alleged that the storage fee, transshipment freight and container detention fee resulted from the goods exceeded the value of the goods in good condition and caused huge economic loss to Norasia Container and SAS, the goods were disposed as wasted paper at the beginning of September 2102 in Malaysia at a price of USD4,000. On July 24, 2013, Ejoy Survey assessed the goods, and held that the ivory board involved, after being contained in the closed containers for more than one year, affected by the temperature and humidity, would occur oxidation, mildew and other chemical and physical phenomena, as a consequence, the ivory board could not be normally used; it only could be recycled as wasted paper for raw material; according to the domestic market inquiry and quotation, the residual value of the goods was USD4,025, the price of wasted paper abroad was basically equal to that at home, so it was reasonable that Norasia Container disposed the goods in Malaysia at a price of USD4,000.

It was also found that Jielong Company and Baolong Company signed an export agency agreement on February 22, 2011. It was agreed that Baolong Company would export corrugated boxes/cartons, cardboard boxes, jewelry boxes and the alike as the agent of Jielong Company. The validity period of the contract was from January 1 to December 31, 2011. On January 4, 2012, Baolong Company issued a certificate confirming that Jielong Company was the actual shipper of the carriage contract, the four containers under No.NDADFDK00 and No.NDADL3800 B/Ls were owned by Jielong Company, Baolong Company was just a trading agent.

The court of first instance held that the case was concerning dispute over a carriage contract of goods by sea, Norasia Container was a company registered in a foreign country, the destination port was St-Petersburg Port, Russia, the case involved with foreign-related element. According to the law of the People's Republic of China, the parties concerned might explicitly choose the applicable law to foreign-related civil legal relationship. Since the parties in the trial chose to apply the law of the People's Republic of China, the court of first instance permitted and determined the applicable law of this case should be the law of the People's Republic of China.

As whether Jielong Company had the right of claim, according to the available evidence, Jielong Company was the shipper recorded in the B/L, Norasia Container was the carrier, SAS was the agent of the carrier, both Jielong Company and Norasia Container confirmed the above identities, Baolong Company, a party not involved in this case, was a trading agent, it confirmed the owner of the goods of the four containers was Jielong Company. The court of first instance held that the carriage contract between Jielong Company and Norasia Container was valid, as the original B/L was not actually issued, the goods were not delivered for circulation, Jielong Company as the shipper under the carriage contract and the owner of the goods involved, it had the right of claim in terms of the compensation according to the carriage contract, the court of first instance did not adopt the defense of Norasia Container and SAS.

As whether Norasia Container and SAS should bear the liability for compensation, Jielong Company claimed that because of the delay in delivery in the transportation, the consignee dissatisfied and delayed in taking delivery of the goods, Norasia Container also transshipped the goods to a third country without the permission of Jielong Company, as a consequence, the consignee could not take delivery of the goods and refused to pay price of goods, Norasia Container and SAS should compensate Jielong Company. Norasia Container and SAS argued that the goods had not been taken delivery at the destination port, in order to protect the interest of Jielong Company, Norasia Container loaded the goods back to the ship, Norasia Container also informed Jielong Company and the consignee to take delivery of the goods for many times, the carrier insisted that it was reasonable to dispose the goods according to the terms under the B/L. The court of first instance confirmed that according to the existing evidence, after the goods arrived at the destination port, the consignee did not take delivery of the goods over almost one year, Norasia Container contacted the consignee for several times, but the mails could not be served on the consignee for wrong address.

Norasia Container had contacted the shipper for several times and asked for the instruction for disposal of the goods, but the shipper did not reply. According to the law, the contract of carriage of goods by sea was a contract agreeing to carry the goods from one port to another port by sea. As the original B/L had not been issued, the goods involved were telex released, the carriage contract was agreed to deliver the goods to a specific third party namely, Z Company, Norasia Container had carried the goods to the port of destination safely and fulfilled the carrier's obligations completely. In the case of non-taking delivery at the port of destination, Norasia Container sent the delivery notice to the consignee's address provided by Jielong Company, Norasia Container also sent the notice of disposal of goods to Jielong Company, it could be seen that Norasia Container had exercised due diligence in taking care of the goods. At the expiry of the temporary storage at the destination port, Norasia Container for the purpose of Jielong Company's interest and avoiding the addition of the storage fee or the warehouse fee, it was reasonable that Norasia Container loaded the goods back to the ship and informed Jielong Company of disposal of the goods.

Jielong Company as the counterpart of the carriage contract, it was obliged to inform Norasia Container accurately about the consignee's address and the name and the other necessary transportation information. Nevertheless, neither Jielong Company told the right contact information to the carrier, nor did it reply Norasia Container regarding to how to dispose the goods, as a result, the goods could not be delivered in a long time, Jielong Company was indolent to exercise the right as the shipper and the owner of the goods, it was obvious Jielong Company's fault, the risks and the losses resulted therefrom should be born by Jielong Company. The goods have not been taken delivery at the destination port, according to the law, the carrier should discharge the goods at an appropriate place or act a lien on the goods carried and apply for an action to the court. It was improper that Norasia Container disposed the goods without going through legal procedures, Norasia Container should bear the corresponding liability.

To sum up, both Jielong Company and Norasia Container had faults in the performance of the contract, which led the goods to be regarded as the garage in the end, the losses resulted therefrom should be shared by Jielong Company and Norasia Container.

As for the defense of Norasia Container that Norasia Container's delay in delivery of the goods caused the delay in taking delivery of the goods by the consignee, the court of first instance held that Jielong Company could not provide relevant evidence to prove whether the goods were delayed in delivery and whether there was a causal relationship between the delay in delivery of goods and the delay in taking delivery of the goods by the consignee, the court of first instance did not adopt the defense. As for the defense of Norasia Container that it disposed the goods in according to the terms under the B/L, the court of first instance held that the original B/Lswere not issued, Jielong Company could not know the content of the terms of the B/Ls, no evidence could prove that the terms have been negotiated and agreed by the parties, so the defense should not be admitted. SAS was the agent of Norasia Container, it was not the party to the contract, so it should not bear the liability for compensation.

As the commercial value and the actual value of the goods, Jielong Company claimed that the sum USD144,778 recorded in the Customs declaration was the value of the goods (the dollar currency translated to renminbi according to the U.S. dollar against RMB exchange rate at 1:6.3381 prevailing on July 26, 2012 was RMB917,617.44), Norasia Container and SAS held that because the goods were none-taken delivery at the destination port, the goods were stored in the containers for more than one year, the value thereof was devaluated, it was proper to disposed the goods as wasted paper. the court of first instance held that the sum recorded in the Customs declaration was expected benefit which would be gained by Jielong Company when the trade contract was accomplished, it was the commercial value of the goods, according to the existing evidence, the goods have been stored in the destination port for several months, Norasia Container tried to contact Jielong Company and Z Company, but there was no reply from them. The goods were under the control of Norasia Container for more than one year, Norasia Container requested Jielong Company for taking delivery or return of the goods, but Jielong Company never replied. Jielong Company did not submit evidence to prove that Z Company or other consignee took delivery of the goods, that Jielong Company did not prove that it could achieve the commercial value of the goods, and obtain the corresponding commercial benefit, according to Ejoy Survey Report, as the goods were contained in the closed containers for a long period, the temperature and humidity would cause derogation of the actual value to some extent.

As for the loss of interest, Jielong Company claimed that it should be calculated from July 26, 2012 to the date that the judgment enters into force according to the deposit interest rate published by the People's Bank of China. As the loss of interest was the fruits derived from delay in payment, the court of first instance confirmed that.

To sum up, the court of first instance held this case was concerning dispute over a carriage contract of goods by sea, Jielong Company had fault in performing the contract, which caused the derogation in the commercial value and the actual value of the goods, besides, it was clearly inappropriate that Norasia Container deposed the goods without legal procedures, it should be reasonable that Jielong Company and Norasia Container should each bear half of the loss in sum of RMB917,617.44. According to Article 304 of the Contract Law of the People's Republic of China, Articles 41 and 48 of the Maritime Code of the People's Republic of China, Article 64 Paragraph 1 of the Civil Procedure Law of the People's Republic of China, the judgment was as follows: 1. Norasia Container should pay RMB458,808.72 yuan and the interest thereon (the interest should be calculated from July 26, 2012 to the date of effectiveness of the judgment at the deposit interest rate published by the Bank of China over the same period) to Jielong Company within ten days from the date of effectiveness of the judgment; 2. reject other claims of Jielong Company.

Jielong Company appealed and requested to revoke the original judgment according to the law, and amend the judgment to support its claims. The main reasons were as follows:

1. The evidence concerning the carrier's performance of the transport contract involved and the handling of the goods was unilaterally made by itself, of which some had not gone through notarization and certification procedure, the court of first instance should not admit that.
2. Where the goods were not taken delivery of after their arrival at the port of destination, the carrier should dispose the goods by means of auction by court or handing over the goods to the Customs at the port of destination and in other lawful ways, but not arbitrarily carried the goods from the port of destination back to Shanghai, and finally disposed the good in Malaysia. Therefore, it should bear the liability for the goods being disposed as waste.
3. Jielong Company should be liable for the storage fee, warehouse fee and containers detention fee at the port of destination of the goods, but it had no default for the loss of the goods. Therefore, the court of first instance's determination of the damage to the goods was incorrect.

Norasia Container appealed and requested to revoke the original judgment according to the law, and amend the judgment to reject the claims of Jielong Company. The main reasons were as follows:

1. The wrong ascertainment on whether the original bill of lading was issued and transferred, which further led to negation of the effectiveness of the terms on the back of the bill of lading and the wrong determination Jielong Company's title to sue, it did not comply with the legal provisions.
2. The original court held that did not handle the goods under legal procedures, it was wrong understanding and application of the law. First of all, the port of destination of the goods involved was Russia, there was no possibility to apply to the local court for auction in light of the maritime law; secondly, after the goods in two containers were shipped back to Shanghai, despite repeated urging, Jielong Company still did not response, Norasia Container, as the carrier, could not arrange clearance, or apply to court for auction according to the maritime law; finally, during more than one year from the goods involved arrived at the port of destination to the time when the goods were sold, the carrier repeatedly contacted the consignee and the shipper, but got no reply, in this case, Norasia Container had to consider to handle the residual goods, it was cautious and had no fault in the whole process.
3. The court of first instance neither examined whether Jielong Company suffered any loss of the actual price nor correctly analyzed whether there was a causal relationship between Norasia Container's handling of the goods and the loss of Jielong Company, misjudged the loss of the goods involved should be assumed by Norasia Container and Jielong half and half, there was no factual or legal basis.

In response to Jielong Company's claims of appeal, Norasia Container argued that:

1. In terms of the ascertainment on the evidence of Jielong Company, Norasia Container had already submitted relevant evidence in the first instance, which had been undergone notarization in Russia.
2. The goods involved arrived at the port of destination designated in the bill of lading, the carrier had completed the obligations under the contract of carriage. Because of the non-taking delivery of goods and no reply of the consignee and the shipper on how to dispose of the goods, the carrier, in order to reduce loss, disposed the goods, the shipper was at fault.

In terms of the appeal of Norasia Container, Jielong Company argued that:

1. The consignee never appeared or claimed delivery of the goods, the case could be confirmed on the opposite side of the contract was Jielong Company, the counterparty to the transport contract could be identified as Jielong Company, Norasia Container requested Jielong Company to bear the responsibility of the owner. So Jielong Company had the title to sue, the ascertainment of the first instance thereon was correct.
2. The terms on the back of the bill of lading involved were standard terms, and they were not explained to the shipper, it was correct that the court of first instance denied the validity of the terms.
3. It was correct that the original court held that Norasia Container did not handle the goods involved under legal procedures was correct, but also held that Jielong Company had fault in the disposal of the goods, it was completely wrong. Norasia Container claimed that it could not auction the goods according to the law of the port of destination, but it did not accomplish the burden of proof. The goods were sold by the carrier arbitrarily without any conformation of the owner or any instructions of the customs or other authorities, it constituted a serious breach of the carrier.
4. The key to the case was whether the carrier was entitled to dispose the goods without authorization. It was obvious wrong that the court of first instance decided equal liability for the loss of the goods.

SAC stated it agreed with the appeal and defense of Norasia Container. And added that its position in the case was the agent of Norasia Container, it should not assume liability in the present case in the case where Jielong Company failed to provide evidence to prove SAC as an agent had fault.

In the second instance, Norasia Container and SAC submitted two sets of original bill of lading and a guarantee letter for telex release, to prove that Jielong Company gave a guarantee letter for telex release and returned two sets of original bill of lading to SAC on July 27 and July 29, 2011. Therefore, the bill of lading had been issued, and Jielong Company should be fully aware of the terms on the back of the bill of lading, Jielong Company should be bounded by the terms.

Jielong Company cross-examined that: the evidence above was not new evidence of second instance; in the meantime, the seal of Jielong Company on the guarantee letter for telex release issued on July 27, 2011 was a copy, and the bar seal was not Jielong Company's, so the authenticity thereof. In addition, even if the guarantee letter for telex release was true, it could only prove that Jielong Company authorized to release the goods subject to telex, but could not prove that SAC actually issued a bill of lading involved and Jielong Company knew the terms on the back of the bill of lading.

SAC did not express any opinion in respect of the evidence.

The court after verification holds that the two sets of bill of lading involved are the originals. Except the seal of Jielong Company, there is a seal of Litong Logistics which is used to agent booking shipping space only. In addition, Jielong Company in the original instance that it was agreed the goods would be released subject to telex. The court admits the authenticity of the above evidence. However, the court will consider whether the bill of lading has been issued and whether the terms on the back of the bill of lading shall be binding upon Jielong Company in combination with other evidence.

After hearing, the court finds that the facts found by the original court are basically true, and can be confirmed.

The court holds that this case is arising from dispute over contract of carriage of goods by sea. Since Jielong Company is the shipper under the bill of lading, it concluded the contract of carriage of goods by sea with the containers. Jielong Company has the right to claim its rights against the carrier Norasia Container on the basis of the contract of carriage of goods by sea. In respect of whether the bills of lading was issued, the court holds that when Jielong Company filed the original lawsuit, the two bills of lading it submitted are copies delivered by Litong Logictics, combined with the date of issuance of the original bill of lading and the guarantee letter for telex release, it can be proved that the bills of lading involved have been actually issued. However, the goods involved were demanded to be released by telex, so the bills of lading have not transferred to the consignee, the consignee does not know the relevant contents of the bill of lading. Similarly, the terms on the back of the bill of lading cannot be binding on the shipper Jielong Company. So the court admits the determination on the terms on the back of the original bill of lading.

Although in the port of destination no one took delivery of the goods involved, Norasia Container had contacted with the consignee and the shipper recorded in the bill of lading for many times, it had fulfilled the obligations and responsibilities of a diligent and prudent carrier. Norasia Container finally sold the goods to a scrap merchant, it violated the law. However, during more than one year from the goods arrived at the port of destination to the time when the goods were sold out, Jielong Company received several notices from Norasia Container, which remanded opinions of handling the goods, but Jielong Company did not make any written reply, it ignored the goods, it was indolent in exercising the right and obligations as the shipper of the goods until the goods were sold. It only claimed its rights after the goods involved were sold, its behavior is also faulty. Accordingly, the original court based on the actual circumstances of this case, determined JieLong Company and Norasia Container should respectively bear half of the loss of goods, there is no impropriety.

In summary, the decision of first instance is not improper. The appeals of Jielong Company and Norasia Container lack factual and legal basis, the court will not support. According to Article 170 Paragraph 1 Sub-paragraph 1 and Article 175 of the Civil Procedure Law of the People's Republic of China, the judgment is as follows:

Dismiss the appeal, and affirm the original judgment.

Court acceptance fee of second instance in amount of RMB8,605 yuan, the Appellant, Shanghai Jielong Industrial Group Co., Ltd. Yutian Packaging and Printing Branch, and the Appellant, Norasia Container Line Limited, shall each pay RMB4,302.50.

The judgment is final.

Presiding Judge: DONG Min
Acting Judge: ZHOU Yi
Acting Judge: XU Yijin

September 1, 2014

Clerk: LUO Gang

Appendix: Relevant Law

1. **Civil Procedure Law of the People's Republic of China**

    Article 172 After hearing an appellate case, the people's court of second instance shall handle the case respectively according to the following circumstances:

    (1) If the facts were clearly found and the law was correctly applied in the original judgment, the appeal shall be rejected by a judgment and the original judgment shall be sustained;
    (2) If the law was incorrectly applied in the original judgment, the judgment shall be amended according to law;
    (3) If in the original judgment the facts were incorrectly found or were not clearly found and the evidence was inconclusive, the judgment shall be rescinded and the case remanded by an order to the original people's court for a retrial, or the people's court of second instance may amend the judgment after investigating and clarifying the facts; or
    (4) If in the original judgment a violation of the prescribed procedure may have affected the correctness of the judgment, the judgment shall be rescinded and the case remanded by an order to the original people's court for a retrial.

    The parties may appeal against the judgment or ruling rendered in a retrial of their case.

    Article 175 The judgments and rulings of a people's court of second instance shall be final.

The Supreme People's Court of the People's Republic of China
Civil Ruling

Shanghai Jielong Industrial Group Co., Ltd. Yutian Packaging and Printing Branch
v.
Norasia Container Lines Limited et al.

(2015) Min Shen Zi No.573

Related Case(s) This is the ruling of retrial, and the judgment of first instance and the judgment of second instance are on page 987 and page 999 respectively.

Cause(s) of Action 202. Dispute over contract of carriage of goods by sea or sea-connected waters.

Headnote Refusing the Plaintiff-shipper's petition for a retrial on the basis of new evidence, affirming lower court decisions that the Plaintiff-shipper and the Defendant-carrier were equally responsible for loss caused by consignee's failure to collect cargo at port of destination, which ultimately led to rerouting and sale of cargo by the Defendant-carrier.

Summary The Plaintiff-shipper, Jielong Company, filed this application for retrial, alleging that it had evidence that was sufficient to overturn the lower courts' judgment that the shipper was at fault for neglecting to respond to the carrier regarding disposal of the goods involved after the consignee had failed to collect them at the port of destination. This new evidence, an e-mail correspondence between Jielong Company's agent *ad litem* and the Defendant-carrier, Norasia Container, was insufficient to overturn the determination that the shipper had failed to adequately inform the carrier about disposal procedures. The Supreme People's Court recognized the lower courts' finding that the Plaintiff-shipper's failure to properly execute its obligations as the shipper under the carriage contract made it liable for half of the loss of the damaged goods. Thus, the court denied the application for retrial.

Ruling

The Claimant of Retrial (the Plaintiff of first instance, the Appellant of second instance): Shanghai Jielong Industrial Group Co., Ltd. Yutian Packaging and Printing Branch
Domicile: No.1, Lane 7076, Chuanzhou Road, Pudong New District, Shanghai, the People's Republic of China.
Person in Charge: WU Jiangming, manager
Agent *ad litem*: CAO Fang, lawyer of Shanghai Allbright Law Office.
Agent *ad litem*: KONG Jingyuan, lawyer of Shanghai Allbright Law Office.

The Respondent of Retrial (the Defendant of first instance, the Appellant of second instance): Norasia Container Lines Limited
Domicile: 18/2 South Street, District 11, Valletta, Republic of Malta.
Legal representatives: Héctor Arancibia Sánchez and José Francisco Munoz, directors.
Agent *ad litem*: CHEN Youmu, lawyer of Shanghai Wintell & Co.
Agent *ad litem*: LIU Yujia, lawyer of Shanghai Wintell & Co.

The Respondent of Retrial (the Defendant of first instance): South American Steamship (China) Shipping Co., Ltd.
Domicile: Room 1901A, 1902-1906, Hongyi International Plaza, No.288 Jiujiang Road, Shanghai, the People's Republic of China.
Legal representative: Andres Roberto Kulka Kuperman, general manager.
Agent *ad litem*: CHEN Youmu, lawyer of Shanghai Wintell & Co.
Agent *ad litem*: LIU Yujia, lawyer of Shanghai Wintell & Co.

Dissatisfied with (2013) Hu Gao Min Si (Hai) Zhong Zi No.132 Civil Judgment rendered by the Shanghai High People's Court with respect to the case airing from dispute over contract of carriage of goods by sea, Shanghai Jielong Industrial Group Co., Ltd. Yutian Packaging and Printing Branch (hereinafter referred to as Jielong Company), petitioned a retrial against the Respondents Norasia Container Lines Limited (hereinafter referred to as Norasia Container) and South American Steamship (China) Shipping Co., Ltd. (hereinafter referred to as SAC). The court formed a collegiate panel to review this case. Now the case has been concluded.

Jielong Company petitioned for retrial and claimed as follows:

1. The ascertainment of the first and second judgments that Norasia Container had no fault in performance of transport contract and handling the goods involved outside the territory of China lacked evidence, and the application of law was wrong.
2. The ascertainment of the first and second judgments on the determination of fault and immediate cause of the damage to the goods involved was in serious logic confusion.
3. The new evidence submitted by Jielong Company, namely, the email sent by CAO Fang, agent *ad litem*, to SAC on March 22, 2012, which was to prove

Jielong Company had responded to the contact and claim of Norasia Container and SAC, but not without reply, it was sufficient to overturn the decision of the original judgment determining Jielong Company had fault.

According to Article 200 Paragraphs 1, 2 and 6 of the Civil Procedure Law of the PRC, Jielong Company requested a retrial of the case.

It was alleged in the submissions referred to by Norasia Container:

1. The letter of attorney submitted by Jielong Company was not new evidence, it was insufficient to prove that Jielong Company had responded to taking delivery and handling of the goods involved. It was proper that the judgment of first instance ascertained that Jielong Company was slack to give instruction to the handling of the goods and then concluded that Jielong Company had fault therein.
2. The evidence which was produced outside China submitted by Norasia Container and SAC had been notarized in Russia, no circumstance of lack of evidence to prove the basic facts existed in this case.
3. The damage to the goods involved should be born entirely by Jielong Company itself, Jielong Company had no basis to application for retrial.

It was alleged in the submissions referred to by SAC:

1. SAC was the agent of Norasia Container, but not the carrier under the contract of carriage involved, it should not bear the liability under the contract of carriage.
2. The so-called new evidence submitted by Jielong Company could not negate the fact that SAC was acting as an agent, and there was no factual and legal basis for Jielong Company to request SAC bear liability for compensation.

Upon examination, the court holds that this case was concerning dispute over carriage of goods by sea. Jielong Company is the shipper set forth in the bill of lading, Norasia Container is the carrier expressed therein, and SAC is the agent of the carrier, the parties concerned have confirmed the facts aforesaid. In the case of Jielong Company's application for retrial, the key points to be reviewed in this case are as follows: (1) whether the evidence submitted by Jielong Company to the court is new evidence that can overturn the original judgment as provided in Article 200 Paragraph 1 of the Civil Procedure Law of the People's Republic of China; (2) whether the facts ascertained by the first and second instances judgments are lack of evidence; (3) whether it is correct that the first and second instances judgments determined Jielong Company should assume half of the liability for loss of goods.

In respect of whether the evidence submitted by Jielong Company to the court is new evidence that can overturn the original judgment as provided in Article 200 Paragraph 1 of the Civil Procedure Law of the People's Republic of China, Norasia Container and SAC did not raise any objection to the authenticity of lawyer's reply to Jielong Company, but challenged the establishment of new evidence and the purpose of proof. However, the e-mail was formed in March 2012, prior to the first instance, and the email was sent the lawyer CAO Fang entrusted by Jielong Company. It is evidence holding by Jielong Company, but Jielong Company did not submit it in the first and second instances. In addition, the contents of the e-mail only expresses it retained the entitlement to claim against the carrier's return transport of the goods, but not involved with how to deal with the goods non-taking delivery of. Obviously, the email cannot prove that Jielong Company has responded to Norasia Container and SAC in respect of how to deal with the goods. The purpose of Jielong Company intended to prove that the facts ascertained in the original judgment were incorrect cannot be established. The evidence does not fall into the new evidence that can overturn the original judgment as provided in Article 200 Paragraph 1 of the Civil Procedure Law of the People's Republic of China.

In respect of whether the facts ascertained by the first and second judgments instances are lack of evidence, first of all, it was found in the original instance that the goods involved arrived at the port of destination on June 30 and August 5, 2011. The carrier its agent of the goods involved sent a notice of demand for taking delivery of goods through the Russian Post to the address of consignee recorded in the bill of lading, but the notice was returned. The Russian Federation Baltic Customs issued a document asking for the reason and related information of the overdue temporary storage of containers. SAC had sent several notices on the handling of the goods involved by courier, but it did not receive any reply from Jielong Company.

Norasia Container and SAC submitted the document issued by the Russian Federation Baltic Customs, the notice of taking delivery of goods and the postal order, the notice of demand for taking delivery of goods and the express sheet to prove the facts mentioned above. The above evidence materials are the originals or copies having been notarized, Jielong Company did not admit the authenticity or the and probative force of the evidence, but it did not submit any evidence to the contrary, the court of first instance admitted the probative force of the evidence aforesaid, as well as the fact that nobody took delivery of the goods after its arrival at the port of destination, Norasia Container and SAC contacted with Jielong Company in terms of the handling of the goods, but got no reply. Such determination is well grounded and proper. Secondly, although the evidence concerning the storage fee, customs inspection fee and other fees submitted by Norasia Container and SAC was declaration or statement made by itself, but the first and second instance judgments only ascertained the fact that Norasia Container and SAC had claimed the fees mentioned above against Jielong Company, and the amount of the loss of the goods as determined by the judgments is the amount recorded in the customs declaration document, which is not affected by the storage fee, customs inspection fee and other fees advocated by the Norasia Container. Therefore, the allegation of Jielong Company that the evidence submitted by Norasia Container and SAC had no probative force and the facts found in the original judgments is short of evidence to prove lacks factual and legal basis.

In respect of whether it is correct that the first and second instances judgments determined Jielong Company should assume half of the liability for loss of goods, according to the facts identified in the original instances, the goods involved were agreed to be released subject to telex, the bill of lading involved is a straight bill of lading, since the goods was not taken delivery of after arriving at the port of destination, Norasia Container sent a notice of demand for taking delivery of goods to the consignee provided by Jielong Company, but the consignee did not settle in the address and the notice was undelivered, Norasia Container issued a notice on how to deal with the goods to the Jielong Company, but got no response. The carrier has fulfilled the obligation of a diligent and prudent carrier.

Jielong Company neither informed the carrier of the correct contact information of the consignee, nor did it contact with the carrier to deal with the goods involved, resulting in failure to deliver the goods for a long term. It has been more than one year since from the goods arrived at the destination port to the final sales, Jielong Company did not respond to how to deal with the goods and only claimed its rights by means of action until the goods were sold, the costs and risks arising therefrom shall be born by itself. Accordingly, it is not disadvantaged to Jielong Company that the first and second instance courts held Jielong Company was slack to exercise the rights and obligations of shipper, and determined Jielong Company should bear half liability for the damage to the goods.

In summary, Jielong Company's application for retrial does not conform to circumstances of retrial as stipulated in Article 200 Paragraphs 1, 2 and 6 of the Civil Procedure Law of the People's Republic of China. According to Article 204 Paragraph 1 of the Civil Procedure Law of the People's Republic of China, the ruling is as follows:

Dismiss the application for retrial filed by Shanghai Jielong Industrial Group Co., Ltd. Yutian Packaging and Printing Branch.

Presiding Judge: HU Fang
Judge: GUO Zhonghong
Judge: YU Xiaohan

July 15, 2015c

Clerk: LI Na

Dalian Maritime Court
Civil Judgment

SHAN Yongzhen et al.
v.
LIANG Mingren

(2014) Da Hai Shi Chu Zi No.121

Related Case(s) This is the judgment of first instance and the judgment of second instance is on page 1022.

Cause(s) of Action 200. Dispute over liability for personal injury at sea.

Headnote Vessel-owner held to be 20% responsible for accidental death of seaman engaged in welding activities as independent contractor; deceased seaman 80% responsible, as he had performed welding activities without appropriate certification, so his family's recovery of damages was reduced accordingly.

Summary The Plaintiffs sued for damages following the death of their family member, WU Zhong, a welder who died following an accidental explosion that happened while he was performing welding work on the Defendant's fishing vessel. The court ruled that the deceased was principally at fault for the accident because he did not have the proper certification to perform the welding work he was contracted to perform. The court also held that, however, that although the Defendant was unaware of WU Zhong's lack of qualifications, he nevertheless contracted him to perform the work and was, therefore, also partially liable for WU Zhong's injury and death following the explosion. Responsibility should be apportioned 80% to WU Zhong and 20% to the Defendant. The Defendant was ordered to pay compensation for 20% of WU Zhong's death and funeral expenses plus emotional damages and living expenses to the Plaintiffs in addition to litigation fees.

Judgment

The Plaintiff: SHAN Yongzhen, female, Han, living in Donggang

The Plaintiff: JIA Xiuli, female, Han, living in Donggang

The Plaintiff: WU Anyang, male, Han, living in Donggang
Joint agent *ad litem* of the three Plaintiffs: WANG Juan, lawyer of Liaoning Fade Law Firm.

The Defendant: LIANG Mingren, male, Han, living in Donggang
Agent *ad litem*: JIANG Qingguo, male, Han, living in Donggang.

With respect to the case arising from dispute over liability for personal injury at sea, the Plaintiffs SHAN Yongzhen, JIA Xiuli and WU Anyang (hereinafter referred to as the three Plaintiffs) filed an action against the Defendant LIANG Mingren, the court, after entertained this case, constituted a collegiate panel and held a hearing in public. The three Plaintiffs and WANG Juan, agent *ad litem*, the Defendant and agent *ad litem*, JIANG Qingguo, appeared in court and participated in the action. Now the case has been concluded.

The three Plaintiffs alleged that: at 1000 h on May 31, 2014, LIANG Mingren informed WU Zhong (the deceased) (son of SHAN Yongzhen, husband of JIA Xiuli, father of WU Zhong) by telephone to weld the oil tank of fishing boat LIAO DAN YU YUN 25099 owned by LIANG Mingren on Risheng Wharf. WU Zhong died due to explosion which was caused by unknown reason during welding process. the Plaintiffs sued to the court, requesting the court to order LIANG Mingren to pay death compensation in amount of RMB604,760, funeral expenses in amount of RMB27,408, living expenses for the dependents in amount of RMB39,403, the fee of depositing corpse in amount of RMB13,912, transportation costs in amount of RMB5,000, the spiritual damage compensation in amount of RMB110,000, the total amount was RMB800,483, and LIANG Mingren should bear the litigation fees.

The Plaintiffs provided the following evidence to support their claims: 1. accident investigation report, to prove the deceased had an employment contractual relationship with the Defendant and died in the employment activity; 2. household status of three Plaintiffs, to prove the identities of the three Plaintiffs; 3. proof of marriage registration, to prove the husband-wife relationship between the deceased and the Plaintiff JIA Xiuli; 4. medical certificate of death, to prove the death of the victim WU Zhong; 5. proof of the village committee, to prove mother–child between the deceased and the Plaintiff SHAN Yongzhen; 6. funeral service contract, to prove the costs of body conserving and cremation.

The Defendant argued that the deceased and the Defendant was not employment contractual relationship, according to the provisions of law, the Defendant should not undertake the liability for compensation. The compensated claimed by the three Plaintiffs should not be protected by law. The Defendant requested the court to reject the claims of the three Plaintiffs.

The Defendant, in support of his defense, provided the following evidence to the court: 1. witness testimony, to prove the deceased and the Defendant established word contract relationship, and after the accident happened, the witness on behalf of the Defendant paid the Plaintiff RMB20,000 yuan; 2. record of inquiries, to prove that the Defendant had no fault; 3. a copy of documentary evidence, to prove that the deceased and the Defendant established word contract relationship; 4. receipt of payment, to prove the costs of shroud the Defendant purchased for the deceased; 5. receipt of medical expenses, to prove the expenses the Defendant paid to rescue the deceased; 6. outpatient medical record, to prove that the Defendant rescued the deceased; 7. practicing certificate, to prove the deceased had a welder qualification certificate; 8. accident report, to prove the course of the accident involved.

After cross-examination and court investigation, the court finds out that:

Fishing boat LIAO DAN YU YUN 25099 was owned by the Defendant, it was registered 30 m in length, 6.7 m in width, 3 m in depth, with gross tonnage of 118 tons, a main engine of 137 kilowatts and hull of steel. (The deceased WU Zhong, when he was alive, he was the son of SHAN Yongzhen, husband of JIA Xiuli, father of WU Anyang)WU Zhong as well as JIA Xiuli, WU Anyang and SHAN Yongzhen were urban residents and SHAN Yongzhen has a total of 5 children. WU Zhong got the Welder Occupation Skill Certificate, of which the number is No.1107061007500714, issued by the Shandong Municipal Labor and Social Security Bureau. The date of issuance was December 27, 2011, but he did not hold a special appliance operator certificate of the People's Republic of China issued by the Liaoning Safety Production Administration. At about 0700 h on May 31, 2014, fishing boat LIAO DAN YU YUN 25099 after returning berthed in Risheng Wharf, Donggang. YU Yonggang, a support personnel of the Defendant who was in charge of the repair and maintenance and of the ship discovered oil leaking from a gap about 10 cm in the front oil tank of cargo hold, telephoned WU Zhong for welding repair. At about 1000 h, WU Zhong arrived at Risheng Wharf, with accompany of WANG Shusheng, the crew of the ship, went down to the oil tank in the front of cargo hold. After WANG Shusheng pointed out the place of leakage WU Zhong immediately started to weld. 3 min later, WU Zhong asked WANG Shusheng to find a flashlight for lighting because the light there was dark. About 2 min later, WANG Shusheng found flashlight but did not come back, the front cargo hold-happened fires and explosion. WANG Shusheng immediately ordered the chief engineer to open the ship auxiliary machine and pump turbine to fight fire. After hearing the sound of explosion, YU Yonggang immediately rushed to the ship and called Fire Alarm 119 and 120 emergency dialing. Then firefighters arrived and rescued WU Zhong from the front cargo hold, found his left arm was blown off and his body was severely burned, WU Zhong still could say some words, and then he was sent by 120 ambulance to Donggang Central Hospital and dead after rescue. The Defendant paid the medical rescue expense. The three Plaintiffs spent the funeral expenses for the deceased WU Zhong in amount of RMB13,912. After the accident happened, Dandong Fishing Port Supervision Department issued *Investigation Report of Donggang Fishing Boat LIAO DAN YU YUN 25099 Welding Operation Explosion Accident* on May 31. The report conformed the course of the above accident and stated analysis on the cause of the accident. Welders WU Zhong welded the oil tank of fishing boat LIAO DAN YU YUN 25099, the working place (the front cargo hold of ship) suddenly happened fires and caused an explosion and then resulted in serious damage to the hull. At the same time, the operator WU Zhong was severely wounded and dead upon rescue.

According to the existing materials, the factors causing the accident of the fire and explosion in the work place remained unclear.

It is also found in the relevant data of standards of compensation for road traffic accident damage in 2014 of Dalian, the amount of per capita disposable income of urban residents was RMB30,238, the amount of per capita consumption expenditure of urban residents was RMB22,516, the amount of funeral expenses was RMB27,408.

The court holds that this case is concerning a dispute over compensation liability in connection with personal injury on the sea. Agent *ad litem* of the three Plaintiffs claimed that the Defendant and the deceased WU Zhong entered into a relationship of employment contract. Therefore, WU Zhongdiedin the activity to accomplish the employer's order, so the Defendant should be liable for compensation. Agent *ad litem* of the Defendant claimed that the relationship between both parties was contract for work. As a contractor, WU Zhong caused his own death during the operation of work. the Defendant should not be liable for compensation as ordering party. In conclusion, agent *ad litem* of the Defendant requested the court to reject the claims of the three Plaintiffs according to law. According to Article 10 of the Interpretation of the Supreme People's Court on Certain Issues concerning the Application of Law in the Trial of Cases involving Compensation for Personal Injury, "if the contractor caused damage to the third person or to himself during the course of completing work, the ordering party shall not be liable for compensation. Where ordering party has fault in manufacturing, ordering, appointment, he shall bear the corresponding liability"; and Article 11provides that "where the employer shall be liable for compensation for personal injury of employee in the employment activities". According to the aforesaid provisions of judicial interpretations, combined with the facts having been identified, WU Zhong received the phone of employee of the Defendant who was responsible for maintenance and repair. Then WU Zhong brought his welding tools and materials to weld on fishing ship owned by the Defendant. In the past, the Defendant settled payment every time WU Zhong finished the welding work. There was no relationship of controlling, dominating and subordination between WU Zhong and the Defendant when WU Zhong was carrying out welding work. How to weld and welding work was not part of operating activities of the fishing ship owned by the Defendant. Consequently, there was no relationship of employment between WU Zhong and the Defendant. the court does not support the claims of the Plaintiffs in connection with the relationship of employment between WU Zhong and the Defendant. According to Article 251 of the Contract Law of the People's Republic of China, "a contract for work is a contract whereby the contractor shall, in light of the requirements of the ordering party, complete certain work and deliver the results therefrom, and the ordering party pays the remuneration therefor. Work includes processing, ordering, repairing, duplicating, testing, inspecting, etc." Article 253 stipulates that: "the contractor shall use its own equipment, skills and labor to complete the main part of the work, except as otherwise agreed upon by the parties". In this case, the victim WU Zhong brought his own welding tools and materials to weld the oil tank according to the requirements of the Defendant. After the welding was finished, the Defendant paid service fee to WU Zhong on the basis of materials, labor and time by WU Zhong. The contract relationship between both parties is in consistence with the features of contract for work. the court supports allegation of the Defendant on relationship of contract for work between both parties. According to Article 23 of the Safety Production Act of the People's Republic of China (2009): "special operation personnel of production and business units must undergo an special training and obtain a special operation certificate according to the relevant regulation before beginning work". In the Article 2.1 Special Operation Directory of the Provisions on the Examination and Management of Safety Technical Training for Special Operation Personnel (No.30 Decree of the State Production Safety Supervision and Administration): fusion welding and hot cutting operation is a work to accomplish welding and cut which refer to the method of using local heating to heat the metal or other material in the position of junction, continuing to the state of melting. It is suitable for cutting and welding, arc welding and carbon arc gouging and submerged arc welding, gas welding, plasma arc welding, electroslag welding, electron beam welding, laser welding, flux cutting, laser cutting, and plasma cutting operations. The victim WU Zhong who was engaged in welding work, which was a special operation, therefore, work could only be started where a person had obtained a qualification certificate before induction pursuant to the stipulations of safety production rules. However, in this case, the victim WU Zhong only obtained the occupation welder skill certificate, he did not have the qualification for post. He had greater fault because of lacking of the qualifications of special operations. During the process of selection of welders, the Defendant was not in-depth knowledge of whether WU Zhong had operation qualification of engaging special operation for welding, and he had oil tank of the ship welded, resulting in the severe accident of explosion and death of welder as well as the damage of fishing ship. Therefore, the Defendant had certain fault in selection of welders. On basis of *Investigation Report of Donggang Fishing Boat LIAO DAN YU YUN 25099 Welding Operation Explosion Accident on May 31*, the specific location of the explosion is the front cargo hold of fishing ship of the Defendant, but the specific object first happened explosion was unclear and the direct cause could not be found. The victim WU Zhong was a welder who has welding occupation skill certificate, and had be engaged in the work for many years. Before the activities of contract for work, WU Zhong should conduct a comprehensive and rigorous inspection on the construction place, construction object and construction conditions to ensure the safety of construction. However, WU Zhong started welding without careful check of the construction place of the former cargo hold, resulting in the severe accident of explosion and fire and his own death. Thus, the victim WU Zhong had responsibility due to lack of appropriate check. In combination of the facts of this case and the responsibilities and the faults of the two parties, the court holds that the victim WU Zhong only got the welder occupation skill certificate, but lacked a qualification certificate for special operations, so he did not have the qualifications for special operations, and he did not inform the Defendant he was lack of qualifications for special operations when the Defendant asked him to weld the oil tank, during the process of performing the contract, he did not perform obligation for careful inspection. During the process of selection of welders, the Defendant was not in-depth knowledge of whether WU Zhong had operation qualifications to engage special operation for welding. Compared the fault between both parties in this case, the victim WU Zhong had a major fault, while the Defendant had the corresponding fault of selection. It was more appropriate that the victim WU Zhong and the Defendant should bear the responsibility in the ratio of 8:2.

The three Plaintiffs and the victim are all urban residents, thus, the calculation standard of the losses of the Plaintiffs shall be based on the standards of Dalian, where the court entertaining this case is located. the Plaintiffs claimed for compensation for spiritual damages, according to Article 11 of the Interpretation on Certain Issues concerning the Determination of Compensation Liability for Mental Damage in Civil Torts of the Supreme People's Court: "if the victim has fault in the facts and the consequences of damage, the liability of infringer for compensation for mental injury can be reduced or exempted according to the degree of fault". According to the Notice of Liaoning High People's Court on Issuing the Minutes of Meeting for Civil Trial of the Courts in the Province [Liao Gao Fa(2009) No.120], the provisions concerning the standard of spiritual damages are as follows: "if right to life and the right to health of natural people is infringed, result in death or disability, or other personality rights is infringed and leading to severe spiritual distress, the victim or his close relative is entitled to compensation for spiritual damage, when calculating the spiritual damage compensation, six factors as stipulated in relevant judicial explanation of the Supreme Court shall be taken into consideration, and based on the per capita disposable income of urban residents and per capita net income of rural residents in the last year, in comparison of Article 50 Sub-paragraph 11 of the Regulations on the Handling of Medical Accidents. If the victim is dead, the maximum length of compensation shall not exceed six years; if the victim is disabled, the maximum length of compensation shall not exceed three years. Therefore, the Plaintiffs shall obtain a spiritual damage compensation in sum of RMB36,285.6 yuan, resulted from the calculation formula: RMB30,238 yuan per year* 6 years * 20% (the Defendant shall bear 20% of liability). According to Article 29 of the Interpretation of the Supreme People's Court on Certain Issues concerning the Application of Law in the Trial of Cases involving Compensation for Personal Injury, when it refers to the compensation for death, the Plaintiffs shall obtain RMB120,952 yuan, RMB30,238 yuan per year * 20 years * 20% (the Defendant shall bear 20%of liability). In respect of the traffic expenses, the three Plaintiffs did not provide relevant documents to support the claims of SHAN Yongzhen, JIA Xiuli and WU Anyang, the court does not support. In respect of the living expenses for dependents, according to the provisions of Interpretation of the Supreme People's Court on Certain Issues concerning the Application of Law in the Trial of Cases involving Compensation for Personal Injury, the Plaintiffs were entitled to claim. The accident happened on May 31, 2014, the dependents was born on July 18, 1941, based on Relevant Data of Standards for Compensation of Traffic Accident Damages of Dalian City in 2014, the living expenses shall be RMB5,481.6 yuan, RMB22,516 yuan per year * 7 years / 5 persons * 20% (the Defendant shall bear 20% of liability). The Plaintiffs claimed that funeral expenses in sum of RMB13,912 yuan to preserve the body and funeral and interment shall be included in the funeral expenses and the court does not support the above claims. All the aforesaid compensation is in total of RMB169,023.68 yuan, the Defendant shall pay to SHAN Yongzhen, JIA Xiuli and WU Anyang. According to Articles 10, 18, 22, 28 and 29 of the Interpretation of the Supreme People's Court on Certain Issues concerning the Application of Law in the Trial of Cases Involving Compensation for Personal Injury, the judgment is as follows:

1. The Defendant LIANG Mingren shall compensate the Plaintiffs SHAN Yongzhen, JIA Xiuli and WU Anyang for death compensations in amount of RMB120,952 within 10 days after the judgment comes into effect;
2. The Defendant LIANG Mingren shall compensate the Plaintiffs SHAN Yongzhen, JIA Xiuli and WU Anyang for spiritual damage compensation in amount of RMB36,285.6 within 10 days after the judgment comes into effect;
3. The Defendant LIANG Mingren shall compensate SHAN Yongzhen for living expenses for dependents in amount of RMB6,304.48 within 10 days after this judgment comes into effect;
4. The Defendant LIANG Mingren shall compensate the Plaintiffs SHAN Yongzhen, JIA Xiuli and WU Anyang for funeral expenses in amount of RMB5,481.6. The amount of the above compensation items is RMB169,023.68 in total;
5. Reject other claims of the Plaintiffs SHAN Yongzhen, JIA Xiuli andWU Anyang.

Court acceptance fee in amount ofRMB11,804 which has been prepaid by the Plaintiffs, RMB9,312 shall be born by the three Plaintiffs, and RMB2,492 shall be born by the Defendant. The Defendant shall pay the above sum to the three Plaintiffs.

In case of dissatisfaction with this judgment, any party may submit an statement of appeal within 15 days upon the service of this judgment, with duplicates in the number of the other parties, to lodge an appeal to the Liaoning High People's Court.

Presiding Judge: SUN Yuchuan
Judge: WANG Lei
People's Juror: WANG Chunyan

April 6, 2015

Clerk: BI Chongdi

Liaoning High People's Court, Civil Judgment

SHAN Yongzhen et al.
v.
LIANG Mingren

(2015) Liao Min San Zhong Zi No.201

Related Case(s) This is the judgment of second instance, and the judgment of first instance is on page 1015.

Cause(s) of Action 200. Dispute over liability for personal injury at sea.

Headnote Affirming lower court decision holding vessel-owner to be 20% responsible for accidental death of seaman engaged in welding activities as independent contractor; deceased seaman 80% responsible, as he had performed welding activities without appropriate certification, so his family's recovery of damages was reduced accordingly.

Summary The court of first instance held that WU Zhong was primarily responsible (80%) for the explosion and fire aboard the vessel that took his life because he did not hold the proper certification to perform the welding work that he was engaged in and which caused the accident. The vessel-owner was found to be comparatively negligent (20%) because he did not verify WU Zhong's qualifications before hiring him to perform the work and was, therefore, ordered to pay damages to WU Zhong's survivors, who brought this appeal. The Appellants claimed that WU Zhong and the vessel-owner had an employment contract, which the court below mistakenly characterized as an arrangement for independent contract work, and that the court misapplied the law in its apportionment of liability for the accident. The appeal court held that WU Zhong was properly described as an independent contractor because, whenever he had done welding work for the vessel-owner in the past, he used his own tools and materials and was paid upon completion of each project. Additionally, the court confirmed the lower court's reasons for finding comparative fault and its apportionment of liability for the payment of damages. Therefore, the original judgment was recognized and the appeal was dismissed with the costs of appeal to be paid by the Appellants.

Judgment

The Appellant (the Plaintiff of first instance): SHAN Yongzhen, female, Han
Agent *ad litem*:WU Anyang, male, Han, grandson of SHAN Yongzhen.
Agent *ad litem*:WANG Juan, lawyer of Liaoning Fade Law Firm.

The Appellant (the Plaintiff of first instance): JIA Xiuli, female, Han
Agent *ad litem*:WU Anyang, male, Han, son of JIA Xiuli.
Agent *ad litem*:WANG Juan, lawyer of Liaoning Fade Law Firm.

The Appellant (the Plaintiff of first instance): WU Anyang, male, Han
Agent *ad litem*:WANG Juan, lawyer of Liaoning Fade Law Firm.

The Respondent (the Defendant of first instance): LIANG Mingren, male, Han
Agent *ad litem*:SUN Baoren, male, lawyer of Liaoning Boyang Law Firm.

Dissatisfied with (2014) Da Hai Shi Chu Zi No.121 Civil Judgment rendered by Dalian Maritime Court with respect to the case arising from dispute over liability for personal injury on the sea or on the sea-connected areas, the Appellants SHAN Yongzhen, JIA Xiuli and WU Anyang lodged an appeal against the Respondent LIANG Mingren before the court. The court, after entertaining this case on May 28, 2015, constituted a collegiate panel according to law, and questioned the parties concerned on July 13, 2015. Now the case has been concluded.

SHAN Yongzhen, JIA Xiuli and WU Anyang alleged in the first instance that: at 1000 on May 31, 2014, LIANG Mingren informed WU Zhong (the deceased) (son of SHAN Yongzhen, husband of JIA Xiuli, father of WU Zhong) by telephone to weld the oil tank of fishing boat LIAO DAN YU YUN 25099 owned by LIANG Mingren on Risheng Wharf. WU Zhong died due to explosion which was caused by unknown reason during welding process. SHAN Yongzhen, JIA Xiuli and WU Anyang sued to the court of first instance, requesting the court of first instance to order LIANG Mingren to pay death compensation in amount of RMB604,760, funeral expenses in amount of RMB27,408, living expenses for the dependents in amount of RMB39,403, the fee of depositing corpse in amount of RMB13,912, transportation costs in amount of RMB5,000, the spiritual damage compensation in amount of RMB110,000, of which the total amount was RMB800,483, and LIANG Mingren should bear the litigation fees.

LIANG Mingren argued in first instance that there was no relationship of employment contract between the deceased and LIANG Mingren, and he should not be liable for compensation according to law. The amount claimed by SHAN Yongzhen, JIA Xiuli and WU Anyang should not be protected by law. LIANG Mingren requested the court of first instance to reject the claims of SHAN Yongzhen, JIA Xiuli and WU Anyang.

After trial, the court of first instance found out that: fishing boat LIAO DAN YU YUN 25099 was owned by LIANG Mingren, it was registered 30 m in length, 6.7 m in width, 3 m in depth, with gross tonnage of 118 tons, a main engine of 137 kilowatts and hull of steel. (The deceased WU Zhong, when he was alive, he was the son of SHAN Yongzhen, husband of JIA Xiuli, father of WU Anyang)WU Zhong as well as JIA Xiuli, WU Anyang and SHAN Yongzhen were urban residents and SHAN Yongzhen has a total of 5 children. WU Zhong got the Welder Occupation Skill Certificate, of which the number was No.1107061007500714, issued by the Shandong Municipal Labor and Social Security Bureau. The date of issuance was December 27, 2011, but he did not hold a special appliance operator certificate of the People's Republic of China issued by the Liaoning Safety Production Administration. At about 0700 h on May 31, 2014, fishing boat LIAO DAN YU YUN 25099 after returning berthed in Risheng Wharf, Donggang. YU Yonggang, a support personnel of LIANG Mingren who was in charge of the repair and maintenance and of the ship discovered oil leaking from a gap about 10 cm in the front oil tank of cargo hold, telephoned WU Zhong for welding repair. At about 1000 h, WU Zhong arrived at Risheng Wharf, with accompany of WANG Shusheng, the crew of the ship, went down to the oil tank in the front of cargo hold. After WANG Shusheng pointed out the place of leakage WU Zhong immediately started to weld. 3 min later, WU Zhong asked WANG Shusheng to find a flashlight for lighting because the light there was dark. About 2 min later, WANG Shusheng found flashlight but did not come back, the front cargo hold happened fires and explosion. WANG Shusheng immediately ordered the chief engineer to open the ship auxiliary machine and pump turbine to fight fire. After hearing the sound of explosion, YU Yonggang immediately rushed to the ship and called Fire Alarm 119 and 120 emergency dialing. Then firefighters arrived and rescued WU Zhong from the front cargo hold, found his left arm was blown off and his body was severely burned, WU Zhong still could say some words, and then he was sent by 120 ambulance to Donggang Central Hospital and dead after rescue. LIANG Mingren paid the medical expense. SHAN Yongzhen, JIA Xiuli and WU Anyang spent the funeral expenses for the deceased WU Zhong in amount of RMB13,912. After the accident happened, Dandong Fishing Port Supervision Department issued *Investigation Report of Donggang Fishing Boat LIAO DAN YU YUN 25099 Welding Operation Explosion Accident on May 31.* The report conformed the course of the above accident and stated analysis on the cause of the accident. Welders WU Zhong welded the oil tank of fishing boat LIAO DAN YU YUN 25099, the working place (the front cargo hold of ship) suddenly happened fires and caused an explosion and then resulted in serious damage to the hull. At the same time, the operator WU Zhong was severely wounded and dead upon rescue. According to the existing materials, the factors causing the accident of the fire and explosion in the work place remained unclear.

It was also found out that: in the relevant data of standards of compensation for road traffic accident damage in 2014 of Dalian, the amount of per capita disposable income of urban residents was RMB30,238, the amount of per capita consumption expenditure of urban residents was RMB22,516, the amount of funeral expenses was RMB27,408.

The court of first instance held that: this case was concerning the dispute over compensation liability in connection with personal injury on the sea. Agent *ad litem* of SHAN Yongzhen, JIA Xiuli and WU Anyang claimed that LIANG Mingren and the deceased WU Zhong entered into a relationship of employment contract. Therefore, WU Zhong died in the activity to accomplish the employer's order, so LIANG Mingren should be liable for compensation. Agent *ad litem* of LIANG Mingren claimed that the relationship between both parties was contract for work. As a contractor, WU Zhong caused his own death during the operation of work. LIANG Mingren should not be liable for compensation as ordering party. In conclusion, agent *ad litem* of LIANG Mingren requested the court to reject the claims of SHAN Yongzhen, JIA Xiuli and WU Anyang according to law. According to Article 10 of the Interpretation of the Supreme People's Court on Certain Issues concerning the Application of Law in the Trial of Cases Involving Compensation for Personal Injury, if the contractor caused damage to the third person or to himself during the course of completing work, the ordering party shall not be liable for compensation. Where ordering party has fault in manufacturing, ordering, appointment, he shall bear the corresponding liability; and Article 11 provided that "where the employer shall be liable for compensation for personal injury of employee in the employment activities". According to the aforesaid provisions of judicial interpretations, combined with the facts having been identified, WU Zhong received the phone of employee of LIANG Mingren who was responsible for maintenance and repair. Then WU Zhong brought his welding tools and materials to weld on fishing ship owned by LIANG Mingren. In the past, LIANG Mingren settled payment every time WU Zhong finished the welding work. There was no relationship of controlling, dominating and subordination between WU Zhong and LIANG Mingren when WU Zhong was carrying out welding work. How to weld and welding work was not part of operating activities of the fishing ship owned by LIANG Mingren. Consequently, there was no relationship of employment between WU Zhong and LIANG Mingren. The court of first instance did not support the claims of SHAN Yongzhen, JIA Xiuli and WU Anyang in connection with the relationship of employment between WU Zhong and LIANG Mingren. According to Article 251 of the Contract Law of the People's Republic of China, "a contract for work is a contract whereby the contractor shall, in light of the requirements of the ordering party, complete certain work and deliver the results therefrom, and the ordering party pays the remuneration therefor. Work includes processing, ordering, repairing, duplicating, testing, inspecting, etc." Article 253 stipulated that: "the contractor shall use its own equipment, skills and labor to complete the main part of the work, except as otherwise agreed upon by the parties". In this case, the victim WU Zhong brought his own welding tools and materials to weld the oil tank according to the requirements of LIANG Mingren. After the welding was finished, LIANG Mingren paid service fee to WU Zhong on the basis of materials, labor and time by WU Zhong. The contract relationship between both parties was in consistence with the features of contract for work. The court of first instance supported allegation of LIANG Mingren on relationship of contract for work between both parties. According to Article 23 of the Safety Production Act of the People's Republic of China (2009): "special operation personnel of production and business units must undergo an special training and obtain a special operation certificate according to the relevant regulation before beginning work". In the Article 2.1 Special Operation Directory of the Provisions on the Examination and Management of Safety Technical Training for Special Operation Personnel (No.30 Decree of the State Production Safety Supervision and Administration): fusion welding and hot cutting operation was a work to accomplish welding and cut which referred to the method of using local heating to heat the metal or other material in the position of junction, continuing to the state of melting. It was suitable for cutting and welding, arc welding and carbon arc gouging and submerged arc welding, gas welding, plasma arc welding, electroslag welding, electron beam welding, laser welding, flux cutting, laser cutting, and plasma cutting operations. The victim WU Zhong who was engaged in welding work, which was a special operation, therefore, work could only be started where a person had obtained a qualification certificate before induction pursuant to the stipulations of safety production rules. However, in this case, the victim WU Zhong only obtained the occupation welder skill certificate, he did not have the qualification for post. He had greater fault because of lacking of the qualifications of special operations. During the process of selection of welders, LIANG Mingren was not in-depth knowledge of whether WU Zhong had operation qualification of engaging special operation for welding, and he had oil tank of the ship welded, resulting in the severe accident of explosion and death of welder as well as the damage of fishing ship. Therefore, LIANG Mingren had certain fault in selection of welders. On basis of *Investigation Report of Donggang Fishing Boat LIAO DAN YU YUN 25099 Welding Operation Explosion Accident on May 31*, the specific location of the explosion is the front cargo hold of fishing ship of LIANG Mingren, but the specific object first happened explosion was unclear and the direct cause could not be found. The victim WU Zhong was a welder who has welding occupation skill certificate, and had be engaged in the work for many years. Before the activities of contract for work, WU Zhong should conduct a comprehensive and rigorous inspection on the construction place, construction object and construction conditions to ensure the safety of construction. However, WU Zhong started welding without careful check of the construction place of the former cargo hold, resulting in the severe accident of explosion and fire and his own death. Thus, the victim WU Zhong had responsibility due to lack of appropriate check. In combination of the facts of this case and the responsibilities and the faults of the two parties, the court of first instance held that the victim WU Zhong only got the welder occupation skill certificate, but lacked a qualification certificate for special operations, so he did not have the qualifications for special operations, and he did not inform LIANG Mingren he was lack of qualifications for special operations when LIANG Mingren asked him to weld the oil tank, during the process of performing the contract, he did not perform obligation for careful inspection. During the process of selection of welders, LIANG Mingren was not in-depth knowledge of whether WU Zhong had operation qualifications to engage special operation for welding. Compared the fault between both parties in this case, the victim WU Zhong had a major fault, while LIANG Mingren had the corresponding fault of selection. It was more appropriate that the victim WU Zhong and LIANG Mingren should bear the responsibility in the ratio of 8:2.

SHAN Yongzhen, JIA Xiuli, WU Anyang and the victim were all urban residents, thus, the calculation standard of the losses of SHAN Yongzhen, JIA Xiuli and WU Anyang should be based on the standards of Dalian, where the court of first instance entertaining this case was located. SHAN Yongzhen, JIA Xiuli and WU Anyang claimed for compensation for spiritual damages, according to Article 11 of the Interpretations on Certain Issues concerning the Determination of Compensation Liability for Mental Damage in Civil Torts of the Supreme People's Court: "if the victim has fault in the facts and the consequences of damage, the liability of infringer for compensation for mental injury can be reduced or exempted according to the degree of fault". According to the Notice of Liaoning High People's Court on Issuing the Minutes of Meeting for Civil Trial of the Courts in the Province[Liao Gao Fa (2009) No.120], the provisions concerning the standard of spiritual damages was as follows: "if right to life and the right to health of natural people is infringed, result in death or disability, or other personality rights is infringed and leading to severe spiritual distress, the victim or his close relative is entitled to compensation for spiritual damage, when calculating the spiritual damage compensation, six factors as stipulated in relevant judicial explanation of the Supreme Court shall be taken into consideration, and based on the per capita disposable income of urban residents and per capita net income of rural residents in the last year, in comparison of Article 50 Sub-paragraph 11 of the Regulations on the Handling of Medical Accidents. If the victim was dead, the maximum length of compensation should not exceed six years; if the victim was disabled, the maximum length of compensation should not exceed three years. Therefore, SHAN Yongzhen, JIA Xiuli and WU Anyang should obtain a spiritual damage compensation in sum ofRMB36,285.6 yuan, resulted from the calculation formula: RMB30,238 yuan per year* 6 years * 20% (LIANG Mingren should bear 20% of liability). According to Article 29 of the Interpretation of the Supreme People's Court on Certain Issues concerning the Application of Law in the Trial of Cases Involving Compensation for Personal Injury, when it referred to the compensation for death, SHAN Yongzhen, JIA Xiuli and WU Anyang should obtainRMB120,952 yuan, RMB30,238 yuan per year * 20 years * 20% (LIANG Mingren should bear 20%of liability). In respect of the traffic expenses, SHAN Yongzhen, JIA Xiuli and WU Anyang did not provide relevant documents to support the claim of SHAN Yongzhen, JIA Xiuli and WU Anyang, the court of first instance did not support. In respect of the living expenses for dependents, according to the provisions of the Interpretation of the Supreme People's Court on Certain Issues concerning the Application of Law in the Trial of Cases Involving Compensation for Personal Injury, SHAN Yongzhen, JIA Xiuli and WU Anyang were entitled to claim. The accident happened on May 31, 2014, the dependents was born on July 18, 1941, based on the Relevant Data of Standards for Compensation of Traffic Accident Damages of Dalian City in 2014, the living expenses shall be RMB5,481.6 yuan, RMB22,516 yuan per year * 7 years / 5 persons * 20% (LIANG Mingren should bear 20%of liability).SHAN Yongzhen, JIA Xiuli and WU Anyang claimed that funeral expenses in sum of RMB13,912 yuan to preserve the body and funeral and interment should be included in the funeral expenses and the court of first instance did not support the above claim. All the aforesaid compensation is in total of

RMB169,023.68 yuan, LIANG Mingren should pay to SHAN Yongzhen, JIA Xiuli and WU Anyang. According to Articles 10, 18, 22, 28 and 29 of the Interpretation of the Supreme People's Court on Certain Issues concerning the Application of Law in the Trial of Cases Involving Compensation for Personal Injury, LIANG Mingren should compensate SHAN Yongzhen, JIA Xiuli and WU Anyang for death compensations in amount of RMB120,952 within 10 days after the judgment came into effect; LIANG Mingren should compensate SHAN Yongzhen, JIA Xiuli and WU Anyang for spiritual damage compensation in amount of RMB36,285.6 within 10 days after the judgment came into effect; LIANG Mingren should compensate SHAN Yongzhen for living expenses for dependents in amount of RMB6,304.48 within 10 days after this judgment came into effect. LIANG Mingren should compensate SHAN Yongzhen, JIA Xiuli and WU Anyang for funeral expenses in amount of RMB5,481.6. The amount of the above compensation items was RMB169,023.68 in total. The court of first instance did not support the other claims of SHAN Yongzhen, JIA Xiuli and WU Anyang. Court acceptance fee of first instance in amount of RMB11,804 which had been prepaid by SHAN Yongzhen, JIA Xiuli and WU Anyang, RMB9,312 should be borne by SHAN Yongzhen, JIA Xiuli and WU Anyang, and RMB2,492 should be borne by LIANG Mingren. LIANG Mingren should pay the above sum to SHAN Yongzhen, JIA Xiuli and WU Anyang.

After the judgment was published, SHAN Yongzhen, JIA Xiuli and WU Anyang refused to accept the original judgment and appealed to the court, the Appellants claimed that:1. the relationship between the deceased WU Zhong and the Respondent LIANG Mingren was relationship of employment contract, it was wrong that the original judgment recognized it as relationship of contract for work; 2. the original judgment violated the principle of fairness in determining the ratio of liability, it constituted incorrect application of law. Summing up the above, the original judgment was unclear in determination of facts, so the Appellants request the court to amend the first-instance judgment according to law or remand for retrial.

LIANG Mingren defended that: the deceased WU Zhong was engaged in individual welding work in Donggang, Dandong. He usually associated business on the shore and did not only provide welding work for the ship of LIANG Mingren, and WU Zhong used his own tools to finish work every time, LIANG Mingren paid WU Zhong every time he finished welding work. Thus, it was proper that the original judgment ascertained the relationship between LIANG Mingren and WU Zhong as work contract. Therefore, the facts were clearly ascertained and the law was correctly applied in the original judgment, the court should dismiss the appeal of SHAN Yongzhen, JIA Xiuli and WU Anyang and affirm the original judgment.

The facts found by the court are consistent with those found by the original judgment.

The court holds that the outstanding issues in this case lie in whether the relationship between LIANG Mingren and WU Zhong is employment contract and whether the ratio of responsibility is properly determined in the original judgment.

Article 215 of the Contract Law of People's Republic of China stipulates that "a contract for work is a contract whereby the contractor shall, in light of the requirements of the ordering party, complete certain work and deliver the results therefrom, and the ordering party pays the remuneration therefor. Work includes processing, ordering, repairing, duplicating, testing, inspecting, etc." According to Article 10 of the Interpretation of the Supreme People's Court on Certain Issues concerning the Application of Law in the Trial of Cases Involving Compensation for Personal Injury, "if the contractor is responsible for any damage or damage to the third person in the course of his work, the contractor shall not be liable for compensation. But the ordering party has fault in manufacturing, ordering, appointment, he shall bear the corresponding liability".

In this case, LIANG Mingren ordered his staff who was in charge of ship repair and maintenance to telephone WU Zhong for repairing oil tank who was responsible for logistic repairing. Then WU Zhong brought his own welding tools and materials to start welding work on ship owned by LIANG Mingren. Judging from the previous settlement of work between LIANG Mingren and WU Zhong, the payment was based on the working results delivered by WU Zhong, such situation is in light with the constructive elements of contract for work. Therefore, it is proper for original judgment to identify the relationship between LIANG Mingren and WU Zhong as relationship of contract for work. As for the ground for relationship of employment contract between LIANG Mingren and WU Zhong alleged by SHAN Yongzhen, JIA Xiuli and WU Anyang in the appeal, the court holds that: there is no relationship of control, domination and subordination between WU Zhong and LIANG Mingren when WU Zhong carried out the welding work. In addition, welding work is not part of operation activities of the fishing ship owned by LIANG Mingren.WU Zhong got the lump sum paid by LIANG Mingren in manner of delivering the welding result. It is not sustainable services that WU Zhong provided to LIANG Mingren for fix income regularly. Thus, there is no existence of relationship of contract for work between WU Zhong and LIANG Mingren, so the court does not support the ground of appeal held by SHAN Yongzhen, JIA Xiuli and WU Anyang.

In respect of the issue whether the ratio of liability is properly determined by the original judgment, the victim WU Zhong should know that he only possessed a welder job skill certificate but not a post qualification. Thus he has greater fault to be actively engaged in welding oil tank in this case in the case where he did not have the qualification of special operation. LIANG Mingren has negligence in the selection of welder, he did not verify whether WU Zhong had the qualification of special operation. In view of the reason of faults of both parties in this case, the victim WU Zhong has great fault and should be mainly responsible for this accident involved, while LIANG Mingren had negligence in selection and shall assume secondary liability. Therefore, it is proper that the original judgment determined that the victim WU Zhong and LIANG Mingren should both assume the responsibility primary and secondary liability within the range in proportion of 8:2.

In conclusion, according to Article 170 Paragraph 1 Sub-paragraph 1 of the Civil Procedure Law of the People's Republic of China, the judgment is as follows:

Dismiss the appeal, and affirm the original judgment.

Court acceptance fee of second instance in amount of 9,312 yuan, shall be born by SHAN Yongzhen, JIA Xiuli and WU Anyang.

The judgment is final.

Presiding Judge: GUO Li
Acting Judge: LIU Shanchao
Acting Judge: ZHANG Yansong

August 17, 2015

Clerk: ZHANG Tong

Guangzhou Maritime Court
Civil Judgment

Shenzhen COSCO Logistics Co., Ltd.
v.
Guangdong Yanlin Energy Limited by Share Ltd.

(2012) Guang Hai Fa Chu Zi No.910

Related Case(s) This is the judgment of first instance and the judgment of second instance is on page 1042.

Cause(s) of Action 212. Dispute over voyage charter party.

Headnote The Plaintiff agent held entitled to recover indemnity from the Defendant for damages the Plaintiff had to pay to third party ship owner as a result of the Defendant's failure to load vessel voyage-chartered by the Plaintiff on the Defendant's behalf.

Summary The Plaintiff was hired by the Defendant to voyage charter a ship in order to transport the Defendant's cargo of coal. The Plaintiff then contracted with a third party, Jaldhi Overseas Pte Ltd., and entered into a voyage charter for one of their vessels that suited the needs of the Defendant. When Jaldhi Overseas Pte Ltd. delivered the ship to the agreed port of loading, the Defendant failed to produce its cargo for loading, causing the Plaintiff to cancel its voyage charter with Jaldhi and to pay damages accordingly. The Plaintiff sued, seeking damages from the Defendant for its breach of its undertaking. The court found that there was a clear breach by the Defendant in not fulfilling its obligations pursuant to the voyage charter and that this directly led to Plaintiff's breach of its voyage charter with Jaldhi. For these reasons, it awarded the Plaintiff compensation for its payment to Jaldhi Overseas Pte Ltd. and interest.

Judgment

The Plaintiff: Shenzhen COSCO Logistics Co., Ltd.
Domicile: No.2501 of Liantai Building, Zhuzilin Road, Futian District, Shenzhen, Guangdong.
Legal representative: ZHANG Bo, executive director of the company.

Agent *ad litem*: FAN shu'an, lawyer of Guangdong Haili Law Firm.
Agent *ad litem*: Hou Fuzhi, lawyer of Guangdong Haili Law Firm.

The Defendant: Guangdong Yanlin Energy Limited by Share Ltd.
Domicile: Room 504, Block 2, China Phoenix Building, No.2 6–3 Central Area, Futian District, Shenzhen, Guangdong.
Legal representative: CAI Jiatong, general manager.
Agent *ad litem*: WANG Yong, lawyer of Beijing Long'an (Shenzhen) Law Firm.
Agent *ad litem*: HUANG Shi, lawyer of Beijing Long'an (Shenzhen) Law Firm.

With respect to the case arising from dispute over contract of voyage charter the Plaintiff Shenzhen COSCO Logistics Co., Ltd. filed the litigation against the Defendant Guangdong Yanlin Energy Limited by Share Ltd. before the court on August 29, 2012. After entertaining this case, the court organized a collegiate panel consisted of Judges XIONG Shaohui, PINGYANG Danke and QU Xin, to try the case according to the law. Judge XIONG Shaohui served as Presiding Judge and Clerk ZENG Huifen served as Clerk. During the trial, Judges of collegiate panel, XIONG Shaohui and QU Xin were replaced by Judges CHANG Weiping and LI Lifei, besides, PINGYANG Danke was appointed to be Presiding Judge. On November 26, 2013, the court summoned all parties to exchange evidence before hearing and held a hearing in public on November 27. FAN shu'an, agent *ad litem* of the Plaintiff and HUANG Shi, agent *ad litem* of the Defendant appeared in court and participated in the hearing. Now the case has been concluded.

The Plaintiff alleged that: on May 10, 2012, the Plaintiff signed the contract of the voyage charter party with the Defendant and agreed that the Plaintiff rent M.V. IVS Kwaito or other substitute vessels to the Defendant, and the vessel would transport 33,000 tons of steam coals from Muara Satui, Kalimantan Island, the south of the Republic of Indonesia to Huizhou Port, Guangdong, China. In order to fulfill the charter party which signed with the Defendant, the Plaintiff and Jaldhi Overseas Pte Ltd. (hereinafter referred to as "Jaldhi Company") established voyage charter party and agreed that Jaldhi Company would charterM.V. "IVS Kwaito" or other substitute vessels to the Plaintiff to transport 33,000 tons of steam coal from Muara Satui, Kalimantan Island, the south of the Republic of Indonesia to Huizhou Port, Guangdong, China. After signing of the above charter party, M.V. "Sentosa" arrived at the loading port on schedule during the loading period which was agreed in the contract. And on the same day of arrival of the vessel (May 21, 2012), a notice of readiness was issued to the Defendant, but the Defendant failed to prepare the goods on schedule. On June 1, for the reason that the Defendant failed to prepare the goods on schedule, the Plaintiff was notified to cancel the charter party. On the same day, the Plaintiff notified Jaldhi Company to cancel the charter party, and this act led to a claim against the Plaintiff submitted by Jaldhi Company. Later Jaldhi Company raised an arbitration against the Plaintiff in Hong Kong International Arbitration Center. The relevant arbitral awards claimed that the losses should be compensated by the Plaintiff to Jaldhi Company, and the Plaintiff had already paid the compensation. But the Defendant failed to prepare the goods pursuant to the provisions of the charter party, and this constituted a fundamental breach of contract, thus the Defendant should compensate all the losses to the Plaintiff for its default. Requesting the court to order that: 1. The Defendant should compensate RMB662,397.97 to the Plaintiff for its breach of contract, including the compensation and its interest USD65,435.82 to Jaldhi Company, after deducting USD8,400 of the prepaid freight paid to the Plaintiff by the Defendant, the amount of compensation and its interest in arbitral awards, which stated that the Plaintiff should pay to the Defendant (calculated by the exchange rate of 1 to 6.1571 for dollar against renminbi on June 28, 2013, amount to RMB351,175.25. The interest according to the loan interest rate of the Bank of China over the same period from June 29, 2013 to the day of payment agreed in the judgment) and 9,192 lb and its interests of lawyer's fee and arbitration fee of Jaldhi Company arising from the arbitration in Hong Kong (calculated by the exchange rate of 1 to 9.3902 for pound against renminbi on June 28, 2013, amount to RMB86,314.72. The interest according to the loan interest rate of the Bank of China over the same period from June 29, 2013 to the day of payment agreed in the judgment), RMB220,000 and the interest of the lawyer's fee of the Plaintiff arising from the arbitration in Hong Kong (the interest according to the loan interest rate of the Bank of China over the same period from October 18, 2013 to the day of payment agreed in the judgment), HKD3,500 of the notarization fee of Hong Kong arbitration award (calculated by the exchange rate of 1 to 0.7880 for renminbi against Hong Kong dollar on October 16, 2013, amount to RMB2,758), and RMB2,150 of the translation fee for relevant documents; 2. the Defendant should compensate the loss of commission fee USD11,550 and its interest to the Plaintiff (the interest according to the loan interest rate of the Bank of China over the same period from the day it was changed into renminbi on June 5, 2012 to the day of payment which was agreed in the judgment); 3. the Defendant should bear all the litigation costs of the case, including the application fee for property preservation.

The Plaintiff submitted the following evidence materials within the time limit of burden of proof: 1. charter party between the Plaintiff and the Defendant, and between the Plaintiff and Jaldhi Company; 2. notice of readiness of the vessel; 3. statement of facts within lay time; 4. notice of withdrawal of the vessel; 5. the lawyer's letter and attachment presented to the Plaintiff offered by Jaldhi Company's agent *ad litem*; 6. Hong Kong arbitration award; 7. e-mails between the Plaintiff and Jaldhi Company, and the payment voucher of compensation which paid by the Plaintiff to Jaldhi Company; 8. agency appointment contract and logging record between the Plaintiff and Guangdong Haili Law Firm, and the payment voucher that the Plaintiff paid to the attorneys; 9.notarization fees of Hong Kong arbitration award and the payment voucher of relevant documents' translation fee.

The Defendant alleged that: 1.the Defendant had no objection to the Plaintiff's plea that the Plaintiff should pay the compensation to Jaldhi Company according to the Hong Kong arbitration award, but it claimed that the compensation should be based on the balance of USD53,996 according to the arbitration award after deducting USD8,400 of the extra prepaid freight which paid by the Defendant, not including the interest of the compensation. Due to the Plaintiff's claims, the lawyer's fee and arbitration fee of Jaldhi Company, the lawyer's fee, notarization fee and translation fee of the Plaintiff, the Defendant assumed that its act of withdrawal of the vessel did not necessarily led to the arbitration in Hong Kong between the Plaintiff and Jaldhi Company, and these fees had no necessary legal relationship with the charter party between the Plaintiff and the Defendant or with the case; 2. with respect to the loss of the commission which was requested by the Plaintiff, the Defendant argued that pursuant to the provisions of the charter party between the Plaintiff and the Defendant, the commission should be USD11,400.55; 3. as for the litigation cost the Plaintiff requested, the Defendant argued that it should be bore based on the proportion of victory ratio between the Plaintiff and the Defendant in this case.

The Defendant submitted the following evidence materials within the time limit for evidence submission: 1.charter party between the Plaintiff and the Defendant; 2. e-mails between the Plaintiff and the Defendant; 3. payment voucher of USD92,400 that the Defendant paid to the Plaintiff; 4. bank foreign exchange record of the Defendant; 5. business license of the translation company that in charge of the Chinese translation according to the above evidence materials.

After the cross-examination of evidence, the Plaintiff and the Defendant had no objection to the authenticity of the evidence which submitted by the Plaintiff and the Defendant to each other, and the court shall confirm it. The Defendant claimed that the charter party submitted by the Plaintiff between the Plaintiff and Jaldhi Company, the lawyer's letter and attachment presented to the Plaintiff submitted by agent *ad litem*, who was entrusted by Jaldhi Company, the agency appointment contract and logging record between the Plaintiff and Guangdong Haili Law Firm, the payment voucher that the Plaintiff paid the lawyer's fee, notarization fees of Hong Kong arbitration award, and the payment voucher about relevant documents' translation fee were lack of relevancy to the case. The court reckons that the above evidence were related to the disputes in this case and confirmed its relevancy. The Plaintiff argued that e-mails between the Plaintiff and the Defendant concerning the record of withdrawal of the vessel should not be accepted, but the court reckoned that the authenticity of this evidence should be confirmed. As to whether the content was sufficient to prove the facts of the case, it was necessary to make a comprehensive judgment on the basis of combining other certain facts and evidence.

According to the facts confirmed by the Plaintiff and the Defendant and the evidence that was confirmed above, the court ascertains the facts as follows:

On May 10, 2012, the Plaintiff and the Defendant signed a charter party based on the form of fixture note, the Plaintiff as the shipowner and the Defendant as the charterer. Both parties agreed that the Plaintiff chartered M.V. "IVS Kwaito" (32,573 tons of the deadweight) or other substitute vessels to the Defendant to transport 29,000 to 33,000 tons of steam coals from Muara Satui, the Republic of Indonesia to Huizhou Port, Guangdong, China. The laydays of goods was from May 15 to 23 and the fee was 14 dollars per ton. The loading and discharging lesser was not responsible for the loading, unloading, stowage and trimming (FIOST BSS 1/1). The charterer should, within 1 day after the conclusion of the contract, pay 20% of the freight to the shipowner in advance, and should pay the freight and the commission excluding the prepaid part to the lesser within 3 days after the loading was completed. The demurrage was USD11,000 per day and the despatch was 50% of the demurrage. And if the demurrage, despatch or dead freight was originated at the loading port, these fees should be paid together with the freight. The charterer should guarantee to prepare the goods and relevant documents before the arrival of the vessel and start loading within 48 h thereafter. The commission should be accounted as 2.5% of the freight/demurrage/despatch. On the same day, the Plaintiff signed a charter party with Jaldhi Company. Jaldhi Company was the charterer and the Plaintiff was the shipowner, and the parties agreed on that Jaldhi Company should charter M.V. "Sentosa" (36,205 tons of the deadweight) to the Plaintiff. And the rest of agreed contents including the quantity, loading and discharging ports, laydays, freight, prepaid freight, demurrage and period of stock by the charterer should be consistent with the charter party between the Plaintiff and the Defendant. On May 11, the Defendant prepaid USD92,400 to the Plaintiff. On May 15, the Plaintiff paid USD84,000 to Jaldhi Company in advance.

On May 21, 2012, M.V. "Sentosa" arrived at the anchorage of Muara Satui, the Republic of Indonesia and the notice of readiness was issued at 1200 h of the local time. On the same day, the Plaintiff notified the Defendant the above information by e-mails, claiming that M.V. "Sentosa" arrived at the loading port and get ready for the pseudo loading of 33,000 tons of goods under the terms of the loading charter party, but the Defendant failed to load the goods within 48 h. On May 26, the Plaintiff sent the Defendant an e-mail claiming that the vessel arrived at the loading port at 1200 h on May 21 and submitted the notice of readiness, but had not received the information about the readiness of the goods from the Defendant. The vessel was still at the loading port and the grab machine was prepared to load goods, thus any delay, damage, and relevant fees caused by faults of the goods preparation by the Defendant shall be paid by the Defendant. On May 28, the Defendant responded to the Plaintiff that M.V. "Sentosa" caused demurrage due to the cargo owner failed to supply the goods. And even till now, the cargo owner had not paid the demurrage yet. So if the Defendant still failed to receive the payment before 1200 h that day, the Defendant should withdraw the vessel and cancel this contract as well. On May 29, the Defendant again sent an e-mail to the Plaintiff, apart from affirming the e-mail content on May 26, it also claimed that if the Defendant failed to load goods within 48 h after the arrival of the vessel, it should notify the Plaintiff in advance and pay the compensation according to the provisions of the fixture note. It required the Defendant to fulfill the obligation according to the contract and provide the logging record of M.V. "Sentosa". On June 1, the Defendant emailed the Plaintiff that due to the fact that the cargo owner failed to supply goods in time, M.V. "Sentosa" now was still in demurrage which should be paid by the cargo owner, but the cargo owner had not paid any compensation, thus the Defendant decided to withdraw the vessel. In the same day, the Plaintiff responded that the Defendant failed to fulfill the fixture note and withdrew the vessel, his act breached the contract, thus the Plaintiff shall require the Defendant to bear all the losses or damages arising therefrom. On June 2, the Plaintiff notified Jaldhi Company to withdraw the vessel. On June 3, M.V. "Sentosa" left Muara Satui, the Republic of Indonesia.

On June 6, 2012, the Plaintiff sent an e-mail to the Defendant claiming that the Plaintiff and the Defendant both signed the charter party. M.V. "Sentosa" arrived at the loading port on schedule, waited for the shipment and got ready the loading machine. But later, the transportation was cancelled by the Defendant due to fact that the delay of the goods, thus the vessel left the loading port on June 3. The Plaintiff has fulfilled the obligation of the lesser and caused much extra fees, amounting to USD287,253.1. Due to the fact that the breach of the charter party by the Defendant, the above fee arising from its breach shall be compensated by the Defendant if the Plaintiff requested.

On July 31, 2012, Jackson Parton Solicitor on behalf of Jaldhi Company sent a lawyer's letter to the Plaintiff, claiming that Jaldhi Company should start an arbitration process against the Plaintiff to claim the loss of breach of contract in amount of USD175,627.40 pursuant to the provisions in the charter party and request the Plaintiff to respond before August 7. On August 5, the Plaintiff sent an e-mail to the Defendant, claiming that the loss that suffered by the Plaintiff under the provisions of the charter party was USD175,627.40. On August 7, the Plaintiff sent an e-mail again to Jaldhi Company, claiming that it was willing to pay USD50,000 to settle the dispute. On August 8, Jackson Parton Solicitor sent an e-mail again to the Plaintiff, claiming that Jaldhi Company would not accept the solution submitted by the Plaintiff and the claim of Jaldhi Company shall add the demurrage in amount of USD82,083.33. So the total loss that the Plaintiff should compensate to Jaldhi Company was USD257,750.73, and the Plaintiff was requested to give a respond before August 17. Otherwise, Jaldhi Company should start the arbitration process against the Plaintiff to claim the above losses.

On September 8, 2012, the Plaintiff and Jaldhi Company jointly appointed a resident of the Hong Kong Special Administrative Region, YANG Liang Yee Philip as the sole arbitrator to arbitrate the disputes between the parties of the voyage charter, according to the Hong Kong Arbitration Ordinance (Chapter 609). In the process of arbitration, Jaldhi Company claimed that the Plaintiff should compensate the loss of USD259,429.05, interests and other charges arising therefrom, for the reason that the Plaintiff breached the charter party and failed to prepare the goods. The Plaintiff admitted its responsibilities, but raised objections to the amount of loss submitted by Jaldhi Company. On March 18, 2013, the sole arbitrator YANG Liang Yee Philip made the final award: (A) the Plaintiff should pay the compensation in amount of USD62,396 to Jaldhi Company; (B) the Plaintiff should pay the interests (from June 5, 2012 to the day of payment, according to a 4.5% annual interest) of the compensation in amount of USD62,396 to Jaldhi Company; (C) the Plaintiff should bear his own relevant expenses and should pay 35% of the recoverable fee in this arbitration of Jaldhi Company (to be negotiated, if the negotiation failed, the arbitrator expressly reserved the arbitrator's jurisdiction and power to evaluate and determine the scope of recoverable fee of Jaldhi Company and made further decisions about the cost); the Plaintiff should bear and pay 60% of the cost of the final award (Jaldhi Company should bear and pay the rest 40% of the cost). The sole arbitrator estimated this final award as HKD99,450 and if any party paid the part beyond its share, thus it should have the right to obtain the payment back from the other party (if arbitration parties did not contact the sole arbitrator about the (C) verdict within 28 days after receiving (C) verdict, (C) verdict would become effective).

From June 13 to 26, 2013, the Plaintiff contacted Jaldhi Company for several times via e-mails to fulfill the above arbitration award and finally negotiated that the Plaintiff paid the compensation in amount of USD62,396 and the interest in amount of USD3,039.82 from June 5, 2012 to June 28, 2013 to Jaldhi Company (total principal and interest were USD65,435.82), the arbitration fee was changed into 5,152 lb from 60% of HKD9,9450, 35% of the recoverable fee, 4,040 lb, of Jaldhi Company (including lawyer's fee in sum of 11,150.50 lb, appointed arbitrator fee of HKD4,000 which equals to 345.28 lb, 49.88 lb of the express fee from Hong Kong region to the Mainland of China). On June 28, the Plaintiff paid Jaldhi Company USD65,435.82 and 9,192 lb. Above foreign currencies were purchased respectively under the exchange rate of 1 to 6.1571 for dollar against renminbi and 1 to 9.3902 for pound against renminbi by the Plaintiff, but in fact it cost RMB402,894.89 and RMB86,314.72.

On August 13, 2012, the Plaintiff entrusted lawyers FAN shu'an and XU Hongkai from Guangdong Haili Law Firm as agents for the voyage charter contract dispute between it and Jaldhi Company. On November 17, 2013, the Plaintiff paid Guangdong Haili Law Firm RMB220,000 as Hong Kong arbitration fee.

On October 16, 2013, the Plaintiff paid Hong Kong Deacons Solicitors & Notaries the notarization fee of arbitration award for HKD3,500. The above Hong Kong dollars, the Plaintiff purchased respectively under the exchange rate of 1 to 0.7880 for renminbi against Hong Kong dollar, but in fact it costed RMB2,758.

On April 15 and October 18, 2013, the Plaintiff respectively paid Shenzhen Daxinya Translation Co., Ltd. and Shenzhen Bilan Translation Co., Ltd. RMB750 and RMB1,400 as the translation fees.

The court, pursuant to the Plaintiff's application for property preservation, rendered (2012) Guang Hai Fa Bao Zi N0.101–2 and (2012) Guang Hai Fa Chu Zi No.910–1 respectively on August 20 and December 18, 2012. The court successively froze the Defendant's bank deposit of RMB1.65 million and RMB590,000. The Plaintiff paid the application fee of property preservation of RMB5,000 and 3,470 to the court in advance. On June 5, 2013, on account of altering claims, the Plaintiff applied to cancel the freeze of the Defendant's bank deposits of RMB590,000, thus relevant deposits were automatically unfroze on June 18. On November 27, on the grounds that the Plaintiff changed his claim, the Plaintiff requested the court to change the amount of the Defendant's frozen bank deposit from RMB1.65 million to RMB750,000. The court approved a Civil Ruling of (2012) Guang Hai Fa Chu Zi No.910–2 and altered the amount of the Defendant's frozen bank deposit to RMB750,000.

The Plaintiff and the Defendant in the trial had the mutual consent for choosing the law of the People's Republic of China to solve the substantive disputes in the case.

The court holds that:

The case is a dispute over the voyage charter party. The voyage charter transportation between the Plaintiff and the Defendant was from Muara Satui, the Republic of Indonesia to Huizhou Port, Guangdong, China, and the transportation contained foreign factors. According to Article 16 of the Some Provisions of the Supreme Court on the Scope of Cases to be Entertained by Maritime Courts, the disputes of voyage charter party belong to the exclusive jurisdiction case of the maritime court. The domicile of the Defendant in this case was in Shenzhen, Guangdong, and was within the jurisdiction of the court. According to Article 2 Paragraph 3 of Chapter 6 of the Special Maritime Procedure Law of the People's Republic of China, "if the lawsuit incurred for the contract dispute of the vessel rental, the case shall be in the jurisdiction of following maritime courts, the place of the port of delivery, port of redelivery, port of registry or forum where the Defendant domicile was located", the court has jurisdiction over the case. The Plaintiff and the Defendant both agreed to solve the substantive disputes of this case pursuant to the laws of the People's Republic of China. According to Article 269 of the Maritime Code of the People's Republic of China, the court applies the laws of the People's Republic of China to solve substantive disputes.

The Plaintiff and the Defendant signed the charter party, agreeing that the Plaintiff shall rent M.V. "IVS Kwaito" or other substitute vessels to the Defendant to load and transport goods from the loading port Muara Satui, the Republic of Indonesia to the discharging port Huizhou Port, Guangdong, China. The Plaintiff was the ship owner and the Defendant was the charterer. The contract was the real intent of the two parties and had no violation to mandatory provisions of laws or administrative regulations. Thus, the contract was lawful and effective, and the two parties shall exercise their rights and perform their obligations according to the provisions of the contract and legal regulations. The Plaintiff rented M.V. "Sentosa" from Jaldhi Company in order to fulfill the above charter party and planned to arrive at the loading port within the laydays and prepared to load goods, but the Defendant failed to provide the goods agreed in the contract on schedule, and this led to the loss of the vessel and the suspension of the charter party. Pursuant to Article 100 Paragraph 2 of the Maritime Code of the People's Republic of China, "if the losses of the charterer was caused by the delay of the goods agreed in the contract, the charterer shall bear the liability to pay the compensation", the Defendant shall bear the corresponding liability for breach of contract, and paid the compensation to the Plaintiff.

The Defendant had no objection to bear the liability for breach of contract to the Plaintiff. The controversy in this case was the scope of loss that the Defendant should pay to the Plaintiff.

The Defendant requested USD57,035.82, which was the balance of USD65,435.82 of the compensation and its interest it paid to Jaldhi Company according to the arbitration award after deducting the extra prepaid freight in amount of USD8,400 paid by the Defendant, and 9,192 lb for the lawyer's fee and arbitration fee of Jaldhi Company, RMB220,000 for the arbitration fee paid by the Plaintiff, and interests of the above fees. The Defendant had no objection in

RMB62,396 of the compensation paid to Jaldhi Company and USD8,400 of the prepaid freight's extra balance paid to the Plaintiff by the Defendant according to the arbitration award, but it argued that the interests of the above compensations shall not be paid by the Defendant. And it claimed that the lawyer's fee and arbitration fee of Jaldhi Company and the Plaintiff's lawyer's fee were not related to the case, and shall not be paid by the Defendant to the Plaintiff. The case was identified that due to the fact that the Defendant failed to deliver the goods agreed in the contract on schedule, which caused M.V. "Sentosa" failed to perform the appointed transportation under the situation that it had arrived at the loading port for the shipment arranged by the Plaintiff. Thus it caused the Plaintiff was charged by Jaldhi Company and shall pay the compensation and interest to Jaldhi Company according to the arbitration awards, bearing 35% of the relevant fees and 60% of the arbitration fee of Jaldhi Company, and bearing the relevant fees of itself. The Plaintiff had paid and bearded the above fees in fact. The Plaintiff requested the balance of the above fees which should deduct the prepaid freight paid by the Defendant. And the factual losses of the Plaintiff for the breach of contract caused by the Defendant, the Defendant shall pay the compensation. Meanwhile, according to the provisions about the quantity and freight of the goods in the charter party between the Plaintiff and the Defendant, if the charter party was fulfilled, the Plaintiff at least can gain USD406,000 of 29,000 tons of goods. After deducting USD92,400 of the prepaid freight that had paid already, the Plaintiff at least shall receive USD313,600. The Plaintiff and the Defendant shall foresee this when they concluded the charter party. Now the Defendant's act of breach of contract caused that the Plaintiff could not receive the above unpaid freight. Pursuant to Paragraph 1 of Article 113 of the Contract Law of the People's Republic of China, "if one party fails to fulfill the obligation in the contract or its activity for the fulfillment of the contract is not accordance with the provisions, which causes losses to the other party, the amount of the compensation shall equal to the loss caused by breach of contract, including the profit obtained if the contract would be fulfilled. But the amount shall not exceed the loss of breach of contract that one party have foreseen or should foresee when signing the charter party." The Plaintiff could claim the loss of the above unpaid freight, but now the Plaintiff requested the Defendant to pay compensation according to the relatively lower amount of the actual loss, which was the performed of its own rights. In conclusion, the request of the Plaintiff was reasonable and should be supported. The Defendant's plea was lack of factual and legal basis, and cannot be established. The Plaintiff requested to respectively exchange USD57,035.82 and 9,192 lb into RMB351,175.25 and RMB86,314.72 according to the exchange rate of 1 to 6.1571 for dollar against renminbi and 1 to 9.3902 for pound against renminbi on June 28, 2013 (in amount of RMB437,489.97). The case was identified that the dollars and pounds paid by the Plaintiff to Jaldhi Company with renminbi was bought by foreign currency pursuant to the above rate, thus the request of the Plaintiff was reasonable, and should be supported. The Defendant shall pay the interests of the above fees. The Plaintiff applied that the above various fees should be respectively calculated from the following day of the actual payment day and the interests by the loan interest rate over the same period. The request was reasonable, and should be supported.

The Plaintiff requested HKD3,500 for the arbitration award and RMB2,150 for the documents' translation fee. The Defendant claimed that the above fees had no relation to the dispute in this case, and the Defendant shall not be responsible for the fee. These costs were costed by the Plaintiff to provide evidence in this case, and shall be paid by the Plaintiff itself. The Plaintiff's request was lack of factual and legal basis, and will not be supported.

The Plaintiff requested a charter party commission fee of USD11,550. The Defendant admitted the charter party commission requested by the Plaintiff, but remained an objection against the amount of the commission. The commission agreed by the Plaintiff and the Defendant in the charter party shall be calculated by the 2.5% of the freight, and both parties had no objection upon the freight should be calculated at USD14 per ton. The Plaintiff claimed to charge USD11,550 for 33,000 tons of goods, but the Defendant claimed to charge USD11,400.55 according to the 32,573 tons of deadweight of M.V. "IVS Kwaito". The Plaintiff and the Defendant agreed in the charter party that the Plaintiff shall rent M.V. IVS Kwaito or other vessels to the Defendant, but in fact, the Plaintiff provided M.V. "Sentosa", of which had the deadweight of 36,205 tons to fulfill the charter party. So the Defendant's request that to calculate commission according to the deadweight of M. V. "IVS Kwait" was lack of factual basis and shall not be supported. The case was identified that the Defendant paid the Plaintiff the freight of USD92,400 in advance. According to the provisions concerning the calculation of the freight and the prepaid freight in the charter party between the Plaintiff and the Defendant, USD92,400 was the prepaid freight of 33,000 tons of goods. And the Plaintiff have already notified to prepare 33,000 tons of cargoes when the Defendant was notified that M.V. "Sentosa" arrived at the loading port and ready for the shipment, and the Defendant had no objection to this. The above facts were sufficient to prove that the Defendant planned to deliver the goods in a quantity of 33,000 tons, thus it is reasonable for the commission submitted by the Plaintiff and shall be supported. Pursuant to the provisions of the charter party between the Plaintiff and the Defendant, the Defendant shall pay the interest loss of the commission. The Defendant shall pay the commission within 3 days after the loading of goods. The laydays agreed in the charter party was from May 15 to 23, 2012, thus the deadline to pay the commission of the Defendant was May 26, 2012. The interest shall be calculated on the next day, after the payment of the commission. It is reasonable for the Plaintiff to claim that the interest shall be calculated from June 5, 2012, which was the performance of its own rights and shall be supported. After exchanging USD11,550 into renminbi with the benchmark exchange rate of 1 to 6.3225 for dollar against renminbi which issued by the Bank of China, the relevant interest was calculated from that day to the day of payment agreed in the judgment according to the loan interest rate of the Bank of China over the same period.

According to Article 38 Paragraph 3 of the Measures on the Payment of Litigation Costs, the Plaintiff could list the application fee for the property preservation in the proceeding. The Plaintiff applied property preservation in order to ensure the execution of the judgment, which was caused by the Defendant's act of breach of contract. Thus the Defendant shall compensate the Plaintiff the application fee RMB8,470.

According to Article 100 Paragraph 2 in the Maritime Code of the People's Republic of China, the judgment is as follows:

1. The Defendant Guangdong Yanlin Energy Limited by Share Ltd. shall compensate the Plaintiff Shenzhen COSCO Logistics Co., Ltd. RMB437,489.97 and its interest (the interest according to the loan interest rate of the Bank of China over the same period from June 29, 2013 to the day of payment agreed in the judgment);
2. The Defendant Guangdong Yanlin Energy Limited by Share Ltd. shall pay the Plaintiff Shenzhen COSCO Logistics Co., Ltd. lawyer's fee in amount of RMB220,000 and its interest (the interest according to the loan interest rate of the Bank of China over the same period from October 18, 2013 to the day of payment agreed in the judgment);
3. The Defendant Guangdong Yanlin Energy Limited by Share Ltd. shall compensate the Plaintiff Shenzhen COSCO Logistics Co., Ltd. USD11,550 and its interest (after exchanging dollars into renminbi with the benchmark exchange rate of 1 to 6.3225 for dollar against renminbi which issued by the Bank of China on June 5, 2012, the interest was calculated from that day to the day of payment agreed in the judgment according to the loan interest rate of the Bank of China over the same period) of the charter party;
4. The Defendant Guangdong Yanlin Energy Limited by Share Ltd. shall pay the Plaintiff Shenzhen COSCO Logistics Co., Ltd. application fee for the property preservation in sum of RMB8,470;
5. Reject other claims filed by the Plaintiff Shenzhen COSCO Logistics Co., Ltd.

The above obligation of payment shall be fulfilled within 10 days after this judgment comes into effect.

If the Defendant fails to fulfill the obligation of payment within the period designated by this judgment, according to Article 253 in Civil Procedure Law of the People's Republic of China, the interest on the debt for the delayed period shall be doubled.

Court acceptance fee in amount of RMB11,159.71, the Plaintiff Shenzhen COSCO Logistics Co., Ltd. shall bear RMB82.75, and the Defendant bear RMB11,076.96.

In case of dissatisfaction with this judgment, the Plaintiff and the Defendant may within 15 days upon the service of this judgment, submit a statement of appeal to the court, together with copies according to the number of the opposing parties, and appeal to the Guangdong High People's Court.

Presiding Judge: PINGYANG Danke

Judge: CHANG Weiping

Judge: LI Lifei

August 28, 2014

Clerk: ZENG Huifen

Guangdong High People's Court
Civil Judgment

Shenzhen COSCO Logistics Co., Ltd.
v.
Guangdong Yanlin Energy Limited by Share Ltd.

(2014) Yue Gao Fa Min Si Zhong Zi No.197

Related Case(s) This is the judgment of second instance, and the judgment of first instance is on page 1031.

Cause(s) of Action 212. Dispute over voyage charter party.

Headnote Voyage charterer held liable to reimburse disponent owner for liability incurred to head charterer as a result of voyage charterer's breach; reimbursement to be in RMB because disponent owner had purchased foreign currency in RMB to pay head charterer; disponent owner not entitled to lawyer's fees for conducting arbitration in Hong Kong with head charterer as not proven that it was necessary to hire lawyers.

Summary The Defendant's breach of a voyage charter party with the Plaintiff caused the Plaintiff to incur liability to a head charterer, the amount of which was determined after arbitration between the Plaintiff and the head charterer in Hong Kong. The court held that: (1) because the Plaintiff had settled its liability to the head charterer by buying foreign currency with RMB, the Defendant should reimburse the Plaintiff in RMB, which is what is usually done between Chinese domestic enterprises; (2) the Defendant was not required to reimburse the Plaintiff its lawyer's fee for the arbitration in Hong Kong because it had not provided sufficient evidence that it was necessary to hire lawyers to conduct the arbitration; (3) the Defendant should pay the costs associated with the Plaintiff's application for an asset preservation order to secure payment of any favourable judgment. The lower court's judgment was recognized on point (1) but reversed on points (2) and (3).

Judgment

The Appellant (the Defendant of first instance): Guangdong Yanlin Energy Limited by Share Ltd.
Domicile: Room 504, Building 2, China Phoenix Mansion, Center of Futian district, Shenzhen, Guangdong.
Legal representative: CAI Jiatong, general manager.
Agent *ad litem*: HUANG Shi, lawyer of Beijing Long'an Law Firm.
Agent *ad litem*: WANG Yong, lawyer of Beijing Long'an Law Firm.

The Respondent (the Plaintiff of first instance): Shenzhen COSCO Logistics Co., Ltd.
Domicile: 2501, Liantai Mansion, Bamboo Forest, Futian district, Shenzhen, Guangdong.
Legal representative: ZHANG Bo, executive director.
Agent *ad litem*: FAN shu'an, lawyer of Guangdong Haili Law Firm.
Agent *ad litem*: JIAO Chunshan, lawyer of Guangdong Haili Law Firm.

The Appellant, Guangdong Yanlin Energy Limited by Share Ltd. (hereafter referred to as Yanlin Energy) refused to accept (2012) Guang Hai Fa Chu Zi No.910 Civil Judgment regarding voyage charter party dispute between Yanlin Energy and the Respondent Shenzhen COSCO Logistics Co., Ltd. (hereafter referred to as COSCO Logistics) made by Guangzhou Maritime Court as final and lodged an appeal to the court. After accepting the case, the court formed a collegiate panel to try the case. Agent *ad litem* of the Appellant Yanlin Energy, HUANG Shi, and agent *ad litem* of the Respondent COSCO Logistics, FAN shu'an, participated the court investigation. Now the case has been concluded.

Yanlin Energy refused to accept the original judgment, appealed to the court and requested that: revoke the first item of the original judgment and commute Yanlin Energy to COSCO LogisticsUSD53,996 for compensation; revoke the second and fourth items; all litigation costs (including case acceptance fees and preservation application fee, etc.) in the case of first instance should be assumed by COSCO Logistics and Yanlin Energy in their respective proportion stipulated by the verdict, all legal costs of the second instance shall be born by COSCO Logistics. The reasons were as follows: firstly, the charter party between Yanlin Energy and COSCO Logistics agreed on the dollar as the settlement currency, and the compensation paid to Gardy Co. Ltd. by COSCO Logistics was also in USD. So Yanlin Energy should compensate to COSCO Logistics in USD rather than in RMB converted by rates on June 28, 2013. Secondly, if COSCO Logistics paid compensation to Gardy timely, and there would not be interest accrued, which meant the compensation interest accrued from improper behavior of COSCO Logistics and there was no causal relationship with contract act of Yanlin Energy. So Yanlin Energy only needed to bear the principal amount of USD53,996, namely the compensation USD62,396 paid to Gardy by COSCO Logistics minus freight prepaid balance of USD8,400. Thirdly, COSCO Logistics arbitrated in Hong Kong to resolve the contract dispute with Gardy. According to the arbitration award, COSCO Logistics should bear some lawyer fees of Gardy as well as arbitration fees 9,192 lb. The fees of this part had no causal relationship with disputes in the case, so it should not be born by Yanlin Energy. Fourthly, COSCO Logistics paid lawyer fees RMB220,000 for its charter party arbitration with Gardy. The lawyer fees were not arising from the disputes of this case, so it should be born on its own. According to the relevant provisions of the law, even though the lawyer fees generated in the case, it shall not be assumed by Yanlin Energy.

COSCO Logistics defended in the second trial: firstly, as a domestic company, COSCO Logistics purchased foreign exchange with RMB to pay Gardy compensation payments, so the company was entitled to claim compensation in the form of RMB from Yanlin Energy. Secondly, it took time to resolve contract disputes between COSCO Logistics and Gardy. It was impossible for COSCO Logistics to pay Gardy any claim directly before an arbitral award was made or without arbitration. There was a long period of time between actually compensation payment of COSCO Logistics and breach of the contract, which was objective demands of dispute settlement. And the fundamental reason was that Yanlin Energy breached the contract with COSCO Logistics. So Yanlin Energy claimed not to bear the interest of compensation payment paid Yanlin Energy by COSCO Logistics, which was unreasonable proposition. Thirdly, Yanlin Energy's breach of contract with COSCO Logistics directly caused COSCO's breach of contract with Gardy, which as a result made the arbitration between COSCO Logistics and Gardy in Hong Kong and the former had to assume total fees 9,192 lb including some arbitration fees and some lawyer fees of Gardy. The two parts of fees were recognized by arbitration agency and had a direct causal relationship with Yanlin Energy's breach of contract, so Yanlin Energy claimed not to pay compensation, which was unreasonable. Fourthly, COSCO Logistics arbitrated in Hong Kong to solve the charter contract disputes with Gardy and paid RMB220,000 for lawyer fees. COSCO's lawyer fees were not substantially different from those of Gardy's, both of them were generated to solve the charter contract disputes and determined by arbitration award, the fundamental reason was Yanlin's default behavior. The arbitration award identified that the attorney fees shall be born by COSCO Logistics itself. So, for COSCO Logistics, this belonged to one of the losses caused by Yanlin Energy's default behavior. As a domestic enterprise, COSCO Logistics did not have the ability to go to Hong Kong to participate in the arbitration, so it was objective necessity to hire professional lawyers to participate in the arbitration instead. And it was very common in practice and accepted internationally. In terms of actual results, the final arbitration award only supported USD62,396 of more than USD350,000 claimed for compensation by Gardy. It could be seen that hiring professional lawyers had an obvious effect on reducing liquidated damages and Yanlin Energy benefited from it directly. It had reached an agreement that the disputes in the charter contract would be arbitrated in Hong Kong, so hiring lawyers participating in the arbitration could be perceived by each other. According to the contract, Yanlin Energy should pay COSCO Logistics over USD400,000 for carriage, which could be predictable in the default. However, the amount of liquidated damages including attorney fees claimed by COSCO Logistics was far less than the above amount. In terms of predictable degree, COSCO Logistics' claims did not exceed the foreseeable range of Yanlin Energy. The original judgment was not anywhere proper, requesting to dismiss the appeal and affirm the original judgment.

Both COSCO Logistics and Yanlin Energy had no objection to the facts ascertained by the original judgment in the court of second instance investigation. It has been proved that there was no anything improper in facts found out by the original judgment, and the court gave confirmation.

According to the property preservation before and in litigation in first instance, the court ascertained and added facts as follows:

To guarantee the execution of effective judgment thereafter, COSCO Logistics put forward the application for property preservation before litigation to the court of first instance, who permitted after examination. The relevant Civil Ruling (2012) Guanghai Bao Zi No.101-2 stated that: the applicant COSCO Logistics bore application fee of property preservation before litigation in sum of RMB5,000. In the first instance trial of the case, COSCO Logistics asked for litigation property preservation and the original court permitted it after investigation. The relevant Civil Ruling (2012) GuangHai Fa Chu Zi No.910-1 stated that: COSCO Logistics burdened application fee of property preservation in sum of RMB3,470, which could be included in litigation request.

According to the charter party between COSCO Company and Gardy Company and the charter party between COSCO Company and Yanlin Energy Company of trial evidence, the court ascertained and added the following facts:

Article 25 of the charter party between COSCO Logistics and Gardy was G/A Arbitration, agreeing on: if any to be settled in Hong Kong with English law to apply in case of disputes between the two sides.

The charter party between COSCO Logistics and Yanlin Energy did not achieved an agreement on the cost commitment of dispute settlement.

In the court of second instance investigation, both COSCO Logistics and Yanlin Energy confirmed that: the two sides did not negotiate or reach consensus on lawyer fees payment of arbitration between COSCO Logistics and Gardy in Hong Kong. COSCO Logistics stated a staff named HU Jian of Yanlin Energy once agreed COSCO Logistics to hire lawyers to participate in arbitration in Hong Kong orally by telephone but failed to provide evidence.

The court holds that: this case belongs to a voyage charter party dispute involving foreign elements. The court affirms the original judgment, of which there was no anything improper on case governing and application of law. The two parties had no objection to the conclusion, performance and breach of the contract in the case and the arbitration as well as the formation of arbitration decision of the charter contract disputes between COSCO Logistics and Gardy in Hong Kong. According to the appeal, defense and the court investigation, the court identified disputes in the case of second instance was the compensation items and specific amount of Yanlin Energy, including default compensation, interest and relevant costs paid to Gardy by COSCO Logistics according to arbitral decision, attorney fees paid by COSCO Logistics for arbitration in Hong Kong, and the burden on the application fees for property preservation.

1. For default compensation, interest and relevant costs paid to Gardy by COSCO Logistics according to arbitral awards.

    From the signing time and content of the charter party between COSCO Logistics and Gardy as well as Yanlin Energy, it could be seen that COSCO Logistics signed charter party with Gardy and had actually used the ships provided by Gardy, while Yanlin Energy's unilateral breach of contract forced COSCO Logistics to violate its agreement with Gardy and terminate the contract eventually, of which there was a direct causal relationship between the former and the later. Conforming to the charter party, COSCO Logistics submitted its dispute with Gardy to the arbitration agency and according to the project and amount determined by arbitration paid Gardy default compensation, interest and relevant expenses, which were caused by Yanlin Energy's default and had actually produced, so Yanlin Energy should be responsible for it. According to the provisions of charter party between COSCO Logistics and Gardy, the dispute shall be settled by arbitration in Hong Kong, and the two sides arbitrated in Hong Kong after the occurrence of dispute. Before the arbitral award was made, the specific liability for COSCO Logistics' compensation to Gardy was not clear and definite. So there was no premise condition for COSCO Logistics to pay for compensation. The arbitral award recognized that the loss of Gardy included the interest of breach of contract and relevant expenses, but only confirmed the calculation method, starting time and the proportion of bearing fees. And at the same time the arbitration indicated that the scope of fees needed to be negotiated or arbitrated further. After arbitration, COSCO Logistics and Gardy put forward clearly the deadline of interest calculation, the specific items and amount of expenses by negotiating. So far, the specific compensation liability born by COSCO Logistics to Gardy had been finally determined. COSCO Logistics performed the payment obligation timely after determination of responsibility, whose behavior was not improper, so the statement that COSCO Logistics did not pay Yanlin Energy timely, generating interest as a result, the interest should not be assumed by Yanlin Energy lacked factual basis and was not supported by the court. The basic reason of the dispute and arbitration in Hong Kong between COSCO Logistics and Gardy was Yanlin Energy's unilateral default. The arbitration, applying to English Law, listed part of arbitration fees and part of recoverable costs including attorney fees of Gardy into the scope of liability of compensation and made it clear that it shall be undertook by COSCO Logistics. However, Yanlin Energy did not give evidence to prove the arbitration was illegal or inappropriate and COSCO Logistics actually paid for it, so Yanlin Energy's statement that part of arbitration fees and Gardy's lawyer's fees totally 9,192 lb had nothing to do with this case and should not assumed by Yanlin Energy lacked factual and legal basis and was not supported. The charter party between COSCO Logistics and Yanlin Energy agreed on calculation of freight in USD but did not make it clear that the two sides must settle in USD. The funds between domestic enterprises are usually settled in RMB. Both COSCO Logistics and Yanlin Energy are domestic enterprises. COSCO Logistics performed compensatory obligations under award of arbitration to the overseas enterprise Gardy in the way of purchasing foreign exchange in RMB. So the requirement of COSCO Logistics paying for the compensation in RMB and calculating according to exchange rates was reasonable. Yanlin Energy claimed that the compensation between two parties shall be settled in USD, which is lack of evidence and was not supported. In conclusion, Yanlin Energy's statement that it only needed to pay COSCO Logistics USD53,996 for the loss lacks factual basis and is not supported. The original judgment on Yanlin Energy paying COSCO Logistics RMB437,489.97 for default loss compensation as well as expenses and the processing of interests was not improper and shall be affirmed.

2. Lawyer's fees spent by COSCO Logistics on the arbitration in Hong Kong.

The facts in the case indicated that neither COSCO Logistics nor Yanlin Energy made an agreement on undertaking the costs of resolving relevant dispute in the charter contract, negotiated and reached consensus on assuming attorney fees for the arbitration between COSCO Logistics and Gardy in Hong Kong during the process of dispute resolution. Moreover, no other facts or evidence in the case showed the rules applicable to the arbitration between COSCO Logistics and Gardy compulsively stipulated that lawyers must participate in arbitration. COSCO Logistics claimed that hiring lawyers to participate in the arbitration on behalf of the company was the international practice and objective necessity, but the company did not provide sufficient and effective evidence to prove it. According to Article 64 Paragraph 1 of the Civil Procedure Law of the People's Republic of China, the party has the responsibility to provide evidence for claims put forward by himself, and Article 90 of the Interpretation of the Supreme People's Court on the Application of the Civil Procedure Law of the People's Republic of China, the facts based on which the parties put forward their claims or refute the other party's claim should be proved with enough evidence, except those facts provided by law. Before making a judgment, the party was unable to provide evidence or evidence was insufficient to prove those claims, the party who had the responsibility for giving evidence should bear adverse consequences. COSCO Logistics should bear the adverse consequences of failing to give proof and his above proposition lacked factual basis. Accordingly, COSCO Logistics' requirement that Yanlin Energy should paid COSCO Logistics lawyer fees for arbitration in Hong Kong lacks promissory or legal basis and is not supported. Yanlin Energy's statement that the company need not assume attorney fees for the arbitration of COSCO Logistics in Hong Kong was reasonable. The decision that Yanlin Energy should pay COSCO Logistics RMB220,000 for lawyer's fees in the original judgment is improper and the court corrects the original judgment.

3. Burden on application fee for property preservation

COSCO Logistics applied to the trial court through separated case for property preservation before litigation and paid RMB5,000 for application fee, the corresponding Civil Ruling made it clear that the charges were for the account of COSCO Logistics. According to Article 10 of the Measures on the Payment of Litigation Costs, a party who, according to the law, makes an application to a people's court with respect to any of the following matters shall pay application fees: ...... (2) the application for preservation measures ......, and Article 38 Paragraph 3, the application fee provided in Article 10 Sub-paragraph 2 of the Measures shall be born by the applicant, where the applicant brings an action, the application fee may be incorporated into the claim. COSCO Logistics listed relevant application fee for property preservation before litigation into the claim at the time it filed the lawsuit of the case, which is legally. Disputes of the present case was resulted from Yanlin Energy's unilateral breach of contract, who should bear compensation liability for the loss suffered by COSCO Logistics. Measures of property preservation before litigation taken by COSCO Logistics to ensure the implementation of effective judgment was not inappropriate, thus COSCO Logistics's request that Yanlin Energy shall compensate the application fee for property preservation before litigation in sum of RMB5,000 was reasonable, and it should be supported. In the first instance of the case, COSCO Logistics applied for litigation property preservation to ensure the enforcement of judgments, thus the corresponding application fee should serve as legal costs of the case, and be addressed according to Article 29 Paragraph 2 of the Measures on the Payment of Litigation Costs, in a case where each party thereto partially loses the case, the people's court concerned shall, in light of the specific conditions of the case, determine the amount of court costs to be born by each party respectively. Judgment of first instance regarded application fee for preservation in litigation in sum of RMB3,470 of this case as compensation from Yanlin to COSCO Logistics, which is improper and should be corrected.

In summary, the facts of the original judgment were basically clear, but the application of law was wrong and the handling results was improper, the court shall correct it. Appeal from Yanlin Energy was partially reasonable, the court supports the reasonable part and did not support the unreasonable part. According to Article 100 Paragraph 2 of the Maritime Code of the People's Republic of China, Article 170 Paragraph 1 Sub-paragraph 1 and Sub-paragraph 2 of the Civil Procedure Law of the People's Republic of China, Article 90 of the Interpretation of the Supreme People's Court on the Application of the Civil Procedure Law of the People's Republic of China, Article 38 Paragraph 3 and Article 29 Paragraph 2 of the Measures on the Payment of Litigation Costs, the judgment is as follows:

1. Affirm item 1, item 3 and item 5 of (2012) Guang Hai Fa Chu Zi No.910 Civil Judgment rendered by Guangzhou Maritime Court.
2. Revoke item 2 of (2012) Guang Hai Fa Chu Zi No.910 Civil Judgment rendered by Guangzhou Maritime Court.
3. Change item 4 of (2012) Guang Hai Fa Chu Zi No.910 Civil Judgment rendered by Guangzhou Maritime Court into Yanlin Energy Company paying COSCO Logistics application fee for property preservation before litigation in sum of RMB5,000.

The obligation for paying money above should be performed within 10 days from the date that the judgment comes into effect.

If the obligor fails to fulfill its obligation to make the said payments within the time limit provided by this judgment, the interest shall be double paid for the period of deferred payment according to Article 253 of the Civil Procedure Law of the People's Republic of China.

Court acceptance fee of first instance in amount of RMB11,159.71 and application fee for litigation property preservation in amount of RMB3,470, totally RMB14,629.71, shall be born by COSCO Logistics and Yanlin Energy, respectively RMB4,388.91 and RMB10,240.8.

Court acceptance fee of second instance in amount of RMB6,302.51, shall be born by Yanlin Energy and COSCO Logistics, respectively RMB2,079.83 and RMB4,222.68. Yanlin Energy actually prepaid RMB6,302.51, RMB4222.68 was given back to Yanlin Energy by the court. COSCO Logistics shall pay the court acceptance fee in amount of RMB4,222.68 for second instance within 10 days from the date the judgment coming into effect.

The judgment is final.

Presiding Judge: DU Yixing
Acting Judge: YU Dan
Acting Judge: MO Fei

April 29, 2015

Clerk: PAN Wanqin

Appendix: Relevant Law

1. **Maritime Code of the People's Republic of China**
   Article 100 The charterer shall provide the intended goods, but he may replace the goods with the consent of the shipowner. However, if the goods replaced is detrimental to the interests of the shipowner, the shipowner shall be entitled to reject such goods and cancel the charter.
   Where the shipowner has suffered losses as a result of the failure of the charterer in providing the intended goods, the charterer shall be liable for compensation.

2. Civil Procedure law of the People's Republic of China

Article 64 A party shall have the responsibility to provide evidence in support of its own propositions.

For the evidence that cannot be obtained by any parties or their litigation representatives because of some realistic reasons or for the evidence that the people's court shall investigate and collect such evidence.

The people's court shall, according to the procedure prescribed by law, collect and examine evidence comprehensively and objectively.

Article 170 After trying a case on appeal, the people's court of second instance shall, in the light of the following situations, dispose of it accordingly:

(1) if the facts were clearly ascertained and the law was correctly applied in the original judgment, the appeal shall be rejected in the form of a judgment and the original judgment shall be recognized;
(2) if the application of the law was incorrect in the original judgment, the said judgment shall be amended according to the law;
(3) if in the original judgment the facts were incorrectly or not clearly ascertained and the evidence was insufficient, the people's court of second instance shall make a written order to set aside the judgment and remand to case to the original people's court for retrial, or the people's court of second instance may amend the judgment after investigating and clarifying the facts; or
(4) if there was violation of legal procedure in making the original judgment, which may have affected correct adjudication, the judgment shall be set aside by written order and the case remanded to the original people's court for retrial.

Th

3. Measures on the Payment of Litigation Costs

Article 6 Court costs that parties shall pay to the people's court include:

(1) Acceptance fees;
(2) Application fees; and
(3) Traveling expenses, lodging expenses, meal expense and compensation for absence from work, which arise from relevant witnesses, expert witnesses, translators or interpreters and adjusters' appearance before courts on the dates as designated by the people's court concerned.

Article 10 A party who, according to the law, makes an application to a people's court with respect to any of the following matters shall pay application fees:

(1) the application for the execution of a legally effective judgment, order, conciliation statement made by the people's court, an award or conciliation statement legally made by an arbitration institution according to the law, or a document evidencing the creditor's rights made enforceable by a notary office according to the law;

(2) the application for preservation measures;
(3) the application for an order of payment;
(4) the application for publicizing a public notice for assertion of claims;
(5) the application for setting aside an arbitration award or ascertaining the validity of an arbitration agreement;
(6) the application for bankruptcy;
(7) the application for a maritime injunction, general adjustment, constitution of a limitation fund for maritime claims, registration of maritime claims or exigency of a maritime lien; and
(8) the applicant for recognition and enforcement of a judgment or order made by a foreign court or of an award made by a foreign arbitration institution.

e partied concerned may appeal against the judgment or written order rendered in a retrial of their case.

Article 29 Court costs shall be born by the party who loses the case, unless the party who wins the case volunteers to pay the costs.

In a case where each party thereto partially loses the case, the people's court concerned shall, in light of the specific conditions of the case, determine the amount of court costs to be born by each party respectively.

Where the parties to a joint action lose the case, the people's court concerned shall, based on their respective interest in the object of action, determine the amount of court costs to be born by each of them.

Article 38 The application fee provided for in Subparagraphs (1) and (8), Article 10 of these Measures shall be born by the party subject to execution.

Where the parties reach a settlement agreement during the process of execution, the bearing of the application fee shall be determined by the parties through consultation; if the consultation fails, the bearing of the application fee shall be determined by the people's court concerned.

The application fee provided for in Subparagraph (2), Article 10 of these Measures shall be born by the applicant; where the applicant brings an action, the application fee may be incorporated into the claim.

The bearing of the application fee provided for in Subparagraph (5), Article 10 of these Measures shall be determined by the people's court concerned according to Article 29 of these Measures.

Tianjin Maritime Court
Civil Judgment

Silvery Dragon Prestressed Materials Co., Ltd. (Tianjin)
v.
Dalian Pei Hua International Logistics Co., Ltd.

(2014) Jin Hai Fa Shang Chu Zi No.698

Related Case(s) None.

Cause(s) of Action 202. Dispute over contract of carriage of goods by sea or sea-connected waters.

Headnote Contracting carrier held liable to the Plaintiff cargo owner for delivering cargo to wrong port; subcontracting actual carrier delivered to port named in its contract with contracting carrier, which was different from port named in contract between contracting carrier and the Plaintiff.

Summary The Plaintiff entered into a contract with the Defendant for the carriage of goods by sea, entrusting Defendant with 50 containers of steel to be shipped from China to Izmir Port in Turkey. The Defendant subsequently signed a contract with United Arab Shipping Co. to carry the goods. However, the bill of lading for this second contract indicated that the port of destination was Aliaga Port rather than Izmir Port. The goods were then transported to Aliaga Port and Plaintiff had to pay to have them transported to Izmir Port. Plaintiff alleged that Defendant breached the contract by delivering the goods to the wrong port, resulting in economic losses for Plaintiff. The court held that the Defendant was in breach of contract and awarded damages to Plaintiff in the amount of RMB386,393.05 plus interest. The court reasoned that the literal interpretation of the terms of the contract as stated in the bill of lading, the purpose of the contract, and standard industry practice all indicated that the ports were in fact distinct and thus the Defendant was in breach of contract by delivering the goods to the wrong port. The Court further concluded that the Plaintiff's losses were foreseeable by the Defendant at the time the contract was signed.

Judgment

The Plaintiff: Silvery Dragon Prestressed Materials Co., Ltd. (Tianjin)
Domicile: Shuangyuan Road No.62, Beichen Economic Development Zone, Tianjin.
Legal representative: XIE Tieqiao, chairman of the company.
Agent *ad litem*: LIU Zuoming, lawyer of Beijing Haitong Law Firm.
Agent *ad litem*: CHANG Jie, staff of Silvery Dragon Prestressed Materials Co., Ltd. (Tianjin).

The Defendant: Dalian Pei Hua International Logistics Co., Ltd.
Domicile: Room 303, Gaoxin Street No.3, the third floor, Qixianling Industrial Base, Dalian High Tech Industrial Park, Dalian, Liaoning.
Legal representative: LIN Youyu, chairman of the company.
Agent *ad litem*: XIA Xiaoping, lawyer of Boss & Young, Attorneys-At-Law (Shanghai).

With respect to the case arising from contract disputes in carriage of goods by sea field by the Plaintiff, Silvery Dragon Prestressed Materials Co., Ltd. (Tianjin) against the Defendant, Dalian Pei Hua International Logistics Co., Ltd., the court entertained the case on August 6,2014, applied summary procedure according to the law, and held a hearing in public according to the applicable ordinary procedure on September 15, 2014. LIU Zuoming, agent *ad litem* of the Plaintiff, XIA Xiaoping, agent *ad litem* of the Defendant, appeared in court and participated in hearing. During the trial, the case transferred to general procedure on October 22, 2014. The court organized a collegiate panel, composed of Presiding Judge CAO Ke, Acting Judge ZHANG Lina, Acting Judge WANG Huiran, who tried the case in public hearing on January 15, 2015. Agents *ad litem* of the Plaintiff were changed to LIU Zuoming and CHANG Jie, LIU Zuoming, agent *ad litem* of the Plaintiff, XIA Xiaoping, agent *ad litem* of the Defendant, took part in the litigious action. Now the case has been concluded.

The Plaintiff alleged that on June 28, 2013, the Plaintiff and the Defendant signed the contract of carriage of goods by sea, the Defendant was a carrier of the 50 containers of steel from China to Turkey. The Defendant issued a bill of lading to the Plaintiff, number of the bill of lading was TMEI13064401ZM, the Plaintiff was the shipper recorded on the bill of lading, the Defendant was the contractual carrier, the recorded unloading port was Izmir Port (Turkey). On June 28, 2013, the Defendant and the actual carrier (UNITED ARAB SHIPPING COMPANY S.A.G, hereinafter referred to as the Emirates Company) signed a contract of carriage. The actual carrier issued another bill of lading to the Defendant. The bill of lading recorded that the shipper was the Defendant, the port of discharge was changed to Aliaga Port. This changes were done by the Defendant unilaterally, and he did not notice the Plaintiff, so the Plaintiff did not know, either. On August 21, 2013, the actual carrier delivered and unloaded the goods to Aliaga Port instead of Izmir Port. Through negotiations with the Defendant, the Defendant argued that there were two berths in Izmir Port, Aliaga is one of the two berths, so Izmir Port and Aliaga Port was the same port, the carrier's unloading behavior did not violate the contract of transportation. In fact, the above two ports were two completely different and independent to each other. In the case of unsuccessful negotiations with the Defendant, the Plaintiff was forced to entrust agent in Turkey to transfer the goods involved from Aliaga Port to agreed Izmir Port on September 17, 2013, and delivered to the consignee, and thus produced a series of charges, including terminal storage fee, inland transfer fee, container demurrage, discharge fee, equal to RMB404,812.78.If the Defendant was subject to the contract, which delivered the goods to the port of discharge stipulated in the bill of lading, then it would not produce the above costs. Therefore, the Plaintiff requested the Court ordered that first, the Defendant compensated the Plaintiff the costs caused by the goods that were not unloaded in the stipulated bill of lading, amounting to a total of 404812.78 yuan and above amounts would calculate the interests since October 30, 2013 to the date of actual payment according to the People's Bank of China the same period of the loan interest rate; second, the case acceptance fee 7,386 yuan should be born by the Defendant.

The Defendant defended that firstly, the port of discharge to which the Plaintiff was entrusted to the Defendant was expressed as "LANDED IZMIR PORT", the Defendant had delivered the goods to Turkey Izmir City according to the Plaintiff's requirement, in the shipping market, the English word "IZMIR" had no special meaning, Izmir city had two ports, the Plaintiff failed to clarify shipped to the which port to the Defendant, so the Defendant had completed the contract obligations no matter how transported to any port. Secondly, the cost requested by the Plaintiff had exceeded which the Defendant should fulfill the obligations according to the contract, the Defendant should not bear the cost of transshipment of the Plaintiff.

According to the Plaintiff's claims and the Defendant's plea, the court summed up the focus of controversy on this case lies: firstly, whether the Defendant had fulfilled obligation in the contract that carrying the goods involved to the agreed port of destination or not. Secondly, if the Defendant was breach of contract, whether it should bear the liability for the loss of the Plaintiff. Thirdly, the Plaintiff's the losses and the specific amount of interest.

The evidence presented by the Plaintiff to support its claims: 1. the bill of lading No.TMEI13064401ZM issued by the Defendant to prove that the unloading port and delivery place recorded on the bill of lading was Turkey Izmir Port, transport clause was CY/CY; 2. the bill of ladingNo.CNXGG062768 issued by the Emirates Company to prove that the unloading port recorded on the bill of lading was Aliaga Port, transport clause was CY/FO; 3. the outsider COSCO Container Lines Co. Ltd. (hereinafter referred to as COSCO Company) in Turkey agent Company Marti Container Services S.A., (hereinafter referred to as Marti Company) sent an e-mail to the Plaintiff's attorney LIU Zuoming lawyer, the e-mail, the notarization of this e-mail, and the registration certificate of Marti Company, all could prove that Izmir Port and Aliaga Port were not the same port, not the one operating Company, not the port authority, and because the consignee of goods involved (T.C. Devlet Demiryollari Isletmesi Genel Mudurlugu Gar Ankara Turkiye, hereinafter referred to as TCDD Company) was the operator of Izmir Port, all the container operating costs of the goods unloaded to Izmir Port were free; 4. two port operators public website information to prove that Izmir Port was exist, the operator was TCDD Company, which was a state-owned enterprise. Aliaga Port is a private Company, which was called Ege Gübre Sanayi A.S.; 5. Turkey local agent EDA Endustriyel Dis Ticaret. A.S. (hereinafter referred to as EDA Company) on behalf of the Plaintiff to pay the payment produced in Aliaga Port, the payment voucher, the e-mail, the invoice to prove that the additional costs happened from August 21, 2013 to September 17 were a total of USD14,714.32; 6. the inland transport fee invoice and payment vouchers to prove that the inland transport fees from Aliaga Port to Izmir Port were 35,518 Turkish Lira; 7. NORA International Forwarding Co., Ltd. (hereinafter referred to as NORA Company) issued the demurrage invoice, demurrage details, EDA payment bank receipts and bank drafts to prove that the demurrage costs from September 10, 2013 to 23 were USD22,160; 8. Unloading fee invoice, payment memo and related email issued by NORA Company to prove that the additional charges paid to NORA Company was USD6,195; 9. the temporary receipt invoices and bank payment memo issued by NORA Company to prove that the additional charges paid to NORA Company was 10,165.41 Turkish Lira; 10. the statement of the facts and the attachment, the evidence was the agent EDA detailed description of the whole event, as well as the letter and reply of EDA Company to the local competent authority for inquiry to prove that Aliaga Port and Izmir Port were not the same port, and the additional costs of the goods because inland transportation from Aliaga Port to Izmir Port; 11. booking note to prove that the port of discharge agreed between the Plaintiff and the Defendant was Izmir Port; 12. the letter of attorney to prove that the Plaintiff authorized EDA Company to deal with the relevant matters of the goods involved in Turkey; 13. on August 28, 2013, the e-mails between the Plaintiff and the Defendant to prove that Aliaga Port was not the port that the Plaintiff specified in the bill of lading, which requested to transport the goods to Izmir Port. The Defendant claimed that the above were just two docks and refused to arrange transport, and requested the consignee to arrange transportation on their own and bear the cost; 14. on August 28, 2013, the e-mail sent by Tianjin branch to agent of the Plaintiff of loading Awot Global (hereinafter referred to as Awot Global Tianjin Corporation) to prove that the Defendant said that the carrying vessel was to Aliaga Port not to Izmir Port, the matter of transport was coordinated by consignee and the shipper; 15. the e-mails between the Plaintiff and the EDA Company; 16. the bill of lading of other two batches of similar goods (number of bill of lading MSCUXH901881, MSCUXR730826), the bill of carrier and bank payment, evidence 15、16 to prove that the Plaintiff had a total of 3 batches of similar goods to Izmir Port, goods involved was the second batch at the same time, it proved that the incurred costs of the first and the third batch of the goods under the terms of the CY/FO at destination port Izmir, and confirmed that all expenses the goods involved produced by the goods were wrongly shipped to Aliaga Port; 17. the e-mail between the Plaintiff and the EDA Company to prove that the English translation of fee invoice of the first and third batch of goods of Izmir was made by the EDA

Company, and the letter inquiry to the Turkey official advisory which mentioned "Ege Gübre" referred to Aliaga port; 18. the confirmation letter of EDA Company to prove that before October 10, 2014, EDA Company had received full payment from the Plaintiff for dealing with transport matters of the goods; 19. exchange rate table of Turkish Central Bank dollar against Turkish lira and exchange rate table of China Bank dollar against RMB to prove the exchange rate of date of payment; 20. the Court according to the application of the Plaintiff, took out the proof issued by Mediterranean Shipping (Shanghai) Co., Ltd. Tianjin Branch to prove according to the similar records as the involved bill of lading, the other two batches of goods which were same as the goods involved were shipped to Izmir Port by Mediterranean Shipping Company S.A. (hereinafter referred to as Mediterranean Shipping), in the system of Mediterranean Shipping, Izmir Port and Aliaga Port were two different ports; 21. the record of inquiry staff of CMA CGM (China) Co., Ltd. Tianjin branch (hereinafter referred to as CMA CGM) to prove that the operation of CMA CGM to the goods and the understanding of the two English words "Izmir Port" and "Aliaga" and corresponding ports; 22. the Plaintiff entrusted agent *ad litem* LIU Zuoming to inquiry EDA Company and the e-mail of the Company's reply to prove that the proof of EDA Company to pay the costs and the facts that the Company name had changed. Evidence 3, 5 to 10 and 12, 18, 20, 21 have the original copies, evidence of 3 and 12 had handled the procedures for notarization, evidence 4 to 10 and 18 had handled the notarized certification procedures.

The cross-examination opinions of the Defendant to the Plaintiff:

1. The Defendant had no objections to the authenticity of evidence 1 and 2. and had objection to the validity of the proof.
2. The Defendant had objections to the authenticity and the validity of evidence 3 he thought that the evidence was only personal point of view from Marti Company's staff Erdal Tokcan, so it did not have the authority.
3. The Defendant recognized the authenticity of the web information of the first page of evidence 4 but the evidence was made by TCDD Company, and it did not have the authority, so the Defendant had objections to the effectiveness of the proof; the Defendant had objections to the authenticity and the effectiveness of the web information of the second page.
4. The Defendant did not recognized the authenticity and the validity of evidence 5 and evidence 6 he thought that it could not prove that the actual cost and the actual amount was reasonable.
5. The Defendant approved of the authenticity of evidence of 7, 8, 9, and confirmed that NORA Company was the agent of the actual carrier Emirates Company, also confirmed that the NORA Company received the above money, but the Defendant did not recognize the effectiveness of evidence, and thought that it could not prove that the cost incurred had causal relationship with the goods that were shipped to Aliaga Port.
6. The Defendant had no objection to the authenticity of evidence 10, but he had objections to the validity of the evidence, he thought that it was the EDA

Company's unilateral views, and did not have the authority, as well as could not prove the Plaintiff's claims.
7. The Defendant had no objection to the authenticity of evidence 11, but had objections to the validity of the evidence, he thought that the Defendant, the Plaintiff had arguments of the port of destination.
8. The Defendant had objections to the authenticity and the validity of evidence 12.
1. The Defendant had no objection to the authenticity of evidence 13, 14, but had objections to the validity of the evidence, he thought that the Plaintiff had no clear agreement on the port of destination when the Plaintiff entrusted them, the Defendant meant that the goods involved had been shipped to the destination.
2. The Defendant had objections to the authenticity and validity of evidence 15, 16, he thought that the different companies had different operating habits, the above evidence had nothing to do with the case.
3. The Defendant did not recognize the authenticity and effectiveness of evidence 17, 18, 19, and 22, he thought that the above evidence was the EDA Company's unilateral statement, and could not prove the Plaintiff's claims, at the same time, the exchange rate was not recognized.
4. The Defendant had no objections to the authenticity of the evidence 20 and 21, but the Defendant thought that the behaviors of Mediterranean Shipping and CMA CGM companies had no the authority, so it could not concluded other shipping companies' practices, therefore the Defendant had objections to the validity of the above evidence.

The evidence presented by the Defendant to support its claims:
1. From June 19, 2013 to June 24, 2013, the e-mails sent between the Defendant and Awot Global Tianjin Corporation to prove that: (1) the Plaintiff's shipping agent Awot Global Tianjin Corporation entrusted the Defendant to inquiry and booking to the shipping Company in terms of the goods involved, the Plaintiff was fully aware of the situation; (2) the Defendant fully implied that the destination was "Izmir", the Plaintiff and the agent, Awot Global Tianjin Corporation, both had no objections; 2. booking note;3. the e-mails sent between the Plaintiff and the Defendant on August 28, 2013; 4. payment guarantee; 5. cost confirmation copy, the above evidence proved that: (1) the Plaintiff booking space for the Defendant that only required the port of destination was "Izmir" and did not specify the port; (2)Awot Global Tianjin Corporation implied that the Defendant the port of destination was "Izmir", and also did not specify the port; 6. the power of attorney of exports of the goods was to prove that the Defendant according to the instructions of the Plaintiff to covey the information of the port of the destination to the shipping Company; 7. the e-mail of Awot Global Tianjin Corporation on August 28, 2013; 8. the Plaintiff writing to the Defendant's lawyer's letter, the above evidence proved that the Plaintiff and the agent were fully aware of the fact that Izmir City, Turkey had two different ports; and 9. The e-mail sent between the staff of the Defendants and NORA Company and the statement of the Defendant to prove that container demurrage, the cargo unloading fees, temporary charges of goods involved all had

been charged by the actual carrier UNITED ARAB SHIPPING COMPANY S.A.G on behalf of NORA Company, the above fees would be charged according to the different rates whether in Izmir or Aliaga port, but under the special circumstances that the consignee of the goods involved was the management party of the port, it may be given concessions or deductions.

The cross-examination opinions of the Plaintiff to the Defendant's evidence: 1. the Plaintiff had no objection to the authenticity and the validity of evidence 1; 2. the Plaintiff had no objection to the authenticity of evidence 2 to 5, but had objections to the effectiveness of the proof, who thought that the evidence just could prove that when booking the port of discharge recorded Turkey Izmir Port, and Izmir port and Aliaga port were not the same port, so it cannot prove the Defendant' claims; 3. the Plaintiff had no objection to the authenticity of evidence 6, but had objection to the validity of the proof, who thought that the Defendant entrusted the actual carrier to appoint the port of destination was not consistent with that the Plaintiff entrusted the Defendant; 4. the Plaintiff had no objection to the authenticity of evidence 7, 8, but had objections to the effectiveness of the proof, which considered that the time of the e-mail was August 28, 2013, and the goods involved had reached at Aliaga Port on August 20, so it could not be presumed the Plaintiff prior knowledge of the port of destination was Aliaga port. The Plaintiff in the lawyer's letter pointed out that Aliaga Port and Izmir Port were two different ports; and 5. the Plaintiff had no objection to the authenticity of evidence 9, but had objections to the validity of the proof, which thought that the Defendant claimed that the discharge fees and temporary charges would be charged at any ports had no evidence to support it.

The ascertainment opinions of the court to the Plaintiff's evidence: 1. the Defendant had no objection to the authenticity of evidence of 1 and 2, the court confirmed the authenticity of the evidence, the above evidence could prove that the Plaintiff and the Defendant had marine goods traffic congruent relationship. The Plaintiff was the shipper, the Defendant was the contractual carrier, UNITED ARAB SHIPPING COMPANY S.A.G was the actual carrier and the content of the rights and obligations of the contract, the court was also confirmed its effectiveness; 2. evidence 3 and evidence 4, 10, 13, 14, 17 could confirm each other to prove that Izmir Port and Aliaga Port were not the same port, the court confirms the authenticity and the effectiveness of the evidence; 3. evidence 5 to 9 were the notarized original copy and could confirm each other with evidence 10 to prove the additional fees paid by the Plaintiff because the goods were shipped to Aliaga Port, the court identifies the authenticity and the effectiveness of the evidence; 4. the Defendant had no objection to the authenticity of evidence 11, and the evidence could prove that the two sides agreed to the port of destination was Izmir Port, the court confirmed its authenticity and effectiveness; 5. evidence 12 and other evidence could confirm each other to prove that EDA Company was the Plaintiff's agent in Turkey, the court confirmed its authenticity and effectiveness; 6. evidence 15, 16 and evidence 20 could confirm each other to prove that there had a total of

3 batches of similar goods that were shipped to Izmir Port, the goods involved were the second batch of goods. According to the similar records with the bill of lading involved, the other two batches of goods were shipped to Izmir Port by the carrier Mediterranean Shipping Company S.A. In Mediterranean Shipping system, Izmir Port and Aliaga Port were two different ports and the expenses of two other batches of goods under the terms of CY/FO at Izmir Port. The court identifies the authenticity and the effectiveness of the evidence; 7. the evidence 18 was the notarized original copy, the sourt confirms its authenticity and effectiveness; 8. evidence 19 was the statistics data published by the bank, the Court confirmed its authenticity, but the translation of the Plaintiff's legal costs should be subject to exchange rate of the date of payment to the EDA, and should not apply to exchange rate that EDA pad payment, the sourt did not recognize its effectiveness; 9. evidence 20, 21 were the original copy, which could prove that Izmir Port and Aliaga Port were different ports, the sourt confirmed the authenticity and the effectiveness of the evidence; 10. Although evidence 22 was not notarized, it could confirm each other with the other evidence of the Plaintiff to prove the necessity of EDA Company to pay the costs, the sourt identifies the authenticity and effectiveness of the evidence.

The ascertainment opinions of the sourt to the Defendant's evidence: 1. the Plaintiff had no objection to the authenticity of the evidence of the Defendant, the sourt also confirms; 2. the Plaintiff had no objection to the validity of the evidence 1, the court confirms; 3. evidence 2 to 5 cannot prove that the Plaintiff and the Defendant agreed to the port of destination was Aliaga Port, the court did not recognize its effectiveness; 4. evidence 6 to 8 could not prove that Izmir Port and Aliaga Port were the same port, as well as could not prove that the Plaintiff knew the port of destination was Aliaga Port, the court did not recognize its effectiveness; 5. evidence 9 can prove that the demurrage fees, unloading charges and temporary charges of the goods involved had been charged by NORA Company on behalf of the actual carrier UNITED ARAB SHIPPING COMPANY S.A.G and under the special circumstances that the consignee was the management party of the port, the fact that the cost may get concessions or deduction, the court identifies its effectiveness.

After trial we found out, the Plaintiff booking to the Defendant by Awot Global Tianjin Corporation on June 2013, which entrusted the Defendant 50 containers of steel shipped from China to Turkey, on June 28, the Defendant issued an order bill of ladingNo.TMEI13064401ZM to the Plaintiff, the bill of lading recorded the shipper was the Plaintiff, the carrier was the Defendant, the notify party was TCDD Company, the voyage number was UMM SALAL 1326 W. The port of loading was Xingang (China Tianjin), the unloading port was LANDED IZMIR PORT, TURKEY, transportation term was CY/CY. On the same day, the Defendant signed a shipping contract with UNITED ARAB SHIPPING COMPANY S.A.G, which entrusted the Company commissioned the actual goods involved, UNITED ARAB SHIPPING COMPANY S.A.G issued No.CNXGG062768 of the straight bill of lading to the Defendant, the bill of lading noted that the shipper was the Defendant, the carrier was UNITED ARAB SHIPPING COMPANY S.A.G, the consignee was NORA Company, the voyage number was UMM SALAL 1326 W, the loading port was Xingang (China Tianjin), the port of discharge was ALIAGA IZMIR, the transportation conditions were the carriers received the FCL at the loading port and shipped the goods to the port of discharge, but was not responsible for unloading (CY/FO). From August 21, 2013 to 22, the cargo involved was unloaded in Turkey Aliaga Port.

In the case of the Defendant refused to transfer, the Plaintiff in order to complete the obligation to deliver the goods, on September 17, 2013, the Plaintiff entrusted the agent in Turkey EDA Company to ship the goods involved to Izmir Port and delivered to the consignee TCDD Company. Meantime, it produced the following additional cost:

1) CUSTOM MOVES IMPORT INSPECTION, IMPORT INSPECTION, DELIVERY and STORAGE in Aliaga Port amounted to USD14,714.32; 2) TRANSPORT paid to inland carrier and DEMURRAGE were a total of 35,518 Turkish Lira; 3) DEMURRAGE paid to pay the NORA Company USD22,160, FREE OUT USD6,195 and TEMPORARY ACCEPTANCE 10,165.41 Turkish Lira. These costs were paid by the EDA Company on behalf of the Plaintiff to the relevant companies on September 2013. On October 10, 2014, EDA Company confirmed that it had received all the fees from the Plaintiff.

In addition, the court found that Izmir Port and Aliaga Port were two independent ports, which belonged to different port authorities and customs authorities. Izmir Port was also known as the Al Sanja J port, it is a state-owned port of Turkey, and was owned by the state-owned Company TCDD Company. Aliaga Port was from 50 km of the north of Izmir city (Turkey). The port was private, and was operated by Private Companies Ege Gübre Sanayi A.S. The operator was known simply as TCEEGE Company. In the case of the consignee as TCDD Company, the cargo that were unloaded to Izmir Port would be exempted from the relevant operating costs.

Besides, the court finds out that the Plaintiff had a total of three batches of steel shipped from China to Turkey and delivered to TCDD Company. The goods involved were the second batch of the goods, the other two batches of goods were shipped respectively on April 28, 2013 and October 26, which were shipped by Mediterranean Shipping and respectively issued order bills of lading No. MSCUXH901881 and No.MSCUXR730826. The bills of lading noted that the shipper was the Plaintiff, notify party was TCDD Company, port of loading was Xingang (China Tianjin), port of unloading was LANDED IZMIR PORT, TURKEY, the transportation term was CY/FO. The two batches of goods were shipped to Izmir Port (Turkey) and delivered to the consignee TCDD Company. In addition to prepare for freight, EDA Company paid the expense items in the unloading port on behalf of the Plaintiff were unloading shipping charges, documentation fees, unloading supervision fees, equipment inspection and control costs and port security charges.

Besides, the court finds out that Marti Company was an agent company of the outsider CIMC Company in Turkey. Erdal Tokcan was the director and vice president of Marti Company. EDA Company was an agent Company of the Plaintiff in Turkey. NORA Company was the agent Company of the Defendant and UNITED ARAB SHIPPING COMPANY S.A.G in Turkey.

The court holds that this case is the dispute over contract of carriage of goods by sea, the Plaintiff was the shipper, the Defendant was the carrier and UNITED ARAB SHIPPING COMPANY S.A.G was the actual carrier. According to the Maritime Code of the People's Republic of China Article 49 Paragraph 1, the carrier shall carry the goods to the port of discharge on the agreed or customary or geographically direct route. In this case, the Plaintiff, the Defendant and UNITED ARAB SHIPPING COMPANY S.A.G did not sign a written contract, so the records of bill of lading became the proof of the content of the contract for carriage of goods by sea of the goods involved. And, because the Defendant issued the bill of lading No.TMEI13064401ZM noted the English text of the port of discharge was LANDED IZMIR PORT, TURKEY, and UNITED ARAB SHIPPING COMPANY S.A.G issued the bill of ladingNo.CNXGG062768 noted the English text of the port of discharge was ALIAGA IZMIR, and the goods involved were actually shipped to Aliaga Port (Turkey), rather than Izmir Port that the Plaintiff claimed. The two ports were also not the same port, so the key point to judge whether the Defendant breach was to clear the meaning of the terms of the port of discharge in the contract of the Plaintiff and the Defendant, namely "IZMIR PORT" referred to Izmir Port or Aliaga Port, the two sides both had great differences in understanding the terms.

According to the Contract Law of the People's Republic of China Article 125 Paragraph 1, in case of any dispute between the parties concerning the construction of a contract term, the true meaning thereof shall be determined according to the words and sentences used in the contract, the relevant provisions and the purpose of the contract, and according to the relevant usage and the principle of good faith. First of all, from the perspective of literal interpretation, English text "IZMIR PORT" literal translation into Chinese referred to Izmir Port, rather than Aliaga Port, English version of Aliaga Port was "ALIAGA". Secondly, from the angle of objective interpretation, the purpose of the Plaintiff and the Defendant signed the contract for carriage of goods by sea was delivered the goods involved to the consignee TCDD Company, the Company was the operator of Izmir Port, so shipped the goods involved to Izmir Port would be more in line with the purpose of the contract. Once again, from the perspective of trading habits, according to guidelines of ports, the statement of EDA Company and the reply of the Turkey port authority, departments in charge and the related companies, the operation practices of Mediterranean Shipping Company S.A., CMA-CGM and other large international shipping corporations, "IZMIR PORT" referred to Izmir Port (Turkey), rather than Aliaga Port. If the bill of lading noted the port of discharge as "IZMIR PORT", then the carrier should ship the goods to the port of Izmir (Turkey), which had been recognized by the shipping practice and became the trading habits of shipping industry. In summary, to explain the Plaintiff and the Defendant agreed the port of discharge clause whether from the angle of the meaning, purpose or the trading habits, the conclusion was that "IZMIR PORT" referred to the port of Izmir (Turkey). In the case of the two sides agreed to the port of discharge was the port of Izmir, the Defendant had shipped the goods to the Port of Aliaga, the behavior violated the obligations of the contract, so the Defendant constituted a breach of contract and shall be liable for breach of contract.

According to the Contract Law of the People's Republic of China Article 113, damages to consumer where a party failed to perform or rendered non-conforming performance, thereby causing loss to the other party, the amount of damages payable shall be equivalent to the other party's loss resulting from the breach, including any benefit that may be accrued from performance of the contract, provided that the amount shall not exceed the likely loss resulting from the breach which was foreseen or should have been foreseen by the breaching party at the time of conclusion of the contract. In this case, due to the Defendant breach of contract, shipped the goods to Aliaga Port where was about 50 km from Izmir Port and refused to transfer. The Plaintiff in order to perform the obligation of delivery the goods to the consignee, so the Plaintiff was forced to transfer goods to the port of Izmir. In this process, the storage fee, inland transportation fees, demurrage and container demurrage inevitably happened, the fee of going out was the Plaintiff taken away the goods involved from Aliaga Port which shall pay to the operator of the port TCEEGE Company. Temporary charges was that the Plaintiff taken away the goods involved from Aliaga Port which shall pay to UNITED ARAB SHIPPING COMPANY S.A.G, which were also the necessary costs in the transport process. With reference to the Plaintiff shipped the goods to Izmir Port to delivered the consignee and the incurred costs of the other two batches of goods of the port operator of TCDD, the different claims of the Plaintiff, in addition to the transfer box fees and import inspection fees could be avoided incurred or be exempted. Therefore, there has a causal relationship between the above costs and the Defendant's breach of contract behavior, the Defendant should compensate the Plaintiff.

As for the unloading charges, the Defendant issued the bill of lading noted that the transport conditions was yard to yard (CY/CY). According to the terms, the Defendant should be responsible for discharging the goods to the port of destination yard and bear the unloading costs, but the Defendant and the actual carrier UNITED ARAB SHIPPING COMPANY S.A.G agreed to transport condition was that the carrier was not responsible for unloading (CY/FO), resulting in the Plaintiff additionally paid unloading charges to UNITED ARAB SHIPPING COMPANY S.A.G, the Defendant shall compensate the Plaintiff for discharge fee losses.

Transfer box fees and import inspection fees were actually the costs charged by Turkey Customs, which were inevitable of import of goods and had nothing to do with the port of discharge, so there was no causal relationship between the loss and the Defendant's breach of contract behavior. The court shall not support the claim that the Plaintiff requested the Defendant to compensate for transfer box fees and the import inspection fees.

The Defendant claimed that the Plaintiff's loss was beyond the predictable range when the Defendant contracted, which the court holds that the Plaintiff's loss should be able to foresee by the Defendant. First of all, from the perspective of the identity, the Defendant, as a specialized in international shipping business logistics Company, which shall know the names, the geographical location, the charging items and standards of the major ports worldwide, this was a quality as a professional Company should have. Even if the Defendant did not know the facts that there were two ports in Turkey Izmir area, as the carrier at least should be clear that shipping the goods to the other port beyond the port of destination would cause additional costs and losses. Secondly, from the perspective of the course of contracting, the e-mail and the booking note between the Defendant and the freight agent Awot Global Tianjin Corporation of the Plaintiff could prove that the Defendant knew that when the Plaintiff booked to them, the port of discharge was Izmir Port and notify party was the port operator TCDD Company. In international shipping carriage, notify party of indicating the bill of lading was usually the consignee or its agent, the Defendant in the case of knowing the consignee may be TCDD Company, which shipped the goods to Aliaga Port, so the Defendant should foresee this behavior may lead to the loss. Therefore, the court did not support the above claims of the Defendant.

With regard to the specific amount of the Plaintiff's loss, all the losses of the Plaintiff shall be certified by a certificate of notarization and authentication, and the amount of the loss of the Plaintiff shall be recognized by the court. The interests the Plaintiff claimed was due to the Defendant delay to pay the interest losses, which should be supported. The date of interest should be calculated from the Plaintiff paid the fees to EDA Company. But the Plaintiff failed to prove the specific time and only could prove that EDA Company had received the all payments from the Plaintiff for dealing with the transport matters of goods involved until October 10, 2013. The interest should be calculated from October 10, 2014, according to the loan interest rate stipulated by the people's Bank of China for the corresponding period to the actual payment date of the Defendant. The court does not supported the Plaintiff's claim that requested respectively calculated the interests from the date of EDA Company advanced the all fees. The loss of the Plaintiff's appeal was calculated in RMB. The cost of EDA Company advanced both in dollars also in Turkish Lira, translations should be paid according to the exchange rate of the actual payment date of the Plaintiff. But the Plaintiff was only able to prove that until October 10, 2014, which had paid all the money to EDA Company and failed to prove the specific payment time, so it should be applicable to the exchange rate of October 10, 2014 for translation. The court did not support the Plaintiff's claim that requested respectively translations according to the exchange rate of date that EDA Company advanced the all costs. Concerning that it could not change RMB directly into Turkish Lira, translation should change Turkish Lira into dollars and then converted into RMB. According to the Turkish lira-dollar rate and RMB-dollar rate on October 10, 2014, calculated the costs losses of the Plaintiff was totaling 386,393.05 yuan.

Pulling the threads together, according to Article 113 Paragraph 1 and Article 125 Paragraph 1 of the Contract Law of the People's Republic of China, Article 49 Paragraph 1 of the Maritime Code of the People's Republic of China and Article 64

Paragraph 1 of the Civil Procedure Law of the People's Republic of China, the judgment is as follows:

1. The Defendant Dalian Pei Hua International Logistics Co., Ltd. shall pay the Plaintiff Silvery Dragon Prestressed Materials Co., Ltd. (Tianjin) RMB386,393.05 for economic loss in ten days from the date of the judgment coming into effect.
2. The Defendant Dalian Pei Hua International Logistics Co., Ltd. shall pay the Plaintiff Silvery Dragon Prestressed Materials Co., Ltd. (Tianjin) the above payments from October 10, 2014 to the actual performance date of the duration of the judgment, according to the loan interest rate of the People's Bank of China for the corresponding period.
3. Reject other claims of the Plaintiff Silvery Dragon Prestressed Materials Co., Ltd. (Tianjin).

If the Defendant fails to perform the obligations of the payment of money in the period specified in this judgment, then the Defendant shall double pay the debts interest of delay in performance according to Article 253 of the Civil Procedure Law of the People's Republic of China.

Court acceptance fee in amount of RMB7386, the Plaintiff shall bear RMB336, the Defendant shall bear RMB7050. In view of the Plaintiff's payment of the fee, the Court will not repay the Plaintiff and the Defendant's share of the fee will be paid by the Defendant together with the above payment to the Plaintiff.

If not satisfy with this judgment, within fifteen days of the date of the judgment be delivered, with seven copies of the original Letter of Appeal, a party can appeal to Tianjin High People's Court. And that party will pay the appeal fee to the Tianjin High People's Court within seven days of the appeal. (Bank Account: Agricultural Bank of China Tiancheng Branch in Tianjin, Number: 02200501040006269, Name: Department of Finance, Tianjin High People's Court.)

Presiding Judge: CAO Ke
Acting Judge: ZHANG Lina
Acting Judge: WANG Huiran

February 3, 2015

Clerk: MA Sai

Qingdao Maritime Court
Civil Judgment

Station Ocean Administration Beihai Branch
v.
WANG Jianlong et al.

(2013) Qing Hai Fa Hai Shang Chu Zi No.986

Related Case(s) None.

Cause(s) of Action 236. Dispute over contract for construction of dock or harbor.

Headnote Fishermen required to reimburse government agency for cost investigating whether government's construction project had damaged fishing nets, because statements made by fishermen were untrue.

Summary The Plaintiffs, agents of the government, sued the Defendant fishermen to recover losses incurred when the Plaintiffs employed a police vessel and diving team to investigate the Defendants' allegations that the Plaintiffs' construction project damaged their fishing nets.

The Plaintiffs contracted with Contractors to build a jetty. Contractors required a temporary dumping ground for dredged materials to complete the construction. Plaintiff selected the temporary dumping grounds. The Defendants claimed their fishing nets, which were located outside the temporary dumping grounds, were damaged by the Plaintiffs' construction project.

To claim for compensation, the Defendants signed a Letter of Commitment, which stated they assume liability for any false statements made to Plaintiffs. After receiving Defendants' claims for compensation, the Plaintiffs employed a police vessel and diving team to investigate the Defendants' claims. The diving team concluded there were no damaged fishing nets where the Defendants claimed there would be.

The Plaintiffs sued the Defendants to recover expenses incurred while employing the police vessel and the diving team. Because no buried fishing nets were found, the Plaintiffs argued the Defendants made false statements in the Letters of Commitment regarding their losses. Because the Defendants made false claims, the Plaintiffs argued, the Defendants should be liable for all expenses incurred.

The court held that the Defendants should compensate the Plaintiffs for the diving inspection but not for the police vessel escort. The court stated that the Plaintiffs provided insufficient proof to show it needed to employ the police vessel escort, and the employing of the police vessel was unreasonable. Defendants were ordered to pay the Plaintiffs proportionately for the diving team expenses.

This case involves a dispute over marine resource exploitation and utilization.

Judgment

The Plaintiff: Station Ocean Administration Beihai Branch.
Legal representative: HONG Fuzhong, director.
Agents *ad litem*: ZHOU Qinglin and LUAN Ke, lawyers of Shandong Wenkang Law Firm.

The Defendant: WANG Jianlong.

The Defendant: WANG Fugang.

The Defendant: WANG Zhenggang.
Agents *ad litem* appointed by the three Defendants: HUO Jifeng and HONG Zuqin, lawyers of Shandong Taicheng Law Firm.

With respect to the case arising from dispute over marine resource exploitation and utilization filed by the Plaintiff, Station Ocean Administration Beihai Branch (SOA Beihai), against the Defendants, WANG Jianlong, WANG Fugang and WANG Zhenggang, the court entertained the case, and formed a collegiate panel to conduct the trial according to the law. Agent *ad litem* of the Plaintiff, ZHOU Qinglin and LUAN Ke, the three Defendants and their agent *ad litem* HUO Jifeng appeared in the hearings and participated in the hearing. Now the case has been concluded.

The Plaintiff alleged that in January 2013, it was allowed to set a temporary ocean dumping site for Qingdao Marine Scientific Research Base in the vicinity of Sha Zi Kou sea area in Qingdao City. In March 2013, the three Defendants claimed that the fixation pile had been set in the ocean dumping sites was buried by nud and claimed for compensation, also, they signed written Letter of Commitment and a Statement for guarantying true information and documents about provided buried fixation pile. If there was any false, they would bear all the economic losses and legal responsibilities. In July 2013, under the acceptation of the three Defendants, the Plaintiff authorized Qingdao Haisheng Diving Service Co., Ltd. (hereinafter referred to as Diving Company) to search relevant sea area underwater for verifying declared information, in which all progress the three Defendants participated in. The underwater work-paper about fixation pile in temporary ocean dumping sites provided by Diving Company showed that: the area searched was all sand without any materials artificially set thereon. Because of untruthful declaration, the Plaintiff lost about RMB152,290. Therefore, the Plaintiff requested the court to rule: the three Defendants bear the joint and several liability for the loss in amount of RMB152,290, and bear the litigation costs of this case.

The Plaintiff submitted the following evidence to support its claims:

1. The statement and its attachments issued by WANG Jianlong on March 14, 2013, to prove that WANG Jianlong provided buried fixation pile sea coordinates for demanding compensation from the Plaintiff, and Letter of Commitment is there any false, they will to bear all the economic loss.
2. The statement and its attachments issued by WANG Fugang on March 14, 2013, to prove that WANG Fugang provided buried fixation pile sea coordinates for demanding compensation from the Plaintiff, and Letter of Commitment is there any false, they will to bear all the economic loss.
3. The statement and its attachments issued by WANG Zhenggang on March 14, 2013, to prove that WANG Zhenggang provided buried fixation pile sea coordinates for demanding compensation from the Plaintiff, and Letter of Commitment is there any false, they will to bear all the economic loss.
4. Notice of statistics work about SOA Qingdao Marine Scientific temporary ocean dumping sites fixation pile, to prove that the Plaintiff released notice about compensation matters to emphasize only fishermen who truly suffered the economic loss could be compensated; ones who misrepresented or made false declaration should be subject to legal liability.
5. Letter of Commitment and Registration form of damaged setting nets issued by WANG Jianlong on April 27, 2013, to prove WANG Jianlong provided the information of the buried pile sea coordinates again for demanding compensation from the Plaintiff, and committed to bear all legal liability for the truth of the documents.
6. Letter of Commitment and Registration form of damaged setting nets issued by WANG Fugang on April 27, 2013, to prove that WANG Fugang provided the information of the buried pile's sea coordinates again for demanding compensation from the Plaintiff, and committed to bear all legal liability for the truth of the documents.
7. Letter of Commitment and Registration form of damaged setting nets issued by WANG Zhenggang on April 27, 2013, to prove WANG Zhenggang provided the information of the buried pile's sea coordinates again for demanding compensation from the Plaintiff, and committed to bear all legal liability for the truth of the documents.
8. Notice of statistics work about SOA Qingdao Marine Scientific temporary dumping sites setting net pile, to prove that the Plaintiff released notice about compensation matters to emphasize only fishermen who truly suffered the economic loss could be compensated; ones who misrepresented or made false declaration should be subject to legal liability.
9. Agreement.
10. Invoice of Diving Company, evidence 9–10 is to prove that for verifying the quantity and distribution of setting nets pile in ocean dumping sites, the Plaintiff entrusted Diving Company to detect and issue the inquest report and costs RMB86,000, and agreed that the Plaintiff provided a diving ship.

11. The Defendant's bill of credit, to prove that the Plaintiff had paid inspection cost in amount of RMB86,000 to Diving Company.
12. The record of commission, to prove WANG Jianlong WANG Fugang WANG Zhenggang and other fishermen took part in the detection process, and it was sure that there was no setting net pile in the underwater detection process.
13. The underwater work-paper of setting net pile in the temporary ocean dumping sites, to prove the underwater work was taken part in by the Plaintiff, the Bureau of Marine and Fishery of Laoshan Distract, Sha Zi Kou community office and community and fishermen representatives all together; Diving Company detected twice, and its concluded that submarine geology is relatively flat and all sand without other artificial placed matters in the detection area.
14. Report about cost of setting net pile detection task, to prove that maritime police vessel 1117 carried out underwater operation, which ensured the safety of navigation, accurate ship positioning, equipment hoisting and power supplying etc. all cost RMB66,290.
15. Notice of usage of temporary ocean dumping sites, to prove that SOA approved set temporary ocean dumping sites at waters near Sha Zi Kou of Qingdao City, and the boundary and the quality of the dumping sites had been announced.
16. Live video of setting net pile at the temporary dumping sites (a CD), to prove that according to the previous agreement that declarers who gave false information after investigation should bear the inspection cost, the two parties took part in the action together, during the period, they made equal consultation and affirmation to the detection plan and position, but in the progress setting net pile had not been found.
17. Qingdao Marine Science Research Base rights protection law enforcement function area's Hydraulic engineering construction contract; Accounting voucher of September 15, 2014, to prove that the Plaintiff as Employer signed construction contract with contractor, CCCC Second; made civil acts; project funds was paid from Human rights law enforcement base renovation project of Project Expenditure of fiscal appropriation.
18. Accounting voucher of January 31, 2014, to prove that the Plaintiff and the fishermen reached an agreement by mutual consultation about the involved dumping sites pile compensation items; compensation payments collected from Sha Zi Kou Human rights law enforcement base renovation project fiscal appropriation. The Plaintiff's acts related to compensation items of involved dumping sites pile were civil acts, which could not use the administrative appropriation of Basic Expenditure.
19. Work Reports, to prove that the Plaintiff convened briefings with sea vessel, Diving Company and fishermen representatives joint, and informed implementation plan; and correspondingly recorded twice sea work content on July 10 and 11.

As for the evidence the Plaintiff provided, the three Defendants held that it had no objection to evidence 1–8 and 15; it had no objection to the authenticity of the evidence 12, 17 and 18, but the items of proof thereof were involved; it had no objection to evidence 9–11, 13, 14 and 19; it had both objection to the authenticity and proof items of the evidence 9–11, 13, 14 and 19; it had no objection to the authenticity of the evidence 16, but it was clipped and incomplete.

The three Defendants all defended that the Plaintiff as a state administrative organ should fulfill its government administrative functions according to the law; under the circumstance that the inaccurate information reported by the Defendants and the detection situation was unclear, the first detection by the Plaintiff using precise poisoning instrument failed but the second time setting net pile was found. The Plaintiff deliberately filed this case based on false declaration of the Defendants, which on purpose of evading the compensation of burying piles. To sum up, the Defendants requested the court to reject the Plaintiff's claims.

The three Defendants, in order to prove its defense, submitted the following evidence the court:

1. A photograph taken by the Defendants in March 2013, to prove that the Plaintiff set dumping sites for dumping mud by dumping ship to majority fishermen include the three Defendants operating waters. Because of dumping mud, the operating waters were buried, which caused tort to the waters. So the Plaintiff should bear the liabilities of compensation according to the law.
2. A photograph taken in July 17, 2013 by JIA Lei who worked for the Plaintiff, to prove that the Plaintiff in July 11, 2013 under the condition that after the detection throughout the maritime police vessel and commissioned divers, and unclear detection condition due to inaccurate GPS position data, the two parties agreed to continue underwater detection for raising efficiency. Thus, in July 17th, the second detection was carried out with the presence of JIA Lei, Marine and Fishery Bureau of Laoshan District's staff, Aquatic Office's of Laoshan District, Sha Zi Kou and the three Defendants and other fishermen; after this detection, it was ascertained that the pile provided by the three Defendants was objective and real existence.
3. The operation plan of the compensation of fishermen as for buried setting net pile in temporary dumping sites of SOA Qingdao Marine Scientific, to prove that the Plaintiff with the Ocean and Fishery Bureau of Laoshan District and Sha Zi Kou community office made compensation plan for buried setting net pile fishermen, and verified the objects of compensation involved 17 fishermen, 205 setting net piles, including three Defendants' 69 setting net piles.
4. Compensation pronouncement, to prove that the other 14 fishermen together with the three Defendants simultaneously reported the data to the Plaintiff were compensated publicly, of which the fisherman QU Baoju who was confirmed as detected object together with the three Defendants at the first detection on July 11, 2013 also was compensated. The Plaintiff claimed compensation also for the detection process of QU Baoju providing the true data, but he signed the compensation agreement with QU Baoju and compensated him instead of filing

a suit, obviously the Plaintiff's claim against the three Defendants could not stand.
5. The statements, letters of commitment and compensation agreement of WANG Zhengyan and QU Minhui, to prove that the setting net piles data provided by the Defendants to the Plaintiff were calculated by WANG Zhengyan's. The basis of data provided by WANG Zhengyan, QU Minhui and the three Defendants was the same. The Plaintiff have signed compensation agreement with WANG Zhengyan and QU Minhui and compensated them, but did not compensate the Defendants' setting net piles, which had no basis.
6. WANG Zhengyan's testimony, to prove that that of WANG Zhengyan calculated the data of the Defendants, whose basis was the same as that of witness WANG Zhengyan, the Plaintiff compensated WANG Zhengyan's buried setting net piles.
7. The coordinate data of WANG Jianlong, WANG Zhenggang and WANG Fugang's setting net piles, to prove that the three Defendants did not provide false coordinates, the differences only due to different positioning tools, but the setting net piles are objective and true realities, so they should be along with all the compensation.
8. Wang Jianhong's certificate from Sha Zi Kou Aquatic Office of Laoshan Distract, Qingdao City, to prove that the Plaintiff provided underwater detection video on July 11, 2013, which was more controversial, then on July 17, 2013 the Plaintiff, the Bureau of Marine and Fishery of Laoshan Distract, Sha Zi Kou community office and fishermen representatives after field salvage, they found fisherman's arc, thus, the objective existence of three Defendants' setting net piles was confirmed. The Plaintiff held the photos and live video documents.

As for the evidence three Defendants provided, the Plaintiff held that it had no objection to evidence 4, 5 and 7, but for the items of proof thereof; it had objection to the authenticity of the evidence 1, 2, 3 and 8; it did not recognize evidence 6 the testimony, due to its inconsistence with the facts.

According to the evidence provided by the two parties, the court ascertains the following facts: As for the evidence the Plaintiff provided, the three Defendants held that it had no objection to evidence 1–8, 12, 15, 16, 17 and 18, the court ascertains the probative force thereof; evidence 9, 10, 11, 13, 14 and 19 all have the originals to be checked, though the three Defendants have objection to the evidence, they did not raise any contrary evidence, so the court ascertains the probative force thereof. In respect of evidence provided by the Defendants, the Plaintiff did not raise any objection to the authenticity of the evidence 4, 5 and 7, so the court ascertains the probative force thereof; evidence 1, 2 and 8 all have the originals to be checked, though the Plaintiff has objection to the evidence, he did not raise any contrary evidence, so the court ascertains the probative force thereof; evidence 3 by the Defendants is a copy which made by the Plaintiff, it partly corroborates with evidence 4, so the court ascertains it; evidence 6 by the Defendants is a testimony, the court will ascertain by combining with other evidence.

According to the evidence raised by both Plaintiff and Defendants and the statements in the hearing, the court ascertains the following facts:

The Plaintiff, in order to implement rights protection and law enforcement function in Qingdao Marine Science Research Base, planned to build the jetty and terminal located at Sha Zi Kou community office of Laoshan Distract, Qingdao City where is located in the west Nanjiang Village and east Xijiang Village. The scale and content of the project is that the 360-m jetty and terminal, the 40-m embankments, the 330-m revetments, about 20,000-squaremeters land back-fill and hydro-power communication supporting fire.

On November 20, 2012, the Plaintiff and CCCC Second Harbour Engineering Company (hereinafter referred to as CCCC Second) signed a marine scientific research base of law enforcement functions of hydraulic engineering construction contract, and agreed that the Plaintiff as the employer has accepted the bidding of the contractor CCCC Second.

CCCC Second for the need of scientific research base construction, set up temporary ocean dumping sites to solve the dredged materials such as soil, mud, stone and etc. in the process of construction upon the application of the Plaintiff to the SOA.

On January 5, 2013, the SOA approved the establishment of the Qingdao marine science research base temporary marine dumping area, that is involved dumping area. On January 17, the Plaintiff on its website issued Notice of usage of temporary ocean dumping sites is that the establishment of the Qingdao marine science research base temporary marine dumping area approved by the SOA, a period of 3 years, the position at the sea area surrounded by the four points of 120°29′22″E 36°02′06″N, 120°31′02″E 36°02′06″N, 120°31′21″E 36°01′34″N, 120°29′22″E 36°01′34″N, the dumping amount controlled in less than 1,308,000 cubic meters.

The Defendant claimed that after the 2013-year Spring Festival, about twelve of the first lunar month, when the Defendant went to sea fishing, he found working vessel dumping so much debris to the location of his setting net piles that buried the pile. Thus, the fishermen, such as the Defendants found the Plaintiff and claimed for compensation.

The Plaintiff claimed in the hearing that the waters of the temporary dumping sites belong to the Marine Functional Reservations where have no fishing or other use function. In the process of the dumping site selection, the Shandong Province Ocean and Fishery Department, Qingdao Maritime Safety Administration and other departments had solicited ideas, but they had no objection to the set of the local dumping sites; during the operations of dredging and dumping, they did not know there are setting net piles. The Plaintiff in the process of selection did not publicize in the local.

The Defendant claimed that part of fishermen of Nanjiang Village and Xijiang Village pile in the sea, every two piles was an arc (called by local fishermen). In the fishing season, usually every arc fastened a buoy with their home logo so that it was convenient to hang nets and distinguish. When not fishing, the arc down in the sea, there is no logo from the surface of the ocean.

According to the fishermen's request, the Plaintiff decided to compensate for the buried matters about the fishermen's setting net piles. The Plaintiff issued a public notice in the local about the requirements of the declaration of the net piles in the temporary dumping sites. Three Defendants and other nearly one hundred fishermen declared.

On March 24, 2013, the three Defendants separately filled contents and signed in the form of a statement issued by the Plaintiff. The main contents of the statement are concerning that the buried of setting net piles by throwing mud during the construction process of Beihai branch in Wharf Engineering in dumping area, compensation was requested therefor. A copy of fishing license, copy of ID card, sea level of buried pile are attached. The Plaintiff committed that the above information was true, and the attachments were true and effective, if there was a false he was willing to bear all the economic losses resulting therefrom, and bear full legal responsibility.

The Plaintiff claimed that due to the existence of a large number of false phenomenon, on April 25, 2013, the Plaintiff issued the Notice of the SOA Qingdao marine scientific research base of temporary dumping area set-net piles' statistical work, the main contents of which are as follows: in order to solve the set-net pile household compensation problems in the SOA Qingdao marine scientific research base construction project in the temporary designation of dumping areas, so that the fishermen who truly suffered real economic losses could get appropriate compensation, ones who misrepresented or made false declaration should be subject to legal liability, and it should be declared again. The applicants should have fishing license promulgated by the administrative department, with fishing methods according to the provisions, and have set-net piles in the said sea areas. The declaration is required to submit the fishing license, the owner ID, set-net pile coordinates, at the same time the signature of the Letter of Commitment.

On April 27, 2013, the three Defendants as the declarants signed in the form of Letter of Commitment by the Plaintiff. The book contents are as follows: "for fitting the bureau of the SOA Qingdao marine scientific research base project construction work, according to the requirements, SOA Beihai, Laoshan District Sha Zi Kou Community office and the Bureau of Marine and Fishery of Laoshan Distract jointly issued the Notice of the SOA Qingdao marine scientific research base of temporary dumping area set-net piles' statistical work, I will declare the number of piles within the sea area of which, and summit the relevant information to your bureau after investigation and verification, all as the payment of compensation basis. To the declaration data, my pledge and commitment are as follows: firstly, I guarantee that I submit to your bureau data is the original written information, the copies of data are the same as the original of that, the signature and stamps in all files are true, and all the content of the documents are objective that can prove the authenticity and objectivity of the declaration, and I will bear all the legal responsibility for the authenticity, accuracy and completeness of the information provided. Secondly, if I misrepresented or made false declaration, after verification, I am willing to bear all legal responsibilities, including but not limited to civil liability and criminal liability of providing malicious false materials for diddling compensation".

On April 30, 2013, the Plaintiff issued the Notice of statistics work about SOA Qingdao Marine Scientific temporary dumping sites setting net pile in every community of Qingdao city Sha Zi Kou community office, publicizing to the 58 fishermen who declared setting net piles, in which 282 of declared net piles is in the dumping sites, 37 of that is in the extension area, and 667 of that is out the dumping sites. There into, the declaration of WANG Jianlong is 12, that of WANG Fugang is 18, that of WANG Zhenggang is 25, the piles declared by three Defendants are all in the dumping sites.

On July 9, 2013, the Plaintiff and Diving Company signed the agreement, agreed to inspect the quantity and distribution of setting nets pile in the temporary dumping sites. The location is the position in the sea area surrounded by the four points of 120°29′22″E, 36°02′06″N,120°31′02″E, 36°02′06″N,120°31′21″E, 36°01′34″N,120°29′22″E, 36°01′34″N. The project content is that through detection and mark of about 100 setting net piles within the selected range to determine the coordinate position, and then issued inspection report subject to actual quantity. The contract amount is RMB86,000.

On July 11, staff of the Plaintiff with the three Defendants, staff of the Bureau of Marine and Fishery of Laoshan Distract and other departments detected underwater to whether the three Defendants declared setting net piles exist objectively by China Maritime Police Vessel 1117. According to the coordinates point by the Defendant, the diving company has diving detected twice found the underwater visibility less than one meter, submarine geology relatively flat and all sand without other artificial placed matters in the detection area.

After the detection, three Defendants claimed that they did not find the net piles, because the Plaintiff's positioning instrument and the Defendants' measuring instrument exist error. According to the request of the Defendants, on July 15, the Bureau of Marine and Fishery of Laoshan Distract and other relevant departments went to the scene inspection again found floater tied to the piles. But the net piles are all outside the dumping area.

On December 26, 2013, the Plaintiff made the implementation scheme of buried piles to fishermen compensation, which proposed compensation 164 piles of 14 fishermen; other reporting piles due to the existence of overlapping pile unreasonable spacing and other phenomenon, so no compensation. On January 17, 2014, the Plaintiff publicized the above compensation matters.

Three Defendants submitted re-measured latitude and longitude of the setting net piles to the court. According to the three Defendants, the deviation is about 200 m east between the latitude and longitude of the Plaintiff and that of the Defendant declared to the Plaintiff, part of the piles outside the dumping area.

The Plaintiff claimed that the reason for using China Maritime Police Vessel 1117 in the first detection is to ensure the safety of the underwater operation. The operation of China Maritime Police Vessel 1117 total costs RMB66,290.

The court holds that the case is the dispute whether the compensation should be done due to the dumping of waste in the temporary dumping area, resulting in customized local fishermen piles buried, the Plaintiff as the subject of compensation with the three Defendants. The outstanding issue is whether the Plaintiff to compensate the piles is civil act; the payment of the Plaintiff detected whether the piles declared by three Defendants is objective existence whether asked three Defendants to pay compensation.

In this case, the Plaintiff is the construction party of Qingdao Marine Science Research Base rights protection law enforcement function area's Hydraulic engineering project (hereinafter referred to as the scientific base project), CCCC Second as the contractor in charge of scientific base project construction. In the process of construction, CCCC Second need dump dredged materials to the sea. Due to the implementation of ocean dumping permission system, CCCC Second as the construction side of the project, applied for the establishment of temporary dumping area. According to the provisions of the Implementation Measures of the Regulations on Management of Ocean Dumping of the People's Republic of China, the departments in charge of sea area organize the selection and demarcation of temporary dumping sites. The Plaintiff, as the agency of the SOA, as the competent department in charge of the sea area involved, is responsible for the selection of the temporary dumping area. Thus, in the course of the construction of the wharf and the selection of the dumping sites, the Plaintiff also has the identity of the civil subject as the terminal construction and the administrative main body of the sea area management and the dumping area.

In respect of the identity of the Plaintiff in the negotiation process with the fishermen on the piles compensation, the court held that according to the relevant provisions, the temporary dumping sites selection procedure is about that the dumping waste owners and dredging engineering departments prior to proposed dumping application to the competent department, the competent department organize the review and put forward the examination opinions, applicants according to the examination opinions for selection report, the competent department proposed preliminary views after the organization of expert reviews and seeking opinions from the relevant departments, then submitted to the SOA approval, finally issued the dumping permit by examination and approval. It is obvious that the Plaintiff, as the administrative department in charge of the dumping sites selection, does not have the duty and obligation to compensate for the dumping of the inner part of the dumping sites. However, as the erector party of the scientific base construction project, the Plaintiff has the duty to compensate for the fishermen with piles in the declared dumping sites, when the construction party CCCC Second applied for the temporary dumping area permit. Therefore, the behavior of the Plaintiff and the fishermen to negotiate the compensation of the net piles is not an act of administrative law enforcement, but a civil act.

According to the law, civil acts shall follow the principles of voluntariness, fairness, compensation for equal value and good faith. The Plaintiff in the construction process of scientific base project, causing fishermen piles buried, shall bear the compensation liability; when the fishermen claimed for compensation, shall truthfully declare the number and coordinate of piles. False declaration or wrong declaration shall bear the losses caused to the Plaintiff.

When the fishermen found buried net piles then claimed for the compensation, the Plaintiff as the erector of the scientific base construction project, shall be equal consultation with the fishermen, jointly determine the inspection methods, compensation standard and error declaration compensation liability and other matters. According to the Defendants' work report, the Plaintiff held a briefing of the fishermen's representatives and relevant departments, before inspection the piles. The Plaintiff commissioned the diving company inspection by China Maritime Police Vessel 1117, which is determined on the briefing. Whether the three Defendants to participate in the briefing, the Plaintiff did not prove. Therefore, that the Plaintiff commissioned the diving company to go to sea inspection is not the result of consultation with the three Defendants, but the Plaintiff's inspection in order to determine the authenticity of piles declaration by all the 58 fishermen.

According to the results of the diving company inspection, in the piles coordinates of the three Defendants declared, none piles was found. It can be found that the three Defendants in the claims of compensation for the net piles, there is a false declaration or error declaration. The three Defendants shall bear the reasonable expenses incurred by the Plaintiff for sea going inspection.

The Plaintiff claims the cost is composed of two parts, one is the cost of coast guard boat in the amount of RMB66,290, the other is the cost of diving company detection in amount of RMB86,000. The Plaintiff calculates sea boat charges unilaterally, and unable to justify the cost reasonable, so the cost will not be supported by the court. As for the detection cost in amount of RMB86,000 paid to the diving company, because the voyage inquest declared 58 fishermen involved, therefore, the three Defendants should bear false declaration caused the Plaintiff costs shall be 1/58, that is RMB1,483.

Upon examination by the judicial committee of the court, according to Article 106 of the General Principles of the Civil Law of the People's Republic of China, the judgment is as follows:

1. The Defendant WANG Jianlong shall pay RMB1,483 to the Plaintiff Station Ocean Administration Beihai Branch within ten days after this judgment comes into effect;
2. The Defendant WANG Fugang shall pay RMB1,483 to the Plaintiff Station Ocean Administration Beihai Branch within ten days after this judgment comes into effect;
3. The Defendant WANG Zhenggang shall pay RMB1,483 to the Plaintiff Station Ocean Administration Beihai Branch within ten days after this judgment comes into effect;
4. Reject other claims of the Plaintiff Station Ocean Administration Beihai Branch.

In case of failure of payment within the period specified in this judgment, the interest on the debt for the delayed period shall be doubled according to Article 253 of the Civil Procedure Law of the People's Republic of China.

Court acceptance fee in amount of RMB3,346, the Plaintiff shall bear RMB3,247 and the Defendants, WANG Jianlong, WANG Fugang and WANG Zhenggang shall separately bear RMB33.

In the event of dissatisfaction with this judgment, the two parties may within 15 days, submit a statement of appeal to the court, together with copies in the number of the opposite party, to lodge an appeal to the Shandong High People's Court.

Presiding Judge: ZHANG Xianli
Judge: LI Hua
Acting Judge: WANG Yan'e

August 14, 2015

Clerk: WANG Xiaojun

Wuhan Maritime Court
Civil Judgment

Suqian Rongxiang Shipping Co., Ltd.
v.
China United Property Insurance Co., Ltd. Jiangsu Branch

(2014) Wu Hai Fa Shang Zi No.01351

Related Case(s) None.

Cause(s) of Action 230. Dispute over marine insurance contract on the sea or sea-connected waters.

Headnote The Defendant insurer held liable to indemnify the Plaintiff shipowner for compensation paid to heirs of crewmember who died suddenly from causes not excluded by the insurance policy.

Summary The Plaintiff-insured shipowner filed suit against the Defendant-insurer seeking indemnification under an insurance policy for amounts it paid out to the legal heirs of one of its crew members. The Plaintiff had procured hull insurance as well as shipowner-employer's liability insurance from the Defendant, which was to last for a period of one year. Towards the end of the insurance period, one of the Plaintiff's crew members suddenly collapsed and later died while the vessel was discharging its cargo. It was officially determined via death certificate that the crew member experienced a sudden death and not one induced from disease, which would have fallen under one of the exclusions contained in the insurance policy. Plaintiff immediately compensated the legal heirs of the crew member and reported the incident to the Defendant. The Plaintiff also requested indemnification, however the Defendant issued a Notice of Refusal on the grounds that the crew member's death fell under the exclusions provision of the policy. The Plaintiff argued that the crew member's death was not by disease, and therefore the Defendant should indemnify Plaintiff for the compensation it paid to the crew member's legal heirs according to the insurance policy. In finding that the Defendant was obliged to indemnify the Plaintiff, the court found that the cause of the crew member's death was not excluded under the policy, meaning the amount paid to the crew member's legal heirs was covered. This was because "sudden death" was medically defined as a naturally occurring incident of death not caused by disease, and that the Defendant could not produce any evidence showing the crew member's death was not a naturally occurring one which would have relieved it from its obligation to indemnify Plaintiff. However, the court disagreed with Plaintiff in regards to when interest was to be calculated, and determined that the interest shall be calculated from when Defendant issued its Notice of Refusal since the Plaintiff's argued calculation date was not correct. The court therefore ordered that the Defendant indemnify the Plaintiff for the amount paid out to the legal heirs of the deceased crew member plus interest on the grounds that the cause of the crew member's death was not excluded under the insurance policy.

Judgment

The Plaintiff: Suqian Rongxiang Shipping Co., Ltd.
Domicile: Room 103, Building No.K, Hao Yu Garden, Suqian City, Jiangsu.
Organization code: 69334685–5.
Legal representative: JIA Cheng, general manager.
Agent *ad litem*: LIANG Kun, lawyer of Jiangsu Suyuan Law Firm.
Agent *ad litem*: WANG Chong, legal worker of Nanjing Pukou District Pancheng Legal Service Office.

The Defendant: China United Property Insurance Co., Ltd. Jiangsu Branch.
Domicile: No.229, Zhu Jiang Road, Nanjing City, Jiangsu.
Organization code: 74682386–3.
Representative: JIANG Yuewu, general manager.
Agent *ad litem*: ZHU Qing, lawyer of Jiangsu Huating Law Firm.
Agent *ad litem*: ZHAO Xiaodan, lawyer of Jiangsu Huating Law Firm.

With respect to the case arising from dispute over marine insurance contract filed by the Plaintiff Suqian Rongxiang Shipping Co., Ltd. (hereinafter referred to as "Rongxiang Company") against the Defendant China United Property Insurance Co., Ltd. Jiangsu Branch (hereinafter referred to as "United Insurance"), the Plaintiff instituted an action to the court on October 26, 2014. This case was concerning dispute over maritime contract and was within the special jurisdiction of maritime court and the place of residence of the Defendant, Nanjing, Jiangsu, was within the court's jurisdiction area, according to Article 24 of the Civil Procedure Law of the People's Republic of China, the court had jurisdiction over this case. The court, after entertaining this case on October 28, 2014, appointed Judge ZHOU Yanhua as sole judge to try this case and held a hearing in public on December 17, 2014. Agent *ad litem* of Plaintiff LIANG Kun and agent *ad litem* of DefendantZHU Qing appeared in court and participated in the action. Upon mediation, this case was not settled successfully. Now the case has been concluded.

It was alleged by the Plaintiff Rongxiang Company that, on September 13, 2012, it effected the insurance with the Defendant United Insurance against "all risks" for its vessel M.V. "Jun Xing 888", and additional risks were shipowner's employer liability insurance and ship carrier's liability insurance. The duration of insurance began from 0000 on September 14, 2012 to 2400 on September 13, 2013.

On August 14, 2013, when M.V. "Jun Xing 888" berthed and discharged cargo at Zhiwei Port, Mayong Nan Zhou Village, Dongguan, Guangdong, its mate LUO Feng suddenly fell in a faint. The attempts at resuscitation by the Dongguan City Mayong Hospital were ineffectual and Mr. Luo died. The cause of Mr. Luo's death diagnosed by the hospital was "a sudden death". At the same day, the Plaintiff Rongxiang Company reported Mr. Luo's death to the police and the Defendant United Insurance. Mr. Luo had five legal heirs, including his mother ZHAO Xi, his wife SUN Huilan, his elder daughter LUO Xinyi and his sons LUO Weidong and LUO Fangze. Through the negotiation with Mr. Luo's legal heirs, the Plaintiff Rongxiang Company compensated the legal heirs altogether RMB299,800. Mr. Luo's mother ZHAO Xi acknowledged receipt of the compensations. The Plaintiff lodged insurance claims against the Defendant United Insurance as provided in the insurance contract, and the Defendant United Insurance issued the Notice of Declination of Claim on April 10, 2014. The Plaintiff Rongxiang Company held that the cause of Mr. Luo's death was not diseases but a sudden death and the Defendant should pay the insurance compensations as provided in the contract and thereby filed the case to the court, and asked the court to order the Defendant United Insurance to pay the insurance compensations of RMB299,800 and the interests accrued thereon (from October 17, 2013 to the day when the Defendant actually compensated the Plaintiff pursuant to the interest rate promulgated by People's Bank of China over the corresponding period) and to order the Defendant United Insurance to bear the court fees.

The Defendant contested that in this case the cause of Mr. Luo's death was a sudden death, which corresponded to the exclusions of the insurance clauses, and the Plaintiff Rongxiang Company failed to prove that it had paid the compensations to the legal heirs, thereof the interests it claimed did not correspond to the stipulations of the Insurance Law, even it was ordered to settle the claim it should reduce or remit compensations. In summary, the Defendant requested the court to reject the litigation claims filed by the Plaintiff.

The Plaintiff Rongxiang Company presented the following evidential documents during the period for adducing evidence:

1. River And Marine Hull Insurance Policy issued by the Defendant United Insurance on September 13, 2012 (original document, policy No.021232982100 110C000012) to prove the Plaintiff arranged the all risks cover-hulls insurance with the Defendant for its M.V. "Jun Xing 888", and additional risks were shipowner's employer liability insurance and ship carrier's liability insurance. The Defendant United Insurance had no objection to the authenticity of the evidence. The court holds that the Defendant United Insurance had no objection to the authenticity of the evidence, so the court admits the evidence.
2. Death Certificate (original document) provided by Dongguan City Mayong Hospital on August 14, 2013, and Certificate (original document) provided by Dongguan City public security bureau Mayong branch office to prove the cause of Mr. Luo's death was a sudden death. The Defendant United Insurance had no objection to the authenticity of the evidence. The court holds that the Defendant

United Insurance had no objection to the authenticity of the evidence, and the source of evidence is lawful and the evidence is relevant to this case, and the two documents can be corroborated mutually, so the court approves their probative force.

3. Seaman's Record Book (copy document) to prove Mr. Luo was the mate of M. V. "Jun Xing 888". The Defendant contested the evidence cannot be verified and not agreed with the evidence. The court holds that although the Seaman's Record Book provided by the Plaintiff Rongxiang Company was copy document, the target the evidence intends to prove has been verified in evidence 2, namely the Certificate provided by public security bureau, so the court affirms Mr. Luo to be a crew member of M.V. "Jun Xing 888".
4. Marriage Registration Review and Treatment Table (with registration seal of the Lin Gao County Civil Affairs Bureau on it), Identify And Household Registration Materials (with Hu Kou special seal of Lin Gao County public security bureau Mei Xia Border police station and villagers' committee seal of Lin Gao County Dong Ying Town Mei Xia village on them) to verify SUN Huilan was the spouse of Mr. Luo and to verify the identities of the legal heirs of Mr. Luo. The Defendant contested that the evidence was not uniform with the identify materials submitted in the first litigation, so it did not agree with the authenticity of the evidence. The court holds that the Plaintiff Rongxiang Company referred copy documents of identify materials to the court in the first litigation and for reason of Acquisition of new evidence, it requested withdrawal of its appeal. By permitting it withdrew its appeal and referred this group of evidence to the court in the litigation of this case and the evidence is original document with relevant department seal on it and its source is lawful, so the court admits the evidence.
5. Receipt (original document) provided by ZHAO Xi, and the Receipt (original document) provided by LUO Ruicheng to prove Mr. Luo's legal heirs had received the compensation of RMB299,800 of Mr. Luo's death paid by the Plaintiff Rongxiang Company. The Defendant did not agree with the authenticity of the evidence. The court holds that this group of evidence was original document and was relevant to this case and had the characteristics of authenticity and validity, and the Defendant did not refer any rebuttal evidence to the court to deny the authenticity of the evidence, so the court approves its probative force.
6. Notice of Declination of Claim (original document) on 10 April 2014 issued by the Defendant United Insurance to the Plaintiff Rongxiang Company to prove that the Defendant United Insurance refused to comply with its duty of compensation. The Defendant United Insurance had no objection to the authenticity of the evidence. The court holds that the Defendant United Insurance had no objection to the authenticity of the evidence, so the court admits the authenticity of the evidence, and it can prove that the Defendant United Insurance's reason of declination was Mr. Luo's sudden death, which they held was the exclusion of the additional risks.

The Defendant United Insurance presented the following evidential documents during the period for adducing evidence:

1. River And Marine Hull Insurance Hull Insurance Slip sealed by the Defendant United Insurance on September 13, 2012 to prove that before concluding a contract, the insurer had provided insurance clause, and the insured had approved the description and suggestion of the terms and conditions, and they had also agreed on the deductibles on the special agreement. The Plaintiff Rongxiang Company had no objection to the authenticity of the evidence but it contested that the Defendant did not made any marks on the deductible excess and deductible rates, so it cannot come into the Plaintiff's notice, and it also did not explained to the Plaintiff, so the Plaintiff shall be not bound to the exception from liability. The court holds that the Plaintiff Rongxiang Company had no objection to the authenticity of the evidence, so the court admits this evidence, which can prove the fact that the Plaintiff procured all risks cover-hulls insurance and relevant additional risks from the Defendant United Insurance.
2. Additional insurance clause of shipowner's employer liability to prove that the insurer shall be not liable on the condition that diseases led to the crew members' death on exclusion. The Plaintiff Rongxiang Company had no objection to the authenticity of the evidence but contested that the exclusion did not list sudden death in it. Though exclusion marked out that the condition of hurt and disability accidents can be deductible, the condition of a sudden death in this case shall not be deductible. The court holds that the Plaintiff Rongxiang Company had no objection to the authenticity of the evidence and this evidence was a part of the insurance contractual relation between the parties in this case and had essential characteristics, so the court admits the evidence.

After the production of evidence, cross-examination and the court's authentication opinions, the court finds out the facts as follows:

On September 13, 2012, the Plaintiff Rongxiang Company affixed its company seal on The River And Marine Hull Insurance Hull Insurance Slip and procured all risks cover-hulls insurance from the Defendant United Insurance for M.V. "Jun Xing 888", and added shipowner's employer liability insurance and ship carrier's liability insurance. At the same day, the Defendant United Insurance issued the River And Marine Hull Insurance Policy, policy No.021232982100110C000012, the insurance policy recorded the main risk of all risks cover-hulls insurance, and the additional risks of shipowner's employer liability insurance and ship carrier's liability insurance and duration of insurance beginning from 0000 on September 14, 2012 to 2400 on September 13, 2013 and so forth. Thereinto, the insurance amount recorded in the added shipowner's employer liability insurance was RMB1,800,000, the insurance amount per person was RMB300,000. The deductible excess/ rate was recorded in the special agreement. The special agreement recorded as follows: this insurance policy adds risks of shipowner's employer liability insurance, compensation limit is RMB1,800,000 (6 persons*RMB300,000 per person). The deductible franchise per accident per person is RMB1,000 or 10%

of the actual losses of the amount, whichever is higher. On the Additional Shipowner's Employer Liability Insurance Clause, in respect of the insurance liability, it was ruled that "the vessel insured had crew members on duty dead or injured on the voyage transportation or the duration of berth, pursuant to the labor contract and the law, the shipowner (the assured) shall undertake the medical fee, hospitalization expenses, disability or death compensation for the crew members, and the insurer shall compensate for the damages". On insurance clause in respect of exclusion (II), conditions listed of "fighting, suicide, self-inflicted injuries, diseases, and death or injuries caused by illegal or criminal actions". And in respect of claim handling (VI), it was agreed that "the deductible excess per crew member at each injury accident shall according to the amount stated in the policy".

On August 14, 2013, when M.V. "Jun Xing 888" berthed and discharged cargo at Zhiwei Port, Mayong Nan Zhou Village, Dongguan City, Guangdong Province, its mate LUO Feng (Male, born on May 26, 1980, domicile at No.16, Wen Ming Street, Mei Xia Village, Dong Ying Town, Lin Gao County, Hai Nan Province, identity card number: 460028198005261612) suddenly fell in a faint. The attempts at resuscitation by the Dongguan City Mayong Hospital were ineffectual and Mr. Luo died, and the Plaintiff Rongxiang Company immediately reported Mr. Luo's death to the police and the Defendant United Insurance. At the same day, Dongguan City Mayong Hospital provided the Death Certificate to prove the cause of Mr. Luo's death was a sudden death and on August 17, 2013 Dongguan City Public Security Bureau Mayong Branch office provided Certificate: LUO Feng, before his death, was the crew member of M.V. "Jun Xing 888", and temporary resided on M. V. "Jun Xing 888", and was initially excluded possibility of homicide, the direct cause of his death is a sudden death.

Mr. Luo's wife named SUN Huilan (identity card number: 460028198411011627), and his mother ZHAO Xi (identity card number: 460028195203051620), and his elder daughter LUO Xinyi (identity card number: 469024200604151629), and his elder son LUO Weidong (identity card number: 469024200807111619), and his second son LUO Fangze (identity card number: 469024201005051612). After this accident, LUO Buwu (identity card number: 460028198009031611), LUO Ruicheng (identity card number: 460028195507031610) on behalf of Mr. Luo's relatives to negotiate compensation with the Plaintiff Rongxiang Company. On August 17, 2013, LUO Buwu and LUO Ruicheng provided a receipt of the compensation of RMB299,800.

After paid of compensation, the Plaintiff Rongxiang Company claimed to the Defendant United Insurance according to the insurance contract. On April 10, 2014, the Defendant United Insurance gave the Plaintiff a Notice of Refusal of Indemnity that the cause of Mr. Luo's death was a sudden death and breached the exclusion (II) "death or injuries caused by diseases" of the Additional Shipowner's Employer Liability Insurance Clause loss so it was not recoverable. The Plaintiff then brought a suit against the Defendant.

The court holds that this case arose from a dispute over insurance contract on the sea and/ or sea-linked waters. The fact that the Plaintiff put forth a proposal for insurance of all risks cover-hulls insurance and additional risks and the Defendant accepted the proposal and issued certificates of insurance meant that the insurance contract had been concluded between the two parties. The assured Rongxiang Company had insurance benefits on the object of insurance, and the contract was a bona fide expression of intention on the basis of free will, and the terms of the contract did not violate laws and regulations. Hence the contract shall be legally concluded and valid. The parties shall strictly use their civil rights according to the insurance contract and laws, and complied with their duty completely and honestly. It's ascertained as truth in the court hearing that the accident of the mate LUO Feng's sudden death happened when M.V. "Jun Xing 888" berthed and discharged cargo, and the Plaintiff reported to the Defendant United Insurance on time and paid compensation RMB299,800 to Mr. Luo's legal heirs. The Defendant's contradiction of that the Plaintiff could not prove its payment to the Mr. Luo's legal heirs had no basis of fact, so the court not admits the evidence.

After the Plaintiff paid the compensation, it had the civil right to claim insurance amount to the Defendant United Insurance according to the insurance contract. The reason the Defendant refused to compensate was that the cause of Mr. Luo was a sudden death and shall apply the exclusion of insurance clause "death or injuries caused by diseases". The Death Certificate in this case verified the cause of Mr. Luo was a sudden death, and in medicine a sudden death was defined as naturally occurrent and unexpected death incident. The cause of a sudden death was incurred more than the condition of diseases, namely, diseases not certainly lead to the inevitability of a sudden death. In this case, Mr. Luo's sudden death could not exclude other non-diseased causes, and the Defendant United Insurance could not submit any evidence to prove that the cause of Mr. Luo's death was diseases, so the defenses, in respect of the condition that sudden death shall according to the diseases condition of the exclusion, of the Defendant United Insurance shall not be supported by the court. The Defendant United Insurance shall pay the insurance compensation to the Plaintiff Rongxiang Company according to the contract agreements.

In respect of the deductible excess at issue, the paragraph (VI) of clause 5 of Additional Shipowner's Employer Liability Insurance Clause prescribed that "the deductible excess deducted in each accident per person shall according to the provisions of the insurance policy", clause of which was labeled in bold black words. The insurance policy recorded that "the deductible franchise per accident per person is RMB1,000 or 10% of the actual losses of the amount, whichever is higher". When the Plaintiff effected the insure to the Defendant, the first step was to read and understand the insurance clauses, according to the notes it can interpret the clauses that the deductible excess shall only be deducted on the condition of the injuries of the crew members but shall not be deducted on the condition of the death of the crew members. Thereafter the insurance policy issued by the Defendant United Insurance was just to make sure the specific amount deductible in such accidents. The Defendant United Insurance emphasized that the deductible excess shall be deducted at each accident including death accidents. Because the insurance contract involved was concluded by standard terms provided by the Defendant Union Company, the other party of contract had another interpretation of whether the terms of deductible excess applies to the condition of crew members' death, and the court according to the law to interpret the provision backing the Plaintiff Rongxiang Company, namely, the terms of deductible excess shall not applies to the condition of crew members' death.

In respect of the interest claimed by the Plaintiff, because the claims of paying compensation by the Plaintiff Rongxiang Company to the Defendant United Insurance was according to the provisions of the contract, and the Defendant United Insurance did not comply with its obligation of paying the compensation in a timely manner, pursuant to Article 23 of the Insurance Law of the People's Republic of China, in addition to the payment of compensation, the Defendant shall compensate the Plaintiff for the damage incurred thereby, so the court shall support this claim of the Plaintiff Rongxiang Company. But the Plaintiff did not submit evidence to prove the specific time of its claim, so its claim of calculating interest from October 17, 2013 had no factual basis, so the court confirms to calculate interest from the time the Defendant issuing the written notice of declination of claim, namely on April 10, 2014, the interest to be calculated at the current fund loan rate in the same currency and in the corresponding period as published by the People's Bank of China.

To sum up, the claims of the Plaintiff Rongxiang Company are lawful and valid, and the court shall support them according to the law. Based on Article 13 and Article 23 and Article 30 of the Insurance Law of the People's Republic of China, Article 142 of the Civil Procedure Law of the People's Republic of China, the judgment is as follows:

The Defendant China United Property Insurance Co., Ltd. Jiangsu Branch shall pay the Plaintiff Suqian Rongxiang Shipping Co., Ltd. the insurance compensation once and for all in amount of RMB299,800 and the interest thereon(the interest to be calculated on April 10, 2014, to the date of payment ascertained in this judgment on basis of the loan interest rate for current funds published by the People's Bank of China for the same period) within 10 days after the date this judgment comes into effect.

Where the Defendant against whom enforcement is sought fails to perform the obligation of pecuniary payment during the period specified in this judgment, based on Article 253 of the Civil Procedure Law of the People's Republic of China, it shall pay double interest for the debt for the period of deferred performance.

Court acceptance fee in amount of RMB5,798, shall be halved to RMB2,899 due to the application of summary procedure. The Defendant China United Property Insurance Co., Ltd. Jiangsu Branch shall undertake the sum.

In case of dissatisfaction with this judgment, any party may within 15 days upon the service of this judgment, submit a statement of appeal to the court, together with copies according to the number of the opposite party, and appeal to the Hubei High People's Court. The Appellant shall, according to the amount of appeal request against this judgment and according to Article 13 Paragraph 1 of the Measures on the Payment of Litigation Costs, pay the entertainment fee for the appeal in advance. The remittance should be made to: non-revenue finance special bank account of Hubei Province financial department. The bank of deposit: Agriculture

Bank of China Wuhan Donghu branch, the account: 052101040000369. If the Appellant pays the fee in the ways of bank transfer or bank exchange, he shall mark "Hubei High People's Court" or the unit code "103001" of Hubei High People's Court on the application blank of the bank receipt. If the appellant does not pay the entertainment fee within 7 days after appeal period expires, it will be regarded as withdrawal of the appeal of his own accord.

Judge: ZHOU Yanhua

January 11, 2015

Clerk: ZHENG Wenhui

(Editor's Note: After this judgement of first instance, China United Property Insurance Co., Ltd. Jiangsu Branch appealed and the appeal court – Hubei High People's Court made the judgement of second instance in 2015 to dismiss the appeal and affirm this judgement of first instance.)

Guangzhou Maritime Court
Civil Judgment

Tai-I Jiangtong (Guangzhou) Co., Ltd.
v.
American President Lines, Ltd.

(2013) Guang Hai Fa Chu Zi No.552

Related Case(s) This is the judgment of first instance and the judgment of second instance is on page 1107.

Cause(s) of Action 202. Dispute over contract of carriage of goods by sea or sea-connected waters.

Headnote Ocean carrier and freight forwarder held not liable for loss caused by detention of goods by Customs authorities because the importer had an obligation under Customs law to be responsible for making correct declarations.

Summary The Plaintiff Tai-I Jiangtong brought suit against Defendants, American President Lines, Ltd., Lokman Shipping Company, and Shenzen International Freight Forwarding Company, and its various agents and subsidiaries for breach of a contract for the carriage of goods by sea. Here, Tai-I Jiangtong was the consignee, American President Lines was the first carrier and Lokman Shipping Company was the second carrier. The Plaintiff alleged due to the input error of Lokman Shipping Company and Guangzhou Lokman Shipping Company, the good information under one of the bills of lading B/L was omitted, which eventually led to Huangpu Xingang Customs of the People's Republic of China seizing all the goods under the two Bills of Lading for more than three months.

However, pursuant to Article 24 Paragraph 1 of the Customs Law of the People's Republic of China: the receiver of import goods and the sender of export goods shall make an accurate declaration and submit the import or export license and relevant papers to the Customs office for examination. The goods involved were import goods, and thus as the consignee, Tai-I Company had the duty of ensuring that proper information was reported to Customs. The court held that Tai-I Company failed to properly disclose to Customs that one its containers held two sets of goods, and thus because of its dishonest conduct, its claims against the Defendants were rejected.

Judgment

The Plaintiff: Tai-I Jiangtong (Guangzhou) Co., Ltd.
Domicile: No.251, Junye Road, Economic and Technology Development Zone East District, Guangzhou, Guangdong, the People's Republic of China.
Legal representative: YANG Zhongji, general manager.
Agent *ad litem*: AI Zongyuan, lawyer of Guangdong Xindesheng Law Firm.
Agent *ad litem*: XUAN Yunjing, apprentice lawyer of Guangdong Xindesheng Law Firm.

The Defendant: American President Lines, Ltd.
Domicile: 16220 N. Scottsdale Road, Suite 300 Scottsdale AZ 85254, United States.
Legal representative: ERIC R. SWETT, Director.
Agent *ad litem*: CAO Yanghui, lawyer of Guangdong Wang Jing & Co.
Agent *ad litem*: LI Jianping, lawyer of Guangdong Wang Jing & Co.

The Defendant: American President Lines(China) Co., Ltd.
Domicile: Room. 2305, 2306, Floor 23, China Resources Building, No.8 Jianguomen North Avenue, Dongcheng District, Beijing, the People's Republic of China.
Legal representative: CHEN Duanqiang, General Manager.
Agent *ad litem*: CAO Yanghui, lawyer of Guangdong Wang Jing & Co.
Agent *ad litem*: LI Jianping, lawyer of Guangdong Wang Jing & Co.

The Defendant: Lokman Shipping Company
Domicile: FLAT/RM 01–02 20/F TINS ENTERPRISES CENTRE 777 LAI CHI KOK ROAD CHEUNG SHA WAN.
Legal representative: CHEN Mengci, director.
Agent *ad litem*: HUANG Hui, lawyer of Guangdong Hengyun Law Firm.
Agent *ad litem*: ZHANG Jing, lawyer of Guangdong Hengyun Law Firm.

The Defendant: Guangzhou Lokman shipping Co., Ltd.
Domicile: Room B816, No.403 Dashadi East Road, Huangpu District, Guangzhou, Guangdong, the People's Republic of China.
Legal representative: XIONG Guowei, manager.
Agent *ad litem*: HUANG Hui, lawyer of Guangdong Hengyun Law Firm.
Agent *ad litem*: ZHANG Jing, lawyer of Guangdong Hengyun Law Firm.

The Defendant: Shenzhen Lokman International Freight Forwarding Co., Ltd. Guangzhou Branch
Domicile: Room B810, B812, No.403 Dashadi East Road, Huangpu District, Guangzhou, Guangdong, the People's Republic of China.
Legal representative: DING Fusheng, manager.
Agent *ad litem*: HUANG Hui, lawyer of Guangdong Hengyun Law Firm.
Agent *ad litem*: ZHANG Jing, lawyer of Guangdong Hengyun Law Firm.

With respect to the case arising from dispute over contract of carriage of goods by sea, the Plaintiff Tai-I Jiangtong (Guangzhou) Co., Ltd. (hereinafter referred to as "Tai-I Company") filed a litigation against the Defendant American President Lines, Ltd. (hereinafter referred to as "President Lines Company"), American President Lines(China) Co., Ltd. (hereinafter referred to as "President Lines China Company"), Lokman Shipping Company (hereinafter referred to as "Lokman Shipping Company"), Guangzhou Lokman Shipping Co., Ltd. (hereinafter referred to as "Guangzhou Lokman Shipping Company") and Shenzhen Lokman International Freight Forwarding Co., Ltd. Guangzhou Branch (hereinafter referred to as "Shenzhen Lokman Freight Forwarding Company Guangzhou Branch"), before the court on May 17, 2013. After entertaining this case on May 27, 2013, the court constituted the collegiate panel consisted of Judge SONG Ruiqiu as Presiding Judge, Judge LI Zhengping and Acting Judge HU Shi according to the law. On September 13, the court organized evidence exchanges among the parties, and held the hearings in public on March 23, July 31, and October 30, 2014 respectively. Tai-I Company replaced agent *ad litem* CHEN Daixi with AI Zongyuan on September 10, 2013, and replaced agent *ad litem* GAO Xin with XUAN Yunjing on July 30, 2014. Agents *ad litem* GAO Xin and AI Zongyuan of Tai-I Company attended evidence exchanges and the first hearing. Agents *ad litem* AI Zongyuan and XUAN Yunjing attended the second and third hearings. LI Jianping, the common agent *ad litem* of President Lines Company and President Lines China Company participated in the evidence exchanges and all the hearings. HUANG Hui and XIANG Wei, the common agents *ad litem* of Lokman Shipping Company, Guangzhou Lokman shipping Company and Shenzhen Lokman Freight Forwarding Company Guangzhou Branch participated in the evidence exchanges, and the common agents *ad litem* HUANG Hui and ZHANG Jing attended the first hearing, and HUANG Hui attended the second and third hearings. Now the case has been concluded.

The Plaintiff Tai-I Company alleged that Tai-I Company purchased electrolytic copper plate from Pansonic Corporation. Pansonic Corporation instructed Pan Pacific Copper Co., Ltd. (hereinafter referred to as "Pan Pacific Company") to deliver the goods directly to Tai-I Company. Pan Pacific Company commissioned President Lines Company to transport the goods from Japan to China Huangpu. On April 23, 2012, President Lines Company issued No.APLU058193457 and No. APLU058193461 bills of lading. President Lines Company was responsible for shipping the goods to Hong Kong, and then Lokman Shipping Company trans-shipped the goods to the outward wharf of China Pudong East River. The goods under the aforesaid two bills of lading arrived at Huangpu Port at the same time. Due to the input error of Lokman Shipping Company and Guangzhou Lokman Shipping Company, the goods information under No.APLU058193461 B/L was missed, which eventually lead to Huangpu Xingang Customs of the People's Republic of China (hereinafter referred to as "Huangpu Xingang Customs") seized all the goods under the two Bills of Lading for more than three months, and during the investigation, the goods involved were weighed. Therefore Tai-I Company suffered losses totally RMB411,389.21, including the Delayed Declaration Fee of

RMB39,090.00, the Administrative Fine of RMB29,000.00, the Container Deposit of RMB34,000.00, the Weighing Charges of RMB2,210.00, the Port Storage Charge of RMB6,552.00 and the loss of Capital Backlog Interest of RMB300,537.21. President Lines Company was the carrier of the goods involved. As the representative of the President Lines Company, President Lines China Company could bear all civil obligations on behalf of President Lines Company. Lokman Shipping Company was the actual carrier from Hong Kong to Huangpu, Guangzhou Lokman Shipping Company and Shenzhen Lokman Freight Forwarding Company Guangzhou Branch were the actor of Manifest Declaration, there existed confusion behaviors among the three parties. To safeguard the lawful rights and interests, the Plaintiff requested the court to rule the five Defendants to jointly and severally compensate the Plaintiff Tai-I Company for the losses in sum of RMB411,389.21, and bear the court fees.

Tai-I Company submitted the following 10 sets of evidence:

1. No.GM000862-C Sales Contract, No.GMX00556-A Invoice, copy of No. LC442131201256 L/C, Confirmation Letter, Import L/C Receipt, External Payment / Acceptance Notice and No.APLU058193457 B/L, to prove the legal relationship between Tai-I Company and President Lines Company and the value of goods under the No.APLU058193457 B/L;
2. No.GM000863-C Sales Contract, No.GMX00555-A Invoice, copy of No. LC442131201255 L/C, Confirmation Letter, Import L/C Receipt, Foreign Payment / Acceptance Notice and No.APLU058193461 B/L, to prove the value of goods under No.APLU058193461 B/L;
3. E-mails and mail attachments between Lokman Shipping Company and Tai-I Company from April 27 to May 7, 2012, to prove the legal relationships between Taiyi Company and Lokman Shipping Company, and the fact that Tai-I Company confirmed the Switched B/L information of goods involved to Lokman Shipping Company;
4. The Hong Kong and Macau Ship Import / Export Manifest declared by Lokman Shipping Company to Huangpu Xingang Customs, to prove that the manifest information declared by Lokman Shipping Company was not accurate;
5. The letters issued by Shenzhen Lokman Freight Forwarding Company Guangzhou Branch on May 22, 2012, Application of Manifest Amendment and Deletion filled by Shenzhen Lokman Freight Forwarding Company Guangzhou Branch, and E-mail received by Tai-I Company from Lokman Shipping Company on July 25, 2012, to prove that the goods involved were seized by customs due to the inaccurate manifest information declared by Lokman Shipping Company and Guangzhou Lokman shipping Company;
6. E-mails between President Lines Company and Tai-I Company from April 23 to April 27, to prove that the legal relationships between President Lines Company and President Lines China Company, and the fact that Tai-I Company confirmed the consignee information to President Lines Company during the transportation of goods involved;

7. Notice of Outbound Receipt issued by Sinotrans Guangdong Dongjiang Warehouse & Terminal Co., Ltd. (hereinafter referred to as "Dongjiang Warehouse & Terminal Company"), the Notice of Delayed Declaration Fee by Huangpu Xingang Customs, Declaration for Import Goods, Bank Deposit Slip, Special Bill for the Administration of Customs, Check stub of Shenzhen Development Bank, the receipt issued by Guangzhou Lokman Shipping Company, Customer Statements, Bank Deposit Slip, Cash Voucher, Application Slip for Mechanical Loading and Unloading Operation, the Invoice of Terminal Weighing Fee, the Invoice of Storage Fee and Billing List, Interest Loss Calculation Table, to prove the losses of Tai-I Company;
8. Xin Guan Ji Gao Zi No.[2013] 1030033 Administrative Punishment Notice and Xin Guan Ji Wei Zi No.[2013] 1030053 Administrative Penalty Written Decision of Huangpu Xingang Customs, and Customs Penalty Confiscation Payment, to prove that Tai-I Company had paid the payment;
9. No.LH12040720 B/L of Lokman Shipping Company stamped by Huangpu Xingang Customs, the Notice of Releottom Cargo issued by Lokman Shipping Company on May 22, 2012, the Receipt of Import Cargo Distributional Card REIF issued by Dongjiang Warehouse &Terminal Company on July 20, 2012, No.LH12050131 B/L of Lokman Shipping Company stamped by Huangpu Xingang Customs, the Notice of Releottom Cargo issued by Lokman Shipping Company on August 1, 2012, the Receipt of Import Container Distributional Card REIF issued by Dongjiang Warehouse &Terminal Company on August 1, 2012, the Notice of Customs Inspection issued by Huangpu Xingang Customs on May 28, 2012 and Situation Description on October 29, 2014, to prove the seized time by Huangpu Customs to check the goods involved and the release time; and
10. Xin Guan Ji Gao Zi No.[2013] 1030086 Administrative Punishment Notice and Xin Guan Ji Wei Zi No.[2013] 1030086 Administrative Penalty Written Decision taken by the court from Huangpu Xingang Customs as Tai-I Company applied, to prove that Guangzhou Lokman Shipping Company was punished by Customs.

The Defendant President Lines Company and President Lines China Company defended that: 1. the action of Tai-I Company shall be dismissed, since the goods involved arrived at Huangpu Port on May 3, 2012 which was more than a year of litigation prescription period; 2. President Lines China Company was the agent of President Lines Company, but was not the proper Defendant of this case; 3.as the carrier of the goods involved, President Lines Company had safely delivered the goods to the port of destination and had fulfilled transportation obligations. Due to the defective customs declaration data, the losses proposed by Tai-I Company shall not be compensated by President Lines Company. For the convenience of customs clearance of Tai-I Company, President Lines Company provided Chinese supplementary information to Lokman Shipping Company and Guangzhou Lokman Shipping Company timely, which was a free service provided by President Lines Company outside the transport obligation. If there was no significant fault,

President Shipping Company shall not bear responsibilities; 4. the reason of being seized by customs was that Tai-I Company was full aware of manifest information was wrong, but still used the incorrect manifest information to declare customs. If Tai-I Company declared customs after manifest correction, the goods shall not be seized by customs. Even if Lokman Shipping Company and Guangzhou Lokman Shipping Company did not verify the relevant documents and containers leading to the incorrect manifest information of the port of destination, Tai-I Company provided the incomplete Chinese supplementary information in two B/L involved caused the misunderstanding of Lokman Shipping Company and Guangzhou Lokman Shipping Company; 5. Because President Shipping Company timely conveyed the Chinese supplementary information of Tai-I Company, Tai-I Company used other materials provided by other three Defendants to declare customs rather than use any materials provided by President Lines Company and President Lines China Company, Consequently, President Lines Company and President Lines China Company had no causal relationship with manifest error behavior of other three Defendants and shall not bear joint and several liability with other three Defendants; 6. Tai-I Company did not take the goods under No. APLU058193457 B/L in time after the customs clearance, also did not actively reflect the situation to the customs to admit declaration errors. Abstain from an act of Tai-I Company led to the goods detained at the port for more than three months after the seizure; 7. according to the provisions of the B/L issued by the President Lines Company, the liability for compensation of President Lines Company was limited to GBP800.00. The Defendant requested the court to dismiss the claims of the Plaintiff Tai-I Company.

The Defendant President Lines Company and President Lines China Company submitted the following 9 sets of evidence:

1. A letter from President Lines Company to Tai-I Company on November 14, 2012;
2. E-mail from Tai-I Company to President Lines Company on April 27, 2012, the above 2 pieces of evidence, to prove that the Chinese supplementary information submitted by Tai-I Company was not complete;
3. The letter from Shenzhen Lokman Freight Forwarding Company Guangzhou Branch to American President Lines(China) Guangzhou Branch Co., Ltd. (hereinafter referred to as "President Lines China Company Guangzhou Branch") on May 31, 2012;
4. E-mails between Shenzhen Lokman Freight Forwarding Company Guangzhou Branch and President Lines China Company from June 2, 2012 to July 18, 2012;
5. E-mail from Tai-I Company to Lokman Company on May 7, 2012;
6. Application of Manifest Amendment and Deletion filled by Shenzhen Lokman Freight Forwarding Company Guangzhou Branch;
7. Special Bill for the Administration of Customs;

8. Storage charge billing list, above 5 pieces of the evidence, to prove that Tai-I Company declaration was wrong and customs had already released the correct 16 container cargo;
9. No.APLU058193461 B/L issued by President Lines Company and Back Clause, to prove that the Limit of Indemnity of President Lines Company.

The Defendant Lokman Shipping Company provided that:

1. The goods involved under the B/L arrived in Hong Kong and was delivered to Tai-I Company, but the date of the complaint of this case was on May 17, 2013, which had exceeded the one-year limitation, and shall dismiss all claims of Tai-I Company according to the law.
2. Tai-I Company claimed that Lokman Shipping Company made operational errors, and missed the goods information under No.APLU058193461 B/L, which was without any factual basis. So Lokman Shipping Company did not make any mistake about it, and shall not bear compensation liability according to the law.
3. Lokman Shipping Company had no obligation to check the carrier's different batches of goods whether existed LCL. Hence Lokman Shipping Company and Guangzhou Lokman shipping Company missing the manifest claimed by Tai-I Company was not obviously formed. Lokman Shipping Company shall not bear compensation liability according to the law.
4. Lokman Shipping Company actively cooperated and promoted the solution of the problems involved, including the amendment of B/L to Huangpu Xingang Customs, which did not mean to waiver any rights and bear responsibility.
5. Tai-I Company claimed that the loss of Capital Backlog Interest of RMB300,537.21 resulted from delayed clearance of goods, which had exceeded the reasonable and foreseeable loss when Lokman Shipping Company signed the contract, and Tai-I Company could not prove the rationality and authenticity of this loss. Hence, Lokman Shipping Company shall not bear such loss. The Defendant requested the court to dismiss the prosecution or claims to Lokman Shipping Company.

Lokman Shipping Company submitted the following 6 sets of evidence:

1. Notice of Releottom Cargo and Proxy, to prove that claim of Tai-I Company had exceeded the limitation of action;
2. E-mails from Lokman Shipping Company to President Lines Company on April 10, 2012, to prove that the records requirements proposed from Lokman Shipping Company to President Lines Company with regard to LCL goods;
3. E-mail from President Lines Company to Lokman Shipping Company on April 26, 2012;
4. E-mail from President Lines Company to Lokman Shipping Company on April 28, 2012, above 2 pieces of evidence, to prove that all the information provided by President Lines Company and Lokman Shipping Company were not mentioned or clearly indicated LCL under 2 B/Ls involved;

5. Fact Statement of Lokman Shipping Company, to prove that Lokman Shipping Company did not make mistake with regard to the goods involved detained in Customs;
6. Booking Information of Kong Hing Agency Co., Ltd. and Yang Ming Marine Transport Corporation, to prove the practice of LCL goods.

The Defendant Guangzhou Lokman Shipping Company agreed to the reply opinions of Lokman Shipping Company and defended that: Guangzhou Lokman Shipping Company was not the carrier under the B/L involved, and the Switched B/L of goods involved was issued by Lokman Shipping Company, Guangzhou Lokman Shipping Company was only the agent of Lokman Shipping Company in Huangpu Port. According to B/L, Tai-I Company claimed compensation for damages according to the law to the carrier under the carriage contract, Guangzhou Lokman Shipping Company had no obligation of compensation for loss of Tai-I Company. The Defendant requested the court to dismiss the prosecution or claims to Guangzhou Lokman Shipping Company.

Guangzhou Lokman Shipping Company submitted the following 3 sets of evidence:
1. Business Registration Certificate; 2. enterprise Industrial and Commercial Registration Information; 3. Shipping Agency Agreement, above 3 pieces evidence, to prove the legal relationship between Guangzhou Lokman Shipping Company and Lokman Shipping Company.

The Defendant Shenzhen Lokman Freight Forwarding Company Guangzhou Branch agreed to the reply opinions of Lokman Shipping Company and defended that: Shenzhen Lokman Freight Forwarding Company Guangzhou Branch was not the carrier under the B/L involved, and the switched B/L of goods involved was issued by Lokman Shipping Company, Shenzhen Lokman Freight Forwarding Company Guangzhou Branch was only the agent of Lokman Shipping Company in Huangpu Port. According to B/L, Tai-I Company claimed compensation for damages according to the law to the carrier under the carriage contract, Shenzhen Lokman Freight Forwarding Company Guangzhou Branch had no obligation of compensation for loss of Tai-I Company. The Defendant requested the court to dismiss the prosecution or claims to Shenzhen Lokman Freight Forwarding Company Guangzhou Branch.

Shenzhen Lokman Freight Forwarding Company Guangzhou Branch submitted the following 3 sets of evidence:
1. Business Registration Certificate; 2. enterprise Industrial and Commercial Registration Information; 3. Shipping Agency Agreement, above 3 pieces of evidence, to prove the legal relationship between Shenzhen Lokman Freight Forwarding Company Guangzhou Branch and Lokman Shipping Company.

Upon hearing and cross-examination, examination and determination of the evidence were as follows:

No.GMX00556-A Invoice, copy of No.LC442131201256 L/C, Import L/C Receipt, External Payment / Acceptance Notice and cope of No.APLU058193457 B/L submitted by Tai-I Company, which were consistent with the original ones through review, probative force shall be ascertained thereof; No.GM000862-C Sales Contract and No.LC442131201256 L/C Confirmation were copies, but corroborating with above 5 pieces of evidence, probative force shall be ascertained thereof; No.GMX00555-A Invoice, copy of No.LC442131201255 L/C, Import L/C Receipt, Foreign Payment / Acceptance Notice and copy of No.APLU058193461 B/L, which were consistent with the original ones through review, probative force shall be ascertained thereof; No.GM000863-C Sales Contract and copy of No. LC442131201255 L/C Confirmation, but corroborating with above 5 pieces of evidence, probative force shall be ascertained thereof; Tai-I Company and Lokman Shipping Company, Guangzhou Lokman shipping Company, Shenzhen Lokman Freight Forwarding Company Guangzhou Branch with regard to the E-mails and mail attachments from April 27 to May 7, 2012 between Tai-I Company and Lokman Shipping Company, the Hong Kong and Macau Ship Import / Export Manifest declared by Lokman Shipping Company to Huangpu Xingang Customs, the letters issued by Shenzhen Lokman Freight Forwarding Company Guangzhou Branch on May 22, 2012, Application of the Manifest Amendment and Deletion Filled by Shenzhen Lokman Freight Forwarding Company Guangzhou Branch, E-mail received by Tai-I Company from Lokman Shipping Company on July 25, 2012, the Court had no objection to authenticity of them and probative force shall be ascertained thereof; Tai-I Company, President Lines Company and President Lines China Company had no objection to E-mails between President Lines Company and Taiyi Company from April 23 to April 27, and probative force shall be ascertained thereof; the five Defendants had no objection to the Notice of Delayed Declaration Fee by Huangpu Xingang Customs, Declaration for Import Goods, Bank Deposit Slip, Special Bill for the Administration of Customs, Check stub of Shenzhen Development Bank, the Receipt issued by Guangzhou Lokman Shipping Company, Customer Statements, Bank Deposit Slip, Cash Voucher, Application Slip for Mechanical Loading and Unloading Operation, the Invoice of Terminal Weighing Fee, the Invoice of Storage Fee and Billing List, Xin Guan Ji Gao Zi No.[2013] 1030033 Administrative Punishment Notice and Xin Guan Ji Wei Zi No.[2013] 1030053 Administrative Penalty Written Decision of Huangpu Xingang Customs, and Customs Penalty Confiscation Payment, Xin Guan Ji Gao Zi No.[2013] 1030086 Administrative Punishment Notice and Xin Guan Ji Wei Zi No. [2013] 1030086 Administrative Penalty Written Decision, the court has no objection to authenticity of them, and probative force shall be ascertained; Tai-I Company submitted Notice of Outbound Receipt issued by Dongjiang Warehouse & Terminal Company which corroborated with Invoice of Storage Fee and Billing List, probative force shall be ascertained thereof. Situation Description issued by Huangpu Xingang Customs on October 29, 2014 had original one to review, probative force shall be ascertained thereof. Although Notice of Releottom Cargo issued by Lokman Shipping Company on May 22, 2012 and August 1, 2012 were the copies, in the absence of contrary evidence submitted by Lokman Shipping Company, probative force shall be ascertained thereof. Notice of Customs Inspection issued by Huangpu Xingang Customs on May 28, 2012, the Receipt of Import Cargo Distributional Card REIF issued by Dongjiang Warehouse

& Terminal Company on July 20, 2012, No.LH12050131 B/L of Lokman Shipping Company stamped by Huangpu Xingang Customs, the Notice of Releottom Cargo issued by Lokman Shipping Company on August 1, 2012, the Receipt of Import Container Distributional Card REIF issued by Dongjiang Warehouse &Terminal Company on August 1, 2012, the Notice of Customs Inspection issued by Huangpu Xingang Customs on May 28, 2012 could corroborate with other evidence that was deemed to be probative, probative force shall be ascertained thereof. The five Defendants all had objection to Interest Loss Calculation Table submitted by Tai-I Company, in the absence of other evidence to be corroborated, probative force shall not be ascertained thereof.

Tai-I Company had no objection to the Letter from President Lines Company to Tai-I Company on November 14, 2012 and Back Clause of No.APLU058193461 B/L issued by President Lines Company and President Lines China Company, probative force shall be ascertained thereof. Lokman Shipping Company, Guangzhou Lokman Shipping Company and Shenzhen Lokman Freight Forwarding Company Guangzhou Branch had no objection to the letter from Shenzhen Lokman Freight Forwarding Company Guangzhou Branch to President Lines China Company Guangzhou Branch on May 31, 2012 and the E-mails between Shenzhen Lokman Freight Forwarding Company Guangzhou Branch and President Lines China Company from June 2, 2012 to July 18, 2012, probative force shall be ascertained thereof.

Tai-I Company had no objection to Notice of Releottom Cargo and Proxy submitted by Lokman Shipping Company, probative force shall be ascertained thereof. President Lines Company and President Lines China Company had no objection to the E-mails from Lokman Shipping Company to President Lines Company on April 10, 2012, the E-mail from President Lines Company to Lokman Shipping Company on April 26, 2012 and the E-mail from President Lines Company to Lokman Shipping Company on April 28, 2012, probative force shall be ascertained thereof. Tai-I Company, President Lines Company and President Lines China Company all had objection to Fact Statement submitted by Lokman Shipping Company, and admitted the fact recorded in Fact Statement which could corroborate with the above evidence with probative force. Booking Information of Kong Hing Agency Co., Ltd. and Yang Ming Marine Transport Corporation submitted by Lokman Shipping Company were not relevant to this case, probative force shall not be ascertained thereof.

Tai-I Company had no objection to Business Registration Certificate and Enterprise Industrial and Commercial Registration Information submitted by Guangzhou Lokman Shipping Company, probative force shall be ascertained thereof. Shipping Agency Agreement submitted by Guangzhou Lokman Shipping Company had original one to review, probative force shall be ascertained thereof.

Tai-I Company had no objection to Business Registration Certificate and Business License submitted by Shenzhen Lokman Freight Forwarding Company Guangzhou Branch, probative force shall be ascertained thereof. International Cargo Transport Agency Agreement submitted by Shenzhen Lokman Freight

Forwarding Company Guangzhou Branch had original one to review, probative force shall be ascertained thereof.

According to the evidence admitted to be probative and the hearing, the Court ascertained the facts of this case as follows:

Tai-I Company purchased electrolytic copper plate with the CIF price terms China Huangpu from Pansonic Corporation, and signed 2 Sales Contracts of No. GM000862-C and No.GM000863-C. With regard to No.GM000862-C Sales Contract, Tai-I Company applied for issuing the No.LC442131201256 documentary L/C, and obtained No.GMX00556-A Invoice issued by Pansonic Corporation through acceptance as well as No.APLU058193457 B/L issued by President Lines Company and endorsed by Pan Pacific Company. According to No.GMX00556-A Invoice, the number of electrolytic copper plate was 405.011 tons, the unit price was USD9,107.28 CIF Huangpu, and the sum was USD3,688,548.58. With regard to No.GM000863-C Sales Contract, Tai-I Company applied for issuing the No. LC442131201255 documentary L/C, and obtained No.GMX00555-A Invoice issued by Pansonic Corporation through acceptance and payment, as well as No. APLU058193461 B/L issued by President Lines Company and endorsed by Pan Pacific Company. According to No.GMX00555-A Invoice, the number of electrolytic copper plate was 19.776 tons, the unit price was USD8,964.00 CIF Huangpu, and the sum was USD177,272.06.

On April 23, 2012, President Lines Company issued two sets of B/Ls, which was No.APLU058193457 B/L and No.APLU058193457 B/L. Two pieces of B/Ls all recorded that the shipper was Pan Pacific Company, the consignee was to order of the shipper, the vessel name was PROTEUS, the notify party was Tai-I Company, the place of receipt was Oita Japan storage yard, the port of loading was Oita Japan, the port of discharge was Huangpu China, and the place of delivery was Huangpu China container yard. There were 16 TEU General Dry Cargo Containers goods under No.APLU058193457 B/L, including APZU3065257, APZU3142604, APZU3278890, APZU3439193, APZU3514701, APZU3605381, APZU3671510, APZU3745819, APZU3907437, APZU3937771, APZU3953561, APZU3974950, APZU3983503, FCIU3843626, TCLU2285111, and TGHU1588051 (hereinafter referred to as "APZU3065257 etc. 16 containers goods"), added to 5.527 tons goods under No.GESU3417158 container, totally 405.169 tons and 158 bundles. The goods under the No.APLU058193461 B/L were the goods under No. GESU3417158 Container, totally 19.784 tons and 8 bundles.

On April 23, 2012, President Lines Company issued Notice of Arrival to Tai-I Company to notify Tai-I Company that the goods under above 2 B/Ls was expected to arrive at Chiwan, and requested Tai-I Company to provide Chinese Shipping Instruction about these 2 B/Ls. In addition, Notice of Arrival shall specify Free Time of General Dry Cargo Container. From the next day of the goods unloaded at the port of destination, free period of General Dry Cargo Container was 10 days, more than 1–5 days after the free period, container demurrage charge was RMB100 per day, 6–10 days were RMB200 every day, and more than 11 days were RMB400 per day. On April 26, Tai-I Company provided Chinese Shipping Instruction of above 2 B/Ls to President Lines Company, including B/L number,

Description of Goods, Name of Consignee, Contact, Contact of Switched B/L, Total Number of Goods, Weight of Goods and Port of Discharge, but B/L No.was not recorded in Chinese Shipping Instruction of goods under No.APLU058193461 B/L. At 17:24 on April 26, President Lines Company sent a letter to commission Lokman Shipping Company to ship the goods under No.APLU058193457 B/L from Chiwan to Huangpu. The attachments of this letter were the copy of this B/L and the copy of Chinese Shipping Instruction of this B/L provided by Tai-I Company. At 0954 on April 27, Lokman Shipping Company notified Tai-I Company to verify the sample manuscript of Switched B/L correspond with No. APLU058193457 B/L. Goods of No.APZU3065257 Container etc. 16 containers were written in this sample manuscript. At 1541 on April 27, Tai-I Company replied to Lokman Shipping Company that Switched B/L correspond with No. APLU058193457 B/L had been checked. On April 30, Lokman Shipping Company shipped the goods under No.APLU058193457 B/L from Chiwan to Huangpu, corresponding Lokman Shipping Company used No.LH12040720 B/L. On May 1, Guangzhou Lokman Shipping Company transferred Manifest of Import Cargo under No.LH12040720 B/L of M.V. "Hui Hailong 158" to Huangpu Xingang Customs. This manifest was stamped by Lokman Shipping Company, including goods under APZU3065257 etc. 16 containers and No.GESU3417158 Container, which aggregated 405.169 tons, excluding the goods under No.GESU3417158 Container of No.APLU058193461 B/L. On May 3, the goods involved under 17 containers shipped to Huangpu. At 1137 on May 3, Lokman Shipping Company issued the Notice of Arrival under the No.LH12040720 B/L to Tai-I Company, notifying Tai-I Company to declare.

At 1717 on April 27, 2012, Tai-I Company issued Chinese Shipping Instruction of No.APLU058193461 B/L again to President Lines Company. At 2030 on April 27, President Lines Company notified Tai-I Company that the goods under No. APLU058193461 B/L would arrive at Chiwan Port on May 1. At 1708 on April 28, President Lines Company sent a letter to commission Lokman Shipping Company to ship the goods under No.APLU058193461 B/L from Chiwan to Huangpu. The attachments of this letter were the copy of this B/L and the copy of Chinese Shipping Instruction of this B/L provided by Tai-I Company. At 1759 on April 28, Lokman Shipping Company issued Tai-I Company to check Switched B/L corresponding with No.APLU058193461 B/L. At 1012 on May 2, Tai-I Company replied to Lokman Shipping Company that Switched B/L corresponding with No. APLU058193461 B/L had been checked. On May 4, Lokman Shipping Company arranged Switched shipment corresponding with No.APLU058193461 B/L, but the docker replied that the number of container was wrong. On 5 May, Lokman Shipping Company inquired President Lines Company about the goods of No. GESU3417158 Container under No.APLU058193461 B/L, President Lines Company replied that such container had been shipped to Huangpu. At 1605 on May 7, Tai-I Company inquired Lokman Shipping Company that Notice of Arrival of Switched B/L corresponding with No.APLU058193461 B/L had not received, where they were. At 1610 on May 7, Lokman Shipping Company replied to Tai-I Company that such B/L was not arranged with a vessel.

On May 9, 2012, Lokman Shipping Company informed Tai-I Company that the goods under No.APLU058193461 B/L had loaded in the No.GESU3417158 Container and were shipped to Huangpu Port. On May 9, Tai-I Company declared to Huangpu Xingang Customs by general trade about electrolytic copper plate of 405.011 tons under No.LH12040720 B/L in 17 containers, but did not declare the goods under No.APLU058193461 B/L in No.GESU3417158 Container.

On May 21, 2012, Huangpu Xingang Customs stamped No.LH12040720 B/L issued by Lokman Shipping Company to release the goods under No.LH12040720 B/L. Because the goods under No.GESU3417158 Container did not declare import formalities, Tai-I Company did not take the goods under No.LH12040720 B/L in 17 containers after the customs clearance. On May 22, Shenzhen Lokman Freight Forwarding Company Guangzhou Branch sent a letter to Huangpu Xingang Customs, and indicated due to company's mistake, B/L of LCL was leaved out, leaving customers unable to declare, and applied Customs to amend the Manifest of Import Cargo. On May 28, Huangpu Xingang Customs notified Guangzhou Yuesui Customs Declaration Company commissioned by Tai-I Company that the goods under No.LH12040720 B/L shall be inspected, notifying Guangzhou Yuesui Customs Declaration Company to contact harbor section and other related department to prepare. On May 29, Huangpu Xingang Customs inspected the goods under APZU3065257 etc. 16 containers and No.GESU3417158 Container, Tai-I Company paid Dongjiang Warehouse &Terminal Company Weighing Charges of RMB2,210.00.

On July 19, 2012, Huangpu customs endorsed on No.LH12040720 B/L of GESU3417158 shall not be released temporarily. On July 20 and 21, Tai-I Company took the goods under APZU3065257 etc. 16 containers from Dongjiang Warehouse &Terminal Company. Dongjiang Warehouse &Terminal Company charged Tai-I Company RMB6096.00 for the storage fee of such 16 containers.

On July 22, 2012, Tai-I Company sent a letter to Shenzhen Lokman Freight Forwarding Company Guangzhou Branch, requesting Shenzhen Lokman Freight Forwarding Company Guangzhou Branch to assist amending manifest information according to the situation of actual arrival of the goods, so that Tai-I Company can successfully declare to customs and take delivery of goods. Before July 25, Huangpu Xingang Customs permitted Lokman Shipping Company to amend manifest. On July 25, Guangzhou Lokman shipping Company issued Notice of Arrival to Tai-I Company, notifying that the goods under No.APLU058193461 B/L had arrived at Huangpu Port on May 2, 2012, and No.LH12050131 B/L was used by Lokman Shipping Company. On July 26, Tai-I Company declared to Huangpu Xingang Customs about 19.776 tons electrolytic copper under No.LH12050131 B/L. On July 27, Huangpu Xingang Customs notified Tai-I Company that Tai-I Company shall pay delayed declaration fee of RMB39,090.00, because Tai-I Company delayed for 70 days when declaring to Huangpu Xingang Customs about the import electrolytic copper. Tai-I Company had paid such delayed declaration fee to Huangpu Customs. On August 1, Huangpu Xingang Customs released the goods under No.GESU3417158 Container. On August 2, Tai-I Company took the goods under No.GESU3417158 Container. Dongjiang Warehouse &Terminal Company charged Tai-I Company RMB456 for the storage fee of such containers.

On May 9, 2012, on behalf of Tai-I Company, Guangzhou Hong Lian Transport Co., Ltd. issued No.00494356 Check of RMB34,000.00 to President Lines China Company as the deposit of 17 containers involved. After taking delivery of the goods, Tai-I Company returned 17 containers involved to President Lines Company. On August 9, President Lines China Company honored such check. On May 14, 2013, Tai-I Company paid RMB34,000.00 to Guangzhou Hong Lian Transport Co., Ltd. to pay off the advanced container demurrage charges of RMB34,000.00 to Guangzhou Hong Lian Transport Co., Ltd. During the hearing, President Lines Company confirmed that acceptance check of RMB34,000.00 was collected as the container demurrage charges.

On May 28, 2013, Huangpu Xingang Customs issued Administrative Punishment Notice to Tai-I Company. On September 27, Huangpu Xingang Customs issued Administrative Penalty Written Decision to Tai-I Company, finding out that declared import electrolytic copper plate by Tai-I Company was 405.011 tons, but the actual arrival of the electrolytic copper plate was 424.787 tons. Huangpu Xingang Customs deemed that dishonest behavior of Tai-I Company declaration had constituted a violation of the provisions of the customs supervision, thus deciding to impose financial penalties of RMB29,000.00 to Tai-I Company. On October 11, 2013, Tai-I Company paid the penalty of RMB29,000.00.

On December 24, 2013, Huangpu Xingang Customs issued Xin Guan Ji Wei Zi No.[2013]1030086 Administrative Penalty Written Decision to Guangzhou Lokman Shipping Company, finding out that on May 3, 2013,Guangzhou Lokman Shipping Company declaration of electrolytic copper plate of 158 bundles and 405.169 tons under No.LH12040720 B/L in No.52020120205010 Voyage of M.V. "Huihai Long 168", Container number were GESU3417158, APZU3065257, APZU3142604, APZU3278890, APZU3439193, APZU3514701, APZU3605381, APZU3671510, APZU3745819, APZU3907437, APZU3937771, APZU3953561, APZU3974950, APZU3983503, FCIU3843626, TCLU2285111, and TGHU1588051, however, within No.GESU3417158 Container, there were not only the goods under No. LH12040720 B/L, but also 8 bundles and 10.784 tons of electrolytic copper plate under No.LH12050131 B/L. Guangzhou Lokman Shipping Company did not declare such 19.784 tons electrolytic copper plate, hence the Customs deemed that electronic data transferred to customs was not accurate, which affected customs supervision, thus deciding to give a warning to Guangzhou Lokman Shipping Company.

Tai-I Company did not provide evidence to prove that the detention of goods involved in the port was bound to lead to the loss of Capital Backlog Interest. The interest reversal of RMB300,537.21 claimed by Tai-I Company was not confirmed.

The business scope of President Lines China Company included providing canvassion, booking, preparation, confirmation, making out and issuing B/L etc. by owned, leased or operated ship of President Lines Company. There existed commission relationship between President Lines Company and President Lines China Company.

Lokman Shipping Company signed Shipping Agency Agreement with Guangzhou Lokman shipping Company. Lokman Shipping Company confirmed that Guangzhou Lokman shipping Company was commissioned to handle the relevant affairs in the transportation of the goods involved. Lokman Shipping Company signed International Cargo Transport Agency Agreement with Shenzhen Lokman Freight Forwarding Company Guangzhou Branch. Lokman Shipping Company confirmed that Shenzhen Lokman Freight Forwarding Company Guangzhou Branch was commissioned to handle the relevant affairs in the transportation of the goods involved.

During the hearings, parties involved all chose to apply mainland law of People's Republic of China to settle the disputes of this case.

The court held that this case is the dispute over contract of carriage of goods by sea. The Defendant, President Lines Company, was a company registered in the United States, and the departure point of the goods involved was Japan, with foreign elements of this case. Pursuant to Article 2 Paragraph 11 of Some Provisions of the Supreme People's Court on the Sccope of Cases to be Entertained by Maritime Courts, this case shall be under the specific jurisdiction of maritime courts. The transport destination Huangpu Port of the goods involved fell within the jurisdiction of the court; Pursuant to Article 6 Paragraph 1 of the Special Maritime Procedure Law of the People's Republic of China and Article 27 of the Civil Procedure Law of the People's Republic of China, the court has jurisdiction over this case. In the litigation, parties involved made a clear choice to apply mainland law of the People's Republic of China, pursuant to Article 269 of the Maritime Code of the People's Republic of China that the parties to a contract may choose the law applicable to such contract, unless the law provides otherwise. this case ensured the rights and obligations of the parties by applying mainland law of the People's Republic of China.

With respect to the five Defendants' legal status in connection with the contract of carriage of goods by sea. President Lines Company issued through bill of lading for the goods involved, Tai-I Company took the goods by B/L, there existed B/L to prove relationship of Contract for Carriage of Goods by Sea between Tai-I Company and President Lines Company. Tai-I Company was the consignee of the goods involved, President Lines Company was carrier. President Lines China Company was the agent of President Lines Company, was not the disputed party of Contract for Carriage of Goods by Sea. Lokman Shipping Company was commissioned by President Lines Company, and was responsible for the second carriage of the goods involved from Chiwan to Huangpu. Lokman Shipping Company was the actual carrier from Chiwan to Huangpu. Guangzhou Lokman shipping Company and Shenzhen Lokman Freight Forwarding Company Guangzhou Branch were all agents of Lokman Shipping Company, and carried out obligations commissioned by Lokman Shipping Company respectively. Guangzhou Lokman shipping Company and Shenzhen Lokman Freight Forwarding Company Guangzhou Branch were not the disputed parties of involved Contract for Carriage of Goods by Sea. On record evidence cannot prove that President Lines China Company, Guangzhou Lokman shipping Company and Shenzhen Lokman Freight Forwarding Company Guangzhou Branch already were aware that the matters entrusted were illegal but still carried them out. President Lines China Company,

Guangzhou Lokman shipping Company and Shenzhen Lokman Freight Forwarding Company Guangzhou Branch were not the responsible carrier or actual carrier of this case in the Contract for Carriage of Goods by Sea.

With respect to the limitation of this case. This case was a dispute of contract for carriage of goods by sea, pursuant to Article 257 Paragraph 1 of the Maritime Code of the People's Republic of China that the limitation period for claims against the carrier with regard to the carriage of goods by sea is one year, counting from the day on which the goods were delivered or should have been delivered by the carrier. Hence, limitation of action was one year that Tai-I Company accused President Lines Company and Lokman Shipping Company. Goods involved arrived at the destination on May 3, 2012, after Tai-I Company filed customs declaration, customs released goods on 21 May. However Tai-I Company did not take all the goods involved, because the parts of the goods in No.GESU3417158 Container were not declared. The day can be regarded as Tai-I Company knew or should know that his rights had been infringed on, which shall be the beginning of limitation. Date of the complaint of Tai-I Company was on May 17, 2013, which did not exceed the limitation of action.

With respect to the reasons for the detention of goods in the port. Tai-I Company claimed that due to the input error of the agent of Lokman Shipping Company, parts of the goods were missed, which eventually led to Huangpu Xingang Customs seized all the goods for more than three months. The court does not confirm such facts claimed by Tai-I Company. The reasons were that: pursuant to Article 24 Paragraph 1 of the Customs Law of the People's Republic of China that The receiver of import goods and the sender of export goods shall make an accurate declaration and submit the import or export license and relevant papers to the Customs office for examination. The goods involved were import goods, as the consignee, Tai-I Company must properly handle the customs clearance of the goods involved according to the law in order to take the goods. The B/L held by Tai-I Company clearly documented that 5.527 tons electrolytic copper under No. APLU058193457 B/L and 19.784 tons electrolytic copper under No. APLU058193461 B/L were loaded in the same container that was No. GESU3417158 Container. As the consignee, Tai-I Company knew or should know that exists LCL before handling the customs declaration of inbound goods. Tai-I Company already knew there exists LCL, but failed to take correct measures to avoid loss, leaving a mistake uncorrected and making the best of it, and then handled the customs declaration of inbound goods in No.GESU3417158 Container, which violated the provisions of the customs, leading to the inspection of all goods involved by customs, until July 25, 2012, customs permitted that Lokman Shipping Company amended the electronic data of the manifest. Hence, the direct cause of 17 container inspected and detained in the port was that such dishonest behavior under the condition of LCL and inaccurate Manifest Declaration.

With respect to claim of fine, weighing charges and storage losses. Article 86 Paragraph 3 of the Customs Law of the People's Republic of China stipulates that Dishonest declaration of imported and exported goods, commodities or transit, transshipment, through goods shall impose a fine, if there is illegal obtained, confiscate the illegal gains. Article 2 of the Administrative Measures of the Customs of the People's Republic of China for the Inspection of Imported and Exported Goods stipulates that The inspection of imported and exported goods as mentioned in these Measures refers to the law enforcement act in which the customs house carries out actual verification of imported and exported goods so as to determine whether the contents declared by the consignee or consignor of imported and exported goods conform to the actual situation of imported and exported goods or to determine the classification, price and producing area of commodities. Article 17 Paragraph 2 of the Administrative Measures of the Customs of the People's Republic of China for the Inspection of Imported and Exported Goods stipulates that Result of inspection of import and export goods moved, opened or sealed packaging and other costs born by the consignor or consignee of imported and exported goods. Due to the reason of Tai-I Company, the goods involved detained in the port of destination. Tai-I Company shall volunteer to undertake fines caused by dishonest declaration, Weighing Charges caused by cargo inspection and storage charges paid to customs.

With respect to claim of container demurrage charges. Arrival time of goods involved in 17 containers was on May 3, 2012, Container free use period was 10 days, so container demurrage charges shall be paid from May 14. Dishonest declaration of Tai-I Company led to the goods detained at ports, so the day taking the goods in batches, actual occupation time of involved containers had exceeded container free use time, the payment of container demurrage charges to President Lines Company cannot less than RMB34,000.00 received by President Lines Company. Hence, Tai-I Company cannot request President Lines Company to return RMB34,000.00 of received container demurrage charges.

With respect to claim of delayed declaration fee. Article 24 Paragraph 2 and Paragraph 3 of the Customs Law of the People's Republic of China stipulates that "declaration of import goods shall be made to the Customs office by the receiver within 14 days of the arrival of the means of transport; Where the receiver fails to declare the import goods within the time limit described in the preceding paragraph, a fee for the delayed declaration shall be imposed by the Customs." Article 14 of the Customs Law of the People's Republic of China stipulates that "when a means of transport arrives at or departs from a place where there is a Customs office, the person in charge of the means of transport shall make a truthful declaration to the Customs, submit the relevant papers for examination and accept customs control and examination." Article 13 of the Administrative Measures of the Customs of the People's Republic of China for Manifests of Inward and Outward Means of Transport stipulates that "if the electronic data of transmissed manifest needs to be changed, the person can directly amend before prescribed transmission time of original manifest and advance manifest, except the owner of the cargo or the goods has go through declaration formalities for the cargo or the goods." Goods arrived at port on May 3, 2012, Tai-I Company shall at least declare to customs on May 16. Due to dishonest declaration behavior carried out by Tai-I Company, there was inconsistent situation between actual arrival and declaration of the goods involved before expiry dates. On May 22, 2012, Lokman Shipping Company applied to amend manifest information, but customs permitted to amend on July 22 after investigation of all the goods involved in the declaration, and imposed different administrative penalty to Tai-I Company and Guangzhou Lokman shipping Company. The facts of the case showed that dishonest declaration of Tai-I Company was the focus of customs supervision. Even Lokman Shipping Company inaccurate declared manifest information behavior happened earlier, due to dishonest declaration behavior carried out by Tai-I Company, Lokman Shipping Company could not amend on before investigation of all the goods involved in the declaration. The cause that 19.784 tons goods under No.APLU058193461 B/L could not handle the declaration formalities for imported goods shall be attributed to Tai-I Company, Tai-I Company shall volunteer to undertake losses of delayed declaration fee.

In conclusion, Article 64 Paragraph 1 of the Civil Procedure Law of the People's Republic of China stipulates that a party shall have the burden to provide evidence for its claims. Article 2 of the Some Provisions of the Supreme People's Court on Evidence in Civil Procedures stipulates that The parties concerned shall be responsible for producing evidence to prove the facts on which their own allegations are based or the facts on which the allegations of the other party are refuted. Where any party cannot produce evidence or the evidence produced cannot support the facts on which the allegations are based, the party concerned that bears the burden of proof shall undertake unfavorable consequences. Tai-I Company cannot provide evidence to prove that the loss of its claim was attributed to the five Defendants, shall bear the adverse consequences that cannot prove evidence. Tai-I Company claimed that five Defendants shall compensate Tai-I Company for RMB411,389.21 of fines, delayed declaration fee, Weighing Charges, storage fee, container demurrage charges and Capital Backlog Interest, because there was no basis in fact, the court did not to support it. According to Article 64 Paragraph 1 of the Civil Procedure Law of the People's Republic of China and Article 2 of the Some Provisions of the Supreme People's Court on Evidence in Civil Procedures, the judgment is as follows:

Reject the claims of the Plaintiff Tai-I Jiang Corp (Guangzhou) Co., Ltd.

Court acceptance fee in amount of RMB7,036.00, shall be born by the Plaintiff Tai-I Jiangtong (Guangzhou) Co., Ltd.

If dissatisfaction with this judgment, the Plaintiff Tai-I Jiangtong (Guangzhou) Co., Ltd., American President Lines (China) Co., Ltd., Guangzhou Lokman shipping Co., Ltd. and Shenzhen Lokman International Freight Forwarding Co., Ltd. Guangzhou Branch shall within 15 days as of the service of this judgment, and the Defendants American President Lines Co., Ltd. and Lokman shipping Co., Ltd. shall within 30 days as of the service of this judgment, submit a statement of appeal to the court, with duplicates in the number of the opposing parties, so as to make an appeal before Guangdong High People's Court.

Presiding Judge: SONG Ruiqiu
Judge: LI Zhengping
Acting Judge: HU Shi

November 27, 2014

Clerk: SHU Jian

Guangdong High People's Court Civil Judgment

Tai-I Jiangtong (Guangzhou) Co., Ltd.
v.
American President Lines, Ltd.

(2015) Yue Gao Fa Min Si Zhong Zi No.24

Related Case(s) This is the judgment of second instance, and the judgment of first instance is on page 1089.

Cause(s) of Action 202. Dispute over contract of carriage of goods by sea or sea-connected waters.

Headnote Affirming first instance decision holding ocean carrier and freight forwarder not liable for loss caused by detention of goods by Customs authorities because the importer had an obligation under Customs law to be responsible for making correct declarations.

Summary The Plaintiff/Appellant Tai-I Jiangtong appealed the judgment of the court of first instance in its dispute against American President Lines Co., Ltd., Lokman Shipping Co., Ltd., Guangzhou Lokman Shipping Co., Ltd and Shenzhen Lokman International Freight Forwarding Co., Ltd. Guangzhou Branch. The court here recognized the court of first instance and supported its finding that Tai-I Jiangtong evidenced dishonest behavior for failing to declare the existence of LCL to customs because of their actual knowledge of LCL, despite the negligence of American President Lines Co. and Lokman Shipping Co. for failing to inform the Plaintiff earlier regarding the LCL.

Judgment

The Appellant (the Plaintiff of first instance): Tai-I Jiangtong (Guangzhou) Co., Ltd.
Domicile: No. 251, Junye Road, Economic and Technology Development Zone, Guangzhou, Guangdong, the People's Republic of China.
Legal representative: YANG Zhongji, general manager.
Agent *ad litem*: AI Zongyuan, lawyer of Guangdong Xindesheng Law Firm.
Agent *ad litem*: XUAN Yunjing, trainee lawyer of Guangdong Xindesheng Law Firm.

The Respondent (the Defendant of first instance): American President Lines Co., Ltd.
Domicile: 16220 N. Scottsdale Road Suite 300 Scottsdale AZ 85254, United States.
Legal representative: ERIC R. SWETT, director.
Agent *ad litem*: CAO Yanghui, lawyer of Guangdong Wang Jing & Co.
Agent *ad litem*: LI Jianping, lawyer of Guangdong Wang Jing & Co.

The Respondent (the Defendant of first instance): American President Lines (China)Co., Ltd.
Domicile: Room 2305, 2306, Floor 23, China Resources Building, No. 8 Jianguomen North Avenue, Dongcheng District, Beijing, the People's Republic of China.
Legal representative: CHEN Duanqiang, director and general manager.
Agent *ad litem*: CAO Yanghui, lawyer of Guangdong Wang Jing & Co.
Agent *ad litem*: LI Jianping, lawyer of Guangdong Wang Jing & Co.

The Respondent (the Defendant of first instance): Lokman Shipping Co., Ltd.
Domicile: FLAT/RM 01–02 20/F ENTERPRISES CENTRE 777 LAI CHI KOK ROAD CHEUNG SHA WAN.
Legal representative: CHEN Mengci, director.
Agent *ad litem*: HUANG Hui, lawyer of Guangdong Hengyun Law Firm.
Agent *ad litem*: ZHANG Jing, lawyer of Guangdong Hengyun Law Firm.

The Respondent (the Defendant of first instance): Guangzhou Lokman Shipping Co., Ltd.
Domicile: Room B816, No. 403 Dashadi East Road, Huangpu District, Guangzhou, Guangdong, the People's Republic of China.
Legal representative: XIONG Guowei, manager.
Agent *ad litem*: HUANG Hui, lawyer of Guangdong Hengyun Law Firm.
Agent *ad litem*: ZHANG Jing, lawyer of Guangdong Hengyun Law Firm.

The Respondent (the Defendant of first instance): Shenzhen Lokman International Freight Forwarding Co., Ltd. Guangzhou Branch
Domicile: Room B810, B812, No. 403 Dashadi East Road, Huangpu District, Guangzhou, Guangdong, the People's Republic of China.
Legal representative: DING Fusheng, manager.
Agent *ad litem*: HUANG Hui, lawyer of Guangdong Hengyun Law Firm.
Agent *ad litem*: ZHANG Jing, lawyer of Guangdong Hengyun Law Firm.

Dissatisfied with Civil Judgment (2013) Guang Hai Fa Chu Zi No.552 rendered by Guangzhou Maritime Court in respect of the case of dispute over contract of carriage of goods by sea in which the Respondents American President Lines Co., Ltd. (hereinafter referred to as "President Lines Company"), American President Lines(China) Co., Ltd. (hereinafter referred to as "President Lines China Company"), Lokman Shipping Company (hereinafter referred to as "Lokman Shipping Company"),Guangzhou Lokman shipping Co., Ltd. (hereinafter referred to as "Guangzhou Lokman shipping Company") and Shenzhen Lokman International Freight Forwarding Co., Ltd. Guangzhou Branch (hereinafter referred to as "Shenzhen Lokman Freight Forwarding Company Guangzhou Branch") were involved, the Appellant Tai-I Jiangtong (Guangzhou) Co., Ltd. (hereinafter referred to as "Tai-I Company") filed an appeal before the court. The court, after entertaining this case, constituted a collegiate panel according to the law and tried this case. AI Zongyuan and XUAN Yunjing, agents *ad litem* of Tai-I Company, and LI Jianping, the common agent *ad litem* of President Lines Company and President Lines China Company, as well as HUANG Hui, the common agent *ad litem* of Lokman Shipping Company, Guangzhou Lokman Shipping Company and Shenzhen Lokman Freight Forwarding Company Guangzhou Branch participated in the investigation of the second instance organized by the court. Now this case has been concluded.

Tai-I Company was dissatisfied with the judgment of first instance, filed an appeal before the court and requested that: 1. the court shall revoke the judgment of first instance; 2. the court shall amend the judgment to that President Lines Company, President Lines China Company, Lokman Shipping Company, Guangzhou Lokman shipping Company and Shenzhen Lokman Freight Forwarding Company Guangzhou Branch shall bear joint and several liability for compensating Tai-I Company for delayed declaration fee of RMB39,090.00, detention fee Deposit of RMB34,000.00, Weighing Charges of RMB2,210.00, Storage Fee of RMB6,552.00, Administrative penalty of customs of RMB29,000.00, and Capital Backlog Interest caused by delay of goods clearance of RMB300,537.21; 3. President Lines Company, President Lines China Company, Lokman Shipping Company, Guangzhou Lokman shipping Company and Shenzhen Lokman Freight Forwarding Company Guangzhou Branch shall bear all litigation fee of the first instance and the second instance.

Main reasons were as follows:

1. There did not exist dishonest declaration of the first shipment of goods by Tai-I Company. The obligation of Tai-I Company was to declare the goods loaded in the container, not to declare the container as a whole. Although there existed LCL of two shipment of goods, two shipment of goods and all cargo papers were independent of each other. There was no provision for LCL cargo must be declared to the customs at the same time, hence Tai-I Company can choose to declare respectively. The declaration information of Tai-I Company was consistent with the real situation of the goods, so there did not exist dishonest declaration.
2. Before the customs inspected the goods involved, Tai-I Company did not declare the second shipment of goods yet. Hence there did not exist dishonest declaration concerning the second shipment of goods.
3. Tai-I Company failed to declare second shipment of goods to the customs timely, simply because of the fault caused by Lokman Shipping Company. Firstly, Lokman Shipping Company was the person of manifest transmission, whose false manifest information transmission, led to the results that Tai-I Company could not declare the second shipment of goods to customs. The actual date of goods involved arrived at the port of destination was on May 3,

2012, but Lokman Shipping Company only transmitted the manifest information of the first shipment of goods, and did not transmit the manifest information of the second shipment of goods, whose behavior violated the provisions of customs. Hence, there existed an obvious fault. Article 9 Paragraph 3 of the Administrative Measures of the Customs of the People's Republic of China for Manifests of Inward and Outward Means of Transport stipulates that, "only after the customs receives the transmission of the major data of the original manifest may the consignee or the enterprise entrusted to declare at the customs handle the customs declaration formalities for the cargoes or articles concerned." Hence, under the condition that Lokman Shipping Company failed to transmit the manifest information of the second shipment of goods, Tai-I Company could not go through the declaration formalities of the second shipment of goods. Secondly, Lokman Shipping Company did not issue required Switched B/L to Tai-I Company, led to the results that Tai-I Company could not declare the second shipment of goods to customs. Lokman Shipping Company issued Notice of Arrival of the second shipment of goods until July 25, 2012, and subsequently issued Switched B/L. So far Tai-I Company could only go through the declaration formalities of the second shipment of goods.
4. The fault of Lokman Shipping Company led to the results that Tai-I Company cannot declare the second shipment of goods, and Tai-I Company could not take the goods of the first shipment. Instead, suffered inspection of goods by customs and detention of the goods in the harbor. Therefore, Tai-I Company bore Weighing Charges, storage fees, fines and other losses caused by inspection and penalty of customs, which shall be bore jointly and severally by President Lines Company, President Lines China Company, Lokman Shipping Company, Guangzhou Lokman shipping Company and Shenzhen Lokman Freight Forwarding Company Guangzhou Branch. In conclusion, the cause of the detention of the goods involved in the port was identified wrongly by the court of first instance, and requested the court of second instance to support a Tai-I Company's appeal according to the law.

In the second instance, President Lines Company and President Lines China Company defended that:

1. As an agent of President Lines Company, President Lines China Company was responsible for external liaison, and only performed agency obligations in the course of the case involved, and shall not bear the responsibility, and agreed with the conclusion drawn by the court of first instance.
2. With regard to LCL, President Lines Company confirmed that Tai-I Company was the consignee, LCL done by the seller. President Lines Company was only responsible for loading. President Lines Company was independent of LCL. As the buyer, Tai-I Company shall realize the reality of LCL. When the goods involved under two B/Ls arrived in Chiwan, President Lines Company transmitted the arrival information to Tai-I Company in order to cooperate with Tai-I Company to declare, and requested Tai-I Company to provide Chinese Shipping

Instruction. On 26 April, Tai-I Company provided the information of the first document, and provided the information of the second document. After receiving two documents, President Lines Company faithfully transferred to the carrier, Lokman Shipping Company. In the process, President Lines Company did not do anything wrong.
3. With regard to declaration, Tai-I Company was the subject of duty. Tai-I Company should declare to the customs after verifying the arrival goods, but he declared to the customs without verification, which led to inconsistency between actual goods and goods listed on the declarations, and led to penalty of customs. In the process of customs clearance, Tai-I Company directly contacted Lokman Shipping Company, Guangzhou Lokman shipping Company and Shenzhen Lokman Freight Forwarding Company Guangzhou Branch, which President Lines Company did not participate in.
4. The goods involved were punished by Customs because Tai-I Company deliberately omitted the goods, which had nothing to do with Lokman Shipping Company. Lokman Shipping Company had been actively cooperated, so could not put that kind of coordination as its fault and requested it bear responsibilities. In conclusion, the company requested the court of second instance to affirm the original judgment according to the law.

In the second instance, Lokman Shipping Company, Guangzhou Lokman Shipping Company, Shenzhen Lokman Freight Forwarding Company Guangzhou Branch defensed that:

1. Tai-I Company knew that there existed LCL and inaccurate manifest declaration, which led to the results that the goods was inspected by customs and was detained at the port. First, it was wrong that, "there was no obligation to declare LCL at the same time but mutually independent two shipment of goods" claimed by Tai-I Company. The imported and exported products assembled in the same container shall be declared for customs supervision. If the consignee only declared the partial assembled goods in the same container, customers would release the full container and it could not be effectively regulated unknowingly. Second, Tai-I Company claimed that," Our company had not made a declaration against the goods of second B/L, so there did not exist false circumstances of declaration, which will not lead to suffer customs inspection as a result of dishonest declaration." It was the one-sided interpretation of the dishonest declaration and the wrong understanding of the cause of the customs inspection. Notice of a penalty decision issued by customs to Tai-I Company clearly pointed out that, the quantity of goods declared by Tai-I Company to the customs was less than the quantity of actual arrival, leading to tax evasion, that was declaration evasion. That is to say, Tai-I Company had already known LCL, but still did not declare one of those, such negative behavior led to customs penalty. Third, Tai-I Company claimed that Lokman Shipping Company failed to properly transmit manifest information, and led to its second goods could not be declared to the customs, which was shirking its responsibility. So-called

failed declaration refers to that Tai-I Company took the initiative to submit declaration materials to declare but ultimately failed to declare successfully. But in this case, in the knowing of the LCL, Tai-I Company did not submit any information of the second shipment declaration. Whether manifest information was right or not, or the declaration was right or not, such behavior cannot exempt Tai-I Company from the legal obligation to truthfully and comprehensively declare to the customs against LCL cargo. The reason of the goods seizes by Customs was that Tai-I Company knew the existence of LCL cargo but only declared partial goods, which constituted declaration evasion, rather than the inaccurate manifest information. Fourth, when Lokman Shipping Company declared to customs against import manifest, Lokman Shipping Company fully complied with Chinese Shipping Instruction provided by Tai-I Company and President Lines Company. There was no fault, Lokman Shipping Company shall not assume any liability. Before accepting the shipment of the first B/L, Lokman Shipping Company was not notified the existence of LCL. Subsequently, Lokman Shipping Company was also not notified the existence of LCL in the shipment of the second B/L, and could not find LCL container involved in Chiwan Terminal. Hence, Lokman Shipping Company could not transmit unloaded manifest information for the second goods was not shipped. In this case, the entire carrier and the consignee did not inform Lokman Shipping Company of LCL information. Lokman Shipping Company had fulfilled its reasonable and prudent duty. In addition, when the LCL goods had arrived at port and Tai-I Company knew the existence of LCL of second B/L, Tai-I Company declared the first B/L in the same container without obtaining the relevant documents of second B/L, and did not explain LCL to customs, at that time, Customs released all the goods, which was the direct cause of inspection of all the goods by customs and detention on the port.
2. Tai-I Company failed to provide evidence to prove that the loss was caused by the fault of Lokman Shipping Company, Guangzhou Lokman shipping Company and Shenzhen Lokman Freight Forwarding Company Guangzhou Branch. In conclusion, the company requested the court of second instance to affirm the original judgment according to the law.

After verification, the court holds that: There existed related evidence to support the facts identified by the first instance, and the parties had not raised any objections and not submitted new evidence.

Hence, the court confirms the facts identified by the first instance. Another facts are identified:

1. Though the evidence submitted by Tai-I Company, it clearly showed that Tai-I Company provided President Lines Company with Chinese Shipping Instruction of Notice of Arrival by e-mail on April 26, 2012, among which the Chinese Shipping Instruction of Notice of Arrival of No.APLU058193457 B/L recorded 158 bundles of electrolytic copper plate, which coincided with the quantity of electrolytic copper plate in the 17 containers under such B/L recorded in Notice

of Arrival issued by President Lines Company to Tai-I Company by e-mail on April 23, and gross weight totally 405,169.00 kg. Another 8 bundles of electrolytic copper plate were recorded in another Chinese Shipping Instruction of Notice of Arrival, but this document did not record B/L number, and recorded that gross weight of the goods was 19,784.00 kg, which coincided with the quantity of electrolytic copper plate in the 8 containers under No. APLU058193461 B/L recorded in Notice of Arrival issued by President Lines Company to Tai-I Company by e-mail on April 23.

2. On September 27, Huangpu Xingang Customs issued Xin Guan Ji Wei Zi No. [2013] 1030053 Administrative Penalty Written Decision. After customs made the Administrative Punishment Notice on May 28, 2013, Tai-I Company pleaded. Hence, after checking, the customs decided to withdraw the origin Administrative Punishment Notice, and released new Administrative Punishment Notice, and reinformed Tai-I Company on July 25, 2013. On July 29, 2013, Tai-I Company defended again on the contents of new Administrative Punishment Notice. After checking, the customs decided to maintain Administrative Punishment Notice. That was identified that on May 9, 2012, Tai-I Company declared 17 containers (including lawsuit No.GESU3417158 container) under the first No.APLU058193457 B/L, and actual arrival electrolytic copper plate was 424,787.00 kg. Though verifying of Customs Department, the dishonest behavior of Tai-I Company led tax evasion, which influenced national tax levy. So, the customs decided to impose fine of RMB29,000.00 of the dishonest behavior of the Tai-I Company.

The court held that:

This case was Contract of Carriage of Goods by Sea. President Lines Company registered legal entity in the United States, and Lokman Shipping Company registered legal entity in Hong Kong Special Administrative Region, in addition, the origin place of the goods involved was in Japan, hence, this case concerned foreign and Hong Kong affairs. Pursuant to Article 269 of the Maritime Code of the People's Republic of China to apply law of the mainland of China adopted by the court of first instance, all disputed parties had no objection to it, and the court confirmed it.

All disputed parties in the second instance had no objection to that Tai-I Company was the consignee of the goods involved, President Lines Company was the carrier of through carriage, Lokman Shipping Company was the carrier of the second carriage, and limitation of action in the judgment of first instance. The court will maintain the above identification. According to the grounds of appeal of Tai-I Company, the court summarized issues in the second instance:1.whether Tai-I Company existed dishonest behavior. 2. Whether the suffered losses of Tai-I Company can be attributed to President Lines Company, President Lines China Company, Lokman Shipping Company, Guangzhou Lokman shipping Company and Shenzhen Lokman Freight Forwarding Company Guangzhou Branch.

With respect to the first focal point of the disputes: Tai-I Company's appeal argued that there did not exist dishonest behavior with respect to first shipment of goods, that is the goods declaration under No.APLU058193457 B/L. With regard to second shipment of goods, that is the goods declaration under No.APLU058193461 B/L, there also did not exist dishonest declaration, thus leading to declaration delay for the omission of Lokman Shipping Company. According to the contents of Xin Guan Ji Wei Zi No.[2013] 1030053 Administrative Penalty Written Decision issued by Huangpu Xingang Customs On September 27, the Customs Declaration of Tai-I Company about 17 containers under No.APLU058193457 B/L of first carriage contained the partial goods of the disputed No.GESU3417158 container, whose quantity was less than the actual delivery. Through verification of Customs department, Tai-I Company's behavior constitutes dishonest declaration. At the same time, Customs still maintained above determination after Tai-I Company exercising the right of defense. Accordingly, Tai-I Company's behavior had been recognized as dishonest declaration by customs. The determination made by Huangpu Xingang Customs was based on the full investigation to Tai-I Company's declaration. Tai-I Company failed to submit relevant evidence to overturn it, the customs administrative punishment should be used as basis of the case. Moreover, the goods under No.GESU3417158 container was LCL cargo, and the goods cannot be divided into different containers in the transportation, the state of the container was only possible for the FCL to the port or not. Tai-I Company only declared the partial of the goods, but not explained the existence of LCL to customs, hence, such behavior itself was inappropriate. Tai-I Company claimed that the obligation of declaration was to declare the goods contained in the container, rather than to declare the container as a whole, which was inconsistent with the existence of LCL. The court did not support it and recognized that the dishonest behavior had constituted dishonest declaration.

With respect to the second focal point of the disputes:

Tai-I Company claimed that because of manifest omission of Lokman Shipping Company, Tai-I Company suffered various losses, such as delayed declaration fee, Administrative Fine, Container Deposit, Weighing Charges, Port Storage Charge, Capital Backlog Interest and so on. Whit regard to the loss of Capital Backlog Interest, Tai-I Company failed to provide evidence to prove there existed inevitable relationship between customs seizures and the goods detention. Moreover, such losses exceeded the foreseeable losses when the carrier signed carriage contract in Contract of Carriage of Goods by Sea, hence, the court did not affirm such losses. In addition to the losses of Capital Backlog Interest, all parties had objection to the amount of other losses, the court recognized that. After verification, there existed the direct relation between the losses of delayed declaration fee, Administrative Fine, Container Deposit, Weighing Charges, Port Storage Charge and declaration behavior of Tai-I Company. And the customs seizure and punishment were one result caused by declaration behavior of Tai-I Company. As previously mentioned, Tai-I Company did exist dishonest declaration, and the key issue of this case was whether the dishonest declaration could be attributed to the others. This made the following analysis: First, the facts of this case showed that as the buyer and consignee of the goods involved, Tai-I Company received two Notice of Arrival issued by President Lines Company, the carrier of through carriage, on April 23, 2012. The notice clearly showed that the No.GESU3417158 container was described in

No.APLU058193457 B/L and No.APLU058193461 B/L respectively, that was the the existence of LCL. On the back of the Notice of Arrival issued by President Lines Company was the blank delivery query form. After receiving the Notice of Arrival and the blank delivery query form, Tai-I Company issued the Chinese Shipping Instruction to President Lines Company by E-mail on April 26, 2012, namely filled the blank delivery query form provided by President Lines Company, among which the Chinese Shipping Instruction of No.APLU058193461 B/L and the Chinese Shipping Instruction of No.APLU058193461 B/L were distinguished from each other, and the Chinese Shipping Instruction of No.APLU058193461 B/L also lacked B/L number. Above facts suggested that Tai-I Company at latest should know the same container was under two B/Ls, namely No.GESU3417158 container existed LCL on April 26, 2012 to provide Chinese Shipping Instruction to President Lines Company. Second, because the No.GESU3417158 container was recorded in No.APLU058193457 B/L and No.APLU058193461 B/L respectively, such container should be shipped to Huangpu with other 16 containers, which did not belong to the transport error under the circumstance that the carrier of through carriage President Lines Company and the consignee Tai-I Company did not make a separate requirement about the LCL and separate transportation to the carrier of the second carriage Lokman Shipping Company. Third, Tai-I Company had known the the existence of LCL, but only declared 2 bundles of electrolytic copper plate in No. GESU3417158 container and did not explain the existence of LCL to customs when Tai-I Company declared the 17 containers under the No.APLU058193457 B/L on May 9, 2012. Because the state of No.GESU3417158 container may only FCL to port or FCL not to port, as the consignee known the existence of LCL, regardless the base of the fact that such container did not reach the port on 7 May or the base of the fact that such container reached the port on May 9, Tai-I Company only declared the partial goods to the customs, which was counterintuitive. Hence, the declaration behavior of Tai-I Company itself existed subjective fault. Although there existed negligence that the carrier of through carriage President Lines Company and the carrier of the second carriage Lokman Shipping Company did not clearly inform Tai-I Company of the existence of LCL when they submitted the Chinese Shipping Instruction, and there also existed negligence that the carrier of the second carriage Lokman Shipping Company did not track the circumstance of the container when was informed of the error of the number of the container in the wharf. Taking account of above analysis, the losses suffered by Tai-I Company cannot be attributed to President Lines Company, Lokman Shipping Company, President Lines China Company, Guangzhou Lokman shipping Company and Shenzhen Lokman Freight Forwarding Company Guangzhou Branch. The appeal of Tai-I Company lacked the factual basis, so the court shall not support it. The court of the first instance made a correct judgment, the court shall affirm it.

In conclusion, the judgment of the first instance identified facts clearly, applied the law correctly, handled the results appropriately, the court should maintain it. Tai-I Company's appeal lacks reasonable evidence, the court shall dismiss it according to the law. According to Article 170 Paragraph 1 Sub-paragraph 1 of the Civil Procedure Law of the People's Republic of China, the judgment is as follows:

Dismiss the appeal, and affirm the original judgment.

Court acceptance fee in amount of RMB7036 of second instance, shall be assumed by the Appellant Tai-I Company.

The judgment is final

Presiding Judge: DU Yixing
Acting Judge: GU Enzhen
Acting Judge: YE Dan

June 1, 2015

Clerk: PAN Wanqin

Appendix: Relevant Law

1. Civil Procedure Law of the People's Republic of China

Article 170 After trial, the people's court of second instance shall handle appeal cases according to the following different circumstances:

(1) Dismissing an appeal and sustaining the original judgment or ruling in the form of a judgment or ruling, if the original judgment or ruling is clear in fact finding and correct in application of law.
(2) Reversing, revoking or modifying the original judgment or ruling according to law in the form of a judgment or ruling, if the original judgment or ruling is erroneous in fact finding or application of law.
(3) Issuing a ruling to revoke the original judgment and remand the case to the original trial people's court for retrial or reversing the original judgment after ascertaining facts, if the original judgment is unclear in finding the basic facts.
(4) Issuing a ruling to revoke the original judgment and remand the case to the original trial people's court, if the original judgment seriously violates statutory procedures, such as omitting a party or illegally entering a default judgment.

Where, after the original trial people's court enters a judgment for a case remanded for retrial, a party appeals the judgment, the people's court of second instance shall not remand the case again for retrial.

Tianjin Maritime Court
Civil Judgment

Tianjin Tianguan Ocean International Freight Forwarding Co., Ltd.
v.
Yantai Fuhai International Ship Management Co., Ltd. et al.

(2014) Jin Hai Fa Shang Chu Zi No.772

Related Case(s) None.

Cause(s) of Action 202. Dispute over contract of carriage of goods by sea or sea-connected waters.

Headnote The Plaintiff cargo-owner's claim to recover non-general-average costs from carrier held to be time-barred by statute of limitations because cause of action arose when it received general average adjustment.

Summary While on a voyage carrying a cargo of steel tubes from Tianjin New Port to Batam, Indonesia, the carrying ship MV "Fuhai No.11" had to put in to the port of Weihai for repairs, as its port side had flooded. Because MV "Fuhai No.11" could not complete the voyage, the shipowner declared general average. The Plaintiff (the shipper's agent) and the Defendants (the shipowner, and the party that had voyage-chartered the ship to the shipper) agreed an "Emergency Disposal Agreement" by which the Plaintiff arranged and paid for transshipment costs and other fees. After a general average adjustment, the cost of transshipment was allocated among the parties. The Plaintiff sued the Defendants to recover that portion of the transshipment costs that was not allowable in general average. The court held that the Plaintiff's claims were barred by the two-year statute of limitations. The Plaintiff's cause of action arose on the date it received the general average adjustment report, which was more than two years before it sued the Defendants. However, the Defendant which had voyage-chartered the ship to the Plaintiff was held liable for the cost of damage to the steel tubes under the voyage charter, as it had not raised the limitation defence in relation to this claim.

Judgment

The Plaintiff: Tianjin Tianguan Ocean International Freight Forwarding Co., Ltd.
Domicile: Door No.6, Apartment No.15, Tai He Hua Yuan, No.19 Xin Cheng West Road, Binhai New District, Tianjin.
Legal representative: WU Shigang, chairman.
Agent *ad litem*: YAN Ping, lawyer of Tianjin Yuanhai Law Firm.
Agent *ad litem*: WU Xiaomei, lawyer of Tianjin Yuanhai Law Firm.

The Defendant: Yantai Fuhai International Ship Management Co., Ltd.
Domicile: Room 63, unit 2, No.12, Xin Zhuang Jie Road, Zi Zheng Area, Yantai City, Shandong.
Legal representative: CHEN Yi, director.
Agent *ad litem*: ZHANG Hongkai, lawyer of Liaoning Feiran Law Firm.
Agent *ad litem*: GAN Hongxia, lawyer of Liaoning Feiran Law Firm.

The Defendant: Hongyang International Limited.
Domicile: Trust Company Complex, Ajeltake Road, Ajeltake Island, Majuro, Majuro Marshall Islands.

The Defendant: Tianjin Zhong Hai Hang International Freight Forwarding Co., Ltd.
Domicile: Floor 5, Gang Ao Buiding, Zhengzhou Dao, He Ping Area, Tianjin.

With respect to the case arising from dispute over contract of carriage of goods by sea the Plaintiff, Tianjin Tianguan Ocean International Freight Forwarding Co., Ltd., filed an action against the Defendants, Yantai Fuhai International Ship Management Co., Ltd. (hereinafter referred to as "Fuhai Company"), Hongyang International Limited (hereinafter referred to as "Hongyang Company"), and Tianjin Zhong Hai Hang International Freight Forwarding Co., Ltd. (hereinafter referred to as "ZHH Company") on September 1, 2014. The court tried this case under general procedure subject to the law after entertainment. The court held a hearing in public on November 17, 2015. YAN Ping and WU Xiaomei, agents *ad litem* of the Plaintiff, and GAN Hongxia, agent *ad litem* of the Defendants, appeared in hearing and participated in the action, but the Defendant ZHH Company did not appear in the hearing after being summoned by the court according to law, the court tried this case by default subject to law. Now the case has been concluded.

The Plaintiff alleged that on March 15, 2010, Tianjin Gangguan International Economic Trade Co., Ltd. (hereinafter referred to as "Gangguan Company"), as the shipper, entrusted the Plaintiff as his agent to sign a charter party with the contract carrier, ZHH Company, who was the agent of Fuhai Company, agreed that 6,500 tons of steel tubes involved would be carried by M.V. "Fuhai No.11", which was owned by the actual carrier Hongyang Company from Tianjin New Port to Batam Port of Indonesia. Accordingly, on April 11, 2010, 28 consignments of goods, 6,514.396 tons of steel tubes in total were loaded on M.V. "Fuhai No.11" for shipment. On April 12, 2010, M.V. "Fuhai No.11" changed her course and called at Weihai Port because her port side was flooded, Fuhai Company therefore declared general average. To avoid breach of the delivery date agreed in the sales contract, upon negotiation, the Plaintiff and the Defendants signed MV Fuhai No.11 Goods Emergency Disposal Agreement (hereinafter referred to as the "Emergency Disposal Agreement") on April 23, 2010, agreeing that the Plaintiff would arrange transshipment for the goods above and pay the cost of transshipment and other fees first, the Defendant should bear joint liability for transshipment fees. On April 26, 2010, Fuhai Company recognized in written that the Plaintiff was obliged to arrange the partial transshipment of all of the goods on M.V. "Fuhai No.11" once again. On April 27, 2010, ZHH Company put forward proposals about general average and claimed that goods owner should pay the transshipment freight in advance. The Plaintiff successfully arranged M.V. "Green Pine" and M.V. "Win Moony" to transport the goods involved, and advanced the transshipment freight and other related fees for the Defendant (including general average fees and non-general average fees) in amount of RMB1,294,150.82 and USD301,264.3. After that, Fuhai Company entrusted the Average Adjustment Department of the China Council for the Promotion of International Trade to make the adjustment of this accident. On May 25, 2012, the Average Adjustment Department issued Average Adjustment Statement, which recognized the accident involved as a general average accident. The fees accounting was as follows: the fees of dealing marine accident and transshipment in amount of USD738,485.07, among which the general average expense was in amount of USD409,533.14. USD226,584.54 of the fees advanced by the Plaintiff, was general average expenses, the other USD165,109.93 and RMB940,492.7 did not fall into non-general average expense, in terms of this part, the Defendant should bear joint and sever liability subject to Article 3 of the Emergency Disposal Agreement. About the non-general average expense, the Defendant had not pay until now, although the Plaintiff had requested. In addition, the insurer refused to compensate the Defendant for the general average expenses according to Emergency Disposal Agreement, the Defendant has filed a lawsuit against the Plaintiff and the insurer, of which the case number was (2013) Jin Hai Fa Shang Chu Zi No.325. The Plaintiff had suffered great losses for advancing the transshipment fees, which should be afforded by the Defendant. Therefore, the Plaintiff filed a lawsuit and requested the court to judge: 1. the three Defendants to pay the Plaintiff for the transshipment fees and other expenses in amount of RMB940,492.7 and USD165,109.93 jointly and severally; 2. the Defendant should afford the court fee.

The Defendants alleged as follows: 1. Fuhai Company and Hongyang Company have no legal relationship with the Plaintiff, Steel Tube Company transferred its litigious rights to the Plaintiff, it infringed legal regulations, so it was invalid, and it has no basis that the Plaintiff filed the charge against letter of authorization, and the Plaintiff has no qualification; 2. even though the Plaintiff had the right to sue, the right was based on the legal relationship of the contract of carriage of goods by sea between Steel Tube Company and Hongyang Company, but the statute of limitation was one year and the Plaintiff's filing the suit on September 2, 2014 had exceeded the statute of limitation, thus, its claims should not be supported by the court; 3. except the freight for transshipment, Fuhai Company and Hongyang Company did not instruct Steel Tube Company to advance any fee, among the fees claimed by the Plaintiff, part thereof fell into general average and was irrelevant with this case, part thereof should be afforded by itself, thus it had no right to claim the Defendants Fuhai Company and Hongyang Company bear several and joint liability for compensation.

The Defendant ZHH Company did not appear in court, nor did it submit written defense.

To support its claims, the Plaintiff submitted 25 pieces of evidence, the Defendants, Fuhai Company and Hongyang Company, submitted 3 group of evidence materials totally, including complete ship certificates and maritime protest, such as bills of lading, inspection report, business license, loading list, ship ownership certificate. All of evidence materials of the Plaintiff and the Defendants, Fuhai Company and Hongyang Company have been expressed and examined in court. The court, after synthetically analyzes the opinions of the parties on the evidence, affirms the authenticity of evidence 1–10, evidence 13–23, and evidence 25 of the Plaintiff, and affirms the authenticity of all evidence submitted by the Defendant. The invoice of cleaning rust and painting fee at the destination port, which is evidence producing abroad, there is no notarization certification form, and the invoice is issued to Tubular Resources Pte Ltd., a party not involved in this case,, cannot prove that the Plaintiff has paid the fee above actually. Travel expenses is interior reimbursement document of a company, it cannot prove that fees have happened actually, and prove the entertainment expenses and taxi expenses are reasonable, the travel expenses have necessity and rationality, the court affirms travel expenses shall be RMB3,000 as appropriate. As for the witness testimony, its authenticity cannot be checked because the witness did not appear in court.

After trial, the court finds out that: on March 15, 2010, the Plaintiff, as the agent of Steel Tube Company, signed a charter party with ZHH Company agreeing that M.V. "Fuhai No.11" owned by the actual carrier Hongyang Company would carry 6,500 tons of steel tubes involved from Tianjin New Port to Batam Port, Indonesia. Accordingly, on April 11, 2010, 28 consignments of goods totally in amount of 6,514.396 tons of steel tubes were carried by M.V."Fuhai No.11". On April 12, 2010, M.V. "Fuhai No.11" changed to call at Weihai Port because the port side appeared a crack, sea water came into goods holds, for the common safety of navigation and goods, Fuhai Company therefore declared general average. M.V. "Fuhai No.11" could not recover to navigate at once, in order to help the consignor to deliver goods on time, and after negotiation, the Plaintiff, three Defendants and Steel Tube Company signed MV Fuhai No.11 Goods Emergency Disposal Agreement (hereinafter referred to as the Emergency Disposal Agreement) on April 23, 2010, the Plaintiff, Steel Tube Company and ZHH Company are party A, Fuhai Company and Hongyang Company are party B. It is agreed therein that: 1. party A shall arrange transshipment for the goods involved, party B should assist and corporate; 2. party A advance the transshipment freight, if this maritime accident is recognized as general average, then expenses of transshipment shall be afforded according to general average adjustment and related rules; 3. party A and party B should obey the Agreement, a party shall bear several and joint liability if any company of the party breaches the agreement. According to the Emergency Disposal Agreement, the Plaintiff arranged M.V. "Green Pine" and M.V. "Win Moony"to transship the goods involved, paid the transshipment freight in amount of USD226,326.64 and port fee, reloading fee, lashing fee, agent fee, lifting fee, lifting chain fee in total amount of RMB354,438.12 and secondary insurance premium of USD14,879.31. Except the transshipment freight and the fees aforesaid, the Plaintiff repaired the damaged steel tubes after the goods involved were unloaded at Weihai Port, there happened repairing costs in amount of RMB225,000, operation fee in amount of RMB466,545.5, materials costs in amount of RMB235,500 and traveling expenses in amount of RMB3,000. After that, Fuhai Company entrusted the Average Adjustment Department of the China Council for the Promotion of International Trade to adjust this accident. On May 25, 2012, the Average Adjustment Department issued an Average Adjustment Statement, which affirms the accident involved is general average. The costs are accounted as follows: the transshipment freight is USD130,202.64 (the total transshipment freight is USD226,326.64, deducting the freight in amount of USD96, 124, which should have be paid by the carrier to finish the navigation after the general accident happened) and the port fee, reloading fee, lashing fee, agent fee, lifting fee, lifting chain fee totally in amount of RMB354,438.12 and secondary insurance premium of USD14,879.31 are general average expenses. The freight of remaining voyage in amount of USD96,124 and the repairing cost in amount of RMB225,000, operation cost of repairing tubes in amount of RMB466,545.5, materials costs of repairing tubes in amount of RMB235,500 are not general average expenses. Steel Tube Company received the general average adjustment report on 14 May 2012, and requested the Defendants, Fuhai Company and Hongyang Company to repay the advanced fees desperately on May 21, 2012, May 22, 2012, May 23, 2012, the Defendants did not reply after May 23, 2012. On May 16, 2013, because the general average contributions could not be recovered, Hongyang Company filed an action with respect to general average contribution against the consignee, Indonesia PT. Tpco Pan Pan Asia and the insurer, Hui Feng Insurance (Singapore) Co., Ltd., (the case number is (2013) Jin Hai Fa Shang Chu Zi No.325). On August 29, 2014, Steel Tube Company transferred his creditor's rights over the advanced payment to the Plaintiff. On November 11, 2014, the notice of transferring creditor's rights was delivered to the three Defendants by e-mail. On May 4, 2015, Hongyang Company withdrew the suit of the case numbered with (2013) Jin Hai Fa Shang Chu Zi No.325.

The court summarizes the outstanding issues of this case based on claims and defenses of each party as follows: 1. the legal status of the Plaintiff and the Defendants; 2. the amount of losses of the Plaintiff; 3. whether the suit filed by the Plaintiff has passed the statute of limitations.

The court holds that this case is arising from dispute over a marine contract. Article 3 of the Law of the Application of Law for Foreign-related Civil Relations of the People's Republic of China stipulates "the parties may explicitly choose the laws applicable to foreign-related civil relations according to the provisions of law." Both the Plaintiff and the Defendants chose to apply Chinese law during the hearing, so Chinese law shall apply to this case. Steel Tube Company has transferred his lawful creditor's rights to the Plaintiff through transfer agreement of creditor's rights, and notified the debtor, such creditor's rights transfer is lawful and valid.

1. The legal relationship between the Plaintiff and the Defendants and the assumption of responsibilities.

   Steel Tube Company signed a voyage charter party with ZHH Company, ZHH Company affixed its official seal on the column of shipowner to confirm the identity of the shipowner, and actually collected the freight, therefore Steel Tube Company and ZHH Company established a relationship of voyage charter party. The goods involved were carried by Hongyang Company actually, therefore Hongyang Company issued the bill of lading numbered with ZT-01–29, both the Plaintiff and the Defendants recognized the fact that a bill of lading in Emergency Disposal Agreement after the accident, although no bill of lading was issued when the goods involved were loaded on ship, therefore, there is relationship of contract of carriage of goods by sea between Steel Tube Company and Hongyang Company. In addition, in the case where the maritime accident happened to M.V. "Fuhai No.11" after the above goods were sailed, to reduce losses and avoid the goods involved being laid in the temporary refuge port for a long time, the Plaintiff, the Defendant and Steel Tube Company signed the Emergency Disposal Agreement, agreeing that: the Plaintiff, Steel Tube Company, and ZHH Company transshipped goods and advanced fees first. Therefore, there is relationship of transshipment contract among the Plaintiff, Steel Tube Company, ZHH Company, Hongyang Company and Fuhai Company.

   In this case, the Plaintiff filed a lawsuit on the basis of the Emergency Disposal Agreement, according to the provisions of Emergency Disposal Agreement: to avoid losses, with respect to the delay of carriage of goods caused by maritime accident, the Plaintiff, Steel Tube Company, ZHH Company shall arrange transshipment for the goods involved, Hongyang Company and Fuhai Company should assist and corporate. The Plaintiff, Steel Tube Company, ZHH Company shall advance the transshipment freight, if this maritime accident is recognized as general average, the expenses of transshipment shall be afforded according to general average adjustment and related rules; in addition, two parties to the contract shall obey the agreement, should obey the Agreement, a party shall bear several and joint liability if any company of the party breaches the agreement. After the Emergency Disposal Agreement was signed, the Plaintiff, Steel Tube Company, ZHH Company arranged the transshipment and paid the transshipment freight actually, however, Hongyang Company, as the counterparty of the contract, shall in light of the transshipment freight clause of the Emergency Disposal Agreement pay the transshipment freight not allowed as general average on the basis of the adjustment report. But Hongyang Company does not pay that, it shall bear the liability for breach. Fuhai Company is also the opposite

party to the contract, so it shall bear several and joint liability for the default of Hongyang Company.
2. Whether the lawsuit filed by the Plaintiff exceeded the statute of limitation
In respect of the transshipment freight, the transshipment freight is in amount of USD130,202.64 and port fee, reloading fee, lashing fee, agent fee, lifting fee, lifting chain fee totally in amount of RMB354,438.12 and secondary insurance premium in amount of USD14,879.31 are allowed as general average, only the freight in amount of USD96,124, which shall be paid by the carrier to finish the voyage after the accident happened is particular average, the Plaintiff advanced that for the carrier and has rights to collect it from Hongyang Company. Subject to the Emergency Disposal Agreement, the two parties has agreed clearly that advanced fees should be contributed directly according to general average adjustment and relevant rules. The Plaintiff has already known the proportion of contribution since receiving the general average adjustment report, and items are clear and the sum is express. Therefore, the Plaintiff has title to sue since it received the general average adjustment report. From the day the Plaintiff received the adjustment report, namely May 14, 2012 and demanded the creditor's rights, May 23, 2012, to the day the Plaintiff filed an action, September 2, 2014, it has passed the statute of limitation (two years). In addition, with respect to the general average contribution, the consignee Indonesia PT. Tpco Pan Pan Asia and its insurer rejected to pay the shipowner for the general average contribution, which made the shipowner file a suit against the consignee and its insurer over the general average contribution on May 16, 2013, of which the case number is (2013) Jin Hai Fa Shang Chu Zi No.325, the court holds the case of general average contribution has no relation with this case, the consignee's rejecting to perform the obligation of general average contribution does not influence the litigation rights of the Plaintiff, nor does it constitute a reason to calculate or suspend statute of limitation of this case. What's more, if the Plaintiff does not recognize the results of adjustment, it should file a lawsuit in respect of the fees it should pay after receiving the adjustment report, but it has exceeded statute of limitation when the Plaintiff filed litigation on 2 September 2014, because it is indolent in exercising the rights to demand and sue, thus the court will not support the claims of the Plaintiff which requested Hongyang Company and Fuhai Company to pay the transshipment freight. In addition, the Plaintiff repaired the damaged steel materials after the goods involved were unloaded at Weihai Port, the repairing tubes cost, operation cost of repairing tubes, materials cost of repairing tubes and traveling expenses are all particular average expenses, it has passed the statute of limitation from the day of the accident happened on April 12, 2010 to the day of filing litigation on September 2, 2014.
Summarizing the reasons above, the Defendants, Hongyang Company and Fuhai Company raised the defense of statute of limitation, the action filed by the Plaintiff against Hongyang Company and Fuhai Company has exceeded the statute limitation, Hongyang Company and Fuhai Company shall not be responsible for the compensation.

3. Losses of the Plaintiff and assumption of expenses

The goods involved were unloaded at Weihai Port temporarily after the accident at sea involved happened. The goods were damaged in the accident by seawater, losses thus happened. To repair the goods, the Plaintiff paid the repairing cost in amount of RMB225,000, operation cost of repairing tubes in amount of RMB466,545.5, materials cost of repairing tubes in amount of RMB235,500 and travel expenses in amount of RMB3,000. In the transshipment freight advanced by the Plaintiff, USD96,124 is the freight which the carrier should have paid to finish the remaining voyage, and shall not be contributed in general average.

As for the fees above, the Plaintiff required the Defendants to be responsible severally and jointly for compensating particular average expenses by cargo-owner such as goods repairing fees, and expenses of removing rust and painting, and the transshipment freight not allowed as general average. First, the carrier, Hongyang Company, stated in the bill of lading, has no several and joint responsibility with the owner under the voyage charter party; secondly, there is no agreement that the three Defendants shall bear several and joint liability in the Emergency Disposal Agreement, therefore, there is no contractual or legal basis for the Plaintiff to require the three Defendants to bear several and joint responsibility for compensation; thirdly,, particular average by goods owner like repairing fees of goods involved, and the transshipment freight not allowed as general average, the creditor's right has exceeded the statute of limitation stipulated by law, the Defendants, Hongyang Company, Fuhai Company shall not be liable for this responsibility. But the Defendant, ZHH Company did not raise a defense on statute limitation, there is relationship of voyage charter party between it and Steel Tube Company, subject to the voyage charter party, it shall take care of the goods properly, and be liable for losses of the goods and repairing costs due to its fault. In addition, as for the transshipment freight not allowed as general average, it has collected all freights, but the fees advanced by the Plaintiff to finish the remaining voyage after the accident happened shall be repaid by ZHH Company.

To sum up, there is a relationship of voyage charter party between the Plaintiff and the Defendant, ZHH Company, and the Defendant shall bear liability for compensation of the fees paid by the Plaintiff. On these grounds, according to Article 92 of the Maritime Code of the People's Republic of China, Article 64 Paragraph 1 and Article 144 of the Civil Procedure Law of the People's Republic of China, the judgment is as follows:

1. The Defendant, Tianjin Zhong Hai Hang International Freight Forwarding Co., Ltd., shall pay the Plaintiff, Tianjin Tianguan Ocean International Freight Forwarding Co., Ltd., the transshipment freight, tubes repairing cost, operation cost, material cost, and travel expenses in amount of RMB930,045.5 with in ten days after the judgment comes into effect.
2. Reject other claims of the Plaintiff.

The obligations of paying the above-mentioned amounts shall be fulfilled within ten days as of the effectiveness of this judgment. Where the Defendant fails to perform the obligation of paying above-mentioned amounts within the period prescribed herein, such party shall, according to Article 229 of the Civil Procedure Law of the People's Republic of China, double pay the interest for the period of delayed performance.

Court acceptance fee in amount of RMB22,415, RMB4,994 shall be born by the Plaintiff, Tianjin Tianguan Ocean International Freight Forwarding Co., Ltd., and RMB17,421 by the Defendant, Tianjin Zhong Hai Hang International Freight Forwarding Co., Ltd.

In event of dissatisfaction with this judgment, the Plaintiff, Tianjin Tianguan Ocean International Freight Forwarding Co., Ltd., the Defendant, Yantai Fuhai International Ship Management Co., Ltd., and the Defendant, Tianjin Zhong Hai Hang International Freight Forwarding Co., Ltd. may, within 15 days upon service of this judgment, and the Defendant, Hongyang International Limited may, within 30 days upon service of this judgment, submit a statement of appeal and seven copies to the court, to lodge an appeal to the Tianjin High People's Court, and pay the appeal fee to Tianjin High People's Court on the basis of the dissatisfied amount against the first instance judgment (account administrator: Agricultural Bank of China Tianjin Tiancheng branch; account name: Tianjin High People's Court; account number: 02200501040006269) within seven days from the date of submitting the appeal, otherwise it will be deemed as to be withdrawn automatically.

Presiding Judge: SHI FuXin
Acting Judge: MA Shijun
Acting Judge: YAN Ping

December 22, 2015

Clerk: LIN Hao

Wuhan Maritime Court
Civil Judgment

WANG Hong
v.
Jiangsu Yuanhai Logistics Co., Ltd. et al.

(2014) Wu Hai Fa Shi Zi No.00040

Related Case(s) None.

Cause(s) of Action 201. Dispute over illegal lien on ship, cargoes carried by ship, bunkers and stores of ship.

Headnote Shipowner successful in his claim for wrongful arrest of his ship, but recovered no damages as he had not proved that the wrongful seizure had caused him loss.

Summary The Plaintiff WANG Hong, owner of M.V. "Yu Xin Yu 11288" brought suit against the Defendants Jiangsui Yuanhai Logistics Co., Ltd., and HU Zheli alleging damages resulting from their illegal seizure of his ship, on which they had no valid lien. The court held that the behavior of the Defendant Yuanhai Company in taking M.V. "Yu Xin Yu 11288" constituted illegally detaining the ship, and therefore that Yuanhai Company should bear the corresponding tort liability, but that because Plaintiff WANG Hong could not prove any losses, Plaintiff could not recover.

Judgment

The Plaintiff: WANG Hong, male, Han, born on November 6, 1977, living in Huaibin County, Henan
Agent *ad litem*: CHANG Wen, lawyer of Jiangsu Tianmao Law Firm.
Agent *ad litem*: ZHANG Lu, lawyer of Jiangsu Tianmao Law Firm.

The Defendant: HU Zheli, male, Han, born on June 6, 1970, living in Pukou District, Jiangsu.

The Defendant: Jiangsu Yuanhai Logistics Co., Ltd.
Domicile: Room 104, Building 1, Shanghai Road 192, Jiangyan Economic Development Zone, Taizhou City, Jiangsu.
Organization code: 55,929,979-5.
Legal representative: HU Zheli, chairman.
Agent *ad litem* of the two Defendants: CHEN Jing, lawyer of Jiangsu Weishide Law Firm.

With respect to the case arising from dispute over liability for damage caused by illegally detaining ship, the Plaintiff WANG Hong filed a litigation against the Defendants HU Zheli and Jiangsu Yuanhai Logistics Co., Ltd. (hereinafter referred to as "Yuanhai Company") before the court on June 3, 2014. The court entertained the case on June 4, 2014, and constituted a collegiate panel consisted of Judge ZHOU Da as Presiding Judge, Acting Judge LI Yan and Acting Judge XIONG Jing according to the law. When the two Defendants submitted the pleadings, they challenged the jurisdiction of the case. After reviewed, the case was a maritime tort dispute, and the place of an infringe act, Nanjing Yangtze River District, is within its jurisdiction. According to Article 1 of the Interpretation of the Supreme People's Court on the Application of the Special Maritime Procedure Law of the People's Republic of China and the provisions of the Notice of the Supreme People's Court on Adjustment of the Jurisdiction and the Scope of Cases Entertained by Dalian, Wuhan and Beihai Maritime Courts, the court had the jurisdiction over this case in light of law. Because the two Defendants objecting to jurisdiction were not tenable in this case, the court issued (2014) Wu Hai Fa Shi Zi No.00040 Civil Ruling on August 6, 2014 and rejected the two Defendants objecting to jurisdiction of the case. Then, due to job changes, the collegiate panel was changed to that Judge LIU Weihong as Presiding Judge, Acting Judge LUO Yan and Acting Judge XIONG Jing participated in the trial. After the ruling on rejecting the two Defendants objecting to jurisdiction came into effect, the court re-designated a period of adducing evidence not less than 30 days, and heard the case in public on October 28, 2014.CHANG Wen and ZHANG Lu, agents *ad litem* of the Plaintiff WANG Hong, CHEN Jing, agent *ad litem* of the two Defendants, appeared in court and participated in the action. The court according to the application of the Parties, made conciliation on the case, but they finally failed to reach agreement because of divergence. Now the case has been concluded.

The Plaintiff WANG Hong alleged that on September 15, 2013, the Defendant HU Zheli, as the legal representative of the Defendant Yuanhai Company, signed a ship trading contract with the Plaintiff WANG Hong, and sold M.V. "Yuanhai Junwei" owned by the Defendant Yuanhai Company to the Plaintiff WANG Hong. The Plaintiff WANG Hong paid the fees of purchasing the vessel in sum of RMB9,468,000 (hereinafter referred to as RMB) to the Defendant Yuanhai Company according to the contract. After the Plaintiff WANG Hong got the ownership, the vessel's name was changed to M.V. "Yu Xin Yu 11288". On November 11, 2013, the Plaintiff WANG Hong signed a charter party with another person. He was ready to deliver the vessel in Wuhu Port, when passed the Nanjing water area, the Defendant HU Zheli instigated several people to go on board forcibly and illegally detained the vessel in Nanjing central island, which resulted in the vessel failing to navigate and manage normally for three months and suffering losses of direct hires of RMB900,000 and the liquidated damages of RMB100,000. The Plaintiff WANG Hong believed that the sales contract was formed according to the law between the Plaintiff and the Defendant. The Defendant Yuanhai Company shall deliver the ship according to the contract, but the Defendant HU Zheli instigated some people to detain M.V."Yu Xin Yu 11288" illegally, which caused the Plaintiff WANG Hong suffering huge economic losses. As a result, the Plaintiff WANG Hong requested the court to judge the two Defendants to pay losses of hires in sum of RMB900,000 and the liquidated damages in sum of RMB100,000 and bear all litigation costs including maintenance costs.

Two Defendants both defended that, firstly, the loss of hire the Plaintiff WANG Hong alleged did not exist. According to the sales contract, due to the Plaintiff WANG Hong had not paid off the balance of the vessel so far, so the Defendant Yuanhai Company still had the ownership and operation of the vessel, and the Plaintiff WANG Hong did not achieve the ownership of the vessel. Secondly, the evidence of the losses of hires and liquidated damages alleged by the Plaintiff WANG Hong was fabricated by himself and the third party Anhui Shengfan Logistics Co., Ltd. (hereinafter referred to as Shengfan Company). The bareboat charter party was an invalid contract, which could not be the basis of facts of the case. Thirdly, it had no legal basis that the Plaintiff WANG Hong asked the two Defendants to assume joint and several liability. The Defendant HU Zheli was the legal representative of Yuanhai Company, the Defendant HU Zheli's behavior was duty behavior and he shall not assume the liability.

In the course of the time limitation for adducing evidence, the Plaintiff WANG Hong submitted the following evidence to support its claim:

1. The ship trading contract was signed by the Plaintiff WANG Hong and the Defendant Yuanhai Company on September 15, 2013 (Without special instructions, below are the original check), the ship delivery certificate was signed by the Plaintiff WANG Hong and the Defendant Yuanhai Company on September 25, 2013, which was to prove the original sales contract was legally formed between the Plaintiff and the Defendant.

   The examination opinion of the two Defendants: they had no objection to its authenticity. Ship trading contract agreed that the location of ship delivery was in Jiangxin Island of Nanjing. The seller was entitled to operate before the buyer had not paid off the ship charges. After the delivery of the ship, the buyer shall pay off the balance within one month. Ship delivery certificate indicated that the ship had been delivered at Taizhou wharf on September 25, 2013.

2. The description of the case issued by ZHANG Maosong on 3 December 2013 (copy), ID card(copy) and savings statement of account(the total sum of RMB100,000), the description of the case issued by ZHANG Qijun on January 9, 2014, ID card(copy) and debit card statement of account(the amount of RMB200,000), the description of the case issued by XU Zhongkui on

November 3, 2013, ID card(copy) and vouchers of bank transfer(the amount of RMB300,000), the receipts issued by the Defendant HU Zheli on September 15, 2013(the amount of RMB900,000) and bank transfer telephone transaction information(the total amount of RMB1,000,000), the description of the case issued by YANG Maojing on December 3, 2013, ID card(copy) and vouchers of bank transfer (the amount was RMB300,000), the description of the case issued by WANG Qiguo on December 4, 2013, ID card(copy) and two bank receipts (the total amount of RMB568,000), the description of the case issued by XU Zhongkui on December 3 2013, ID card(copy) and vouchers of bank transfer (the amount of RMB200,000), the description of the case issued by CHEN Haoyu on December 4, 2013, ID card(copy) and two vouchers of bank transfer (the total amount of RMB200,000), two descriptions of the case issued by SHI Zhenjia on December 4, 2013, ID card (copy), the transfer transaction receipt (the amount of RMB600,000) and a set of liquidation(the total amount of RMB6,000,000), the proof issued by Nanjing Hongkai Logistics Co., Ltd. (hereinafter referred to as Hongkai Company) on December 5, 2013(the amount of RMB100,000),which were to prove that the Plaintiff WANG Hong had paid the debts in full to the Defendant HU Zheli.

The cross-examination opinions of the two Defendants: the Defendant HU Zheli acknowledged to receive RMB9,368,000, but according to the agreement of ship trading contract, the Plaintiff WANG Hong still had the debts of RMB100,000 not to be paid. Although the Defendant HU Zheli issued the receipt of RMB900,000 on September 15, but actually received only RMB800,000. The two descriptions of the case on December 4, 2013 issued by third Party SHI Zhenjia shall be forged because the signatures at the end were obviously different, so they had objection to the their authenticity. The proof issued by Hongkai Company belonged to witness testimony. The Company shall give testimony as the witness and accept the inquires of the court. The recorded contents referred to a tripartite agreement which the two Defendants did not know. If the Plaintiff WANG Hong could not adduce evidence to prove the agreement, then it proved that the proof was fabricated by the Plaintiff WANG Hong. They had objection to the authenticity, legality and relevancy of evidence. They recognized the authenticity of other evidence in this set of evidence.

3. Ship ownership certificate of M.V. "Yu Xin Yu 11288", nationality certificate (copy) and inspection certificate (copy), to prove that the Plaintiff WANG Hong legally obtained the ownership of M.V. "Yu Xin Yu 11288" and had the all necessary navigation statutory certificates.

Cross-examination opinions of the two Defendants: they had no objection to the authenticity, legality, relevancy of evidence. While from the contents recorded in the nationality certificate, the Plaintiff WANG Hong obtained the certificate on December 4, 2013, but signed a bareboat charter party with others on November 8, 2013, in other words, the Plaintiff WANG Hong signed a bareboat

charter party with others before he obtained the nationality certificate, which was neither reasonable nor legal.
4. (2014) Wu Hai Fa Qiang Zi No.00001 Civil Ruling of the court, maritime injunction and inquiry records(copy) made by Nanjing Public Security Bureau Water Branch Water Sanchahe police station against the Defendant HU Zheli on November 11, 2013, to prove that the Defendant HU Zheli illegally detained M. V. "Yu Xin Yu 11288", the Plaintiff WANG Hong had paid RMB9,268,000 by bank transfer and RMB100,000 in cash (a clear record of inquiry records at the last page) to the Defendant HU Zheli, and deposit RMB100,000 the intermediary reserved, a total amount of RMB9,468,000.

Cross-examination opinions of the two Defendants: they had no objection to the authenticity of the inquiry records, but had objection to the purpose of proofs. The inquiry records could not prove that the Defendant HU Zheli illegally detained M.V. "Yu Xin Yu 11288". Instead, the inquiry records could prove that when the Defendant Yuanhai Company was in normal operation at Zhenjiang waters on November 8, 2013, the Plaintiff WANG Hong and the third party SHI Zhenjia and other people boarded the ship forcibly and detained all the items of the Defendant Yuanhai Company, drove the crew away and sailed to Nanjing arbitrarily. The Plaintiff WANG Hong did not paid off the ship price, and the Defendant Yuanhai Company still had the right to operate according to the contract. To retrieve items of the ship, the Defendant HU Zheli boarded. Then due to the disputes, until the police came, the parties of the case were all stayed on board, and the Defendant HU Zhelidid not detain the ship illegally. They had no objection to the authenticity of civil ruling and maritime injunction. But maritime injunction was made on December 22, 2013, and the Defendant HU Zheli left the ship once receiving the injunction on February 18, 2014, which could not prove the Defendant HU Zheli detained the ship illegally, either.
5. The bareboat charter party was signed by the Plaintiff WANG Hong and the third party Shengfan Company on November 8, 2013, supporting to prove that the Plaintiff WANG Hong obtained the ownership of M.V. "Yu Xin Yu 11288" on September 25, 2013. The original period of bareboat charter was from November 12, 2013. Because the ship was illegally detained, the Plaintiff WANG Hong breached the contract to third Party, as a result, the Plaintiff suffered losses of hires and liquidated damages.

Cross-examination opinions of the two Defendants: they had no objection to the authenticity of the apparent contract, but had objection to the relevancy and legality. Shengfan Company had not yet obtained waterway transportation license, one of the buyers of the involved ship, SHI Zhenjia, was the shareholder of the Company. The contract agreed that bareboat hires were RMB300,000 per month, which was far RMB10,000 per month higher than the normal operating incomes of the same type of ship.
6. The receipt issued by the Plaintiff WANG Hong on November 8, 2013,to prove that the Plaintiff WANG Hong received the deposit RMB100,000 from Shengfan Company.

Cross-examination opinions of the two Defendants: they had objection to the authenticity, legality and relevancy. Shengfan Company paid the deposit not through bank transfer, Shengfan Company's shareholder SHI Zhenjia was one of the buyers of the involved ship, had an interest relationship with the Plaintiff WANG Hong. The receipt was the evidence that the Plaintiff WANG Hong colluded with the third party SHI Zhenjia to make, so it was not true and objective and had no demonstrability.

The court ascertains the evidence submitted by the Plaintiff WANG Hong: the two Defendants had no objection to the authenticity of evidence No.1,3,4, these three pieces of evidence was regarded as the basis of the case. Evidence No.5,6 was associated with the rebuttal evidence submitted by the two Defendants, which would be certified later. The two Defendants defended that they did not detain the involved ship illegally, and alleged the Plaintiff WANG Hong did not suffer claimed loss due to the involved dispute. The focus of controversy involved in this case would be judged in the judgment below.

Evidence 2 was related to ship trading price of RMB9.468 million, there was a bank transaction voucher in the amount of RMB9.468 million, but the Defendant HU Zheli only acknowledged receiving RMB9.368 million. The differences were mainly reflected in the following three pieces of the evidence: the receipt in the amount of RMB900,000 issued by the Defendant HU Zheli on September 15, 2013, the telephone banking transfer transaction details in the amount of RMB100,000 on September 15, 2013, the proof issued by Hongkai Company on December 5, 2013 that the two Defendants still had RMB100,000 to receive.

The two Defendants defended that the Plaintiff WANG Hong still had RMB100,000 to pay the ship price, and although the Defendant HU Zheli issued the receipt of RMB900,000, but actually he only received RMB800,000. Therefore, the court held that according to evidence 1 about the agreement of ship trading contract on the deposit of RMB100,000,0, combined the receipt of RMB900,000 issued by the Defendant HU Zheli, the banking transfer telephone transaction details in the amount of RMB100,000,0 with the proof issued by Hongkai Company, especially the proof issued by Hongkai Company, which recorded that the Plaintiff WANG Hong transferred RMB100,000,0 to Hongkai Company by using POS machines of Hongkai Company on September 15, 2013. Hongkai Company transferred RMB800,000 to the Defendant HU Zheli on that day. The Plaintiff WANG Hong and the two Defendants, each of the party held RMB100,000 as the deposits, hence the Defendant HU Zheli issued the receipt of RMB900,000 although he only received RMB800,000 on September 15, 2013. The two Defendants defended that the proof issued by Hongkai Company referred to the tripartite agreement that they did not know, they had objection to the authenticity, legality, relevancy of the proof, the Court shall not accept it. This evidence is mainly the testimony of witnesses, though the witnesses including Hongkai Company did not testify in the Court, but the evidence can be interacted and form a chain of evidence, the Court regards evidence 2 as the basis of identifying the fact of the case. In addition, the two Defendants defended that the two descriptions of the case issued by the third party SHI Zhenjia were forged evidence because of the distinctly different signatures at the end of the paper. Objection to the authenticity of the two descriptions of the case. Because there was no evidence to prove, so the court did not accept it.

In order to justify its demurrer, the two Defendants submitted the following evidence within the time period for producing evidence:

1. The ship trading contract and ship sales contract signed by the Plaintiff WANG Hong and the Defendant Yuanhai Company, to prove that the Plaintiff WANG Hong did not obtain the ownership of M.V. "Yu Xin Yu 11288" according to the contract.

   The cross-examination opinions of the Plaintiff WANG Hong: it had no objections to the authenticity. The two copies of contracts could prove that the Plaintiff WANG Hong had obtained the ownership of the ship after he paid the ship price.

2. The inquiry records made by Jiangxin Island police station, Jianye substation Public Security Bureau, Nanjing, Jiangsu Province against the third party SHI Zhenjia(stamped with the seal of copies of Nanjing Jianye District People's Court), the inquiry record against the Defendant HU Zheli, the third party Deng Yonggang, the third Party DENG Zhaokuo and the Plaintiff WANG Hong (stamped with the seal of Nanjing Jianye District People's Court), color photographs that the Defendant HU Zheli was injured, Nanjing Jianye District People's Court (2014) Jian Xing Chu Zi No.35 criminal judgment, to prove that the third Party SHI Zhenjia ever used violence and other illegal means to try to force the two Defendants to delivery the ship.

   Cross-examination opinions of the Plaintiff WANG Hong: it had no objection to the authenticity of the apparent contract, but had objection to the relevancy. The third Party SHI Zhenjia hurt people on November 2, 2013, and it had nothing to do with the case on detaining ship illegally.

3. The business license of Shengfan Company, registration information inquiry form and list of shareholders were all from Wuhu Industrial and Commercial Bureau in Anhui province, to prove that Shengfan Company had no waterway cargo transport qualification, SHI Zhenjia was one of the shareholders of the Company.

   Cross-examination opinions of the Plaintiff WANG Hong: it had no objection to the apparent authenticity, but had objection to the relevancy. Whether Shengfan Company had waterway cargo transportation qualification or not did not affect to charter M.V. "Yu Xin Yu 11288", and it had nothing to do with the case on detaining the ship illegally. Even if Shengfan Company's shareholder, SHI Zhenjia and SHI Zhenjia was the same person, and the SHI Zhenjia was the shareholder of Shengfan Company, it did not affect Shengfan Company as a independent legal person to exercise its rights.

4. ID card of SHI Zhenjia and SHI Zhenjia(copy), the letter of complaints and accusation issued by the Defendant HU Zheli to Dantu substation Public Security Bureau, Zhenjiang City, Jiangsu on July 10, 2014 and the reply on July

31, 2014, to prove that the aforementioned person that received criminal penalties and the shareholder of Shengfan Company, SHI Zhenjia was the same person.

Cross-examination opinions of the Plaintiff WANG Hong: it had no objections to the apparent authenticity, but to the relevancy. It has nothing to do with the case on detaining the ship illegally.

5. Lian Shun 918 operating income statement issued by Yichang Lian Shun Shipping Co., Ltd, Chang Lian Hai 2198 income statement issued by Changzhou Chang Lian Hai Shipping Co., Ltd. and M.V. "Yuanhai Junwei" operating income statement issued by the Defendant Yuanhai Company, to prove that the Plaintiff WANG Hong claimed the loss of hires in the amount of RMB900,000 was unreasonable.

Cross-examination opinions of the Plaintiff WANG Hong: it had objection to the authenticity, the legality and the relevancy. The three copies of statements were unilateral statements, and there was no other evidence to back up.

6. The proof of receiving alarm record issued by the Zhenjiang Public Security Bureau Water Branch water Zheng Run Zhou police station on November 4, 2014, the statement of alarming issued by the Yangtze River Shipping Public Security Bureau Zhenjiang substation Yangzhou police station on November 3, 2014, to prove SHI Zhenjia and the other persons boarded forcibly in Yangtze River Zhenjiang waters and delivered the ship. When it happened the dispute, the relevant public security bureau policed on November 9, 2013. The Plaintiff WANG Hong enforced to delivery the ship before he paid off the ship price, the two Defendants did not constitute unlawfully detaining the ship.

Cross-examination opinions of the Plaintiff WANG Hong: it had no objection to the authenticity, but it could not prove that SHI Zhenjia and other persons boarded forcibly, on the contrary, the dispute of the case was caused because the two Defendants did not delivery the ship according to the contract.

7. The registration of alarming of Nanjing Public Security Bureau Water Branch Water Sanchahe police station, to prove that on November 11, 2013, SHI Zhenjia took over the ship forcibly in Zhenjiang and sailed to Nanjing Pukou water plant nearby waters, the Defendant HU Zheli and the companions heard the news and rushed to claim the money of purchasing ship, and then it happened the dispute, the local public security policed. The Plaintiff WANG Hong did not paid off the money of purchasing the ship, the two Defendants did not constitute unlawfully detained the ship.

The cross-examination opinions of the Plaintiff WANG Hong: it had no objection to the authenticity. WANG Yan, the family member of the Plaintiff WANG Hong, was injured in the dispute because the Defendant HU Zheli gathered several people and boarded to hurt her.

8. Two color photos, to prove SHI Zhenjia discarded a part of items belonged to Yuanhai Company from his controlled ship in Nanjing waters, the Defendant Yuanhai Company's staff pulled them away by car. The Plaintiff WANG Hong

enforced to deliver the ship before paying off the money of purchasing ship, the two Defendants did not constitute illegally detained the ship.

Cross-examination opinions of the Plaintiff WANG Hong: it had no objection to the authenticity. After the Defendant HU Zheli illegally detained the ship, he towed away items of the ship forcibly.

The court ascertains the evidence submitted by both Defendants: the Plaintiff WANG Hong had no objection to the authenticity of evidence No.1,2,3,4,6,7,8, evidence 7 was as the basis of judging the facts of the case. Although the Evidence No.5 was the original document, the three income statements were made by unilateral party, two of which had no identity information, one was issued by the Defendant Yuanhai Company, data calculation had errors, and statistical time of three copies of statements was not clear, which could not be confirmed with each other, so they could not be regarded as the basis of judging the facts of the case.

On the basis of certification on the rebuttal evidence summitted by the two Defendants, the court ascertains on evidence 5,6 submitted by the Plaintiff WANG Hong: although the two Defendants held that the two copies of evidence was colluded by the Plaintiff WANG Hong and the third party SHI Zhenjia, but they did not submit evidence to prove. Shengfan Company was a legal person of independent personality. Whether the Company had the waterway transportation license did not affect bareboat charter party signed with the Plaintiff WANG Hong. SHI Zhenjia, as the financing party of purchasing the involved ship and the small shareholder of Shengfan Company (10% invested), the two Defendants did not proved there was confusion of personality between SHI Zhenjia and Shengfan Company, either. The bareboat charter party signed by Shengfan Company and WANG Hong did not breach the prohibitive provisions of the law, which shall be a legal and valid contract, and the two Defendants had no objection to the apparent authenticity of evidence 5. Evidence 6 was the original, the two sets of evidence can confirm each other, the Court confirmed the authenticity of evidence 5,6.

On the basis of adducing evidence, cross examination and the Court investigation, the court ascertains the following facts:

Firstly, the signing of the involved ship sales contract.

On September 15, 2013, the Defendant Yuanhai Company and the Plaintiff WANG Hong signed a ship transaction contract by the introduction of the ship trading agency Hongkai Company. Tripartite agreement: the Defendant Yuanhai Company sold its M.V. "Yuanhai Junwei" to the Plaintiff WANG Hong at the price of RMB9.468 million yuan. The Plaintiff WANG Hong shall have paid the purchasing ship deposit in the amount of RMB100,0000 to the Defendant Yuanhai Company on September 15, 2013, the Defendant Yuanhai Company shall give the intermediary the ship ownership certification to custody or pay deposit. The Plaintiff WANG Hong shall return to registered port to handle the letter of ship acceptance and hand over it to the intermediary before September 18, 2013. The intermediary shall notice the Defendant Yuanhai Company after receiving the letter of acceptance within 24 h. The Plaintiff WANG Hong shall pay the money of purchasing ship in the amount of RMB100,000,0 to the Defendant Yuanhai Company. After the Defendant Yuanhai Company received money, the intermediary would issue the transactions certification, the Defendant Yuanhai Company shall return to the original port to finish the ship registration cancellation and cancellation of operation certificate before September 25, 2013. After receiving the cancellation procedures of the Defendant Yuanhai Company, the intermediary shall notice the Plaintiff WANG Hong to carry the balance to the intermediary for the ship handover procedures at that day. The Plaintiff WANG Hong shall go to the intermediary for the ship handover before the date of October 25, 2013. After the transfer was completed, the Plaintiff WANG Hong, the Defendant Yuanhai Company shall pay the 2% agency fee of total turnover to the intermediary respectively, the intermediary would issue the ship handover certification. Ship transfer location was appointed in Nanjing Riverbank. In addition, they had special supplementary agreement that the Defendant Yuanhai Company firstly assisted the Plaintiff WANG Hong to transfer the ownership to facilitate loans. After the Plaintiff WANG Hong paid off the money of purchasing ship, the Defendant Yuanhai Company would deliver the ship. The Defendant Yuanhai Company would guarantee the Plaintiff WANG Hong successfully register the ship in Xinyang, Henan province. The Plaintiff WANG Hong's loan time was within one month after the success of the registration. If at the time the loan was not successful, the Defendant Yuanhai Company had the right to run. During the operation, all the responsibility was undertaken by the Defendant Yuanhai Company. Business contract also noted the Defendant HU Zheli's receipt account of Agricultural Bank of China number 8111. The Defendant HU Zheli as the legal representative of the Defendant Yuanhai Company, signed the ship trading contract with the Plaintiff WANG Hong and the intermediary Hongkai Company.

On September 15, 2013, the Plaintiff WANG Hong and the Defendant Yuanhai Company had also signed another sales contract of the ship. Except the aforementioned contents of ship trading contract, the two parties also agreed the deposit RMB200,000,0, before the Plaintiff paid off the money of purchasing ship in the amount of RMB9.468 million yuan, the ownership and operation of the vessel were owned by the Defendant Yuanhai Company.

Third Party SHI Zhenjia and the Plaintiff WANG Hong jointly purchased M.V. "Yuanhaijunwei", and he claimed that he was the agent of purchasing the ship by the Plaintiff WANG Hong in the involved criminal cases of public security investigation.

Second, the fulfillment of the involved ship sales contract.
On September 15, 2013, the Plaintiff WANG Hong paid RMB100,000,0 to the Hongkai Company by POS machines of ship trading agency, Hongkai Company. Hongkai Company transferred RMB800,000 to the Defendant HU Zheli on the same day. The two parties both charged RMB100,000 as the deposit including the intermediary costs, the Defendant HU Zheli issued the receipt of RMB900,000. Thereafter, according to the Plaintiff WANG Hong's instructions, the following 10 people remitted 18 sums of money to the Defendant HU Zheli, totally RMB8.468 million yuan. WANG Qiguo remitted RMB300,000 on September 17 of the same

year, YANG Maojing remitted RMB300,000 on September 18, ZHANG Maosong remitted 3 sums of money in the total amount of RMB100,000 on September 19, ZHANG Qijun remitted RMB200,000 on September 24, XU Zhongkui remitted RMB300,000 on October 21, CHEN Hao remitted 2 sums of money in the total amount of RMB200,000 on November 1, SHI Zhenjia remitted 6 sums of money in the total amount of RMB600,000,0 on November 1, SHI Zhenjia remitted RMB600,000 again on November 2, WANG Qiguo remitted RMB268,000 again on November 3, and XU Zhongkui remitted RMB200,000 on November 3. Before the date of November 3, 2013, the Plaintiff WANG Hong and the third party SHI Zhenjia paid RMB100,000 to the Defendant HU Zheli personally in China Postal Savings Bank Taizhou Jiangyan Branch.

On September 25, 2013, by the authentication of Taizhou Thai liner ship trading center, the acceptance and the agreement of the Defendant Yuanhai Company and the Plaintiff WANG Hong, M.V. "Yuanhai Junwei" was delivered at 15:20 on that day in Taizhou pier. Technical conditions and equipment performance of the ship matched the contractual conditions. Taizhou Thai Liner Trade Center issued the ship delivery certificate. On October 8, M.V."Yuanhai Junwei" changed to be registered as M.V. "Yu Xin Yu 11288" in local maritime bureau in Xinyang City, Henan Province, and obtained the ownership of the registration certificate. Certificate showed the person of the ownership was the Plaintiff WANG Hong, the ownership acquisition date was on September 25, 2013. On October 12, Henan Ship Survey Registration Xinyang Ship Inspection Department issued the inspection certificate of inland ship for M.V."Yu Xin Yu 11288". On October 23, the Plaintiff WANG Hong registered the mortgage of the ship in local maritime bureau in Xinyang, Henan, and the mortgagee was Huaibin Rural Credit Cooperative Union. On December 4, M.V. "Yu Xin Yu 11288" obtained nationality certificate, which noted the operator was Huaibin Xin Yu shipping Co., Ltd.

Thirdly, M.V. "Yu Xin Yu 11288"happened dispute because of poor delivery.
On November 1, 2013, ship trading agency Hongkai Company informed buyers and sellers to deliver the ship in Nanjing Riverbank. The next day, the Defendant HU Zheli told SHI Zhenjia to change as delivering the ship in Jiujiang, Jiangxi province. Due to the two sides did not ascertain the place and the time of delivery, SHI Zhenjia firstly hurt the Defendant HU Zheli in the office of ship trading center of Hongkai Company, which caused the Defendant HU Zheli injured, the Defendant HU Zheli was sent to the hospital after he called the police. By identification, the Defendant HU Zheli was comminuted fracture of the left nasal bone, fracture of the left frontal process of maxilla, which constituted the secondary minor injuries. After the trial of Nanjing Jianye District People's Court, the court made (2014) Jian Xing Chu Zi No.35 criminal judgment, SHI Zhenjia was sentenced to ten months imprisonment, suspended for one year because of crime of intentional injury.

From morning November 8 to 9, 2013, the third party SHI Zhenjia brought some people to board M.V. "Yu Xin Yu 11288" in Jiangsu Zhenjiang Gaozi port, and practically controlled of the liner. On November 10, the original crew of the ship was driven away, and the ship sailed from Zhenjiang to Nanjing. After the

Defendant HU Zheli knew this fact, he convened a number of people including his own relatives and friends to board M.V. "Yu Xin Yu 11288" at about 3:00 on November 11 in the waters near the Nanjing Pukou waterworks. He claimed SHI Zhenjia also defaulted him the balance of purchasing the ship in sum of RMB100,000, and required him to stop the ship. The Defendant HU Zheli and the third party SHI Zhenjia happened dispute and physical altercations, SHI Zhenjia's wife was injured in the dispute, SHI Zhenjia and the Defendant HU Zheli both called the police. M.V. "Yu Xin Yu 11288" was actual controlled by the Defendant HU Zheli, and could not leave but berthed in Nanjing riverbank.

On November 8, 2013, the Plaintiff WANG Hong signed the bareboat charter party with Third Party Shengfan Company, agreed on November 12, 2013 to deliver the ship in Wuhu Port, the charter period was from November 12, 2013 to November 11, 2014, lump sum of hires of RMB300,000 per month, deposit 100,000 yuan. After signing the contract, the Shengfan Company paid to the Plaintiff WANG Hong deposit of RMB100,000 in cash, and the Plaintiff WANG Hong issued the corresponding receipt.

On December 20, 2013, the Plaintiff WANG Hong applied for a maritime injunction to the court, demanded the Defendant HU Zheli to immediately deliver M.V. "Yu Xin Yu 11288" to him. The court made (2014) Wu Hai Fa Wu Qiang Zi No.00001 Civil Ruling on December 22, 2013, and permitted the application of the Plaintiff WANG Hong. At the same time, the president of the court issued (2014) Wu Hai Fa Wu Qiang Zi No.00001 maritime injunction, ordered the Defendant HU Zheli to immediately deliver M.V. "Yu Xin Yu 11288" to the Plaintiff WANG Hong. The Defendant HU Zheli left M.V. "Yu Xin Yu 11288" after receiving the order on February 18, 2014.

Fourthly, the facts related to the case.

Shengfan Company was a limited liability company with a registered capital of RMB1 million, of which the third party Wang Yu invested RMB900,000, the third party SHI Zhenjia invested RMB100,000. Wang Yu was the legal representative of the company, SHI Zhenjia was the supervisor of the company. The company mainly engaged in the operation of general merchandise items as road transport, general cargo stowage, warehousing services, domestic waterway cargo transportation agency business and domestic shipping agency business.

The court holds that:

This case is a dispute over damage liability caused by detaining the ship illegally because the Defendant Yuanhai Company sold M.V. "Yu Xin Yu 11288" to the Plaintiff WANG Hong. According to the certified facts and the allegation and defense of the parties, the court concluded the issues of the dispute of the case: firstly, whether the ship trading price had been paid off; secondly, whether the two Defendants constituted illegally detaining the ship and the corresponding responsibility; thirdly, economic losses the Plaintiff WANG Hong suffered.

Firstly, whether the ship trading price had been paid off.

The Plaintiff WANG Hong had paid off the full price of the ship in the amount of RMB9.468 million yuan before November 3, 2013, and the Defendant HU Zheli had received in full as the legal representative of the Defendant Yuanhai Company. The reasons were as follows: First, according to the second sets of evidence submitted by the Plaintiff WANG Hong, the Defendant HU Zheli received RMB9.268 million yuan by another bank transfer directly. In the above, it mentioned that the Plaintiff WANG Hong paid the deposit of RMB100,000 to the Hongkai Company on behalf of the Defendant Yuanhai Company on the date of signing the ship trading contract, so the Defendant HU Zheli issued the receipt of RMB900,000 (including the deposit of RMB800,000 paid by the Hongkai Company for the Plaintiff WANG Hong), and Hongkai Company also issued the proof for this fact. According to the fourth sets of evidence issued by the Plaintiff WANG Hong, the Defendant HU Zheli stated on November 11, 2013 in the public security case of the public security bureau on investigating his hurting Shi Zhe Jia's wife, the Plaintiff WANG Hong and the third party SHI Zhenjia had ever paid RMB100,000 in cash personally in China Postal Savings Bank Taizhou Jiangyan Branch. Secondly, according to the second sets of evidence summited by the two Defendants, Deng Yonggang, DENG Zhaokuo, as the employees of ship trading agency Hang Kai Company, when the public security authorities investigated SHI Zhenjia's suspicion of intentional assault, it had been mentioned that up to November 3, 2013, the Plaintiff WANG Hong had paid off the balance of the ship. Third, Hang Kai Company charged RMB200,000 to be used as the deposit of intermediary costs of buyers and sellers, of which RMB100,000 was paid by the Plaintiff WANG Hong on behalf of the Defendant Yuanhai Company. Although the two Defendants defended that they did not know this fact, but the signature of the ship trading contract and ship sales contract in this case, the Plaintiff WANG Hong paid deposit of RMB100,000 to the Company by POS machines of Hongkai Company, Hongkai Company transferred to the Defendant HU ZheliRMB800,000, the Defendant HU Zheli issued the receipt of RMB900,000, all these relative facts were happened on September 15, 2013, the two Defendants did not prove that they had paid the intermediary costs to Hongkai Company, and the Defendant HU Zheli was also impossible to issue the receipt of RMB900,000 hastily after actually receiving only RMB800,000 on September 15, 2013 under the condition of unknowing the Plaintiff WANG Hong had paid RMB100,000 to Hongkai Company as the deposit of intermediary costs on behalf of the Defendant Yuanhai Company. Therefore, the two Defendants only acknowledged received RMB9.368 million yuan and defended that the Plaintiff WANG Hong still had the debts of RMB100,000 to pay, which the court would not adopted.

Secondly, whether the two Defendants constituted illegally detaining the ship and the corresponding responsibility.

The Plaintiff WANG Hong had paid off the full price of the ship in the amount of RMB9.468 million yuan to the Defendant Yuanhai Company before the date of November 3, 2013, the Defendant HU Zheli had received in full as the legal representative of the Defendant Yuanhai Company. According to the agreement of ship trading contract and the ship sales contract, the Plaintiff WANG Hong had obtained the ownership and operation rights of M.V. "Yu Xin Yu 11288" completely since November 4, 2013 after paying off the price of the ship. The Plaintiff WANG Hong, as the owner of M.V. "Yu Xin Yu 11288", could exercise the rights of possession, use, proceeds and disposal of the ship. Meanwhile, according to the agreement of ship trading contract and the ship sales contract, the place of deliver the ship shall be in Nanjing riverbank. Although the third party SHI Zhenjia brought people to board on M.V. "Yu Xin Yu 11288" from morning November 8 to 9, 2013 in Zhenjiang, Jiangsu, using radical means to achieve the purpose of actually controlling the ship shall not get legal positive evaluation. However, given that the ship had arrived at the place of delivery that contract agreed, Nanjing, the Defendant Yuanhai Company shall have fulfilled the obligation to deliver the ship.

The Defendant HU Zheli convened a number of people including his own relatives and friends to board M.V. "Yu Xin Yu 11288" in the waters near the Nanjing Pukou waterworks around at 3:00 on November 11, 2013, controlled the liner and did not make the liner leave. Up to February 18, 2014, the ship left after the Defendant HU Zheli received a maritime injunction of the Court. The Defendant HU Zheli as the legal representative of the Defendant Yuanhai Company, held that the Defendant Yuanhai Company still had the ownership and operation rights of M.V."Yu Xin Yu 11288". The purposes and results of snatching and controlling the liner all pointed to the business interests of the Defendant Yuanhai Company over M.V. "Yu Xin Yu 11288", so the Defendant HU Zheli's the behavior of controlling the ship was official conduct, which shall be considered as the behavior of the Defendant Yuanhai Company. Given that the two Defendants did not have any right to M.V. "Yu Xin Yu 11288", therefore, the Defendant Yuanhai Company snatched and controlled M.V. "Yu Xin Yu 11288", which had constituted unlawfully detaining the ship and directly caused the Plaintiff WANG Hong could not use the ship as the owner of the liner. According to Article 2 of the Tort Liability Law of the People's Republic of China, "Those who infringe upon civil rights and interests shall be subject to the tort liability according to this law. Civil rights referred in this Act, including the regulations of right of life, right of health, right of name, right of reputation, right of honor, right of portrait, right of privacy, right of marital autonomy, right of guardianship, the usufructuary right, real rights for security, copyright, patent right, exclusive right to use trademark, right of discovery, stock rights, inheritance and other personal or property interests", the Defendant Yuanhai Company infringed the ownership of the ship of the Plaintiff WANG Hong, and shall bear tort liability.

Thirdly, the economic losses the Plaintiff WANG Hong suffered.
On October 14, 2014, because M.V. "Yu Xin Yu 11288" was detained, the Plaintiff WANG Hong requested the Court to entrust the qualified appraisal department to evaluate losses for detention he suffered in three months in the lawsuit. First, the losses for detention were the money that the charterer failed to complete loading and discharging in the agreed time but paid to the shipowner. In

dispute over ship collision, generally, loss of earning is calculated on the basis of average net profits of two voyages before and after the collision or that of other corresponding voyages. This case was a dispute over damage liability caused by detaining the ship illegally, the Plaintiff WANG Hong claimed the ship hires and liquidated damages, which were different from losses for detention obviously. Second, after the Plaintiff WANG Hong bought M.V. "Yu Xin Yu 11288", he did not put it into operation, so it could not be identified the losses for detention happened in the dispute through the identification. Accordingly, the Court did not permit the application that the Plaintiff WANG Hong requested to evaluate the losses for detention in three months of M.V. "Yu Xin Yu 11288".

The Plaintiff WANG Hong claimed the two Defendants to bear compensation liability for tort because M.V. "Yu Xin Yu 11288" was detained, which caused he could not put it into operation in time and suffered economic losses. However, the Plaintiff WANG Hong requested calculating the losses of ship hires and liquidated damages according to the bareboat charter party signed by the Plaintiff WANG Hong and the Third Party Shengfan Company, which belonged to resulting from the third person infringed the ownership and claimed for compensation for the expected creditor's rights were damaged, the claim has no legal basis and the loss did not actual occur, the court shall not sustain such request.

To sum up, the behavior of the Defendant Yuanhai Company snatching and controlling M.V. "Yu Xin Yu 11288" constitutes illegally detaining ship, and it shall bear the corresponding tort liability. But the losses of the ship hires and liquidated damages alleged by the Plaintiff WANG Hong had no legal basis, the court shall not sustain such request. According to Article 64 Paragraph 1 and Article 124 of Civil Procedure Law of the People's Republic of China, the judgment is as follows:

Reject all the claims of the Plaintiff WANG Hong.

Court acceptance fee in amount of RMB13,800, shall be born by the Plaintiff WANG Hong. According to Article 6 and Article 14 of the Measures on the Payment of Litigation Costs, the application fee in amount of RMB5,000 of maritime injunction applied by the Plaintiff WANG Hong belonged to litigation expenses. Because the Defendant Yuanhai Company shall bear the tort liability of detaining ship, so the application fee in amount of RMB5,000 of maritime injunction shall be born by the Defendant Yuanhai Company.

If dissatisfied with this judgment, any party shall within fifteen days as of the service of this judgment, submit a Statement of Appeal to the court, with duplicates in the number of the opposing parties, so as to make an appeal before Hubei High People's Court. Appeal entertainment fee shall be paid in advance when submitting the Statement of Appeal according to Article 13 Paragraph 1 of Measures on the Payment of Litigation Costs. Name of account: non-tax revenue settlement account of Hubei Finance Department; number of account: 052101040000369–1; deposit bank: Wuhan Agricultural Bank of China East Lake Branch. The payer paid by bank transfer or bank remittance should mark in the credential column "Hubei High

People's Court" or the Hubei High People's Court Unit code "103001". If the fee is not paid within seven days after the period of appeal expires, the appeal will be automatically recalled.

Presiding Judge: LIU Weihong
Acting Judge: LUO Yan
Acting Judge: XIONG Jing
March 5, 2015
Clerk: WANG Fang

Dalian Maritime Court
Civil Judgment

WANG Jun
v.
Dalian Tiger Beach Tourism Development Co., Ltd.

(2013) Da Hai Shi Chu Zi No.78

Related Case(s) None.

Cause(s) of Action 196. Dispute over liability for damage of ship pollution.

Headnote The Plaintiff abalone farmer held entitled to recover damages for pollution caused by Defendant's land reconstruction project to Plaintiff's embryonic abalone, but only for damage until Plaintiff discovered the pollution.

Summary The Plaintiff, WANG Jun, was a farmer using an area of rented land for aquaculture for the purpose of growing abalone. The Defendant, Dalian Tiger Beach Tourism Development Co., Ltd., obtained permission from local authorities to perform a land reconstruction project. The Plaintiff contacted the Defendant once he knew what the project entailed and told him it would cause pollution and destroy his ability to conduct abalone farming. The Defendant nonetheless proceeded with the project. The court found that the Plaintiff's farming behavior was legal. The Defendant caused the pollution resulting in the Plaintiff suffering damages as determined by the measure of the cost of the embryo abalone and their market value on the market had they survived the pollution. Lastly, the Court ruled that while there was causation between the Defendant's pollution and the Plaintiff's damages, the Plaintiff did not mitigate his damages. Therefore, the Plaintiff was able to recover the loss of value from his lost abalone during the period of time he did not know about the Defendant's operation, but not for the damages he suffered after he obtained knowledge of the pollution.

Judgment

The Plaintiff: WANG Jun, male, Han.
Agent *ad litem*: LIU Zhi, male, Han, employee.
Agent *ad litem*: WEI Jide, lawyer of Liaoning Dongya Law Firm.

The Defendant: Dalian Tiger Beach Tourism Development Co., Ltd.
Domicile:No.3, Hutan Road, Zhongshan District, Dalian.
Legal representative: YANG Lin, manager.
Agent *ad litem*: HU Liang, male, Han, employee.
Agent *ad litem*: HAO Wei, lawyer of Liaoning Haiwen Law Firm.

With respect to the case arising from dispute over liability for marine pollution, the Plaintiff WANG Jun filed litigation against the Defendant Dalian Tiger Beach Tourism Development Co., Ltd., before Dalian Maritime Court and the case was entertained, the court formed collegiate panel by law, and heard the case in curia. The Plaintiff and his agents *ad litem* LIU Zhi and WEI Jide, Defendant's agents *ad litem* HU Liang and HAO Wei appeared in the court and participated in the action. Now the case has been concluded.

The Plaintiff alleged in the Statement of Claim: in May 2011, the Plaintiff used sea water to farm abalones and carried out other production industry in Dalian Tiger Beach Shi Cao Pump Station(he alleged in the hearing that he started the aquaculture since October 2010). When the Defendant carried on the land reclamation project, it made pollution on the Plaintiff's aquaculture products, and caused the death of all seeds of abalones and semi-finished abalones. In this respect, the Plaintiff requested the court to order the Defendant to compensate the losses in sum of RMB13,600,000 yuan, and bear the case entertainment fee.

The Defendant defended that:

1. The cause of action should be the compensation dispute of relocation of the use of sea areas, rather than marine pollution liability dispute. Since the establishment of the project, the environmental assessment of it and construction of it, Defendant's land reclamation project had been strictly enforced according to the national law, and accepted supervision and administration from administrative departments in charge of marine, marine controllers, marine fisheries, environmental protection, etc. The project was properly constructed in the boundary point coordinates' sea area, which had already been approved. Besides, the project was legal, there was no intention or negligence under the construction, and it never caused the marine pollution.
2. Before the Defendant started the project, Dalian Zhongshan District Relocation and Cleaning office had already provided appropriate relocation compensation and proper arrangements for those people, who was involved in this project and used this area legally. For the reasons that the Plaintiff did not have certificates of sea areas utilization and aquaculture, and never paid fees of his utilization, so

the Plaintiff used the sea areas illegally, and should not be involved in the compensation.
3. The losses claimed by the Plaintiff had no basis. The Plaintiff did not offer legal financial and tax certificates, and he did not have scientific appraisal evidence. The photos and witness testimony, which were provided by the Plaintiff, cannot proof the quality, specifications, quantity and value of his farming abalones. The testing report about quality and the sample of the water was taken by the Plaintiff himself. He just did the detection of suspended substance of the water sample, without other physical and chemical index detection, and also no identification about the cause of the death of abalones. Besides, the risk of farming industry was tremendous, a variety of factors could cause the death or reducing production of abalones.
4. Pursuant to the Plaintiff's application, the appraiser did the calculation report about the amount of the farming, ignoring these basic facts. The appraiser just relied on the area of the seeds pond and the temporary farming pond, repeatedly calculating the area for the water from seeds pond and the temporary pond. This appraiser relied on an operating principle for the production technology from a company in Fuzhou, which had a vast distance between the farming conditions in Dalian, rather than choosing that principle in Shandong province, which farming area was near to Dalian's farming area. So the quantity of seeds of abalones and semi-finished abalones was unscientific; the evaluation report which was done on the basic of above date and the IOUs which was only issued by the Plaintiff, without any other valid financial evidence and other relevant evidence supporting that, so the assessment of the sum of losses RMB9,500,000 yuan was also unscientific.
5. The Defendant's land reclamation project did not start suddenly, but has already been constructed for several months, the Plaintiff cannot farming, reduce the quantity of farming, sell his abalones which were farmed in interior room, or take other measures to prevent or redoes the losses. However, the Plaintiff still farmed his abalones under the circumstances that he had already known this sea area would be used by the land reclamation project, and could not farm any more, so what he did was contrary to the common sense.

The court reckons that: on March 10, 2010, Dalian Government had convened a conference about the environment reform for Dalian Tiger Beach, which confirmed that the government of Zhongshan District, Dalian City (hereinafter referred to as "the Zhongshan district government") had the authority to undertake the relocation and removal project, which would remodel the outside area of the Tiger Beach Ocean Park(land, waters). On April 19, 2010, Dalian City Construction and Management Bureau sent the letter to Zhongshan district government, stating that the relocation and removal departments, which involved in the land relocation and removal project and was undertaken by the Zhongshan district government, involving Dalian Grease Chemical Plant. On August 13, 2010, the Defendant was turned to undertake the main responsibility to that project, which was agreed by the Dalian Government. On November 29, 2010, the Zhongshan district government made a farming assessment to the waters of Dalian Fishery Research Institute and the waters of Dalian Tiger Beach Fishery, when it verified whether the farming enterprises had legal formalities and other relevant information about that, and then provided the compensation for them. On July 13, 2011, Liaoning Marine and Fishery Department sent the "With regard to the opinions of approval about "the Reports about the Influence of the Dalian Tiger Beach Environment Reforming Project and land reclamation Project on Marine Environment" to the Defendant, and the documents stated that this report basically meet the requirements of the national marine environmental protection standards. Therefore, it reached the agreement that this project could be constructed, and requested that the following work should be done in the process of the construction: the sea land reclamation project should use the method that cofferdam first and then filling the land; cofferdam and backfilling should be given the greatest extent of control, in order to prevent the sediment from being stirring, and reduce the amount of the suspended substance. The Defendant took the method that cofferdam first and then filling the land to this land reclamation project. On December 12, 2011, the Liaoning Marine and Fishery Department sent the notification to the Defendant that it has agreed the Defendant to take construction under the land reclamation project of the Dalian Tiger Beach environment reforming project, and request the Defendant to fill the application of completion acceptance before thirty days of the completion of the land reclamation project, the certificate of the right to use sea areas would be given by the Liaoning Marine and Fishery Department to the Defendant. In August 2013, National Marine Environment Monitoring center issued the *Dalian Tiger Beach Environment Reforming Project and Completion Acceptance Report About the Right To Use Sea Areas Under the land reclamation Project(Draft to be approved)*, besides, in *Report of Project Completion (The East Bank)*, which indicated that the construction should be stared on November 25, 2010, and the date of completion of the project was December 10, 2012. On August 12, 2013, the Defendant got the certificate of the right to use sea areas under Dalian Tiger Beach environment reforming project and land reclamation project. On September 13, 2013, Liaoning Marine and Fishery Department sent the notification to the Defendant, which indicated that the project was qualified and has been completion accepted, which meant that the Defendant could use the certificate of the right to use sea areas to go through the land registration formalities.

On March 5, 2010, the Plaintiff got the business license for his Dalian San Ba Long De aquatic product individual business, stating that: business operator was Plaintiff, the place of business was No.4, No.2 building of Dalian San Ba Long De aquatic, the scope and manner of business was wholesaling and retailing of aquatic products, and aquaculture. On June 30, 2010, the Plaintiff rent 4,000 square meters of the yard and the plant in the Small Shi Cao, Zhongshan District, Dalian(the former was water pump station of the Dalian Grease Chemical Plant) from Dalian Grease Chemical Plant, the yard was used to aquaculture, and the duration of right to use was one year. The method which was used by the Plaintiff to farming the abalones was to extract the sea water and transported to the indoors by the sea. On April 6, 2011, the land where the water pump station existed has been auctioned by the Xigang District Court of the People's Republic of China, Dalian (hereinafter referred to as "Xigang District Court"). Before the auction, this land has been seized because the Dalian Grease Chemical Plant was involved in other cases, and the Plaintiff successfully bought it. After that, the Plaintiff filed the litigation against Dalian Grease Chemical Plant before Xigang District Court (the Plaintiffdid not provide relevant documents of judgment).

In 2010, when the land which was involved in cases was in the process of relocation and examining, the Defendant accompanied with the people of relocation department to examine the water pump station, and the Defendant also connected with Xigang District Court and Dalian Grease Chemical Plant for the reason that this land was seized by the court. The Defendant alleged that due to the fact that there were national defence engineerings, which cannot be relocated, near this land, so this land was not in the list of relocation. Since that land has been seized by Xigang District Court, the Defendant believed that the water pump station which was involved in cases was an idle one. The Plaintiff alleged that: he has connected with the Defendant in the duration of relocation and examining, and raised the comments that the Defendant's land reclamation project would make the marine pollution, which would cause the losses of abalones. Around January 2011, the Plaintiff tried to prevent the Defendant from performing land reclamation project by blocking the Defendant's soil car, since the Defendant have started his project from Shicao. However, the Plaintiffdid not succeed. From March to April in 2011, the Plaintiff contacted with the Defendant for the reason that the water around the water pump station gradually became turbid. From July to August in 2011, the Plaintiff also contacted with the Defendant due to the fact that the condition of farming abalones became abnormal, after that, the Defendant asked other people to take pictures of the died abalones.

The Plaintiff alleged something about the process of seeds and death of the farming stuffs: in October 2010, the Plaintiff bought 3200 abalones seeds in order to farming them. The sum price was RMB680,000 yuan. And in January 2001, these seeds became 4 million abalones. From June to July in 2011, those seeds gradually died, however, the normal rate of death was 20%. From March to April in 2011, the Plaintiff bought 1,104,000 semi-finished abalones(more than 5 cm) in order to farming. And those abalones also became abnormal from June to July 2011, and also gradually died after 2 to 3 months.

The facts mentioned above, two parties adduced the relocation documents from Dalian government and relevant departments, the documents which were approved by the Liaoning Marine and Fishery Department, the report from National Marine Environment Monitoring center, the certificate of the right to use sea areas, business license of individual business, the court recognized, "tenancy contracts", photos as well as other evidence, and statement on trial. After cross-examination, the court affirms and uses the volume to support the evidence.

When the case at bar, the Plaintiff applied identification to the following information: 1. based on the Plaintiff's site and farming facilities, whether he can farming 4 million abalone seeds (the abalone will group from the size of 0.1–0.2 cm to 1.8–1.9 cm) and 1.1 million self-finished abalones(will group from the size of

5 cm to 7 cm); 2. the market value(the area of Dalian, in 2011) of annual output of abalone seeds(1.8–1.9 cm) and the self-finished abalones(7 cm), which was based on the expert conclusion of the first prong. the court entrusted the judicatory appraisal center of Dalian Maritime University School to test the first prong, and this center held the report of the amount of farming abalones, the conclusion was that: based on the seeds pond and the temporary farming pond, which was examined in scene, and pursuant to the procedure of abalone production technical operation in the Fuzhou Ri Xing Food Co., Ltd. The amount of seeds of interior corrugated abalones was 6,875,669; pursuant to the temporary farming pond, the procedure of corrugated abalone technical operation, the amount of interior corrugated abalones(the length of body was about 5 mm) was 3,708,800, the amount of the abalones, which was longer than 5 cm, in the interior seeds pond and the temporary farming pond was 1,426,461. After that, the court entrusted the Dalian ShenMing Capital Rating Office to assess the value of abalones. The report of value assessment, which was held by this office, came to the conclusion that: compared the amount of farming abalones in the said report, with the output of abalones, which was applied by the Plaintiff. The office stated that the amount of the output: 4 million abalone seeds which was 1.8–1.9 cm and the 1.1 million self-finished abalones, which was 5 to 7 cm, can only be used as the assessment evidence under this assessment purposes. If based on the market value of the base date of assessment on October 12, 2011, the value of abalone seeds was RMB4,000,000 yuan, the value of self-finished abalones was RMB5,500,000 yuan, the sum of them was RMB9,500,000 yuan. the Plaintiffdid not have dissent to these two reports. However, the Defendant had the dissent on both (the dissent is in the brief), but the Defendant did not apply the cross-examination with the appraiser.

The court holds that, the Plaintiff alleged that the Plaintiff's farming abalones' death was caused by the reason that the Defendant's land reclamation project polluted the sea waters, so the case is concerning dispute over the liability for marine pollution damages. Pursuant to the Articles 65 and 66 of the Tort Liability Law of the People's Republic of China, the Plaintiff should first prove he is the legal infringed, the fact that this area of sea was polluted, the tortfeasor who made the pollution, and the loss of damages caused by the pollution. Then the burden of proof shifts to the Defendant, the Defendant should prove that there is no causation between the situation of immunity or reducing liability and the damages. So the outstanding issues are as follows: 1. whether the Plaintiff's farming behavior is legal or not; 2. whether the Defendant made the pollution or not; 3. whether the Plaintiff has suffered the damages; 4. the causation between the pollution and the damages. The court comes to the following decisions:

Firstly, whether the Plaintiff's farming behavior is legal or not.

Although the business license for the individual business, which was provided by the Plaintiff, could prove that he has the right to operate the aquaculture, the San Ba Mall, which was the place of business, does nothing with this case at bar. Since June 30, 2010, the Plaintiff rent the land and the buildings in the yard of water pump station, and the yard was used to aquaculture, the duration of right to use was one year. With regard to the certificate of the right to use sea areas and the certificate of aquaculture, the Article 2 Paragraph 1 of the Law of the People's Republic of China on the Administration of the Use of Sea Areas stipulates that the sea areas refer to the sea surface, water volume, seabed and subsoil of the inland waters and territorial seas of the People's Republic of China. Pursuant to the Article 3 Paragraph 2 thereof, Any entity or individual that intends to use the sea areas is required to obtain the right to their use according to law. Under the Article 11 Paragraph 1 of the Fishery Law of the People's Republic of China, the used must obtain the certificate of aquaculture, if the individual or the company needs to use the sea areas and the intertidal zone, which was owned by the public and planned by the nation in order to run the farming industry. The land and the plants in the yard of water pump station, which were rent by the Plaintiff, should not be included in the sea areas and the intertidal zone. The Defendant alleged that the Plaintiffdid not have the certificate of the right to use sea areas and the certificate of aquaculture, meanwhile, did not pay the fees for using sea areas, all those behaviors violated the law, but the Defendant did not offer the evidence. In our county, there is no relevant law which expressly stipulates that the Plaintiff's farming behavior needs relevant certificates, so we conclude that the Plaintiff's farming behavior is legal.

Secondly, Whether the Defendant made the pollution or not.

On December 12, 2011, the Liaoning Marine and Fishery Department sent the notification to the Defendant that it has agreed the Defendant to take construction under the land reclamation project of the Dalian Tiger Beach environment reforming project. However, the Defendant started the land reclamation project from November 25, 2010. So the Defendant lack the necessary constructing conditions when he started the construction in advance without permission. On July 13, 2011, Liaoning Marine and Fishery Department sent the "with regard to the opinions of approval about "the Reports about the Influence of the Dalian Tiger Beach Environment Reforming Project and land reclamation Project on Marine Environment" to the Defendant, and this opinions of approval cannot prove that the Defendant has already operating the construction strictly according to opinions. Besides, it also cannot conclude that this project will not pollute the Plaintiff's aquaculture stuff. And the relevant evidence which showed that the project was qualified and has been completion accepted, cannot draw this conclusion. The Defendant took the method that cofferdam first and then filling the land to the adjacent sea area of land, and this method will inevitably make the sea water turbidity. Then it blocked up the entry which was used by the Plaintiff for extracting the sea water, and in order to farming the abalones. So the Defendant's land reclamation project made the pollution on the waters in the area of cofferdam.

Thirdly, whether the Plaintiff has suffered the damages.

The Plaintiff rent the land and plants in order to farming abalones, the Defendant's land reclamation project made the pollution on the waters in the area of cofferdam. Ultimately, it blocked up the entry which was used by the Plaintiff for extracting the sea water, and this caused the abalones gradually died for the reason that the quality of water turned turbid, and caused the Plaintiff cannot continue farming abalones. So the Plaintiff suffered the loss.

Fourthly, the causation between the pollution and the loss.

The disputes as talked above determine the causation between the pollution, which made by the Defendant's land reclamation project, and the Plaintiff's farming damages. Considering whether the Defendant can get the immunity, the Plaintiff alleged in the court that: he has connected with the Defendant in the duration of relocation(from April to November 2010) and examining, and raised the comments that the Defendant's land reclamation project would make the marine pollution, which would cause the losses of abalones. Around January 2011, the Plaintiff tried to prevent the Defendant from performing land reclamation project by blocking the Defendant's soil car, since the Defendant have started his project from Shicao. From March to April in 2011, the Plaintiff contact with the Defendant for the reason that the water around the water pump station gradually became turbid. However, the Plaintiff made the following statement about the process of farming in court: in October 2010, the Plaintiff bought abalone seeds in order to farming them. And in January 2001, these seeds became 4 million abalones. From June to July in 2011, those seeds gradually died. From March to April in 2011, the Plaintiff bought semi-finished abalones(more than 5 cm) in order to farming. And those abalones also became abnormal from June to July 2011, and also gradually died after 2 to 3 months. Those statements indicate that, the Plaintiff connected with the Defendant when he knew this land would be used for relocation, and the negotiation was about the land reclamation project's effect on the farming industry. But the Plaintiff knew about the relocation project does not represent that he knew the starting time of the Defendant's land reclamation project. So in October 2011, the Plaintiff's behavior that bought the abalone seeds and farmed them in the field and plants was rational. The Defendant should be liable for paying the damages, which the Plaintiff suffered because of the land reclamation project. the Plaintiff should foresee the land reclamation project will cause the damages of his farming, after in October 2010 the Plaintiff knew the Defendant started the land reclamation project. However, from the March to April 2011, the Plaintiff still bought the semi-finished abalones for farming. So the Plaintiff also has the comparative fault on the damages which caused by the Defendant's land reclamation project, and the Defendant should not be liable for this damages.

With regard to the fact that the sum of the damages which caused by the Plaintiff buying the abalone seeds in the October 2010. The report of the amount of farming abalones, based on the seeds pond and the temporary farming pond, which were examined on scene, concluded that the amount of abalone seeds was 4 million; the assessment report which was based on the market value of the base date of assessment on October 12, 2011, concluded the value of that 4 million abalone seeds, which were 1.8–1.9 cm, was RMB4,000,000 yuan. We held that, the report of the amount of farming abalones just determined the amount of the field and plants' ability to farm the abalones, but never determined the real amount of abalones, which was farmed by the Plaintiff. The assessment report just confirmed the value of abalones, but not assessed the damages of farming abalones, so it cannot determine the amount of damages that the Plaintiff real suffered. The Plaintiff also did not offer ample evidence to prove the quantity and the value of his seeds.

However, considering that the Plaintiff rent the field and the plants in order to farm the abalones, the Plaintiff cannot abandon this field and plants under the normal circumstances, unless there is the evidence that can prove the Plaintiff was willful. Now the Defendant did not prove the Plaintiff was willful, so we held that the Plaintiff farmed the abalones in this filed and plants in reality. However, based on the Plaintiff's statement, in the beginning of 2011, when the Plaintiff knew the Defendant started the land reclamation project, the amount of the abalones has already been 4 million, the Plaintiff should foresee that these seeds will be suffered the marine pollution, so he should took the measures to reduce the damages in time, for example, the Plaintiff could find other plants to continue his farming industry, or sold to other individuals who also farmed the abalones, rather than not interfering and let those abalones died gradually. Due to the emergency situation, if the Plaintiff cannot find other fields to continue farming nor sell them in market price, he can also reduce the price and sell them. So the court based on the amount of the available farming abalones and the value assessment, and considered about the normal death rate in farming as well as the rational situation that the Plaintiff should sell them in a lower price, the court holds the compensation should be reduced and the damages should be determined as RMB1,600,000 yuan. All in all, the court recognized the Plaintiff's appeal that the Defendant should pay the compensation about RMB1,600,000 yuan to the Plaintiff, for the reason that the Defendant's land reclamation project made the pollution on the Plaintiff's farming abalones. Pursuant to Article 2 Paragraph 1 and Article 3 Paragraph 2 of the Law of the People's Republic of China on the Administration of the Use of Sea Areas, Article 11 Paragraph 1 of the Fishery Law of the People's Republic of China, Articles 26, 65 and 66 of the Tort Liability Law of the People's Republic of China, the judgment is as follows:

1. The Defendant Dalian Tiger Beach Tourism Development Co., Ltd. within ten days as of the effective day of this judgment, compensate the Plaintiff WANG JunRMB1,600,000 yuan;
2. Reject other claims made by the Plaintiff WANG Jun.

If the Defendant Dalian Tiger Beach Tourism Development Co., Ltd. fails to fulfill its obligation to make the said payments within the time limit provided by this judgment, the interest shall be double paid for the period of deferred payment according to Article 253 of the Civil Procedure Law of the People's Republic of China.

Court acceptance fee in amount of RMB103,400 yuan (the Plaintiff has prepaid), the Plaintiff should shall bear RMB91,235, the Defendant should bear RMB12,165 yuan.

If dissatisfied with this judgment, the Plaintiff WANG Jun and the Defendant Dalian Tiger Beach Tourism Development Co., Ltd. shall within fifteen days as of the service of this judgment, submit 10 Statement of Appeal to the court, so as to make an appeal before Liaoning High People's Court.

Presiding Judge: SUN Guang
Judge: XIN Xin
Acting Judge: DONG Shihua
May 29, 2015
Clerk: BIAN Xin

Wuhan Maritime Court
Civil Judgment

WU Guangbao et al.
v.
Anqing City Yingjiang District Xinzhou Country Ferry Station

(2015) Wu Hai Fa Shang Chu Zi No.00827

Related Case(s) None.

Cause(s) of Action 205. Dispute over ship operation contract.

Headnote The Plaintiffs who claimed damages for breach of a ship management contract were held not to be the real owners of ship involved, and not parties to the ship management contract with the Defendant, so their claims were rejected.

Summary The six Plaintiffs claimed that they had suffered loss because of the Defendant's breach of a ship operation and management contract. The court held that the six Plaintiffs had not provided any evidence that they were actually party to the contract, nor that they were investors, nor that they actually paid for M.V. "Wan An Qing Du 18" to be built. Thus, the six Plaintiffs were not real owners of M.V. "Wan An Qing Du 18". The court also held that the six Plaintiffs did not have a contractual relationship with the Defendant, and that the Defendant was therefore not liable for breach of contract as alleged by the six Plaintiffs. Therefore, the Court dismissed all the claims of the six Plaintiffs.

Judgment

The Plaintiff: WU Guangbao

The Plaintiff: ZHA Xianzhong

The Plaintiff: CHENG Jinmao

The Plaintiff: WU Youping

The Plaintiff: MIU Yubing

The Plaintiff: WU Xiaoheng

Representative of action: WU Xiaoheng.

Agent *ad litem* of the Plaintiffs: ZHENG Guoping, legal worker of Anqing YIngjiang Jianshe Legal Service Office.

The Defendant: Anqing City Yingjiang District Xinzhou Country Ferry Station

Domicile: Qinglong village, Xinzhou Country, Yingjiang District, Anqing City, Anhui.

Legal representative: WU Liangyi, master.

With respect to the dispute over contract of operation and management of ship, the Plaintiffs WU Guangbao, ZHA Xianzhong, CHENG Jinmao, WU Youping, MIU Yubing and WU Xiaoheng (hereinafter referred to as "the six Plaintiffs") filed litigation against the Defendant Anqing City Yingjiang District Xinzhou Country Ferry Station (hereinafter referred to as "Ferry Station") before the court. After entertaining this case on June 4, 2015, the court applied the summary procedure by law, appointed Acting Judge REN Nina as the solo judge, and held a hearing in public on July 28, 2015. The six Plaintiffs and their agent *ad litem* ZHENG Guoping, the legal representative of Defendant Ferry Station WU Liangyi appeared in court and participated in the hearing. Now the case has been concluded.

The six Plaintiffs alleged that: in 2006, all six Plaintiffs raised fund Renminbi (hereinafter referred to as "RMB") 125,800 yuan to build the ship named "Wan An Qing Du 18". In November 2008, the Transport Department of Yingjiang District, Anqing City, Anhui Province, held a special conference for the operation and management of M.V. "Wan An Qing Du 18", confirming the ship would be operated and managed by the Defendant Ferry Station. This ship's certificate and the annual inspection formalities were all operated by the Defendant Ferry Station, in order to warrant M.V. "Wan An Qing Du 18" to navigate normally, and the six Plaintiffs paid the management fees to Ferry Station every year regularly. In 2013, the Defendant did not conduct the annual inspection without any excuse, and made M.V. "Wan An Qing Du 18" out of action. In order to reduce the loss, the six Plaintiffs sold M.V. "Wan An Qing Du 18" to others at a price of RMB30,000. In this respect, the Plaintiff requested the court to order the Defendant compensate the losses in sum of RMB95,800 for discard of M.V. "Wan An Qing Du 18", and bear the case entertainment fee.

The Defendant defended that: the six Plaintiffs were not proper Plaintiffs, because the registered shipowner of M.V. "Wan An Qing Du 18" was LU Zhenyuan, so the six Plaintiffs could not obtain the title to sue in terms of the losses. Ferry Station's behavior did not lead to the result that M.V. "Wan An Qing Du 18" suspended the navigation and was discarded. From the November in 2008 to the October in 2013, the Defendant performed contractual obligations faithfully, actively assisted M.V. "Wan An Qing Du 18" to attend to the ship's annual inspection, and held the responsibility to coordinate and handle the relevant affairs for the ship's operation. On October 24, 2012, the government of Anqing City YingJiang District ChangFeng Country (hereinafter referred to as Changfeng County Government) issued *Report on Request of Strengthening Supervision and Coordination of Hidden Risks in "Wan An Qing Du 18 (Ya Er Gou——dam)"* by Competent Authority (hereinafter referred to as Report), which focused on the coordination and supervision of the hidden risks in M.V. "Wan An Qing Du 18" [ChangZheng (2012) No.67], requesting that the prohibitive hidden risks of M.V. "Wan An Qing Du 18", which existed in the operation, should be corrected within the time limit. For the overdue correction, the ship would be ordered to suspend the navigation and temporarily seize the ferry tool. On February 2, 2013, the Maritime Safety Department of Niutou Mountain in Anqing, for the reasons that M.V. "Wan An Qing Du 18" navigated in the fog without approval under the circumstance that the ship did not lift the ban of prohibition of departure, and issued the Circular on the Decision of the Navigation in Frog of M.V. "Wan An Qing Du 18" without Approval [Anhai Niutou Mountain (2013) No.1] (hereinafter the Circular), implementing RMB1,000 maritime administrative penalty fine on M.V. "Wan An Qing Du 18", and ordered the ship not to carry passengers without approval under the circumstances that the ship did not lift the ban of prohibition of departure. According to the Article 5 of Ship Commissioned Management Contract, in the period of commissioned management, the bailee's ship should be warranted to maintain seaworthy, the ship was prohibited from navigating without approval, and make sure that the information was available, the hidden risks should be corrected in time, if the ship refused the correction, the bailee had the right to terminate the commissioned management contract. According to Article 2 of the Minutes of Meeting of the Transport Department of Yingjiang District Anqing City, the shipowner of M.V. "Wan An Qing Du 18" should make the Commissioned Management Contract with the Defendant, the contract should be concluded every year, and the Yingjiang Transport Department, the Changfeng Government, the Xinzhou Country Government should issue the opinions on the contract, the contract would be effective when it is stamped. In November 2013, the Defendant seriously refused to renew the Commissioned Management Contract in terms of M.V. "Wan An Qing Du 18". Meanwhile, the ship never submitted the Application for Operation Inspection of Anhui Province Ship Inspection Bureau (hereinafter the Application), and never asked the bureau to assist them to handle the ship annual inspection, the ship insurance and the relevant formalities. So it was the Plaintiff's own fault that the ship did not have the annual inspection, and the Plaintiff itself should burden the loss.

In order to prove the claim, the six Plaintiffs submitted following evidence:

1. The six Plaintiff's certificates of citizen identification, certificates of seafarer, the company information of the Defendant Ferry Station, to prove that the Plaintiffs and the Defendant are proper Plaintiffs.
2. Ferry's construction contract, the statement, to prove that M.V. "Wan An Qing Du 18" was constructed by the six Plaintiffs, and the six Plaintiffs are the actual owners of this ship.
3. Minutes of Meeting for Commissioned Operation and Coordination of M.V. "Wan An Qing Du 18" of the Ya Er Gou Ferry Station (hereinafter the Minutes of Meeting), the Ship Commissioned Management Contract, to prove that every year the six Plaintiffs have paid the management fees to the Defendant until 2013, the Defendant should perform the contract's obligation, and handle the ship's annual inspection and the relevant formalities.
4. Information of registration number of M.V. "Wan An Qing Du 18", to prove that the ship was operating legally.
5. Certificate of the ship's registered ownership, the ship's operation and transport certificate, nationality papers of ship, to prove that the "Wan An Qing Du 18" was registered under LU Zhenyuan.
6. Endorsement Book of Vessel, to prove that the annual inspection of M.V. "Wan An Qing Du 18" until October 2013, the Defendant is the registered commissioned management operator.
7. Request for Cancellation of Ya Er Gou Ferry Station in Changfeng County of Anqing City Yingjiang District Changfeng Country (hereinafter the Cancellation Request) [ChangZheng (2014) No.46], which was issued by the Changfeng County Government, and an Agreement, to prove that M.V. "Wan An Qing Du 18" did not pass the annual inspection, and the ship was required to stop navigation by the transport and maritime administration, and the Changfeng Government considered the status of the ferry, applying the District government to ban Ferry Station, so the six Plaintiffs sold M.V. "Wan An Qing Du 18" in order to reduce the loss.

Evidence adduced by all the Plaintiffs, the Defendant's cross-examination opinions are as follows: the Defendant had no objection to the authenticity of evidence 1, 2, 3, 4, 5, 6 and Cancellation Request, which was issued by the Changfeng County Government, in evidence 7. However, the Defendant considered the shipowner of M.V. "Wan An Qing Du 18" was LU Zhenyuan, not the six Plaintiffs, and the six Plaintiffs had the unclear relationship with LU Zhenyuan, had no relevancy with this case. The Defendant had objection to the authenticity and relevancy of the Agreement in evidence 7.

The court's opinions are as below: the court admits the authenticity of evidence 1, 2, 3, 4, 5, 6 and Cancellation Request in evidence 7, but whether those evidence can achieve the purposes of proof, the court elaborates the determinations in detail below. The form of the Agreement in evidence 7 is a copy, so the Defendant did not recognize the authenticity thereof, and in its content, YE Ping is the undisclosed bargainee. The six Plaintiffs also did not provide other evidence to prove the authenticity of sales of the ship, so the court did not confirm the relevancy of this evidence with this case.

In order to prove the defense opinion, the Defendant submitted the evidence as follows:

1. Organization Code Certificate, business license, water transport license and WU Liangyi's certificate of identification, to prove the Defendant is the proper defendant.
2. Ownership Registration Certificate of M.V. "Wan An Qing Du 18", to prove that the shipowner of M.V. "Wan An Qing Du 18" is LU Zhenyuan, the six Plaintiffs are not proper Plaintiffs.
3. Minutes of Meeting, which was issued by the Transport Department of Anqing City Yingjiang District, and the Ship Commissioned Management Contract, to prove that M.V. "Wan An Qing Du 18" was entrusted to the Defendant to operate.
4. Statement receipts of Anhui Province administrative institutional organization, and 4 receipts, to prove that commissioned operation fees arising from M.V. "Wan An Qing Du 18" have been paid the to the Defendant.
5. Inland Water Passenger Quota Certificate, inland water ship's load line certificate, inland water ship seaworthy certificate, inland water ship pollution prevention certificate, ship's minimum safe manning certificate, ship's annual inspection certificate, to prove that the Defendant actively perform its contractual obligations in the period of commissioned management, and assisted M.V. "Wan An Qing Du 18" to handle the ship's annual inspection and other relevant formalities until October 20, 2013.
6. Report, which was issued by the Changfeng County Government, and the Circular, to prove that M.V. "Wan An Qing Du 18" navigated under the danger when it was unseaworthy. From October 2013, the Defendant terminated the operation and management of this ship, and did not renew the contract.

Evidence adduced by the Defendant Ferry Station, the six Plaintiffs' cross-examination opinions are as follows: there is no objection to the authenticity thereof. However, the six Plaintiffs held they were the actual owners of M.V. "Wan An Qing Du 18", LU Zhenyuan was the person who was just liable to communicate and handle the relevant affairs, and the six Plaintiffs had paid the fees for management until October 2013, so the contract kept valid. The Defendant just accepted the management fees but never assisted to instruct the navigation, so the Defendant's was responsible for the hidden risks of M.V. "Wan An Qing Du 18". Besides, the document was issued in 2012 by the Changfeng County Government and in 2013, the Defendant still handled the annual inspection for M.V. "Wan An Qing Du 18", so the Defendant did not follow the requirements of the Minutes of Meeting to perform the obligation that the Defendant should manage and operate the ship, and the minutes of meeting was issued by the Transport Department of Anqing City YingJiang District, so the Defendant should be liable for that.

The court reckons that: the court confirms the authenticity of the evidence, but whether the evidence can achieve the purpose of proof, the court will elaborate the determination in detail.

In consideration the investigation on trial, the court finds the facts as follows:

On December 14, 2006, Changfeng Shipping Co., Ltd. (hereinafter referred to as Changfeng Company) (Party A) signed the Shipbuilding Contract with Anqing Ning Jiang Shipyard (hereinafter referred to as Ningjing Shipyard) (Party B), and the parties reached the agreement that a ship which would be made from steel by Ningjing Shipyard, and the value of the ship would be RMB124,800. If the Party B can deliver the goods on time, the Party A will give RMB1,000 to the Party B as bonuses, and in the contract, the parties also came into agreement about the blueprint, construction, inspection, schedule and the method of payment. LU Zhengyuan and JIN Renbing respectively represented Changfeng Company and Ningjing Shipyard signed the contract, and CHAO Xiping, YOU Baobei who are parties not involved in the case, as well as the four Plaintiffs CHENG Jinmao, ZHA Xianzhong, WU Youping and WU Xiaoheng signed as witnesses. On November 12, 2007, LU Zhengyuan (the name is displayed) issued the statement, stating that: CHENG Jinmao, ZHA Xianzhong, WU Xiaoheng and other people collected the funds to build a new ship, and entrusted LU Zhengyuan to handle the relevant ship construction affairs. On December 24, 2006, he signed the Shipbuilding Contract with ship constructor JIN Renbing from Ningjing Shipyard. In consideration that the ship construction was not proper, so the delivery of the ship was delayed, JIN Chengmao and other people communicated with ship company about the issue of delivery.

On November 10, 2008, the Transport Department of Anqing City Yingjiang District held the meeting for commissioned operation and coordination of M.V. "Wan An Qing Du 18" of the Ya Er Gou Ferry Station. In the meeting, the Defendant was confirmed to be entrusted to operate M.V. "Wan An Qing Du 18", the shipowner should sign the Ship Commissioned Management Contract with the Defendant, the contract should be signed every year, and the Transport Department, the Changfeng Government and the Xinzhou Country Government should sign the opinions on the contract, then the contract would come into effect after the contract was affixed a seal. On November 7, 2008, the Defendant signed the Ship Commissioned Management Contract with LU Zhengyuan, reaching an agreement that M.V. "Wan An Qing Du 18" was entrusted to the Defendant to operate, LU Zhengyuan was liable for safety responsibility which would happen in the daily operation, and he would be supervised and instructed by the Defendant Ferry Station. The Defendant would assist LU Zhengyuan to handle the annual inspection, insurance and relevant formalities. In the period of commissioned management, M.V. "Wan An Qing Du 18" should keep in seaworthy, and was not allowed to navigate in danger, the hidden risks should be corrected timely as soon as being discovered, otherwise the Defendant had the right to terminate the Ship Commissioned Management Contract. Besides, the contract also agreed that LU

Zhengyuan should pay RMB2,800 as the commissioned management fees every year, and the fees should be totally paid at the time when the contract was signed. The period of the contract was one year, from November 1, 2008 to October 30, 2009. After LU Zhengyuan and the Defendant signed the contract, the Transport Department, the Changfeng Government and the Xinzhou Country Government also should sign and affix a seal then the contract would come into effect.

After the contract came into effect, the Defendant assisted M.V. "Wan An Qing Du 18" to handle relevant certificates, including the certificate of ship registered ownership, nationality papers of ship, the inland water passenger quota certificate, inland water ship's load line certificate, inland water ship seaworthy certificate, inland water ship pollution prevention certificate, ship's minimum safe manning certificate, ship's annual inspection certificate, and the Defendant assisted M.V. "Wan An Qing Du 18" to handle the annual inspection every year, the last time of the ship's qualified annual inspection was on 6 December 2012, and the period of validity was from December 6, 2012 to October 20, 2013. The Defendant confirmed that it had the factual commissioned management relationship with LU Zhengyuan within the period of time from October 31, 2009 to October 20, 2013, and in those four years, LU Zhengyuan have paid RMB2,800 to it every year as the management fees.

On October 24, 2012, the Changfeng Government issued the Report, requesting that the prohibitive hidden risks of M.V. "Wan An Qing Du 18", which existed in the operation, should be corrected within the time limit. For the overdue correction, the ship would be ordered to suspend the navigation and temporarily seize the ferry tool. Changfeng Country government suggested that the ship should be banned, and the wharf should be cancelled.

On February 3, 2013, the Maritime Safety Department of Niutou Mountain in Anqing City, for the reasons that M.V. "Wan An Qing Du 18" navigated in the fog without approval under the circumstances that the ship did not lift the ban of prohibition of departure, and issued the Circular, implementing the RMB1,000 penalty fine of maritime administrative on M.V. "Wan An Qing Du 18", and ordered the ship that under the circumstance that the ship did not lift the ban of prohibition of departure, the ship cannot carry passengers without approval.

On August 4, 2014, the Cancellation Application, which was issued by the Changfeng Government. For the reason that M.V. "Wan An Qing Du 18" did not pass the annual inspection, and the ship was required to stop navigation by the transport and maritime authority, and the Changfeng Government considered the status of the ferry, applying to the District government for banning Ferry Station.

Through investigation, it is found LU Zhenyuan was the shipowner of M.V. "Wan An Qing Du 18" on the certificate of ship registered ownership, nationality papers of ship, the certificate of ship operation and navigation, but the signature in the statement and the Commissioned Management Contract both were LU Zhengyuan. During the trial, the Plaintiffs and the Defendant did not object to the fact that LU Zhenyuan and LU Zhengyuan was the same person, so the court affirms this fact.

The court reckons as follows:

This case is concerning dispute over the ship operation and management contract. The six Plaintiffs considered the Defendant violated the agreements in the operation and management contract and caused the loss, so the Plaintiffs proved the capacity of plaintiffs, the contractual relationship of operation and management, the Defendant's behavior of violating the contract and the sum of the loss.

With respect to the capacity of six Plaintiff Appellants. The court reckons that: in consideration of the record in certificate of ship registered ownership of M.V. "Wan An Qing Du 18" and the Shipbuilding Contract, the registered ship owner was LU Zhenyuan. The six Plaintiffs alleged that they were the actual owner of M.V. "Wan An Qing Du 18", so they should offer the relevant evidence to prove. The evidence submitted by the six Plaintiffs was the Shipbuilding Contract and the statement. With respect to the Shipbuilding Contract, the court reckons that the Shipbuilding Contract was signed by LU Zhengyuan and the Anqing Ningjiang Shipyard, and there were only four of the six Plaintiffs (the four Plaintiffs were CHENG Jinmao, ZHA Xianzhong, WU Youping, WU Xiaoheng) have signed as the witnesses, however, the other two people (CHAO Xiping and YOU Baobei) were undisclosed. So the six Plaintiffs were not the clients of that contract, and also from the content of the contract, the six Plaintiffs cannot be regarded as the buyer or bailee in the Shipbuilding Contract, besides, the court cannot find other relevant contractual rights and obligations from the contract's content. With respect to the statement, the court reckons that the statement just figure out that in the six Plaintiffs, the ship was built under the collection of funds from CHENG Jinmao, ZHA Xianzhong, WU Xiaoheng, and those people do not correspond to the witnesses' names in the Shipbuilding Contract. The statement stated that "on December 14, 2006, Changfeng Company signed the Shipbuilding Contract with Ningjing Shipyard", this does not correspond to the time, which the Shipbuilding Contract was signed on December 14, 2006. Meanwhile, LU Zhengyuan was undisclosed and he did not appear in the court to receive the confronting. Besides, the six Plaintiffs did not submit the evidence that they collected funds and bought M.V. "Wan An Qing Du 18", so the court cannot hold that the new ship which was stated in the statement is M.V. "Wan An Qing Du 18", the court also cannot hold that the six Plaintiffs are investor, nor did the six Plaintiffs actually pay the RMB125,800 to build M.V. "Wan An Qing Du 18". So the court shall not affirm the fact that the six Plaintiffs are the real owners of M.V. "Wan An Qing Du 18".

With respect to the relationship of management and operation in this case, the court reckons that the Defendant just signed the Ship Commissioned Management Contract in written with LU Zhengyuan once, and the contract period is one year, from November first in 2008 to October 30 in 2009. From 2009 to 2012, the Defendant just recognized that it has the factual commissioned management relationship for M.V. "Wan An Qing Du 18" with LU Zhengyuan, and LU Zhengyuan paid the commissioned management fees in sum of RMB2,800 to it every year. The six Plaintiffs did not sign the written Commissioned Management Contract with the Defendant, they did not prove that they have entrusted LU Zhengyuan to sign the Ship Commissioned Management Contract with the Defendant, nor did they provide other evidence to prove that they had the actual commissioned management relationship with the Defendant, so there is no basis in fact that the six Plaintiffs alleged that they have the commissioned management relationship with the Defendant, the court shall not affirm this fact.

With respect to whether the Defendant had the nonperformance of the contract, the court reckons that based on the document of the Transport Department, the Commissioned Management Contract would be signed every year, and the contract should be signed and affixed the seal by the Transport Department, the Changfeng County Government, the Xinzhou Country Government. Besides, in 2012 and 2013, the ship was ordered to suspend the navigation by the government and the maritime department, for the reasons that M.V. "Wan An Qing Du 18" had the hidden risks and navigated in danger. So it is not the Defendant's own reason that let it terminate the operation and management of M.V. "Wan An Qing Du 18", so the Defendant shall not burden the liability for breach of contract as alleged by the six Plaintiffs.

With respect to the loss of the ship, the court reckons that the sum of loss should be based on the current value of the ship, namely the difference by deducting the effective sales price of the ship. It has already been 8 years from M.V. "Wan An Qing Du 18" was built in 2007 to the six Plaintiffs filed a suit, but the six Plaintiffs did not prove the current value of the ship, so there is no basis for the Plaintiffs to calculate the sum of loss which is based on the value of the ship in 2007. Besides, there is also no effective evidence proving that the behavior of sale ship and the price of sale ship, so the court does not support the six Plaintiffs' claim.

In sum, the six Plaintiffs did not have ample evidence to prove that they had the contractual or torts relationship with the Defendant Ferry Station, and they also did not prove there were other legal relationships, so there is absence of fact and legal basis in constitution of litigation, the court does not affirm. According to Article 64 Paragraph 1 and Article 142 of the Civil Procedure Law of the People's Republic of China, and Article 92 Paragraph 2 of the Interpretation of the Supreme People's Court on the Application of the Civil Procedure Law of the People's Republic of China, the judgment is as follows:

Reject the claims of the Plaintiffs WU Guangbao, ZHA Xianzhong, CHENG Jinmao, WU Youping, MIU Yubing, and WU Xiaoheng.

Court acceptance fee in amount of RMB2,195, due to application of the summary procedure, the sum is reduced to RMB1,097.5, the six Plaintiffs should shall bear the fee.

If dissatisfied with this judgment, the Plaintiffs shall within fifteen days as of the service of this judgment, submit an original Statement of Appeal, with 5 duplicates of the counterparties to the court, so as to appeal to the Hubei High People's Court.

The Appellant should prepay the case entertainment fee when submitting the Statement of Appeal, the sum of entertainment fee shall be based on the dissatisfied amount of this judgment, and Article 13 Paragraph 1 of the Measures on the Payment of Litigation Costs. The fees shall be paid to the bank: Agricultural Bank of Wuhan City East Lake Branch; payee: nontax revenue of financial account of Hubei Province Department of Finance; number of account: 052101040000369-1, and noting in the column of the use by the bank "Hubei High People's Court" or "103001", in order to let the receiving bank confirm the use of funds. If the appellant fails to prepay the case entertainment fee within seven days after the expiration of the appeal period, automatic appeal withdrawal shall govern.

Acting Judge: REN Nina
August 10, 2015
Clerk: WANG Peilin

Wuhan Maritime Court
Civil Judgment

Wuhan Ling Da Compressor Co., Ltd.
v.
Falcon Insurance Company (Hong Kong) Limited

(2014) Wu Hai Fa Shang Zi No.01268

Related Case(s) None.

Cause(s) of Action 230. Dispute over marine insurance contract on the sea or sea-connected waters.

Headnote The Defendant marine insurer held not liable to pay indemnity for damage to goods occurring during land transportation, which was beyond the scope of the policy.

Summary The Plaintiff bought four machines and insured the items under a marine insurance policy with the Defendant. The goods were damaged during the truck transport of the container that the goods were shipped in. The Plaintiff sued the Defendant to recover the damages as stated in the insurance policy. The court held that the Defendant was not liable for the damages to the goods because the insurance policy did not extend to land transport.

Judgment

The Plaintiff: Wuhan Ling Da Compressor Co., Ltd.
Domicile: No.26 Chuang Ye Road, 1C1 Plot, Wuhan Economic-Technological development Area, Wuhan City, Hubei.
Organization Code: 57491565-6.
Legal representative: DONG Mingzhu, chairman.
Agent *ad litem*: TAN Yaolin, male, Han, staff of Wuhan LingDa Compressor Co., Ltd.
Agent *ad litem*: WANG Zhenxing, lawyer of Guangdong Feifan Law Firm.

The Defendant: Falcon Insurance Company (Hong Kong) Limited
Domicile: Floor 6, Li Shan Building, No.18, Zhe Da Road, Medium Ring, Hong Kong Special Administration Region.
Representative: Lau Soh Har, Senior Vice President.
Agent *ad litem*: XU Jianfeng, lawyer of Guangdong Wang Jing & Co. Shanghai Office.
Agent *ad litem*: XIE Yihan, lawyer of Guangdong Wang Jing & Co. Shanghai Office.

With respect to the case arising from dispute over marine insurance contract, the Plaintiff Wuhan Ling Da Compressor Co., Ltd. (hereinafter referred to as Lingda Company), filed a litigation against the Defendant Falcon Insurance Company (Hong Kong) Limited (hereinafter referred to as Falcon Company), before the court on September 15, 2014. After entertaining this case, the court constituted the collegiate panel consisted of Judge XU Zemin as the Presiding Judge, Judge XIONG Wenbo and Judge PI Weining. The Defendant Falcon Company raised the jurisdiction objection to the court during the time period for filing the statement of answer in the reason that the Defendant Falcon Company and the Plaintiff Lingda Company had reached an agreement of jurisdiction in Hong Kong Special Administrative Region. The court dismissed the Plaintiff Lingda Company's objection on December 20, 2014. After the Plaintiff Lingda Company made an appeal, Hubei High People's court held that the court had the jurisdiction over this case. So the court ruled to revoke the civil ruling of the first instance and ordered the court to keep hearing. Due to job changing, the court reorganized the collegiate panel consisted of Judge WANG Jianxin, as Presiding Judge, Acting Judge LUO Yan and Acting Judge Chen Rong. The court organized an evidence exchange between both parties and held a hearing in public. TAN Yaolin and WANG Zhenxing, agents *ad litem* of the Plaintiff Lingda Company, XU Jianfeng and XIE Yihan, agents *ad litem* of the Defendant Falcon Company, appeared in court and participated in the action. Now the case has been concluded.

The Plaintiff Lingda Company alleged that the Plaintiff Lingda Company bought four high-speed precision presses from the NEW WAY COMPANY by the trading way of "CIF Wuhan" and the unit price was ninety one million yen. The manufacture was AIDA ENGINEERING CO., LTD (hereinafter referred to as Aida Company). The transportation full insurance of equipment was insured by the seller New Way Company according to 110% of CIF price. Three of the equipment aforementioned arrived at the factory of the Plaintiff Lingda Company in middle June 2012. The forth equipment left arrived in Wuhan Yangluo Port on November 5, 2012 and was divided into three containers for transportation. When the goods arrived at the factory of the Plaintiff Lingda Company on November 15 of the same year, it was found that the outside containers were deformed and the inside equipment was damaged severely. It was ascertained that the goods were damaged by traffic accident during the transportation. In order to minimize the loss, the Plaintiff Lingda Company transported this equipment to the maintenance base of the manufacture for repair and paid the cost of repair RMB (unless specially notified, all RMB)1,821,946. As the insurer, the Defendant Falcon Company should take the insurance compensation liability of this goods damage during the period of insurance. So, the Plaintiff Lingda Company requested to order the Defendant Falcon Company to compensate for the losses in sum of RMB1,898,305.90 (including the cost of equipment repair in sum of RMB1,821,946 and transportation fee of RMB76,359.90) and bear all the litigation fees for the subject case.

The Defendant Falcon Company defended that: firstly, the Plaintiff Lingda Company did not prove it had ownership of the goods involved and was not the lawful holder of the involved insurance policy. So it had no access to claim for the right under the insurance policy. Secondly, according to the front side of the involved insurance policy, the goods voyage was from the Yokohama Port, Japan to the Wuhan Port, China. So the goods damage was happened out of the insurance liability period and the Defendant Falcon Company shall not bear the insurance compensation liability. Third, London Institute Cargo Clauses (A) (hereinafter referred to as London Insurance Clauses) was not the constituent part of the involved insurance policy. Even if, the damage shall be regarded as the exception of liability and the Defendant Falcon Company was irresponsible for the liability of the insurance compensation. Fourth, the Plaintiff did not prove the value of goods and the rationality of the repair cost, so the insurance liability shall deduct the deductible of 0.5% of goods insurance value.

In order to support its claims, the Plaintiff Lingda Company submitted the following evidence to the court:

Evidence 1: beneficiary's certificate (copy, unless specially notified, all original) and translation, to prove that the Plaintiff Lingda Company was the beneficiary of the involved insured object.

Evidence 2: invoice and translation, to prove the value of the involved insured object.

Evidence 3: certification of quantity and translation, to prove the particular conditions of the involved insured object.

Evidence 4: insurance policy and translation, to prove that the Defendant Falcon Company was the insurer of the involved insured object.

Evidence 5: bill of lading and translation, to prove that the involved insured object was translated by Shanghai Fan Ya Shipping Co., Ltd. and give the bill of lading according to the order.

Evidence 6: inspection report from the Shanghai Dong Fang Tianxiang Inspection Service Co., Ltd. (hereinafter referred to as Tianxiang Company), to prove that the damage process details and damage fact of the involved insured object.

Evidence 7: repair report, to prove the fact that the involved insured object was repaired by Shanghai Aida Engineering Technology Co., Ltd. (hereinafter referred to as Shanghai Aida Company).

Evidence 8: invoice of repair cost, to prove that the cost of equipment repair was RMB1,821,946.

Evidence 9: three transfer vouchers of repair cost and three official invoices of repair cost, to prove the fact that the Foshan City Shunde Area New Way Pressing Co., Ltd. (hereinafter referred to as Foshan New Way Company) paid Shanghai Aida Company the repair cost.

Evidence 10: two invoices of transportation cost, to prove that the transportation cost to and from was happened when the Plaintiff Lingda Company transported the involved insured object from factory to the Shanghai Aida Company, which cost was RMB76,359.90 (43,759.2 + 32,600.7).

Evidence 11: London Insurance Clauses, to prove that the period of insurance liability started from the manufacture warehouse to the warehouse of the Plaintiff Lingda Company.

Evidence 12: Statement and attachment, to prove the fact that the Foshan New Way Company was consigned by the Plaintiff Lingda Company to pay the repair cost.

Evidence 13: (2013) E Wu Jing Kai Min Wai Chu Zi No.00001 Civil Judgment and second instance judgment issued by Wuhan Economic-Technological Development Area Court, to prove the fact that the Plaintiff Lingda Company took procedures against Wuhan Tian Lun Logistics Co., Ltd. (hereinafter referred to as Tian Lun Company).

The Defendant Falcon Company gave cross-examination opinions on the aforementioned evidence:

The Defendant Falcon Company had no objection to the authenticity, legality and relevancy of evidence 4 and Evidence 6; had objection to the authenticity and relevancy of evidence 1. It was a copy and was not submitted during settlement of claim, so the authenticity and relevancy could not be judged; had no objection to the authenticity of evidence 2 but had objection to the translation. The "CIF WUHAN PORT, CHINA" in translation, shall not be translated into "CIF WUHAN, CHINA"; had objection to the authenticity and legality of evidence 3. It was issued by the Japan Aida Company and was not submitted during settlement of claim, so the authenticity could not be judged.

The Defendant Falcon Company had no objection to the authenticity of evidence 5, but alleged that this evidence could not prove that the Plaintiff Lingda Company was the legal holder of this bill of lading. Because the back of bill of lading did not have the endorsement, and no other evidence can prove that the Plaintiff Lingda Company was the legal holder of this bill of lading; had no objection to the authenticity of evidence 7 and evidence 8, but had objection to the legality and relevancy. It alleged that the issue of repair lacked a bidding process as well as the item and price details of repair cost were unknown. So the relevancy to the involved insured object could not be judged and the rationality of the repair cost could not be identified; had no objection to the authenticity of evidence 9 and had objection to the target of evidence. It alleged that the repair cost was not actually paid by the Plaintiff Lingda Company, so the existence of relevant loss could not be proved; had no objection to the authenticity of evidence 10, but had objection to the relevancy. It alleged that the relevancy between this invoice and the involved insured object could not be proved.

The Defendant Falcon Company had no objection to the authenticity of evidence 11, but had objection to the relevancy. It alleged that the London Insurance Clauses were not the attachment of insurance policy, so the Plaintiff Lingda Company could not invoke the regulations of insurance liability period in this clause; had no objection to the authenticity of evidence 12, but had objection to the target of evidence. According to business registration information, the investor of the Foshan New Way Company was Xin Yi Enterprise Co., Ltd. (hereinafter referred to as Xin Yi Company), so the doubt on the authenticity of the content was reasonable. And according to the statement, Foshan New Way Company paid in advance for the repair cost until the litigation dispute between the Plaintiff Lingda Company and the third party Tian Lun Company was settled. The Plaintiff Lingda Company won the suit in the first instance in Wuhan Economic-Technological Development Area Court and did not perform the duty of paying repair cost, so the fact that the repair cost actually happened and it was undertaken by the Plaintiff Lingda Company could not be proved; had no objection to the authenticity, legality and relevancy of evidence 13, but it could not prove the rationality of the repair cost of the goods involved and could not prove the fact that it was expended actually. The Plaintiff Lingda Company had the obligation to apply execution after winning the suit. The prosecution against the Defendant Falcon Company obeyed the principle of indemnity, so even the execution was improper, it did not belong to the insured items of insurance contract.

According to the cross-examination opinions of evidence 7 and Evidence 8 from the Defendant Falcon Company, the Plaintiff Lingda Company alleged: the involved insured object was special merchandise. It was imported from Japan and no other domestic enterprise had the repair capability, so it only could be repaired by Shanghai Aida Company which was ordered by the manufacture in Japan. This was the most reasonable and necessary measure to reduce loss and recover manufacture. So the repair could not be requested through a bidding procedure.

According to the cross-examination opinions of evidence 9 from the Defendant Falcon Company, the Plaintiff Lingda Company alleged: the Plaintiff Lingda Company had frequent connections with the New Way Company as well as its subsidiary company in China the Foshan New Way Company. After the involved insured object was damaged, because the Plaintiff Lingda Company was short of current capital, paying the repair cost in advance by the Foshan New Way met the commercial conventions.

According to the cross-examination opinions of evidence 12 from the Defendant Falcon Company, the Plaintiff Lingda Company alleged: it can be known according to the open cover evidence submitted by the Defendant Falcon Company during jurisdiction objection that the New Way Company and the Yi Xin Company were the same company.

According to the cross-examination opinions of evidence 13 from the Defendant Falcon Company, the Plaintiff Lingda Company alleged: in the second instance, (2013) E Wu Jing Kai Min Wai Chu Zi No.00001 Civil Judgment issued by the Wuhan Economic-Technological Development Area Court was recognized and it was a judgment came into effect.

In order to justify its demurrer, the Defendant Falcon Company submitted the following evidence to the court:

The receipt of open cover, No.MOC/512/12 open cover and the insurance declaration sheet. The purpose of evidence was: 1. to prove that New Way Company acknowledged receiving the No.MOC/512/12 open cover on July 1, 2012. The open cover specified that New Way Company was one of the insured; 2. in October 2012, New Way Company declared the involved insured object to the Defendant Falcon Company. The declaration form in the insurance policy recorded that the involved insured object was transported from the Yokohama Japan to the Wuhan Port China by M.V. "ZI YA HE". The Plaintiff Lingda Company had no objection to the authenticity of aforementioned evidence but had objection to the purpose of the evidence. It alleged that the receipt of open cover and No.MOC/512/12 open cover only proved the authenticity of the forms of documents but the authenticity of the contents of documents could not be identified. The Plaintiff Lingda Company could not judge the authenticity of the content of the aforementioned evidence. Moreover, according to the No.MOC/512/12 open cover, the insured included New Way Company and Xin Yi Company, which stated that New Way Company and Xin Yi Company were the same company. And this evidence proved evidence 12 submitted by the Plaintiff Lingda Company.

The certification opinions of the court towards the evidence submitted by both parties:

The Defendant Falcon Company had no objection to evidence 4 and Evidence 6 submitted by the Plaintiff Lingda Company, so the court regarded it as admissible; Although evidence 1 was a copy, the Plaintiff Lingda Company had documents including the transferred bills of lading, invoices and packing lists which met the trade practice. So the court confirmed the probative force of evidence and the Plaintiff Lingda Company was the beneficiary of the involved insured object; evidence 2 was an original copy and the court confirmed the authenticity of it. This evidence proved that the value of the goods involved was ninety one million yen and the actual port of discharge was Yangluo Port, which belongs to the Wuhan Port. "CIF WUHAN PORT" should not be translated into "CIF WUHAN"; evidence 3 was an original copy. The name of goods "MSP-3000-230" and the model "#12830-3510" can be corroborated with evidence 6 mutually. Although the Defendant Falcon Company denied its authenticity, it failed to submit rebuttal evidence. So the court confirmed the authenticity of it. This evidence was issued by the equipment manufacture Japan Aida Company and can prove that the ex-factory condition of goods met the contract.

Evidence 5 was an original copy and the court confirmed the authenticity of it. The back of the order bill of lading had the shipper's blank endorsement, which indicated that this order bill of lading was endorsed by the shipper. The Plaintiff Falcon Company stated that re-transferring this order bill of lading should be endorsed in blank, so the defense that the Plaintiff Lingda Company was not the legal holder of bill of lading lacked factual and legal basis. Combining evidence 1 with evidence 6, the Plaintiff Lingda Company was the consignee of the goods involved and held the bill of lading legally. Evidence 7 and evidence 8 were original copies and the Defendant Falcon Company had no objection to their authenticity. The correlative data and the test report had no conflict with the fact confirmed by the (2013) E Wu Jing Kai Min Wai Chu Zi No.00001 Civil Judgment (entered into force). The court confirmed the authenticity of it. The Defendant Falcon Company did not submit any evidence to prove that the actual repair cost exceeded the reasonable range, and did not submit any evidence to prove that the repair should have a bidding procedure. The court regarded the fact that the Plaintiff cost RMB1,821,946 for equipment repair was admissible.

Evidence 9 and evidence 12 were original copies. The Defendant Falcon Company had no objection to the authenticity of evidence 9 and had no objection to the authenticity of the form of evidence 12. The court alleged that the evidence submitted by the Defendant Falcon Company No.MOC/512/12 open cover listed Xin Yi Company and New Way Company as the insured. The involved insurance policy also recorded that the insured included New Way Company. Foshan New Way Company expressed in the Statement that "this company was the subsidiary in China of the damaged high-speed precision press seller New Way Company (Xin Yi Company)". This expression was not unsuitable. The Defendant had objection to the authenticity merely due to the fact that Xin Yi Company was the registered investor in China of the Foshan New Way Company. This was inconsistent with the objective fact. Two evidence proved the fact that Foshan New Way Company paid the repair cost in advance and the court regarded it as admissible. Evidence 10 was an original copy and the Defendant Falcon Company had no objection to its authenticity. The court confirmed the authenticity of this evidence; the freight of transporting goods to a specific place for repair by the Plaintiff Lingda Company for reducing loss, belonged to the reasonable and necessary cost caused by rescue measure. The court confirmed the fact that the Plaintiff Lingda Company cost RMB76,359.90 for return freight due to equipment repair.

Evidence 11 was the London Insurance Clauses. The Defendant Falcon Company had no objection to the authenticity and the court confirmed it. The involved insurance policy was standard insurance policy which was unilaterally printed by the Falcon Company in advance and the face of bill of lading was generally incorporated into the insurance clause. The regulation about the insurance liability period was binding on both the Plaintiff Lingda Company and the Defendant Falcon Company. The court confirmed this evidence. Evidence 12 was an original copy. Verified by the court, Wuhan Intermediate People's Court recognized the original judgment, so the (2013) E Wu Jing Kai Min Wai Chu Zi No.00001 Civil Judgment was an effective judgment. The facts related to this case and confirmed by this judgment, the court regarded it as admissible because the Defendant did not submit reverse evidence.

The evidence submitted by the Defendant Falcon Company were overseas evidence. After notarization, the Plaintiff Lingda Company had no objection to the authenticity and legality of the form of evidence. The court confirmed their authenticity and legality. Although the Plaintiff Lingda Company denied the authenticity of their content, but it did not submit rebuttal evidence. The court confirmed the fact that New Way Company was the insured and the involved insured object recorded in the insurance declaration form was transported from Yokohama Port Japan to Wuhan Port China by M.V. "ZI YA HE".

After trial, the court ascertains:

The Plaintiff Lingda Company bought one(four in actual, another three have been delivered) high-speed precision press (MSP-3000-230) from New Way Company through the trading way of CIF WUHAN PORT CHINA(CIF WUHAN PORT CHINA, that is to say, cost, insurance and freight to WUHAN PORT CHINA)with the price of 91 million yen. The manufacture was Japan Aida Company. On October 26, 2012, the goods involved loaded on M. V. "ZI YA HE" was transported from Yokohama Port Japan. Shanghai Fan Ya Shipping Limited Company as the carrier issued No.PASU5120907470 bill of lading for this shipment. It stated that NET INTERNATIONAL CORP was the shipper, which endorsed in blank. Consignee according to the order. Lingda Company was notify party. Loading port was the Yokohama Port Japan. Unloading port was the Wuhan Port China. The shipper loaded and counted one MSP-3000-230 press. The mode of transportation is container transport. On October 30, 2012, M. V. "ZI YA HE" arrived in Shanghai transfer port. The goods involved was barged to another ship to continue the transportation on the next day. It arrived in Wuhan Yangluo Port on November 6, 2012.

On November 15, 2012, the goods involved was consigned to Tian Lun Company by the Plaintiff Lingda Company to transport from port to factory by trunk. When delivering the goods, it was found that the outside containers were deformed and the inside equipment was damaged severely. The damage to goods was caused by the rollover accident in trunk transportation. After receiving the case, the Defendant Falcon Company entrusted Tianxiang Company to exam the damaged goods. And it was ascertained that the damage was caused in the period of trunk transportation. In order to minimize the loss, the Plaintiff Lingda Company, following the confirmation of New Way Company, authorized by Japan Aida Company which produced the equipment, sent the equipment for repair to Shanghai Aida Company, which repaired the high-speed precision press in China. The cost of equipment repair RMB1,821,946 and transportation fee RMB76,359.90 were paid in advance by Foshan New Way Company for the Plaintiff Lingda Company.

On May 30, 2012, the Defendant Falcon Company issued No.MOC/512/12 open policy and schedule for New Way Company as the insured. It stated that the insurance period had been valid since April 15, 2012 in condition that it passed the annual check. It was not forbidden for the insured or the assignee to transfer the insurance policy. On July 1, 2012, the insured New Way Company received the open cover. And in October of the same year, it declared marine transportation insurance to the Defendant Falcon Company for the goods involved. On October 25, the Defendant Falcon Company issued the insurance policy regarding the involved goods as the insured object. And the insured was New Way Company or on behalf of NEW WAY COMPANY O/B HONOUR EASE ENTERPRISE LIMITED. The insured object was a high-speed precision press (MSP-3000-230). The insurance amount was 10.01 million yen. The carried ship was M. V. "ZI YA

HE". The voyage was from Yokohama Port Japan to Wuhan Port China. The insurance policy stated that the insurance condition included "London Insurance Clauses" revised on 1 January 1982. On October 26, the New Way Company issued a certificate that the involved full set of original bill of lading, commercial invoice and packing list were transferred to the Plaintiff Lingda Company.

According to the front page of insurance policy, it was agreed by the both parties of the insurance contract to choose "London Insurance Clauses" as covered conditions. As is prescribed in Clause 8, this insurance attaches from the goods leave the warehouse or place of storage at the place named herein for the commencement of the transit, continues during the ordinary course of transit and terminates either. As is prescribed in Clause 8.1.1, on delivery to the consignees' or other final warehouse or place of storage at the destination named herein. As is prescribed in Clause 8.2, if, after discharge overside from the oversea vessel at the final port of discharge, but prior to termination of this insurance, the goods are to be forwarded to a destination other than that to which they are insured hereunder, this insurance, whilst remaining subject to termination as provided for above, shall not extend beyond the commencement of transit to such other destination.

The court also ascertains:

On September 17, 2013, after the Plaintiff Lingda Company found the damage to goods, it prosecuted Tian Lun Company and Wuhan An Ke Lai Company to Wuhan Economic-Technical Developing Area People's Court due to the dispute over land transportation contract. After trial, the court issued (2013) E Wu Jing Kai Min Wai Chu Zi No.00001 Civil Judgment on July 7, 2014. The court ordered Tian Lun Company to compensate the Plaintiff Lingda Company for the losses of goods and transportation fee in sum of RMB1,898,305.9, including repair fee of RMB1,821,946 and transportation fee of RMB76,359.9. Tian Lun Company was dissatisfied with the judgment and appealed. Wuhan intermediate people's court recognized the original judgment as the final judgment on May 25, 2015.

The court holds:

This case regards dispute over marine transportation insurance contract. The domicile of the Defendant Falcon Company is Hong Kong. Therefore this case belongs to dispute related to Hong Kong. According to Article 41 of the Law of the Application of Law for Foreign-related Civil Relation of the People's Republic of China and the Article 19 Interpretation of the Supreme People's Court on Several Issues Concerning the Application of the Law of the Application of Law for Foreign-related Civil Relation of the People's Republic of China (I), parties in the contract related to Hong Kong can choose law for settling the dispute. During the court trial, the Plaintiff Lingda Company chose to apply the laws of the Mainland. And the Defendant Falcon Company made a written approval to apply the laws of the Mainland after the trial. The laws of the Mainland were applied to this case due to the agreement from both the Plaintiff and the Defendant.

The issues of the dispute in this case included three aspects: firstly, whether the Plaintiff Lingda Company had right to prosecute the Defendant Falcon Company;

secondly, whether the damage to goods happened in the period of insurance liability of the Defendant Falcon Company; thirdly, whether it was reasonable for the damage to goods claimed by the Plaintiff Lingda Company. After analyzing synthetically, the court holds as follows:

Firstly, whether the Plaintiff Lingda Company had right to prosecute the Defendant Falcon Company.

The Plaintiff Lingda Company held that: beneficiary certificate, bill of lading and insurance policy had proved that the Plaintiff Lingda Company was the buyer and the consignee of the goods involved, who shall gain the legal right under the insurance policy. Therefore Lingda Company had right to prosecute the Defendant Falcon Company.

The Defendant Falcon Company held that: the Plaintiff Lingda Company did not provide the evidence of import contract and customs declaration. There was no any information about the bill of lading on beneficiary certificate. There was no endorsement of New Way Company on the back of bill of lading. Therefore Lingda Company had no right to prosecute the Defendant Falcon Company.

The court holds that: the bill of lading was the certificate of the ownership of goods. The involved bill of lading was an order bill of lading. The blank endorsement can be transferred. The Plaintiff Lingda Company gained the documents including the bill of lading, insurance policy and the commercial invoice in normal trade channel, which proved that it had the ownership of goods involved. Unless the party had the opposite evidence, the fact recognized by the effective judgment can be regarded as the evidence to ensure the fact. The civil judgment which came into effect by Wuhan Economic-Technical Developing Area People's Court recognized Tian Lun Company was responsible for the compensation of the losses of goods caused in transportation for the Plaintiff Lingda Company. The judgment can also prove the Plaintiff Lingda Company owned the goods and was the goods importer.

The insured recorded in the involved insurance policy was New Way Company (the seller). New Way Company transferred the involved insurance policy to the Plaintiff Lingda Company (the buyer). And the No.MOC/512/12 open policy issued by the Defendant Falcon Company was not forbidden for the insured or the consignee to transfer the insurance policy. The Plaintiff Lingda Company, as the consignee of the goods involved, owned the insurance policy, which met the international trade convention and did not obey the agreement of open policy contract. According to the laws of Mainland, the insurance policy of marine transportation can be endorsed or transferred in other way by the insured. The right and the obligation of the contract were transferred with it. The Plaintiff Lingda Company had the ownership of the goods, and transferred the insurance policy according to law and gained the equal legal status to the insured. It had insurance benefit to involved insured object, and has right to prosecute the Defendant Falcon Company.

Secondly, whether the damage to goods happened in the period of insurance liability of the Defendant Falcon Company.

The Plaintiff Lingda Company held that: the involved insurance policy applied the "London Insurance Clauses". The Clause 8 should be the basis to ensure the insurance period in this case, which was the meaning that that insurance period was from the warehouse at the place of commencement to the warehouse of the consignees. The voyage recorded in insurance policy was different from insurance period. It had the moral risk if ensuring the period of insurance by voyage. So the insurance liability period could not be ensured by the concept of voyage. It fitted the basic rule of "being beneficial for the insured and beneficiary to explain" to ensure the domicile of the Plaintiff Lingda Company as the termination of the insurance period.

The Defendant Falcon Company held that: marine transportation insurance was voyage insurance. The involved policy insurance recorded from Yokohama Port Japan to Wuhan Port China, and did not record the involved trunk number and the address where installing the equipment. The period of insurance liability was clear, not including the land transportation. The trade terms of the commercial invoice between the Plaintiff Lingda Company and New Way Company was "CIF WUHAN PORT CHINA", not including the land transportation. New Way Company had no obligation to buy land transportation insurance for Lingda Company. Whether the "London Insurance Clauses" was applied in this case or not, damage to goods was out of the period of insurance liability and it was out of exclusions.

The court holds that: the issue of this case is the period of insurance liability. It required the professional knowledge of marine transportation insurance and international trade convention to analysis synthetically to judge the period of insurance liability for this case.

Firstly, the primary evidence to ensure the period of insurance liability was the insurance policy. According to the law, the policy holder has the obligation to inform the basic information of goods transportation to the insurer. The policy holder New Way Company did not know the basic transportation information of the transfer after the goods arrived in the destination port. Therefore it had no way to inform the transportation information to the Defendant Falcon Company. The Defendant Falcon Company knew nothing about land transportation information and its risk and could not cover, which was the basic condition to form the insurance law relationship. Therefore only the accordance between the period of insurance liability and the transportation tool and the transportation section may fit the agreement of policy holder and the insurer. The Plaintiff Lingda Company was the consignee with rights and obligations. The period of insurance liability cannot be more than the one on the insurance policy which was agreed by the policy holder and the insurer. The involved insurance policy was called marine transportation insurance policy. Ship was used to transport goods. The transportation period was from Yokohama Port Japan to Wuhan Port China, not including the land transportation part. The principle "being beneficial for the insured and beneficiary to explain" claimed by the Plaintiff Lingda Company was applied in controversial standard clause. And the period of insurance liability in this case was clear. So this rule did not fit in this case.

Secondly, even though the "London Insurance Clauses" was incorporated in the front page of involved insurance policy, the clause stated that the termination of the insurance liability was on delivery to the consignees' or other final warehouse or place of storage at the destination named herein. If the goods were to be forwarded to a destination other than that to which they are insured hereunder, this insurance, whilst remaining subject to termination as provided for above, shall not extend beyond the commencement of transit to such other destination. This clause does not point out the specific place of departure. The place of departure and the destination stated in insurance policy should be combined to ensure the period of insurance liability. The destination stated in the policy was Wuhan Port China, so the termination of the insurance liability shall be Wuhan Port. According to related clause. It was easy to judge that "London Insurance Clauses" was not to redefine the period of the insurance liability but to redefine the obligation between the policy holder and the insurer during the period of the insurance liability. After the goods was transported to Wuhan Port, it was transferred by land transportation. according to the Clause 8.2, the period of the insurance liability of the Defendant Falcon Company terminated since the transfer started.

Thirdly, the trading way of the Plaintiff Lingda Company was CIF WUHAN PORT CHINA. International Rules for Interpretation of Trade Terms in 2000 is generally accepted international convention in international shipping and trade. According to the definition of "CIF" in this rule, "CIF" is only applied in marine transportation and inland river transportation, not for transportation other than water transportation. "CIF" does not include land transportation after discharging in the port. New Way Company made a consistence of insurance of goods, freight and insurance fee. The trading way of the Plaintiff Lingda Company was CIF WUHAN PORT CHINA. The claim in the period of the insurance liability was beyond the range of trade risk undertaking and transportation liability period, which did not fit the basic rule of "CIF".

Fourthly, "morality" in modern society is the behavior and value standard identified by society. And it is the inner law of people. Morality can make up for law, but not replace the law. These two make up for each other. The period of insurance liability in this case was consistent with the bill of lading, insurance policy and the trading way. It was also consistent with the predictable risk of the policy holder and the insurer, which fit the basic moral standard. The Plaintiff Lingda Company used moral risk as defense reason, which had no factual basis. The court does not approve.

Thirdly, whether it was reasonable for the loss claimed by the Plaintiff Lingda Company.

The Plaintiff Lingda Company held that: the involved object had certain particularity. After the loss happened, it was the most feasible way for the Plaintiff Lingda Company to minimize the loss to contact with the relative factory pointed by New Way Company. Due to the short of fund of the Plaintiff Lingda Company, it was logical for Foshan New Way Company to pay the repair fee in advance.

The Defendant Falcon Company held that: The Plaintiff Lingda Company did not provide the repair detail and did not have the process of bidding, which cannot prove the specific contents of repair and it related to the loss in transportation. The repair fee was paid by other companies actually. The Plaintiff Lingda Company did not provide the payment voucher of repair.

The court holds that: the involved object was the equipment imported from Japan. It was reasonable to transport the equipment to the pointed maintenance base in order to minimize the loss. The Plaintiff Lingda Company had adduced evidence for repair process and cost. The Defendant Falcon Company had examined as well. The fact of the damage to goods had been confirmed by the valid judgment of other court. According to the law, parties have the obligation to adduce evidence for disapproving. The Defendant Falcon Company defended that the generation of repair fee was not reasonable. This should be through bidding. But it had no evidence to support and no legal basis. The court did not regard it as admissible. Therefore the court ascertains the rationality of repair fee.

To sum up, the goods damage in this case did not occur during the period of insurance liability. The right of insurance compensation of the Plaintiff Lingda Company had no legal basis and lacked basic constitutive requirements. So the Defendant Falcon Company was irresponsible for the liability of insurance compensation. According to Article 229 of the Maritime Code of the People's Republic of China, Article 10 of the Insurance Law of the People's Republic of China and Article 142 of the Civil Procedure Law of the People's Republic of China, the judgment is as follows:

Reject all the claims of the Plaintiff Wuhan Ling Da Compress Co., Ltd.

Court acceptance fee in amount of RMB21,884, shall be assumed by the Plaintiff Lingda Company.

If dissatisfied with this judgment, the Plaintiff Lingda Company shall within fifteen days as of the service of this judgment, the Defendant Falcon Company shall within thirty days as of the service of this judgment, submit a Statement of Appeal to the court, with duplicates in the number of the opposing parties, so as to make an appeal before Hubei High People's Court.

Appeal entertainment fee shall be paid in advance when submitting the Statement of Appeal according to Article 13 Paragraph 1 of the Measures on the Payment of Litigation Costs. Name of account: non-tax revenue settlement account of Hubei Finance Department; number of account:052101040000369–1; deposit bank: Wuhan Agricultural Bank of China East Lake Branch. The payer shall pay by bank transfer or bank remittance with mark in the credential column "Hubei High People's Court" or the Hubei High People's Court Unit code "103001". If the fee is not paid within seven days after the period of appeal expires, the appeal will be deemed withdrawn automatically.

Presiding Judge: WANG Jianxin
Acting Judge: CHEN Rong
Acting Judge: LUO Yan

August 20, 2015

Clerk: WANG Peilin

Wuhan Maritime Court Civil Judgment

WU Jinya
v.
Nanjing Haijing Shipping Co., Ltd.

(2015) Wu Hai Fa Shang Chu Zi No.00123

Related Case(s) None.

Cause(s) of Action 245. Dispute over ownership of ship.

Headnote Dispute between registered owner of a ship and person claiming to be the true owner resolved in favor of the latter, who had financed the construction of the ship; registered owner was merely ship manager.

Summary The Plaintiff WU Jinya brought an action against Nanjing Haijing Shipping Co., Ltd. in a dispute over ownership of M.V. "Minguang 3". The Plaintiff registered the ownership of M.V."Minguang 3" under the name of the Defendant Haijing Company because of business management needs, and filed this petition asking the court to declare him the owner of the vessel. The Defendant Haijing Shipping averred that Plaintiff failed to pay fees related to their business venture. Third party ZHOU Dongzhong argued that the vessel was actually owned by Defendant Haijing Shipping. The court held that the Plaintiff was the owner of the vessel and ordered the Defendant to pay court expenses. The court said that the Defendant's request for unpaid fees did not arise from the same relationship as the ownership registration agreement, and that the third party was unable to sustain the argument that Plaintiff was not the true owner of the vessel because he did not fully pay shipbuilding costs.

Judgment

The Plaintiff: WU Jinya, male, Han, born on March 13, 1952, living in Daishan County, Zhejiang
Agent *ad litem*: WANG Chong, legal worker of Jiangsu Nanjing Pukou District Legal Service Office.

The Defendant: Nanjing Haijing Shipping Co., Ltd.
Domicile: Room 542, No.300, Emeishan Road, Xiongzhou Street, Liuhe District, Nanjing, Jiangsu.
Legal representative: ZHANG Xingguo, chairman.
Agent *ad litem*: WANG Liang, male, Han, born on February 5, 1979, living in Xuanwu District, Nanjing, Jiangsu, staff of the company.

The Third Party: ZHU Jianmin, male, Han, born on September 20, 1967, living in Xuanwu District, Nanjing, Jiangsu
Agent *ad litem*: DING Ke, lawyer of Jiangsu Gaode Law Firm.
Agent *ad litem*: CHOU Huijuan, lawyer of Jiangsu Gaode Law Firm.

The Third Party: ZHOU Zhongdong, male, Han, born on October 8, 1968, living in Gulou District, Nanjing, Jiangsu
Agent *ad litem*: FA Renfei, lawyer of Beijing Dentons Law Firm (Nanjing).

With respect to the case arising from dispute over ship ownership, the Plaintiff WU Jinya filed a litigation against the Defendant Nanjing Haijing Shipping Co., Ltd. (hereinafter referred to as Haijing Company), the Third Party ZHU Jianmin and ZHOU Zhongdong, before the court on January 9, 2015. Because his case belonged to maritime dispute and was exclusively governed by maritime court, so according to Article 21 Paragraph 1 of the Civil Procedure Law of the People's Republic of China, the court had jurisdiction over the case. After the court entertained the case on January 12, 2015, it constituted a collegiate panel consisted of Judge ZHOU Yanhua as Presiding Judge, Acting Judge CHEN Nan and Acting Judge ZHENG Wenhui according to the law. The court held a hearing in public on April 21, 2015. WANG Chong, agent *ad litem* of the Plaintiff WU Jinya, WANG Liang, agent *ad litem* of the Defendant Haijing Company, DING Ke and CHOU Huijuan, agents *ad litem* of the Third Party ZHU Jianmin, and FA Renfei, agent *ad litem* of the Third Party ZHOU Zhongdong, appeared in court and participated in the action. Now the case has been concluded.

The Plaintiff WU Jinya alleged that he had authorized CHEN Yuguo to sign an Berth Lease Agreement with Xinzhou Ship Building and Repairing factory in Jiangning District, Nanjing (hereinafter referred to as Xinzhou Repairing Factory), made an agreement to lease the berth of Xinzhou Ship Building and Repairing Factory so as to build a 16,000 tons of coastal bulk cargo ship. As soon as the Plaintiff WU Jinya signed a contract, he began to purchase equipment and organize personnel to construct, and he finished ship construction on November 11, 2009. In order to register the port of registry in Nanjing to obtain operational qualification. The Plaintiff WU Jinya, signed ship commission management contract with Nanjing Hengshunda Shipping Co., Ltd. (hereinafter referred to as Hengshunda Company), put the involved ship to be managed under the name of Hengshunda Company, and the ship was named as M.V."Minguang 3". M.V."Minguang 3"was changed to under the name of Haijing Company, and Haijing Company confirmed the ownership of the ship was owned by WU Jinya. The Plaintiff WU Jinya held that the ship was constructed and invested by himself, the Defendant Haijin

Company and the Third Party had no rights and interests to the ship. In order to safeguard his rights and interests, the Plaintiff requested the court to confirm the Plaintiff WU Jinya was the actual owner of M.V."Minguang 3", and the Defendant Haijing Company should bear the court fees.

The Defendant Haijing Company defended that the ownership of M.V."Minguang 3" has been registered under the name of the Defendant Haijing Company, and was affiliated business. The actual owner of the ship was the Plaintiff WU Jinya, the Plaintiff WU Jinya failed to pay related affiliated fees during the period of affiliated business.

The Third Party ZHU Jianming stated that judging the standard of the ownership of ship was subject to registration, after M.V."Minguang 3"was established, it was registered under the name of Hengshunda Company. After that the ship was mortgaged to the Bank of Jiangsu, because the Plaintiff WU Jinya could not prove that he had paid all shipbuilding fees, he shall not have full ownership of the ship. ZHU Jianmin requested the court to reject the claim of the Plaintiff WU Jinya.

The Third Party ZHOU Dongzhong claimed that the construction fund of M.V."Minguang 3"was paid by Hengshunda Company, who loaned money from the bank on August 12, 2009, the Plaintiff WU Jinya was the responsible person of the shipbuilding party Xinzhou building and repairing factory, after that, Hengshunda Company sold the ship to Haijing Company, consequently, the ownership of M.V."Minguang 3" belonged to the Defendant Haijing Company. Because of lack of sufficient evidence, in order to avoid the implementation, the Plaintiff filed a false litigation, so it requested the court to reject his claims.

In the course of the time limitation for adducing evidence, the Plaintiff submitted the following evidence:

1. The Plaintiff WU Jinya signed *Ship Commission Management Contract*(original copy) with the Defendant Haijing Company on July 23, 2013, to prove that both sides agreed the Plaintiff WU Jinya affiliated M.V."Minguang 3"under the name of the Defendant Haijing Company. The ship ownership all belonged to the Plaintiff WU Jinya, the Defendant Haijing Company could not sell, offset a debt, transfer, demise, mortgage or invest this ship without the consent of the Plaintiff WU Jinya.
   The Defendant Haijing Company had no objection to the authenticity of the evidence.
   The Third Party ZHU Jianmin had objection to the authenticity of the evidence as it was inconsistent with the ownership register of M.V."Minguang 3".
   The Third Party ZHOU Zhongdong held that the evidence was fake, because it was contradict to the ownership and mortgage of M.V."Minguang 3".
2. Three receipts (original copies), to prove when the ship was affiliated under the name of Hengshunda Company, it has paid all affiliation and management fees according to the requirement of the company.
   The Defendant Haijing Company had no objection to the authenticity of the evidence.

The Third Party ZHU Jianmin had objection to the authenticity of the evidence, and he held the opinion that the Plaintiff WU Jinya should not pay money for this ship. The Third Party ZHOU Dongzhong had objection to the authenticity and relevancy of evidence. Hengshunda Company and the Defendant Haijing Company were the same legal representative. The evidence was fake. It was made and colluded by the Plaintiff WU Jinya and the Defendant Haijing Company.

3. Hengshunda Company issued the ownership statement of M.V."Minguang 3" (original copy) on September 12, 2014, to prove the original owner of this ship, Hengshunda Company, confirmed that it was constructed by the Plaintiff WU Jinya himself, and the Plaintiff WU Jinya had ownership of the ship, so it had no relation to Hengshunda Company and the Defendant Haijing Company.

The Defendant Haijing Company had no objection to the authenticity of the evidence.

The Third Parties ZHU Jianmin and ZHOU Zhongdong had no objection to the authenticity of the evidence, and they thought that Hengshunda Company had stake with this case, and the content was contradict to many of the facts of this case.

4. *Berth Lease Agreement* signed on October 21, 2007 and product sales contract (all original copies), to prove that the Plaintiff WU Jinya leased a berth of Xinzhou building and repairing factory to build M.V."Minguang 3", and he also arranged ZHANG Lianghu (male, the Han nationality, born on March 14, 1950, domicile: Huang Hua Guan Village Huang Hua Country, Yueqing City, Zhejiang and ZHANG Xingfu purchased the host, air conditioning equipment, generator, hatch propeller shafting and rudder system and so on used for shipbuilding.

The Defendant Haijing company had no objection to the authenticity of evidence.

The Third Parties ZHU Jianmin and ZHOU Zhongdong had objection to the authenticity and relevancy of the evidence, they believed that the Plaintiff WU Jinya had no relationship with M.V."Minguang 3", and there was a big gap between document price and total value of the ship.

5. List of shipbuilding personnel and equipment, application submitted by Xinzhou Repairing Factory to Nanjing Ship Inspection Bureau on March 23, 2008, M.V."Minguang 3" Water Operation Plan submitted by Xinzhou Repairing Factory to the Nanjing Maritime Safety Administration and so on (all original copies, totally 18 pages) to prove that the Plaintiff WU Jinya was the shipowner, and WU Jinya, ZHANG Lianghu and ZHANG Xingfu participated in the construction and launching work of the ship.

The Defendant Haijing Company had no objection to the authenticity of evidence.

The Third Party ZHU Jianmin, ZHOU Zhongdong had objection to the authenticity and relevancy of the evidence, they believed the registered owner of M.V."Minguang 3'"' was Hengshunda Company, and Wu Yajin was not the one who submitted applications to maritime bureau, consequently, the evident was unauthentic.

6. Shipbuilding statement of M.V."Minguang 3", the berth lease agreement the same as evidence 4) and the business license of Xinzhou Repairing Factory (all original copies), to prove the whole process that the Plaintiff WU Jinya leased the berth of Xinzhou Repairing Factory to construct the ship. Xinzhou Repairing Factory confirmed that they only had contact with the Plaintiff WU Jinya and its designated personnel during the period of constructing the ship, and they did not have any contact with the Defendant Haijing Company and Hengshunda Company.

The Defendant Haijing Company had no objection to the authenticity of evidence.

The Third Parties ZHU Jianmin and ZHOU Zhongdong had objection to the authenticity and relevancy of evidence, they believed that WU Jinya was not construction commission party of involved ship. And there was evidence that Xinzhou Repairing Factory had a close contact with Hengshunda Company, and also had a close relationship with the Plaintiff WU Jinya.

7. The testimony and identity information of ZHANG Lianghu and ZHANG Xingfu (original copies) to prove that they were responsible for the purchase of host, generator, air conditioning, hatch equipment, shafting and rudder system and participated in the work of ship launching under the arrangement of WU Jinya.

The Defendant Haijing Company had no objection to the authenticity of the evidence.

The Third Parties ZHU Jianmin and ZHOU Zhongdong had no objection to the authenticity and relevancy of the evidence, and they believed the evidence did not met the rules of evidence.

8. Certificate of ownership of ship and sea ship inspection certificate of M.V."Minguang 3", to prove M.V."Minguang 3" was registered under the name of Haijing Company., and the shipbuilding factory was Xinzhou Repairing Factory.

The Defendant Hainjing Company and the Third Parties ZHU Jianmin and ZHOU Zhongdong had no objection to the authenticity of the evidence.

9. Crew wage list from May 2013 to May 2015 of M.V."Minguang 3" (original copy), to prove the wage of the staff of M.V."Minguang 3" were paid after WU Jinya examined, which proved that the owner of this ship was WU Jinya instead of the Defendant Haijing Company and Hengshunda Company.

The Defendant Haijing Company had no objection to the authenticity of the evidence.

The Third Parties ZHOU Zhongdong and ZHU Jianmin had objection to the authenticity and relevancy of the evidence, they thought that they could not confirm the evidence was the wage of ship crew, so the ownership of the ship could not proved by operating behavior.

10. *Certificate of Competency* and the crew certificates (original copies), to prove that current crew of M.V."Minguang 3" were all recruited by the Plaintiff WU Jinya, the wages were also paid by WU Jinya, and the ship was operated and owned by the Plaintiff WU Jinya, instead of Hengshunda Company and the Defendant Haijing Company.

    The Defendant Haijing Company had no objection to the authenticity of the evidence.

    The Third Parties ZHU Jianmin and ZHOU Zhongdong had no objection to the authenticity and relevancy of the evidence, and they thought the evidence could not prove the ship owner was the Plaintiff WU Jinya.

11. Business contract of M.V."Minguang 3" (original copy) (from March 2013 to December 2014), to prove that the real operator of M.V."Minguang 3"was the Plaintiff WU Jinya. The business contract was signed and stamped by WU Jinya himself, freight was transmitted into ZHANG Xingfu's personal account arranged by the Plaintiff WU Jinya, and it had nothing to do with Hengshunda Company and the Defendant Haijing Company.

    The Defendant Haijing Company had no objection to the authenticity of the evidence, and made it clear that it did not participate in operating M.V."Minguang 3".

    The Third Parties ZHU Jianmin and ZHOU Zhongdong had objection to the authenticity and relevancy of the evidence, they thought it could not prove the ship owner of M.V."Minguang 3" was the Plaintiff WU Jinya.

12. Transaction details of ZHANG Xingfu's Agricultural Bank of China card (original copy) from May 2013 to December 2015, to prove that all the freight of M.V. "Minguang 3" was transferred into ZHANG Xingfu's personal account, and it had nothing to do with Hengshunda Company and the Defendant Haijing Company.

    The Defendant Haijing Company had no objection to the authenticity of the evidence.

    The Third Parties ZHU Jianmin and ZHOU Zhongdong had no objection to the authenticity and relevancy of the evidence, and they held the opinion that the transaction details could not prove there was relationship with the ship freight. It had no probative force.

13. Bank account information and part of the transaction details of the Defendant Haijing Company (original copies), to prove that the Defendant Haijing Company had never paid money for M.V."Minguang 3". The ship sales contract of M.V."Minguang 3" signed by the Defendant Haijing Company with Hengshunda Company on July 1,2013 did not exist a real ship sales transaction, just in order to solve the problem of affiliated relationship and register the ship to sign the contract,, so the Defendant Haijing Company was not the real owner of the involved ship.

    The Defendant Haijing Company had no objection to the authenticity of the evidence, and admitted the fact that it did not pay for this ship.

The Third Party ZHU Jianmin and ZHOU Zhongdong did not recognize the authenticity and relevancy of the evidence, they held the opinion that the proof could not prove the owner of the ship was the Plaintiff WU Jinya.

14. Witness SUN Jun, male, Han, born on January 1, 1976 crew of M.V. "Minguang 3" testified in court, to prove that the ship was operated by the Plaintiff WU Jinya, the crew of the ship were recruited by himself, and the freight was also charged by WU Jinya himself.

The Defendant Haijing Company did not made any cross-examination opinions for they did not participate in the operation of the involved ship.

The Third Parties ZHU Jianmin and ZHOU Zhongdong believed that the testimony of the witness could not prove that the Plaintiff WU Jinya was the real owner of this ship.

15. ZHANG Lianghu, a witness, testified in court, to prove that WU Jinya paid money for the construction of this ship, the ship was operated by the Plaintiff WU Jinya, the crew of the ship were recruited by himself, and the freight were also charged by WU Jinya himself.

    The Defendant Haijing Company had no objection to the testimony of witness. The Third Party ZHU Jianmin thought that the content of testimony was contradictory and had no legal effect.

    The Third PartyZHOU Dongzhong thought that the testimony was not specific enough to prove that the Plaintiff WU Jinya was the owner of the involved ship.

16. ZHANG Xingfu, as the witness, appeared in court, to prove that WU Jinya paid money for the construction of this ship, the ship was operated by the Plaintiff WU Jinya, the crew of the ship were recruited by himself, and the freight were also charged by WU Jinya himself.

    The Defendant Haijing Company had no objection to the testimony of witness. The Third Parties ZHU Jianmin and ZHOU Zhongdong believed that the evidence could not prove the claim of the Plaintiff WU Jinya.

17. Vouchers and bank receipt (all original copies, totally 39 pages), to prove that steel (including hatch) for construction was purchased by the Plaintiff WU Jinya, documents amount was RMB1,704.41795 million yuan.

The Defendant Haijing Company had no objection to the evidence.

The Third Party ZHU Jianmin thought the procedures of vouchers were not very clear, so they did not recognize the relevancy authenticity and legality of the evidence.

The Third Party ZHOU Zhongdong recognized the authenticity of the voucher but he did not recognize the authenticity and relevancy of vouchers.

The court ascertains that among evidence 1, 2, 3, 8, 13 mentioned above submitted by the Plaintiff WU Jinya, each of the parties had no objection to the authenticity of evidence 8. The evidence was issued by National Maritime Department, real and believable, so the Court confirmed its authenticity. Evidence 1 was the Commissioned Management Contract of M.V."Minguang 3", evidence 2 was the affiliation management fees of M.V."Minguang 3", Evidence 3 is the ownership statement of M.V."Minguang 3", and evidence 13 was the bank account information of the Defendant Haijing Company. The contents of the four sets of evidence were related to the case, and the evidence were legal and could be confirmed with each other. Meanwhile, the contents of evidence 1, 2, 3, 13 not only met the current situation of ship operation and management in China but also had no contradiction with ship ownership acquisition and mortgage establishment, and it was not unreasonable to write the payment unit as M.V."Minguang 3", therefore the objection of the Third Party could not be established. The Defendant Hainjing Company had no objection to the authenticity of evidence 1, 2, 3, 13, the Third Party did not submit evidence to prove that the four sets of evidence were false, and the four sets of evidence were original copies, therefore the court confirmed the probative force of the four sets of evidence according to the law. Evidence 1, 2, 3, 8, 13 submitted by the Plaintiff WU Jinya could prove he entrusted Hengshunda Company and the Defendant Haijing Company to manage M.V."Minguang 3", WU Jinya registered the ship under the name of Hengshunda Company and the Defendant Haijing Company in order to establish affiliated business relationship, and paid affiliation and management fees. Hengshunda Company and the Defendant Haijing Company confirmed the fact that the Plaintiff WU Jinya possessed the full ownership to this ship.

Evidence 4, 5, 6, 17 submitted by the Plaintiff WU Jinya were original copies, it gave a relatively comprehensive reflection of the whole construction process of M. V."Minguang 3", and the contents of evidence could be mutually confirmed with evidence 1, 2, 3 submitted by he, was authentic and believable, and it had a close relationship to the case. The Defendant Haijing Company had no objection to the authenticity of the four sets of evidence, the Third Party did not provide further evidence to deny the authenticity and relevancy of it, and the action that Xinzhou Repairing Factory submitted the launching operation plan to Maritime Safety Administration conformed to management regulations of shipbuilding industry. Therefore, the court confirmed the probative force of the four sets of evidence. The four sets of evidence could prove the fact that the Plaintiff WU Jinya constructed M. V."Minguang 3" (original name was M.V. "Dong Xu 3").

Meanwhile, evidence 9, 10, 11, 12 submitted by the Plaintiff WU Jinya were all original copies and in light of the law, and the contents of the evidence referred to the actual operating situation of M.V."Minguang 3", which was associated with the case. As evidence 9 and evidence 10 could be confirmed with each other that wages distributed by WU Jinya were the wages of crew from the involved ship. Evidence 11and 12 could prove that the consistency between transportation contract and freight charge, therefore the defense opinions of the Third Party on "it was unable to confirm the evidence was the wages of crew from the involved ship and transaction details, which could not prove it had any relationship to the freight of involved ship." could not be established. The Defendant Haijing Company had no objection to the authenticity of the four sets of evidence, and the Third Party did not provide related evidence to deny the authenticity and relevancy of the four sets of evidence, therefore, the court admitted the authenticity of the four sets of evidence.

The four sets of evidence could prove the fact that the Plaintiff WU Jinya operated M.V."Minguang 3".

Besides, evidence 7, 14, 15, 16 submitted by the Plaintiff WU Jinya belonged to testimony of witness, the witness had testified in court legally, the contents of testimony were confirmed with evidence related to the construction and management of M.V. "Mingguang 3". The Defendant Haijing Company had no objection of the evidence, so the court confirmed the probative force of the four sets of witness testimony legally, and the four sets of evidence further proved that Plaintiff WU Jinya was the ship builder and actual operator of the involved ship.

The Defendant Haijing Company and the Third Party did not provide related evidence to the court.

In the course of the time limitation for adducing evidence, the Third Party ZHOU Zhongdong submitted the following evidence:

1. *Basic Situation of Ship* of M.V."Minguang 3"in July 2013 and *Certificate of Ship Ownership Registration* (which were the same as evidence 8 submitted by the Plaintiff WU Jinya), to prove that the ownership of M.V."Minguang 3" was neither the Plaintiff WU Jinya nor Hengshunda Company.

The Plaintiff WU Jinya had no objection to the authenticity of the evidence, but stressed that he registered the ownership of M.V."Minguang 3" under the name of the Defendant Haijing Company because of the affiliated business needs.

The Defendant Haijing Company had no objection to the authenticity of the evidence but had objection to the purpose of evidence and pointed out that the Plaintiff WU Jinya affiliated the ship under the name of the Defendant Haijing Company because of business needs.

The Third Party ZHU Jianmin had no objection to the authenticity and relevancy of the evidence.

2. On July 1, 2013, Hengshunda Company signed *Ship Sales Contract* with the Defendant Haijing Company, to prove that the Defendant Haijing Company had gained the ownership of M.V."Minguang 3" with the price of RMB12 million legally.

The Plaintiff WU Jinya had objection to the evidence, and pointed out he signed the contract because he needed to handle an affiliated procedure, and the buyer, the Defendant Haijing Company did not pay money for purchasing the ship.

The Defendant Haijing Company agreed to the cross-examination of the Plaintiff WU Jinya.

The Third PartyZHU Jianmin had no objection to the authenticity and relevancy of the evidence.

3. *Basic Situation of Ship* of M.V."Minguang 3"in October 2009 and *Certificate of Ship Ownership Registration*, to prove that the initial owner of M.V."Minguang 3"was Hengshunda Company, and the ship had no common owner, and Hengshunda Company knew about it.

The Plaintiff WU Jinya had objection to the evidence, and he pointed out he registered and affiliated the ship under the name of Hengshunda Company because of business needs after the involved ship was constructed. Hengshunda Company also issued relevant evidence to prove the real owner of the involve ship was the Plaintiff WU Jinya.

The Defendant Haijing Company stressed that it was not the actual owner of the involved ship.

The Third Party ZHU Jianmin had no objection to the authenticity and relevancy of the evidence.

4. *Shipbuilding Contract* to prove that Xinzhou Repairing Factory built M.V."Minguang 3" for Hengshunda Company. The Plaintiff WU Jinya was the agent of Xinzhou Repairing Factory, and he made a false litigation for evading debts.

The Plaintiff WU Jinya and the Defendant Haijing Company had objection to the evidence, and thought the contract was signed due to the affiliated registration needs, Both parties of the contract had issued evidence to prove the owner of M.V."Minguang 3" was the Plaintiff WU Jinya.

The Third Party ZHU Jianmin had no objection to the authenticity and relevancy of the evidence.

5. *Loan Contract and Mortgage Contract* signed by Hengshunda Company and Nanjing Rural Credit Cooperatives, to prove the funding sources of Hengshunda company purchasing M.V."Minguang 3" and the fact that Hengshunda Company exercised the right of mortgage guarantee, so the ownership of M.V."Minguang 3"did not belong to the Plaintiff WU Jinya.

The Plaintiff WU Jinya had objection to the evidence, and he pointed out that ship was built in 2009, and the contract had no relation to the case.

The Defendant Haijing Company thought that the evidence was not related to the case.

The Third Party ZHU Jianmin stated that Hengshunda Company borrowed money from him after the deadline of the loan contract came, and he had no objection to the evidence.

The court ascertained that evidence 1 and 3 submitted by the Third Party ZHOU Zhongdong was copied from Maritime Administration Copy, so the source of evidence was legal. The contents of the two sets of evidence was about registration situation of the ship owner, and it was related to the case. The Plaintiff WU Jinya and the Defendant Haijing Company and the Third Party ZHOU Zhongdong had no objection to the authenticity of the two sets of evidence. However, the Plaintiff WU Jinya and the Defendant Haijing Company had objection to the aim of evidence, and the court acknowledged the authenticity of the two sets of evidence according to the law, The two sets of evidence could prove the fact that the owner of M.V."Minguang 3"was registered under the name of Hengshunda Company and the Defendant Haijing Company.

Evidence 2 and 4 submitted by the Third Party ZHOU Zhongdong was ship sales and shipbuilding contract about M.V."Minguang 3", and the contract was related to the case. The other parties had no objection to the authenticity of the evidence, the court acknowledged the authenticity of the two sets of evidence legally, but the purpose of the two sets of evidence "the Defendant Haijing Company bought the ship to get the ownership of the involved ship, the involved ship was constructed by Xinzhou Ship Building and Repairing Company for Hengshunda Company, and the Plaintiff WU Jinya was merely agent of Xinzhou Ship Building and Repairing Company" were contradict with the evidence submitted by WU Jinya related to the actual construction. Due to evidence 2 that the two parties of the contract denied the sales fact, evidence 4 that the two parties of the contract denied the construction fact, and the counterparty of the contract claimed signing the sales and construction contract was to meet the needs of handling affiliated business procedures. The Third Party ZHOU Zhongdong cannot submit relative evidence to prove the actual performance of the contract, therefore the probative force of the two sets of evidence was less than the probative force of the evidence about actual construction of M. V."Minguang 3" submitted by the Plaintiff WU Jinya. The court does not accept the purpose of the two sets of evidence. The two sets of evidence originated from ship registration and archive information of Maritime Bureau, to prove the fact that the parties signed sales and construction contract in the process of dealing with affiliated business of the involved ship.

Evidence 5 submitted by the Third Party ZHOU Zhongdong was involved in the following evidence investigated by court, here was no longer a separate certification. According to the Third Party ZHOU Zhongdong's application in court, the court take two mortgage information of M.V."Minguang 3"from Nanjing Maritime Safety Administration, there were "Loan contract", "Mortgage Guarantee Contract", "Ship Mortgage Registration Certificate", "Loan Settlement Certificate", "Ship Cancellation Registration Certificate". The Third Party ZHOU Zhongdong thought that the evidence could prove the funds sources of the involved ship and the fact that Hengshunda Company exercised mortgage right for couple of times and the current owner of the ship was the Defendant Haijing Company. The Plaintiff had no objection to the authenticity of the evidence, but he believed the funds involved in this set of evidence was loan of Hengshunda Company for turnover, and it had no relation to the case, which cannot prove that Hengshunda Company was the actual owner of the ship.

The Defendant Haijing Company had no objection to the authenticity of the evidence, but held that it cannot prove that the construction funds of the involved ship was originated from Hengshunda Company, which had no relation to the case. The Third Party ZHU Jianmin believed that the court certificated that because the parties had no objection to authenticity of evidence, and the source of evidence was legal, so the court recognized its authenticity legally. The contents of evidence only referred to mortgage loan information of the involved ship, which cannot prove the purpose of construction funds of the vessel involved. The evidence could prove the fact that Hengshunda Company loaned money from the bank by mortgaging the ship twice due to the capital turnover when it was the registered owner of M.V."Minguang 3"and after paying off the loan, handled the mortgage cancellation registration procedures, and the current registered owner of the ship was the Defendant Haijing Company.

The court ascertains that CHEN Yuguo entrusted by the Plaintiff WU Jinya signed a Berth Lease Agreement with Xinzhou Building and Repairing Factory on October 21, 2007, they reached an agreement that the Plaintiff WU Jinya chartered building berth to build a 16,000 tons of coastal bulk cargo ship, WU Jinya prepared qualified drawings, ship equipment and materials, brought tools and organized personnel to construct, and assume the lease fees of RMB80 million / ship and gantry crane of RMB30 million; Xinzhou Repairing Factory was responsible for providing building berth and ensuring electricity and gas for the Plaintiff WU Jinya to use, helped WU Jinya to finish the check of drawings and inspection work and was responsible for a series of work after the ship's launching. After signing the contract, the Plaintiff WU Jinya arranged workers to construct in Xinzhou Repairing Factory. Xinzhou Repairing Factory submitted *List of Ships Construction Personnel and Equipment* to maritime department, and made it clear a series of details, such as the ship named as "Dong Xu No.3" and the owner was WU Jinya, the shipbuilding factory was Xinzhou Repairing Factory. In the shipbuilding process, the Plaintiff WU Jinya purchased steel, cabin cover (the two costs were RMB17.0441795 million yuan) from XU Shunqing, YE Haiwu and Shanghai Ocean Wave Ship Equipment Co., Ltd., and he arranged ZHANG Lianghu and ZHANG Xingfu responsible for purchasing the host, generator, air conditioning, hatch equipment, shafting and rudder system and so on for the construction of ship. On March 23, 2008, Xinzhou Repairing Factory submitted application to Nanjing Ship Inspection Bureau, which specified since investing funds to build a 13,800 ton of cargo ship, the drawings of this ship were designed by Taizhou Haishun Marine Design Co. Ltd. And approved by Zhejiang Province Ship Inspection Bureau, the ownership of this ship belonged to WU Jinya and it was operated by East Port Shipping Co., Ltd. In Daishan County, Zhejiang Province, the ship was named as M.V. "Dong Xu 3", the nationality of the ship was Zhoushan. In the process of shipbuilding, in order to register the ship at the port of Nanjing and obtain the qualification of the operation of the ship, the Plaintiff WU Jinya signed a *Ship Commissioned Management Contract* with Hengshunda Company. They reach an agreement to affiliate the ship under the name of Hengshunda Company, the ship was named as M.V."Minguang 3", Xinzhou Repairing Factory submitted the Launching Operation Scheme of M.V."Minguang 3" to Nanjing Maritime Safety Administration, which clarified the ship was 140.19 m long, 20 m wide, 10.50 m deep, 4.3 m draft tail, weighing about 4,500 tons and other information of M.V."Minguang 3". Xinzhou Repairing Factory made an application for maritime boat escort to the Nanjing Maritime Safety Administration on July 18, 2009. M. V."Minguang 3" was built on November 11, 2009.

In order to apply for a ship affiliation and management procedures, Hengshunda Company signed a *Shipbuilding Contract* (dated on March 2, 2008) and submitted it to Nanjing Maritime Safety Administration. Nanjing Maritime Safety Administration conferred certificate of ship ownership registration to Hengshunda

Company on November 25, 2009, the certificate recorded the owner and operator of the ship was Hengshunda Company. Since that, M.V."Minguang 3" was managed by the Plaintiff WU Jinya until now. It was WU Jinya that recruited crew and paid wages, he also charged the freight of the ship. The Plaintiff WU Jinya paid the affiliation and management fees to Hengshunda Company regularly. During that period of time, Hengshunda Company loaned money from the bank by mortgaging the ship twice due to the capital turnover and after paying off the loan, handled the mortgage cancellation registration procedures, ownership statement of M.V."Minguang 3"was issued by Hengshunda Company on December 12, 2004; M.V."Minguang 3" was 13,800 tons of coastal bulk cargo ship constructed by WU Jinya who rented the berth of Xinzhou Ship Building and Repairing Factory. Neither did my company put a penny nor participated in the process of construction. For the reason that WU Jinya did not have a permanent residence in Nanjing, M.V."Minguang 3" was affiliated under the name of our company, the whole ownership of the ship belonged to WU Jinya, except charge affiliation and management fees of the ship from WU Jinya, our company did not participate in business. After that, due to the management problem in our business, the ship was registered under the name of Haijing Company in July 2013, and WU Jinya was informed about these. Xinzhou Repairing Factory issued the construction statement of M.V."Minguang 3" at the same time: WU Jinya, who is from Zhejiang province, came to our company to negotiate leasing 16,000 tons of berth for shipbuilding, our Company signed a Berth Lease Agreement with CHEN Yuguo entrusted by WU Jinya on October 21, 2007, the personnel and equipment for shipbuilding were provided and organized by WU Jinya, he had paid all the money according to the agreement, M.V."Minguang 3" had been handed over to WU Jinya, and according to WU Jinya's designation, our company signed Ship Handing over Agreement with Hengshunda Company, and our company only had contact with WU Jinya and his designated personnel in the process of taking over and shipbuilding.

On July 23, 2013, because of management needs, the Plaintiff WU Jinya agreed Hengshunda Company to change the ownership and operator of M.V."Minguang 3"under the name of Haijing Company, and WU Jinya signed a *Ship Commission Management Contract* with the Defendant Haijing Company, they reached an agreement that the whole ownership of M.V."Minguang 3"belonged to WU Jinya, and Haijing Company were not permitted to buy and sell, offset, transfer, rent, mortgage or invest ship without written permission of the Plaintiff WU Jinya. The ship was operated by WU Jinya independently, WU Jinya paid management fees (including operating expenses) to Haijing Company at the price of 0.8 yuan per month per ton. In order to apply for affiliated business procedures, Hengshunda Company signed a *Ship Sales Agreement* (dated July 1, 2013) with the Defendant Haijing Company and submitted it to the Nanjing Maritime Safety Administration. Nanjing Maritime Safety Administration issued *Certificate of Ship Ownership Registration* to the Defendant Haijing Company on July 11, 2013, and the certificate recorded the owner and operator of the ship was the Defendant Haijing Company. On December 4, 2014, in the implementation of the dispute over loan contract with application executor ZHOU Dongzhong, ZHU Jianmin and Haijing

Company, the court detained M.V."Minguang 3"according to the law. The Third Party, the Plaintiff WU Jinya in the case, brought the lawsuit to the court, when he raised objection to execution.

And also ascertained the basic information of M.V."Minguang 3": steel cargo ship, ship identification number was CN20081212498 and port of registry was Nanjing, the navigation area was offshore, 140.19 m long, 20 m wide, 10.50 m deep, with a total tonnage of 8,376 tons, 4,690 tons of net tons, the host was the internal combustion engine, and the main engine power of 2,970 kilowatts.

The court holds that the case is a dispute over the ownership of the ship, in the current domestic shipping market, in order to obtain the ship operating qualification, registration in different places or apply for bank loans, the individual owner registers all or part of the ownership of a ship under the name of company which possesses ship operating qualification by way of affiliation. When handling the registration of the ownership of the ship, the maritime registration authority only has a formal examination, the situation of the registered owner of the ship is not conformed with the actual owner will happen. In this case, M.V."Minguang 3" was funded, constructed and operated by the Plaintiff WU Jinya, who had always been the owner, user, beneficiaries of the ship, it reflected that the Plaintiff WU Jinya obtained and enjoyed the ownership of this ship legally. His deeds that he affiliated the ship under the name of Hengshunda Company and Haijing Company met the current situation of ship management in China. The related parties Hengshunda Company, the Defendant Haijing Company and Xinzhou Repairing Factory were all approved that the actual ownership of M.V."Minguang 3" belonged to WU Jinya. Handling the affiliation procedure was out of ship operation. Therefore, the Plaintiff WU Jinya's claim that he was the actual owner of M.V."Minguang 3" was reasonable and legal, so the court supports his claim. The defense of the Defendant Haijing Company that the Plaintiff WU Jinya did not pay enough affiliated expenses, was not the same legal relationship, so the court would not make a combined trial in light of law. The defenses of the Third PartyZHU Jianmin and Zhong Dongzhou that the Plaintiff WU Jinya cannot prove that he had paid all the payment of all shipbuilding, and the construction fund of the involved ship was paid by Hengshunda Company who loaded money from the bank, and the Plaintiff WU Jinya was the agent of Xinzhou Repairing Factory, and Hengshunda Company sold the ship to the Defendant Haijing Company were contradict to the fact what the court found out, so the court was inadmissible to these. Hengshunda Company loaned money from the bank by mortgaging M.V."Minguang 3"twice, it was based on the fact that Hengshunda Company was the registered owner of the ship and exercised civil rights legally, which did not affect the determination of the actual owner of the ship. Meanwhile, according to Article 7 and Article 9 of the Maritime Code of People's Republic of China regarding on getting the ownership of the ship, combining Article 24 of the Property Law of the People's Republic of China regarding on "ship the establishment, alteration, transfer and elimination, without registration shall not challenge any bona fide Third Party", stated that the ship ownership change of our country implements the registration system and non registration system. When registered ship owner and the actual ship owner happened at the same time, there should be based on the actual owner to determine the ship ownership, but because the actual ship owner did not be registered, one shall not oppose the bona fide Third Party (bona fide Third Party of property right, should not be expanded to ordinary creditors). Accordingly, according to Article 7 and Article 9 of the Maritime Code of People's Republic of China and Article 24 and 39 of the Property Law of the People's Republic of China, and Article 142 of the Civil Procedure Law of People's Republic of China, the judgment is as follows:

The Plaintiff WU Jinya was the actual owner of M.V."Minguang 3", but the property was not registered, so he shall not oppose the bona fide Third Party.

Court acceptance fee in amount of RMB1,000, shall be born by the Defendant Nanjing Haijing Shipping Co., Ltd.

If dissatisfied with this judgment, any party shall within fifteen days as of the service of this judgment, submit a Statement of Appeal to the court, with duplicates in the number of the opposing parties, so as to make an appeal to the Hubei High People's Court. Appeal entertainment fee shall be paid in advance when submitting the Statement of Appeal according to Article 13 Paragraph 1 of the Measures on the Payment of Litigation Costs. Name of account: non-tax revenue settlement account of Hubei Finance Department; number of account:052101040000369–1; deposit bank: Wuhan Agricultural Bank of China East Lake Branch. The payer shall pay by bank transfer or bank remittance with mark in the credential column "Hubei High People's Court" or the Hubei High People's Court Unit code "103001". If the fee is not paid within seven days after the period of appeal expires, the appeal will be deemed withdrawn automatically.

Presiding Judge: ZHOU Yanhua
Acting Judge: CHEN Nan
Acting Judge: ZHENG Wenhui

May 29, 2015

Clerk MO Junchao

Xiamen Maritime Court
Civil Judgment

Xiamen Yida Sihai Import & Export Co., Ltd.
v.
A.P. Moller—Maersk A/S Co., Ltd.

(2014) Xia Hai Fa Shang Chu Zi No.583

Related Case(s) None.

Cause(s) of Action 202. Dispute over contract of carriage of goods by sea or sea-connected waters.

Headnote Ocean carrier held not liable for loss of goods seized and auctioned by police authorities at port of destination after consignee claimed to the authorities that it had been defrauded by Plaintiff shipper.

Summary Through an agent, Plaintiff arranged with the Defendant Maersk Xiamen for carriage of five containers of pomelos from Tianjin to Riga, Latvia. The containers were carried to Riga under five bills of lading issued on behalf of Defendant A.P. Moller-Maersk. The Latvian consignee was not able to take delivery of the goods in Riga, because it had not received the original bills of lading from Plaintiff. The consignee had paid 80% of the purchase price in advance after receiving emails which appeared to come from Plaintiff. Plaintiff said that the emails were a scam, that it had received none of the purchase price, and so it could not transfer the original bills of lading to the consignee. The goods were sold at auction by the Latvian authorities after the consignee complained that it had been defrauded. The Plaintiff sued the Defendants for delivering the goods without presentation of the original bills of lading. The Court held that the Defendant A. P. Moller-Maersk had not delivered the goods without presentation of the original bills, because the goods had been seized and auctioned by Latvian authorities. Although the goods had been lost while in the carrier's period of responsibility under the bills of lading, Defendant A.P. Moller-Maersk was not liable for that loss, which arose from the excluded cause "Act of the government or competent authorities, quarantine restrictions or seizure under legal process". The Defendant Maersk Xiamen was not liable as it had no contract of carriage with Plaintiff.

Judgment

The Plaintiff: Xiamen Yida Sihai Import & Export Co., Ltd.
Domicile: Room 311, 329 Jiahe Road, Siming District, Xiamen City, Fujian, the People's Republic of China.
Legal representative: YE Weirong, general manager.
Agent *ad litem*: YANG Yuejin, lawyer of Fujian Jiuxin Law Firm.

The Defendant: A.P. Moller – Maersk A/S Co., Ltd.
Domicile: 50 Esplanaden, 1098 CopenhagenK, Denmark.
Representative: Jacob Stausholm, member of corporate executive board.
Agent *ad litem*: CAO Fang, lawyer of Shanghai All Bright Law Office.
Agent *ad litem*: KONG Jingyuan, lawyer of Shanghai All Bright Law Office.

The Defendant: Maersk Line (China) Co., Ltd. Xiamen Branch.
Domicile: Unit A-E, Building 19, International Bank Center, No.8 Lujiang Avenue, Siming District, Xiamen City, Fujian, the People's Republic of China.
Representative: ZHANG Weiliang, manager.
Agent *ad litem*: CAO Fang, Shanghai All Bright Law Office.
Agent *ad litem*: KONG Jingyuan, Shanghai All Bright Law Office.

With respect to the case arising from dispute over a contract of carriage of goods, by sea, the Plaintiff, Xiamen Yida Sihai Import & Export Co., Ltd. (hereinafter referred to as Yida Company), lodged an action against the Defendants, A. P. Moller-Maersk A/S Co., Ltd. (hereinafter referred to as Maersk) and Maersk Line (China) Co., Ltd. Xiamen Branch (hereinafter referred to as Maersk Xiamen) before the court on November 12, 2014. The court, after entertaining this case, organized the collegiate panel according to the law to try this case. Maersk Xiamen challenged the jurisdiction within the period of submitting defense. The court made a ruling, rejecting the application for challenging jurisdiction on December 10, 2014. Maersk Xiamen dissatisfied with the aforementioned ruling and lodged an appeal thereto. Fujian High People's Court rendered (2015) Min Min Zhong Zi No.319 Civil Ruling, which dismissed the appeal and affirmed the original ruling on February 28, 2015. The court held hearings in public to try this case respectively on May 19, 2014 and June 18, 2014, YANG Yuejin, agent *ad litem* of the Plaintiff, and KONG Jingyuan, the agent *ad litem* of the Defendants, appeared in court and participated in the hearings. Now the case has been concluded.

The Plaintiff alleged that it signed a pomelo sales contract, the price of which was USD74,601.6, with its foreign client SIA "DANEKS" on September 26, 2013. It entrusted Jiahong International Transport Agency Co., Ltd. Xiamen Branch (hereinafter referred to as Jiahong Company) to book space and handle the export customs declaration for the goods involved against the Defendant, Maersk Xiamen. The total volume of the declared goods was 98.16 tons, the total price of the declared goods was USD74,601.6, the name of transport method was M.V. "MAERSK MC-KINNEY MOLLER/1304"; the export date stated in the customs declaration was October 15, 2013. After the goods involved were shipped, Maersk Xiamen, as the agent of Maersk, issued the bills of lading in terms of the goods involved. The title of the bills of lading stated "MAERSK LINE". The signature in the bottom right corner of the bills of lading stated "signed as the agent of A. P. Moller" in print. The numbers of the bills of lading were No.561490586, No.561490590, No.561490587, No.561490588 and No.561490620. The bills of lading stated that the shipper was Yida Company, the carrying vessel was M.V. "MAERSK MC-KINNEY MOLLER/1304", the port of loading was Xiamen Port, the port of discharging was Riga Port, both the consignee and the notify party were SIA DANEKS, the goods were delivered by means of CY to CY, the Plaintiff paid the freight and miscellaneous charges to Maersk Xiamen. On November 22, 2013, the Plaintiff requested to change the destination port to KLAIPEIDA, and submitted a guarantee for such change, promising to bear the relevant expenses and responsibilities caused by changing the port of discharging. The Defendant took back the aforementioned five original bills of lading due to the request of changing document of Maersk Xiamen. Maersk Xiamen did not return the new or the original bills of lading to the Plaintiff afterwards. The Defendant Maersk Xiamen knew that the goods of the Plaintiff involved had been auctioned at Riga Port through its agent Jiahong Company on December 30, 2013. Maersk, as the carrier, was obliged to deliver the goods to the appointed port and properly and carefully care for the goods. However, Maersk expressly accepted the request of transfer of bills of lading before the goods arrival, and released the goods without an original bill of lading and authorization by the Plaintiff, which caused total loss of the Plaintiff's goods involved. Due to the high relevancy between the two Defendants, and subject to the fact that Maersk Xiamen engaged in cargo canvassing and issued bills of lading on behalf of Maersk, Maersk Xiamen and Maersk should be jointly and severally liable for the loss of goods of the Plaintiff. The default of the Defendants, namely, they delivered goods without an original bill of lading, caused huge loss to the Plaintiff. The Plaintiff alleged subject to the relevant regulations of the Maritime Code of the People's Republic of China and the Contract Law of the People's Republic of China, the Defendants, as the carrier, should compensate for the aforementioned losses of goods and freight together the interest thereon.

Consequently, the Plaintiff requested the court to rule: 1. the Defendants should compensate the losses of goods in sum of USD72,246.99 (the amount should be translated to RMB458,650.6 at the exchange rate of 1:6.148), as well as the interest thereon (the interest should be calculated to the actual payment day at the bank loan interest rate over the same period); 2. the Defendants should compensate the loss of freight in sum of RMB72,246.99, as well as the interest thereon (the interest should be calculated to the day when the Defendants paid off the sum at the bank loan interest rate over the same period). The total amount of the losses mentioned above was RMB530,897.59 and the interest thereon.

To support its claims, the Plaintiff submitted the following evidence:

1. *Sales Contract*, to prove that the value of the goods involved was USD74,601.6;
2. Export customs declaration;
1. Commercial invoice, to prove that the Plaintiff was the shipper, the carrying vessel was owned by Maersk, and the goods price was USD74,601.6;
2. Invoices of freight, to prove that the goods had been loaded and shipped, and the Plaintiff had paid the freight in sum of USD18,152.5;
3. Five copies of the bills of lading;
4. Notarial certificate and recording disc (enclosing transcriptions);
5. The notice on upgrading and data migration of Maersk's website;
6. Chinese office of Maersk and its contact details;
7. Statement, evidence 1–9 to prove that establishment of relationship of contract of carriage of goods by sea between the Plaintiff and the Defendant Maersk, the Maersk Xiamen was the issuer of the bills of lading; the Plaintiff returned the original bills of lading to the carrier on December 13, 2013;
8. Data of the container website, to prove that the containerized goods involved had been discharged, and this containers had been transferred; the Defendant Maersk definitely accepted the request of transfer of bills of lading before the goods arrival, and released the goods without original bills of lading and authorization from the Plaintiff, it caused total loss of the Plaintiff's goods involved;
11. *Port-changing Entrustment*, to prove that the Plaintiff promised to bear extra expenses and liabilities arising from changing port according to the instructions of the Defendant.

The two Defendants contended in the trial that:

1. The goods involved were auctioned ex officio by the authorities of destination port. The carrier could exempt its liabilities under this circumstance. The fact that the Plaintiff returned the original bills of lading did not mean that carrier accepted the application for changing port.
2. The Plaintiff did not prove its loss. The Plaintiff had received at least 30% or 80% of the payment of the goods, the customs declaration provided by the Plaintiff was under CNF terms, which included the freight. Thus, the second claim of the Plaintiff should not be supported.
3. The Plaintiff should only claim for the interest on deposit.
4. The Defendant Maersk Xiamen, as the agent of port of lading, should not bear the responsibility for the losses at the port of destination.

The two Defendants submitted the following evidence to support their allegations:

1. Emails and the translation thereof, to prove that the Riga Customs of the Republic of Latvia prohibited the containerized goods involved leaving from Riga port.

2. (1) Application of SIA DANEKS and the translation thereof to the police station at the port of destination; (2) notification of the police station at the port of destination to SIA DANEKS and the translation thereof; (3) final documents of the police station at port of destination and the translation thereof; (4) the sales contract in terms of the auctioned goods involved between the National Guarantee Administration and the buyer; (5) the documents of the handing-over procedure and the translation thereof after the goods were auctioned according to the law; the aforementioned evidence was to prove the fact that the goods involved were detained and auctioned by the local authorities.
3. Business license and industrial and commercial registration information of Maersk Xiamen, to prove that the Defendant Maersk Xiamen, just as the agent at the port of loading of the Defendant Maersk, should not bear the liability for the delivery of the goods at the port of destination.
4. Qualification of the translation company, to prove that the translation company which provided the translations of the evidence possessed relevant qualification.
5. *Service Agreement*, which was screen shot of No.695694 system affixed with seal and the translation thereof, to prove that the two parties clearly stated import service charges and destination terminal handling charges under the terms of No.695694 Service Agreement. Consequently, Yida Company should pay the aforementioned charges where no one took delivery of the goods at the destination port.
6. Emails from December 4, 2013 to December 11, 2013 and the translation thereof, to prove that Maersk informed Yida Company of the fact in time that the goods involved had been put on file for investigation and prosecution by the police station and would be auctioned by the authorities at any time.

Upon adducing evidence and cross-examination, the court analyzes and ascertains the evidence as follows:

In respect of the evidence submitted by the Plaintiff and the relevant cross-examination opinions of the Defendants and the facts the court ascertained are as follows:

The two Defendants' cross-examination opinions were as follows: as to evidence 1, the two Defendants did not recognized the authenticity, legality and relevancy. But combined with the evidence submitted by the Defendants, it could prove that the Plaintiff had received at least 30% or 80% of the payment for the goods. As to evidence 2 and 3, the two Defendants confirmed the authenticity, legality and relevancy. The trade terms of the goods involved was DNF, which contained the freight, thus, it suggested USD74,610 was the value of the goods involved instead of the Plaintiff's loss of payment for goods. As to evidence 4, it was irrelevant to the Defendants. As to evidence 5, the two Defendants confirmed its authenticity, legality and relevancy. As to evidence 6, the two Defendants confirmed the authenticity, and did not recognized the content the evidence to prove due to the illegal obtaining of this evidence. As to evidence 7 and 8, the two Defendants confirmed the authenticity, legality and relevancy. As to evidence 9, the two Defendants confirmed the authenticity, but did not recognized the purpose the evidence to prove. As to evidence 10, the two Defendants confirmed the authenticity, but did not recognized the purpose the evidence to prove. The goods involved were disposed by the destination port authorities rather than released by the carrier, thus, there was no direct causal relationship between the Plaintiff's losses and the Defendants. As to evidence 11, the two Defendants confirmed the authenticity but did not recognized the purpose the evidence to prove. The application for changing the destination port was unilaterally issued by the Plaintiff, and did not constitute the two-party acceptance or a new port-changing contract.

The court holds that: evidence 1 is a copy, there is no original to verify, the court disaffirms the authenticity thereof; but the court ascertains the following facts in view that the two Defendants had no objection to the price terms, trade practice, email address or the website address stated in evidence 1. The court ascertains the authenticity and the probative force of evidence 2, 3, 5, 7 and 8, and admits the aforementioned evidence as the basis to ascertain the facts of this case. The court ascertains the authenticity and the probative force of evidence 4, 6, 9- 11, and admits the aforementioned evidence as the basis to ascertain the facts of this case; due to the fact that the items the evidence to prove were controversial between both sides, they shall be comprehensively ascertained by the court according to details of the case and other evidence.

The evidence submitted by the two Defendants and the relevant cross-examination opinions of the Plaintiff and the ascertainment of the court are as follows: as to evidence 1 and 2, the Plaintiff confirmed the authenticity, but did not recognized the legality thereof; as to evidence 3, the Plaintiff confirmed the authenticity, but did not recognized the contents of proof thereof; as to evidence 4, the authenticity cannot be confirmed; as to evidence 5, the Plaintiff did not recognized the authenticity thereof. It was unilaterally provided by Maersk, the relevant details such as the counterparty and time of contract was unclear. As to evidence 6, the authenticity cannot be confirmed, the fact should subject to the statement Jiahong Company issued to the court.

The court holds that: evidence 1 and 2 was formed overseas having undergone the notarial certification procedures. Thus, the court ascertains the authenticity and the probative force thereof, and admits the aforementioned evidence as the basis to ascertain the facts of this case. The court ascertains the authenticity of evidence 3 and 4. Evidence 5 is a printed document of the computer system of Maersk, although it was sealed by Maersk Line (China) Co., Ltd. Shanghai Branch, it does not meet the requirements of the form of evidence. Thus, the court disaffirms the authenticity of evidence 5. Evidence 6 is emails between Jiahong Company and Maersk Line (China) Co., Ltd. (hereinafter Maersk China). Since the parties have dispute over the fact of this evidence purports to prove, it shall be comprehensively ascertained by the court according to details of the case and other evidence.

Based on the aforementioned evidence having been ascertained and the investigation in the hearing, the court finds the following facts:

Yida Company signed a pomelo sales contract, of which the contract price was USD74,601.6 with the Latvian client SIA "DANEKS" on 26 September 2013, in which it was stated that Yida Company sold 98.16 tons of pomelo to SIA

"DANEKS" (hereinafter referred to as the consignee); the trade term was CNF; the payment method was: 30% of the price as the deposit to be paid in advance when signing the contract via TT, 50% of the price to be paid within 3 days after receiving the scanned copy of the bill of lading, and 20% of the price as final payment to be paid within 7 days after the goods delivered to the consignee's warehouse. The email address and website address of Yida Company were enclosed to the contract. Yida Company handled the export customs declaration formalities for the aforementioned goods on 12 October 2013. According to the statement of the customs declaration and the commercial invoices, the goods involved were respectively loaded in five containers, the total value of the goods was USD74,601.6. In the hearing, Yida Company confessed that it had received 30% of the price in advance from the consignee. The total value of the goods included the freight.

Jiahong Company, as the agent of the goods involved, booked space from Maersk Xiamen. The goods was loaded in five 40' refrigerated container, and shipped at Tianjin Port on October 15, 2013. Maersk China, as the agent of the carrier Maersk, issued five full set original bills of lading on October 16, 2013, which respectively numbered with No.561490586, No.561490587, No.561490588, No.561490590 and No.561490620. According to the statement of the bills of lading, the shipper was Yida Company, the carrying vessel was M.V. "MAERSK MC-KINNEY MOLLER/1304", the loading port was Xiamen Port, the discharging port was Riga Port, the consignee and the notify party both were SIA "DANEKS", the goods was delivered by means of CY to CY. The goods arrived at the destination port Riga on November 24, 2013, and was unloaded at Riga Baltic Sea Container Terminal Company. The consignee failed to take delivery of goods after the goods arrived at the destination port due to Yida Company's failing to submit the original bill of lading involved to the consignee. The consignee applied to the police office of the capital of Latvia, Riga on September 26, 2013, said: the consignee signed a sales contract with Yida Company, agreeing Yida Company transported 98.16 tons pomelo to Riga by sea, the total contract price was USD74,601.6; the first payment was 30% of the contract price, namely USD22,435.2, which had been transferred to Yida Company; the second payment was 50% of the contract price, namely USD37,246.08, which should have been paid on November 12, 2013, the consignee received an email from the same mail address, which said it demand the payments to be sent to its partner's bank account, attached with the new power of attorney; on November 8, 2013, the consignee received an email from the same mail address of Yida Company, demanding the payments to be sent to its partner's bank account, and attached with a new authorization; on November 12, 2013, the consignee transferred USD37,246.08 to the bank account designated therein. After the payment, the consignee contact the Yida Company demanded its submitting original documents of the goods and failed; on November 21, 2013, the consignee received an email from Yida Company, in which Yida Company said its mailbox had been illegally used by unauthorized people and it had reported to the police that someone used mailbox of Yida Company for scams against the consignee and Yida Company had not received the payment in amount of USD37,246.08, consequently it cannot submit original documents of the goods to the consignee; on November 25,2013, the container loading the goods involved arrived at Riga Port and were detained because the trade involved fraud; thus, the consignee requested to execute judicial procedures and bring frauder to justice.

On December 2, 2013, the consignee was informed by the Third Investigation Bureau of the Riga Criminal Investigative Bureau of the Republic of Latvia (hereinafter the Third Investigation Bureau), that this case was determined as a fraud according to its application and the relevant documents; on December 11, 2013, the Third Investigation Bureau informed the consignee that this case was referred to court on December 10, 2013.

On December 10, 2013, a procurator of No.1 Squad No.1 Squad of No.3 Bureau of the Riga Police Criminal Station of the National Police of the Republic of Latvia issued the Decision on Auction and Release of the Evidence in respect of the goods loaded in the aforementioned five containers sealed by police officer at Riga Baltic Sea Container Terminal Company on December 4, 2013, deciding to unload the containerized goods and deliver the goods to the National Bureau of Guarantee for auction. On December 20, 2013, the National Bureau of Guarantee signed *Sales Agreement of the Subject Matter* with the buyer SLA "ZAAO SYSTEMS", agreed that the buyer purchased the goods involved with LATU 12,300, and shall bear all the costs relevant to the subject matter, including all the duties, taxes, fines, etc.

It is also found that on November 22, 2013, Yida Company requested Jiahong Company to change the destination port to Klaipeda, Lithuania, while such change failed subject to the confirmation of Maersk Xiamen; on November 27, 2013, Yida Company requested Jiahong Company to change the destination port to Rotterdam. On December 4, 2013, Maersk Xiamen asked for returning full set original bills of lading in order to change destination port; on December 5, 2013, Yida Company applied officially to Maersk Xiamen to change the destination port stated in the bills of lading to Rotterdam through Jiahong Company, and sent the full set original bills of lading to Jiahong Company; on December 9, 2013, Yida Company informed Jiahong Company of pausing the operation of changing destination port due to an emergency situation at Riga Port; on December 12, 2013, Maersk Xiamen informed Jiahong Company that it should submit the documents for changing destination port; on December 13, 2013, Jiahong Company submitted five copies of full set original bills of lading to Maersk Xiamen.

On December 18, 2013, Maersk Latvia Co., Ltd., as the agent at the destination port of Maersk, consulted the Riga Customs of the Republic of Latvia about whether it would approve the shipment of the five containers' goods out of Riga Port; on the same day, the Customs of Riga replied and did not approve due to the aforementioned containers' goods was under criminal procedures, and on December 10, 2013, No.3 Bureau of the Riga Police Criminal Station decided to detain and auction the good.

The court holds that the case is concerning dispute over a contract of carriage of goods by sea. According to Article 6 Paragraph 2 Sub-paragraph 2 of the Special Maritime Procedure Law of the People's Republic of China and Article 27 of the

Civil Procedure Law of the People's Republic of China, "an action arising from a dispute over a contract of carriage by sea shall be under the jurisdiction of the maritime Court of the place where the Defendant has his domicile or the port of shipment, destination, transshipment is located", the port of shipment of the goods involved was Xiamen Port, thus the court as the maritime court located in the port of shipment has jurisdiction over this case according to the law. The Defendant Maersk, the carrier of the goods, is a Danish legal person, so this case is foreign-related civil legal dispute. Yida Company and Maersk did not reached an agreement on the applicable law when entered into a contract of carriage of goods by sea, but the Plaintiff cited Chinese Law to claim its rights and the Defendants cited Chinese Law to defend, it shows both sides have actually agreed the application of the law. Pursuant to Article 41 of the Law of the Application of Law for Foreign-related Civil Relations of the People's Republic of China and Paragraph 2 of Article 8 of the Interpretation of the Supreme People's Court on Several Issues concerning the Application of the Law of the Application of Law for Foreign-related Civil Relations of the People's Republic of China (I), the court decides to apply the law of the People's Republic of China in solving the substantial disputes of this case. The outstanding issues in this case are as follows:

1. Whether the Defendant delivered the goods without original bills of lading

   Yida Company entrusted Maersk to transport five 40' refrigerated containers' goods from Xiamen Port, China to Riga Port, the Republic of Latvia. Maersk China, the carrier, issued straight bills of lading as the agent of Maersk, in which Yida company was the shipper. Consequently, Yida Company and Maersk established contractual relationship of carriage of goods by sea. In this case, Yida Company returned five copies of full set original bills of lading to the carrier due to the requirement of changing the destination port, only submitted copies of the bills of lading in the hearing, but Maersk confirmed Yida Company was the lawful holder of the bills of lading involved, thus the rights of Yida Company under the bills of lading should be protected.

   Yida Company submitted the evidence on the five 40' refrigerated containers which loaded the goods involved had been transferred to other shipment, to prove that Maersk delivered the goods without original bills of lading. Maersk confirmed the fact that the five 40' refrigerated containers which loaded the goods involved had been transferred to other shipment, but denied it delivered the goods without presentation of original bills of lading, it argued that the goods involved had been detained and auctioned by authorities at the destination port due to the consignee's reporting of the fraud to the Riga Police Station, and Maersk submitted the relevant evidence. It is known now that after the goods involved had arrived in Riga, the destination port, Yida Company refused to submit the bills of lading to the consignee for the reason it had not received payment. Therefore, the consignee reported to the Riga Police Station, and police seized the goods involved. The Riga Criminal Investigation Bureau determined this case as a fraud and submitted this case to the local court; then, a procurator of No.1 Squad of No.3 Bureau of the Riga Police Criminal Station issued the Decision on Discharge of Evidence and Auction, which decided to discharge the containerized goods and delivered them to the National Bureau of Guarantee for auction. The court holds that Maersk has submitted sufficient evidence to rebut and to prove the fact that goods involved were detained and auctioned by authorities at the destination port, the fact which Plaintiff claimed that the carrier Maersk delivered the goods without original bills of lading, cannot be established.

2. Whether the Defendant shall bear the liability for compensation for the carriage of goods or not

Maersk, after accepting commission of containers shipment from Yida Company, pursuant to Article 46 and 48 of the Maritime Code of the People's Republic of China, Maersk shall bear obligations to transport the goods properly and carefully from the port of loading, Xiamen Port to the port of discharge, Riga Port, and the responsibility of the carrier covers the period during which the carrier is in charge of the goods, starting from the time of loading of the goods onto the ship until the time the goods are discharged therefrom. During the period the carrier is in charge of the goods, the carrier shall be liable for the loss of or damage to the goods, except as otherwise provided for in the Maritime Code of the People's Republic of China. Moreover, Article 51 of the Maritime Code of the People's Republic of China also provided 12 causes that the carrier shall not be liable for the loss of or damage to the goods happened during the period of carrier's responsibility arising or resulting from them, and provided that the carrier who is entitled to exemption from the liability for compensation as provided for in the preceding paragraph shall, with the exception of the causes of fire, bear the burden of proof. In this case, Maersk submitted relevant evidence, such as the Consignee's Reporting Application, Decision of Case-filing issued by the No.3 Bureau of the Riga Police Criminal Station, the Decision on Discharge of Evidence and Auction issued by procurator of No.1 Squad, No.3 Bureau of Riga Police Criminal Station of the National Police of the Republic of Latvia. etc., it is sufficient to prove that Yida Company's losing control of the goods was caused by "Act of the government or competent authorities, quarantine restrictions or seizure under legal process" according to Article 51 Paragraph 5 of the Maritime Code of the People's Republic of China, it was entitled to exemption from the liability as prescribed in the law. Accordingly, the court holds that Maersk shall not bear the liability for damages of the goods involved.

The Defendant Maersk Xiamen accepted the export shipment operation from Yida Company including space booking and arrangement of shipment, it was the agent of the carrier Maersk. There was no contractual relationship of carriage of goods by sea between Yida Company and Maersk Xiamen, thus the claim of Yida Company that Maersk Xiamen should bear the liability for damages under the transport contract lacked factual and legal basis, the court will not support it.

Moreover, Yida Company also alleged that Maersk had clearly accepted the request for changing port before the arrival of the goods involved and should bear the compensation liability for damages to the goods. The court holds that Yida

Company proposed the request for changing destination port to its agent Jiahong Company earliest on November 22, 2013, then Maersk confirmed that the destination port could not be changed. On November 27, 2013, Yida Company proposed to Jiahong Company for changing the destination port to Rotterdam, in the meantime the goods had been delivered to the destination port under the bills of lading and discharged in Baltic Sea Container Terminal Company of the Riga Port. On December 9, 2013, Yida Company informed Jiahong Company of pausing operation of changing destination port due to the emergency situation at Riga Port, which showed that Jiahong Company had been aware of the actual situation that the goods were under the control of judicial authorities due to the report by the consignee. Since then, Maersk still made attempt to change destination port for Yida Company until receiving the clear reply of the Riga Customs of the Republic of Latvia on December 18, 2013, which stated that the aforementioned containerized goods were under criminal procedures, the Riga Government Criminal Police Station determined to detain and auction the goods, and application for changing destination port should not be approval. In summary, the operation of Maersk in dealing with the request for changing destination port of Yida Company is proper. There was no connection between the detainment and auction of goods involved at the destination port and the destination-port-changing operation of Maersk. The claim of Yida Company that Maersk should bear the liability for compensation on basis of changing port had no factual or legal basis, the court will not support.

Pursuant to Article 64 Paragraph 1 of the Civil Procedure Law of the People's Republic of China, and Article 2 of the Some Provisions of the Supreme People's Court on Evidence in Civil Procedure, the judgment is as follows:

Reject the claims of the Plaintiff Xiamen Yida Sihai Import & Export Co., Ltd.

Court acceptance fee in amount of RMB9,109, shall be born by Xiamen Yida Sihai Import & Export Co., Ltd.

In event of dissatisfaction with this judgment, the Plaintiff Xiamen Yida Sihai Import & Export Co., Ltd. and the Defendant Maersk Line (China) Co., Ltd. Xiamen Branch may, within 15 days upon service of this judgment, and the Defendant A.P. Moller- Maersk A/S Co., Ltd. may, within 30 days upon service of this judgment, submit a Statement of Appeal to the court, with duplicates in the number of the opposing parties, to lodge an appeal to the Fujian High People's Court.

Presiding Judge: LIN Jing
Judge: CHEN Ya
Acting Judge: ZHENG Xinying

August 3, 2015

Clerk: CHEN Yu

Appendix: Relevant Law

1. **Civil Procedure Law of the People's Republic of China**
   Article 64 Paragraph 1 It is the duty of a party to an action to provide evidence in support of his allegations.
2. **Several Provisions of the Supreme People's Court on Evidence in Civil Procedure**
   Article 2 The parties concerned shall be responsible for producing evidence to prove the facts on which their own allegations are based or the facts on which the allegations of the other party are refuted.
   Where any party cannot produce evidence or the evidence produced cannot support the facts on which the allegations are based, the party concerned that bears the burden of proof shall undertake unfavorable consequences.

Haikou Maritime Court
Civil Judgment

XIE Hongjian
v.
WENG Kaiheng

(2015) Qiong Hai Fa Shang Chu Zi No.80

Related Case(s) This is the judgment of first instance and the judgment of second instance is on page 1214.

Cause(s) of Action 210. Dispute over ship dismantling contract.

Headnote The Plaintiff held entitled to recover damages for the Defendant's breach of ship dismantling contract; delays in completion caused by the Defendant's failure to cooperate in the process.

Summary The Plaintiff XIE Hongjian sued Defendant WENG Kaiheng for breach of contract. Plaintiff alleged that Defendant breached a ship dismantling contract made between them for payment of RMB150,000 for dismantling two old ships. Plaintiff argued that the Defendant failed to perform its obligations of payment and cooperation and asked the court to terminate the contract and order the Defendant to finish the payment. The Defendant counter-argued that the Plaintiff breached the contract by its failure to dismantle the two ships on time and asked the court to order the Plaintiff to complete the remaining project within one month. The Defendant's arguments failed and the court found fully in favor of the Plaintiff. The court ordered the contract to be terminated from May 12, 2015 and that the Defendant should complete its payment as required under the contract, dismissing any remaining claims against the Defendant.

Judgment

The Plaintiff: XIE Hongjian, male, born on August 10, 1971, Han, living in Gangnan District, Guigang City, Guangxi Zhuang Autonomous Region

The Defendant: WENG Kaiheng, male, born on June 28, 1976, Han, living in, Lingshan County, Guangxi Zhuang Autonomous Region
Agent *ad litem*:HUANG Guanjun.

With respect to the dispute over ship dismantling contract, the Plaintiff XIE Hongjian, filed an action against the Defendant WENG Kaiheng, with this court on April 20, 2015. The court accepted the case on April 22, 2015 and appointed a sole Judge CHEN Yunhong to hear the case. On June 10, July7, July 10 and July14, 2015, this court held three hearings to try this case. The Plaintiff XIE Hongjian, agent *ad litem* of the Defendant WENG Kaiheng, HUANG Guanjun, attended the court hearings. Now the case has been concluded.

The Plaintiff alleged that: on June 29, 2014, the Plaintiff and the Defendant signed an *Old Ship Dismantling Contract*. The Plaintiff contracted the project to dismantle two old ships contracted out by the Defendant. The old ships dismantling project was located at the beach opposite the Fudao Hotel, Basuo Town, Dongfang City. The general contract price was RMB150,000. The Plaintiff contracted the project and the Defendant paid the Plaintiff slotting allowances in the sum of RMB5,000 and living expenses in the sum of RMB3,000 in advance. With the progress of the dismantling project, the Defendant, WENG Kaiheng, and the manager hired by him paid the Plaintiff RMB75,500 in total. According to the contract, the Defendant still owed the Plaintiff RMB74,500. There remained a small part of the ship dismantling project yet unfinished, however the Defendant did not answer the telephone and the uncompleted project could not be finished without his cooperation. The dismantling fees that were owed to the Plaintiff were still unpaid. In order to safeguard its lawful rights and interests, the Plaintiff applied to this court, requesting the court to judge that: discharge *Old Ship Dismantling Contract* signed by the Plaintiff and the Defendant; the Defendant should pay the outstanding dismantling fees in the sum of RMB74,500; and the Defendant should bear the court acceptance fee.

The Defendant, WENG Kaiheng, argued in written that: the two parties signed *Old Ship Dismantling Contract* on June 29, 2014. Thereafter, he actively cooperated with the Plaintiff's work and paid on behalf of the Plaintiff the material cost and electricity fees in the sum of RMB20,097, which included the pulling line of the electric generator, distributing and electricity fees according to the requirement of the Plaintiff, and paid the Plaintiff for the living expenses and progress payments in the sum of RMB77,000. The Defendant, in order to cooperate with the Plaintiff to finish the work, paid in total RMB97,097, during the period from June 25, 2014 to February 2, 2015, and appointed two workers to the scene. The Plaintiff's work was slow and not fully complete, which caused serious delays in the dismantling period because there was only one person who conducted the disassembling work. Additionally, the Defendant suffered heavy losses because the price of scrap steel fell from RMB1,900 per ton to RMB 900 per ton. Meanwhile the Defendant actively paid the Plaintiff 80% of the contract price as stipulated in the contract. The Defendant had planned to pay the actual shortages, amounting to about RMB7,000 to the Plaintiff when the Plaintiff returned to work after the Spring Festival, however the Plaintiff did not resume working and contact with him was lost. Therefore, the Defendant requested this Court to overrule the claim of the Plaintiff and order the Plaintiff to fulfill the dismantling work stipulated in the contract within a month.

The Plaintiff submitted the following evidential materials to the court to support his claims:

1. *Old Ship Dismantling Contract*, to prove the Plaintiff and the Defendant signed the *Old Ship Dismantling Contract* on June 29, 2014, the total contract price is in sum of RMB 150,000.
2. No.5013934 receipt, to prove the manager of the Defendant WENG Kaiheng paid the Plaintiff for work payment in sum of RMB10,000 on November 3, 2014.
3. No.0001357 receipt, to prove the Defendant WENG Kaiheng paid the Plaintiff for work payment in sum of RMB25,000 through HE Zhongliang on January 6, 2015.
4. No.005699 receipt and No.5005700 receipt, to prove the manager of the Defendant of WENG Kaiheng,GUO Daguang, paid the Plaintiff for work payment in sum of RMB10,000 and RMB7,000 severally on January 31 and February 21, 2015.
5. 15 scene pictures of the dismantling project, No.1-No.14 pictures of which are used to prove the project was nearly completed, and no one removed the steels that were cut down. No.15 picture is the picture of the ship before dismantling, to prove the appearance of the ship before dismantling.
6. Six call recordings and translation versions (both sides of the call used the local dialect of Guangxi-vernacular), to prove the Plaintiff connected to the Defendant or the workers recruited by the Defendant for many times to require the Defendant to cooperate at the construction scene and pay the work payment, the Defendant neither went to the construction scene to cooperate with the Plaintiff to complete the remaining project, nor did he pay the outstanding work payment.

Agent *ad litem* of the Defendant WENG Kaiheng cross-examined the evidence submitted by the Plaintiff and held that: No.1 to No.4 evidence are consistent with the original, but he could not propose the cross-examination opinion because he have not seen these evidence. The No.1–No.14 pictures of the evidence 5 were pictures of the scene of the ship dismantling, No.15 picture was picture of the ship before dismantling. As for the evidence 6, the agent *ad litem* of the Defendant thought it was a fact that the call between him and the Plaintiff, but some contents that were harmful to the Plaintiff have not been written down in the translation version. As for the call between the Plaintiff and the Defendant, cause he did not know the Defendant and the call between the Plaintiff and the Defendant, he held the authenticity thereof was inadmissible. But similarity, the contents adverse to the Plaintiff have not been written down in the translation version.

The Defendant submitted the following evidence to support his pleas:

1. *Old Ship Dismantling Contract*, to prove the Plaintiff and the Defendant signed the *Old Ship Dismantling Contract*, the total contract price is RMB150,000, 80% thereof was paid by progress, and the balance payment would be paid off within 5 days when the dismantling finished.

2. No.5013934, No.0001357, No.5005699 and No.5005700 receipts, to prove the Defendant WENG Kaiheng paid the Plaintiff for the construction fees in sum of RMB5,2000.
3. Receipts, to prove WENG Kaiheng paid the Plaintiff the construction fees and living expense in sum of RMB5,000, RMB2,500, RMB3,000, RMB2,000, RMB5,000, RMB500, RMB500, RMB1,500, RMB5,000 severally on June 25, July 4, July 21, July 21, August 3, August 13, August 30, September 6, September 15, October 2, 2014, the total amount of the payment above is RMB25,000.
4. Pieces of No.1921236, No.1049893, No.1049892, No.1049906, No.1049894, No.8018389, No.7018663, No.6000924, No.8016710, No.2544984, No.6020384, No.2545197, No.6024759, No.7813709, No.1005477 and No.7016668 receipts, total 8 pieces of receipt, 3 pieces of electricity receipt (August: RMB900, October: RMB1,243.05, December: RMB316.13), a piece of repair receipt, a piece of delivery note, to prove WENG Kaiheng paid on behalf of the Plaintiff the material costs, electricity fees, etc. total in sum of RMB20,097.
5. Four scene pictures, to prove the project remains unfinished.

The cross-examination opinions of the Plaintiff on the evidence submitted by the Defendant that:

The Plaintiff raised no contest to evidence 1, 2, 3 and 5, but did not confirm the first 16 receipts, cause there was not my signature, also he did not asked them to purchase, the 3 pieces of electricity receipts were unclear, he would bear it if they were true, otherwise he would not. He did not confirm the repair receipt because it was not his responsibility. He did not confirm the delivery note cause it was not him to ask others to delivery the goods.

In terms of the evidence adduced by the Plaintiff, the attestation of this Court are as follows:

As for evidence 1-4 submitted by the Plaintiff, the agent ad litem of the Defendant neither saw them before, nor presented the cross-examination opinion, but the Defendant submitted the same evidence and the Plaintiff raised no objection, so this Court confirms the authenticity and the relevance of evidence 1-4 submitted by the Plaintiff. The resource of the evidence is lawful, so this court confirms the demonstrated content and the effect. As for Evidence 5 submitted by the Plaintiff, the Defendant admitted that they were the scene pictures of the ship before dismantling and the ship after dismantling, specifically the 14 pictures of the ship after dismantling which are basically consistent with the situation that this Court has investigated. Accordingly, this court confirms the authenticity, relevance, and the legitimacy of evidence 5 submitted by the Plaintiff as well the demonstrated content and the probative effect of the evidence. As for evidence 6, the original recording of the call recorded on the phone between the Plaintiff and the Defendant or the worker recruited by the Defendant (agent *ad litem* HUANG Guanjun), because it is hard for the Plaintiff to cheat and the Defendant did not deny the authenticity of the recording, despite there being some content not having been written down in the translated version, after checking and supplementing the recording in this court Evidence 6 could essentially prove that the Plaintiff had contact with the Defendant or the workers recruited by the Defendant at least 6 times to ask them to cooperate in dismantling the ship and pay the work payment. Therefore this court confirms the authenticity and the relevance of the evidence. Although the Plaintiff did not tell the other side or obtain an agreement, it did not violate the privacy or other rights of the opposing side, so the record is lawful and effective. This court confirms the legitimacy, demonstrated content, and the probative force of Evidence 6.

In terms of the evidence adduced by the Defendant, the attestation of this court are as follows:

This court confirms the authenticity and the relativity of evidence 1, 2, 3, and 5 because the Plaintiff did not raise an objection. It also confirmed the demonstrated content and the probative effect of the evidence because the original is lawful. The receipt No. 1921236 did not indicate the drawee and the propose of it being meals, the Defendant did not prove that he had to pay for the meals and it is related to *Old Ship Dismantling Contract*. Although there is the official seal on the receipt and it is indicated for electronic connection in writing, this court believes the evidence is irrelevant to the case. This court does not admit the relevance and the legitimacy of two receipts, No. 1049893 and No. 1049892, because there is no signature or seal of the payee, nor is there a signature of the payee. "Cigarette" was written in the column for the name of the goods and the Defendant did not prove the relevance between the cigarettes he purchased and *Old Ship Dismantling Contract*. Additionally, the lower case and the capitals of the amount of the money are different. This Court does not admit the relevance or the legitimacy of two receipts, No. 1049906 and No. 1049894, because there is no signature or seal of the payee. "Aqi" was written down in the column of the payee, and, according to the investigation, "Aqi" is the nickname of the Defendant WENG Kaiheng. The court does not admit the relevance of the receipt No.7813709. A 400w electric cooker was written down in the column of name and specifications and the Defendant did not prove that the electric cooker was related to *Old Ship Dismantling Contract*. Additionally, the capitals and the lower case are different. The court does not admit the authenticity, relevance and the legitimacy of the repair receipt (January 7, 2015), because there is no signature or seal on the receipt, and it is indicated that the deposit could return. The court did not confirm the authenticity, relevance, and legitimacy, because there is no signature or seal of the payee, or the name of the payee. Also, these two receipts indicate an air compressor or consumables of an air compressor. As for the receipt of the cost of the air compressor, this judgment will be discussed later. The court confirms the authenticity, legitimacy, and relevance of nine receipts and delivery note No.8018389, No.7018663, No.6000924, No.8016710, No.2544984, No.6020384, No.2545197, No.6024759, and No.6001018 because there is a seal of payee on each paper. Although these are not formal receipts, it is hard to meet such an extravagant demand. The evidence above is used to fix or purchase the spare parts of the electric machinery or the air compressor, and this Court will discuss who should bear the cost later. This Court does not admit the authenticity of three electricity receipts (indicated in writing:

August: RM 900, October: RMB1,243.05, December: RMB316.13), because these three receipts are printed copies and the handwriting is too unclear to identify. The Defendant also did not submit the receipt of the electricity supply unit to prove it.

Identifications on the main issues: the Plaintiff and the Defendant had no dispute over the facts that *Old Ship Dismantling Contract* was signed on June 29, 2014 and the project remained unfinished.

1. After signing the contract, whether the Defendant did not cooperate with the Plaintiff to finish the uncompleted project, or the Plaintiff did not finish the work actively and delayed the construction period.
   The recording submitted by the Plaintiff could prove that during the period from November 3, 2014 to April 30, 2015, the Plaintiff had contacted the Defendant and the worker recruited by the Defendant many times, but the Defendant never cooperated and paid the work compensation, which resulted in the Plaintiff being unable to conduct the ship dismantling work. Therefore, the court accepts the opinion of the Plaintiff that the Defendant neither cooperated with the Plaintiff to finish the uncompleted project nor did he pay the outstanding work payment. The court does not accept the opinion of the Defendant that the Plaintiff did not aggressively finish the project, delayed the construction period, and never contacted him, because he failed to prove as much.
2. How many work payment the Plaintiff has paid to the Defendant?
   The Plaintiff argued in the civil complaint that the Defendant completely paid the work payment in the sum of RMB75,500, the Defendant argued that he paid the living costs and the progress payment in the sum of RMB77,000. Currently the Plaintiff raised no contest to the allegation in the civil complaint that the Defendant has paid the Plaintiff RMB77,000, therefore the court accepts the fact that the Defendant has paid the Plaintiff RMB77,000.
3. Who should the bear the fees in sum of RMB20,097?
   The court does not confirm the receipts No.1921236 and the payment receipts No.1049893, No.1049892, No.1049906, No.1049894, No.7813709, and the repair receipt (January 7, 2015) and receipts No.1005477, No.7016668, three electricity receipts, and other evidence, because there are many different flaws. Therefore this court does not accept the fees corresponding to the contract in the sum of RMB 12,669.18. Although this Court confirms the authenticity, legitimacy, and the relevance of the nine receipts No.8018389, No.7018663, No.6000924, No.8016710, No.2544984, No.6020384, No.2545197, No.6024759, No.6001018, the articles stated in the receipts were used to fix and maintain the generator, air compressor and other electric equipment. According to Article 3 of *Old Ship Dismantling Contract*, "Party A (the Defendant) shall provide generator and air pressure places (shrink) machine, Party B (the Plaintiff) is responsible for the purchase of diesel oil". Now that the Defendant provided the generator and air compressor, the Defendant should bear the responsibility to fix and maintain the machinery, therefore the Defendant should bear the fees corresponding to the receipts above in the sum of RMB6,632. The court does not admit the opinion of the Defendant that the Plaintiff should bear

the material fees and electricity fees in the sum of RMB20,097 (only RMB19,301.18 in fact after calculating by the court according to the evidence submitted by the Defendant).

4. How many uncompleted project?

In the dismantling project of the two ships, the larger ship was finished at the end of the January or the beginning of February 2015, the sum of the work payment being RMB130,000, to which neither party has a disagreement. As for the smaller ship, the corresponding money is in the sum of RMB20,000 and still unfinished, a point for which both sides also have no disagreement. The Plaintiff asserted that the uncompleted project accounts for 30% of the small ship dismantling project, while the Defendant counters that the uncompleted project accounted for 10% of the total project, which, converted to work payment, is RMB15,000, an amount that is comparable to the 75% of the work payment of the small ship at the first hearing. In the second hearing, the Defendant argued that the unfinished portion of the small ship was 70%. The court holds that the uncompleted portion of the small ship is 70% and the corresponding work payment is RMB14,000. The Plaintiff did not fully prove that the unfinished portion of the small ship dismantling project is 30%, and the Defendant admitted the uncompleted project was 70%. This, combined with the site investigation by the court and the pictures of the ship before being dismantled and after being dismantled submitted by the Plaintiff, as well as, considering that the difficulty of dismantling the portion sunken in the water and buried by sand far outweighs that of the part that had not been submerged by water and buried by sand. The court holds that the uncompleted quantity of the small ship project is 70% and the corresponding work payment shall be RMB14,000.

After trail, this Court ascertains the following facts: the Plaintiff and the Defendant signed *Old Ship Dismantling Contract* on June 29, 2014, both sides agreed: 1. the contract price was RMB150,000 for the ship plate of the big ship which had not been dismantled (including the amount of the small ship in the sum of RMB20,000). 2. The main engine of the ship would be removed by a contracted party, as a whole without dismantling. 3. Party A (the Defendant, hereinafter) provided the generator and air compressor, Party B (the Plaintiff, hereinafter) was responsible for purchasing the diesel oil. 4. Party A provided the accommodation for free. 5. Party B took the tools of dismantling themselves. 6. Party B cut every part to weigh less than 2 tons or a suitable weight to load according to the requirement of Party A. Party B was not responsible to load or unload. The payment method: Party A should pay slotting allowance in the sum of RMB5,000 in advance and then pay living costs in the sum of RMB 5,000 after entering the site. During the project, 80% of the price should be paid by progress, and the remaining payment would be paid off within 5 days of finishing the dismantling project. After signing the contract, both parties could fulfill their obligations at the beginning. Since December 3, 2014, the Defendant did not cooperate with the Plaintiff to gradually finish the dismantling project, which caused the dismantling project to come to a standstill. About February 3, 2015, the dismantling project of the big ship was completed and 30% of the small ship dismantling project has been completed to date, making the whole project at a 90.67% completion status. The amount of the corresponding work payment is RMB136,000. The Defendant has paid the Plaintiff the work payment in the sum of RMB77,000.

The court held that: the Plaintiff and the Defendant signed *Old Ship Dismantling Contract* which is the declaration of their intention, and does not violate the prohibitive provisions of the laws and regulations. Although the Plaintiff did not sign the contract, the Plaintiff admitted to the effect of the contract and had fulfilled the 90.67% of the contractual obligations as agreed, therefore the contract shall be lawful and valid and both parties should voluntarily abide by the contract and fulfill the contractual obligations. Still, the Defendant had been demanded payment by the Plaintiff many times since December 2014. He neither cooperated with the Plaintiff at the construction scene, nor did he pay the work payment, which caused the project to be unable to proceed and the purpose of the contract unable to be achieved. Therefore, the Plaintiff is entitled to dissolve the contract. It was hard for both parties to work together and discharging the contract was inevitable, due to the conflict between the two sides deepening day by day. Although the Plaintiff did not notify the Defendant to discharge the contract, the first claim of the civil complaint submitted by the Plaintiff had clearly proposed such an action, and this Court had sent the copy of the civil complaint to the Defendant on May 12, 2015. The law did not stipulate clearly for the form of notification to discharge the contract, so the Plaintiff sent the civil complaint to this Court and which in turn sent it to the opposite party. The effect of sending the copy of the civil complaint through the court is equal or even prior to the effect of the party sending the notice of discharging the contract. As long as the civil complaint recording discharging the contract was sent to the Defendant by this Court, the discharging of the contract comes into effect. Therefore, *Old Ship Dismantling Contract* signed by the Plaintiff and the Defendant was discharged on May 12, 2015. The Defendant could require this Court or an arbitration organization to ensure the effect of discharging the contract be met if he has a disagreement with it. The Defendant, WENG Kaiheng, neither filed a counterclaim nor had it filed for litigation or arbitration within the statute of limitation. As for the project the Plaintiff had finished before the contract was discharged, the Defendant should pay the corresponding work payment in the sum of RMB136,000. After deducting the work payment in the sum of RMB77,000 the Defendant had paid, the Defendant should still pay the Plaintiff the outstanding work payment in the sum of RMB 59,000. In accordance with the provisions of the Paragraph 4 of Article 94, Paragraph 1 of Article 96 and Article 97 of the Contract Law of the People's Republic of China, the judgment is as follows:

1. *Old Ship Dismantling Contract* signed by the Plaintiff, XIE Hongjian, and the Defendant, WENG Kaiheng, on June 29, 2014 shall be deemed as discharged on May 12, 2015;
2. The Defendant, WENG Kaiheng, shall pay the Plaintiff the outstanding work payment in the sum of RMB59,000 within ten days of the effectiveness of this judgment; and

3. Reject other claims of the Plaintiff XIE Hongjian.

   If the Defendant fails to fulfill its obligation to make the said payments within the time limit provided by this Judgment, the interest shall be double paid for the period of deferred payment in accordance with Article 253 of the Civil Procedure Law of the People's Republic of China.

   Court acceptance fee in amount of RMB831, the Plaintiff, XIE Hongjian, shall bear RMB173 and the Defendant WENG Kaiheng bear RMB658.

   If dissatisfy with this Judgment, any party shall within fifteen days of the service of this judgment submit a Bill of Appeal to this Court, with copies according to the number of the opposing parties, so as to make an appeal before Hainan High People's Court.

Judge: CHEN Hongyun

July 14, 2015

Clerk: LI Zhicheng

Hainan High People's Court
Civil Judgment

XIE Hongjian
v.
WENG Kaiheng

(2015) Qiong Min San Zhong Zi No.84

Related Case(s) This is the judgment of second instance, and the judgment of first instance is on page 1205.

Cause(s) of Action 210. Dispute over ship dismantling contract.

Headnote Affirming lower court decision that Plaintiff was entitled to recover damages for Defendant's breach of ship dismantling contract but modifying award of damages.

Summary Plaintiff at first instance (Respondent) was held entitled to recover damages for Defendant's breach of ship dismantling contract; delays in completion caused by were held to be caused by Defendant's failure to cooperate in the process. Defendant in (Appellant) filed this appeal. Appellant asked the Court to set aside the judgment of first instance and dismiss Respondent's claims. Appellant argued that the facts found in the first instance were unclear and the law was misapplied, and the contract should not be terminated. Respondent counter-argued that the court of first instance found the facts clearly and applied the law correctly. The Court held that it was appropriate for the court of first instance to determine that the purpose of the contract was defeated and the contract should be discharged according to Article 94 of the Contract Law of the People's Republic of China, but the ascertainment of the sum of work payment was wrong. Therefore, the Court amended the judgment of first instance regarding the sum of work payment and upheld the other portion.

Judgment

The Appellant (the Defendant of first instance): WENG Kaiheng, male, born on June 28, 1976, Han, living in Lingshan District, Guigang City, Guangxi Zhuang Autonomous Region.
Agent *ad litem*: LU Qiaoshi, lawyer of Hainan Dongfang Guoxin Law Firm.

The Respondent (the Plaintiff of first instance): XIE Hongjian male, born on August 10, 1971, Han, living in Gangnan District, Guigang City, Guangxi Zhuang Autonomous Region.
Dissatisfied with the Civil Judgment of (2015) Qiong Hai Fa Shang Chu Zi No.80 rendered by Haikou Maritime Court with respect to the dispute over a ship dismantling contract, the Appellant XIE Hongjian filed an appeal against the Respondent WENG Kaiheng with the court on July 7, 2015. The court entertained this case and constituted the collegiate panel, and held a hearing in public on October 9, 2015 to try this case. The Appellant WENG Kaiheng and his agent *ad litem* LU Qiaoshi, and the Respondent XIE Hongjian, appeared in court and participated in the action. Upon mediation, the case has been concluded.

XIE Hongjian held that WENG Kaiheng defaulted the dismantling project price, and requested the court of first instance to rule that *Old Ship Dismantling Contract* signed by them should be discharged and WENG Kaiheng pay the outstanding project price in sum of RMB74,500 yuan, and bear the court acceptance fee. WENG Kaiheng alleged that XIE Hongjian was slack to work, actually, the contract price was only short of RMB7,000 yuan, he requested the court to dismiss the claims of XIE Hongjian, and requested him to fulfill the obligation for dismantling the ships within one month as agreed.

The court of first instance found out that: XIE Hongjian and WENG Kaiheng signed *Ship Dismantling Contract* on June 29, 2014, agreeing: 1. the contract price was in sum of RMB150,000 for the ship plate of the big ship which had not been dismantled (including the amount of the small ship in sum of RMB20,000); 2. the main engine of the ship should be removed as a whole without dismantling by the contracting-out party; 3. Party A (WENG Kaiheng, similarly hereinafter) provided the generator and air compressor, Party B (XIE Hongjian, hereinafter similarity) was responsible to purchase the diesel oil; 4. Party A provided the accommodation for free; 5. Party B prepared the tools of dismantling;6. Party B cut every part less than 2 tons or suitable to load according to the requirement of the Party A. Party B were not responsible to load and unload. Payment method: Party A should pay slotting allowance in sum of RMB5,000 in advance and then pay living costs in sum of RMB5,000 after entering the site, during the project, 80% of the price should be paid by progress, and the balance payment would be paid off within 5 days when the dismantling finished. After signing the contract, both parties could fulfill their obligations at the beginning. Since from December 3, 2014, WENG Kaiheng did not cooperate with XIE Hongjian to finish the dismantling project gradually, which caused the dismantling project came to standstill gradually. On February 3, 2015, the dismantling project of the big ship was totally finished, 30% of the small ship dismantling project had been completed so far, the whole project was finished 90.67%, the amount of corresponding work payment is RMB136,000. WENG Kaiheng has paid XIE Hongjian the work payment in sum of RMB77,000.

The court of first instance held that XIE Hongjian and WENG Kaiheng signed *Ship Dismantling Contract*, which had been fulfilled 90.67%, should be lawful and valid WENG Kaiheng had been demanded payment by XIE Hongjian for many times since December 2014, he neither cooperated with XIE Hongjian at the construction scene, nor did he pay the work payment, which caused the project unable to proceed and the purpose of the contract unable to achieve. Therefore XIE Hongjian was entitled to dissolve the contract. It was hard for both parties to work together and discharging the contract was unstoppable, because the contradiction between two sides was deepened day by day, even fights happened. Although XIE Hongjian did not notify WENG Kaiheng to discharge the contract, but the first claim in the civil complaint submitted by XIE Hongjian had clearly proposed, and the court of first instance had sent the copy of the civil complaint to WENG Kaiheng on May 12, 2015. The law did not stipulate clearly for the form of notification to discharge the contract, so XIE Hongjian sent the civil complaint to the court of first instance and then the court of first instance sent it to the opposite party, the effect of sending the copy of the civil complaint through the court of first instance was equal or even prior to the effect of the party sending the notice of the discharging of the contract. As long as the civil complaint recording discharge of the contract was sent to WENG Kaiheng by the court of first instance, the discharge of the contract came into the effect. So *Ship Dismantling Contract* signed by XIE Hongjian and WENG Kaiheng should have been discharged on May 12, 2015. WENG Kaiheng could require the court of first instance or arbitration organization to ensure the effect of discharging the contract if he has disagreement with it, WENG Kaiheng in the case neither filed a counterclaim nor had it filed a litigation or arbitration within the statute of limitation. As for the project XIE Hongjian had finished before the contract was discharged, WENG Kaiheng should pay the corresponding work payment in sum of RMB136,000, after deducting the work payment in sum of RMB77,000 WENG Kaiheng had paid, WENG Kaiheng should still pay XIE Hongjian the outstanding work payment in sum of RMB59,000. according to Article 94 Paragraph 4, Article 96 Paragraph 1 and Article 97 of the Contract Law of the People's Republic of China, the court of first instance judged as follows: 1. *Ship Dismantling Contract* signed by XIE Hongjian and WENG Kaiheng on June 29, 2014 should be identified as discharged on May 12, 2015; 2. WENG Kaiheng should pay XIE Hongjian the outstanding work payment in sum of RMB59,000 within ten days as of the effectiveness of this judgment; 3. reject the said payments within the time limit provided by this judgment, the interest should be double paid for the period of deferred payment according to Article 253 of the Civil Procedure Law of the People's Republic of China. Court acceptance fee of first instance in amount of RMB831, XIE Hongjian should bear RMB173 and WENG Kaiheng bear RMB658.

WENG Kaiheng requested in the appeal that: 1. revoke the judgment of first instance, and reject the claims of XIE Hongjian; 2. XIE Hongjian should bear the court fees of the first and second instances. Facts and reasons are as follows:

1. The facts found in the first instance were unclear, *Old Ship Dismantling Contract* signed by the two parties was legal and effective, WENG Kaiheng for the purpose of performing the contract had paid nearly RMB10 million yuan, but XIE Hongjian was slack to carry out the project, as a result, the price of

scrapped steel WENG Kaiheng suffered great losses and conflicts happened. XIE Hongjian should fully perform the contract, and complete the remaining dismantling work, so that WENG Kaiheng would sell the scrapped steel then pay corresponding price. WENG Kaiheng agreed to pay the full amount of the balance payment when XIE Hongjian complete the work, otherwise it would recourse its liability for compensation.

2. The application of law in the first instance was wrong, XIE Hongjian's filing the suit did not equal to a notice of discharging contract, the contract involved should not be discharged. The contract prescribes WENG Kaiheng should generators and air compressors for XIE Hongjian free use, but expenses and electricity charges incurred by maintenance should be born by XIE Hongjian, and XIE Hongjian should ensure the equipment in good condition at the time of return. In order to cooperate with XIE Hongjian to dismantle the old ship, WENG Kaiheng paid maintenance fees and electricity charges more than RMB20,000 yuan, such sum should born by XIE Hongjian.

XIE Hongjian defended that the court of first instance found the facts clearly and applied the law correctly, XIE Hongjian called WENG Kaiheng, but the later did not reply long after the call, after typhoon came, the electric box was flooded, wires were stolen, the work was not attended to, as a result, XIE Hongjian could not continue to work, XIE Hongjian requested the court to uphold the judgment of first instance.

During the second instance, WENG Kaiheng submitted six invoices of electricity charges to the court (August 2014: RMB901.59 yuan, September 2014: RMB2,572.78 yuan, October 2014: RMB1,244.62 yuan, November 2014: 880.04 yuan, December 2014: RMB343.04 yuan, August 2015: RMB128.91 yuan), to prove that he advanced the electricity charges. XIE Hongjian examined the evidence and held the amount of the electricity charges WENG Kaiheng differed with that claimed in the first instance, electricity was from a nearby bar, some fees were generated by the bar business. XIE Hongjian returned to Guangxi in April 2015, he only admitted the sum of August, November and December in 2014.

The court ascertains that: the six invoices WENG Kaiheng submitted in the second instance were evidence adduced exceeding the designated period, but they are relevant with the basic facts of this case, according to Article 102 of the Interpretations of the Supreme People's Court on the Application of the Civil Procedure Law of the People's Republic of China, the court hereby adopts. The above invoices are the originals, the court admits the authenticity, relevancy and probative force of the invoices of August 2014 to December 2014, but as XIE Hongjian was not in the site in August 2015, the court does not admit the relevancy and probative force of the invoice of that month.

On October 27, 2015, the court went to the site in East Basuo and surveyed and take photos of the site which were enclosed to the files. Seen from the site, even at the time of low tide, only a piece of rusty steel of the small ship was immersed in seawater. The main body was under water, and the bottom was almost all trapped in the sand, the part having been dismantled were discarded not far from the beach, the remaining part of the scrap has not been removed.

It is found in the second instance that WENG Kaiheng and XIE Hongjian admitted ship dismantling work had been completed in a total of 90.67% of the project, and the corresponding work payment should be RMB136,005 yuan. WENG Kaiheng had actually paid RMB77,000 yuan to XIE Hongjian. The operating machine was changed from a diesel generator to an electric power engine, WENG Kaiheng advanced the electricity charges ship dismantling operations in sum of RMB5,942.07 yuan, the part of the ship having not been dismantled was trapped into the sand, the part having been dismantled is still remained in the site on the beach but not carried away for sale.

Other facts ascertained by the court are consistent with that ascertained in the first instance, the court hereby ascertains other facts found in the first instance.

The court holds that this case is concerning dispute over a ship dismantling contract. The Old Ship Dismantling Contract signed by WENG Kaiheng and XIE Hongjian is declaration of real intention of the two parties, it is not against the compulsory provisions of law, and it is a valid contract, the two parties shall perform the contract as agreed. The outstanding issue in this case is the amount of project price when the contract was discharged.

In respect of whether the contract signed by the two parties should be discharged, according to Article 94 Paragraph 4 of the Contract Law of the People's Republic of China, "the other party delays performance of its obligations, or breaches the contract in some other manner, rendering it impossible to achieve the purpose of the contract", it is agreed in the Old Ship Dismantling Contract signed by WENG Kaiheng and XIE Hongjian: "Party A should pay slotting allowance in sum of RMB5,000 in advance and then pay living costs in sum of RMB5,000 after entering the site, during the project, 80% of the price should be paid subject to progress, and the balance payment would be paid one-off within 5 days when the dismantling project finished". WENG Kaiheng and XIE Hongjian admitted the ship dismantling work had been completed 90.67%, corresponding to work payment of RMB136,005 yuan, Wengkai Heng should timely pay 80% of the progress payment to XIE Hongjian, namely RMB136,000 yuan*80% = RMB108,804 yuan, and pay one-off the remaining amount within five days following the completion of the work. However, WENG Kaiheng has only paid a total of RMB77,000 yuan to XIE Hongjian, far less than the due amount, and some scrapped steel were not removed to sell in the sand, XIE Hongjian was slack to fulfill his contractual obligations. Judging from the possibility of contract performance, the two parties were in deep contradiction, and the remaining part of the small ship having not been dismantled was almost trapped into the sand, if the contract continues to fulfill, the sale of scrapped steel can hardly make up the increased costs, it was not inappropriate that the court of first instance accordingly determined that the purpose of the contract could not be achieved and the contract should be discharged. The claim of WENG Kaiheng that the contract should continue to be fulfilled has no merit, the court does not support.

In respect of the amount of project price WENG Kaiheng should pay to XIE Hongjian, the amount of the amount of the project. As prescribed in Article 3 of *Old Ship Dismantling Contract*: "Party A shall provide generator and air pressure places (shrink) machine, Party B is responsible for the purchase of diesel oil." Since the two parties changed the diesel generator to electric engine to operate, the corresponding electricity charges should be on the account of XIE Hongjian, WENG Kaiheng has paid the electricity charges for the dismantling construction in sum of RMB5,942.07 yuan. As mentioned above, the payment for the quantity completed by XIE Hongjian is RMB136,005 yuan, deducting the work payment WENG Kaiheng has paid namely RMB77,000 yuan and electricity charges in sum of RMB5,942.07 yuan he advanced, Weng Kai shall pay the outstanding sum of RMB53,062.93 yuan to Heng Xie Hengjian.

In summary, in the judgment of first instance, the application of law is correct, but the ascertainment of facts is wrong, the judgment shall be amended. According to Article 170 Paragraph 1 Sub-paragraph 2 of the Civil Procedure Law of the People's Republic of China, the judgment is as follows:

1. Affirm the first item of (2015) Qiong Hai Fa Shang Chu Zi No.80 Civil Judgment rendered by Haikou Maritime Court;
2. Revoke the second item of (2015) Qiong Hai Fa Shang Chu Zi No.80 Civil Judgment rendered by Haikou Maritime Court;
3. WENG Kaiheng shall pay the outstanding work payment in sum of RMBRMB53,062.93 yuan within ten days as of the effective date of this judgment;
4. Reject other claims of XIE Hongjian.

If WENG Kaiheng fails to perform the pecuniary obligation within the period designated in this judgment, the interest on the debt shall be double paid over the delayed period according to Article 253 of the Civil Procedure Law of the People's Republic of China.

Court acceptance fee of first instance in amount of RMB831, and court acceptance fee of second instance in amount of RMB1662, in aggregate amount of RMB2,493,XIE Hongjian shall bear RMB590, WENG Kaiheng shall bear RMB1,903.

The judgment is final.

Presiding Judge: WANG Hao
Judge: GAO Junhua
Judge: LIN Da
November 4, 2015
Clerk: LIU Xiaoxia

Appendix: Relevant Law

1. Civil Procedure Law of the People's Republic of China

Article 172 After hearing an appellate case, the people's court of second instance shall handle the case respectively according to the following circumstances:

(1) If the facts were clearly found and the law was correctly applied in the original judgment, the appeal shall be rejected by a judgment and the original judgment shall be sustained;
(2) If the law was incorrectly applied in the original judgment, the judgment shall be amended according to law;
(3) If in the original judgment the facts were incorrectly found or were not clearly found and the evidence was inconclusive, the judgment shall be rescinded and the case remanded by an order to the original people's court for a retrial, or the people's court of second instance may amend the judgment after investigating and clarifying the facts; or
(4) If in the original judgment a violation of the prescribed procedure may have affected the correctness of the judgment, the judgment shall be rescinded and the case remanded by an order to the original people's court for a retrial.

The parties may appeal against the judgment or ruling rendered in a retrial of their case.

Beihai Maritime Court
Civil Judgment

XUE Haibing et al.
v.
Sun Shell Shipping Co., Ltd.

(2015) Hai Shi Chu Zi No.3

Related Case(s) None.

Cause(s) of Action 193. Dispute over liability for ship collision damage.

Headnote Allocation of fault in relation to a collision in the People's Republic waters and determination of which expenses were recoverable as being caused by the collision and which were not, disallowing (for example) recovery for cost of taking damaged vessel to a distant shipyard when closer ones were available.

Summary The Plaintiffs' vessel and the Defendants' vessel, which was registered in Taiwan region, collided near a the People's Republic port. The Defendants' vessel had not been granted entry permission by the People's Republic maritime safety administration, but the vessel has been issued a certificate of seaworthiness. After the collision, a the People's Republic inspection report indicated Defendants could sail their vessel to a shipyard in Ningbo; however, there were several other shipyards closer to the collision location. Among the services provided to the Defendants' vessel in Ningbo, the vessel was repainted and de-rusted.

The issues before the court were as follows: 1) what was the division of fault between the parties; 2) what were Plaintiffs' losses; 3) what damages do Defendants owe Plaintiffs?

The court adopted a the People's Republic maritime safety administration's report, which indicated Plaintiffs were 80% at fault and Defendants were 20% at fault. The court reasoned that the Defendants' vessel's lack of the People's Republic entry documents did not contribute to any assumptions of fault. Further, each party will be liable in proportion to its fault.

When assessing Plaintiffs' liability, the court held not all repair costs incurred by Defendants' vessel were directly caused by the collision. For instance, Plaintiffs cannot be liable for the repainting or de-rusting of Defendants' entire vessel. Further, Defendants' vessel should have been repaired at the nearest shipyard unless Defendants could prove that traveling to a further shipyard could reduce losses or save cost. Because Defendants proved neither, Plaintiffs cannot be liable for the fuel consumption costs incurred during Defendants' vessels' voyage to Ningbo.

Additionally, the court held that the post-repair inspection fees for Defendants' vessel are auxiliary expenses associated with the repairs. As such, Plaintiffs are responsible for those inspection fees. Further, the crew maintenance fees incurred because of the collision were maintenance fees for which Plaintiffs are liable. Defendants, shipowner, are liable to Plaintiffs in proportion to their fault, which is 20%.

Judgment

The Plaintiff: XUE Haibing
Agent *ad litem*: ZHENG Xueping, lawyer of Grandall Law Firm (Fuzhou).
Agent *ad litem*: TANG Jiafeng, lawyer of Grandall Law Firm (Fuzhou).

The Plaintiff: Ningbo Libaida Shipping Co., Ltd.
Legal representative: XUE Chenghong, general manager.
Agent *ad litem*: ZHENG Xueping, lawyer of Grandall Law Firm (Fuzhou).
Agent *ad litem*: TANG Jiafeng, lawyer of Grandall Law Firm (Fuzhou).

The Defendant: Sun Shell Shipping Co., Ltd.
Legal representative: WANG Shuqin, chairman.
Agent *ad litem*: ZHOU Chongyu, lawyer of GUANGYU & CO.
Agent *ad litem*: LIAO Min'er, lawyer of GUANGYU & CO.

With respect to the case arising from the dispute over the liability for damage caused by ship collision between the Plaintiffs XUE Haibing and Ningbo Libaida Shipping Co., Ltd. (hereinafter referred to as "Libaida Company") and the Defendant Sun Shell Shipping Co., Ltd. (hereinafter referred to as "Sun Shell Company"), the court accepted the case on January 4, 2015 and formed a collegiate panel according to the law, and conducted a public trial on January 28, 2015. Agent *ad litem* of the Plaintiffs TANG Jiafeng, and agents *ad litem* of the Defendant ZHOU Chongyu and LIAO Miner, attended the hearing. Now the case has been concluded.

The two Plaintiffs alleged that: on January 13, 2013, while she was entering the Fuzhou Port, the Defendant's M.V. "Yong Shun 66" collided with the Applicants' departure M.V. "Li Bai Da 6", which resulted in multiple serious deformation towards the hull of M.V. "Li Bai Da 6", and affected the normal production and operation of the Plaintiffs seriously. The accident caused the Plaintiffs economic losses of RMB501,802, including the vessel repair fee RMB275,067, the vessel inspection fee RMB18,572, the crew's wages maintenance fee RMB170,370, the oil consumption RMB37,793. M.V. "Yong Shun 66" navigated over the navigating area. As a general cargo ship, she loaded containers, which inevitably affected the lookout and maneuverability of the vessel, so she was unseaworthy and was not entitled to enjoy the right of limitations of liability for maritime claims. M.V. "Yong Shun 66" was a ship registered in Taiwan region. According to the Maritime

Traffic Safety Law of the People's Republic of China, vessels of foreign nationality navigating in internal water need the approval of the Maritime Authorities and must be navigated by a pilot. However, there was no pilot on the vessel and no approval from the maritime authorities, which shall be deemed as escaping regulation. Moreover, the crews of the vessel were not competent. Therefore, M.V. "Yong Shun 66" should assume all the liability for the collision, and the Defendant should assume the liability of compensation for the loss happened to M.V. "Li Bai Da 6". To this end, the court should judge that: 1. the Defendant should compensate the two Plaintiffs for economic loss RMB501,802 and the interest until the date of payment (the interest should begin to be calculate since January 14, 2013 according to the loan interest rate of the bank for the corresponding period, temporarily RMB30,000 until the time of prosecution); 2. the property preservation fee and litigation fee of this case should be assumed by the Defendant.

The Defendant argued that:

1. Regarding to the responsibility of the collision accident in this case. After the accident, Fuzhou Maritime Safety Administration investigated the collision accident and issued *Water Traffic Accident Identification* on June 20, 2013, which established that M.V. "Li Bai Da 6" is mostly liable and M.V. "Yong Shun 66" is secondarily liable for the accident. M.V. "Li Bai Da 6" and M.V. "Yong Shun 66" were sailing in the Minjiang River and constituting a head-on situation. M.V. "Li Bai Da 6" caused intense situation for she did not keep sailing at the starboard side of channel. In addition, she violated navigation rule and took a turn to the portside, which resulted in the collision, M.V. "Li Bai Da 6" should take at least 80% of responsibility of the collision.
2. Libaida Company claimed an overlarge damage. 1) Regarding to the vessel repair fee. Both parties established that the damaged parts of M.V. "Li Bai Da 6" were all above the waterline. Customarily, there was no need to enter the dock for repairing the damaged parts that above the waterline. In the repair list of Libaida Company, most of the repair fees are dock repair fee which is not belong to the scope of loss in this case. 2) Regarding to the vessel inspection fee. The inspection authority is the Ship Inspection Bureau of Zhejiang, Ningbo Branch. However, the receipt submitted by Libaida company was issued by Ninghai County Department of Shipping Management. Hence, the receipt was irrelevant to this case. Moreover, the inspection time also did not show its connection with this case.
3. Regarding the loss of the crews' wages. In case of collision of ships, only the reasonable wages lost during the repair period should be bore. The loss of crews' wages for 42 days claimed by Libaida Company is not according to the fact. Moreover, the wage calculation standards they used are far higher than market standards. These sailors in the corresponding ship wages for RMB3000 per month or so. The captain's salary of the 70,000 tons of ocean-going ship is about RMB40,000.
4. Regarding to the extra oil consumption. Relevant judicial interpretations regulate that collided ship should be repaired nearby to avoid or reduce the loss.

M.V. "Li Bai Da 6" did not need to be repaired in the dock. The circumstance that there was no dock in Mawei, Xiamen so that the vessel need to sail to Ningbo for repairing did not exist. Hence, the oil consumption for sailing back to Ningbo for repair was an extra loss caused by Libaida Company's failure to fulfill their obligation of nearby repair and should not be supported.

The two Plaintiffs submitted the following evidence to the court to support their claims:

Evidence 1: certificate of ship's nationality, to prove the owners and the managers of M.V. "Li Bai Da 6";

Evidence 2: seaworthiness certificate of sea cargo ship;

Evidence 3: inspection report;

Evidence 2-3: to prove that M.V. "Li Bai Da 6" was seaworthy when the accident happened and the ship inspection department allowed to empty the vessel and repair it in Ningbo after the site inspection;

Evidence 4: site inspection memorandum, to prove the conditions of the damaged parts of M.V. "Li Bai Da 6" when being inspected in the shipyard;

Evidence 5: ship repair contract;

Evidence 6: ship repair budget;

Evidence 7: ship repair SOA;

Evidence 8: payment receipt;

Evidence 5-8: to prove that the ship repair fee caused by the collision accident was RMB275,067;

Evidence 9: vessel inspection fee, to prove the ship inspection fee caused by the collision accident was RMB18,572;

Evidence 10: voyage ship visa application form;

Evidence 11: minimum safety manning certificate for ships.

Evidence 12: payroll of M.V. "Li Bai Da 6";

Evidence 10-12: to prove that the crew's wages maintenance fee caused by the collision accident was RMB170,370;

Evidence 13: oil consumption of the accident, to prove that the extra oil consumption caused by the collision accident was RMB37,793;

Evidence 14: assessment inspection report of the collision accident of M.V. "Li Bai Da 6" (expert witness JIN Ningfeng appearing in court), to prove the circumstance of the occurrence, the subsequent processing and the loss towards the two vessels of the collision accident.

The Defendant cross-examined: affirming the authenticity, legality and relevancy of evidence 1 and 2, but holding that the certificate issued on February 26, 2014 has no relevancy with the accident in this case, it cannot prove the seaworthiness of the vessel when the accident was happening. Affirming the authenticity, legality and relevancy of evidence 3 but holding that according to the inspection report, the damaged part of the vessel was the hawse of the bow, there was no any damage happened to the part under waterline, the loss was slight, Affirming the authenticity, legality and relevancy of evidence 4, but holding that it proved there was no damage below the waterline and the repair in the dock was unnecessary. Regarding to evidence 5, the contract was signed not because of this collision accident. The second item of repair scope was obviously degusting and painting the whole ship, it was the reason for the ship to be repaired in the dock. Hence, it was irrelevant to this case. Affirming the authenticity of evidence 6, but dissenting from the legality and relevancy thereof. Among evidence 6: dissenting from item 1-9, holding that because it's unnecessary to repair the damage caused by the accident in the dock, the fee of going in and out of the dock should not be support; affirming the fee of ironwork part in assessment report submitted by the Plaintiffs; regarding to the item 25- electronic fee, the time of power consuming should be distinguished, it won't cost more than 5 days to change the plate, so electricity charges should only be calculated for 5 days; not affirming item 26-27, holding that the repaired area was 12.4 square meters, and the unit price is RMB1500 per square meter which was too high and far beyond the market price. Affirming other items of this evidence. Affirming the authenticity of evidence 7, but dissenting from the legality and relevancy thereof. Affirming the authenticity of evidence 8, but dissenting from the content to be proved, holding that there should be a corresponding proof of the remittance certificate. Affirming the authenticity of evidence 9, but dissenting from the relevancy thereof, holding that the ship inspection institution should be the Ship Inspection Bureau of Zhejiang, Ningbo branch, however, the beneficiary of the inspection fee was Ninghai County Department of Shipping Management which is irrelevant to this case. Hence, the vessel inspection fee was also irrelevant to this case. Dissenting from evidence 10. Evidence 11 is subject to the Maritime Safety Administration. Dissenting from the authenticity and legality of evidence 12, holding that the crew's wage was unreal because it went far beyond the wage of crew of 3,000 tons of seagoing ships; moreover, the calculation time of the payroll was unreasonable, only 5 days for repairing shall be calculated into the payroll, crew wage happened during suspending sailing period because repairing other items was irrelevant to this case; the signatures of chief engineer officer DAI Mingfeng, chief officer XUE Ruixiao, sailor HUANG Da were inconsistent with the signatures in the record of the maritime investigation, hence the payroll might be made by the shipowner unilaterally after the accident, instead of actually being signed by the crews. Dissenting from the authenticity of Evidence 13, holding that it was an unilateral statement of Libaida Company and no corresponding mainframe document to support; moreover, according the relevant judicial interpretations of the Supreme People's Court, vessels should be repaired nearby, M.V. "Li Bai Da 6" could be repaired in Xiamen and there was no need to sail back to Ningbo; also no need to replace the plate over the waterline in the dock. The only reason for Libaida Company to sail the vessel back to Ningbo was degusting and painting the whole ship, hence, the repair fee in the dock was irrelevant to this case. Affirming the authenticity of Evidence 14, but dissenting from the verdict of the assessment report, holding that verdict of the assessment issued by the assessment agency was not supported by corresponding evidence.

The Defendant submitted the following evidence to the Court to support the pleas:

Evidence 1: certificate of ship's nationality of M.V. "Yong Shun 66", to prove that the Plaintiff was the owner of M.V. "Yong Shun 66", the vessel was built in June 2008 with a gross tonnage of 1,685;

Evidence 2: ownership certificate of registration of M.V. "Li Bai Da 6", to prove that the owner of the vessel is the Plaintiff XUE Haibing:

Evidence 3: certificate of seaworthiness (certificate of ship inspection), holding that M.V. "Yong Shun 66" got the certificate of inspection issued by Kaohsiung Port Authority of Taiwan region on May 27, 2009, the certificate would be valid until February 1, 2014, to prove that the vessel was seaworthy before the accident happened;

Evidence 4: water traffic accident report of M.V. "Yong Shun 66", to prove that on January 13, 2013, M.V. "Yong Shun 66" was sailing from Mazu to Mawei, when she was passing by Tingjiang anchorage, M.V. "Li Bai Da 6" crashed into her;

Evidence 5: water traffic accident identification, notice of accepting the investigation and handling, to prove that after the collision accident, inspected by the Fuzhou Maritime Safety Administration, the extent of faults of M.V. "Li Bai Da 6" exceeded the extent of faults of M.V. "Yong Shun 66", and the port bow, amidships and the under waterline part of M.V. "Yong Shun 66" was damaged severely;

Evidence 6: investigation report of Fuzhou "1.13" – the collision accident about M.V. "Yong Shun 66" and M.V. "Li Bai Da 6", to prove that M.V. "Li Bai Da 6" should take the main responsibility because she caused intense situation by not fulfilling the obligation to sail at starboard side of the channel and caused collision directly; M.V. "Yong Shun 66", a ship specially engaged in petty trade, should be deemed as a domestic sailing vessel, no need to apply for import and export visas, and was not applicable for the requirements of international navigation according to the relevant regulations;

Evidence 7: certificate of ship's nationality of M.V. "Li Bai Da 6", minimum safety manning certificate for ships, book of certificate of ship's inspection, certificate of tonnage for seagoing ships, certificate of preventing oil pollution of seagoing ship and the attachments; certificate of load line for seagoing ships, certificate of seaworthiness for seagoing cargo ship; visa book of ships, voyage ship visa application form, crew list and crew certificates, to prove the basic information of M.V. "Li Bai Da 6";

Evidence 8: certificate of ship's nationality of M.V. "Yong Shun 66", loadline certificate, certificate of registry, international tonnage certificate, ship radio license, minimum safety manning certificate for ships, ship inspection certificate and inspection records, ship safety equipment table, crew competency certificates and accreditation certificates, to prove the basic situation of M.V. "Yong Shun 66". All the certificates had been recognized by the Maritime Safety Administration and the vessel was seaworthy. Rules for certification in Taiwan region is different from the mainland and the mate of Taiwan region can serve as captain according to their different grades;

Evidence 9: on - the - spot investigation record of water traffic accident, to prove the collision facts and extent of damage;

Evidence 10: inquiry record of water traffic accident, to prove the facts relating to the case, the basic material of Maritime Investigation Report;

Evidence 11: video material from Maritime Safety Administration, to prove that M.V. "Li Bai Da 6" should bear full responsibility, because she illegally sailed and caused the collision; and

Evidence 12: introduction of Mawei Shipbuilding Co., Ltd., introduction of Fujian Pingtan Eagle Shipyard Co., Ltd., introduction of Fujian Huadong Shipyard Co., Ltd., introduction of Fujian Southeast Shipyard, to prove that there were many shipyards which could repair the damaged ship in Fuzhou, M.V. "Li Bai Da 6" was not repaired in the shipyard nearby but sailed to Ningbo and incurred unnecessary fees, it was inconsistent with the proximity principle for repair.

The two Plaintiffs cross-examined: dissenting from the authenticity and legality of evidence 1 and evidence 3, holding that the evidence was not original and as evidence formed in the outbound, it was not notarized and certified. The evidence revealed that M.V. "Yong Shun 66" was a general cargo ship, the navigation area allowed was Taiwan region waters; affirming evidence 2; dissenting from the authenticity, legality of evidence 4, holding that the evidence was an unilateral statement of the Plaintiffs and was inconsistent with the facts; affirming the authenticity and legality of Water Traffic Accident Identification in evidence 5, but dissenting from the identification of collision liability, holding that M.V. "Yong Shun 66" should entirely responsible for the accident because she was unseaworthy and the crew was incompetent; could not affirm the authenticity of notice of accepting the investigation and handling in evidence 5; affirming the authenticity of evidence 6-11 which was retrieved by the court applied by the Defendant, but not affirming the matter it purposing to prove; affirming the certifications of ship of the Plaintiffs. Do not cross-examine evidence 12 submitted by the Defendant after the court hearing, because the time limited for adducing evidence has expired.

The court reckons that the Defendant did not dissent from the authenticity of evidence 1, 3-9, 14 submitted by the two Plaintiffs, and only dissented from the relevancy thereof, therefore, it should be taken as the basis for ascertaining the facts of the case, regarding to the relevancy, credibility and the divergent items, the court heard the case comprehensively, combined with the parties' statements and the whole evidence, reckons that the certificates in evidence 2, 11 submitted by the two Plaintiffs were issued after the accident and were irrelevant to this case therefore, shall not be adopted as evidence in this case; the voyage ship visa application Form issued on January 13, 2013 in evidence 10 is as identical as evidence 7 submitted by the Defendant, which would be accepted, and the other two visas were issued after the collision accident, therefore were irrelevant to this case; the list of crew was not fully consistent with the crew information retrieved by Maritime Safety Administration in the accident investigation, and the signature of the crew in the signed column is obviously inconsistent with the signature of the crew in the record of the maritime investigation, without the reasonable explanation of the two

Plaintiffs, it shall have less credibility, and constitute an isolated evidence without other corroborative proof to support, the court will not accept it; evidence 13 is a unilateral statement made by the two Plaintiffs about the claimed loss of fuel consumption by the ship, which cannot be reckoned as evidence.

Evidence 1-11 submitted by the Defendant were authentic, legitimate and relevant, the Court reckons it as evidence. Evidence 12 is rebuttal evidence, regarding to the proof the Defendant claimed, the court, as appropriate, allowed the Defendant to adduce evidence within 7 days after the court's hearing, the Plaintiffs also can adduce evidence within 7 days after the court hearing. This is consistent with Article 99 Paragraph 3 of the Interpretation of the Supreme People's Court on the application of the Civil Procedure Law of the People's Republic of China, which stipulates "after expiration of time limit for adducing evidence, the Court may reaffirm the time limit for adducing evidence, if the parties apply for adducing rebuttal evidence or rectifying defects with respect to the sources, format etc. of the evidence towards the evidence they have adduced. The time limit shall not be restricted by the preceding paragraph". Hence, the court approves the authenticity and legality of the format of evidence 12 and will make a comprehensive judgment on its credibility with considering other pieces of evidence in combination.

The court ascertains that:

On January 13, 2013 around 2100, when the Taiwan region registered and trading M.V. "Yong Shun 66" was entering into Fuzhou Mawei Old Port Wharf, collided with the departure M.V. "Li Bai Da 6", a bulk cargo vessel registered in Ningbo, within the nearby waters of Tingjiang port channel in Mingjiang River. Specified as follows: the accident happened in the nearby waters of Tingjiang anchorage, where a large number of vessels navigating, anchoring. The weather of the nearby waters when the accident happened was: sunny, north easterly force 6-7 wind, good visibility, high tide, flow rate of about 2-3 knots. M.V. "Yong Shun 66" set sail from Taipei port at 1700 on January 12, 2013, mid-range port of Matsu for managing transit procedures, at 1740 on January 13 departed from Matsu, planned to bound for the 10,000-ton wharf of Mawei Old Port. Before the accident happened, the vessel did not go through the procedures of applying for entering the port and getting approval. M.V. "Li Bai Da 6" departed from the port in ballast at 1930 on January 13 after discharge completed at the Mawei Old Port Wharf, planned to bound for Taizhou Damayu Port to load. During the accident there were four crews on the bridge. On January 13 at 1900, M.V. "Yong Shun 66" arrived at Minjiang estuary, light buoy D1, hand steering into the port. When sailing into the Minjiang estuary, a report had been sent to the VTS of the port of Fuzhou, there were 4 crews, including the Captain QIAO Xiangyi, on the bridge, VHF set in 09,16 channel. it was the first time for Captain QIAO Xiangyi to come to the Mawei Port, so he was unfamiliar with the navigation environment of Minjiang River. At 1950, M.V. "Li Bai Da 6" departed from the 10,000-ton wharf of Mawei Port after sending a report to the VTS of Fuzhou Port. At 2045, M.V. "Li Bai Da 6" was located near the Songmen Port, heading 005 degrees / speed of 8.5 knots. M.V "Yong Shun 66" was going through the Langqi Bridge under construction,

Captain QIAO Xiangyi saw 3 nautical miles away there was a departure vessel, name unknown, but could see the red navigation lights of the coming vessel. At 2050, M.V. "Yong Shun 66" arrived at the nearby waters of the Tingjiang Long-handle Light Buoy at a speed of 9.7 knots or so, heading about 210 degrees, 2 nautical miles away from the departure M.V. "Li Bai Da 6", the red navigation lights of the departure M.V. "Li Bai Da 6" were visible. At 2055, M.V. "Li Bai Da 6" was located in Chenshi Beacon Light, navigating along the middle channel, heading 030 degrees, speed 8.4 knots. At 2057, M.V. "Yong Shun 66" was located near the Tingjiang Xinfeng No.1 Light Buoy, speed 9.7 knots, heading about 210 degrees, and about 0.95 nautical miles away from the departure M.V. "Li Bai Da 6", the red navigation lights of the departure M.V. "Li Bai Da 6" were visible. M.V. l "Li Bai Da 6" was located in Tingjiang anchorage No.3 pontoon, heading about 031 degrees, speed 8.4 knots, she could see the starboard navigating lights of the coming vessel (green), and continued keeping sailing along the left side of the channel at the same direction and speed. At 2059, M.V. "Li Bai Da 6" sailed along the west and outside of the channel, and her body had passed the Tingjiang No.1 pontoon, sailing about 034 degrees, speed 7.8 knots. The starboard navigating lights of the coming M.V. "Yong Shun 66" was visible (green), two vessels were about 0.3 nautical miles away from each other, then M.V. "Li Bai Da 6" adjusted the heading to the starboard to 044 degrees. M.V. "Yong Shun 66" speed 9.5 knots, 0.3 nautical miles away from the departure M.V. "Li Bai Da 6", the captain ordered port to port, saw that M.V. "Li Bai Da 6" adjust the course to left. At 2100, the distance between the two vessels was about 0.1 nautical miles, M.V. "Li Bai Da 6" with speed of 5.9 knots, and turn left, after seeing M.V. "Yong Shun 66" turn right, M.V. "Li Bai Da 6" altered a sharp right course at once, followed by the left side of her bow colliding the left side of the bow of M.V. "Yong Shun 66". Pursuant to the statement of the crew on duty in the bridge of M.V. "Yong hun 66" said, when noticing the departure M.V. "Li Bai Da 6" at 2045, until 2100 when two vessels collided, M.V. "Yong Shun 66" could not, at all the time, establish effective contact with the opposing vessel to coordinate avoidance actively. After the collision, at about 2103, the host of M.V. "Yong Shun 66" stopped, and she was out of control and drifting. Under the influence of wind, her port side amidships collided with the bow of M.V. "Lian He 10" which was anchoring in Tingjiang anchorage. The accident caused severe collapse of the port side bow of M.V. "Yong Shun 66", the fore peak tank under the waterline was broken and flooded, the port side amidships under the water line was damaged. Hold No.1 and Hold No.2 were damaged to some extend and flooded, Hold No.1 flooded with much more water; the bow above the waterline of M.V. "Li Bai Da 6" was dented and damaged, the left hawsepipe was deformed but no water flooded, the left hawsehole was damaged, the anchor could not be tossed as common; the starboard shell plate above the bow waterline of M.V. "Lian He 10" was dented and damaged with 3.6 m^2 but no water flooded. The accident did not cause loss of goods, casualties and water pollution. Fuzhou Maritime Safety Administration carried out an investigation on the collision accident and made a Water Traffic Accident Identification on June 20, 2013. It was concluded that M.V. "Li Bai Da 6" met M.V. "Yong Shun 66" head-on while they were sailing in the channel of the Mingjiang River, the navigator was negligent in lookout, failed to sail at a safe speed, when the departure M.V. "Li Bai Da 6" did not try to keep sailing at the right side of the channel and causing an intense situation between the two vessels, both of the two vessels did not take effective measures to avoid collision in time, and the measures of collision avoidance took by both vessels in the immediate danger were absonant, which was the direct causation of the collision accidents; this accident was a regular grade of water traffic accidents, the faults of M.V. "Li Bai Da 6" exceeded the faults of M.V. "Yong Shun 66", M.V. "Li Bai Da 6" undertook the main responsibility and M.V. "Yong Shun 66" undertook the secondary responsibility.

After the accident, the Plaintiff XUE Haibing applied to the Ship Inspection Bureau of Zhejiang for appointing a surveyor to take an additional inspection on M.V. "Li Bai Da 6" on January 16, 2013 and the surveyor made an inspection report. The report stated: in the region (about 3,300 × 2,200 mm) of the bow plate above the main deck of the vessel, there was deformation and cracks due to the collision. The deformation area was about 10 m^2, and of the three cracks, the longest one was about 500 mm, The corresponding hull structures of the damaged part incurred different degrees of deformation and damage; the left hawsehole bored, the anchor could not be tossed as common, the right hawsehole was also damaged but could be tossed as common; there was no leakage phenomenon in the fore peak tank under the main deck collision bulkhead, the corresponding shell plates and components were not found to be abnormal. The inspection concluded: 1. agree that the vessel to sail back to the registry port Ninghai, Ningbo Port with unloading condition in a single voyage to carry out restorative repair, the Certificate of Seaworthiness was valid until January 26, 2013; 2. when the vessel was on voyage the master should always pay attention to vessel conditions, and have relevant measures to prevent leakage from the cracked parts of the bow, carefully navigating to ensure safe navigation. Item 1 of this inspection report was also recorded in the visa book of the vessel. On January 19, M.V. "Li Bai Da 6" sailed to Ningbo Ninghai, arrived on January 21. On January 27, the Plaintiff "Libaida Company" and Ninghai Shengli Shipyard signed a vessel repair contract, agreed to repair the collided M.V. "Li Bai Da 6", the scope of repair including repatching the hawsepipe and the area over the hawsepipe, derusting and painting towards the whole vessel and so on. On January 28, M.V. "Li Bai Da 6" sailed into the dock of the Ninghai Shengli Shipyard for repairing, totally used 25 days; the estimated repair price was RMB230,000, the actual settlement price equalled as the contract price plus or minus the repair cost of the additional or subtractive project; after the contract coming into effect, the "Libaida Company" should prepay RMB69,000. The vessel's budget and settlement of the repair project were all made on January 19, 2013, totally 27 repair items, repair costs amounted to RMB275,067. On February 3, Ninghai Shengli Shipyard issued a receipt of the repair fee. On February 28, the Plaintiff paid the inspection fee of the vessel and the marine products for RMB18,572 to the Ninghai County Department of Shipping Management.

M.V. "Li Bai Da 6" was covered by the China Life Property & Casualty Insurance Company Limited, Ningbo Branch, after the collision accident, the company entrusted Fujian New Ocean Insurance Loss Adjusters Co., Ltd to investigate and examine the accident on January 15, 2013,, and to verify the loss caused by the accident. On the same day, the inspectors of New Ocean Insurance Loss Adjusters Co., Ltd took an inspection towards the damage condition of M.V. "Li Bai Da 6". During the repair period, the aforesaid company also conducted a follow-up inspection, and finally concluded that the repair cost happened in this accident of M.V. "Li Bai Da 6" was RMB201,460 in the assessment report.

When the collision accident happened, there were 13 people in M.V. "Li Bai Da 6", 12 of which were crews, 1 was chef, the voyage in accident met the requirement of minimum safety manning. The crew list as follows: Captain XUE Ruibing, mate XUE Ruixiao, third mate WU Hongqian, sailor XUE Guohui, sailor ZHANG Xiaohuan, sailor HUANG Da, full-time GMDSS general operator WANG Mingyi, chief engineer DAI Mingfeng, second engineer TONG Wenjun, third engineer MAO Yongjun, mechanic QIU Zhufeng and ZHANG Jipeng.

It is also ascertained, M.V. "Li Bai Da 6" was named as "Yong Yao 6? before, and was a steely bulk cargo ship. When the collision accident happened, Plaintiff XUE Haibing was the shipowner, Plaintiff Li Bai Da Company was the operator, the port of registry was Ningbo port, length 88 m, breath 13.20 m, depth 6.20 m, GT 1,985 t, NT 1,112t, total power 735 KW, coastal navigation area A1 + A2. There were 13 people in the vessel when the accident happened, consistent with the minimum safety manning requirements. The vessel and crew certificates were valid, and the equipment on the bridge worked normally at the time when the accident happened. M.V. "Yong Shun 66" was a steely general cargo ship, construction completed in June 2008, registered on February 16, 2009. When the accident in dispute happened, the shipowner was the Defendant, the registry port was Keelung, The total length was 74.80 m, breath 12.60 m, depth 6.48 m, GT 1,685 t, NT 1063 t, and the power of the main machine was 720 KW. The minimum safety manning certificate of the vessel stated that the navigating area was within 300 miles of the navigation ports between Taiwan region and the Mainland of China. When the accident happened, the manning of the vessel was in compliance with the requirement of the Taiwan region Port Navigation Department. The vessel and crew certificates were valid, and the equipment on the bridge worked normally at the time when the accident happened. M.V. "Yong Shun 66" did not apply to Fuzhou Maritime Safety Administration for entering, and without any entry approval from 2012 to January 14, 2013. On May 13, 2014, the Defendant sold the vessel to Yongshun Shipping Co., Ltd., on May 19, the registry shipowner of this vessel was changed to Yongshun Shipping Co., Ltd.

Near the location for the accident, Fuzhou Mawei Port, there were Mawei Shipbuilding Co., Ltd., Fujian Pingtan Eagle Shipyard Co., Ltd, Fujian Huadong Shipyard Co., Ltd., Fujian Southeast Shipyard etc.

The court holds this a dispute over the liability of damage caused by ship collision. The Defendant comes from the Taiwan region, and M.V. "Yong Shun 66" has Taiwan region registration, therefore, the case belongs to Taiwan-related civil cases. Pursuant to Article 1 of the Regulations Made by the Supreme People's Court for the Application of Laws relating to Hearing the Taiwan-related Civil and Commercial Cases, "when hearing the Taiwan-related civil and commercial cases, the People's Court shall apply the relevant provisions of the laws and judicial interpretations". Article 44 of the Law of the Application of Law for Foreign-related Civil Relations of the People's Republic of China: "the laws at the place of tort shall apply to liabilities for tort, but if the parties have a mutual habitual residence, the laws at the mutual habitual residence shall apply. If the parties choose the applicable laws by agreement after any tort takes place, the agreement shall prevail." The Plaintiffs and the Defendant unanimously chose to apply the laws of the People's Republic of China in the court hearing, therefore, this case shall apply to the laws of P.R.C and refer to the international conventions, such as the Maritime Code of the People's Republic of China, the Convention on the International Regulations for Preventing Collisions at Sea, 1972. Integrating the pleas of the Plaintiffs and the Defendant, the Court reckons that the issues in this case are that: (1) how to divide the proportion of responsibility of the collision accident; (2) how to determine the loss of M.V. "Li Bai Da 6" in this collision; (3) whether the Defendant should bear the responsibility for the damage caused by the collision and how to bear the loss.

Firstly, regarding to the issue of how to divide the proportion of responsibility of the collision accident.

The court reckons, the Fuzhou Maritime Safety Administration conducted a survey on the collision accident and concluded that the extent of faults of M.V. "Li Bai Da 6" exceeded M.V. "Yong Shun 66" thereof, M.V. "Li Bai Da 6" undertook the main responsibility, and M.V. "Yong Shun 66" undertook the secondary responsibility. This conclusion is consistent with facts and laws, the Court will adopt.

The faults of M.V. "Li Bai Da 6" in the accident was mainly as the following five aspects:

1. Failed to strengthen lookout while departing from the port, failed to maintain a safe speed, her sailing speed was maintained at 7.7-8.4 knots from the time she passed the Songmeng Wharf to the collision happened, and when the collision was inevitable, she still could not stop in time;
2. M.V. "Li Bai Da 6" kept sailing along the left side of the departure channel from the time when it was near the Chen Shi dangerous buoys to Tingjiang waters and colliding with M.V. "Yong Shun 66", she failed to comply with Rule 9 (a) "a vessel proceeding along the course of a narrow channel or fairway shall keep as near to the outer limit of the channel or fairway which lies on her starboard side as is safe and practicable", Rule 14 (a) "when two power-driven vessels are meeting on reciprocal or nearly reciprocal courses so as to involve risk of collision each shall alter her course to starboard so that each shall pass on the port side of the other" of the International Regulations for Preventing Collisions at Sea, 1972; and Article 15 of the Maritime Traffic Safety Management Regulations of Fuzhou City "a vessel entering or departing a port shall keep sailing as near the right side of the channel as is safe, and maintain a safe navigation speed" to keep sailing along the right side of the channel. Moreover, she sailed to the outer edge of the left side of the channel (the west side) after she passed the Tingjiang No.2 pontoon, which, resulted in an intense situation between the entering M.V. "Yong Shun 66";

3. The vessel failed to establish effective contact with the entering vessel before it's too late and make timely coordination to avoid collision. At about 2055, the vessel found the entering M.V. "Yong Shun 66", but she did not adjust her course until 2059. Till the two vessels collided with each other at 2100, she could not establish effective contact with the counter vessel to coordinate avoiding the collision actively;
4. After the intense situation was formed, the vessel did not take the avoidance action in time, including turn right to restore sailing along the right channel, substantially slowdown, stop and even reverse etc.; and
5. In the intense situation, the vessel took an incongruous avoidance measures, first turned to the right course, then turned to the left, which were opposite to the counter vessel, resulting in collision accident unavoidable.

When M.V. "Yong Shun 66" departed along the course of a narrow channel at night, she could sail along the right side of the entering channel as far as possible, during the whole procedure of head-on after the intense situation was formed, she fulfilled the obligation of avoidance, objectively. But the vessel in the accident still has faults as the following three aspects:

1. Captain was not familiar with the port channel within the estuary of the Minjiang River, when sailing at night in a water area with larger traffic density, he did not strengthen the lookout. After the vessel passed the No.1 Xinfeng lighted buoys till the two vessels collided with each other, she kept entering the port at a speed of more than 9 knots, resulting in failing to stop the vessel in time when the collision happening, therefore, the vessel failed to maintain a safe speed of navigation;
2. Vessel failed to establish effective contact with the counter vessel before it's too late and make timely coordination to avoid collision;
3. after collided with M.V. "Li Bai Da 6", the vessel failed to observe a good seamanship, and collided with M.V. "Lian He 10" which was anchored at Tingjiang anchorage, resulting in damage to the vessel's amidships, increased the amount of water entering No.2 cargo hold.

Two Plaintiffs claimed that M.V. "Yong Shun 66" sailed in an ultra-navigation area, but the Court reckons that the legal navigation area of this vessel was within 300 miles of the navigation ports between Taiwan region and the Mainland of China, therefore, she was not sailed in an ultra-navigation area. Moreover, whether it belongs to an ultra-navigation area or not, it shall fall into the category of administrative management and supervision of the maritime departments of the China mainland and Taiwan, instead of having any relevancy with the civil liability for compensation in this collision accident.

The two Plaintiffs claimed that M.V "Yong Shun 66" was a general cargo vessel but loaded with containers, it shall inevitably affect the lookout and manoeuvrability, so she was unseaworthy. But they failed to provide sufficient basis and reason to prove that general cargo vessel shall not load container; moreover, the certificates of M.V. "Yong Shun 66" were completed, the maritime department did not identify the vessel to be unseaworthy after the investigation, and the fact that the vessel was loaded with containers was not take into account when the identification of responsibility was made. The Court reckons that the Plaintiffs did not provide evidence to prove that there was causality between the fact of loading containers and the occurrence of the collision in the present case, so the claim was dismissed.

The two Plaintiffs claimed that M.V. "Yong Shun 66" entered the port without being piloted by a domestic pilot was a violation of relevant provisions, it was an obvious fault. The court reckons, as for the regulation of compulsory pilotage for foreign ships entering or departing from port, it is an administrative management regime implemented by the Port and Harbor Superintendence Departments towards the foreign ships in order to demonstrate national sovereignty, maintain the order of the port or coastal waters and navigation safety. Violating the compulsory pilotage obligation, the harbor supervision departments can inflict corresponding punishment, but there is no necessary connection with the assumption of responsibility for collision accident in this case. The court has identified that M.V. "Yong Shun 66" had faults on lookout, navigating speed, and establishing contact with the counter vessel, the Plaintiff failed to prove the negligence of non-pilot which may lead to the collision accident, therefore, the claim was not accepted.

The two Plaintiffs claimed that the crew of M.V. "Yong Shun 66" is ineligible, the Court reckons that it's not in conformity with the identified facts in this case, it shall not be adopted.

In conclusion, the court reckons that: collision process happened when the two ships were in sight of one another, the negligent acts of M.V. "Li Bai Da 6" in the accident mainly violated the relevant provisions of the International Regulations for Preventing Collisions at Sea 1972 with respect to the look-out, safe speed, narrow channels navigation rules, risk of collision judgments, the action to avoid collisions and so on, particularly, she seriously violated the rules of navigation in narrow channels, and took the uncoordinated avoidance measures in face of immediate danger; the negligent acts of M.V. "Yong Shun 66" in the accident mainly violated the relevant provisions of the International Regulations for Preventing Collisions at Sea 1972 with respect to the look-out, safe speed, risk of collision judgments and so on. It's obvious that the content and extent of violation of the International Regulations for Preventing Collisions at Sea 1972 for M.V. "Li Bai Da 6" exceeded M.V. "Yong Shun 66" thereof. Therefore, M.V. "Li Bai Da 6" should bear the main responsibility for the accident, and M.V. "Yong Shun 66" should bear the secondary. Accordingly, the Court hereby reckons that M.V. "Li Bai Da 6" and M.V. "Yong Shun 66" should bear the collision responsibility respectively with 80% and 20% for this accident.

Secondly, regarding to the issue of how to ascertain the loss of M.V. "Li Bai Da 6" caused by this collision accident.

The court reckons that: according to Article 3 Paragraph 2 of the Provisions of the Supreme People's Court on the Trial of Compensation for Property Damage in Cases of Collision and Contact of Ships, the loss of M.V. "Li Bai Da 6" caused by this collision accident includes:

1. Repair cost of the ship. After the collision, the Plaintiffs took M.V. "Li Bai Da 6" to Ninghai Shengli Shipyard for repair, the Ship Repair SOA and the Payment Receipts issued by the Shipyard specified that the repair cost was RMB275,067.

The court holds that the repair costs could not be all identified as loss caused by the collision accident. the reasons are as follows:

(1) According to Article 3 Paragraph 2 of the Provisions of the Supreme People's Court on the Trial of Compensation for Property Damage in Cases of Collision and Contact of Ships, the ship shall be repaired nearby unless the Appellant can prove that the repair in other places could further reduce the losses and save the cost, or for other reasonable reasons. There are several shipyards around the port of Mawei Fuzhou where the accident happened, the Plaintiffs did not choose these nearest shipyards, but chose Ninghai Port to repair which would took nearly two days to reach, and the Plaintiffs did not provide evidence to prove that repair of the Ninghai Shengli Shipyard could reduce more losses and save more cost; meanwhile, due to the damages to M.V. "Li Bai Da 6" was not serious, the ship inspection department agreed her to take a single voyage in ballast back to Ninghai Port, Ningbo to have a recovery repair, but this is a safety confirmation for the single voyage, rather than a confirmation for whether the choice of repair place was reasonable, therefore, it cannot be a reasonable excuse for the Plaintiffs to choose to repair in Ningbo Port. Hence, The measure that Plaintiff let the ship sail to the port of Ninghai, Ningbo to repair did not meet the principles of the nearest repair

(2) According to Article 3 Paragraph 2 of the Provisions of the Supreme People's Court on the Trial of Compensation for Property Damage in Cases of Collision and Contact of Ships, the compensation shall be limited only to the loss and cost happened in repairing the damaged part due to this collision if the repairment of collision parts is accompanied with the repairment made by the Appellant to ensure the worthiness of the ship, or the repairment caused by another accident, or the routine examine and repair. From the content of the ship repair contract signed by the Plaintiff Libaida Company and Ninghai Shengli Shipyard, the scope of ship repair not only includes the repair of the hawsepipe and the hawssepipe upper hull which were damaged by the collision, but also includes the entire ship derusting and painting. Hence, the repair cost of the SOA issued by the Ninghai Shengli Shipyard must include the cost apart from the repair of the damaged parts of the collision.

(3) According to the ship repair contract, the Plaintiff should pay the advance payment of RMB69,000, but they did not adduce evidence to prove that, instead, they only provided a receipt as the proof of payment of the repair costs, there was no other evidence, such as commercial invoice, bank transfer certificate, etc. The receipt is an isolated evidence which has a limited force of proof, and it cannot be used alone as the evidence of a proof that the Plaintiff had actually paid RMB275,067 to repair the ship, therefore, the Court shall not accept the evidence.

According to the Defendant's statement in the trial, they had no objection to the repair cost of the Ship Repair SOA issued by Ninghai Shengli Shipyard from the tenth item to the twenty-fourth item, the cost of this part was totally RMB73,237, the Court confirms. For the 26, 27 item, the Defendant held that the scope of repair was not beyond the damaged parts of the collision, but only the cost was calculated too high, and the Assessment Report issued by Fujian New Ocean Insurance Loss Adjusters Co., Ltd, which was presented by the Plaintiff, also indicated that repair costs of the 26, 27 item were too high, it should be counted as RMB7200. Therefore, combining the Defendant's statement and the Assessment Report issued by Fujian New Ocean Insurance Loss Adjusters Co., Ltd., the court discretionarily recognized that the total painting cost of the repair parts of the items 26, 27 was RMB7,200. Regarding to items 4, 7 and 8 of the SOA, both the Defendant and the Assessment Report issued by Fujian New Ocean Insurance Loss Adjusters Co., Ltd held that they shall not be charged, and the court adopts. For the settlement, entering and exiting dock fee RMB5040 on item 1, the tugboat fee RMB15,000 on item 3, the water sealing test fee RMB3000 on item 9, because the Defendant failed to provide rebuttal evidence to prove that it's unnecessary for M.V. "Li Bai Da 6" to be repaired in the dock, the court confirms. For the settlement of item 2 of dock rent fee RMB125,000, the item 5 of fire on duty fee RMB5000, the item 6 of electricity consumption fee for living RMB4950 and the item 25 of electricity fee for rehabilitation work RMB12,500, totaling RMB147,450, belongs to the common cost of repairing the hawsepipe and the hawssepipe upper hull and derusting and painting the entire ship, the court holds at discretion that 50% of the total cost, that is RMB73725 (50% * 154,990), is the necessary cost for repairing damaged parts due to the collision,.

To sum up, the court confirms that the damage of ship repairing costs happened to M.V. "Li Bai Da 6" caused by the collision was RMB177,202 (RMB73c237 + RMB7,200 + RMB50,000 + RMB15,000 + RMB73c725).

2. Fees for ship inspection

After M.V. "Li Bai Da 6" was repaired, the Plaintiffs paid the survey fee of RMB18,572. The court reckons that this fee belongs to the "Auxiliary Expenses" regulated in Article 3 Paragraph 2 of the Provisions of the Supreme People's Court on Trial of Compensation for Property Damage in Cases of Collision and Contact of Ships, according to Article 16 Paragraph 6 of the same Provisions, "Auxiliary Expenses" means the reasonable expenses incurred for the purpose of repair, including but not limited to the necessary docking costs, cleaning and degassing fee, discharge of oil polluted water treatment fee, port charges, pilotage fees, inspection fees and dock charges during the ship's repairing, wharfage and so on, hence, it belongs to the scope of damages. The Defendant argued that the fees for ship inspection was a cost of regular routine test of M.V. "Li Bai Da 6", but he did not provide the contrary evidence to refute, therefore, the Court will not adopt his defense.

3. Necessary crew wages during the period of ship repairing. According to Article 16 Paragraph 7 of the Provisions of the Supreme People's Court on the Trial of Compensation for Property Damage in Cases of Collision and Contact of Ships "Maintenance Charge means the cost of daily consumption of the ship and crew, including the consumption of fuel, materials, fresh water and supplies and crew wages during the period of the ship repair", it belongs to the scope of damage. The court reckons, according to the actual situation of the case, no crew was repatriated from M.V. "Li Bai Da 6" during the repair, crew wages will occur inevitably and objectively, although the Plaintiffs failed to fully prove it, the maintenance charges should still be considered as appropriate. Combining the factors of the repair time and the number of crew on ship, the court set it RMB80,000 at discretion.

On the loss of fuel consumption. The Plaintiffs did not claim the loss of fuel consumption during the repair of the ship, but only claimed the loss of fuel consumed by M.V. "Li Bai Da 6" from Fuzhou Mawei Port to Ningbo Ninghai Port, without adducing evidence to prove the facts of refueling; moreover, the purpose for the vessel to bound for Ninghai Port is to repair, however, the Plaintiff's choice of repair site violated the principle of repair nearby, they should bear their own expense for the fuel consumption. Therefore, the Plaintiff's claim about the fuel consumption lacks factual and legal basis, the court rejects it.

In conclusion, the court confirms that the losses M.V. "Li Bai Da 6" incurred is RMB275,774 (RMB177,202 + RMB18,572 + RMB80,000).

On the Plaintiff's claim for interest loss, according to Article 7 and Article 13 of the Provisions of the Supreme People's Court on the Trial of Compensation for Property Damage in Cases of Collision and Contact of Ships "in addition to compensation for the principal, interest loss should also be compensated", "Interest loss calculation: the interest of loss of ship value, from the day of stop counting loss for detention to the day of payment is due indicated by the judgment or mediation; interest loss of other items shall be calculated from the day loss occurring or cost arising to the day indicated by the judgment or mediation that payment is due; interest is calculated at the coterminous rate of the principal", it shall be calculated from the day in which all the above losses happened, namely February 28, 2013, per the bank lending rate of the corresponding period announced by the People's Bank of China.

Thirdly, regarding to the issue of whether the Defendant should bear the liability and how to bear about the losses of M.V. "Li Bai Da 6" caused by collision accidents.

The court reckons, M.V. "Li Bai Da 6" should bear 80% of the responsibility for the collision accident, and M.V. "Yong Shun 66" should bear the left 20%. According to Paragraph 1 and 2 of Article 169 of the Maritime Code of the People's Republic of China, "If the colliding ships are all in fault, each ship shall be liable in proportion to the extent of its fault", "the ships in fault shall be liable for the damage to the ship, the goods and other property on board pursuant to the proportions prescribed in the preceding paragraph", and Article 4 of the Provisions of the Supreme People's Court on the Trial of Certain Issues in Cases of Disputes over Collision of Ships, "the compensation liability happened due to ship collision shall be undertook by the ship owner, for colliding ship during the bareboat charter period and is legally registered, the bareboat charterer shall undertake", the Defendant, as the owner of M.V. "Yong Shun 66" at the time when accident happened, should bear 20% of the compensation liability for damages. Therefore, with respect to the loss M.V. "Li Bai Da 6" incurred for RMB275,774, the Defendant should compensate the Plaintiff XUE Haibing for RMB55,154.80 (RMB275,774 × 20%). The Plaintiff Libaida Company is not the owner or the registered bareboat charterer of M.V. "Li Bai Da 6", it is not liable for the accident and also not entitled to gain the compensation.

According to Paragraph 1 and 2 of Article 169 of the Maritime Code of the People's Republic of China, Article 4 of the Provisions of the Supreme People's Court on the Trial of Certain Issues in Cases of Disputes over Collision of Ships, Paragraph 1 of Article 64 of the Civil Procedure Law of the People's Republic of China "a party shall have the responsibility to provide evidence in support of its own proposition", the judgment is as follows:

1. The Defendant Sun Shell Shipping Co., Ltd. should compensate the Plaintiff XUE Haibing for property loss RMB55,154.80 and interest(calculate from February 28, 2013 to the last day of the time limit for performance ascertained by this judgment in force in this case, per the working capital loan rate of the corresponding period announced by the People's Bank of China, if the performance was advanced, it shall be calculated till the actual payment date);
2. Reject other claims made by the Plaintiff Ningbo Libaida Shipping Co., Ltd.;
3. Reject other claims made by the Plaintiff XUE Haibing.

Court acceptance fee in amount of RMB8818, the Plaintiffs, XUE Haibing and Ningbo Libaida Shipping Co., Ltd., shall bear RMB7849, and the Defendant Sun Shell Shipping Co., Ltd. shall bear RMB969.

The debt in this case shall be fulfilled within 10 days by the obligor, in case of overdue payment, interest on the debt for the delayed period shall be doubled. The obligee may apply to the court for execution within two years from the last day of the performance deadline stipulated in the judgment in force in this case.

In the event of dissatisfaction with this judgment, the Plaintiff XUE Haibing and Ningbo Libaida Shipping Co., Ltd. may within 15 days upon the service of this judgment, and the Defendant Sun Shell Shipping Co., Ltd. may within 30 days upon the service of this judgment submit an original statement of appeal to the court, together with copies in the number of the opposite party, to lodge an appeal to Guangxi Zhuang Autonomous Region High People's Court, and the Appellant shall pay the litigation fee for appeal in advance within seven days after expiration of appeal period (Receiving units: Guangxi Zhuang Autonomous Region High

People's Court, Account number: 20 × 77, Account name: Agricultural Bank Nanning Wanxiang Branch). If the party overdue and without presenting the deferred application, the appeal will be deemed to be withdrawn automatically.

Presiding judg: HUANG Siqi
Judge: YANG Ding
People's Juror: HUANG Xiuxing

November 20, 2015

Clerk: YANGQian

Qingdao Maritime Court
Civil Judgment

Yantai Maritime Safety Administration of the People's Republic of China
v.
China People's Property Insurance Co., Ltd. Qingdao Branch

(2011) Qing Hai Fa Shang Chu Zi No.187

Related Case(s) This is the judgment of first instance and the judgment of second instance is on page 1250.

Cause(s) of Action 231. Dispute over contract for protection and indemnity insurance on the sea or sea-connected waters.

Headnote Maritime safety administration held entitled to recover costs of wreck removal from P&I Club that was insurer of sunken ship.

Summary The Plaintiff, Yantai Maritime Safety Administration, sued Defendant, China People's Property Insurance Co., for USD3,500,000 owed under a Protection and Indemnity Insurance (P&I) Contract signed between the Defendant and Shuntong Shipping S.A. Plaintiff argued it was entitled to the full amount insured under the contract for its efforts in wreck removal of Shuntong's sunken M.V. "Chang Tong" the insured vessel, after its collision with M.V. "Hanjin Goteborg" on the sea area near Yantai, Shandong Province. The Court held: (1) the Defendant was the insurer of M.V. "Chang Tong" and had a duty to pay for the expenses for the salvage and cleaning of the wreckage, giving the Plaintiff the right to sue the Defendant; (2) the suit brought by the Plaintiff was within the statute of limitations for compensation of a third party to the insurer of a vessel; and (3) the Defendant should pay the insurance indemnity in the sum of USD3,500,000 which should be paid to Shuntong Company directly to the Plaintiff.

Judgment

The Plaintiff: Yantai Maritime Safety Administration of the People's Republic of China
Domicile: No.8 Huanhai Road, Yantai City, Shandong.
Legal representative: XU Zengfu, president.
Agent *ad litem*: LI Cheng, lawyer of Shandong Binhai Zhengda Law Firm.
Agent *ad litem*: LIU Jianzheng, director of the Supervision Bureau of Yantai Maritime Safety Administration.

The Defendant: China People's Property Insurance Co., Ltd. Qingdao Branch
Domicile: No.66 Hong Kong Middle Road, Qingdao, Shandong.
Person in charge: WU Changkui, general manager.
Agent *ad litem*: ZHU Hailin, lawyer of Shangdong Hailin & Co.

With respect to the case arising from dispute over subrogation under a marine insurance contract, the Plaintiff Yantai Maritime Safety Administration of the People's Republic of China filed an action against the Defendant China People's Property Insurance Co., Ltd. Qingdao Branch before the court on May 18, 2011. After entertaining this case, the court organized the collegiate panel and held a hearing in public. LI Cheng, agent *ad litem* of the Plaintiff, and ZHU Hailin, agent *ad litem* of the Defendant, appeared in court and participated in the hearing. Now the case has been concluded.

The Plaintiff alleged during the court session that, the Defendant offered Protection Indemnity (P&I) Insurance for M.V. "Chang Tong" of Shuntong Shipping S.A (hereinafter referred to as Shuntong Company) and issued the Policy. M.V. "Hanjin Goteborg" had a collision accident with M.V. "Chang Tong" on 15 September 2007. And M.V. "Chang Tong" sank on September 20, 2007. After the collision accident, the Plaintiff organized and implemented dregs catching, dregs pollution preventing and the sunken vessel raising. Shuntong Company should pay for the related expenses and carried out responsibilities. The payment from Shuntong Company to the Plaintiff was far beyond USD3,500,000. Considering that the compensation was within the limit of the Defendant, and according to related provisions, the Plaintiff had the right to directly claim the Defendant for compensation. The Plaintiff would claim the Court to award that the Defendant indemnified for USD3,500,000 (about RMB22,925,000) and related interests to the Plaintiff, and paid for costs of this case.

The Defendant argued as follows: 1. the Plaintiff did not have the just claim, and had no right to claim compensation for salvage and clearing up; 2. Regarding the dispute from maritime insurance contract, the statute of limitations of the lawsuit against the Defendant had expired; and 3. the Plaintiff lacked fact and legitimate basis for the compensation amount, so the court shall not support. Thus, it requested the Court to turn down the suit from the Plaintiff or reject the claims of the Plaintiff.

The Plaintiff, in order to prove its claims, submitted the following evidence to the court, the Defendant's cross-examination opinions and the authentication opinions of the court are as follows:

1. Insurance policy of M.V. "Chang Tong", the bank receipt of premium, notice of premium, the statement of the third and fourth instalments of premium, copies from the files of (2009) Qing Hai Fa Yan Hai Chu Zi No.94 case, which was provided by Shuntong Company, to prove that the Defendant undertook P&I insurance of M.V. "Chang Tong", the policy records "premium paid according to the arrangements", and the premium has been paid as required by the Defendant.
2. Claim form, a copy from the files of (2009) Qing Hai Fa Yan Hai Chu Zi No.94 case, which was provided by Shuntong Company, to prove the after the collision accident, Datong Shipping Co., Ltd. on behalf of Shuntong Shipping Co., Ltd. informed the Defendant.
3. Civil complaint and pre-trial evidence exchange transcripts, copies from the files of (2009) Qing Hai Fa Yan Hai Chu Zi No.94 case, which was provided by Shuntong Company, to prove that the Defendant undertook insurance for M.V. "Chang Tong", and issued a policy, and the premium had been paid as agreed.
4. The four faxes concerning entrustment of detection and refloating of M.V. "Chang Tong", which were issued by the Defendant, to prove that the Defendant set about arrangement for detection and refloating of the wreck after the sinking of M.V. "Chang Tong", detection and refloating of wreck fell into the insurance coverage, indicating that the Defendant was the insurer of M.V. "Chang Tong", and its insurance liability had commenced.
5. Application for withdrawal of suit of (2009) Qing Hai Yan Shang Zi No.94, and civil ruling permitting withdrawal of suit, copies from the files of (2009) Qing Hai Fa Yan Hai Chu Zi No.94 case, to prove that Shuntong Company withdrew the suit against the Defendant, it was slack to demand the insurer to assume insurance liability.
6. (2008) Qing Hai Yan Bao Zi No.18 Civil Ruling issued by Qingdao Maritime Court, to prove that the Plaintiff had taken pre-suit property preservation measures on the Defendant's insurance compensation in sum of USD 3.5 million.
7. (2008) Qinghai Fasha Shangchu Zi No.46 Civil Judgment issued by Qingdao Maritime Court, to prove the payment for removal of wreck of M.V. "Chang Tong" by Shuntong Company to the Plaintiff.
8. The announcement published by Qingdao Maritime Court on the People's Daily on 21 September 2011, to prove that the civil judgment referred to in Evidence 7 had been served within six months from the announcement day, that was to say, it came into force on 20 March 2012.
9. (2008) Qing Hai Fa Yan Hai Shang Chu Zi No.11 Civil Mediation Agreement, civil complaint, mediation agreement, to prove that the Defendant abandoned all substantial and procedural rights against because of the collision between

M.V. "Chang Tong" and M.V. "Hanjin Goteborg", including rights of claim, subrogation and the like.
10. The Shipowners' Protection & Indemnity Insurance Clauses (as amended on 1 January 1993), established by the People's Insurance Company of China, to prove that: the insurer covered the liability and expenses of removal of wreck; the insurer assumed liability for compensation in the case of a claim being raised within one year to after the insured settled the case with the Appellant.

The Defendant recognized the authenticity of the evidence, the court hereby admits the authenticity and legality as well as the relevancy of the evidence above.

The Defendant submitted the following two pieces of evidence in support of its allegations, the cross-examination opinions of the Plaintiff and the authentication opinions of the court are as follows:

1. (2008) Qing Hai Fa Yan Hai Shi Chu Zi No.1 Civil Ruling and the letter Shun Tong Company's Letter to Qingdao Maritime Court, copied from the files of (2008) Qing Hai Yan Hai Shi Chu Zi No.1 case, to prove that Shun Tong Company, without the consent of the Defendant, agreed to withdraw the suit against the owner of M.V."Hanjin Goteborg" with Qingdao Maritime Court, and give up all rights airing from the ship collision against M.V. "Hanjin Goteborg", it damaged the Defendant's right of subrogation.
2. Yantai Salvage Bureau provided the shipowner with an unsigned shipwreck refloating contract in October 2007, before the Plaintiff decided to take compulsory refloating to remove the wreck of M.V. "Chang Tong". The total contract price was RMB195,010,000 yuan, that is to say, if the shipowner of M. V. "Chang Tong" actively salved the ship, it only needed to pay RMB19.5 million yuan, rather than the subsequent compulsory refloating costs in sum of RMB67,494,465.26 yuan.

The Plaintiff raised no objection to the authenticity of the evidence 1, the court hereby admits. The Plaintiff denied the authenticity of evidence 2, due to the absence of official seal on the contract. In the case where the Defendant has no other supporting evidence, the court shall not admit the authenticity of evidence 2.

Upon hearing, the court finds the following facts:

The Defendant paid P&I insurance premium for M.V. "Chang Tong" of Shuntong Company, and issued No.PCAE2007370291070000074 Policy. As stated in the Policy, the insured was Shuntong Company, its vessel named M.V. "Chang Tong", with a gross tonnage of 20,700; the vessel was registered at Panama and was built in 1978. Insurance conditions: the Defendant covered P&I Risks according to the shipowner's guarantee and liability for compensation the Insurance Clauses (1993.1.1), and the compensation amount was limited to USD3,500,000 for each accident; insurance period or the voyage: from 2000 h on 20 February 2007 to 2000 h on 20 February 2008 (Beijing time); insurance amount: as arranged.

As a result of the investigation, regarding the shipowner's guarantee and liability for compensation under the Insurance Clauses (1993.1.1) as stated in this Policy, the insurer should take the liability to compensate for wreckage salvage and cleaning. The agreed the Insurance Clauses in this Policy was PICC P&C shipowner's guarantee and liability for compensation the Insurance Clauses (1993.1.1) (hereinafter referred to as the Insurance Clauses), in which Section IV (3) that related to claim and statute of limitations provided that "...unless proved in written, the company shall not take liability to compensate in the following situations... (2) The insured did not claim the company for compensation within 1 year after the case between the insured and claim party or any other parties was over".

Section III related to risks for accepting insurance in the Insurance Clauses provided that "the company shall accept insurance and compensate for the insured's following responsibilities, loss and expenses according to this section...".

On September 15, 2007, M.V. "Hanjin Goteborg" had a collision accident with M.V. "Chang Tong" on sea area around Yantai, Shandong Province. On September 20, 2007, M.V. "Chang Tong" sank around the 2nd guidance quarantine anchorage in Yantai Port. After this accident, the Plaintiff commanded and organized Yantai Salvage Bureau, Yantai Bihai Sea Co., Ltd. (hereinafter referred to as Bihai Company) etc. to implement pollution cleaning, pollution defending and vessel salvage.

And on September 16, 2007, Shuntong Company informed the Defendant of the accident.

As required by the Plaintiff to carry out the salvage as soon as possible, on October 7, 2007, the Defendant entrusted Yantai Salvage Bureau to implement search before the salvage and draft a salvage plan including time and expenses, and it should be reported to related department for approval. At the same day, the Defendant telephoned M.V. "Chang Tong" and required the shipowner to entrust salvage company as required by Maritime Bureau to implement salvage as soon as possible within 15 days, and reported to related departments for approval. On January 11, 2008, the Plaintiff issued Decision on Salvage and Cleaning up of M.V. "Chang Tong" Compulsively, and decided to salvage and clean up M.V. "Chang Tong" compulsively. the Defendant, as the insurer of M.V. "Chang Tong", sent a notice to Yantai Salvage Bureau, and entrusted it to implement search process before the salvage.

On January 12, 2008, the Defendant called the Plaintiff, and explained that it had received the notice on Decision on Salvage and Cleaning up of M.V. "Chang Tong" Compulsively, and would coordinate actively with related parties. On January 16, 2008, the Plaintiff issued Proxy on Salvage and Cleaning up of M.V. "Chang Tong" Compulsively to Yantai Salvage Bureau, and entrusted the concrete project of salvage and cleaning up. The salvage of bow block finished on August 4, 2008 and the salvage of stern block finished on May 11, 2010.

On August 14, 2009, Shuntong Company formally sued the Defendant, claiming for USD3,500,000 to compensate the shipowner's guarantee and liability insurance proceeds. On November 10, 2010, Qingdao Maritime Court approved the withdrawal of lawsuit by Shuntong Company according to (2009) Qing Hai Fa Yan Hai Shang Chu Zi No.94 Ruling.

On January 16, 2008, the Plaintiff applied Qingdao Maritime Court for property preservation before the lawsuit, and requested to freeze the compensation in sum of

USD3,500,000 which Shuntong Company should have acquired from the Defendant. Qingdao Maritime Court ruled this approval by (2008) Qing Hai Fa Yan Bao Zi No.18, and issued an assistant execution notice to the Defendant.

After finishing the salvage, since entrusted and organized by the Plaintiff, Yantai Salvage Bureau and Bihai Company who participated in the salvage, agreed the Plaintiff to recover salvage and cleaning expenses from Shuntong Company.

The Plaintiff sued Shuntong Company, and on April 20, 2011, according to (2008) Qing Hai Fa Hai Yan Shang Chu Zi No.46 Civil Judgment, Qingdao Maritime Court judged that Shuntong Company paid the Plaintiff for RMB67,494,465.26 and related interests and expenses. The judgment defined the salvage of M.V. "Chang Tong" was a dispute over expenses on salvage and cleaning up compulsively. The Plaintiff, as a Chinese maritime competent authority, had the right to claim Shuntong Company to perform statutory duty of salvage and cleaning up on the ground that the sunken M.V. "Chang Tong" threatened safe navigation and pollution of the marine environment according to the law. After receiving the related notice and written reprimands from the competent authority, Shuntong Company did not perform the duty of salvage and cleaning up within the ruled period. The Plaintiff had the right to take actions on salvage and cleaning up compulsively according to the law. The Plaintiff organized and completed the work of salvage and cleaning up, and the related expenses should be paid by Shuntong Company. After this case came into existence, the involved organizations agreed to claim for. indemnity on salvage and cleaning represented by the Plaintiff.

In addition, the Plaintiff charged RMB5,356,296 during the auction on wreckage of M.V. "Chang Tong".

The court holds that there are three outstanding issues in this case, namely, 1. whether the subject of action of the Plaintiff is qualified, and whether the Plaintiff has the title to sue; 2. whether the sue from the Plaintiff was beyond the statute of limitations; 3. the calculation of losses of the Plaintiff.

1. The Defendant was the insurer of M.V. "Chang Tong", and had duty to pay for the expenses on salvage and cleaning of the wreckage, the Plaintiff had right to prosecute the Defendant. According to the Insurance Clauses stated in the Policy, the insurer should take the liability to compensate for wreckage salvage and cleaning up. The insurance contract was signed before the Revised Insurance Law [hereinafter referred to as the Insurance Law (2009)] was carried out, but according to the Interpretation of the Supreme People's Court on Several Issues Concerning the Application of the Insurance Law of the People's Republic of China (I), as provided in Article 1, "the dispute over insurance contract arising after the implement of Insurance Law, would apply the provision of Insurance Law. The dispute over insurance contract arising before the implement of Insurance Law, apart from the provision in this Explanation, would apply the provision in the law at that time. If no provision in the law, applicable provision of Insurance Law should be referred to." As for the provision on the third party directly sue the insurer in Article 65 of the Insurance Law (2009), there was no clear stipulation in the old Insurance Law [hereinafter referred to as Insurance Law (2002)]. And according to

the judicial interpretation above, this case could refer to provision of Article 65 of the Insurance Law (2009).

According to Article 65 of the Insurance Law (2009), the Plaintiff had the right to directly charge the Defendant for insurance indemnities.

According to Interpretation of the Supreme People's Court on Several Issues Concerning the Application of the Insurance Law of the People's Republic of China (I), as provided in Article 3, "the insurance contract establishes before the implement of Insurance Law, while the behaviors or incidents such as transfer of insurance object, insurance accident, settlement of claim and subrogation arise after the performance of Insurance Law, the provision of Insurance Law shall be applied." The occurrence date of insurance accident for third-party liability insurance was the date on which the liability of the insured to the third party was determined. Only when the liability was determined, could the insurance company start the settlement of claim. In this case, the insurance liability of Shuntong Company, the shipowner of M.V. "Chang Tong" was confirmed until March 21, 2012, when the judgment came into effect. At that time, the Insurance Law (2009) had come into force, so the insurance accident and claim settlement happened after the implementation of the Insurance Law (2009), and the provision of the Insurance Law (2009) shall apply to this case.

Since Shuntong Company (the insured) withdrew the lawsuit and got slack in claiming the insurer (the Defendant) for compensation, the third party (the Plaintiff) had the right to directly prosecute the insurer, which was not unfair to the insurer. The subject of the Plaintiff was qualified and enjoyed the right to suit.

2. The suit of the Plaintiff was within the statute of limitations. This case was a suit for compensation that the Plaintiff as the third party directly filed against the insurance company, the legal basis was Article 65 of the Insurance Law (2009). So the statute of limitations should be determined according to the provisions of the article. As provided in Paragraph 2 of this Article, "if the insured of liability insurance causes damage to the third party, and the liability for compensation that the insured should pay for the third party, the insured should pay the insurance money directly to the third party, according to the request from the insured. If the insured slacks the request, the third party has the right to claim the insured for insurance money directly on the money that the insured should have paid." Therefore, the starting point of the statute of limitations should meet two requirements, firstly, confirm the compensation liability that the insured should pay for the third party; secondly, the insured slacks the request. In this case, the liability confirmation date of the insured was on March 21, 2012, that was the date when the judgment came into force, and after this date, the insured had always slacked to claim the insurer to pay the insurance money, so March 21, 2012 should be the starting point of the lawsuit. the Plaintiff filed a lawsuit before the court on May 18, 2011, so the lawsuit was within the statute of limitations.

In addition, the lawsuit against the Defendant was within the statute of limitations, according to the provision in the insurance contract. As provided in Section IV (3) "Claims and Limitation" of this insurance contract, "…Unless the company agrees in writing, the company shall not be liable to the insured for any of the following situations. (2) The insured does not claim the company for compensation within one year after the case between the insured and claim party or any other parties was over." In this case, the closing date of this lawsuit between the insured and the Appellant, that was, the responsibility determination date of the insured was on March 21, 2012, but the Plaintiff filed the lawsuit on May 18, 2011, which was within the statute of limitations.

In addition, as provided both in Article 50 of the Insurance Law (2002) and Article 65 of the Insurance Law (2009) that, "...Liability insurance refers to insurance that makes the liability to indemnities of the insured to the third party as the object." Section III related to "risks for accepting insurance" in the Insurance Clauses provided that "the company shall accept insurance and compensate for the insured's following responsibilities, loss and expenses according to this section...". According to the law provisions and insurance terms, the insurance object of the third party's liability insurance was the liability that the insured shall bear for the third party, only when the liability that the insured shall pay for the third party was determined, can the insurance accident of the third party's liability insurance be constituted, then the insured shall claim the insurer for compensations, that was, the date that the insurance accident of the third party's liability insurance happened, was the date on which the liability was confirmed that the insured shall pay for the third party. In this case, the date when the liability was confirmed was on March 21, 2012, so the date that the insurance accident happened as provided in the Article 264 of the Maritime Code should be March 21, 2012, rather than September 15, 2007 when the ship had a collision accident. the Plaintiff filed a lawsuit before the court on May 18, 2011, so the lawsuit was within the statute of limitations.

The Defendant alleged that the collision accident was the third party's liability insurance accident, but the collision accident did not necessarily lead to liability insurance accident. After the collision accident, only the liability of the insured to the third party was determined, would happened the third party liability insurance accident.

No.256 Response to Claim Limitation and Related Questions made by China Insurance Regulatory Commission (CIRC) (1999) which the Defendant had referred to, was only the industry explanation, could not be the basis for hearing the case.

As for the value assessment that the Plaintiff had lost, the Defendant held that when the insurance company paid the insurance money, the wreckage value should be deducted, according to the Insurance Clauses. "Firstly deduct the insured vessel's wreckage" was referred to in Section III Paragraph 13 "Liabilities on Wreckage Cleaning", the deduction meant the wreckage value should be deducted from the total salvage and cleaning expenses that the insurer should have taken. Since the amount of deducted costs was still much higher than USD3,500,000, the statute of limitations which the Defendant should pay for compensations under the policy, so the liability of the Defendant in the case shall not be affected by "deduction of wreckage value".

On the one hand, the Defendant had waived any rights against M.V. "Hanjin Goteborg" on the collision accident, including the right of claim, the right of action, the right of debt, the right of subrogation, etc. On the other hand, it proposed that Shuntong Company (the insured) had harmed it is right of subrogation against shipowner of M.V. "Hanjin Goteborg". This propose shall not be supported according to the law.

The Defendant should pay the insurance indemnity in sum of USD3,500,000 which should be paid to Shuntong Company directly to the Plaintiff.

The related interests loss that the Plaintiff had requested, shall be counted from the next day with its clear claim right to prosecute to the date that the Defendant paid actually, same as the interests in the bank in the same period.

According to Article 65 of the Insurance Law of the People's Republic of China and Article 237 and 238 of the Maritime Code of the People's Republic of China, the judgment is as follows:

The Defendant China People's Property Insurance Co., Ltd. Qingdao Branch shall pay an insurance compensation in sum of USD3.5 million and the interest (the interest shall be calculated from May 19, 2011 to the day the Defendant actually pays the sum aforesaid) to the Plaintiff Yantai Maritime Safety Administration of the People's Republic of China within ten days as of the effectiveness of this judgment.

Where the Defendant China People's Property Insurance Co., Ltd. Qingdao Branch fails to perform the obligation of paying within the period prescribed herein, it shall, according to Article 253 of the Civil Procedure Law of the People's Republic of China, double pay the interest for the period of delayed performance.

Court acceptance fee in amount of RMB156,426, shall be born by the Defendant China People's Property Insurance Co., Ltd. Qingdao Branch. Since the Plaintiff Yantai Maritime Safety Administration of the People's Republic of China has paid in advance, the court will not return, it shall be paid back to the Plaintiff by the Defendant directly.

In event of dissatisfaction with this judgment, a party may, within 15 days upon service of this judgment, submit a statement of appeal and six copies to the court, to lodge an appeal to the Shandong High People's Court.

Presiding Judge: LIU Minggao
Judge: YU Wenbin
Judge: QIN Tao

January 13, 2014

Clerk: WANG Ning

Shandong High People's Court
Civil Judgment

Yantai Maritime Safety Administration of the People's Republic of China
v.
China People's Property Insurance Co., Ltd. Qingdao Branch

(2014) Lu Min Si Zhong Zi No.107

Related Case(s) This is the judgment of second instance, and the judgment of first instance is on page 1241.

Cause(s) of Action 231. Dispute over contract for protection and indemnity insurance on the sea or sea-connected waters.

Headnote Maritime authority permitted to bring direct action against shipowner's insurer to recover costs it incurred after shipowner failed to perform a proper post-collision clean-up; direct action was permitted even though the law making it possible was passed after the marine insurance contract between the shipowner and its insurer was made.

Summary The Defendants insured Owner's vessel, and Owner's vessel was involved in a collision. Plaintiffs, maritime authority, incurred expenses related to the collision because Owners did not perform proper post-collision clean up. Owners gave up all rights it had against Defendants, and Plaintiffs sued Defendants to recover costs, which Owners would have owed Plaintiffs.

Allowing the Plaintiff to sue Defendant directly, the court held a law in force after the signing of the underlying marine insurance contract applied. With marine insurance cases, the Maritime Code of the People's Republic of China applies first, then Insurance law of the People's Republic of China in force at the time of the contract signing, then PRC Insurance Law not in force at the time of the contract signing may be applied if it provides an applicable provision not found in the two aforementioned sets of laws.

According to the new Insurance Law of the People's Republic of China, a third party can directly sue an insurer when an insurer's assured's liability to the third party is confirmed. The court held Defendants' (insurers) assured's liability to Plaintiffs was confirmed on the date of a judgment holding same. The date of confirmation is the correct date from which to assess time bar.

Judgment

The Appellant (the Defendant of first instance): China People's Property Insurance Co., Ltd. Qingdao Branch
Domicile: No. 66, Hong Kong Middle Road, Qingdao, Shandong.
Person in charge: WU Changkui, general manager.
Agent *ad litem*: ZHU Hailin, lawyer of Shandong Hailin & Co.
Agent *ad litem*: LIU Guogang, lawyer of Shandong Hailin & Co.

The Respondent (the Plaintiff of first instance): Yantai Maritime Safety Administration of the People's Republic of China
Domicile: No. 8, Huanhai Road, Yantai, Shandong.
Legal representative: XU Zengfu, president.
Agent *ad litem*: LI Cheng, lawyer of Shandong Binhai Zhengda Law Firm.
Agent *ad litem*: LIU Jianzheng, division chief of Inspection Department of Yantai MSA.

The Appellant, China People's Property Insurance Co., Ltd. Qingdao Branch (hereinafter referred to as PICC Qingdao), refused to accept (2011) Qing Hai Fa Shang Chu Zi No.187 Civil Judgment made by Qingdao Maritime Court, and lodged an appeal before the court, regarding the dispute arising from subrogation right on maritime insurance contract with Yantai Maritime Safety Administration of the People's Republic of China (hereinafter referred to as Yantai MSA). After accepting this case, the court formed a collegiate panel and hearings in public on September 16, 2014 and November 3, 2014. ZHU Hailin and LIU Guogang, agent *sad litem* of the Appellant PICC Qingdao, LI Cheng and LIU Jianzheng, agents *ad litem* of the Respondent Yantai MSA, appeared in court and participated in the hearing. Now the case has been concluded now.

Yantai MSA alleged during the court session that, PICC Qingdao offered Protection Indemnity (P&I) Insurance for M.V. "Chang Tong" of Shuntong Shipping S.A (hereinafter referred to as Shuntong Company) and issued the Policy. M.V. "Hanjin Goteborg" had a collision accident with M.V. "Chang Tong" on September 15, 2007. And M.V. "Chang Tong" sank on September 20, 2007. After the collision accident, Yantai MSA organized and implemented dregs catching, dregs pollution preventing and the sunken vessel raising. Shuntong Company should pay for the related expenses and carried out responsibilities. The payment from Shuntong Company to Yantai MSA was far beyond USD3,500,000. Considering that the compensation was within the limit of PICC Qingdao, and according to related provisions, Yantai MSA had the right to directly claim PICC Qingdao for compensation. The Plaintiff would requested the court to award that PICC Qingdao indemnified for USD3,500,000 (about RMB22,925,000) and related interests to Yantai MSA, and paid for costs of this case.

PICC Qingdao argued as follows: 1. Yantai MSA did not have the just claim, and had no right to claim compensation for salvage and clearing up. 2. Regarding the dispute from maritime insurance contract, the statute of limitations of the lawsuit against PICC Qingdao had expired. 3. Yantai MSA lacked fact and legitimate basis for the compensation amount, so the court shall not support. Thus, it requested the court to reject the lawsuit of Yantai MSA or reject the claims of Yantai MSA.

The court of first instance found out the following facts after the hearing:

PICC Qingdao paid P&I insurance premium for M.V. "Chang Tong" of Shuntong Company, and issued No.PCAE200737029107000074 Policy. As stated in the Policy, the insured was Shuntong Company, its vessel named M.V. "Chang Tong", with a gross tonnage of 20,700; the vessel was registered at Panama and was built in 1978. Insurance conditions: PICC Qingdao covered P&I Risks according to the shipowner's guarantee and liability for compensation Insurance Clauses (1993.1.1), and the compensation amount was limited to USD3,500,000 for each accident; insurance period or the voyage: from 2000 h on February 20, 2007 to 2000 h on February 20, 2008(Beijing time); insurance amount: as arranged.

As a result of the investigation, regarding the shipowner's guarantee and liability for compensation Insurance Clauses (1993.1.1) as stated in this Policy, the insurer should take the liability to compensate for wreckage salvage and cleaning. The agreed Insurance Clauses in this Policy was PICC P&C shipowner's guarantee and liability for compensation Insurance Clauses (1993.1.1) (hereinafter referred to as Insurance Clauses), in which Section IV(3) that related to claim and statute of limitations provided that "...unless proved in written, the company shall not take liability to compensate in the following situations... (2)The insured did not claim the company for compensation within 1 year after the case between the insured and claim party or any other parties was over".

Section III related to risks for accepting insurance in the Insurance Clauses provided that "the company shall accept insurance and compensate for the insured's following responsibilities, loss and expenses according to this section...."

On September 15, 2007, M.V. "Hanjin Goteborg" had a collision accident with M.V. "Chang Tong" on sea area around Yantai, Shandong. On September 20, 2007, M.V. "Chang Tong" sank around the 2nd guidance quarantine anchorage in Yantai Port. After this accident, Yantai MSA commanded and organized Yantai Salvage Bureau, Yantai Bihai Sea Co., Ltd. (hereinafter referred to as Bihai Company) etc. to implement pollution cleaning, pollution defending and vessel salvage.

And on September 16, 2007, Shuntong Company informed PICC Qingdao of the accident.

As required by Yantai MSA to carry out the salvage as soon as possible, on October 7, 2007, PICC Qingdao entrusted Yantai Salvage Bureau to implement search before the salvage and draft a salvage plan including time and expenses, and it should be reported to related department for approval. At the same day, PICC Qingdao telephoned M.V. "Chang Tong" and required the shipowner to entrust salvage company as required by Maritime Bureau to implement salvage as soon as possible within 15 days, and reported to related departments for approval. On 11 January 2008, Yantai MSA issued Decision on Salvage and Cleaning up of M.V. "Chang Tong" Compulsively, and decided to salvage and clean up M.V. "Chang Tong" compulsively. PICC Qingdao, as the insurer of M.V. "Chang Tong", sent a notice to Yantai Salvage Bureau, and entrusted it to implement search process before the salvage.

On January 12, 2008, PICC Qingdao called Yantai MSA, and explained that it had received the notice on Decision on Salvage and Cleaning up of M.V. "Chang Tong" Compulsively, and would coordinate actively with related parties. On January 16, 2008, Yantai MSA issued Proxy on Salvage and Cleaning up of M.V. "Chang Tong" Compulsively to Yantai Salvage Bureau, and entrusted the concrete project of salvage and cleaning up. The salvage of bow block finished on August 4, 2008 and the salvage of stern block finished on May 11, 2010.

On August 14, 2009, Shuntong Company formally sued PICC Qingdao, claiming for USD3,500,000 to compensate the shipowner's guarantee and liability insurance proceeds. On November 10, 2010, Qingdao Maritime Court approved the withdrawal of lawsuit by Shuntong Company according to (2009) Qing Hai Fa Yan Hai Shang Chu Zi No.94 Ruling.

On January 16, 2008, Yantai MSA applied Qingdao Maritime Court for property preservation before the lawsuit, and requested to freeze the compensation in sum of USD3,500,000 which Shuntong Company should have acquired from PICC Qingdao. Qingdao Maritime Court ruled this approval by (2008)Qing Hai Fa Yan Bao Zi No.18, and issued an assistant execution notice to PICC Qingdao.

After finishing the salvage, since entrusted and organized by Yantai MSA, Yantai Salvage Bureau and Bihai Company who participated in the salvage, agreed Yantai MSA to recover salvage and cleaning expenses from Shuntong Company.

Yantai MSA sued Shuntong Company, and on April 20, 2011, according to (2008) Qing Hai Fa Hai Yan Shang Chu Zi No.46 Civil Judgment, Qingdao Maritime Court judged that Shuntong Company paid Yantai MSA for RMB67,494,465.26 and related interests and expenses. The judgment defined the salvage of M.V. "Chang Tong" was a dispute over expenses on salvage and cleaning up compulsively. Yantai MSA, as a Chinese maritime competent authority, had the right to claim Shuntong Company to perform statutory duty of salvage and cleaning up on the ground that the sunken M.V. "Chang Tong" threatened safe navigation and pollution of the marine environment according to the law. After receiving the related notice and written reprimands from the competent authority, Shuntong Company did not perform the duty of salvage and cleaning up within the ruled period. Yantai MSA had the right to take actions on salvage and cleaning up compulsively according to the law. Yantai MSA organized and completed the work of salvage and cleaning up, and the related expenses should be paid by Shuntong Company. After this case came into existence, the involved organizations agreed to claim for. indemnity on salvage and cleaning represented by Yantai MSA.

In addition, Yantai MSA charged RMB5,356,296 during the auction on wreckage of M.V. "Chang Tong".

The court of first instance held that there were three outstanding issues in this case., namely, 1. whether the subject of action of Yantai MSA was qualified, and whether Yantai MSA had the title to sue; 2. whether the sue from Yantai MSA was beyond the statute of limitations; 3. the calculation of losses of Yantai MSA.

1. PICC Qingdao was the insurer of M.V. "Chang Tong", and had duty to pay for the expenses on salvage and cleaning of the wreckage, Yantai MSA had right to prosecute PICC Qingdao. According to the Insurance Clauses stated in the Policy, the insurer should take the liability to compensate for wreckage salvage and cleaning up. The insurance contract was signed before the Revised Insurance Law [hereinafter referred to as the Insurance Law (2009)] was carried out, but according to Interpretation of the Supreme People's Court on Several Issues Concerning the Application of the Insurance Law of the People's Republic of China (1), as provided in Article 1, "the dispute over insurance contract arising after the implement of Insurance Law, would apply the provision of Insurance Law. The dispute over insurance contract arising before the implement of Insurance Law, apart from the provision in this Explanation, would apply the provision in the law at that time. If no provision in the law, applicable provision of Insurance Law should be referred to." As for the provision on the third party directly sue the insurer in Article 65 of the Insurance Law (2009), there was no clear stipulation in the old Insurance Law [hereinafter referred to as Insurance Law (2002)]. And according to the judicial interpretation above, this case could refer to provision of Article 65 of the Insurance Law (2009).

According to Article 65 of the Insurance Law (2009), Yantai MSA had the right to directly charge PICC Qingdao for insurance indemnities.

According to Interpretation of the Supreme People's Court on Several Issues Concerning the Application of the Insurance Law of the People's Republic of China (I), as provided in Article 3, "the insurance contract establishes before the implement of Insurance Law, while the behaviors or incidents such as transfer of insurance object, insurance accident, settlement of claim and subrogation arise after the performance of Insurance Law, the provision of Insurance Law shall be applied." The occurrence date of insurance accident for third-party liability insurance was the date on which the liability of the insured to the third party was determined. Only when the liability was determined, could the insurance company start the settlement of claim. In this case, the insurance liability of the Shuntong Company, the shipowner of M.V. "Chang Tong" was confirmed until March 21, 2012, when the judgment came into effect. At that time, the Insurance Law (2009) had come into force, so the insurance accident and claim settlement happened after the implementation of the Insurance Law (2009), and the provision of the Insurance Law (2009) shall apply to this case.

Since Shuntong Company (the insured) withdrew the lawsuit and got slack in claiming the insurer (Defendant in this case) for compensation, the third party (Yantai MSA) had the right to directly prosecute the insurer, which was not unfair to the insurer. The subject of Yantai MSA was qualified and enjoyed the title to sue.

2. The suit of Yantai MSA was within the statute of limitations. This case was a suit for compensation that Yantai MSA as the third party directly filed against the insurance company, the legal basis was Article 65 of the Insurance Law (2009). So the statute of limitations should be determined according to the provisions of the article. As provided in Paragraph 2 of this Article, "if the insured of liability insurance causes damage to the third party, and the liability for compensation that

the insured should pay for the third party, the insured should pay the insurance money directly to the third party, according to the request from the insured. If the insured slacks the request, the third party has the right to claim the insured for insurance money directly on the money that the insured should have paid." Therefore, the starting point of the action limitation should meet two requirements, firstly, confirm the compensation liability that the insured should pay for the third party; secondly, the insured slacks the request. In this case, the liability confirmation date of the insured was on March 21, 2012, that was the date when the judgment came into force, and after this date, the insured had always slacked to claim the insurer to pay the insurance money, so March 21, 2012 should be the starting point of the lawsuit. Yantai MSA filed an lawsuit on May 18, 2011, so the lawsuit was within the limitation.

In addition, the lawsuit against PICC Qingdao was within the limitation, according to the provision in the insurance contract. As provided in Section IV (3) "Claims and Limitation" of this insurance contract, "…Unless the company agrees in writing, the company shall not be liable to the insured for any of the following situations. (2)The insured does not claim the company for compensation within one year after the case between the insured and claim party or any other parties was over." In this case, the closing date of this lawsuit between the insured and the Appellant, that was, the responsibility determination date of the insured was on March 21, 2012, but Yantai MSA had filed the lawsuit on May 18, 2011, which was within the statute of limitations.

In addition, as provided both in Article 50 of the Insurance Law (2002) and Article 65 of the Insurance Law (2009) that, "…Liability insurance refers to insurance that makes the liability to indemnities of the insured to the third party as the object." Section III related to "risks for accepting insurance" in the Insurance Clauses provided that "the company shall accept insurance and compensate for the insured's following responsibilities, loss and expenses according to this section…"According to the law provisions and insurance terms, the insurance object of the third party's liability insurance was the liability that the insured shall bear for the third party, only when the liability that the insured shall pay for the third party was determined, can the insurance accident of the third party's liability insurance be constituted, then the insured shall claim the insurer for compensations, that was, the date that the insurance accident of the third party's liability insurance happened, was the date on which the liability was confirmed that the insured shall pay for the third party. In this case, the date when the liability was confirmed was on March 21, 2012, so the date that the insurance accident happened as provided in the Article 264 of the Maritime Code should be March 21, 2012, rather than September 15, 2007 when the ship had a collision accident. Yantai MSA filed a lawsuit on May 18, 2011, so the lawsuit was within the statute of limitations.

PICC Qingdao claimed that the collision accident was the third party's liability insurance accident, but the collision accident did not necessarily lead to liability insurance accident. After the collision accident, only the liability of the insured to the third party was determined, would happened the third party liability insurance accident.

No.256 Response to Claim Limitation and Related Questions made by China Insurance Regulatory Commission (CIRC) (1999) which PICC Qingdao had referred to, was only the industry explanation, could not be the basis for hearing the case.

3. About the value assessment that Yantai MSA had lost, PICC Qingdao held that when the insurance company paid the insurance money, the wreckage value should be deducted, according to Insurance Clauses. "Firstly deduct the insured vessel's wreckage" was referred to in Section III Paragraph 13 "Liabilities on Wreckage Cleaning", the deduction meant the wreckage value should be deducted from the total salvage and cleaning expenses that the insurer should have taken. Since the amount of deducted costs was still much higher than USD3,500,000, the limitation which PICC Qingdao should pay for compensations under the policy, so the liability of PICC Qingdao in the case shall not be affected by "deduction of wreckage value".

On the one hand, PICC Qingdao had waived any rights against M.V. "Hanjin Goteborg" on the collision accident, including the right of claim, the right of action, the right of debt, the right of subrogation, etc. On the other hand, it proposed that Shuntong Company (the insured) had harmed it was right of subrogation against shipowner of M.V. "Hanjin Goteborg". This propose shall not be supported according to the law.

PICC Qingdao should pay the insurance indemnity in sum of USD3,500,000 which should be paid to Shuntong Company directly to Yantai MSA.

The related interests loss that Yantai MSA had requested, shall be counted from the next day with its clear claim right to prosecute to the date that PICC Qingdao paid actually, same as the interests in the bank in the same period.

According to Article 65 of the Insurance Law of the People's Republic of China and Article 237 and 238 of the Maritime Code of the People's Republic of China, the court judged that, PICC Qingdao shall pay Yantai MSA for insurance compensation in sum of USD3,500,000 and related interests within 10 days since the judgment came into force, and the interests shall be counted from May 19, 2011 to the date on which PICC Qingdao paid the compensation actually. The fees for acceptance in sum of RMB156,426 shall be born by PICC Qingdao.

PICC Qingdao refused to accept the court's decisions, firstly, it argued that Yantai MSA did not have the right of claim against PICC Qingdao according to the law. According to the provisions in the Insurance Law (2009), the provisions in Maritime Code shall apply to maritime insurance, if there are no provisions in the Maritime Code, the provisions of the Insurance Law shall apply. Just as provided in Maritime Code, only the third party who suffered a loss from the oil pollution damage can claim directly the insurer for compensation under the oil pollution compulsive liability insurance, and the third party under other liability insurances shall not have the right to claim directly the insurer for compensation. According to the principle of non-retroactivity of the law, the present case shall apply the provisions of Insurance Law (2002) when the insurance contract was concluded. Article 50 of Insurance Law (2002) has provided the conditions for payment to a third party. Yantai MSA did not meet the above requirements for claiming PICC

Qingdao for insurance compensation. The insured waived the right to claim M.V. "Hanjin Goteborg" for claims without the consent of PICC Qingdao, the insured had already no right to claim PICC Qingdao for insurance indemnity, and Yantai MSA had no right to claim PICC Qingdao for insurance indemnity, either. Secondly, the lawsuit from Yantai MSA against PICC Qingdao had been beyond the statute of limitations. The insurance accident in marine insurance refers to the maritime accident agreed by the insurer and insured, and the insurer only takes responsibilities for the loss of the subject and related compensation which is caused by the agreed insurance accident. In this case, the civil judgment that the third party sued the insured came into force, which did not belong to any one of the insurance accidents in the agreed clauses. And the original judgment ruled that March 21, 2012, the date that the judgment Yantai MSA sued the insured came into force, was the date when the insurance accident took place, which was obviously violated above provisions of Maritime Code. The court of first instance did not take into account the fact that the insurance period provided in the insurance contract was from February 20, 2007 to February 20, 2008 and made the judgment that PICC Qingdao was responsible for the insurance accident happened after the expiration of the insurance period, which obviously violated the basic principle of insurance contract. This had led PICC Qingdao to take responsibility for accidents which did not occur during the insurance period. This action from the court of first instance was a deliberate favor for Yantai MSA. Thirdly, there was a clear error in the original judgment as for the facts. 1. The original judgment identified that the liability of PICC Qingdao shall not be affected by "deduction of the wreckage value", which was an obvious error. 2. The original judgment identified that PICC Qingdao had given up the right of claim against M.V. "Hanjin Goteborg", which further made it had no right to claim that the insured had damaged its subrogation, which also was an error. Therefore, PICC Qingdao requested the court of second instance to revoke the original judgment and commute that PICC Qingdao shall not take responsibility for any liability or remand this case. The fees for this lawsuit shall be born by Yantai MSA.

Yantai MSA argued that, firstly, Yantai MSA had the right of claim. The provisions of Maritime Code shall apply to maritime insurance in priority. If the Maritime Code did not provide, the provisions of Insurance Law shall apply. The Maritime Code did not provide the compensation system that the insurer shall pay to the third party. However, the Insurance Law before and after the amendment both provided that "the liability insurer can directly pay the third party the insurance compensation". The insurance contract in this case was signed before the performance of the Insurance Law (2009), and PICC Qingdao did not claim even after the performance of Insurance Law (2009). The occurrence date of the third party liability insurance accident referred to the date when the liability of the insured to the third party was confirmed. In this case, the liability of the insured was confirmed until March 21, 2012, at this time the Insurance Law (2009) has already came into force. So the court of first instance concluded that the insurance accident, claim, etc. took place after the performance of the Insurance Law (2009), and concluded that this case shall apply the new Insurance Law (2009), which was correct. The original judgment that Yantai MSA had the right of claim against PICC Qingdao and shall apply the law was correct. "The insured waived the right of claim against M.V. "Hanjin Goteborg" without the consent of PICC Qingdao" which PICC Qingdao had referred to did not match the objective fact. Secondly, it was correct that the original judgment concluded that the lawsuit from Yantai MSA was within the statute of limitations. Yantai MSA had the direct right of claim against PICC Qingdao. Whether the insured's request against the insurer was within the statute of limitations shall not affect the statute of limitations that Yantai MSA sued the PICC Qingdao. Even if the statute of limitations that Yantai MSA sued PICC Qingdao was coherent with the statute of limitations that the insured sued PICC Qingdao, the lawsuit from Yantai MSA against PICC Qingdao was still within the statute of limitations since the right of request for compensation from the insured against PICC Qingdao was within the statute of limitations.

1. According to the provisions in Section V of the Insurance Clauses on "Claims and Limitation", the insured shall make a claim within one year since the conclusion of the case. In this case, the date of conclusion was also the date when the judgment came into force, which was on March 21, 2012. Request for compensation within one year since this date shall comply with the provisions in the Insurance Clauses. Yantai MSA filed a lawsuit on May 18, 2011, according to this date, it was correct for the court of first instance to conclude that the lawsuit from Yantai MSA was within the statute of limitations.
2. According to the provisions of the Insurance Law before and after modification on the "liability insurance" and agreement on the coverage in the Insurance Clauses, the insured object of the third party liability insurance was the responsibility that the insured should have taken for the third party. The court of first instance concluded that it was correct about "the occurrence date of the insurance accident of the third party liability insurance referred to the date when the insured's liability against the third party was confirmed", and it was according to the law.
3. Even according to the view of PICC Qingdao, to refer September 15, 2007, the date when the collision accident happened as the date that the insurance accident happened, the lawsuit from Yantai MSA still was within the statute of limitations. After the collision on September 15, 2007, Yantai MSA filed a lawsuit against the insured in January 2008 over the dispute of compulsory salvage and cleaning. However, since the court did not rule for a long period, the liability that the insured should have taken against Yantai MSA has not been confirmed. According to provisions about statute of limitations in the Maritime Code and the General Principles of the Civil Law, in the last six months of the statute of limitations, there was "obstacle" to exercise the right of claim, namely the statute of limitations was terminated on March 15, 2009. The elimination date on which the reason for the statute of limitations was terminated, namely on March 21, 2012, when the reliability of M.V. "Chang Tong" the insured was confirmed, six months later since this date, namely September 21, 2012, shall be the expiration day of the lawsuit limitation.

However, Yantai MSA sued before the court on May 18, 2011, so the lawsuit was within the statute of limitations. Thirdly, the facts that the court of first instance concluded was correct.

1. The provision in Article 13 Section III of the policy in this case, referred to deduct firstly from "the liability or expenses that the insured should have taken during the process of disposing the wreckage", rather than to deduct wreckage value from the insurer's liability. So it was correct that the court of first instance concluded that the liability of the insurer shall not be affected by "wreckage deduction value".
2. In (2008) Qing Hai Fa Yan Hai Shi Chu Zi No.1 case, the insured only withdrew the claim request, without giving up all its rights against M.V. "Hanjin Goteborg". However, in (2008) Qing Hai Fa Yan Hai Shi Chu Zi No.11 case, in Article 2 of Conciliation Agreement which was signed by PICC Qingdao on March 8, 2011, what PICC Qingdao had given up was all entity rights and procedural rights against M.V. "Hanjin Goteborg", including but not limited to the right of claim, the right of creditor, the right of request, the right of subrogation, etc., it was not only limited to the rights about the hull loss in this case. It was correct that the original judgment concluded that PICC Qingdao had no right to claim the insured had damaged its right of subrogation.

To sum up, the facts from the original judgment were clear, and had applied the right law. Yantai MSA here requested the court to maintain the judgment according to the law.

The facts that the court found was the same as what the court in first instance found.

The court holds that this case was arising from the third party's lawsuit against the insurer for insurance compensation, due to the insured under the insurance contract had a collision accident, and this accident caused loss of the third party. According to arguments from both parties, the issues in this case were as follows. Firstly, whether Yantai MSA had the right of claim; secondly, whether the lawsuit from Yantai MSA against PICC Qingdao is within the limitation; thirdly, since the insured Shuntong Company have reached a settlement with M.V. "Hanjin Goteborg", and given up all its rights against M.V. "Hanjin Goteborg", whether this action shall affect the liability that PICC Qingdao should have taken; fourthly, if PICC Qingdao shall take responsibility for the compensation, whether the money in sum of RMB5,356,296 from the auction of M.V. "Chang Tong" wreckage shall be deducted.

1. Whether Yantai MSA can directly sue the insurer and whether Yantai MSA can directly sue PICC Qingdao depends on two conditions, the first one was the liability and loss confirmation that the insured Shuntong Company had caused to Yantai MSA; the second one was, Yantai MSA shall apply the provisions in Article 65 of the Insurance Law (2009), to directly sue PICC Qingdao.

About the first question. As recorded in (2008)Qing Hai Fa Yan Hai Shang ChuZi No.46 Civil Ruling which had come into force from Qingdao Maritime

Court, on September 15, 2007, M.V. "Chang Tong" had a collision with M. V."Hanjin Goteborg" and sank around 2nd guidance quarantine anchorage in Yantai Port. Yantai MSA organized and implemented the salvage and cleaning, which cost RMB67,494,465.26. Therefore, Yantai MSA filed a lawsuit before Qingdao Maritime Court against the shipowner of M.V. "Chang Tong", and requested the court to order Shuntong Company pay for the above expenses.

As for the second issue, this case is concerning whether the third party can directly claim the insurer for compensation which was caused by marine insurance contract. Both parties claimed or argued through invoking the provisions in maritime insurance contract of the Maritime Code, the Insurance Law (2002) and the Insurance Law (2009) separately. Therefore, to ascertain the rights and obligations between the both parties, it was crucial to clarify the relationship among the above laws. According to provisions in Article 184 of the Insurance Law (2009) and Article 1 of the Provisions of the Supreme People's Court on Several Issues about the Trial of Cases concerning Marine Insurance Disputes, the hearing of maritime insurance contracts shall give priority to the provisions of the Maritime Code, if the Maritime Code does not provide, the provisions in the Insurance Law shall apply. In addition, according to the provisions in Article 1 of the Interpretation of the Supreme People's Court on Several Issues Concerning the Application of the Insurance Law of the People's Republic of China (I), the disputes arising from the insurance contracts which was signed before the implementation of the Insurance Law shall be governed by the laws at that time; the relevant provisions of the applicable insurance law shall be referred to if there is not provision in the law at that time. Since the insurance contract was established before the implementation of the Insurance Law (2009), if the maritime law does not provide, the provisions of the Insurance Law (2002) shall be applicable. Therefore, this case shall firstly apply the provisions in the Maritime Code, then the provisions in the Insurance Law (2002), If there is no provision in the above law, it then shall apply the provisions in the Insurance Law (2009). The provision on the direct right of request in Article 65 Paragraph 2 of the Insurance Law (2009), was a newly added provision, which was not provided in the amended Insurance Law and the Maritime Code. This provision on the third party's right of direct request could be referred to in this case. According to this provision, Yantai MSA could directly claim for insurance compensation against PICC Qingdao.

Secondly, about whether this case had been beyond the limitation. As provided clearly in Article 252 of the Maritime Code on subrogation in maritime insurance contract, after the insurer paid the insurance compensation, the insured's right to claim for. compensation shall transfer to the insurer. If Yantai MSA had the right to claim compensation from PICC Qingdao in this case, it did not exercise the subrogation right as provided in the Maritime Code. According to provisions in Article 65 Paragraph 2 of the Insurance Law (2009), only the liability that the insured should have taken for the third party was confirmed, then could the insured have the right of request for compensation. In this case, the limitation of the third party Yantai MSA claiming the insurer PICC Qingdao for insurance compensation should be counted from the date when (2008) Qing Hai Fa Hai Yan Shang Chu Zi

No.46 Civil Judgment came into force, namely March 21, 2012. And Yantai MSA filed the lawsuit on May 18, 2011, which did not exceed the two-year statute of limitations provided in Article 264 of the Maritime Code.

Thirdly, about whether the insured's giving up the right of claim against M.V. "Hanjin Goteborg" shall affect the insurance liability that the insurer should bear. On March 8, 2011, Shuntong Company issued a statement to Qingdao Maritime Court, declaring to give up all the entity rights and procedural rights against the shipowner, the carrier, the operator of M.V. "Hanjin Goteborg". On the same day, PICC Qingdao and the shipowner of M.V. "Hanjin Goteborg" signed a mediation agreement, and waived the same rights. Shuntong Company waived its rights without the consent of PICC Qingdao, but in view of PICC Qingdao waived the same rights on the same day, therefore, the action of Shuntong Company did not hinder PICC Qingdao to exercise its right of subrogation, and the request to deduct the insurance compensation from PICC Qingdao could not be established, the court shall not support.

Fourthly, about whether the money that Yantai MSA have got from the wreckage auction should be deducted from the insurance compensation. Calculation of the insurance compensation should firstly confirm the amount of compensation, and the amount of insurance is the maximum limit of the liability insurance. In this case, if the wreckage value was deducted from the amount of insurance, the insurance amount shall lose its significance as the maximum for insurance indemnity. Although it was agreed that the wreckage value of the insured vessel shall be deducted firstly in the part of "Responsibility of Wreckage Cleaning" provided in Article 13 Section III of the Insurance Clauses in this case, it did not provide clearly that the wreckage value should be deducted from what kind of amount, and this also should be an advantage explanation for the insured. Therefore, the ground that PICC Qingdao requested to deduct the wreckage value shall not be established. The Court shall not support.

In addition, there are clear provisions on subrogation right in maritime insurance and subrogation right in insurance contract in Article 252 of the Maritime Code, Article 44 of the Insurance Law (2002) and Article 60 of the Insurance Law (2009). Article 73 of the Contract Law also had relevant provision on the subrogation right. The provision that the third party directly claimed the insurer for insurance compensation in Article 65 Paragraph 2 of the Insurance Law (2009) was a special provision in liability insurance, which was different from the provision on subrogation in the Maritime Code, the Insurance Law or the Contract Law. Therefore, the cause of this case shall be confirmed as a dispute over maritime insurance contract, while the court of first instance confirmed the cause as a dispute over the subrogation under an insurance contract, it shall be corrected.

Overall, the grounds that PICC Qingdao filed the appeal cannot be established, and the claims of appeal shall not be supported. The facts were clearly found in the original judgment, the law was properly applied, and the judgment shall be maintained. According to Article 170 Paragraph 1 of the Civil Procedure Law of the People's Republic of China, the judgment of the Judicial Committee of the court is as follows:

Dismiss the appeal and affirm the original judgment.

Court acceptance fee of second instance in amount of RMB156,426, shall be born by PICC Qingdao.

The judgment is final.

Presiding Judge: Zhao Tong
Judge: DONG Bing
Acting Judge: WANG Lei
December 23, 2015

Clerk: ZHAO Fei

Guangzhou Maritime Court
Civil Judgment

Yue Hai (Fan Yu) Petrochemicals Storage Transportation Development Co., Ltd.
v.
Shanghai Port Fuxing Shipping Co., Ltd.

(2014) Guang Hai Fa Zhong Zi No.55

Related Case(s) None.

Cause(s) of Action 194. Dispute over liability for contact of vessel.

Headnote Port authority held to have priority over other claims against limitation fund for damage caused by vessel allision.

Summary The Plaintiffs (the port operator and its insurer) sued the Defendant (the vessel-owner) for damages because of an allision accident. The Defendant argued that (1) its vessel was a barge without self-navigability and the Defendant had no control over its operation when the accident took place; (2) the Plaintiff as the port operator had no standing to claim for damages; (3) the amount of damages was unreasonable in consideration of the losses and causation. The court found in favor of the Plaintiffs, affirming their priority of claim in the limitation fund for maritime claims liability for most of its claims, but rejecting their claims for the loss of operation due to lack of evidence.

Judgment

The Plaintiff: Yue Hai (Fan Yu) Petrochemicals Storage Transportation Development Co., Ltd.
Domicile: No.1 Yue Hai Road, Huang Ge County, Nan Sha Town, Guangzhou, Guangdong.
Legal representative: ZHANG Lei, general manager.
Agent *ad litem*: HUANG Shao, lawyer of Guangdong Zhengda Union Law Firm.
Agent *ad litem*: YANG Meihua, lawyer of Guangdong Zheng Da Union Law Firm.

The Plaintiff: PICC Property and Casualty Company Limited Guangzhou Branch.
Domicile: Floor 2, 6, 7, 8, 14, 22, West of No.303, 305 first floor, Guangzhou Da Dao Road, Yue Shou Town, Guangzhou City, Guangdong.
Representative: YE Jiangming, general manager.
Agent *ad litem*: WEN Shaodong, lawyer of Guangdong Yonghang Law Firm.
Agent *ad litem*: CHEN Leiming, lawyer of Guangdong Yonghang Law Firm.

The Defendant: Shanghai Port Fuxing Shipping Co., Ltd.
Domicile: Room 2701, 2702, No.908, Dong Da Ming Road, Hongkou District, Shanghai.
Legal representative: ZOU Fangzhong, general manager.
Agent *ad litem*: CHEN Longjie, lawyer of Shanghai Wintell & Co.(Guangzhou).
Agent *ad litem*: LIU Yun, lawyer of Shanghai Wintell & Co.(Guangzhou).

With respect to the case arising from dispute over damage compensation of ship collision filed by the Plaintiff, Yue Hai (Fan Yu) Petrochemicals Storage Transportation Development Co., Ltd. (hereafter referred to Yue Hai Company) against the Defendant, Shanghai Port Fuxing Shipping Co., Ltd. to confirm the rights on July 16, 2014 after registration of the claims under the court. The court entertained the case on October 28, organized the collegiate panel and held hearings. The Plaintiff, PICC Property and Casualty Company Limited Guangzhou Branch (hereafter referred to PICC Guangzhou), as the insurer of the Plaintiff, Yue Hai Company, who had paid partial insurance money, claims to be the co-Plaintiff involved, the court made the grant on January 27, 2015. The court summoned parties to exchange evidence on January 28, convened four pretrial conferences respectively on March 4, April 17, June 15, June 27, and held hearings in public on July 1 and September 11 respectively. HUANG Shao and YANG Meihua, agents *ad litem* of the Plaintiff Yue Hai Company, WEN Shaodong and CHEN Leiming, agents *ad litem* of the Plaintiff PICC Guangzhou, CHEN Longjie and LIU Yun, agents *ad litem* of the Defendant, appeared in the hearings and participated in the proceedings. Now the case has been concluded.

The Plaintiff, Yue Hai Company alleged that on July 24, 2012, M.V. "Dong Guan Tuo 03" and M.V. "Dong Guan Tuo 08", which are owned by Dong Guan City Sheng Hai Towing Ship Co., Ltd., towed M.V. "Hai Gang Te 001" to avoid typhoon, then collided the port of the Plaintiff, Yue Hai Company, and caused severe losses to its port, so the Defendant shall be liable for all the collision accident involved. The Plaintiff, Yue Hai Company suffered total loss in amount of RMB12,593,047.66, deducting RMB4,277,082.96, which the Plaintiff PICC Guangzhou has paid, the Defendant shall compensate the Plaintiff Yue Hai Company in amount of RMB8,315,964.70. The Defendant set up a Limitation of Fund for this accident, the court granted registration of the claims application. The Plaintiff Yue Hai Company requested the court to affirm that it is entitled to require the Defendant to pay it in amount of RMB8,315,964.70 and the interest (calculate according to RMB loan benchmark interest rate of the People's Bank of China over the same period, from the commencement of general expenses to the date of the decision determines to pay, deducting which the Plaintiff PICC Guangzhou will claim), and the claiming right shall be paid in advance in the Limitation of Liability Fund, in amount of SDR1,217,263, which the Defendant set up and its interest, and the Defendant shall afford the entertainment cost, claim registration cost and other court fees of this case.

The Plaintiff, Yue Hai Company submitted the following evidence during the period of producing evidence to support its claims:

1. Port Operation License Certification;
2. Ship Ownership Registration Certification;
3. Accident Investigation Report of Collision Accident between M.V. "Hai Gang Te 001" and Yue Hai Porton7.24 in Guangzhou(hereinafter referred to the Accident Investigation Report)and other related materials;
4. Invoices, certificate of payment and sale contract of production of quick cable-releasing hook;
5. Detection service contract of port structure, supplemental agreement on port construction detection, the invoice of detection cost, certificate of payment, and detection report;
6. Consultation service contract, marine accident consultation service special report on berth 1# in Yue Hai Xiao Hu Petrochemical Base, invoice, certificate of payment;
7. Consultation contract of safety evaluating program on recovery of No.1–7 pier production, the safety evaluating report on the port of dangerous cargo operation recovery after marine accident of berth 1# (from 1# pier to 7# pier), invoice, certificate of payment;
8. Contract of construction design, project design instruction, berthing capacity accounting report of port 1, invoice and certificate of payment;
9. Sales contract of rubber fenders, invoice and certificate of payment;
10. Construction contract of port-repairing, engineering certification list, final statement of port-repairing program, invoice and certificate of payment;
11. Contract of pipeline pressure testing and removing, engineering certification list, pipeline pressure testing report, project settlement sheet, invoice and certificate of payment;
12. Principal-agent contract for civil lawsuits, invoice and certificate of payment;
13. Navigation safety evaluating contract of berth 1# in Yue Hai Xiao Hu Petrochemical Base repairing project, invoice and certificate of payment;
14. Contact of pipeline repairing, book of project estimates, design drawing, supplemental designing instruction, invoice and certificate of payment;
15. Consultation contract of cost of construction, budget report book of repairing, budget report book of pipeline repairing project, invoice and certificate of payment;
16. Contract of port structure repairing, project quoted book, construction journal/log, statement, invoice and certificate of payment;

17. Supervision contract of construction, notice of supervisors entering into site, supplemental agreement of program supervision, supervision record, typhoon record, invoice and certificate of payment;
18. Measuring contract of harbor basin depth about Yue Hai Xiao Hu petrochemical port, invoice and certificate of payment;
19. Construction contract of pipeline repairing, urban construction repairing archives, final statement of project, invoice and certificate of payment;
20. Control point measuring agreement, invoice and certificate of payment;
21. Asset appraisal agreement, invoice and certificate of payment;
22. Port 1#-5# pier construction contract, engineering certification list, invoice and certificate of payment;
23. Technology consultation contract of safety evaluation program on dangerous cargo operations at port, report of safety evaluation on dangerous cargo operations at port, invoice and certificate of payment;
24. Navigation safety report of port 1# after marine accident in Xiao Hu petrochemical base, the navigation safety report of repairing of port 1# in Xiao Hu petrochemical base, invoice and certificate of payment;
25. Notice of audit fee payment, and invoice thereof;
26. Acceptance book on construction repairing;
27. Expenses statistics of handling pipeline after M.V. "Hai Gang Te 001" collision and port damage, list of expenses details on handling port pipeline and related voucher;
28. Special auditor's report on average net profit of port 1#, which is owned by Yue Hai (Fan Yu) Petrochemicals Storage Transportation Development Co., Ltd., from April to June 2012, and the special auditor' report on average net profit of port 1#, which is owned by Yue Hai (Fan Yu) Petrochemicals Storage Transportation Development Co., Ltd., from July to December;
29. Approval certificate of dangerous cargo operation port;
30. Construction quantities tab of dredging about harbor basin and turning section of Yue Hai XIao Hu Dao Petro Port;
31. Clarification letter;
32. Industrial and commercial registration information of enterprise;
33. Check submission of Guangzhou Port Authority; and
34. Reply of recovering dangerous cargo port operation of berth 1#, which is owned by Yue Hai (Fan Yu) Petrochemicals Storage Transportation Development Co., Ltd., after average accident.

The Plaintiff, Yue Hai Company, asked for the witnesses, WANG Jinliang, LIN Xueyao, TU Kaijun, and the expert witness WANG Xianjun to appear in court and testify.

The Plaintiff PICC Guangzhou alleged that the Plaintiff PICC Guangzhou has insured property including the port of the Plaintiff Yue Hai Company, against all risks, the total sum insured is RMB562,470,587.08, the period insured is from June 16, 2012 to June 15, 2013. M.V. "Hai Gang Te 001", which is owned by the Defendant, collided and damaged the port, which is owned by the Plaintiff Yue Hai

Company during anchorage to avoid typhoon on July 24, 2012. The Plaintiff PICC Guangzhou paid the Plaintiff Yue Hai Company for the insurance money in a total amount of RMB4,277,082.96 on September 28, 2014 and on December 25, 2014 respectively. The Defendant set up a Limitation of Liability Fund in the court and the Plaintiff Yue Hai Company instituted legal proceeding of affirming its claiming right against the Defendant, because of that, the Plaintiff PICC Guangzhou is entitled to commence legal proceeding on behalf of the insured under the insurance money aforesaid. The Plaintiff PICC Guangzhou requests the court to affirm that it is entitled to require the Defendant to pay it in amount of RMB277,082.96 and the interest (calculate according to the People's Bank of China over the same period of RMB loan benchmark interest rate, RMB2,000,000 of which from the commencement of September 29, 2014, and RMB2,277,082.96 of which from the commencement of December 26, 2014 to the date of the decision determines to pay), and the Appellant's right shall be paid in advance in the Limitation of Liability Fund, SDR1,217,263, which the Defendant has set up and its interest, and the Defendant shall afford the entertainment cost, claiming right registration cost and other court fees of this case.

The Plaintiff PICC Guangzhou submitted the following evidence during the period of producing evidence to support its claims: 1.the policy;2. the confirmation letter of bank payment information; 3. the calculation book of indemnity money; 4. the business license of Shenzhen Xin Cheng Union Insurance Public Evaluation Co., Ltd., public evaluation business license, price assessment organization quality certificate of which, and the public evaluation practitioners practicing certificates; 5. the report of public evaluation.

The Defendant defended as follows:

1. The Defendant has no relation to accident involved at all, and is not liable for any indemnity of two Plaintiffs. M.V. "Hai Gang Te 001" is a barge which has no self-navigability, and it is chartered by Tong Bao (Hong Kong) Sea Engineering Co., Ltd. (hereinafter referred to Tong Bao Company) from its operator, Shang Gang Group Logistics Co., Ltd. (hereinafter referred to Shang Gang Logistics Company), and it is sub-chartered by Chinese Gang Wan Engineering Co., Ltd.(hereinafter referred to Gang Wan Engineering Company) from Tong Bao Company. The Defendant, as the owner of M.V. "Hai Gang Te 001", does not actually control and use it, and has no fault on the collision accident involved, has no responsibility of indemnity according to law.
2. The two Plaintiffs are not entitled to claim indemnity of losses of the accident involved. The Plaintiff Yue Hai Company, fails to prove he is the owner of this port because he only submits the Port Operation License Certification as the basis of claiming indemnity, so the Plaintiff Yue Hai Company has no right to ask for claim with respect to losses of port involved, nor the Plaintiff PICC Guangzhou on behalf of him. To say the least, the Plaintiff PICC Guangzhou can only perform the right of subrogation under indemnity sum RMB2352395.63, which is 55% of co–insurance.

3. The lost amount is unreasonable, which claimed by the two Plaintiffs.1.The damage of port involved is not completely caused by the collision of M.V. "Hai Gang Te 001", it was also caused by the second collision of M.V. "GINGA CARACAL" before repairing the port, so M.V. "Hai Gang Te 001" shall not afford all the losses; 2.there is no need to repair the pipeline in the process of the port repairing construction because pipeline suffers no damage, the designing and repairing cost of pipeline shall be afforded by the Plaintiff Yue Hai Company himself; 3. the bidding procedure of port repairing project is unlawful, it is lack of due quantities and costs checking, cost of dredging about harbor basin is irrelevant with this accident, and lifetime of the anticorrosive mental accessories of 8# and 9#'s caissons and rubber fenders has changed from 8 to 10 years, and adds construction quantities like adding 1 M stones-casting quantities at the front of caissons, the cost of port construction repairing is unreasonable; 4. except for costs including the consultation cost of special safety evaluating program on putting No.1–7 pier back on production RMB80,000, rubber fenders payment RMB17,500, payment against the port-repairing construction program RMB19,511.84, payment against pipeline testing pressure and removing RMB61,937, service cost of the navigation safety evaluating of repairing berth 1# project RMB130,000, payment of supervision RMB165,000, payment of the measuring of harbor basin depth RMB15,000, cost of the navigation safety report of repairing project of port 1# after average accident RMB130,000, other cost of lost is unreasonable; 5. accident involved does not influence the general operation of port, the Plaintiff Yue Hai Company suffers no operating losses, two Plaintiffs have no right to claim for operating losses.

The Defendant submitted the following evidence during the period of producing evidence: 1. the correspondence among attorneys; 2. Emails; 3. the bidding documents; 4. the design quotation book; 4. the design instructions of construction drawing; 5. the survey and inspection report of the accident about M.V. "Hai Gang Te 001" collision port, which is owned by Yue Hai Company on July 24, 2012, the survey and inspection supplemental report of the accident about M.V. "Hai Gang Te 001" collision port, which is owned by Yue Hai Company on July 24, 2012; 5. the business license of Shanghai Hen Liang Public Evaluation Co., Ltd., public evaluation business license, and the public evaluation practitioners practicing certificates; 6. the documents calling for a bid; 7. the contract of damage detecting of Za Pu Gang Phase 3 Common Port and its invoice; 8. the contract of damage detecting of Tai Cang Gang Phase 3 Port and its invoice; 9. the information of vessel.

The Defendant ask for expert witnesses, WU Houliang, PU Qingjie to appear in court and give opinions on special issues.

The Defendant and two Plaintiffs have no objection to the authenticity of evidence submitted by the other party, and they can be recognized to be basis to identify case facts involved. The Defendant and two Plaintiffs have some objection to the relevancy of evidence submitted by the other part, the court will identify facts comprehensively according to facts which two parties have no objection and trial investigation together.

The court finds out facts as follows:

1. Basic information of the port involved

    The Plaintiff Yue Hai Company was founded on 20 October 1992, it has 5 first class loading-discharging berths of dangerous cargo, namely berth 1#, 2#, 3#, 4#, 5#. The Port Operation License Certification, No.(Yue Hui) Gang Jing Zheng (0024), which is licensed by Guangzhou Harbor Authority, states the operating area of Yue Hai Company is berth 1#, 3#, 4#, 5# of port, which is owned by Guangzhou Harbor Nan Sha Harbor Section Yue Hai (Fan Yu) Petrochemicals Storage Transportation Development Co., Ltd.

    Berth 1# is located in the east of Xiao HuIsland, Nan Sha Town, Guangzhou City, and is founded in 1995, it is a 30,000-ton oil production wharf, 296 m long, cylinder caisson pier structure. There are 11 piers in this port from south to north, namely pier 1#, 2#, 3#, 4#, 5#, 6#,7#, 8#, 9#, 10#, among those piers 10# lays easternmost, the scope of 6A#-10# inside is berth 5#.

    Berth 2# starts to be founded in December 1992, was designed to be 5,000-tonclass, but later be granted to be 20,000 ton-class, and gets finished in August 2004, the inspection of it is still undergoing, now it adopts "one vessel one discussion" principle to deal with the dangerous cargo operation.

2. Facts related to the collision accident

    According to the statements on Accident Investigation Report, which is issued by China Nan Sha Maritime Safety Administration, accident involved happened as follows: on July 23, 2012, M.V. "Hai Gang Te 001" called at berth 5#, container wharf, Dong Guan Hu Men Port, after finishing the loading of large stent steel board pile (stent steel board pile weighs 2,394 tons, lateral area scales 3,273.8 square meters). At 1441 h on July 23, inner harbor of Guangzhou Port hangs and flies typhoon signal No.2 wind ball, and the force is getting stronger gradually, influenced by periphery of typhoon No.201208 "Wei Sen Te". At 1610 h on July 23, Guangzhou City Observatory released that "there is no change for inner harbor of Guangzhou Port hangs and flies typhoon signal No.2 wind ball, but outside harbor of Guangzhou Port needs to change to hang and fly typhoon signal No.3 wind ball". At 1745 h on July 23, M.V. "Hai Gang Te 001" was towed from berth 5#, container wharf, Dong Guan Hu Men Port for anchorage to avoid typhoon outside with the help of M.V. "Dong Guan Tuo 03", M.V. "Dong Guan Tuo 06", and M.V. "Dong Guan Tuo 08" together. At 1830on July 23, M.V. "Hai Gang Te 001" arrived at the anchorage 66DH, Guangzhou Port with the help of three tugs above said, cast single anchor, let go starboard anchor ten sections in water. After that, M.V. "Dong Guan Tuo 08" leaves with towing rope open, M.V. "Dong Guan Tuo 06" and M.V. "Dong Guan Tuo 03" stay with M.V. "Hai Gang Te 001" to watch and supervise. At 1940 on July 23, M.V. "Hai Gang Te 001" found it was not enough to just cast single anchor on the site, and adjusts anchor chain at once to cast double anchors, after lifting starboard anchor to five sections let go port anchor five sections in water, starboard anchor eight sections in water mooring to avoid typhoon. Around 1955 after casting double anchors, M.V. "Dong Guan Tuo 06" opens towing rope and turns to the other side to watch and supervise M.V. "Hai Gang Te 001" with M.V. "Dong Guan Tuo 03". At 0109 on July 24, Guangzhou City Observatory released that "there is no change for inner harbor of Guangzhou Port hangs and flies typhoon signal No.3 wind ball, but outside harbor of Guangzhou Port needs to change to hang and fly typhoon signal No.4 wind ball from now". At 0330 on July 24, M.V. "Dong Guan Tuo 06" was appointed to arrive to a ship yard of COSCO's to tow another vessel to avoid typhoon from the dispatching phone of its company, and M.V. "Dong Guan Tuo 08" would replace it on the site. At 0350, M.V. "Dong Guan Tuo 06" leaves M.V. "Hai Gang Te 001", leaving M.V. "Dong Guan Tuo 03" to watch and supervise M.V. "Hai Gang Te 001" on the site. At 0400on July 24, M.V. "Dong Guan Tuo 03" finds M.V. "Hai Gang Te 001" is dragging anchor, and notifies M.V. "Hai Gang Te 001" with HF (high frequency) at once, and starts itself to tow M.V. "Hai Gang Te 001" going against the wind. At that time the force of wind has gone up to grade 7–8, the height of waves was 2–3 m. At 0410 on July 24, M.V. "Dong Guan Tuo 08" has arrived and tow M.V. "Hai Gang Te 001" with towing rope. After taking the towing rope, M.V. "Dong Guan Tuo 08" tugs the starboard of bow section, and M.V. "Dong Guan Tuo 03" tugs the starboard of stern of M.V. "Hai Gang Te 001" to avoid typhoon with all their strength. At 0430 on July 24, when the two tugs towed M.V. "Hai Gang Te 001" to avoid typhoon with all their strength, they move with the wind to where the stern of M.V. "Hai Gang Te 001" is about 20 m away Yue Hai Port, the stern towing rope of M.V. "Dong Guan Tuo 03", who towed the stern, was broken, left with only the front towing rope. At 0440, the stern of M.V. "Hai Gang Te 001" hits toward berth 1# of the Plaintiff, Yue Hai Company's port. At that time, the force of wind has gone up to grade 8–9`. At 0442 on July 24, the stern towing rope of M.V. "Dong Guan Tuo 08", who tugs the bow, was broke as well, the bow of M.V. "Hai Gang Te 001" hits toward berth 1# of the Plaintiff, Yue Hai Company's port again. About 0447 on July 24, two tugs take on towing ropes again, tried to tow M.V. "Hai Gang Te 001" away from the port, but failed. After that, with the joint help with M.V. "Dong Guan Tuo 01" and M.V. "Dong Guan Tuo 09" appointed by the tugs company, at 0615 on July 24, M.V. "Hai Gang Te 001" was towed away from the port, and at 0730, to mooring place to avoid typhoon. After that, the four tugs, M.V. "Dong Guan Tuo 08", M.V. "Dong Guan Tuo 03", M.V. "Dong Guan Tuo 09", M.V. "Dong Guan Tuo 01" stayed on the site to watch and supervise and to avoid typhoon, at 0820, M.V. "Dong Guan Tuo 01" and M.V. "Dong Guan Tuo 08" finish the work and leave. Accident Survey Report concludes that, the accident involved is a single party responsibility accident influenced by the bad weather, sea circumstances, not good preparation of avoiding typhoon for a vessel, and incorrect actions to avoid typhoon, M.V. "Hai Gang Te 001" shall be liable for all the responsibility of this accident. Every party has no objection to the Accident Survey Report issued by China Nan Sha Maritime Safety Administration.

On April 2, 2013, M.V. "Jin Jia Mao" collided the same part of berth 1# once, before the repairing construction of the port involved. The Plaintiff, Yue Hai Company states in the hearing, he does not report this collision accident to Maritime Safety Administration because it has no influence to the repairing plan and it happened after detection and construction design finished, so he does not recognize the detection and repairing design again, nor ask M.V. "Jin Jia Mao" for claim.

3. Facts about M.V. "Hai Gang Te 001"

M.V. "Hai Gang Te 001" is a barge which has no power, grossly weighs 6,789 tons, net weighs 2,036, both the registered owner and operator are the Defendant. Accident Survey Report states the using of M.V. "Hai Gang Te 001", on 25 March, the vessel was assigned to Shang Gang Logistics Company to maintain and operate by the Defendant's parent company, Shanghai International Port, but until the accident happened, the owner of the vessel is the Defendant. On March 1, 2012, it is chartered by Tong Bao Company from Shang Gang Logistics Company. On the same day, it is sub-chartered by Hang Wan Company from Tong Bao Company. Before the accident, the vessel is used and controlled by Gang Zhu Ao Bridge Hong Kong Seaport Manmade Island Lattice Steel Board Piles Project Department.

4. Facts about the insurance indemnity

The Plaintiff, Yue Hai Company buys the property insurance of all risks over port assets including the damaged berth involved from the Plaintiff PICC Guangzhou, on July 11, 2012, the Plaintiff PICC Guangzhou issues the policy after accepting the insurance application. The policy states the insurer is the Plaintiff PICC Guangzhou, the insured is the Plaintiff Yue Hai Company, the total insurance amount is RMB562,470,587.08, the insured period is from 0000 June 16 2012 to 2400 June 15, 2013. List of special agreement of policy states that this insurance is co-insurance, PICC Property and Casualty Company Limited Guangzhou City Dong Shan Branch has 55%, China Ping An Property Insurance Stock Co., Ltd. has 45%.

After the accident involved, two Plaintiffs jointly entrusted Shenzhen Xin Cheng Union Insurance Public Evaluation Co., Ltd. (hereinafter referred to Xin Cheng Public Evaluation Company) to do the inspection work, damage cause identification, damage losses identification, evaluation and adjustment, and to issue the report of public evaluation. Xin Cheng Public Evaluation Company issues the "2012–7-24" damage caused by vessel collision public evaluation report of Yue Hai (Fan Yu) Petrochemicals Storage Transportation Development Co., Ltd.(hereinafter referred to public evaluation report) on December 20, 2014 after finishing the entrusted work, it explains the accident causes, damage, insurance adjustment, etc., and finally ascertains the damage is RMB4,277,082.96. Xin Cheng Public Evaluation Company has insurance public evaluation business license and price assessment organization quality certificate. Public evaluating individuals, LI Shijun, XIE Xiaofeng have the public evaluation practitioners certificates.

On December 18, 2014, two Plaintiffs makes an insurance indemnity agreement, which writes the Plaintiff PICC Guangzhou affords insurance indemnity of accident involved totally is RMB4,277,082.96, as his final insurance responsibility in the policy. Two parties agree with the distribution of recourse getting from responsible party as follows: 1. if the Limitation of Liability Fund is less than losses of accident involved decided(mediated) by the court, the sum of compensation getting by the Plaintiff PICC Guangzhou(Limitation of Liability Fund / losses sum of accident involved decided(mediated) by the court)* RMB4,277,082.96, and the left will be given to Yue Hai Company; 2. if the Limitation of Liability Fund is more than losses sum of accident involved decided(mediated) by the court, the Plaintiff Yue Hai Company shall give the compensation payment RMB4,277,082.96 back to the Plaintiff PICC Guangzhou, and the left will be given to Yue Hai Company. The Plaintiff PICC Guangzhou pays the Plaintiff Yue Hai Company for insurance compensation RMB2,000,000 on September 28, 2014, on December 25 pays the Plaintiff Yue Hai Company for insurance compensation RMB2,277,082.96. On December 18, 2014, the Plaintiff Yue Hai Company issued a letter of subrogation, the Plaintiff Yue Hai Company transfers all the rights and interests of the insurance subject matter of payment RMB2,277,082.96 to the Plaintiff PICC Guangzhou.

In the hearings, two Plaintiffs affirm the way of distribution in insurance indemnity agreement, agree with the way of distribution of losses sum of accident involved decided (mediated) by the court as aforesaid, two Plaintiffs did not distinguish damage losses claimed by them clearly.

5. Facts about losses

After the accident involved happened, the insurer of Shang Gang Group Logistics Co., Ltd. Engineering Logistics Branch, China Continent Property Insurance Co., Ltd. Shanghai Branch entrusts Shanghai High-level Insurance Public Evaluation Co., Ltd. (hereinafter referred to High-level Public Evaluation Company) to do the public evaluation work about accident involved on July 26, 2012. On January 20, 2015, High-level Public Evaluation Company finishes the survey and inspection report of the accident about M.V. "Hai Gang Te 001" collision port, which is owned by Yue Hai Company on July 24, 2012 (hereinafter referred to the survey and inspection report) according to partial evidence submitted by Yue Hai Company and information getting from inspection of early accident on site, tracking and inspection of accident disposal, and gives public evaluating opinions to every loss claimed by two Plaintiffs. On June 25, 2015, High-level Public Evaluation Company finishes the survey and supplemental inspection report of the accident about M.V. "Hai Gang Te 001" colliding port, which is owned by Yue Hai Company on 24 July 2012 (hereinafter referred to the survey and supplemental inspection report) according to evidence materials submitted by the Plaintiff PICC Guangzhou and other evidence materials submitted by the Plaintiff Yue Hai Company, and does the supplemental public evaluation on accident losses claimed by two Plaintiffs. The Defendant agrees with public evaluating opinions in survey and inspection report and the survey and supplemental inspection report, and gives specific identifying opinions on every loss claimed by two Plaintiffs according to High-level Public Evaluation Company's public evaluating opinions.

With respect to every loss item claimed by two Plaintiffs, the Defendant affirms eight costs claimed by two Plaintiffs consisting of the technology consultation cost of special safety evaluating program on putting No.1–7 pier back on production RMB80,000, rubber fenders payment RMB17,500, payment against the port-repairing construction program RMB19,511.84, payment against pipeline testing pressure and removing RMB61,937, service cost of the navigation safety evaluating of repairing berth 1# project RMB130,000, payment of supervision RMB165,000, payment of the measuring of harbor basin depth RMB15,000, cost of the navigation safety report of repairing project of port 1# after average accident RMB130,000. Among which, the Plaintiff Yue Hai Company pays RMB40,000 twice for the technology consultation cost of special safety evaluating program on putting No.1–7 pier back on production on September 17 and October 18, 2012 respectively, on October 19, 2012 pays RMB17,500 for rubber fenders payment, on July 31, 2013 pays RMB15,000 for the measuring of harbor basin depth. The Defendant has no objection to assets evaluating cost RMB3,000, lawyer cost RMB200,000, auditing cost RMB80,000 paid by the Plaintiff, Yue Hai Company, but the three costs are reasonable or not, this will be left to the court to ascertain subject to law. Among which, the cost of assets evaluation is producing from that the Plaintiff, Yue Hai Company entrusts Guangzhou Guang Cheng Min Assets Evaluating Co., Ltd. to evaluate his house assets used as mortgage to perform his guarantee obligation of property preservation before lawsuit involved. Lawyer cost RMB200,000 is producing from that the Plaintiff, Yue Hai Company entrusts the lawyer of Guangdong Zhengda Union Law Firm to be the lawyers of lawsuit involved.

As for the other lost claimed by two Plaintiffs, the court finds out facts as follows:

1. The payment of mooring bollard of pier 5#

   On July 25, 2012, the Plaintiff Yue Hai Company signs the sales contract of quick cable-releasing hook with Lian Yun Gang Bu Sheng Machine Co., Ltd. (hereinafter referred to Bu Sheng Company), agree with that the Plaintiff Yue Hai Company will buy one quick cable-releasing hook from Bu Sheng Company in total amount of RMB42,000, not including cost of installation and commission, and the delivery date will be August 25, 2012. The Plaintiff Yue Hai Company pays for goods RMB39,900 on September 6, 2012, and the remaining payment is paid on October 31, 2012. This quick cable-releasing hook is installed by Guangzhou Nan Sha Town Cheng Wei Construction earth-rock Project Team (hereinafter referred to Cheng Wei Project Team), the installing cost is included in payment against port repairing RMB19,511.84, which is recognized by the Defendant, the construction period of port repairing including the installation aforesaid starts from July 1, 2012 to September 30, 2012. The Plaintiff Yue Hai Company pays Cheng Wei Project Team for payment against construction RMB19,511.84 on November 26, 2012. The Plaintiff Yue Hai Company alleged he ordered the quick cable-releasing hook aforesaid at once after the accident to put back berth 1# pier 1#-7# into producing as soon as possible. The public evaluating report affirms this cost.

The Defendant alleged that, this item was bought on the next day of the accident, which is the ordinary repairing project purchase, has no relation with this accident, considering the fact that berth 1# pier 5# of this port is damage to mooring bollard, purchase cost of ship column is RMB3,300.

2. Inspection fees

On July 24, 2012, Guangzhou Gang Wan Engineer Quality Inspection Co., Ltd. (hereinafter referred to Gang Wan Company) entrusted by the Plaintiff Yue Hai Company, issues a "7/24" marine accident structure inspection plan of port of Yue Hai (Fan Yu) Petrochemicals Storage Transportation Development Co., Ltd. the inspection plan states the scope of this accident's structure inspection is total 160 M section of port structure from pier 5# to pier 10 of berth 1#, specific inspecting items consist of port main structure over water component appearance condition inspection, port foundation under water feeling inspection, concrete crack depth of structure above component inspection by ultrasound, the degree of inclination inspecting of pier, the degree of inclination inspecting of caisson, relative horizontal displacement of pier and connection bridge cope line measuring, relative vertical displacement of pier and connection bridge top surface measuring, components of structure joints misplacement measuring, petroleum pipeline inspection, accessories of port inspection, estimation of influence on operational aspect of port structure caused by the accident, estimation of influence on safety of port structure caused by the accident, repairing and reinforcing suggestion. The inspection plan gives a quotation RMB645,964 after inspecting quantities, measuring methods and in details.

On July 31, 2012, the Plaintiff signs with Gang Wan Company on the contract named Yue Hai (Fan Yu) Petrochemicals Storage Transportation Development Co., Ltd. Port "7/24"detection service of port structure, agree that the Plaintiff Yue Hai Company entrusts Gang Wan Company to do marine accident inspection of port structure involved, technology service consist of 13 items, namely port main structure over water component appearance condition inspection, port foundation under water feeling inspection, concrete crack depth of structure above component inspection by ultrasound, the degree of inclination inspecting of pier, the degree of inclination inspecting of caisson, relative horizontal displacement of pier and connection bridge cope line measuring, relative vertical displacement of pier and connection bridge top surface measuring, components of structure joints misplacement measuring, petroleum pipeline inspection, accessories of port inspection, estimation on influence of port structure operations caused by the accident, estimation on influence of port structure safety caused by the accident, repairing and reinforcing suggestion, technology service cost is RMB600,000. The Plaintiff pays Gang Wan Company for technology service costs RMB300,000, RMB200,000, RMB100,000 on August 2, August 10, August 22, 2012 respectively. The evaluating report affirms this cost.

The Defendant alleged that the contents and scope of inspecting plan were about the specific damage condition of berth 1# of this port and evaluate the influence of accident involved on operation and safety of port structure, it is reasonable for handling this accident, but the quotation of inspecting plan is too high, after High-level Public Evaluation Company checks, the reasonable cost is RMB286,200. Staff of High-level Public Evaluation Company stated that, the sum of RMB286,200 is based on the opinion of Shanghai Zhong Jiu Engineer Inspection Co., Ltd. (hereinafter referred to Zhong Jiu Company) about Gang Wan Company's inspecting plan, but Zhong Jiu Company checks the price based on written material, does not appoint individual to accident site.

On August 28, 2012, the Plaintiff made a supplemental agreement with Gang Wan Company named "Yue Hai (Fan Yu) Petrochemicals Storage Transportation Development Co., Ltd. Port '7/24'detection service of port structure agreement", agreed that in order to know about how the accident influence structure from pier 5# to pier 10#, the Plaintiff entrusts Gang Wan Company again to inspect the structure from pier 1# to pier 4# according to the previous inspection taken from pier 5# to pier 10# of berth 1 of this port based on previous technology service contract and inspecting report, items inspected consist five items, namely port main structure over water component appearance condition inspection, port foundation under water feeling inspection, the degree of inclination inspecting of pier, relative horizontal displacement of pier and connection bridge cope line measuring, relative vertical displacement of pier and connection bridge top surface measuring, and the inspecting cost is RMB98,000, after finishing inspection on the site, the result is combined with inspection result of pier 5# to pier 10#, forming the accident inspection report of berth 1# of the port. The Plaintiff pays Gang Wan Company for the supplemental inspection cost RMB98,000 on September 11, 2012. Public evaluation report revealed that pier 1# to pier 4# was not collided by vessel, nor obvious sign of damage, this inspection cost does not belong to the scope of this accident, shall not be recognized to be one of damage loss insured.

The Defendant held, the first inspection has specified the extent and scope of damage, it is unreasonable to do the supplemental inspection from pier 1# to pier 4#, which is beyond the damaged part, so the Plaintiff, Yue Hai Company shall afford the inspecting cost himself.

Gang Wan Company issued the port structure test report on August 26, 2012 after he finished the entrusted work. The report sets out the test findings as follows: 1. there are more cracks of non-durability in surface and stringer of ferry-bridge 7#, 8#; pier 5#, 6#, 8# and 10# each has one place of concrete peeling; ferry-bridge 7#'s edge and junction disconnected; other piers and ferry-bridges have no cracks of non-durability due to the accident; 2. the junction of cylinder below pier 8# and river bank has a slight shift; body of 9# cylinder barrel has scratch, cylinder sea front toe front coastal bed has been found one riverbed cutting phenomena, river bed stones have a displacement, another cylinder below the pier looks good; 3. ferry-bridge 7#, 8# longitudinal beams' crack depth value of the sampling is greater than the design value.

Sampling of surface crack depth value is greater than the ferry-bridge 8# pavement thickness design value; 4. the inclination of pier 8# is -16.3 per thousand percent and the inclination of pier 9# is -67.3 per thousand percent. They are both greater than 5 per thousand percent and do not meet regulatory requirements. The inclination of other piers is less than 5 per thousand percent, so meet regulatory requirements; 5. The inclination of the cylinder below 8# pier and 9# pier is -18.6 per thousand percent and -68.9 per thousand percent respectively, they are both greater than 4 per thousand percent and do not meet regulatory requirements. The inclination of the cylinder of the other piers is all not greater than 4 per thousand percent and meet regulatory requirements; 6. the flatness deviations of the measurement point of the pier 8# are respectively -338 mm and -371 mm, the flatness deviation of the measurement point of the 8# are -462 mm and -744 mm respectively, the flatness deviation of the measurement point of the pier 9# are -1,068 mm and -1,054 mm respectively. Pier 8#, ferry-bridge 8#, pier 9# straightness has large deviation; 7. ferry-bridge 7#, pier 8#, ferry-bridge 8#, pier 9#, ferry-bridge 9#'s height and design elevation have large deviation, maximum of positive deviation is 345.9 mm, the maximum of negative deviation is -338.0 mm; Same section along the height has large difference before and after, maximum positive deviation is 328.4 mm, the maximum negative deviation is -169.2 mm; 8. the deformation of structural joint between ferry-bridge 7#,8# ferry-bridge and piers is large, structural joint dislocation largest value is 37 cm, the maximum value of seam width is 38 cm and the maximum height is 21 cm; 9. pipelines look as usual, joint position does not crack and fracture and dislocation; 10. pier 5# is lack of bollards, other pier bollard has fine appearance; the rubber fender on the left side of the pier 5# cracked, the rubber fender under pier deformed, other fenders look good; the curb between pier 5# and pier 7# have massive broken, bars are exposed and broken; steel platform creates significant lateral and vertical deformation; 11. pier 8#, 9#, ferry-bridge 7#, 8#, 9# are largely affected by the accident, security and usability were considered D-level; damage to the pier 7# does not influence the safety of its structure; pier 1#-6#, 6A#, 7#, 10#, ferry-bridge 1#-6#, ferry-bridge 6A# are affected small by the accident, safety and usability were considered B-level.

Test report, according to results of test, combined with actual facts of the port, made recommendations of reinforcement as follows: 1. to deal with the foundation of pier 5# mooring bollard, and then install the same specification bollard; 2. using polymer mortar to repair concrete peeling position of pier 5# and pier 6# and pier 10#; 3. chipping damage concrete in pier 5#, ferry-bridge 5#, pier 6#, ferry-bridge 6#, pier 6A#, ferry-bridge 6A# and pier 7#'s kerbs, repairing welding steel of the reinforcement fracture location, and using polymer mortar to repair kerb; 4. dismantling and replacing of the ferry-bridge 7#, 8# and 9#; force analysis and accounting for the pier 8# and pier 9# will be made by design intelligence units, combined with using conditions of port, the actual situation on the site, studying the repairing method of the pier 8# and pier 9# in order to determine final repairing plan of pier 8# and pier 9#. Gang Wan Company is an engineering testing institution with A-qualification structure engineering in water transport, and holds a measurement certificate.

3. Consultation service cost

On August 14, 2012, the Plaintiff Yue Hai Company signs the contract of consultation service with Guangzhou Shi Le Maritime Consultation Co., Ltd. (hereinafter referred to Shi Le Company), agree that Shi Le Company supplies consultation service related to evaluation of repairing port involved, scope of consultation service includes but not limits to invite exports to appraise putting the berth undamaged back into work, organize appraising meetings to appraise projects related to repairing (Shi Le Company has no obligation to issue reports, nor the consultation cost in this contract includes consultation cost of evaluation), Shi Le Company affords the consultation cost of related exports, meeting place cost, dinner cost, the Plaintiff, Yue Hai Company pays Shi Le Company for consultation cost RMB108,000, RMB33,000 paid within three months after putting the berth undamaged back into work, the remaining paid within three months after supplying all of consultation service aforementioned. Shi Le Company issues an invoice RMB33,000 on August 21, 2013, the Plaintiff, Yue Hai Company pays Shi Le Company RMB33,000 by bank transfer on August 30, 2013. Shi Le Company issues an invoice RMB75,000 on March 17, 2014, the Plaintiff, Yue Hai Company pays Shi Le Company RMB75,000 in cash, Shi Le Company issues a collection receipt on November 14, 2014.

After finishing the entrusted work, Shi Le Company issues the special report of marine accident consultation service about berth 1# in Yue Hai Xiao Hu Petrochemical Bas on November 12, 2014. All steps of appraising meetings stated in the special report and service of which supplied by Shi Le Company are as following:

1. The first meeting is an expert appraising meeting about the special safety evaluating report on resuming dangerous cargo port operation of pier 1# -pier 7#, on September 20, 2012, in Lan Hai Building, notify party of meeting is Guangzhou Harbor Authority, and contents of the meeting are eight appraising reports exports called the special safety evaluating report on resuming dangerous cargo port operation of pier 1# -pier 7# of berth 1# of Yue Hai (Fan Yu) Petrochemicals Storage Transportation Development Co., Ltd., etc.
2. The second meeting is an expert appraising meeting about port structure repairing project design plan, on December 4, 2012, in Hai LI Garden Hotel, notice party of meeting is Guangzhou Harbor Authority, the appointed party of meeting is the Plaintiff, Yue Hai Company, and contents of the meeting is an export appraisal on Yue Hai (Fan Yu) Petrochemicals Storage Transportation Development Co., Ltd. Yue Hai Xiao Hu Petrochemical Base port 1# structure repairing project design plan.
3. The third meeting is an export appraising meeting about port construction drawing design, on January 23, 2013, in Jiang Wan Hotel, notice party of

meeting is Guangzhou Harbor Authority, the appointed party of meeting affairs is the Plaintiff, Yue Hai Company, and contents of the meeting is an export appraisal on Yue Hai (Fan Yu) Petrochemicals Storage Transportation Development Co., Ltd. Yue Hai Xiao Hu Petrochemical Base port 1# construction drawing design.
4. The fourth meeting is an appraising meeting about the navigation safety report of repairing project of port after marine accident, on March 21, 2013, in Xiang Jiang Hotel, notice party of meeting is Guangzhou Maritime Safety Administration, the appointed party of meeting affairs is Guangzhou Jia Wen Above Water Engineer Technology Service Co., Ltd.(hereinafter referred to Jia Wen Company), and contents of the meeting is to check the navigation safety report of repairing project of Xiao Hu Petrochemical Base port 1# after marine accident.
5. The fifth meeting is an appraising meeting about the navigation safety checking conference of repairing project of port after marine accident, on June 27, 2014, in Xiang Jiang Hotel, notify party of meeting is Guangzhou Maritime Safety Administration, the appointed party of meeting affairs is Jia Wen Company, and content of the meeting is the navigation safety checking of repairing project of port after marine accident of Yue Hai (Fan Yu) Petrochemicals Storage Transportation Development Co., Ltd. Yue Hai Xiao Hu Petrochemical Base port 1#.
6. The sixth meeting is an appraising meeting about port structure repairing project after marine accident acceptance check conference, in September 10, 2014, in Guangzhou Nan Sha Ao Yuan Yang Sheng Hotel, notice party of meeting is the Plaintiff, Yue Hai Company, the appointed party of meeting affairs is the Plaintiff, Yue Hai Company, content of the meeting is structure repairing project acceptance check of Yue Hai (Fan Yu) Petrochemicals Storage Transportation Development Co., Ltd. Yue Hai Xiao Hu Petrochemical Base port 1#.

The Defendant alleged according to the contract between the Plaintiff, Yue Hai Company and Shi Le Company aforementioned, Shi Le Company affords the consultation cost of related exports, meeting place cost, dinner cost, in the condition that the Plaintiff, Yue Hai Company does not supply any proof to certify Shi Le Company has paid costs above, consultation cost claimed by the Plaintiff, Yue Hai Company will not to be recognized. To say the least, among six meetings above, meeting affairs cost of meeting two, three, six shall be afforded by the Plaintiff, Yue Hai Company dependently, there is eight owners in meeting one totally, they shall share the cost, costs of meeting four, five shall be afforded by Jia Wen Company, the appointed party of meeting affairs and report writing party. In addition, the Plaintiff Yue Hai Company has not submitted the payment instrument RMB75,000, that the Plaintiff Yue Hai Company has paid the bill or not actually is unclear.

In addition, according to the contract of the navigation safety evaluation of repairing project of Yue Hai Xiao Hu Petrochemical Base port 1#, the Plaintiff, Yue Hai Company entrusts Jia Wen Company to write the navigation safety evaluation report of repairing project of Yue Hai Xiao Hu Petrochemical Base port 1#, Jia Wen

Company shall finish draft for approval of navigation safety evaluation report before January 10, 2013, and make it into electronic edition for appraisal conference use of maritime Safety Administration, the lump sum of writing the navigation safety evaluation report and exports appraising meeting is RMB130,000, lump sum of meeting affairs is just limited to appraising meetings opening in Guang Dong Province, if beyond Guang Dong, charges of meeting affairs shall be negotiated. The Plaintiff, Yue Hai Company pays Jia Wen Company RMB130,000 on April 15, 2013.

According to the contract of the navigation safety evaluation report of repairing project of Yue Hai Xiao Hu Petrochemical Base port 1# after marine accident signed between the Plaintiff Yue Hai Company and Jia Wen Company, the Plaintiff Yue Hai Company entrusts Jia Wen Company to write the navigation safety evaluation report of repairing project of Yue Hai Xiao Hu Petrochemical Base port 1# structure after marine accident, Jia Wen Company finishes draft for approval of navigation safety evaluation report within ten days after receiving complete materials, and makes it into electronic edition for appraisal conference use of maritime Safety Administration, the lump sum of total meeting affairs of writing navigation safety evaluation report and navigation safety exports checking conference is RMB130,000. The Plaintiff Yue Hai Company pays Jia Wen Company RMB130,000 on July 23, 2014.

7. Cost of port structure repairing design

    On August 31, 2012, the Plaintiff Yue Hai Company signs a contract with Zhong Jiao fourth Hang WU Engineer Survey Design Institute Co., Ltd. (hereinafter referred to Zhong Jiao Design Institute), named Yue Hai Xiao Hu Petrochemical Base berth 1# berthing capacity reasoning and construction design of repairing project, agrees that the Plaintiff Yue Hai Company entrusts Zhong Jiao Design Institute finish Yue Hai Xiao Hu Petrochemical Base berth 1# berthing capacity reasoning and construction design of repairing project, main work includes accounting report of berthing capacity of berth 1# pier 1#-7#,repairing plan of berth # damage part (almost pier 8#, pier 9#, ferry bridge 8#-9#, ferry bridge 7#-8#), construction drawing design of berth # damage part (almost pier 8#, pier 9#, ferry bridge 8#-9#, ferry bridge 7#-8#); the negotiating design price between two parties is RMB750,000, based on and calculating upon local and national related laws and regulations, if no, two parties will negotiate; the Plaintiff Yue Hai Company will pay Zhong Jiao Design Institute RMB200,000 within seven working days after receiving the port berthing capacity amounting report, will pay RMB250,000 within seven working days after receiving repairing plan, will pay RMB300,000 within seven working days after receiving construction drawing designing paper. The Plaintiff Yue Hai Company pays RMB200,000 on September 19, 2012, pays RMB250,000 on November 13, pays RMB300,000 on July 16, 2013. Public evaluating report affirms this cost.

After finishing the entrusted work, Zhong Jiao Design Institute issues Yue Hai (Fan Yu) Petrochemicals Storage Transportation Development Co., Ltd. Yue Hai Xiao Hu Petrochemical Base port 1# berthing capacity amounting report, the marine accident repairing project plan instruction of Yue Hai (Fan Yu) Petrochemicals Storage Transportation Development Co., Ltd. Yue Hai Xiao Hu Petrochemical Base port 1#, the construction drawing design instruction of the marine accident repairing project of Yue Hai (Fan Yu) Petrochemicals Storage Transportation Development Co., Ltd. Yue Hai Xiao Hu Petrochemical Base port 1#. Zhong Jiao Design Institute is an engineer design institute, which is comprehensive qualification in Class A of engineer design and engineer survey comprehensive class A, and has engineer consultation institute certificate.

Main conclusions of berthing capacity accounting report of port 1# consist of: (1) 224-m-long port structure from pier 1# to pier 7# will be used to tie and stay vessels, length of berth is able to satisfy oil ship of 30,000 tons class or chemical ship of 30,000 tons class (ship type in current guide regulations) and the largest vessel arriving at port actually to call at, the largest vessel shall not exceed 188 m; (2) current soft pipe technology settings can be adapted to requirements of discharge safety and uploading and discharge operations for oil ship of 30,000 tons class or chemical ship of 30,000 tons class; (3) after replacing fender and mooring bollard of pier 5#, pier 1#-7# of port structure are able to satisfy requirements of oil ship of 30,000 tons class or chemical ship of 30,000 tons class to tie and call at safely during ordinary operation.

Instructions of plan port 1# repairing project after marine accident states contents of structure repairing as following, accident of port being collided mainly causes structure damage, technology of port, water supply and drainage, fire-fighting pipeline and electrical equipment, controlling system are in good condition, therefore contents of structure repairing this time mainly is structure of pier 8#, pier 9#, ferry bridge 7#, ferry bridge 8#, ferry bridge 9#. When structure is repaired, it needs to temporarily remove devices like process pipeline of structure creature of ferry-bridge 7# and pier 8#, lay process pipeline again after finishing repairing structure. Removing pipeline will be arranged by its owner instead be included in repairing plan work. The repairing project mainly does such work, removing and remaking and reinstalling ferry bridge 7#, 8#, removing and re-cast-in site pier 8#, 9#, meanwhile, polishing, consolidating, leveling machine tools in pier 8#, 9# again. Replace mooring bollards of pier 8#, 9#, replace and reinstall fenders of pier 8#, 9#. Reuse circular caisson of under-part of pier 8#, 9# and ferry-bridge 9#.

Repairing plan shall repair according to original design structure in principle, on the assumption of satisfaction of safety and usability, try to be economic, construction performance shall be simply and convenient. Repairing design plan is as follows in brief:

1. Pier 8#, pier 9# and foundations thereof. Piers and caissons are in severe inclined condition, fundamental foundations of throw stone are damaged thereof, it is prior for repairing plan to replace pier, draw backfill sand inside caisson out, lift caisson, single caisson weights about 380 tons net, so it is good

for 500-ton crane ship to lift. Fill and temp foundations of throw stone after lifting caisson, replace original caisson after checking foundations, pour steel concrete pier once again. Reuse original prefabricated caisson structure, do not damage original prefabricated caisson structure when removing piers, so given taking machine-cutting and piece-lift method to remove pier. It is required to undergo underwater and clean coverings before lifting caisson away.
2. Ferry-bridge 7#, 8#, 9#. There are many cracks on surface layer and longer-on of ferry-bridge 7#, 8#, cracks are new, and all of them are nondurable, depth value of cracks of longer-on spot checked is bigger than protecting layer depth design value, depth value of cracks of surface layer of ferry-bridge spot checked is bigger than protecting layer depth design value, therefore ferry bridge 7#, ferry bridge 8# cannot be reused, consider remove and abandon them, then prefabricate longer-on, pouring surface layer of ferry bridge 7#,8# again. As for the condition that ferry bridge 9# only inclines, has no cracks and does not influence structure in force, consider it can be reused, ferry bridge 9# is made of one longer-on, lift it away to place first, reinstall ferry bridge 9# after repairing pier.
3. To prevent apparent small cracks on caisson's surface caused by port be collided, it will influence caisson's durability, it is needed to do anti-corrosion coating handling to lateral wall of caisson.
4. To sweep sea after finishing construction.
5. To repair concrete kerb damaged according to original structure, the damaged mooring bollard of pier 5# is needed to be replaced. There is pipeline in ferry bridge 7#, pier 8#, they needed to be replaced and installed temporarily when structure is repairing, until now, pipeline thereof have been replaced by owner himself, owner will arrange laying process pipeline work once again after finishing structure repairing. When construction is going on, the constructing party shall try his best to watch out port's safety, if it is needed to avoid port loading and discharge operation, it is better to coordinate mutual relationship to insure the safety of construction and port loading and discharge operation, period of construction is about five months tentatively estimating. The estimated total budget of project is RMB8,997,900, consisting of engineering cost RMB6,138,000, the other cost RMB2,431,400 and reserving cost RMB428,500.

The construction drawing design instruction of the marine accident repairing project of port 1# specifies requirements of every constructive technology, it is needed to do anti-corrosion coating handling to lateral wall of caisson 8#,9#, service life of anticorrosion is 20 years, coating system shall be subject to concrete coating regulations provided in (JTJ275-2000) 7.1 section in sea port project concrete structure anticorrosion technology regulations; all mental accessories supplied by rubber fender factory shall be adapted to sea circumstances, all is needed to satisfy anticorrosion requirements, life of anticorrosion protection shall be more than ten years; it is required to do rigid seabed-sweeping after finishing construction; two permanent observing points will be set up in this repairing project section to regularly observe port distortion; permanent observing points shall subject to measuring related regulations, be set in the front of port, work of burying and subsequent period of observation has been done during construction by related entity entrusted by owners. The construction drawing design instruction points out when evaluating navigation safety, that removing and pouring pier 8#, 9#, prefabricating and reinstalling ferry bridge 7#,8#, reinstalling 9#, lifting and reinstalling caissons are main contents of port repairing project constructing work; construction of lifting and reinstalling ferry bridge and caissons are the important construction item of this repairing project, according to common construction experience of gravity type caisson, the constructive party has rich experience in this operation and it is simple, and this work will occupying limited water area, mainly around piers, since construction will occupy little water area, it will not influence navigation circumstances of channel; since construction area is around port, construction operation will influence relatively little of the navigation safety in outer channel; because original foundation is required to be rebuilt for repairing this port, foundation of pier, ferry bridge and accessories over part also, construction area is narrow, constructive vessels have difficulty to do work on the site, so most of construction items will be performed in back of port, area influenced is just limited to northern port, and has little influence to navigation in Guangzhou Petrochemical port and channels area; the total construction quantities are small in port repairing operation, it may use surface water performing vessels when repairing foundation underwater, but construction quantities are small, quantities and scale of vessels used are little too, generally construction performance will have little influence to navigational circumstances.

The Defendant argued that, engineering design above is needed, but cost is unreasonable, according to project survey design charge management regulations, the reasonable cost is RMB132,193.50 calculated on budget standard RMB5,000,000 and some adjust factors.

8. Construction cost of port structure repairing project
   According to the structure detection and construction design aforementioned, the Plaintiff Yue Hai Company begins bidding on port marine accident repairing project in January 2013. the main repairing contents stated in the tender documents stated in the port 1# marine accident repairing project plan instructions and contents stated in the port 1# marine accident repairing project construction drawing design instruction, also includes dredging project of harbor pool and turning section of berth 1#, 5# berth, the deadline of bidding is on February 17, 2013. Yue Hai Company received 3 formal bidding documents after he issues the bidding documents. The quotation of Guang Dong Hang Da Engineering Co., Ltd. (hereinafter referred to as Hang Da Company) is RMB7,805 7,805,616.37, including project cost of harbor dredging RMB1,749,880, specific for dredging mud of 79,540 cubic meters, per cubic meter at RMB22. The quotation of Zhong Jiao Fourth Navigation Bureau the Second Engineering Co., Ltd. is RMB8,672,773, including project cost of harbor dredging RMB2,123,900, specific for dredging mud of 84,956 cubic meters, per cubic meter price at RMB25. The quotation of Zhong Hai Engineering Zong Ju is

RMB8,142,718.50, including project cost of harbor dredging RMB1,924,72, specific for dredging mud of 78,560 cubic meters, per cubic meter at RMB24.5. The Defendant's attorney, before the deadline, submits the bidding documents (which has not been stamped with the company seal) of the Guang Dong Dian Bai Construction Group Co., Ltd. (hereinafter referred to as Dian Bai Company). The quotation of Dian Bai Company is RMB7,053,400, including project cost of harbor dredging RMB2,070,000, specific for dredging mud of 90,000 cubic meters, per cubic meter at RMB23. Because Dian Bai's bidding documents do not meet the requirements, the Plaintiff Yue Hai Company does not accept them. After evaluation of bid, the Plaintiff Yue Hai Company accepts Hang Da Company as the winning bidder. After further negotiation between the Plaintiff Yue Hai Company and Hang Da Company, they determine the final contract price is RMB7,600,000. The project quotation proposal (the confirmed price after negotiations) signed between the Plaintiff Yue Hai Company and Hang Da Company, states costs of all project items, including harbor dredging and rigid seabed-sweeping of 79,540 cubic meters, per cubic meter at RMB22, a total of RMB1,749,880. About the concrete construction quantities of harbor dredging and seabed-sweeping, according to the statistical graph of dredging quantities of harbor pool and turning section in Yue Hai Xiao Hu Petrochemical port issued by Hang Da Company, berth 1# turning area is 45,966.30 square meters, dredges for 27,870.90 cubic meters; berth 1# harbor pool area is of 12,975.10 square meters, dredges for 7,591.95 cubic meters; berth 5# harbor pool area is of 2,728.50 square meters, dredges for 3,696.60 cubic meters; berth 5# turning area is of 5,693.90 square meters, dredges for 13,374.75 cubic meters; excavation area of 834.97 square meters of piers 8# and 9# is needed for sea measurement construction, the excavation volume is of 834.97 cubic meters; the excavation area of 2,728.50 square meters of piers 8# and 9# is needed for bank measurement construction, Project volume is of 17,735.25 cubic meters; bank measured construction of piers 8# and 9# needs to dig slope in the amount of 7,069.88 cubic meters; construction quantities of dredging and rigid bed-sweeping around piers 8# and 9# is of 1,365.70 cubic meters; the total construction quantities of eight dredging projects above is 79,540 cubic meters.

On February 22, 2013, the Plaintiff Yue Hai Company and Hang Da Company signed construction contract named Yue Hai (Fan Yu) Petrochemicals Storage Transportation Development Co., Ltd. Yue Hai Xiao Hu Petrochemical Base port 1# marine accident repairing project, agreed the Plaintiff Yue Hai Company entrusts Hang Da Company to complete Xiao Hu Petrochemical Base port berth1# marine accident repairing project, contents thereof are mainly based on construction drawing (include design modification), consist of (1) disassembly and assembly three oil-pipe walls; (2) remove, prefabricate and reinstall ferry-bridge 7#, 8#; (3) remove and report pier 8#, 9#; (4) polish, compact and level beddings of pier 8#, 9#; (5) replace mooring bollard of pier 8#, 9#, replace and reinstall all fenders of 9#, 8# to reuse; (6) remove and reinstall circular caissons in lower part of the original pier 8#, 9# and ferry-bridge 9#; (7) dredge harbor pool and turning section of port

1#,5#, harbor pool of port 1# in -12 m, turning section in -11.5 m, turning section of port 5# in -6 m, -0.5 m in super deep, super wide processed according to relevant regulations; and (8) increase caisson anti-corrosion of 8#, 9# according to the new construction drawings, life of steel component anti-corrosion is 10 years, increase 1 m wide of throwing stone foundation bed around pier 8# and 9#; contract construction duration is of five months, the project starts from the date of getting construction work permit above water and under water certificate issued by the port supervision and construction permit certificate approved by harbor bureau; total lump sum of this project is RMB7,600,000, including cost of construction quantities increased of caisson 8#, 9# anti-corrosion, changing anti-corrosion life of rubber fender metal accessories from 8 to 10 years and increasing 1 m throwing stones in the front of caissons etc., adjusting factors of contract price includes only changing of engineering (design), other than any factor, cost of construction quantities of changing of engineering (Design) will not be adjusted within the contract price plus or minus 2%, part beyond plus or minus 2% of cost of construction quantities will be calculated according to actual amount when completion of clearing; 20% of project payment will be paid within seven days after the contract is signed, monthly payment will be paid according to 85% of the actual completion of project amount, the advance payment for project will be deducted from the monthly payment three times, 95% of the contract amount will be paid after complication and project acceptance qualified for this project, the left 5% will be the project quality guarantee deposit, the quality guarantee life is twelve months, dredging project has no warranty terms of repairing; contractor's work includes determining benchmark and coordinate control points, to submit to opposite contractor to inspect on the site in written. On May 15, 2014, a settlement confirmation is signed among the Plaintiff, Yue Hai Company, Hang Da Company and the supervising entity, Guangzhou Hai Jian Engineering consultation Co., Ltd. (formerly known as Guangzhou Hai Jian Engineering Supervision Company, hereinafter referred to as Hai Jian Company), confirms the total contract price of complement is RMB7,600,000, plus the increased cost of avoiding typhoon RMB40,000, the total settlement price is RMB7,640,000. The Plaintiff, Yue Hai Company pays Hang Da Company for payment against construction RMB7,540,000 during the period from April 7, 2013 to June 11, 2015, specifically RMB1,520,000 on April 7, 2013, RMB1,496,835 on August 28, RMB321,356.21 on November 27, RMB200,000 on December 10, RMB800,000 on December 25, RMB300,000 on January 22, 2014, RMB200,000 on January 28, RMB200,000 on February 20, RMB279,107.70 on March 10, RMB200,000 on March 26, RMB200,000 on April 15, RMB200,000 on May 5, RMB400,000 on May 21, RMB200,000 on July 8, RMB200,000 on July 30, RMB250,000 on August 21, RMB150,000 on September 24, RMB140,701.09 on October 21, RMB282,000 on June 11, 2015.

Public evaluation report held that, the scope of harbor pool dredging and rigid bed-sweeping is too large, and its cost is unreasonable, the cost of harbor pool dredging and rigid bed-sweeping shall be adjusted into RMB612,458, other project repairing cost and expenses of avoiding typhoon will be recognized.

The Defendant held that, the bidding time decided by the Plaintiff, Yue Hai Company is not consistent with regulation in the bidding law of the People's Republic of China, the bidding procedure is unreasonable. The construction contents include increased construction quantities unrelated with this accident like dredging harbor pool and turning section of port 1#, 5#, increasing caisson anti-corrosion of 8#, 9#, changing life of steel component anti-corrosion from 8 to 10 years, increasing 1 m wide of throwing stone foundation bed in the front of caisson, cost related above shall be afforded by the Plaintiff Yue Hai Company himself. The quotation price of Dian Bai Company is RMB7,053,400 of port 1# marine accident repairing project, excluding harbor pool dredging cost RMB2,070,000, construction cost of port 1# marine accident structure repairing project is RMB4,983,400. The reasonable construction cost of port 1# marine accident structure repairing project involved is RMB4,983,400, the Defendant will affirm it.

9. Project cost consultation cost

    The Plaintiff Yue Hai Company signs a construction project cost consultation contract of Yue Hai (Fan Yu) Petrochemicals Storage Transportation Development Co., Ltd. Yue Hai Xiao Hu Petrochemical Base port 1# marine accident structure repairing project with Guangzhou Jian Hai Engineering Supervision consultation Co., Ltd. (hereinafter referred to as Jian Hai Company) on February 6, 2013, agree that Jian Hai Company supplies the service of construction project budget of project costs to the Plaintiff Yue Hai Company, consultation cost is RMB20,000, the Plaintiff Yue Hai Company pays for this once clearly when Jian Hai Company submits the documents of consultation results. The Plaintiff Yue Hai Company pays for Consultation service cost RMB20,000 on March 26, 2013. the public evaluating report affirms this cost.

After finishing the entrusted work, Jian Hai Company issues a budget book of Yue Hai (Fan Yu) Petrochemicals Storage Transportation Development Co., Ltd. Yue Hai Xiao Hu Petrochemical Base port 1# marine accident structure repairing project and a budget book of Yue Hai (Fan Yu) Petrochemicals Storage Transportation Development Co., Ltd. port 1# pipeline repairing project after "7*24" accident respectively on January 29, 2013 and on March 8, held that total project cost of marine accident repairing project is RMB1,171,661.19, the budget price of pipeline repairing project is RMB1,261,367.21.

The Defendant held port berth 1# repairing project has been in the bidding procedure when the contract is signed, so it has no need to consultation project cost, what's more, port pipeline rebuilt project included in consultation items has no relation with accident, the cost of this item shall be afforded by The Plaintiff, Yue Hai Company himself. As for this, the Plaintiff, Yue Hai Company alleged the budget of project cost is required by related administration department when performing report of construction.

10. Measuring cost of controlling points

    On March 26, 2013, the Plaintiff Yue Hai Company signs a project measurement agreement with Guangzhou Ying Yi Mapping Technology Co., Ltd.

(hereinafter referred to as Ying Yi Company), agreed that the Plaintiff, Yue Hai Company entrusts Ying Yi Company to measure three controlling points to be used for project construction, each price at RMB3,512, the total cost is RMB1,536, Ying Yi Company submits two measuring materials within ten working days after the Plaintiff Yue Hai Company supplies related materials, the Plaintiff Yue Hai Company shall pay off by one time within seven days after Ying Yi Company submits qualified related measuring materials to him. the Plaintiff Yue Hai Company pays for measuring cost RMB10,536. the public evaluation affirms this cost.

The Defendant held that, main repairing contents of subsection seven of section two in bidding book about Yue Hai (Fan Yu) Petrochemicals Storage Transportation Development Co., Ltd. Yue Hai Xiao Hu Petrochemical Base port 1# marine accident repairing structure project marks the bidding price includes every inspection cost, and costs of handling underwater construction work permitting certificate and service charges of other departments etc. the construction contract of marine accident repairing structure project has been signed when the Plaintiff Yue Hai Company signs a project measurement agreement with Ying Yi Company, this operation work of measuring project as preparation before construction shall be included in construction contract, this cost shall be afforded by the winning bidder of repairing project. To say the least, the Plaintiff Yue Hai Company must set permanent surveying points when building port, because the rebuilding is caused by the Plaintiff Yue Hai Company failing to maintain, this cost shall be afforded by himself, too.

11. Supplemental supervising cost

    On February 25, 2013, the Plaintiff, Yue Hai Company signs a contract of entrusted supervising construction project with Hai Jian Company, agree that Hai Jian Company supplies supervision service of Yue Hai (Fan Yu) Petrochemicals Storage Transportation Development Co., Ltd. Yue Hai Xiao Hu Petrochemical Base port 1# marine accident repairing structure project, period of supervision service is 150 calendar days, from the day the Plaintiff, Yue Hai Company notices him to come into site to the day of finishing the project settlements and ending of warranty period, reward of contract supervision is RMB165,000, the Final settlement supervision fees will be charged downward float 20% calculating by the development and reform price No.[2007]670, unless the delay is caused by supervisor, the Plaintiff Yue Hai Company agrees to pay for reward of supervision service additionally according to the amount of payment of contract payment divided by days of the supervision service, and multiplied by the additional working days. the Plaintiff, Yue Hai Company pays respectively on March 26, 2013, June 8, July 25, October 16, January 8, 2014 RMB49,500, RMB21,450, RMB21,450, RMB42,900 and RMB21,450.

On April 19, 2013, the Plaintiff Yue Hai Company gives notice of coming into the site to Hai Jian Company in written. According to the supervision diaries made by Hai Jian Company, Hai Jian Company on the same day comes into the site to supervise.

On December 25, 2013, the Plaintiff Yue Hai Company signs supplemental item supervision agreement of Yue Hai Xiao Hu Petrochemical Base port 1# marine accident structure repairing project with Hai Jian Company, agree that service of supervision will be delayed, continuing from September 20, 2013 to the project finished to be accepted, according to the cost of continuing supervision in the entrusting supervision contract of the construction project, the reward of extension of the supervision will be the working days of the supervision multiplied by RMB1100, the supervision charges will be paid one time a month, the monthly payment will be RMB3,000. The Plaintiff Yue Hai Company pays Hai Jian Company for reward of extended supervision RMB99,000. The public evaluation report affirms this cost.

On December 26, 2013, construction entity, Hang Da Company submits Project postponed report confirmation to the Plaintiff Yue Hai Company and Hai Jian Company, stating that the planning construction period in the contract is five months, starting date is on May 18, 2013, subject to the date of Guangzhou Maritime Bureau issuing the activities under and above water permitting certificate, the planning completion date is on October 19, 2013, but the actual completion date is on December 25, 2013, the project duration delays for a total of 67 days; factors of project duration postponed include the influence of typhoon for 29 days, rain and fog weather for 17 days, safety inspection by Harbor Survey and Port Affairs Authority for 10 days, production operation of the construction units for 10 day.

The Defendant argued that, according to the urban construction archives named Xiao Hu Petrochemical Base port 1# marine accident structure repairing project construction diaries, which is made by Hang Da Company, the project construction starts from May 25, 2013, for 150 calendar days shall be calculated to November 1, 2013, the actual extension of supervision service starts from November 2, 2013 to the date actual completion on December 25, 2013, it actually postponed for 54 days, expecting urban construction archives of repairing project stating that it stops construction from July 10, 2013 to July 15, 2013 by flood season, and the shutdown, on August 15, 16, September 19–21, affected by the typhoon, other cost of postponing service producing from delaying caused by other reasons of construction party shall be afforded by himself.

As for construction starting date, the Plaintiff Yue Hai Company alleged it is on April 19, 2013, the starting date of construction is stated on May 25, 2013 in urban construction archives of repairing project because activities under and above water permit certificate and construction permit certificate of port structure repairing project have not been gotten at that time, and the starting date is May 2013 stated in project survey acceptance submission.

12. Design and repairing cost of pipeline

   On October 31, 2012, the Plaintiff Yue Hai Company signs a supplemental pipeline removed and pressure test contract of Yue Hai port 1#-5# with Guangzhou Xin Guan Equipment Install and Repair Co., Ltd.(hereinafter referred as Xin Guan Company), agree that the Plaintiff Yue Hai Company entrusts Xin Guan Company to remove and test pressure of pipeline of collided berth 1#, 5#,construction starts from August 1, 2012 to September 8, 2012, Xin Guan Company will supply materials to the construction and do this project himself, the project cost is RMB61,937. After finishing this entrusted work, Xin Guan Company issues a report of pipeline pressure test Yue Hai port 1#, results of pressure test are all as usual. The Plaintiff Yue Hai Company pays Xin Guan Company RMB61,937 on November 23, 2012.

On January 5, 2013, the Plaintiff Yue Hai Company signs a design contract of Yue Hai (Fan Yu) Petrochemicals Storage Transportation Development Co., Ltd. port 1# repairing pipeline project after "7*24" accident with Shenzhen Tian Yang Design Co., Ltd. (hereinafter referred as Tian Yang Company), agree that the Plaintiff Yue Hai Company entrusts Tian Yang Company to do design work of Yue Hai (Fan Yu) Petrochemicals Storage Transportation Development Co., Ltd. port 1# repairing pipeline project after "7*24" accident, the design cost is RMB60,000, contents and scope thereof include: 1. formulate budget estimates of the demolition, installation, pipe rack of pipelines damaged by "7*24" accident and the mounting and dismounting of three sets of oil transfer arm and other equipments etc., and change the original pipe pier laying to pipe rack laying of pipelines on the north side of the port berth 1# (including oil, a common line, fire pipe, steam pipe etc. 18 pipes); 2. the structure design of the pipe rack, the stress check of the wharf is responsible by the original design unit of the port. The Plaintiff Yue Hai Company pays for the design costs RMB20,000 and RMB40,000 respectively on January 31, February 27, 2013.

After finishing the entrusted work, Tian Yang Company issues design drawing paper and budget estimates of project in January 2013, forecasting the project construction cost is RMB1,661,815.83. On March 13, 2013, the design supplemental instructions issued by Tian Yang Company states, original pipeline of port is built and designed in 1995, subject to regulations in that time, but the original pipeline lays in pier along the surface of port, lacking of pipeline intensive, safe escape and fire exits, this repairing design needs to meet the current regulations requirements, according to the provisions of current "fire protection design code of loading and discharging oil port" JTJ237-99 article 5.2.2.4, on the assumption of not changing the original function, pipelines will be changed to overhead laying between port berth 1# ferry-bridge 5# to pier 8.

On April 10, 2013, the Plaintiff Yue Hai Company signs construction contract of Yue Hai (Fan Yu) Petrochemicals Storage Transportation Development Co., Ltd. port 1# repairing pipeline project after "7*24" accident with Sichuan Chemicals Construction Co., Ltd. (hereinafter referred to as Sichuan Chemicals Company), agreed that the Plaintiff Yue Hai Company entrusts Sichuan Chemicals Company to perform construction of Yue Hai (Fan Yu) Petrochemicals Storage Transportation Development Co., Ltd. port 1# repairing pipeline project after "7*24" accident, payment against construction is RMB1,140,000, and will be paid 30% within seven days after contract signature, monthly payment will be paid according to 85% of the actual completion of engineering amount, 95% will be paid after the acceptance of the project and handling settlement of completion, the remaining 5% of the payment against project will be quality guarantee deposit, the guarantee period is for 12 months, the scope of the project includes removal and reinstallation of pipelines, removal and reinstallation of pipeline foundation and sand blasting, corrosion protection, testing and pressure testing of pipeline, construction duration is of 5 month. On May 13, 2014, the Plaintiff Yue Hai Company signs construction settlement book with Sichuan Chemicals Company, the payment against project of settlement is RMB1,140,000. The Plaintiff Yue Hai Company pays Sichuan Chemicals CompanyRMB342,000, RMB200,000, RMB233,200, RMB200,000, RMB107,800 respectively on May 23, 2013, November 19,2013, November 22,2013, July 8, 2014 and July 30,2014.

On April 28, 2013, the Plaintiff Yue Hai Company signs construction contract of port repairing in supplement with Cheng Wei construction team, agree that the Plaintiff Yue Hai Company entrusts Cheng Wei construction team to remove pipelines and repair pipe piers in the construction area, the payment against project is RMB8,943.22. The Plaintiff Yue Hai Company pays Cheng Wei construction team for the payment against project RMB8,943.22.

The public evaluating report affirms cost of design of repairing pipeline RMB60,000 and the payment against project of construction of port repairing RMB8,943.22, as well as the necessary of repairing pipelines project, but held that in the process of repairing pipeline, it shall try to reuse old pipelines to reduce repairing cost, so the cost of repairing construction shall be recognized RMB922,181.77.

The Defendant held that, the inspection report issued by Gang Wan Company states appearance of pipeline is normal, no crack, breakage and dislocation is found in joint position of pipeline. The results of the pipeline pressure test by Xin Guan Company is as usual, the plan instruction of port 1# marine accident repair project issued by Zhong Jiao Design Institute states that when the structure is repaired, it is required to temporarily remove original process pipeline device in structures of ferry-bridge 7#, pier 8, again lay process pipeline after completion of repairing structure, etc., so port pipelines is just required to be removed and reinstalled as original design, no need to design again. Current wharf pipelines are changed from laying in piers into overhead laying, cost of pipeline design and the payment against project of construction of port repairing thereof shall be afforded by the Plaintiff Yue Hai Company himself. Because two Plaintiffs failed to provide evidence to prove removing and installing cost of original process pipeline device in structures of ferry-bridge 7#, pier 8, the Defendant agrees to compensate for related costs of removing and installing construction and materials according to costs of removing and pressure test RMB61,937.

13. Cost of safety assessment after repairing

    On December 2, 2013, the Plaintiff Yue Hai Company signs a technology consultation contract with Guang Dong Jing An Safety Assessment consultation Co., Ltd. (hereinafter referred as Jing An Company), agree that the Plaintiff

Yue Hai Company entrusts Jing An Company to supply technology consultation service of Yue Hai (Fan Yu) Petrochemicals Storage Transportation Development Co., Ltd. safety assessment item of dangerous cargo operation at port, consultation cost is RMB90,000, including the assessment cost of Guangzhou Port Authority, will pay 50% within 5 working days after signing the contract, will pay 50% within 5 working days after the safety evaluation report reviewed by Harbor Affairs Authority and passed. The Plaintiff Yue Hai Company pays RMB45,000 respectively on December 25, 2013 and on July 15, 2014. The public evaluating report affirms this cost.

After finishing the entrusted work, Jing An Company issues a safety assessment report of dangerous cargo operation at port of Yue Hai (Fan Yu) Petrochemicals Storage Transportation Development Co., Ltd. (edition for record). Report states in the preface: according to related regulations provided in safety producing law of the People's Republic of China, harbor law of the People's Republic of China and requirements of Guangzhou Harbor Affairs Authority, after the completion of Yue Hai Xiao Hu Petrochemical Base port 1# marine accident structure repairing project, berth 1# ferry-bridge 7# - ferry-bridge 9# structure section are be put into reuse, berth 1# recovers the port dangerous cargo operation in the length of design and recovering the port dangerous cargo operation of berth 5# shall take the safety assessment, in addition, according to the Plaintiff Yue Hai Company's requirements, port dangerous cargo operation of all loading and discharging berths (berth 1#, 2#, 3#, 4#, 5#) owned by this company shall take special safety assessment. The report is divided into two parts, the first part is the safety assessment of berth 1# and berth 5# port dangerous cargo operation involved in berth 1# marine accident repairing project, assessment of the geographical area is the section from ferry-bridge 7# - ferry-bridge 9# of berth1#, dangerous cargo operation area of berth 1#, 5#, and berthing and leaving waters at the front of berth 1#, 5#, land area in the back of port and dangerous cargo operation area of berth 2#, 3#, 4# are not included; The second part is safety assessment of port dangerous cargo operation of Yue Hai (Fan Yu) Petrochemicals Storage Transportation Development Co., Ltd., the assessing geographical area is loading and discharging area from the front of berth 1#, berth 2#, berth 3#, berth 4#, berth 5# to the roots of ferry-bridge, not including land part at the back of every berth.

The Defendant argued that, because the safety assessment of the port dangerous cargo operations includes the entire port and those not involved in this accident, the Defendant only needs to bear 1/3 of the cost, namely RMB30,000.

14. Cost of handling pipeline emergency

The Plaintiff Yue Hai Company argues, In this case, the accident caused pier 8# and pier 9# to displace and incline, and the T type beam between the two piers may fall into sea at any time, part of pipelines on the surface of the wharf is of displacement and deformation, to avoid causing greater loss and the leakage of materials pollution accident, he immediately starts the emergency plan to rescue and the resumption of production preparation work, producing material cost and operating cost RMB182,182,155.20 totally. The Plaintiff Yue Hai Company submitted cost statistics of processing pipeline, fee schedule of processing port pipeline and some material documents after M.V. "Hai Gang Te 001" collision and damage port, which are made by its own party for this. The public evaluating report does not approve this cost because it is not belonging to the scope of insurance liability.

The Defendant argued that, that the port has been in a state of avoiding typhoon when accident involved occurs, no ship is loading and discharging cargo, materials in pipelines of port has been swept to storage, and the accident did not cause partial process pipelines laying on the surface of wharf in deformation or replacement, reasons of handling emergency stated by the Plaintiff Yue Hai Company does not match actual conditions of damaged port after being collided, so this cost will not be recognize.

15. Operating losses

After accident involved happened, berth 1# stops all operations on July 24, 2012. On September 21, 2012, 224 m long of pier 1#-7# section of berth 1# recovers operation. According to the replying letter made by Guangzhou Harbor Affairs Authority Hai Gang Branch about recovery of port dangerous cargo operation after marine accident of Yue Hai (Fan Yu) Petrochemicals Storage Transportation Development Co., Ltd. berth 1# on October 12, 2012, after 224 m long section of pier1#-7# of berth 1# recovers the operation, the operating range is unchanged, the Plaintiff Yue Hai Company shall arrange necessary test of berthing operation, and gradually make it recover to the maximum berthing ship. On September 10, 2014, port repairing project passes the acceptance.

To prove the operating losses, the Plaintiff Yue Hai Company applies the court to entrust a certifying agency to audit the average net profit of berth 1# 3 months before suffering the accident. The court selects Shenzhen Chai An Partnership Accounting Firm (hereinafter referred to as Chai An Firm) as the certifying agency for the authentication matter aforementioned according to legal procedures, the Plaintiff Yue Hai Company pays Chai An Firm for auditing cost RMB25, 000 on April 4, 2014. After finishing the entrusted work, Chai An Firm issues special audit report on average net profit from April to June in 2012 of Yue Hai (Fan Yu) Petrochemicals Storage Transportation Development Co., Ltd. berth 1# on July 14, 2014, stating that the total revenue of the Plaintiff Yue Hai Company from April to June 2012 is RMB21,768,515.55, total revenue of berth 1# is RMB3,835,189.71, daily average net profit of berth 1# is RMB5,995.95. Because part of berth 1# is in operation and has income, the Plaintiff Yue Hai Company applies the court to entrust a certifying agency to audit the average net profit of berth 1# 5 months before suffering the accident. The court selects Chai An Firm as the certifying agency for the authentication matter aforementioned according to legal procedures, the Plaintiff Yue Hai Company pays Chai An Firm for auditing cost RMB55, 000 on June 4, 2015. After finishing the entrusted work, Chai An Firm issues special audit report on average net profit from July to December in 2012 of Yue Hai (Fan Yu) Petrochemicals Storage Transportation Development Co., Ltd. berth 1# on July 7, 2015, stating that the total revenue of the Plaintiff Yue Hai Company from August to September 2012 is RMB13,928,357.66, total revenue of berth 1# is RMB506,134.46, daily average net profit of berth 1# is RMB740; the total revenue of the Plaintiff Yue Hai Company from October to December 2012 is RMB22,504,411.48, total revenue of berth 1# is RMB4,259,954.73, daily average net profit of berth 1# is RMB5,453.75; in addition, according to the financial information got from auditing the average net profit from July to December 2012, considering influence of land use tax, house property tax and annual double wage on net profit from April to June 2012, daily average net profit of berth 1# from April to June 2012 will be adjusted for RMB5,633.38. The Plaintiff Yue Hai Company claims that daily average net profit loss of 1# berth is RMB6,735.95 (5,995.95 + 740) during 68 days from July 24, 2012 to September 30, 2012, the operating losses is RMB458,458,044.60; day daily average net profit loss of berth 1# during 709 days from October 1, 2012 to September 10, 2014 is RMB542.20 (5,995.95–5,453.75), the operating loss is RMB384,419.80.

The Defendant argued that, the reducing amount of daily average net profit of berth 1# before and after the accident as the basis of operating losses is unreasonable, which the Plaintiff Yue Hai Company bases on, the reducing amount of daily average net profit of entire port shall be the basis of operating losses of the Plaintiff Yue Hai Company. From the perspective of the entire port operating conditions, ships who berth here do not reduce after the accident, the total income does not reduce significantly, nor the Plaintiff actually suffered operating losses.

16. Other facts

With respect to losses caused by accident involved, the Defendant applies to the court to set up a Limitation of Liability Fund on September 3, 2013, after acceptance, the court publishes it three times in people's court newspaper from October 22, 2013 to October 24, 2013, limiting related claimants to register maritime rights within 60 days from the next day of the last publishing with respect to claiming rights related to this fund. The Plaintiff Yue Hai Company applies to the court to register Appellant's rights on November 12, 2013, and pays the court for the registration cost RMB1,000, no other claimants come to register the claim. After the court and Guangdong High People's Court approved the establishment of the fund, the Defendant set up a Limitation of Liability Fund on May 26, 2014 in the court, the amount of the Limitation of Liability Fund is SDR1,217,263 and its interest (calculate according to RMB loan benchmark interest rate of one year of financial institutions over the same period determined by the People's Bank of China, from July 24, 2014 to May 26, 2014). On July 10, 2014, the court awards that approve the Plaintiff Yue Hai Company's registration application of claimant's rights.

The court contends that:
This case is a dispute over the liability for damages arising from ship allision.

1. As for the right of claim of the two Plaintiffs
   According to the Port Operation License Certification, No.(Yue Hui) Gang Jing Zheng (0024), which is licensed by Guangzhou Harbor Authority, the Plaintiff Yue Hai Company is the operator of berth 1#, 3#, 4#, 5# of port, which is owned by Guangzhou Harbor Nan Sha Harbor Section Yue Hai (Fan Yu) Petrochemicals Storage Transportation Development Co., Ltd., he has property rights of berths of port above. When property rights above mentioned is damaged, the Plaintiff Yue Hai Company has rights to claim the infringer to bear tort liability, and claims the infringer to pay losses like port repairing cost and so on caused by accident involved.
   The Plaintiff PICC Guangzhou issues a policy of which the insured is the Plaintiff Yue Hai Company after accepted property against all risk applied by the Plaintiff Yue Hai Company with respect to property of port berths above mentioned, a relationship of insurance contract is established between the Plaintiff Yue Hai Company and the Plaintiff PICC Guangzhou. That M.V. "Hai Gang Te 001" touches and damages berth 1# of port in this case is covered by this insurance, belongs to insurance accident, The Plaintiff PICC Guangzhou pays the Plaintiff Yue Hai Company for insurance compensation RMB4,277,082.96 after the insurance accident happened subject to laws, as well as the Plaintiff Yue Hai Company issued a letter of rights and interests subrogation, the Plaintiff Yue Hai Company transferred all the rights and interests of the partial insurance subject matter of payment RMB4,277,082.96 to the Plaintiff, PICC Guangzhou. According to the provision of subsection 1 Sect. 60 of insurance law of the People's Republic of China "where an insured incident occurs for any damage caused by a third party to the subject-matter insured, the insurer shall, from the day when it pays insurance proceed to the insured, subrogate the insured's claim for indemnity against the third party within the extent of the insurance proceed", the Plaintiff PICC Guangzhou shall have the right to claim the right of subrogation in the range of insurance claims paid, and the right to claim compensation from the infringer. Because the Plaintiff Yue Hai Company claims the Defendant to compensate for his failure to obtain compensation insurance losses on the grounds of the loss amount more than RMB4,277,082.96, according to the provision of subsection 3 Sect. 60 of insurance law of the People's Republic of China "the insurer's right of subrogation to a claim for indemnity as prescribed in Paragraph 1 of this Article shall not prejudice the insured's right to claim indemnity against the third party for the part of loss which the insured has not been indemnified for", the Plaintiff Yue Hai Company may claim the infringer to compensate losses which he does not obtain. The two Plaintiffs are not entitled to claim indemnity of losses of the accident involved. The Defendant defenses that the Plaintiff, Yue Hai Company, fails to prove he is the owner of this port, so the Plaintiff, Yue Hai Company has no right to ask for compensation with respect to losses of port involved, nor the Plaintiff PICC Guangzhou has the right of subrogation, because it lacks of factual and legal basis, so will not be supported. The Defendant defenses that the Plaintiff PICC Guangzhou can only perform the right of subrogation under indemnity sum RMB2,352,395.63, which is 55% of

co-insurance, which will not influence the relationship of insurance contract between the Plaintiff Yue Hai Company and the Plaintiff PICC Guangzhou, because the Plaintiff Yue Hai Company only applies property insurance of all risks to the Plaintiff, PICC Guangzhou, so the Plaintiff PICC Guangzhou is the only insurer of this insurance contract, insurance payment RMB4,277,082.96 is paid by the Plaintiff PICC Guangzhou to the Plaintiff Yue Hai Company, co-insurance business is the inter relationship between the Plaintiff, PICC Guangzhou and China Pin An Property Insurance Stock Co., Ltd., so the Plaintiff PICC Guangzhou is entitled to exercise the right of subrogation within RMB4,277,082.96 based on the relationship of insurance contract between the Plaintiff Yue Hai Company and the Plaintiff PICC Guangzhou, then this defense of the Defendant lacks of factual and legal basis, so will not be supported.

The two Plaintiffs made an agreement of the way of distribution in insurance indemnity, this agreement does not violate the mandatory provisions of laws and administrative regulations, its effectiveness will be recognized. two Plaintiffs agree that they will not distinguish damage losses items claimed by them clearly, every loss claimed by two of the Plaintiff will be taken a unified recognition by the court, and then be distributed according to the agreement reached by the two Plaintiffs.

2. Whether the Defendant needs to be liable for the responsibility

   The Defendant, as the owner of M.V. "Hai Gang Te 001", has been registered in the vessel certificates and registration has the effect of publicity. The Defendant argues that, M.V. "Hai Gang Te 001" is a barge which has no power, has been chartered by Tong Bao Company from Shang Gang Logistics Company and it is re-chartered by Gang Wan Company from Tong Bao Company, but there is no evidence to prove it is bareboat charter above mentioned, none party has done the bareboat charter registration, that cannot oppose the Plaintiff Yue Hai Company as the infringed, and thus cannot oppose the Plaintiff PICC Guangzhou who exercise the right of subrogation. It shall seek other access to solve the liability problem among the Defendant and Shang Gang Logistics Company, Tong Bao Company, Gang Wan Company. Chinese Nan Sha Marine Safety Administration concludes that, the accident involved is a single party responsibility accident influenced by the bad weather, sea circumstances, not good preparation of avoiding typhoon for a vessel, and incorrect actions of avoiding typhoon, M.V. "Hai Gang Te 001" shall be liable for all the responsibility of this accident. According to Article 6 Paragraph 1 of the Tort Liability Law of the People's Republic of China, the Defendant shall be liable for his M.V. "Hai Gang Te 001" collision the port. The Defendant defenses that it does not control and operate M.V. "Hai Gang Te 001" actually although he owns it, so it has no fault for the collision accident involved, shall not be liable for compensation responsibility subject to law, this defense of the Defendant lacks of legal basis, so will not be supported.

   The two Plaintiffs agreed that the Defendant can enjoy the maritime limits of compensation liability for accident involved, the sum of Limitation of Liability

Fund is SDR1,217,263 and its interest (calculate according to RMB loan benchmark interest rate of one year of financial institutions over the same period determined by the People's Bank of China, from July 24, 2014 to May 26, 2014), the court affirms it.

3. Whether the loses is enlarged by the second collision of M.V. "GINGA CARACAL"

After the collision accident involved happened, the Plaintiff Yue Hai Company firstly entrusted entrusts Gang Wan Company to do technology inspection of port structure, then entrusts Zhong Jiao Design Institute to do design of repairing project. The Plaintiff, Yue Hai Company organized the construction biding of port marine accident repairing project in January 2013. According to the result of the bidding, the Plaintiff, Yue Hai Company signs the construction contract Hang Da Company on February 22, 2013, two parties agree with contents and payment against construction thereof. On April 2, 2013, M.V. "GINGA CARACAL" collided the same part of berth 1# once, before the repairing construction of the port involved.

The collision accident of M.V. "GINGA CARACAL" happened after completion of inspection and construction design, at that time the Plaintiff, Yue Hai Company has signed the construction contract with Hang Da Company, Hang Da Company did not ask for increasing payment against construction due to any increased construction amount caused by the second collision accident. Hang Da Company completed the repairing project according to the original construction design drawing, as well as according to the construction contract handled settlements of main contents and payment against construction thereof. As we can see, the collision accident of M.V. "GINGA CARACAL" caused no new losses, the Plaintiff, Yue Hai Company did not pay for payment against construction of repairing project beyond that agreed in the original contract. The Defendant argued that the damage of port involved is not completely caused by the collision of M.V. "Hai Gang Te 001", so M.V. "Hai Gang Te 001" shall not afford all the losses, this defense of the Defendant lacks of factual and legal basis, so will not be supported.

4. As for every loss item claimed by two Plaintiffs

(1) Eight items of costs which the Defendant has no objection. With respect to every loss item claimed by the two Plaintiffs, the Defendant affirms eight costs claimed by two Plaintiffs consisting of the technology consultation cost of special safety evaluating program on putting No.1–7 pier back on production RMB80,000, rubber fenders payment RMB17,500, payment against the port-repairing construction program RMB19,511.84, payment against pipeline testing pressure and removing RMB61,937, service cost of the navigation safety evaluating of repairing berth 1# project RMB130,000, payment of supervision RMB165,000, payment of the measuring of harbor basin depth RMB15,000, cost of the navigation safety report of repairing project of port 1# after average accident RMB130,000, because the Defendant has no objection, the court affirms them.

(2) Payment of mooring bollard of pier 5#.Gang Wan Company presented to process the foundation of mooring bollard of pier 5# in the inspecting report, and then install the same size mooring bollard. berthing capacity accounting report of port 1# issued by Zhong Jiao Design Institute points out that, port structure from pier 1# to pier 7# will be able to satisfy oil ship of 30,000 tons class or chemical ship of 30,000 tons class to tie and call at, after the replacement of the damaged fenders and mooring bollard of pier 5#. So, it is necessary to repair mooring bollard of pier 5#. The Plaintiff, Yue Hai Company installed quick cable-releasing hook to replace original mooring bollard, this is inconsistent with suggestions of repairing and consolidation given by Gang Wan Company, because it realized the upgrade of mooring equipment pier #. The Plaintiff Yue Hai Company argued that installing the quick cable-releasing hook in pier 5# is to recover the operation of pier 1# - pier 7# of pier 5# as soon as possible. However, to see from the actual situation, it takes more than two months from the accident happened to recovering producing of pier 1# -pier 7# of pier 5#, the Plaintiff Yue Hai Company has enough time to handle the foundation of mooring bollard of pier 5# and install the same size bollard, so this claim of the Plaintiff, will not be supported. Because two Plaintiffs did not supply evidence to prove the needed costs of handling the foundation of mooring bollard of pier 5# and installing the same size bollard, and the Defendant has recognized the cost of installation of quick cable-releasing hook in pier 5#, he shall compensate the payment of the same size mooring bollard. Because two Plaintiffs did not supply evidence to prove the cost of the payment of the same size mooring bollard, the court affirms the cost of the payment of the same size mooring bollard is RMB3,300 given out by the Defendant according to the report of survey and inspection and the supplemental report of survey and inspection. In summary, the Defendant needs to compensate the two Plaintiffs for purchase cost of mooring bollard of pier 5# RMB3,300.

(3) Inspection fees. After the collision accident happened, the Plaintiff, Yue Hai Company entrusted Gang Wan Company to inspect the structure between pier 5# to pier 10 of the damaged berth 1# of this port, Gang Wan Company gives a quotation RMB645,964, and by mutual agreement, the determined inspecting price is RMB600,000,the Plaintiff Yue Hai Company has actually paid Gang Wan Company for the inspecting cost RMB600,000. The Defendant held, the contents and scope of inspection is consistent with the requirements of handling accident, but the reasonable cost of inspection is RMB286,200. The Defendant only supplied the public evaluating opinions of High-level Public Evaluation Company to support his argument aforesaid, and the public evaluating opinions of High-level Public Evaluation Company is based on the price-check opinion of Zhong Jiu Company, because neither the public evaluating opinions nor price-check opinion has enough evidence to prove, this defense of the Defendant lacks of factual basis, so will not be supported. In the condition that the Defendant has not submitted enough evidence to prove the inspecting cost RMB600,000 is unreasonable, the court

will affirm this inspecting cost. In order to know about how the accident influence structure from pier 5# to pier 10#, the Plaintiff entrusts Gang Wan Company once more to inspect complementally the structure from pier 1# to pier 4# according to that inspection has been taken to pier 5# -pier 10# of berth 1 of this port, and pays Gang Wan Company for this RMB98,000. This supplemental inspection is necessary for the Plaintiff, Yue Hai Company to know about the influence of accident on the structure from pier 1# to pier 4# and the recovery of pier 1#-pier 7#, In the condition that the Defendant has not submitted enough evidence to prove the inspecting cost RMB98,000 is unreasonable, the court will affirm this inspecting cost as well. The Defendant argued that the first inspection has specified the extent and scope of damage, it is unreasonable to do the supplemental inspection of part from pier 1# to pier 4#, which is beyond the damaged part, this defense of the Defendant lacks of factual basis, so it will not be supported.

(4) Consultation service cost. According to the special report of marine accident consultation service about berth 1# in Yue Hai Xiao Hu Petrochemical Base issued by Shi Le Company, the contents of Shi Le Company's consultation service mainly is organizing six appraising meetings, among which the appointed party of meeting affairs is Jia Wen Company of the appraising meeting about the navigation safety report of repairing project of port after marine accident and the appraising meeting about checking conference on the navigation safety of repairing project of port after marine accident. according to the contract of the navigation safety evaluation of repairing project of Yue Hai Xiao Hu Petrochemical Base berth 1# and the contract of the navigation safety evaluating report of marine accident repairing project of Yue Hai Xiao Hu Petrochemical Base port 1#, costs of two meeting affairs above is included in the lump sum charge which has paid by the Plaintiff, Yue Hai Company to Jia Wen Company, the Plaintiff, Yue Hai Company has no need to pay for this cost again. Because the export appraising meeting about the special safety evaluating report on resuming dangerous cargo port operation of pier 1# -pier 7# is held with other owners, related costs may be divided for each owner to afford as appropriate. The Plaintiff, Yue Hai Company paid Jia Wen Company for the Consultation service costs RMB108,000, the average cost of per meeting was RMB18,000, deducting costs of two meetings which the Plaintiff Yue Hai Company has no need to afford, and as appropriate deducting some cost producing from the export appraising meeting about the special safety evaluating report on resuming dangerous cargo port operation of pier 1# -pier 7, the court affirms the reasonable consultation cost is RMB66,000. As for the Defendant argued that the Plaintiff, Yue Hai Company did not submit any evidence to prove he has paid the bill to Shi Le Company, because a consultation service contract has been signed between the Plaintiff, Yue Hai Company and Shi Le Company, Shi Le Company has wrote contents of appraising meetings clearly in the special report, and attached related evidence materials on the special report, so it can be recognized that Shi Le Company has finished the consultation service work, the Plaintiff Yue Hai Company

shall pay related costs, the obligation to pay of the Plaintiff Yue Hai Company has no relation with that Shi Le Company has paid related costs of meeting affairs, this defense of the Defendant lacks of factual basis, so will not be supported.

(5) Cost of port structure repairing design. to recover the production and repair the damaged part of pier 1# -pier 7# of berth 1#, the Plaintiff, Yue Hai Company entrusted Zhong Jiao Design Institute to do the work of Yue Hai Xiao Hu Petrochemical Base berth 1# berthing capacity reasoning and construction design of repairing project, and has paid him for this RMB750,000. The Defendant argued, engineering design above is needed, but cost is unreasonable, according to project survey design charge management regulations, the reasonable cost is RMB132,193.50 calculated on budget standard RMB5,000,000 and some adjusting factors. According to the Section 2 provided in project survey design charge management regulations "the charges of the survey and design of the projects in china are applied to this regulation standard of project survey charge and standard of project design charge" engineering design in this case is subject to project survey design charge management regulations and standard of project survey charge and standard of project design charge. According to the Section 2 provided in project survey design charge management regulations "the charges of the survey and design of projects is subject to the amount of investment, which could be divided into government guidance prices and market-regulated prices. The charges of the survey and design of projects will be introduced by government guidance prices when the total estimated investment is RMB5,000,000 and above; The charges of the survey and design of projects will be introduced by market-regulated prices when the total estimated investment amount is below RMB5,000,000."and Section 6 "apart from the seventh of these rules otherwise provides, floating range for the upper and lower 20%. the contractor, the surveyor and the designer should decide the charges in the provisions of the floating range depended upon the special situation. The charges of the survey and design of the projects which is introduced by market-regulated prices, the charges should be bargained by the contractor, the surveyor and the designer". The total budget estimate of project of design plan involved is in amount of RMB8,997,900, so design involved shall be bonded by government guidance prices. standard of project design charge provides the ascertaining of charge of project design in details, among which involving many adjusting factors, all of the ascertaining of these adjusting factors has relations with professional matters of design, the ascertaining of different adjusting factors will influence the amount of design cost directly. The design cost RMB132,193.50 given by the Defendant and High-level Public Evaluation Company is calculated on budget standard RMB5,000,000 after ascertaining adjusting factors by their own, however, the budget standard they based on is obviously lower than that ascertained in the design plan, adjusting factors ascertained by their own has no enough evidence to prove neither, and lack of objective basis, so it cannot be used as a basis for the determination of design cost. the Plaintiff, Yue Hai

Company has paid for RMB750,000, in the condition that the Defendant has not provide any evidence to prove this cost is not consistent with project survey design charge management regulations or is higher than marketing price obviously, the court will affirm this design cost.

(6) Construction cost of port structure repairing project. After the structure detection and construction design aforementioned, the Plaintiff Yue Hai Company begins bidding with respect to port marine accident repairing project involved, and choose Hang Da Company as the construction party of the repairing project through bidding procedure, and determined the contract price RMB7,600,000 after business negotiation with Hang Da Company. As for the Defendant argued the bidding time decided by the Plaintiff Yue Hai Company is not consistent with regulation in the bidding law of PRC, the bidding procedure is unreasonable, because the port repairing project in this case does not belong to the items that must take bidding procedure provided in Article 3 of the Bidding Law of the People's Republic of China, it does not need to ascertain the bidding date according to this law, and within the bidding duration, three companies submitted qualified bidding documents, and finally chose Hang Da Company as the winner bidder through this bidding procedure, in the condition that the Defendant has not submitted any evidence to prove the bidding procedure is unreasonable, so this defense of the Defendant will not be supported. After finishing this repairing project, the Plaintiff Yue Hai Company, Hang Da Company and the supervising entity, Hai Jian Company made the settlement, the total settlement price is RMB7,640,000 due to the increased cost of avoiding typhoon RMB40,000. to see from the settlement confirmation and construction contract signed between the Plaintiff Yue Hai Company and Hang Da Company, the payment against construction is RMB7,640,000 includes the cost of harbor pool dredging and rigid bed-sweeping RMB1,749,880. The public evaluation report held that, the scope of harbor pool dredging and rigid bed-sweeping is too large, the cost of harbor pool dredging and rigid bed-sweeping shall be adjusted into RMB612,458. The Defendant held dredging harbor pool and turning section of port 1#, 5# has no relation with this collision accident involved, cost of which shall be afforded by the Plaintiff Yue Hai Company himself. The court holds that, according to that it shall sweep sea after finishing construction stated in Instructions of plan of port 1# repairing project after marine accident issued by Zhong Jiao Design Institute and it is required to do rigid bed-sweeping after finishing construction, which stated in the construction drawing design instruction of the marine accident repairing project of port 1#, so the port repairing project involved shall do the necessary rigid bed-sweeping and sea-sweeping. As for the project of dredging project of harbor pool and turning section of berth 1#, 5# berth is extended the reasonable beyond which the Plaintiff, Yue Hai Company actually performed, because the instruction of plan of repairing project and the construction drawing design instruction do not point out the area of rigid bed-sweeping and sea-sweeping clearly, it shall be recognized other facts and evidence

comprehensively. To see from the results of navigation safety evaluation in the construction drawing design instruction of the marine accident repairing project of port 1# issued by Zhong Jiao Design Institute, this work involved occupied limited water area, mainly around piers and wharf, the total construction quantities are small in port repairing operation, quantities and scale of vessels used are small. Combined with facts that pier 1#-7# before construction has resumed production, the harbor pool and turning section of berth 1# are in the normal use, it can be identified that the influenced scope of the project involved is mainly around pier 8#-9# and port's surrounding, so the reasonable area of rigid bed-sweeping and sea-sweeping shall be around pier 8#-9# and port's surrounding. According to the statistical graph of dredging quantities of harbor pool and turning section in Yue Hai Xiao Hu Petrochemical port issued by Hang Da Company, the excavation volume is of 834.97 cubic meters of piers 8# and 9# is needed for sea measurement construction; Project volume is of 17,735.25 cubic meter of piers 8# and 9# is needed for bank measurement construction; Bank measured construction of piers 8# and 9# needs to dig slope in the amount of 7,069.88 cubic meters; construction quantities of dredging and rigid bed-sweeping around piers 8# and 9# is of 1,365.70 cubic meters; The total construction quantities aforesaid is of 27,005.80 cubic meters, RMB22 per cubic meter, the total payment against construction is RMB594,127.60. As for the dredging quantities of berth 1# turning area, berth 1# harbor pool area, berth 5# harbor pool area and berth 5# turning area stated in the statistical graph of dredging quantities of harbor pool and turning section in Yue Hai Xiao Hu Petrochemical port, the Plaintiff, Yue Hai Company has not provided enough evidence to prove the project of dredging has relation with the collision accident involved, so the costs producing from this will not be recognized. As for the defense that contents of construction include dredging harbor pool and turning section of port 1#, 5#, increasing caisson anti-corrosion of 8#, 9#, changing life of steel component anti-corrosion from 8 to 10 years, increasing 1 m wide of throwing stone foundation bed in the front of caisson, which have none relation with the collision accident involved, because several projects aforesaid all are included in contents of repairing stated in instructions of plan of port 1# repairing project after marine accident and the construction drawing design instruction of the marine accident repairing project of port 1# issued by Zhong Jiao Design Institute, not the additional construction quantities, this argument of the Defendant will not be recognized neither. The Defendant has not provided evidence to prove costs of other repairing projects of Hang Da Company are unreasonable either, the court will affirm other costs deducting unreasonable part of cost of rigid bed-sweeping and sea-sweeping. As far, after deducting the unreasonable part of cost of rigid bed-sweeping and sea-sweeping, the construction cost of the port structure repairing project involved is RMB648,247.60. the quotation price of port 1# marine accident structure repairing project is RMB4,983,400 given by Dian Bai Company, which the Defendant depends on to argue the construction cost of port 1# marine accident structure repairing project involved is RMB4,983,400, this defense of the Defendant lacks of factual basis, so will not be supported.

(7) Project consultation cost. The Plaintiff Yue Hai Company entrusted Jian Hai Company to supply the service of construction project budget of project costs, paid for consultation service RMB20,000. The Plaintiff Yue Hai Company alleged the budget of project cost is required by related administration department when performing report of construction, but he did not submit related evidence to prove, so he shall be liable for the result of none evidence, the court will not affirm this cost.

(8) Measuring cost for controlling points. The Plaintiff Yue Hai Company entrusted Ying Yi Company to measure three controlling points to be used for project construction, and paid Ying Yi Company for measuring cost in sum of RMB10,536. According to the construction contract signed by the Plaintiff Yue Hai Company and Hang Da Company, the Plaintiff Yue Hai Company shall determine benchmark and coordinate control points and submit to Hang Da Company to inspect on the site in written, so this cost is the necessary cost which the Plaintiff Yue Hai Company must to pay to perform obligation of construction contract, it shall be recognized. The Defendant held that, this operation work of measuring project as preparation before construction shall be included in construction contract, this cost shall be afforded by the winning bidder of repairing project, this defense of the Defendant lacks of factual basis, so will not be supported. The Defendant argued that it must set permanent surveying points when building port, its rebuilding is caused by the Plaintiff Yue Hai Company failing to maintain, but the Defendant has not submitted related evidence to prove, so this defense will not be supported.

(9) Supplemental supervising cost. According to the contract of entrusted supervising construction project, period of supervision service is 150 calendar days, from the day the Plaintiff Yue Hai Company notices him to come into site. On April 19, 2013, the Plaintiff Yue Hai Company gives notice of coming into the site to Hai Jian Company in written, Hai Jian Company on the same day comes into the site to supervise, period of supervision service shall be calculated from this date. However, according to the construction contract signed by the Plaintiff, Yue Hai Company and Hang Da Company, the starting date of construction shall be calculated on the complication of activities under and above water permit certificate and construction permit certificate checked and issued by Harbor Affairs Bureau, so the date of May 25, 2013 stated in the urban construction archives named Xiao Hu Petrochemical Base port 1# marine accident structure repairing project construction diaries, which is made by Hang Da Company cannot be the starting date of period of supervision service. The extension of service of supervision will be calculated from September20, 2013 agreed in supplemental item supervision agreement by the Plaintiff Yue Hai Company and Hai Jian Company, which is consistent with the original contract of entrusted supervising construction project, will be recognized. the actual date of completion of the repairing project is on December 25, 2013, extension of supervision service is beyond three months,

the Plaintiff Yue Hai Company paid Hai Jian Company for the 3 months cost of supervision service, will be recognized by the court. From current evidence of this case to see, 5 months is expected construction duration and factors of the delay are flood season, weather, examination of administrative department and the coming and leaving of ships port operation etc., there is no sufficient evidence to show that the delay is caused by the fault of the Plaintiff Yue Hai Company and Hang Da Company. The Defendant argues, excepting that it stops construction from July 10, 2013 to July 15, 2013 by flood season, and the shutdown, on 15, 16 August, 19–21 September affected by the typhoon stated in urban construction archives of repairing project, other cost of postponing service producing from delaying caused by other reasons of construction party shall be afforded by construction party, but the Defendant has not submitted related evidence to prove, so this defense will not be supported. The Plaintiff Yue Hai Company has paid Hai Jian Company for the supplemental cost of supervision service RMB99,000, this payment is reasonable and necessary, will recognized.

(10) Design and repairing cost of pipeline. Xin Guan Company issues a report of pipeline pressure test Yue Hai port 1#, results of pressure test are all as usual. The inspection report issued by Gang Wan Company states appearance of pipeline is normal, no crack, breakage and dislocation is found in joint position of pipeline. The plan instruction of port 1# marine accident repair project issued by Zhong Jiao Design Institute states that when the structure is repaired, it is required to temporarily remove original process pipeline device in structures of ferry-bridge 7#, pier 8, lay process pipeline again after completion of repairing structure, etc. According to results of pressure test and inspection about pipelines in berth 1# aforesaid, pipelines are not damaged, it is just required to temporarily remove original process pipeline before construction, lay them again after completion of repairing structure, no need to renew pipelines or change the way of lying. The Plaintiff Yue Hai Company argued, repairing pipelines needs to meet the current regulations requirements of "fire protection design code of loading and discharging oil port", so pipelines will be changed to overhead laying from laying in piers. According to Section 1.0.2 provided in "fire protection design specification code of loading and discharging oil port" about "this specification is applicable to the fire protection design of the new, rebuilt and expanded crude oil, refined oil terminal and the normal temperature pressure type liquefied petroleum gas terminal. The fire protection design of temporary oil production port shall be implemented by reference. Excepting the option of fire extinguisher, the liquid chemicals production port may be implemented by reference of this specification", "fire protection design specification code of loading and discharging oil port" is applicable to new, renovation and expansion projects, and project of this case belongs to the repairing work, does not apply to the specification of course, the Plaintiff Yue Hai Company invoked this regulation as the basis to change pipelines into overhead laying from laying in pier, which lacks legal basis, so will not be supported. The wharf pipelines are changed from laying in

piers into overhead laying, which realizes upgrade of functions, cost of pipeline design and the payment against project of construction of port repairing thereof shall be afforded by the Plaintiff Yue Hai Company himself, the increased cost of repairing pipelines project shall be afforded by the Plaintiff Yue Hai Company himself as well. Because two Plaintiffs failed to provide evidence to prove removing and installing cost of original process pipeline device, the Defendant agrees to compensate for related costs of removing and installing construction and materials according to costs of removing and pressure test RMB61,937, so the court will affirm cost of removing and installing pipeline is RMB61,937.

(11) Cost of safety assessment after repairing. The Plaintiff Yue Hai Company entrusts Jing An Company to supply technology consultation service of safety assessment item of dangerous cargo operation at port, and pays Jing An Company for the consultation cost RMB90,000. From the safety assessment report of dangerous cargo operation at port (edition for record) issued by Jing An Company to see, the report is divided into two parts, namely the safety assessment of berth 1# and berth 5# port dangerous cargo operation involved in berth 1# marine accident repairing project and safety assessment of port dangerous cargo operation. The first part, the safety assessment of berth 1# and berth 5# port dangerous cargo operation involved in berth 1# marine accident repairing project is a special safety assessment of damaged berth for reuse, the second part is safety assessment of port dangerous cargo operation of all berths at port, which has no direct relation with the accident, therefore, this item of cost paid by the Plaintiff Yue Hai Company shall be shared properly, and considering the report is consisted of two parts, the court affirms the reasonable consultation cost RMB45,000.

(12) Cost of handling pipeline emergency. The Plaintiff Yue Hai Company alleged he immediately started the emergency plan to rescue and the resumption of production preparation work, producing material cost and operating cost RMB182,155.20 totally and he submitted cost statistics of processing pipeline, fee schedule of processing port pipeline and some material documents after M.V. "Hai Gang Te 001" allision and damage port. Because main evidence above to prove this loss is made by its own party, the Defendant did not recognize any of them, the court cannot affirm this cost according to evidence aforesaid. Considering facts that the port is a chemicals port, the accident in this case leads port to damage, as well as part of pipeline need demolition and pressure test, it is reasonable for the Plaintiff Yue Hai Company to start the emergency plan to rescue and the resumption of production preparation work at once. Because the emergency plan to rescue and the resumption of production preparation work are only done by the Plaintiff Yue Hai Company, and he failed to supply any evidence of third party to prove the happened cost of handling pipeline emergency, thus, the court affirms the cost of emergency treatment is RMB50,000, taking comprehensive consideration of the emergency, professional, risk and other factors of this operation.

(13) Operating losses. From two audit reports issued by Chai An Firm to see, the average monthly of the total income of the Plaintiff Yue Hai Company has been reduced by little scope in August, September 2012 than that in April – June, and because berth 1# stops operation, the average monthly of the total income of berth 1# has been reduced by much scope in August, September 2012 than that in April –June, after berth 1# recovers the operation, the average monthly of the total income of the Plaintiff Yue Hai Company and berth 1# in 10–12 month 2012 is close to that in 4–6 month 2012, the facts aforesaid show this accident involved has influenced the operations of entire port and berth 1#, the Defendant shall compensate the Plaintiff Yue Hai Company for the operating losses caused by this. According to Article 12 provided in the Provisions of the Supreme people's Supreme Court on the Trial of Compensation for Property Damage in Cases of Collision and Contact of Ships "calculation: time limited of compensation for facilities damages: limit to actual duration of stop using deducting duration of routine maintenance; facilities' part damage or loss, respectively shall be calculated by the reasonable cost of repairing or re construction, after deducting the period of depreciation cost; loss of income by using the facilities, shall be calculated according to the actual reduction in net income, namely according to the average net profit of the first three months after stop using; the use of part and has benefits shall be deducted", the Plaintiff claims the operating losses based on the reducing of average net profit daily berth 1# before and after the collision accident, which is according to law and will be supported. The Defendant argued that, the reducing amount of daily average net profit of entire port shall be the basis of operating losses of the Plaintiff Yue Hai Company but he does not supply enough facts and laws to support it, so this defense will not be recognized. The collision accident involved happened at 0440 on July 24, 2012, berth 1# stops the operation since that day, and resumes operation until September 21, so the average net profit of berth 1# from July 24 to July 31, should be ascertained according to that of 8–9 month. the loss of the average net profit in total of 68 days from July 24 to September 30 can be worked out RMB433,389.84, by daily average net profit of berth 1# in 4–6 month RMB5,633.38 plus that in 8–9 month RMB-6,373.38. The average daily net profit loss in 10–12 month 2012 period in a total of 92 days is RMB179.63, the income loss in the period can be calculated RMB1,525.96. Part of 1# berth is in use and has income from January 1, 2013 to September 10, 2014, but two Plaintiffs failed to supply proof to prove earnings during the period, shall bear the legal consequences of the failure of burden of proof, operating losses in that period claimed by two Plaintiffs shall not be supported.

(14) Audit cost, To prove the operating losses he suffered, the Plaintiff Yue Hai Company applied the court to entrust a certifying agency to audit the average net profit in 4–6 months 2012 and 8–12 months 2012, and the Plaintiff Yue Hai Company pays for auditing cost RMB80, 000, the producing of auditing cost has direct cause relation with accident involved, the Defendant shall

compensate this. Therefore, auditing cost RMB80,000 claimed by the Plaintiff Yue Hai Company will be recognized.

(15) Asset appraisal fee and lawyer fee. There is no direct cause and effect relationship between the occurrence of the asset appraisal fee and the lawyer fee and the accident involved. The two Plaintiffs claim the two items of cost, which lacks of legal basis, so will not be supported.

(16) In a sum, the Defendant shall compensate two Plaintiffs the technology consultation cost of special safety evaluating program on putting No.1–7 pier back on production RMB80,000, rubber fenders payment RMB17,500, payment against the port-repairing construction program RMB19,511.84, payment against pipeline testing pressure and removing RMB61,937, service cost of the navigation safety evaluating of repairing berth 1# project RMB130,000, payment of supervision RMB165,000, payment of the measuring of harbor basin depth RMB15,000, cost of the navigation safety report of repairing project of port 1# after average accident RMB130,000, payment of mooring bollard of pier 5# RMB3,300, cost of inspection RMB698,000, consultation cost is RMB66,000, design of port repairing project RMB750,000, construction cost of the port structure repairing project involved is RMB648,247.60, measuring cost of controlling points RMB10,536, supplemental supervising cost RMB99,000, costs of removing and installing pipelines RMB61,937, Cost of safety assessment after repairing RMB45,000, cost of handling pipeline emergency RMB50,000, operating losses RMB449,915,80, auditing cost RMB80,000, a total of losses above is RMB9,416,885.24. The Defendant shall also be liable for the loss of interest from the date of payment or the date of production to the date of distribution of the fund. Due to the total amount of costs and interest do not exceed the amount of Limitation of Liability Fund which the Defendant has set up in the court, according to the agreement of the insurance indemnity made by two Plaintiffs, the Defendant shall compensate for the Plaintiff PICC Guangzhou RMB4,277,082.96 and the interest, the Defendant shall compensate for the Plaintiff Yue Hai Company RMB5,139,802.28 and the interest. It is reasonable that the Plaintiff PICC Guangzhou claimed the interest of RMB2000,000 should be calculated from September 29, 2014, the interest of RMB2,277,082.96 shall be calculated from December 26, 2014, according to the loan benchmark interest rate of the People's Bank of China over the same period, and it will be supported. It is reasonable that the Plaintiff Yue Hai Company claims the interest of every cost shall be calculated from when it has been paid or it has produced according to the loan benchmark interest rate of the People's Bank of China over the same period, and it will be supported. Specifically, the interest of what the Plaintiff Yue Hai Company has paid shall be calculated according to the loan benchmark interest rate of the People's Bank of China over the same period, RMB300,000 from August 2, 2012, RMB200,000 from August 10, 2012, RMB100,000 from August 22, 2012, RMB3,300 from September 6, 2012, RMB98,000 from September 11, 2012, RMB40,000 from September 17, 2012, RMB200,000 from September 19,

2012, RMB40,000 from October 18, 2012, RMB17,500 from October 19, 2012, RMB250,000 from November 13, 2012, RMB61,937 from November 23, 2012, RMB19,511.84 from November 26, 2012, RMB49,500 from March 26, 2013, RMB1,520,000 from April 7, 2013, RMB10,536 from April 8, 2013, RMB130,000 from April 25, 2013, RMB61,937 from May 23, 2013, RMB21,450 from June 8, 2013, RMB300,000 from July 16, 2013, RMB21,450 from July 25, 2013, RMB15,000 from July 31, 2013, RMB1,496,835 from August 28, 2013, RMB33,000 from August 30,2013, RMB42,900 from October 16, 2013, RMB321,356.21 from November 27, 2013, RMB200,000 from December10, 2013, RMB800,000 from December 25, 2013, RMB45,000 from December 25, 2013, RMB21,450 from January 8, 2014, RMB99,000 from January 22, 2014, RMB300,000 from January 22, 2014, RMB200,000 from January 28, 2014, RMB200,000 from February 20, 2014, RMB279,107.70 from March 10, 2014, RMB200,000 from March 26, 2014, RMB25,000 from April 9, 2014, RMB200,000 from April 15, 2014, RMB200,000 from May 5, 2014, RMB400,000 from May 21, 2014, RMB166,948.69 from July 8, 2014, RMB130,000 from July 23, 2014, RMB33,000 from November 14, 2014, RMB55,000 from June 4, 2015. The cost of handling pipeline emergency and operating losses do not belong to cost the Plaintiff Yue Hai Company actually paid, the interest of them shall be calculated from when they produced or has be ascertained, as well according to loan benchmark interest rate of the People's Bank of China over the same period, namely cost of handling pipeline emergency in sum of RMB50,000 from July 24, 2012, the operating losses in sum of RMB43,389.84 from September 30, 2012, RMB16,525.96 from December 31, 2012. The above interest claimed by the Plaintiff Yue Hai Company shall be calculated to the date of allocating the fund, then deduct interest claimed by the Plaintiff PICC Guangzhou.

According to Article 6 Paragraph 1 of the Tort Liability Law of the People's Republic of China, Article 64 Paragraph 1 of the Civil Procedure Law of the People's Republic of China, Article 116 of the Special Maritime Procedure Law of the People's Republic of China, the judgment is as follows:

(1) Affirm that the Plaintiff, China People's Property Insurance Co., Ltd. Guangzhou Branch has the right to claim against the Defendant, Shanghai Port Fuxing Shipping Co., Ltd. for RMB4,277,082.96 and the interest thereon (among which the interest on RMB2,000,000 shall be calculated from 29 September 2014, the interest on RMB2,277,082.96 shall be calculated from 26 December 2014, to the date of allocating the fund, according to RMB loan benchmark interest rate of the People's Bank of China over the same period), this claim can be paid in prior in the Limitation of Liability Fund, SDR1,217,263 and its interest, which Shanghai Port Fuxing Shipping Co., Ltd. has set up;

(2) Affirm the Plaintiff, Yue Hai (Fan Yu) Petrochemicals Storage Transportation Development Co., Ltd. has the right to claim against the Defendant, Shanghai Port Fuxing Shipping Co., Ltd. For RMB5,139,802.28 and the interest thereon, this claim can be paid in prior in the Limitation of Liability Fund, SDR1,217,263 and its interest, which Shanghai Port Fuxing Shipping Co., Ltd. has set up;
(3) Reject other claims of the Plaintiff, Yue Hai (Fan Yu) Petrochemicals Storage Transportation Development Co., Ltd., against the Defendant, Shanghai Port Fuxing Shipping Co., Ltd.

Court acceptance fee in amount of RMB106,677, the Plaintiff, Yue Hai (Fan Yu) Petrochemicals Storage Transportation Development Co., Ltd., shall bear RMB26,906 and the Defendant shall bear RMB79,771. The right registration fee in amount of RMB1,000 shall be afforded by the Defendant. Upon the two Plaintiffs' consent, the Defendant shall pay entertainment fee RMB106,677 and the right registration cost in sum of RMB1,000 to the two Plaintiffs directly, which it shall bear, the court will not repay to the two Plaintiffs otherwise.

The judgment is final.

Presiding Judge: XU Yuanping
Judge: WU Guining
People's Juror: FANG Tonglin

November 5, 2015

Clerk: CHEN Di

Guangzhou Maritime Court
Civil Judgment

Zhuhai Jiaxun Saite Electronic Co., Ltd.
v.
Shenzhen Shi Chang Freight Co., Ltd. et al.

(2015) Guang Hai Fa Chu Zi No.182

Related Case(s) None.

Cause(s) of Action 202. Dispute over contract of carriage of goods by sea or sea-connected waters.

Headnote Ocean carrier held liable for misdelivery of goods contrary to instructions for "telex release" to receiver; freight forwarder held not liable for same misdelivery as it had complied with its instructions from shipper.

Summary The Plaintiff-Shipper filed suit against the Defendant-Freight Forwarder and the Defendant-Carrier in a dispute over a contract for the carriage of goods. The Plaintiff sold tuners and cable TV splitters to a party located in Jordan. It subsequently contacted the Freight Forwarder to get booking space for a container holding the goods. Both parties agreed that the goods would be delivered according to a telex release issued by the Plaintiff. The other Defendant-Carrier accepted the booking space from the Freight Forwarder aboard its vessel, and was notified via email that the release method would be subject to a telex release instruction. The vessel arrived at the port of discharge in Jordan, and the Defendant-Freight Forwarder sent the telex release instructions. The Defendant-Carrier sent the delivery instructions to the port agent, but then the Defendant-Freight Forwarder immediately sent another email stating that delivery should not be arranged yet. The Defendant-Carrier subsequently delivered the goods to the consignee anyway.

The Plaintiff alleged that both Defendants were liable for the loss of goods and both should compensate it for such loss. The Defendant-Carrier was found liable for the Plaintiff's losses because the Defendant-Carrier agreed to carry the Plaintiff's goods through the Defendant-Freight Forwarder, and it entered into the contract of carriage with the Defendant-Freight Forwarder knowing that the Plaintiff was the principal entity. The Court also held that the Defendant-Carrier was the sole party liable for the loss of the Plaintiff's goods because the Defendant-Carrier was responsible for the subject goods from when it took over the container until the goods were delivered. Since the Defendant-Carrier delivered the goods after receiving the email stating not to arrange for delivery, it breached its obligation to follow the instructions of the telex release and is liable for the value of the goods lost. The Defendant-Freight Forwarder was not found liable for the Plaintiff's loss since it fulfilled its obligations as the agent of the Plaintiff.

Judgment

The Plaintiff: Zhuhai Jiaxun Saite Electronic Co., Ltd.
Domicile: High-tech Zone,Zhuhai, Guangdong.
Legal representative: YANG Shengping, chairman.
Agent *ad litem*: LEI Zhengqin, lawyer of Guangdong Shengtang Law Firm.
Agent *ad litem*: ZHANG Lan, trainee lawyer of Guangdong Shengtang Law Firm.

The Defendant: Shenzhen Shi Chang Freight Co., Ltd.
Domicile: 18th floor of Haiwai Lianyi Building, Yingchun Road, Luohu District, Shenzhen City, Guangdong.
Legal representative: XU Jun, general manager.
Agent *ad litem*: XU Xiaolu, lawyer of Beijing Huaiqiu(Shenzhen) Law Firm.

The Defendant: COSCO Container Lines Co., Ltd.
Domicile: Room428, BuildingA of Lingang Management and Service Center, No.188, Ye Shen Road, China (Shanghai) Pilot Free Trade Zone.
Legal representative: YE Weilong, chairman.
Agent *ad litem*: WU Yong, lawyer of Henry & Co.
Agent *ad litem*: YAN Chanjuan, practicing attorney of Henry & Co.

With respect to the case arising from dispute over contract of carriage of goods by sea, the Plaintiff Zhuhai Jiaxun Saite Electronic Co., Ltd. filed an action against the Defendant Shenzhen Shi Chang Freight Co., Ltd. (hereinafter referred to as "Shichang Company") as well as COSCO Container Lines Co., Ltd. (hereinafter referred to as COSCO) to the court on January 21, 2015. The court entertained the case and organized the collegiate panel according to the law. The court held a hearing publicly on April 15 and April 23 and summoned all parties concerned to exchange evidence before trial. LEI Zhengqin and ZHANG Lan, agents *ad litem* of the Plaintiff, XU Xiaolu, agent *ad litem* of Shichang Company, and WU Yong, agent *ad litem* of COSCO appeared in court and evidence-exchange twice.

Now the case has been concluded.

The Plaintiff alleged that it sold a batch of tuners and cable TV splitters to Jordan ANAS GHAZZAW Company on December 25, 2013. The value of the goods was USD101,710 on FOB terms. After the Plaintiff booked shipping space from Shichang Company on February 28, 2014, the later accepted booking and then sent the shipping order to the Plaintiff as well as told the Plaintiff the booking note number, the time of breaking bulk, receiving container, submitting supplement information and the estimated time of departure as well. On March 19, Shichang Company sent the detailed expenses notification to the Plaintiff and claimed that the Plaintiff should pay for freight, telex release surcharge and other fees, among which the freight was USD950 and telex release surcharge was RMB450. On March 31, the Plaintiff paid the freight, telex release surcharge and other fees in sum of USD950 and RMB5,380.38 yuan in total. On March 8, the goods involved were loaded onto M.V. "COSCO Qingdao", a ship owned by COSCO. Then, COSCO issued a Master bill of lading of which the number was COSU6092186080. According to the bill of lading, the Plaintiff was shipper, voyage number was 096 W, port of discharge was Aqaba Jordan, container number was CBHU3499718 and freight was prepaid. The Plaintiff and Shichang Company had an agreement that goods would be telex released to order of the Plaintiff. Shichang Company received the Master bill of lading issued by COSCO but did not issue House bill of lading to the Plaintiff. M.V."COSCO Qingdao" which loaded the container involved set sail on March 8 and arrived at Aqaba Jordan, the port of discharge on March 26. Before April 13, on condition that the Plaintiff did not send an instruction of releasing the goods by telex, the consignee took the delivery of the goods involved, Shichang Company and COSCO, respectively was carrier and actual carrier of goods involved. The instruction in the mail from Shichang Company to COSCO was not clear and COSCO delivered the goods without the instruction of telex releasing the goods. These two reasons caused the loss of the Plaintiff's goods. Two Defendants had fault and should compensate for loss of the Plaintiff. The Plaintiff claimed that: (1) the two Defendants should pay for the losses of the goods in sum of USD101,700, and the loss of ocean freight in sum of USD950 as well as interest thereon (from April 13, 2014 to the actual payment date on the basis of the loan interest rate promulgated by the People's Bank of China over the same period, USD dollars shall be converted into RMB on the basis of the renminbi-dollar central parity rate on January 19, 2015; (2) the two Defendants should bear the court fees jointly and severally.

During the time limit for adducing evidence, the Plaintiff submitted the following four set of evidence. The first set including three files: 1. industrial and commercial registration information of Shichang Company; 2. industrial and commercial registration information of COSCO; 3. industrial and commercial registration information of the Plaintiff, to prove the capacity of all parties concerned. The second set including the following files: 4. sample of COSCO's bill of lading and its translation; 5. shipping order; 6. notice of Shichang Company on charging the Plaintiff the ocean freight and other fees; 7. payment voucher, to prove the Plaintiff had paid the freight; 8. freight invoice issued by Shichang Company; 9. QQ chat records; 10. email of previous trades between Shichang Company and the Plaintiff to prove that the transportation contract relationship between Shichang Company and the Plaintiff, that was to say, Shichang Company was carrier, COSCO was actual carrier. Shichang Company had received ocean freight in sum of USD950, the freight and miscellaneous charges in sum of RMB5,380.38. The third set including the following files: 11. transfer record of the container involved; 12. emails between the Plaintiff and the consignee; 13. emails between Shichang

Company and the Plaintiff and its translation; 14. Power of attorney concerning telex release goods of the Plaintiff; 15. emails between Shichang Company and the Plaintiff to prove that goods involved released the goods against the Plaintiff instruction and the consignee took the delivery of the goods before April 13, 2014. The last set of evidence includes: 16. confirmation of invoice issued by the Plaintiff and its translation; 17. Export Goods Customs Declaration; 18. goods packing list; 19. export goods invoice, to prove that the value of the goods involved was USD101,710.

The Defendant Shichang Company argued that, 1. according to the sample record of bill of lading involved submitted by the Plaintiff and Shichang Company, the shipper of goods involved was the Plaintiff, the carrier was COSCO, and Shichang Company was freight forwarder other than carrier; 2. Shichang Company had required COSCO not to release goods without the instruction of telex release and Letter of Guarantee. In this case, Shichang Company did not send telex release instruction, so Shichang Company shall not be liable for the loss of goods involved; 3. the Plaintiff's claim for the loss of goods and freight had no basis. It requested the court to reject all the claims of the Plaintiff.

The Defendant Shichang Company defended as follows: 1. according to the record of the sample bill of lading involved, the shipper was the Plaintiff, COSCO was the carrier, Shichang Company was the freight forwarder rather than the carrier; 2. Shichang Company had requested COSCO not to release the goods in the event of no guarantee for telex release and instruction of telex release, therefore, it should not bear any liability for compensation; 3. the Plaintiff's claiming the losses of goods and freight lacked factual basis. Shichang Company requested the court to dismiss all the claims of the Plaintiff.

During the time limit for adducing evidence, the Defendant submitted the following evidence: 1. emails between Shichang Company and COSCO on March 5, 2014, to prove that Shichang Company sent the documents involved to COSCO, and notified COSCO to wait for its instruction of telex release; 2. emails between Shichang Company and COSCO on March 7, 2014; 3. amendment advice; 4. emails between Shichang Company and COSCO on March 26, 2014, to prove that the shipper of goods involved was the Plaintiff, the carrier was COSCO; 5. invoice of freight and miscellaneous charges, to prove that Hua Nan COSCO International Freight Co., Ltd. charged freight and miscellaneous charges on COSCO's behalf; 6. Emails between Shichang Company and COSCO on March 28 and June 20, 2014, to prove that Shichang Company had notified COSCO should not release the goods without the letter of guarantee issued by Shichang Company and required COSCO to withhold the goods; 7. the letter sent to Shichang Company issued by the Plaintiff, to prove that the Plaintiff confessed it could not receive the freight in sum of USD91,700; 8. emails between Shichang Company and COSCO on January 7, 2014, to prove that during the previous trades, it was a practice that COSCO always underwent telex release formalities; 9. emails between Shichang Company and COSCO on June 30, 2014, to prove that had fault and should be liable for the loss of goods. 10. QQ chat records between Shichang Company and COSCO, to prove that the Plaintiff confirmed it had received the sample of bill of lading issued by COSCO.

The Defendant COSCO argued as follow:

1. Shichang Company accepted booking from the Plaintiff, COSCO accepted booking from Shichang Company. So in this case, the Plaintiff was shipper, Shichang Company was contracting carrier and COSCO was actual carrier.
2. Though Shichang Company was freight forwarder of goods involved, the method of delivery the goods was telex release according to the instruction of Shichang Company. COSCO released the goods after receiving the telex release instruction issued by Shichang Company at 1619 on March 28, 2014 through mail. So COSCO should not be liable for the loss of goods to the Plaintiff because it had no fault. Shichang Company should be liable for the goods because it sent telex release instruction in the wrong time.
3. Though the Plaintiff lost the goods, considering the freight of goods in the sum of USD10,000 was pre-paid and COSCO charged actual freight in the sum of USD700, the Plaintiff's claim for the loss of goods and freight had no merit. COSCO request ed the court to dismiss all the claims of the Plaintiff.

During the time limit for adducing evidence, the Defendant COSCO submit the following evidence: 1. the email sent to COSCO from Shichang Company; 2. the emails between COSCO and its agent at the port of destination, to prove that Shichang Company had sent telex release instruction in terms of goods involved to COSCO, after COSCO received the instruction, it notified the agent at the port of destination to release the goods; 3. Emails between Shichang Company and COSCO and the booking note, to prove that Shichang Company booked space with COSCO; 4. the mail sent to COSCO from Shichang Company on March 5, 2014, to prove that Shichang Company had told COSCO to wait for its telex release notification of the goods; 5. emails between Shichang Company and COSCO, to prove that any changes to the transportation and any fees should be confirmed by both parties; 6. emails between COSCO and its agent at the port of destination, to prove that COSCO should notify its agent at the port of destination in case of any change to the transportation; 7. invoice for Shichang Company issued by COSCO, to prove that COSCO had charged the freight of the goods involved from Shichang Company.

After the court hearing, the court ascertains the evidence as follows:

As to the evidence submitted by the Plaintiff, the two Defendants raised no objection to the evidence in the first set, evidence 4, 6 and 8 in the second set, and evidence 11 and 15 in the third set. The Plaintiff and COSCO raised no objection to evidence 1 to 7 submitted by Shichang Company. The Plaintiff and Shichang Company raised no objection to evidence 4 and 7 submitted by COSCO. So the court ascertains the above evidence.

Shichang Company objected the authenticity of evidence 5 of the Plaintiff. The two Defendants objected the authenticity, legality and relevancy of evidence 7, 9 and 10 in the second set of evidence, evidence 12 to 14 in the third set of evidence and the fourth set of evidence. The court holds the contents of the shipping order in evidence 5 of Plaintiff and the sample bill of lading in evidence 4 of the Plaintiff and evidence 1 of Shichang Company corroborate each other. Though Shichang Company objected the authenticity, it did not submit evidence to the contrary, thus the court ascertains its probative force. As for evidence 7, the contents of payment requisition for freight and miscellaneous charges cannot be corroborated with other evidence, so the court do ascertain its probative force. As for evidence 9, QQ chat records do not show the QQ number of each other, and the chat subjects are uncertain, so the court does not ascertain its probative force. As for evidence 10, the contents of the emails concerning the previous trades between the Plaintiff and Shichang Company have no relevancy with this case, so its probative force cannot be ascertained. As for evidence 12 in the third set of the Plaintiff's evidence, the emails between the Plaintiff and the consignee, its probative force can be ascertained because COSCO confirmed the fact of releasing goods. As for evidence 13, the mail addresses of the emails between the Plaintiff and Shichang Company are owned by the Plaintiff and Shichang Company respectively, and had relevancy with the case, so its probative force can be ascertained. As for evidence 14, the form of telex release letter of authorization has no relevancy with the case, so its probative force cannot be ascertained. As for the fourth set of the Plaintiff's evidence, evidence 17 customs declaration for goods and evidence 19 the export invoice, have original to verify, and can be corroborated, the two Defendants objected them, but did not submit any evidence to the contrary, so the probative force thereof shall be ascertained.

The Plaintiff and COSCO raised no objection to the authenticity of the emails between two Defendants in evidence 8 and 9 submitted by Shichang Company. The court ascertains the authenticity thereof. But whether it can support Shichang Company's claim or not shall be determined on the basis of overall evidence. Evidence 10 submitted by Shichang Company, QQ chat record between it and the Plaintiff, the latter raised no objection to its authenticity, and the chat contents have relevancy with this case, so the court ascertained its probative force.

The Plaintiff raised no objection to evidence 1 to 3, 5 and 6 submitted by COSCO. Shichang Company objected its authenticity. The court holds that the mail address used in the emails between two Defendants in evidence 1, 3 and 5 are owned by the two parties, and the contents have relevancy with this case, Shichang Company objected thereto but it failed to provide evidence to the contrary, so the probative force of three pieces of evidence can be ascertained. The contents of the emails between COSCO and its agent at the port of destination in evidence 2 and page 18 of evidence 6 submitted by Shichang Company can be corroborated, so the probative force thereof shall be ascertained. Evidence 6 submitted by COSCO and the emails with its agent at the port of destination and the email address in evidence 2 can be corroborated, and the contents of the emails had relevancy with this case, Shichang Company objected to that, but it had no evidence to the contrary, so the court ascertains the probative force thereof.

The court confirms the following facts: on December 25, 2013, Plaintiff sold a batch of tuners and cable TV splitters to Jordan ANAS GHAZZAW Company. According to the record of the export goods customs declaration and Guangdong

Province export goods invoice submitted by the Plaintiff, the value of the goods was USD101,710 on FOB basis. The Plaintiff confirmed that it had received buyer's deposit in the sum of USD10,000 in the hearing.

In February 2014, the Plaintiff contacted with Shichang Company for booking space. Both parties reached an agreement on the delivery terms: according to the telex release instruction issued by the Plaintiff. Then, Shichang Company charged the Plaintiff ocean freight (prepaid) in the sum of USD950, telex release surcharge in the sum of RMB450. On February 26, 2014, Shichang Company in its own name sent the booking note to COSCO through email. According to the records of the booking note, Shichang Company was the co-signer, consignee and notify party were to order, place of receipt was Shekou Port, place of delivery was Port of Aqaba, goods was one 20-Foot container DISEQC SWITCH, gross weight was 10 tons, the booking note was affixed with Shichang Company seal on shipper column. COSCO accepted booking from Shichang Company and issued a shipping order. This Confirmation Letter recorded following information: booking note number: COSU6092186080, container: 20-Foot, goods name: DISEQC SWITCH, place of receipt: Guangdong Shekou Port, the port of discharge: Aqaba Jordan, carrying vessel and voyage: M.V. "COSCO Qingdao" and 096 W voyage. On March 5. Shichang Company sent an instruction to COSCO through email, requiring COSCO to record the shipper as the Plaintiff, the consignee as GHAITH ALSAHRAA and the notify party as EST on the bill of lading. The container number and seal number was CBHU3499718 and W70496 respectively. The goods were 374 boxes of cable TV DISEQC SWITCH. Transportation method was CY/CY. The port of loading, port of destination, carrying vessel and voyage should be consistent with the shipping order. The release method of goods was subject to Shichang Company's telex release instruction. On March 7, COSCO issued a sample bill of lading of which number was COSU6092186080 to Shichang Company through email. The shipper, the consignee, the notify party, the carrying vessel, the voyage, the container number, the port of loading, the port of destination, transportation method and the goods in the sample bill of lading were consistent with the shipping instruction submitted by Shichang Company. The column of carrier is filled with COSCO. Shichang Company sent the sample bill of lading to the Plaintiff through QQ later.

On March 8, M.V. "COSCO Qingdao" which was loaded with container involved set sail from Shekou Port. On March 25, the Plaintiff sent amendment advice to Shichang Company, requiring COSCO to change the consignee and the notify party recorded in the bill of lading into SAFENAT AL-SAHRAA EAT. Then Shichang Company sent the amendment advice to COSCO. On March 26, COSCO issued a sample bill of lading numbered with COSU6092186080 to Shichang Company after amendment. This bill of lading, except the consignee and the notify party was amended as required, other contents are consistent with that issued on March 7. Shichang Company sent sample bill of lading to the Plaintiff after amended later. COSCO charged Shichang Company the ocean freight in the sum of USD700 and telex release surcharge in the sum of USD450 of the goods involved.

On March 26, M.V. "COSCO Qingdao" arrived at Aqaba Jordan, the port of discharge. At 1619 on March 28, Shichang Company notified COSCO to telex release No.COSU602186080 bill of lading through email. After COSCO received the email, it sent an instruction of delivering goods to the agent at the port of destination at 1730. At 1742, Shichang Company notified COSCO again via email that Shichang Company did not submit letter of guarantee for telex release, thus COSCO should not arrange delivery of the goods. On April 12, COSCO delivered the goods involved to the consignee.

Upon investigation, according to the RMB central parity rate authorized to be published by the China Foreign Exchange Trading Center, the renminbi-dollar central parity rate was USD100 for RMB614.95 on April 11, 2014. The renminbi-dollar central parity rate was USD100 for RMB612.3 on January 19, 2015.

During the trial, all parties concerned chose to solve this substantial according to the laws of the People's Republic of China.

The court holds that: the goods involved were transported from Shekou Port, China to Aqaba Jordan by sea. The Plaintiff claimed compensation for loss of the goods under the contract of carriage of goods by sea. So, this case is concerning dispute over the contract of carriage of goods by sea. Both the Plaintiff and the Defendants chose to solve the substantial dispute according to the laws of the People's Republic of China. According to Article 269 of the Maritime Code of the People's Republic of China, this case shall apply the laws of the People's Republic of China.

The outstanding issues of this case: 1. the legal relationship between the Plaintiff and the two Defendants; 2. the liabilities for the loss of the goods involved; 3. the amount of the loss of the goods.

As for the legal relationship between the Plaintiff and the two Defendants, the Plaintiff claimed that it concluded relationship of contract of carriage of goods by sea with Shichang Company, but the evidence can only prove that the Plaintiff connected Shichang Company in terms of booking space, released goods subject to instruction and Shichang Company charged freight and miscellaneous charges, but cannot prove that Shichang Company as the carrier reached an agreement with the Plaintiff on the carriage of goods by sea. Shichang Company did not issue transportation documents such as bill of lading. Before the shipment, the sample of bill of lading issued by Shichang Company sent to the Plaintiff shows that the carrier is COSCO. So the Plaintiff's claim that it concluded a contract of carriage of goods by sea with Shichang Company cannot stand because of lacking factual and legal basis. Shichang Company accepted the Plaintiff's consignment, booked space for the Plaintiff and charged corresponding fees. The Plaintiff and Shichang Company established a relationship of freight forwarding contract. The Plaintiff was the principal and Shichang Company was the agent.

After Shichang Company accepted the Plaintiff's consignment, it booked space from COSCO in its own name. COSCO accepted booking from Shichang Company and bore the responsibility for the transportation of goods. Later, Shichang Company notified COSCO in the shipping instruction that the sample of bill of lading recorded the Plaintiff as shipper. Shichang Company also sent COSCO's sample of bill of lading to the Plaintiff. After the goods involved arrived at the port of destination, the Plaintiff issued the amendment advice to Shichang Company, requiring COSCO to amend the consignee as recorded in the bill of lading. The aforementioned facts are sufficient to prove that though Shichang Company concluded the contract of carriage of goods by sea in its own name with COSCO, Shichang Company, as the agent, disclosed COSCO to the Plaintiff. The Plaintiff had already known COSCO was the carrier of the goods involved. There is no evidence to prove that when COSCO and Shichang Company concluded the transportation contract, COSCO would not conclude the contract if it had known the Plaintiff was the principal of Shichang Company. According to Article 403 Paragraph 1 of the Contract Law of the People's Republic of China, "under a contract concluded by the agent in the agent's name with a third party that is not aware of the proxy relationship between the agent and the principal, when the agent fails to perform obligations toward the principal because of the third party, the agent shall disclose the third party to the principal, and the principal may then exercise the rights of the agent vis-a-vis the third party, except that the third party is unwilling to enter into the contract if it is aware of the principal while making the contract with the agent", the Plaintiff may exercise the rights of Shichang Company against COSCO. COSCO was the carrier of the carriage of goods by sea. Shichang Company, as the agent of the Plaintiff, booked space with COSCO. The Plaintiff was shipper. This contract of carriage of goods by sea is declaration of real intentions of both parties and does not violate any mandatory provision of any law or administrative regulation. So the contract shall be lawful and valid. Both parties shall exercise the rights and fulfill obligations according to the contract and the law.

As for the liabilities for the loss of the goods, the responsibilities of the carrier, COSCO, with regard to the goods carried in containers covers the entire period during which the carrier is in charge of the goods, starting from the time the carrier has taken over the goods at the port of loading, until the goods have been delivered at the port of discharge. Shichang Company, as the agent of the Plaintiff, had a deal with COSCO that the delivery terms was telex release to order when booking space with COSCO, therefore COSCO has the obligations to deliver the goods or not according to the Shichang Company's instruction. In this case, the telex release instruction of the bill of lading numbered with COSU602186080 issued by Shichang Company at 1619 on March 28, 2014 to COSCO through email, it shall be deemed as Shichang Company had clearly instructed COSCO to deliver the goods. But at 1742 on the same day, Shichang Company notified COSCO should not release the goods without the letter of guarantee. It belongs to variation of instruction. COSCO had the obligation to follow the instruct and notify the agent at the port of destination not to deliver the goods. The actual delivery time of the goods to the consignee was on April 12. Although COSCO notified the agent at the port of destination not to deliver the goods at 1730 on March 28. After COSCO received the email concerning not delivering the goods, it still had enough time to notify agent at the port of destination not to deliver the goods. But COSCO did not follow the instruction of Shichang Company nor prove that it lost control of the goods after sending the instruction of delivery of the goods to the agent at the port of destination. COSCO delivered the goods to the consignee without the new instruction of releasing the goods issued by Shichang Company. Finally, the Plaintiff lost the control of the goods and could not require COSCO to perform the contract of carriage of goods by sea. So the goods involved shall be deemed as total lost. According to provision of Paragraph 1 of Article 46 of the Maritime Code of the People's Republic of China, "the responsibilities of the carrier with regard to the goods carried in containers covers the entire period during which the carrier is in charge of the goods, starting from the time the carrier has taken over the goods at the port of loading, until the goods have been delivered at the port of discharge. The responsibility of the carrier with respect to non-containerized goods covers the period during which the carrier is in charge of the goods, starting from the time of loading of the goods onto the ship until the time the goods are discharged therefrom. During the period the carrier is in charge of the goods, the carrier shall be liable for the loss of or damage to the goods, except as otherwise provided for in this Section". COSCO did not prove the loss of goods was caused by the legal exemptions provided in Article 51 of the Maritime Code of the People's Republic of China, the Plaintiff has the right to demand COSCO to compensate for the loss of the goods.

Shichang Company, as the agent, had already performed the obligations such as booking space, charging and paying fees under freight forwarding contract, it instructed to release the goods and amended quickly. So it has no causality or fault in the loss of the goods. The loss of the goods was caused by COSCO. The claim of the Plaintiff and COSCO that Shichang Company should be liable for the loss of the goods was lack of factual and legal basis, and shall not be supported.

As for the amount of loss of goods, the value of the goods involved equals to USD101,710 on FOB basis, after deducting the deposit paid to the Plaintiff, the actual loss of the goods is USD91,710. The Plaintiff paid ocean freight in sum of USD950 to Shichang Company. Shichang Company paid ocean freight in sum of USD700 to COSCO. The ocean freight that Shichang Company charged the Plaintiff includes the ocean freight and agency fee the carrier COSCO charged. So, the loss of the goods shall be calculated as the actual ocean freight in sum of USD700 that COSCO charged. According to Article 55 of the Maritime Code of the People's Republic of China, as prescribed in Paragraph 1 "the amount of indemnity for the loss of the goods shall be calculated on the basis of the actual value of the goods so lost" and as prescribed in Paragraph 2 "the actual value shall be the value of the goods at the time of shipment plus insurance and freight", COSCO shall pay USD92,410 to the Plaintiff for the loss of the goods.

As for the interest, the Plaintiff's claim for the loss of interest complies with the law. COSCO confirmed the goods involved was delivered to the consignee on April 12, 2014. The Plaintiff's claim to calculate the interest from April 13 is reasonable. The interest shall be calculated from April 13 to the date of payment ascertained by the judgment on the basis of the loan interest rate over the same period promulgated by the People's Bank of China and dollars should be converted into RMB at the renminbi-dollar central parity rate published by the People's Bank of China on

April 13. Since April 13 was Sunday, the central parity rate on April 13 shall be substituted by the central parity rate published by the People's Bank of China on April 11. But the Plaintiff required to calculate at the rate on January 19, 2015 which was lower than that on April 11. It was disposal of its own right by the Plaintiff, so the court will support that.

In according with Article 46 Paragraph 1, Article 55 Paragraphs 1 and 2 of the Maritime Code of the People's Republic of China, the judgment is as follows:

1. The Defendant COSCO Container Lines Co., Ltd. shall pay USD92,410 for the loss of the goods and the interest thereon to the Plaintiff Zhuhai Jiaxun Saite Electronic Co., Ltd. [The interest shall be calculated from April 13, 2014 to the payment day designated by this judgment on the basis of the loan benchmark interest rate promulgated by the People's Bank of China over the same period; USD dollars shall be converted into RMB on the basis of the renminbi-dollar central parity rate (USD100 for RMB612.3) promulgated by the China Foreign Exchange Trading Center on January 19, 2015];
2. Reject other claims of the Plaintiff Zhuhai Jiaxun Saite Electronic Co., Ltd.

The pecuniary obligation mentioned above shall be fulfilled within 10 days after this judgment comes into force.

If the Defendant fails to fulfill its obligation to make the said payments within the time limit provided by this judgment, the interest for the deferred period shall be double paid according to Article 253 of the Civil Procedure Law of the People's Republic of China.

Court acceptance fee in amount of RMB10,562.59, the Plaintiff Zhuhai Jiaxun Saite Electronic Co., Ltd. shall pay RMB1,700.96 and the Defendant COSCO Container Lines Co., Ltd. shall pay RMB8,861.63.

If dissatisfied with the judgment, any party may, within 15 day upon service of the judgment, submit a Statement of Appeal to the court, with duplicates in the number of the opposing parties, so as to make an appeal before Guangdong High People's Court.

Presiding Judge: LI Lifei
Acting Judge: XU Chunlong
Acting Judge: WANG Xin

September 11, 2015

Clerk: ZHOU Xi

Haikou Maritime Court
Civil Judgment

Zhuhai Xiangzhou Haiyun Co., Ltd.
v.
Sanya Hongrui Engineer Co., Ltd. et al.

(2014) Qiong Hai Fa Shang Chu Zi No.80

Related Case(s) This is the judgment of first instance and the judgment of second instance is on page 1337.

Cause(s) of Action 213(1) Dispute over time charter party.

Headnote Owner and time charterer both held liable for breach of charter when work for which vessel had been chartered was terminated because the crew's work permits were confiscated by authorities; owner was in breach because its crew did not have adequate work permits, but charterer was in breach for failing to get correct permits for crew, and for failing to pay hire.

Summary The Plaintiffs and Defendants Hongrui entered into a charterparty that provided Defendants Hongrui would charter two vessels from Plaintiffs that would be used to repair a PRC military breakwater. The charterparty provided that Defendants Hongrui will pay monthly hire and entry, exit and dispocsal fees charged to Plaintiffs' vessels. Defendants Hongrui partially paid, and Plaintiffs released its vessels for Defendants Hongrui's use. Thereafter, Defendants Hongrui did not timely pay the aforementioned hire and fees.

Plaintiffs' vessels had certificates of seaworthiness, but the vessels' crews were not equipped with adequate certification. After entering the area to repair the PRC military breakwater, the PRC military took the crews' identification documents. As a result, the crew went on strike, which delayed the breakwater's repair.

Defendants Hongrui verbally instructed Plaintiffs' crews and vessels to withdraw, but the crews did not comply. Defendants Hongrui then issued a notice of withdrawal demanding the vessels cease operations. The notice of withdrawal stated Plaintiffs' vessels were no longer needed because construction had been completed. The notice also contained a handwritten note stating Plaintiffs' crane operators disobeyed orders. Plaintiffs' crews did not sign the notice of withdrawal. When Defendants Hongrui issued the notice of withdrawal, half the materials used to repair the breakwater were still onboard. Consequently, Plaintiffs did not withdraw its vessels immediately.

Defendants Zhongjiao's wholly owned subsidiary, Zhonghang, contracted with the PRC military to perform the breakwater construction. Plaintiffs alleged Defendants Zhongjiao contracted to award the breakwater construction project to Defendants Hongrui.

Plaintiff sued Defendants Hongrui for owed hire and sought to hold Defendants Zhongjiao jointly and severally liable. Defendants Hongrui counterclaimed against Plaintiffs for despatch and asked the court to verify that Defendants Hongrui's notice of withdrawal constituted a repudiation of the charterparty because Plaintiffs' vessels were unable to perform tasks as provided in the charterparty.

The issues before the court were as follows. (1) Whether there was a breach of the charterparty between Plaintiffs and Defendants Hongrui; (2) What was the nature of Defendants Hongrui's notice of withdrawal and whether the charterparty had been cancelled; (3) Whether Plaintiffs must return partial payments made by Defendants Hongrui; and (4) Whether Defendants Zhongjiao are jointly and severally liable to Plaintiffs for Defendants Hongrui's debt.

The court ultimately decided both Plaintiffs and Defendants Hongrui breached the charterparty. The court held Plaintiffs breached because its crews had insufficient certification documents, but the court also held Defendants Hongrui were partially liable because it did not ensure Plaintiffs' crew had adequate certification after accepting Plaintiffs' vessels. The court held Defendants Hongrui breached when it did not timely remit hire payments and entry, exit and disposal fees. The court rejected Defendants Hongrui's argument that Plaintiffs' vessels inadequately performed because Defendants Hongrui offered insufficient evidence to prove same.

The court also held Defendants Hongrui were responsible for the crew strike because it was the party charged with the responsibility of securing the vessels' personnel entry and exit permits according to the PRC military's requirements. When the PRC military confiscated Plaintiffs' crews' identification cards, which caused the strike, Defendants Hongrui did not actively remedy the situation.

Because there were no records indicating Plaintiffs' vessels had mechanical problems prior to Defendants Hongrui's issuing a notice of withdrawal, the court held Plaintiffs' inability to discharge half the materials onboard used to repair the breakwater was not a breach of charterparty.

The court determined the notice of withdrawal issued by Defendants Hongrui was a request to end the charterparty prematurely since Plaintiffs had completed the task set forth in the charterparty. The court rejected Defendants Hongrui's argument that the notice was a request for charterparty termination. As a result, the charterparty was not cancelled, and the court rejected Defendants Hongrui's argument that the charterparty should be cancelled because Plaintiffs' vessels could not perform the required construction.

The court declared both parties are responsible for losses caused by their breaches. In denying Defendants Hongrui's request for its partial entry fee reimbursement, the court held Plaintiffs' breach did not cause Defendants Hongrui's alleged loss, the partial entry fee. Rather, Defendants Hongrui were ordered to pay Plaintiffs the unpaid hire that Plaintiffs requested.

The court determined Defendants Zhongjiao were not jointly and severally liable for Defendants Hongrui's unpaid hire because Defendants Zhongjiao and its parent company, Zhonghang, were separate, independent companies.

Judgment

The Plaintiff (the counterclaim Defendant): Zhuhai Xiangzhou Haiyun Co., Ltd.
Domicile: Floor 1, Building No.9, No.8 Mingyue Road, Xiangzhou District, Guangdong.
Legal representative: ZHAN Huixia, general manager.
Agent *ad litem*: XU Bingshi, lawyer of Hainan Yanbixin Law Firm.

The Defendant (the counterclaim Plaintiff): Sanya Hongrui Engineer Co., Ltd.
Domicile: Room 2A13, Shang Shui Yun Tian Flat, East Xihe Road, Sanya City, Hainan.
Legal representative: WANG Dexian, manager.
Agent *ad litem*: HUANG Suting, lawyer of Hainan Jiatian Law Firm.
Agent *ad litem*: WU Changjiang, lawyer of Hainan Jiatian Law Firm.

The Defendant: China Communications 2nd Navigational Bureau 2nd Engineering Co., Ltd.
Domicile: No.27 Changjiang Road, Yuzhong District, Chongqing.
Legal representative: HUANG Tao, general manager.
Agent *ad litem*: WU Xiaolong, employee.
Agent *ad litem*: LIU Fengming, employee.

With respect to the case arising from the dispute over a charter party, the Plaintiff (the counterclaim Defendant) Zhuhai Xiangzhou Haiyun Co., Ltd. (hereinafter referred to as "Xiangzhou Company"), filed an action against the Defendants (the counterclaim Plaintiff) Sanya Hongrui Engineer Co., Ltd. (hereinafter referred to as "Hongrui Company") and China Communications 2nd Navigational Bureau 2nd Engineering Co., Ltd. (hereinafter referred to as "Zhongjiao Company"), before the court on July 9, 2014. The court entertained the case on the same day, constituted the collegiate panel consisted of Acting Judge WANG Weimin as Presiding Judge, People's Jurors TIAN Shihong and XU Guozhen according to the law. On September 5, Hongrui Company filed a counterclaim against Xiangzhou Company, the court entertained the case on the next day and decided to merge with the principal claim. On October 21, the court held a hearing in public. Agent *ad litem* XU Bingshi of the Plaintiff Xiangzhou Company, the legal representative WANG Dexian of the Defendant Hongrui Company and its agent *ad litem*, HUANG Suting, LU Huimin, agent *ad litem* LIU Fengming of the Defendant Zhongjiao Company, appeared in court and participated in the action. Now the case has been concluded.

Xiangzhou Company claimed that: the charterparty had been concluded between Hongrui Company and Xiangzhou Company on May 16, 2014, where the Hongtong28 tugboat; the despatch cost of both vessels was in the sum of RMB360,000 and the monthly hire was in amount of RMB290,000. The hire shall be counted for three months when the period of charter was less than three months, and the hire shall be calculated by the actual time if the period of charter exceeded three months; After Xiangzhou Company had paid one month's hire and the despatch cost in amount of RMB650,000, the vessels was manoeuvred to the nominated water area for working. Xiangzhou Company was required by Hongrui Company to manoeuvre vessels for working upon merely payment of an amount of RMB180,000, who warrantied that the rest amount of RMB470,000 will be paid in one installment upon the arrival of vessels to the place of working. Vessels had been manoeuvred by Xiangzhou Company to the place of working in Sanya on May 30 and all stones necessary for reinforcing the breakwater had been carried and discharged till June 17. However, Hongrui Company failed to pay the hire and despatch cost pursuant to the charterparty, and forced vessels and mariners to be away. Under this circumstance, Xiangzhou Company raised a claim against Hongrui Company and Zhongjiao Company for the joint payment of hire of vessels and the despatch cost in amount of RMB1,050,000 and the court fees should be born by Hongrui Company and Zhongjiao Company.

Hongrui Company argued and counterclaimed that: firstly, Xiangzhou Company was not entitled to claim the despatch. While the article 6 of the charterparty provided that vessels shall be manoeuvred to the nominated place upon the payment of the first-month hire and the despatch in amount of RMB650,000, a verbal agreement was in fact reached through negotiation of both parties, that Xiangzhou Company might manoeuvre vessels to the nominated place if the despatch in amount of RMB180,000 was paid in advance and the despatch should be paid upon the completion of performance of the charterparty, and the hire should be still paid pursuant to the charterparty. Hongrui Company paid the despatch in amount of RMB180,000 according to the verbal agreement, Xiangzhou Company manoeuvred vessels to the nominated place for working, until then the verbal agreement was confirmed by both parties' actual performance. The delay and several times of repairing of vessels and strikes failed to achieve the purpose of the charterparty in the performance of the charterparty, where the entire working time was merely 50 h and Hongrui Company required to repudiate this charterparty and the despatch should be born by Xiangzhou Company. The request of payment of the despatch by Xiangzhou Company was groundless and shall be rejected.

Secondly, Xiangzhou Company was not entitled to claim the hire. "the hire shall be counted for three months if the period of charter is less than three months" set forth in the article 4 of the charterparty meant that hires shall be paid for three months in case the charterparty completed smoothly and the engineer worked out in less than three months. Since Xiangzhou Company breached the charterparty, failed to provide seaworthy vessels and repaired vessels in several times and the strike happened, the entire working time was merely 50 h, which made Xiangzhou Company fail to complete the work. Xiangzhou Company never provided the debit note to Hongrui Company signed by itself, whereas the charterparty provided that Hongrui Company shall make payment after three day upon the supplement of the debit note and receipt by Xiangzhou Company to be signed by Hongrui Company according to the charterparty. Therefore, the claim of hire of three months by Xiangzhou Company was groundless and shall be rejected.

Thirdly, Hongrui Company required the Court to confirm the repudiation of the charterparty and the loss suffered by Hongrui Company as the result of the failure of performance and Xiangzhou Company shall reimburse the despatch in amount of RMB180,000.

Hongrui Company issued the order of dismiss on June 24, 2014 and ordered Xiangzhou Company to get away given the Xiangzhou Company breached the charterparty to fail to provide seaworthy vessel for the requirement of working and did not possess the capability of performance of charterparty. The contract between both parties had been repudiated upon the issue of notice of dismiss and the severe breach of contract of Xiangzhou Company resulted in another charterparty for working, where the loss suffered therefrom shall be born by Xiangzhou Company.

In light of the above, Hongrui Company required the court to refute the request of Xiangzhou Company. Meanwhile, Hongrui Company required the court to confirm the repudiation of contract between both parties and to decide that Xiangzhou Company shall reimburse the despatch costs in amount of RMB180,000 and bear all court fees for the legal interest of Hongrui Company.

Zhongjiao Company argued that Xiangzhou Company shall not be identified as a proper Defendant since it was Zhongjiao Company Second Harbor Engineering Ltd. (hereinafter referred to as Zhonghang Company) rather than Zhongjiao Company that concluded the contract with Army 91,003. Zhongjiao Company, as the whole owning company of Zhonghang Company, shall be identified as a independent entity and shall not bear relevant responsibility.

Xianghzou Company, as the Defendant in the counter-claim, argued that: firstly, the delay and consecutive repairing of vessels and strikes of mariner did not occur to Xiangzhou Company. Hongrui Company made a merely payment in amount of RMB180,000 on May 21, 2014, and informed Xiangzhou Company of the rest amount of RMB470,000 in three day by call. However, Hongrui Company failed to pay the aforesaid amount and undertook to Xiangzhou Company that Hongrui Company would pay off the rest amount on the date of the arrival of vessels at Tielu Port of Sanya. Under this circumstance, vessels were manoeuvred to set off, on the basis of trust to Hongrui Company, from Wanzai port of Zhuhai city at 11 a.m. on 25 May and arrived at Tielu port at 2 a.m. on May 30, whereas Hongrui Company failed to pay off the rest fund. Vessels of Xiangzhou Company spared no effort to work upon arrival at the nominated port, and all stones necessary for reinforcing the breakwater had been carried and discharged till June 17, whereas the rest of stones had no place to discharge and all stones were discharged until July 9. The claim of Hongrui Company as to the delay and repairing in several times of vessels as well as the strike of mariners was not true. Besides, the contract temporarily set the time of working on April 23, 2014 and the accurate time shall be subject to the written notice issued by Hongrui Company, whereas the aforesaid written notice was not sent to Xiangzhou Company.

Secondly, Xiangzhou Company failed to produce loss to Hongrui Company. The delay of vessels resulting in another charter of vessels and unnecessary loss claimed by Hongrui Company was not in compliance with the truth. Vessels hired by Hongrui Company were not equipped with grapple and did not possess the function to discharge stones for working, and were only used for loading and discharging components of the breakwater. Two vessels provided by Xiangzhou Company were equipped with special grapple, which could grab stones to the breakwater 30 m away therefrom. When vessels came into this nominated place, actual loss did not occur to Hongrui Company given that the discharging had been completed till June 17. Thus, the hire of other vessels was not related to Xiangzhou Company.

The despatch cost in amount of RMB360,000 was provided in the contract and the costs actually happened. Two vessels of Xiangzhou Company, the speed of which were 4 miles/hour, shall normally took 5 days from Zhuhai to Sanya, the distance of which was 450 miles and oil consumption of which was 20 tons. Thus the despatch in amount of RMB360,000 was the actual costs happened. However, Hongrui Company not only failed to pay the dismiss costs in amount of RMB180,000, but also required Xiangzhou Company to reimburse the approach costs in sum of RMB180,000, which was absolutely groundless. In light of the above, Xiangzhou Company required the Court to refute the request of Hongrui Company in the counterclaim.

For supporting the request, Xiangzhou Company adduced the evidence as follows (evidence 1,2,3,4,5,6 were adduced in the period of adducing evidence and evidence 8,9,10,11 were adduced on October 20, 2014): 1. the charterparty concluded between Xiangzhou Company and Hongrui Company; 2. the safety agreement concluded between Xiangzhou Company and Hongrui Company; 3. the first certificate issued by Guo Songgen and other five mariners on June 29, 2014; 4. the second certificate issued by Guo Songgen and other five mariners on June 29, 2014; 5. certificate of nationality and minimum safety manning and inspection of M.V. "28", and certificate of nationality and maritime vessel inspection and seaworthiness; 6. registry material of Hongrui Company; 7. sixteen photos; 8. time of approach and confirmation of oil; 9. document of fuel; 10. log book of M.V. "28"; and 11. bank remittance slip of ICBC in amount of RMB180,000.

The examination argument of Hongrui Company as to the evidence adduced by Xiangzhou Company were as follows: Hongrui Company confirmed the authenticity, legality and relevancy of evidence 1,2,6,11. Hongrui Company refused to recognize the authenticity of evidence No.3,4,5,8,10 and argue that evidence 3,4 had no probative force given that the witnesses were mariners who had interests in this case and shall not be identified as witness of the case. Meanwhile, since evidence 5 was not consistent with the status of vessels, which had been repaired for several times and were not seaworthy, the authenticity of certificates including certificate of quality of inspection may not be confirmed, which meant vessels provided by Xiangzhou Company were likely to be deck vessels rather than the vessels on those certificate; The data of oil in evidence 8 was written by Jing Hua as the person in charge and the rest data was added by Xiangzhou Company itself; evidence 10 was fake since evidence recorded that vessels stayed in Tielu port for 15 days, whereas Tielu port was not a working port, which meant that vessels may not stay in Tielu port for 15 days; Hongrui Company confirmed the authenticity of evidence No.7, but refused to recognize the legality hereof given that this evidence was not capable to prove the actual working of vessels and the failure of discharging stones was attributable to the strike of mariners rather than Hongrui Company. Hongrui Company refused to recognize the relevancy of evidence 9 since the date of issuing the receipt was from July 26 to July 28, which meant the fueling was not in connection with this case.

The failure of Zhongjaio Company to exam the evidence adduced by Xiangzhou Company shall be deemed as a waiver of its right as to the examination of the aforesaid evidence.

Regarding the evidence provided by Xiangzhou Company, the court considers that:

Firstly, Hongrui Company recognized the authenticity, legality and relevancy of evidence 1,2,6,11, and the court accepted it.

Secondly, as regards evidence 3,4, the court held that the two affidavits provided by mariners employed by Xiangzhou Company who experienced all incidents, combined with the court hearing, were consistent with other evidence. The court decided to accept both of the evidence.

Thirdly, with reference to evidence 5, Hongrui Company refused to recognize its authenticity since vessels provided by Xiangzhou Company had been repaired for several times and might be deck vessels. The court held that the aforesaid evidence were issued by national statutory authorities and the repairing of vessels was normal, so the refutation shall be groundless. Besides, Hongrui Company failed to adduce evidence to prove the existence of deck vessels. Therefore, the court confirms evidence 5.

Fourthly, in respect of evidence 7, Hongrui Company recognized its authenticity whereas it refused to recognize its legality. The court held that the content was associated with the breakwater and its working vessels, while this evidence derived from the place of armies. Thus, the content of this evidence was not illegal and the method to achieve did not infringe others' legal interests or violate legally prohibiting provisions. Thus, the court accepted this evidence.

Fifthly, with regard to evidence 8, Hongrui Company refused to recognize its authenticity and considered that the data of oil was merely confirmed by its employee and that other contents like the approach time and the person in charge were absolutely forged. In this respect, the court held that the data of oil and the approach time shall be of essence in the performance of the contract, and only after the confirmation of the rest of the data of oil and the approach time in practice may vessels of Xiangzhou Company proceeded to work; Besides, this evidence was original and had no amendment, and evidence 3,4, also proved that vessels arrived at Tielu port and stones was loaded on May 30, 2014. As far as three evidence concerned, these three evidence were capable to be consistent with each of them, and Hongrui Company proved that "LAO Li" was the mariner to discharge stones and "SUN Gong" was the person to manoeuvre in the court hearing. Therefore, the Court confirmed this evidence.

Sixthly, with regard to evidence 9, Hongrui Company refused to recognize its relevancy. In this respect, the court held that the date of issuing invoices to Xiangzhou Company commenced from July 26 to 28, 2014, and Xiangzhou Company explained that the oil was purchased before the date of issuing invoices and this invoice was issued for supplement in the court hearing. This evidence may prove that the oil of vessels was purchased in Hainan for Hainan affiliate of Sinopec was the company to issue this invoice, which referred to the despatch costs and had connection with this case. Therefore, the court confirmed this evidence.

Seventhly, regarding evidence 10 Hongrui Company refused to recognize its authenticity and held that this evidence was forged since the record in respect of the period of 15 days in Tielu port was not true. In this regard, the court was of the view that the log book was the statutory and original source recording the navigation and working status by mariners in duty. The log book of M.V. "28" recorded the circumstances relating to the set-off and the time of port as well as the working. According to the log book, it was clear that the action against the typhoon "Weimaxun" in Tielu port after the working was consistent with the actual situation and evidence No.3,4. Besides, Hongrui Company failed to bear the burden of proof to prove the aforesaid log book was forged. Thus, the court accepted this evidence.

Xiangzhou Company claimed the mariners on M.V. "28" and M.V. "6" all had effective certificate in the court hearing but failed to submit them to the Court.

For supporting its argument and its claims in the counterclaim, Hongrui Company submitted the following evidence as below (evidence 1,2,3,4 were submitted during the period of adducing evidence, and the evidence 5 was submitted in the court hearing):

1. The working record of M.V. "28" and M.V. "6"; 2. certificate of army No.91003 of PRC; 3. charterparty between M.V. "Fengwang 8" and M.V. "Suyunhaiji 187"; 4. The notice of dismissing; 5. The working record of M.V. "Fengwang 8" and M.V. "Suyunhaiji 187".

Xiangzhou Company refused to recognize the authenticity, legality and relevancy of all of evidence rendered by Hongrui Company. Xiangzhou Company was of the view that in the evidence No.1 the managing department of China Communications 2nd Navigational Bureau 2nd Engineering Co., Ltd. (hereinafter referred to as "Second Department") was not conversant with the situation of working, and the circumstance relating to the discharging of stones was not consistent with the actual circumstance; In the evidence No.2 the army was not conversant with the working situation and was unlikely to issue certificate in connection with the working circumstance; In the evidence No.3 when discharging the stones, only vessels of Xiangzhou Company furnishing grapples satisfied the required conditions; In the evidence No.4 the notice of dismissing was never received by Xiangzhou Company. The evidence No.5 was not relating to this case.

The failure of Zhongjiao Company to exam the evidence submitted by Hongrui Company shall be deemed as the waive of its rights of examination.

For the evidence that Hongrui Company submitted, the court considered that:

1. With regard to evidence No.1, the court considered that: the evidence was formed on 29 August, 2014, after XiangZhou Ship Company filed the litigation, but there were only the stamp of program department of the Second Shipping Office and the signature of Hongrui Company's employee, without the confirmation of the construction side Xiangzhou Shipping, which was contrary to common sense. Hongrui also did not provide the original record of document with the confirmation by the construction side. The evidence recorded the time for the entry of the Xiangzhou Shipping's ship, May 31, 2014, it did not match the identified entry time stated in the oil confirmation sheet, and the ultimate throwing stone time did not match the time recorded in the navigation logbook. As a result, the court shall not confirm the authenticity of the evidence.
2. With regard to evidence 2 Xiangzhou Shipping considered that the troops did not know the construction situation well, the troops could not issue the relevant construction and other content of the proof. Therefore, Xiangzhou Shipping did not approve the reality. The court considered that: the content of this evidence was basically same as evidence 1 submitted by Hongrui Company. However, there was no detailed record of 91,003 troops on the construction situation, such as daily working hours and construction quantity. The court shall not confirm this evidence.
3. With regard to evidence 3 Xiangzhou Shipping believed that only their own ship achieved the conditions of the project at that time. The court held that this evidence and evidence 5 confirmed each other, Xiangzhou Shipping did not provide contrary evidence to prove, the court shall affirm the authenticity of this evidence.
4. With regard to evidence 4 Xiangzhou Shipping said it had never received the "Withdrawal notice of the ship". The Court considered that: under Article 2 of the charter party to terminate the lease in advance or Article 12 in respect of the early termination of the contract shall be notified in writing. The evidence was not supported by the evidence signed by Xiangzhou Shipping, but in the trial both sides confirmed the fact that Hongrui company had sent to Xiangzhou Shipping the Withdrawal notice of the ship orally on June 17, 2014. Therefore, Hongrui company informed Xiangzhou Shipping of the exit in writing accorded with common sense, and the reason for Xiangzhou Shipping did not sign had been noted. The Court recognized the authenticity of the evidence and the fact that Hongrui Company had issued Withdrawal notice of the ship to Xiangzhou Shipping Company.
5. With regard to evidence 5, Xiangzhou Shipping did not affirm the authenticity of this evidence. The court held that this evidence and evidence 5 confirmed each other, Xiangzhou Shipping did not provide contrary evidence to prove, the court shall affirm the authenticity of this evidence.

In support of its defense, China Communications Construction Company Ltd. (Zhongjiao Company) submitted an evidence, namely the Contract of Construction

Framework for Repairing Yalong Bay's South Breakwater. Xiangzhou Shipping had no objection to authenticity, relevancy and legality of the evidence, but considered that Zhongjiao Company, as the specific construction side of the project, should bear the relevant responsibilities. Hongrui Company had no objection to authenticity and legality except relevancy, according to the principle of privity of contract, China National Aviation Corporation (Zhonghang Company) and Zhongjiao Company were not eligible Defendants in this case. The court considered that: the project under construction of Xiangzhou Shipping and Hongrui Company was the same one project under the Contract of Construction Framework for Repairing Yalong Bay's South Breakwater in the case, there was a clear correlation between the evidence and the case. The court shall affirm the evidence.

According to the above-mentioned evidence, the certification, combined with the facts of the trial and argument of the parties, the court concluded the following facts:

On May 16, 2014, Xiangzhou Shipping and Hongrui Company signed the charter party, and agreed in the contract: Due to the project needs of repairing HaiNan Sanya Yalong Bay breakwater, Xiangzhou Shipping rented Vessel No.28 and Vessel No.6 to Hongrui company. The entry and exit fess of the vessels was RMB360,000, the hire per month was RMB290,00, if the charter period was less than three months, the rate will calculated for three months; more than three months, the hire will be calculated according to the actual number of days. The charter period was agreed tentatively for three months and the entry time was agreed tentatively at April 23 of the same year, the specific time was subject to the written notice of Hongrui Company. Hongrui Company shall notify Xiangzhou Shipping in written form three days in advance if the change of construction process or the change of construction period of the project required advancing or delaying termination of the charter period, the termination time of the written notice shall be the final lease time. If Hongrui Company confirmed that XiangZhou Boat had lost the ability to perform the contract, Hongrui shall have the right to notify XiangZhou Ship to terminate the contract. Xiangzhou Shipping must receive the hire for first month and the fee for entry and exist field totally in amount of RMB650,000 all at once before the transfer of the ship to the designated transfer place, the rest hire was settled per month, Hongrui shall pay within 3 days upon receiving the settlement signed by itself and the receipt issued by Xiangzhou Shipping. Two sides shall settle the final settlement upon completion of the leasing of the vessel, Hongrui Company shall pay the balance of the hire within 3 working days upon receiving the receipt issued by Xiangzhou Shipping. Xiangzhou Shipping should provide the seaworthy ship with valid certificate issued by seaworthiness and maritime departments and the corresponding certificate, and fully man the crew with certificate of competency. The ship should be ready to work 24 h a day, at least 8 h a day. The hire shall not be deducted if the vessels stop working within 4 days due to the default of vessels, and the hire shall be deducted according to the converted hire for the time more than 4 days. Hongrui Company should provide convenience in life to Xiangzhou Shipping. Both the parties did not agree on breach penalty.

On May 21, 2014, Hongrui Company paid the vessel entry fee in sum of RMB180,000 to Xiangzhou Shipping after signing the contract. In the condition that Hongrui Company did not pay the balance in sum of RMB470,000, Xiangzhou Shipping dispatched Vessel No.28 and Vessel No.6 to proceed from Wanzai Port, Zhuhai on May 25, arrived in Tielu Port, Sanya at 2:00 on 30th May. In the morning, Hongrui Company arranged Jinghua, the leader of stone quarry, embarked on the measurement of remaining oil and the record of entry time, and arranged the vessels to ship stone near Tielu Port. After the loading of stone, the ship arrived at the military breakwater for normal construction operations on the same day. On the one hand, on June 7, 91,003 troops took the ID cards of crew for handling the pass, which led to inconvenience to the crew's in and out, resulted in difficulties in supply of the ship. On the other hand, due to delays of Hongrui Company in the payment of the remaining dispatch fee and the hire for first month, on June 17, Xiangzhou Shipping crew went to strike collectively, and then the ID cards were returned to the crew on the same day because of the coordination of Hongrui company, Vessel No.28 and Vessel No.6 resumed construction on the same day. On the same day, Hong Rui company informed the crew orally, requested the ships to leave, and no longer arranged construction work. On June 24, Hongrui Company issued a "withdrawal notice of the ship" to Xiangzhou Shipping, required the ships to exit on the same day and withdraw from the construction site within 3 days. There was the signature of Hongrui company site person in charge of the project in the notice, but no Xiangzhou ship's stamp or signature of the responsible person. Because half-ship of stones had not been cast, Xiangzhou Shipping did not withdraw the ships. On 8 July, the responsible on-site person of Hongrui Company arranged the ships to dump the remaining stones in the designated location of the breakwater next day, the stone was cast on the 9th, after that, they left the military breakwaters on July 10 and arrived at Tielu Port, Sanya on the same day. Due to the Typhoon "Vimasson", the ship refueled and took precautions against typhoons in Sanya on 15 July, and left Hainan on 23th July. The two sides disputed over the vessel disposal fee, hire and construction issues and etc., then failed in negotiations, so sued to the court.

The court had ascertained that, Vessel No.28 held a valid certificate of nationality of the ship, the ship minimum safe manning certificate, coastal boat inspection certificate. Vessel No.6 held a valid certificate of nationality of the ship, certificate of inspection of ships at sea, seaworthiness certificate. The above certificates showed that the two vessels had been inspected and were in the seaworthy condition.

On November 21, 2013, 91,003 troops units and Zhonghang Company signed the Yalong Bay Harbor breakwater repair works construction contract. Zhongjiao Company was a wholly-owned subsidiary of Zhonghang Company, which was an independent legal entity.

The court held that this case was the dispute arising from the charter party. The charter party signed by Xiangzhou Shipping and Hongrui Company was the true meaning of two parties, and did not violate the laws and the mandatory provisions of administrative regulations, constituted a valid contract, legally bounded the parties.

The key dispute of this case were as follows: whether there was a breach of contract between Xiangzhou Shipping and Hongrui Company, the nature of the Withdrawal notice of the ship and whether the contract had been canceled, whether Hongrui Company should pay the ship entry, exit fees and the balance of hire and whether Xiangzhou Shipping should return the entry fee in sum of RMB180,000 of the vessels, whether Zhongjiao Company should be jointly and severally liable.

1. Whether there was a breach of contract between Xiangzhou Shipping and Hongrui Company

1) Hongrui Company failed to pay the ship entry, exit fees and the hire for first month in full and on time, whether this was a breach of contract.

According to Article 6 Paragraph 2 of charter party, Xiangzhou Shipping dispatched the vessels to the designated transfer point, the precedent condition of which was that Hongrui Company paid the hire for first month and the fee for entry and exist field totally in sum of RMB650,000 all at once. Xiangzhou Shipping dispatched the ship to the designated transfer point and started construction works according to the requirements of Hongrui Company in the cases while Hongrui Company paid only RMB180,000, which did not violate the contract and was conducive to Hongrui Company, the obligation to pay the ship entry and exist the field and the balance of the hire for first month totally in sum of RMB470,000 in full of Hongrui Company cannot be exempted according to the contract. Xiangzhou Shipping can request Hongrui company to pay the balance in sum of RMB470,000 at any time. Hongrui company did not pay RMB470,000 on time to Xiangzhou Shipping, which constituted breach of the contract. Article 5 of the charter party stipulated the settlement and payment, which was not inconsistent with the stipulations in Article 6 (2) concerning the conditions for dispatch of vessels. Hongrui Company invoked Article 5 of the charter party, advocated that the ship exit and dispatch fees shall be settled after the completion of the contract, the hire were settled per month, which lacked facts and legal basis, shall be dismissed.

2) Xiangzhou Shipping did not equip the vessel with crew in possession of appropriate certificates of competency, whether this was a breach of contract.

According to Article 9 (2) of the charterparty, Xiangzhou Ships shall provide an seaworthy vessel with valid seaworthiness certificate and other corresponding ship certificates and meet the need of 24-h operation at all times, and shall equip the vessels with sufficient crew in possession of appropriate certificates of competency. In the lawsuit, Xiangzhou Shipping only proved that Vessel No.28 and Vessel No.6 had valid seaworthiness certificates, but failed to provide the crews with valid certificates of competency, should be liable for the failure on burden of proof. Xiangzhou Shipping did not equip the crew with valid certificates of competency, which constituted a breach of contract. Hongrui Company accepted and disposed Vessel No.28 and Vessel No.6 for construction operations without inspecting of the valid certificate of crew, should bear some fault liability.

2. Whether there were breaches of contract such as a number of maintenance of the vessels delayed the construction schedule in the construction process, worked less than 8 h per day, worked cumulatively less than 50 h.

Log Book showed that the vessels of Xiangzhou Shipping were in normal working condition from May 30, 2014 to June 16, 2014 before Hongrui informed Xiangzhou of exit orally on June 17, there were no situations such as delayed in the construction schedule, worked less than 8 h a day, worked cumulatively time less than 50 h and so on due to maintenance. Hongrui Company claimed that Xiangzhou Shipping had breaches as aforesaid, the main base were the accounting records of Vessel No.28 and Vessel No.6 which had not been recognized by the court. Even according to the accounting records, the cumulative downtime of the vessels of Xiangzhou Shipping due to maintenance did not exceed 4 days without deduction of rent which agreed in contract, and the 50 h Hongrui Company recorded was not accurate, the time required for the necessary steps of construction, such as "connecting and drawing", "anchor positioning" and "reloading", should reasonably be calculated within the construction time, but Hongrui Company had not recorded. Whether daily operating time of Vessel No.28 and Vessel No.6 was up to 8 h, not only depended on the ship maintenance and crew's attitude, but also depended on the Hongrui Company's construction work arrangements. In this case, in addition to the crew dispute happened on June 17 between two parties, the vessels had been under construction according to the requirements of Hongrui Company all the time, there was no rejection of construction or situations contrary to the construction arrangements of Hongrui Company. Hongrui Company's defense was not established, the court shall not support it.

3. The responsibility of strike among crew of Xiangzhou Shipping

Because the project involved in the case was in the military camp, according to Article 9.4.1 of the charter party, Hongrui Company shall provide the Xiangzhou Shipping Company with the convenience of handling personnel entry and exit documents. On June 7, 2014, after 91,003 troops taking the crew's ID card for handling the pass, Hongrui company should have coordinated with the troops actively to return the crew's ID cards as soon as possible or let the crew out for supply. Hongrui company did not fulfill the obligations actively, resulting in difficulties in ship supply, and Hongrui Company did not pay the balance of the entry, exit and disposal fees of ship and hire on time, resulting in the collective strike among crew of Vessel No.28 and Vessel No.6 on June 17, the fault liability was in the Hongrui Company.

4. The responsibility for Xiangzhou Shipping who had not cast half - ship stones

On June 17, 2014, Hongrui company informed the crew orally, requested the ships to leave, and issued Xiangzhou Shipping a "withdrawal notice of the ship" on June 24, required ships to exit on the same day. At this time, half-ship stone materials had not been cast, the stones were placed in the troop rock breakwater until July 9. Xiangzhou Shipping company said after the strike happened on June 17, Hongrui company asked the ship to exit, and no longer arranged the work and the location of cast, which led to the stone be thrown on July 9 the same year. Hongrui Company contradicted that because the Xiangzhou Shipping's ship had mechanical failure, resulted in the failure to throw the stones in time. The court held that, according to the logbook records, Hongrui's staff boarded the ship on July 8 of the same year and asked to cast the remaining stones to the designated location of the military breakwater next day, there was no record that Hongrui requested to cast, which can prove that Hongrui Company did not make arrangements in time, resulted in the failure to throw the stones in time. Xiangzhou Shipping said the Hongrui Company did not promptly arranged, resulted in the failure to throw the half-ship stones in time, the court supported the argument. Before June 17 the ship worked properly, then the ship's stoppage was not due to the ship's breakdown, but due to the reason that Hongrui Company asked the ship to stop working, Hongrui also failed to issue evidence to prove Xiangzhou Shipping's vessels cannot cast stone after a mechanical failure on June 17 in the same year, it should be liable for the failure on burden of proof, Hongrui Company's defense was not established, the court did not support.

5. The nature of the withdrawal notice of the ship and whether the contract had been cancelled

According to "due to the work of the contract has been completed, we hereby notify you that the vessel Hongtong 28, Shunxing 6 shall exit today" and "the ships are in good condition" recognized in the "withdrawal notice of the ship" by Hongrui Company, it should be recognized that the reason for Xiangzhou Shipping's exit was that Xiangzhou Shipping had completed the construction task according to the contract. Hongrui Company said the withdrawal notice was based on Article 12 of the contract that Xiangzhou Shipping had lost the ability to perform the contract, so Hongrui Company notified the Xiangzhou Shipping to terminate the contract and asked the ship to exit. Clearly, this claim did not meet the above content Hongrui recognized in withdrawal notice of the ship, and Withdrawal notice of the ship did not mention the cancellation or termination of contract.

"Withdrawal notice of the ship" added handwritten note in the margin, "the ship crane did not obey the site arrangements, did not listen to the command, was ordered to exit, the ship refused to sign", literally, it can be interpreted as the reason for the principal of Xiangzhou Shipping refused to sign, and also can be understood that Xiangzhou Shipping's vessels did not obey the site arrangements and command, Hongrui company asked it to exit. In the performance of the contract, in addition to a brief strike among the crew due to the dispute between two parties on June 17, 2014, and the crew resumed construction immediately after the resumption of identity documents, there was no the situation where Xiangzhou Shippping's vessels did not listen to site arrangement and command of Hongrui Company. Hongrui Company on the day of resumption of work informed Xiangzhou Shipping to stop working and exit orally, and did not arranged Xiangzhou Shipping any construction task until June 24 when issued "withdrawal notice of the ship", Xiangzhou Shipping should not be held responsible. The latter understanding of the contents of the "withdrawal notice of the ship" was obviously inconsistent with other contents confirmed by Hongrui Company, and was inconsistent with the situation where Xiangzhou Shippping's vessels did not listen to site arrangement and command of Hongrui Company. The contents of the handwritten note shall be deemed to be the explanation of the reasons for the refusal of the principal of Xiangzhou Shippping to sign the "withdrawal notice of the ship".

In summary, the "withdrawal notice of the ship" shall be regarded as Hongrui Company considered that Xiangzhou Shipping Company had completed the construction task and sent a written notice to Xiangzhou Shipping requesting to terminate charter period in advance according to Article 2 of the charter party, rather than the written notice that Hongrui Company requested to terminate the contract. The allegation that Hongrui requested to confirm that the "ship charter party" had been lifted lacked facts and legal basis, the court shall not support.

6. Whether Xiangzhou Shipping should return RMB180,000 to Hongrui Company and whether Hongrui Company should pay the ship entry, exit fees and the balance of hire.

According to Article 120 of the Contract Law of the People's Republic of China, if both parties breach a contract, each party shall bear its own respective liabilities. In this case, both parties had a breach of contract. Xiangzhou Shipping did not equip the vessels with the crew with valid certificates of competency, breached the contract, but it had completed the construction task required by Hongrui Company, and Hongrui Company did not provide evidence to prove the actual losses alleged suffered, both parties did not make an agreement on liquidated damages. Even if Hongrui Company proved the actual losses caused by the breach of Xiangzhou Shipping, Xiangzhou was responsible for the actual loss, rather than the responsibility to return the entry fees in sum of RMB180,000. The allegation that Hongrui requested Xiangzhou Shipping to return RMB180,000 lacked facts and legal basis, the Court shall not support.

According to Article 60 Paragraph 1 of the Contract Law of the People's Republic of China, each party shall fully perform its own obligations as agreed upon. In this case, Xiangzhou Shipping had completed the construction work according to the requirements of Hongrui Company, and Hongrui Company shall perform the obligation to pay the vessel's entry, exit fees and hire according to the contract. Vessel No.28 and Vessel No.6 of Xiangzhou Shipping entered and completed the construction tasks till the exit according to the requirements of Hongrui, the period of which was less than three months, the obligations that according to the Article 4 Paragraph 1 of charter party,"the rate of hire per month is RMB290,00, if the charter period is less than three months, the rate will be calculated for three months" cannot be exempted. Accordingly, Hongrui Company should pay the hire in sum of RMB870,000 and the ship entry and exit fees of the vessels in sum of RMB360,000 to Xiangzhou Shipping according to the contract. In the performance of the contract, Hongrui Company had paid RMB180,000 to Xiangzhou Shipping. Therefore, Hongrui Company should pay Xiangzhou Shipping entry and exit fees and hire in sum of RMB1,050,000. The allegation that Xiangzhou Shipping requested Hongrui to pay entry and exit fees and hire in sum of RMB1,050,000 shall be supported by the Court.

7. Whether Zhongjiao Company should be jointly and severally liable

Who signed with the troop 91,003 the Contract of Construction Framework for Repairing Yalong Bay's South Breakwater was Zhonghang Company, its wholly-owned subsidiary, Zhongjiao Company, was an independent enterprise legal person. Xiangzhou Shipping did not provide evidence that Zhongjiao Company contracted award the project to Hongrui Company, the allegation that Xiangzhou Shipping requested Zhongjiao Company to be jointly and severally liable for the debt of Hongrui Company shall not be supported by the court.

In summary, according to Article 44 and Article 60 Paragraph 1 of the Contract Law of the People's Republic of China, the judgment is as follows:

1. The Defendant Hongrui Company shall, within ten days as of the effective day of this judgment, pay the Plaintiff Xiangzhou Shipping the entry and exit fees and hire in sum of RMB1,050,000;
2. Reject other claims made by the Plaintiff Xiangzhou Shipping;
3. Reject claim of the counterclaim Plaintiff Hongrui Company;

The parties have the obligation to make the said payments within the time limit provided by this judgment, the interest shall be double paid for the period of deferred payment according to Article 253 of the Civil Procedure Law of the People's Republic of China.

Court acceptance fee in amount of RMB14,250, counterclaim court acceptance fee in amount of RMB7,125, a total of RMB21,375, shall be born by Hongrui Company.

In the event of dissatisfaction with this judgment, the Plaintiff may within 30 days upon the service of this judgment, and the Defendants may within 15 days upon the service of this judgment submit a statement of appeal to the court, together with copies in the number of the opposite party, to lodge an appeal before Hainan High People's Court of the People's Republic of China.

Presiding Judge: WANG Weimin
People's Juror: XU Guozhen
People's Juror: TIAN Shihong

December 16, 2014

Clerk: HUANG Haijun

Hainan High People's Court
Civil Judgment

Zhuhai Xiangzhou Haiyun Co., Ltd.
v.
Sanya Hongrui Engineer Co., Ltd. et al.

(2015) Qiong Min San Zhong Zi No.25

Related Case(s) This is the judgment of second instance, and the judgment of first instance is on page 1321.

Cause(s) of Action 213(1) Dispute over time charter party.

Headnote Dispute about whether time charter had been terminated by charterer on ground that vessel could not perform chartered work held resolved in favour of owner.

Summary This case is an appeal of the (2014) Qiong Hai Fa Shang Chu Zi No.80 judgment. Plaintiffs prevailed below, and Defendants filed this appeal. Defendants alleged the court below admitted improper evidence and refused to admit valid evidence. Defendants argued the vessel leasing contract between Defendants and Plaintiffs was terminated due to dissolution by appointment, statutory dissolution and/or dissolution by agreement. Because the vessel leasing contract was terminated, Defendants argued Plaintiffs should refund Defendants' partial payment. Furthermore, Defendants argued it was not responsible for disposal fees or hire because the vessel leasing contract's purpose had been frustrated due to Plaintiffs' vessels working an insufficient amount of time.

The court concluded the lower court improperly admitted evidence, but the lower court's error did not affect the final judgment. The remaining issues before the court were as follows. 1) Whether the vessel leasing contract between Plaintiffs and Defendants had been terminated by dissolution by appointment, statutory dissolution or dissolution by agreement and whether Plaintiffs should return Defendants' partial payment. 2) Whether Defendants should pay the vessels' disposal fees and hire.

The court ultimately recognized the judgment below and found the vessel lease agreement had not been terminated and held Plaintiffs did not have to refund Defendants' partial payment. Defendants argued the agreement had been dissolved by appointment because the agreement allowed Defendants to terminate it if Plaintiffs' vessels could no longer perform. The agreement stipulated that Defendants should fully pay the first month's hire before using Plaintiffs' vessels. Defendants argued the parties agreed to a different payment plan when Plaintiffs allowed Defendants to initially pay partial vessel hire and use the vessels thereafter. The court held Defendants could not prove the parties agreed to a different payment plan, and Defendants breached because they did not initially pay the first month hire in full. The court reasoned the agreement had not been dissolved by appointment because Defendants, the breaching party, unilaterally chose not to perform.

When a breaching party frustrates the contract's purpose, statutory dissolution allows a non-breaching party to terminate the contract. Because Defendants did not pay the first month's hire according to the agreement, the court held Defendants could not take advantage of statutory dissolution to terminate the agreement.

Even though Defendants sent a withdrawal notice to Plaintiffs, the court held the agreement had not been dissolved by agreement because the parties had not agreed to terminate the contract nor did Plaintiffs sign the withdrawal notice.

Ultimately deciding the contract's purpose had not been frustrated, the court ordered Defendants to pay for Plaintiffs' vessels' disposal fees and hire. The agreement provided that, if the vessel hire time was less than three months, three months of hire would be paid. Even though Plaintiffs' vessels worked far less than three months, the court reasoned Defendants unilaterally decided not to perform and breached the agreement. according to the agreement's plain language, the court ordered Defendants pay the vessels' disposal fees and three months of hire to Plaintiffs.

Judgment

The Appellant (the Defendant of first instance, the counterclaim Plaintiff of first instance): Sanya Hongrui Engineer Co., Ltd.
Domicile: Room 2A13, Shang Shui Yun Tian Flat, East Xihe Road, Sanya City, Hainan.
Legal representative: WANG Dexian, manager.
Agent *ad litem*: HUANG Suting, lawyer of Hainan Jiatian Law Firm.
Agent *ad litem*: WU Changjiang, lawyer of Hainan Jiatian Law Firm.

The Respondent (the Plaintiff of first instance, the counterclaim Defendant of first instance):Zhuhai Xiangzhou Haiyun Co., Ltd.
Domicile: Floor 1, Building No.9, No.8 Mingyue Road, Xiangzhou District, Guangdong.
Legal representative: ZHAN Huixia, general managerm.
Agent *ad litem*: XU Bingshi, Lawyer of Hainan Yanbixin Law Firm.

The Defendant of first instance: China Communications 2nd Navigational Bureau 2nd Engineering Co., Ltd.
Domicile: No.27 Changjiang Road, Yuzhong District, Chongqing.
Legal representative: HUANG Tao, General Manager.

With respect to the case arising from the dispute over the charter party between the Appellant Sanya Hongrui Engineer Co., Ltd. (hereinafter referred to as "Hongrui Company"), the Defendant of first instance, China Communications 2nd Navigational Bureau 2nd Engineering Co., Ltd. (hereinafter referred to as "Zhonghang Company") and the Respondent Zhuhai Xiangzhou Haiyun Co., Ltd. (hereinafter referred to as "Xiangzhou Company"), the Appellant Hongrui Company refused to accept the (2014) Qiong Hai Fa Shang Chu Zi No.80 Civil Judgment made by Haikou Maritime Court, filed an appeal before the court. After accepting the appeal on April 8, 2015, the court constituted a collegiate panel and held an open hearing on May 12, 2015. Legal representative of the Appellant Hongrui Company, WANG Dexian, and agent *ad litem* HUANG Suting, agent *ad litem* of the Respondent Xiangzhou Company, XU Bingshi, appeared in court and attended the hearing. Zhongjiao Company, by legal summon of the court, without justifiable reasons, did not appear in court and attend the hearing. The court heard by default. Now this case has been concluded.

Hongrui Company appealed that: 1. revoke (2014) Qiong Hai Fa Shang Chu Zi No.80 Civil Judgment made by Haikou Maritime Court; 2. according to law confirmed that the charter party signed between Hongrui Company and Xiangzhou Company had been cancelled, Xiangzhou Company shall return the property in sum of RMB180,000 yuan to Hongrui Company; 3. Litigation costs shall be born by Xiangzhou Company.

Facts and reasons: firstly, the first trial verdict with false evidence ascertained the facts unclearly.

1. The first-instance judgment accepted "the proof of (1) and (2) issued by Guo Songgen and other five crew members on June 29, 2014" provided by Xiangzhou Company, which violated Article 69 of the Supreme People's Court about civil action evidence rule "the following evidence cannot be regarded as the basis to determine the case facts alone: ... (2) the testimony issued by the witnesses relating to one party or his agent; ... (5) the testimony of witnesses without justifiable reasons not to testify." The two evidence was issued by the so-called "crew" who had employment relationship with Xiangzhou Company and did not appear in court to testify; after the Hongrui Company applied, the first-instance court during the trial clearly required Xiangzhou Company to provide several crew members' effective certificate in three days, but Xiangzhou Company had not submitted the crew certificate, so the evidence shall not be accepted.
2. The logbook of M.V. "No.28" provided by Xiangzhou Company was perjury. First of all, the evidence was provided by Xiangzhou Company in the court, which did not give Hongrui Company necessary time for cross-examination of evidence. And in the first trial, a people's jurors in court said, "I have been a crew for 25 years, had never seen such a clean logbook, and I ask Xiangzhou Company side to provide navigation diary and operation diary", Xiangzhou Company claimed that they had only logbook and no navigational diary, and it did not match ship operating procedures. After the court, Hongrui Company

online queried the historical weather of Sanya from 5 to 7 month, which showed the weather conditions were not consistent with the records of the logbook. For the most obvious example, Sanya on June 11 to 13 were heavy rain, and the weather recorded in the logbook on June 11 to 13 were sunny, apparently the logbook was not recorded at the time, but forged afterwards to cope with the trial.
3. According to relevant provisions of the Secrecy Law of People's Republic of China and the Security Regulations of People's Liberation Army, force camps are not allowed to use the camera to shoot, or will be held criminally responsible. Photos provided by Xiangzhou Company cannot show the shooting time and place, and may involve confidentiality, however, the evidence was admitted in judgment of first instance, and the court of first trial identified Xiangzhou Company could not exit because Hongrui Company did not allow it to cast the stones. The real reason for Xiangzhou Company could not exit was ships of Xiangzhou Company cannot work, and the crew refused to work and had been delayed, refusing to exit.
4. The approach time and oil amount confirmation slip provided by Xiangzhou Company had obvious suspects. First of all, "approach time" was written on the top of the whole paper, rather than fixed in the paper horizontal line, which did not match to the writing habits of ordinary people. In addition, in the oil record part, the staff "Jinghua" of Hongrui Company signed confirmation, apparently "Jinghua" only confirmed the oil part, the entry time recorded in the paper was not written by Jinghua, and he did not sign to confirm. Because Xiangzhou Company had forged the logbook and instigated the crew to do false proof, Hongrui Company had reason to question the authenticity of "the approach time and oil amount confirmation slip", and filed to perform a handwriting identification in court. The first trial adopted the evidence, and accordingly did not adopt forces evidence provided by Hongrui Company, which was obviously contrary to the rules of evidence.
5. Certificate of nationality of ship provided by Xiangzhou Company showed "ship owner" and "ship operator" of M.V. "No.28"and M.V. "No.6" were Zhuhai Shun Xing Shipping Co., Ltd. It was reported that the common phenomenon of the deck of the ship existed in rental line, Hongrui Company expressed doubts on whether the evidence was involved in the inspection certificate of the ship. And issue time of Coastal Boat Inspection Certificate of M.V. "No.28" was on October 12, 2013, which can only prove that the ship was seaworthy at that time and cannot prove whether the ship afterwards was in damage, maintenance and so on. Hongrui Company had provided sufficient evidence to prove the fact that the ship had been repaired for many times. The Court of First Instance did not consider the proof of the effectiveness of evidence, namely, "two ships had been tested qualified and were seaworthy," was ascertaining the facts wrongly.
6. The first instance did not give reasonable grounds to refuse to accept the on-site operating account of M.V. "No.28" and M.V. "No.6" and People's Liberation Army 91,003 unit proof provided by Hongrui Company, which violated Article 73 of several provisions of the supreme people's court on evidence in civil

procedures that where both parties concerned produces contradicting evidence to prove a same fact but neither has enough evidence to rebut the evidence of the other party, the people's court shall determine which evidence are obviously more forceful than the other evidence by taking the case into consideration, and shall affirm the evidence that are more forceful. The operation ledger was issued by the project department in the project after the completion of the project and when settling, with the Hongrui Company, and was sealed by both sides to confirm. The evidence did form on August 29, 2014, the two sides also signed the date, it was not forged. This case involved the force breakwater project, the troops had strict control for the entry and exit of personnel and ships and had a detailed record, but the information was confidential, which the troops cannot let Hongrui Company copy, but the proof issued by the troops was the best description of the real situation. The authenticity of the two pieces of evidence should be recognized by the court. The Court of First Instance denied the two evidence was inconsistent with the entry time recorded in the "Confirmation of Entry Time and Quantity of Oil" provided by Xiangzhou Company, the authenticity of which was not confirmed by Hongrui Company, which violated Article 77 of Some provisions of the supreme people's court on Evidence in Civil Procedures that the forcefulness of more than one evidence concerning a same fact may be determined by the people's court according to the following principles: 1. the documents formulated by state organs or social bodies according to their respective functions are, as a general rules, more forceful than other written evidence;...... "The probative force of the above two evidence was clearly superior to that of the evidence provided by Xiangzhou Company, the two evidence should be admitted. Certificate and Site Operation Account clearly showed that Xiangzhou Company failed to provide seaworthy vessels, bad management, crew strike, accumulated work time was less than 50 h, and the purpose of the contract was not realized. Hongrui Company had the right to cancel the contract, without the payment of exit fees and rent, and ask the Xiangzhou Company to return RMB180,000 yuan prepaid.

7. Notice of Disembarkation of Ships provided by Hongrui Company was the format form used by Hongrui Company for the exit of the ship after completion of the operation. Although there were words like "hereby informs you that the ship is leaving at the same day for the contract work have been completed", "the ship in good condition" and other words, but the following remarks were the ship crane did not obey the site arrangements, did not listen to command, was ordered to exit, the ship refused to sign. Obviously, the following endorsement was the reason why Hongrui Company required Xiangzhou shipping to exit, which also just proved the authenticity of the evidence. Because Hongrui Company believed that the court can make the problem clear, believed that law was just, otherwise, without signature of Xiangzhou Company, Hongrui Company can re-create a more favorable exit notice. If under the condition of "work has been completed within the contract", "ship in good condition", Xiangzhou Company was asked to exit, Xiangzhou Company had no reason to refuse to sign. The first-instance judgment distorted understanding of Notice of

Disembarkation of Ships, and accordingly found that Xiangzhou Shipping Company had completed the work in the contract and supported all the claims of Xiangzhou Company, which was wrong. Second, application of law was erroneous in judgment of first instance. According to Article 6 Paragraph 2 of charter party about the Marine disposal responsibility, disposal fees. After Hongrui Company paid the ship into, exit disposal fee and the first month's rent in sum of RMB650,000 in full, Xiangzhou Company could dispatch ship to the designated place. In the case, Hongrui Company only paid RMB180,000 yuan, Xiangzhou Company dispatched ships to reach the designated transfer point, it was clear that the two sides reached a new payment agreement. The act shall be regarded as a change of the contents of the original contract, namely, separate payments shall be made for the expenses of entry and exit, and the rent shall be carried out according to *Charging Methods for Charters* stipulated in the contract. According to Article 77 of the Contract Law of the People's Republic of China and the relevant judicial interpretations of the Supreme People's Court, if the content stipulated in the contract is inconsistent with the actual performance, the actual performance shall prevail. On May 21, 2014, Hongrui Company paid RMB180,000 yuan, and Xiangzhou Company ship sailed from Zhuhai on May 25, there was no problem about fulfilling the contractual obligations in advance by Xiangzhou Company. If Xiangzhou Company did not agree that Hongrui Company only paid RMB180,000 yuan for slotting allowance, it can refuse to dispose of the ship and ask to terminate the contract. The court of first trial abused the discretion, violated the principle of party autonomy and found that Hongrui Company breached the contract, the law application of which was wrong. Throughout the charter party, Article 4 "charter costs calculation", Article 5 "settlement and payment", Article 6 "ship disposal responsibilities, disposal costs", Article 9 (2) "Party B" and Article 12 "termination of the contract", the premise of the smooth implementation of the contract was Xiangzhou Company provided seaworthy ship to ensure that the ship at any time was in the seaworthiness to meet the needs of construction and production, and shall comply with scheduling of Hongrui Company, and actively cooperate with the construction. If the construction period was less than three months, the rent would be calculated on the basis of three months if the contract was successfully carried out and the project was successfully completed. In the case of Xiangzhou Boat, the delay of entry, repeated maintenance and crew strike resulted in accumulated work less than 50 h, which could not meet the need of construction and production. The purpose of the contract was not fulfilled and Hongrui Company was entitled to terminate the contract without paying expenditure and rent. According to Paragraph 1 Article 125 of the Contract Law of the People's Republic of China, if the parties have any dispute about the terms of the contract, they shall, according to the terms used in the contract, the relevant provisions of the contract, the purpose of the contract, Credit principles, to determine the true meaning of the terms. The first trial understood the terms of the contract unilaterally, in the circumstance that the purpose of the contract cannot be achieved, still required Hongrui Company to pay disposal fees and rents of three months, which was contrary to the contract, the law and fair and equitable principle. Third, Hongrui Company's claim was consistent with the facts and legal basis. As mentioned above, M.V. "No.28" and M.V. "No.6" of Xiangzhou Company should have entered the yard on May 23, 2014, but they did not enter the field, affecting the construction progress. In order to ensure the progress of the project. On May 26, 2014, Hongrui Company signed a charter party with Lianyungang Eastern Airlines Shipping Company, and rent "Feng Wang 8" and "Su Yunhai 187" with a high price. On May 29, 2014 and May 30, 2014, after the signing of the contract, "Feng Wang 8" and "Su Yunhai 187" entered the yard to complete the loading, cast of stones and other operations. While two vessels of Xiangzhou Company did not enter the yard until May 31, 2014, and began to be repaired after the approach, for three consecutive days without construction, and then tinkering, the cumulative construction work time was only 50 h, and from June 17 stopped working and did not coordinate with the work, which made Hongrui Company suffer heavy economic losses. On June 24, 2014, Hongrui Company issued a notice of exit, ordering the ship and equipment of Xiangzhou Company to transfer from the scene. Because Xiangzhou Company broke the contract, Hongrui Company, in order to avoid delaying in the duration, rent ships to continue the work with high-cost, and therefore increased the cost, so Xiangzhou Company should pay the commitment. Hongrui Company had the right to request the Xiangzhou Company to refund RMB180,000 that has been paid. To sum up, Hongrui Company requested the court to support its requirements.

The Respondent Xiangzhou Company argued:

Firstly, the fact of first-instance judgment was clear, the application of law was correct.

1. Facts of this case. In May 2014, Zhonghang Company subcontracted the sea breakwater project in Sanya Yalong Bay to Hongrui Company. Hongrui Company leased all the two vessels of Xiangzhou Company to complete the task of sea stone transportation and construction. The two parties signed the charter party on May 16, 2014. The contract stipulated that the rent of the two vessels of Xiangzhou Company was RMB290,000 yuan per month and the ship into, exit disposal fee was 360,000 yuan. Once the rental period of the ship was less than three months, the rent shall be calculated according to three months; if more than three months, the rent shall be calculated according to the actual number of days. Only after Hongrui Company remitted the rent and disposal fee of the first month in sum of 650,000 into Xiangzhou Company's account all at once, Xiangzhou Company shall dispatch ships to the designated location. On May 21, 2014, Hongrui Company remitted RMB180,000 yuan to Xiangzhou Company's account and called to pay the balance within 3 days. May 24, Xiangzhou Company still did not receive the balance, Hongrui Company called to request Xiangzhou Company to enter yard and promised to pay the balance one the day the ship arrived in Sanya Tielu Port. As the ship leasing was introduced by the leadership of the company both sides were familiar with, Xiangzhou Company dispatched the ship according to the

requirements of Hongrui Company reluctantly. Two vessels of Xiangzhou Company sailed from Wanchai Port in Zhuhai on May 25, 2014 and arrived at Sanya Tielu Port in early morning of May 30, 2014. On the same day, crews of the both sides began to work after measuring the oil content of the ship. Under the command of the staff of Hongrui Company, the ship was working continuously until June 17, 2014, and all the stones needed to reinforce the breakwater dam had been transported and dumped in place. During this period, Xiangzhou Company had been discussing with Hongrui Company for the rent and disposal fees in arrears. On June 24, 2014, Hongrui Company uncharacteristically, not only did not pay rent or disposal fee according to the agreement, but forcibly evicted the crew of Xiangzhou Company and ship with half a ship of unspent stones to exit. Xiangzhou Company threw away unused half-ship stones on July 9, 2014 in the place designated Hongrui Company. Hongrui Company promised Xiangzhou Company it would pay all the arrears after steering two ships from the construction site to the Sanya Tielu Port, and then it went back to its words again.

2. Hongrui Company should pay Xiangzhou Company the default balance in sum of 1.05 million yuan according to the agreement of contract. Firstly, the ship into, exit disposal fee in sum of RMB360,000 yuan was the contractual and actual costs incurred. The two vessels of Xiangzhou Company sailed from Wanchai Port, Zhuhai to Tielu Harbor, Sanya, on the actual range of 450 nautical miles. The speed of the 28-wheeled ship belt unpowered 6 wheeled barge was about 4 knots under normal sea conditions. It took 5 days to tow the ship. Ship towing fuel consumption was 200 L per hour. And it was about 20 tons of fuel consumption from Zhuhai to Sanya. The in and exit cost in sum of RMB360,000 yuan was the actual cost, which shall be paid by Hongrui Company. Second, the rent 870,000 yuan was the amount agreed and recognized in the contract. The charter party signed by Xiangzhou Company and Hongrui Company was based on the equality and voluntariness of both sides and was the true meaning of the two sides. Article 60 of the Contract Law of People's Republic of China provided that: each party shall fully perform its own obligations as agreed upon. Hongrui Company shall pay the balance of RMB1.05 million yuan in arrears according to the agreement of contract.

3. Hongrui Company stressed to apply Article 77 of the Contract Law of People's Republic of China to decide the case because of its one-sided understanding of its legislative purpose. Article 77 of the Contract Law provided that: a contract may be modified if the parties reach a consensus through consultation. If the parties agree on the change, the change will replace the contents of the original contract; once a party without the other party's consent to arbitrarily change the content of the contract, the change after the other party is not binding, and it is a breach of contract, shall be liable for breach of contract. The two sides did not negotiate on the ship handling fees and rent, there was no change in the terms of the contract, Hongrui Company's claim that the terms of contract were changed could not be established.

Secondly, the reason why Hongrui Company appealed was not established, and its purpose was to refuse to pay arrears balanced.

1. Xiangzhou Company had no delay in the case. Xiangzhou Company and Hongrui Company agreed in Article 6 Paragraph 2 of the contract that Hongrui Company firstly paid RMB650,000 yuan, then Xiangzhou Company transferred the vessel to the designated handover place. On May 21, 2014, Hongrui Company only made a remittance of 180,000 yuan, and had not yet paid the agreed payment. The contract agreed that the ship lease contract tentatively fixed the time for entering the yard on April 23, 2014, according to the written notice by Hongrui Company. Hongrui Company did not write notification to Xiangzhou Company, and Xiangzhou Company had no delay in entering the yard.
2. Two vessels of the Xiangzhou Company entered the port on May 30, there were no three consecutive days for maintenance construction with no construction after entrance. On May 30, 2014, at two o'clock in the morning, Hongrui Company arrived at the Tielu Port of Sanya, at 8 o'clock in the morning, it sent a person in charge named "Jinghua" to the two ships of Xiangzhou Company to measure the remaining oil, immediately after measurement commanded ships of Xiangzhou to start loading stones, until June 17, 2014, the stones for reinforcement of the breakwater dam had all been transported, unloaded in place, and the remaining half ship stones had been put off until July 9 to finish unloading because of no places to be discharged.
3. There were no employees of Xiangzhou Company threatening to strike to increase wages counterclaimed by Hongrui Company in the first instance. According to Paragraph 2 article 4 of the contract, the agreed crew wages were clear, namely: the rent included ship equipments of Xiangzhou Company and the salary of operating people, bonus, various allowances. There was no condition that Hongrui Company shall pay wages to Xiangzhou Company's crew so they were impossible to threaten Hongrui Company to strike to increase wages. On June 17, the crew strike of 2 h happened because Hongrui Company violated item 4, Article 9 (1) of the ship lease contract signed by both parties, Hongrui Company should have provided convenience to Xiangzhou Company such as handling pass of people. On June 7, the troops took crew's ID cards to deal with pass cards and had not returned to the crew, which caused difficulty in ship supply, in addition, Hongrui Company refused to pay the balance owed, the crew struck to struggle their rights.
4. Hongrui Company said it further rent M.V. "FengWang 8" and M.V. "SuYunhai machine 187" to be used in casting stones, which was contrary to the facts. Since May 30, 2014, two vessels of Xiangzhou Company began to cast stones, on June 17, 2014 completed the stone cast task required by the reinforcement of breakwater dam. Only M.V. "No.28" of Xiangzhou Company had the special function to throw and fill stones in the construction site. With lifting arm more than 40 m long, the ship was equipped with "grab" to load and unload the stones, which can throw the stones into the breakwater dam more than 30 m high after grabbing the stones. The other crane ship rent by Hongrui Company in construction was used for hanging and unloading "king used pieces of cement casting" of the dam, although the lifting arm was longer, had more power, if it

was not equipped with grab of loading and unloading the stones, it would be overqualified and lose their significance to play a bigger role. Thus, as Hongrui Company said, it rent M.V. "Fengwang 8" and M.V. "Su Yunhai machine 187" ship to use in casting and filling stones, which was not practical, and it provided only a contract and did not provide detailed information that the two ships were used to throw and fill after grabbing the stones.
5. Hongrui Company denied the evidence with improper reason. Approaching time and fuel confirmation slip was the certificate jointly signed by head of stone field Jinghua, the stone casting member on the scene "Old Li", and "Sun Gong", with signature of Hongrui Company's employee. The content of Notice of vessel's exit was very clear, that was: "because the contract work has been completed, now inform your ship Hongtong 28, shun xing 6 to exit on the day (June 24, 2014), and withdrawal from the construction site in 3 days". According to Article 41 of the Contract Law of People's Republic of China, where there are two or more kinds of interpretation, an interpretation unfavorable to the party supplying the standard terms shall prevail. Xiangzhou Company took the scene photos used as evidence, which did not involve any secrets of troops. Though Hongrui Company recognized it as scene shooting photos on the site, but they were not approved for areas with no legal grounds in the army.
6. The contents of navigational common-sense shall not be approved. Logbook was the original record to reflect the shipping production work and one of the important legal documents necessary to ship, and an important content for port authorities to inspect the ship in and out of the port. First, Hongrui Company used the with the juror's word that "I have been crew for 25 years but I have never seen such a clean logbook" to deny the content recorded by the logbook, which was not objective. Whether the logbook was clean or not cannot judge whether it was true or false, the clean logbook stated store men's cherish, it was also connected with the short inlet and exit time and the few and unitary content needed to record. Secondly, Hongrui Company denied the content recorded in the logbook by the weather forecast of Sanya inquired on the net, which was unrealistic. Sanya's climate was tropical Marine monsoon climate, hot and humid in summer, especially in typhoon seasons of May and November, the weather change unpredictably, the actual situation that sun in the east while rain in the west often appeared. In addition, the weather forecast had obvious error which cannot reflect the weather truly.
7. Hongrui Company provided evidence with much loopholes, which was contradict to each other and did not tally with the actual fact. One is "proof" issued by Hongrui Company in the name of the unit 91,003 on August 28, 2014. First of all, Xiangzhou Company entered the yard on May 30 2014, but "proof" was written as on May 31, 2014. Secondly, Xiangzhou Company exited on July 9, 2014, but "proof" was written as on July 6, 2014. Thirdly, Forces contracted the project with Zhonghang Company, then Zhonghang Company contracted the project with the Hongrui Company, then Hongrui Company rent the ships and staff of Xiangzhou Company to work, forces were not able to work in the construction site, the proof issued without understanding of the circumstances

was clearly forged. Fourthly, standing book of M.V. "Shunxing 6" and M.V. "Hongtong 28" issued by Hongrui Company in the name of Yalong Bay Project Department of Zhonghang Company on August 29, 2014. First of all, the into and out of time of Xiangzhou Company's ships was wrongly recorded in the standing book. Nextly, the standing book formed after the first instance prosecution (first instance lawsuit date was June 30, 2014), was not the real-time records at that time, there was only the seal of Zhonghang Company and the signature of the staff of Hongrui Company in it, which was not confirmed by the staff of the concrete operation operator (Xiangzhou Company).

Moreover, Zhonghang Company subcontracted the project to Hongrui Company, it was impossible to record the relevant content. To sum up, Xiangzhou Company requested the court to find out the fact and reject the request of Hongrui Company to maintain the original verdict.

In the second court hearing, Hongrui submitted the weather conditions from May to August in Sanya, which was printed from a weather website (www.15tianqi.cn). It was used to prove that the weather conditions recorded in the logbook of Xiangzhou 28 were incorrect, and then inferred that Logbook was false evidence. While the cross-examination opinions of Xiangzhou was that the evidence was not a new one and the record according to a weather website cannot reflect real conditions of weather. The court held that: firstly, Hongrui did not submit the evidence in regard to the accuracy and authority of weather records on this weather website; Secondly, weather is changeable, different weather conditions may exist in different areas of a same city. The logbook only recorded the weather conditions of the construction site, while the weather information recorded on the website reflected a wider range of areas in Sanya and it was too general. Thirdly, the website recorded weather conditions generally and the logbook recorded weather conditions based on the time of 8:00. Therefore, two kinds of records were not comparable and the evidence of the website cannot deny the authenticity of the logbook. The court did not accept the evidence in this respect.

The Appellant Hongrui appealed that the first-instance court rejected the evidence sealed by Troops 91,003 of People's Liberation Army and standing book of M.V. "Shunxing 6" and M.V. "Hongtong 28", which, was incorrect. The court held that the Evidential Document sealed by Troops 91,003 of People's Liberation Army was not a state official document issued for the purpose of exercising state administrative function and it was documentary evidence in general. according to Article 115 of the Interpretation of the Supreme People's Court on the Application of the Civil Procedure Law of the People's Republic of China, the evidentiary materials produced by an entity to a people's court shall be signed or sealed by the person in charge and the preparer of the entity, with the seal of the entity to be affixed. A people's court may conduct an investigation of the evidentiary materials on the entity and the preparer of the evidentiary materials. If necessary, the preparer of the evidentiary material may be requested to appear in court as a witness. There was no signature of the producer or the head of unit and the Evidential Document only sealed by the unit cannot fully support the authenticity of the evidence. The standing book of M.V. "Shunxing 6" and M.V. "Hongtong 28" were vessel working records of Xiangzhou which should be confirmed by Xiangzhou, whereas the standing book was not signed by their staff. Therefore, the first-instance court did not adopt the aforesaid evidence, which was correct.

Hongrui held that, photographs taken by Xiangzhou and Entrance Time and Oil Volume Confirmation adopted by the first-instance court were incorrect. The judgment of the first-instance court has reasoned it detailedly and the adoption was acceptable.

The Appellant Hongrui appealed that the logbook and evidential document provided by crews adopted by the first-instance court was incorrect. The court held that the logbook was original and necessary document for every vessel to record daily conditions. Recording the logbook was an important item in daily work of vessels. In the absence of any sufficient contrary evidence provided by Hongrui, the logbook accepted and adopted by the first-instance court was not improper. In respect of the evidential document provided by crews, although there were signatures on it, Xiangzhou did not submit identity materials of these crews and they did not appear in court as witnesses either. Therefore, the authenticity of the evidence cannot be confirmed, the adoption of the first-instance court was obviously improper. The evidential document provided by crews showed that the conditions on May 30, June 7, June 17, June 24, July 8, July 9 etc. were basically consistent with the logbook, the facts in respect of that can be confirmed. Therefore, although the evidential document provided by crews adopted by the first-instance court was improper, it did not affect the affirmation of the facts in this case.

The Appellant Hongrui appealed that the Ship's Notice of Exit adopted by the first-instance court was not correct. In respect of the facts that Hongrui requested Xiangzhou to exit from the field according to the Ship's Notice of Exit, the parties had no objection; but there was a sharp disagreement between the parties regarding to the reason for exiting. according to the printed part of the Ship's Notice of Exit which provided: "Whereas the contract work has been completed and now inform you that the vessel of Hongtong 28, Shunxing 6 to exit today…" and followed with a handwritten part, "The floating cranes did not follow the arrangement and command, was ordered to withdraw, whereas the shipowner refused to sign." The notice was unilaterally made by Hongrui, was a paradox, did not constitute self-admission; The notice failed to constitute a contract, generally cannot be interpreted and explained according to standard terms. As a result of the paradox made by Hongrui in respect of the reason for exiting, the notice cannot be adopted unilaterally as the legal evidence of the reason for exiting. The court confirmed the facts that Hongrui requested Xiangzhou to exit according to the notice, did not confirm the reason for exiting.

After hearing, the court ascertains that, the reason for exiting according to the evidential document provided by crews and the Ship's Notice of Exit cannot be adopted as evidence in this case, the court did not confirm the reason for exiting according to the Ship's Notice of Exit. Other facts ascertained by the first-instance court were corroborated by relevant evidence, which should be confirmed by the court.

The court holds that, this case was a case regarding dispute over contract of vessel leasing and the key disputes in the case were as follows: I. Whether the Vessel Lease Contract concluded between Hongrui and Xiangzhou had been terminated, and whether Xiangzhou should refund Hongrui the disposal cost of RMB180,000; II. Whether Hongrui should pay Xiangzhou the disposal cost and rent.

1. On the nature and validity of the contract. The Vessel Lease Contract concluded between Hongrui and Xiangzhou on May 16, 2014 was a genuine intention expressed by the parties, did not violate the mandatory provisions of laws and regulations. It was lawful and valid, all parties shall exercise due diligence in performing the contract.
2. On whether the contract had been terminated, and whether Xiangzhou should refund Hongrui the disposal cost of RMB180,000. according to the facts ascertained in this case, M.V. "No.28" and M.V. "No.6" of Xiangzhou Company arrived at the construction field and began to work on May 30, 2014; After strike of crews on June 17, Hongrui informed Xiangzhou orally to shut down and thereafter had no further working arrangements for the vessels involved in this case; On June 24, the Ship's Notice of Exit was sent to Xiangzhou, Hongrui requested M.V. "No.28" and M.V. "No.6" of Xiangzhou Company to exit. Hongrui held that it had requested Xiangzhou Company to exit, namely it had terminated the contract, and requested the court to confirm the termination of contract. Firstly, Hongrui claimed that the contract had been terminated, this claim should be proved by Hongrui that the expressed intention to terminate the contract shall have expressly notified to Xiangzhou according to Article 96 of the Contract Law of the People's Republic of China which provided: "A party demanding termination of a contract according to the provisions of Paragraph 2 of Article 93 and Article 94 of this Law shall notify the other party". Whereas the Ship's Notice of Exit provided that Hongrui requested the vessels of Xiangzhou to exit, the words of which were not related to the contract, it cannot absolutely derive that facts that Hongrui had notified Xiangzhou to terminate of the contract. Secondly, Hongrui claimed that the contract had been terminated, which should be proved by substantial conditions for the termination namely dissolution by appointment, dissolution by statutory and dissolution by agreement, the detailed analysis was as follows:

    (1) Dissolution by appointment. Hongrui claimed that the contract was terminated according to Clause 12 of the charter party which provided: "When Party A (Hongrui) confirms that Party B (Xiangzhou) has lost the ability to perform the contract, Party A shall have the right to notify Party B to terminate the contract.", the causes of the affirmation of involved vessels losing the ability to perform the contract were: delayed entrance of vessels, repeated repairs, disobeying orders and strikes, which resulted in the no subsequent performance of contract. The specific entrance time stipulated in

the contract shall be subject to the written notice of Hongrui, but Hongrui did not send the notice, therefore the reason for delayed entrance of the vessels was untenable. Xiangzhou provided the Ship Certificates of Inspection which proved the seaworthiness of the vessels involved. The involved vessels began to work immediately after arrival. Before the dispute was raised on June 17, Hongrui had no doubt about the performance and seaworthiness of the vessels and could not sufficiently prove that the vessels were not suitable for the operation. Therefore, the vessels of Xiangzhou conformed to the terms agreed upon in the contract. In respect of issues that the crews of involved vessels disobeyed orders and struck, according to the contract, Hongrui should pay RMB650,000 to Xiangzhou in advance before it sent vessels. Hongrui claimed that the mode of payment had been changed by the parties, but there was no evidence to support it. Hongrui paid only RMB18,000 and there was still RMB470,000 to pay, it breached the contract first and should also take responsibility for the strike of crews. The strike was settled down at the end of the day and was of short duration. The strike was not enough to hinder the subsequent performance of the contract, it cannot be determined that the vessels of Xiangzhou had lost the ability to perform the contract. Hongrui ordered crews to suspend on the day of the strike and no longer arranged work for vessels thereafter. Therefore, the vessels suspended the work after June 17, the main fault lay in Hongrui. This case did have the condition for dissolution by appointment, the expressed intention unilaterally made by Hongrui to no longer perform the contract cannot constitute termination of the contract.

(2) Dissolution by statutory. The right of dissolution by statutory applies when the breaching party seriously breaches the contract and thus the purpose of contract cannot be achieved, in such circumstance, the non-breaching party is vested with the right to terminate the contract. In this case, there was no evidence to prove that Xiangzhou had fundamental breach of contract. Hongrui did not settle the payment according to the contract and broke the contract first, therefore Hongrui cannot exercise the right to terminate the contract according to Article 94 of the Contract Law of the People's Republic of China.

(3) Dissolution by agreement. Although the Ship's Notice of Exit was sent by Hongrui on June 24, the parties did not reach a consensus on the termination of the contract and Xiangzhou did not sign on the notice, therefore the parties did not constitute a dissolution by agreement on that day.

In sum, the Ship's Notice of Exit sent by Hongrui on June 24 was not the expressed intention to terminate the contract and this case was not under the circumstances of dissolution by appointment, dissolution by statutory or dissolution by agreement. Hongrui claimed to confirm that the contract had been terminated for the parties since the Ship's Notice of Exit was sent, which cannot be supported, and Hongrui's claim that Xiangzhou should refund the disposal cost of RMB180,000 had no basis either. The judgment of the first-instance court on these issues was correct, the court affirms the original ruling about that.

3. On the disposal cost and rent. The Appellant Hongrui appealed that the actual construction time of Xiangzhou was short, it had breach of contract which caused the purpose of contract cannot be achieved, Xiangzhou therefore could not claim the disposal cost and rent of 3 months. On the issue of breach of contract for the parties, the first-instance court has detailedly analyzed and held that Xiangzhou was not under the circumstance of breach of contract which caused the purpose of contract cannot be achieved. This case was a case regarding dispute over contract of vessel leasing, Xiangzhou as the lessor had liability to deliver vessels and crews and Hongrui as the lessee had liability to pay the disposal cost and rent. The time of performance and the calculation of rental were defined by the lease term in vessel leasing contract. The parties reached a temporary agreement that the time of performance was 3 months, it can be perceived that 3 months started after entrancing of the vessels of Xiangzhou, that is, from May 30 to August 30, 3 months as the minimum limit for rent. The exit of the vessels of Xiangzhou in temporary time of performance resulted from the requirement to shut down and exit rendered by Hongrui, and there was no obvious fault for Xiangzhou in no longer continuing to perform the contract. In the temporary time of performance, Hongrui unilaterally proved that it did not continue to perform the contract, constituted a breach of contract, according to Article 108 of the Contract Law of the People's Republic of China: "Where one party express explicitly or indicates by its conduct that it will not perform its obligations under a contract, the other party may demand it to bear the liability for the breach of contract before the expiry of the performance period.", and Article 107 which provides that: "if a party fails to perform its obligations under a contract, or its performance fails to satisfy the terms of the contract, it shall bear the liabilities for breach of contract such as to continue to perform its obligations, to take remedial measures, or to compensate for losses." In this case, although the temporary time of performance was less than 3 months, Xiangzhou had the right to claim the disposal cost and rent against Hongrui according to the contract. The disposal cost of Xiangzhou's vessels for entering and exiting was the actual cost of the ship to arrive and depart. according to the contract, Hongrui should pay Xiangzhou the disposal cost of RMB360,000; Hongrui had paid RMB180,000 and it had RMB180,000 to be paid. In respect of the rent, although the construction time of Xiangzhou's vessels was less than 3 months, according to the contract which provided that when the lease term was less than 3 months, the rent was calculated on a three-month basis, therefore Xiangzhou had the right to claim RMB870,000 of three-month rent against Hongrui. The judgment of the first-instance court on the issue that Hongrui should pay Xiangzhou the disposal cost and rent totally in sum of RMB1,050,000 was correct, the court maintained the original ruling

about that. The appellant Hongrui appealed that the appointed clause of rental violated the principle of fairness and the principle of making compensation for equal value, whereas the clauses of the contract were concluded on the basis of equal negotiation and free will, there was no evidence in this case to prove that at the time when concluding the contract, either party had fraud, coercion or other circumstances which violated the compulsory provisions of laws. Therefore, there was no legally prescribed cause for Hongrui to deny the clauses of the contract. The grounds of appeal that Hongrui refused to pay the disposal cost and hire cannot be established according to law, the court rejected the appeal about that.

Moreover, Hongrui and Xiangzhou had no dispute on the fact that Zhongjiao Company was not a party of this case and should not bear any liability. The facts that the first-instance court rejected the appeal of Xiangzhou against Zhongjiao Company were clear, the court maintained the original ruling about that.

In conclusion, although part of the admissibility of evidence in the first-instance judgment were improper, the ascertainment of the facts was basically clear, the application of law and the trial results were correct. According to Article 170 Paragraph 1 Sub-paragraph 1 of the Civil Procedure Law of the People's Republic of China, the judgment is as follows:

Dismiss the appeal, and affirm the original judgment.

Court acceptance fee of first-instance judgment shall be executed according to the judgment of first instance and the AppellantSanya Hongrui Engineer Co., Ltd. shall bear court acceptance fee of the second-instance judgment in amount of RMB21,375.

The judgment is final

Presiding Judge: LIN Da
Judge: ZENG Ruizhen
Acting Judge: GAO Junhua

June 15, 2015

Clerk: LI Yuanyong

Appendix: Relevant Law

1. Contract Law of the People's Republic of China

Article 93 The parties may terminate a contract if they reach a consensus through consultation.

The parties may agree upon conditions under which either party may terminate the contract. Upon satisfaction of the conditions, the party who has the right to terminate may terminate the contract.

Article 94 The parties to a contract may terminate the contract under any of the following circumstances:

(1) it is rendered impossible to achieve the purpose of contract due to an event of force majeure;
(2) prior to the expiration of the period of performance, the other party expressly states, or indicates through its conduct, that it will not perform its main obligation;
(3) the other party delayed performance of its main obligation after such performance has been demand, and fails to perform within a reasonable period;
(4) the other party delays performance of its obligations, or breaches the contract in some other manner, rendering it impossible to achieve the purpose of the contract;
(5) other circumstance as provided by law.

Article 95 Where the laws stipulates or the parties agreed upon the time limit to exercise the right to terminate the contract, and no party exercises it when the time limit expires, the said right shall be extinguished.

Where neither the law stipulates nor the parties make an agreement upon the time limit to exercise the right to terminate the contract, and no party exercise it within a reasonable time period after being urged, the said right shall be extinguished.

Article 96 A party demanding termination of a contract according to the provisions of Paragraph 2 of Article 93 and Article 94 of this Law shall notify the other party. The contract shall be terminated upon the receipt of the notice by the other party. If the other party objects to such termination, it may petition the People's Court or an arbitration institution to adjudicate the validity of the termination of the contract.

Where the laws and administrative regulations so provide, the approval and registration procedures for the termination of the contract shall be gone through according to such laws and regulations.

Article 107 If a party fails to perform its obligations under a contract, or its performance fails to satisfy the terms of the contract, it shall bear the liabilities for breach of contract such as to continue to perform its obligations, to take remedial measures, or to compensate for losses.

Article 108 Where one party express explicitly or indicates by its conduct that it will not perform its obligations under a contract, the other party may demand it to bear the liability for the breach of contract before the expiry of the performance period.

2. Civil Procedure Law of the People's Republic China

Article 170 After trying a case on appeal, the people's court of second instance shall, in the light of the following situations, dispose of it accordingly:

(1) if the facts were clearly ascertained and the law was correctly applied in the original judgment, the appeal shall be rejected in the form of judgment and the original judgment shall be recognized;
(2) if the facts were wrongly ascertained or the application of law was incorrect in the original judgment, the said judgment shall be amended according to the law;
(3) if the basic facts were not clearly ascertained in the original judgment, the people's court of second instance shall make a written order to set aside the original judgment and remand the case to the original people's court for retrial, or the people's court of second instance may amend the judgment after investigating and clarifying the facts; or
(4) if there was serious violation of legal procedures such as omitting any party or making an illegal absentee judgment in the original judgment, the said judgment shall be set aside by a written order and the case remanded to the original people's court for retrial.

If the party files an appeal against the judgment made in the retrial by the court originally tried the case, the people's court of second instance shall make a judgment according to the law.

Wuhan Maritime Court
Civil Judgment

Zhumadian South China Sea Shipping Co., Ltd.
v.
People's Insurance Company of China Property and Casualty Co., Ltd. Zhumadian Branch

(2014) Wu Hai Fa Shang Chu Zi No.00795

Related Case(s) This is the judgment of first instance and the judgment of second instance is on page 1377.

Cause(s) of Action 230. Dispute over marine insurance contract on the sea or sea-connected waters.

Headnote The Defendant insurer held not entitled to rely on exclusion clause in hull insurance policy because insurer had not adequately explained the effect of the clause to the assured.

Summary The Plaintiff's ship collided with two other vessels and sank. The Plaintiff requested the Defendant to cover the loss under the hull insurance policy. However, the Defendant refused to pay the requested amount citing an exemption clause. The Plaintiff sued, seeking to make the Defendant liable for the loss. The court held that the exemption clause relied on by the Defendant was void, because the Defendant had not fully explained the effect of the exemption clause to the Plaintiff.

Judgment

The Plaintiff: Zhumadian South China Sea Shipping Co., Ltd.
Domicile: Yard of Shenzhai Township Government, Suiping City, Henan Province, China. Organization Code:66,887,749–4.
Legal representative: GENG Li, general manager.
Agent *ad litem*: ZHANG Jianbing, lawyer of Hubei Jintian Law Firm.

The Defendant: People's Insurance Company of China Property and Casualty Co., Ltd. Zhumadian Branch
Domicile: No.145, Chunxiao Road, Zhumadian City, Henan Province, China.
Organization Code:87,586,506–6.
Legal representative: LIU Sihu, general manager.
Agent *ad litem*: WANG Rong, lawyer of Hubei Xiaoyang Law Firm.
Agent *ad litem*: LI Rui, lawyer of Hubei Siyang Law Firm.

With respect to the dispute over the contract of insurance of sea waters, the Plaintiff Zhumadian South China Sea Shipping Co., Ltd. (hereinafter referred to as "Nanhai Company"), filed litigation against the Defendant People's Insurance Company of China Property and Casualty Co., Ltd. Zhumadian Branch (hereinafter referred to as "Insurance Company") on July 8, 2014. The case is regarded as Maritime dispute, and the subject matter insured is means of transportation. The shipping destination and place of the insurance accident (Jiangsu Jiangyin waters of Yangtze River) are both within the jurisdiction of the court. Pursuant to Article 2 of the Notice of the Supreme People's Court on Adjustment of the jurisdiction and the Scope of Cases Entertained by Dalian, Wuhan and Beihai Maritime Courts and Article 25 of the Interpretation of the Supreme People's Court on the Application of the Civil Procedure Law of the People's Republic of China, the court has jurisdiction of this case. The court rendered the case, applied to the summary procedure according to the law and heard by a single agency judge Xiong Jing on the same day of the appeal. On August 18 and September 18, 2014, the court opened the court hearing to try this case. Agent *ad litem* of the Plaintiff Nanhai Company, ZHANG Jianbing, agent *ad litem* of the Defendant Insurance Company, WANG Rong, attended the court hearing. In respect of the two parties' application, the case was presided to mediation by the court. For many of the differences, there was no agreement achieved. Now the case has been concluded.

The Plaintiff Nanhai Company alleged in the Statement of Claim: on July 23, 2013, the Plaintiff Nanhai Company effected insurance with Insurance Company against all risks of inland ships for M.V. "Yu Nanhai 0168". The Defendant Insurance Company issued insurance policy of No.PCEJ201341280000000203. It was stated in the policy that the insured value and amount was RMB5,010,000 (the followings are all RMB), the period of the insurance was from 0 o'clock July 24, 2013 to 24 o'clock July 23. When the up-bound M.V. "Yu Nanhai 0618" sailed to the place of Mue Island Baideng ship in the Yangtze River, it collided with the down-bound vessel M.V. "Ming Tai 89", later it collided with the following up-bound M.V. "Yuan Dong 907". The collision accident led to M.V. "Yu Nanhai 0168" sinking after the sea water pouring into the damaged hull with aggravated damages. Subsequent to the collision accident, the Plaintiff Nanhai Company reported immediately to the Defendant Insurance Company for the settlement of claims, the Defendant Insurance Company had arranged staff to set loss exploration to the accident and vessel, while it is unpaid till now. After the salvage of M.V. "Yu Nanhai 0168", it needed depot repair, thus caused the losses of salvage and repair charges. The Plaintiff Nanhai Company stood that they were entitled to request the

Defendant Insurance Company to pay the insurance regarding the items of the contract. The Plaintiff Nanhai Company requested the court to order the Defendant Insurance Company to pay for the insurance compensation in sum of RMB3,628,428 (among which the charge for salvageing amounted to RMB730,000, tuggage and charges for drainage on the dock was RMB90,000, the emergency cost was RMB103,000, cleaning expense was RMB16,000, decoration fee was RMB177,620, charge paid for the turbine mechanical and electrical equipment installation amounted to RMB238,600, charge paid for the repair of the main engine of the ship was in sum of RMB113,698, repair to ship of Gangda Company was RMB1,681,243, repair to ship of Chuyu Company was RMB85,000, losses of the ship's supply amounted to RMB10,527, fueling charge was RMB56,120, losses of the household application for the ship were RMB55,380, losses of the ship's article were RMB86,240, charge for the paint was RMB185,000) and the interest (calculated from November 15, 2013 to the effective date of relevant judgment as per the loan interest rate published by People's Bank of China during the corresponding period) and all the litigation costs of the case.

The Defendant Insurance Company argued that:

1. It was not opposed to the facts that they had insurance contractual relationship with the Plaintiff Nanhai Company and on November 15, 2013 M.V. "Yu Nanhai 0168" sank as the result of the inland waters traffic accident with the water pouring into the damaged port. With respect to the special agreement of the insurance contract, if the accident was within the scope of the insurance responsibility, the Defendant Insurance Company enjoyed the right of the 10% deductible of hull damages of M.V. "Yu Nanhai 0168".
2. The Defendant Insurance Company did not have any attitude of delaying the claims. On the contrary, they actively entrusted the assessment institution to involve into the investigation of liability and the affirmation of the damages after the accident.
3. The Defendant Insurance Company was cautiously skeptical of the Plaintiff Nanhai Company's claim of PA, and they accepted the claims of salvageing charge of RMB730,000, tuggage fee of RMB80,000, repairs fee of RMB1,176,587.52. The ship owner of M.V. "Ming Tai 89" had paid in advance the salvageing charges in sum of RMB500,000 for the Plaintiff Nanhai Company, and the expense should deduct the evaluated residual value in sum of RMB76,959.08 which was wrote in the Survey Report of the first period (hereinafter referred to as Survey Report) submitted by the Defendant Insurance Company. For the emergency charges of M.V. "Jiang Yun 19", M.V. "Wan Fuyang Gong 753" and M.V. "Huanggang Huo 656" and the decoration fee, supplies and fuel costs were not in the scope of the insured subject matter, so they were not accepted. Losses which did not have legal evidence and severely surpassed the market value were not accepted and they should depend on the evaluated amount of the Survey Report. The interest calculated from November 15, 2013 to the effective date of relevant judgment as per the loan interest rate

published by People's Bank of China during the corresponding period which was claimed by the Defendant was not accepted.

4. The probative force of the Survey Report is greater than that of the evidence surrendered by the Plaintiff Nanhai Company.

In order to support its procedural claim, the Plaintiff Nanhai Company submitted the following evidence to the court:

1. Certification for inland ships (original copy, if there was no clear notice, hereinafter were all referred to as original copy), certificate of registration of ownership of ship, certificate of the transport and operating of the ship, certificate of competence of seafarer on the day of the accident happened(copy), to prove the Plaintiff Nanhai Company was the shipowner and operator of M.V. "Yu Nanhai 0168", the ship was seaworthiness when the accident happened.

The cross-examination of the Defendant Insurance Company: it did not object to the authority of the first evidence, the original of certificate of registration of ownership was kept by the mortgage bank, and they claimed that there was only four sailors left when the accident happened, which did not meet the minimum standard of the allocation of sailors.

2. Inland ship insurance policy of No.PCEJ201341280000000203, to prove the Plaintiff Nanhai Company had already effected insurance with the Defendant Insurance Company against all risks of inland ships, the period of the insurance was from 0 o'clock July 24, 2013 to 24 o'clock July 23, the insurance amount was RMB5,010,000.

The cross-examination of the Defendant Insurance Company: it did not object to the authority of the second evidence. The relationship of insurance contract between the Plaintiff and the Defendant should be proved by both the insurance policy and the insurance items, the Defendant Insurance Company enjoyed the right of the 10% deductible of hull damages of M.V. "Yu Nanhai 0168".

3. Conclusions of investigation of the inland traffic accident drawn by Maritime Office of Yangluo, Wuhan on December 18, 2013, to prove the collision accident was insurance accident, the Defendant should compensate the Plaintiff within the scope of insurance liability.

The cross-examination of the Defendant Insurance Company: it had no objection to the authority of evidence 3.

Authorized opinion of the court: the Defendant Insurance Company had no objection to evidence 1, 2, 3, and the three evidence were regarded as the basis of the case fact. Unless established evidence to the contrary, conditions of seafarer's competency and seaworthiness of the ship shall subject to the investigation of Maritime Office of Yangluo, Wuhan.

4. *Salvage Contract* signed between the Plaintiff Nanhai Company and Hubei Province Huanggang City Tuanfeng Town Salvage Engineering Co. (hereinafter referred to as Salvage Company) on November 16, 2013, and two transfer vouchers of ABC, to prove that the Plaintiff Nanhai Company had entrusted Salvage Company to salvage the ship and paid RMB730,000 for salvaging the ship.

The cross-examination of the Defendant Insurance Company: it had no objection of the authority of evidence 4, accepted the truth of salvaging, but had objection of the relevancy of the evidence. The salvaging charges RMB730,000 consisted two part which were RMB530,000 of the salvage of sunken ship and RMB200,000 of the salvage of the cargo. The salvage charges of the cargo were not within the scope of the insurance liability, so it shall not be compensated by the Insurance Company. The money transfer of the Plaintiff Nanhai Company to the accounts of individuals infringed the relevant provisions of the financial regulations of the company, the paid amount was inconsistent with the agreement of the salvage contract. In addition, the shipowner of M.V. "Ming Tai 89" also paid in advance RMB500,000 of the salvage charges of this accident.

Authorized opinions of the court: the Defendant Insurance Company had no objection to the authority of the evidence 4. The court regarded the evidence as the basis of the facts of this case. Whether to support the claim of the salvage charges concerned the controversial issues of this case, it would be commented in the following paragraph.

5. The agreement of towing and escorting signed between the Plaintiff Nanhai Company and the Salvage Company on November 25, 2013, to prove that the ship was aggravated damaged and it cannot float itself after the salvage of M.V. "Yu Nanhai 0168". The Plaintiff Nanhai Company entrusted the Salvage Company to escort the ship to the repair factory and paid tuggage in sum of RMB80,000 and charges for drainage on the dock in sum of RMB10,000.

The cross-examination of the Defendant Insurance Company: it had no objection to the authority of evidence 5. But it cannot be confirmed whether the Plaintiff Nanhai Company had paid the amount of the money. It accepted the tuggage in sum of RMB80,000, and not accepted charges for drainage on the dock in sum of RMB10,000 for M.V. "Yu Nanhai 0168" had settle on the bottom of the sea.

Authorized opinions of the court: the Defendant Insurance Company had no objection to the authority of the evidence. The court regarded the evidence as the basis of the facts of this case. Whether to support the tuggage and charges for drainage on the dock concerned the issues of this case, it would be commented in the following paragraph.

6. The agreement for emergency of sunken ships signed between the Plaintiff Nanhai Company and the operating party of M.V. "Wan Fuyang Gong 753", the receipt, certificate concerning the rescue charges of the floating cranes issued by XU Zhangming on August 22, 2014, and copies of his ID card, to prove that the Plaintiff Nanhai Company entrusted XU Zhangming to use M.V. "Wan Fuyang Gong 753" for rescuing and paid in cash of RMB50,000.

7. Rescue contract issued solely by BAI Shijie on November 28, 2013, a receipt, certificate concerning rescue charges of M.V. "Jiang Yun 19" issued by BAI Shijie on August 25, 2014, and copies of his ID card, to prove that for purpose of saving the vessel and cargoes, the Plaintiff Nanhai Company entrusted BAI Shijie to rescue by M.V. "Jiang Yun19" and paid in cash for the charges of RMB50,000 for the rescue service.

8. Receipt issued by XIONG Shengan on November 21, 2013, introductions of the conditions issued by Maritime Office of Yangluo, Wuhan on September 1, 2014, to prove F.V. "Wan Fuyang Gong 753", M.V. "Jiang Yun 19", M.V. "Huanggang Huo 656" had participated in the rescue service after the collision accident and the Plaintiff Nanhai Company paid XIONG Shengan RMB3,000 for the rescue charges of M.V. "Huanggang Huo 656".

The cross-examination of the Defendant Insurance Company: it had no objection of the authority of the introduction of the conditions, and accepted the fact that F.V. "Wan Fuyang Gong 753", M.V. "Jiang Yun 19", M.V. "Huanggang Huo 656" had participated in the on- site rescue operation. Except for these facts, they rejected the authority, legality and relevancy of evidence 6, 7, 8. XU Zhangming and BAI Shijie should be testified in court as the witness. The rescue was mainly upon the goods, it had nothing to do with the ship, the subject matter of the insurance. The cargo owner had already paid the charges of salvaging the goods in sum of RMB200,000 in advance, and it cannot be confirmed that the Plaintiff Nanhai Company had paid the related charges.

Authorized opinions of the court: the Defendant Insurance Company had accepted the fact that M.V. "Wan Fuyang Gong 753", M.V. "Jiang Yun 19", M.V. "Huanggang Huo 656" had participated in the rescue service. XU Zhangming and BAI Shijie tried to prove that the two ships had accepted the entrustment of the Plaintiff Nanhai Company to participate in the rescue and been charged and they had issued a corresponding receipt of fee for the Plaintiff Nanhai Company through issuing written testimony respectively as the operating party of M.V. "Wan Fuyang Gong 753" and M.V. "Jiang Yun 19". The court identified evidence 6 and 7. The introductions of condition issued by Wuhan Yangluo Maritime Office can superficially support the facts that M.V. "Huanggang Huo 656" had participated in the on-site rescue which was reflected in the receipt of the evidence 8. It was reasonable that the holder of "Huanggang Huo 656 " had charged RMB3,000 for the rescue expenses, and the court accepted. The Defendant Insurance company said F.V. "Wan Fuyang Gong 753", M.V. "Jiang Yun 19", M.V. "Huanggang Huo 656" had participated in the rescue of cargoes and the cargo owner paid in advance for the salvage charges in sum of RMB20,000. The court held that, except the holder of M.V. "JiangYun19" mentioned of rescuing the cargoes in the Rescue Contract, there was no other evidence to support the facts that M.V. "Wan Fuyang Gong 753" and M.V. "Huanggang Huo 656" had rescued the cargo and no evidence to show that the cargo owner paid in advance for the salvage charges in sum of RMB20,000, so the court rejected the cross-examination. Whether the Defendant Insurance company should compensate the rescue expenses charged by the holder involved was related to the controversial dispute, so it will be reviewed in the following paragraph.

9. Agreement for the hull cleaning signed between the Plaintiff Nanhai Company and CHEN Dongliang on December 3, 2013. Two receipts (RMB2,000 plus 14,000), to prove that the Plaintiff Nanhai Company had entrusted CHEN Dongliang to do the cleaning operation for M.V. "Yu Nanhai 0168 ", and paid RMB16,000.

The cross-examination of the Defendant Insurance Company: it had objection to the authority of the evidence 9, because the fact cannot be confirmed. If the hull had been cleaned, it should be referred to in the survey report, while the Plaintiff Nanhai Company had never referred the fact to the Min Tai An property and casualty survey Co., Ltd. (hereinafter referred to as survey company).

Authorized opinions of the court: the court accepted the authority of evidence 9, because it was the original and it can form the chains of evidence.

10. Installation Contract for the ship turbines, mechanical and electrical equipment and lines signed between the Plaintiff Nanhai Company and Wenzhou CSIC ship equipment Ltd. (hereinafter referred to as Zhongchuan Co.) on December 28, 2013. Lists of sale product. Two invoices. IOU (copy, the amount was RMB150,000). Certificate concerning the charges of the ship turbines, mechanical and electrical equipment and lines issued by Zhongchuan Co. on August 20, 2014, ID card (and copies) of HU Chujun. Two invoices of RMB80,000 and RMB70,000. Money transfer receipt of ABC (RMB150,000). Certificate of the organization code of Zhongchuan Co. and business license of legal personality enterprise, to prove the Plaintiff Nanhai Company had entrusted Zhongchuan Co. to dismantle, stall and maintain the ship turbines, mechanical and electrical equipment and lines. HU Chujun, the general manager of Zhongchuan Co. Wuhan branch office, signed the contract for the ship turbines, mechanical and electrical equipment and lines with the Plaintiff Nanhai Company on behalf of the Zhongchuan Co. and the total amount of the contract was RMB238,600. Money was paid to HU Chujun by the Plaintiff Nanhai Company directly. The Plaintiff Nanhai Company paid RMB50,000, RMB38,600, RMB150,00 on November 28, 2013, January 12, 2014, August 19, 2014 respectively.

The cross-examination of the Defendant Insurance Company: it had no objection of the authority of the invoices of the evidence 10. But the four invoices were written by hand and the form did not meet the legal regulations. Two invoices of RMB150,000 were formulated after the first trial. They cannot prove that they paid for the repair of the collision accident, so their legality and relevancy were not identified. The behavior of transfer which was behaved between privacy on behalf of the company did not meet the related financial institutions and laws. The Defendant Insurance Company cannot confirm the authority of the contract, the list of product, IOU, proof and other evidence, for the Plaintiff Nanhai Company did not inform the Defendant Insurance Company or survey company to fix the unite and lines and how to deal with the repaired was not clear, and there may still be residual values, so the proof submitted by the Defendant Insurance Company was not approved.

11. Contract of the ship decoration signed between the Plaintiff Nanhai Company and YANG Baoyu on December 11, 2013. Transfer of ABC (RMB30,000). Receipt of transfer in sum of RMB20,000. Two receipts (RMB20,000 and RMB16,000). IOU (RMB100,000). Introductions issued by YANG Baoyu on August 20, 2014 and his ID card copies. IOU (RMB11,620). Transfer of ABC (RMB100,000). Two invoices (RMB87,620 and RMB90,000), to prove that the Plaintiff Nanhai Company had entrusted YANG Baoyu to decorate

M.V. "Yu Nanhai 0168". The total amount of the contract was RMB16,000 (tax not included). Because the Plaintiff Nanhai Company required issuing invoice of it, the tax was RMB11,620, the total amount payment was RMB177,620.

The cross-examination of the Defendant Insurance Company: it accepted the authenticity of the introductions, IOU (RMB11,620), transfer of ABC (RMB100,000), two invoices and ID card of YANG Baoyu. The six evidence were formulated after the first trial, so they cannot prove the related charges was related to the collision accident, the relevancy of them was not approved. The authority, legality and relevancy of other evidence of evidence 11 were not accepted. (The charges paid for the indoors decorations of the ship were not the insured subject matter, for the renovation of the ship was not repair). Even though the above charges belonged to the losses of the insured subject matter, the Plaintiff Nanhai Company had not reported to the Defendant Insurance Company or Survey Company. Transfer of the Plaintiff Nanhai Company and the contractor of the indoors decorations happened between individuals, so it did not meet the financial regulations and administrative laws.

The cross-examination of the court: in evidence of 10, 11 group, the two groups of evidence can confirm each other respectively and form a chain of evidence. The Court accepted the authority of the two groups of evidence. The invoice in evidence 10 was filled in by hand, and the invoice itself did not indicate handwriting was invalid. Part of the transfer vouchers, invoices and certificates in evidence 10, 11 were submitted after the first trial in this case, it was beyond the time limit established by the court. According to Article 65 Paragraph 2 of the Civil Procedure Law of the People's Republic of China, the people's court shall, according to the claims of the parties and the situations of the trial, determine the evidence that the parties should provide and the time limit thereof. If the parties have genuine difficulty in providing evidence within the time limit, they may apply to the people's court for a prolongation; the people's court may prolong the time limit properly according to the application of the parties. Where a party provides evidence beyond the time limit, the people's court shall order him to explain the reasons; if he refuses to do so or the reasons are untenable, the people's court may, according to different situations, not accept the evidence, or accept the evidence but impose an admonition or fine upon him. The Plaintiff Nanhai Company was still in implementation of the relevant ship repair and decoration contract, and paid their arrears of repairs and decoration fees after the first trial. After receiving the money, Zhongchuan Co., YANG Baoyu issued receipts which were corresponding to the bills, contracts and IOUs. So the court accepted the transfer vouchers, invoices and certificates which were submitted by the Plaintiff Nanhai Company after the first instance. The Defendant Insurance Company regarded that the transfer behavior of the representative of the company did not comply with the financial regulations and legal requirements. The court held that Xue Lanwei accepted the entrustment of the Plaintiff Nanhai Company to repair M.V. "Yu Nanhai 0168", signed a contract with CSSC and YANG Baoyu and paid the consideration. HU Chujun accepted the payment on behalf of CSSC and was recognized by the Company. YANG Baoyu issued machine-printed invoices as personal service provider, and their behavior was in line with the relevant provisions of the law and invoice issuance rules. The court did not accept the cross-examination of the Defendant Insurance Company.

12. Three sales lists, the receipt issued by Nanjing Zibai Power Equipment Sales Co., Ltd. on December 28, 2013, to prove that for maintenance of main engine of M.V. "Yu Nanhai 0168", the Plaintiff Nanhai Company spent a total amount of RMB113, 698.

The cross-examination of the Defendant Insurance Company: it accepted the fact that the main engine had been repaired which was reflected in evidence 12. The form had flaws for the receipt was stamped with special seal. The repair costs of the motor was similar with the new motor's market price, and the relevant charges was too high. The Plaintiff Nanhai Company did not notify the survey company of the repair affairs in advance. The Plaintiff Nanhai Company did not provide the corresponding repair certificate when the survey company was accounting after the repair was completed.

The authorized opinions of the court: evidence 12 was the original, the Defendant Insurance Company regarded that the corresponding charges was too high, but they cannot provide enough evidence to refute, the court accepted evidence 12.

"Yu Nanhai 0168" dock repair order (the amount was RMB1,681,243) issued by Ezhou Guang Da Shipbuilding Co., Ltd. (hereinafter referred to as Guang Da Co.) ship repair branch on January 13,2014. Four transfers of ABC (the amount were all RMB200,000). Transfers receipt of ICBC (the amount was RMB100,000). Introductions concerning the dock repair costs issued by Guang Da ship repairing branch on August 22, 2014. Invoices issued by Guang Da Co. (the amount was RMB1,681,243) and a copy of its business license. YU Haixiang's ID card (copy), transfer receipt of ABC (the amount was RMB781,243), to prove that the Plaintiff Nanhai Company had entrusted China Guang Da Co. to repair M.V. "Yu Nanhai 0168" into the dock.YU Haixiang was the director of Guang Da Co. ship repair branch. "Yu Nanhai 0168" dock repairs in amount of RMB1,681,243(excluding tax) was paid to YU Haixiang through transfer. In order to issue invoice, the Plaintiff Nanhai company also paid to the Guang Da Company about RMB50,000 for taxes.

The cross-examination opinions of the Defendant Insurance Company: the Insurance Company recognized the dock repair facts reflected from evidence 13, but had dissension on statements and forming time of the invoices, and the invoices were issued after the first trial, cannot prove that the relevant costs were associated with the collision accident of this case. Meanwhile, the Defendant Insurance company viewed that transfer happened between individuals, which did not meet the relevant legal requirements and financial system. The Insurance company had no objection to the authenticity of Guang Da Company's business license, but the relationship between the Guang Da Company and Guangda company repair branch was not clear, and it cannot be confirmed whether YU Haixiang was manager of Guang Da Company or not. The repair was not reported to the Defendant insurance company, and the cost was far more than the market price, the repair costs were not accepted.

14. Lists and receipts (RMB85,000) issued by Wuhan Chuyu Ship Building and Repairing Co., Ltd. (hereinafter referred to as Chuyu Company) on February 16, 2014, and the proof of maintenance of Chuyu Company and copy of business license issued by Chuyu Company on August 28, 2014, copy of ZHAN Caishuang's ID card, to prove that the Plaintiffs Nanhai Company entrusted Chuyu Company for repair of ship, and pay for repair costs in cash in sum of RMB85,000 for hatch coaming, poop deck, hull and electric equipments (including the repainted works for the repair part), ZHAN Caishuang was director of Chuyu Company.

Cross-examination opinions of the Defendant insurance company: ZHAN Caishuang was not legal representative of Chuyu Company, the proof issued by him was not recognized. And the insurance company had no objection to the authenticity of evidence 14, but the transfer between individuals to pay repair costs did not meet the relevant legal requirements and financial system, and the repair costs shall be based on survey report.

The authorized opinions of the court: evidence 13 can form a chain of evidence, and the Defendant Insurance company recognized the fact that M.V. "Yu Nanhai 0168" was repaired in the dock and it must produce the corresponding repair costs, Guang Da Company had requested tax authorities to issue invoices, and they acknowledged the repair by Guang Da Company repair branch, the court confirmed the repair costs. The Evidence 14 can form another chain of evidence, ZHAN Caishuang was not the legal representative of Chuyu Company, But the proof of Chuyu Company's maintenance costs was stamped with the unit seal, it proved that ZHAN Caishuang can represent Chuyu Company, the court approved the repair costs of M.V. "Yu Nanhai 0168" by Chuyu Company.

15. Receipt, two sales receipts and receipts, accessories bill of materials and receipts, two sales lists and receipts, accessories list and receipt of receipt, Two TCL Legrand International E zhou store list and receipt of receipts, to prove that the Plaintiff NanHai Company purchased boat supplies amounted to RMB10,527.

16. Receipt and ICBC Personal Business Certificate, copy of logbook of M.V. "Yu Nanhai 0168", to prove that before the collision, the lubrication of oil tank was 53 cm by M.V. "Yu Nanhai 0168", and after collision, all the diesel in the fuel tank leaked, after the vessel had been salvaged, the oil costed RMB56,120.

Cross-examination opinions of the Defendant insurance company: because the form of the bill was not appropriate, the authenticity of Evidence 15 was not acknowledged, and they had no objection to basic facts of this group of evidence, but the amount of the loss shall be based on the amount in the survey report. The authenticity of the Evidence 16 cannot be confirmed, the Defendant insurance company viewed that diesel was not the subject matter of insurance, oil costs had nothing to do with the case. In addition, the MSA held that the collision did not cause pollution and should not produce diesel costs.

The authorized opinions of the court: the group of Evidence 15 were original documents, mainly reflected purchase of the ship accessories, material hardware during the repair of M.V. "Yu Nanhai 0168", the court accepted this group of evidence. In group of Evidence 16, the logbook was copy, though receipt and ICBC

Personal Business Certificate were original documents, the place of receiving units was stamped "E oil 169" ship chapter and the identity of recipient WANG Jingjing was unknown, which cannot prove the relevancy with case, the court did not recognize the Evidence 16.

In order to support its defense, the Defendant insurance company submitted the following evidence to the court:

1. The copy documents of the insurance policy against all risks of inland ships, insurance slip, Inland Waterway Cargo Insurance Clauses(2009) (hereinafter referred to as Insurance Clause 2009, a handwriting of the insurance policy, to prove that the Plaintiff NanHai Company on July 23, 2013 covered M.V. "Yu Nanhai 0168" with the Defendant insurance companies against all risks, the insurance period was one year, from July 24, 2013 to July 23, 2014, and the insurance amount was RMB5,010,000; each accident deducts RMB5,000 or 10%, whichever is higher, the Defendant Insurance Company enjoyed the right of the 10% deductible of hull damages of M.V. "Yu Nanhai 0168" of the Plaintiff NanHai company in this accident; the insurance content was losses of the insured vessel and necessary salvage costs, the payment by the Defendant Insurance Company for the salvage and rescue costs, when related to the common security of the ship and cargo, was limited to the proportion that the value of the salvaged ship accounted for the total value of the salvaged ship, cargo and freight. The insurance contract was subject to the insurance clause.

Cross-examination opinions of the Plaintiff NanHai Company: it had no objection to authenticity of policy of insurance, insurance slip, a handwriting of the insurance policy, but cannot confirm the authenticity of Insurance Clause2009, and did not recognize the insurance coverage and content by Insurance Clause 2009.

2. The survey report issued by Survey Company on August 15, 2014, to prove that the Defendant Insurance Company actively entrusted the Survey Company to check and investigate the cause of the accident after the insurance accident, there was no delay in the case of claims; survey report could confirm the repair costs and salvage costs of M.V. "Yu Nanhai 0168" in amount of RMB1,909,628.44, included the salvage charges of RMB730,000, the towage charges of RMB80,000, repair costs of RMB1,176,587.52 by salvage company, and then deducted the residual value in sum of RMB76,959.08, deducted the losses which were not insured or seriously exceeded the market price.

Cross-examination opinions of the Plaintiff NanHai Company: it cannot confirm the authenticity of survey report, the survey report was entrusted by the Defendant insurance company unilaterally and on its own, the Plaintiff NanHai Company did not participate. The contents and conclusions of the Survey report had flaws, in particular, there were accounting errors on pages 11, 15 and 17 of the report, the survey company was involved in whole repair of vessel, however, it did not recognize some part of losses, which did not conform to objective facts.

3. Vessel's main item single page (copy) from ship inspection certificate of M.V. "Yu Nanhai 0168", to prove that the subject matter of insurance in this case was the hull and equipment of M.V. "Yu Nanhai 0168".

Cross-examination opinions of the Plaintiff NanHai Company: it had no objection to authenticity, but had objection to proof object, the NanHai Company viewed that the direct losses covered by all risk insurance included hull and goods.

The authorized opinions of the court: the Plaintiff NanHai Company had no objection to authenticity of evidence 1 (included policy of insurance, insurance slip, insurance copy list). Therefore, the court recognized the evidence. As for the Insurance Clause 2009 in evidence 1, because it was the standard format clause of the inland waterway insurance clause of the People's Property Insurance Company of China. Therefore, the court recognized the authenticity of Insurance Clause. Evidence 2 were original documents, though the court recognized the authenticity that the survey company involved in the collision accident investigation and processing. But the report was mainly used for the Defendant insurance company to approve the loss, in the report the basis of approving the loss were not clear enough, the market inquiry situation was not clear enough, and the existence of waste recycling situation during the repair of vessel was not proved, there were no factual and legal basis to deduct residual value. Therefore, the court did not recognize the amount of loss and approved loss in evidence 2.

The parties adduced and examined the evidence. With the investigation and authentication opinions of the court, the court had concludes the following facts:

On July 23, 2013, the Plaintiff NanHai Company covered M.V. "Yu Nanhai 0168" with the Defendant Insurance Company against all risks of inland river vessel and propeller and other separate loss insurance liability insurance, and signed the insurance slip No.TCEJ20134128000000047. The insurance slip recorded that in view of the insured had been insured to the insurer against all risk insurance of inland river ship, and delivered the premium according to the insurance contract, the insurer agreed to bear the insurance liability according to the terms of the agreement, and this policy of insurance was proof. The Defendant Insurance Company signed the policy of insurance No.PCEJ201341280000000203 and gave it to the Plaintiff NanHai Company. The above insurance slip and policy of insurance stated that: the insured was NanHai Company, the insured vessel was M.V. "Yu Nanhai 0168", the main risks was all risk of inland river vessel, and additional propeller and other separate damage insurance liability, both the value of insurance and the amount of insurance were RMB5,010,000. Insurance conditions and special agreement: RMB5,000 per accident deductible or 10%, whichever was higher. The period of insurance was from 0:00 on July 24, 2013 to 24:00 on July 23, 2014.

The involved Insurance Clause 2009 was in a separate page, the main contents were as follows: Article 1, this insurance contract shall be composed of insurance clauses, insurance policies, insurance slip, insurance certificates, and approval documents, all the stipulations in this insurance contract shall be in writing; Article 2, "ship" as referred to in this insurance contract included the ship hull, equipment and navigational aids specified in the certificate of inspection of ships and vessels, which are registered legally in the People's Republic of China and engaged in inland navigation. Article V of the ship all risk of the provisions of the collision, touch and caused by overturning, sinking, etc. caused by the loss of the insurance ship or the total loss of the collision, touch and rescue, rescue responsibility and Costs, the insurer according to the insurance contract is responsible for compensation. With regard to salvage and rescue, Article V also provides that the insurance is responsible for compensating the insured person in the event of an insurance accident, the insurance of the navigation safety expenses necessary reasonable expenses, including in order to determine the reasonable cost of the text and valuation that the nature and degree of the insurance accident, and the expenses incurred for the execution of the special notice of the insurer, the insurer shall pay in addition to the loss of indemnity in respect of the insured ship. The insurer shall pay the expenses prescribed in this subparagraph to the extent that the cargoes are jointly safe and the value of the rescued insurance ship shall be limited to the proportion of the total value of the salvaged ship, freight and freight, and shall not exceed the insured amount; Article 6, Article 7, Article 8, Article 9 are the provisions on the exclusion of liability, the unseaworthiness (unto worthiness) of the ship, including the improperly equipped personnel, the technical condition, the navigation area and the use of the insured vessel do not conform with the navigation (towage) rules or the goods are loaded incorrectly, from the date of such occurrence, the insurer shall not be liable for any liability, loss and expense arising from any cause during the period of insurance. The insurer shall not be liable for the loss, liability and expense of the goods carried on the insured ship during the insurance period. The insurer is not liable for any loss, liability or expense not covered by the insurance policy; Article 17, paragraph 2, the insured apply to the Company for compensation and provide information required for claims, the Company shall be within 60 days for approval. In the case of an insurance liability, the Company shall fulfill the obligation of indemnity within 10 days after reaching an agreement with the Insured for compensation or payment of the insurance benefit; Article 18, in case of full insurance under all risks, the partial loss of the ship shall be compensated according to the actual losses incurred, and shall be limited to the insurance amount. When the amount of insurance is greater than or equal to the value of salvage of the insured ship, the salvage and rescue costs incurred shall be compensated according to the actual costs; Article 21, in addition to the liability for total loss, touch and collision, the insurer shall make a deduction corresponding to the deductible amount or deductible rate stipulated in the insurance policy for each accident; Article 22, the residual value after the ship suffered a total loss or partial loss shall be negotiated by the parties of the insurance.

At 05:50 on November 15, 2013, M.V. "Ming Tai 89" was down to the Mu E Island waterways Baideng ship in Yangtze River (the lower reaches of the Yangtze River waterway mileage of 997 km) and collided with up-bound M.V. "Yu Nanhai 0168", then M.V. "Yu Nanhai 0168" made a large alteration of course to portside, at 05:51, collided with the trailing up M.V. "Yuan Dong 907". The accident led to prow and the portside of M.V. "Yu Nanhai 0168" damaged and water penetration, after emergency beaching, settled on the bottom on the Mu E Island Baideng ship 100 m outside the channel edge, only with the compass deck on the water.

Marine Office of Yangluo Wuhan identified the cause of the accident by the investigation:

1. M.V. "Ming Tai 89", in the case of restricted visibility, sailed without high vigilance, without correct use of sound signal and VHF, sailed without proper ship lookout, and did not unify the make way intention with the up-bound ship, without safe speed and proper selection of waterway route, which was the main cause of collision.
2. M.V. "Yu Nanhai 0168", in the case of restricted visibility, sailed without high vigilance, without correct use of sound signal and VHF, without proper ship lookout, did not unify the make way intention with up-bound ship, and turned left blindly for avoidance in the danger of collision with the down-bound vessel, which was the secondary cause of collision.
3. M.V. "Yuan Dong 906", in the case of restricted visibility, sailed without high vigilance, and without correct use of sound signal and VHF, sailed without proper ship lookout, without safe speed, without keeping safe distance when following the former vessel and without taking effective measures to avoid collision when suspecting the trend of the former vessel, which was another reason of the collision.
4. The channel of the accident water was meandering, narrow and the fog was thick when the accident happened, which were unfavorable objective factors for collision.

After accident on November 15, 2016, the Plaintiff NanHai Company reported and claimed to the Defendant Insurance Company, on the same day, the Defendant Insurance Company entrusted the survey company to investigate the accident and conduct follow-up on-site tracking and survey of the ship during the maintenance period, on August 15, 2014, the Survey Company issued survey report. Survey Company viewed that the accident was caused by collision, so it was within the scope of liability of Defendant Insurance Company against all risk of inland ship. Survey company verified M.V. "Yu Nanhai 0168" produced the salvage costs, tuggage and repairs costs, there were residual during the repair of the ship, and cargo rescue costs (relating to F.C "Wan Fuyang Gong 753", M.V. "Jiang Yun 19", M.V. "Huanggang Huo 656"), fuel costs, loss of personal effects, household appliances and other losses were not approved.

After accident, the Plaintiff NanHai Company entrusted Xue Weilan to deal with rescue, salvage, dredging, repair of M.V. "Yu Nanhai 0168".

On November 15, 2013, the Plaintiff NanHai Company signed the agreement of rescue of sunken ship with XU Zhangming, the occupier of M.V. "Wan Fuyanggong 758", agreed that M.V. "Wan Fuyang Gong 753" rescued M.V. "Yu Nanhai 0168", rescue fee was RMB50,000 and shall be paid in full after the completion of rescue. On November 16, 2013, the Plaintiff NanHai Company paid RMB50,000 in cash for XU Zhangming. From 08:30 of November 15, 2013 to November 28, 2013, BAI Shijie accepted the entrustment of the Plaintiff NanHai Company to rescue the goods, and two parties agreed the rescue fee was RMB50,000. On August 24, 2014, the Plaintiff NanHai Company paid BAI Shijie RMB50,000 in cash. On November 21, 2013, the Plaintiff NanHai Company paid the rescue fee in amount of RMB3,000 to Xiong Sheng'an, the occupier of M.V. "Huang Gang Huo 656".

On November 16, 2013, the Plaintiff NanHai Company signed salvage contract with salvage Company, the salvage Company shall be responsible for salvage of M. V. "Yu Nanhai 0168", and agreed the salvage fee was RMB730,000, and RMB200,000 shall be paid when contract was made, and the balance shall be paid one-time when the ship was salvaged out of water. M.V. "Yu Nanhai 0168", after being salvaged out of water, cannot be self-floating due to serious damage, the Plaintiff Nanhai Company signed a towed escort agreement with the salvage company on November 25, 2013, entrusted the salvage company escort M.V. "Yu Nanhai 0168" to the Guang Da Company, and towing fee was RMB80,000, drain and dock fee was RMB10,000. The Plaintiff Nanhai Company paid salvage, towing and drainage on dock fee in sum of RMB200,000 and RMB120,000 at twice to the salvage company on November 16, 2013, and on December 26, 2013.

After M.V. "Yu Nanhai 0168" being salvaged out of water, the Plaintiff NanHai Company signed Hull Cleaning and Dredging Agreement with CHEN Dongliang on December 3, 2013, and CHEN Dongliang agreed to clean the four compartments of M.V. "Yu Nanhai 0168". After completed the clean-up operations by CHEN Dongliang, on December, 2013, and December 23, 2013, the Plaintiff Nanhai Company at twice paid clean-up fee in sum of RMB2,000 and RMB14,000.

On December 12, 2013, the Plaintiff Nanhai Company signed the ship decorating contract with YANG Baoyu, agreed that YANG Baoyu shall be responsible for interior decoration of M.V. "Yu Nanhai 0168", the contract amount was RMB166,000. The Plaintiff NanHai Company paid RMB30,000 on December 14, 2013, paid RMB20,000 on December 29, and paid RMB16,000 on January 20, 2014. Because the Plaintiff Nanhai Company required YANG Baoyu to issue the corresponding invoice, the contract (included the tax) price was changed into RMB177,620. On August 20, 2014, YANG Baoyu received the balance in sum of RMB111,620 and issued two invoices in amount of RMB87,620 and RMB90,000 for the Plaintiff Nanhai Company.

On December 28, 2013, the Plaintiff signed the Contract of Marine Mechanical and Electrical Equipment and Line Installation with Zhongchuan Company. Zhongchuan Company disassembled, repaired and installed the mechanical and electrical equipment, cable and lighting equipment of M.V. "Yu Nanhai 0168". The Amounted of contract was RMB238,600. HU Chujun, general management of Zhongchuan Company's Wuhan office, was responsible for direct check-out with Plaintiff Nanhai Company, and the Plaintiff NanHai Company paid RMB50,000 on 28 November 2013, paid RMB38,600 on January 12, 2014, paid RMB150,000 on August 19, 2014. Zhongchuan Company issued four invoices in amount of RMB50,000, RMB38,600, RMB80,000, RMB70,000.

On December 28, 2013, the Plaintiff Nanhai Company gave the main engine of M.V. "Yu Nanhai 0168" to Nanjing Province Zibai Power Equipment Sales Co., Ltd. to repair, spent a total of RMB113,698.

On January 13, 2014, Guangda company repair branch issued dock repair statement of M.V. "Yu Nanhai 0168", illustrated that M.V. "Yu Nanhai 0168" costed RMB1,681,243 for repair in dock. YU Haixiang was manager of Guangda company repair branch, the Plaintiff NanHai Company paid repair fee at five times, namely paid for RMB200,000 on December 2, 2013, paid for RMB100,000 on December 10, 2013, paid for RMB200,000 on December 29, 2013, paid for RMB200,000 on December 31, 2013, and paid for RMB200,000 on January 3, 2014. As of August 22, 2014, the Plaintiff Nanhai company paid off the balance in sum of RMB781,243. Guangda company requested the tax authorities to issue invoices in amount of RMB1,681,243.

On February 16, 2014, the Plaintiff NanHai Company paid RMB85,000 for Chuyu Company in cash for repair of hatch coaming, poop deck, hull and electric equipments (including the repainted works of the repair part) of M.V."Yu Nanhai 0168". ZHAN Caishuang was the manager of the company.

From November 25, 2013 to January 3, 2014, the Plaintiff Nanhai Company purchased the spare parts of submersible pumps, cables, plugs and sockets that above all were necessary as ship accessories and paid a total of RMB10,527.

The port of registry of M.V. "Yu Nanhai 0168" was Henan Zhumadian, and the ship was a bulk cargo ship, with a total length of 83.60 m, a width of 14.20 m, a depth of 4.97 m, a gross tonnage of 1962 and a net tonnage of 1,098. The ship-owner and operator was the Plaintiff NanHai Company. The deadweight was 2,500 tons. Granted permission to sail in the waters of the Three Gorges reservoir area of Sichuan and A-level; J2 navigation area (route). A-level area was for 2400 tons of cargo for reference, B, C-class reference area were for 2,500 tons of cargo for reference.

The minimum safety manning certificate of M.V. "Yu Nanhai 0168" recorded the minimum safe manning of 7 persons, namely 1 captain of first class, 1 chief engineer officer of first class, 1 mate of first class, 1 s engineer of first class, 2 sailors, 1 mechanism. In the case of the accident, there were crew of 4 people on board.

The court holds that the case was ship-sea water insurance contract dispute due to the collision. According to facts approved by the court and the litigation and argument of the parties, the court will summarize the controversy of the case as follows: 1. on the validity of the insurance clause 2009, and the composition of the insurance contract; 2. the scope and amount of compensation by the Defendant insurance company for the losses suffered by the Plaintiff Nanhai company; 3. whether the Defendant insurance company was entitled to deduct.

1. Effect of Insurance Clause 2009, and element of the insurance contract

The insurance contract in the case should consist of insurance slip and insurance policy and insurance documents such as Insurance Clauses 2009. However, the Insurance Company neither had separately submitted the insurance clause to the Plaintiff Nanhai Company to sign and affirm, nor attached the insurance clause to the insurance slip and insurance policy on the back and prominently reminded the Plaintiff Nanhai company on the front, the Court held that the Defendant did not fulfill the obligation to fully explain the obligations of exemption to the Plaintiff Nanhai Company. According to Article 17 of the Insurance Law of the People's

Republic of China, where an insurance contract is concluded using the standard clauses of the insurer, the insurer shall provide an insurance policy with the standard clauses attached and explain the contents of the contract to the insurance applicant. For those clauses exempting the insurer from liability in the insurance contract, the insurer shall sufficiently warn the insurance applicant of those clauses in the insurance application form, the insurance policy or any other insurance certificate, and expressly explain those clauses to the insurance applicant in writing or verbally. If the insurer fails to make a warning or express explanation thereof, those clauses shall not be effective, the clause in the Insurance Clause 2009 which excluded the liability of the insurer did not take effect. The insured vessel was M.V. "Yu Nanhai 0168", the Plaintiff Nanhai Company was the insured, the Defendant Insurance Company was the insurer. The insurance contractual relationship between the parties was genuine intention of the parties, was in compliance with the compulsory law and social ethics and was lawful and effective. The contract was constituted of the insurance slip, insurance policy and the most fundamental clauses of Insurance Clause 2009.

2. The scope and amount of compensation by the Defendant insurance company for the losses suffered by the Plaintiff Nanhai company

The accident was caused by NanHai's M.V. "Yu Nanhai", which successively collided with M.V. "Ming Tai 89" and "Yuan Dong 907" at the place of white light boat of Mu Ezhou in the Changjiang River. If the losses suffered by the Plaintiff Nanhai Company were in conformity with the partial loss, rescue, salvage responsibility and charges suffered by the insured vessel due to collision and sinking arising from it provided in Section 5 All risks of Insurance Clause 2009, the Insurance Company shall be liable for the compensation according to the charter party, the details were as follows:

(1) Retrieval expense, salvage, tow, drainage on the dock fee.

Rescue charges claimed by Nanhai Company including salvage charges of M.V. "Wan Fuyang Gong 753", M.V. "Jiang Yun 19", M.V. "Huanggang Huo 656". The court held, whether paid the holder of M.V. "Jiang Yun 19" for the rescue of the goods on board, or paid the holder of M.V. "Jiang Yun 19" or M.V. "Huanggang Huo 656" for rescue of the insured vessel, sinking of M.V. "Yu Nanhai 0168" after collision was the direct reason for payment of this kind of charges, the losses were caused by collision and were within the scope of all risks. Insurance Company argued that rescue of goods was within the scope of all risks by invoking provision of excluded liability of Insurance Clause 2009, the insurer shall not be liable for the loss, liability and expense of the goods carried on the insured ship during the insurance period. But the relevant clauses of excluded liability did not take effect. The court would dismiss this argument.

Insurance Company agreed that because M.V. "Yu Nanhai 0168" sank and submersed, the vessel should be salvaged with expense. M.V. "Yu Nanhai 0168" did not have ability of self-floating because the cabin was broken after salvage. So the vessel needed to be repaired in dock, and sleeper in cabin should be drained.

The fee was necessary and reasonable, so Section 5 of Insurance Clause 2009 was applicable (Section 5: charges for navigating safely is necessary and reasonable). According to the contract, the above four expenses were limited to the proportion the value of the salvaged ship accounted for the total value of the salvaged ship, cargo, freight and they did not exceed the insurance amount. The Defendant insurance company shall pay to the Plaintiff Nanhai Company in addition to the indemnity of the insured ship, namely the rescue fee in sum of RMB103,000 paid by the Plaintiff to Floating crane "Wan Fuyang Gong 753", M.V. "Jiang Yun 19", M.V. "Huanggang Huo 656" and RMB320,000 for salvage, tow, drainage on the dock fee paid by the Plaintiff to the third party.

(2) Clean-up cost, decoration, line installation fee for electromechanical equipment, mainframe repair costs, repair costs for Guang Da Company, and Chuyu Company, maritime material expenses.

Because M.V. "Yu Nanhai 0168" sank and submersed after collision, that was necessary and in line with salvage work to clean-up and repair the cabin. And, above 7 losses of Nan Hai company had corresponding contracts (list, statement), invoice(receipt) and assignee's evidence, which could be able to explain the corresponding costs. According to Article 18 of Insurance Clause 2009, in case of full insurance under all risks, the partial loss of the ship shall be compensated according to the actual losses incurred, and shall be limited to the insurance amount. The Plaintiff had paid clean-up cost in sum of RMB16,000, decoration fee in sum of RMB177,620, line installation fee for electromechanical equipment in sum of RMB238,600, mainframe repair costs in sum of RMB113,698, repair costs for Guang Da Company in sum of RMB1,681,243, repair costs for Chu Yu company in sum of RMB85,000, maritime material expenses in sum of RMB10,527, totally in sum of RMB2,322,688, it did not exceed the insurance amount of RMB5,100,000 and should be compensated by the Defendant insurance company. In addition, Article 22 of the Insurance Clause 2009 listed, the residual after the insured ship suffered a total loss or partial loss would be negotiated by the two sides of insurance. The Defendant insurance company quoted the conclusion in the assessment report that the replaced ship accessories had residual value during the repair of M. V. "Yu Nanhai 0168", required to deduct the residual value in the repair cost claimed by the Plaintiff Nanhai Company. However, because the Defendant insurance company did not prove the treatment of the discarded ship fittings, the calculation of residual value had no basis, and the Plaintiff Nanhai Company did not recognize, the court shall not be adopt the Defendant's claim for deduction of residual value.

(3) Bunker fees, marine appliances losses, losses of ship goods, paint cost.

The bunker fees and marine appliance loss claimed by the Plaintiff Nanhai Company were not within the scope of the All Risks; losses of vessel goods, paint and the above-mentioned marine supplies costs, repair costs were repeated. For the bunker costs, loss of marine appliances, vessel goods loss, paint costs, the Plaintiff Nanhai Company did not provide the appropriate evidence to prove their losses.

According to Article 64 Paragraph 1 of the Civil Procedure Law of the People's Republic of China, a party shall have the burden to provide evidence for its claims. The court shall not support the bunker fees, loss of marine appliances, loss of vessel goods, paint costs claimed by the Plaintiff Nanhai Company.

(4) Interest losses.

In this case, Article 17 Paragraph 2 of the Insurance Clauses listed, the insured shall, within 60 days after the company seeks compensation and provide the information required for the settlement of claims, the company shall, within 60 days, verify the insurance liability, within ten days after reaching an agreement for compensation or payment of the insurance benefit, which was inconsistent with Article 23 Paragraph 1 of the Insurance Law of the People's Republic of China, which listed, after receiving an insured's or beneficiary's claim for paying indemnity or insurance benefits, the insurer shall adjust the claim in a timely manner. If the circumstances are complex, the insurer shall complete the adjustment within 30 days, unless it is otherwise agreed upon in the insurance contract. The insurer shall notify the insured or beneficiary of the adjustment result. For a claim which falls within the insurance coverage, the insurer shall perform the obligation of paying indemnity or insurance benefits within 10 days after reaching an agreement on payment of indemnity or insurance benefits with the insured or beneficiary. If the insurance contract provides for a time limit for payment of indemnity or insurance benefits, the insurer shall perform the obligation of paying indemnity or insurance benefits as agreed upon. The period for insurers to approve liability of insurance in Article 17 Paragraph 2 of the Clause was longer than the statutory period. Because of lacking of explanation or promoting by the company, the term was ineffective between the parties.

According to Article 25 of the Insurance Law, where an insurer cannot determine the amount of indemnity or insurance benefits to be paid within 60 days after receiving a claim for indemnity or insurance benefits and the relevant certificates and materials, it shall first pay the amount which may be determined according to the available certificates or materials, and after it finally determines the amount of indemnity or insurance benefits to be paid, pay the difference, the Plaintiff Nanhai Company had sued the Defendant insurance company on November 15, 2013, and the Defendant insurance company should make compensation or pay in advance at latest on January 14, 2014. But the Defendant insurance company had not compensated for the Plaintiff Nanhai Company, nor reached an agreement on paying the insurance money in advance, so the Defendant did not fulfill insurance obligation of timely payment, occupied the funds of the Plaintiff Nanhai company objectively, resulting in its loss, the Plaintiff Nanhai Company had the right to claim the corresponding interest losses since January 15, 2014.

The losses of the Plaintiff Nanhai Company happened before (not included) the January 15, 2014 were as follows: paid the first sum of retrieval expense ¥50,000 and first sum of salvage, tow, drainage on the dock fee RMB200,000 on November 16, 2013; paid the second sum of retrieval expense RMB3,000 on November 21, 2013. On November 28, paid the first sum of line installation fee for electromechanical equipment RMB50,000. On December 2, 2013, paid the first sum of repair fee ¥200,000 for GuangDa Company. On December 3, paid the first sum of clean-up cost ¥2,000. On December 10, paid the second sum of repair fee RMB100,000 for GuangDa Company. Paid the first sum of decoration fee ¥30,000 on December 14. Paid the second sum of clean-up cost RMB14,000 on December 23. On December 26, paid the second sum of salvage, tow, drainage on the dock fee RMB120,000. On December 28, paid mainframe repair costs RMB113,698. On December 29, paid second sum of decoration fee RMB20,000, and the third sum RMB200,000. On December 31, paid the fourth sum of repair costs RMB200,000. And on January 3, 2014, paid the fifth sum of repair costs RMB200,000 for GuangDa Company and before (included) this day, paid shipping materials costs RMB10,527. On January 12, paid second sum of line installation fee for electromechanical equipment RMB386,00. The total amount of the above-mentioned expenses shall be RMB15,518,250, which shall be calculated from the next day of the deadline for the payment of the insurance premium by the Defendant namely January 15, 2014, at the benchmark lending rate announced by the People's Bank of China, until the date of payment determined in this judgment, to protect the interest losses of the Plaintiff Nanhai Company.

For the losses incurred by Plaintiff Nanhai Company after January 15, 2014 (including the same day), the details were as follows: on January 20,2014, paid the third sum of decoration fee RMB16,000. On February 16, 2014, paid repair fee ¥85,000 for Chuyu Company. On August 19, paid the third sum of line installation fee for electromechanical equipment RMB150,000. And on August 20, paid the fourth sum of decoration fee RMB111,620. On August 22, paid the sixth sum of repair costs RMB781,243 for GuangDa Company. On August 24, paid the third sum of retrieval expense RMB50,000. The aforesaid expenses shall be calculated from the next day of the respective payment timetables, on the basis of the interest rate of the loan at the same period announced by the People's Bank of China, until the date of payment determined by this judgment, to protect the interest losses suffered by the Plaintiff Nanhai Company.

3. Whether the Defendant Insurance Company had right to indemnify.

Manning of the vessel. When accident of M.V. "Yu Nanhai 0168" happened, there actually 4 seamen on the ship, which did not meet the minimum standard of 7 approved by the minimum safety manning certificate of the vessel, constituted the problem of insufficient manning. However, the maritime safety authorities concluded in the accident investigation that M.V. "Yu Nanhai 0168" in the case of poor visibility, sailed without a high degree of vigilance and correct use of sound and VHF radiotelephone, without keeping a proper lookout, without maintaining a safe speed, without unifying make way intention with the down bound vessel and turned to the left to avoid collision in danger of collision with the down bound vessel, which was the secondary cause of collision accident, it could be seen that insufficient manning of M.V. "Yu Nanhai 0168" did not lead to the accident. In addition, as aforesaid, the exclusion of liability insurance clause of the insurance contract did not take effect, the Defendant claimed that insufficient manning of M.V. "Yu Nanhai 0168" affected its compensation, the Court shall not adopt.

"Insurance deductible RMB5,000 or 10%, whichever is higher" listed in the insurance slip and insurance policy, was the exemption of insurer's liability clause of Article 17 Paragraph 2 of the Insurance Law of the People's Republic of China. As stated above, according to Article 17 of the Insurance Law, the record of the deductible was not clearly marked in the front of the insurance slip and the insurance policy, it could not catch the attention of the policy holder, the Defendant insurance company failed to prove that it had stated the contents of the deductible clearly in written or oral form to the policy holder. Therefore, the terms "5,000 or 10% of each accident deductible, whichever is higher" was ineffective. The Defendant insurance company did not enjoy the right to indemnify for the accident.

In summary, the Defendant insurance company should pay compensation in sum of RMB2,745,688 to the Plaintiff NanHai Company, included: retrieval expense in sum of RMB103,000; salvage, tow, drainage on the dock fee in sum of RMB320,000; clean-up cost in sum of RMB16,000; decoration fee in sum of RMB177,620; line installation fee for electromechanical equipment in sum of RMB238,600; mainframe repair costs in sum of RMB113,698; repair costs for GuangDa Company in sum of RMB1,681,243; repair costs for Chuyu Company in sum of RMB85,000; loss of vessel goods in sum of RMB10,527, and the corresponding interests.

According to Article 23 Paragraph 1 and Paragraph 2, Article 25 of the Insurance Law of the People's Republic of China, and Article 142 of the Civil Procedure Law of the People's Republic of China, the judgment is as follows:

1. The Defendant People's Insurance Company of China Property and Casualty Co., Ltd. Zhumadian Branch within 10 days after the judgment takes effect shall pay the Plaintiff Zhumadian South China Sea Shipping Co., Ltd. insurance premium in sum of RMB2,745,688;
2. The Defendant shall pay within 10 days after the judgment takes effect the Plaintiff the interest on RMB1,551,825 from January 15, 2014 to the execution day designated by this judgment on the basis of the benchmark loan interest rate promulgated by the People's Bank of China;
3. The Defendant within 10 days after the judgment takes effect shall pay Plaintiff the interest on RMB16,000 from January 21, 2014 to the execution day designated by this judgment on the basis of the benchmark loan interest rate promulgated by the People's Bank of China;
4. The Defendant within 10 days after the judgment takes effect shall pay the Plaintiff the interest on RMB85,000 from February 17, 2014 to the execution day designated by this judgment on the basis of the benchmark loan interest rate promulgated by the People's Bank of China;
5. The Defendant within 10 days after the judgment takes effect shall pay Plaintiff the interest on RMB150,000 from 20 August 2014 to the execution day designated by this judgment on the basis of the benchmark loan interest rate promulgated by the People's Bank of China;

6. The Defendant within 10 days after the judgment takes effect shall pay Plaintiff the interest on RMB111,620 from August 21, 2014 to the execution day designated by this judgment on the basis of the benchmark loan interest rate promulgated by the People's Bank of China;
7. The Defendant within 10 days after the judgment takes effect shall pay Plaintiff the interest on RMB781,243 from August 23, 2014 to the execution day designated by this judgment on the basis of the benchmark loan interest rate promulgated by the People's Bank of China;
8. The Defendant within 10 days after the judgment takes effect shall pay Plaintiff the interest on RMB50,000 from August 25, 2014 to the execution day designated by this judgment on the basis of the benchmark loan interest rate promulgated by the People's Bank of China;
9. Reject other claims of the Plaintiff Zhumadian South China Sea Shipping Co., Ltd.

In case of failure to perform the obligation of payment according to the period specified in this judgment, the Defendant shall, according to Article 253 of the Civil Procedure Law of the People's Republic of China, double pay interest for the period of deferred payment.

Court acceptance fee in amount of RMB35,827, due to the summary procedure, is halved to receive RMB17,913.5, the Plaintiff Zhumadian South China Sea Shipping Co., Ltd. shall bear RMB4,358, the Defendant People's Insurance Company of China Property and Casualty Co., Ltd. Zhumadian Branch shall bear RMB13,555.5.

If dissatisfied with this judgment, any party shall within fifteen days as of the service of this judgment, submit a Statement of Appeal to the court, with duplicates in the number of the opposing parties, so as to make an appeal before Hubei High People's Court.

When the Appellant files an appeal, he also need to prepay appeal litigation costs according to amount of the appeal request and Article 13 Paragraph 1 of the Measures on the Payment of Litigation Costs. Remit to HuBei High People's Court (Bank: Agricultural Bank of China, Wuhan Donghu branch; Payee: Finance Department of Hubei Province, non - tax revenue fiscal account; Number: 052101040000369-1. The column of bank's proof application shall be indicated: Hubei High People's Court or unit code 103,001). If the Appellant fails to prepay the appeal fee within seven days after the expiration of the appeal period, the appeal shall be withdrawn automatically.

Acting Judge: XIONG Jing

September 23, 2014

Clerk: WANG Fang

Hubei High People's Court
Civil Judgment

Zhumadian South China Sea Shipping Co., Ltd.
v.
People's Insurance Company of China Property and Casualty Co., Ltd. Zhumadian Branch

(2015) E Min Si Zhong Zi No.00058

Related Case(s) This is the judgment of second instance, and the judgment of first instance is on page 1355.

Cause(s) of Action 230. Dispute over marine insurance contract on the sea or sea-connected waters.

Headnote Affirming lower court decision that Defendant insurer was not entitled to rely on exclusion clause in hull insurance policy because insurer had not adequately explained the effect of the clause to the assured.

Summary The Plaintiff's ship collided with two other vessels and sank. The Plaintiff requested the Defendant insurer to cover the loss under their insurance contract. However, the Defendant refused to pay the requested amount due to an exemption clause, causing the Plaintiff to file suit. The court of first instance held that the Defendant failed to fully explain the exemption clause to the Plaintiff so the exemption clause was void. The Defendant appealed and alleged that the exemption clause including "unmanned vessel" was valid and that the Plaintiff's unmanned vessel caused the collision. Therefore, the insurer should be exempt from liability. However, the appellate court rejected such claim under de novo review. No evidence suggested the unmanned vessel caused the collision. Therefore the court dismissed the appeal.

Judgment

The Appellant (the Defendant of first instance): People's Insurance Company of China Property and Casualty Co., Ltd. Zhumadian Branch.
Domicile: No.145, Chunxiao Road, Zhumadian City, Henan Province, China.
Organization Code: 87,586,506–6.
Legal representative: LIU Sihu, general manager.
Agent *ad litem*: WANG Rong, lawyer of Hubei Xiaoyang Law Firm.
Agent *ad litem*: LI Rui, lawyer of Hubei Siyang Law Firm.

The Respondent (the Plaintiff of first instance): Zhumadian South China Sea Shipping Co., Ltd.
Domicile: Yard of Shenzhai Township Government, Suiping City, Henan Province, China. Organization Code: 66887749–4.
Legal representative: GENG Li, general manager.
Agent *ad litem*: ZHANG Jianbing, lawyer of Hubei Jintian Law Firm.

Dissatisfied with the Civil Judgment (2014) Wu Hai Fa Shang Chu Zi No.00795 rendered by Wuhan Maritime Court in respect of the case of dispute over an insurance policy of navigable waters in which the Appellant People's Insurance Company of China Property and Casualty Co., Ltd. Zhumadian Branch (hereinafter referred to as "PICC Zhumadian Branch") and the Respondent Zhumadian South China Sea Shipping Co., Ltd. (hereinafter referred to as "Nanhai Company") were involved, the Appellant PICC Zhumadian Branch files an appeal before the court. After accepting the appeal on April 3, 2015, the court formed a collegiate panel which was composed of the presiding judge SU Jiang, Acting Judges OU Haiyan and HU Zhengwei, and held an open hearing on May 12, 2015. WEI Qingsong and LI Feng as the common agents *ad litem* of PICC Zhumadian Branch, ZHANG Jianbing as agent *ad litem* of South China Sea Company, participated in the hearing. Now the case has been concluded.

Nanhai Company pleaded the court to sentence that PICC Zhumadian Branch pay for the insurance indemnity RMB3,628,428 and the interest (start from November 15, 2013 to the day that the execution is completed, calculate per the loan rate on the same period published by the People's Bank of China) and bear all litigation costs of this case.

The first instance ascertained after trial: on July 23, 2013, Nanhai Company covered M.V. "Yu Nanhai 0168" with PICC Zhumadian Branch against all risks of inland river vessel and propeller and other separate loss insurance liability insurance, and signed the insurance slip No.TCEJ20134128000000047. The insurance slip recorded that in view of the insured had been insured to the insurer against all risk insurance of inland river ship, and delivered the premium according to the insurance contract, the insurer agreed to bear the insurance liability according to the terms of the agreement, and this policy of insurance was proof. PICC Zhumadian Branch signed the policy of insurance No.PCEJ201341280000000203 and gave it to Nanhai Company. The above insurance slip and policy of insurance stated that:

the insured was Nanhai Company, the insured vessel was M.V. "Yu Nanhai 0168", the main risks was all risk of inland river vessel, and additional propeller and other separate damage insurance liability, both the value of insurance and the amount of insurance were RMB5,010,000. Insurance conditions and special agreement: RMB5,000 per accident deductible or 10%, whichever was higher. The period of insurance was from 0:00 on July 24, 2013 to 24:00 on July 23, 2014.

The involved Insurance clause 2009 was in a separate page, the main contents were as follows: Article 1. this insurance contract shall be composed of insurance clauses, insurance policies, insurance slip, insurance certificates, and approval documents, all the stipulations in this insurance contract shall be in writing; Article 2. "ship" as referred to in this insurance contract included the ship hull, equipment and navigational aids specified in the certificate of inspection of ships and vessels, which are registered legally in the People's Republic of China and engaged in inland navigation. Article 5. of the ship all risk of the provisions of the collision, touch and caused by overturning, sinking, etc. caused by the loss of the insurance ship or the total loss of the collision, touch and rescue, rescue responsibility and Costs, the insurer according to the insurance contract is responsible for compensation. With regard to salvage and rescue, Article 5. also provides that the insurance is responsible for compensating the insured person in the event of an insurance accident, the insurance of the navigation safety expenses necessary reasonable expenses, including in order to determine the reasonable cost of the text and valuation that the nature and degree of the insurance accident, and the expenses incurred for the execution of the special notice of the insurer, the insurer shall pay in addition to the loss of indemnity in respect of the insured ship. The insurer shall pay the expenses prescribed in this subparagraph to the extent that the cargoes are jointly safe and the value of the rescued insurance ship shall be limited to the proportion of the total value of the salvaged ship, freight and freight, and shall not exceed the insured amount; Article 6, Article 7, Article 8, Article 9 are the provisions on the exclusion of liability, the unseaworthiness (unto worthiness) of the ship, including the improperly equipped personnel, the technical condition, the navigation area and the use of the insured vessel do not conform with the navigation (towage) rules or the goods are loaded incorrectly, from the date of such occurrence, the insurer shall not be liable for any liability, loss and expense arising from any cause during the period of insurance. The insurer shall not be liable for the loss, liability and expense of the goods carried on the insured ship during the insurance period. The insurer is not liable for any loss, liability or expense not covered by the insurance policy; Article 17 Paragraph 2, the insured apply to the Company for compensation and provide information required for claims, the Company shall be within 60 days for approval. In the case of an insurance liability, the Company shall fulfill the obligation of indemnity within 10 days after reaching an agreement with the Insured for compensation or payment of the insurance benefit; Article 18. in case of full insurance under all risks, the partial loss of the ship shall be compensated according to the actual losses incurred, and shall be limited to the insurance amount. When the amount of insurance is greater than or equal to the value of salvage of the insured ship, the salvage and rescue costs incurred shall be compensated according to the actual costs; Article 21. in addition to the liability for total loss, touch and collision, the insurer shall make a deduction corresponding to the deductible amount or deductible rate stipulated in the insurance policy for each accident; Article 22. The residual value after the ship suffered a total loss or partial loss shall be negotiated by the parties of the insurance.

At 05:50 on November 15, 2013, M.V. "Ming Tai 89" was down to the Mu E Island waterways Baideng ship in Yangtze River (the lower reaches of the Yangtze River waterway mileage of 997 km) and collided with up-bound M.V. "Yu Nanhai 0168", then M.V. "Yu Nanhai 0168" made a large alteration of course to portside, at 05:51, collided with the trailing up M.V. "Yuan Dong 907". The accident led to prow and the portside of M.V. "Yu Nanhai 0168" damaged and water penetration, after emergency beaching, settled on the bottom on the Mu E Island Baideng ship 100 m outside the channel edge, only with the compass deck on the water.

Marine Office of Yangluo Wuhan identified the cause of the accident by the investigation: 1. M.V. "Ming Tai 89", in the case of restricted visibility, sailed without high vigilance, without correct use of sound signal and VHF, sailed without proper ship lookout, and did not unify the make way intention with the up-bound ship, without safe speed and proper selection of waterway route, which was the main cause of collision. 2. M.V. "Yu Nanhai 0168", in the case of restricted visibility, sailed without high vigilance, without correct use of sound signal and VHF, without proper ship lookout, did not unify the make way intention with up-bound ship, and turned left blindly for avoidance in the danger of collision with the down-bound vessel, which was the secondary cause of collision. 3. M.V. "Yuan Dong 906", in the case of restricted visibility, sailed without high vigilance, and without correct use of sound signal and VHF, sailed without proper ship lookout, without safe speed, without keeping safe distance when following the former vessel and without taking effective measures to avoid collision when suspecting the trend of the former vessel, which was another reason of the collision. 4. The channel of the accident water was meandering, narrow and the fog was thick when the accident happened, which were unfavourable objective factors for collision.

After accident on November 15, 2016, Nanhai Company reported and claimed to PICC Zhumadian Branch, on the same day, PICC Zhumadian Branch entrusted the survey company to investigate the accident and conduct follow-up on-site tracking and survey of the ship during the maintenance period, on August 15, 2014, the Survey Company issued survey report. Survey Company viewed that the accident was caused by collision, so it was within the scope of liability of Defendant Insurance Company against all risk of inland ship. Survey company verified M.V. "Yu Nanhai 0168" produced the salvage costs, tuggage and repairs costs, there were residual during the repair of the ship, and cargo rescue costs(relating to F.C "Wan Fuyang Gong 753", M.V. "Jiang Yun 19", M.V. "Huanggang Huo 656"), fuel costs, loss of personal effects, household appliances and other losses were not approved.

After accident, Nanhai Company entrusted Xue Weilan to deal with rescue, salvage, dredging, repair of M.V. "Yu Nanhai 0168".

On November 15, 2013, Nanhai Company signed the agreement of rescue of sunken ship with XU Zhangming, the occupier of M.V. "Wan Fuyanggong 758", agreed that M.V. "Wan Fuyang Gong 753" rescued M.V. "Yu Nanhai 0168", rescue fee was RMB50,000 and shall be paid in full after the completion of rescue. On November 16, 2013, Nanhai Company paid RMB50,000 in cash for XU Zhangming. From 08:30 of November 15, 2013 to November 28, 2013, BAI Shijie accepted the entrustment of Nanhai Company to rescue the goods, and two parties agreed the rescue fee was RMB50,000. On August 24, 2014, Nanhai Company paid BAI Shijie RMB50,000 in cash. On November 21, 2013, Nanhai Company paid the rescue fee in amount of RMB3,000 to XIONG Sheng'an, the occupier of M.V. "Huang Gang Huo 656".

On November 16, 2013, Nanhai Company signed salvage contract with salvage Company, the salvage Company shall be responsible for salvage of M.V. "Yu Nanhai 0168", and agreed the salvage fee was RMB730,000, and RMB200,000 shall be paid when contract was made, and the balance shall be paid one-time when the ship was salvaged out of water. M.V. "Yu Nanhai 0168", after being salvaged out of water, cannot be self-floating due to serious damage, Nanhai Company signed a towed escort agreement with the salvage company on November 25, 2013, entrusted the salvage company escort M.V. "Yu Nanhai 0168" to GuangDa company, and towing fee was RMB80,000, drain and dock fee was RMB10,000. The Plaintiff Nanhai Company paid salvage, towing and drainage on dock fee in sum of RMB200,000 and RMB120,000 at twice to the salvage company on November 16, 2013, and on December 26, 2013.

After M.V. "Yu Nanhai 0168" being salvaged out of water, Nanhai Company signed Hull Cleaning and Dredging Agreement with CHEN Dongliang on December 3, 2013, and CHEN Dongliang agreed to clean the four compartments of M.V. "Yu Nanhai 0168". After completed the clean-up operations by CHEN Dongliang, on December 3, 2013, and December 23, 2013, Nanhai Company at twice paid clean-up fee in sum of RMB2,000 and RMB14,000.

On December 12, 2013, Nanhai Company signed the ship decorating contract with YANG Baoyu, agreed that YANG Baoyu shall be responsible for interior decoration of M.V. "Yu Nanhai 0168", the contract amount was RMB166,000. Nanhai Company paid RMB30,000 on December 14, 2013, paid RMB20,000 on December 29, and paid RMB16,000 on January 20, 2014. Because Nanhai Company required YANG Baoyu to issue the corresponding invoice, the contract (included the tax) price was changed into RMB177,620. On August 20, 2014, YANG Baoyu received the balance in sum of RMB111,620 and issued two invoices in amount of RMB87,620 and RMB90,000 for Nanhai Company.

On December 28, 2013, the Plaintiff signed the Contract of Marine Mechanical and Electrical Equipment and Line Installation with Zhongchuan Company. Zhongchuan Company disassembled, repaired and installed the mechanical and electrical equipment, cable and lighting equipment of M.V. "Yu Nanhai 0168". The Amounted of contract was RMB238,600. HU Chujun, general management of Zhongchuan Company's Wuhan office, was responsible for direct check-out with Plaintiff Nanhai Company, and Nanhai Company paid RMB50,000 on November

28, 2013, paid RMB38,600 on January 12, 2014, paid RMB150,000 on August 19, 2014. Zhongchuan Company issued four invoices in amount of RMB50,000, RMB38,600, RMB80,000, RMB70,000.

On December 28, 2013, Nanhai Company gave the main engine of M.V. "Yu Nanhai 0168" to Nanjing Province Zibai Power Equipment Sales Co., Ltd. to repair, spent a total of RMB113,698.

On January 13, 2014, GuangDa company repair branch issued dock repair statement of M.V. "Yu Nanhai 0168", illustrated that M.V. "Yu Nanhai 0168" costed RMB1,681,243 for repair in dock. YU Haixiang was manager of GuangDa company repair branch, Nanhai Company paid repair fee at five times, namely paid for RMB200,000 on December 2, 2013, paid for RMB100,000 on December 10, 2013, paid for RMB200,000 on December 29, 2013, paid for RMB200,000 on December 31, 2013, and paid for RMB200,000 on January 3, 2014. As of August 22, 2014, Nanhai Company paid off the balance in sum of RMB781,243. GuangDa Company requested the tax authorities to issue invoices in amount of RMB1,681,243.

On February 16, 2014, Nanhai Company paid RMB85,000 for Chuyu Company in cash for repair of hatch coaming, poop deck, hull and electric equipments (including the repainted works of the repair part) of M.V. "Yu Nanhai 0168". ZHAN Caishuang was the manager of the company.

From November 25, 2013 to January 3, 2014, Nanhai Company purchased the spare parts of submersible pumps, cables, plugs and sockets that above all were necessary as ship accessories and paid a total of RMB10,527.

The port of registry of M.V. "Yu Nanhai 0168" was Henan Zhumadian, and the ship was a bulk cargo ship, with a total length of 83.60 m, a width of 14.20 m, a depth of 4.97 m, a gross tonnage of 1,962 and a net tonnage of 1,098. The ship-owner and operator was Nanhai Company. The deadweight was 2,500 tons. Granted permission to sail in the waters of the Three Gorges reservoir area of Sichuan and A-level; J2 navigation area (route). A-level area was for 2,400 tons of cargo for reference, B, C-class reference area were for 2,500 tons of cargo for reference.

The minimum safety manning certificate of M.V. "Yu Nanhai 0168" recorded the minimum safe manning of 7 persons, namely 1 captain of first class, 1 chief engineer officer of first class, 1 mate of first class, 1 s engineer of first class, 2 sailors, 1 mechanism. In the case of the accident, there were crew of 4 people on board.

The court of first instance held that the case was ship-sea water insurance contract dispute due to the collision. According to facts approved by the court and the litigation and argument of the parties, the court summarized the controversy of the case as follows: 1. on the validity of the insurance clause 2009, and the composition of the insurance contract; 2. the scope and amount of compensation by PICC Zhumadian Branch for the losses suffered by Nanhai Company; 3. whether PICC Zhumadian Branch was entitled to deduct.

1. Effect of Insurance Clause 2009, and element of the insurance contract.

  The insurance contract in the case should consist of insurance slip and insurance policy and insurance documents such as Insurance Clauses 2009. However, the Insurance Company neither had separately submitted the insurance clause to Nanhai Company to sign and affirm, nor attached the insurance clause to the insurance slip and insurance policy on the back and prominently reminded Nanhai Company on the front, the court of the first instance held that PICC Zhumadian Branch did not fulfill the obligation to fully explain the exemption to Nanhai Company. According to Article 17 of the Insurance Law of the People's Republic of China, where an insurance contract is concluded using the standard clauses of the insurer, the insurer shall provide an insurance policy with the standard clauses attached and explain the contents of the contract to the insurance applicant. For those clauses exempting the insurer from liability in the insurance contract, the insurer shall sufficiently warn the insurance applicant of those clauses in the insurance application form, the insurance policy or any other insurance certificate, and expressly explain those clauses to the insurance applicant in writing or verbally. If the insurer fails to make a warning or express explanation thereof, those clauses shall not be effective, the clause in the Insurance Clause 2009 which excluded the liability of the insurer did not take effect. The insured vessel was M.V. "Yu Nanhai 0168", Nanhai Company was the insured, PICC Zhumadian Branch was the insurer. The insurance contractual relationship between the parties was genuine intention of the parties, was in compliance with the compulsory law and social ethics and was lawful and effective. The contract was constituted of the insurance slip, insurance policy and the most fundamental clauses of Insurance Clause 2009.

2. The scope and amount of compensation by PICC Zhumadian Branch for the losses suffered by Nanhai Company.

  The accident was caused by Nanhai's M.V. "Yu Nanhai", which successively collided with M.V. "Ming Tai 89" and "Yuan Dong 907" at the place of white light boat of Mu Ezhou in the Changjiang River. If the losses suffered by Nanhai Company were in conformity with the partial loss, rescue, salvage responsibility and charges suffered by the insured vessel due to collision and sinking arising from it provided in Section 5 All risks of Insurance Clause 2009, the Insurance Company shall be liable for the compensation according to the contract, the details were as follows:

(1) Retrieval expense, salvage, tow, drainage on the dock fee.

  Rescue charges claimed by Nan Hai company including salvage charges of F.V. "Wan Fuyang Gong 753", M.V. "Jiang Yun 19", M.V. "Huanggang Huo 656". The court held that, whether paid the holder of M.V. "Jiang Yun 19" for the rescue of the goods on board, or paid the holder of M.V. "Jiang Yun 19" or M.V. "Huanggang Huo 656" for rescue of the insured vessel, sinking of M.V. "Yu Nanhai 0168" after collision was the direct reason for payment of this kind of charges, the losses were caused by collision and were within the scope of all risks.

Insurance Company argued that rescue of goods was within the scope of all risks by invoking provision of excluded liability of Insurance Clause 2009, the insurer shall not be liable for the loss, liability and expense of the goods carried on the insured ship during the insurance period. But the relevant clauses of excluded liability did not take effect. The court would dismiss this argument.

Insurance Company agreed that because M.V. "Yu Nanhai 0168" sank and submersed, the vessel should be salvaged with expense. M.V. "Yu Nanhai 0168" did not have ability of self-floating because the cabin was broken after salvage. So the vessel needed to be repaired in dock, and sleeper in cabin should be drained. The fee was necessary and reasonable, so Section 5 of Insurance Clause 2009 was applicable (Section 5: charges for navigating safely is necessary and reasonable). According to the contract, the above four expenses were limited to the proportion the value of the salvaged ship accounted for the total value of the salvaged ship, cargo, freight and they did not exceed the insurance amount. PICC Zhumadian Branch shall pay to Nanhai Company in addition to the indemnity of the insured ship, namely the rescue fee in sum of RMB103,000 paid by the Plaintiff to Floating crane "Wan Fuyang Gong 753", M.V. "Jiang Yun 19", M.V. "Huanggang Huo 656" and RMB320,000 for salvage, tow, drainage on the dock fee paid by the Plaintiff to the third party.

(2) Clean-up cost, decoration, line installation fee for electromechanical equipment, mainframe repair costs, repair costs for Guang Da Company, and Chuyu Company, maritime material expenses.

Because M.V. "Yu Nanhai 0168" sank and submersed after collision, that was necessary and in line with salvage work to clean-up and repair the cabin. And, above 7 losses of Nan Hai company had corresponding contracts (list, statement), invoice(receipt) and assignee's evidence, which could be able to explain the corresponding costs. According to article 18 of Insurance Clause 2009, in case of full insurance under all risks, the partial loss of the ship shall be compensated according to the actual losses incurred, and shall be limited to the insurance amount. The Plaintiff had paid clean-up cost in sum of RMB16,000, decoration fee in sum of RMB177,620, line installation fee for electromechanical equipment in sum of RMB238,600, mainframe repair costs in sum of RMB113,698, repair costs for Guang Da Company in sum of RMB1,681,243, repair costs for Chuyu Company in sum of RMB85,000, maritime material expenses in sum of RMB10,527, totally in sum of RMB2,322,688, it did not exceed the insurance amount of RMB5,100,000 and should be compensated by PICC Zhumadian Branch. In addition, Article 22 of the Insurance Clause 2009 listed, the residual after the insured ship suffered a total loss or partial loss would be negotiated by the two sides of insurance. PICC Zhumadian Branch quoted the conclusion in the assessment report that the replaced ship accessories had residual value during the repair of M.V. "Yu Nanhai 0168", required to deduct the residual value in the repair cost claimed by Nanhai Company. However, because PICC Zhumadian Branch did not prove the treatment of the discarded ship fittings, the calculation of residual value had no basis, and Nanhai

Company did not recognize, the court shall not be adopt PICC Zhumadian Branch's claim for deduction of residual value.

(3) Bunker fees, marine appliances losses, losses of ship goods, paint cost.

The bunker fees and marine appliance loss claimed by Nanhai Company were not within the scope of the All Risks; losses of vessel goods, paint and the above-mentioned marine supplies costs, repair costs were repeated. For the bunker costs, loss of marine appliances, vessel goods loss, paint costs, Nanhai Company did not provide the appropriate evidence to prove their losses. According to Article 64 Paragraph 1 of the Civil Procedure Law of the People's Republic of China, a party shall have the burden to provide evidence for its claims. The court shall not support the bunker fees, loss of marine appliances, loss of vessel goods, paint costs claimed by Nanhai Company.

(4) Interest losses.

In this case, Article 17 Paragraph 2 of the Insurance Clauses listed, the insured shall, within 60 days after the company seeks compensation and provide the information required for the settlement of claims, the company shall, within 60 days, verify the insurance liability, within ten days after reaching an agreement for compensation or payment of the insurance benefit, which was inconsistent with Article 23 Paragraph 1 of the Insurance Law of the People's Republic of China, which listed, after receiving an insured's or beneficiary's claim for paying indemnity or insurance benefits, the insurer shall adjust the claim in a timely manner. If the circumstances are complex, the insurer shall complete the adjustment within 30 days, unless it is otherwise agreed upon in the insurance contract. The insurer shall notify the insured or beneficiary of the adjustment result. For a claim which falls within the insurance coverage, the insurer shall perform the obligation of paying indemnity or insurance benefits within 10 days after reaching an agreement on payment of indemnity or insurance benefits with the insured or beneficiary. If the insurance contract provides for a time limit for payment of indemnity or insurance benefits, the insurer shall perform the obligation of paying indemnity or insurance benefits as agreed upon. The period for insurers to approve liability of insurance in article 17 Paragraph 2 of the Clause was longer than the statutory period. Because of lacking of explanation or promoting by the company, the term was ineffective between the parties.

According to Article 25 of the Insurance Law, where an insurer cannot determine the amount of indemnity or insurance benefits to be paid within 60 days after receiving a claim for indemnity or insurance benefits and the relevant certificates and materials, it shall first pay the amount which may be determined according to the available certificates or materials, and after it finally determines the amount of indemnity or insurance benefits to be paid, pay the difference, Nanhai Company had sued PICC Zhumadian Branch on November 15, 2013, and PICC Zhumadian Branch should make compensation or pay in advance at latest on January 14, 2014. But PICC Zhumadian Branch had not compensated for Nanhai Company, nor reached an agreement on paying the insurance money in advance, so PICC

Zhumadian Branch did not fulfill insurance obligation of timely payment, occupied the funds of Nanhai Company objectively, resulting in its loss, Nanhai Company had the right to claim the corresponding interest losses since January 15, 2014.

The losses of Nanhai Company happened before(not included) the January 15, 2014 were as follows: paid the first sum of retrieval expense RMB50,000 and first sum of salvage, tow, drainage on the dock fee RMB200,000 on November 16, 2013; paid the second sum of retrieval expense RMB3,000 on November 21, 2013. On November 28, paid the first sum of line installation fee for electromechanical equipment RMB50,000. On December 2, 2013, paid the first sum of repair fee RMB200,000 for GuangDa Company. On December 3, paid the first sum of clean-up cost RMB2,000. On December 10, paid the second sum of repair fee RMB100,000 for GuangDa Company. Paid the first sum of decoration fee RMB30,000 on December 14. Paid the second sum of clean-up cost RMB14,000 on December 23. On December 26, paid the second sum of salvage, tow, drainage on the dock fee RMB120,000. On December 28, paid mainframe repair costs RMB113,698. On December 29, paid second sum of decoration fee RMB20,000, and the third sum RMB200,000. On December 31, paid the fourth sum of repair costs RMB200,000. And on January 3,2014, paid the fifth sum of repair costs RMB200,000 for GuangDa Company and before(included) this day, paid shipping materials costs RMB10,527. On January 12, paid second sum of line installation fee for electromechanical equipment RMB386,00. The total amount of the above-mentioned expenses shall be RMB15,518,250, which shall be calculated from the next day of the deadline for the payment of the insurance premium by PICC Zhumadian Branch namely January 15, 2014, at the benchmark lending rate announced by the People's Bank of China, until the date of payment determined in this judgment, to protect the interest losses of Nanhai Company.

For the losses incurred by Nanhai Company after January 15, 2014 (including the same day), the details were as follows: on January 20, 2014, paid the third sum of decoration fee RMB16,000. On February 16, 2014, paid repair fee RMB85,000 for Chuyu Company. On August 19, paid the third sum of line installation fee for electromechanical equipment RMB150,000. And on August 20, paid the fourth sum of decoration fee RMB111,620. On August 22, paid the sixth sum of repair costs RMB781,243 for GuangDa Company. On August 24, paid the third sum of retrieval expense RMB50,000. The aforesaid expenses shall be calculated from the next day of the respective payment timetables, on the basis of the interest rate of the loan at the same period announced by the People's Bank of China, until the date of payment determined by this judgment, to protect the interest losses suffered by Nanhai Company.

3. Whether PICC Zhumadian Branch Had Right to Indemnify.

Manning of the vessel. When accident of M.V. "Yu Nanhai 0168" happened, there actually 4 seamen on the ship, which did not meet the minimum standard of 7 approved by the minimum safety manning certificate of the vessel, constituted the problem of insufficient manning. However, the maritime safety authorities concluded in the accident investigation that M.V. "Yu Nanhai 0168" in the case of poor visibility, sailed without a high degree of vigilance and correct use of sound and VHF radiotelephone, without keeping a proper lookout, without maintaining a safe speed, without unifying make way intention with the down bound vessel and turned to the left to avoid collision in danger of collision with the down bound vessel, which was the secondary cause of collision accident, it could be seen that insufficient manning of M.V. "Yu Nanhai 0168" did not lead to the accident. In addition, as aforesaid, the exclusion of liability insurance clause of the insurance contract did not take effect, PICC Zhumadian Branch claimed that insufficient manning of M.V. "Yu Nanhai 0168" affected its compensation, the court shall not adopt.

"Insurance deductible RMB5,000 or 10%, whichever is higher" listed in the insurance slip and insurance policy, was the exemption of insurer's liability clause of Article 17(2) of the Insurance Law of the People's Republic of China. As stated above, according to Article 17 of the Insurance Law, the record of the deductible was not clearly marked in the front of the insurance slip and the insurance policy, it could not catch the attention of the policy holder, PICC Zhumadian Branch failed to prove that it had stated the contents of the deductible clearly in written or oral form to the policy holder. Therefore, the terms "5,000 or 10% of each accident deductible, whichever is higher" was ineffective. PICC Zhumadian Branch did not enjoy the right to indemnify for the accident.

In summary, PICC Zhumadian Branch should pay compensation in sum of RMB2,745,688 to Nanhai Company, included: retrieval expense in sum of RMB103,000; salvage, tow, drainage on the dock fee in sum of RMB320,000; clean-up cost in sum of RMB16,000; decoration fee in sum of RMB177,620; line installation fee for electromechanical equipment in sum of RMB238,600; mainframe repair costs in sum of RMB113,698; repair costs for GuangDa Company in sum of RMB1,681,243; repair costs for Chuyu Company in sum of RMB85,000; loss of vessel goods in sum of RMB10,527, and the corresponding interests.

According to Article 23 Paragraph 1, Paragraph 2, Article 25 of the Insurance Law of the People's Republic of China, and Article 142 of the Civil Procedure Law of the People's Republic of China, the judgment was as follows: 1. PICC Zhumadian Branch China People's Property Insurance Co., Ltd. Zhu Madian City Branch within 10 days after the judgment takes effect shall pay the Plaintiff Zhumadian Nanhai Shipping Co., Ltd. insurance premium in sum of RMB2,745,688; 2. PICC Zhumadian Branch shall pay within 10 days after the judgment takes effect the Plaintiff the interest on RMB1,551,825 from January 15, 2014 to the execution day designated by this judgment on the basis of the benchmark loan interest rate promulgated by the People's Bank of China; 3. PICC Zhumadian Branch within 10 days after the judgment takes effect shall pay Plaintiff the interest on RMB16,000 from January 21, 2014 to the execution day designated by this judgment on the basis of the benchmark loan interest rate promulgated by the People's Bank of China; 4. PICC Zhumadian Branch within 10 days after the judgment takes effect shall pay the Plaintiff the interest on RMB85,000 from February 17, 2014 to the execution day designated by this judgment on the basis of the benchmark loan interest rate promulgated by the People's Bank of China; 5. PICC Zhumadian Branch within 10 days after the judgment takes effect shall pay

Plaintiff the interest on RMB150,000 from August 20, 2014 to the execution day designated by this judgment on the basis of the benchmark loan interest rate promulgated by the People's Bank of China; 6. PICC Zhumadian Branch within 10 days after the judgment takes effect shall pay Plaintiff the interest on RMB111,620 from August 21, 2014 to the execution day designated by this judgment on the basis of the benchmark loan interest rate promulgated by the People's Bank of China; 7. PICC Zhumadian Branch within 10 days after the judgment takes effect shall pay Plaintiff the interest on RMB781,243 from August 23, 2014 to the execution day designated by this judgment on the basis of the benchmark loan interest rate promulgated by the People's Bank of China; 8. PICC Zhumadian Branch within 10 days after the judgment takes effect shall pay Plaintiff the interest on RMB50,000 from August 25, 2014 to the execution day designated by this judgment on the basis of the benchmark loan interest rate promulgated by the People's Bank of China; 9. reject other claims of the Plaintiff Zhumadian Nanhai Shipping Co., Ltd.

The Appellant PICC Zhumadian Branch appealed that:

1. The exemption clause in the Insurance Clauses 2009 should be legal and effective. PICC Zhumadian Branch has fulfilled the obligations of reminder and clarification according to the Interpretation 2 of the Supreme People's Court on Several Issues concerning the Application of the Insurance Law of the People's Republic of China.
2. When M.V. "Yu Nanhai 0168" encountered the collision accident, the actual number of crew in board was only four, not reaching the statutory minimum standard of seven, which constituted an insufficient manning, therefore PICC Zhumadian Branch should not bear the insured liability pursuant to the exemption clause in the Insurance Clauses 2009.
3. According to Article 52 of the Insurance Law of the People's Republic of China, at the beginning of the voyage, M.V. "Yu Nanhai 0168" was sailed on understaffed condition, the criticality of the subject-matter insured was significantly increased while Nanhai Company did not fulfill the obligation of timely informing, therefore, PICC Zhumadian Branch should not be liable for the insurance indemnity.

At the trial of the appeal, PICC Zhumadian Branch supplemented some grounds for appeal:

1. M.V. "Yu Nanhai 0168" was insufficiently manned, which caused the Insurance Policy being automatically terminated from the beginning of the voyage according to the Insurance Clauses 2009.
2. The first-instance judgment was wrongly ruled in ascertaining the amount of damage, the 10% excess involved in the case should be valid.
3. The salvage charges of cargoes carried by M.V. "Yu Nanhai 0168" (for M.V. "Jiangyun 19" RMB50,000 and clearance charges for warehouse RMB200,000) should be deducted from the insurance compensation.

4. Pursuant to Article 25 of the Insurance Law of the People's Republic of China, the PICC Zhumadian Branch should pay the insurance indemnity within 60 days from the date Nanhai Company submitted the compensation claim and the evidentiary materia. The first-instance judgment only ordered PICC Zhumadian Branch to bear the interests of insurance about RMB1,550,000 starting from January 15, 2014, the calculation of interest was obviously incorrect, for the costs incurred after January 15, 2014, the court of first instance did not calculate the sixty days grace period for fulfillment. Even if PICC Zhumadian Branch should bear the corresponding interest, the starting point for calculating interest should start from the day PICC Zhumadian Branch received the relevant claim materials and evidence, deducting 60 days of performance period. In summary, requesting the court of second instance to revoke the original judgment, commute that dismiss all claims of Nanhai Company, and all the litigation costs in this case should be born by Nanhai Company.

Nanhai Company defended: PICC Zhumadian Branch submitted two different petitions of appeal successively, the former inscribed one confirmed the Insurance Assessment Report it submitted and part of the insurance amount the court of first instance recognized, while the later inscribed one completely denied the Insurance Assessment Report it submitted in the first instance, which was lack of any basis. The insufficient manning was not the cause of the collision accident and was not related to an inappropriate lookout. The insufficient manning was not the condition for exemption of liability of the PICC Zhumadian Branch and did not necessarily increase the risk. On the effectiveness of the 10% excess, the judgment of first instance was entirely correct. When a collision happened, dealing with the goods was inevitably during cargo handling and salvage of the ship, these two were inseparable. In summary, requesting the court of second instance to reject the appeal and affirm the original judgment.

During the time-limit of evidence specified by the court, neither PICC Zhumadian Branch nor Nanhai Company had submitted any new evidence.

After verification, the court holds that the facts found by the court of first instance are true and the court confirms it.

It is also ascertained that the first part of the insurance policy involved in this case stated "The insured has been covered by the insurer on all risks of the inland river ships, and has paid the premiums according to the insurance contract, the insurer agrees to bear the insurance responsibility according to the terms of the insurance contract, with this insurance policy as a certificate." On the back of the insurance policy that PICC Zhumadian Branch delivered to Nanhai Company, the Insurance Clauses 2009 was not attached.

On November 16, 2013, Nanhai Company and Shifa Salvage Engineering Co., Ltd. of Tuanfeng County, Hubei issued a Contract of Wrecking, the contract agreed that the salvage charge of M.V. "Yu Nanhai 0168" was RMB500,000, if there was cargo in the wreck, the clearance charges would be RMB200,000. On the same day, PICC Zhumadian Branch commissioned Mintaian Property Insurance Surveyors & Loss Adjusters Co., Ltd. to adjust the loss of the collision accident involved in this case. The Contract of Rescue issued on November 28, 2013 stated that from 8:30 on November 15, 2013 to November 28, 2013, BAI Shijie, the shipowner of M.V. "JiangYun 19", accepted a commission from Nanhai Company to salvage cargoes, and the rescue charges was RMB50,000.

Mintaian Property Insurance Surveyor & Loss Adjusters Co., Ltd. provided the first phase of the Insurance Assessment Report on August 15, 2014, stated: the accident was caused by a collision, belong to the scope of insurance coverage of PICC on all risks of the inland river ships, the loss in coverage of the subject ship under the Policy was assessed to be RMB1,909,628.44.

The issues of disputes in this case of the second instance: 1. the effectiveness of the Insurance Contract involved; 2. the insurance liability of PICC Zhumadian Branch.

1. The effectiveness of the Insurance Contract involved.

The PICC Zhumadian Branch claimed that the Insurance Contract involved was automatically terminated at the beginning of the voyage according to Article 52 of the Insurance Law of the People's Republic of China, Article 12 and 14 of Insurance Clauses 2009, PICC Zhumadian Branch undertook no indemnity liability.

Paragraph 1 of Article 52 of the Insurance Law of the People's Republic of China regulates "During the effective period of the contract, in case the criticality of the subject matter insured increased significantly, the assured shall promptly notify the insurer according to the contract, the insurer may increase the insurance premium or cancel the contract according to the contract." Paragraph 3 regulates "if the assured failed to perform the obligation of notification as stipulated in the preceding paragraph, the insurer shall not be liable for indemnity towards the insured accident happened due to the criticality of the subject matter insured significantly increased." The court holds, Wuhan Maritime Safety Administration (2013) No.08006 Survey Conclusion of Inland River Traffic Accident recognized the reason of this collision accident involved, when it referred to the part of M.V. "Yu Nanhai 0168", it did not specify that insufficient manning was one of the reasons for collision accident. There was no causality between the insufficient manning and the occurrence of the collision accident. Therefore, when the collision accident happened, 4 crews in the ship could not meet the minimum safety manning requirement, but this does not belong to the situations that insured accident happened due to the "criticality of the subject-matter insured increased significantly". Meanwhile, in the first instance, PICC Zhumadian Branch submitted the Insurance Assessment Report which approved the collision belonged to the scope of insurance coverage of PICC on all risks of the inland river ships, and in the second instance, it submitted the petition for appeal on 10 January 2015 which also recognized the insurance compensation was RMB1,909,628.44, therefore, the submission PICC Zhumadian Branch stressed in the supplementary petition for appeal that it undertook no insurance liability due to the insurance contract involved was statutorily canceled clearly violates the principle of good faith.

Meanwhile, PICC Zhumadian Branch also asserted that under the Insurance Clauses 2009, the insurance contract involved had been canceled since the beginning of the voyage. Because PICC Zhumadian Branch did not deliver the Insurance Clauses 2009 to the assured Nanhai Company, Nanhai Company could not base on the content of the insurance contract involved to know that the insured items involved in this case shall apply to the Insurance Clauses 2009, meanwhile, PICC Zhumadian Branch did not submit evidence to prove that necessary explanations or tips about the content of the Insurance Clauses 2009 were given to Nanhai Company, so PICC Zhumadian Branch is not entitled to invoke the provisions of the insurance clause so as to claim that the insurance contract has been canceled. In summary, PICC Zhumadian Branch, either invoking the provisions of the Insurance Law of the People's Republic of China, or under the provisions of the Insurance Clauses 2009, is not entitled to claim that the insurance contract has been canceled before sailing.

2. The Insurance Liability of PICC Zhumadian Branch.

The amount of insurance compensation, for the appellate reasons supplemented by PICC Zhumadian Branch in the trial of the second instance, analyzes as follows:

1) Regarding to the effectiveness of the 10% excess in the "Special Agreement" of the insurance policy involved. The court reckons, according to Article 9 of the Interpretation of the Supreme People's Court on Several Issues concerning the Application of the Insurance Law of the People's Republic of China (II), Liability exemption clauses, deductibles, excess, proportional compensations or payments, etc. that exempting or reducing the insurer's liability regulated in the format contract provided by the insurer, can be identified as "the terms of exempting the insurer's liability" regulated in Paragraph 2 Article 17 of the Insurance Law of the People's Republic of China (II), which reads "As to the terms of the insurance contract to exempt the insurer's liability, the insurer, while signing an insurance contract, shall make a reminder that can sufficiently attract the attention of the assured on the insurance slip, insurance policy or any other insurance certificate, and make a clear explanation to the assured about the contents of the terms in written or oral form; failing which, this term shall not have any effect." According to the aforesaid regulations, the excess of the insurance policy is a term that can exempt the liability of the insurer, this term is not necessarily to be valid. As to the All Risks Insurance Policy of the Inland River involved in this case, the "Special Agreement" stated "The absolute deductible is RMB5000 or 10% of the damage per event, whichever is higher", this term was not in bold or black so as to sufficiently attract attention of Nanhai Company, and PICC Zhumadian Company also failed to adduce evidence to prove that it had made explicit interpretation to Nanhai Company either in writing or in oral form, therefore, the agreement regarding to the excess is not valid towards Nanhai Company.

2) Regarding to the issue of cargo salvage and deduction of clearance costs. PICC Zhumadian Branch appealed that M.V. "Jiang Yun 19" clearly agreed that

RMB50,000 was for the goods, not for M.V. "Yu Nanhai 0168", it should be deducted.

The court reckons that, according to Article 57 of the Insurance Law of the People's Republic of China, "in the event of an insurance accident, the assured shall endeavor to take necessary measures to prevent or reduce the loss. After the insurance accident happened, the necessary and reasonable costs the assured took to prevent or reduce the loss of the subject-matter insured shall be born by the insurer". When the collision accident happened, the cargo M.V. "Yu Nanhai 0168" carried were iron ore powder. On the day when the accident happened, M.V. "Jiang Yun 19" participated in cargo salvage and rescue at once, the cargo salvage and rescue was based on the consideration of ship safety, it was a preparation for the subsequent salvage of the ship, and was an operation to prevent or reduce the loss of the subject-matter insured., the costs used was necessary and reasonable. PICC Zhumadian Branch should compensate. Similarly, M.V. "Yu Nanhai 0168" and Shifa Salvage Engineering Co., Ltd. Tuanfeng County, Hubei Province, signed a "Salvage Contract" involving RMB200,000 of the clean-up costs, although the costs relates to the wreck cargo, the costs of the clearance of goods from holds are the necessary and reasonable expenses for reducing loss of the ship and shall not be deducted from the insurance indemnity.

3) Regarding to the issue of interest of the insurance. PICC Zhumadian Branch alleged that the compensation claim was received on November 15, 2013, but the judgment of first instance recognized that the interest of insurance should be born since January 15, 2014, the calculation of the interest was obviously wrong. According to the law, Nanhai Company should submit evidence of claim, and the days for calculating the interest of insurance compensation should start from the date of submitting the claim and evidence materials, and then deduct 60 days of grace period. However, there was no 60-day grace period for costs incurred after January 15, 2014.

The court reckons, according to Article 25 of the Insurance Law of the People's Republic of China, "the insure shall pay in advance the ascertainable amount according to the evidence or materials it has got, if the compensation or payment of insurance cannot be ascertained, within 60 days starting from the date of receiving the insurance claims and related evidence and materials", the above-mentioned provisions only expressly requires the insurer, within 60 days, to pay in advance with respect to a claim for compensation that is supported by preliminary evidence. However, PICC Zhumadian Branch claimed that under this provision, the insurer was entitled to have a 60-day grace period upon payment of the insurance indemnity, and interest shall not be calculated for that period, this allegement is lacking of legal basis. In fact, Nanhai Company has paid RMB1,551,825 in instalments from November 16, 2013 to January 12, 2014 due to the collision accident, the interests should be calculated from the next day of the actual payment date, however, the judgment of the first instance uniformly calculated the interests of every instalment from January 15, 2014, this calculation is essentially beneficial to PICC Zhumadian Branch. As Nanhai Company has not appealed to this section, the starting point for the interest calculation of RMB1551,825 is no longer adjusted.

In summary, all of the appeal grounds of PICC Zhumadian Branch cannot be established. The facts ascertained by the first instance were basically clear, the trial process was legal, the entity was handled properly. According to Article 170 Paragraph 1 Sub-paragraph 1 of the Civil Procedure Law of the People's Republic of China, the judgment is as follows:

Dismiss the appeal, and affirm the original judgment.

Court acceptance fee of second instance in amount of RMB35,827, shall be born by PICC Zhumadian Branch.

The judgment is final.

Presiding Judge: SU Jiang
Acting Judge: OU Haiyan
Acting Judge: HU Zhengwei

June 12, 2015

Clerk: CHENG Jianxiao

Beihai Maritime Court
Civil Judgment

ZHONG Kangqiu
v.
Fujian Chengxing Fuel Oil Co., Ltd.

(2014) Hai Shang Chu Zi No.203

Related Case(s) None.

Cause(s) of Action 201. Dispute over illegal lien on ship, cargoes carried by ship, bunkers and stores of ship.

Headnote Bunker supplier held to be unable to arrest ship to which it had supplied bunkers, because the ship was actually owned by someone other than the vessel operator/registered owner with whom the bunker supplier had contracted.

Summary The Plaintiff purchased a vessel but registered the vessel in Third Party's name. Third Party was the vessel operator and registered owner. Defendants sued Third Party over a bunker price dispute. After Defendants secured a favorable judgment, Third Party did not comply with the judgment. Consequently, Defendants moved to arrest Plaintiff's vessel because Third Party was the vessel's registered owner and operator. Plaintiff was not a party to the underlying lawsuit between Defendants and Third Party. Here, the Plaintiff asked the Court to verify its actual ownership of the vessel and stop the procedures that would lead to vessel arrest.

The issues before the court were as follows: 1) is Plaintiff the actual owner of the vessel involved, 2) can Plaintiff stop the prior judgment's execution and thereby prevent the vessel from being arrested?

The court held that the Plaintiff was the actual vessel owner despite the vessel being registered in Third Party's name. The court reasoned that the Plaintiff was the actual vessel owner upon the vessel's delivery to the Plaintiff. It does not matter that the vessel was never registered in Plaintiff's name.

The court further held that the Plaintiff was entitled to prevent the prior judgment's execution because Plaintiff is the actual vessel owner and not the obligor under the prior judgment. The court confirmed it had the authority to confirm the rights of a non-party to the original lawsuit (namely, Plaintiff).

Judgment

The Plaintiff: ZHONG Kangqiu
Agent *ad litem*: LIANG Kun, lawyer of Jiangsu Suyuan Law Firm.

The Defendant: Fujian Chengxing Fuel Oil Co., Ltd.
Legal representative: LIN Ming, general manager.
Agent *ad litem*: LI Ling, lawyer of Beijing Yingke (Fuzhou) Law Firm.

The Third Party: Guangxi Fangchenggang Shunxin Shipping Co., Ltd.
Legal representative: SHI Meijin, chairman.

With respect to the case arising from dispute over challenge of a party not involved to enforcement, the Plaintiff ZHONG Kangqiu, filed litigation against the Defendant Fujian Chengxing Fuel Oil Co., Ltd. (hereinafter referred to as Chengxing Company), with the Third Party, Guangxi Fangchenggang Shunxin Shipping Co., Ltd. (hereinafter referred to as Shunxin Company) being involved in. After entertaining this case on October 16, 2014, the court organized the collegiate panel to try this case according to the law, and heard this case in public on December 10. LIANG Kun as agent *ad litem* of the Plaintiff, LI Ling as agent *ad litem* of the Defendant and SHI Meijin as legal representative of the Third Party Shunxin Company appeared in court and participated in the hearing. Now the case has been concluded.

The Plaintiff alleged in the Statement of Claim as follows: on August 20, 2011, *Ship Sales and Purchase Contract* was concluded by and between it and ZHUO Shiyi, a party not involved in this case. Pursuant to the contract, the Plaintiff purchased M.V. "Shun **" owned by ZHUO Shiyi and operated the ship in the name of Shunxin Company. The Plaintiff signed *Ship Affiliation Agreement* and *Agreement on Share Holding* with Shunxin Company on September 1, 2011. Xiamen Maritime Court made (2013) Xia Hai Fa Shang Chu Zi No.333 Civil Judgment with respect to the dispute over bunker price of M.V. "Shun **" filed by the Defendant Chengxing Company against the Third Party Shunxin Company. The Defendant applied to the court for compulsory execution of the judgment. On March 24, 2014, Beihai Maritime Court arrested M.V. "Shun **".

The Plaintiff alleged that the dispute over bunker price between the Defendant Chengxing Company and Shunxin Company, which was unrelated to M.V. "Shun **" and the Plaintiff. M.V. "Shun **" was owned by the Plaintiff, so the court should not arrest it. The executive board of the Supreme People's Court made a reply to [2011] No.384 Request for Instructions concerning Whether People's Court Can Compulsorily Execute against Ships Affiliated to and Registered in the Name of the Person Subject to Execution of Hubei Province Prime People's Court, made it clear that whether there was actual owner of the ship should be found before executing the ship registered in the name of the person subject to execution. If there was evidence which could prove the ship was registered in the name of the person subject to execution based on the affiliation operation relationship between the actual owner and the person subject to execution, and execution measures should not be taken against the ship when the actual owner of the ship was inconsistent with the person registered as the owner of the ship. M.V. "Shun **" was registered in the name of Shunxin Company, but the Plaintiff had sufficient evidence to prove that the ship belonged to the Plaintiff and the ship was actually owned by the Plaintiff who was not the person subject to execution. The court should not arrest M.V. "Shun **". The Plaintiff requested the court to order: 1. stop the execution of M.V. "Shun **" and confirm M.V. "Shun **" was owned by the Plaintiff.

The Defendant Chengxing Company defended that it was not the proper Defendant in this case and it was only the Third Party who had an interest. Whether there was real ship sales and purchase relationship and affiliation relationship between the Plaintiff and Shunxin Company was unrelated to Chengxing Company's application for execution. Even though there was an affiliation relationship, the affiliated person and the affiliated ship engaged in operation activities in the name of the affiliated unit. The affiliated unit, which was represented by the actual owner, should bear the responsibility for the operation activities. Therefore, it was proper that the court arrested the ship. The reply of the Executive Board of the Supreme People's Court, which was only aimed at the very case, but not a judicial interpretation, had no universal binding force. The Defendant requested the court to reject the claims of the Plaintiff.

The Third Party Shunxin Company alleged that M.V. "Shun **" was just affiliated to it, but it was owned by the Plaintiff, so Shunxin Company had no challenge to the claims of the Plaintiff.

The Plaintiff submitted the following evidence to the court to support his claims:

1. Enforcement Ruling, to prove that the Plaintiff filed an challenge to the execution court;
2. Ship Sales and Purchase Contract, to prove that M.V. "Shun **" was purchased by the Plaintiff at a price of RMB1,680,000 yuan from ZHUO Shiyi on 20 August 2011;
3. 5 copies of receipt, to prove that the Plaintiff paid total purchase price in sum of RMB1,680,000 yuan;
4. *Ship Affiliation Agreement* and *Agreement concerning Share Holding*, to prove that the Plaintiff affiliated M.V. "Shun **" to Shunxin Company, and Shunxin Company confirmed the Plaintiff had the ownership;
5. Receipt, to prove that the Plaintiff paid affiliation charge to Shunxin Company; and
6. Bank voucher, to prove the payment made by the Plaintiff.

The Defendant Chengxing Company had no challenge to authenticity, legality or relevancy of evidence 1; it did not confirm authenticity of evidence 2 as well as evidence 3, and held there was no actual payment; it did not confirm the authenticity of evidence 4-5; it had no challenge to authenticity or legality of evidence 6, and held that the bank voucher could not reflect the payment for the ship.

The Third Party Shunxin Company had no challenge to authenticity, legality or relevancy of evidence 1-6.

The Defendant Chengxing Company and the Third Party Shunxin Company did not submit any evidence.

The court holds that the Defendant Chengxing Company and the Third Party Shunxin Company had no challenge to authenticity, legality or relevancy of evidence 1 and 6, the evidence can be admitted as the basis to find the facts of the case. As for evidence 4, *Ship Affiliation Agreement* and *Agreement concerning Share Holding* provided by the Plaintiff, which were signed by the Plaintiff and the Third Party Shunxin Company, the Plaintiff provided the original to check and Shunxin Company confirmed the authenti City, so the court confirms the authenticity thereof and they can be admitted as the basis to find the facts of this case. Evidence 5 is a receipt issued by Shunxin Company who received affiliation charge form the Plaintiff. There is an original to verify and Shunxin Company confirmed authenticity, and this evidence and evidence 4 form a chain of evidence. The court confirms the Plaintiff and the Third Party Shunxin Company formed ship affiliation relationship. Evidence 2 Ship Sales and Purchase Contract was signed by the Plaintiff and actual shipowner ZHUO Shiyi, the Third Party Shunxin Company confirmed authenticity thereof. Evidence 3 receipt and evidence 6 Bank voucher can mutually confirm the Plaintiff's purchase of ship and his payment; even though the Defendant Chengxing Company did not confirm authenticity thereof, it did not provide evidence to the contrary; the court confirms the authenticity thereof. The relevancy shall be comprehensively determined in combination with the facts and the whole evidence.

Accordingly, the court finds out and confirms the following facts: on September 5, 2013, with respect to the dispute over ship material supply contract between the Defendant Chengxing Company and the Third Party Shunxin Company, Xiamen Maritime Court made (2013) Xia Hai Fa Shang Chu Zi No.333 Civil Judgment. In accordance to the judgment Shunxin Company should pay fuel cost RMB637,860 yuan and the interest thereon. Because Shunxin Company did not fulfill the obligation for such payment, Chengxing Company applied for execution and Xiamen Maritime court transferred the case to the court. In May 2014, the court made (2014) Hai Fa Zhi Zi No.1-2 of Civil Ruling and arrested M.V. "Shun **". On May 12, the Plaintiff alleged that it was the actual owner of M.V. "Shun **" and put forward a written challenge against (2014) Hai Fa Zhi Zi No.1-2 Enforcement Ruling made by the court. On May 23, the court made Hai Fa Zhi Zi No.3 Civil Ruling to reject the Plaintiff's challenge. The Plaintiff refused to accept such decision and filed an action of challenge over enforcement.

It is also found that on April 26, 2007, Fangchenggang City Fuxin M.V. "Shun **"ping Co., Ltd. (hereinafter referred to as Fuxin Company) signed a shipbuilding contract with Wenling City Qing Gang Ship Repair and Building Yard (hereinafter referred to as Wenling Shipyard), Fuxin Company commissioned Wenling Shipyard to build a 500 GT steel dry cargo ship. On July 20, Fuxin Company applied M.V. "Shun **" as the ship's name, and it was approved by Guangxi Maritime Safety Administration. On 15 September, Wenling Shipyard issued a

Certificate of Merchandise in terms of the steel ship and alleged that Fuxin Company commissioned the yard to build a ship 52.80 meters long, 8.80 meters wide, 4.08 meters deep, with a main power of 218 kilowatts, the ship was named with "Fu **", the ship was qualified according to the inspection by Tai Zhou City Ship Inspection Department, and was allowed to leave the shipyard. On the same day, Wenling Shipyard signed the Protocol of Delivery and Acceptance with Fuxin Company, and Wenling Shipyard delivered M.V. "Fu **" to Fuxin Company. On 28 September, Fangchenggang Maritime Safety Administration issued No.100307000114 Certificate of Ship Ownership. The certificate records: the name of the ship is "Fu **", the port of registry is Fangchenggang, the ship type is dry cargo carrier, the material of hull is steel, the building place is Wenling, Zhejiang Province, and the shipyard is Wenling Shipyard. Built date: September 7, 2007, length: 52.80 meters, width: 8.80 meters, depth: 4.08 meters, gross tonnage: 498 GT, net tonnage: 278 tons, total power: 218 kilowatts. The owner of the ship is Fangchenggang City Fuxin M.V. "Shun **"ping Co., Ltd., the legal representative thereof is WU Meiguan, the date of acquisition of ownership is 15 September 2007, and the ship not a jointly owned one.

On October 9, 2007, Fuxin Company signed an Agreement on Confirmation of Ownership and Operation with ZHANG Chongliang, who lives at Wukeng Village Songmen Town, Wenling City. It was confirmed that in order to handle relevant procedures and ship operation management, the owner of M.V. "Fu **" was registered as Fuxin Company. However, Fuxin Company did not actually fund the construction of the ship and shipbuilding price was paid by ZHANG Chongliang who actually owned the ship. There is no co-ownership. The ship affiliated to Fuxin Company to operate and ZHANG Chongliang needs to pay a management fee in sum of RMB10 thousand yuan every year.

On July 10, 2009, ZHANG Chongliang signed *Ship Sales and Purchase Contract* with YU Lingjun, who lives at No.95 Wenhua Road, Songdong Village, Songmen Town, Wenling City and sold M.V. "Fu **" to YU Lingjun at a price of RMB1,648,800. On 11 October, YU Lingjun signed an Agreement on Confirmation of Ownership and Operation with Fuxin Company. It was confirmed that the owner of ship was YU Lingjun and the ship was affiliated to Fuxin Company for operation.

On April 13, 2011, YU Lingjun sold M.V. "Fu **" to Zhou Ming, who lives at No.90 Wenhua Road, Waitian Village, Qishui Town, Leizhou City, Guangdong Province at RMB1,650,000 yuan. On April 15, the two parties signed the Protocol of Delivery and Acceptance, and delivered the ship to ZHOU Ming formally. At the same time, YU Lingjun and WU Meiguan, the legal reprensentative of Fuxin Company signed a statement and declared that the ship was re-soled to ZHOU Ming, the rights and obligations of the two parties were terminated and the ship was owned by ZHOU Ming continuously. On the same day, ZHOU Ming signed the *Agreement on Confirmation of Ownership and Operation* with Fuxin Company, and affiliated M.V. "Fu **" to Fuxin Company.

On May 10, 2011, ZHOU Ming signed *Ship Sales and Purchase Contract* and *Protocol of Delivery and Acceptance* with ZHUO Shiyi, who lived in Tumu

County, Tangjia Town, Leizhou City, Guangdong Province, re-soled M.V. "Fu **" to ZHUO Shiyi at RMB1,650,000 yuan and delivered the ship on the same day. At the same time, ZHOU Ming signed the *Termination Agreement (Agreement on Confirmation of Ownership and Operation)* with Fuxin Company. Both parties thereto confirmed the actual owner of M.V. "Fu **" was ZHUO Shiyi, and it was irrelevant to Zhou Ming. When ZHUO Shiyi took over the ship, and the ship was no longer affiliated to Fuxing Company, but Shunxin Company. Therefore, Fuxing Company signed a Ship Sales and Purchase Contract and a Protocol of Delivery and Acceptance, re-affiliated M.V. "Fu **" to Shunxin Company. On May 16, Fangchenggang Maritime Safety Administration cancelled the registration of M.V. "Fu **", changed the ship's name to M.V. "Shun **" and registered it in the name of Shunxin Company.

On August 20, ZHUO Shiyi as Party A signed *Ship Sales and Purchase Contract* with Party B, the Plaintiff ZHONG Kangqiu. It is agreed that Party A transferred M.V. "Shun **" to party B at RMB1,680,000 yuan. On the same day, ZHONG Kangqiu paid a deposit of purchase in sum of RMB30 thousand yuan to ZHUO Shiyi at Qishui Village, Leizhou City, Zhenjiang, Guangdong Province. On August 26, the Plaintiff took his postal saving card to Leizhou City Qishui Town Postal Savings Bank Qishui Village Sub-branch and remitted RMB250 thousand yuan and RMB300 thousand yuan to ZHUO Shiyi. The Plaintiff took his postal savings card to Beihai City Postal Savings Bank and withdrew cash in sum of RMB500 thousand yuan and gave that money to ZHUO Shiyi as the fourth instalment. As for the fifth instalment, the Plaintiff withdrew cash in sum of RMB500 thousand yuan at Zhanjiang City Binghai Road Postal Savings Bank and delivered that to ZHUO Shiyi. On August 30, ZHUO Shiyi issued two piece of receipts in amount of RMB1 million yuan each. On August 31, the Plaintiff paid RMB100 thousand yuan in cash to ZHUO Shiyi. The Plaintiff paid RMB1,680,000 yuan in total to ZHUO Shiyi to purchase M.V. "Fu **". For each payment, ZHUO Shiyi issued a receipt with signature and stamp to the Plaintiff. After the payment of the ship, ZHUO Shiyi delivered the ship to the Plaintiff. On September 1, the Plaintiff ZHONG Kangqiu signed the Ship Affiliation Agreement, agreed that M.V. "Shun **" bought by the Plaintiff was affiliated to Shunxin Company. It was operated by the Plaintiff, and the operation income, costs, claims and debts and maritime disputes and other legal liabilities occurring during the operation should be born by the Plaintiff. On the same day, the two parties signed an Agreement on Share Holding. It is stated that according to the relevant provisions, the Plaintiff as an owner of the Guangdong nationality cannot be registered in Guangxi Province directly. The Plaintiff registered the ship in the name of Shunxin Company at Fangchenggang Maritime Safety Administration. However, Shunxin Company did not invest the ship and confirmed the actual owner of M.V. "Shun **" was the Plaintiff. After the ship was put into operation, all the economic benefits and debts were all born by the Plaintiff, irrelevant with Shunxin Company. On December 10, Shunxin Company issued receipts to the Plaintiff, which stated that "we receive affiliation charge in sum of RMB17,000 yuan in terms of M.V. "Shun **" (from September 2011 to September 2012).

The court holds that this case is concerning dispute over challenge over execution filed by a party not involved in this case. Synthesizing both sides of the argument, the outstanding issues in this case lie in that whether the Plaintiff is the actual owner of M.V. "Shun **" and whether the Plaintiff is entitled to application for stopping the execution of M.V. "Shun **" and discharging the arrest of the ship.

1. Whether the Plaintiff is the actual owner of the ship

The court holds that the registered owner of M.V. "Shun **" is Shunxin Company, but it is only the affiliated company for the purpose of operation, but it is not the actual owner of the ship. The name of ship is "Fu **" and the actual owner originally is ZHANG Chongliang who affiliated the ship to Fuxing Company. After that ZHANG Chongliang transferred the ship to Zhou Ming and Zhou Ming re-sold the ship to ZHUO Shiyi. ZHUO Shiyi took over M.V. "Fu **" and affiliated it to Fuxing Company but Shunxin Company and changed the name from "Fu **" to "Shun **". Three months later, ZHUO Shiyi signed the sales and purchase contract of M.V. "Shun **" with the Plaintiff, both parties have fulfilled the signed contract, the Plaintiff paid ZHUO Shiyi RMB1,680,000 for the ship, and ZHUO Shiyi delivered M.V. "Shun **" to the Plaintiff, the ships continuously affiliated to Shunxin Company, therefore the registered owner is Shunxin Company. According to Article 132 of the Contract Law of the People's Republic of China (hereinafter referred to as the Contract Law), sale of the subject matter shall be owned by or rightfully disposed by the seller. ZHANG Chongliang originally acquired the ownership of the ship by means of construction, YU Junling, ZHOU Ming and ZHUO Shiyi derivatively acquired the ownership of the ship via respective purchase, they were the secondary actual owners of the ship and have the right to dispose the ship. The Plaintiff ZHONG Kangqiu bought the ship from ZHUO Shiyi who was the lawful owner.

According to Article 133 of the Contract Law, the ownership over a targeted matter is transferred upon the delivery of the targeted matter. The Plaintiff paid the ship price, ZHUO Shiyi delivered the ship, the ownership of the ship has been transferred to the Plaintiff since the ship was delivered. The Plaintiff affiliated the ship continuously to Shunxin Company, it was operated in the name of Shunxin Company to the outsiders, he paid affiliation charge to Shunxin Company during period of affiliation operation of the ship, it proves that the Plaintiff has the rights to possess, use, benefit from and dispose the ship. Combined with the sales and purchase contract, payment voucher, receipts and other evidence submitted by parties, it can be determined that there is a real contract relationship between the Plaintiff ZHONG Kangqiu and ZHUO Shiyi, the Plaintiff has paid the price in full and actually possessed the ship and has the actual ownership. What's more, the Plaintiff has an affiliation relationship with Shunxin Company. This is an objective fact.

According to Article 9 of the Maritime Code of the People's Republic of China, "the acquisition, transference or extinction of the ownership of a ship shall be registered at the ship registration authorities; no acquisition, transference or extinction of the ship's ownership shall act against a third party unless registered".

China's ship registration adopts the publicity system, rather than the taking effectiveness upon registration system. In this case, although the ship is not registered in Plaintiff's name, it does not deny that the Plaintiff has acquired the ownership thereof. Where the nominal owner is inconsistent with real owner, the real owner's rights shall prevail, the ownership shall not be determined on the basis of the nominal owner. In this case, the Plaintiff purchased M.V. "Shun **"through lawful sales, paid the price in full and took delivery of the ship, he shall acquire actual ownership of the ship.

2. Whether the Plaintiff shall have the right to apply for stopping execution and discharge the seizure of the ship

The court holds according to Article 227 of the Civil Procedure Law of the People's Republic of China, "where a party not involved in this case raises a challenge with respect to the object matter subjected to execution in the course of execution, the execution officer shall examine the challenge according to the procedure prescribed by the law. If the reasons for the challenge are untenable, the challenge shall be rejected, otherwise, the execution shall be suspended with the approval of the president of the court. If a party not involved in this case or a party refuses the written ruling and considers the original judgment or written ruling is improper, it shall be dealt with according to the procedure for trial supervision. If the refusal does not relate to the original judgment or written ruling, the party not involved in this case or the party may bring an action before the people's court within 15 days upon service of the written order. In this case, in order to fulfill (2013) Xia Hai Fa Shang Chu Zi No.333 Civil Judgment made by Xiamen Maritime Court, the Defendant Chengxing Company applied for execution of Shunxin Company's ship M.V. "Shun **". In the course of execution, the Plaintiff made a written challenge to the execution of M.V. "Shun **", the court made (2014) Hai Fa Zhi Zi No.3 Executive Ruling, rejecting the Plaintiff's challenge. The Plaintiff was dissatisfied with the ruling, but the given reason is not related to the original judgment or ruling, the Plaintiff brought an action of party not involved the subject case's challenge over execution before the court within 15 days upon the service of (2014) Haifa Executive Judgment No.3 according to the provisions of Article 227 of the Civil Procedure Law, the Plaintiff exercised the right of suit according to the law, it shall be supported. Given the above, The Plaintiff shall have the actual ownership of M. V. "Shun **" according to law. He is neither the obligor under Xiamen Maritime Court (2013) Hai Fa Shang Chu Zi No.333 Civil Judgment or the person subject to execution of (2014) Hai Fa Zhi Zi No.1 rendered by the court. The Plaintiff proposed to stop the execution of M.V. "Shun **", it has merits, the court shall support.

To sum up, in this case, the Plaintiff and ZHUO Shiyi signed the contract of purchase and sales of ship based on the declaration of real intentions, the contract is legal and valid. The Plaintiff paid the price for the purchase of the ship, the ship was delivered, the Plaintiff actually possessed and dominated the ship, and the Plaintiff actually acquired the ownership of the ship, although the registration of change of ownership was not carried out, the ownership is a substantive right that is sufficient to prevent executing M.V. "Shun **".According to Article 312 of the Interpretations of the Supreme People's Court on the Application of the Civil Procedure Law of the People's Republic of China (hereinafter the Interpretations), "in terms of an action of a challenge over execution filed by a party not involved the subject case, the people's court shall handle according to the following circumstances: (1) make a judgment to reject the execute the subject matter, where the party not involved the subject case has sufficient civil rights which can exclude the compulsory execution; (2) make a judgment to reject the claims, where the party not involved the subject case has not sufficient civil rights to exclude the execution. Where the party not involved the subject case files a claim for conformation of his litigation rights in the meantime, the people's court may make a decision in the judgment". The execution of M.V. "Shun **" shall be stopped.

This case is concerning an action of a party not involved the subject case's challenge over execution filed according to the Civil Procedure Law, pursuant to Article 307 of the Interpretations, where a party not involved the subject case initiates an action for challenge over execution, the person applying for the execution shall be the Defendant; where the person subject to execution objects the challenge of the party not involved the subject case, he shall be the co-Defendant; where the person subject to execution does not object to the challenge of the party not involved the subject case, he shall be listed as a third party. The person subject to execution, Shunxin Company raised no objection to the challenge of the party not involved the subject case in this case, so its litigious status in this case shall be the Third Party. The Defendant Chengxing Company as the applicator for execution, its legal status is the Defendant in this case, the Defendant Chengxing Company argued it was not a qualified Defendant but a party not involved the subject case, whether there was real relationship of ship sales and affiliation operation between the Plaintiff and Shunxin Company was not related to the application for compulsory execution filed by Chengxing Company, such argument lacks evidence, the court shall not support.

Therefore, according to Article 132 and Article 133 of the Contract Law of the People's Republic of China, Article 9 of the Maritime Code of the People's Republic of China, Article 227 of the Civil Procedure Law of the People's Republic of China, Article 304, Article 307 and Article 312 of the Interpretations of the Supreme People's Court on the Application of the Civil Procedure Law of the People's Republic of China, the judgment is as follows:

1. The Plaintiff ZHONG Kangqiu is the actual owner of M.V. "Shun **";
2. Stop the enforcement of M.V. "Shun **".

Court acceptance fee in amount of RMB100, shall be born by the Defendant Fujian Chengxing Fuel Oil Co., Ltd.

If dissatisfied with this judgment, any party may within fifteen days as of the service of this judgment and submit a Statement of Appeal to the court, with duplicates in the number of the counterparties, so as to file an appeal before

Guangxi Zhuang Autonomous Region High People's Court. The appeal fee shall be paid within seven days of the time limitation of appeal, (Beneficiary of Remittance: the Guangxi Zhuang Autonomous Region High People's Court; Account Number: 20-017301040003777; Bank of Deposit: Agricultural Bank of China Nanning City Wanxiang Branch), otherwise the appeal shall be deemed as automatically withdrawn.

> Presiding Judge: WANG Mingsheng
> Judge: SU Weiling
> Acting Judge: WEI Zhenbin
> March 25, 2015
> Clerk: LING Chen